DATE DUE

*Rivers
of the
United States*

Rivers of the United States

VOLUME I
ESTUARIES

Ruth Patrick

FRANCIS BOYER CHAIR OF LIMNOLOGY
THE ACADEMY OF NATURAL SCIENCES OF PHILADELPHIA

JOHN WILEY & SONS, INC.

New York • Chichester • Brisbane • Toronto • Singapore

Library of Congress Cataloging in Publication Data:
Patrick, Ruth.
    Rivers of the United States / Ruth Patrick.
        p.   cm.
    Contents: v.   1. Estuaries
    ISBN 0-471-30345-3
    1. Rivers – United States.   I. Title.
GB1215.P29   1994
551.48′3′0973 – dc20   CIP

Printed in the United States of America

10 9 8 7 6 5 4 3 2 1

This book in dedicated to the family and friends of Ruth Patrick who made this book possible.

Preface

Riverine systems are the most important source of potable surface waters for human beings and other animals that inhabit this planet. Despite this, very few books have been written concerning the species that form the ecosystems through which nutrients and energies are transferred. It is the functioning of these ecosystems that maintains the quality of water suitable for the use of humans and many other organisms.

Many papers have been written on primary and secondary production and detritus processing. Others have listed species found in various areas of rivers. However, integrating this information into the structure of communities and how they function has rarely been done. Certainly this information has not been integrated into a series of books which have included how human use has affected these ecosystems.

Hutchinson has brought together such information, in a remarkable fashion, for lakes. It is hoped that this series of books will produce a better understanding of riverine systems.

When one examines the topography of the country it is evident that the extent and numbers of riverine systems in the contiguous United States is very large. Therefore, one must develop a system of selection of rivers. To do this selecting, 18 watersheds have been designated by the U.S. Water Resource Council (USGS open file report 78-200). They have grouped the rivers in the watersheds of the country into five groups based on dissolved solids. The groupings are 0–250 mg L^{-1}, 251–500 mg L^{-1}, 501–1000 mg L^{-1}, 1001–2500 mg L^{-1}, and 2501–26,000 mg L^{-1}. For this study I selected for inclusion rivers of different types in each of the watersheds. The limiting factor was information on species composition of the ecosystems in a particular river. Since I was interested in the ecosystem approach, information on algae and invertebrates, including insects, and fish, was needed. Too often there would be information on fish or insects but not on algae. Therefore, they were excluded unless information on a chemically and physically similar nearby stream or estuary was available. Often, only one type of river in a watershed is discussed.

The riverine systems are divided into sections: headwaters, main stem, and in some cases, estuaries are also present. Headwater streams are streams that merge near the origin of a river to form the main channel. They are often first to fifth order, particulary in the eastern half of the United States.

Estuaries were selected primarily to represent geohydrological types of estuaries: for example, fjords, drowned river basins, barrier island estuaries, submerged grass meadows (southern Florida), mangrove estuaries, and tectonic-formed estuaries. The limitation to the study was lack of sufficient biological data. However, if there was a similar estuary close by that had been studied, these data were sometimes incorporated.

This series of books should be of interest to people seeking a variety of information. They should be of value to students and researchers seeking information on the structure and factors affecting the functioning of ecosystems in riverine systems. They contain information of value to the planner and the conservationist interested in managing the river or estuary for sustainable development. Without the knowledge contained in this book, correct management would be impossible. For people who enjoy recreating on or near water, these books contain a great deal of interesting information.

Many people have helped me in the preparation of these books: some in providing information; these I will acknowledge in each volume. I will also recognize in each volume people who have assisted me in gathering important scientific information and have helped in the technical writing of the book. I will acknowledge with each volume the very important financial assistance of individuals, foundations, and industries. These monies have been used to pay for my scientific assistants. Without their help this series would not have been possible.

Philadelphia, Pennsylvania   RUTH PATRICK
July 1994

Acknowledgements

This book has been written over several years and through the years many people have provided information that has enabled me to write this volume. I particularly want to thank Dr. W. C. Boicourt who has provided me with information concerning the effects of wind on water movement. I also want to thank numerous other people who have provided information particularly Dr. Boswick H. Ketchum (deceased), Dr. Donald W. Pritchard, Dr. Howard Saunders, Dr. Eugene Odum, Dr. William Odum (deceased), Dr. Robert J. Livingston, Dr. James Sanders, Dr. Larry Pomeroy, Dr. John Hobbie, Dr. Thomas Edmondson and Dr. Frank John Vernberg. I particularly want to recognize the help and encouragement the late Professor G. E. Hutchinson gave me in the preparation of these books.

In the bringing together of references and in some cases abstracting them, I wish to particularly thank Heiden Rochester and Martha Farr-Kent. I want to thank for technical editing and typing of the manuscript Lee Anderson and Susan Durdu. I want to acknowledge the help of the Academy of Natural Sciences Library and my many colleagues. I also want to thank Philip C. Manor and Diana Cisek of John Wiley & Sons, Inc. for their helpful suggestions in the preparation of this volume.

Financial support has been very important for it would not have been possible to write this book without the help of the Rockefeller Foundation and the money from the John and Alice Tyler Award. Also assisting have been the E. I. DuPont Company, Procter and Gamble Company, Phoebe W. Haas Charitable Trust B, and Marian B. Stroud.

Contents

CHAPTER 1

Introduction

O ver the last several years I have been studying headwaters, main stems, and estuaries of riverine systems of the United States. From these studies I have learned a great deal about the complexity of functioning and structuring of these systems. I have been greatly impressed by the importance of biodiversity in the maintaining of the natural functioning of these systems. This has led me to write this series of books on the structure and functioning of ecosystems in riverine systems. These studies have resulted in six volumes: (1) Estuaries, (2) Headwaters and Main Stems of Rivers of Eastern and Southern United States, (3) Riverine Systems in the Mississippi Valley and Great Lakes, (4) Western Riverine Systems, and (5) The Effects of Chemicals in Water on the Ecosystem and the Effect of Anthropogenic Pollution on the Biodiversity and Functioning of the System. This information, which I have obtained from my many studies, has been supplemented by the knowledge in a large number of pertinent papers and books. It is realized that all papers and books have not been read. But it is hoped that the information from those that I have studied plus my own experience will provide enough pertinent information to elucidate how eco-systems are structured and how they function.

Although much information exists in lists and distribution of species and in studies of primary and secondary production and detritus processing, I do not believe that the integration of biodiversity at the species level into the structure and functioning of ecosystems in specific areas in riverine systems has been done. Much of the information in these volumes has been accumulated from my studies at the Academy of Natural Sciences of riverine systems in the United States plus information from the literature.

I have based the presentation in these books on the watersheds designated by the U.S. Geological Survey (USGS). Furthermore, it should be pointed out that the USGS has designated five types of waters that might potentially be in each of these watershed units, based on the concentration of dissolved solids, as follows: $0-250\,mg\,L^{-1}$, $251-500\,mg\,L^{-1}$, $501-1000\,mg\,L^{-1}$, $1001-2500\,mg\,L^{-1}$, and $2501-26,000\,mg\,L^{-1}$. Using this as a basis, we have divided the United States into riverine systems in the eastern and southern United States; riverine systems in the Mississippi drainage basin, which has much more variable water than in the eastern and southern United States; and riverine systems of the western United States, a set of riverine systems with highly variable water concentrations, being low in dissolved solids in areas west of the Rocky Mountains and through the Snake River system and highly variable in other parts of the west. Those riverine systems with the largest amounts of dissolved solids were in Texas, New Mexico, Oklahoma, and parts of Kansas and Colorado.

We were particularly careful to select reaches of the river for study that were not affected adversely by pollution. It would be almost impossible to say that no anthropogenic substances entered several sections of the river which we included. However, the biodiversity and functioning of the community seem to be characteristic of natural systems. Occasionally, it was not possible to find all the biological information necessary from a given reach of the river. However, if we included this information, it was because we were able to find information from nearby, chemically similar rivers. One could infer that probably they supported the same type of ecosystem as the one under study.

Wherever possible we have described the association of organisms in specific habitats, such as those associated with vegetation, those associated with ripples in pools, and those associated with pools. Environment seems to be one of the major factors that determines the type of association present. A great deal of time has been devoted to determining the species that were present in specific habitats. For each list of species we have used the original names, resulting from the identifications of the authors, and have included the reference to the original article. No attempt has been made to reclassify the species into present-day systems. This can be risky if one does not really know the characteristics of the species in question.

It is all-important that one understand how natural ecosystems function and the role that many species that compose the system have in securing an efficient and effective method of nutrient transfer. This approach to understanding the aquatic life in riverine systems has not been done to any great extent except that lists of species have been composed, and functions such as primary and secondary production and detritus processing have been studied thoroughly. The two have not been put together in an extensive way as I have tried to do in this book. Of course, there have been individual areas in which such an approach has been used.

This first volume is devoted to the study of estuaries. I want particularly to thank the Rockefeller Foundation, whose financial help made possible this as well as other volumes by providing the money for the salary of my scientific assistants, Mr. Hayden Rochester and Miss Martha Farr. I also want to thank the Academy of Natural Sciences, which provided the salary of my technical assistant at various times: Lee Anderson, Robin Davis, and Susan Durdu.

In selecting the estuaries for study, I have tried to select those that represent different types of ecosystems: for example, fjords such as those found in New England and in Puget Sound; estuaries that are open mouth; as well as those that are characterized as barrier island estuaries. Each of these types of estuaries often supports large grassland marshes; particularly unique are the mangrove estuaries around southern Florida and parts of the Gulf and the underwater grass estuaries that surround southern Florida. These are mainly beds of *Thalassia*. The estuaries formed by the movement of tectonic plates are on the west coast in southern California. These estuaries have been modified structurally to some extent by human activities but seem to be functioning fairly normally. However, they do represent a distinct type of estuary.

Many people have provided help in developing this volume. I want to particularly thank Dr. Boicourt of the Oxford Laboratories for his aid in bringing up to date the section on the movement of water in estuaries. I also want to thank Dr. Jonathan Sharp of the University of Delaware Estuary Laboratories and Dr. John Vernberg of the Barruch Laboratories of South Carolina, as well as many others who helped provide pertinent literature.

Emphasis in these books is on the importance of large numbers of species belonging to many philogenetic groups working together to form functional communities that are able to maintain themselves over changing conditions and to function under many different environments. This is the reason why there are so many species in an estuary. It is this great amount of biodiversity that produces resilience of the system to sudden change. It is also the mechanism by which many ecosystems are able to exist in a great variety of microhabitats in the ever-changing conditions that exist in an estuary. Diversity is realized not only in the ability of species to utilize many different physical habitats, such as mud, sand, decaying vegetation, and so on, but also in their ability to utilize the changing chemical conditions of the water and the flow rates, which are highly variable. The way in which the species cope with adversity is also very diverse. For example, some form cysts, some go into diapause, some hybernate, but all have a way of reducing their demands on the immediate environment when it becomes too severe. Species in estuaries must have this capability, for there are no bodies of water in the world that are subject to more natural changes than those that exist in estuaries.

The challenge today is: Will this high biodiversity be able to maintain itself in the face of the complex and highly variable pollution that is entering our estuaries not only through water, but also from the drainage of the land and from fallouts of the atmosphere? As human society becomes more complex and the emissions from our society more diverse and more potent, the challenge is to maintain this diversity, which is so necessary to ensure the functioning of the oceans as well as maintenance of the naturalness of the continental waters. Can this biodiversity of species survive? It is only by seeking to understand more clearly the demands of our highly diverse ecosystems that humankind will learn how to cope with anthropogenic effects and yet maintain a sustainable, functional water quality for the uses of society's ever-increasing population.

Although many books have been written about the ecosystems—about the organisms living in estuaries and how they function—I do not believe that there is any single book that has tried to address the problem of biodiversity and its importance in the riverine systems throughout the contiguous United States.

It is obvious that one cannot describe all estuaries, nor do we have the knowledge of the species living in them and how they function to accomplish this task. We have therefore selected representative estuaries of different physical structure, in different parts of the country, to elucidate how the diverse ecosystems in estuaries function.

CHAPTER 2

Physical Characteristics of Estuaries

In this discussion, various classifications of estuaries are set forth. The general characteristics of these bodies of water and examples of the principal types of estuaries in the continental United States are given. Emphasis is on their hydrology, sedimentation, marshlands, and delta formations, as these are the processes that affect aquatic life habitats directly or indirectly. A discussion of the effects of human perturbations on estuaries is included.

The definition of *estuary* used in this work is a modification of that of Pritchard (1967a): An estuary is a semienclosed coastal body of water that has free connection with the open sea and within which seawater is measurably diluted with fresh water derived from land drainage. Excluded from consideration are those strictly freshwater areas not under tidal influence. An exception is the inclusion of the fauna and flora from a non-tidal area adjacent to a freshwater area under tidal influence where the natural fauna and flora have been eliminated by pollution.

Estuaries can be classified on the basis of the following characteristics:

1. Formation and general characteristics of estuaries.
2. Water movement in the estuary—salinity distribution and flow characteristics.
3. Dominant driving mechanisms—tide, wind, or river.
4. Types of ecosystems based on energy flow as a common denominator among the biological, geological, chemical, and physical features (Odum and Copeland, 1972).

TYPES OF ESTUARIES

Existing estuaries are geologically young. Approximately 18,000 years ago the sea level started to rise and rose at about the rate of 10 m per 1000 years until around 9000 years ago. The rate of sea-level rise slowed to a little less than 3 m per 1000 years during the next 6000 years. In the last 3000 years the rate of rise has been less than 1 m per 1000 years. Pritchard (1967a) recognized that estuary basins are formed by the drowning of old river valleys, glacial gouging (fjords), the action of water currents (barrier island estuaries), and tectonic processes.

Estuaries vary in the time of their formation, although the present configurations in most cases have existed for only a few thousand years (Schubel, 1971a). Most estuary shapes change over time as a result of erosion or the accretion of sediments. The estuaries that change the least are the fjords, whereas those that change most have been formed in unconsolidated rock. Estuaries along the eastern Atlantic and southern coasts of the United States lie in unconsolidated rock. The faulted estuaries of the California coast show variable sediment accumulation.

Sediments accumulating in estuaries in unconsolidated substrates cause the channel to assume a V-shape in cross section. The accumulated sediments from extensive salt marsh areas are dominated by grasses on the east coast and by grasses or mangroves on the Gulf coast. An extreme example of sediment accretion is Mobile Bay, which three millennia ago was a large open water estuary. Today the estuary is composed of marshlands and swamps.

Perhaps the best example of sediments forming deltas in our country is at the mouth of the Mississippi River. Atchafalaya Lake is now almost extinct due to the accumulation of deltaic sediments brought down mainly by the Mississippi River, although other rivers have contributed to these formations. The most spectacular example of estuary filling due to delta formation is that of the Amazon, where such filling has occurred over a distance of about 1500 miles (2414 km). Deltas are formed by submarine deposits, as contrasted to the formation of swamplands and some marshlands due to the erosion of subaerial sediments, although many marshlands are a combination of both subsurface or marine deposits and subaerial deposits.

Drowned River Estuaries

Estuaries that are drowned river valleys are sometimes referred to as coastal plains estuaries, although they may occur in other regions. These estuaries are formed in the channels of rivers that extended onto the continental shelf when the sea level was lower. The maximum depth of these estuaries is seldom as much as 30 m. The central channel is often sinuous, and extensive mud flats and marshes may occur along the edges of the open water. The entire estuary is usually floored with varying thicknesses of recent sediments, which tend to be muddy in the upper reaches and to become increasingly sandy toward the mouth.

Drowned river estuaries resemble subaerial valleys that deepen and widen toward their mouths and may be modified by spits. In outline as well as in cross section, drowned river estuaries are triangular. The width-to-depth ratio varies depending on the type of rock cut by the valley. A remarkable characteristic of some of these estuaries is that the increase in cross-sectional area toward the mouth is exponential. This may reflect a long-term equilibrium adjustment between sedimentation and erosion by tidal currents (Dyer, 1973).

Drowned river valley estuaries are most often found in temperate latitudes. In the United States they are most common along the Atlantic and Gulf coasts. Some better known examples of these drowned river estuaries throughout the world are Chesapeake Bay and Delaware Bay (United States), Thames River estuary (England), Ems estuary (Germany), Seine estuary (France), Si-Kian estuary (Hong Kong), and Murray estuary (Australia).

Fjord Estuaries

Fjord estuaries fill glacial troughs gouged out by the tongues of continental glaciers moving down preexisting valleys. In their movement the glaciers increased the depth of the valleys irregularly and steepened their sides to produce the characteristic narrow, steep-sided trough, U-shaped in cross section, and relatively straight and long. Some fjords reach 200 km in length with a common width-to-depth ratio of 10:1. Fjord estuaries have rocky floors or a very thin veneer of sediments, and deposition is generally restricted to the head of the fjord, where the main river enters. The river discharge is small compared to the total fjord volume, but as many fjords have restricted tidal ranges within their mouths, the river flow is often large with respect to the tidal prism.

The tidal prism is blocked by sills aross the mouth of the fjord. The sills may be at rather shallow depths (in Norway they average 4.5 m) and restrict the free exchange of water. The only estuarine flow characteristics are in the upper part of the water column above the sill because the lower waters are trapped and remain stagnant for long periods of time. In contrast, in British Columbia, the depth to the sills below the surface of the water may be 40 to 150 m, thus allowing the estuarine characteristics of flow to be much better developed, approaching more nearly the circulation pattern of a true estuary.

Fjords typically occur in high latitudes and often in mountainous regions. They are among the most picturesque estuaries of the world. Consider, for instance, the Loch Etive fjord in Scotland, the Sogne fjord in Norway, the Alberni Inlet in British Columbia, Puget Sound in Washington, and the Milford Sound in New Zealand (Dyer, 1973).

Barrier Island Estuaries

Barrier island estuaries usually are found on coastal areas where deposition is prominent. Usually, one or more rivers enter the estuary, but the total freshwater input is relatively small. These basins are usually broad and contain considerable amounts of sediments. Some of the sediments are deposited during high river flows while others are derived from the sea. The barrier island that forms across the estuary is interrupted at one or more places, allowing free access to the sea. Inlets may vary in shape and position, depending on the effects of storms on the barrier island.

Tidal currents through inlets are usually quite strong because the inlets are generally small compared to the embayment area. However, behind the barrier island the tidal action is considerably reduced, as is the flow, due to tidal activity. Barrier island or bar-built estuaries are generally found along the east and Gulf coasts of the United States in areas with active coastal deposition of sediments (Dyer, 1973). Examples of such barrier island estuaries are Albermarle Sound and Pamlico Sound in North Carolina and the Galveston Bay region of Texas.

In New England barrier islands are found across the mouths of many estuaries, as is the case in the Merrimack embayment. The elements of topography in most of the northern New England estuaries are sand bodies: primarily point bars, flood tidal deltas, mussel banks, intertidal mud flats, intertidal sandy mud flats, and flat surfaces of the high salt marsh. Tidal channels sometimes have current in only one direction; they are either ebb or flood channels. By far the most spectacular topographic features of the New England estuaries are the large flood tidal deltas. These sand bodies form just inside the inlets, where sand is deposited by the waning flood tidal currents as they flow away from the restricted tidal inlets (Hayes, 1971a).

Tectonic-Formed Estuaries

Tectonic processes may form estuary basins by faulting, land slides, or volcanic eruptions. San Francisco Bay, at least in part, is an example of an estuary produced by a tectonic process, in this case by slippage of fault blocks. The upper reaches of San Francisco Bay estuary were formed, however, by the drowning of the lower reaches of the San Joaquin and Sacramento River systems. Winds are often the driving force in the water circulation pattern in a tectonic-formed estuary, in contrast to tidal action or river flows that dominate circulation patterns in other types of estuaries (Conomos and Peterson, 1976).

WATER MOVEMENT IN ESTUARIES: SALINITY DISTRIBUTION AND FLOW CHARACTERISTICS

Highly Stratified Water (Type A)

A highly stratified estuary may occur in the presence of a salt wedge or in fjords. In a salt wedge estuary, for example the Mississippi River estuary, the river flow is dominant and a saltwater tongue extends upstream along the bed of the estuary. The extent of the tongue becomes longer and the tip sharper if the freshwater flow decreases. If the freshwater flow increases, the saltwater tongue becomes shorter and its tip blunter. In many estuaries in the United States salt water extends farther upstream in the summer than in the spring, when the river discharge is greatest. The upstream extension of the saltwater tongue is also influenced by the shape of the estuary.

The presence of a saltwater tongue determines the type of benthic species that may be present. Species that are continuously under the influence of the tongue are marine or euryhaline species, where as those that live in the area where the salinity shifts seasonally are typically euryhaline species. At the same time that the deep-water species typically belong to a marine fauna and flora, species that live in fresh or nearly fresh water may dominate the shallow water and plankton fauna and flora.

Stratification Other Than Fjords. Typically, the velocity of the freshwater decreases toward the sea. Due to the velocity of the salt water, a shear force develops at the interface which, if or sufficient intensity, causes waves to form and break on the interface. As a result, salt water is mixed with surface fresh water and entrainment occurs. If the fresh water does not mix with the salt water, the salinity of the tongue remains nearly constant.

The two dominant forces in the saltwater balance are horizontal and vertical advection. At quasi-steady state the salt balance equation (Pritchard and Carter, 1971) is approximately

$$0 = u\frac{\partial s}{\partial x} - w\frac{\partial s}{\partial z} \tag{1}$$

where u = component velocity
　　　s = concentration of salt
　　　x = longitudinal distance
　　　z = vertical distance
　　　w = width

Vertical mixing within the upper layer may be expressed by

$$\frac{\partial}{\partial z}\left(K\frac{\partial s}{z\,\partial z}\right)$$

where K is the diffusivity coefficient in the axial direction. This mixing of salt water into the freshwater layer due to the shear effect blends the tip of the salt-water wedge and the interface becomes fuzzy. Salt water lost by mixing is replaced from the sea. Typical velocity and salinity profiles are shown in Figure 2.1.

In a highly stratified estuary the ratio of river flow to tidal flow is large and the width-to-depth ratio is relatively small. For example, in the Mississippi River the mean range of the diurnal tide was 70 cm and the river discharge ranged between 2.8×10^5 and 8.5×10^5 m s^{-1}. In the dredged Southwest Pass of the Mississippi, the upstream flow of the salt wedge was maintained regardless of tidal cycles, whereas in the shallower South Pass the upstream flow occurred in the flood tide at the same time as a downstream flow occurred in the wedge on the surface. During ebb tide the flow in the wedge may reverse and the current can be in a seaward direction at all depths (Wright, 1971; Dyer, 1973).

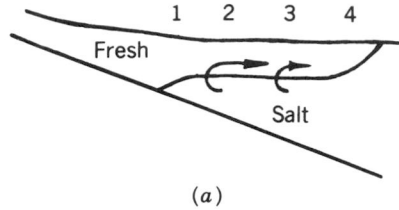

(a)

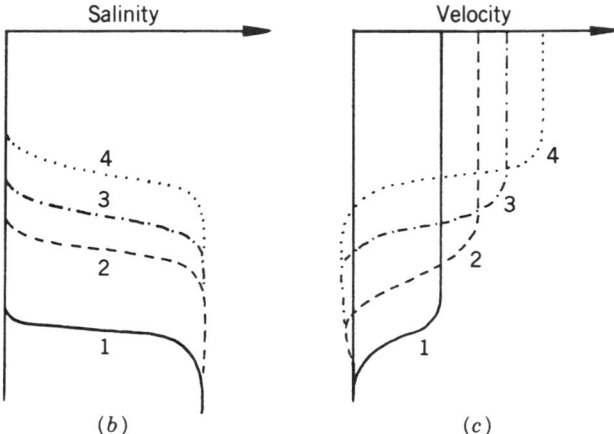

(b)   (c)

FIGURE 2.1. Salinity and velocity profiles at various points along the longitudinal axis of a salt wedge estuary similar to the Mississippi. Numbers on sketch (a) indicate positions in the estuary at which different profiles are to be found. (From Dyer, 1973.)

Stratification in Fjords. The type of stratification found in a fjord estuary was caused by a deep, almost isohaline layer of salt water which had infrequent renewal. Its depth was dependent on the depth of the sill. The river flow in the surface waters was greater than the tidal flow, and entrainment by the mixing of fresh and salt water occurred (Figure 2.2a). Thus the upper layer of water was usually almost the same from headwater to mouth, but discharge increased toward the mouth. In some fjords the thickness of the upper layer of water was restricted to the sill depth. If the river discharge was high, the surface layer was almost homogeneous and the maximum salinity gradient occurred close to the surface (Pickard, 1961; Dyer, 1973). Figure 2.2b relates increase in velocity to the salinity profile of various regions designated in Figure 2.2a.

Because of the larger tidal velocities and weaker stratification, the circulation over the sills may be very different from that within the fjords (Figure 2.2c) (Dyer, 1973). The inflow over the sills is a mixture of coastal and outflow waters. The saline inflow is best developed in summer when the river flow is largest, entrainment is most active, and density differences between the coastal waters and deep fjord water are greatest (Figure 2.2) (Dyer, 1973).

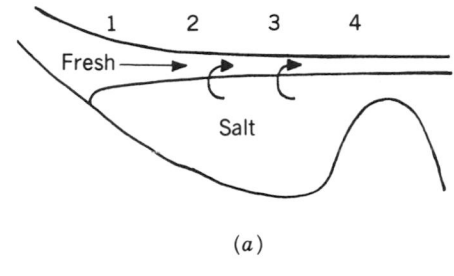

(a)

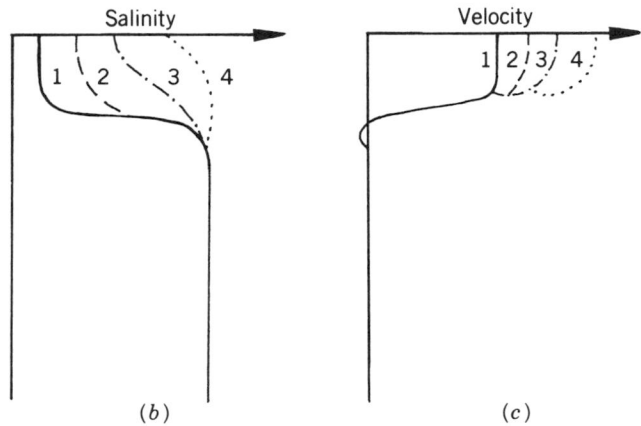

(b)   (c)

FIGURE 2.2. Salinity and velocity profiles at various points along the longitudinal axis of a fjord. Numbers on sketch (a) indicate positions in the estuary at which different profiles are to be found. (From Dyer, 1973.)

Partially Mixed Water (Type B)

In estuaries where the tide is sufficiently strong to prevent the river flow from dominating the circulation pattern, salt water is mixed upward and fresh water is mixed downward by advection and turbulence. These actions effectively erase the salt wedge.

Typically, the salinity of the surface water increases toward the mouth of the estuary, and the salinity of the bottom water decreases toward the head of the estuary. A vertical cross section of the estuarine water will show the surface and bottom layers to be almost homogeneous with a high salinity gradient at about middepth. In shallower water the homogeneous bottom layer may be missing and the maximum salinity gradient may occur near the bottom. The upper layers become thinner toward the sea, and the bottom layers are less deep toward the head of the estuary.

Lateral gradients of salinity may be present in broad estuaries where the Coriolis force causes a horizontal separation of the flow. In the northern hemisphere the boundary between the upper layer having a net seaward flow, and the lower layer, having a net flow up the estuary, is slightly tilted. On the right side facing seaward, the upper layer is deeper and stronger, whereas the flow up estuary is nearer the surface and stronger on the left side (Pritchard and Carter, 1971).

In this type of estuary, under steady-state conditions, the important terms in the salt balance equation are horizontal advection, vertical advection, and vertical diffusion. The salt balance equation is

$$0 = -u\frac{\partial s}{\partial x} - w\frac{\partial s}{\partial z} + \frac{\partial}{\partial z}\left(K\frac{\partial s}{z\partial z}\right) \tag{2}$$

The energy involved in the circulation of the water is considerable, and is dissipated primarily against frictional forces on the bottom, producing turbulence. Energy is lost by viscous dissipation, which creates heat. The kinetic energy of the turbulent eddies is lost by working against density gradients, which increase the potential energy of the water column. These eddies mix salt water upward and fresh water downward (Dyer, 1973).

The tidal amplitude, tidal currents, and salinity in partially mixed water estuaries produce various tidal patterns and hence variable salinities. Ketchum (1953) plotted the variation of salinity with distance for four Atlantic coast estuaries (Figure 2.3).

If the estuary is of appropriate depth and length, the tidal wave entrance, reflection from the upstream end, and return may be in a time equal to a harmonic of the tidal period. A standing-wave system may be established in the estuary, and the reflected wave will then interfere with the entering wave. Often, the node is produced near the mouth of the estuary with the antinode near the head; however, in longer estuaries several nodes and antinodes may be present (Dyer, 1973). If a single node is at the mouth, the tidal amplitude increases toward the head of the estuary. Throughout the estuary high and low water and the time of turning are simultaneous with the maximum currents occurring near the mouth (Figure 2.4a). The tidal amplitude and salinity variations are 90° out of phase.

The tidal wave may be solely progressive if the energy of the tidal wave is completely dissipated before reflection. In such cases the amplitude of the tide and the speed of the current diminish toward the head and the time of high and low tide, and the turn of the current is progressive along the estuary. Under such conditions the maximum flood currents would occur at high water as the tidal amplitude and current velocity would be in phase (Figure 2.4b).

Although the tidal current may be symmetrical outside the estuary, it tends to become asymmetrical inside, because each part of the tidal wave travels at a speed that depends on water depth, with the crest traveling faster than the trough. This causes the water to rise more quickly than it falls. Toward the head of the estuary, which is narrower and more shallow, the tidal amplitude will tend to increase because of convergence but decrease because of friction. If the tidal range is normally large, the tidal amplitude may be very large and

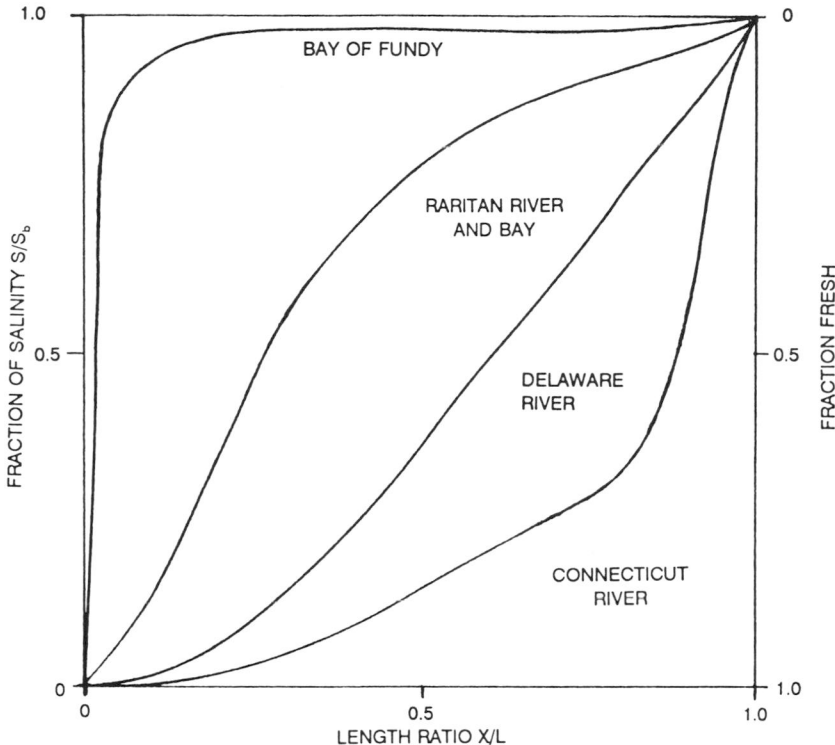

FIGURE 2.3. Distribution of salinity along the length of four estuaries. The length ratio, X/L, is determined by dividing the distance downstream, X, by the total length of the estuary, L. The salinity ratio, S/S_b, is obtained by dividing the chlorinity of seawater, S, by the chlorinity of freshwater S_b. Note that the salinity ratio is the reciprocal of the fraction fresh. (From Ketchum, 1953.)

a bore may develop, because the asymmetry becomes very marked. An excellent example is the Bay of Fundy in Nova Scotia, Canada.

The velocity of tidal wave propagation is much less in long, shallow estuaries, and several progressive tidal waves may be present at the same time (Dyer, 1973). In most estuaries there is a mixture of a standing wave with variable magnitudes of contributions of progressive waves, and the tidal amplitude and timing of events vary along the estuary.

When the river flow is confined primarily to the surface in partially mixed estuaries, the ebb flow starts on the surface at the head of the estuary as soon as the pressure of incoming high water diminishes and progresses downstream. The water will continue to flow out at the mouth of the estuary until a pressure gradient stops it. The current then turns and progresses upstream. Consequently, at the beginning of flood tide the bottom current is landward, and the surface currents ebb before the bottom current. If these effects are measured in the middle of the estuary, there is a significant difference in the amplitudes of tidal velocity fluctuation at the top and bottom (Figure 2.4c). The average or mean

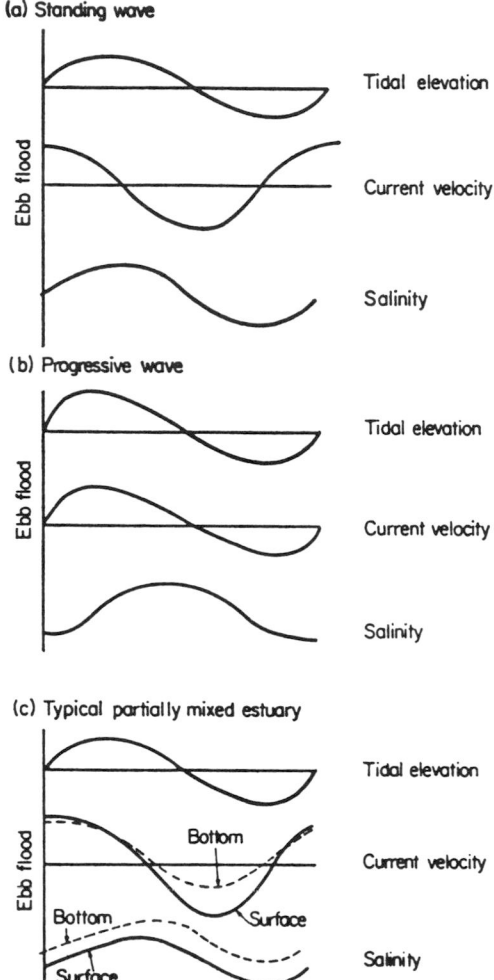

FIGURE 2.4.   Tidal response in estuaries: (*a*) standing wave; (*b*) progressive wave; (*c*) typical partly mixed estuary. (From Dyer, 1973.)

current over the complete tidal period is in the flood direction at the bottom and in the ebb direction at the top. The landward residual flow in the bottom layer diminishes toward the head of the salt intrusion and a null point is produced.

At the null point there is a zone of maximum turbidity caused by suspended matter trapped by the water circulation, and shoaling may occur (Dyer, 1972, 1973). The most rapid shoaling is normally between the flood and ebb positions of the limit of seawater intrusion. For example, in Chesapeake Bay the sedimentation rate is probably an order of magnitude greater in the upper reaches of the "estuarine circulation regime" than in the seaward section of the bay. Rapid shoaling may also occur where the tidal flow of the estuary is interrupted by entering tributaries as in Charleston Harbor.

Homogeneous Water (Type C)

Vertically Homogeneous. A vertically homogeneous estuary occurs when the volume and forces of tidal mixing are great enough to eradicate the vertical salinity gradient. It is difficult to be sure that vertically homogeneous estuaries really exist, as small vertical variations may be lost in the averaging process. Although the vertical gradient may apparently be lost, the longitudinal salinity gradient remains with the salinity increasing seaward.

If sufficiently wide, these estuaries may be laterally inhomogeneous, largely because of the Coriolis force. In the northern hemisphere the net flow is upstream on the left side (as one faces seaward) and downstream on the right side of the estuary. The circulation is in a horizontal plane, which is not typical of other types of estuaries. This results in the salinity being higher on the left side than on the right side, and has considerable effect on the kinds of aquatic life that one finds on the two sides of the estuary. On both sides the salinity increases seaward. Excellent examples of this type of estuary are the Chesapeake estuary in Maryland and the lower reaches of the Delaware estuary of Delaware and New Jersey.

Under steady-state conditions the vertical terms disappear and the salt balance equation is

$$0 = -u\frac{\partial s}{\partial x} - v\frac{\partial s}{\partial y} + \frac{\partial}{\partial y}\left(K\frac{\partial s}{y\,\partial y}\right) \tag{3}$$

where v is the velocity (Pritchard and Carter, 1971).

During periods of high flow the importance of the rivers entering the estuary increases and an estuary may change from a type C (homogeneous) to a type B (partially mixed) estuary (Schubel, 1971b).

According to theory, shoaling can be expected to be most severe at the limits of saltwater intrusion on the left side of an estuary. Studies of the Thames in England have shown that there is an upstream movement of sediments on the left side and a flux of sediments on the right side. Simmons (1966) states that in this type of estuary, available field evidence indicates that shoals generally form in regions of excessive cross section adjacent to islands and channel bifurcation.

Laterally Homogeneous. A laterally homogeneous estuary is homogeneous horizontally and has a longitudinal salinity gradient. It may be vertically homogeneous or vertically stratified. Schubel (1971b) questioned whether a truly sectional homogeneous estuary exists. Dyer (1973) stated that if the width is small and the lateral shear is sufficient to create laterally homogeneous conditions, such an estuary might exist. The salinity would increase evenly toward the mouth, and the mean flow throughout the cross section would be seaward. This would tend to drive salt water out of the estuary except for an upstream turbulent exchange of salt associated with tidal flow.

Various estuarine conditions may exist in the same estuary under varying flow and tidal prism conditions. Pritchard (1955) points out that estuarine depth and width are important factors in typing an estuary. For example, if the river flow and tidal range (prism) are kept constant and the estuarine width is increased, the ratio of tidal volume to river flow is changed. This produces an effect similar to a decrease in river flow, resulting in a more completely mixed estuary. Where tidal velocities are higher in constricted sections of estuaries, the estuary tends to be well mixed, whereas in wider sections it becomes more stratified. For example, in the region where the Hudson River empties into New York Harbor, the abrupt widening causes the estuary to shift from a well-mixed to a partially mixed estuary. In such estuaries one would expect shoaling if the slow net seaward flow were interrupted by tributaries or obstacles (Schubel, 1971b; Dyer, 1973).

BASIC PRINCIPLES OF CIRCULATION AND MIXING

The circulation and mixing of water of various densities in estuaries are accomplished principally by freshwater flow from riverine sources and unchannelized land runoff; by advection caused by tides, wind, and unusual atmospheric conditions such as hurricanes; and by diffusion. Bowden (1967) has formulated equations to express the basic principles controlling circulation and mixing. These are expressed by equations of motion of water, continuity of volume of water, and mass of salt.

Consider a horizontal plane with the Ox axis being along the axis of the estuary; the Oy, the axis across the estuary. Add to this the Oz axis, which is vertical downward. "Let u, v, w be the components of mean velocity at the point (x, y, z) at time t. Then the equations of motion may be written

$$\frac{Du}{Dt} - fv = -a\left(\frac{\partial p}{\partial x} + \frac{\partial \tau_{xx}}{\partial x} + \frac{\partial \tau_{yx}}{\partial y} + \frac{\partial \tau_{zx}}{\partial z}\right) \tag{4}$$

$$\frac{Dv}{Dt} + fu = -a\left(\frac{\partial p}{\partial y} + \frac{\partial \tau_{xy}}{\partial x} + \frac{\partial \tau_{yy}}{\partial y} + \frac{\partial \tau_{zy}}{\partial z}\right) \tag{5}$$

$$0 = -a\frac{\partial p}{\partial z} + g, \tag{6}$$

where

$$\frac{D}{Dt} = \frac{\partial}{\partial t} + \left[u\left(\frac{\partial}{\partial x}\right)\right] + \left[v\left(\frac{\partial}{\partial y}\right)\right] + \left[w\left(\frac{\partial}{\partial z}\right)\right]$$

$f = 2w \sin \phi$ is the Coriolis parameter

$p =$ pressure

a = specific volume ($a = 1/\rho$ where ρ is the density

g = acceleration due to gravity

τ_{xy} = stress on a plane perpendicular to Ox acting in an Oy direction

"In these equations the stress components τ_{xy}, etc., are nearly always the result of turbulent stresses since, except very near the boundaries, the stresses due to molecular viscosity are several orders of magnitude smaller.

"Then, if u', v', w' are the components of turbulent velocity at any instant, $\tau_{xx} = p(u'^2)\tau_{xy} = (\langle u'v' \rangle)$, etc. where $\langle\ \rangle$ denotes an average over the time taken to compute the mean velocity. The remaining Coriolis terms and the vertical acceleration may be shown to be negligible and have been omitted.

"The continuity of volume equation

$$\frac{\partial u}{\partial x} + \frac{\partial v}{\partial y} + \frac{\partial w}{\partial z} = 0 \tag{7}$$

"The equation of salt conservation may be written

$$\frac{Ds}{Dt} = \frac{\partial}{\partial x}\left(K_x \frac{\partial S}{\partial x}\right) + \frac{\partial}{\partial y}\left(K_y \frac{\partial s}{\partial y}\right) + \frac{\partial}{\partial z}\left(K_z \frac{\partial s}{\partial z}\right) \tag{8}$$

$K_x, K_y,$ and K_z are coefficients of eddy diffusion in the x, y, z directions, respectively. The molecular diffusivity can nearly always be neglected as in the case of viscosity (Bowden, 1967).

"It is often assumed in an estuary that transverse velocities are very small compared with those along the estuary so that the terms involving v in the above equation may be neglected.

"From equation (6), the hydrostatic equation, the pressure at z depth is given by

$$p = P_a + g \int_{-\zeta}^{z} p\, dz \tag{9}$$

P_a = atmospheric pressure

ζ = elevation of the free surface above the level surface taken as reference

"If P_a is uniform, then

$$\frac{\partial p}{\partial x} = gP_s \frac{\partial \zeta}{\partial x} + g \int_0^z \frac{\partial p}{\partial x}\, dz \tag{10}$$

P_S = density at the surface.

"There is a similar equation for $\partial p/\partial y$.

"The density of p_s is a function of salinity S, temperature θ and pressure P:

$$\rho = p(S_1 \Theta_1 P) \tag{11}$$

In an estuary the variation of ρ (density) with P (pressure) may be neglected, and very often the dependence on Q is of little importance compared with that of S. In this case it is sufficient to take ρ (density) as being a linear function of S (salinity), that is,

$$\rho = p_0 + aS \tag{12}$$

where a is a constant.

"The complete solution of the estuarine circulation problem would involve solving equations (4) through (8) with (10) and (11) or (12). The velocity components depend on the pressure gradients which are a function of density distribution. The density is a function of salinity and the distribution of salinity depends on the velocities, thus completing the system" (Bowden, 1967).

Various workers have recognized the difficulty of quantitatively estimating the circulation and mixing patterns of estuaries (Bowden, 1967; Pritchard, 1967b; Dyer, 1977). Pearson and Winter (1977) computed the tidal flow in homogeneous estuaries with irregular boundary configurations and arbitrary depth. Pritchard (1954, 1955, 1956), Hansen (1967), and Abood and Bourodimos (1976) formulated equations for salt balance and circulation in partially mixed estuaries. Rattray (1967) presented equations for estimating the dynamics of circulation in fjords. Virta (1977) developed equations for estimating salt budgets of a stratified estuary. Long (1976) gave equations for estimating fluxes of brackish and ocean water out of and into an estuary as well as for the depth of the halocline. Numerical models have been developed for estuarine circulation (Blumberg, 1977) and for stratified estuarine flows (Hodgins et al., 1977). Elliott and Reid (1976) developed a model for bar-built estuaries such as those found on the Gulf coast.

Various writers have pointed out the great difficulty of real-world information or predictions from many of the equations and models that have been developed. Bowden (1967) said that most of the studies of the large changes that occur in river discharges and the resulting changes in estuaries have been made considering a series of steady states rather than a continuous changing state. This is because studies have been made at various intervals rather than as a continuous record of conditions. In some estuaries the large seasonal variation in river flow results in different patterns of salinity. Temperature changes due to varying heat budgets may produce significant effects; for example, the increased temperature in surface layers during the summer months may reduce vertical mixing because of increased stratification. Increased river flow tends to produce greater vertical gradients of density, which lead to intense vertical mixing and more horizontal mixing than would be expected from the horizontal salinity gradient. These processes result in a change in the volume of water accumulated in the estuary.

An adequate method of dealing with the variable state is one of the problems of describing estuarine circulation accurately.

INDICES AND EQUATIONS FOR CLASSIFYING ESTUARIES BY WATER MIXING

Schubel (1971b) gave the simplest mixing index (MI) in an estuary, but as Dyer (1973) pointed out, this type of index is not always applicable.

Mixing index (MI) = volume of freshwater entering during $\frac{1}{2}$ tidal period

In a highly stratified estuary, MI $\geqslant$ 1. In a partially mixed estuary, MI $\ll$ 1. (In the Chesapeake Bay of Maryland it is $\frac{1}{25}$; in the Savannah River estuary of Georgia, $\frac{1}{10}$.) In a vertically homogeneous estuary, MI $\lll$ 1.

Pritchard (1955), Pritchard and Carter (1971) classified estuaries based on the advection–diffusion equation for the salt, also called the balance equation.

$$\frac{\partial s}{\partial t} = -u\frac{\partial s}{\partial x} - v\frac{\partial s}{\partial y} - w\frac{\partial s}{\partial z} + \frac{\partial}{\partial x}\left(K_x\frac{\partial s}{\partial x}\right) + \frac{\partial}{\partial y}\left(K_y\frac{\partial s}{\partial y}\right) + \frac{\partial}{\partial z}\left(K_z\frac{\partial s}{\partial z}\right) \quad (13)$$

$$\frac{\partial s}{\partial t} = \text{local time of change of salinity} \quad (14)$$

$$-u\frac{\partial s}{\partial x} - v\frac{\partial s}{\partial y} - w\frac{\partial s}{\partial z} = \text{advection of salt} \quad (15)$$

$$\frac{\partial}{\partial x}\left(K_x\frac{\partial s}{\partial x}\right) + \frac{\partial}{\partial y}\left(K_y\frac{\partial s}{\partial y}\right) + \frac{\partial}{\partial z}\left(K_z\frac{\partial s}{\partial z}\right) = \text{diffusion of salt} \quad (16)$$

and where s is the concentration of salt; u, v, w the component velocities; and K_x, K_y, K_z the diffusivities in the axial direction.

Ippen and Harleman (1961) and Dyer (1973) developed a stratification number that increases as mixing increases and becomes lower as stratification increases. The stratification number is developed as follows:

$$\tan \sigma = -\tan kx \tan h\mu x \quad (17)$$

where $\tan \sigma_t^H$ = time of high water relative to high water at estuary head
$k = 2\pi/\lambda$
k = wave number
λ = wavelength of tidal wave
x = longitudinal distance from head of estuary
h = estuary depth
μ = damping coefficient $(\phi/2\pi)k$
ϕ = dissipation constant

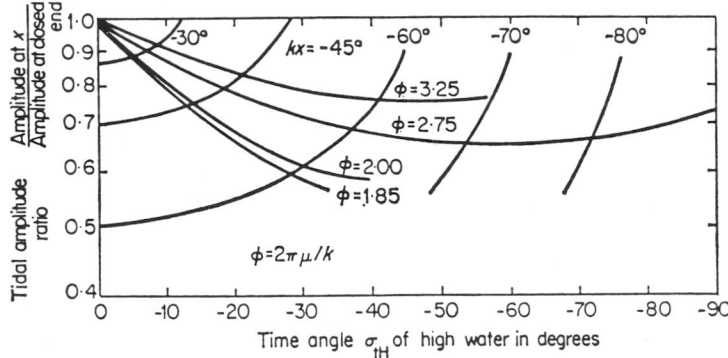

FIGURE 2.5. Nomogram for determination of μ and k from tidal amplitudes and time of high water. (From Dyer, 1973.)

The rate of transport of tidal energy (Px) across any section (Dyer, 1973)

$$Px = -cbg\rho A_0^2 \sin h\, 2\mu x \qquad (18)$$

$c = 2\pi/Tk$
T = tidal period
b = the breadth
ρ = water density
A_0 = tidal amplitude at the estuary head

For a standing wave without any progressive component $\mu = 0$.

Total energy flux = 0

Rate of energy dissipation between x_1 and x_2 (a portion of the channel) is $Px_1 - Px_2$ and the rate of energy dissipation per unit mass of water

$$G = (Px_1 - Px_2/\rho bh(x_1 - x_2) \qquad (19)$$

as a water unit of mass moves toward the sea, the rate of gain of potential energy per unit mass over the entire length of the estuary L is

$$J = g\left(\frac{\Delta\rho}{P}\right)hu_f/L$$

$\Delta\rho$ = density difference between fresh and ocean water
μ_f = mean density of fresh water over L
L = length of the estuary

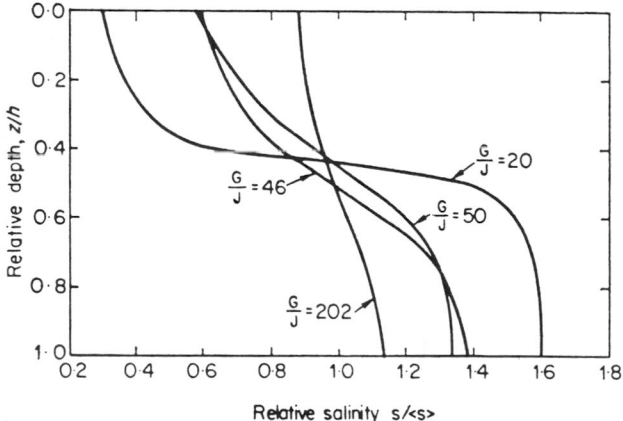

Relative salinity s/<s>

FIGURE 2.6. Vertical salinity gradients in relation to stratification number, G/J, derived from model experiments. The relative depth, z/h, is the ratio of depth in the profile, z, to the total depth of the estuary at that point, h. Relative salinity, $s/\langle s \rangle$, is the ratio of the salinity at a given depth, s, to the depth mean salinity, $\langle s \rangle$. (From Dyer, 1973.)

For a given estuary J is only effected by variation in the river discharge.

G = amount of energy dissipated from tide that can mix with water or be liberated as heat.

G/J = stratification number—a measure of the amount of energy lost by the tidal wave relative to that used in mixing the water column.

Figure 2.6 gives the vertical salinity gradient in relation to the stratification number (Dyer, 1973).

Hansen and Rattray (1966) developed a stratification–circulation diagram. They used two dimensionless parameters, a circulation parameter and a stratification parameter:

u_s/u_f = ratio of net surface current to mean cross-sectional velocity   (20)

where u_s = longitudinal time/mean velocity at the surface $z = 0$

u_f = integral mean velocity

R = (cross-sectional area of estuary) river discharge rate

and

$$\partial S/S_0 \qquad (21)$$

where ∂S = ratio of the difference of top to bottom salinity

S_0 = cross-sectional mean salinity

In Figure 2.7 the proposed classification for several estuaries is illustrated.

Type 1   The net flow is seaward at all depths and the upstream salt transport is by diffusion. Type 1a has slight stratification and coincides with the

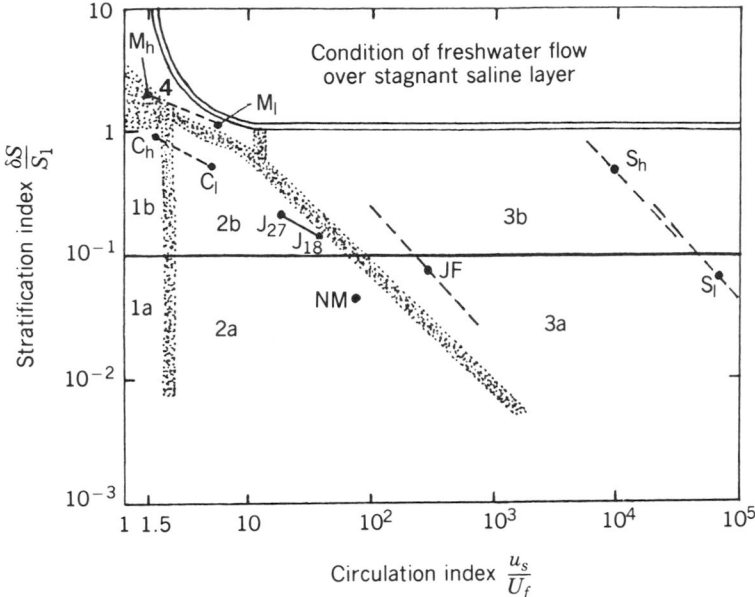

FIGURE 2.7. Estuary classification diagram, with examples. Station code: M, Mississippi River mouth; C, Columbia River estuary; J, James River estuary; NM, Narrows of the Mersey estuary; JF, Strait of Juan de Fuca; S, Silver Bay. Subscripts h and l refer to high and low river discharge, respectively. Numbers on James River plot indicate kilometers from the mouth. Notation and estuary types are explained in the text. (After Hansen and Rattray, 1966.)

laterally homogeneous well-mixed estuary. In type 1b there is appreciable stratification.

Type 2   The flow reverses at depth and corresponds to a partially mixed estuary. Both advection and diffusion contribute to the upstream salt flux.

Type 3   The salt transfer is primarily advective, with a small amount of diffusion. Type 3a are estuaries that are comparatively well mixed. In type 3b circulation does not extend to the bottom (as in fjords).

Type 4   The stratification is of the intense, salt wedge type (Dyer, 1973).

CLASSIFICATION OF ESTUARIES BY ENERGY INPUT

Odum and Copeland (1972) developed an ecological clasification of coastal ecosystems that has as one of its most important bases the type of energy input to the system (Table 2.1). They recognized light, organic fuels, and mechanical energy as being generally dominant in coastal systems. Light energy drives photosynthesis of plants and supports the food chains that support biological populations. Organic fuels serve as food for bacteria and higher animals. Some of these organic fuels, carried by rivers as organic load, are wastes from human energy systems; others are entirely natural, such as organic matter from swamps

TABLE 2.1.　*Classification of Coastal Ecological Systems and Subsystems According to Characteristic Energy Sources*

Category	Type	Characteristic Energy Source or Stress
		High-stress energies
A. Naturally stressed systems of wide latitudinal range	1. Rocky sea fronts and intertidal rocks	Breaking waves
	2. High-energy beaches	Breaking waves
	3. High-velocity surfaces	Strong tidal currents
	4. Oscillating temperature channels	Shocks of extreme temperature range
	5. Sedimentary deltas	High rate of sedimentation
	6. Hypersaline lagoons	Briny salinities
	7. Blue-green algal mats	Temperature variation and low nighttime oxygen
		Light and little stress
B. Natural tropical ecosystems of high diversity	1. Mangroves	Light and tide
	2. Coral reefs	Light and current
	3. Tropical meadows	Light and current
	4. Tropical inshore plankton	Organic supplements
	5. Blue water coasts	Light and low nutrient
		Sharp seasonal programming and migrant stocks
C. Natural temperate ecosystems with seasonal programming	1. Tide pools	Spray in rocks, winter cold
	2. Bird and mammal islands	Bird and mammal colonies
	3. Land-locked seawaters	Little tide, migrations
	4. Marshes	Lightly tidal regimes and winter cold
	5. Oyster reefs	Current and tide
	6. Worm and clam flats	Waves and current, intermittent flow
	7. Benthic vegetation (eelgrass and benthic algal bottoms)	Light and current
	8. Olighaline systems	Saltwater shock zone, winter cold
	9. Medium salinity plankton estuary	Mixing intermediate salinities with some stratification
	10. Sheltered and stratified estuary	Geomorphological isolation by sill
	11. Kelp beds	Swells, light, and high salinity
	12. Neutral embayment and shore waters	Shelf waters at the shore
		Winter ice, sharp migrations, and seasonal programming

Continued

TABLE 2.1.   (*Continued*)

Category	Type	Characteristic Energy Source or Stress
D. Natural arctic ecosystems with ice stress	1. Glacial fjord	Icebergs
	2. Turbidity outwash fjord	Outflow of turbid ice-water lens
	3. Ice stressed intertidal zones	Winter exposure to freezing
	4. Sea ice	Ice, low light
	5. Under-ice plankton	Low light
		New but characteristic man-made energy sources and/or stresses
E. Emerging new systems associated with humans	1. Sewage waste	Organic and inorganic enrichment
	2. Seafood wastes	Organic and inorganic enrichment
	3. Pesticides	An organic poison
	4. Dredging spoil	Heavy sedimentation by humans
	5. Impoundment	Blocking of current
	6. Thermal pollution	High and variable temperature discharges
	7. Paper mills waste	Wastes of wood processing
	8. Sugarcane waste	Organics, fibers, soils of sugar industry wastes
	9. Phosphate wastes	Wastes of phosphate mining
	10. Acid waters	Release or generation of low pH
	11. Oil shores	Petroleum spills
	12. Pilings	Treated wood substrates
	13. Salina	Brine complex of salt manufacture
	14. Brine pollution	Stress of high salt wastes and odd element ratios
	15. Petrochemicals	Refinery and petrochemical manufacturing wastes
	16. Radioactive stress	Radioactivity
	17. Multiple stress	Alternating stress of many kinds of wastes in drifting patches
	18. Artificial reef	Strong currents
F. Migrating subsystems that organize areas		Some energies taxed from each system

Source: Odum and Copeland (1972), Table 1, pp. 26–27.

or mangrove coasts or from fields and forests through which the river passes. Mechanical energy is the absorption of fluid momentum of the winds, waves, and tides and is another environmental source of energy that is responsible for many phenomena of the system. A beach, for example, receives the pounding of incoming waves that dominate the system. Sedimentation, the organismal adaptations, and the chemical phenomena are all determined by and coupled to mechanical energy sources.

Tides

Ocean tides are one of the most important energy sources influencing the waters of estuaries. Tides influence not only the current structure but also the chemical characteristics of the water. These factors, in turn, greatly affect the structure of aquatic communities which one finds in various parts of the estuary. The range of the tides and the degree to which salt water penetrates an estuary are two of the most important factors affecting aquatic life.

Tidal Ranges. Table 2.2 lists the mean range and highest and lowest tides for a number of locations on the Atlantic coast. The mean range is the difference in height between the mean high water and the mean low water. Heights for highest tides are above the local datum of mean high water, while heights for lowest tides are below the local datum of mean low water. The average yearly highest and lowest tides represent the mean of the highest tide of each year and the mean of the lowest tide of each year, covered by a series of observations (Disney, 1955). From Table 2.2 it is apparent that on the Atlantic coast the average yearly highest tide varies from 1.5 to 4 ft (0.46 to 1.22 m) above the mean high water, whereas the average yearly lowest tide varies from 1 to 3.7 ft (0.3 to 1.13 m) below mean low water. In places such as Key West, Florida, where the movement of water is largely unrestricted, the heights are not materially affected by storms. In contrast, in areas with hydrological characteristics such as those at Providence, Rhode Island, very high water levels may be encountered.

The range between the average yearly highest tide and the average yearly lowest tide for each location in Table 2.2 may readily be obtained by adding the heights of the average yearly highest and lowest tides to the mean range for each location. For example, at Eastport, Maine, this range is $4 + 3.7 + 18.2 = 25.9$ ft $(1.22 + 1.13 + 5.55 = 7.9$ m).

The extreme low water levels at the various places do not show the wide variation displayed between extreme high water levels. The lowest tide recorded along the Atlantic coast occurred at Philadelphia, the height being 5.1 ft (1.55 m) below mean low water. Along other sections of the coast the extreme low water varied from this value to 1.4 ft (0.43 m) in the Miami–Key West, Florida, area.

On the Pacific coast of the United States the datum of sounding for nautical charts is mean lower low tide (MLLT). This datum is used because of the large diurnal inequalities in the tides, particularly in the low waters around the days of maximum north and south declination of the moon. The practical importance of this characteristic is indicated by the fact that at Seattle, Washington, on

TABLE 2.2. *Mean Range and Highest and Lowest Tides: Atlantic Coast*

| Place | Series | Mean Range (ft) | Highest Tides (ft) Above Mean High Water | | | Lowest Tides (ft) Below Mean Low Water | | |
| | | | Average Yearly Highest | Extreme High | | Average Yearly Lowest | Extreme Low | |
				Height	Date		Height	Date
Eastport, Me.	1930–1953	18.2	4.0	5.0	Nov. 20, 1945	3.7	4.2	Jan. 7, 1943
Portland, Me.	1912–1953	8.9	3.0	4.3	11/30/44, 11/20/45	2.6	3.2	10/8/15, 4/3/23, 1/7/43
Portsmouth, N.H.	1927–1953	8.1	2.9	3.9	Nov. 30, 1944	2.4	2.8	Mar. 14, 1930
Boston, Mass.	1922–1953	9.5	3.1	4.3	Apr. 21, 1940	2.8	3.5	1/25/28, 3/24/40
Woods Hole, Mass.	1933–1953	1.8	2.8	7.8	Sept. 21, 1938	1.8	2.5	Jan. 24, 1936
Newport, R.I.	1931–1953	3.5	2.9	10.3	Sept. 21, 1938	1.9	2.6	Jan. 25, 1936
Providence, R.I.	1938–1947	4.6	3.3	15.6	Sept. 21, 1938	2.4	3.0	May 11, 1945
New London, Conn.	1938–1953	2.6	3.5	8.5	Sept. 21, 1938	1.9	3.0	Dec. 11, 1943
Willets Point, N.Y.	1932–1953	7.2	4.0	9.9	Sept. 21, 1938	2.9	3.8	Mar. 24, 1940
Fort Hamilton, N.Y.	1893–1932	4.7	2.8	4.0	2/5/20, 11/10/32	3.0	4.1	Feb. 2, 1908
New York (Battery), N.Y.	1920–1953	4.4	3.1	5.5	Nov. 7, 1953	2.8	3.8	Mar. 8, 1932
Sandy Hook, N.J.	1933–1953	4.6	3.1	5.6	Nov. 7, 1953	2.7	3.7	Jan. 24, 1936
Atlantic City, N.J.	1912–1920, 1923–1953	4.1	2.9	5.4	Sept. 14, 1944	2.6	3.5	Mar. 8, 1932
Philadelphia, Pa.	1900–1920, 1922–1953	5.8	2.4	4.8	Nov. 25, 1950	3.0	5.1	Jan. 25, 1945
Baltimore, Md.	1902–1953	1.1	2.7	7.2	Aug. 23, 1933	2.9	4.5	Jan. 24, 1908
Washington, D.C.	1931–1953	2.9	3.1	8.6	Oct. 17, 1942	2.7	3.4	2/15/40, 3/1/49
Norfolk (Sewell Pt.), Va.	1928–1953	2.5	2.8	6.3	Aug. 23, 1933	1.8	2.7	Jan. 23, 26, 1928
Southport, N.C.	1933–1953	4.1	2.4	3.4	Nov. 2, 1947	1.2	1.9	June 28, 1934
Charleston, S.C.	1922–1953	5.1	2.6	5.6	Aug. 11, 1940	2.1	2.8	Feb. 15, 1953
Fort Pulaksi, Ga.	1936–1953	6.9	2.8	4.5	Oct. 15, 1947	2.7	4.1	Mar. 20, 1936
Fernandina, Fla.	1897–1924, 1939–1953	6.1	2.7	7.8	Oct. 2, 1898	2.4	3.7	Jan. 24, 1940
Miami Beach, Fla.	1931–1951	2.5	1.9	3.9	Oct. 18, 1950	1.1	1.4	Mar. 24, 1936
Key West, Fla.	1926–1953	1.3	1.5	2.6	Oct. 18, 1944	1.0	1.4	Feb. 19, 1928
Cedar Key, Fla.	1914–1925, 1939–1953	2.5	2.5	3.5	Feb. 15, 1953	2.6	4.6	Sept. 18, 1947
Pensacola, Fla.	1923–1953	1.3	1.8	7.8	Sept. 20, 1926	1.3	2.0	Jan. 6, 1924
Galveston, Texas	1908–1953	1.0	2.8	10.1	Aug. 16–17, 1915	2.3	4.9	Jan. 11, 1908

Source: From Tide heights along the coasts of the United States, L. P. Disney, Proceedings of the American Society of Civil Engineers, no. 81, 1955. Reproduced by permission of ASCE.

26

TABLE 2.3. Diurnal Range and Highest and Lowest and Tides: Pacific Coast

Place	Series	Diurnal Range (ft)	Highest Tides (ft) Above Mean Higher High Water			Lowest Tides (ft) Below Mean Lower Low Water		
			Average Yearly Highest	Extreme High Height	Extreme High Date	Average Yearly Lowest	Extreme Low Height	Extreme Low Date
San Diego, Calif.	1906–1953	5.8	1.9	2.5	Dec. 17, 18, 1914	1.9	2.6	Dec. 17, 1933
La Jolla, Calif.	1925–1953	5.2	1.9	2.3	Dec. 17, 1952	1.9	2.5	Dec. 17, 1933
Los Angeles, Calif.	1924–1953	5.4	1.9	2.2	Jan. 25–26, 1948	1.9	2.6	12/26/32, 12/17/33
Santa Monica, Calif.	1933–1953	5.4	2.0	2.3	12/27/36, 7/17/51	1.7	2.5	Dec. 17, 1933
San Francisco, Calif.	1898–1953	5.7	1.7	2.5	Dec. 24, 1940	1.9	2.5	12/26/32, 12/17/33
Crescent City, Calif.	1933–1953	6.9	2.5	3.1	Dec. 29, 1951	2.3	2.5	5/12/33, 5/4/50
Astoria, Oreg.	1925–1953	8.2	2.7	3.9	Dec. 17, 1933	1.9	2.8	Jan. 16, 1930
Neah Bay, Wash.	1935–1953	8.2	2.8	4.0	Nov. 30, 1951	3.0	3.6	Nov. 29, 1936
Seattle, Wash.	1899–1953	11.3	2.3	3.4	Feb. 6, 1904	3.9	4.6	Jan. 4, 1916
Friday Harbor, Wash.	1934–1953	7.7	2.4	3.3	Dec. 30, 1952	3.2	3.9	Jan. 7, 1947
Alaska								
Ketchikan	1918–1953	15.4	4.4	5.4	Nov. 2, 1948	4.5	5.2	Dec. 8, 1919
Juneau	1936–1941, 1944–1953	16.6	4.1	5.2	Nov. 2, 1948	5.1	5.9	Dec. 29, 1951
Skagway	1945–1953	16.9	4.5	5.8	Oct. 22, 1945	5.4	6.1	Dec. 28–29, 1951
Sitka	1938–1953	9.9	3.3	4.5	Nov. 2, 1948	3.3	4.0	June 19, 1951
Yakatut	1940–1953	10.0	3.5	4.5	Nov. 2, 1948	3.4	4.3	Dec. 29, 1951
Seward	1925–1938	10.5	3.4	4.1	Oct. 13, 1927	3.6	4.3	Jan. 14, 1930
Anchorage	1918, 1922–1925	29.6	4.5	5.8	Oct. 12, 1923	4.3	4.9	June 19, 1924
Dutch Harbor, Unalaska I.	1934–1939, 1946–1953	3.7	2.0	2.9	Jan. 14–15, 1938	2.0	2.7	Nov. 13, 1950
Sweeper Cove, Adak I.	1943–1953	3.7	2.2	2.6	Jan. 5–6, 1951	2.2	2.9	Nov. 11, 1950
Massacre Bay, Attu I.	1943–1953	3.3	1.5	1.9	Jan. 27, 1949	1.8	2.5	Nov. 12–13, 1950

Source: From Tide heights along the coasts of the United States, L. P. Disney, Proceedings of the American Society of Civil Engineers, no. 81, 1955. Reproduced by permission of ASCE.

certain days one low water level of the day may be 10 ft (3.3 m) lower than the other low water level. On the Pacific coast, therefore, mean high or high water, mean low or low water, and the range between these two levels has specific significance. The difference in height between the mean higher high water and the mean lower low water is known as the diurnal range. Table 2.3 gives the diurnal range and the highest and lowest tides for a number of locations on the Pacific coast. The heights of the highest tides are above the local datum of mean higher high water, while the heights for the lowest tides are below the local datum of mean lower low water. The average yearly highest and lowest tides represent the mean of the highest tides of each year and the mean of the lowest tides of each year covered by a series of observations (Disney, 1955).

The table shows that along the Pacific coast of the continental United States (exclusive of Alaska) the average yearly highest tide varies from 1.7 to 2.8 ft (0.5 to 0.85 m) above the mean of the higher high water, while the average yearly lowest tide varies from 1.7 to 3.9 ft (0.5 to 1.19 m) below the mean of the lower low water. For Alaska, the average yearly highest tide varies from 1.5 to 4.5 ft (0.46 to 1.37 m) above the mean of the higher high water and the average yearly lowest tide varies from 1.8 to 5.4 ft (0.55 to 1.65 m) below the mean of the lower low water. Comparison of Tables 2.2 and 2.3 shows that the storm effects on water levels on the Atlantic coast are substantially greater than they are on the Pacific coast (Disney, 1955).

Yearly Variation in Sea Level.   Considerable interest has been evidenced in recent years in the slow changes taking place in the relation of land and sea. An example of determinations of the trends in the relative elevations of land and sea along the coast of the United States is shown in Figures 2.8 through 2.10. These figures present the yearly variation in sea level and the changes for a number of places. The change for each place is indicated by the heavy straight line, which was computed by the method of least squares. A long series of observations on the Pacific and Atlantic coasts indicates a rise of 0.005 ft (0.152 cm) per year on the Pacific coast, which is about half that on the Atlantic coast (Disney, 1955).

Winds

Wind may be an important force in the movement and mixing of water in an estuary. In the Chesapeake Bay, the lower layer of water may respond as a barotropic counterflow to the upper layer flow, which is driven directly by wind. Because the bay is so long, surface movement set up by longitudinal wind stress may appreciably lag the water stress. The response to this pressure gradient occurs first near the bottom of the estuary and progresses upward. Viera (1986) and Pritchard and Viera (1984) believe that this upward phase propagation is caused by a gradually increasing dominance of the surface slope-driven barotropic flow over the direct effect of the wind stress from above.

Further work is needed to determine the dependence of response of the surface and internal wave speed. It is believed that cases may occur where the internal

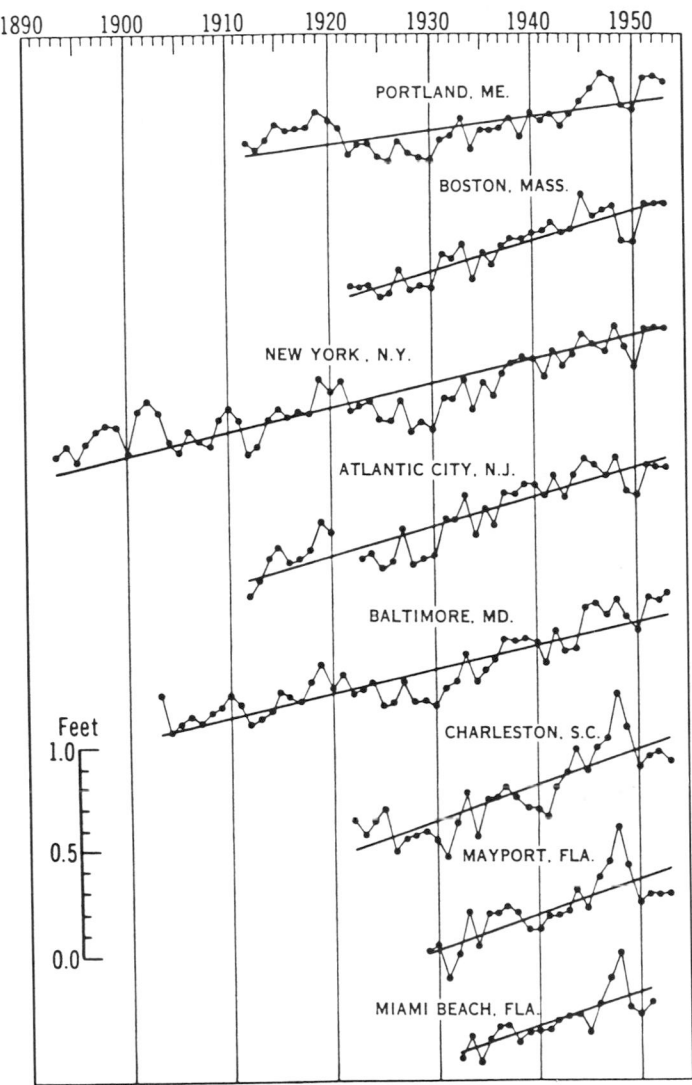

FIGURE 2.8. Variation in sea level, Atlantic coast. (From Tide heights along the coasts of the United States, L. P. Disney, Proceedings of the American Society of Civil Engineers, no. 81, 1955. Reproduced by permission of ASCE.)

phase speed is sufficiently fast and the channel length is sufficiently short to allow a baroclineic response to the longitudinal wind stress (Boicourt, in press).

Stress caused by wind may also excite other modes of motion. Subtidal oscillations in the Chesapeake Bay were found to occur with periods less than 4 days of wind-induced seiche (Wang, 1979). As to the origin of the 2-day oscillations, Chuang and Boicourt (1989) found a burst of seiche activities in the Chesapeake in April 1986. They suggested that this quarter-wave seiche was almost in

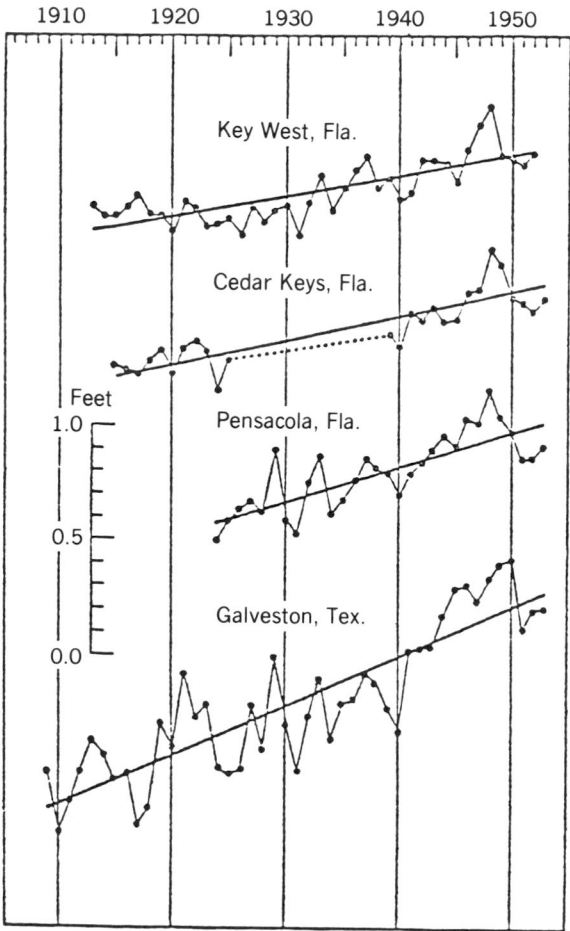

FIGURE 2.9. Variation in sea level, Gulf coast. (From Tide heights along the coasts of the United States, L. P. Disney, Proceedings of the American Society of Civil Engineers, no. 81, 1955. Reproduced by permission of ASCE.)

resonance and was forced by winds over the lower fourth of the bay. Another interpretation could be that the seiche was more a damped force oscillation with strong forcing rather than a free oscillation resonance phenomenon. Regardless of the solution to this question, in large areas such as the Chesapeake, the quarter-wave seiche seems to be a primary mode of variability in the water movement.

At any season the kinetic-energy spectra show a peak near the free-oscillation period. This mode of motion may be a significant additional contribution to

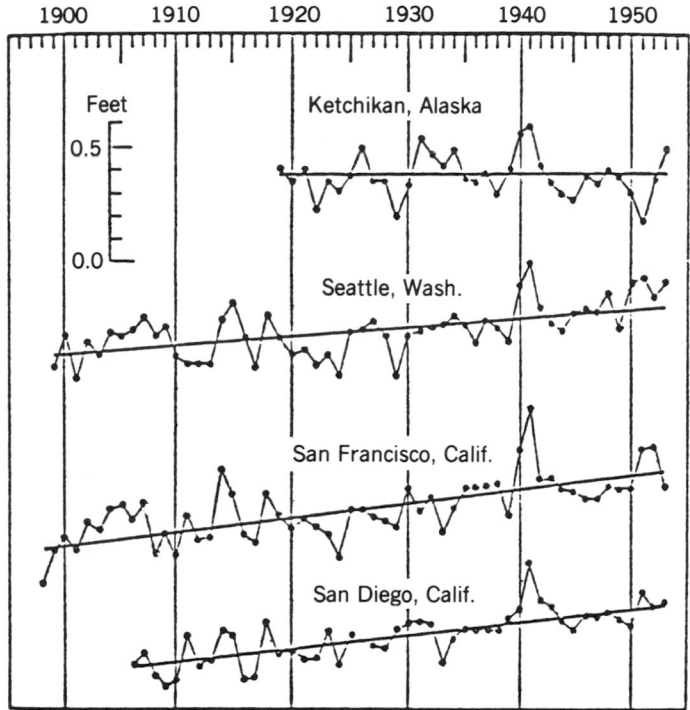

FIGURE 2.10. Variation in sea level, Pacific coast. (From Tide heights along the coasts of the United States, L. P. Disney, Proceedings of the American Society of Civil Engineers, no. 81, 1955. Reproduced by permission of ASCE.)

estuary-shelf exchange, supplementing the exchange by gravitational circulation and the tides (Goodrich, 1988).

Wind mixing seems to be on the same order of magnitude as that produced by tidal interactions with the bottom topography. In fjords and coastal plain estuaries, it seems to reduce stratification. A good example of wind mixing in estuaries was destratification of the Chesapeake Bay by cold air outbreaks within 2 days of the autumnal equinox (Goodrich et al., 1987). Large velocity shear preceded destratification events, suggesting a dynamic instability mechanism at the pycnocline for the primary mixing process. During high stratification the response is two-layered, but following destratification the upper and lower layers move in unison, with only a frictional fall-off with depth. The establishment of the details of transition between these two states needs to be studied (Boicourt, in press).

Of particular interest is the intertidal mixing process in the Frazier River, which is a salt wedge estuary (Geyer and Smith, 1987; Geyer and Farmer, 1988). Shear instabilities were found to occur during ebb tide, where water from both the upper and lower layers was entrained into the pycnocline. Destabilization was brought about by the combined mean velocity shear and shear due to internal waves. Internal wave shear was thought to be sufficiently constant within the zone of instability that an effective Richardson's number (0.33) derived only from mean velocity and density gradients worked well in predicting the instability threshold. Internal waves have been thought to play a critical role in the mixing of both salt wedge estuaries and partially mixed estuaries.

In Knight's Inlet, a fjord estuary, dramatically large-amplitude lee waves were observed at the entrance sill during both flood and ebb tides. Both lee waves and freely propagated internal waves have been identified in partially mixed estuaries (Dyer and New, 1986; Brandt et al., 1986; New et al., 1987; New and Dyer, 1988).

Internal Waves

There have been few quantitative assessments of the influence of internal waves on turbulence and mixing (Kranenburg, 1988; Jay and Smith, 1990). Abraham (1988) believes that during slack water the mixing processes are primarily internal, while for maximum tidal currents, the turbulence is external, emanating from tidal interactions with the boundaries. This breakdown probably does not apply to all estuarine types. Geyer and Farmer (1988) show that the shear instabilities are active throughout the ebb cycle in the Frazier estuary. In partially mixed estuaries, substantial differences occur in the intertidal variation and mixing processes between macrotidal estuaries such as the Columbia River and estuaries with a weaker tide, such as the Chesapeake Bay (Jay and Smith, 1990; Boicourt, in press).

In the Chesapeake Bay, internal tides are evidenced as lateral excursions of the pycnocline, possibly as near-resonant lateral seiches driven by the tide (Sanford et al., 1990; Boicourt, in press). Fortnightly variations in stratifications of the York River seem to involve special gradients in tidal mixing and phased advection in tributary main-stem interactions (Hayward et al., 1982; Ruzecki and Evans, 1988).

Gravity Currents

Gravity currents have been found to represent a high-frequency limit of gravitational circulation. For example, in the Frazier River, the flood-tide advance of the salt wedge is a gravity current whose progress is arrested on the ebb tide. In narrow estuaries with strong tidal currents, tidal intrusion fronts are set up by a balance on the flood tide between the gravity currents of the outflowing water and the entering tidal currents (Simpson and Nunes, 1981; Simpson and Turrell, 1986). In Puget Sound, during the fortnightly renewal process, high-salinity water propagates into the inner basin as a gravity current (Geyer and Cannon, 1982). In addition, wind can force breaches of entrance sills, where saline water propagates into estuaries or into tributaries protected by sills as a gravity current (Sanford and Boicourt, 1990).

The two-layer wind response set up gravity currents even in partially mixed estuaries. Recently, Armi and Farmer (1986) and Farmer and Armi (1986) have shown that a combination of geometry and stratification can produce hydraulic controls on flow and density structure, especially of the transition in channel depths or cross-sectional areas. Whereas hydraulic controls were thought to be solely a phenomenon of strongly stratified and fjord estuaries, Sanford and Boicourt (1990) have found that they are active in the Chesapeake Bay, a partially mixed estuary. Hydraulic controls may not only arrest the propagation of gravity current transits but also constrict the steady-state gravitational circulation (Boicourt, in press). It has been found that in well-mixed estuaries with strong tidal currents, sectionally driven secondary flows can create axial convergence (Nunes and Simpson, 1985; Simpson and Turrell, 1986).

Constriction in flow in a tidal inlet can change the tidal spectra considerably as the tide propagates through the inlet (Aubrey and Speer, 1985). Research concerning the exploration of residual currents arising from the interaction of the oscillary motion of tides with bottom topography has expanded in the past decade. Perhaps the simplest form of this interaction is the Stokes drift associated with an incoming progressive or partially progressive tidal wave. This component of motion is important in the balance for estuaries, for example in the Columbia River, which has a 3-m tidal range. Hansen's (1965) decomposition of salt and water transport of the Columbia showed that the Stokes drift term is a first-order contributor to the cross-sectional mean water flux. As Pritchard (1980) has explained, a longitudinal slope in the surface elevation is created by *Stokes drift*, which, in turn, drives an Eulerian seaward flow (Jay and Smith, 1988).

Stokes drifts associated with tidal elevation variations have been incorporated in the analyses of estuarine flow for some time. Only recently have Stokes drift and the Lagrangian residual currents resulting from "horizontal" gradients in velocity been incorporated in the theory and analyses of transport processes in an estuary. In estuaries with large tidal excursions and large topographic variability, these flows cannot be ignored for an accurate description of transport, which is an inherently Lagrangian process (Boicourt, in press).

The correct relationship may be expressed by the following equation:

Lagrangian residual current
= Eulerian mean velocity + Stokes drift velocity + Lagrangian
drift velocity (22)

Fronts

Fronts (tide lines) are ubiquitous features of the estuary environment. Until recently there has been little systematic or quantitative investigation of these structures. Part of the reason is the obvious observation difficulties. Fronts have small space scales and are often mobile and ephemeral, appearing only in a portion of the tidal cycle. Fronts represent a singularity of convergence and associated vertical transport, whose physical and ecological importance to the estuary as a whole has not yet been properly assessed (Boicourt, in press).

Recently, there has been accelerated research on the interaction of estuaries with the adjacent Continental Shelf. Estuary plumes often are a mechanism for rapid transport of chemicals to the ocean, short-circuiting the Continental Shelf. The buoyancy flux associated with these plumes increased stratification on the shelf, occasionally to the point where anoxic or hypoxic regions develop along the plume axis, as in the Mississippi River plume. For estuaries, fluctuations in Continental Shelf circulation can profoundly influence not only the character of the inflowing water but also estuarine circulation itself. Upwelling, storm surges, and Continental Shelf waves can produce significant variation in the boundary conditions at the entrance to the estuary. In addition, the portion of the outflowing water returning to the estuary is determined by circulation and mixing on the shelf. For the Continental Shelf, the buoyant outflowing water represents a set of discrete circulations, the most common of which is the upper-layer plume and associated coastal currents flowing in the direction of Kelvin wave propagation (Boicourt, 1980; in press).

These circulations appear only loosely coupled with ambient shelf circulation. In the lower layers the estuarine inflow may create a perturbation on the shelf circulation that can extend 20 to 30 km offshore (Boicourt, in press).

Estuarine plumes often create narrow coastal currents or "jets" that flow with little apparent coupling to the lower layer. However, on a larger scale and at some distance downstream from a point or distributed source of low salinity, these flows can coalesce to form a coastal current that spans the majority of the shelf width. The scale and dynamics of the transition between these local flows and large-scale buoyancy forcing, such as the 5000-km-long current terminating at Cape Hatteras, are highly uncertain (Boicourt, in press).

Strong fronts may be associated with the estuary plumes. They define lateral boundaries that may stretch on the order of 100 km from the plume source. Often, only the offshore boundary is marked for these fronts. In both the initial turning region and the coastal current, these fronts propagate seaward with approximately the internal wave phase speed. Such fronts are not only restricted to the Continental Shelf region. In partially mixed estuaries and fjords, tributary estuaries and rivers entering the main stem discharge water that is often lower salinity than the upper layer water of the receiving water body (Boicourt, in press).

Effects of Wind on Water Circulation.   Wind can produce a net transport of water because of the stress exerted on the surface. This transport of surface water is mainly in the direction of the wind. If the wind is blowing up the estuary, the seaward flow of water will be decreased or even reversed, depending on the strength of the wind. In deeper water, compensating currents occur. The waves generated by the wind will increase the intensity of vertical mixing, which may bring about a breakdown in the normal pattern of stratification (Bowden, 1967).

Examples of the effects of wind have been shown by Ketchum et al. (1951) in the New York Bight. They found intense mixing during storms, with normal circulation restored in about 2 days.

Pickard and Rodgers (1959) studied the effect of wind on Knights Inlet (Canada). Data were collected from the sill of this fjord, which lay at a depth of about 75 m, and from water of about 350 m in depth in the inner basin. The maximum tidal range was about 5 m. On the sill, the currents showed tidal oscillations at all depths, with the peaks midway between high and low flow; however, there were irregularities in current at all depths. The amplitude of currents at all depths was about 50 cm sec^{-1}. During the first 24 hours when the wind was light, an outward flow of water extended down to 40 m. Below 40 m the water flowed landward. When the up-inlet wind increased to 6 m^{-1} s^{-1}, there was a surface flow landward to a depth of 6 m and a seaward flow from 6 to 55 m. Below this, the flow was slightly up-inlet (Figure 2.11) (Dyer, 1973).

Weisberg (1976) studied the effects of wind on water velocity fluctuations in the partially mixed estuary of the Providence River, Rhode Island. He used as the basis of his study velocities recorded 2 m from the bottom over a period of 51 days with time scales between steady-state gravitational convection and tidal oscillations. He found that the mean speed along the channel axis was steady and landward at 11.7 cm s^{-1}. The total axial current variance was 166.9 cm s^{-1}; 48% resided in subtidal frequencies and 45% in semidiurnal tide. Over the most energetic portion of the axial current spectrum (4- to 5-day periodicities), 97% of the variance was coherent, with the wind velocity component lying along the direction of maximum fetch, with the current lagging the wind by about 4 hours. River runoff and atmospheric pressure were ineffective in exciting an axial current response; however, they should be important in extreme storm events. Along the wind-induced transport there occurred upwelling (or downwelling) capable of redistributing mass over the entire water column. Weisberg concluded that wind-induced motions can permeate the entire water column of a partially mixed estuary and can provide an equal, if not larger portion of the total circulation than tidal currents or gravitational convection (Weisberg, 1976).

Storms

Effects of Hurricanes on Sediment Transport.
Hurricanes frequently breach barrier islands and other shorelines where the vegetation is poorly developed, and there is an absence of well-developed fore-island dunes. Sand is readily transported across narrow barrier islands, whereas on broad barrier islands sand accumulates within a short distance of the bayward terminus of the storm channel and forms washout fans. These washout fans are typically composed of sand and finer sediments. The geologic history of an area and the type of

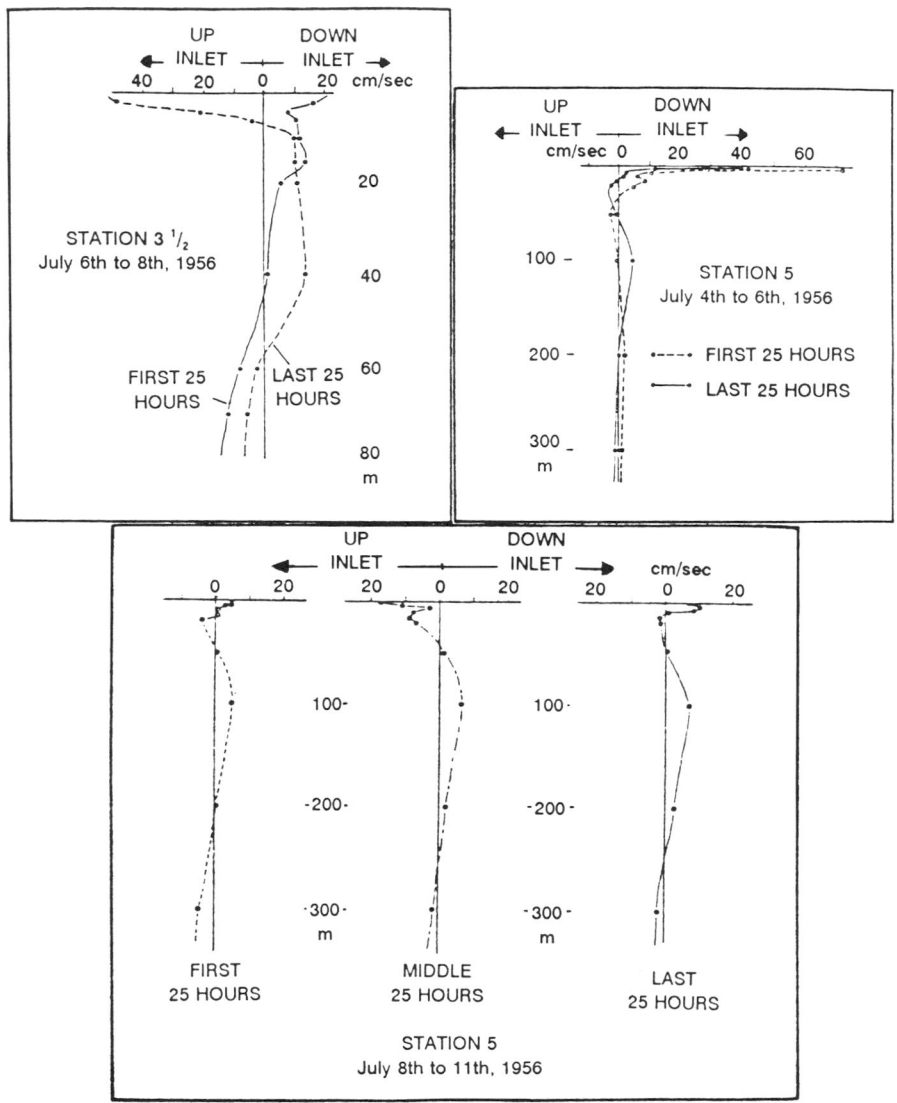

FIGURE 2.11.   Net current profiles for varying wind conditions in Knight Inlet, British Columbia. (From Pickard and Rodgers, 1959.)

sediments (shell or sand) affect the erodibility of these areas under the stress of hurricanes. The blowout of poorly vegetated dunes and the transport of sands greatly affect the amount of transport of sediments and their ultimate position. Subsequent erosion of beaches often takes place, and the scour of hurricanes frequently removes sediments and causes inlets or channels to be formed across the barrier islands (McGowan and Scott, 1975).

On the Texas coast where hurricanes are most frequent, the ability of these storms to erode barrier islands and transport sediments through breaches to bays and lagoons depends mostly on the density of the vegetation, the degree of fore-island dune development, and the width of the barrier island. For example, Hurricane Carla, with 10 to 11 ft (3 to 3.4 m) of storm surge in the Matagorda, Texas area cut a peninsula into numerous small islands separated by channels of scour widths to 1700 ft (518 m). The shoreline was cut back as much as 800 ft (244 m). Sediments scoured from the shelf, shore face, beach, and channel areas were carried across the peninsula and deposited in Matagorda Bay as much as half a mile (0.8 km) beyond the bay margin. These deposits are called washover deltas (Shepard and Wanless, 1971).

Hurricane Agnes, which occurred in June 1972, greatly affected the suspended solids in the northern Chesapeake area. Schubel (1974) found that the storm caused suspended solids to exceed 10,000 mg m^{-3}, and in a 1-week period the sediment discharge was greater than in the past several decades. The bulk of this sediment was deposited in the upper 40 km of the bay.

Effects of Hurricanes on Water Quantity and Quality. Flooding from hurricanes is usually abetted by a large amount of rain. This large quantity of fresh water reduces the salinity in an estuary. The salinity of Chesapeake Bay was decreased by 33% due to Hurricane Agnes. Salinity was reduced to less than 0.5 ppt from the surface to the bottom throughout the upper 60 km of the bay. The surface salinity was less than 1 ppt in the upper 125 km of the bay. The salinities remained low through most of the summer but recovered to nearly normal levels by September (Schubel, 1974).

The great decrease in salinity resulted in large oyster kills throuhout Chesapcake Bay. Oysters were particularly vulnerable because their normal development depends on an increase in salinity during the summer, not the drop in salinity provided by rains from Hurricane Agnes (June 1972). Academy of Natural Sciences studies (1974) in Chesapeake Bay before and after Hurricane Agnes clearly showed the effects of freshened water, and its chemical components, on the aquatic life.

As a result of the storm the salinity of bay waters dropped from averages of 10 to 12.6 ppt in June and 11.9 to 13.6 ppt in August (measured 1969 to 1971) to an average of 1.5 ppt in June and 7.3 ppt in August 1972. A bed of soft clams, *Mya arenaria*, disappeared from the area. The rooted aquatic plants also decreased. Productivity showed a huge drop and the number of species present in study areas decreased by 30%. These statistics validate the fact that species that were adapted to salinities of about 10 ppt would be eliminated. Species adapted to fresh and slightly brackish waters increased in population with the decrease in salinity (ANSP, 1974).

In barrier island estuaries, such as along the Gulf coast, a large tidal flow across barrier islands often results in much higher salinities in marshlands behind the barriers. If the more saline water is trapped for fairly long periods of time, severe damage may be inflicted on the vegetation and aquatic organisms. If standing water accumulates in areas as a result of hurricane action, anaerobic conditions may become severe due to increased deposition of organic matter, and the increased hydrogen sulfide may subsequently kill aquatic life (Schubel, 1974).

Effects of Hurricanes on Vegetation. The effects of hurricanes on vegetation along the Gulf coast have been recorded extensively for Hurricanes Audrey and Camille, although some data are also available concerning other hurricanes. The effect of Hurricane Audrey was to destroy the existing vegetation, which resulted in an open marsh. This was revegetated by annuals, which greatly increased in the area compared to conditions before the hurricane. Following this increase in annuals, the revegetation of other species began, and considerable restoration of the original conditions were noted in about a year.

Chabrek and Palmisano (1973) had made a study of the marshes of the Mississippi delta just before Hurricane Camille in 1969. A resurvey was made 2 weeks and again a year after the storm. Although the hurricane reduced vegetation drastically, after a year the plant coverage in the delta marshes approached the pre-hurricane levels of abundance. Recovery was slow in the ponds and lakes. The main vegetational damage was due to the uprooting and dismemberment of plants caused by the sweeping action of wind and water.

The effects of the increase of salinity on vegetation did not seem to be very important. *Bacopa monnieri* was virtually unaffected, and *Phragmites communis* and *Spartina alterniflora* were reduced only slightly. *Myriophyllum spicatum*, *Panicum repens*, and *Alternanthera philoxeroides* were severely reduced by the storm, and after one year only *Alternanthera* had shown significant recovery. The floating plants in the ponds and lakes seemed to be particularly vulnerable, as they were mostly washed out. The development of hydrogen sulfide due to organic decay did not seem to damage the vegetation, as recorded in Florida by Craighead and Gilbert (1962) [according to Chabreck and Palmisano (1973)].

Hurricane Donna in southern Florida caused the loss of woody plants, presumably as a result of hydrogen sulfide generation from the anaerobic digestion of organic matter in the newly deposited silt. Webert (1956; according to Chabreck and Palmisano, 1973) recorded that Hurricane Flossy, in 1956, which flooded the Mississippi delta area, resulted in the washing out of *Alternanthera philoxeroides* and *Eichhornia crassipes*. The flood water was so deep that wave action produced little damage to the turf, and high rainfall reduced the effects of salinity. The washing out of these two types of vegetation was only temporary (O'Neil, 1949; according to Chabreck and Palmisano, 1973). O'Neil found that in the Louisiana delta marshes the September hurricane of 1947 swept away considerable loose debris, which caused about a 10% increase in open water areas. The destructive effect of this hurricane on vegetation was believed to be due largely to seawater being trapped behind the levees.

In New England the effect of the 1938 hurricane was to cause deforestation in the watersheds of the Connecticut and Merrimack Rivers. This deforestation resulted in an increase in annual runoff flow of about 5 in. during the first year after the hurricane. Another 5 in. of increased flow runoff occurred at diminishing rates during the next 2 to 3 years. At least half of this flow increase occurred in July, August, and September, when the streams were naturally at their lowest levels. After 5 years the regrowth of the forest was well under way, and there was no indication of increased flow (Patrick, 1974).

FLUSHING AND EFFECTS ON POLLUTION

The time it takes a molecule of water to move out of an estuary is the time required to "flush" the estuary. This movement is greatly influenced by the force of flow of fresh water and the periodic opposing force of the tidal waters. Because tides may slow the exit of water from the estuary, water can receive many inputs from nonpoint or point sources of effluents, and thus change the chemical characteristics of the water to a greater degree than would happen if the flow was once through a given point. The lag in flushing time caused by tides is very important in considering the quality of water as it affects aquatic life.

Dyer (1973) has given an excellent discussion of some of the better known equations for calculating the flushing time of estuaries and for estimating the fate of conservative (those that do not decay or change) and nonconservative pollutants.

Flushing

The flushing time is the time required to replace the existing fresh water in an estuary at a rate equal to discharge of the river (Dyer, 1973). Flushing time can be calculated in several ways (Dyer, 1973).

Method Based on Fraction of Fresh Water. The mean fraction of fresh water in a segment may be expressed as

$$f = \frac{S_s - S_n}{S_s} \tag{23}$$

where f = fractional fresh water concentration
S_s = salinity of undiluted seawater
S_n = mean salinity in a given segment

The total volume (Q) for the segment is found by multiplying f by the volume of the estuary segment.

Tidal Prism Method. The tidal prism method states that the flushing time in tidal cycles is

$$T = \frac{V + P}{P} \tag{24}$$

where T = flushing time in tidal cycles
$\quad\quad V$ = low tide volume
$\quad\quad P$ = intertidal volume (tidal prism)

Ketchum (1951a) modified this method by dividing the estuary into volume segments, defined horizontally by the estuary width, and lengthwise by the average excursion of a water particle on flood tide. The inner section is where the intertidal volume P_0 is supplied by river flow R. Thus $P_0 = R$. The low-tide volume of this segment is V. The limit of the next section is $V_1 = V_0 + P_0 = V_0 + R$, and so on. The low-tide volume in each segment equals the total tidal prism within the adjacent upstream segment plus the low-tide volume in segment 0, or

$$V_n = V_0 + R + \sum_{1}^{n-1} P \tag{25}$$

If the mixing is complete at high tide, the proportion of water removed on the ebb tide is the ratio between the local intertidal volume and the high-tide volume. The exchange ratio can be defined for any segment n as

$$r_n = \frac{P_n}{P_n + V_n} \times \frac{D}{H} \tag{26}$$

where D = average depth
$\quad\quad H$ = depth of mixed layer

The flushing time in a tidal cycle is $1/r_n$.

If the river flow is constant, each segment receives R volume of river water per tidal cycle. The amount of river water removed on the ebbing tide will be $r_n R$, and the amount remaining is $(1 - r_n)R$.

Since this process has been going on for many tidal cycles, there will be contributions of water from previous cycles to the water removed and to the water remaining. This can be summarized as follows:

Age in tidal cycle	*River water removed*	*River water remaining*
1	rR_1	$(1-r)R_1$
2	$r((1-r)R_2$	$(1-r)^2 R_2$
3	$r(1-r)^2 R_3$	$(1-r)^3 R_3$
m	$r(1-r)^{m-1}R_m$	$(1-r)^m R_m$

The total volume of water accumulated in the segment n (Q_n) will be the sum of the last column plus one volume of river flow that has not been removed,

Dyer (1973).

$$Q_n = R[1 + (1 - r_n) + (1 - r_n)^2 + \cdots + (1 - r_m)^m] \tag{27}$$

The sum of this geometric progression is

$$\frac{R}{r_n}[1 - (1 - r_n)^{m+1}] \tag{28}$$

when M is large $(1 - r_n)^{m+1}$ approaches 0 when r_n is less than 1, so that

$$Q_n = \frac{R}{r_n} \tag{29}$$

Similarly, the amount of river water removed is

$$R[r_n + r_n(1 - r_n) + r_n(1 - r_n)^2 + \cdots + r_n(1 - r_n)^{m-1}] = R \tag{30}$$

Thus one may calculate the flushing time $(1/r_n)$ for any section, and if the salinity of undiluted seawater is known, the high water salinity in each segment can be calculated. For incomplete mixing at high tide, exchange ratios can be adjusted by multiplying by $\bar{h}/\bar{H}$, where $\bar{h}$ is the average depth of the segment and $\bar{H}$ is the average depth of the mixed layer. The total flushing time of the estuary will be the sum of the flushing times for the separate segments.

This is a useful method of calculating the flushing time and salinity distribution, as it only requires data for river flow, tidal range, and the estuary topography. Some idea of current velocities within the estuary can be obtained, since the segment length is equivalent to the tidal excursion (Dyer, 1973).

This method had been found to agree reasonably well with field data for several estuaries (Ketchum and Keen, 1953). For other estuaries, such as the Severn, the agreement is not as good (Stommel, 1953).

Pollution Dispersion Prediction
Near the mouth of the estuary the freshwater fraction is relatively low. On each low tide enough water must escape so that the volume of fresh water equivalent to the river flow is removed. The escaping volume may be an order of magnitude or more greater than the river flow. It is this larger volume of water for dilution that is often an important factor in making estuaries more desirable locations for the discharge of pollutants than are the tributary streams.

Flushing Conservative Pollutants. The maximum concentration of conservative pollutants will be near the point of discharge, but tidal mixing will distribute it upstream and downstream. If the pollutant acts in the same way in fresh or salt water, the distribution of the pollutant will be related directly to the salinity distribution once a steady state is achieved. Predictions can be based on a knowledge of freshwater distribution (Dyer, 1973).

A fractional freshwater method for the prediction of the concentration of the pollutant was developed by Ketchum (1955). Let C_0 be the cross-sectional average concentration at the outfall after steady-state conditions have been obtained (Dyer, 1973). Then

$$C_0 = \frac{P}{R} f_0 \tag{31}$$

where P = rate of supply of effluent
$\quad R$ = river discharge
$\quad f_0$ = cross-sectional fractional freshwater concentration

The pollutant must pass through a cross section (x) downstream at the same rate it is discharged from the outfall (Dyer, 1973).

$$C_x = C_0 \frac{f_x}{f_0} = \frac{P}{R} f_x \tag{32}$$

The quantity of the pollutant carried upstream of the outfall with saline water will balance that carried downstream by the mean flow. Its distribution will be directly proportional to the salinity distribution and inversely proportional to the freshwater fraction. Thus

$$C_x = C_0 \frac{S_x}{S_0} \tag{33}$$

where S_0 = the salinity or chlorinity of fresh water up stream
$\quad S_x \equiv$ salinity of tidal water

The steady-state distribution is shown in Figure 2.12. If the discharge point is moved downstream, the concentration at points seaward will not be affected, but the upstream concentrations are greatly reduced and those in the immediate vicinity of the outfall are also reduced (Dyer, 1973).

Pritchard (1969) has developed a method for predicting pollution distribution which is particularly applicable to partially mixed extuaries. Figure 2.13 shows Pritchard's two-dimensional box model.

$(Q_u)_{n-1,n}$ is the volume flow rate from the $(n-1)$th segment into the nth segment of the upper layer.

$(Q_n)_{n,n-1}$ is the flow in the lower layer from the nth to the $(n-1)$th segment.

$(Q_u)_{n,n+1}$ will be the upper layer flow rate from the nth to the $(n+1)$th segment, etc.

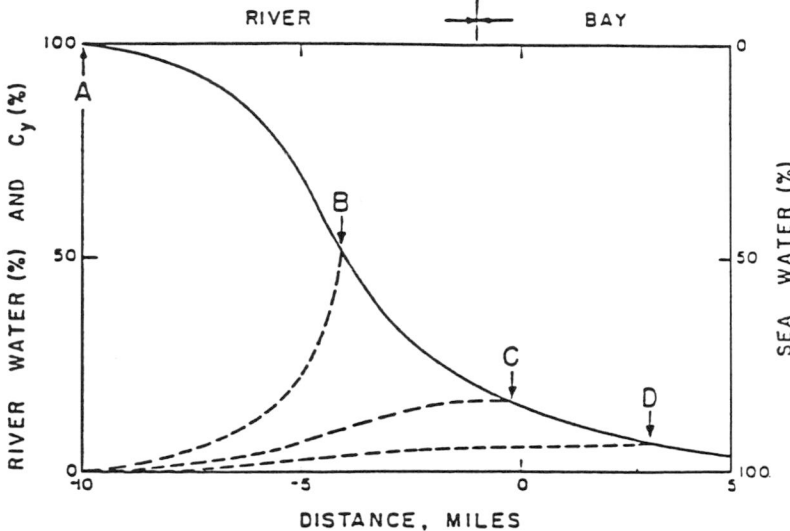

FIGURE 2.12. Observed average distribution of river water, and calculated distribution of a conservative pollutant (C_y) in Raritan River and Bay for four outfall locations. (From Ketchum, 1955.)

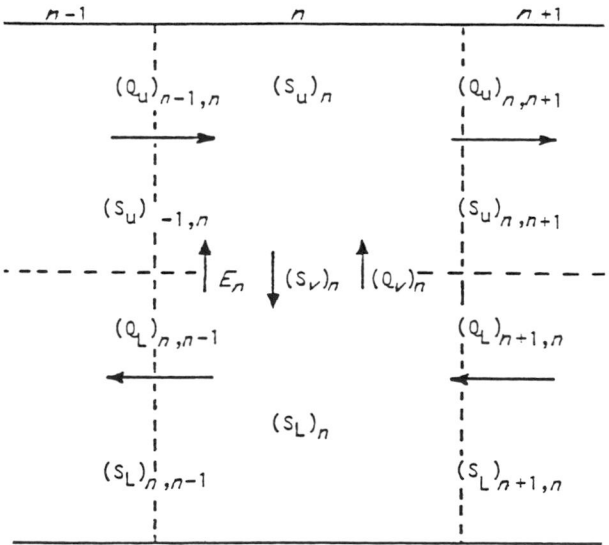

FIGURE 2.13. Definition diagram for two-dimensional box model. (From Dyer, 1973.)

There will be a volume rate of flow in the nth segment from the lower into the upper layer $(Q_v)_n$ because of vertical advection, and a vertical exchange coefficient representing the vertical diffusion E_n. $(S_u)_n$ and $(S_L)_n$ represent the salinity of the upper and lower layers. The salinity at the boundary between them is $(S_v)_n$. The salinity at the other boundaries will be $(S_L)_{n-1,n}$; $(S_L)_{n+1,n}$; and so on. Homogeneity is assumed in each box.

The steady-state equilibrium in segment n for the upper layer is (Dyer, 1973)

$$(S_u)_{n,n+1} \cdot (Q_u)_{n,n+1} = (S_u)_{n-1,n} \cdot (Q_u)_{n-1,n} + E_n[(S_L)_n - (S_u)_n] + (Q_v)_n \cdot (S_v)_n \quad (34)$$

from volume continuity:

$$(Q_v)_n = (Q_u)_{n,n+1} - (Q_u)_{n-1,n} \quad (35)$$

for similar equations for the lower layer:

$$Q_u = R \frac{S_L}{S_L - S_u} \qquad Q_L = R \frac{S_u}{S_L - S_u} \quad (36)$$

If the salinity distribution and freshwater flow are known, the horizontal volume flow rates can be calculated using equation (36). The vertical flow rates can be calculated from equation (24) and equation (34) solved for E_n.

If the conservative pollutant is introduced in the surface layer of the kth segment at a rate P, and the concentration C of the pollutant is assumed uniform in each subsection and at the boundaries the concentration is equal to the average between adjacent segments, then for the upper layer the pollutant balance is

$$(Q_u)_{n,n+1} \frac{(C_u)_n + (C_u)_{n+1}}{2} = (Q_u)_{n-1,n} \frac{(C_u)_{n-1} + (C_u)_n}{2} + E_n[(C_L)_n - (C_u)_n]$$

$$+ (Q_v)_n \frac{(C_u)_n + (C_L)_n}{2} \quad (37)$$

For the lower layer:

$$(Q_L)_{n,n+1} \frac{(C_L)_n + (C_L)_{n+1}}{2} = (Q_L)_{n,n-1} \frac{(C_L)_{n-1} + (C_L)_n}{2} + (Q_v)_n \frac{(C_L)_n + (C_u)_n}{2}$$

$$+ E_n[(C_L)_n - (C_u)_n] \quad (38)$$

In the upper layer of the kth segment, the input term P should be added to equation (37).

Using equations (35), (37), and (38) yields

$$(C_u)_{n-1} \cdot (Q_u)_{n-1,n} - 2(C_u)_n E_n + (C_L)_n[2E_n + (Q_v)_n] - (C_u)_{n+1} + (Q_u)_{n,n+1} = 0 \quad (39)$$

and

$$(C_L)_{n+1}(Q_L)_{n+1,n} - 2(C_L)_n E_n + (C_u)_n [2E_n - (Q_v)_n] - (C_L)_{n-1}(Q_L)_{n,n-1} = 0 \quad (40)$$

In the kth segment equation (39) will again have an additional P term. Using the boundary conditions that upstream C goes to zero and S goes to zero and that downstream $(C_L)_m = 0$, these equations can be solved for the distribution of pollutant concentration for a given input if one assumes that the vertical exchange coefficient is the same for the pollutant as it is for salt (Dyer, 1973).

Flushing Nonconservative Pollutants. Prediction is difficult for nonconservative (degradable) pollutants because they diminish with time as well as mixing. For coliform bacteria in sewage, the change is exponential because of mortality. This can be represented by

$$C_t = C_0^{e^{kt}} \quad (41)$$

where k is a constant that is negative.

Ketchum (1955) states that the pollution decreases to $\frac{1}{10}$ in $1\frac{1}{2}$ to 3 days in the Raritan River. He assumes that all the decrease in concentration is due to mixing, mortality, and grazing by zooplankton. These effects are represented by

$$C_n = (C_0)_n \frac{r_n}{1 - (1 - r_n)e^k} \quad (42)$$

where r_n is the exchange ratio in segment n. If the mortality rates and exchange ratios are equal in the segments in the estuary, then downstream from the outfall

$$C_n = C_0 \frac{f_n}{f_0} \left[\frac{r}{1 - (1 - r)e^k} \right]^n \quad (43)$$

and upstream

$$C_n = C_0 \frac{S_n}{S_0} \left[\frac{r}{1 - (1 - r)e^k} \right]^n \quad (44)$$

where n is the number of segments from the outfall, the segments being defined by the analysis of the modified prism. If the coefficient of mortality is zero, then $e^k = 1$ and the equations equal those of a conservative pollutant.

The effect of mortality is

$$\frac{C_n}{C_x} = \left[\frac{r}{1 - (1 - r)e^k} \right]^n \quad (45)$$

Larger exchange rates result in larger populations for a given rate of mortality, because the water is mixed faster and less mortality occurs.

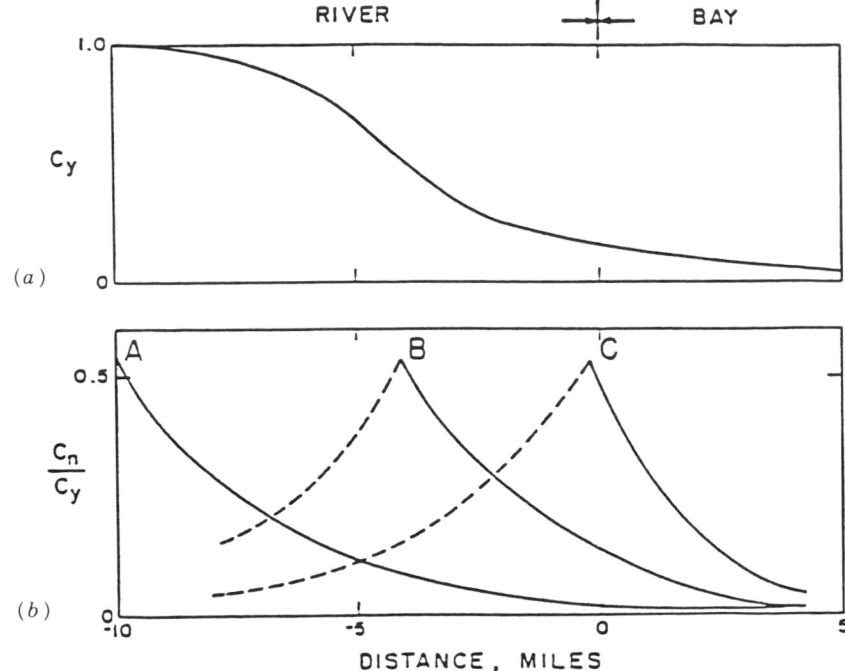

FIGURE 2.14.   Relative size (C_n/C_y) of a population of coliform bacteria calculated for three possible outfall locations in Raritan River and Bay, New Jersey. C_n is the actual population size independent of dilution; C_y is the concentration as it is affected by dilution. (From Ketchum, 1955.)

Figure 2.14 is that of Ketchum (1955) for the distribution of a nonconservative pollutant where the exchange ratio is 0.34. The curve in Figure 2.14a shows the effects of dilution alone on a conservative pollutant discharged at A. The three curves in Figure 2.14b are for fractions of populations expected when $k = 0.578$ tide^{-1}, and the relative populations at the outfall locations are A = 0.538, B = 0.278, and C = 0.092.

The downstream movement of the outfall decreases the peak concentration more than for a conservative pollutant (Ketchum, 1955). In contrast to the conservative pollutant, moving the point of discharge upstream reduces the concentration downstream.

SEDIMENTS

Size and Characteristics of Sediments
Sediments in estuaries have been roughly classified as follows. The smallest particles are silts and clays and very fine organic particles. These are often colloidal in size and difficult to precipitate. However, if they aggregate, they may flocculate and settle out when the current is reduced. This qroup of very small

particles may also include small organisms such as bacteria, viruses, and very small flagellates. Larger organisms may be difficult to precipitate because of their physiological or motile activities.

Larger particles are in suspension but settle out as the current slows down. These particles form most of the bulk of the suspended solids load. The largest particles (rocks, rubble, pebbles, and some sands) move as a bedload and are suspended only during storms.

Flocculation

Factors Effecting Flocculation Differential. Current and salinity are important factors in the flocculation of particles of colloidal and semicolloidal dimensions (Postma, 1967). The stability of a suspension is correlated with its electrolytic potential. Clay particles of colloidal size may have a negative electrical charge. The negative charge may be explained by (1) preferential adsorption of anions, especially hydroxyl ions; (2) cationic substitution within the particle's crystal lattice; and (3) residual valences (broken bonds at the particle edges). The negative charge on these particles is balanced by a double layer of hydrated cations which tend to move away from the surface of the clay mineral, although electrostatic attraction prevents a complete escape.

The thickness of the double layer of hydrated cations depends on the valence of the sorbed ions, the total concentration of those ions in the surrounding medium, temperature, and pH. In water with a small electrolytic content a thick double layer may be formed around each clay particle and the suspensions are stable. If more electrolyte is added, the thickness of electrolytic potential of the double layer decreases and the possibility for two particles to unite increases. Cations in the solution are exchanged for cations in the double layer. The effect of the cation is in accordance with its valence; thus cations with a double valence have a greater effect than cations with a single valence. As a result, clay particles coagulate and flocculate in seawater, especially under the influence of magnesium and calcium ions. The electrolytic coagulation process is in most instances reversible, and marine floccules carried upstream in fresh water may be deflocculated.

It is customary to characterize floccules by their apparent or equivalent grain size—that is, to assume that all particles are spherical and have specific weights of quartz. Because the diameter of the floccule is usually much greater than that of the individual components, it tends to settle more rapidly. It should be noted, however, that much water is included in the flocculates, so that increase in settling time may not be as great as one would expect from the size of the particles. For example, a unit particle with a diameter of 5 μm and a specific weight of 2.7 has a settling velocity in seawater of $0.002 \, \text{cm s}^{-1}$. A particle of 500 μm at the same density sinks at $20 \, \text{cm s}^{-1}$, but a flocculate of clay particles of the same size, containing 95% water, settles with the velocity of only $0.4 \, \text{cm s}^{-1}$, or as slowly as a quartz sphere of about 20 μm (Postma, 1967).

Differential Flocculation of Particles. Different kinds of clay particles flocculate at different rates. Illite particles are usually smaller than kaolinite but are

TABLE 2.4.   *Representative Settling Velocities of Clay Mineral Types in Artificial Seawater[a]*

Clay Mineral	Settling Velocity (cm min^{-1} × 10^{-2}) for Chlorinity (%):					
	0.5	1.0	2.0	6.0	10.0	18.0
Illite	89.1	90.1	105.0	110.0	110.0	110.0
Kaolinite	80.1	80.5	81.1	81.2	81.2	81.2
Montmorillonite	0.23	0.36	0.78	4.06	7.55	8.77

Source: Postma (1967), Table 1, p. 161; after Whitehouse et al. (1960).
[a] Pipette method, 26 °C, pH 8.2.

considerably larger than montmorillonite. This might in itself lead to differential settling, but the physical–chemical differences are important. Experiments have shown that flocculation of kaolinites and illites is generally completed at very low chlorinity, whereas flocculation of montmorillonite increases gradually with increased chlorinity because of the very stable double layer around montmorillonite. Table 2.4 shows the relationship between chlorinity and settling velocity. The liqht transmission of these clays increases with an increase in chlorinity (Postma, 1967).

In rapidly moving water clay minerals of the same particle size may be transported without differentiation, but at low current velocities illite and kaolinite may be deposited, whereas montmorillonite remains in suspension. The difference in transport velocities may be greater in fresh and brackish water than in salt water. A summary of the settling rates of random clays is given in Figure 2.15.

Meade (1972) sugests that although salt flocculation is important in the process of flocculation of colloids, it is not the only important force. Particles must be brought together and once they collide, they must cohere. Meade believes the important factors causing coherence to be salinity, decomposition, concentration of the suspended matter, and agitation of the water. In addition, he emphasizes the importance of organic interactions in bringing about agglomeration.

Organisms and Flocculation.   Many filter-feeding organisms, such as oysters, agglomerate particles of fine-grained suspended matter into pellets whose settling velocity is many times greater than that of the constituent particles. In considering the importance of this process, one can say that due to the activities of these organisms, most of the fine-grained material that is eventually incorporated into estuarine bottom sediments has been ingested or otherwise affected by more than one organism. We do not know the importance of this process relative to other factors that may influence deposition of sediments in estuaries. For example, Lund (1957a), studying the oyster, *Crassostrea virginica*, has shown that oysters take in a great deal of the fine suspended matter and then excrete it as agglomerated fecal pellets which vary in length from 1 to 5 mm. The material they do not eat is ejected from the gills in loose clumps that have been aggregated by mucus.

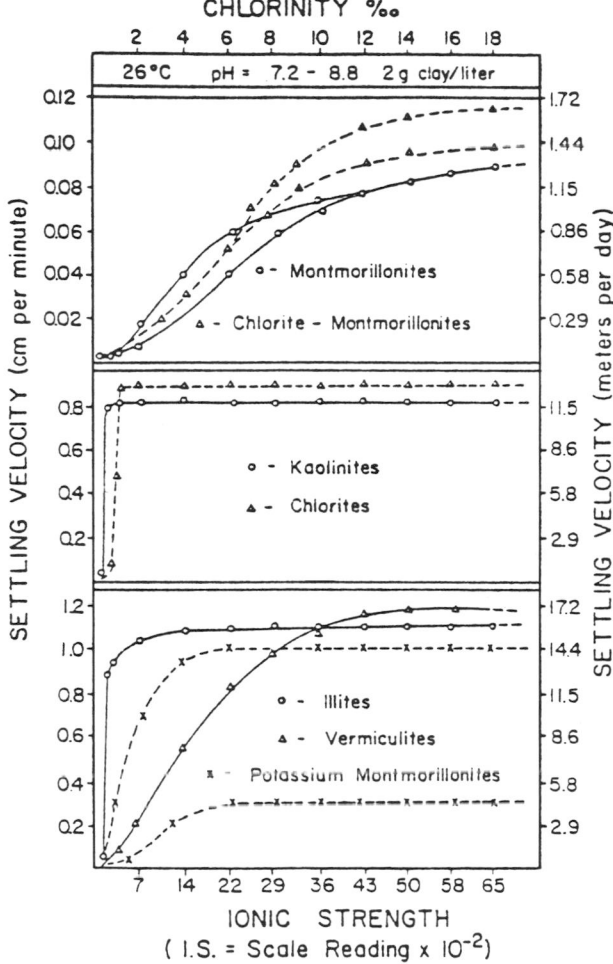

FIGURE 2.15.   Settling velocities of clay minerals in seawater at various chlorinities. (From Postma, 1967.)

Figure 2.16 shows the results of laboratory experiments on clearing of saltwater suspensions by filter-feeding estuarine molluscs. Lund (1957b) has estimated that a single continuous layer of oysters could deposit 12 metric tons of sediment per hectare per week. In a perhaps more realistic estimate, Haven and Morales-Alamo (1966) have calculated that the typical commercial oyster bed in the lower York River, Virginia would deposit 1 to 2 metric tons dry weight of solids per hectare per week. Rhoads (1963) estimated that the clam, *Yoldia*, even though it constituted less than 10% of the total bottom fauna, was able to rework bottom sediments in Buzzards Bay and Long Island Sound faster than they can accumulate. Over a large portion of Buzzards Bay, Rhoads and Young (1970) found

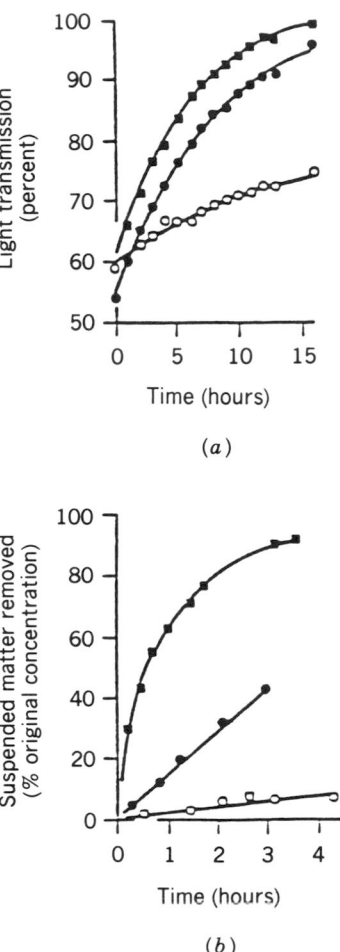

(a)

(b)

FIGURE 2.16.   Results of laboratory experiments on clearing of saltwater suspensions by filter-feeding estuarine molluscs. (a) Removal of suspended fuller's earth by oysters; light transmission measured by Fisher turbidimeter; dark squares represent suspensions cleared by two different groups of oysters; open circles represent control suspensions in oyster-free tank. (b) Removal of suspended graphite by scallop, *Pecten latiauratus*; dark squares and circles represent control suspensions in scallop-free tanks. (From Meade, 1972.)

that the upper centimeter or so of bottom sediments consisted mostly of fecal pellets.

Agglomerated material, such as feces or pseudofeces of oysters, may be a food source for bacteria, and thus their content may be resuspended. The importance of this process needs further investigation in regard to the ultimate deposition of agglomerated sediments (Haven and Morales-Alamo, 1972).

Organic aggregates may take on two forms. One form is transparent, almost colorless, mostly 10 to 25 μm in size and has definitely sharp edges. The other form, which is colonized by bacteria, is less transparent, is 20 to 40 μm in size, and has fuzzy edges. Both forms have been found as suspended particles (Riley, 1963; Wangersky, 1965). Other organic processes that tend to increase the permanence of sedimentation are bacterial slimes within the sediments, algal growths, and the precipitation of calcium carbonates, which tend to bring about agglomeration.

Clay Deposits. The physical–chemical characteristics of clay deposits are determined by estuarine circulation and salinity differences. However, a gradual downstream change in mineral composition of clays often occurs. In the Chesapeake area this change is caused, in part, by the sediments in the rivers entering the bay, which are relatively rich in kaolinite and contain variable amounts of illite, very little montmorillonite, and no chlorite. An example from the Rappahannock River estuary is given in Table 2.5. The downstream change in composition is in part due to a transformation of one clay mineral into another by the transition from fresh to salt water. These changes are also, in part, caused by differential flocculation and the behavior of the mineral types supplied by the river when the minerals encounter salt water.

The cations in the water column also affect the behavior of the colloids (Mueller, 1964). If calcium ions predominate in fresh and slightly brackish water, sediments with adsorbed calcium will be found in fresh and slightly brackish waters of the estuary. However, in brackish sediments where the saline content is high, the effect of seawater causes magnesium to be more commonly adsorbed than calcium. Sodium is the principal adsorbed ion, although monovalent ions have only a small bonding energy in seawater because the concentration of sodium ions is much higher than that of magnesium or calcium ions.

Erosion, Transportation, and Deposition of Sediments

The relation between erosion, transportation, deposition velocities, and the grain size of sediments was developed by Hjulstrom and reexamined by Sundborg

TABLE 2.5 *Changes in Mineral Composition in the Rappahannock Estuary According to Nelson (1960)[a]*

	Upper River	Lower River	Upper Estuary	Middle Estuary	Lower Estuary
Kaolinite	×	×	×	×	×
Unorg. Illite	×	×	×	×	×
Vermiculite	×	×	×	×	×
12.4-Å Montmorillonite		×	×	×	×
14.2-Å Montmorillonite			×	×	×
Illite			×	×	×
Chlorite					×
Feldspar					×

Source: Postma (1967), Table 3, p. 177.
[a] Presence of a mineral is indicated by a cross.

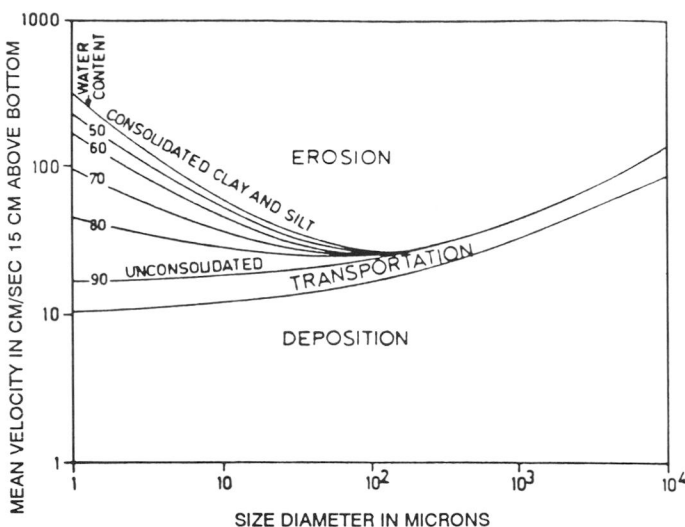

FIGURE 2.17.   Erosion, transportation, and deposition velocities for different sediment grain sizes.
The diagram indicates possible values for various stages of consolidation. (From Postma, 1967.)

(1956). The critical erosion velocity is the minimum current velocity at which
sediments of a particular size begin to move. The movement stops at a flow
velocity called the lowest transportation velocity, or the deposition velocity.
Figure 2.17 shows curves of critical velocities for different particle sizes at a
distance about 15 cm above the bottom.

The critical values depend on current velocity only indirectly. The important
factors are the tractive forces acting on the bottom, the roughness of the bottom,
the turbulence, and so on. From a size of 0.2 to 0.3 mm upward, the critical
erosion velocity increases with increasing grain size. (A 0.3-mm particle is
assumed to be quartz sand with a specific weight of 2.65.) The deposition velocity
is slightly smaller and is usually about two-thirds of the erosion velocity. The
difference in the velocity between erosion and deposition is of great importance
for the behavior of suspended material in tidal streams. For grains with a lower
density, the curves move downward. If the density is higher, the curves are located
above those shown on the graph. For diameters smaller than 0.2 mm and
especially below 0.5 mm, one set of curves is sufficient to describe the relationships.

Cohesiveness and the duration of consolidation are important. Differences
between erosion and transportation velocities are much larger for consolidated
than for unconsolidated clays. Consolidation is a process that essentially results
from the expulsion of water from the interstices between soil grains under load.
The water escapes through microscopic channels that connect the interstices.
During this process the particles form a more closely packed sediment of greater
density and lower water content. The rate at which this process occurs is

dependent on the type of clay mineral and the degree of flocculation. Recently deposited fine-grained matter is often unconsolidated, very loosely cohesive, and may be carried away easily by a small change in current velocity. When the material has been deposited for a longer time, it gradually loses water and becomes increasingly difficult to erode. The increase in cohesive forces generated by the bonds of thin layers of oriented water molecules around the particles and by electrostatic attraction increases the erosion velocity with decreased water content. These forces are largely dependent on the physical and mineralogical properties of the clays.

Transport by Estuarine Circulation. The transport of suspended matter in estuarine circulation systems usually refers to the transport that occurs when both fresh and salt water are present. In the head of the estuary, typically the whole flow is fresh water and unidirectional. Below this area is a freshwater area where little tidal influence is felt. This area merges into an area composed of fresh and brackish water which may be highly stratified, mixed, or homogeneous. The relative mixture of fresh and salt water varies with the structure of the estuary, freshwater flow, tidal influence, and such catastrophic processes as wind and storm. For the most part it is the density difference between fresh and salt water that sets up the estuarine circulation system.

In areas where saltwater flow does not penetrate farther upstream, sediments within the saltwater wedge will precipitate. At the same time, fresh water overflowing the salt water wedge contains particulates that may settle out upon interaction with salt water, and thus a sediment trap is formed. The limits of this sediment trap may vary as the salt water wedge fluctuates within a tidal cycle and with seasonal shifts in flow. The settling velocity of the sediments involved also influences the quantity of sediment reaching the mouth of the estuary.

These sediment traps are often the area of greatest water turbidity, although high turbidity may be found due to other causes at the mouth of the estuary. The magnitude of the turbidity is dependent on the amount of suspended matter in the river flow and the saltwater tongue that penetrates the estuary. The explanation for the higher turbidity in the sediment trap is, according to Schubel (1971d), the continual resuspension of bottom sediments in the sediment trap produced by the net nontidal estuary circulation and newly introduced material. For example, maximum turbidities found in Chesapeake Bay are indicated in Figure 2.18. The suspended particle population is determined .by physical processes or local resuspension and net nontidal circulation, which combine to produce the turbid zone.

In the Chesapeake Bay's turbid zone the particle population is composed of two subpopulations. One of these subpopulations is a natural background of suspended sediments that increase with depth and the presence of which at any depth is relatively constant over time scales of weeks and months. This natural background is made up of very fine-grained particles whose settling times are long compared to the mixing time. A constant level of sediment is attributable in part directly to runoff, and in part to resuspension, primary production, and shore erosion (Schubel, 1971d).

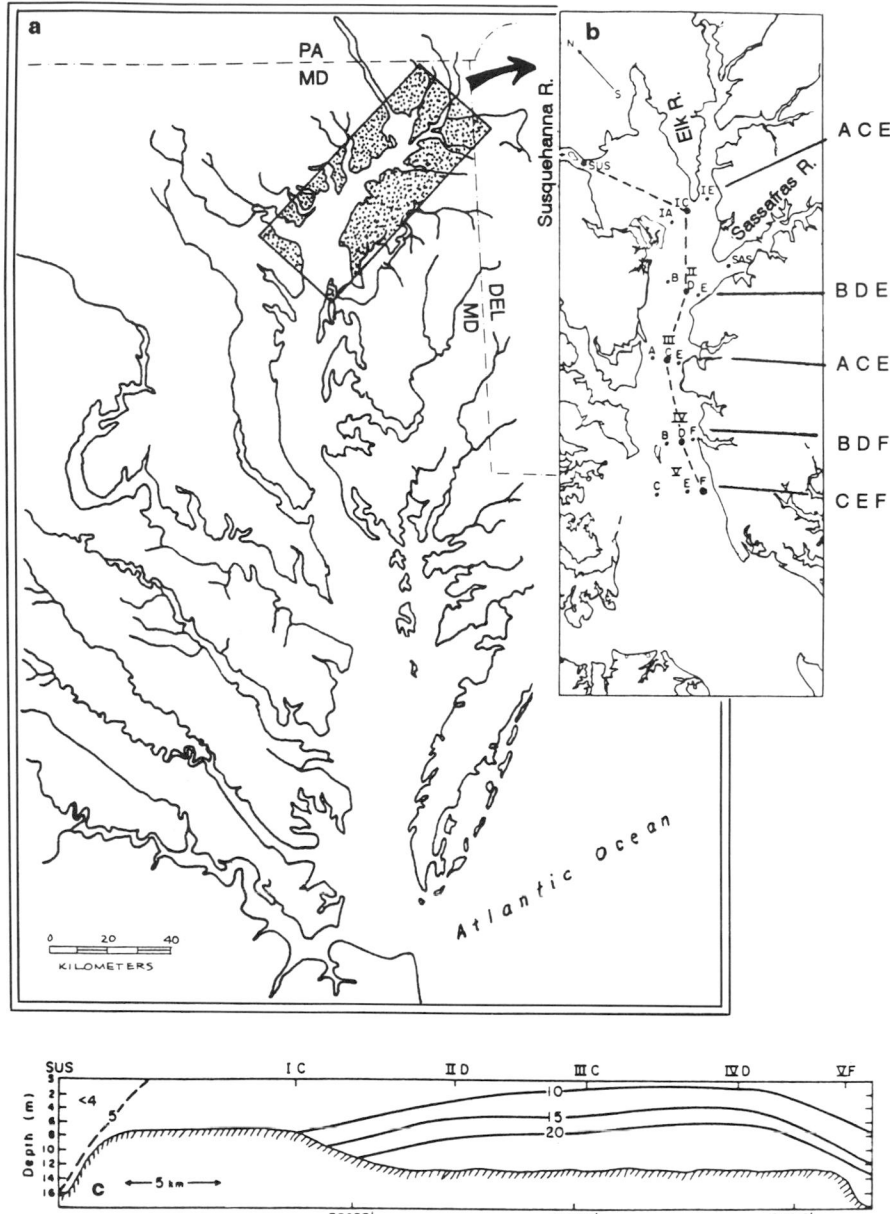

FIGURE 2.18.   Area of maximum turbidity in the Chesapeake Bay: (*a*) part of the bay in which turbidity maxima are typically found; (*b*) detail of area shown in (a), showing the sampling locations used for turbidity determinations; (*c*) longitudinal distribution of suspended sediment in the area of maximum turbidity (units: mg L^{-1}). (After Schubel, 1971d. Reprinted with permission of the American Geological Institute.)

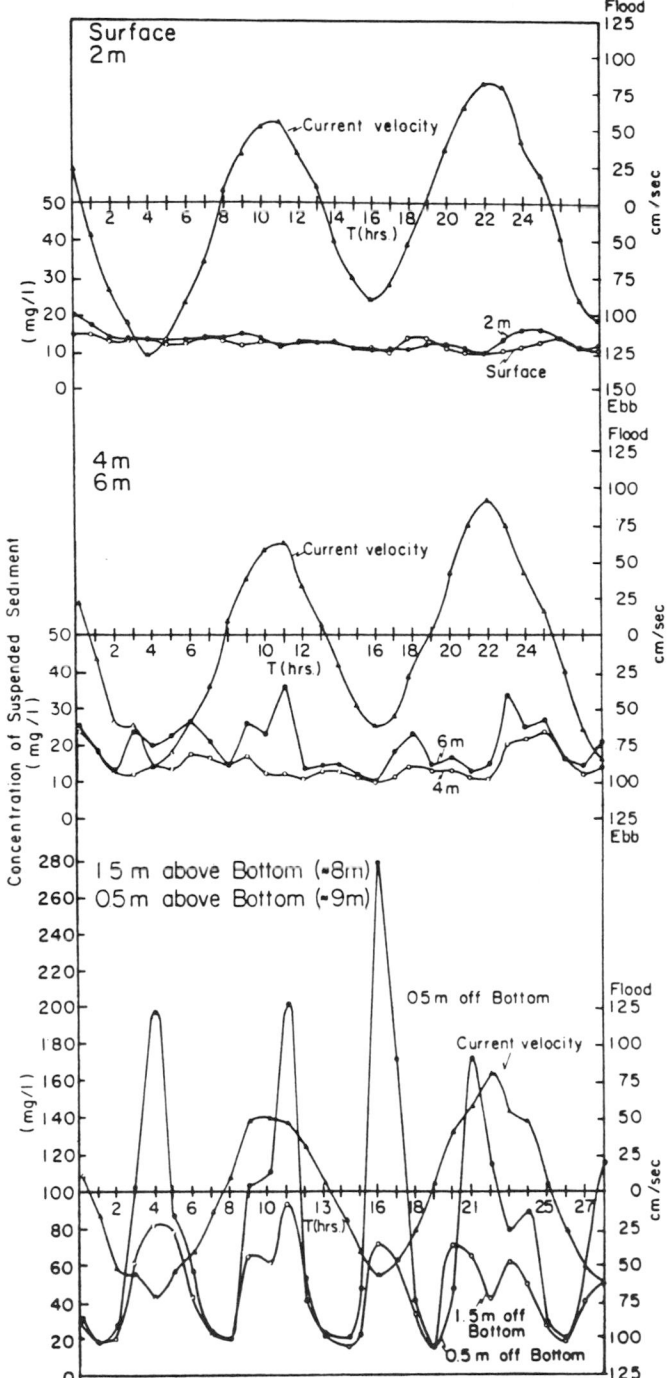

FIGURE 2.19. Variation of current velocity and suspended sediment concentration in July 1967 in Chesapeake Bay (see Figure 2.18) at about the level of Baltimore. Measurements were made hourly at six depths. (From Schubel, 1971d. Reprinted with permission of the American Geological Institute.)

The second subpopulation consists of particles that are alternately suspended and deposited. The presence of this subpopulation is made manifest by semitidal fluctuations of concentrations of suspended sediments in water deeper than about 4 m and throughout the water column in shallower areas (Figure 2.19). Fluctuations in the presence of this sediment are marked by changes in volume, size distribution, and density near the sediment source (Schubel, 1971d).

Very low river discharges may be detrimental to the development of turbidity maxima, since the estuarine circulation may practically disappear. Hence in a constant tidal regime a certain volume of river discharge will be optimal for the formation of the turbid zone (Postma, 1967).

Upstream from the peak of the turbidity maximum, the silt content of water gradually decreases. However, this decrease in sediments does not end when the water becomes completely fresh. It is evident that suspended silt can be infiltrated from the turbidity maximum against the residual flow into fresh water (Demerara Coastal Investigation, 1962). This upstream diffusion is influenced by the tide. The suspended matter carried upstream by the flood temporarily settles during the ebb and is subsequently carried farther upstream by the following flood. This process works only as long as the tidal influence is strong enough to cause a reversal of the current. Thus it is apparent that the deposition of marine mud can take place above the level of salt penetration in a river. This has been validated by the presence of marine diatoms in freshwater deposits (Brockman, 1908, 1929; Postma, 1967).

From this discussion it is apparent that particles flocculated in salt water may be deflocculated in fresh water, and this process for the same particle may be repeated many times before the particle eventually moves downstream or consolidates on the riverbed.

Transport by Tidal Currents.   In shallow water the vertical tidal movement is accompanied by ebb and flood currents, which sometimes have a maximum velocity of $300 \, \mathrm{cm \, s^{-1}}$ in narrow tidal inlets. Rarely is the back-and-forth movement of the tide symmetrical in shape. If it were symmetrical, the amount of water carried through a certain point over an ebb tide would equal that carried over a flood tide. This condition is not often realized, and in coastal seas the amount of water carried over the flood often exceeds that of the ebb. In very shallow waters, slack water coincides with high and low tides. This is particularly true in small tidal gullies that occur on tidal flats. In deeper water the turn of the tide falls behind high and low tides. The time lag may vary from 20 minutes in water 5 m deep to up to 3 hours in water 30 m deep.

Tidal currents are usually sufficiently strong and turbulent to set into motion considerable amounts of suspended matter. The quantities and grain size of the material at a fixed point fluctuate with the current velocity as shown in Figure 2.20. The turbulent motion of water may carry even coarse sand into the surface layers, especially when tides are at the maximum (Postma, 1967).

Transport Within Estuarine Bays.   The movement and deposition of sediments and the factors causing various patterns of sedimentation have been mapped and described by Folger (1972). The sediments transported and deposited in

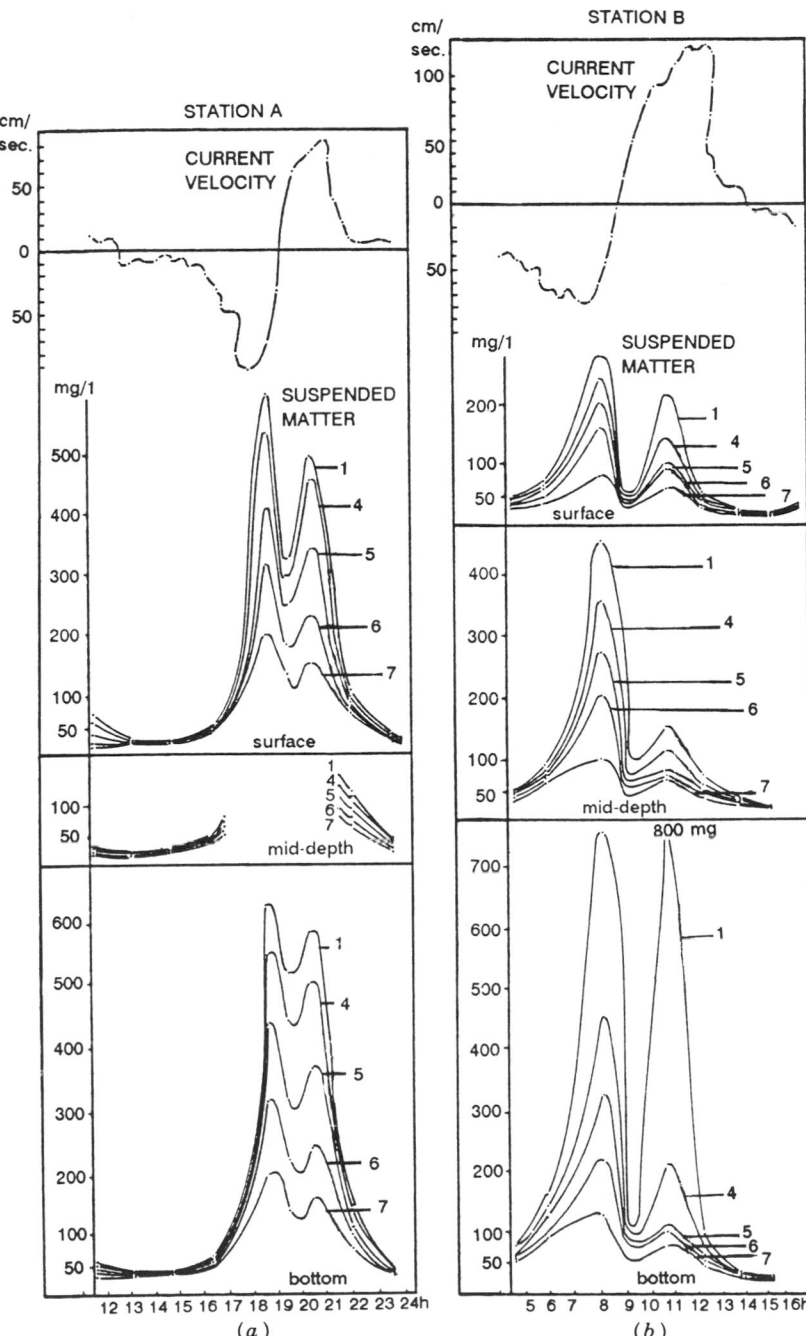

FIGURE 2.20. Current velocities at middepth and contents of suspended matter at three depths. Observations at two fixed points (a) and (b) in the Wadden Zee (Ameland area of Holland). Flood currents are shown above and ebb currents below the horizontal line in the "current velocity" portion of the figures. The curves for suspended matter refer to the following grain-size fractions: 1, total suspended matter; 4, fraction below 64 μm; 5, fraction below 32 μm; 7, fraction below 8 μm. High-water depth at (a) is 4.5 m; at (b) is 7.3 m. (From Postma, 1967.)

estuaries are primarily from four sources: erosion of the watershed, scouring within the estuary, erosion of the estuary banks, and sediments transported in by tidal and wave action.

The effect of horizontal spreading of water over a large area at high tide in tidal flats and the confining of this water to tidal channels at low tide results in more suspended matter being deposited at high tide than at low tide, causing most of the sediments carried landward with the flood to be deposited on the bottom. Owing to settling lag or scouring lag or both effects together, the material is not picked up by the body of water that carried it landward but by water located farther landward. The net result is a landward shift of particles as each high tide shifts the particles closer to the shore.

In shallow coastal areas the tide does not simply move back and forth but tends to rotate. Often, this is aided by the Coriolis force. This tends to bring particulate matter inward and deposit it near the head of the estuary because of clockwise rotation. Asymmetry of the time–velocity curve also affects the deposition of sediments. In an area where tidal current decreases from the open sea to the coast, the period of low current velocities is longer around high tide than around low tide. It has further been shown that the tidal velocity curve at a fixed point in a small tidal channel is in fact asymmetrical, having its maximum nearer the low tide than the high tide. This holds for the ebb as well as the flood phases (Figure 2.20) (Postma, 1967).

Sediment eroded from the landscape is the predominant source of inorganic sediments. Weil (1977) estimates 5.27×10^6 metric tons (mts) of sediment enter the Delaware estuary annually, of which 0.77×10^6 mts enter the Delaware River above Philadelphia, 0.23×10^6 enter from the mouth of the Schuylkill River at Philadelphia, and 4×10^6 mts yr^{-1} are contributed by other natural and anthropogenic sources. The 0.77×10^6 mts yr^{-1} entering the Delaware above Philadelphia (the upper estuary) are quite similar to the 0.758×10^6 mts yr^{-1} entering the upper Chesapeake.

Of the 5.27×10^6 mts entering the Delaware each year, 3.4×10^6 mts are deposited in the ship channel and anchorage areas between Philadelphia and Delaware Bay. There is little sedimentation above this point to Trenton, and virtually no deposition along the axis of the lower bay (Weil, 1977). Biggs (1970) states that most of the sediments entering upper Chesapeake Bay are deposited near their point of entry. Less than 40% escape seaward beyond the first 35 km or so of the upper bay (Figure 2.21). Considerable sediment enters the mid-Chesapeake from erosion of the shoreline, but only 0.11×10^6 tons per year are carried beyond the mouth of the Potomac River.

Schubel (1971c) gives the annual sediment load entering estuaries in various regions of the United States and nearby areas in Table 2.6. Table 2.7 is a summary of estuarine circulation characteristics and sedimentation patterns.

The sediments in the lower part of an estuary typically are derived from the sea and often are sand. Deposition of ocean-derived sediments, usually caused by tide and wave action, contribute to the general structural characteristics of many estuaries.

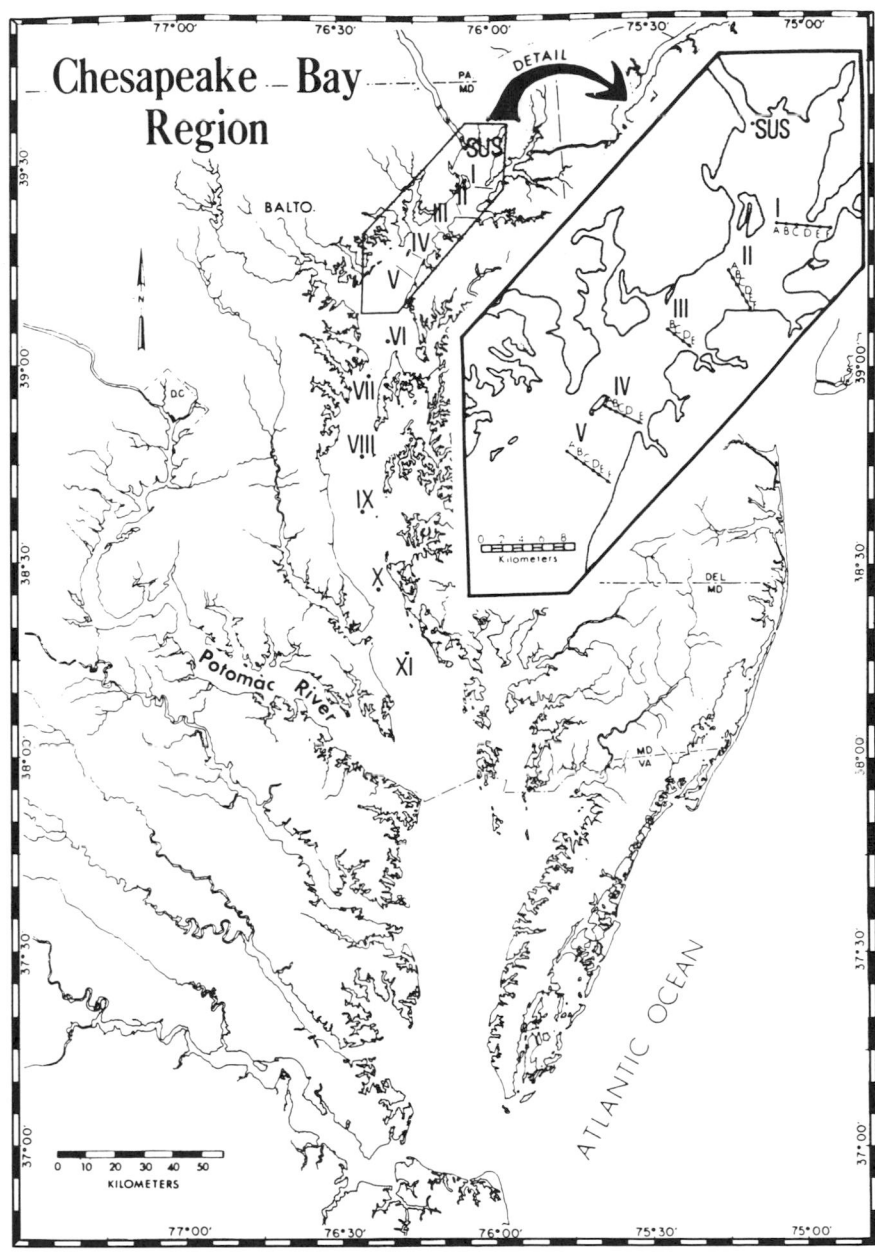

FIGURE 2.21. Map of Chesapeake Bay region showing northern part of estuary studied by Biggs. (From Biggs, 1970.)

TABLE 2.6.   *Characteristics of Sediment Loads Entering and Sediments Resident in the Estuarine Zone*

Biophysical Region	Average Annual Suspended Sediment Load		Number of Rivers Sampled	Kinds of Sediments in the Estuarine Zone
	Tons per Square Mile	Tons		
North Atlantic	[a]	[a]	0	Glacial debris—little input from rivers; clay silt in deep areas; sand, gravel around edges
Middle Atlantic	220.0	15,300,000	5	Silt, clay in deep areas; fine sand elsewhere
Chesapeake Bay	130.0	8,640,000	3	Silt, clay in deep areas; fine sand elsewhere
South Atlantic	389.0	58,100,000	1	Fine sand predominates; organic silt in rivers and swamps
Caribbean	[a]	[a]	0	Fine sand, except for coral reefs and mangroves
Gulf				
Excluding Mississippi	124.0	57,600,000	7	Silts and clays with sands abundant around margins only
Mississippi	244.0	305,000,000	1	Fine silts and clays, covered with fine sand where delta making is inactive
Pacific Southwest				
Pacific slopes	398.0	21,000,000	2 ⎱	Fine sand in channels, silts and clays around
Central Valley	71.4	3,000,000	2 ⎰	edges and on tidal flats
Pacific Northwest				
Pacific slopes	3610.0	98,000,000	3 ⎱	Fine sand in channels, silts and clays around
Columbia	112.0	29,000,000	2 ⎰	edges and on tidal flats
Alaska	[a]	[a]	0	Mixture of gravel, silt, and general glacial debris on southeast, south; extremely fine "flour" on some parts of south and southwest
Pacific Islands	[a]	[a]	0	Sand, coral slight amounts of silt near rivers

Source: National Estuarine Pollution Study (1970), Table IV.1.2, p. 74. Data from the National Estuarine Inventory and the U.S. Geological Survey.
[a]Not available.

TABLE 2.7. *Estuarine Circulation Characteristics and Sedimentation Patterns in Relation to Mixing Type*

	Type A: Highly Stratified	Type B: Partially Mixed	Type C: Vertically Homogeneous	Type D: Laterally Homogeneous
Primary influence on estuarine circulation system	River-dominated circulation system	Tidal influence of river-dominated circulation system	River influence on tide-dominated circulation system	Tide-dominated circulation system
Flow Characteristics	Net downstream flow on surface; net upstream flow near bottom	Net downstream flow on surface; net upstream flow near bottom	Upstream on right side of flood direction; downstream on right side of ebb	Slow net seaward flow at all depths
Relative volume of ebb and flood flow	Flow volume up the estuary during flood less than 10 × freshwater flow	Flow volume up the estuary during flood greater than 10 × freshwater flow	Flow volume up the estuary during flood greater than 10 × freshwater flow	Not known
Nature of salt water–fresh water boundary	Bottom salt wedge thinning upstream	Intense mixing across fresh water–salt water interface	No vertical salinity gradient; lateral gradient due to Coriolis force	Laterally and vertically homogeneous with longitudinal salinity gradient
Mixing pattern	Salt water mixes upward	Salt water mixes upward and fresh water downward	Extensive vertical and lateral mixing	Upstream diffusion
Controls on upstream limit of salt	Related directly to river discharge	River discharge dominates over tidal effects	River discharge over "long" term and tidal cycle over "short" term	Dominated by tidal excursion
Locus of rapid shoaling	In the vicinity of the salt wedge tip	Between ebb and flood limits of salt intrusion (the "turbidity maximum") at the mouths of tributaries	Near upper limit of salt intrusion (on right side of channel going upstream) in channel section with excessive cross-sectional area	Channel section with excessive cross-sectional areas
Examples	Mississippi River	Chesapeake Bay, James River, Savannah River, Charleston Harbor, Miramichi River, Delaware Bay, Gironde Estuary	Thames estuary, Raritan Bay, Gironde estuary, Delaware Bay	Merrimack estuary, Piscataqua estuary

Source: Weil (1977), Table 6, p. 111; summarized from Schubel (1971b) and Schubel and Pritchard (1972).

Classification of Estuaries by Sediment Deposition and Tidal Range
Hayes (1975), using the classification of Davies, divides estuaries as follows:

Small tidal range, microtidal estuaries. Mean tidal range is 0 to 2 m. Coarse-grained sediment accumulation. Wave action and storm deposition are more important in this class than in any other. *Example*: Galveston Bay, Texas (Figure 2.22).

Medium tidal range, mesotidal estuaries. Mean tidal range is 2 to 4 m. Coarse-grained sediment accumulation. Tidal deltas and tidal current-formed sand bodies increase noticeably in this class. *Examples*: Some of the estuaries on the New England coast, South Carolina, and Georgia coasts (Figure 2.23).

Large tidal range, macrotidal estuaries. Mean tidal range is 4 m or more. Coarse-grained sediment accumulation. These are funnel-shaped, wide-mouth estuaries that contain linear sand bodies, which are the most common type of deposit in these areas. *Examples*: Bristol Bay, Alaska and the Ord estuary, Australia (Figure 2.24).

Wide-mouth estuaries. Delaware and Chesapeake bays, the two largest estuaries on the east coast, are wide-mouth estuaries which fit none of the first three categories. Delaware Bay has linear sand shoals composed of coarser material near the mouth of the bay (Figure 2.25) but has a tidal range of only 5.8 ft (1.77 m). Chesapeake Bay lacks coarse sediments (Table 2.6), has no linear shoals, and its mean tidal range is 2.5 ft (0.76 m) at Norfolk, Virginia, near the mouth of the bay.

In Figure 2.26 the characteristics of microtidal, mesotidal, and macrotidal estuaries are compared as to the variation of morphology of coastal plain shoreline. All of these are estuaries formed on moderate-to-low energy shorelines.

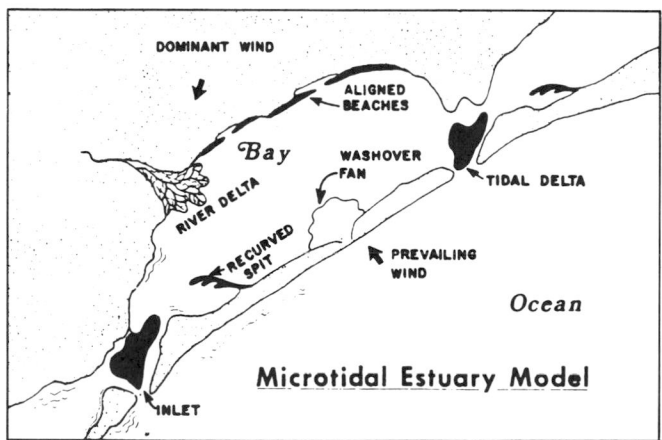

FIGURE 2.22. Microtidal estuary model. Sand bodies in the estuary are mostly storm- or river-generated (washover fans, river deltas) or wave-generated (aligned beaches, recurved spits). Tidal deltas are usually small. Most of the estuaries in the Gulf of Mexico are of this type. (From Hayes, 1975.)

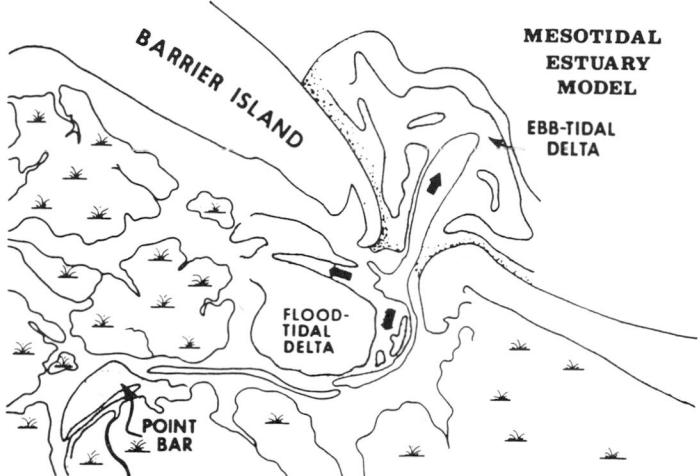

FIGURE 2.23. Mesotidal estuary model. Tidal deltas and point bar deposits are the principal sand bodies. Most estuaries on the New England shoreline and on the Wadden Sea of Holland are mesotidal. (From Hayes, 1975.)

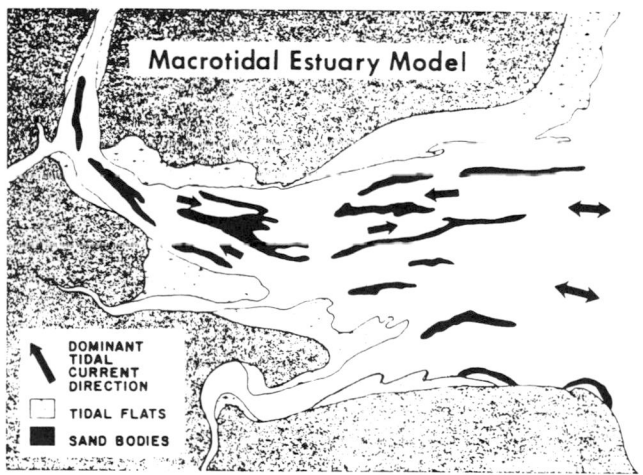

FIGURE 2.24. Macrotidal estuary model. The principal sand bodies are linear sand bars built by tidal currents in the central portion of the estuary. (From Hayes, 1975.)

The Pacific coast of the United States in many areas is a high-energy coastline. The bays are deeper than on the Gulf coast probably because of the narrow and deeper continental shelves on the Pacific coast. Barrier islands are rare or absent, and embayments may be open to the sea or have constricted inlets between bluffs or coastal mountains. A few estuaries in southern California, such as Mugu Lagoon and Newport Bay, are abandoned mouths of major streams which

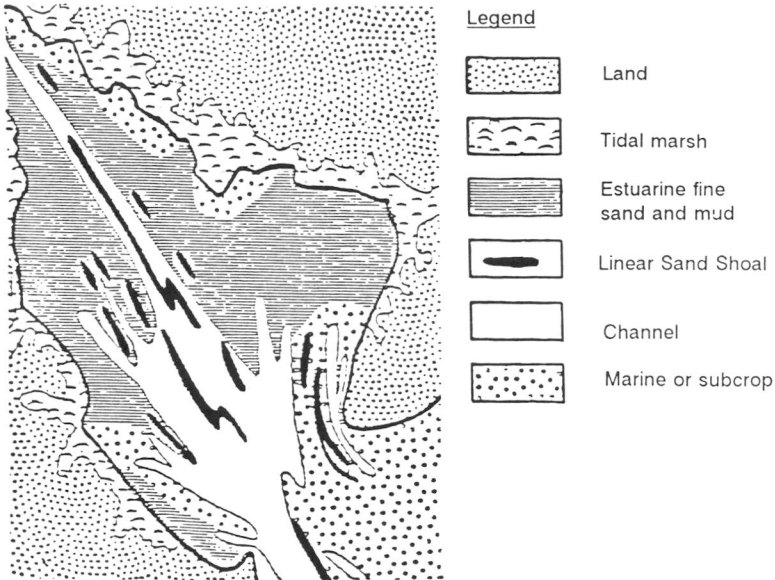

FIGURE 2.25.   Present surface sediment types in Delaware Bay. (From Weil, 1977.)

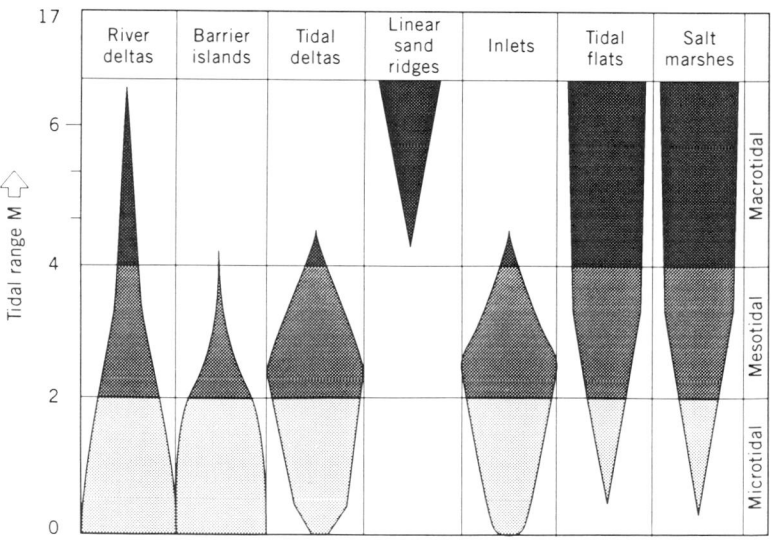

FIGURE 2.26.   Variation of morphology of coastal plain shorelines with respect to differences in tidal range. River deltas and barrier islands are most common in microtidal areas. Tidal deltas and tidal inlets are most common in mesotidal areas. Linear sand ridges (sand ridges deposited on shallow continental shelf by tidal currents), tidal flats, and sand marshes are most common in macrotidal areas. (From Hayes, 1975.)

have been closed off by long shore drift and later opened to the sea by artificial channels. Other southern California estuaries, such as San Diego Bay, Mission Bay, and Moro Bay, are separated from the sea by spits and tombolos.

On the Pacific coast, in arid to semiarid climate, winds provide a transport for sand into lagoons. Washovers are not characteristic of the Pacific barriers, nor is rapid vegetative growth a stabilizing force. Estuaries fed by intermittent streams are dominated by tidal incursions from the ocean (Gorsline, 1967).

Sediments Associated with Inlets

"Noreasters," storms that approach the New England coast obliquely from the northeast, have a dominant influence on coastal sedimentation. Waves generated by storms set up a net littoral drift to the south in most areas (Hayes, 1971b). At most New England inlets, the barrier beach downdrift of the inlet extends farther seaward than the one on the updrift side. Wave refraction around the ebb-tide deltas influences the accumulation of sand on the downdrift side of these inlets. This reversal of wave direction on the downdrift side tends to promote the accumulation of sand, and the beach builds seaward at this point.

Kaczorowski (1971) states that the most common type of inlet in the eastern United States is of the downdrift offset variety and may be found, generally, along the eastern and Gulf coasts. Exceptions are four of the six inlets on the south shore of New York Harbor, where the updrift side of the inlet is offset seaward of the downdrift side.

Inlet Stability. Bruun and Gerritsen (1960) distinguish three kinds of inlet stability: (1) bypassing stability, in which current through the inlet consistently deflects littoral drift from the updrift shore to the downdrift shore; (2) location stability, in which there is a low rate of migration of the inlet as a whole or of individual channels in the shoals; and (3) cross-sectional stability, in which a certain cross section or at least a certain cross-sectional area is maintained.

Battjes (1967) says that inlet stability is a state of dynamic equilibrium between antagonistic agencies. The agencies involved are littoral drift and the ebb and flow currents that transport sand through the inlet. Bruun and Gerritsen (1960) liken the back-and-forth movement of sediments through an inlet to a rolling carpet. Part of this carpet is continually deposited at both ends—that is, in the bay and in the ocean.

Coarse sand is usually the bottom material of inlets. Fine sand and silt are winnowed out by strong currents and carried to tidal flats, where they settle out as current velocity decreases. At the turn of the tide, current velocity is zero and suspended silt values are at their lowest. After the turn of the tide, the water mass moves in the opposite direction but carries less sediment seaward since the current is weaker. The effect of inlet scouring and of sediments settling during this lag at the turn of the tides is that fine particulate matter is deposited landward of a barrier in a complete tidal cycle (Postma, 1967).

Mathematics of Inlet Stability. Bruun and Gerritsen (1960, 1961) analyzed a great many inlets and found the following:

$\Omega/M > 300$ indicates a high degree of stability.
$\Omega/M < 100$ indicates a lower degree of stability.
$M/Q_m > 200$ to 300 indicates predominant bar bypassing.
$M/Q_m < 10$ to 20 indicates predominant tidal flow bypassing.

In these relations

Ω = tidal prism expressed in cubic units per half tide cycle
M = mean annual amount of littoral drift in cubic units per year
Q_m = maximum discharge through the inlet during an average
       spring tide expressed in cubic units per second.

Three factors must be considered in applying these criteria, according to Battjes (1967):

1. Omega (Ω) and Q are proportional to one another. For a simple harmonic tide $\Omega = Q_m T/\pi$, where T is the tidal period. Deviations from this relationship are minor compared to uncertainties and approximations involved in the criteria.

2. Tidal flow should not be used to indicate the flushing power of an inlet, but rather as an expression for the actual movement of material. For example, the maximum rate of sand transport through the inlet in the absence of littoral drift is V_0, and Ω or Q_m could be substituted because for natural conditions V_0 is roughly proportional to Ω or Q_m.

3. The parameter describing the littoral drift should be the rate of movement of material along the adjacent shores regardless of direction. Battjes proposes M', the mean total transport from both sides, instead of M, the mean net transport. Thus he would substitute M'/V_0 for Ω/M and M/Q_M as a dimensionless parameter indicative of the overall stability of the inlet as well as the mode of bypassing the littoral drift.

Sands and Coarse-Grained Material
The transportation of coarser sediments in an estuary has not been the subject of much study. It is well known that they generally move as a bedload and are moved primarily by strong tides, wind, and storms. The energy required to suspend coarse sediments is much greater than that required to suspend the finer particulate matter. Sand settles quickly and the velocity necessary to resuspend it is greater than the velocity that will resuspend fine particles.

One of the most important characteristics of sandy estuaries is the existence of separate ebb and flood channels. The flood channels gradually shoal landward, whereas the ebb channels typically follow a meandering course. The sand deposits brought in by tide and wave action are most commonly found near the mouths of estuaries and in the sea adjacent to the mouth of the estuary. The barrier islands, described above, and some of the linear islands formed in mouths of estuaries are due to the accumulation of such sediments.

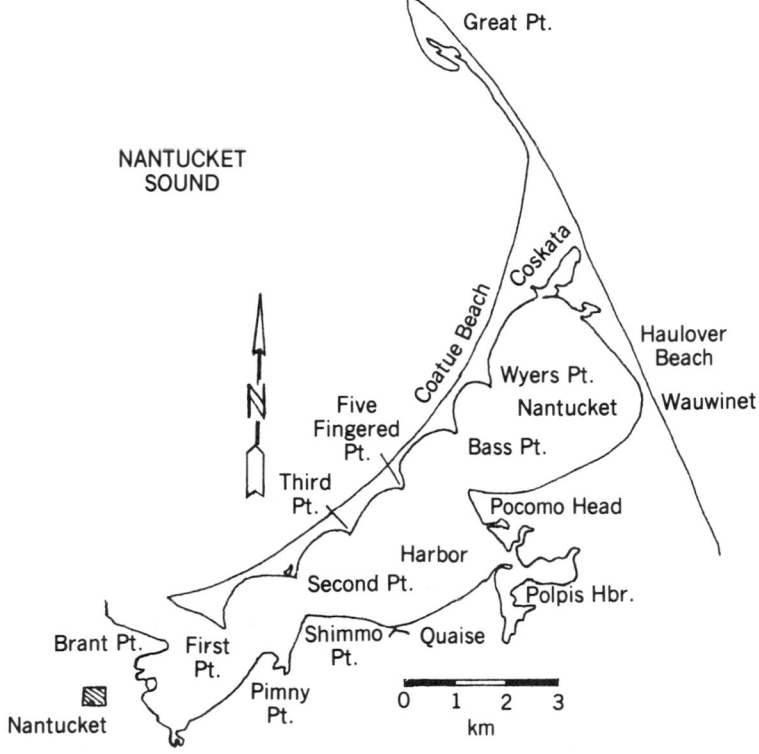

FIGURE 2.27. Cuspate spit shoreline behind Coatue Beach, Nantucket Harbor, Massachusetts. (From Rosen, 1975.)

Cuspate Spits

Sometimes, cuspate spits form in estuaries as a result of reorientation of the shoreline to the approach of the dominant wave (Zenkovich, 1959, according to Rosen, 1975). If the dominant wave is perpendicular to the shore in an elongate lagoon, there will be a point where the longshore sediment transport is constant. If anything obstructs the sediment load, the capacity will decrease, because of the decreased wave approach angle, and deposition will occur. A spit will begin to form from the shore at an angle of about 45°. Waves from the opposite direction will act similarly on the opposite side of the spit, which results in the cuspate form. Examples of such spits occur in Nantucket Harbor, Massachusetts (Figure 2.27).

DELTAS

Formation of Deltas

The sediments that accumulate in the delta region where a river enters the sea are a combination of fluvial and marine sediments. If the river is large and carries heavy suspended solids loads regularly or at irregular intervals, the fluvial sediments will predominate in such deposits. If the contribution of the river is small and/or the tidal and wave actions are strong, marine sediments will predominate.

The size and shape of such deposits are determined by many factors. Zenkovich (1967) states that the process of delta formation results in the deposition of alluvial material of various sizes in the sea and the extension of the river which flows over this material and branches into secondary water courses or channels. The most important factors controlling the size and types of deltas are (1) the relation of the amount of solid load to the wave regime of the sea, (2) the effects of tidal phenomena and swell on the structure of the delta, and (3) the past and present relative vertical movements of the surrounding area. When analyzing deltas the interaction of biological and pedological factors, size of material, climatic conditions affecting the nature of flooding, wind effects, and icing phenomena should be considered (Zenkovich, 1967).

The formation of deltas is dependent on the discharge and the sediment load that a river carries. Rivers that have discharges of less than 500 cfs ($14 \, m^3 \, s^{-1}$) usually do not develop deltas. Those with discharges of about 15,000 cfs ($425 \, m^3 \, s^{-1}$) develop cuspate deltas without distributary channels. If the discharge is upward of 50,000 cfs ($1416 \, m^3 \, s^{-1}$), large distributary systems are initiated and maintained. The major deltas of the world, such as the Amazon and the Nile, are characterized by deltas with distributary channels.

Major Factors Affecting Delta Formation. Coleman and Wright (1973) studied approximately 400 parameters of delta formation in 55 estuaries. Figure 2.28 diagrammatically illustrates what they consider the major process controls in the various parts of a riverine system. They defined the more important process parameters and the major controls they exert as follows:

1. *Climate.* Rainfall and evaporation determine the characteristics of the runoff in an alluvial valley; the in situ deposits within the alluvial valley and subaerial delta plain of several environments have significant effects on the sediment concentration reaching the river mouth.

2. *Relief in basin.* Within any climatic zone in a river basin, the higher the relief, the greater the sediment yield. Normally, high relief in the drainage basin is associated with steep channel gradients, and produces braided channel patterns and abundant sediment trading.

3. *Water discharge.* The more erratic the annual discharge, the greater the tendency toward channels that are braided, unstable, and shifting. Erratic discharges produce many overbank crevasse splays. Less erratic discharges are usually associated with meandering channels.

4. *Sediment yield.* High-bedload rivers have braided and rapidly shifting channels that form widespread sheets of sand. Low-bedload rivers normally have meandering patterns and well-formed "meander belt" sand bodies. High-suspended-load rivers usually have more stable channels.

5. *River mouth processes.* The geometry of distributary mouth bar deposits is strongly controlled by the relationship between bouyant, frictional, and

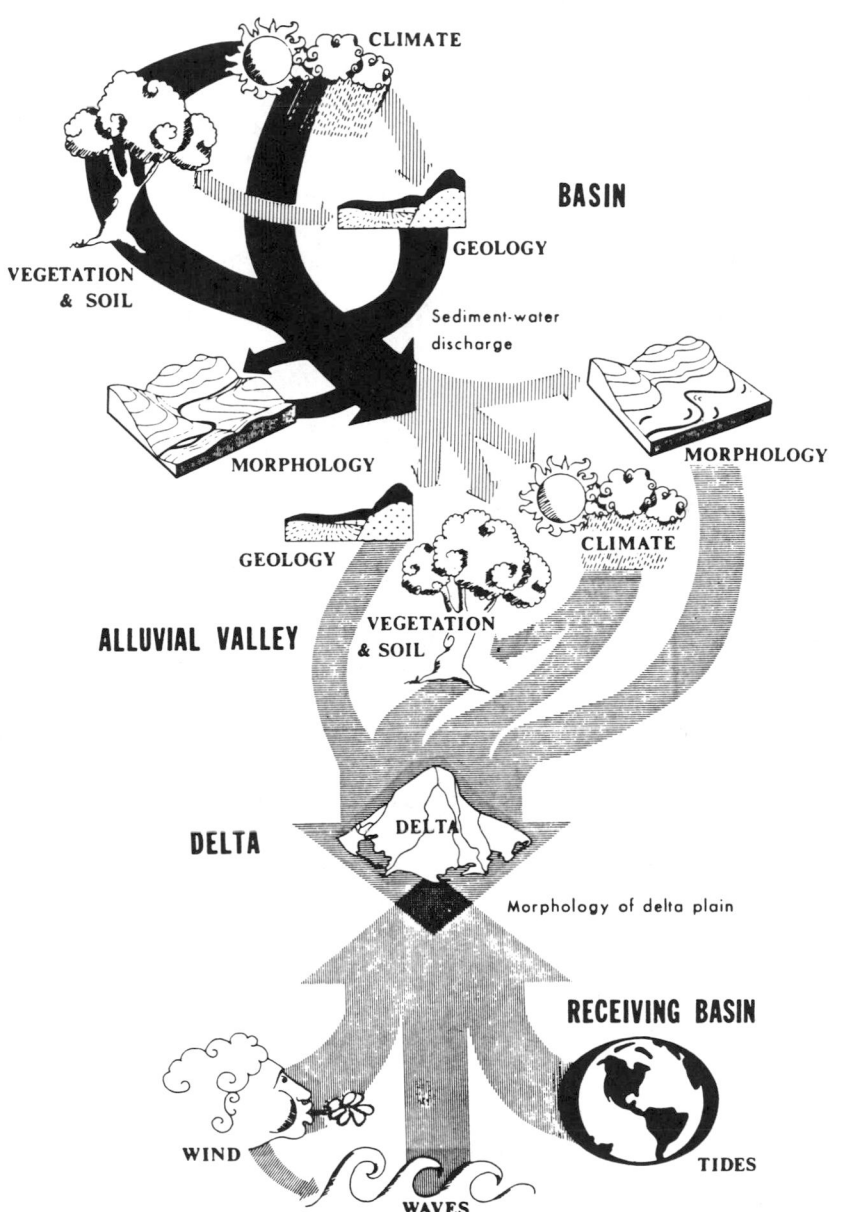

FIGURE 2.28. Diagrammatic illustration of major process controls in a river system. (From Coleman and Wright, 1973.)

inertial forces, and several distinct types may be formed. The channel patterns in the delta plain are formed to a large extent by the forces that control effluent plume geometry (sediment dispersal patterns), which are responsible for initiating several distinctive types of almost contemporaneous sediment deformational features.

6. *Wave power.* The higher the wave power, the greater the tendency toward the formation of nearshore sand bodies, which have a characteristic internal geometry. The distribution and geometry of nearshore sand bodies are strongly influenced by the phase relationships between wave power and river discharge maxima. River discharge may drastically modify deep-water wave power that may exert a strong control over nearshore discharge. High shoreline wave power commonly is associated with steep concave offshore slopes, and low wave power is more characteristic of low, convex offshore slopes and elongate "dirty" deltaic sand bodies. Widespread clean, highly quartzose deltaic sand bodies are characteristic of higher-wave-power environments. Wave-power variations at the shoreline provide distinctive channel patterns in the deltas.

7. *Tide.* The higher the tide range, the greater the tendency for distributary channels to be sand-filled. If the tidal prism is modified, the geometry and lateral continuity of the channel sand bodies may be greatly affected. Tidal range and channel gradient interactions control the distribution, shape, and abundance of overbank crevasse splays in deltas. Tidal modifications upriver greatly influence channel migration patterns in the lower part of the alluvial valley. High tide ranges in association with broad channel mouths produce linear offshore sand bodies.

8. *Alongshore currents.* The orientation and lateral continuity of deltaic and nearshore sand bodies are greatly affected by the intensity of these currents. Mechanisms responsible for generating currents produce and control distinctive relationships between sand body orientation and current directional properties. Often, a well-defined and distinctive zonation of biological communities results from strong coastal drift associated with low wave power. Without strong drift, an offshore–onshore zonation results.

9. *Wind system.* The relationship between wind systems and shoreline orientation strongly influences nearshore current patterns and the resulting geometry of sand bodies. Specific wind systems produce characteristic subaerial delta plain environments.

10. *Shelf slope.* Low-sloping continental shelves often are associated with shifting delta lobes, and steep offshore slopes are associated with channel "jumps" (Figure 2.29). A wide variety of subaqueous mass movement deformations result from river systems dumping sediments onto deep continental margins. If river-borne detritus is funneled through rivermouth submarine canyons on the continental shelf into deeper water, large deep-water deltaic fans are formed.

11. *Receiving basin geometry.* Strong control on delta configuration and delta switching patterns is exerted by the geometry of the receiving basin. The range of variability of delta types formed in a single depositional basin is often determined by the basin shape.

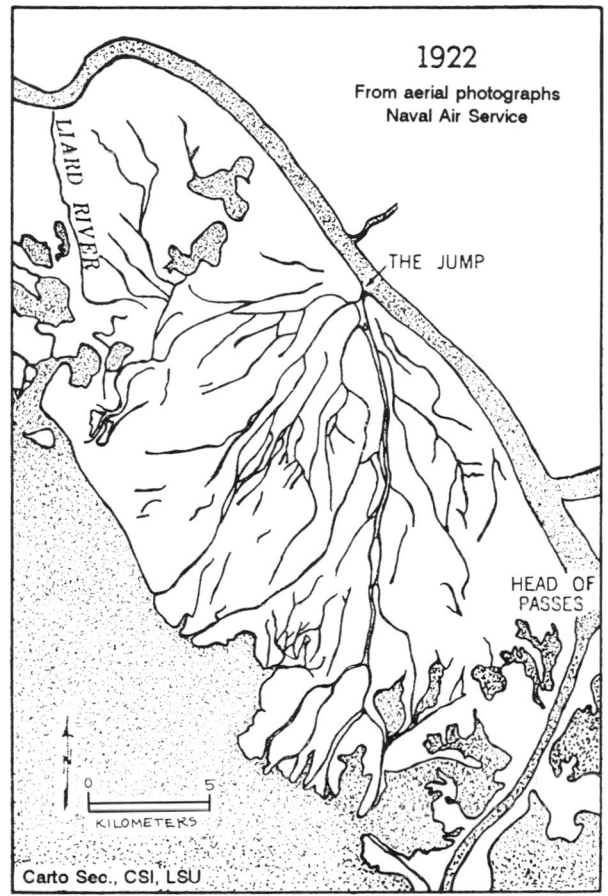

FIGURE 2.29. The Jump (West Bay, Mississippi delta) subdelta near height of depositional activity. (From Morgan, 1967.)

12. *Tectonic nature of the receiving basin.* The rate of subsidence greatly influences the thickness of the deltaic facies. The penecontemporaneous deformation of deltaic facies (diaprism, growth of faulting, mass wasting) is more common in basins displaying high subsidence rates.

Coleman and Wright (1973) found that even though a large number of delta facies might result from the interaction of these processes, a few models could be made to represent net sand distribution patterns resulting from their interaction (Figure 2.30).

Large River Deltas: Alluvial Sediments Dominate. If the river is as large as the Mississippi or the Volga, and flows into a shallow sea, the bed of the channel merges smoothly with the surrounding floor without marked change in depth or widening of the mouth. Deposits will be laid down outside the mouth and

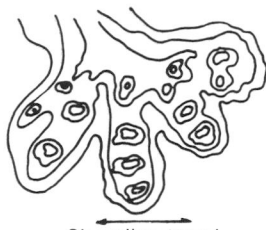

Shoreline trend

1. Low wave energy; low
   littoral drift; high
   suspended load.

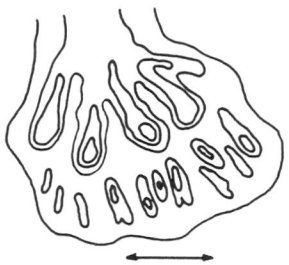

2. Low wave energy; low
   littoral drift; high
   tide.

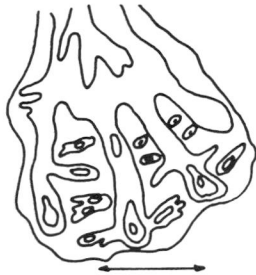

3. Intermediate wave
   energy; high tide; low
   littoral drift.

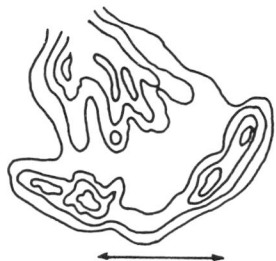

4. Intermediate wave
   energy; low tide.

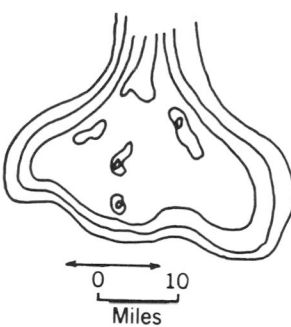

0   10
  Miles

5. High wave energy; low
   littoral drift; steep
   offshore slope.

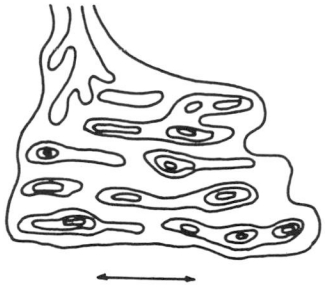

6. High wave energy; high
   littoral drift; steep
   offshore slope.

FIGURE 2.30. Schematic representation of net sand distribution patterns resulting from combinations of specific processes. Examples of each type include the following: 1, Mississippi (United States) and Magdalena (Colombia); 2, Ord and Victoria (Australia), Ganges–Brahmaputra (India–Pakistan), and Shatt al Arab (Iraq–Iran); 3, Irrawaddy (Burma), Mekong (Vietnam), and Burdekin (Australia); 4, Sagavanirktok (Alaska), Horton (Canada), and Apalachicola (United States); 5, Sao Francisco and Paraiba (Brazil) and Rhone (France); 6, Senegal (Senegal) and Marowyne (French Guiana–Surinam). (From Coleman and Wright, 1973.)

two channels will be formed. Subsequent growth of the delta with the accompanying effects of tidal and wave action will result in subdivision of the delta by many smaller channels and the formation of channel banks. The larger the delta becomes and the more irregular its contour over time, the more lagoons, marshes, and channels will develop, with subsequent complete separation of parts of the former delta into small islands (Figure 2.31).

Small River Deltas: Marine Sediments Dominate. Most of the rivers emptying on the coast of the United States are relatively small and marine sediments dominate in the formation of barrier islands, spits, and so on. Hayes (1975) has described the types of deltas found in microtidal estuaries (tidal range 0 to 2 m) and mesotidal estuaries (tidal range 2 to 4 m). As seen in Figure 2.31, small river-mouth deltas and flood-tide deltas may be formed within the inlet mouths.

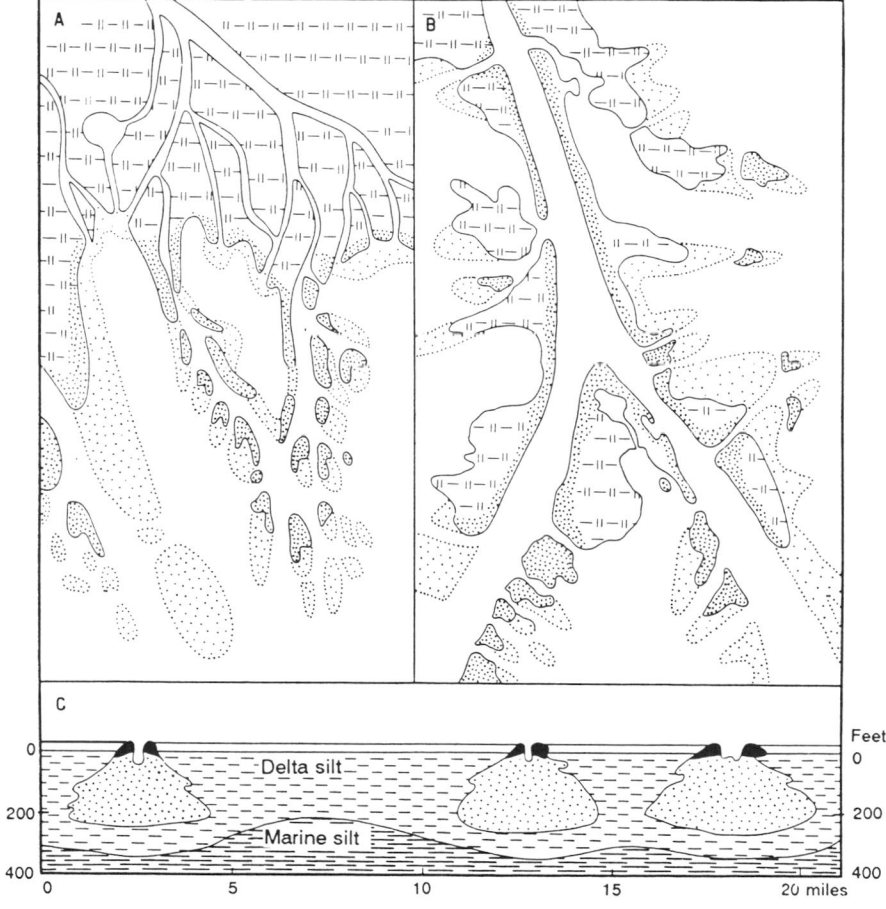

FIGURE 2.31. Structure of a delta: (*A*) the Volga; (*B*) the Mississippi; (*C*) section through the Mississippi delta obtained by drilling. Each channel of the river is denoted by a patch of sand; the black patches denote channel banks. (From Zenkovich, 1967.)

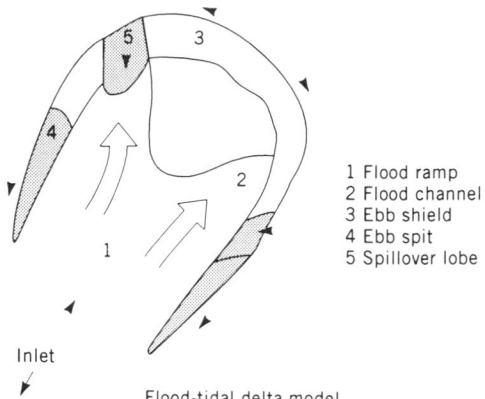

FIGURE 2.32.   Model of morphology of flood-tide delta. Arrows indicate dominant direction of tidal currents. Based on studies of tidal inlets on the coasts of New England, South Carolina, Alaska, and Baja California by the Coastal Research Division, University of South Carolina. (From Hayes, 1975.)

The flood-tide delta (Figure 2.32) consists of (1) a flood ramp, which is a seaward-facing slope on a sand body over which the main force of the flood current is directed; (2) flood channels, which are channels dominated by flood currents that bifurcate off the flood ramp; (3) ebb shields, which are high rims or margins around the tidal delta that protect it from modification by ebb currents; (4) ebb spits, which are formed by ebb tide currents; and (5) spillover lobes, which are lobate bodies of sediment formed by unidirectional currents.

In mesotidal estuaries flood deltas are formed as described above and shown in Figure 2.32. Ebb-tide deltas are formed that are outside barrier islands. In the formation of ebb tide deltas, ebb tide currents dominate over the flood-tidal currents.

Channel-margin linear bars flank the sides of the main ebb-tide channel, and are built by the interaction of ebb- and flood-tidal currents and wave-generated currents to form levee-like deposits. A relatively steep terminal lobe with a seaward slope is at the end of the main channel. Broad sheets of sand (swash platforms) flank both sides of the main channel. Swash bars are often built on swash platforms by the wash of wave action. Marginal flood-tide channels usually occur between the swash platform and adjacent downdrift and updrift beaches.

MARSHES

Marshlands are under tidal influence: lowland marshes are flooded during each tidal cycle, whereas upland marshes are usually flooded only once or twice a year during extreme high tides. In these areas the water table is very close to the surface and there are depressions that may remain flooded.

The most extensive marshlands are found in drowned river valley and barrier island estuaries, although marshes do occur on the west coast, where there have

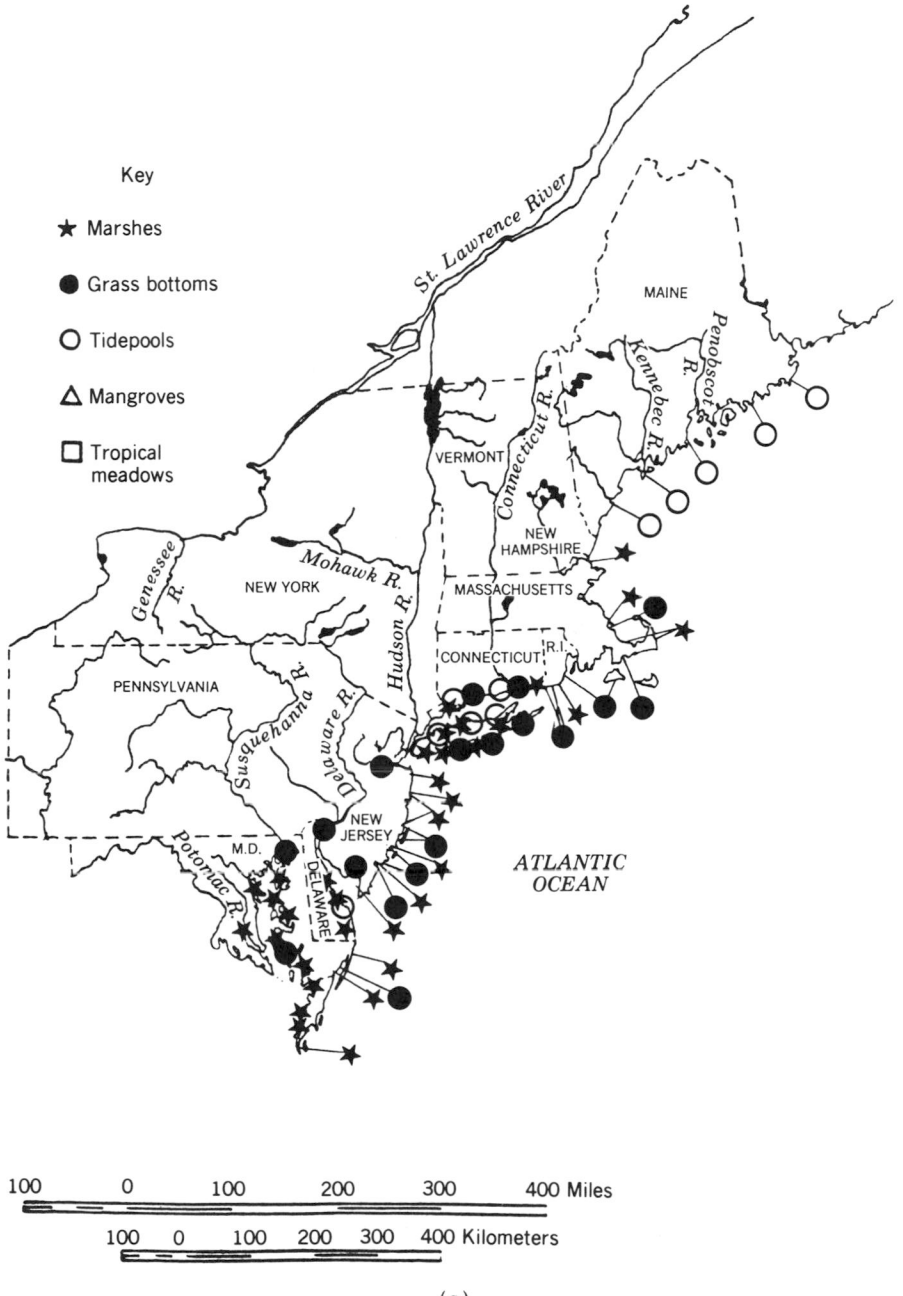

Key

★ Marshes

● Grass bottoms

○ Tidepools

△ Mangroves

☐ Tropical meadows

(a)

FIGURE 2.33. Different types of wetlands occurring on (a) the northern Atlantic coast of the United States; (b), the southern Atlantic coast of the United States, exclusive of Florida; (c) the Gulf of Mexico and the coast of Florida; and (d) the Pacific coast of the United States, including Alaska. (All after Copeland and Odum, 1974.)

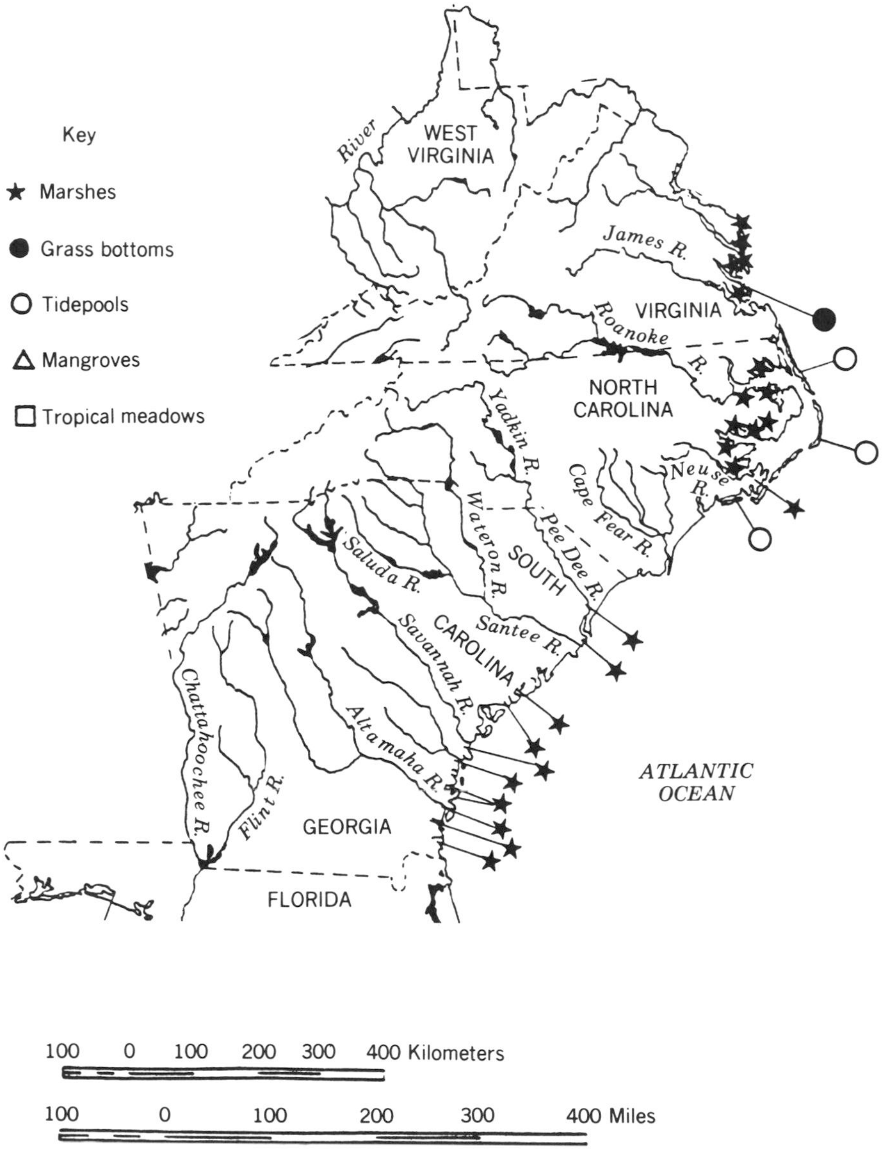

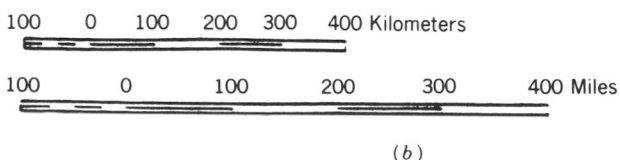

Key

★ Marshes

● Grass bottoms

○ Tidepools

△ Mangroves

□ Tropical meadows

WEST
VIRGINIA

River

James R.

VIRGINIA

Roanoke R.

NORTH
CAROLINA

Yadkin R.

Wateron R.

Cape Fear R.

Pee Dee R.

Neuse R.

Saluda R.

SOUTH

Santee R.

CAROLINA

Savannah R.

Chattahoochee R.

Flint R.

Altamaha R.

GEORGIA

FLORIDA

ATLANTIC
OCEAN

100   0   100   200   300   400 Kilometers

100   0   100   200   300   400 Miles

(b)

FIGURE 2.33.   (Continued)

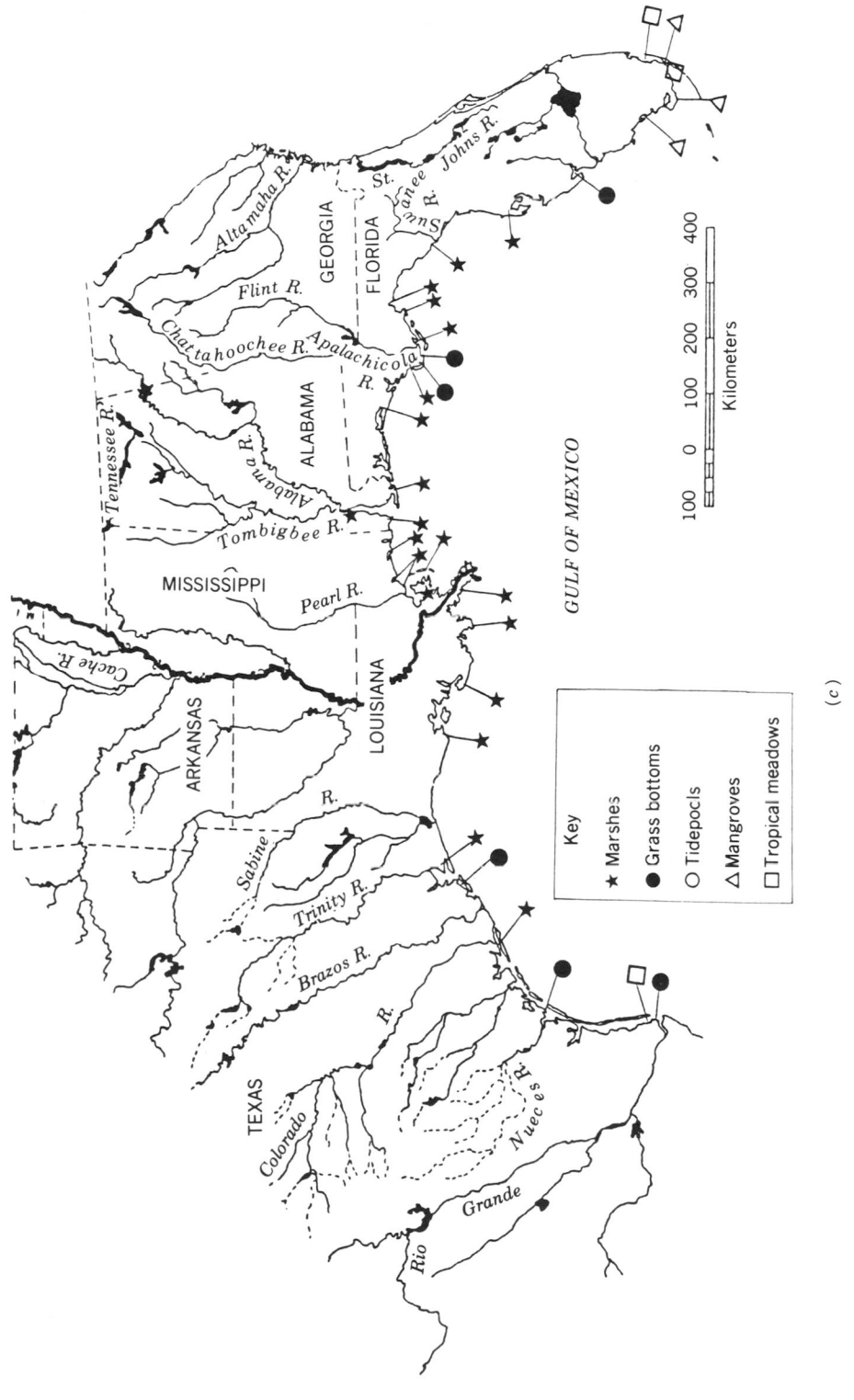

FIGURE 2.33. (Continued)

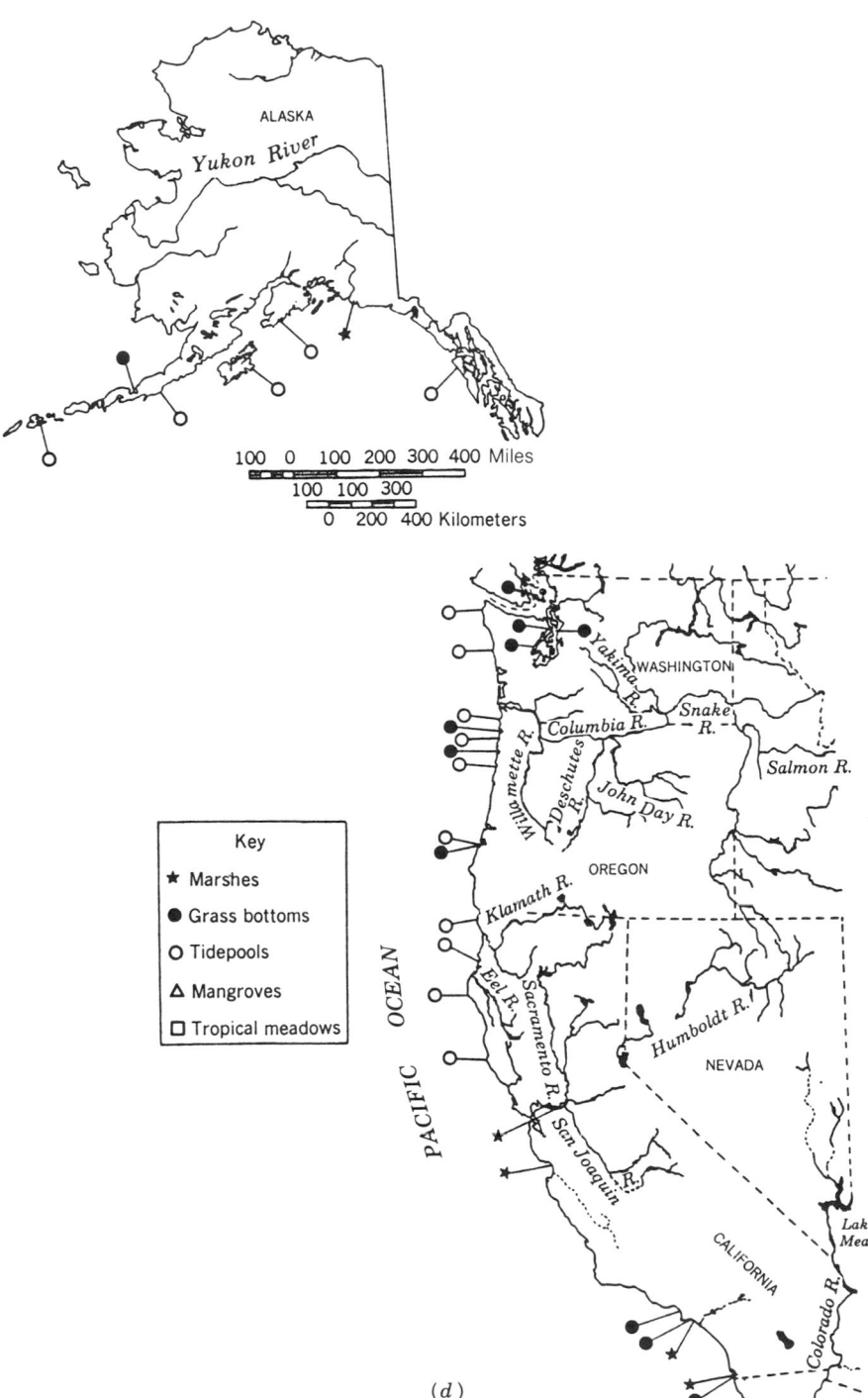

FIGURE 2.33.   (*Continued*)

been tectonic slippages. Grassy marshlands characterize the Atlantic coast, portions of the Gulf coast, and the west coast of the United States. Mangrove forest marshes are more characteristic of semitropical conditions along the Gulf coast and some parts of the east and west coasts of Florida. Figure 2.33 gives the location of U.S. marshlands. [Flint (1971) points out that the rise in sea level started about 10,000 years ago and that at first the rise was much faster than it has been in the last 5000 years (Figure 2.34).]

New England Marshes

Redfield (1967) states that the main forces involved in the salt marshes in New England are the range of tide, the growth physiology of peat–producing plants, sedimentation processes in open tidal flats and within the marsh itself, and long-term increases in the relative sea level. Bloom and Ellis (1965) recognize three main types of marshlands on the Connecticut coast.

Estuarine Freshwater Marshes. Estuarine freshwater marshes form along rivers which are subject to alternate acceleration and deceleration of current in

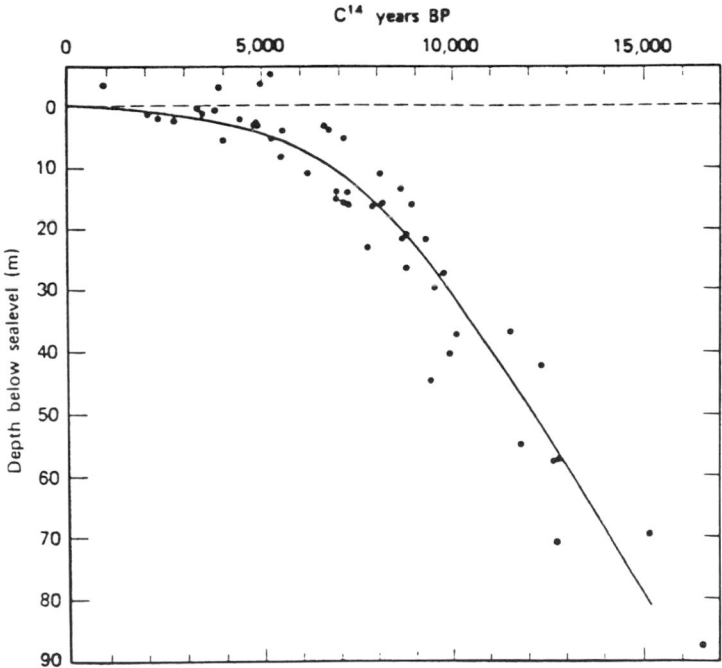

FIGURE 2.34. Submergence curve based on nearly 50 ^{14}C-dated samples of organisms taken from growth positions judged to have been close to sea level. Samples are from various depths along or off several coasts thought to have been "relatively stable." ^{14}C ages are plotted against depths. Curve reflects progressive submergence, believed to be chiefly eustatic. (From Glacial and Quaternary Geology, R. F. Flint. Copyright © 1971 by John Wiley & Sons, Inc. Reprinted by permission of John Wiley & Sons, Inc.)

response to tide, but have sufficient flow to hold back saltwater intrusion. The salinity is low and nutrients are abundant in the water. Peat production keeps pace with submergence, so a thick layer of sedge peat builds up, with its surface at the local high-tide level. An example is the marsh in Quinnipiac River valley at Hamden, in which over 15 ft of peat has accumulated.

Deep Marshes.   Deep marsh [9 to 50 ft (2.7 to 15.25 m) deep] development began with deglaciation when the rise of sea level was rapid, and many coastal valleys became flooded. For the last 3000 years the sea level has risen slowly, so that the sedimentation rate in the early bays and lagoons has exceeded the increase in depth. A typical stratigraphic section of these salt marshes is composed of a veneer of muddy salt marsh peat 9 ft (2.7 m) or less thick, overlying a thick wedge of mud that has an open-bay fauna. Below the mud in many marshes is a thin layer of sedge peat, in sharp contrast with the substratum. This peat represents the fringe of freshwater rushes and reeds that grew at the transgressing shoreline. An example of this is the Hammock River marsh near Clinton, Connecticut.

Shallow Marshes.   Shallow [less than 9 ft (2.7 m) deep] marshes were not affected by submergence prior to 3000 years ago. Many shallow marshes on the coastal lowlands, especially outwash plains, are of this type. They slope gently seaward for a mile (1.6 km) or more beyond the high-water line. Many of these areas were marshy even before submergence raised the water table. The stratigraphy of this type of marsh resembles that of the deep bay marsh except that lenses and tongues of sedge peat alternate in a complex way with the salt marsh peat. The alternations reflect variations in runoff or tidal height that changed the position of the boundary between the salt marsh and the freshwater marsh. Deeper parts of the marsh were apparently depressions present in the outwash plain before submergence.

New England Example of a Shallow Coastal Marsh.   The Barnstable estuary in Massachusetts, which has been analyzed extensively by Redfield (1959, 1967) and Redfield and Rubin (1962), is of the shallow type. Studies of the present-day marsh included coring of sediments and ^{14}C dating. The results of these studies showed that vegetation in the Barnstable Marsh, as in most grassland marshes on the eastern and southern coasts of the United States, was characteristic of high marshes and intertidal marshes.

Redfield (1972) recognized five stages in the colonization and early succession of the intertidal marsh.

1. Colonization of bare sand flats by *Spartina alterniflora* seedlings, including clump development and subsequent expansion by rhizome growth.
2. Development of a juvenile marsh of pure unbroken stands of *S. alterniflora*.
3. Panne marsh formation in bare areas where unequal sedimentation has produced poor drainage, thus killing the *S. alterniflora*.
4. Slough marsh development in which ridges covered with *S. alterniflora* develop between the pannes [the relative depth difference between panne bottoms and ridge tops is greater than in the early panne stage, and the marsh as a whole is about 1 ft (0.3 m) higher in elevation].

5. Ridges in those areas less than 3 ft (1 m) below mean high water broaden to fill in pannes as elevation increases. The relative amount of vegetated area increases but the *S. alterniflora* does not grow as tall.

Figure 2.35 is a contour map of Barnstable estuary showing low intertidal areas, high marsh areas, sand dunes, and upland areas. Figure 2.36 is a block diagram showing the depth of the peat along various sections across the head of the marsh at Barnstable. Figure 2.37 is a reconstruction, from coring, of the appearance of this area at various times in the past. The earliest age that has been reconstructed is 1300 B.C. when the sea level was 18 ft (5.5 m) below its present elevation. The marsh itself at the earliest stages consisted of isolated pockets of peat which occupied indentations in the uplying areas that are similar to those existing today along the shore of the open harbor east of Calves Pasture Point (Figure 2.35). The extension of the sand spit and the accumulation of sediments in the protected basin resulted in the marginal marsh becoming continuous and extending as an intertidal marsh in this enclosure. As the sea level rose, the marsh invaded the uplands, particularly the valley and the area of low relief to the west (Redfield, 1967).

The subsequent reconstruction, shown in Figure 2.37c and e, indicated that the marsh grew out into the basin as tongues whose beginnings were evident at the earlier stage. They occupied positions where, presumably, sand flats had built up. The marsh expanded by the establishment of vegetation on these flats. The vegetation subsequently became continuous, and the process can be seen taking place on intertidal flats today. The development of these marshy tongues resulted in the separation of the open water into broad sounds that narrowed progressively to define the position of the present major creeks. A comparison of Figure 2.37c, d, and e suggests that the sounds narrowed by the spreading of intertidal marsh onto sand flats where a meandering channel system was already developed. The marsh peat seems to have stabilized in a meandering pattern that has remained with little alteration as the peat has built up to the present high marsh level.

Goldthwait (1937) noted the stability of the meandering pattern of the channels of these tidal creeks. The various hydraulic forces appear to have developed a quasi-equilibrium between the processes of accretion and erosion. The bottoms of these channels that drain the marshlands are sand, and the banks of the creeks are high marsh that controls the pattern of the creeks, the quasi-equilibrium between the width, the quality of water, and the response of the marshlands to the rhythm of the tides. In a tidal estuary the width, depth, and velocity of flow vary with the power of the mean discharge, Q. The main difference in the hydraulic characteristics of an estuary and a freshwater stream is that the estuary has a much more rapidly changing velocity with discharge than that of the stream (Myrick and Leopold, 1963; Langbein, 1963).

Mid-Atlantic Shallow Coastal Marsh. An example of a shallow marsh in the middle Atlantic states is the marshland drained by the Broadkill River into the lower Delaware estuary. DeWitt (1974) found that the Broadkill River was divided into three portions: the lower portion, the upper estuarine portion, and

FIGURE 2.35.   The Barnstable estuary, showing the distribution of depth of peat in the high marsh. Contour intervals, 6 ft (1.83 m). (After Redfield, 1967.)

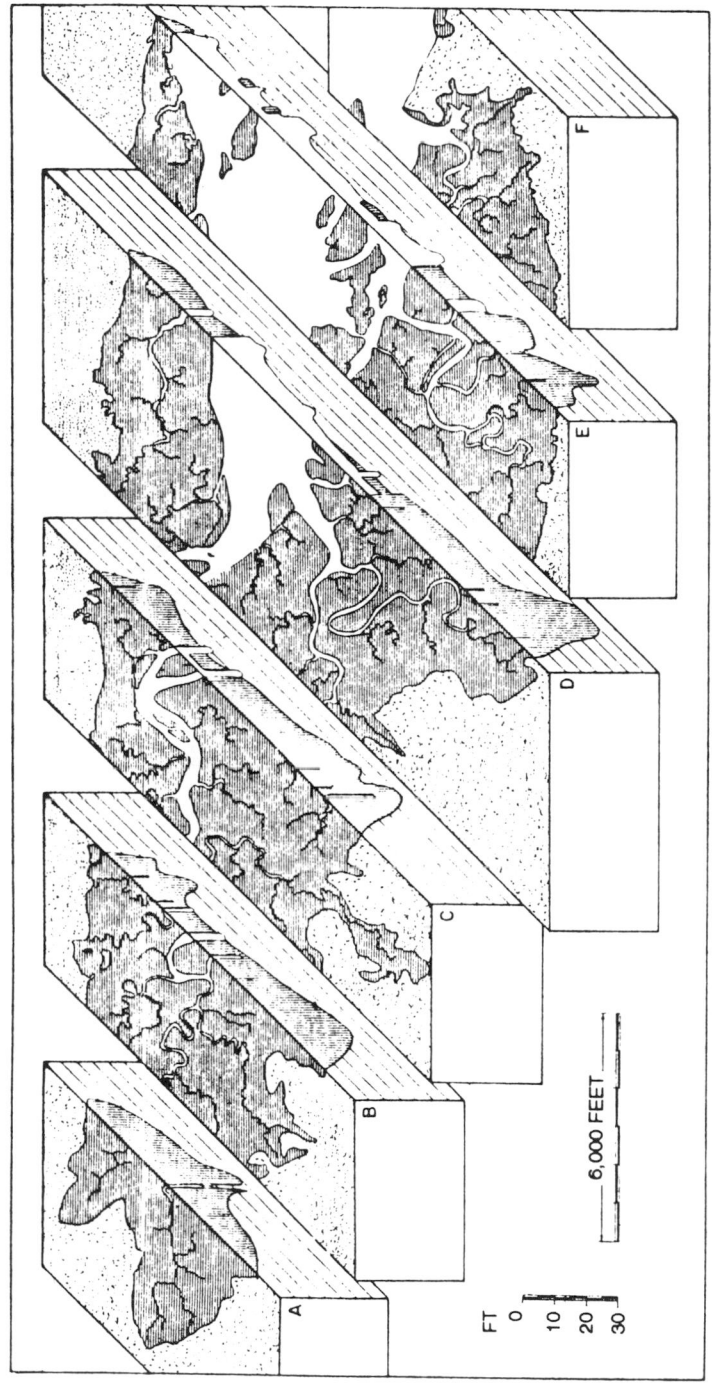

FIGURE 2.36. Block diagram showing the depth of peat along sections across the marsh at Barnstable. (From Redfield, 1967.)

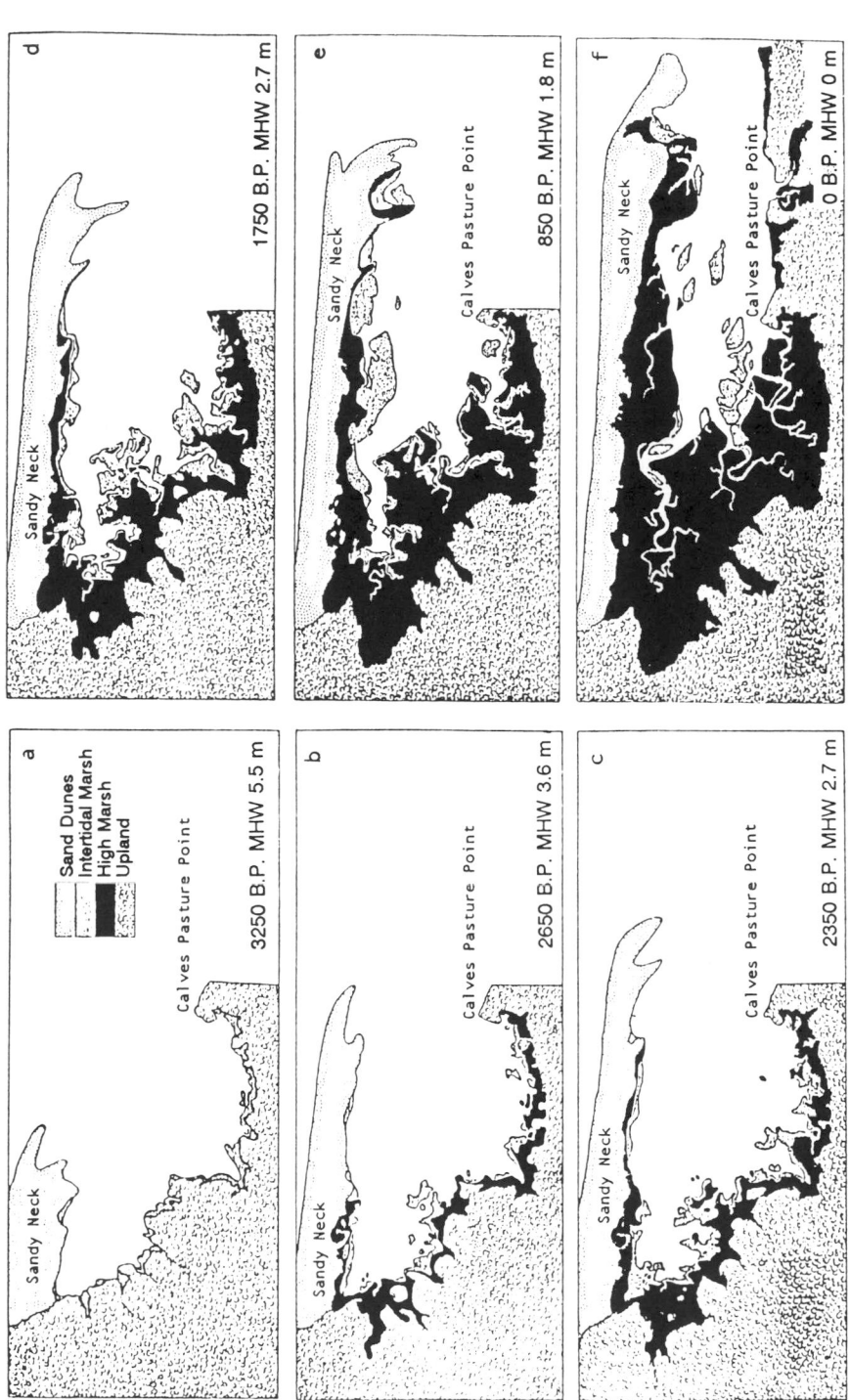

FIGURE 2.37. Reconstruction of the history of the Barnstable Marsh, Massachusetts. Dates are years before present (A.D. 1950); depths are in reference to present mean high water, in feet. (After Redfield, 1965.)

84

the river portion. In the lower part of the stream the salinity variations were directly related to tidal amplitude, but at various seasons of the year the salt concentration could be greatly influenced by runoff. For example, in the summer, when runoff was high, the salinity was much less than in the winter, when runoff was low. The salinity of the water was homogeneous both laterally and vertically, except for a salt wedge that existed at the mouth of the stream at the beginning of the flooding cycle. The ebbing velocities were stronger than the flooding velocities.

The upper estuary portion of the system was stratified as to salinity at high slack water. The mean current velocity in this section was less than in the lower part of the river. In this section the ebbing currents were stronger than the flooding currents in all parts of the water column.

In the riverine section, which was not directly under the salinity influence of tidal flow, there was only seasonal variation in salinity, which was correlated with runoff. The velocity of the current in this area was least, and the ebbing and flooding waters had about equal current.

Southeastern Marshes
The most extensive marshlands in the United States are found south of Chesapeake Bay, on the Atlantic coast, and along the Gulf shores. In southeastern Florida and along the Gulf states the grassland marshes often give way to the mangrove forest marsh.

The outer banks of North Carolina form a barrier behind which brackish-water sounds and their accompanying marshes develop. Similar sounds can be found from Virginia through the Carolinas, where flooding is irregular and tidal amplitudes are usually less than 1 ft (0.3 m). Rapid changes in wind direction and velocity accompany the movement of weather fronts in this region and drive the high tides that cause flooding. Marshall (1974) estimated that these irregularly flooded swamp marshes covered 205,750 acres (833 km^2) in North Carolina.

Gulf Coast Marshes
Another type of salt- or brackish-water marsh is formed in deltas. The work of Coleman and Smith (1964) in the western part of the Mississippi deltaic plain produced evidence, based on peat deposits, of a 4700-year-old Mississippi delta in the vicinity of Marsh Island, Louisiana. The deltaic mass covered by this marshy peat deposit accumulated when the rising sea was 10 ft (3.05 m) below its present level. Subsequent depositions have coalesced to form vast marshlands that extend many miles east of the older delta. As long as the river provides depositional sediments and the erosion by tidal action is not too great, these marshlands will continue to exist. However, a decrease in river flow or subsidence of the coastline will cause the compact natural sediment levees along the channels to slump, and their subsidence often causes the inflow of water to form elongated ponds parallel to the outer or stronger natural levee. Thus the large marshy

areas become open water. An example of such an embayment area extends inland between the distributary systems of the present Mississippi level and the abandoned distributaries of the older LaFourche–Mississippi delta.

A complex interconnected baylike network extends inland from brackish Barataria Bay through less brackish Little Lake into freshwater Lake Salvador and Lake des Allemands. This entire lake and bay complex with interconnecting bayous traverses a low, generally marshy basin. The Barataria–Salvador basin has been deprived of active sedimentations since the LaFourche–Mississippi system deteriorated in favor of the modern delta about 700 years ago. In much of the basin, vegetation growth has kept pace with slow regional subsidence, forming broad expanses of floating marsh, but most ponds, lakes, and bays have gradually enlarged as a result of wave action on their marshy shores (Russell, 1942). As the ponds enlarge they coalesce to form lakes, which in turn are able to generate waves even more effective in accelerating erosion of the banks. By subsidence and erosion of unconsolidated sediments, such interdeltaic estuaries gradually enlarge and the marshlands deteriorate (Morgan, 1967).

The marshlands of Matagorda Bay, Texas, usually have been formed by sediment-deposited deltas from Garcitas Creek, Lavaca River, and the Colorado River of Texas. They have also been formed by the breaking of logjams in the Colorado River (McGowen and Brewton 1975).

The extent of the marshes has varied greatly over the last 100 years under the influence of accretion of sediments discharged by the rivers and the erosion caused by the effects of wind, hurricanes, and wave action. Marshes can be buried beneath sediments during hurricanes or can be damaged by drought. Human beings have also brought about the burial of wetlands by the deposition of dredge spoil. In some cases new wetlands have been created by spoil outwash and by changing river regimes, which have resulted in a change in the volume of fresh water and sediments delivered to the bay margins.

During the period 1856 to 1957, approximately 2650 acres (10.72 km^2) of land were lost by erosion along the bay side of Matagorda Peninsula. Erosion accounted for almost half of the loss of the marsh area. The marsh area was reduced at a rate of about 26 acres (0.1 km^2) per year through shoreline erosion. Burial beneath outwash deposits, possibly in conjunction with the droughts in 1950, accounted for approximately 3150 acres (12.75 km^2) of marsh reduction. In the region of the Pass Cavallo tidal delta and along the bay side of Matagorda Island, approximately 1925 acres (7.8 km^2) was lost. Of this lost marsh area, approximately 475 acres (1.92 km^2) was destroyed by erosion along Pass Cavallo, and approximately 1450 acres (5.87 km^2) was destroyed by burial beneath sediments and perhaps by drought conditions. Within the area bounded on the east by Caney Creek and extending to the northwest boundary of Brown Cedar Cut there were some large patches of marsh that had been destroyed by drought (McGowan and Brewton, 1975).

In some areas marshlands have increased. There has been an increase of about 130 acres (0.53 km^2) at the mouth of Garcitas Creek and also an increase of about 55 acres (0.22 km^2) at the mouth of Lavaca Creek. Flood-tidal deltas totaling about 340 acres (1.54 km²) have also been formed at Brown Cedar Cut and at Greens Bayou. The Lake Austin area has also had an increase in wetland area of about 835 acres (3.38 km²), primarily as a result of subsidence of the Brazos–Colorado delta (McGowan and Brewton, 1975).

Human beings have also brought about the burial and creation of wetlands by the deposition of dredge spoil. The removal of some 46 miles (74 km) of logjam along the lower Colorado River changed the river regime and released a large volume of sediments into Matagorda Bay. Rapid deltation resulted in the creation of about 7910 acres (32 km²), of which 4000 acres (16.19 km²) was marshland. Along the northern shore of Matagorda Bay there are two areas of spoil outwash that are now inhabited by marsh plants. These are east of the Colorado delta and south of McNab Lake, about 316 acres (1.28 km²); and west of the Colorado delta and south of Freshwater Lake, about 265 acres (1.07 km²). Thus it is evident that erosion, both natural and human-made, has decreased marshlands in the Matagorda Bay area at the same time that natural forces and human activities have increased marshlands. The overall shift in marshlands of this area continues (McGowan and Brewton, 1975).

West Coast Marshes

The marshlands of the west coast are far more limited than those on the Atlantic or Gulf coasts and have been studied much less. Most marshes are formed on sediments deposited in small embayments in rivers. In the southern part of the west coast, rivers have seasonal flow and empty directly into the ocean or into heavily dredged areas that were once small embayments.

Originally, marshes were scattered along the edges of San Francisco Bay, but most of them have been eliminated. Marshes in San Francisco Bay are built on alluvial fans produced by streams running out of the nearby Santa Cruz mountains and by freshwater flow from the San Joaquin and Sacramento river systems. The soil is composed mainly of fine-grained sediments. In Washington and Oregon the marshlands are confined to the borders of some estuaries and to points of inflow of small streams, as in the Olympic Peninsula.

Mangrove Forest Marshes

The tide is of great importance to the development of mangrove forests, as it makes possible highly variable salinity and by this variation it encourages mangroves and keeps out other plants that might compete with them. Where tidal ranges are small, the wind often forces seawater into the shallow basins, and thus produces highly variable salinity gradients.

It has been found that mangroves can live in areas in Puerto Rico where the tidal range is less than $\frac{1}{3}$ m (Biebl, 1962), as well as in Australia in areas where the tidal range exceeds 3 m (Macnae, 1967). Mangroves also line the upper reaches of rivers in the Everglades where the tidal ranges are very small. Mangroves may become established in silicious and marl sands that are more commonly found associated with marl gravel and marl rock.

EXAMPLES OF HYDROLOGY, CIRCULATION, AND
SEDIMENTATION PATTERNS OF ESTUARIES IN
THE UNITED STATES

New England Estuaries.   Most New England estuaries have relatively small
inlets, restricted outlets, and limited influx. The volume of fresh water entering
an estuary relative to the volume of the tidal prism is critical in determining
whether salt-fresh water stratification will occur. The total discharge of the
stream divided by the total tidal volume provides a ratio for determining the
degree of stratification in estuaries. When the ratio exceeds approximately 10%,
the estuary becomes stratified (Farrell, 1971).

   Merrimack River Estuary.   The Merrimack estuary (Figure 2.38) is a partially
mixed estuary that receives an annual discharge of approximately 7000 cfs
($198 \, m^3 \, s^{-1}$) (Hartwell and Hayes, 1969). When the tide floods during periods
of normal and high runoffs, a sharp, slightly tilted boundary develops between
the intruding saltwater mass and the overriding fresh water. The salt water
from the ocean is deflected to the north side of the estuary, and freshwater
ponds develop on the south side, where significant amounts of suspended solids
and pollutant loads carried by the river are deposited.

   The hydrology of this estuary reveals the presence of horizontal or entwined
boundary stratifications during average flow periods—the ratio is 11.8%. During
high freshwater flows the ratio equals 38.7% and the discharge virtually excludes
the salt wedge. At low freshwater flow the ratio is 2.86%. The lack of fresh
water prevents a freshwater layer from developing. "When the discharge drops
below approximately 3000 cfs (about $85 \, m^3 \, s^{-1}$) the stratification disappears and
the estuary becomes partially mixed. Maximum ebb current velocities are
frequently twice as strong as flooding current velocities. They are concentrated
in the upper portion of the water column, whereas the maximum flood current
velocities occur near the bottom" (Hartwell, 1970).

   Parker River Estuary.   The Parker River estuary, which is situated behind
Plum Island, Massachusetts (Figure 2.38), contains large meander loops in the
main channel, large point bars on the loops, and a complex flood-tidal delta
system. Numerous tributary creeks branch off the main body of the estuary.
The ebb currents are stronger than flood currents in the main channel, whereas
flood currents are stronger than ebb currents in the flood bifurcations off the
main channel and over the tidal flats.

   Salinities.   There is an average freshwater influx of 112 cfs ($3.17 \, m^3 \, s^{-1}$)
and the estuary is predominantly horizontally and vertically mixed. There is
some tendency toward a slight horizontal salinity stratification that becomes
more pronounced during ebb tide in the upper reaches of the estuary. The
maximum salinity difference between surface and bottom waters is 4% (DaBoll,
1969, cited in Hayes, 1971a). Most New England estuaries resemble the
hydrographic makeup of the Parker River estuary.

   Saco River and Royal Estuaries.   In his studies of the Saco River and Royal
estuaries (Maine), Farrell (1971) showed that excellent stratification occurred
under average flow conditions—that is, ratios of 27% and 10.5%, respectively.

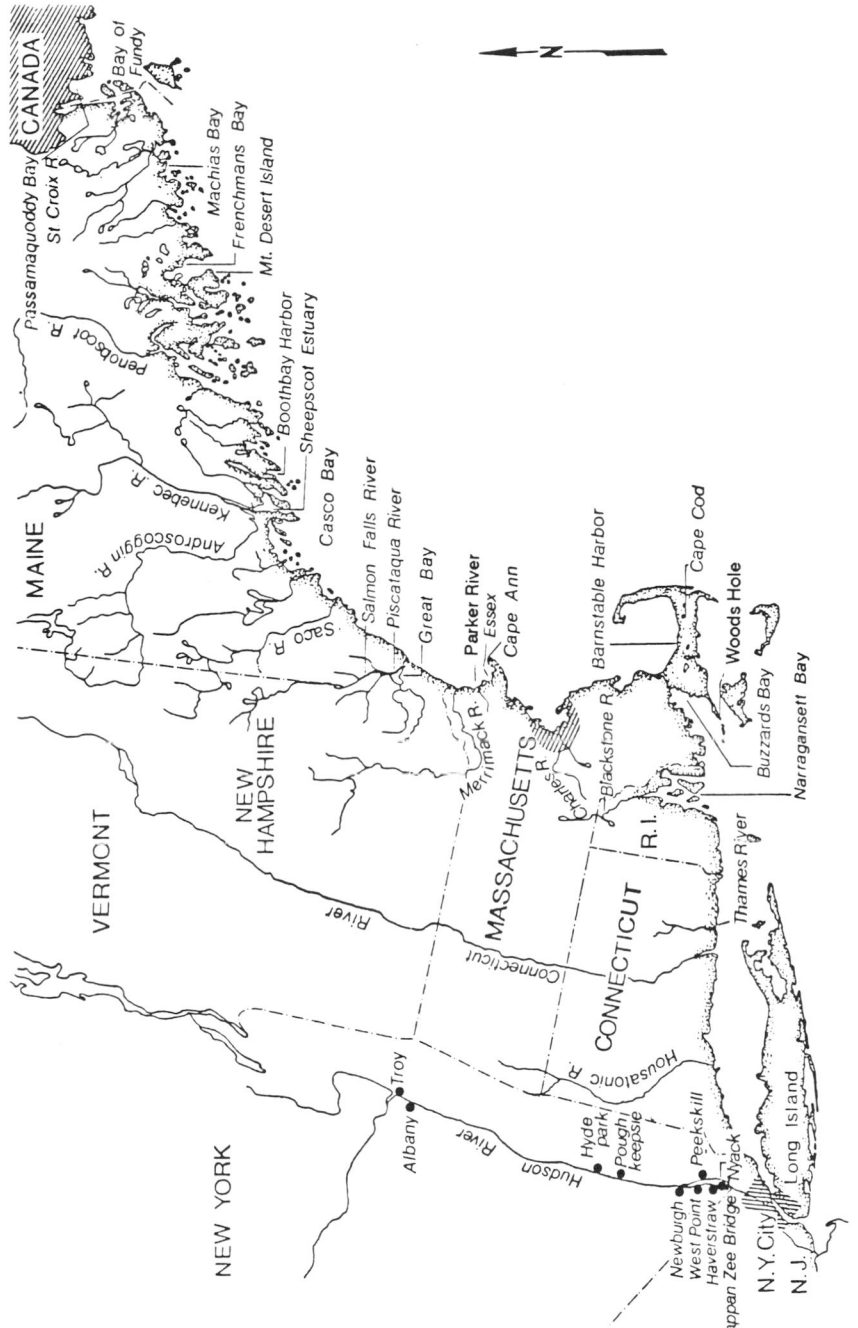

FIGURE 2.38. Location of selected estuaries on the New England coast. (After Kuenzler, 1974.)

Connecticut River Estuary

Salinities. The distribution of temperature and salinity in the Connecticut River estuary has been described by Garvine (1975). The Connecticut River is the largest New England river, with a mean discharge of fresh water of $560 \, m^3 \, s^{-1}$, and is comparable with major rivers, such as the Hudson and Delaware, of the Atlantic coastal plain of the United States.

In contrast to these rivers, the lower valley of the Connecticut is tightly constricted by hills of crystalline bedrock. Consequently, the estuary serves as a long, narrow conduit to tidal currents induced by the rise and fall of adjacent waters in Long Island Sound. Tidal currents, but not tidal flux, are perceptible nearly 100 km upstream. The tidal flux is relatively small; the ratio of the tidal influx to freshwater flow volume during flood portions of the tidal cycle is about 0.5 for mean conditions, compared to ratios of 10 and 140 for the Hudson and Delaware rivers (Ketchum, 1951b).

Largely because of its relatively low tidal volume flux, the Connecticut River estuary is of the salt wedge type. As such, it is unique among the major rivers of the United States, and in general character it is comparable only to the conditions at South Pass on the stem of the Mississippi River within its delta (Wright and Coleman, 1971).

During times of discharge above the mean, the estuarine portion of the Connecticut River is nearly free of salt at all depths, even during flood times. When discharge levels are well below the mean, salt water from Long Island Sound penetrates upstream nearly 20 km above the mouth. Figure 2.39 shows the isohalines at ebb tide for high slack water and for low slack water.

Meade (1966) showed in his studies of salinity that under low-tide conditions winds could affect the salinity within the river by acting on the local sea level. Garvine (1975) studied the temperature and salinity at 0.5 m depth. He found that the low temperature was about 1 °C within the river in 1972 and was about 3 °C in February 1973. The high temperature in the river climbed to about 25 °C in August 1972, whereas the summer peak in Long Island Sound was 22 °C. In general, the annual temperature cycles in the river and the sound were similar but a little more extreme in the river during winter and summer.

The results of these studies clearly showed that the temperature distribution was highly correlated with salinity distribution. A simple linear relationship between temperature and salinity permits the prediction of temperature distribution with good accuracy, given the salinity fraction distribution and the temperature of the freshwater and saltwater masses. The yearly cycles of temperature seemed to be predominantly seasonal, whereas the yearly cycles of salinity were correlated with freshwater discharge. The major controlling parameters governing the horizontal salinity and hence temperature distribution are stream flow, tidal flow, and tidal phase (Garvine, 1975).

Middle Atlantic Estuaries

Delaware River Estuaries. Most studies of the Delaware River have been in the stretch between Trenton and the Appoquinimink River. The studies of the Delaware Bay are much less in number.

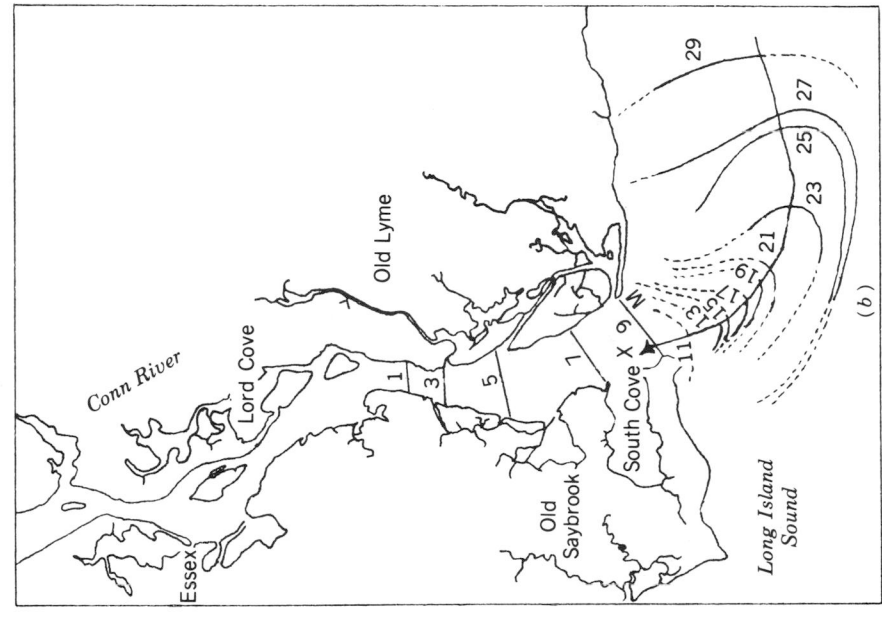

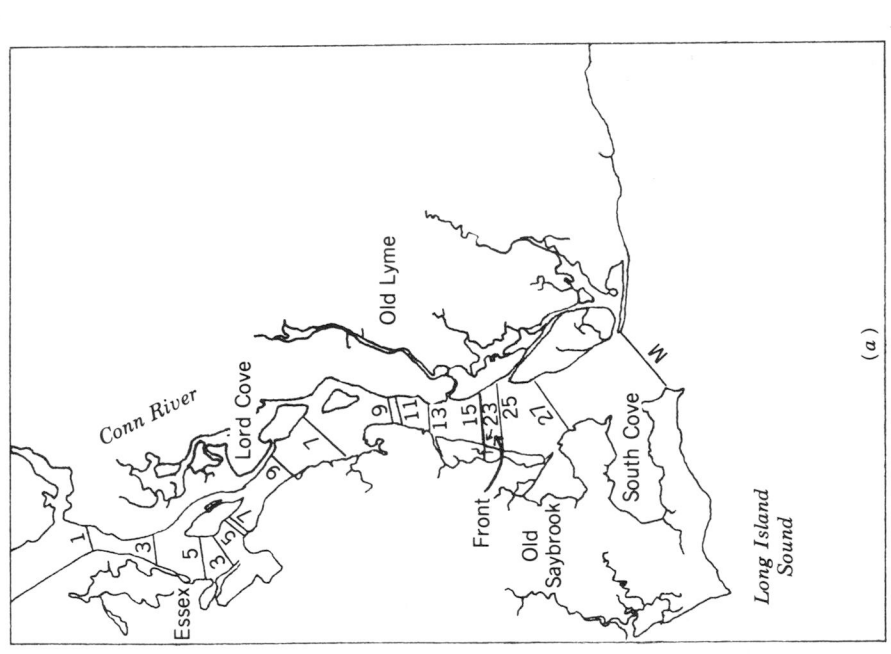

FIGURE 2.39. Connecticut Estuary isohalines in parts per mil at 0.5 m depth for July 29, 1973, at (a) high slack water and (b) low slack water. The plume axis coordinate, X, is indicated. (After Garvine, R. W. Journal of Geophysical Research No. 80, pp. 1176–1183, 1975, Copyright by the American Geophysical Union.

The length of the estuary from Trenton to the Appoquinimink River is about 78 miles (125.5 km). Trenton is the upper end of tidal influence; however, saltwater penetration rarely occurs above the Walt Whitman Bridge, which is approximately 44 miles (70.8 km) from the Appoquinimink River. The Delaware River is approximately 810 m wide at the Walt Whitman Bridge, 1980 m wide at the Delaware Memorial Bridge, and 3690 m wide at Reedy Point, near the Appoquinimink River.

Salinities. The maximum concentration of dissolved solids, which is approximately the Delaware River's salinity, occurs between June and October when the freshwater flow is lowest. The lowest concentration of salinity occurs between October and June. At Philadelphia the river level and salinity are mainly a function of freshwater flow in March and April; whereas in August, September, and October, they are mainly a function of sea level. The most important factors affecting the extent of salinity are freshwater flow and the seawater level.

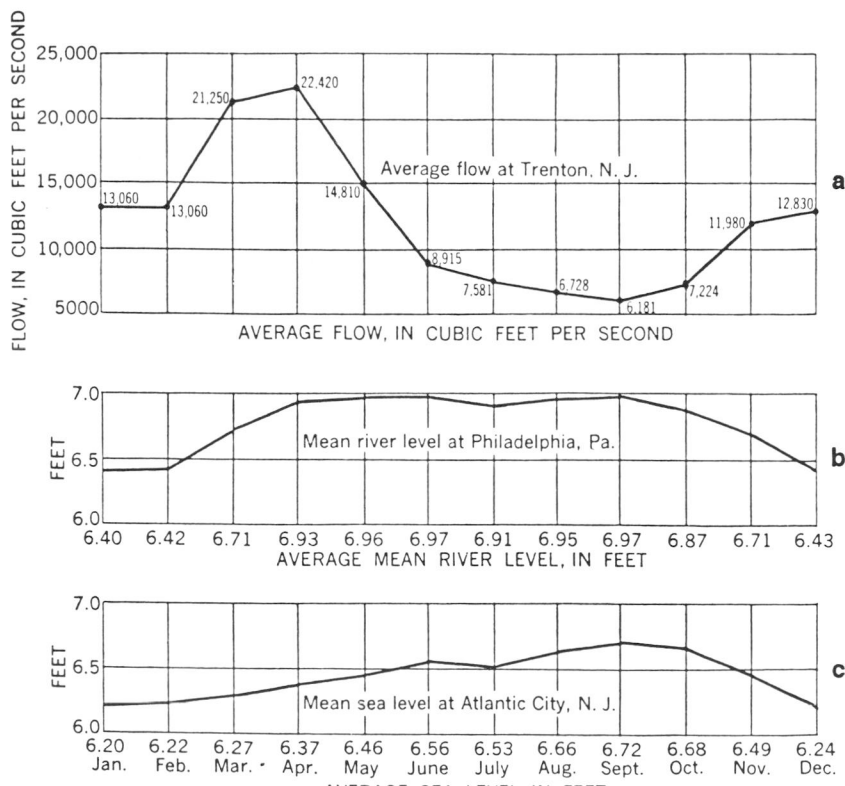

FIGURE 2.40. (a) Curves of average flow in the Delaware River at Trenton, New Jersey; (b) mean river level at Philadelphia; (c) mean sea level at Atlantic City, New Jersey. (On the basis of 33 years of record, 1923 to 1955.) (From Cohen and McCarthy, 1966.)

The relationship between the average river flow in cubic feet per second, the average mean river flow in feet at Philadelphia, and the average sea level in feet is given in Figure 2.40. Usually, the dominant effect on river water level in the Delaware estuary is that of changes in sea level, and only under very heavy freshwater flows (early spring) does the river flow affect the river level. Therefore, usually when the mean river water level increases, quantities of salt water are moving into the river and generally increase the salinity of the river. The converse is true when the mean river level is falling. Ebb and flood tides occur very close to slack water ebb and slack water flood times. In a tidal cycle salinity is at a maximum at approximately the time of high slack water and at a minimum at approximately the time of low slack water. In general, the salt water in the estuary increases toward the mouth, and the gradient of salinity becomes more pronounced (Figure 2.41).

Biggs (1972) reported on the research carried out on the deposition of sediments in the Delaware estuary and correlated this with pH and redox potentials (Eh), as shown in Figure 2.42. He found that sands were characteristically found in the center portion of the middle bay, whereas sediments with larger percents of silt and clay formed belts near the Delaware side of the bay and seemed to parallel it. This suggests that silt and clay sources were present along the Delaware shore and/or that the Delaware side was the prime deposition site for fine sediments.

Clay particulate matter often carries down with it organic matter, and this organic matter may have an oxygen demand since it is easily digested by bacterial activity. A lower redox potential with lower oxygen is often found in deposits of fine-grained sediments.

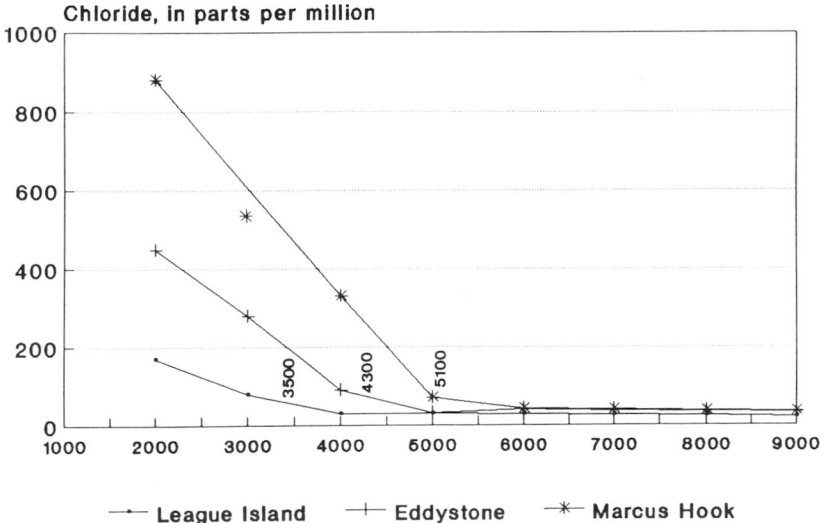

FIGURE 2.41.   Discharge and chloride concentration at three locations in the Delaware River, August 1949 to December 1963. (From Keighton, 1966.)

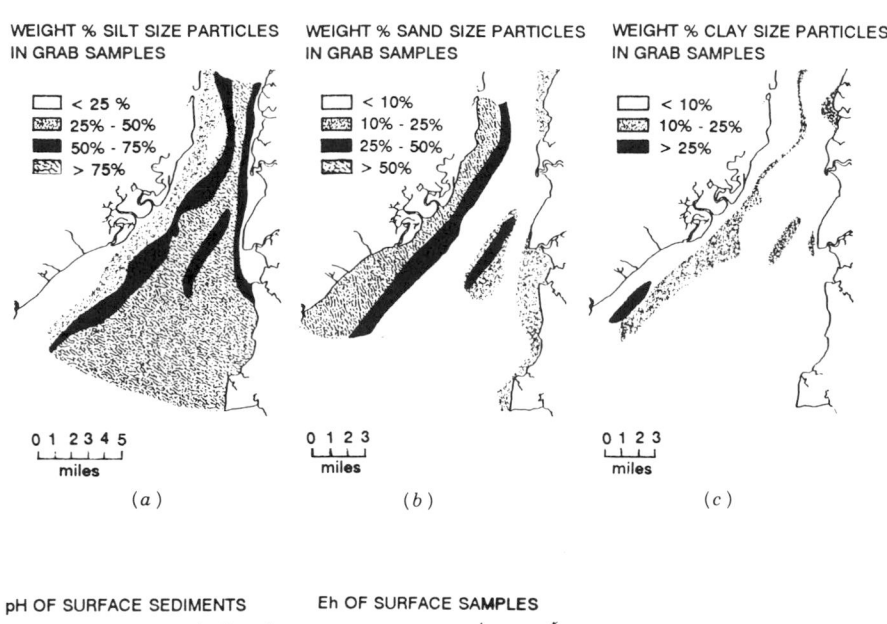

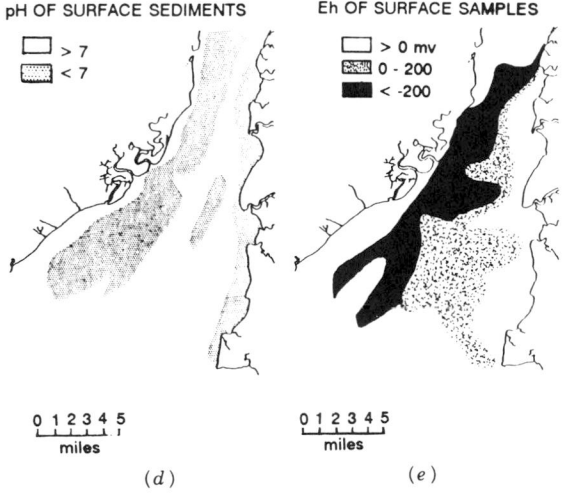

FIGURE 2.42. Delaware Bay: (*a*) distribution of silt in the surface sediments (contour interval 25%, with area less than 10% shown); (*b*) distribution of sand in the surface sediments (contour interval, 25% by weight); (*c*) distribution of clay sized particles in the surface of sediments, (*d*) generalized pH distribution in surface sediments; (*e*) generalized Eh distribution in surface sediments. (From Biggs, 1972.)

Since clays and silt often have electrically active surfaces and sorb onto their surfaces many other substances, certain heavy metals and various other pollutants may be concentrated on them. The presence of certain elements sorbed onto colloids may also tend to lower the pH of the waters. This relationship between particle size and lower pH and Eh is valid when viewed on a gross scale. For example, there is some correlation between these three factors in the Delaware Bay (Figure 2.42). It is interesting to note that oyster beds are found on the east side of the bay where less clay is present.

Chesapeake Bay and Its Tributaries. The Chesapeake Bay and its tributaries are the best studied estuaries in the world, largely due to the work of D. W. Pritchard and to the work of others, such as Nash (1947) on the Patuxent, Haas (1977) on the York and Rappahannock, and Elliott (1976) on the Potomac.

The Chesapeake estuary is a drowned river and it is partially mixed. The depths are relatively shallow (Figure 2.43), so that mixing of at least moderate magnitude extends to the depths. In the total estuary approximately 50% of the system is less than 20 ft (6 m) deep, 35% has depths greater than 30 ft (9 m), 18% greater than 40 ft (12 m), and only 8% greater than 60 ft (18.3 m). For the Chesapeake Bay proper, about 57% of the area is greater than 20 ft (6 m) in depth, 44% greater than 30 ft (9 m), 24% greater than 40 ft (12 m), and 10% greater than 60 ft (18.3 m) (Pritchard, 1952).

The Chesapeake Bay is approximately 165 nautical miles (305.58 km) long, extending from the mouth of the Susquehanna River at Havre de Grace, Maryland, to the Virginia capes. The area of the estuary that is influenced by measurable saltwater intrusions is approximately 11,681 km^2.

The Susquehanna River contributed 49% of the annual freshwater inflow into the bay, and the Potomac River, as the second largest contributor, provides 18%. The salt intrusion in measurable quantities extends for nearly 60 miles (96.54 km) upstream from the Chesapeake Bay. About 16% of the annual contribution of fresh water is supplied by the James River, about 4% by the Rappahannock River, and 2% by the York River. Only about 7% of the riverine contribution comes from the eastern shore of the bay; the remaining 4% is supplied by small streams entering from the western shore. Figure 2.43 shows the relative depths of estuaries entering the bay.

Tides. Tidal currents constitute the most obvious water movements and are considered here as being primarily responsible for supplying the energy needed for the vertical and horizontal mixing. The tidal currents in the estuary are of a reversing type directed up and down its longitudinal axis. The observed net horizontal current is obtained by averaging the total current observations over one or more complete tidal cycles.

Salinities. The typical horizontal salinity distribution is shown in Figure 2.44. The distribution of salinity governs the structure and dynamic circulation pattern (Pritchard, 1952). The salinity increases from zero at the head of the estuary to nearly that of seawater at the mouth.

In the upper Chesapeake Bay and in each tributary estuary there are considerable seasonal variations in salinity which diminish in magnitude toward the mouths of these estuaries. In the spring the high river flow is reflected in minimal salinities throughout the estuary, while in summer and fall the decreased river flow results in maximum salinity during the fall season. The isohalines are not perpendicular to the $x - 1$ axis, but run rather obliquely across the estuary, the salinities on the right side being slightly lower than those on the left (Figure

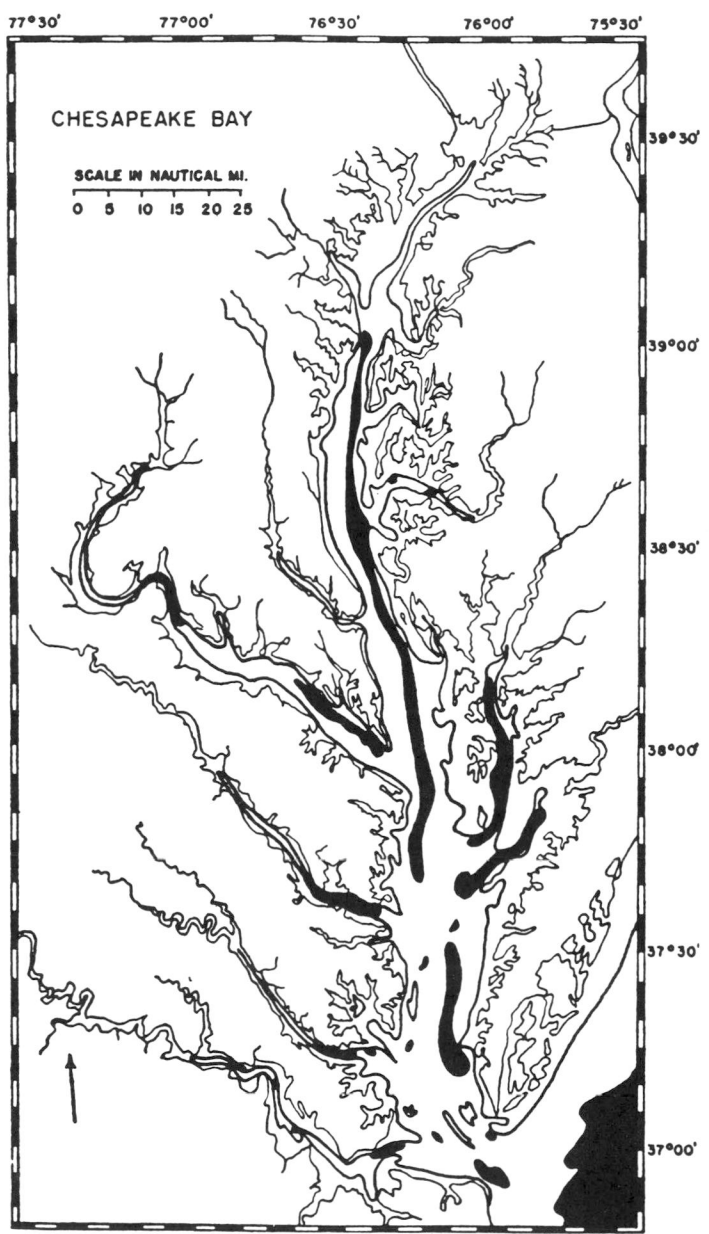

FIGURE 2.43.   Depth contours of the Chesapeake Bay estuarine system. The heavy line is the 20-ft
(6-m) contour. Black areas represent depths greater than 60 ft (18.3 m). (From salinity distribution
and circulation in Chesapeake Bay estuarine system, D. W. Pritchard, Journal of Marine Research,
No. 11, pp. 106–123, 1952, Copyright by the American Geophysical Union.)

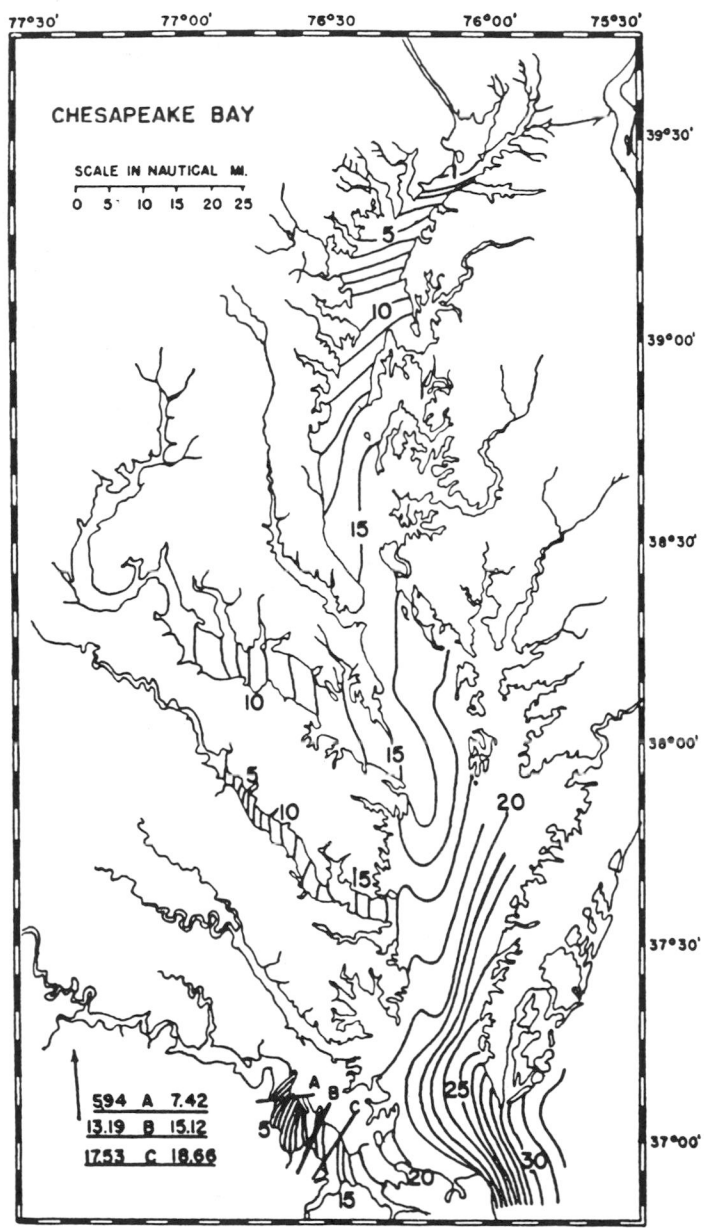

FIGURE 2.44. Typical surface salinity pattern in the Chesapeake Bay estuarine system. (From salinity distribution and circulation in Chesapeake Bay estuarine system, D. W. Pritchard, Journal of Marine Research, No. 11, pp. 106–123, 1952, Copyright by the American Geophysical Union.)

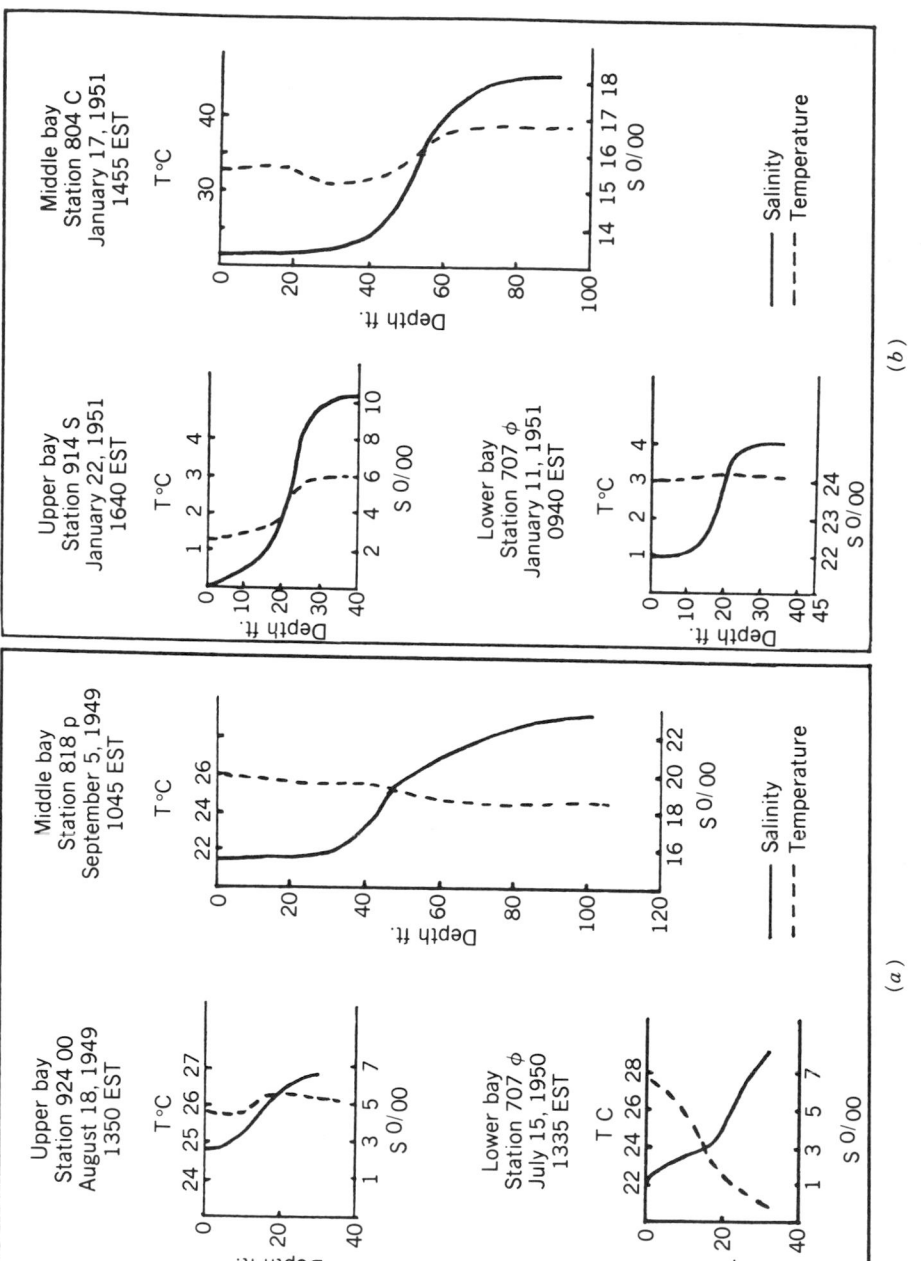

FIGURE 2.45. Examples of vertical profiles of temperature and salinity in the Chesapeake Bay: (a) summer; (b) winter. (After salinity distribution and circulation in Chesapeake Bay estuarine system, D. W. Pritchard, Journal of Marine Research, No. 11, pp. 106–123, 1952, Copyright by the American Geophysical Union.)

2.44). A characteristic feature of this distribution is the obliqueness of the isohalines. This, of course, is in part due to the greater flow of fresh water on the right-hand side of the estuary facing toward the mouth, and to the Coriolis force.

In contrast to the fairly regular salinity field, the temperature distribution over much of the year shows no clear-cut pattern. The summer temperature distribution indicates that the temperatures are controlled primarily by local weather conditions. In winter the surface isotherms show a more regular pattern, with temperatures increasing from the head of the estuary toward the mouth.

In Figure 2.45 are examples of summer and winter temperature and salinity curves in the Chesapeake Bay. Throughout the year the salinity depth curve has the general shape of an inverse tangent function and departs from its general shape near the bottom, and to a lesser extent near the surface, which is caused by boundary effects. There may be an inflection point at middepth. The temperature curves frequently show a positive gradient at the depth of maximum salinity change, particularly in winter.

From the standpoint of physical structure and circulation the estuary may be considered as having two layers; in the upper layer there is a net horizontal flow down the estuary; in the lower, a net horizontal flow up the estuary. The boundary between the two layers has a slight lateral slope, with the right side deeper than the left. The net velocity depth curve is exponential in character. In the upper layers it decreases from a maximum on the surface to zero at the boundary between the two layers. In the lower layer the horizontal component of velocity is directed in the negative $x - l$ direction. Its magnitude increases with depth until the frictional layer at the bottom is reached. The boundary between the two layers occurs close to, but does not necessarily coincide with, the middepth inflection point on the salinity depth curve. Thus the upper layer must exceed the volume of flow in the lower layer by an amount equal to the inflow of fresh water from the river.

Although the salinity distribution shows a seasonal variation, it may be considered to be in a steady state during any particular season (Pritchard, 1952). Since the upper layer is transporting seaward a net amount of fresh water equal to the inflow, there must be a flow of salt water into the upper layer to maintain the salinity distribution. This is accomplished by a net transfer of water of relatively higher salinity from the lower to the upper layer. Hence there must be a negative vertical velocity across the boundary between the two layers. The volume of flow in the upper layer increases toward the mouth, and the lower layer decreases toward the head.

Patuxent River Estuary. Nash (1947) summarized the data available on the Patuxent between 1936 and 1946: a single period of stratification from March to August and a single period of overturn from September to February. This pattern occurred throughout the length of the river and in the region of the Chesapeake Bay opposite its mouth. Temperature ranges and the earliness of their seasonal changes increased progressively upstream. On the average surface water was 0.5° warmer than air. The temperature ranges were greater at the water surface than at the bottom. The greatest relative temperature stratification of the inflowing river and bay waters occurred in the middle third of the estuary, although the surface-to-volume differentials increased downstream because of increasing depth.

Salinities. The salinity range was greatest in the surface waters. Salinity is lower in the spring and summer and higher in the fall and winter. The river level is lower in the winter and higher in the summer. Winds as well as stream flow were important factors in influencing the salinity pattern. The effect of seasonal changes of stream flow and river level was diminished by opposing seasonal changes in wind direction. The depth of light penetration was closely correlated with salinity, both seasonally and longitudinally. Peculiarly, the depth of light penetration seemed to vary inversely with seasonal changes in solar radiation.

Potomac River Estuary. Circulation and salinity distribution in the upper Potomac estuary indicate that this partially mixed estuary possessed an internal circulation with reverse flow. Between Douglas Point and Morgantown, river flow dominated. Reverse flow was greatly decreased and usually eliminated (Elliott, 1976).

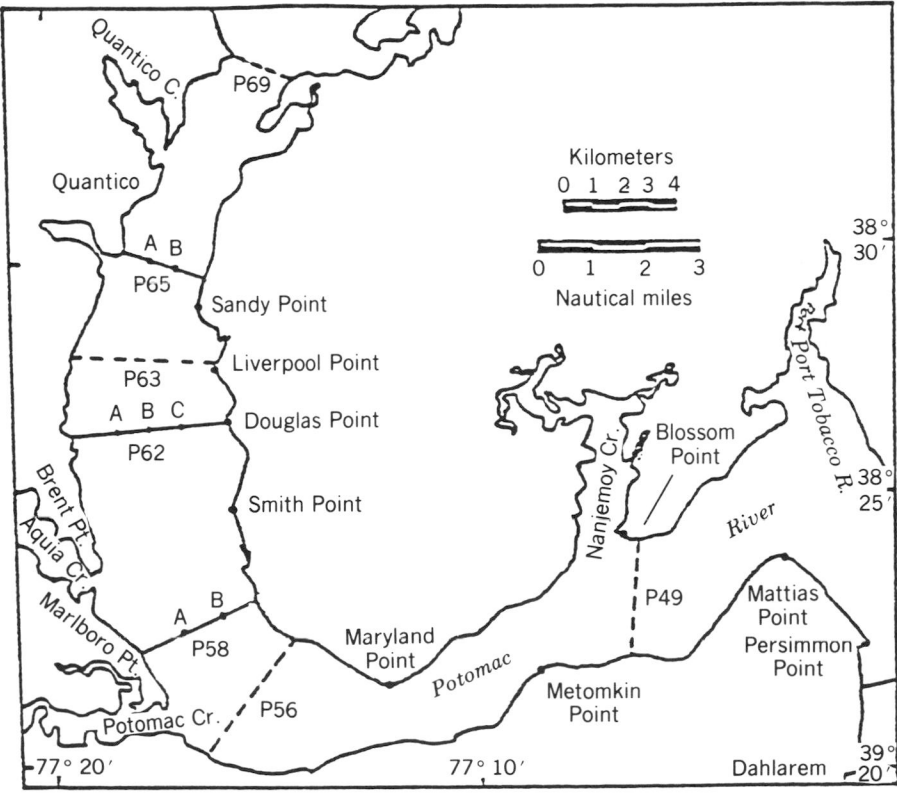

FIGURE 2.46.   Station positions for salinity study on the upper Potomac estuary. (After Elliott, 1976.)

The data from studies made in October 1973 and April 1974 (Figure 2.46) indicate that the net flow was seaward at all depths sampled. There was no evidence of a reversal of flow due to internal circulation; however, the magnitude of the flow did decrease significantly with depth (Figures 2.47 and 2.48).

The results of Elliott's studies (1976) for two northern sections, at Sandy Point and Douglas Point, showed that the laterally averaged flow was on the order of 2 to 3 cm s^{-1} and was relatively constant with depth until reaching a bottom friction layer. The net flux at Sandy Point, Douglas Point, and Marlboro Point was 348, 505, and 354 m^3 s^{-1}, respectively. This gave a corrected mean figure of 366 m^3 s^{-1}.

Rappahannock River and York River Estuaries. The Rappahannock River is tidal to the fall line at Fredericksburg, Virginia, a distance of 130 km from its

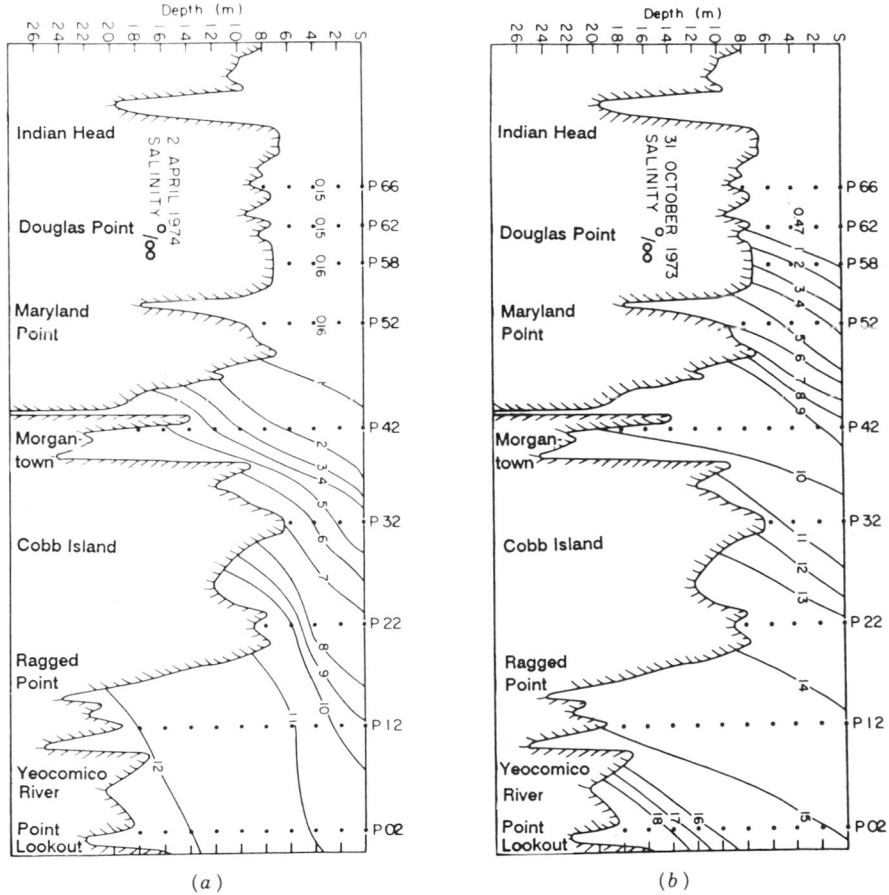

FIGURE 2.47. Salinity sections for the Potomac River estuary on (a) October 31, 1973, and (b) April 2, 1974. (From Elliott, 1976.)

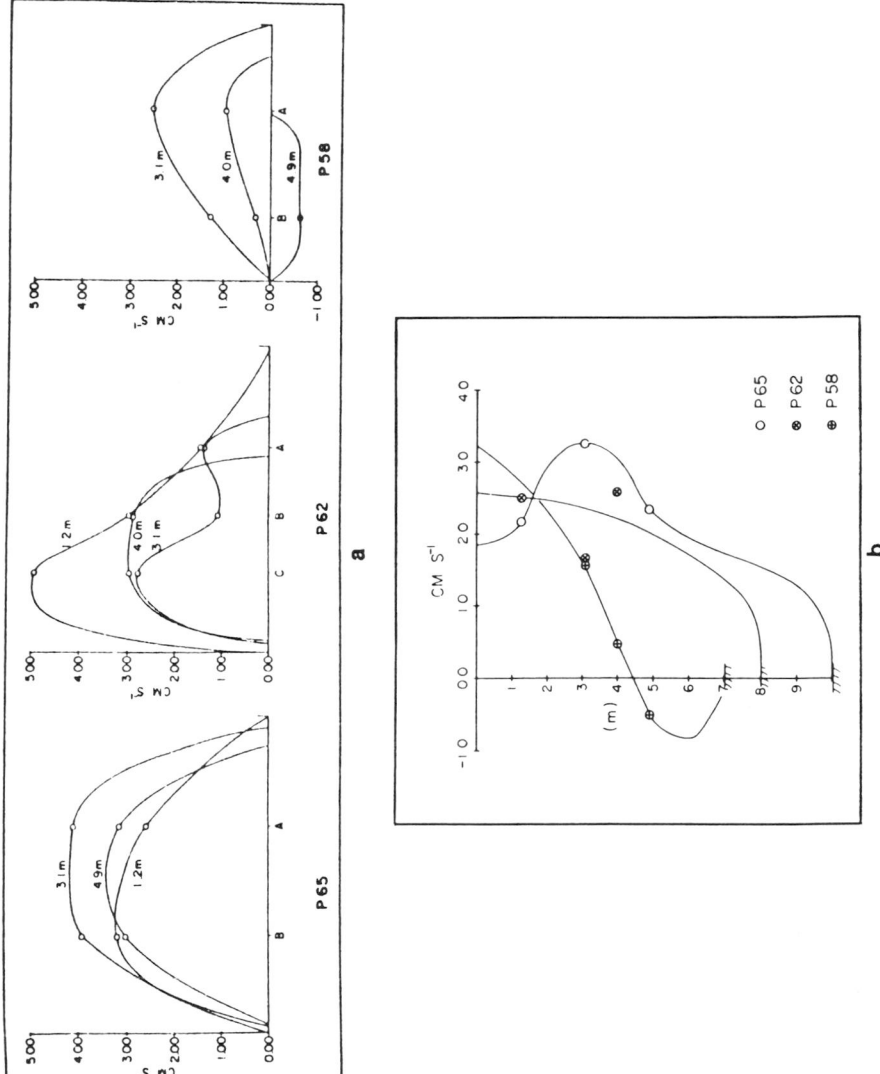

FIGURE 2.48. Net flow for the Potomac River, November, 1973. (a) lateral distribution of net flow. (b) laterally averaged net flow. (From Elliott, 1976.)

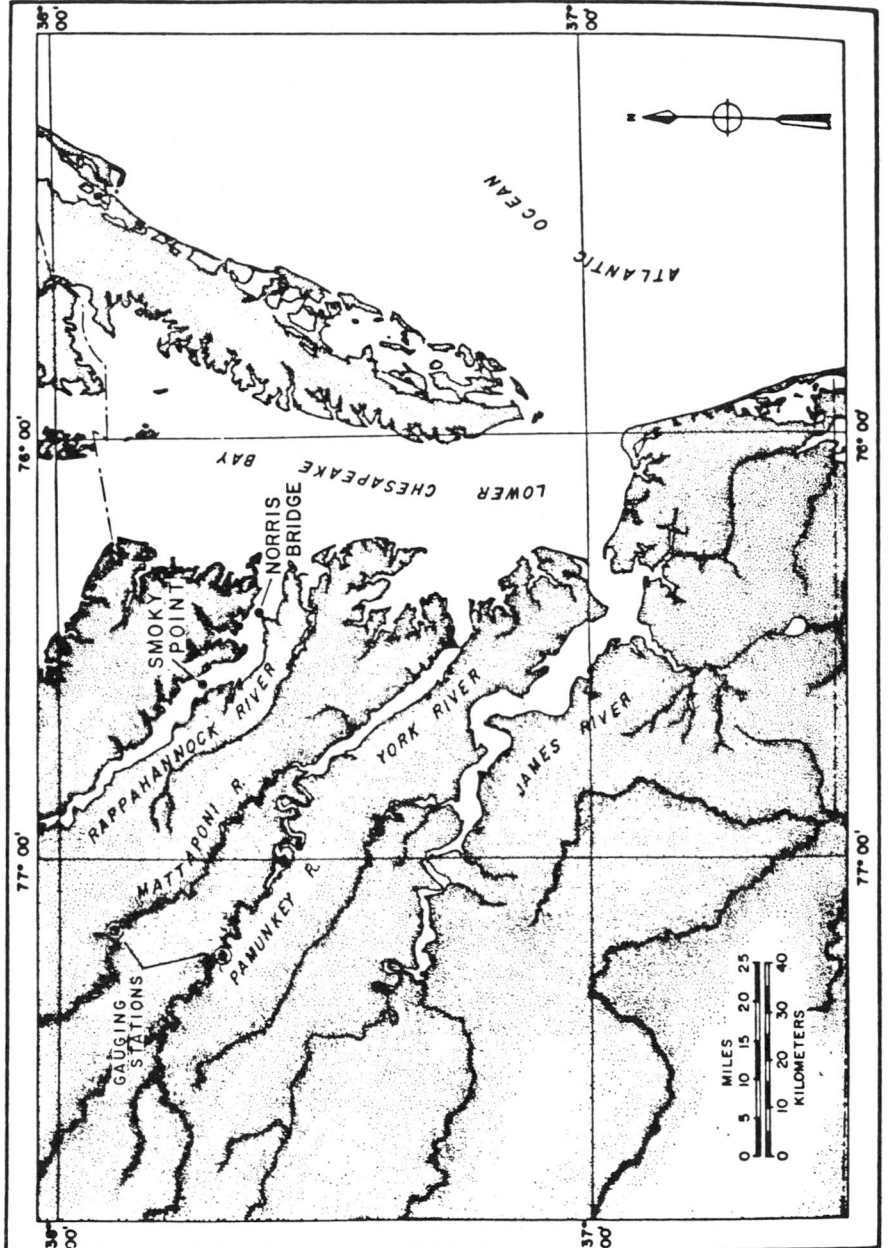

FIGURE 2.49. Lower Chesapeake Bay showing the James, York, Rappahannock, Mattaponi, and Pamunkey rivers. (From Haas, 1977.)

mouth. The 1% isohaline is normally 75 to 90 km upriver. The mean tidal range and surface salinities at the mouth are 0.4 m and 12 to 18 ppt, respectively.

The Rappahannock varies from being a stratified estuary to being almost homogeneous. The maximum homogeneity occurs 1 to 6 days following the higher monthly spring tides. The best correlation of homogeneity with the monthly spring tides is about 4 days after high tide. A similar correlation of stratification exists for neap tide. There appears to be a regular oscillation in the estuary between correlation of vertical homogeneity and stratification in conjunction with the monthly spring–neap tide cycle (Haas, 1977).

The York River is formed by the confluence of the Pamunkey and Mattaponi rivers about 50 km from the York's point of entry into the Chesapeake Bay (Figure 2.49). The York River is tidal throughout its entire length, and the 1-ppt isohaline is normally found 65 to 90 km from its mouth. The mean tidal range at the mouth is 0.7 m, and the surface salinities at this point range between 15 and 24 ppt. The lower York River is delimited at the upstream end by constriction at Gloucester Point.

Salinities.   A plot of surface and bottom salinities for the York River for the period from mid-June to August shows that similar periods of homogeneity lasted only up to 4 days; otherwise, the water column was stratified. During the year 1974 vertical salinity homogeneity was observed in the lower York River on 12 occasions (Figure 2.50). Three periods of homogeneity observed in the lower Rappahannock River coincided with periods of homogeneity observed in the lower York River (Figure 2.50). However, the duration of homogeneity appears longer in the lower Rappahannock and the magnification of stratification less (Haas, 1977).

James River Estuaries.   The James River is a tidal estuary for a distance of 170 km from its mouth, and the 1 ppt isohaline is normally located 55 to 95 km

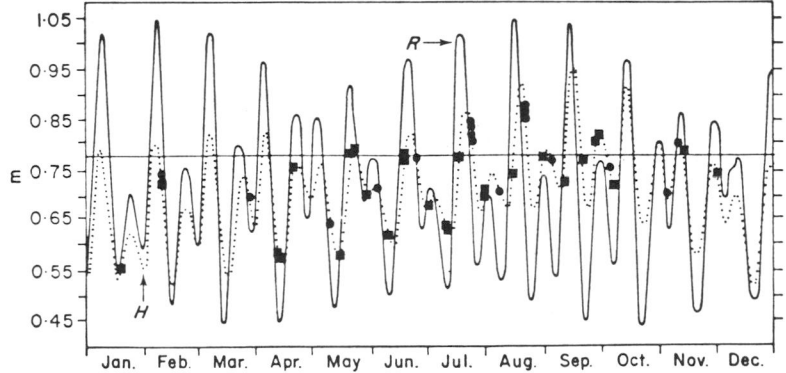

FIGURE 2.50.   Mean daily tidal range, *R*, shown as solid line, and mean daily high-tide height, *H*, shown as dotted line, in the lower York River for 1974. Circles indicate days on which vertical salinity homogeneity was observed. Squares are vertical salinity stratification observations. The horizontal line indicates a tidal magnitude of 0.78 m. (From Haas, 1977.)

upriver. The mean tide range and surface salinities at the mouth are 0.8 m and 15 to 25 ppt, respectively. The hydrography of the James River is the most thoroughly studied of the Chesapeake estuary.

Studies were made in the James River in the summer of 1950. The observations were made at three sections for three periods of time, each 4 to 11 days in length. The sections were located at approximately 20 km above the mouth, where the salinity was about 17 ppt; 31 km above the mouth, where the mean salinity was about 12.5 ppt; and at approximately 44 km above the mouth, where the mean salinity was about 5 ppt. The data from the middle station were used to develop the figures; however, the major features were similar at all three sections for all three periods (Pritchard, 1967b).

Salinities.   Figure 2.51 shows the general salinity pattern of the James River in the area of the three stations. There was an evident increase in salinity in the seaward direction, and a lateral variation, with lower-salinity water being on the

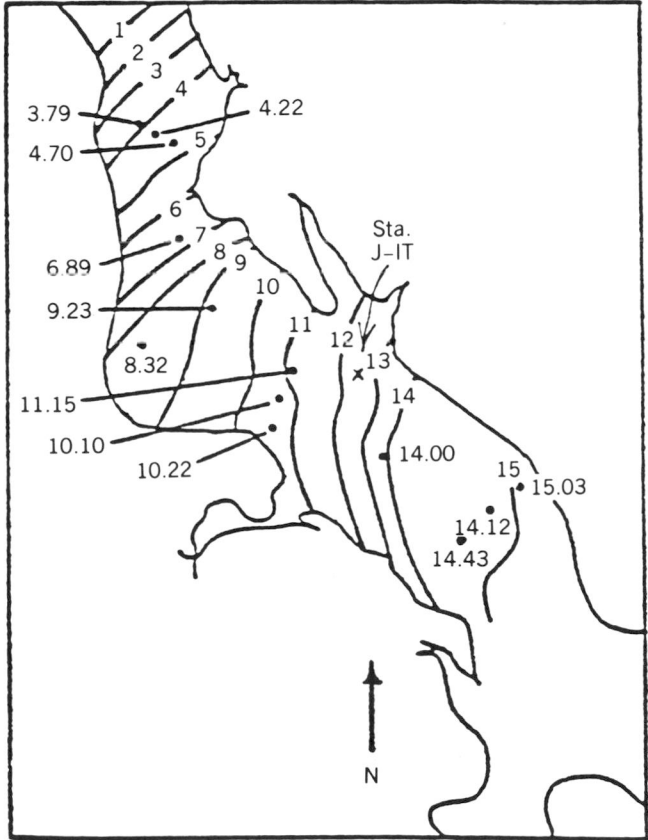

FIGURE 2.51.   Salinity distribution (in ppt) at the surface of a portion of the James River estuary. (From Pritchard, 1967b.)

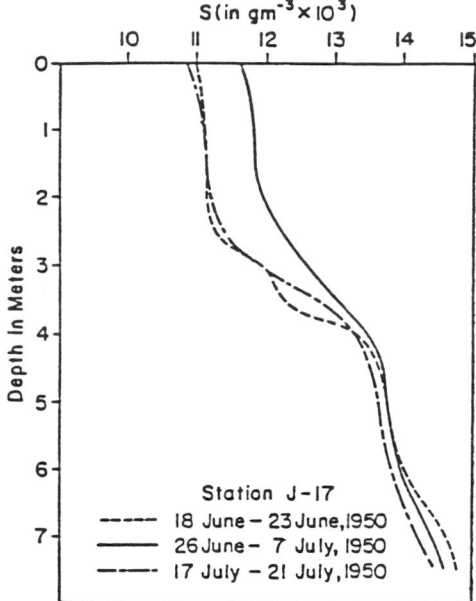

FIGURE 2.52. Mean vertical salinity profile at station J-17 in the James River estuary. (From Pritchard, 1967b.)

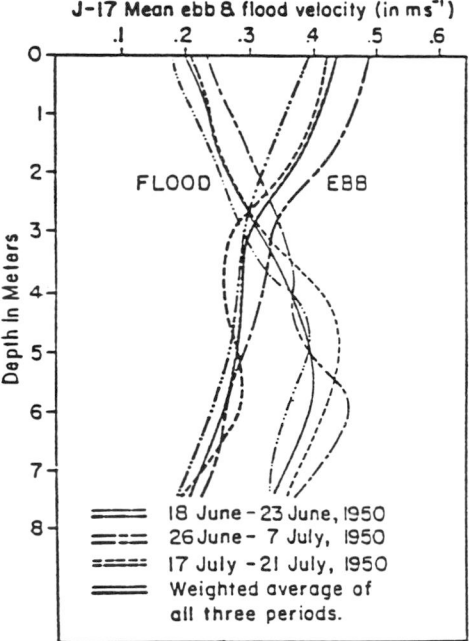

FIGURE 2.53. Vertical profile of mean ebb and flood currents at station J-17 in the James River estuary. (From Pritchard, 1967b.)

right side of the estuary when facing downstream. The horizontal pattern was similar at subsurface depths, although at any one point the salinity increased with depth. The vertical variation is shown in Figure 2.51 by the mean salinity profiles for the three periods of study. The surface layers showed a weak vertical gradient. Below this was an intermediate layer in which the rate of salinity change with depth reached a maximum. A deeper layer had a less rapid change of salinity with depth (Pritchard, 1967b).

The vertical profiles of the mean ebb currents and the mean flood currents for the three periods of study are given in Figure 2.52. The ebb flow was at a maximum at the surface and decreased with depth. The current velocity during the flood period was minimum at the surface and increased with depth until near the bottom, where friction apparently had some influence. The net tidal velocity is plotted as a function of depth in Figures 2.53 and 2.54. Positive values indicate downstream estuary flow and negative values, upstream flow (Pritchard, 1967b).

The mean strength of the ebb and flood current was about 0.35 m s^{-1}. In the surface layer the vertical mean of the net nontidal velocity directed down-estuary was 0.066 m s^{-1}, or about 19% of the average tidal current. In the lower half of the water column, the net upstream velocity had a vertical mean value of 0.07 m s^{-1}, which was about 20% of the average tidal velocity. The net nontidal velocities were much larger than the mean sectional velocity. The mean sectional

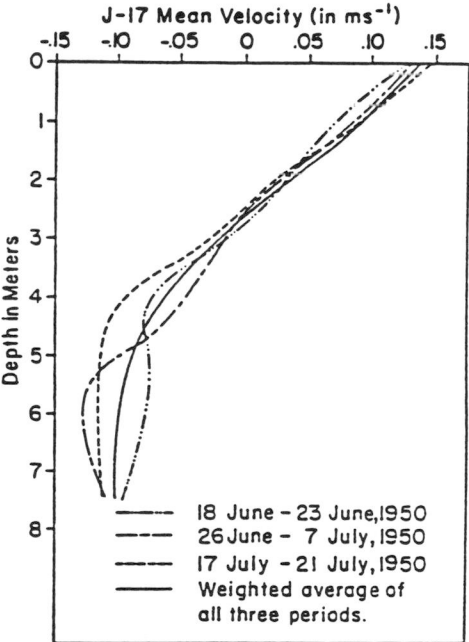

FIGURE 2.54. Vertical profile of net nontidal velocity at station J-17 in the James River estuary. Net flow is seaward in the upper layer (positive values) and up-estuary in the lower layer (negative values). (From Pritchard, 1967b.)

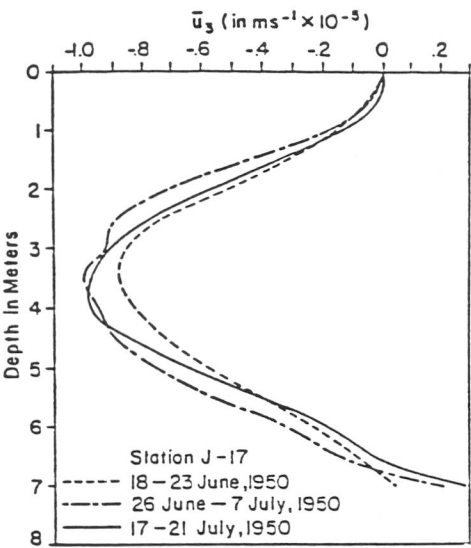

FIGURE 2.55. Average vertical velocity ($\bar{u}_3$) as a function of depth at station J-17 in the James River estuary. (From Pritchard, 1967b.)

velocity required to transport the volume of inflowing water seaward was computed to be $0.0073 \, \text{m s}^{-1}$, or 11% of the net nontidal surface velocity.

Since current observations were made at three sections, it is possible, through a numerical, stepwise integration of the equation of continuity, to compute the average vertical velocity as a function of depth. This is given in Figure 2.55. The equations are given in Appendix A of Pritchard's paper, reproduced as Appendix A to the present chapter.

Southeastern Estuaries

South Edisto River Estuary. Cummings (1968) described the temperature, tidal height, discharge, and salinity pattern of the South Edisto River estuary in South Carolina. The penetration of the saltwater influence is about 25 miles (40.2 km) up the river to near the town of Jacksonboro. As shown in Figure 2.56, this estuary is long and narrow.

Temperatures. The temperature during this study varied from 31 °F (-0.5 °C) to about 89 °F (31.67 °C). As shown in Figure 2.57, half the time the temperature equaled or exceeded 68 °F (20 °C) at the lower station and 64 °F (17.78 °C) at the upper station (Cummings, 1968).

Tides. The height of the tide, as seen in Figure 2.58, is usually fairly large, more than 6 ft (1.8 m) 70 to 80% of the time and over 8 ft (2.4 m) about 5% of the time. High tides, together with low discharges, undoubtedly account for the very high salinities shown in Figure 2.59 for a short period of time during August.

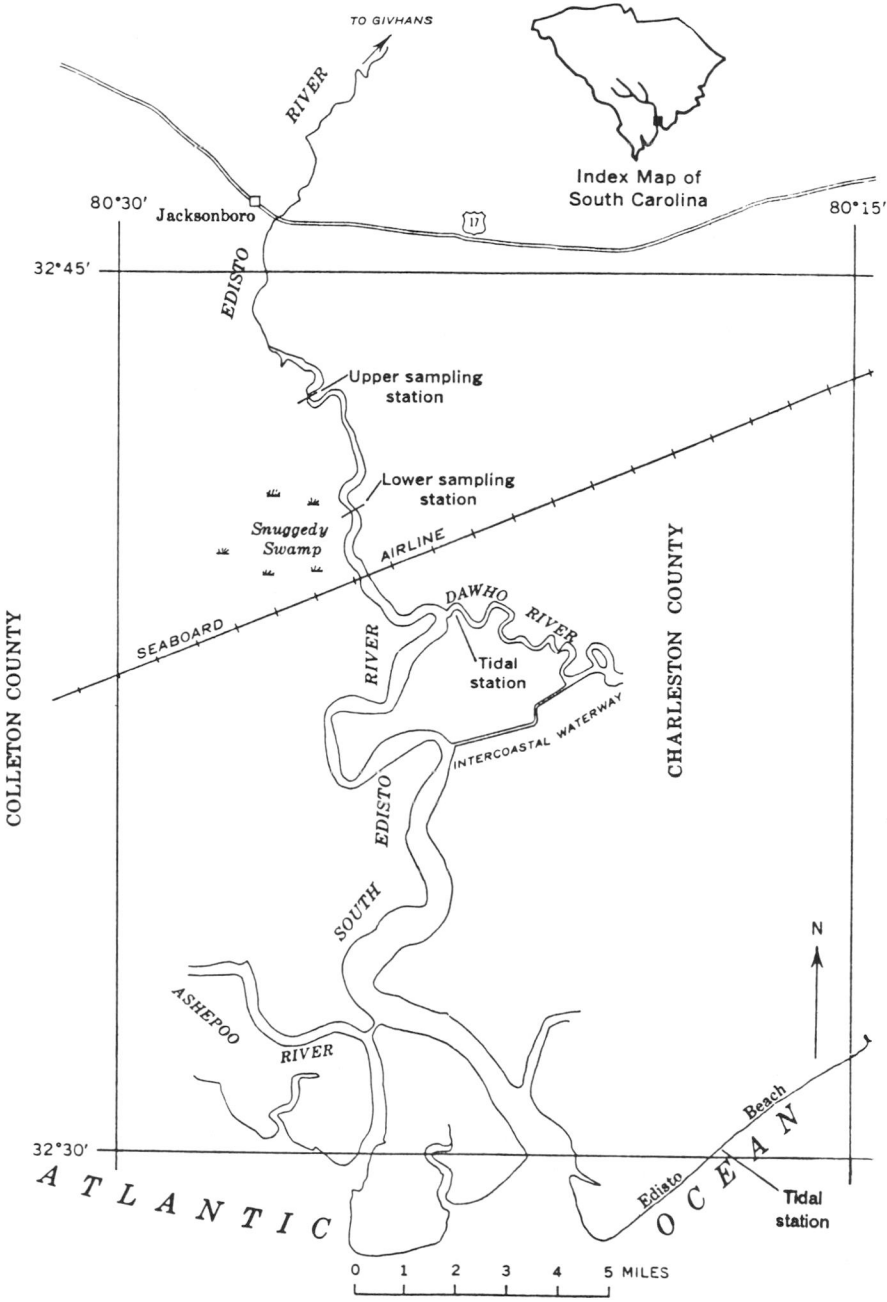

FIGURE 2.56.   Map of the South Edisto River estuary in South Carolina. (From Cummings, 1968.)

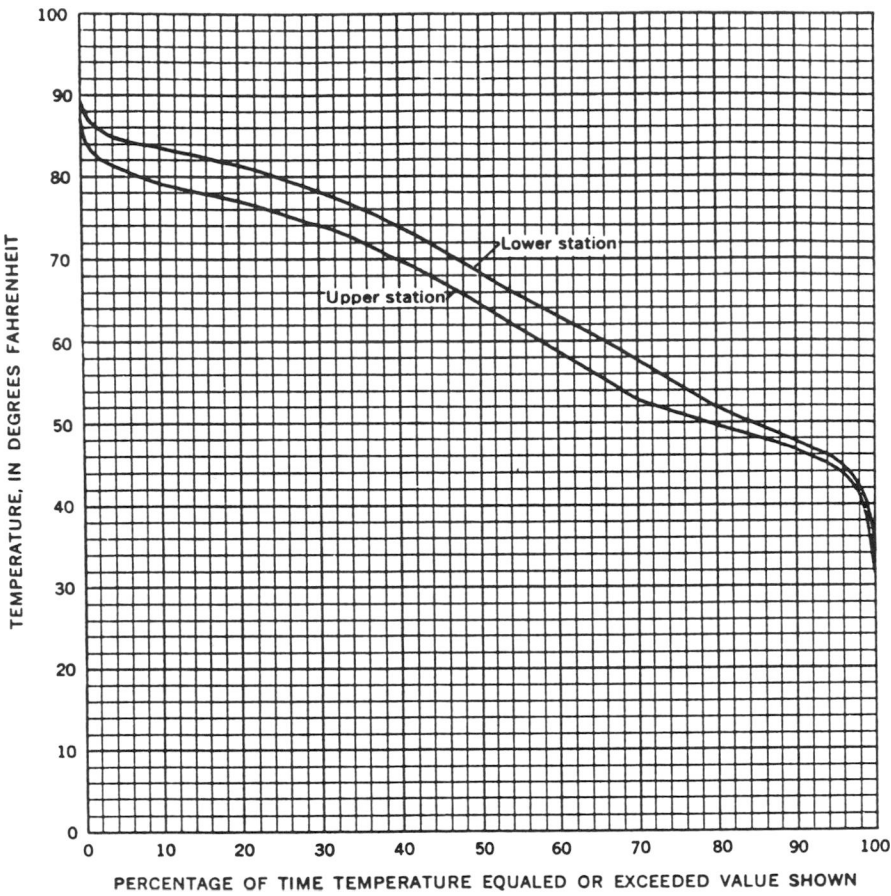

FIGURE 2.57. Frequency curves for temperature of water at high tide at Edisto River near Jacksonboro, January 1958 to September 1962. (From Cummings, 1968.)

The correlation of salinity with the height of tide is clearly seen in Figure 2.60. At Jacksonboro, half of the time the chlorides exceed 10 ppm at the upper station.

Salinities. The effects of salinity are generally expressed as specific conductance. In Figure 2.61 chlorides and dissolved solids are correlated with the specific conductance. It can be seen from Figure 2.62 that the mean monthly discharge of the Edisto River at Givhans is greatest in February, March, and April, and lowest in June, July, and November. The saltwater penetration, and the effect of salinity was greatest near Jacksonboro in August following the lower water flows of June and July (Figure 2.59). The relation of specific conductance (salinity) to discharge at high tide in the Edisto River near Jacksonboro is seen in Figure 2.63.

St. John's River Estuary. The St. John's River, Florida, is approximately 300 miles (482.7 km) long and the influence of spring tides may be felt 283 miles

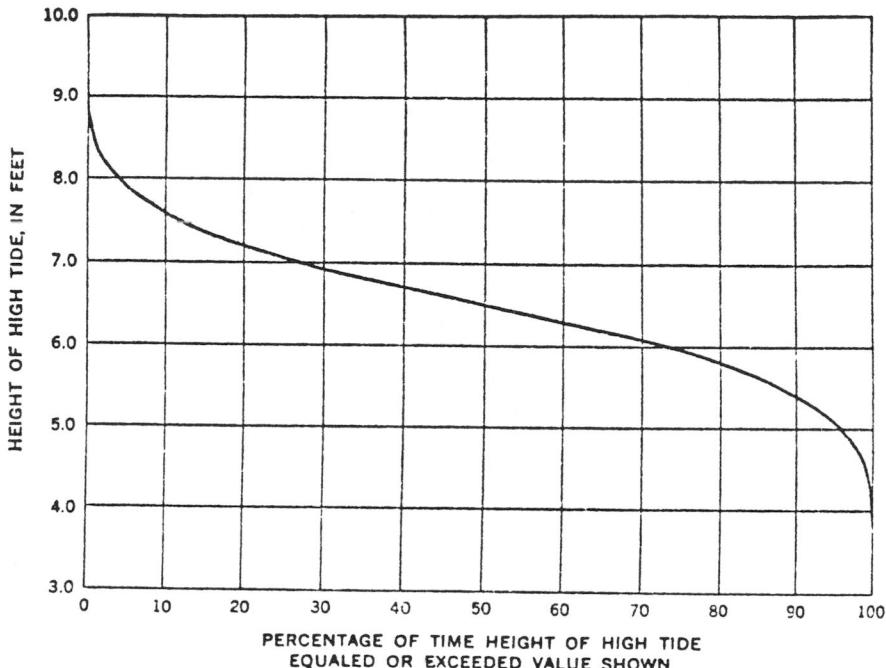

FIGURE 2.58. Frequency curve for height of high tide at Dawho River entrance to the South Edisto River, January 1958 to September 1962. (From Cummings, 1968.)

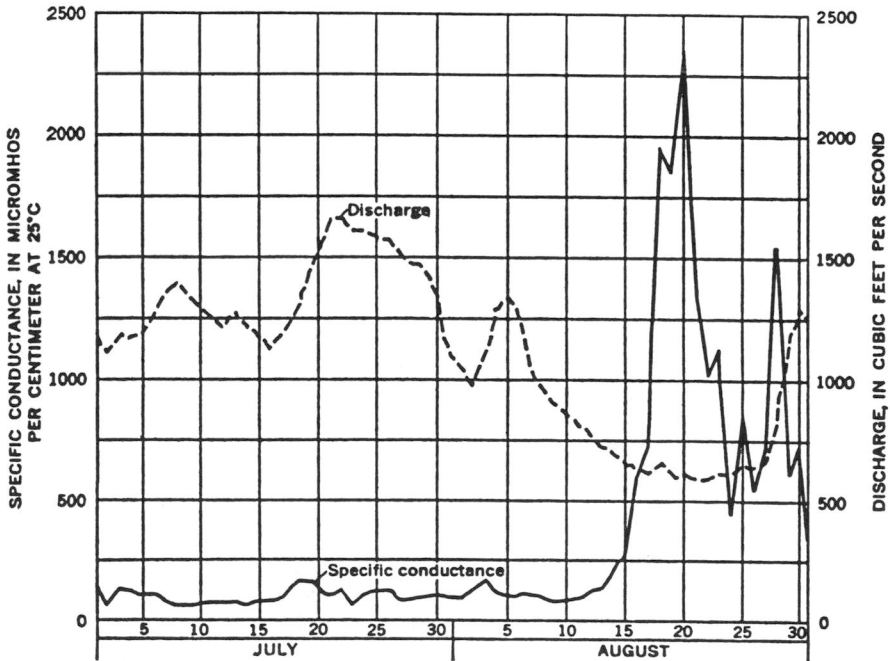

FIGURE 2.59. Variations of specific conductance and discharge at high tide at Edisto River near Jacksonboro, July and August 1958. (From Cummings, 1968.)

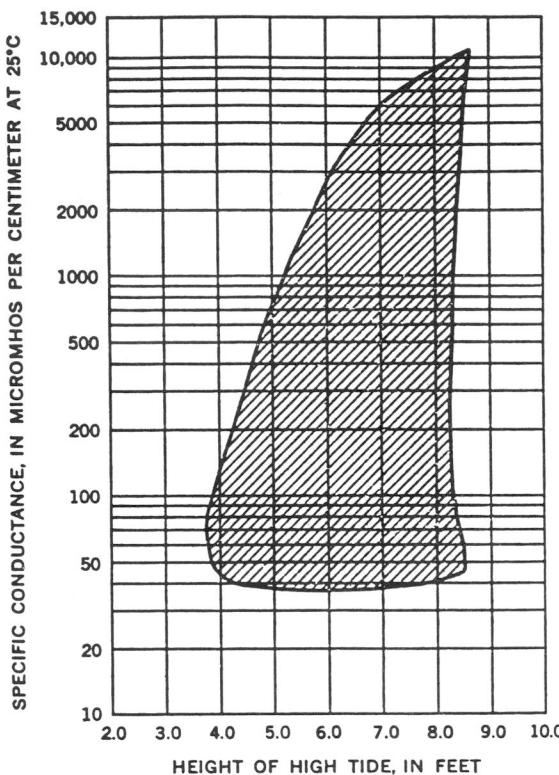

FIGURE 2.60.   Relation of specific conductance at high tide at Edisto River near Jacksonboro to the height of high tide at Dawho River entrance, January 1958 to September 1962. Shaded area includes all data obtained. (From Cummings, 1968.)

(455.35 km) from its mouth. This great penetration of salt is made possible by the low gradient of the river. Normally, this river is tidal for at least 80 miles (128.7 km) from its mouth. Hydrologic studies are complicated by the presence of numerous wetlands in the drainage basin and limestone sinks, fissures, springs, and subsurface rivers, some of which are saline. The net flow of the river is often negative over a 24-hour period—that is, the river actually flows upstream due to the tides more than it flows downstream in a tidal cycle.

Gulf Coast Estuaries
   Tampa Bay and Its Tributaries.   The Tampa Bay system (Florida) is a shallow estuary with a modal depth of only 9.7 ft (3 m) and a maximum depth of 57 ft (17.4) near the mouth (Simon, 1974). The system includes Old Tampa Bay, Hillsborough Bay, Tampa Bay, and Boca Ciega Bay (Figure 2.64). In addition to direct rainfall, nine major streams and numerous smaller ones, draining a total area of 2235 square miles (5788 km), supply the estuary with fresh water.

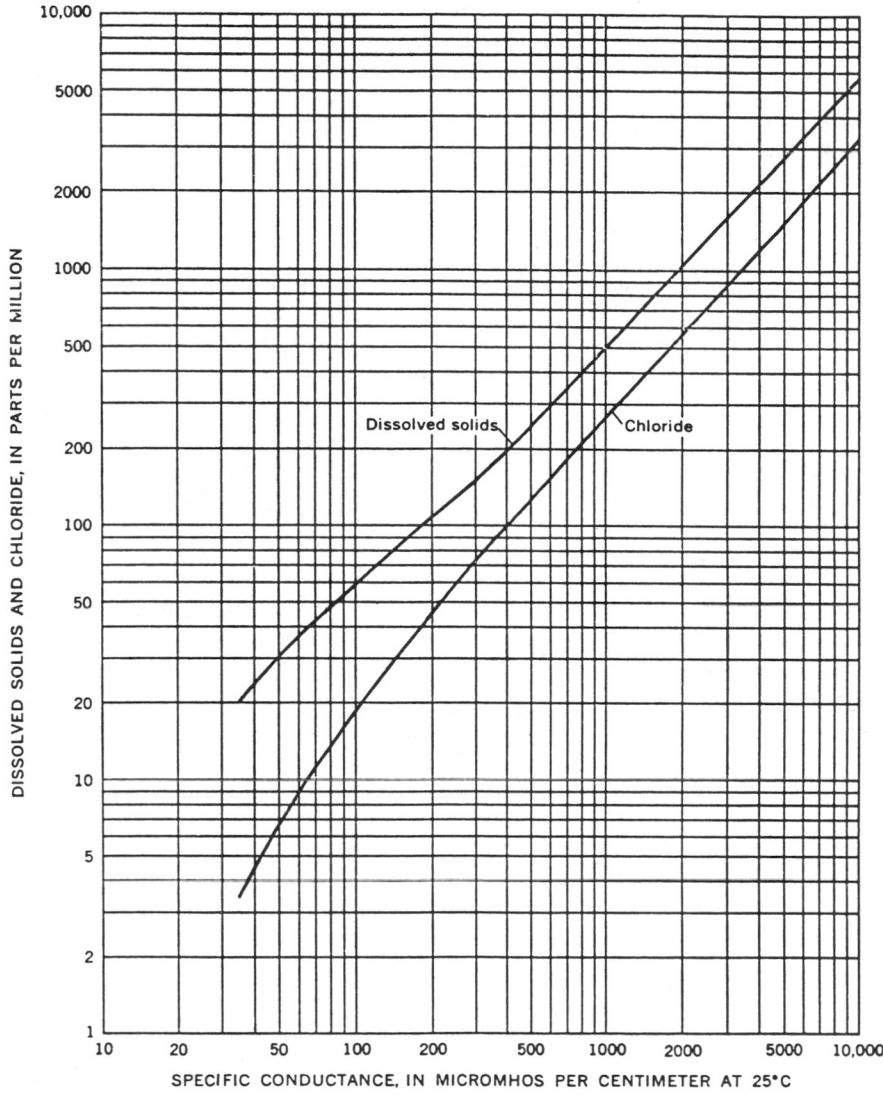

FIGURE 2.61. Relation of dissolved-solids content and chloride to specific conductance at high tide at Edisto River near Jacksonboro, January 1958 to September 1962. (From Cummings, 1968.)

Tides. Tides are mixed, a combination of diurnal and occasional semidiurnal components; the average tidal range is 2.3 ft (0.7 m), with a range of about 3.5 ft (1 m). Hurricanes reported since 1848 have caused several high tides ranging up to more than 14 ft (4 m). Maximum currents at the mouth of the bay are greater than 6.0 ft (1.8 m) s^{-1} on ebb tide, under 3.5 ft (1 m) s^{-1} on flood tide. In the surrounding small component bays, the currents are considerably weaker.

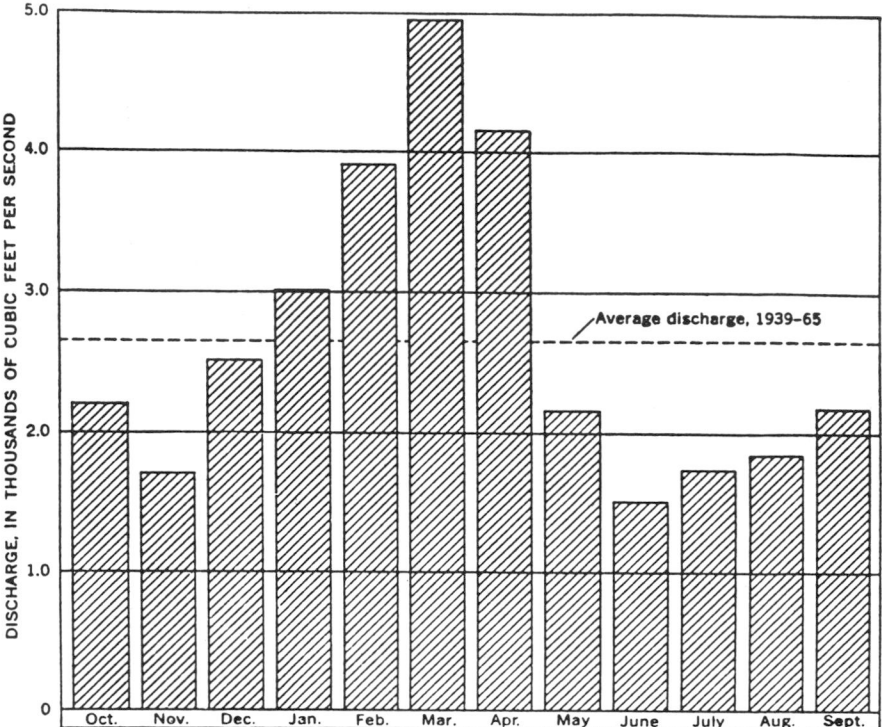

FIGURE 2.62. Mean monthly discharge at Edisto River near Givhans, 1939 to 1965. (From Cummings, 1968.)

Hillsborough Bay has little circulation, a condition that causes pollution accumulation problems.

Salinities. Salinity within the system is quite variable, being affected especially by rainfall and runoff levels. Upper Old Tampa Bay and Hillsborough Bay have the lowest salinity due to freshwater contributions from several sources (McNulty et al., 1972). Vertical salinity gradients are known to exist but have been little studied.

Dragovich and May (1962) found that salinity was inversely related to runoff in the main rivers feeding Tampa Bay (Figure 2.65). The Hillsborough River had the greatest tendency to stratify, as indicated by the large differences between surface and bottom salinities.

Sediments. Coastal currents converge at the entrance to Tampa Bay. Littoral drift from north to south in the north of the bay, and from south to north in the south of the bay cause extending sand spits that almost close the mouth. Sediment inputs from Tampa Bay streams are small, but dissolved material inputs from tributaries are considerable (Dragovich and May, 1962). Many areas are subjected to drifting dredge spoil material and organic effluents from treatment plants. Sedimentation occurs in many dead-end inlets and in canals.

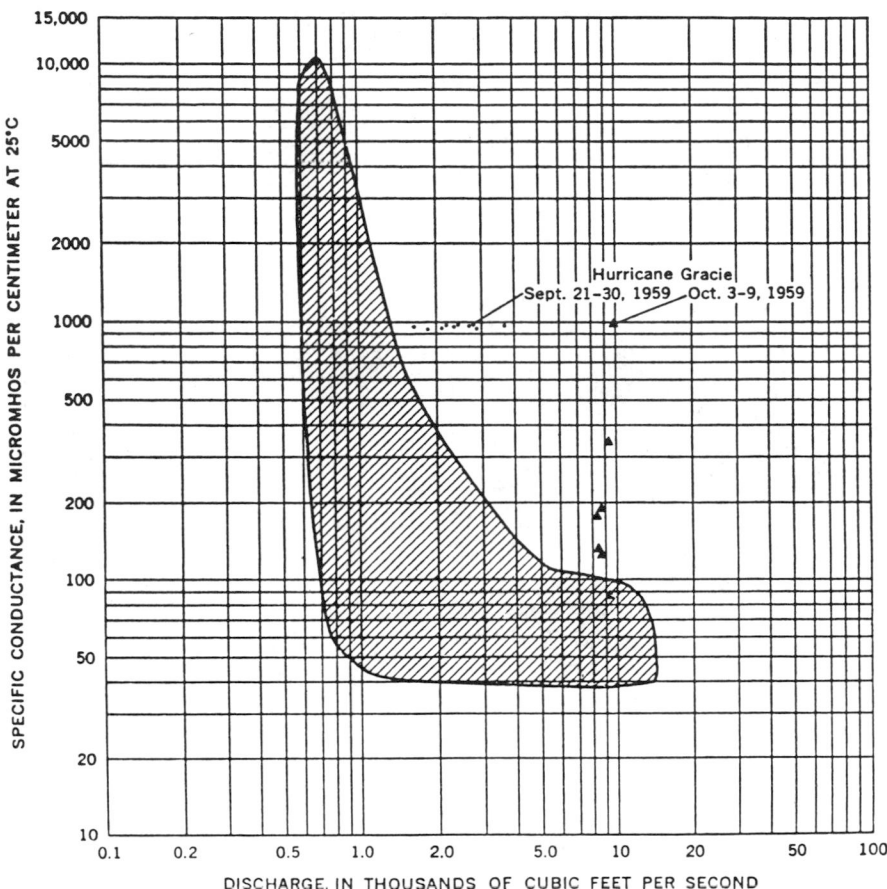

FIGURE 2.63. Relation of specific conductance to discharge at high tide at Edisto River near Jacksonboro, January, 1958 to September 1962. Shaded area includes all data except those affected by Hurricane Gracie. Points represent single days. (From Cummings, 1968.)

Apalachicola Bay Estuary. The Apalachicola Bay system (Florida) is a complex of riverine wetlands with both freely flowing and vegetated parts (Livingston et al., 1974). Apalachicola Bay is a shallow coastal estuary contained by a series of barrier islands. Its average depth is 2.7 m at mean low water. Four major rivers, the Flint, Chattahoochee, Apalachicola, and Chipola, and many small streams contribute fresh water to the bay (Figure 2.66). According to Brooks (1973), most of the sediment carried into the bay from upland rivers remains in the bay.

Tides. Tides in Apalachicola Bay are semidiurnal and exhibit diurnal inequality. Maximum tidal range is about 1 m; the usual range is 0.5 to 0.7 m. Tides are affected by winds and can be modified by periods of prolonged high winds (Gorsline, 1963).

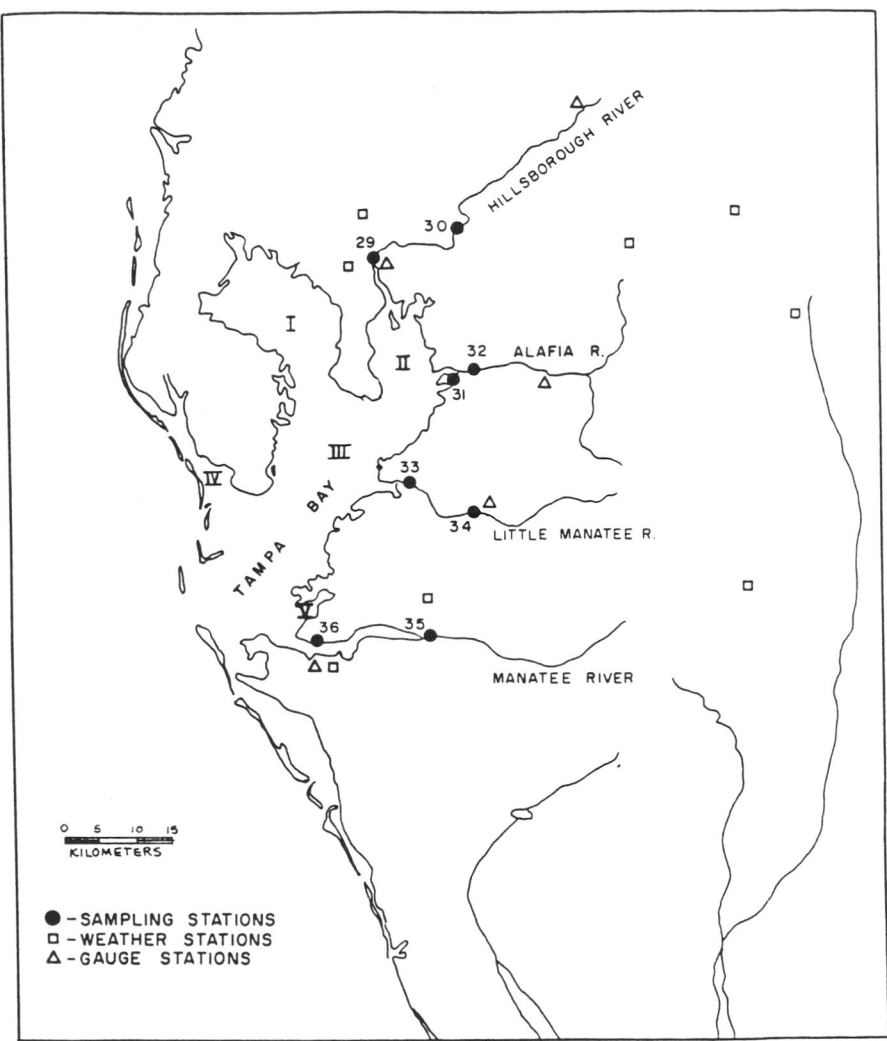

FIGURE 2.64.   Tampa Bay estuarine system in Florida. I, old Tampa Bay; II, Hillsborough/MacKay Bay; III, Tampa Bay proper; IV, Boca Ciega Bay; V, Terra Ceia Bay. (After Dragovich and May, 1962.)

Salinities.   The salinity distribution in Apalachicola Bay is controlled by the freshwater discharge from the Apalachicola River in combination with wind speed and direction. Winds sometimes mix the entire water column, or occasionally mix only the upper part, thus uncoupling bottom salinity from surface salinity (Estabrook, 1973). Frequently, penetrations of highly saline water extend into the bay through cuts, as shown in Figure 2.67. Figure 2.68 shows the average seasonal patterns of surface and bottom salinities.

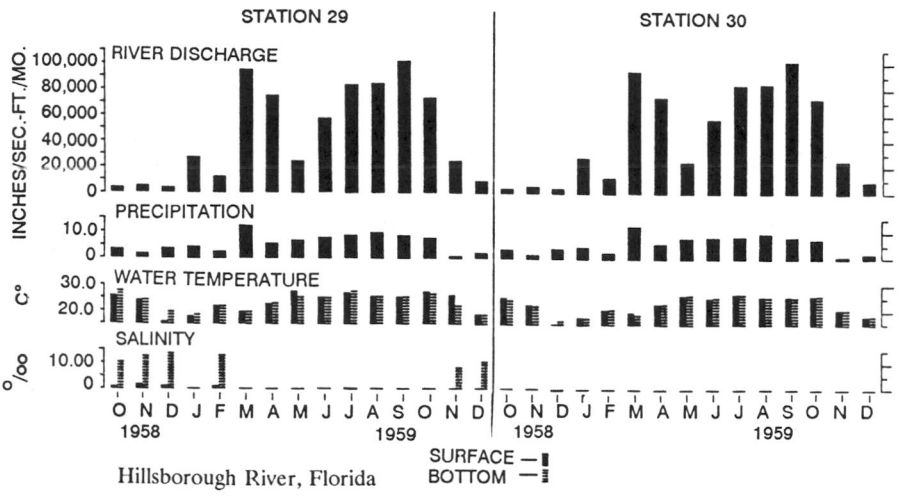

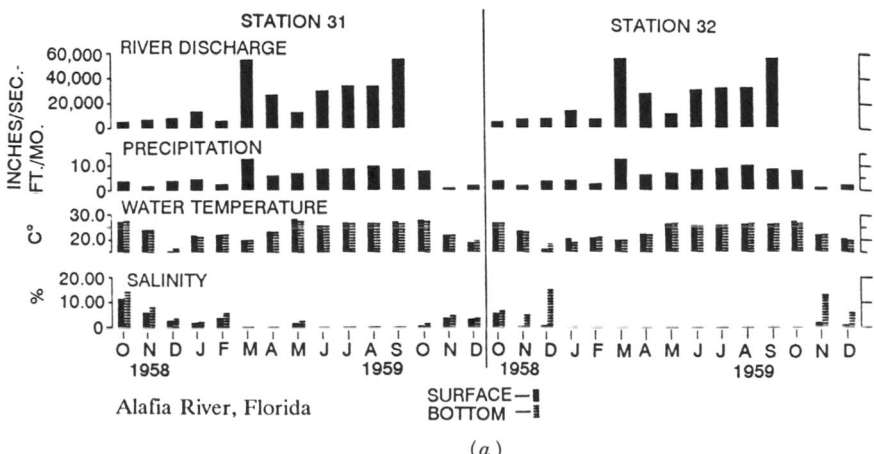

(a)

FIGURE 2.65. River discharge, precipitation, temperature, and salinity of major Tampa Bay tributaries, October 1958 to December 1959. (From Dragovich and May, 1962.)

Mobile Bay and Its Tributaries. The main components of the Alabama coastal zone are, from east to west, Perdido Bay and Wolf Bay, Little Lagoon, Mobile Bay and its component estuaries, including the Mobile Delta (Alabama and Tombigbee confluence), and the eastern end of Mississippi Sound (Figure 2.69) (Chermock, 1974).

Tides. Tides in Alabama estuaries are diurnal, with one high and one low water level occurring each day. South winds tend to raise tides by driving ocean water against the shore, whereas north winds lower tides. Hurricanes have raised

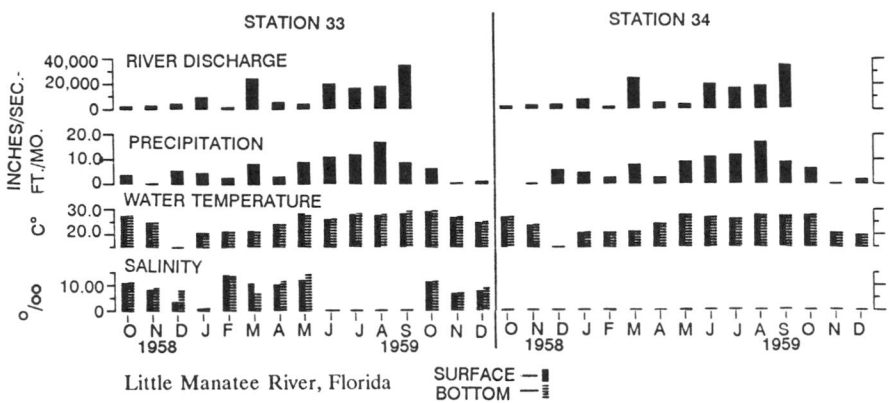

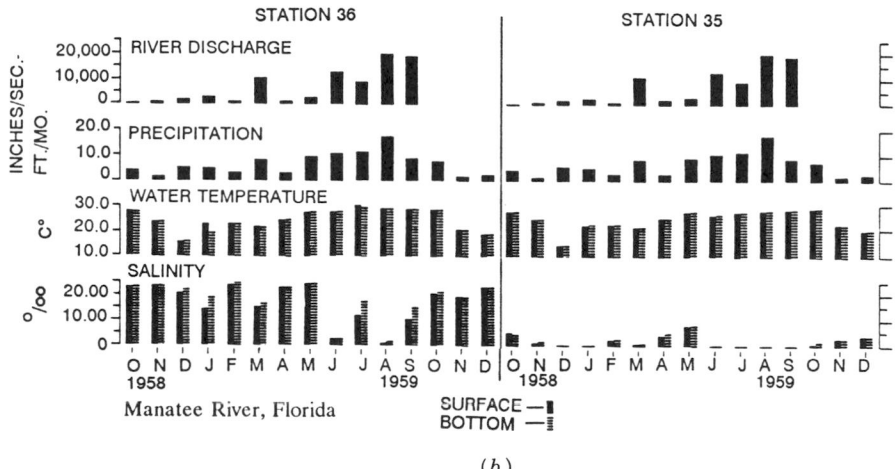

(*b*)

FIGURE 2.65.   (*Continued*)

tides to as much as 11.6 ft (3.4 m) and depressed water level to 9.7 ft (nearly 3 m) below mean low water. Tides have also been raised by the flooding of streams in the Mobile River basin.

Tidal currents in Alabama estuaries reverse about every 6 hours, with periods of slack water between reversals. Discharge of fresh water affects the speed of the flood and ebb currents. Figure 2.70 illustrates the paths of tide flow in Mobile Bay. Note the tendency of currents to move to the right (east on flood tide, west on ebb tide) as expected from the Coriolis effect. Austin (1954), using Ketchum's method, calculated that the flushing time for Mobile Bay was 45 days, whereas observed data and nontidal drift estimates indicate a figure of 54 days. Because of daily fluctuations in river discharge, the flushing time is considered to be between these values.

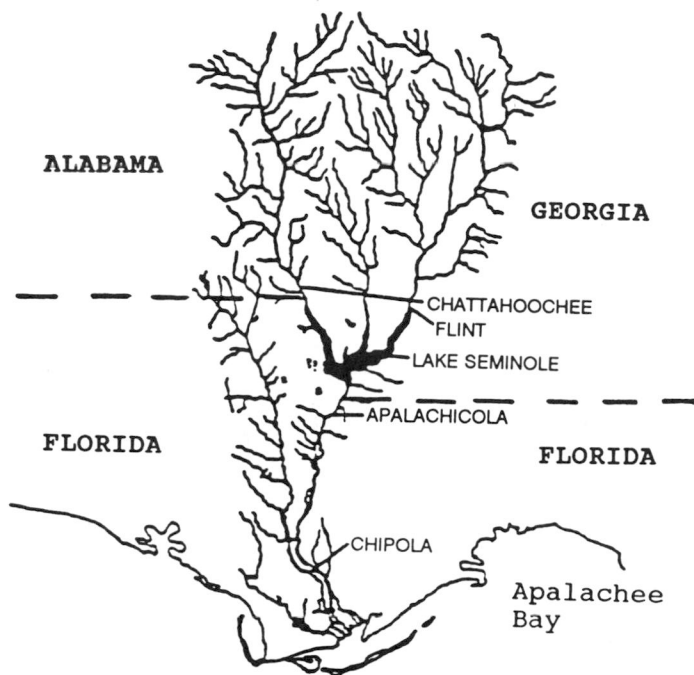

FIGURE 2.66.   Lower portion of the Apalachicola drainage system of Florida, including the major rivers that contribute to the Apalachicola Bay estuarine system. (After Livingston et al., 1974.)

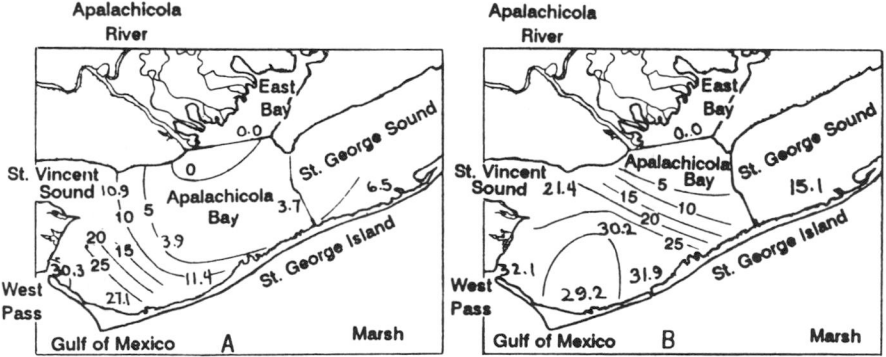

FIGURE 2.67.   Comparison of surface and bottom salinities in Apalachicola Bay, on May 19, 1973: (A) surface; (B) bottom. At the time of sampling, winds were S to SW at 8 to 12 knots, and tide was at flood stage. Contour interval = 5 ppt. (After Livingston et al., 1974.)

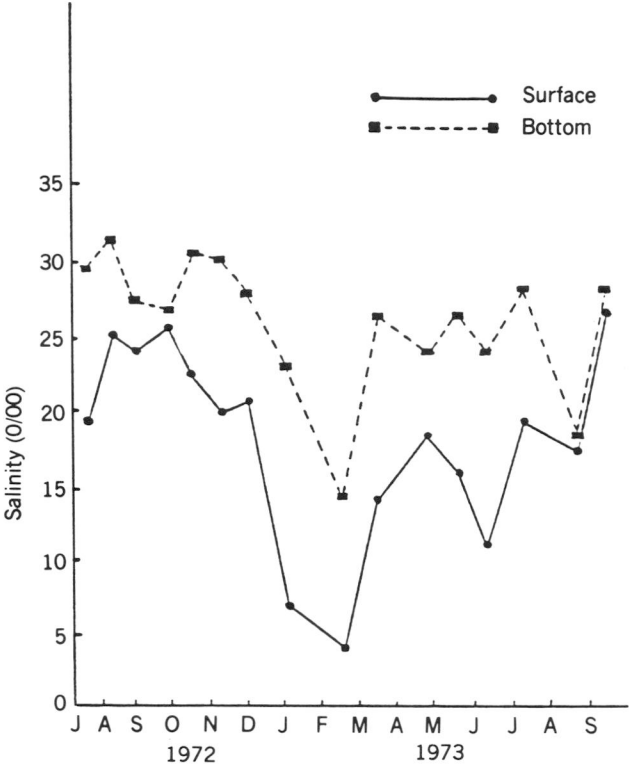

FIGURE 2.68.   Average seasonal variation in salinity for Apalachicola Bay in 1972 and 1973. (After Livingston et al., 1974.)

Salinities.   Generally, there is a salt wedge in Mobile Bay when salinities are higher in July through October and when river discharges are less. Increased river discharges tend to cause increased mixing. Lateral salinity patterns in Mobile Bay and the adjacent Mississippi Sound are shown in Figures 2.71 (surface) and 2.72 (bottom). Comparison of the two figures illustrates clearly how the salt wedge pushes through the passes between barrier islands, whereas the low-salinity water arises mainly in the delta region. The change in shape of the salt wedge in the lower Mobile Bay ship channel during tide changes is illustrated in Figure 2.73.

Laguna Madre.   The Laguna Madre area of Texas is characterized by very shallow bays behind barrier islands. The landscape is almost flat, so that slight changes in water level can either expose or inundate large areas of coastal flats (Copeland et al., 1968). Studies using a recording anemometer and a tide gage simultaneously have shown that water levels can be markedly affected by winds, which can raise or lower water levels more than the lunar tides in the area. At a site about 40 miles (64.4 km) south of Corpus Christi Bay, winds blowing toward the north raised water levels, whereas winds blowing toward the south

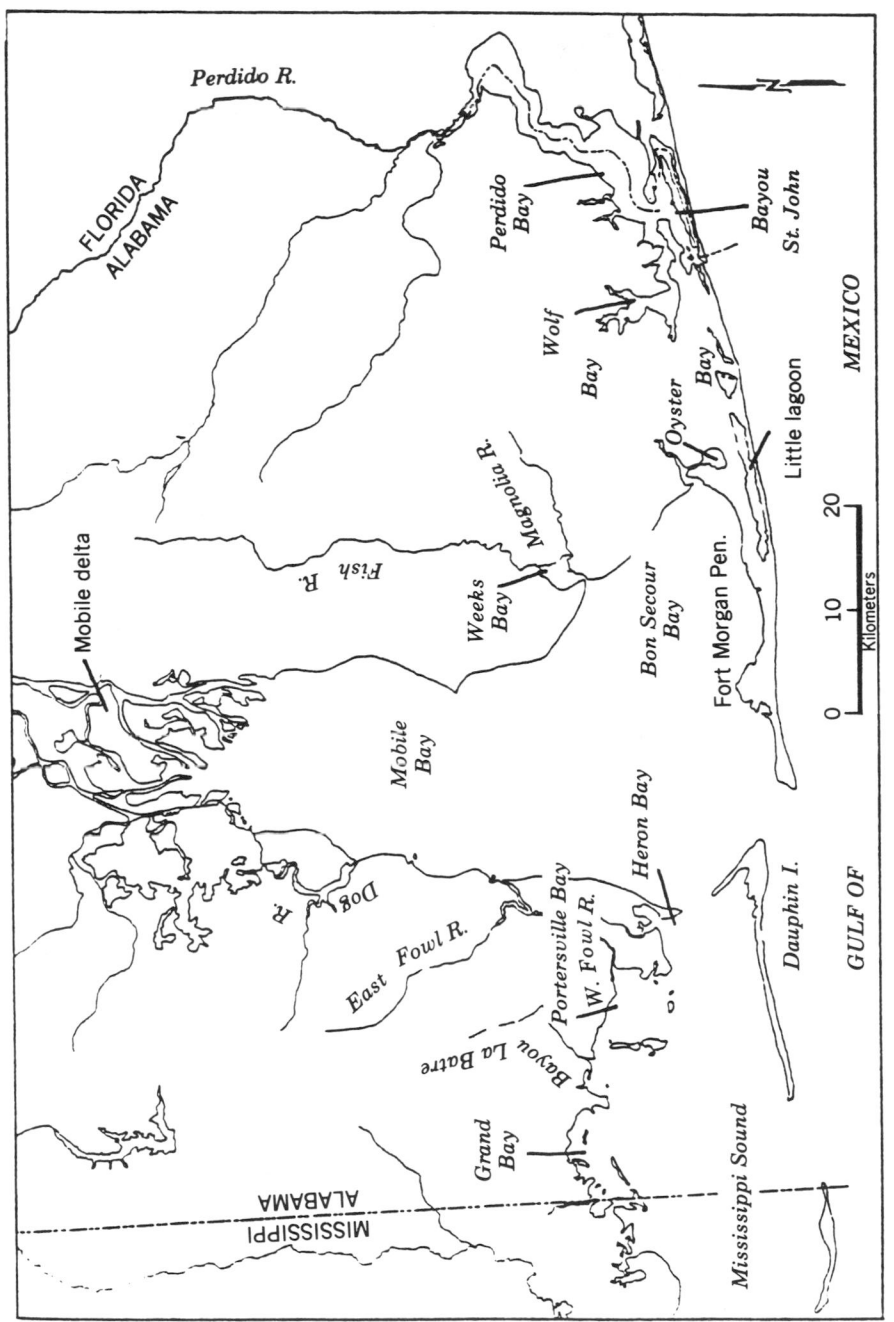

FIGURE 2.69. Alabama coastal zone. (From Chermock, 1974).

121

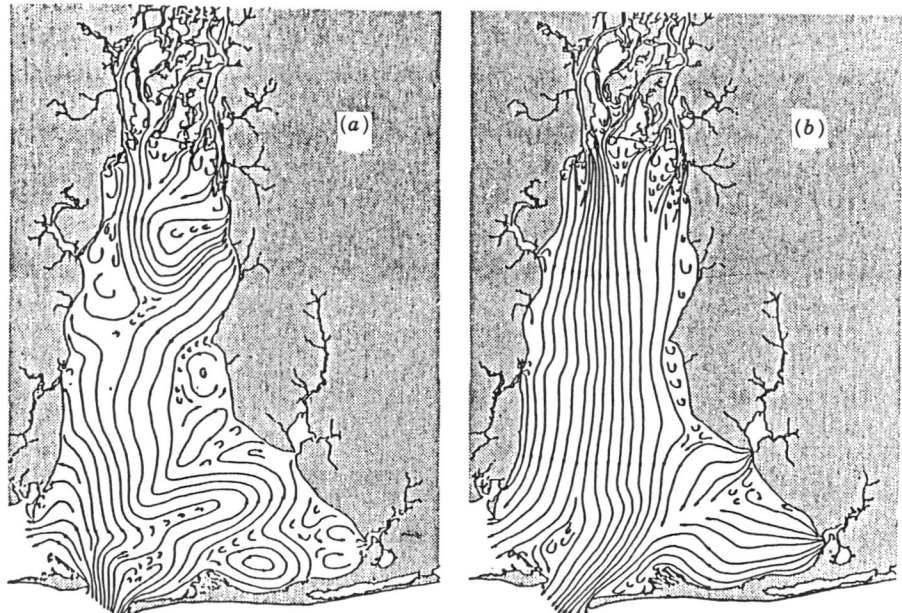

FIGURE 2.70.   Tidal currents in Mobile Bay, Alabama in October 1954: (*a*) flood tide; (*b*) ebb tide. (From Chermock, 1974.)

lowered them (Figure 2.74). The reaction to wind is more immediate in the case of winds blowing toward the north, and water level was related to both strength and direction of wind.

Sediments.   The deposition of sediments on the Gulf coast has largely been accomplished by wave and tidal action forming islands, or by river sediments producing deltas. The major factors affecting changes on the Texas coast seem to be a deficit of sediments due to a deficit of discharge from the rivers, changing sea level, and compactional subsidence. Studies indicate that the changes in the shoreline and vegetation line are largely the result of natural processes, perhaps expedited by human activities. On the Texas Gulf coast between Sabine Pass and Bolivar Roads the Texas shoreline is retreating, aggravated by the opening of Bolivar Pass (Figure 2.75). The only exceptions are accretions associated with jetties (Morton, 1975).

Pacific Coast Estuaries
San Diego Bay.   San Diego Bay (California) is a crescent-shaped estuary that is almost completely enclosed (Smith, 1976). The entrance to the bay is a narrow channel that blocks the action of the open sea. Bay water is well mixed, has no significant density-induced currents, and is fed by three relatively small rivers, the San Diego, Sweet Water, Otay, and a number of smaller streams (Figure 2.76).

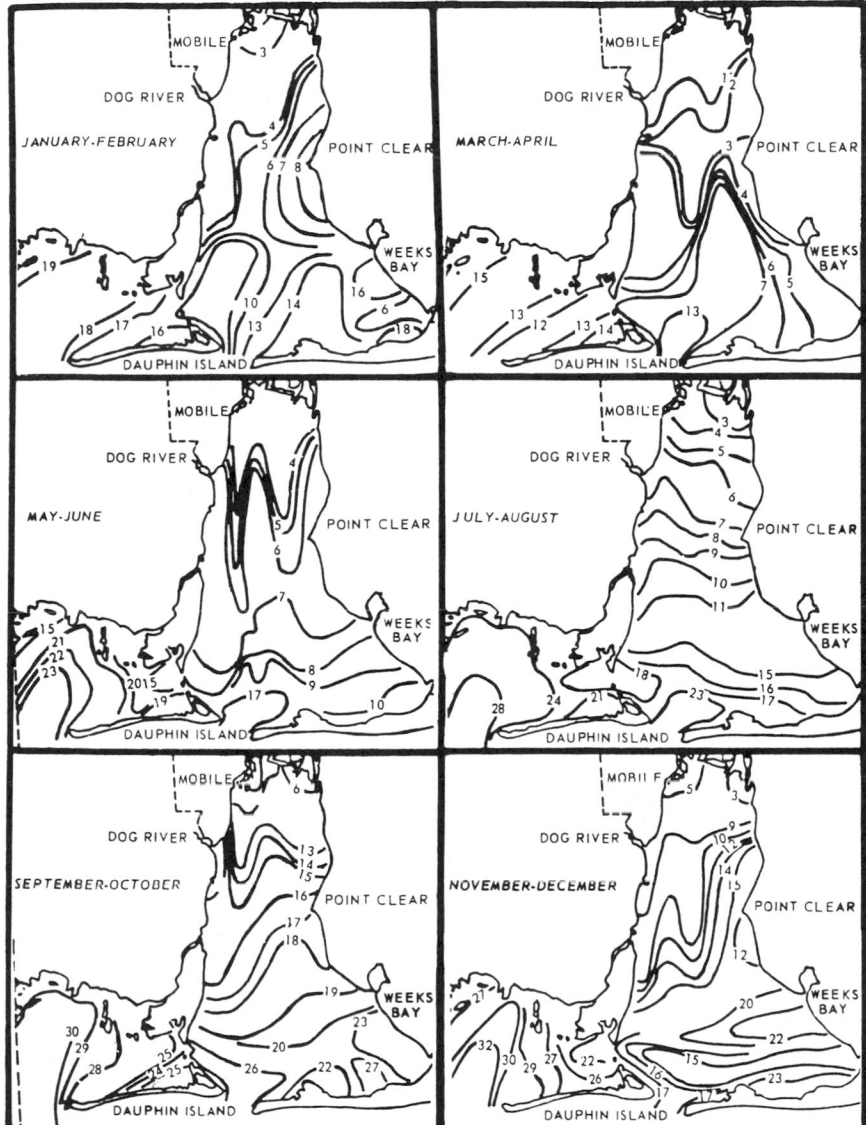

FIGURE 2.71. Bimonthly surface isohaline maps of Mobile Bay and Mississippi Sound. (From Chermock, 1974.)

The bay receives minimal freshwater runoff from the rivers and has a high evaporation rate. Local winds generate short-period waves or chop.

Tides. Tides are mixed and diurnal. The mean range is 1.3 m and the extreme range is 3.2 m.

Sediments. Sediment contribution to San Diego Bay is minimal from all sources. Prior to diversion and damming of local rivers, sediment inputs had been

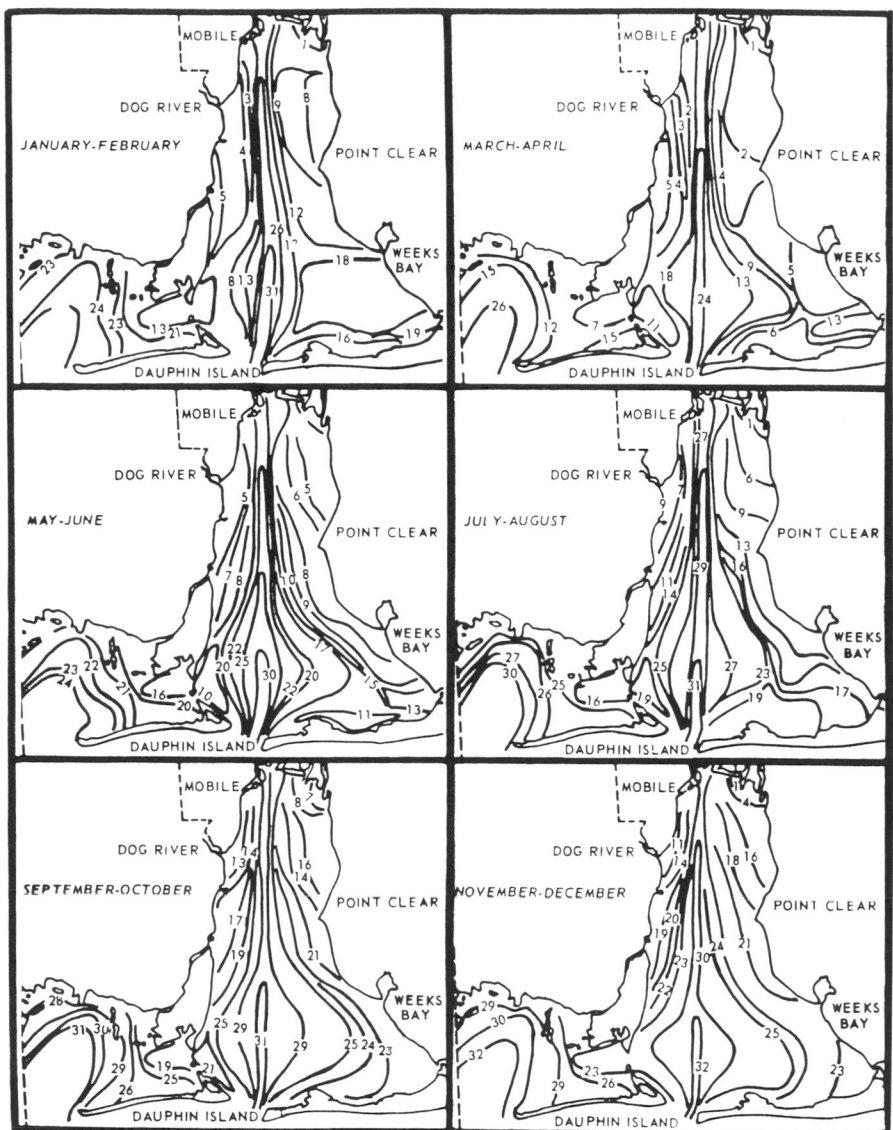

FIGURE 2.72. Bimonthly bottom isohaline maps of Mobile Bay and Mississippi Sound. (From Chermock, 1974.)

considerable, but present velocities in the lower reaches of these rivers are not great enough to produce scouring. Sedimentation before human intervention was 0.8 to 1.1×10^6 m^3. After alteration of the natural stream flow, sedimentation levels dropped to 1.4 to 1.9×10^5 m^3. Because of the shape of the bay and the nature of the Pacific Ocean there is very little sedimentation from other sources. The protection afforded the bay entrance by Point Loma makes littoral transport

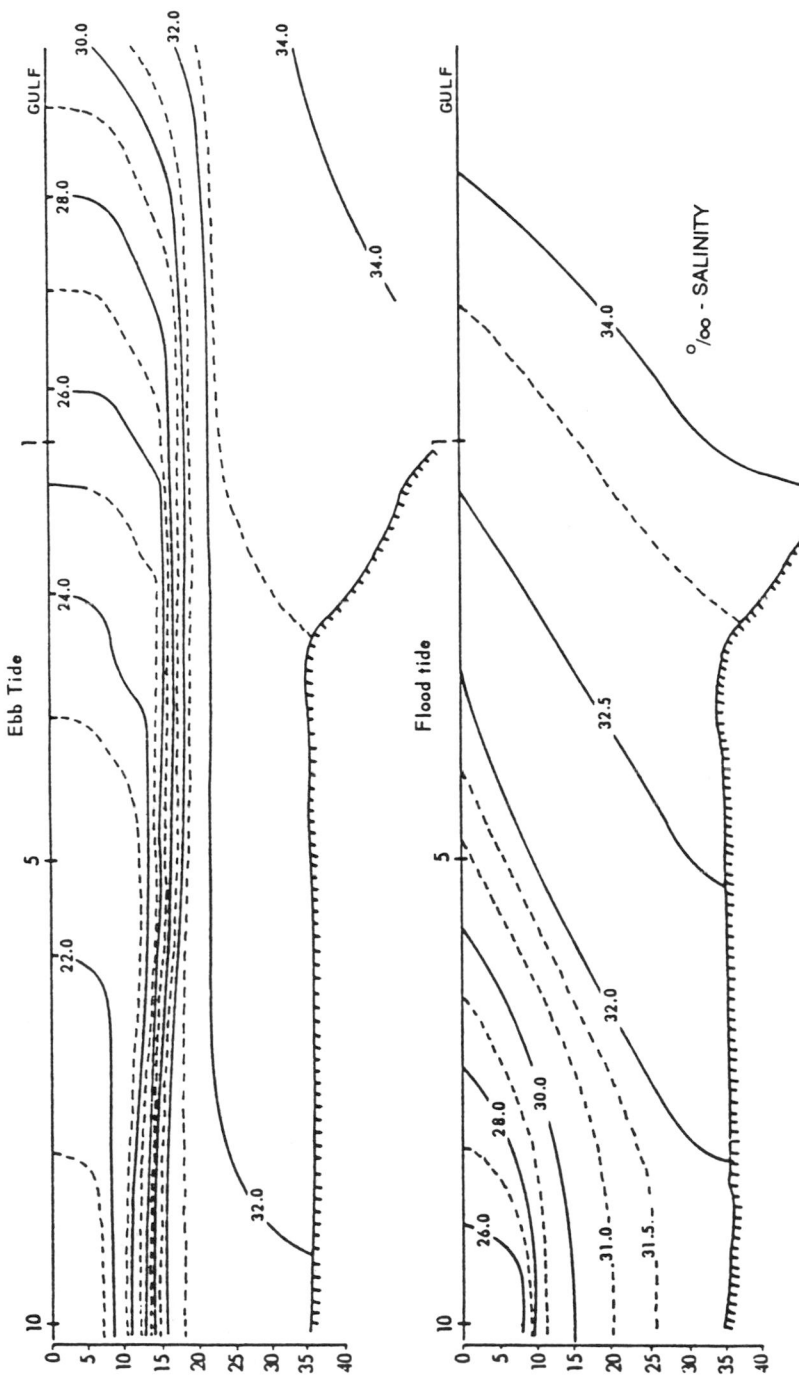

FIGURE 2.73. Longitudinal section along the lower Mobile Bay ship channel, showing salinity profiles. (From Chermock, 1974.)

125

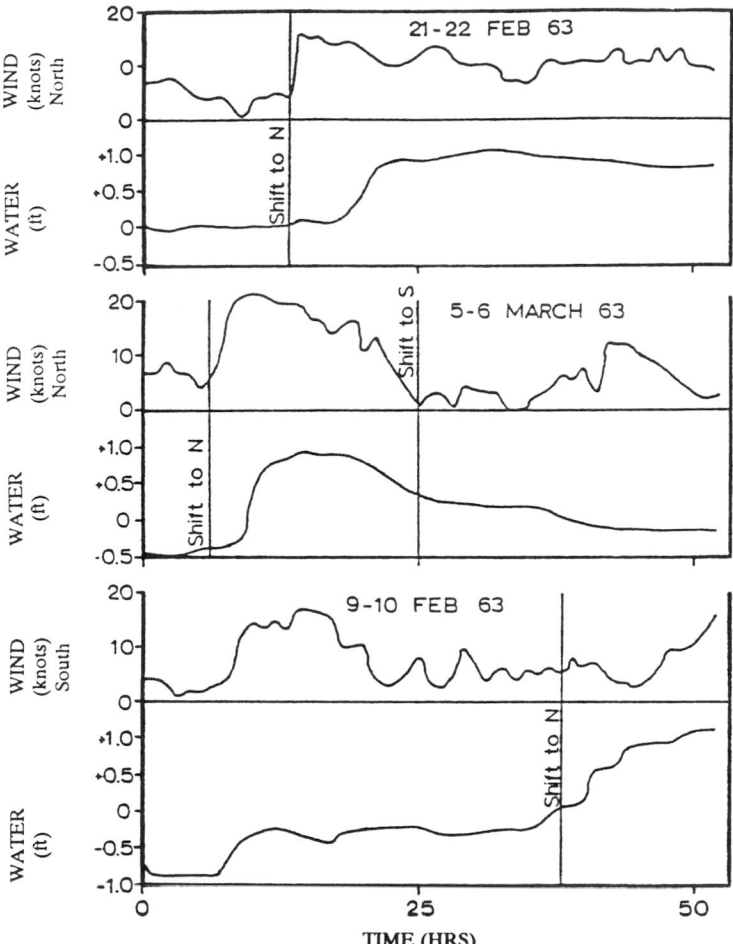

FIGURE 2.74. Examples of changes in water level due to wind shifts in the Texas Laguna Madre in 1963. Water levels are in relation to the mean tide level of the Gulf of Mexico. Vertical lines mark the times of a major shift in wind direction. (From Copeland et al., 1968.)

negligible. Storm washovers and wind transport across the Silver Strand are very rare. Most of the shoreline within the bay is protected from erosion by bulkheads and the like, and for those unprotected areas, the fetch of the wind is insufficient to cause erosion. San Diego Bay is highly developed, as reflected in the pattern of marginal filling (Figure 2.77).

Mugu Lagoon. Mugu Lagoon is located in southern California at the foot of the Santa Monica Mountains (Figure 2.78A). The inlet, and therefore sedimentology, is controlled by tides and seasonal conditions (Warme et al., 1976). The lagoon extends about 7 km parallel to the coast behind a narrow barrier beach. Waves approach mainly from the northwest.

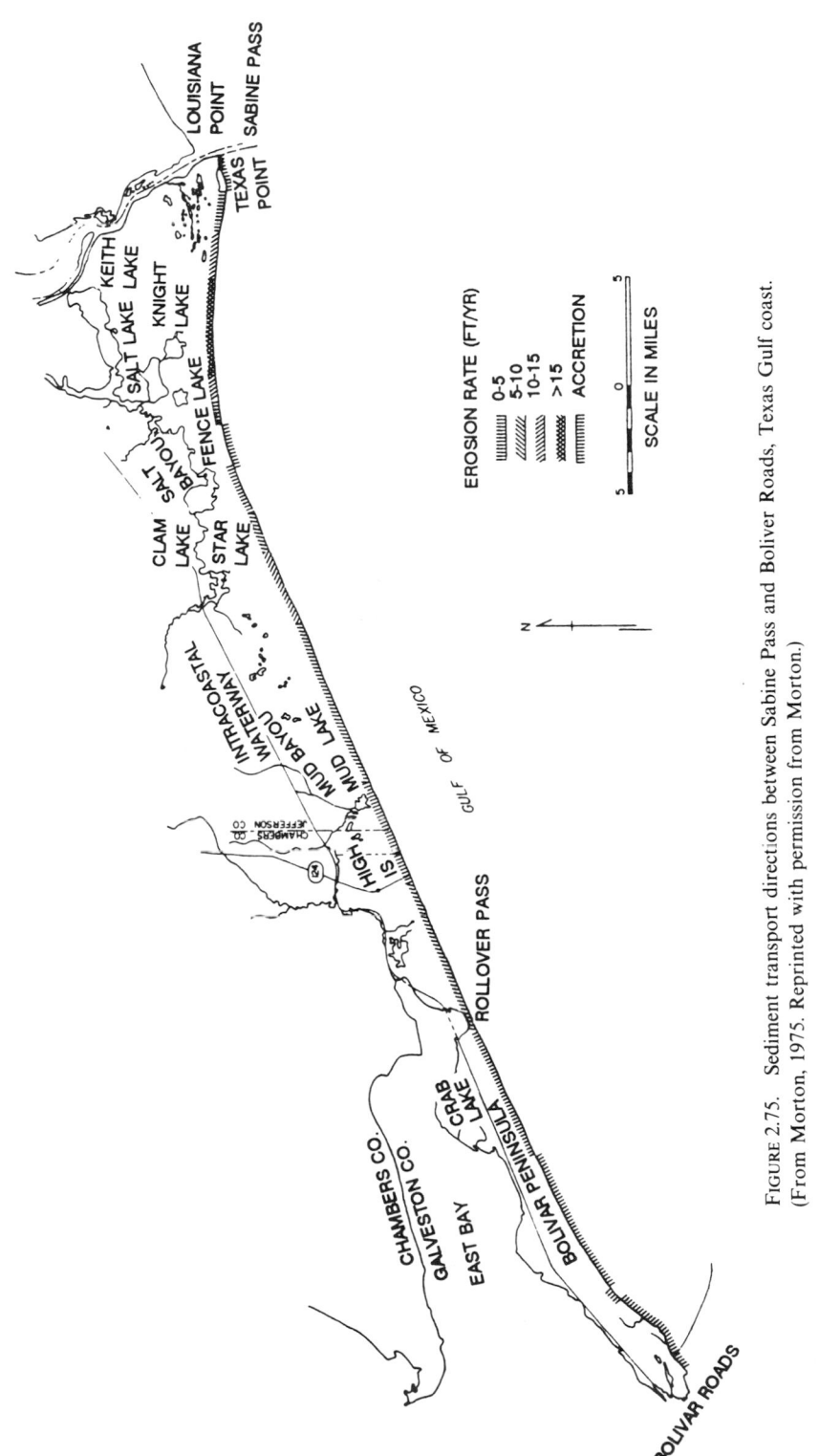

FIGURE 2.75. Sediment transport directions between Sabine Pass and Boliver Roads, Texas Gulf coast. (From Morton, 1975. Reprinted with permission from Morton.)

127

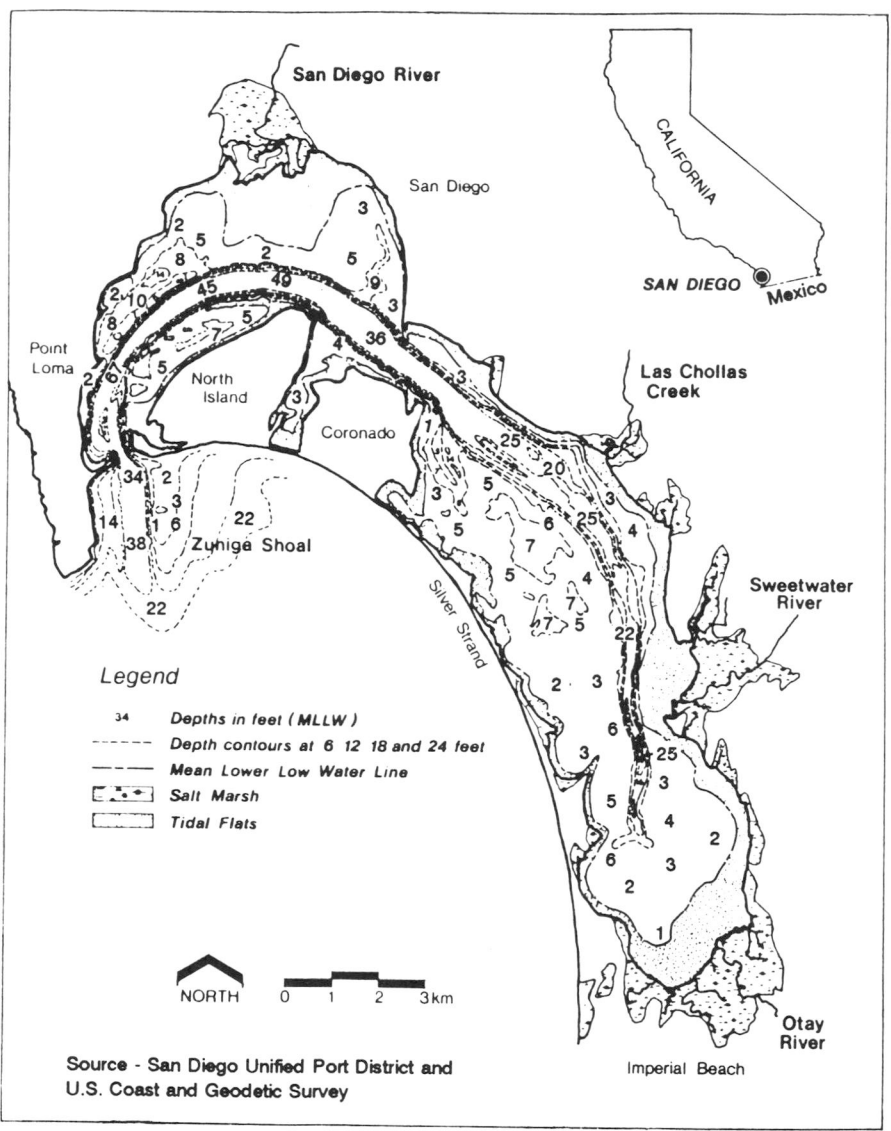

FIGURE 2.76. San Diego Bay, California, in 1857, before large-scale human intervention. (From Smith, 1976.)

Tides. Tides are mixed and diurnal; the spring tidal range is about 2 m. The inlet of the lagoon is maintained around mean sea level, so only the upper half of the tidal spectrum affects it. Maximum water exchange occurs during spring tides. As a result of these irregular tides, water levels, and currents, slack water durations are extremely variable. The lagoon has a very narrow inlet channel, and the maximum tidal current velocities occur there. Velocity decreases as the currents disperse toward the distal parts of the lagoon.

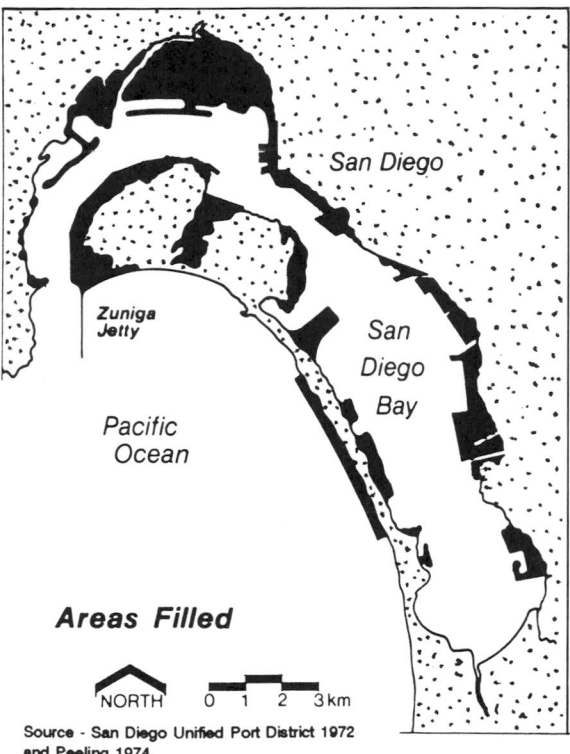

FIGURE 2.77. San Diego Bay, showing the areas filled during the period 1914 to 1971. (From Smith, 1976.)

Tidal currents are most important in the distribution of sediment in the lagoon. Mugu Lagoon's inlet has a natural open and closed cycle. Neap tides and a high rate of sand deposition act to close it. The effects of tidal currents are naturally eliminated when the inlets are closed. The lagoon may remain closed for long periods of time, and high storm waves, high runoff, or both, coupled with high water level in the lagoon, are necessary to reopen the inlet (Warme et al., 1976).

Sediments. Net longshore transport of sediments is to the southwest. Sand is transported in and out.of the lagoon with the tide, and some of it is deposited in the lagoon. In the Mugu Lagoon, the most important processes affecting sediment distribution are tidal currents, barrier washover, and wind. Runoff from Calleguas Creek and the Santa Monica Mountains has less effect on sediment distribution. The sand supplied by longshore drift is transported into Mugu Lagoon from the beach. Mud is introduced by Calleguas Creek or transported from turbid offshore waters after storms. Once mud has entered the lagoon, it is moved away from the inlet by the tide and deposited in areas where the current slows (Warme et al., 1976).

San Francisco Bay Estuary System. The Sacramento and San Joaquin estuary system expands into Suisun Bay and San Pablo Bay and enters the

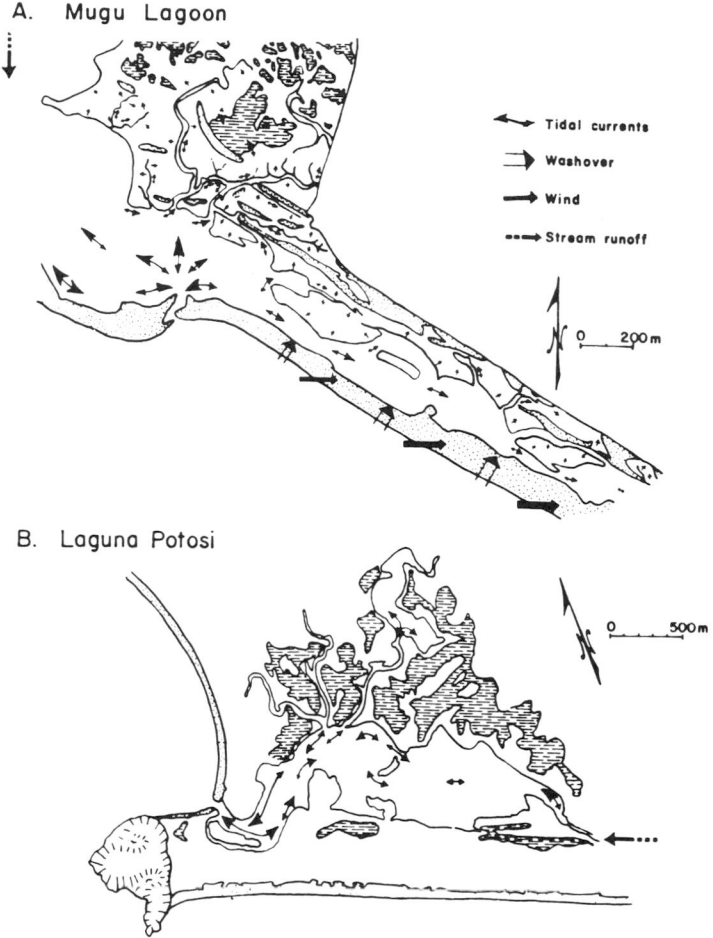

FIGURE 2.78.   Sediment transport pathways in Mugu Lagoon. Arrow azimuths indicate directions of transport; lengths represent relative current velocities; sizes of arrows or their heads show relative amount of sediment transported in a given direction. (After Warme et al., 1976.)

northern part of San Francisco Bay. The bay connects to the Pacific Ocean through the Golden Gate (Figure 2.79). The Sacramento, San Joaquin, and Mokelumne rivers provide most of the runoff into the estuary. The Sacramento contributed more than twice the flow of the other two rivers in any given month of the years 1963 and 1964. Highest flows in all the rivers were in winter and spring (Kelley, 1966). The San Joaquin and Mokelumne rivers are both affected by extensive water diversion for irrigation and municipal uses.

Tides.   Tides are diurnal, having two low phases and two high phases in every lunar day (about 24.8 hours). Tidal ranges are as shown in Table 2.8. Currents tend to be strong throughout the estuary. Both tides and winds contribute to

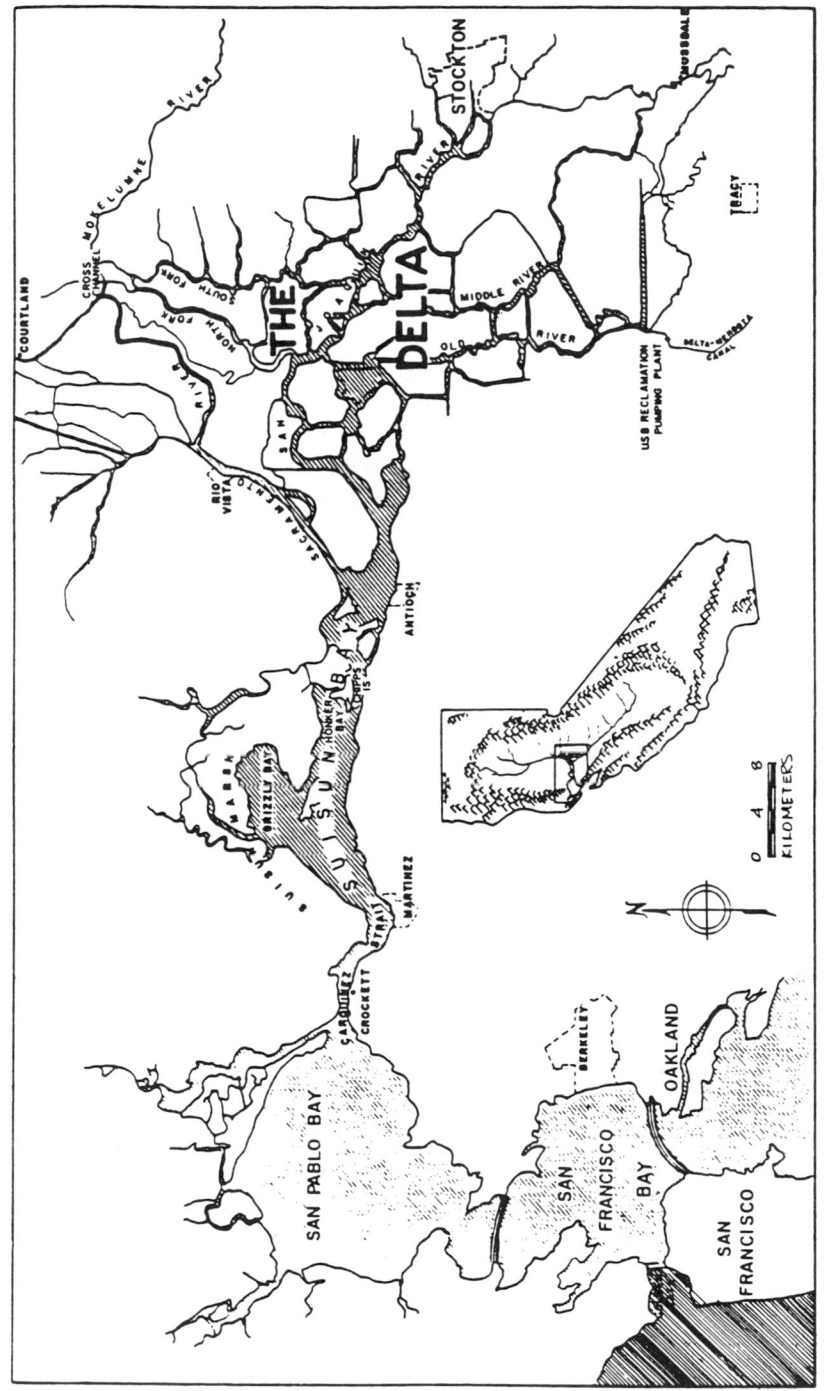

FIGURE 2.79. Sacramento–San Joaquin estuary system, California. (From Kelley, 1966, California Department of Fish and Game.)

131

TABLE 2.8.   *Tidal Ranges in the Component Basins of the San Francisco Bay*
Area

Basin	Mean High to Mean Low (ft)	Mean High High to Mean Low Low (ft)
South San Francisco Bay	6.5	8.4
North San Francisco Bay	4.0	5.7
San Pablo Bay	4.4	6.1
Carquinez Strait	4.4	5.9
Suisun Bay	3.9	5.3
Delta	2.7	3.3

Source: Kelley (1966), Table 3, p. 11. California Department of Fish and Game.

currents. Currents in the Golden Gate and Carquinez Strait reach 8 ft $(2.5 \text{ m}) \text{s}^{-1}$, whereas currents in the main channel of San Pablo Bay sometimes reach 5 ft $(1.5 \text{ m}) \text{s}^{-1}$, and in the shallow part of the bay the currents are rarely over 1.5 ft (0.5 m).

In the three-year study, releasing surface and seabed drifters bimonthly verified the fact that the northern reach ocean section has a permanent estuarine circulation cell maintained by density differences between the Sacramento–San Joaquin river water and sea water. As a result of the density differences, a constant net landward bottom flow of dense sea water was present in opposition to a less dense river water seaward flow. A null zone was produced by these currents having equal and opposite effect. The place where this effect occurs is known as the null zone and is graphically portrayed by the convergence of the seabed drifters in Figure 2.81.

In the southern reach, because of the small supply of river water inflow, there was weaker salinity stratification and the two-layer estuary circulation was not exhibited. However seasonally the near-bottom and surface currents reversed. Strong prevailing winds in the summer altered any weak density in these circulations and controlled the nontidal drift (Figure 2.81). Except in dead-end channels, currents in the delta are commonly 2.5 ft $(0.76 \text{ m}) \text{s}^{-1}$ on ebb flow. Currents in the delta depend on tides, river flow, and the operation of the U.S. Bureau of Reclamation's cross channel at Walnut Grove and the pumping plant near Tracy (Figure 2.79).

Salinities.   The salinity gradient extends for about 50 miles (80 km) from the western edge of the delta formed by the Sacramento and San Joaquin rivers to mid-San Francisco Bay. The gradient is steepened during floods, and its location moves according to flow of the rivers. Figure 2.80 shows how the salinity values and zones changed through 1963 and 1964 at several locations along the estuary. Releases of fresh water from upstream reservoirs along the Sacramento River are used to keep salt water out of the delta. The estuary is generally well mixed. Differences of even 2 to 4 ppt between surface and bottom water are rare. During periods of flood, a mass of fresh water may override the salty water in San Pablo

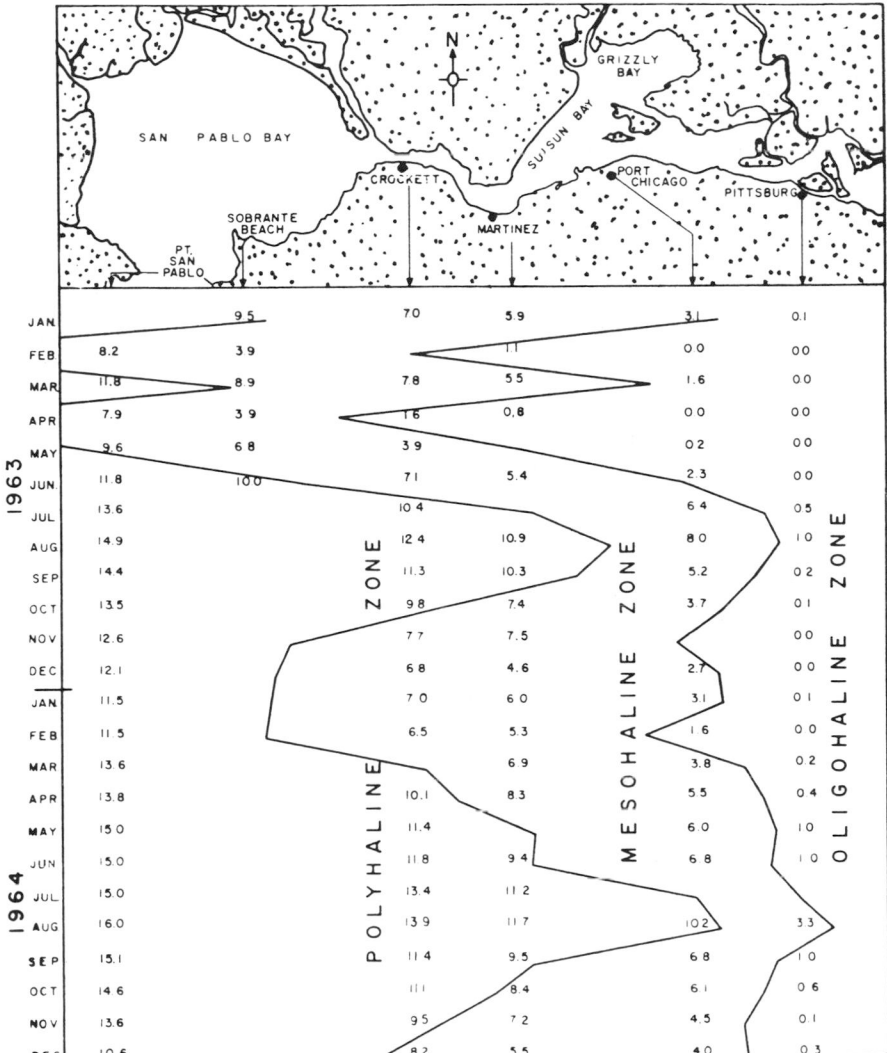

FIGURE 2.80. Release and recovery points for (*A*) surface and (*B*) seabed drifters in the San Francisco Bay system and adjacent ocean. Drifter movements are shown as arrows drawn from release points to recovery locations and portray simplified paths of movement occurring within 2 months of release. Winter release: December 1970; summer release: September 1971. Data are typical of 18 releases over a 3-year period, from 1970 to 1973. (From Conomos and Peterson, 1976.)

and San Francisco bays. Constant mixing by tides and winds is the rule in this system. Alterations by human beings have brought the usual salinity of the Suisun Bay to somewhat higher levels than was probably natural, but the same alterations have prevented saline intrusions far into the delta as had often happened in very dry years.

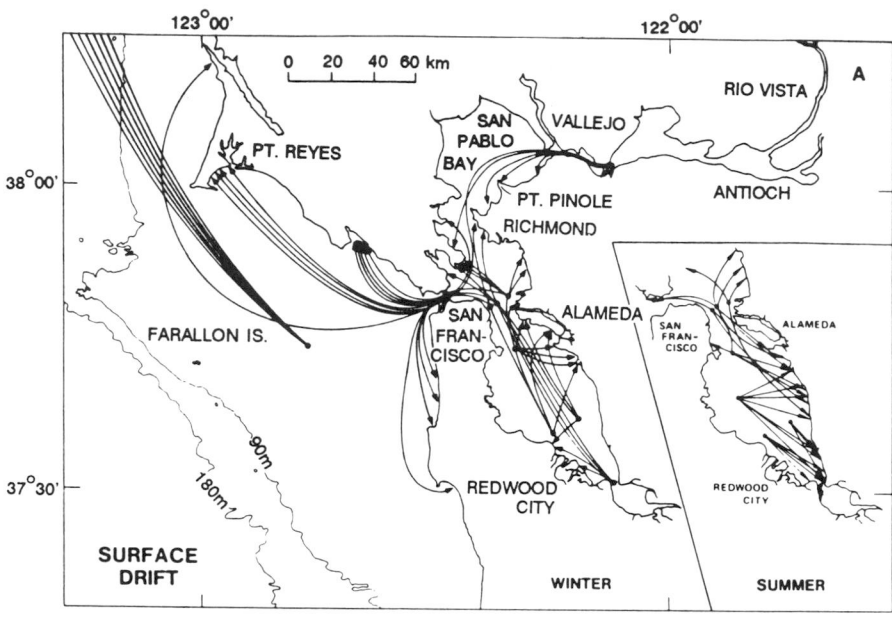

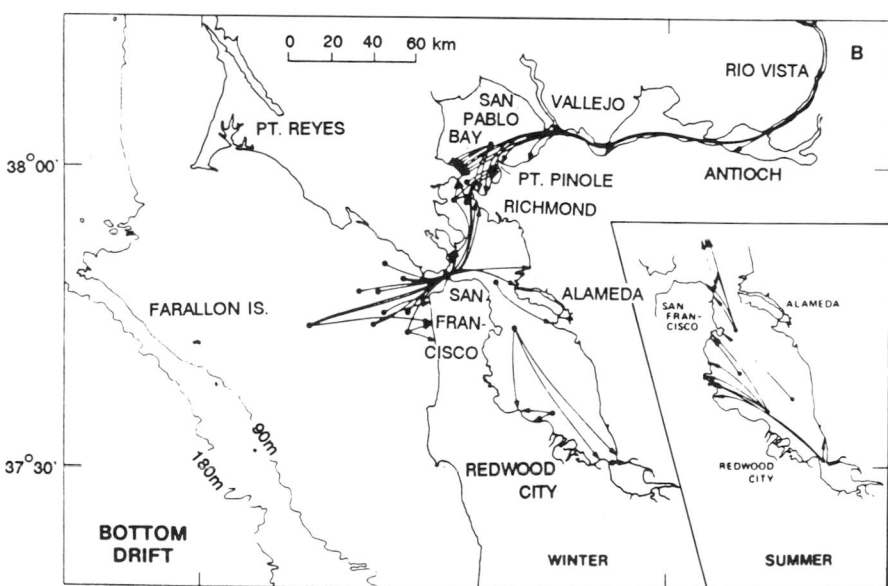

FIGURE 2.81.   Seasonal changes in salinity in the Sacramento–San Joaquin estuary system during 1963 and 1964. Values are parts per million chlorides. (From Kelley, 1966, California Department of Fish and Game.)

Sediments. Sedimentary conditions in the San Francisco Bay are influenced by winds, tides, river input, and density-driven circulation. Winds from the west and northwest predominate and are stronger and more variable in the summer than in the winter, although there are biweekly storms in the winter. Tides are mixed and mostly semidiurnal. The bay is a high-energy system with strong currents caused by a large tidal prism (about 24% of the bay volume) and large waves and nontidal currents caused by winds.

The Sacramento and San Joaquin rivers release into the northern part of San Francisco Bay 90% of the bay's freshwater and sediment input. The bay's salinity distribution is also dependent on the inflow of these large northbay rivers. The annual river inflow is large (three times the volume of the bay) and causes estuarine circulation in the northern bay and density-induced advection in the southern bay. The large volume of sediment inflow and the relative shallowness of the bay coupled with these environmental conditions cause quite a bit of mobility in the bay. The dispersal of the sediments is seasonal, with 80% of the sediment supplied and most of the deposition occurring during the winter. Resuspension and redeposition are predominant during the summer.

During the winter the heavier portion of the large sediment load that enters the northern bay is deposited soon after entry. Some of it is resuspended periodically by tidal currents. The deposited sediments cause shoaling in the San Pablo Bay (the null zone) during the winter. Sediments are unable to escape from this area, which acts as a trap. The sediment portion that remains suspended constitutes the turbidity maximum. This turbidity maximum is maintained by density-induced currents, and its concentration changes seasonally. Most of the near-surface sediment flowing seaward is carried through the Golden Gate. In the southern reach, where sediment is from local streams, what is not deposited is either carried out the Golden Gate in the surface layer or transported to the northern reach. Considerable material is resuspended due to the shallowness of the southern bay and the frequency of winter storms (Conomos and Peterson, 1976).

In summer, a decrease in sediment flow and an increase in wind velocity cause much more resuspension of bottom material than deposition of new material. Resuspended material in the northern reach is transported to the turbidity maximum and the null zone, which has migrated into the Suisun Bay region. The southern reach probably loses sediment to the northern reach and there is some erosion of marginal mud flats as well.

Studies have shown that most of the near-surface suspended sediments are transported through the Golden Gate to the ocean, and that all those moving on the bottom actually moved landward of the Golden Gate. Seaward-floating sediments are clay or fine-grained silt. Once out in the ocean they seem to by-pass the Gulf of Fallarones, dispersing beyond it, or are carried back into the bay in inflowing bottom current (Conomos and Peterson, 1976).

Pistol River Estuary

Tides. The tidal range and timing within the basin may differ markedly from that in the ocean outside. A constricted inlet to the basin establishes a hydraulic level that lies alternately above and below the tidally varying level of the adjacent ocean. In such a basin the two water levels correspond twice each tidal cycle for only a short time, once during the rising tide and once during the falling tide. At high tide the estuarine level lies below the adjacent sea level. Water therefore continues to pour in from the ocean during the initial fall of the tide. This inflow may continue for more than an hour after high tide occurs in the ocean.

Sediments. In the course of a year the Pistol River (Oregon) passes through all the various types of sediment deposition of smaller streams entering the Pacific in Oregon. During flood stage the Pistol River has a discharge of a few hundred cubic meters per second and behaves as a large stream flowing without deflection into the ocean. At such times the sediments of the bed consist of seaward-moving sand and gravel. At the mouth of the river a layer of fine mud may be deposited in the channel at high tide when downstream currents diminish and bedload movement ceases. Although the water is relatively turbulent, silt and clay may flocculate from suspension and form a film over the bottom. This layer may inhibit further sand transport, and if the bed is not eroded, more than a centimeter of additional mud may be deposited at successive high tides (Clifton et al., 1972).

As the flood stage passes, the discharge drops to about $10 \, cm^3 \, s^{-1}$. At this time a rivermouth bar becomes obvious near the beach and the stream is deflected to either the north or south. The deflection may cause the development of a new channel rather than a new channel being formed as a lateral shift in the main channel. With further waning of stream discharge the combination of waves and tides creates a topographic sill to the channel above low-tide level in the lower reaches of the stream. The first sill may develop at the time of the development of lateral channels or may be formed later within the channel. The development of a sill (mostly from marine sediments) produces a configuration common to streams with summer discharges of about 0.1 to $1 \, m^3 \, s^{-1}$. This characteristic configuration consists of a broad estuarine basin lying immediately inshore from a narrow outlet to the ocean. The basin may be 100 to 200 m across and extend upstream for several kilometers into the larger streams. Maximum water depth in the basins ranges from 2 to 3 m, in contrast to the outlet depth, which is usually less than a meter (Clifton et al., 1972).

The presence of the sill at the mouth of the estuary profoundly affects the orientation of the directional structures in the channel. The discharge from the estuary during ebb flow should generally exceed that entering during tidal flood by the amount of river discharge in the estuary, but once the topographic sills develop, upstream-facing megaripples within the channel upstream from the sill become persistent features (Clifton et al., 1972).

During 1972 the Pistol River developed three separate sills. The first of these exceeded a meter in height and apparently formed when the main channel was blocked and a more shallow lateral channel developed. Stratification upstream from this sill was quite noticeable, and landward-facing megaripples persisted upstream from it throughout the tidal cycle.

A second sill, about 0.5 m high, developed in mid-July approximately halfway between the first sill and the ocean. Prior to the development of this sill, megaripples in the channel downstream from the first sill reversed orientation as the tide changed. Once the second sill was formed, upstream-facing megaripples 30 to 40 cm high became persistent bedforms upstream from it.

A third sill developed near the mouth of the Pistol River on July 19, 1972, and the low tide within the estuary rose a half meter over its position the previous day. The discharge from the estuary dropped from $1.3\,m^3\,s^{-1}$ on July 19 to $0.012\,m^3\,s^{-1}$ at low tide on July 20. With the development of this third sill, ripples and megaripples faced upstream in all parts of the stream except the final outlet. In the outlet, downstream-facing ripples constituted the dominant bedform, as they generally do in streams of this size. Once the third sill had been developed and the outlet to the sea greatly diminished by the increased sill height, water loss from the estuary was by seepage. Measurements of discharge in the Pistol River above the range of tidal influence compared to that in the mouth of the estuary just before damming indicate that as much as $1\,m^3\,s^{-1}$ may seep from the estuary. Once the river mouth becomes dammed, water stratification in the estuary breaks down and it becomes a homogeneous water column. This great change in salinity greatly affects the marine benthos (Clifton et al., 1972), which was established when daily fresh ocean water entered the estuary.

Accretion occurs in this estuary, and this is evidenced not only by the gradient of salinity but also by the temperature gradient. Sediments can also be introduced into the estuary from its margins by berm overwash and wind. (A berm, or ridge, develops between the mouth of a laterally deflected stream and the ocean. Overwash usually occurs during high spring tides or particularly large waves.)

Sediment is transported from the beach and deposited on an avalanche slip face that extends from water level to the stream floor at the edge of the estuary. Additional overwash causes the slip face to migrate, producing cross-bedding that dips, usually landward, in the direction of the overwash. An actively flowing stream may soon erode these deposits, but if the stream is dammed, the deposits will be preserved, at least until the next large flood (Clifton et al., 1972).

Windblown sand may also enter the estuary from the side. On the Oregon coast eolian transport of sand is predominantly by northerly and northwesterly summer winds. Continuous additions of sand produce avalanche slip faces at the estuary margin similar to those produced by berm overwash.

The two types of deposits differ in their orientation, position, and grain size. Material brought in by berm overwash consists of sand and fine gravel. It lies along the seaward margin of the estuary in large-scale foresets that dip predominantly to the south and southeast. Sand brought in by the wind is better sorted and large deposits lie on the northern and northwestern side of the estuary. Where the channel or estuarine shoreline lies oblique to wind direction, the foresets will strike parallel to the shoreline, which is not normal to wind direction. Such deposits will build at a lower rate than where the wind is normal to the shore. This degree of lateral deposition differs from year to year, but rarely fills the entire estuary.

Once the river mouth is dammed, it may overflow occasionally during the summer and cut a new channel through the beach. Flow in such a channel is intense but generally short-lived. The next series of high tides or large waves will tend to rebuild the berm and redam the stream. Ultimately, increased runoff due to fall or winter rains will raise the stream level to the point where it breaks through. Winter and spring floods erode much of the previously deposited sediments and start a new cycle (Clifton et al., 1972).

Coos Bay. Burt and Queen (1957) stated that Coos Bay, Oregon, was a "positive, vertically homogeneous estuary with the principal movement of salt water upstream being caused by eddy diffusion." There was little variation in salt content with depth throughout the estuary, and a linear increase occurs in concentration from seawater at the mouth to fresh water of the Coos River at the estuary head.

Tides. The tidal pattern was usually as follows: higher high water–lower low water–lower high water–higher low water. Salinity data demonstrated that the tidal excursion was greater in the surface due to frictional resistance of the bottom. With the flood tide, surface water moved upstream faster than the bottom water, and a salinity inversion was produced. The result was the two layers became mixed, causing an instability. This condition occurs during flood and high water. On the ebb tide, the surface flow is faster, but turbulent vertical mixing seems to prevent the formation of strong vertical stability.

The process described above is called tidal overmixing by Burt and Queen (1957). This phenomenon aids in movement of salt upstream against the mean flow of the river. It also ventilates the bottom waters and presumably mixes oxygen, nutrients, plankton, pollutants, and any other suspended materials. The whole water column is well mixed on every tidal cycle.

Yaquina Bay

Tides. Yaquina Bay, Oregon, has a mixed semidiurnal tide, the typical pattern along the Pacific coast (Neal, 1966). The greatest tide range (higher high water) is from 2.6 to 2.8 m, depending on distance upstream. The least tide range (lower low water) is from 2.1 to 2.2 m, which varies with distance upstream. The maximum tidal range observed is 2.38 m at Criteser's Marina, the farthest point upstream from the mouth from which data are available (Figure 2.82).

Currents decrease sharply in the upstream direction whether they are flood-tide or ebb-tide currents. The maximum recorded surface current is $78 \, \text{cm} \, \text{s}^{-1}$ on an ebb tide. Ebb-tidal flows are always greater than the flood currents, and bottom currents are weaker than surface currents (Figure 2.83). Current velocity follows a sinusoidal pattern, being approximately 90° out of phase with the tide (Figure 2.84).

Columbia River Estuary. Hubbell et al. (1971) define the Columbia River estuary as the part of the river between the mouth and river mile 66, near Longview, Washington. They report that the saline intrusion reaches Harrington Point, at about river mile 23 (Figure 2.85). Between Harrington Point and the sea, the estuary is from 2 to 10 miles (3.2 to 16 km) wide.

Flow of the Columbia River near its mouth has varied historically from 65,000 cfs ($1841 \, \text{m}^3 \, \text{s}^{-1}$) to 1,200,000 cfs ($33,984 \, \text{m}^3 \, \text{s}^{-1}$). Maximum flows (average about 660,000 cfs or ($18,691 \, \text{m}^3 \, \text{s}^{-1}$) are typically in the months of May, June, and July,

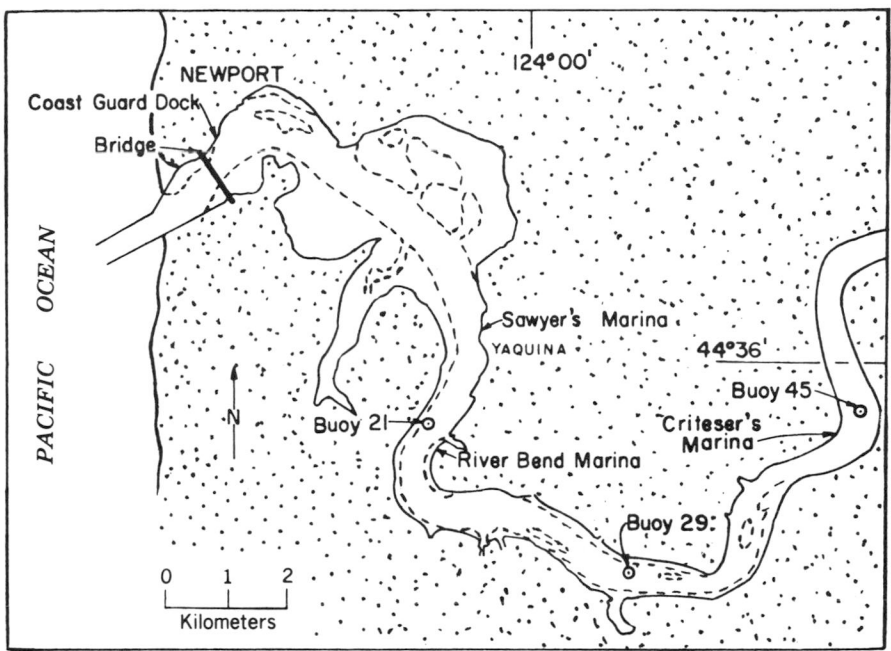

FIGURE 2.82.   Yaquina Bay, Oregon. Dashed line marks mean lower low water. (After Neal, 1966.)

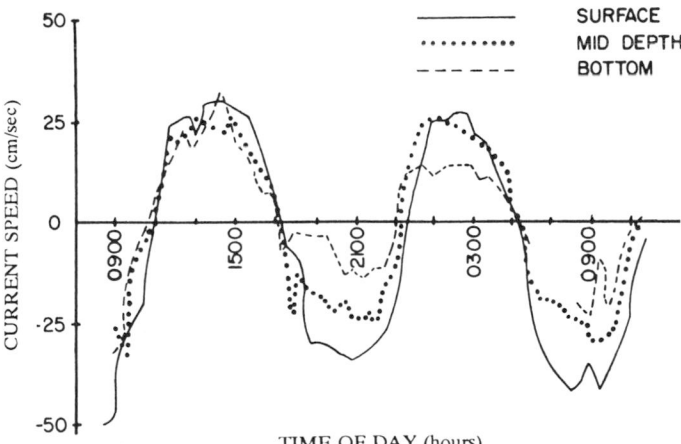

FIGURE 2.83.   Currents recorded at buoy 29 (see Figure 2.82) in the Yaquina Bay estuary. Flood currents are positive, ebb currents negative. (From Neal, 1966.)

due to melting snows in the headwater areas. Lowest flows are usually found in September through March, and the average in 1951 was about 70,000 cfs (1982 m^3 s^{-1}) (Hickson and Rodolf, 1951). Dams on the river under construction in 1963 were estimated to limit maximum flows to about 600,000 cfs (16,992 m^3 s^{-1}) and increase minima to about 150,000 cfs (4248 m^3 s^{-1}) (Lockett, 1963).

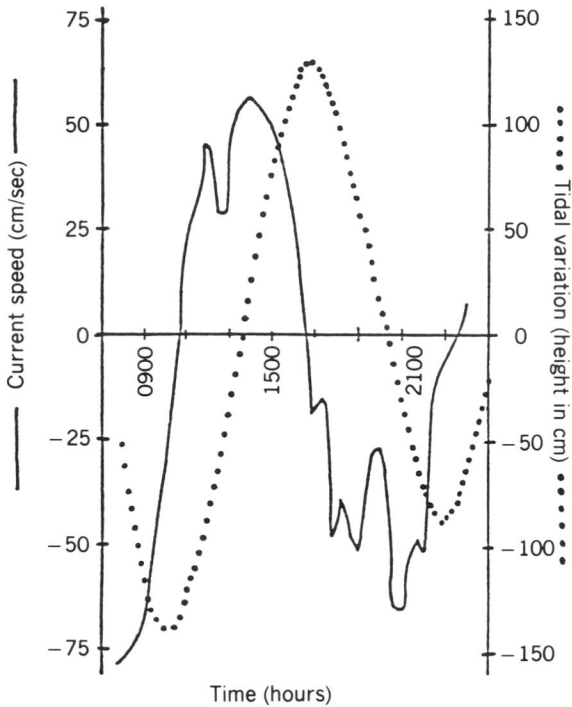

FIGURE 2.84. Phase relationships of tide and currents at buoy 21 in the Yaquina Bay estuary. (After Neal, 1966.)

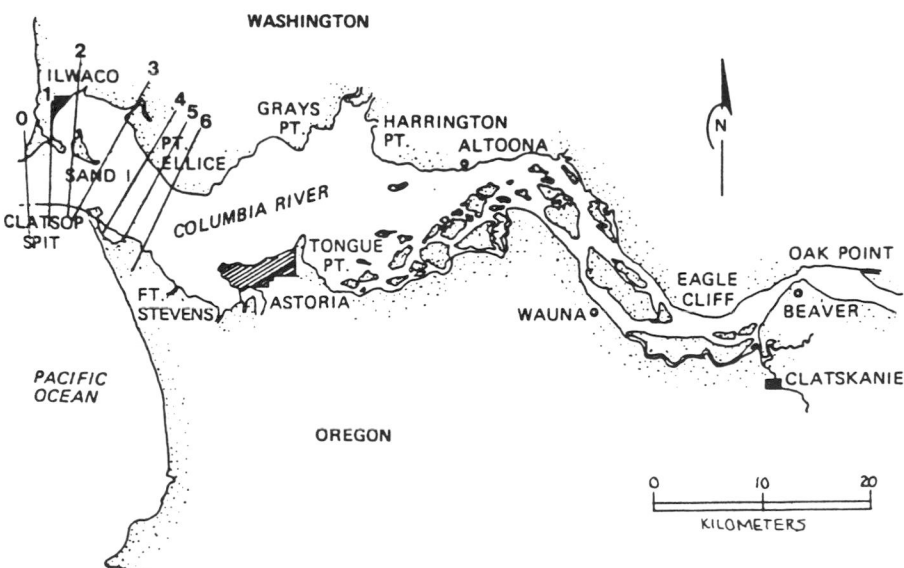

FIGURE 2.85. Columbia River estuary, Oregon and Washington. (From Neal, 1972.)

Tides. Tides at the estuary mouth are of the mixed semidiurnal type usually found on the Pacific coast (Neal, 1972). The mean tidal range at the mouth is 6.5 ft (2 m), the mean range between lower low water and higher high water is 8.5 ft (2.6 m). The lowest low water has been estimated at 3.0 ft (1 m) below mean lower low water, and the highest high water was 11.6 ft (3.5 m) above lower low water, the result of a combination of storm and high tide (Lockett, 1963). Tides influence waters of the Columbia River Estuary by causing water-level fluctuations, reversal of river flow, and mixing of seawater with river water.

Tidal effects on reversal of flow.   Reversal of the hydraulic flow occurs up to 40 km from the mouth throughout the year according to the U.S. Army Corps of Engineers (Clark and Snyder, 1969). The reversal point is farther upstream during low discharge. Since change in height of river surface is perceptible as far upstream as Bonneville Dam, slight changes in flow rate due to tides are found as far upriver as 225 km (Neal, 1972).

During the time of filling of the John Day Dam in April, 1968, Clark and Snyder (1969) observed dye travel after release at river km 109 (near Cowlitz River confluence). During this period of very low discharge, when the flow (2390 m³ s⁻¹) was less than one-third mean annual discharge, reversal occurred after a slight rise in river level coinciding with a decrease in downstream flow velocity. The reversal lasts about 4 hours. This means that in a 24-hour period, the flow is reversed for 8 hours.

The study raised questions about the advisability of placing a thermal discharge source on the river, since the reversal may cause a particular mass of

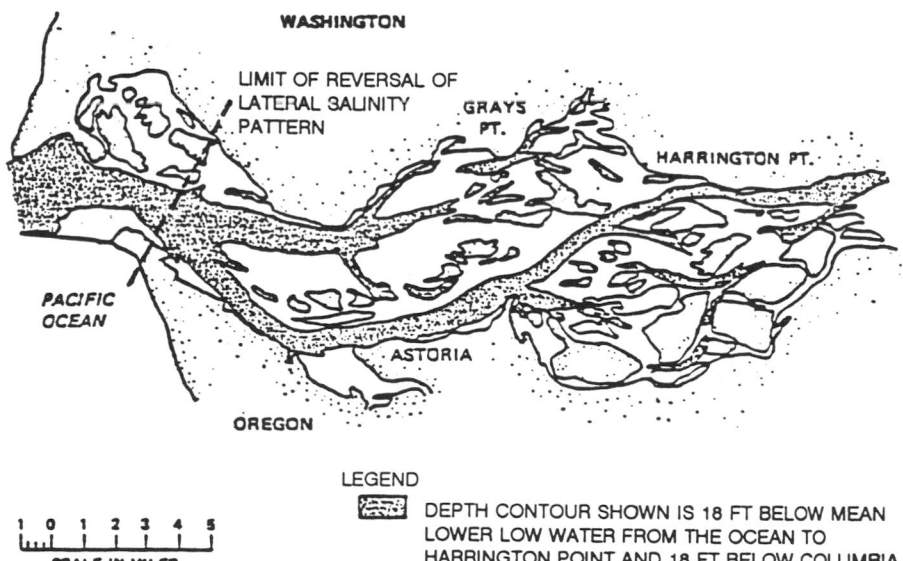

FIGURE 2.86.   Two main channels near the mouth of the Columbia River. Dashed line indicates the limit of reversal of the lateral salinity pattern. (Neal, 1972.)

water to be reheated after discharge and thus attain temperatures much higher than expected.

The configuration of the channel bottom profoundly affects the current direction and strength of tidal flows. There are two channels near the mouth of the Columbia (Figure 2.86). Flood-tide currents should be greatest on the south side, due to the Coriolis effect, and ebb-tide currents should be strongest on the north side. The expected relationship is reversed because the north channel is more directly aligned with the mouth, whereas the south channel has a continuous connection with the river but the north does not, so the south channel carries the ebb (downstream) flow more effectively (Neal, 1972).

Salinities. The maximum extent of seawater intrusion is generally less than 23 miles (37 km). The maximum intrusion is about 6 miles (9.7 km) less during low water than during higher water. When river flow is high, saltwater intrusion distance is reduced. Maximum salinity at a given site is usually about 1 hour behind peak high tide (Figure 2.87). The lag is seen throughout the estuary and is apparently related to the river flow, which causes the surface water to start ebbing while the bottom water is still flooding (Neal, 1972).

Salinity gradients show unexpected lateral distributions on ebb and flood tide due to the same effects of the estuary's two-channel structure as described above for maximum currents. That is, while the Coriolis effect should normally produce high salinities on the south side of the estuary during flood tide, salinities are actually higher on the north side, due to more direct alignment of the north channel with the mouth. An observation in September 1959 (low flow) and one in June 1959 (high flow) both showed higher salinities on the north side (Figure 2.88) above nautical mile segment number 4 even though the entrance salinity

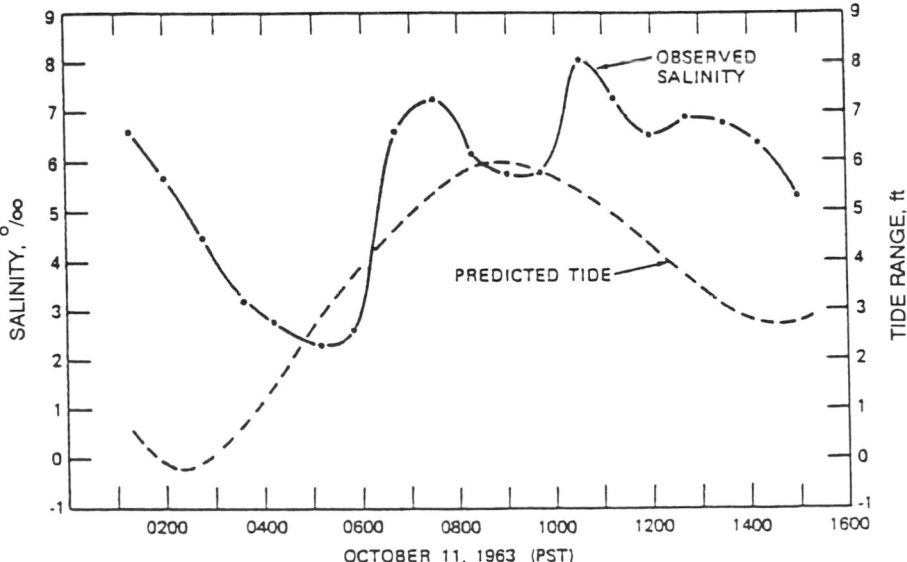

FIGURE 2.87. Observed surface salinity of the Columbia River compared with the predicted tide at Astoria, Oregon. (From Neal, 1972.)

distribution is as expected when the Coriolis effect is considered. The vertical salinity distribution varies with tidal stage, being affected by river stage and distance from the ocean (Figure 2.88) (Neal, 1972). The haloclines may be sharply inclined during high tide and high river flow (Figure 2.89).

Flow velocities near the surface during flood tides range from zero to about 4 fps (1.2 m s^{-1}), and during ebb tides range from zero to about 8 fps (2.4 m s^{-1}),

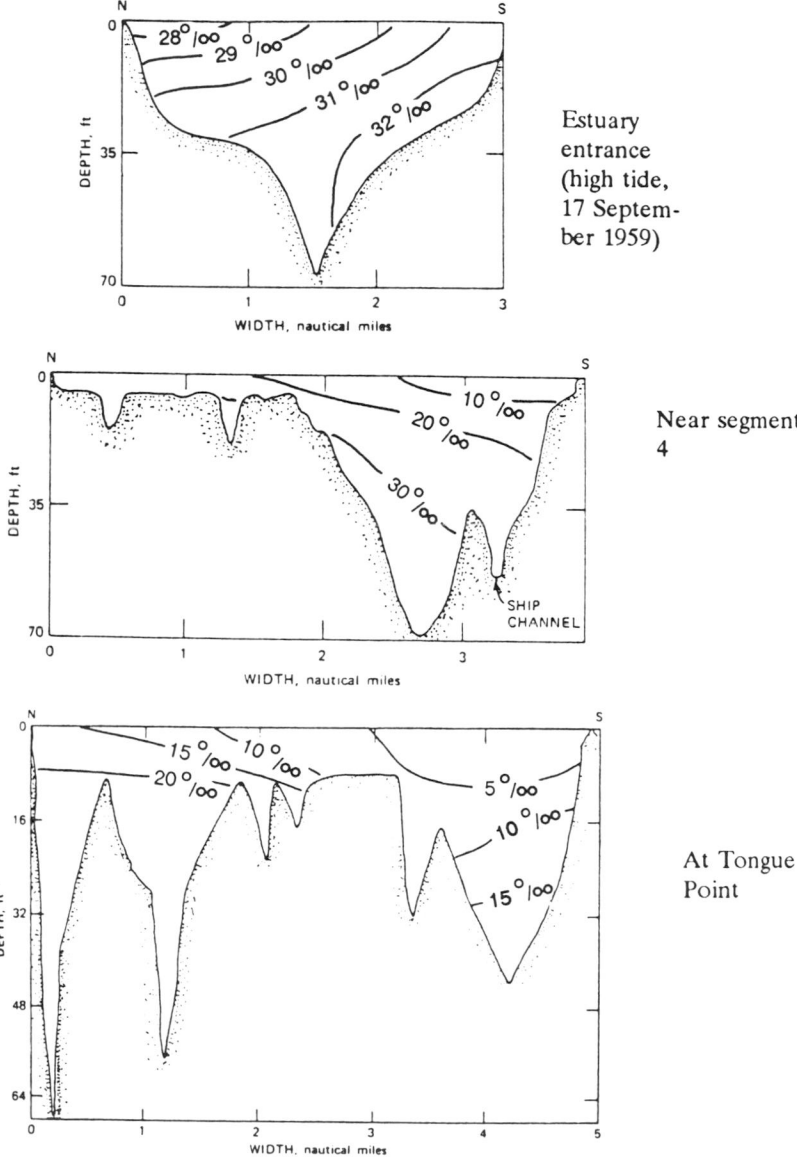

FIGURE 2.88. Cross-channel salinity distributions at different cross sections along the Columbia estuary. (From Neal, 1972.)

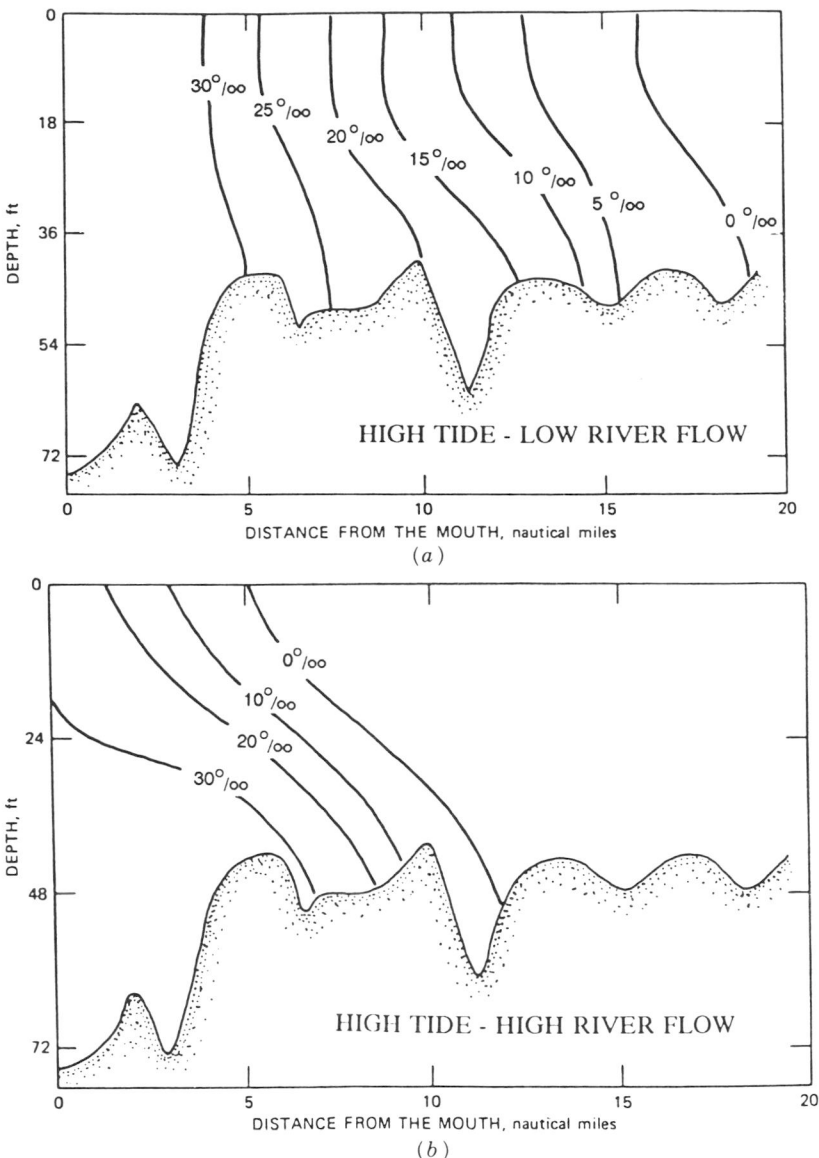

FIGURE 2.89.   Longitudinal salinity distribution in the Columbia River estuary for (*a*) low and (*b*) high river flow conditions. (From Neal, 1972.)

depending on location (Hubbell et al., 1971). Suspended sediment concentrations also vary over a relatively wide range in response to these velocities.

Sediments.   In the part of the estuary having estuarine circulation, the turbidity is maximum because of the resuspension of sediments wherever velocities are sufficient. At the null point of flow, current velocity is low and sediments accumulate, shifting seaward or landward with the ebb and flow of the tides. Sediment movement along the bottom in this part of the estuary is also greatly influenced by estuarine circulation. The sediments tend to move landward in the deep channels and seaward in the shallow areas. The landward transport of sediments along the bottom tends to cause coarse sediments to be trapped in the estuary. The fine sediments move along the edges in the more shallow water, and about 30% of these fine sediments transported into the estuary by the river are retained in the estuary.

Figure 2.90 illustrates the relations among depth, salinity, and total suspended sediment at points located in the turbidity maxima for high and low river flow. Peak suspended sediment concentrations are apparently associated with high ebb and high flood periods, which are very roughly associated with times of higher salinity. The relationship between salinity and tides is closer than that between tides and sediment concentrations.

The Columbia River estuary is a positive coastal plain estuary. Table 2.9 shows how the estuarine classification changes according to river stage.

Grays Harbor Estuary. Grays Harbor is a large estuary located on the Pacific coast of Washington about 50 miles (80.5 km) north of the Columbia River (Beverage and Swecker, 1969). The Chehalis, Wishkah, and Hoquiam rivers are the major freshwater sources (Figure 2.91).

Tides. Tides are of the mixed type typical of the Pacific coast. At Aberdeen, near the point where the Chehalis River widens to form the harbor, the mean and diurnal tidal ranges are 7.8 ft (2.4 m) and 9.9 ft (3 m), respectively. These values decrease both toward the mouth of the harbor and upstream.

Beverage and Swecker (1969) found that vertical maximum mean velocities varied from about 3 fps (1 m s^{-1}) on the flood tides to about 4.5 fps (1.4 m s^{-1}) on ebb tides. Distortion from a simple harmonic function exhibited by the mean velocity curves may be attributable to channel geometry and frictional effects. On ebbing tides, 0.1 velocities (velocities at 20% of total depth) were always greater than 0.8 velocities (80% of total depth). Near low tide, the bottom water

TABLE 2.9. *Classification of Salinity of the Columbia River Estuary, Washington and Oregon*

	Low River		High River	
	Minimum Salinity (ppt)	Maximum Salinity (ppt)	Minimum Salinity (ppt)	Maximum Salinity (ppt)
	Near the Mouth			
Surface salinity	5.8	30.5	1.3	18.7
Bottom salinity	20.0	32.5	5.9	30.3
Classification	B	D	B	B
	Near Tongue Point			
Surface salinity	Insufficient	6.3	0.0	0.0
Bottom salinity	data	15.9	0.0	20.0
Classification		B	0.0	A

Source: Neal (1972), Table 2.1, p. 29.

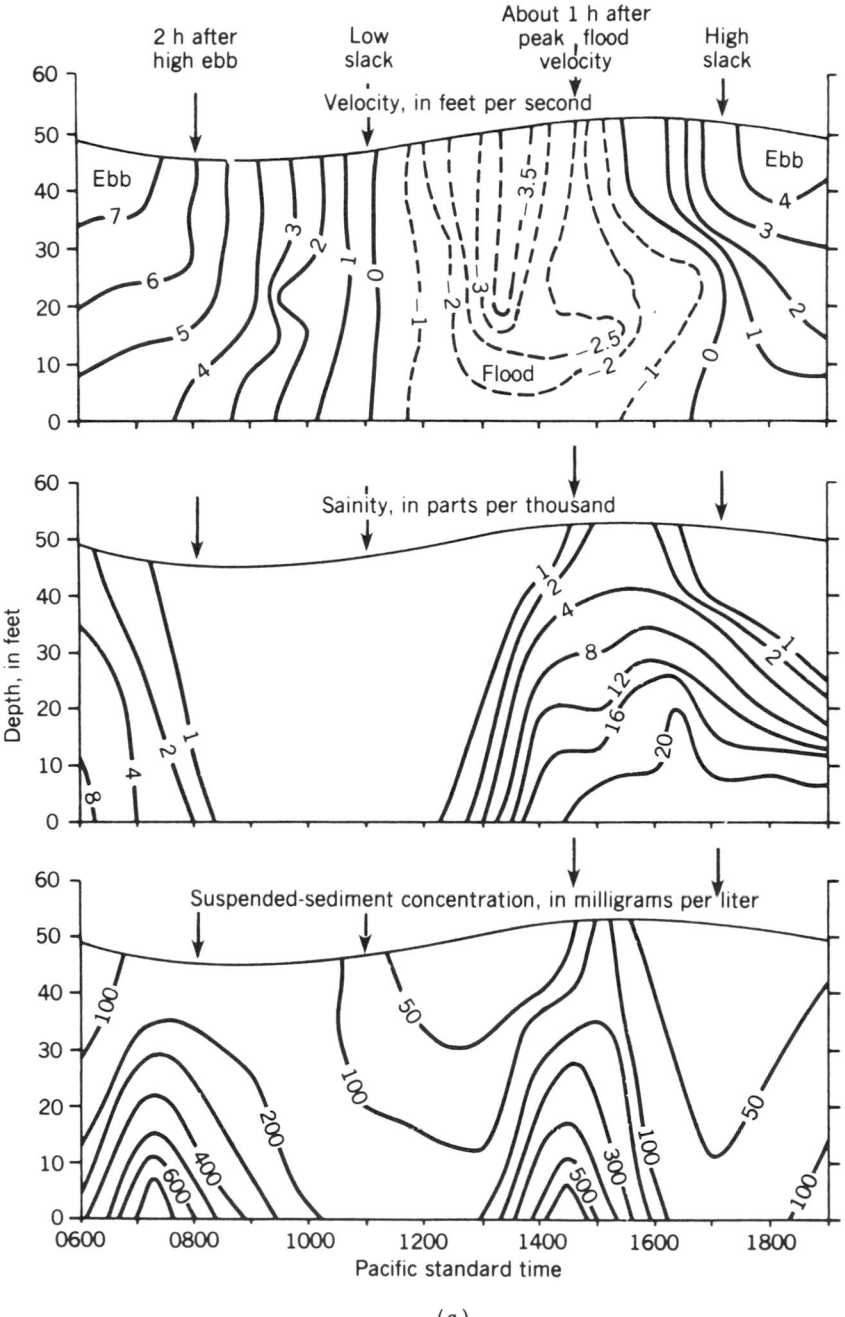

FIGURE 2.90.   Vertical distributions of velocity, salinity, and suspended sediment concentration in the Columbia River: (*a*) at river mile 8.5 on May 23, 1970, with discharge at Astoria, Oregon (river mile 13) of 468,000 cfs; (*b*) at river mile 16.2 on September 14, 1969, with discharge at Astoria, Oregon, of 231,000 cfs. (After Hubbell and Glenn, 1971.)

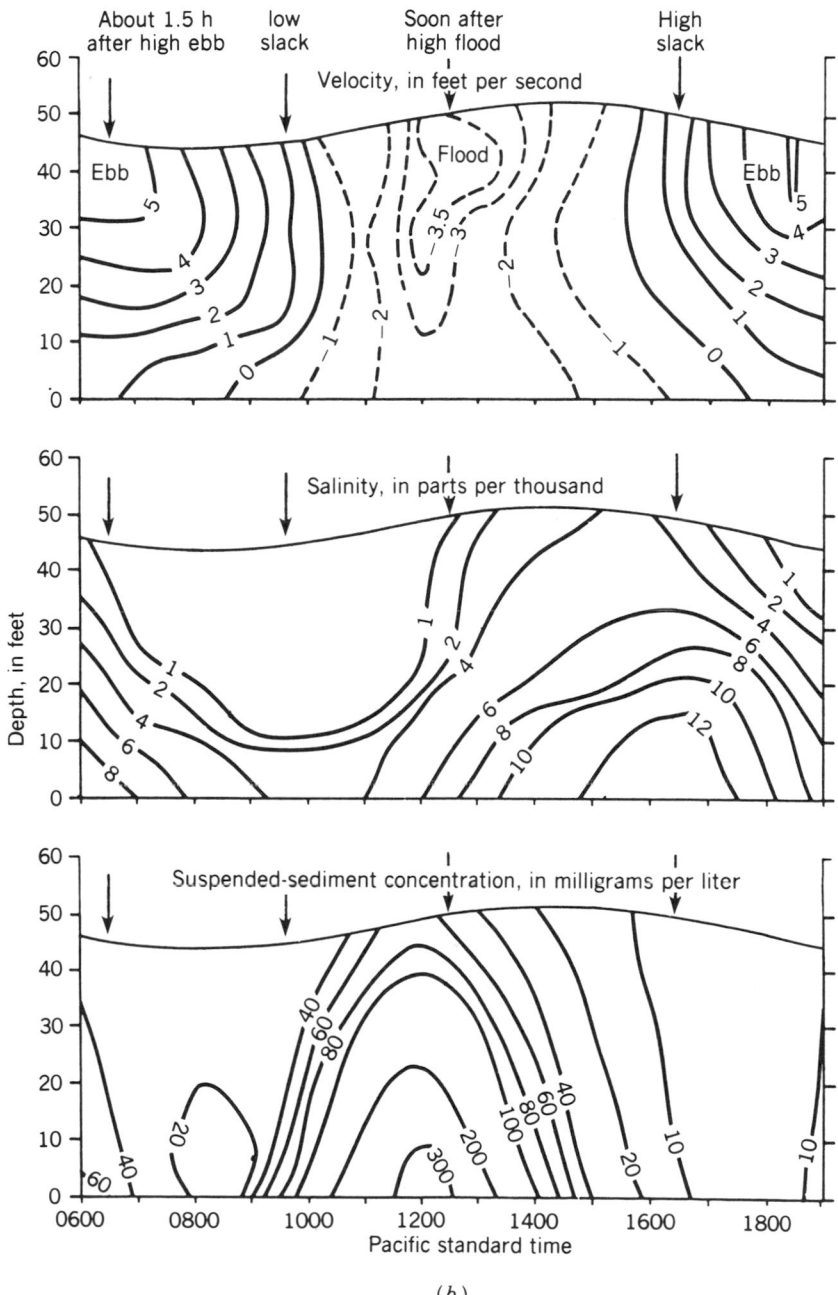

(*b*)

FIGURE 2.90. (*Continued*)

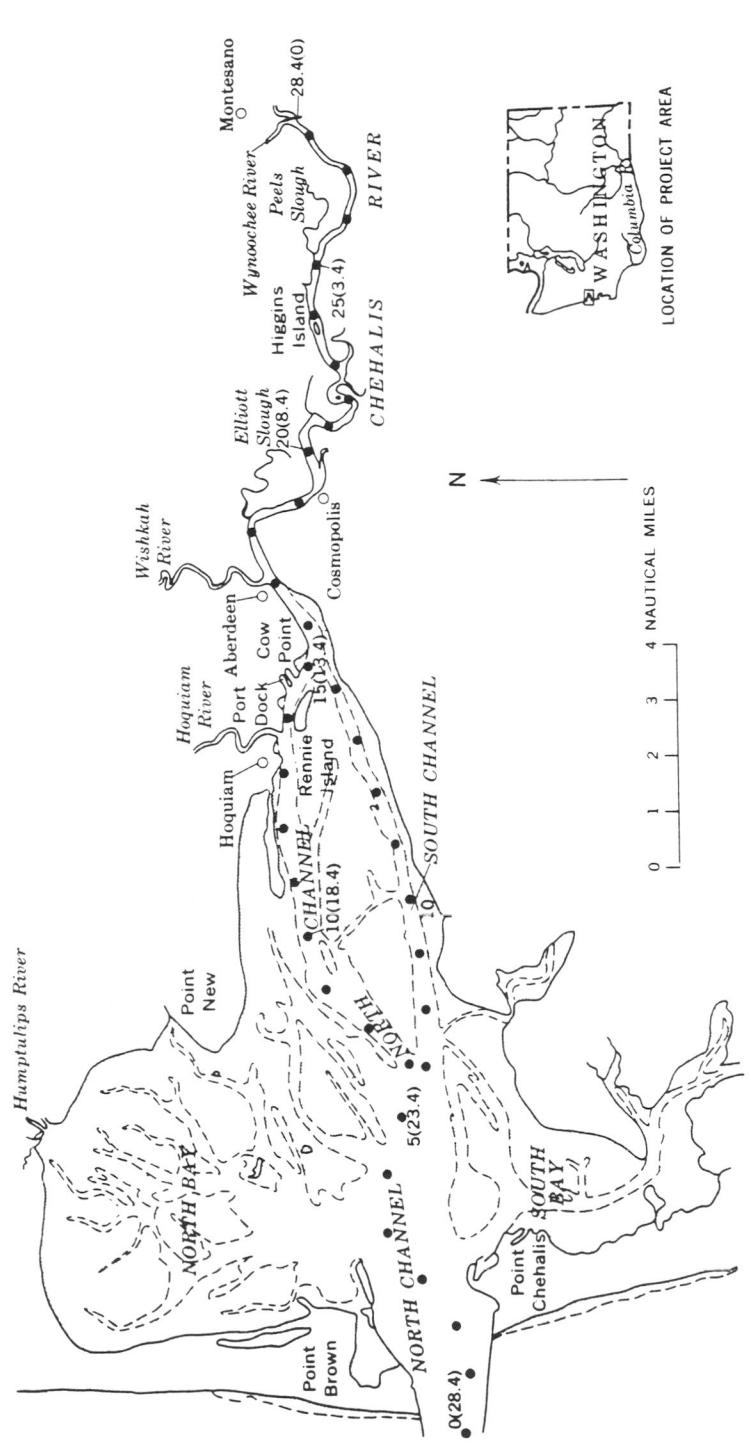

FIGURE 2.91. Grays Harbor, Washington. Dots mark 1-mile intervals, starting at the mouth of the harbor. Numbers outside parentheses indicate distance along the navigation channel from the mouth. Numbers in parentheses indicate distances downstream from a highway bridge south of Montesano. Shaded areas are tidal flats. (From Beverage and Swecker, 1969.)

reverses first, the surface water following after an interval. On flooding tides, the 0.2 and 0.8 velocities were about the same, and near high tide the surface water reverses first and the bottom water follows.

Salinities. Grays Harbor has a well-mixed vertical salinity distribution during low-flow periods of several weeks. The ratio of top to bottom salinity difference to mean vertical salinity, $\Delta s/s$, increases with increasing discharge (Figure 2.92). Longitudinal distribution of mean salinity for 1966 is shown in Figure 2.93. The figures illustrate how the saline water is forced farther upstream during higher tides. In addition, during the higher-discharge periods, the saline intrusion is less on both high and low tides (Beverage and Swecker, 1969).

Dye studies were used to determine the movement of water in the upper part of Grays Harbor. Water traveled up the estuary 7.7 to 8.6 nautical miles (14.3 to 16 km) on average ebb tides, and 5.7 to 8.8 nautical miles (10.5 to 16.3 km) on average flood tides. The largest excursions for flood tides were associated with

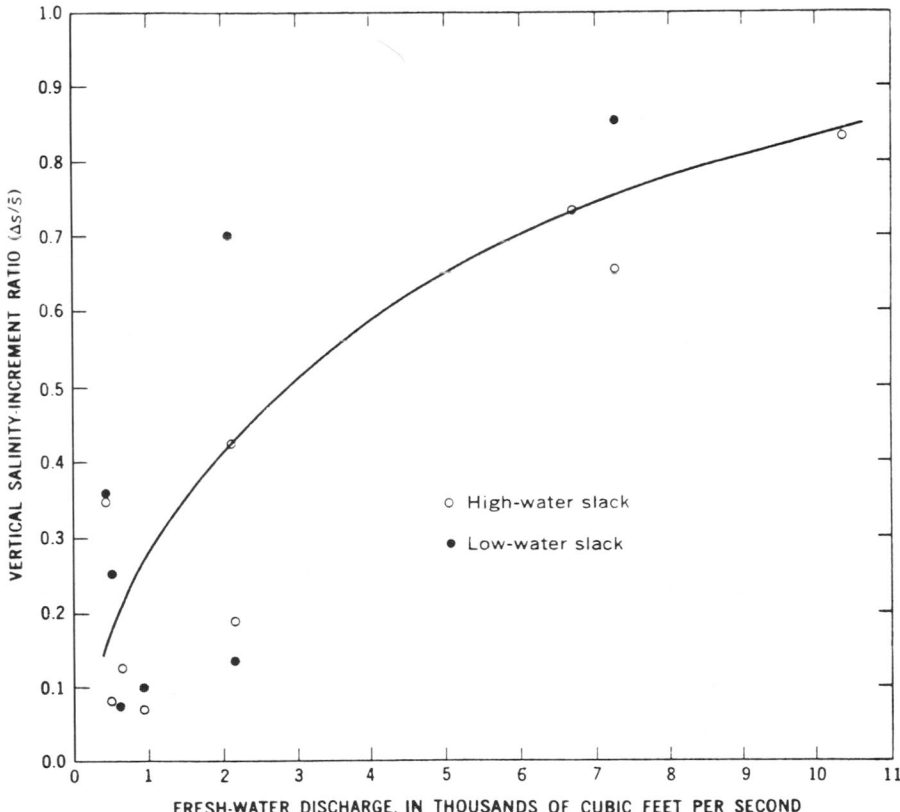

FIGURE 2.92.   Relation between vertical salinity-increment ratio ($\Delta s/\bar{s}$) at Cow Point (Grays Harbor, Washington) and freshwater discharge. Off-scale ratio of 3.36 at 10,400 cfs (low-water slack) is not shown. (From Beverage and Swecker, 1969.)

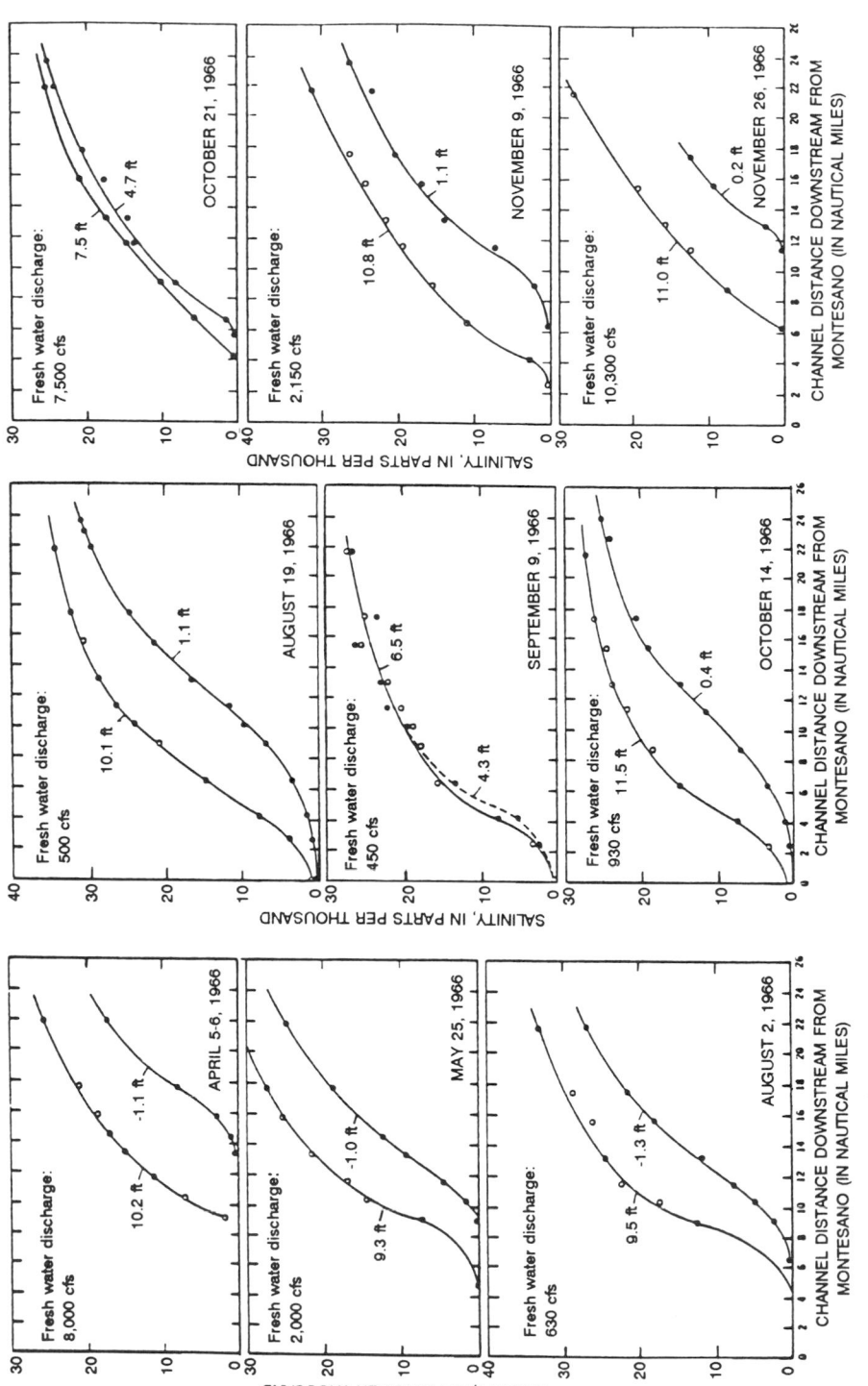

FIGURE 2.93. Longitudinal salinity profiles of Grays Harbor at different tide stages throughout 1966. ○, High-water slack; ●, low-water slack. Distance shown is downstream from Montesano (see Figure 2.96). (From Beverage and Swecker, 1969.)

150

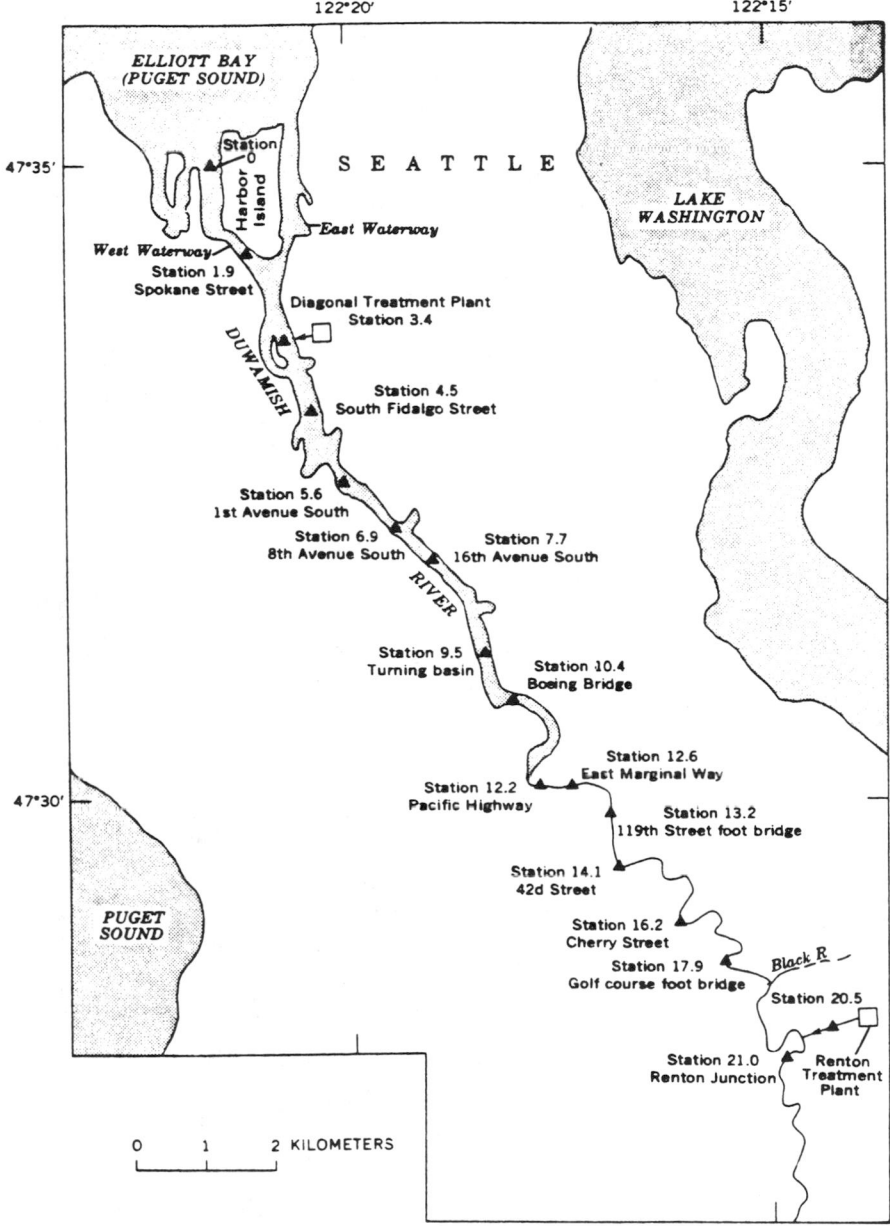

FIGURE 2.94. Duwamish River estuary, Washington, showing location of sampling stations. (From Santos and Stoner, 1972.)

low freshwater discharge and wide tidal range, and the largest excursions for ebb tides were associated with high discharge and wide tidal range. The distance traveled also depended on where the dye was injected (Beverage and Swecker, 1969).

Duwamish River Estuary. The Duwamish River basin drains an area of 483 square miles (1251 km) in east central Washington. The estuary is a relatively narrow one with an island at its mouth where it empties into Elliott Bay in Puget Sound (Figure 2.94).

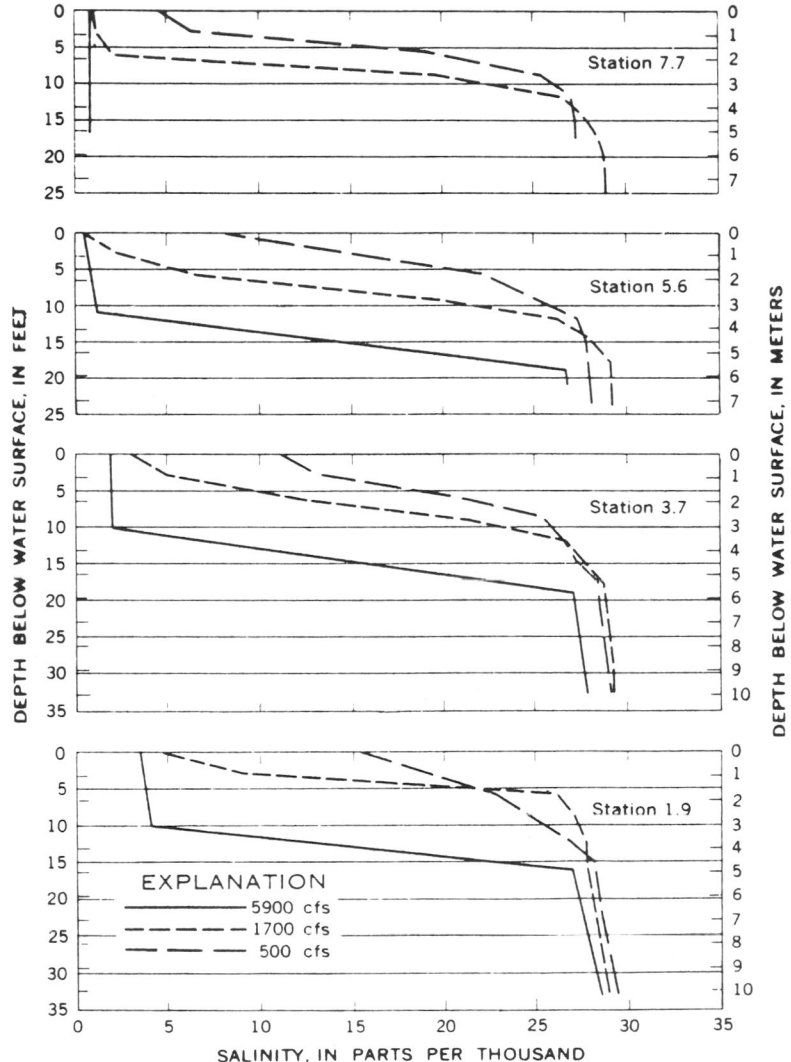

FIGURE 2.95. Vertical salinity profiles at selected stations on the Duwamish River, for various rates of freshwater inflow. (From Santos and Stoner, 1972.)

Tides.   The mean range of tide is 7.5 ft (2.3 m). mean diurnal range is 11.1 ft (3.4 m), and the extreme range is from −4.6 to 14.7 ft (−1.4 to 4.5 m).

Salinities.   The salinity distribution in the estuary varies longitudinally, laterally, and vertically (Santos and Stoner, 1972). Longitudinal and vertical variations depend primarily on freshwater discharge and tidal flow. Lateral variation is dependent primarily on the shape of the estuary. In this case there is little variation in salinity across the estuary because width is insufficient for a Coriolis force influence. In contrast, the vertical distribution is nonuniform, taking the form of a saline wedge, which is typical of a stratified estuary (Figure 2.95). The fresh water–salt water interface is sharply defined where the influx of fresh water is the greatest. Below, where freshwater flows decrease, the stratification breaks down. Longitudinal distribution depends on tides and the rate of freshwater flow (Figure 2.96).

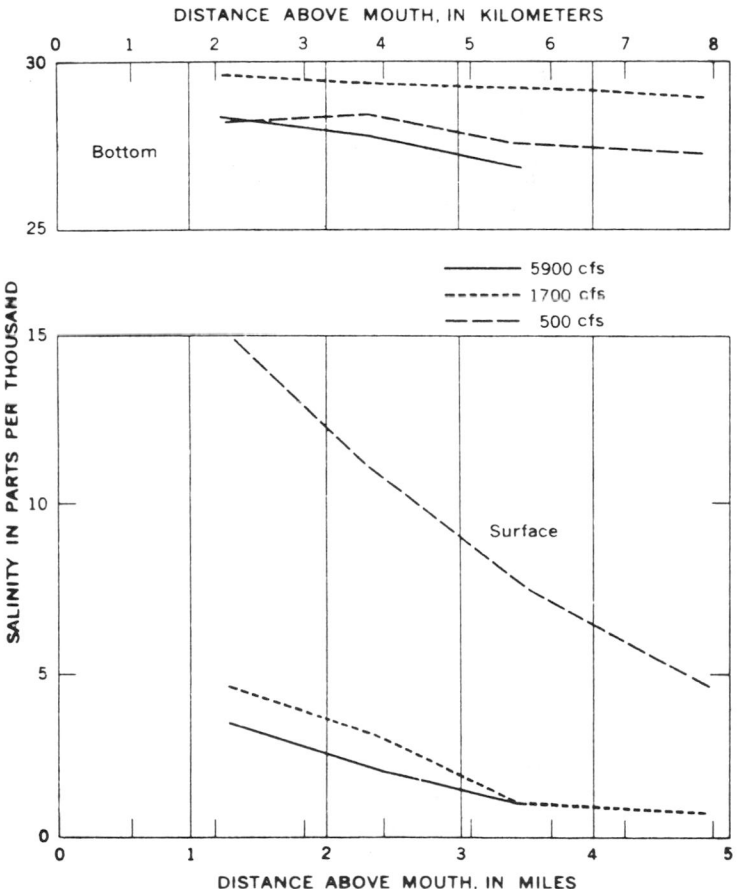

FIGURE 2.96.   Longitudinal salinity profiles of the Duwamish River, for selected rates of freshwater inflow. (From Santos and Stoner, 1972.)

   Salinity in the salt wedge remains fairly constant longitudinally except near the
upstream end. Slight decreases in salinity in this direction are probably due to
slow diffusion, and slight decreases throughout the salt wedge are due to an
increase in freshwater flow. An increase in flow greater than 100 cfs ($2.8 \, \text{m}^3 \, \text{s}^{-1}$)
prevents the wedge from intruding higher than about 5.5 km upstream. A very
low tide and high rates of freshwater inflow may push the tip of the wedge a
considerable distance downstream, while extremely high tides and low flow rates
can push the salt wedge tip around 16 miles upstream above the mouth. In the
surface layer salinity increases in a downstream direction and is controlled
primarily by the rate of freshwater inflow.

   Santos and Stoner describe the pattern of circulation in the Duwamish estuary
as the classical salt wedge defined by Pritchard (1955). Most of the mixing that
occurs is at the salt water–fresh water interface, where salt water is entrained
upward into the freshwater layer. The net movement of water in the saline wedge
is in an upstream direction, to replace the water that was lost to the freshwater
layer. Surface and bottom velocities are plotted in Figure 2.97.

   Juan de Fuca Strait.   Juan de Fuca Strait is a channel of water connecting
the Pacific Ocean, at Cape Flattery, with the channels of the San Juan
Archipelago. It consists of two basins separated by a sill (Figure 2.98).

   Tides.   Tides in the Strait of Juan de Fuca are mixed with semidiurnal
inequality. Tidal velocities are strongest at half tides, flow is in the direction of
the rising tide, and ebb and flood occurs at all depths. If this were not true, the
fresh water entering the system would be trapped. Water below this level (residual
current) moves inward, replacing the water entrained outward by the upper zone.

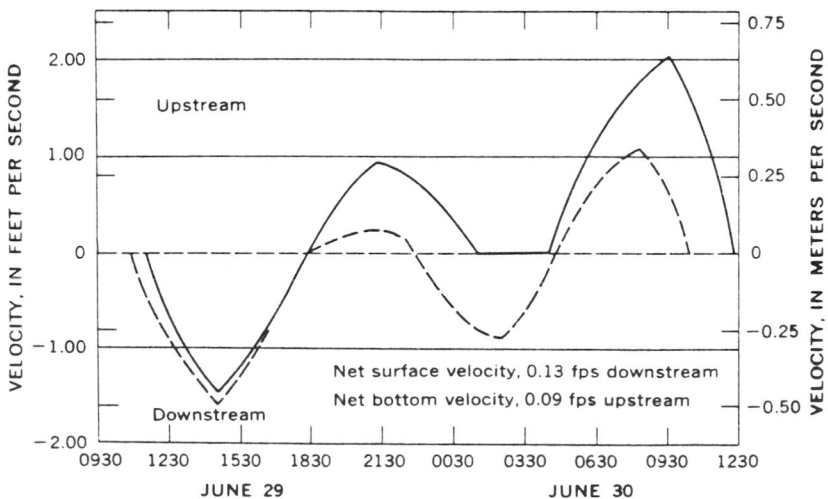

FIGURE 2.97.   Variations in surface and bottom velocities at station 7.7 in the Duwamish river,
June 29–30, 1965. Solid line indicates surface velocity; dashed line shows bottom velocity. (From
Santos and Stoner, 1972.)

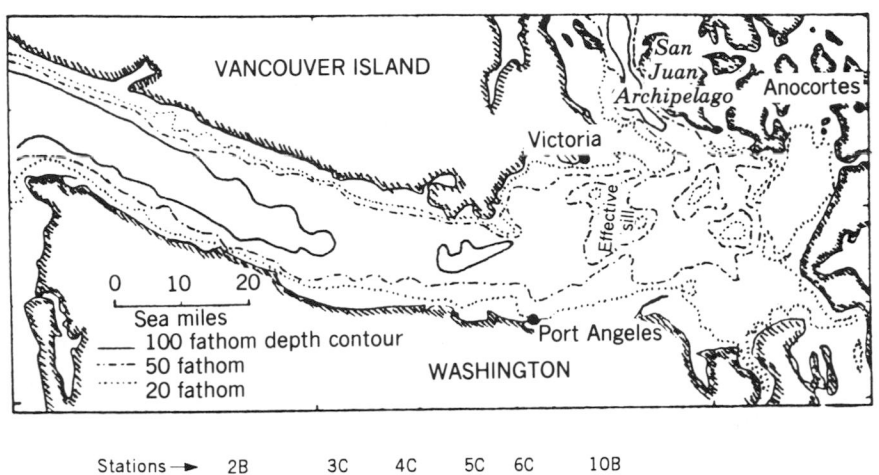

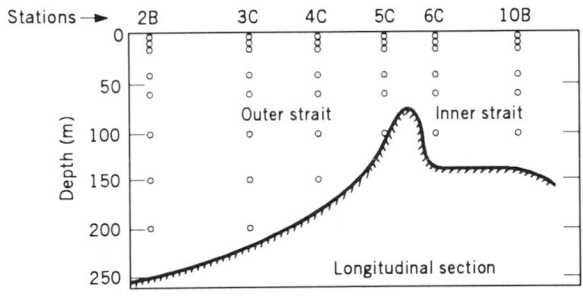

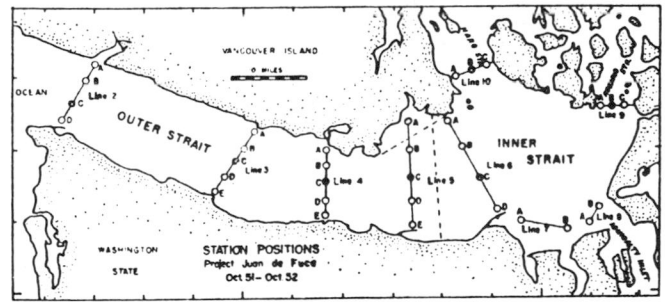

FIGURE 2.98. Juan de Fuca Strait, showing bottom topography and location of observations. (After Herlinveaux and Tully, 1961.)

Thus there is always a region of water with no net movement between these two zones.

Figure 2.99 shows current patterns during a flood flow. Ocean water intrudes up the outer strait. The flow of fresher water in the upper zone is reversed. The greatest flood-tide velocity occurs in the lower layers because the effect of freshwater flow is absent. Flow is influenced toward the southern side of the strait by a combination of the Coriolis and centrifugal forces, so that flow slackens first

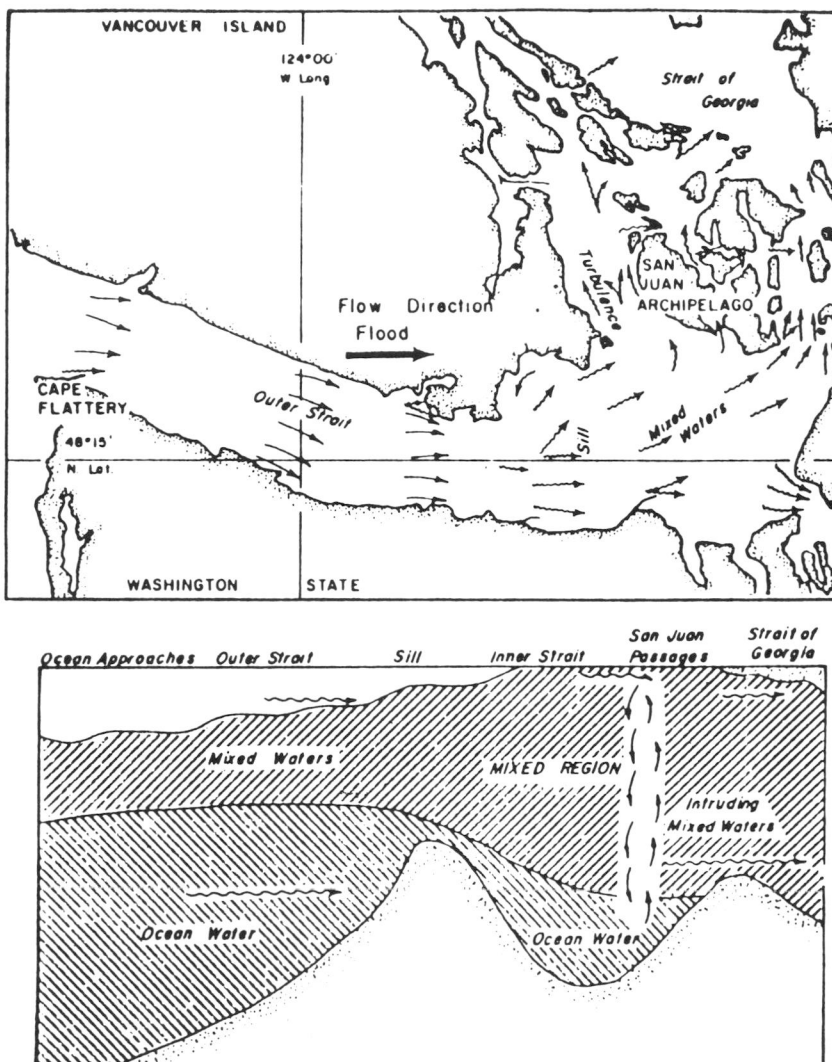

FIGURE 2.99.   Movements of flood-tide water during tide flows in Juan de Fuca Strait and its approaches. (From Herlinveaux and Tully, 1961.)

on the northern side. The ocean water proceeds over the sill, most of it going over the southern end, where it is deepest. Since the channel is constricted vertically by the sill, velocity is increased. This, plus the cascading of the water over the sill, produces turbulence and mixing of the upper and lower layers, destroying the halocline. The flow momentum is dissipated as it enters the San Juan passage and the Strait of Georgia, resulting in great turbulence evident at the surface (Herlinveaux and Tully, 1961).

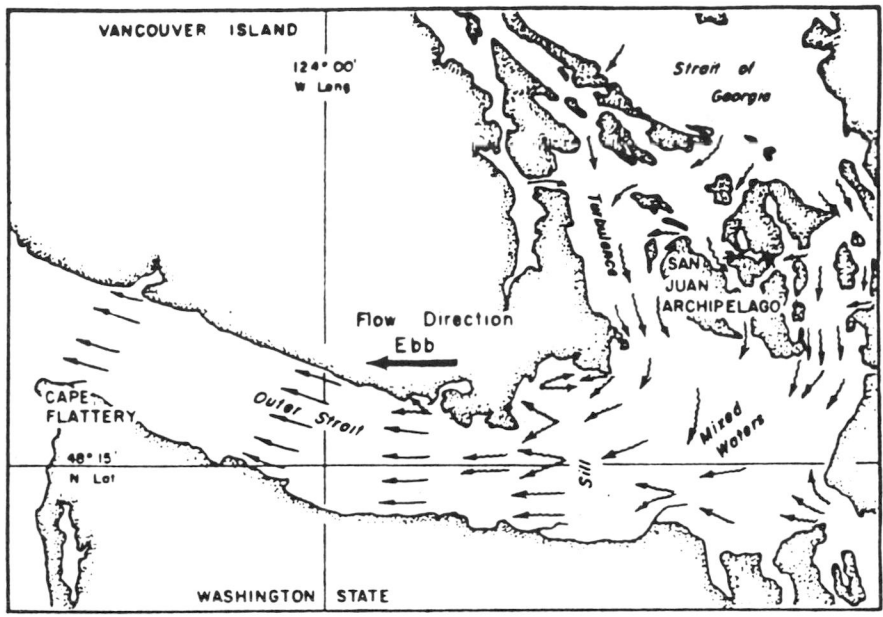

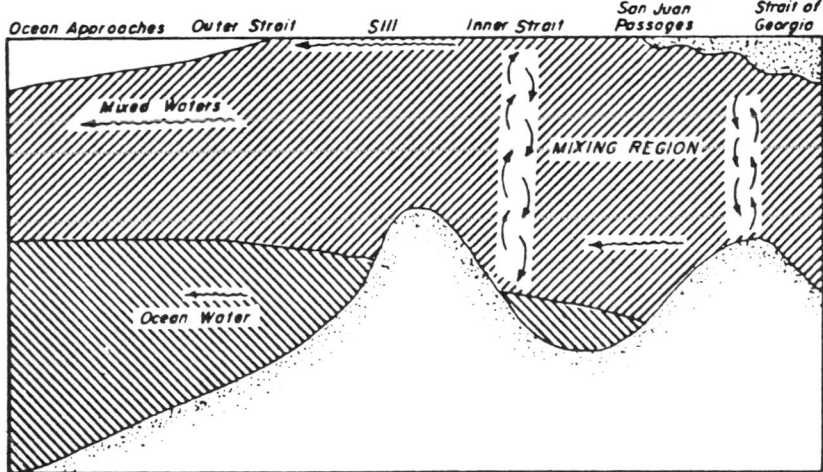

FIGURE 2.100. Movements of ebb-tide water during tide flows in Juan de Fuca Strait and its approaches. (From Herlinveaux and Tully, 1961.)

Ebb-flow patterns are shown in Figure 2.100. There is great turbulence and eddying in the Inner Strait, due to the jets of water issuing from the San Juan passage and the Strait of Georgia and the constriction caused by the sill. The mixed surface waters run over the sill, and flow velocity is reduced in the outer strait. The layered structure is reestablished as the mixed waters flow over the dense ocean water. Here, the upper portion of the halocline is composed of the

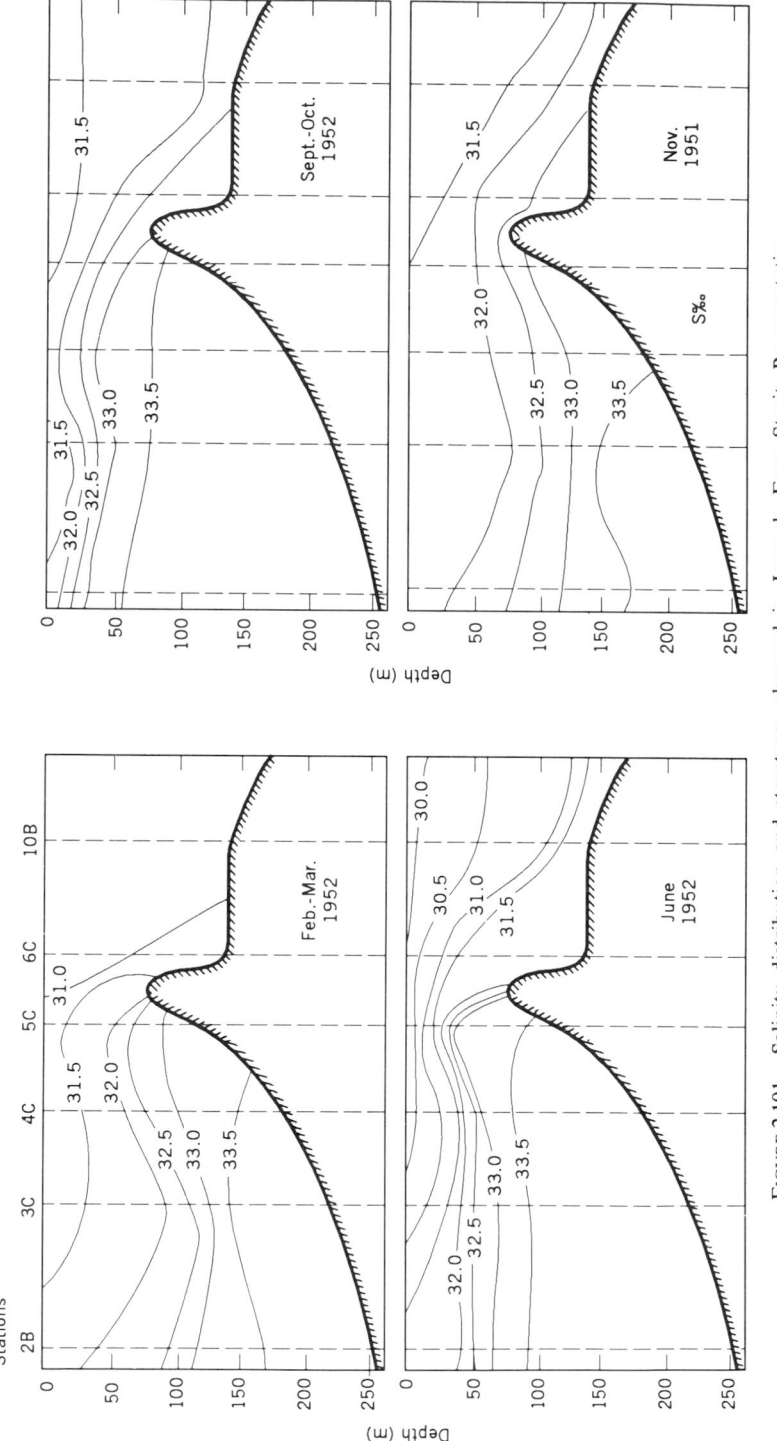

FIGURE 2.101. Salinity distribution and structures observed in Juan de Fuca Strait. Representative seasonal salinity structures are shown. (After Herlinveaux and Tully, 1961.)

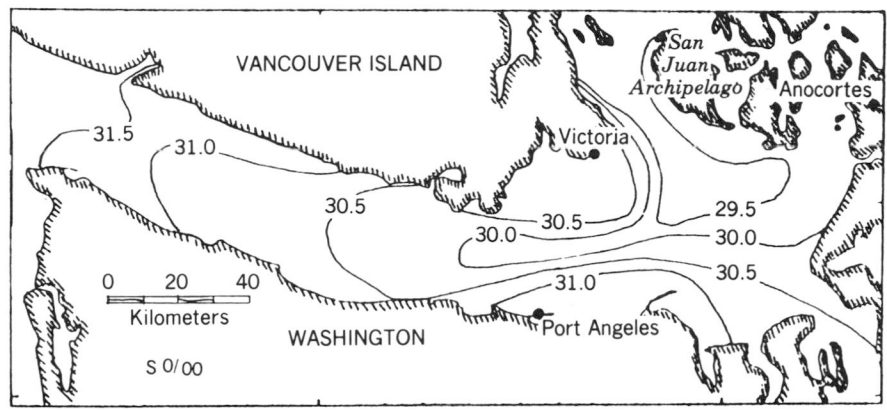

FIGURE 2.102.   Surface salinity distribution for June 1952. (After Herlinveaux and Tully, 1961.)

waters from the inner strait, and the lower part is composed of ocean waters which were entrained in the wake stream at the sill. Seaward flow is at first confined to the northern side of the strait, but as it develops it spreads to the southern side. When flow reaches the ocean it forms a wake stream which veers to the right due to the Coriolis force and is dissipated along the coast of Vancouver Island. This mechanism acts as a tidal pump and is important in limiting the salt budget in the Strait of Georgia (Herlinveaux and Tully, 1961).

   Salinities.   Herlinveaux and Tully (1961) report that the lowest salinities occur around the San Juan passage and through the inner part of the strait. Salinity increases toward the Pacific Ocean (Figures 2.101 and 2.102). Transverse and longitudinal sampling showed salinity increasing with depth, with lower salinities found on the north side of the strait than on the south side. Salinity structure differed in the inner and outer straits. In the inner strait, water down to 150 m depth was less than 32% saline. This water was continuous over the sill with a layer in the outer strait that was only 50 m deep. This distinct upper zone was separated by a halocline from deep water with greater than 33.5% salinity. The halocline was the result of internal mixing and extended to the surface in the absence of wind. Fresh water entering the strait moved persistently seaward in the upper zone, entraining some seawater from the lower zone. In general, the fresh water was in the upper layer while the lower zone contained only intruding seawater (Tully, 1958).

APPENDIX A

Through a numerical, stepwise integration of the equation of continuity, it is possible to compute the average vertical velocity in an estuary as a function of depth. In performing the integration, the kinetic boundary condition is applied at the surface. If the bottom were perfectly horizontal, the vertical velocity should be almost zero at the bottom; the slight departure of the computed value from zero probably reflects the accumulated error in the data, but it is interesting that the sign is correct considering the local bottom slope. The vertical velocity is directed upward at all depths except very close to the bottom and has a maximum value of $1 \times 10 \, \mathrm{m \, s}^{-1}$ at middepth. This is a very small number, but it provides a volume rate of flow, from the lower layers which are moving up the estuary into the upper layers which are moving seaward, equal to the total inflow from the river in each 4 km of length of the estuary. These data are also used to determine indirectly the longitudinal and vertical eddy flux terms from the salinity balance equations (Pritchard, 1967b). Neglecting the lateral advective and nonadvective terms, the salt balance equation can be written

$$\frac{\partial s}{\partial t} = -\frac{\partial(wu_1 s)}{\partial x_1} - \frac{\partial(wu_3 s)}{\partial x_3}$$

$$+ \left(\frac{1}{w}\frac{\partial}{\partial x}\right)w(u_1' s') + \left(\frac{1}{w}\frac{\partial}{\partial x_3}\right)w(u_3' s') \tag{1}$$

where s = tidal mean salinity at x_1, x_3
u_1 = longitudinal component of the tidal mean velocity
u_3 = vertical component of the tidal mean velocity
w = width of the estuary at the section X and depth X
u_1', u_3' = turbulent velocity deviations
s' = turbulent salinity deviation
$\langle\ \rangle$ = time mean

These determinations showed that the salt balance is dominated by the horizontal advective terms and vertical eddy flux terms, except near middepth, where the vertical advective term becomes more important. Classically, the eddy flux terms have been assumed to be equal to the product of an eddy's diffusivity times the mean salient gradient; thus

$$u_3' s' = -K_3 \frac{\partial s}{x_3} \tag{2}$$

Using this relationship, the vertical eddy diffusivity (K) can be computed. Figure 2.103 gives K related to depth. The minimum in this curve occurring at middepth is associated with the high vertical stability in the halocline.

The appropriate time-mean longitudinal equation of motion for a point along the central axis of the estuary can be written

$$\frac{\partial u_1}{\partial t} + u_1 \frac{\partial u_1}{\partial x_1} + u_3 \frac{\partial u_1}{\partial x_3} + \frac{\partial}{\partial x_1}(u_1, u_1) + \frac{\partial}{\partial x_3}(u_1, u_3) = a\frac{\partial p}{\partial x} - \frac{\partial}{\partial x_3}(u_1', u_3') \tag{3}$$

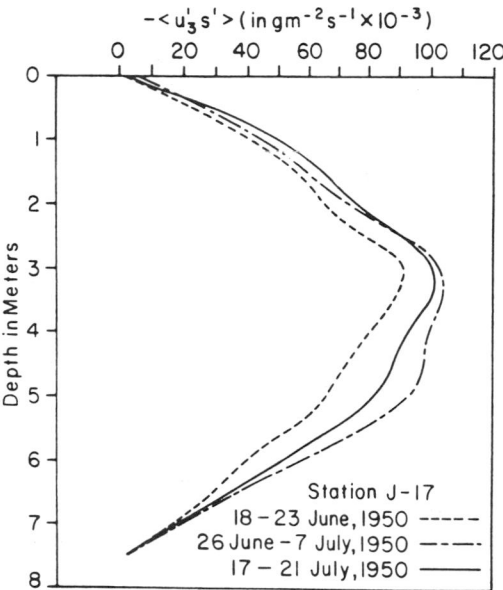

FIGURE 2.103. Vertical eddy flux of salt ($v_3's'$) as a function of depth at Station J-17. (After Herlinveaux and Tully, 1961.)

The corresponding lateral equation is

$$0 = -\left\langle a \frac{\partial p}{\partial x_2} \right\rangle \tag{4}$$

The instantaneous velocity is assumed to be composed of a mean tidal term (u_1, u_3).

Harmonic term of the tidal period: (u_1, u_3)
Turbulent deviation term: (u_1', u_2', u_3')
Tidal mean pressure forces: $\langle a(\partial p/\partial x_1) \rangle$ and $\langle a(\partial p/\partial x_3) \rangle$
Coriolis parameter: f

Except for an undetermined constant representing the slope of the water surface, one can determine $\langle a(\partial p/\partial x) \rangle$ and $\langle a(\partial p/\partial x_3) \rangle$ from observation of temperature and salinity using the hydrostatic equation. A constant term representing the surface slope can be obtained from vertically integrated equations using the equation of continuity with reasonable values of boundary stress. Stepwise vertical integration then gives the values of the eddy flux momentum (u_1', u_3') and (u_2', u_3').

These computations show that in the longitudinal equation the important terms balancing the pressure force are the vertical eddy friction term and the term involving the longitudinal change in tidal current amplitude. In the lateral equation the pressure term is very nearly balanced by the Coriolis term—that is, even in the estuary there is very nearly geostrophic balance if only the component of the pressure force perpendicular to the horizontal velocity is considered.

The vertical variation in slope of the pressure surfaces is also determined by the procedure outlined above. The water surface slopes down toward the ocean and also from the right side of the estuary to the left. Below the water surface the pressure surfaces decrease in slope until at about middepth a level pressure surface occurs. Below the middepth, pressure surfaces slope downward toward the river from the ocean and from the left side of the estuary to the right (Pritchard, 1967b).

SUMMARY

In this book we defined an estuary as a semienclosed coastal body of water that has free connections with the open sea and within which seawater is measurably diluted with fresh water derived from land drainage. Excluded are those strictly freshwater areas not under tidal influence. An exception is the inclusion of the fauna and flora from an area adjacent to an area under tidal influence where the natural fauna and flora have been eliminated by pollution. Estuaries can be classified on the basis of the following characteristics: formation and general characteristics of the estuary; water movements in the estuary; and dominant driving mechanisms (tide, wind, or river). Types of ecosystems are based on energy flow as a common denominator among the biological, geological, chemical, and physical features. In the United States there are roughly four types of estuaries: fjords, barrier island estuaries, drowned river estuaries, and those formed by tectonic movement. Estuaries are geologically young. Estuary basins are formed by the drowning of old river valleys, glacial gorging as in fjords, the action of the wind currents, and tectonic processes. The movement of water is of many different types. The water may be highly stratified, partially mixed water or homogeneous (vertically homogeneous, laterally homogeneous, or homogeneous in one of these directions). Water in an estuary is continually circulating and mixing. Estuaries may be classified as to the type of water mixing. They may also be classified by energy inputs, such as tides, yearly variation in sea level, wind, internal waves, gravity currents, and fronts. The circulation of water may be affected by winds and by storms such as hurricanes.

Naturally, due to tidal action, estuaries flush. Pollution may alter this flushing pattern; for example, the concentration of chemicals as a result of flushing may be altered. The flushing time of estuaries may be determined in various ways. One method is based on the fraction of fresh water present. Another method is the tidal prism method, which describes the flushing time in tidal cycles. Or the dispersion of pollution may be used to determine the flushing time. This, of course, varies depending on the type of pollution: conservative or nonconservative.

The sediments in an estuary are of many different types. Flocculation time may be very different depending on the size and chemical constituents of the flocculent.

Organisms often affect the flocculation time. Consolidated materials such as sand flocculate much faster than clay particles, which are often in a colloidal state.

Movement of sediments in estuaries has very important effects on aquatic life and their habitats. Sedimentation may take place in varying manners. The strength and height of the tide may have substantial effect on the movement of sediment. The effects of storms and winds on sediment movement may be very pronounced, particularly if waves of varying size are generated. Inlet stability is discussed. Movement of various-sized particles of sediment is a major factor in their deposition and effects on the structure of the estuary. Wave movement as well as tidal movement are very important in the ultimate fate of sediment loads. The formation of deltas and their stability are the result of the movement of sediments. Discussion then followed concerning marshes and their structure. The chapter concluded with examples of hydrological circulation and sedimentation patterns in estuaries of the United States.

BIBLIOGRAPHY

Abood, K. A., and E. Bourodimos. 1976. Evaluation of circulation in estuaries. J. Hydraul. Div. Proc. Am. Soc. Civ. Eng. 102 (HY9): 1211–1224

Abraham, G. 1988. Turbulence and mixing in stratified tidal flows, pp. 149–180. *In:* J. Dronkers and W. van Leussen, eds, Physical processes in estuaries. Springer-Verlag, Berlin.

Academy of Natural Science of Philadelphia (ANSP). 1974. Oyster tray studies on the Chesapeake Bay; for Baltimore Gas and Electric Company. Philadelphia, Pa. Unpaginated.

Armi, L., and D. M. Farmer. 1986. Maximal two-layer exchange through a contraction with barotropic net flow. J. Fluid Mech. 164: 27–51

Aubrey, D. G., and P. E. Speer. 1985. A study of non-linear tidal propagation in shallow inlet/estuarine systems. Part I. Observations. Estuarine Coastal Shelf Sci. 21: 185–205.

Austin, G. B. 1954. On the circulation and tidal flushing of Mobile Bay, Alabama Part 1. Texas A&M Univ. Dep. Oceanogr. Coll. Res. Found. Proj. 24, Tech. Rept. 12. 28 pp.

Battjes, J. A. 1967. Quantitative research on littoral drift and tidal inlets, pp. 185–190. *In* G. H. Lauff, ed., Estuaries. AAAS. Publ. 83.

Bault, E. I. 1972. Hydrology of Alabama estuarine area. Ala. Mar. Resour. Bull. 7. 25 pp.

Belevich, E. F. 1958. Fluctuations of the level of the Caspian and formation of the Volga delta. Tr. Astrakh. Zapov. 4.

Beverage, J. P., and M. N. Swecker. 1969. Estuarine studies in upper Grays Harbor, Washington. U.S. Geol. Surv. Water-Supply Pap. 1873-B. 90 pp.

Biebl, R. 1962. Protoplasmatisch-okologische Untersuchungen an Mangrovealgen von Puerto Rico. Protoplasm 55: 572–606.

Biggs, R. B. 1970. Sources and distribution of suspended sediment in northern Chesapeake Bay. Mar. Geol. 9: 187–201.

Biggs, R. B. 1972. Sedimentation on shell banks in Delaware Bay. Univ. Del. Coll. Mar. Sci. Publ. 2 GL-059. 56 pp.

Bloom, A. L., and C. W. Ellis, Jr. 1965. Postglacial stratigraphy and morphology of coastal Connecticut. State Geol. Natur. Hist. Surv. Conn. Guidebook 1. 10 pp.

Blumberg, A. F. 1977. Numerical model of estuarine circulation. J. Hydrual. Div. Proc. Am. Soc. Civ. Eng. 103(HY3): 295–310.

Boicourt, W. C. 1980-NASA

Bowden, K. F. 1967. Circulation and diffusion, pp. 15–36. *In* G. H. Lauff, ed., Estuaries. AAAS Publ. 83.

Brandt, A., C. C. Sarabun, H. H. Seliger, and M. A. Tyler. 1986. The effects of a broad spectrum of physical activity on the biological processes in the Chesapeake Bay, pp. 361–384. *In* J. C. J. Nihoul, ed., Marine interfaces ecohydro-dynamics. Elsevier, Amsterdam.

Brockman, C. 1908. Uber das Verhalten der Plankton-diatomeen des Meeres bei herabsetzung der Konzentration der Meereswassers und uber das Vorkommen von Nordseediatomeen im Brackwasser der Wesermundung. Wiss. Meeeresunters. Helgol. 8:1–18.

Brockman, C. 1929. Das Brackwasser der Flussmündungen als Heimat und Vernichter des Lebens. Senckenberg am Meer 29. Natur Museum 59:404–414.

Brooks, H. K. 1973. Geological oceanography. *In* J. L. Jones, R. E. Ring, M. O. Rinkel, and R. E. Smith, eds., A summary of knowledge of the eastern Gulf of Mexico. State Univ. System, Florida Institute of Oceanography, St. Petersburg. Fla.

Bruun, P., and F. Gerritsen. 1960. Stability of coastal inlets. North-Holland, Amsterdam.

Bruun, P., and F. Gerritsen. 1961. Natural bypassing of sand at coastal inlets. Trans. Am. Soc. Civ. Eng. 126(IV):823–854.

Burt, W. V., and J. Queen. 1957. Tidal overmixing in estuaries. Science 126:973–974.

Chabreck, R. H., and A. W. Palmisano. 1973. The effects of Hurricane Camille on the marshes of the Mississippi River delta. Ecology 54:1118–1123.

Chermock, R. L. 1974. The environment of offshore and estuarine Alabama. Geol. Surv. Ala. Inf. Ser. 51. 135 pp.

Chuang, W. S., and W. C. Boicourt. 1989. Resonant seiche motion in the Chesapeake Bay. J. Geophys. Res. 94:2105–2110.

Chute, N. E., and R. L. Nichols. 1941. Geology of northeastern Massachusetts. Mass. Dep. Publ. Works U. S. Geol. Surv. Coop. Geol. Proj. Bull. 7. 48 pp.

Clark, S. M., and G. R. Snyder. 1969. Time and extent of a flow reversal in the lower Columbia River. Limnol. Oceanogr. 14:960–965.

Clifton, H. E., R. L. Phillips, and R. E. Hunter. 1972. Depositional structures and processes in the mouths of small coastal streams, southwestern Oregon, pp. 115–140. *In* D. R. Coates, ed., Coastal geomorphology, Proceedings of the 3rd annual geomorphology symposium series, Binghamton, N. Y., Sept. 28–Oct 3, 1972. Publications in Geomorphology, SUNY, Binghamton, N. Y.

Cohen, B., and L. T. McCarthy, Jr. 1966. Salinity of the Delaware estuary. U.S. Geol. Surv. Water-Supply Pap. 1586-B:B1–B847.

Coleman, J. M., and W. G. Smith. 1964. Late recent rise of sea level. Geol. Soc. Am. Bull. 75:833–840.

Coleman, J. M., and L. D. Wright. 1973. Variability of modern river deltas. Trans. Gulf Coast Assoc. Geol. Soc. 23:33–36.

Conomos, T. J., and D. H. Peterson. 1976. Suspended-particle transport and circulation in San Francisco Bay: an overview, pp. 82–97. *In* M. Willey, ed., Estuarine processes. Vol. II. Circulation, sediments, and transfer of material in the estuary. Academic Press, New York.

Copeland, B. J. and H. T. Odum. 1974. Ecological systems by state. pp. 104–123. *In:* H. T. Odum, B. J. Copeland, and E. A. McMahan. eds. Coastal ecological systems of the United States. Vol. 1. The Conservation Foundation, World Wildlife Fund. Washington, D.C. For Copyright Information, Contact WWF.

Copeland, B. J., J. H. Thompson, Jr. and W. B. Ogletree. 1968. The effects of wind on water levels in the Texas Laguna Madre. Tex. J. Sci. 20:196–199

Craighead, F. C., and V. C. Gilbert. 1962. The effects of Hurricane Donna on the vegetation of southern Florida. Q. J. Fla. Acad. Sci. 25:1–28.

Crommelin, R. O. 1940. De herkomst van het zand van de Waddenzee. Tijdschr. Koninkl. Ned. Aardi. Gen. 57:347–361.

Cummings, T. R. 1968. Salt-water encroachment in the South Edisto River estuary, South Carolina. U. S. Geol. Surv. Water-Supply Pap. 1586-1. 19 pp.

DaBoll, J. M. 1969. Holocene sediments of the Parker River estuary, Massachusetts. M. S. thesis. Univ. Massachusetts, Amherst. Coastal Research Contrib 3-CRG. 138 pp.

Demerara Coastal Investigation. 1962. Report on siltation of Demerara Bar Channel and coastal erosion in British Guiana. Delft Hydraulics Laboratory, Delft, The Netherlands.

deWitt, W., III. 1974. Hydrography, pp. 106–112. *In* H. T. Odum, B. J. Copeland, and E. A. McMahan, eds., Coastal ecological systems of the United States, Vol. 2. The Conservation Foundation, Washington, D.C.

Disney, L. P. 1955. Tide heights along the coasts of the United States. Proc. Am. Soc. Civ. Eng. 81:666–1 to 666–9.

Dragovich, II., and B. Z. May. 1962. Hydrological characteristics of Tampa Bay tributaries. U. S. Fish Wildl. Serv. Fish. Bull. 62(205):163–176.

Dyer, K. R. 1972. Sedimentation in estuaries, pp. 10–33. *In*. R. S. K. Barnes and J. Green, eds., The estuarine environment. Applied Science, London.

Dyer, K. R. 1973. Estuaries: a physical introduction. Wiley, New York. 140 pp.

Dyer, K. R. 1977. Lateral circulation effects in estuaries, pp. 22–29. *In* Geophysics of estuaries panel; estuaries, geophysics, and the environment, National Academy of Sciences, Washington, D.C.

Dyer, K. R., and A. L. New. 1986. Intermittency in estuarine mixing, pp. 321–339. *In* D. A. Wolfe, ed., Estuarine variability. Academic Press, Orlando, Fla.

Elliott, A. J. 1976. The circulation and salinity distribution of the Upper Potomac estuary. Chesapeake Sci. 17(3): 141–147.

Elliott, B. A., and R. O. Reid. 1976. Salinity induced horizontal estuarine circulation. J. Waterways Harb. Coastal Eng. Div. Proc. Am. Soc. Civ. Eng. 102(WW):425–442.

Estabrook, R. H. 1973. Phytoplankton ecology and hydrography of Apalachicola Bay. M. S. thesis. Florida State Univ., Tallahassee.

Farmer, D. M., and L. Armi. 1986. Maximal two-layer exchange over a sill and through the combination of a sill and contraction with barotropic flow. J. Fluid Mech. 164:53–76.

Farrell, S. C. 1971. Estuary stratification, a function of the ratio of stream discharge to tidal volume. Geol. Soc. Am. Abstr. Progr. 3(1):27.

Fisk, H. N., E. McFarlan, Jr., C. R. Kolb, and L. J. Wilbert, Jr. 1954. Sedimentary framework of the modern Mississippi delta. J. Sediment Petrol. 24:76–99.

Flint, R. F. 1971. Glacial and quaternary geology. Wiley, New York. 892 pp.

Folger, D. W. 1972. Characteristics of estuarine sediments of the United States. U.S. Geol. Surv. Prof. Pap. 742. 94 pp.

Garvine, R. W. 1975. The distribution of salinity and temperature in the Connecticut River estuary. J. Geophys. Res. 80:1176–1183.

Geyer, W. R., and G. A. Cannon. 1982. Sill dynamics related to bottom water renewal in a fjord. J. Geophys. Res. 87:7985–7996.

Geyer, W. R., and D. M. Farmer. 1988. Time induced variation of the dynamics of a salt wedge estuary. J. Phys. Oceanogr. 28:1060–1073.

Geyer, W. R., and J. D. Smith. 1987. Shear instability in a highly stratified estuary. J. Phys. Oceanogr. 17:1668–1679.

Goldthwait, J. W. 1937. Unchanging meanders in tidal creeks. Proc. Geol. Soc. Am. 1936:73–74.

Golley, F. B., H. T. Odum, and R. F. Wilson. 1962. The structure and metabolism of a Puerto Rican red mangrove forest in May. Ecology 43:9–19.

Goodrich, D. M. 1988. On meteorologically induced flushing in three U. S. east coast estuaries. Estuarine Coastal Shelf Sci. 26:111–121.

Goodrich, D. M., W. C. Boicourt, P. Hamilton, and D. W. Pritchard. 1987. Wind-induced destratification in Chesapeake Bay. J. Phys. Oceanogr. 17:2232–2240.

Gorsline, D. S. 1963. Oceanography of Apalachicola Bay, pp. 69–96. *In*: T. Clements, ed., Essays in marine geology in honor of K. O. Emery. Univ. California Press, Los Angeles.

Gorsline, D. S. 1967. Contrasts in coastal bay sediments on the Gulf and Pacific coasts pp. 219–225. *In* G. H. Lauff, ed., Estuaries. AAAS Publ. 83.

Haas, L. W. 1977. The effect of the spring-neap tidal cycle on the vertical salinity structure of the James, York, and Rappahannock rivers, Virginia, U.S.A. Estuarine Coastal Mar. Sci. 5:485–496.

Hansen, D. V. 1965. Currents and mixing in the Columbia River estuary. Ocean Sci. Ocean Eng. 2:943–955.

Hansen, D. V. 1967. Salt balance and circulation in partially mixed estuaries, pp. 45–51. *In* G. H. Lauff, ed., Estuaries. AAAS Publ. 83.

Hansen, D. V., and M. Rattray, Jr. 1965. Gravitation circulation in straits and estuaries. J. Mar. Res. 23:(2)104–122.

Hansen, D. V., and M. Rattray, Jr. 1966. New dimensions in estuary classification. Limnol. Oceanogr. 11(3):319–326.

Hartwell, A. D. 1970. Hydrography and holocene sedimentation of the Merrimack River estuary, Massachusetts. Univ. Mass. Coastal Res. Cent. Contrib. 5. 166 pp.

Hartwell, A. D., and M. O. Hayes. 1969. Hydrography of the Merrimack River estuary, pp. 218–244. *In* Coastal Research Group, Univ. Massachusetts, Field trip guidebook: coastal environments of northeastern Massachusetts and New Hampshire. Geol. Dept. Univ. Mass. Amherst Contrib. 1-CRG.

Haven, D. S., and R. Morales-Alamo. 1966. Aspects of biodeposition by oysters and other invertebrate filter feeders. Limnol. Oceanogr. 11:487–498.

Haven, D. S., and R. Morales-Alamo. 1972. Biodeposition as a factor in sedimentation of fine suspended solids in estuaries. *In* B. W. Nelson, ed., Environmental framework of coastal plain estuaries. Geol. Soc. Am. Mem. 133:121–130.

Hayes, M. O. 1971a. Geomorphology and sedimentation of some New England estuaries, pp. XII-1 to XII-71. *In* J. R. Schubel, convenor, The estuarine environment: estuaries and estuarine sedimentation. AGI Short Course Lect. Notes, Oct. 30–31, 1971, Wye Institute, Md. American Geological Institute, Washington, D.C.

Hayes, M. O. 1971b. Geomorphology of tidal inlets, pp. XIII-1 to XIII-17. *In* J. R. Schubel, convenor, The estuarine environment: estuaries and estuarine sedimentation. AGI Short Course Lect. Notes, Oct. 30–31, 1971, Wye Institute, Md. American Geological Institute Washington, D.C.

Hayes, M. O. 1975. Morphology of sand accumulation in estuaries: an introduction to the symposium, pp. 3–22. *In* L. E. Cronin, ed., Estuarine research. Vol II. Geology and engineering. Academic Press, New York.

Hayward, D., C. S. Welch, and L. W. Haas. 1982. York River destratification: an estuary–subestuary interaction. Science 216:1413.

Heald, E. J. 1969. The production of organic detritus in a south Florida estuary. Ph.D. dissertation. Univ. Miami, Miami, Fla. 110 pp.

Herlinveaux, R. H., and J. P. Tully. 1961. Some oceanographic features of Juan de Fuca Strait. J. Fish Res. Board Can. 18:1027–1071.

Hickson, R. E., and F. W. Rodolf. 1951. History of the Columbia River jetties, pp. 283–298. *In* Proceedings of the first conference on coastal engineering. Council on Wave Research, The Engineering Foundation. Mexico City, Mexico.

Hodgins, D. O., T. R. Osborn, and M. C. Quick. 1977. Numerical model of stratified estuary flows. J. Waterway Port Coastal Ocean Div. Proc. Am. Soc. Civ. Eng. 103(WW1):25–42.

Howard, C. S. 1940. Salt-water intrusion in the Connecticut River. Trans. Am. Geophys. Union 21:455–457.

Hubbell, D. W., and J. L. Glenn. 1971. Distribution of radionuclides in bottom sediments of the Columbia River estuary. U. S. Geol. Surv. Open-file Rept. 136 pp.

Hubbell, D. W., J. L. Glenn, and H. H. Stevens, Jr. 1971. Studies of sediment transport in the Columbia River estuary, pp. 190–226. *In* J. N. Nath and L. S. Slotta, eds., Proceedings of the 1971 technical conference on estuaries of the Pacific northwest. Eng. Exp. Stn. Oreg. State Univ. Corvallis, Circ. 42.

Ippen, A. T., and D. R. F. Harleman. 1961. One-dimensional analysis of salinity intrusion in estuaries. U.S. Army Corps Eng. Comm. Tidal Hydraul. Tech. Bull. 5.

Jay, D. A., and J. D. Smith. 1988. Residual Circulation and classification of shallow stratified Estuaries. *In* Physical Processes in Estuaries Edited by J. Dronkers and W. van Leussen, pp. 19–41. Springer Verlag, New York.

Jay, D. A., and J. D. Smith, 1990. Residual circulation in shallow estuaries. 2. Weakly stratified and partially mixed narrow estuaries. J. Geophys. Res. 95:733–748.

Jorgensen, C. B. 1960. Efficiency of particle retention and rate of water transport in undisturbed lamellibranchs. J. Cons. Permanent Int. Explor. Mar. 26:94–116.

Kaczorowski, R. T. 1971. Offset tidal inlets, Long Island, New York. Second coastal and shallow water conference, Univ. Delaware, Newark, Del., Oct. 9–10, 1971.

Keighton, W. B. 1966. Fresh-water discharge–salinity relations in the tidal Delaware River. U.S. Geol. Surv. Water-Supply Pap. 1586-G:G1–G16.

Kelley, D. W. 1966. Ecological studies of the Sacramento–San Joaquin estuary. Part 1. Zooplankton, zoobenthos, and fishes of San Pablo and Suisun bays, zooplankton and zoobenthos of the delta, Calif. Dep. Fish Game Fish Bull. 133.

Ketchum, B. H. 1950. Hydrographic factors involved in the dispersion of pollutants introduced into tidal waters. J. Boston Soc. Civil Eng. 37:296–314.

Ketchum, B. H. 1951a. The exchanges of fresh and salt water in estuaries. J. Mar. Res. 10:18–38.

Ketchum, B. H. 1951b. The dispersion and fate of pollutants discharged into tidal waters, and the viability of enteric bacteria in the sea. Woods Hole Oceanogr Inst. Ref. 51–11.

Ketchum, B. H. 1953. Circulation in estuaries, pp. 65–76. *In* J. W. Johnson, ed., Proceedings of the 3rd conference on coastal engineering, Oct. 1952. Council on Wave Research, The Engineering Foundation Cambridge, MA.

Ketchum, B. H. 1955. Distribution of coliform bacteria and other pollutants in tidal estuaries. Sewage Ind. Wastes 27:1288–1296.

Ketchum, B. H., and D. J. Keen. 1953. The exchanges of fresh and salt waters in the Bay of Fundy and in Passamaquoddy Bay. J. Fish. Res. Board Can. 10:97–124.

Ketchum, B. H., A. C. Redfield, and J. C. Ayers. 1951. The oceanography of the New York bight Pap. Phys. Oceanogr. 8:1–46.

Kranenburg, C. 1988. On internal waves in partially mixed and stratified tidal flows, pp. 213–238. *In* J. Dronkers and W. van Leussen, eds., Physical processes in estuaries. Springer-Verlag, Berlin.

Kuenzler, E. J. 1974. Mangrove swamp ecosystems, pp. 346–371. *In:* H. T. Odum, B. J. Copeland, and E. A. McMahan. Coastal ecological systems of the United States. Vol. I. The Conservation Foundation, World Wildlife Fund, Washington, D.C. For Copyright Information, Contact WWF.

Kulm, L. D., and J. V. Byrne. 1967. Sediments of Yaquina Bay, Oregon, pp. 226–238. *In* G. H. Lauff, ed., Estuaries. AAAS Publ. 83.

Langbein, W. B. 1963. The hydraulic geometry of a shallow estuary. Bull. Int. Assoc. Sci. Hydrol. 8:84–94.

Livingston R. J., R. L. Iverson, R. H. Estabrook, V. E. Keys, and J. Taylor, Jr. 1974. Major features of the Apalachicola Bay system: physiography, biota, and resource management. Fla. Sci. 37:245–271.

Lockett, J. B. 1963. Phenomena affecting improvement of the lower Columbia estuary and entrance, pp. 695–755. *In* Proceedings of the 8th conference on coastal engineering. Council on Wave Research, The Engineering Foundation. Mexico City, Mexico.

Long, R. R. 1976. Mass and salt transfers and halocline depths in an estuary. Tellus 28:460–472.

Lund, E. J. 1957a. A quantitative study of clearance of a turbid medium and feeding by the oyster. Univ. Texas Inst. Mar. Sci. Publ. 4:296–312.

Lund, E. J. 1957b. Self-silting by the oyster and its significance for sedimentation geology. Univ. Texas Inst. Mar. Sci. Publ. 4:320–327.

Macnae, W. 1967. Zonation within mangroves associated with estuaries in North Queensland, pp. 432–444. *In* G. H. Lauff, ed., Estuaries. AAAS Publ. 83.

Marshall, H. L. 1974. Irregularly flooded marsh, pp. 150–170. *In* H. T. Odum, B. H. Copeland, and E. A. McMahan, eds., Coastal ecological systems of the United States. Vol. 2, The Conservation Foundation, Washington, D.C.

Mason, W. D., and W. H. Pietsch. 1940. Salinity movement and its causes in the Delaware River estuary. Trans. Am. Geophys. Union 21:457–463.

Mcdonald, K. B. 1969. Quantitative studies of salt marsh faunas from the North American Pacific coast. Ecol. Monogr. 39:33–60.

McGowen, J. H., and J. L. Brewton. 1975. Historical changes and related coastal processes, gulf and mainland shorelines, Matagorda Bay area, Texas. Univ. Texas Austin Bur. Econ. Geol. 72 pp.

McGowen, J. H., and A. J. Scott. 1975. Hurricanes as geologic agents on the Texas coast, pp. 23–46. *In* L. E. Cronin, ed., Estuarine research. Vol. 2, Geology and engineering. Academic Press, New York.

McNulty, J. K., W. N. Lindall, Jr., and J. E. Sykes. 1972. Cooperative Gulf of Mexico estuarine inventory and study, Florida. Phase 1, area description. NOAA, Natl. Mar. Fish. Serv. Tech. Rep. NMFS Circ. 368. 126 pp.

Meade, R. H. 1966. Salinity variations in the Connecticut River. Water Resour. Res. 2:567–579.

Meade, R. H. 1972. Transport and deposition of sediments in estuaries. *In* B. W. Nelson, ed., Environmental framework of coastal plain estuaries. Geol. Soc. Am. Mem. 133:91–120.

Morgan, J. P. 1967. Ephemeral estuaries of the deltaic environment, pp. 115–128. *In* G. H. Lauff, ed., Estuaries. AAAS Publ. 83.

Morton, R. A. 1975. Shoreline changes between Sabine River Pass and Bolivar Roads: an analysis of historical changes of the Texas Gulf shoreline. Univ. Texas, Austin Bur. Econ. Geol. Circ. 75-6. 43 pp. Reprinted with permission from Morton.

Mueller, W. 1964. Unterschiede in den chemischen und physikalischen Eigenschaften von fluviatilen, brackischen und marinen Sedimenten. Proceedings of the sedimentological congress, Amsterdam.

Myrick, R. M., and L. B. Leopold. 1963. Hydraulic geometry of a small tidal estuary. U.S. Geol. Surv. Prof. Pap. 422-B:B1–B18.

Nash, C. B. 1947. Environmental characteristics of a river estuary. J. Mar. Res. 6:147–174.

National Estuarine Pollution Study. 1970. Report of the Secretary of the Interior to the United States Congress pursuant to Public Law 89–753, the Clean Water Restoration Act of 1966. 91st Congress, 2nd Session, U.S. Senate Doc. 91–58. 633 pp.

Neal, V. T. 1966. Tidal currents in Yaquina Bay. Northwest Sci. 40(2):68–74.

Neal, V. T. 1972. Physical aspects of the Columbia River and its estuary, pp. 19–40. *In* A. T. Pruter and K. L. Alverson, eds., The Columbia River estuary and adjacent ocean waters. Univ. Washington Press, Seattle, Wash.

Nelson, B. W. 1960. Clay mineralogy of the bottom sediments, Rappahannock River, Virginia, pp. 135–147. *In* Proceedings of the 7th National conference on clays and clay minerals.

New, A. L., and K. R. Dyer. 1988. Internal waves and mixing in stratified estuaries, pp. 239–254. *In* J. Dronkers and W. van Leussen, eds., Physical processes in estuaries. Springer-Verlag, Berlin.

New, A. L., K. R. Dyer, and R. E. Lewis. 1987. Internal waves and intense mixing periods in a partially stratified estuary. Estuarine Coastal Shelf Sci. 24:15–33.

Nunes, R. A., and J. H. Simpson. 1985. Axial convergence in a well-mixed estuary. Estuarine Coastal Shelf Sci. 20:637–649.

Odum, E. P. 1959. Fundamentals of ecology, 2nd ed. W. B. Saunders, Philadelphia. 546 pp.

Odum, H. T., and B. J. Copeland. 1972. Functional classification of coastal ecological systems of the United States. *In* B. W. Nelson, ed., Environmental framework of coastal plain estuaries. Geol. Soc. Am. Mem. 133:9–28.

Odum, H. T., B. J. Copeland, and E. A. McMahan. 1974a. Coastal ecological systems of the United States. Vol. IV. The Conservation Foundation, World Wildlife Fund, Washington, D.C. 470 pp. For Copyright Information Contact WWF.

Odum, H. T., B. J. Copeland, and E. A. McMahan. 1974b. Coastal ecological systems of the United States. Vol. 1. The Conservation Foundation, World Wildlife Fund, Washington, D.C. For Copyright Information, Contact WWF.

O'Neil, T. 1949. The muskrat in Louisiana coastal marshes. Louisiana Wildl. Fish. Comm., New Orleans, La. 195 pp.

Patrick, J. H. 1974. River flow increases in central New England after the hurricane of 1938. J. For. 72:21.

Patrick R. 1988. Changes in the chemical and biological characteristics of the upper Delaware River estuary in response to Environmental Laws Chap. 23, 28 pp. *In* S. K. Majumdar, E. W. Miller and Louis E. Sage Editors. Ecological Restoration at the Delaware River Basin.

Pearson, C. E., and D. F. Winter. 1977. On the calculation of tidal currents in homogeneous estuaries. J. Phys. Oceanogr. 7: 520–531.

Pestrong, R. 1965. The development of drainage patterns on tidal marshes. Stanford Univ. Publ. Geol. Sci. 10: 1–87.

Pickard, G. L. 1961. Oceanographic features of inlets in the British Columbia mainland coast. J. Fish. Res. Board Can. 18: 907–999.

Pickard, G. L., and K. Rodgers. 1959. Current measurements in Knight Inlet, British Columbia. J. Fish. Res Board Can. 16(5): 635–678.

Postma, H. 1954. Hydrography of the Dutch Wadden Sea. Arch. Neerl. Zool. 10: 405–511.

Postma, H. 1961. Suspended matter and Secchi disc visibility in coastal waters. Neth. J. Sea Res. 1: 359–390.

Postma, H. 1967. Sediment transport and sedimentation in the estuarine environment, pp. 158–179. *In* G. H. Lauff, ed., Estuaries. SCIENCE 83. Copyright 1967 by the AAAS.

Pritchard, D. W. 1952. Salinity distribution and circulation in Chesapeake Bay estuarine system. J. Mar. Res. 11: 106–123.

Pritchard, D. W. 1954. A study of the salt balance in coastal plain estuary. J. Mar. Res. 13: 133–144.

Pritchard, D. W. 1955. Estuarine circulation patterns. Proc. Am. Soc. Civ. Eng. 8: 717–1 to 717–11.

Pritchard, D. W. 1956. The dynamic structure of a coastal plain estuary. J. Mar. Res. 15: 33–42.

Pritchard, D. W. 1967a. What is an estuary: physical viewpoint, pp. 3–6. *In* G. H. Lauff, ed., Estuaries. AAAS Publ. 83.

Pritchard, D. W. 1967b. Observations of circulation in coastal plains estuaries, pp. 37–44. *In* G. H. Lauff, ed., Estuaries. SCIENCE 83. Copyright 1967 by the AAAS.

Pritchard, D. W. 1969. Dispersion and flushing of pollutants in estuaries. Proc. Am. Soc. Civ. Eng. 95(HY1): 115–124.

Pritchard, D. W. 1980. A note on the Stokes transport in tidal estuaries, pp. 217–226. *In* B. Patel, ed., Management of environment. Wiley, Bombay.

Pritchard, D. W., and H. H. Carter. 1971. Estuarine circulation patterns, pp. IV-1 to IV-17. *In* J. R. Schubel, convenor, The estuarine environment; estuaries and estuarine sedimentation. AGI Short Course Lect. Notes, Oct. 30–31, 1971, Wye Institute, Md. American Geological Institute, Washington, D.C.

Pritchard. D. W., and M. E. C. Viera. 1984. Vertical variations in residual current response to meteorological forcing in the mid-Chesapeake Bay, pp. 27–65. *In* V. S. Kennedy, ed., The estuary as a filter. Academic Press, Orlando, Fla.

Rattray, M. Jr. 1967. Some aspects of the dynamics of circulation in fjords, pp. 52–62. *In* G. H. Lauff, ed., Estuaries. AAAS Publ. 83.

Redfield, A. C. 1959. The Barnstable Marsh, *In* Proceedings of the salt marsh conference, Univ. Georgia Marine, Institute, Athens, Ga, pp. 37–39.

Redfield, A. C. 1965. The ontogeny of a salt marsh estuary. SCIENCE 147(3653): 50–55. Copyright 1967 by the AAAS.

Redfield, A. C. 1972. Development of a New England salt marsh. Ecol. Monogr. 42(2): 201–237.

Redfield, A. C., and M. Rubin. 1962. The age of salt marsh peat and its relation to recent changes in sea level at Barnstable, Massachusetts. Proc. Natl. Acad. Sci. 48: 1728–1735.

Rhoads, D. C. 1963. Rates of sediment reworking by *Yoldia limatula* in Buzzards Bay, Massachusetts, and Long Island Sound. J. Sediment. Petrol. 33: 723–727.

Rhoads, D. C., and D. K. Young. 1970. The influence of deposit-feeding organisms on sediment stability and community trophic structure. J. Mar. Res. 28: 150–178.

Riley, G. A. 1963. Organic aggregates in seawater and the dynamics of their formation and utilization. Limnol. Oceanogr. 8: 372–381.

Rosen, P. S. 1975. Origin and processes of cuspate spit shorelines, pp. 77–92. *In* L. E. Cronin, ed., Estuarine Research. Vol. 2. Geology and engineering. Academic Press, New York.

Russell, R. J. 1942. Flotant. Geogr. Rev. 32: 74–98.

Ruzecki, E. P., and D. A. Evans. 1988. Temporal and spatial sequencing of destratification in a coastal plain estuary, pp. 368–389. *In* M. J. Bowman, C. M. Yentsch, and W. T. Peterson, eds. Lecture Notes on coastal and estuarine studies. Springer-Verlag, Berlin.

Sanford, L. P., and W. C. Boicourt. 1990. Wind forced salt intrusion into a tributary estuary. J. Geophys. Res. 48: 567–590.

Sanford, L. P., K. G. Sellner, and D. L. Breitburg. 1990. Covariability of dissolved oxygen with physical processes in the summertime Chesapeake Bay. J. Mar. Res. 48: 567–590.

Santos, J. F., and J. D. Stoner. 1972. Physical, chemical and biological aspects of the Duwamish River estuary, King County, Washington, 1963–1967. U.S. Geol. Surv. Water-Supply Pap. 1837-C: C1–C74.

Schubel, J. R. 1971a. The origin and development of estuaries, pp. III-3 to III-7. In J. R. Schubel, convenor, The estuarine environment; estuaries and estuarine sedimentation. AGI Short Course Lect. Notes, Oct. 30–31, Wye Institute, Md. American Geological Institute, Washington, D.C.

Schubel, J. R. 1971b. Estuarine circulation and sedimentation, pp. VI-1 to VI-17. *In* J. R. Schubel, convenor, The estuarine environment; estuaries and estuarine sedimentation. AGI Short Course Lecture Notes, Oct. 30–31, 1971, Wye Institute, Md. American Geological Institute, Washington, D.C.

Schubel, J. R. 1971c. Sources of sediments to estuaries, pp. V-1 to V-19. *In* J. R. Schubel, convenor, The estuarine environment; estuaries and estuarine sedimentation. AGI Short Course Lect. Notes, Oct. 30–31, 1971, Wye Institute, Md. American Geological Institute, Washington, D.C.

Schubel, J. R. 1971d. Some notes on turbidity maxima, pp. VIII-1 to VIII-28. *In* J. R. Schubel, convenor, The estuarine environment; estuaries and estuarine sedimentation. AGI Short Course Lect. Notes, Oct. 30–31, 1971, Wye Institute Md. American Geological Institute, Washington, D.C.

Schubel, J. R. 1974. Effects of tropical storm Agnes on the suspended solids of the northern Chesapeake Bay. *In* R. J. Gibbs, ed., Suspended solids in water. Mar. Sci 4: 113–132.

Schubel, J. R., and D. W. Pritchard. 1971. What is an estuary? pp. I-1 to I-11. *In* J. R. Schubel, convenor, The estuarine environment; estuaries and estuarine sedimentation. AGI Short Course Lect. Notes, Oct. 30–31, 1971, Wye Institute, Md. American Geological Institute, Washington, D.C.

Schubel, J. R., and D. W. Pritchard. 1972. The estuarine environment. Part 1. J. Geol. Educ. 20: 60–68.

Shepard, R. P. 1963. Thirty-five thousand years of sea level, pp. 1–10. *In* Essays in honor of K. O. Emery. Univ. Southern California Press, Los Angeles.

Shepard, F. P., and H. R. Wanless. 1971. Our changing coastlines. McGraw-Hill, New York, 579 pp.

Simmons, H. B. 1955. Some effects of upland discharge on estuarine hydraulics. J. Hydraul. Div. Proc. Am. Soc. Civ. Eng. 81: 792–1 to 792–20.

Simmons, H. B. 1966. Field experience in estuaries, pp. 673–690. *In* A. T. Ippen ed., Estuary and coastline hydrodynamics. McGraw-Hill, New York.

Simon, J. L. 1974. Tampa Bay estuarine system: a synopsis. Fla. Sci. 37: 217–244.

Simpson, J. H., and R. A. Nunes. 1981. The tidal intrusion front: an estuarine convergence zone. Estuarine Coastal Shelf Sci. 13: 257–266.

Simpson, J. H., and W. R. Turrell. 1986. Convergent fronts in the circulation of tidal estuaries, pp. 139–152. *In* D. A. Wolfe, ed., Estuarine variability. Academic Press, Orlando, Fla.

Smith, D. D. 1976. Dredging and spoil disposal: major geologic processes in San Diego Bay, California, pp. 150–166. *In* M. Wiley, ed., Estuarine Processes. Vol. 2. Circulation, sediments, and transfer of material in the estuary. Academic Press, New York.

Steers, J. A. 1977. Physiography, pp. 31–60. *In* V. J. Chapman, ed., Ecosystems of the world. 1. Wet coastal ecosystems. Elsevier, New York.

Stommel, H. 1951. Recent developments in the study of tidal estuaries. Woods Hole Oceanogr. Inst. Tech. Rep. 51–53.

Stommel, H. 1953. Computation of pollution in a vertically mixed estuary. Sewage Ind. Wastes 25: 1065–1071.

Sundborg, F. A. 1956. The river Klaralven, a study on fluvial processes. Geogr. Ann. Arg. 37: 125–316.

Tabb, D. C. 1963. A summary of existing information on the fresh-water, brackish water, and marine ecology of the Florida Everglades region in relation to fresh-water needs of Everglass National Park. Report to the Superintendent, Everglades National Park and Fort Jefferson National Monument.

Tully, J. P. 1958. Structure, entrainment and transport in estuarine embayments. J. Mar. Res. 17: 523–535.

Van Stratten, L. M. 1960. Transport and composition of sediments. *In* Symposium Ems-Estuarium, Nordsee. Verhandel. Koninkl. Ned. Geol. Mijnbouwk. Geoot. Geol. Ser. 19.

Viera, M. E. C. 1986. The meteorologically driven circulation in mid-Chesapeake Bay. J. Mar. Res. 44: 473–493.

Vitra, J. 1977. Estimating the water and salt budgets of a stratified estuary. Nord. Hydrol. 8: 11–32.

Wang, D. P. 1979. Subtidal sea level variations in the Chesapeake Bay and relations to atmospheric forcing. J. Phys. Oceanogr. 9: 413–421.

Wangersky, P. J. 1965. The organic chemistry of sea water. Am. Sci. 53: 358–374.

Warme, J. E., L. A. Sanchez-Barreda, and K. T. Biddle. 1976. Sedimentary patterns and processes in West Coast lagoons, pp. 167–181. *In* M. Wiley, ed., Estuarine processes. Vol. 2. Circulation sediments, and transfer of material in the estuary. Academic Press, New York.

Webert, F. J. 1956. Hurricane damage to the fur industry. La. Conserv. 10–13: 20–21.

Weil, C. B. 1977. Sediments, structural framework, and evolution of Delaware Bay, a transgressive estuarine delta. Univ. Delaware Sea Grant Tech. Rep. DEL-SC-4-77. 199 pp.

Weisberg, R. H. 1976. The nontidal flow in the Providence River of Narragansett Bay: a stochastic approach to estuarine circulation. J. Phys. Oceanogr. 6: 721–734.

Whitehouse, U. G., L. M. Jeffrey, and J. D. Debrecht. 1960. Differential settling tendencies of clay minerals in saline waters, pp. 1–79. *In* Proceedings of the 7th national conference on clays and clay minerals.

Wright, L. D. 1971. Hydrography of South Pass, Mississippi River. Proc. Am. Soc. Civ. Eng. 97. (WW3): 491–504.

Wright, L. D., and J. M. Coleman. 1971. Effluent expansion and interfacial mixing in the presence of a salt wedge, Mississippi River delta. J. Geophys. Res. 76: 8649–8661.

Zenkovich, V. P. 1959. On the genesis of cuspate spits along lagoon shores. J. Geol. 67: 269–277.

Zenkovich, V. P. 1967. Processes of coastal development. *In* J. A. Steers, ed., assisted by C. A. M. King; D. G. Fry, transl. Oliver & Boyd, London. 739 pp.

CHAPTER 3

Northern New England Estuaries

T he shoreline, in which New England estuaries occur, varies greatly from the northern to the southern part of New England. In the northern part, the shoreline is rugged, consisting of older resistant rocks that make up the rocky shoreline throughout Maine and New Hampshire (U.S. Geological Survey, 1970). In Massachusetts, the rocky shore includes pocket beaches with pebble and sand, except for the Charles River front, which is largely human-made, and becomes at Cape Cod a coast that is almost entirely sand. South of Cape Cod to New York City, pocket beaches are often present in the older, resistant rock. Barrier island estuaries, common along Long Island, present habitats that differ from those of some of the open-mouth estuaries.

The main estuaries north of Cape Cod are Passamaquoddy Bay, St. Croix River estuary, the Penobscot River estuary, Casco Bay, and the estuaries of the Androscoggin, Kennebec, and Eastern rivers and the Sheepscot River, and the Saco River estuaries in Maine. South of Cape Cod are Salmon Falls–Piscataqua River estuary (Narragansett Bay) in Rhode Island, and the Thames and Connecticut River estuaries in Connecticut (Figure 3.1). The Hudson River estuary is the principal estuary in New York State.

The tides in northern New England estuaries are semidiurnal; that is, there are two nearly high waters and two nearly equal low waters during each tidal day (U.S. Geological Survey, 1970). The height of the tides is variable in New England. Around Passamaquoddy Bay, the maximum range is about 3.7 m. About 220 km farther south the range decreases to 3.1 m. From Muscongus Bay, Maine, to Cape Cod's northern shore, the maximum tide range is about 3 m.

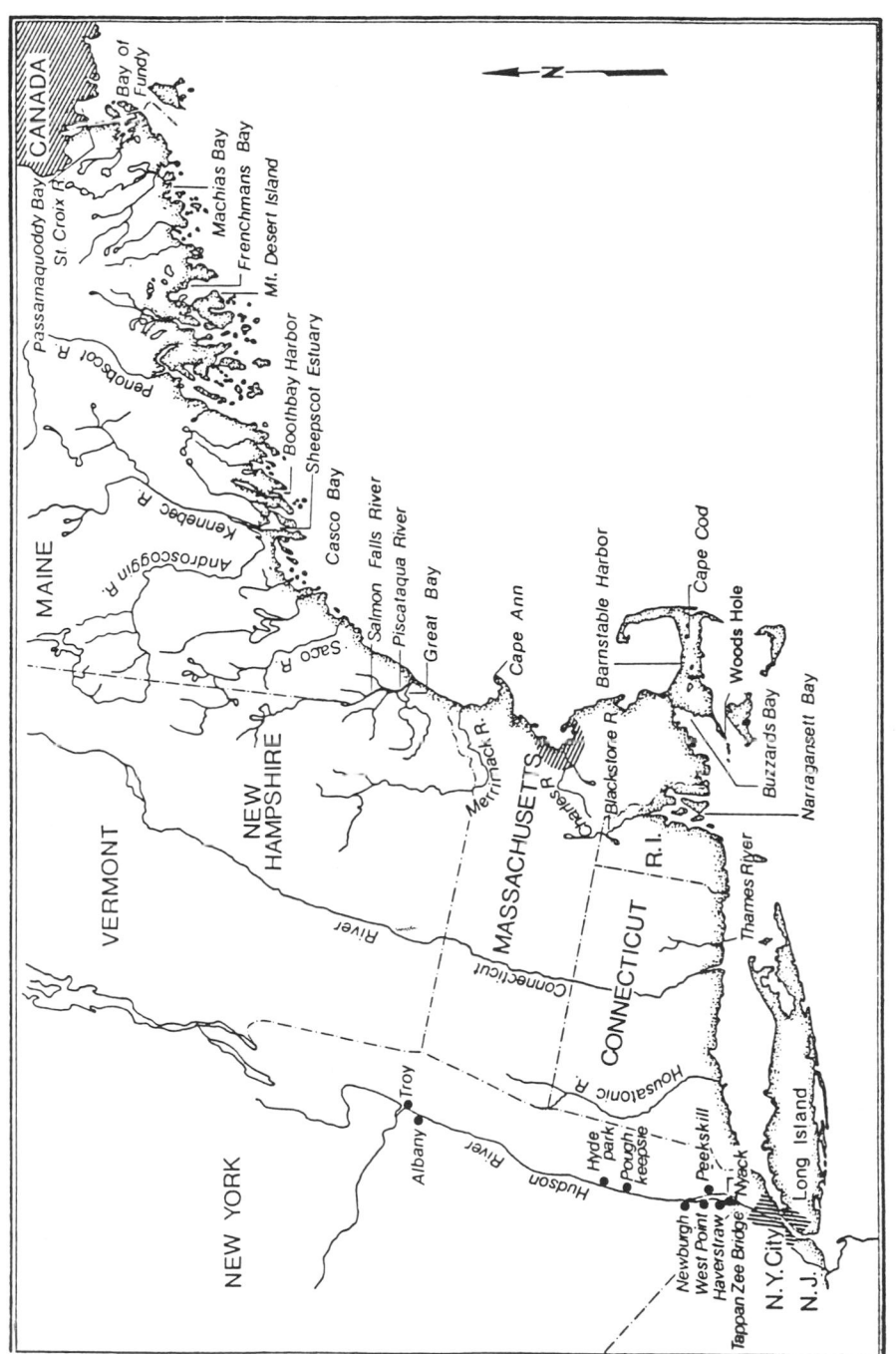

FIGURE 3.1. Map of New England showing rivers, estuaries, and towns mentioned in Chapter 3. (After Kvenzler, 1974.)

Characteristics of the water current and temperature of the oceanic waters bordering the New England states divide the coastal area, more or less, into two regions: estuaries entering the Atlantic Ocean above Cape Cod, and estuaries entering the Atlantic Ocean below Cape Cod. Above Cape Cod, the estuaries are greatly influenced by the cooler oceanic temperatures, and therefore the fauna is more Acadian in type. South of Cape Cod a mixture of Acadian and Virginian oceanic fauna is found (Ray, 1975).

The main associations of organisms commonly found in these northern New England estuaries are pelagic communities composed of plankton and nekton organisms. Intertidal associations occur on or in rocky substrates, sandy bars and flats, sandy-mud and mud flats, and salt marshes. The amount of exposure and salinity gradients cause major shifts in the species comprising these various communities. The submerged benthic fauna and flora are also important components of aquatic life.

COMMUNITIES OF AQUATIC LIFE

Most studies in northern New England estuaries have been confined to brackish water and marine estuary areas. Therefore, it is not possible to set forth the communities and species interactions in the freshwater reaches of the estuaries.

Submerged Fauna and Flora
Submerged fauna and flora consist of plankton, nekton, and the benthic communities, which include eelgrass beds and sand and mud flats.

Plankton.   Temperature, nutrients, and water current patterns seem to be important in determining the abundance of phytoplankton and zooplankton.

Phytoplankton.   Phytoplankton communities in New England are dominated by diatoms, although small amounts of other algae are often present. Dinoflagellates are also very common, sometimes rivaling diatoms in abundance. If pollution is present, dinoflagellates may become more abundant than the diatoms.

Zooplankton.   The zooplankton consists of protozoans, microcrustaceans, megacrustacean larvae, and fish larvae. One of the most common of the crustacea is *Calanus finmarchicus*. Nauplii larvae of crustaceans (mysid shrimp, *Malacostraca*) and veliger larvae (*Mollusca*) are fairly common. In a study by Johnson (1925), *Calanus finmarchicus* averaged 39.9% of the total specimens collected from April to September along the coast of Maine, and 35.5% of the specimens from the Bay of Fundy.

Zooplankton populations seemed to be related to temperature, nutrients, and stability of water mass. Generally, the zooplankton populations tended to be larger offshore west of Mount Desert Island, and smaller in the headlands east of Mount Desert Island and in Passamaquoddy Bay. In general, the abundance of coastal zooplankton seemed to decline from the western southern part near the end of the Gulf of Maine, to the eastern end of the Gulf of Maine (i.e., Machias Bay) (Sherman, 1970). Copepods were the dominant group at all seasons.

Fish larvae were often quite common in the plankton. Chenoweth (1973) found 22 different types of fish larvae in Maine estuaries. The larvae of a few common species, hatched from demersal eggs, were dominant in winter and early spring and remained concentrated in the upper estuaries. In spring and summer, the larval population consisted of less abundant species, hatched from pelagic eggs, and was not concentrated in the upper estuary. The larvae of the herring (*Clupea harengus harengus*) were common in many New England estuaries. In the Boothbay Harbor area in Maine, most of the mortality of the hatching eggs occurred in late fall or early winter and the larvae seemed to be in the poorest condition during the winter.

Sometimes the plankton or suspended organisms consist of a great variety of forms. A plankton haul taken in September 1945 in Cape Ann estuary (Massachusetts) on a strong outgoing current contained abundant *Calanus finmarchicus* (a copepod) and smaller quantities of green algae fragments, ostracods, nauplius larvae, mysid larvae, veliger larvae, rhabdocoele turbellarians, very small clams, and fragments of bryozoan and hydrozoan colonies. Quantities of large jellyfish usually appeared in the plankton near Cape Ann in late summer. The two most common medusae were *Aurelia aurita* and *Cyanea capillata*. Many crustaceans, belonging to the genus *Hyperia*, were commensal on jellyfish.

Nekton. The nekton consists primarily of fish in New England estuaries, although some invertebrates are also present. In the inlet of Cape Ann (Dexter, 1947), the more important pelagic species were Atlantic mackerel (*Scomber scombrus*), Atlantic herring (*Clupea harengus harengus*), pipefish (*Syngathus peckianus*), pollock (*Pollachius virens*), alewife (*Alosa pseudoharengus*), butterfish (*Poronotus triacanthus*), bluefish (*Pomatomus saltatrix*), silver hake (*Merluccius bilinearis*), rainbow smelt (*Osmerus mordax*), common squid (*Loligo pealii*), harbor seal (*Phoco vitulina*), and the jellyfish mentioned above.

Of the anadromous fish, the most common are salmon and shad. The migration of Atlantic salmon smolts in the Penobscot River estuary starts when the water temperature is above $5\,°C$, and the full expression of the migratory behavior is evident at temperatures above $9\,°C$. Most of the fish movement seems to be passive; however, fish have been observed moving actively and holding positions against a current (Fried et al., 1978). The rate of movement varies with the strength of the current. In open water in the Penobscot River estuary the average rate of travel is $1.85\,km\,h^{-1}$ for $25.3\,km$ of the estuary (Labar et al., 1978).

American shad (*Alosa sapidissima*) runs used to be more common in New England than they are today. Between 1896 and 1960, the shad disappeared from the Kennebec and Penobscot rivers, but they are still present in the Merrimack as far upstream as Lawrence, Massachusetts. Table 3.1 shows a comparison of the lengths of shad runs during 1896 and 1960 in these three rivers. The shad ascend the river in the spring when the water temperature is between 5 and $23\,°C$, with the peak movement of the run occurring in the temperature range 13 to $16\,°C$ (Walburg and Nichols, 1967).

TABLE 3.1. *Historical Distances of Shad (Alosa sapidissima) Runs Up Three New England Rivers*

River	Length (km) of River from Source to Coastline	Distance (km) Traveled Upriver by Runs of Shad		
		Original (undated)	1896	1960
Merrimack	225	201	32	32
Kennebec	249	174	71	No shad
Penobscot	410	145	56	No shad

Source: After Walburg and Nichols (1967), Table 1.

Benthic Communities. The communities of aquatic life found in shallow, submerged areas of the estuary were best described by Dexter (1947) in his account of the Cape Ann estuary. Here he found, on the sand and sandy mud and bare sediments of the channel floor, many transient animals, such as crabs (*Cancer, Pagurus, Carcinus*), the snail (*Polinices*), the horseshoe crab (*Limulus*), and shrimp (*Crangon*). The most prevalent ground fish were squirrel hake (*Urophycis*), flounder (*Pseudopleuronectes*), sculpins (*Myoxecephalus*), skates (*Raja*), and the eel (*Anguilla*). Also present were invertebrates such as starfish (*Asterias*), sea urchins (*Strongylocentrotus*), and the sand dollar (*Echinarachnius*). Within the substrate proper are amphipods, annelids, and bivalves belonging most frequently to the genera *Tellina* and *Certastoderma*. Shorey (1973) reported that in the sediments of these shallow waters, polychaetes (*Scolecolepides viridis*) and bivalve molluscs (*Macoma balthica* and *Mya arenaria*) were common. In more granular substrates polychaete worms such as *Prionospio malngrini* and crustacea such as *Corophium volutator* were present.

Kelps (*Laminaria digitata* and *L. saccharina*) were found in the deepest part of the channel attached to solid substrate. Dense growths of *Laminaria* impede water currents and reduce light intensity. This easing of harsh conditions allowed other plants and invertebrates to flourish. Algae holdfasts are a microhabitat for an important bottom community of small animals, including sea squirts (*Molgula* and *Botryllus*); mat-forming bryozoans; sponge colonies (*Haliclona*); small sea anemones (*Metridium*); the bivalve, *Saxicava*; and small forms known as seeds of the blue mussel, *Mytilus*. Among the *Laminaria* holdfasts on the channel floor were other algae, such as tufts of *Chondrus*; masses of the green algae, *Chaetomorpha*; and strings of the brown algae, *Chorda. Chaetomorpha* often harbored the bivalve, *Gemma*; the shrimp, *Crangon*; and the amphipod, *Caprella*. Many immature annelids as well as crustacea occurred among these algae. Sometimes colonies of sponge (*Chalina*) and hydroids (*Abietinaria*) were attached to the islands of algae. The sponge, in turn, harbored small worms, amphipods, bivalves, and sometimes the brittle star, *Ophiopholis*.

Many small animals of the community move about over the stipes of the *Laminaria*. This mobile group includes amphipods such as *Gammarus*, isopods, worms (*Lepidonotus* and *Nereis*), crabs (*Neopanope*, *Cancer*, and *Carcinus*), small sea urchins (*Strongylocentrotus*), brittle stars (*Ophiopholis*), flatworms (*Leptoplana*), periwinkles (*Littorina littorea*), and fish fry.

Attached to the algal stipes and fronds were hydroid colonies (*Sertularia*, *Tubularia*, *Obelia*), crustose bryozoans (*Lichenopora* and *Bugula*), algae (*Ectocarpus*), annelid worms (*Spirobis*), small amphipods, starfish (*Asterias*), and snails.

The snail, *Nassarius triviattata*, is often found in shallow, muddy, and sandy areas. On shelly, rocky bottoms many specimens of the sea anemone, *Metridium*; the boat shell, *Crepidula fornicata*; and molluscs such as *Aemaea* and *Anomia* were found. The species forming these associations varied with the salinity of the habitat and also its degree of protection.

Eelgrass Associations. In very protected areas of shallow bottoms, one often finds beds of eelgrass (*Zostera*). Eelgrass was very common in the New England area before 1930, then disappeared between 1930 and 1935, and reappeared in the early 1950s. In Goose Cove, Cape Ann (Massachusetts) estuary, the eelgrass association was reestablished by 1949 (Dexter 1950). The periwinkle, *Littorina littorea*, was in great abundance, peppering the leaves throughout the stand. Other molluscs in the association were *Littorina saxatilis*, *L. obtusata*, *Lacuna vincta*, *Cingula aculeus*, *Gemma gemma*, and seed of *Mytilus edulis*. Crustaceans found in the eelgrass were the isopod, *Idotea balthica*, and the shirmp, *Crangon septemspinos* (and an unidentified amphipod). A tube-building annelid, *Spirobis spirillum*, was found on eelgrass leaves. The lobster, *Homarus americanus*, and the American eel, *Anguilla rostrata*, have been captured in traps set in the cove. The fry of the mummichog, *Fundulus heteroclitus*, and the three-spined stickleback, *Gasterosteus aculeatus*, were collected with a dip net.

Food Web. The algae living on the estuary bed (i.e., the *Laminaria*, *Chaetomorpha*, *Ulva*, *Chondrus*) are food for many snails, crustacea, and fishes. Herbivorous snails are devoured by the carnivorous snails (*Polinices* sp. and *Nassarius trivittata*), and both of these types are eaten by crabs and fish. The smaller fish are in turn eaten by larger fish and also by diving birds such as terns and kingfishers. Plankton and detritus are consumed by filter-feeding mussels and other bivalves. These in turn are attacked by various carnivorous animals, such as snails, the horseshoe crab, the king crab, decapod crabs, starfish, annelids, and bottom fish such as flounder, sculpins, skate, and squirrel hake. Carnivores also consume almost all of the invertebrate enemies of bivalves. The plankton-eating fish (mackerel, herring, pollock, and pipefish), are devoured by the predacious bluefish, butterfish, and silver hake or by diving birds. Coelenterates, sponges, and bryozoans feed on the plankton and detritus, and they are eaten by crustaceans and fish. Annelid worms and shrimp feed on organic matter (often referred to as marine humus) in the bottom sands and mud. In turn, the worms and shrimp are dug up and eaten by the king crab; rock, hermit, and green crabs; and by bottom-dwelling fish. Dead animal bodies and other organic refuse are eaten by scavenging snails, crabs, arthropods, and fish. At the base of the food web are algae, organic debris, bacteria, and plankton, a combination

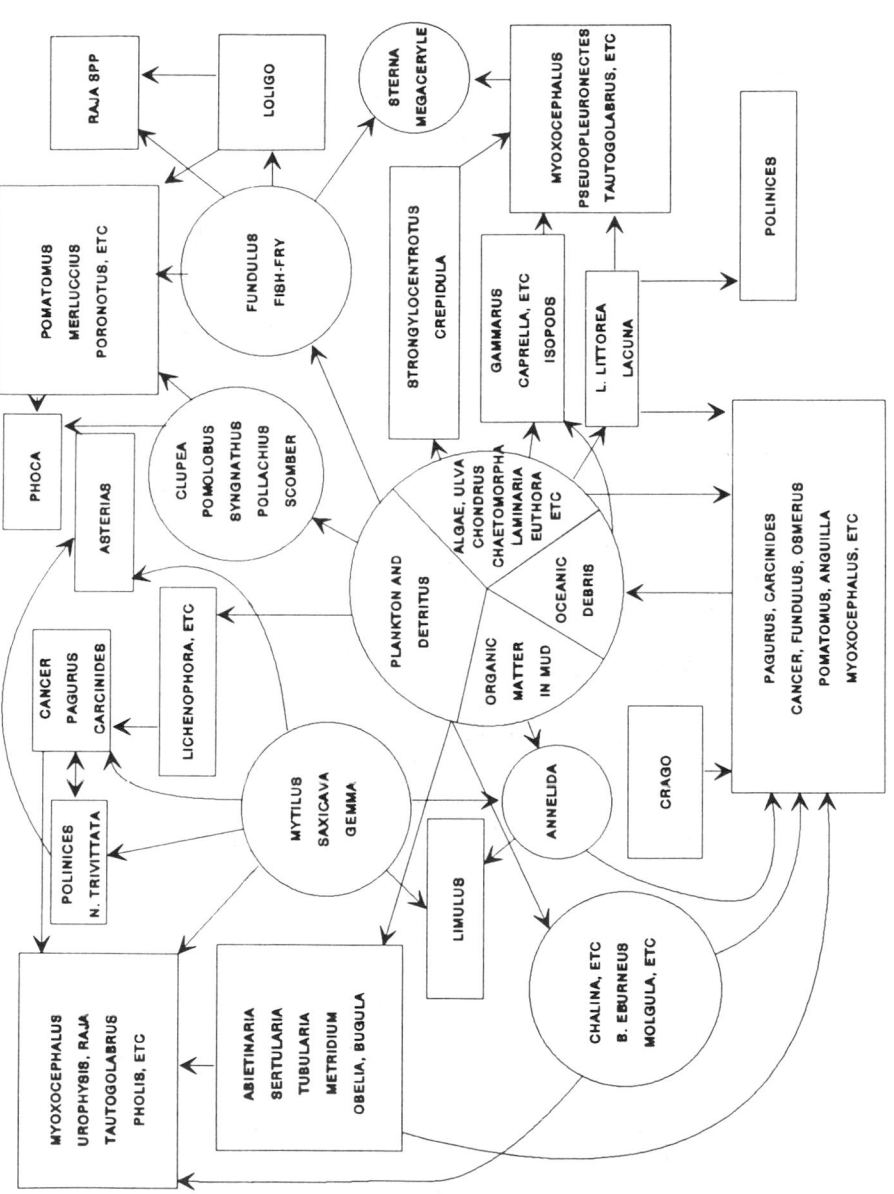

FIGURE 3.2. Food coactions of the subtidal *Laminaria–Cancer* faciation at Cape Ann, Massachusetts. (After "The marine communities of a tidal inlet at Cape Ann, Massachusetts: a study in bioecology" by R. W. Dexter, *Ecological Monograph*, 1947, **17**, 261–294. Copyright © 1947 by the Ecological Society of America. Reprinted by permission.)

connecting benthic, nektonic, and pelagic communities. Interrelationships of these various species are set forth in Figure 3.2.

Intertidal Areas

In the northern part of New England, precipitous, rocky shores are often present and form the hard substrates of the intertidal zone. As one proceeds southward and the topography of the landscape becomes less rugged, these rocky shores tend to be less steep. Here one also finds flats, which occupy the area between the subtidal zone and the saltwater marsh, and bars of various types. These bars and flats may be sandy, mud and sand, or mainly mud. Typically, the muddy flats and bars occur in the more sheltered areas and at or about the saltwater interface, that is, nearer the head of the estuary. As one progresses toward the mouth of the estuary, the sediments tend to become coarser.

The highest portion of the intertidal zone offers the harshest habitat and supports the fewest species. The species living in this region are exposed to longer periods of desiccation and greater temperature changes than are species in the other intertidal areas. The intertidal zone and the low tidal zone support more diverse fauna and flora. Species found in the low part of the intertidal and subtidal zones often are the same.

Rocky Shore Habitat.   The rocky shore habitats in New England generally consist of fairly steep cliffs or headlands with occasional ledges possessing tidal pools. These upper reaches of rocky, intertidal areas have the harshest environment because organisms are exposed to the drying air for the longest period of time. Because of this exposure, they are also subject to the greatest seasonal variation in temperatures. Summer high temperatures may be excess of 37 °C and winter temperatures can sink below -34 °C (personal communication, 1984, National Climatic Center, North Carolina).

Upper Intertidal.   In the upper intertidal area the following algae were found: *Ascophyllum nodosum, Fucus vericulosis, F. filiformis, Porphyra umbilicalis, Rhizoclonium tortuosum,* and *Enteromorpha minima.* The most common invertebrate was the barnacle, *Balanus balanoides.* For the most part, the populations of algae, as well as barnacles, were relatively spotty.

Mid Intertidal.   The mid-intertidal zone supported a much richer fauna and flora. Those algae found in the upper intertidal zone were also found in the intermediate intertidal zone. Growth of *Fucus vericulosus* and *F. filiformis* and *Ascophyllum nodosum* was usually more extensive in the middle intertidal zone. These algae formed a shelter for several species of invertebrates. The most common invertebrates were the barnacle, *Balanus balanoides,* and the mussel, *Mytilus edulis.* Common in this zone was the predator snail, *Thais lapillus.* Where wave shock is severe and the growth of algae sparse, this predator had little influence on community structure and fed only in crevices. In more sheltered areas, however, it fed on the surface of substrates and was an important factor in controlling the community's structure (Menge, 1978a).

The barnacle had the smallest populations under the canopies of *Fucus vesiculosus* and where it had to compete with the mussel, *Mytilus edulis.* The mussels seemed to exert a competitive dominance over the barnacles by covering available recruitment space, but they, too, were subject to heavy loss when winter storm waves removed dense patches in exposed communities. Dexter (1947) states that in Cape Ann estuary, the periwinkles, *Littorina littorea* and *L. obtusata*, were associated with the algae. Associated with the mussels, barnacles, and seaweeds on the rocks was the insect, *Anurida maritima*. Beneath the seaweeds and intermingled among them were the amphipod, *Gammarus lacusta*, and the coelenterate (hydroid), *Sertularia clava*. Crabs (*Neopanope* and *Cancer*) were found occasionally under loose rocks and among bunches of seaweed.

Lower Intertidal. The lower intertidal zone contained many species also found in the subtidal areas. The chief algae was *Chondrus crispus*, accompanied by *Chordaria flagelliformis*, *Ectocarpus littoralis*, *Fucus furcatus*, *Gigartina mammillosa*, *Halosaccion ramentaceum*, *Petalonia fascia*, *Ralfsia verucosa*, *Rhodymenia palmata*, *Scytosiphon lomentarius*, *Spongomorpha arcta*, *S. spinescens*, and *Ulva lactuca*.

Mussels seemed to dominate the low, rocky intertidal area exposed to wave shock, whereas the Irish moss, *Chondrus crispus*, dominated protected sites (Lubchenco and Menge, 1978). In and among the *Chondrus crispus* and *Ulva lactuca* were annelids belonging to the genus *Spriobis*, and bryozoans, *Gemellaria* and *Schizoporella*, which encrusted many of the rocks (Dexter, 1947).

Tide Pools. Tide pools on ledges of the rough, rocky shores generally had fauna and flora characteristic of the intertidal zone in which they were located. For example, in the lower tide pools, subtidal algae such as *Alaria esculenta*, *Corallina officinalis*, *Laminaria digitata*, *Melobesia lenormandi*, and *Saccoriza dermatodea* were found. Close to the subtidal area, tide pools contained invertebrate animals such as the anemone, *Metridium*; the periwinkle, *Littorina littorea*; many worms; and brittle stars, *Ophiopholis*, which lived on the bottom of the pool.

Algae that were found only in tide pools and not in other areas of the rocky habitat (except subtidally) were *Ceramium botryocarpum*, *Leathesia difformis*, *Rhizoclonium tortuosum*, *Spongomorpha hystrix*, and *Chaetomorpha melagonium*. Rarely, the algae, *Agrum turneri*, *Cladophora constricta*, and *Enteromorpha intestinalis*, were found in the tide pools (Dexter, 1947).

Predator–Prey Relationships. Lubchenco and Menge (1978) found that predation was the most important factor in maintaining community structure. *Asterias forbesi*, *A. vulgaris*, and *Thais lapillus* preyed upon the mussel, *Mytilus edulis*. The diet preferences of *Thais lapillus* and *Asterias vulgaris* are set forth in Table 3.2. The preferred prey was *Mytilus edulis*, which was, by far, the most abundant herbivore at both the sites studied.

Thais lapillus seemed to be the most important predator of the invertebrates in the mid-intertidal rocks of the New England coast (Menge 1978a). Predation intensity exerted by *Thais lapillus* did not seem to be dependent on its population size on rocky, intertidal community substrates. Six other factors seemed to be more important: prey abundance and productivity, other predators, canopy of

TABLE 3.2.   *Percent of Prey Species in the Diets of Predators in the Low Intertidal at Two New England Study Sites*

| | Percent in Diet at: | | |
| | Grindstone Neck | | Chamberlain: |
Prey Species	*Asterias vulgaris*[a]	*Thais lapillus*[b]	*Thais lapillus*[b]
Mytilus edulis (mussel)	47.3	96.6	89.1
Balanus balanoides (barnacle)	38.2	2.9	8.7
Lacuna vincta (gastropod)	7.0	0	0
Acmaea testudinalis (limpet)	1.6	0	0
Unidentified amphipod (crustacean)	1.0	0	0
Littorina obtusata (gastropod)	0.9	0	0
Margarites sp. (gastropod)	0.7	0	0
Thais lapillus (gastropod)	0.7	0.3	1.1
Littorina littorea (gastropod)	0.6	0	0
Saxicava sp. (bivalve)	0.6	0.3	1.1
Balanus crenatus (barnacle)	0.6	0	1
Asterias vulgaris (sea star)	0.4	0	0
Unidentifiable	0.4	0	0
Prey items eaten (N)	696	350	92
Species eaten (N)	12+	4	4

Source: (From "Community development and persistence in a low, rocky intertidal zone," by J. Lubchenco and B. A. Menge, *Ecological Monograph*, 1978, **48**, 67–94. Copyright © 1978 by Ecological Society of America. Reprinted with permission.)

[a]Data from summers and autumns 1971–1974.

[b]Data from summers 1972–1974.

[c]Data from summer 1973.

algae, wave shock, desiccation stress, and snail phenotype (Menge, 1978a). It would appear that the snail's predation was enhanced by a thick algal canopy, freedom from desiccation, and low wave shock. There appeared to be an inherited difference in the predatorial effectiveness of the snail. Dexter (1974) outlined the food web relationships of this type of biome at low and high tides (Figure 3.3).

At sheltered sites, *Littorina littorea*, the periwinkle, was effective in controlling the ephemeral abundance of algae but had little or no effect on *Chondrus crispus*. *Littorina* did not seem to graze on *Chondrus crispus*; thus it limited the competing algae but not *Chondrus* itself. In laboratory experiments (Table 3.3) this snail strongly preferred ephemeral algae, such as the green algae, *Enteromorpha*, *Spongomorpha*, *Ulva*, and *Monostroma*; the brown algae, *Petalonia* and *Scytosiphon*; and the red algae, *Ceramium* and *Porphyra*. Limpets and sea urchins had a negligible role in limiting *Chondrus*. On exposed sites, *Littorina littorea* was less abundant and thus the seasonally abundant algae could compete more effectively against *Chondrus*. Also on exposed sites, predators did not seem to be able to control *Mytilus* very well, so it was often almost completely dominant.

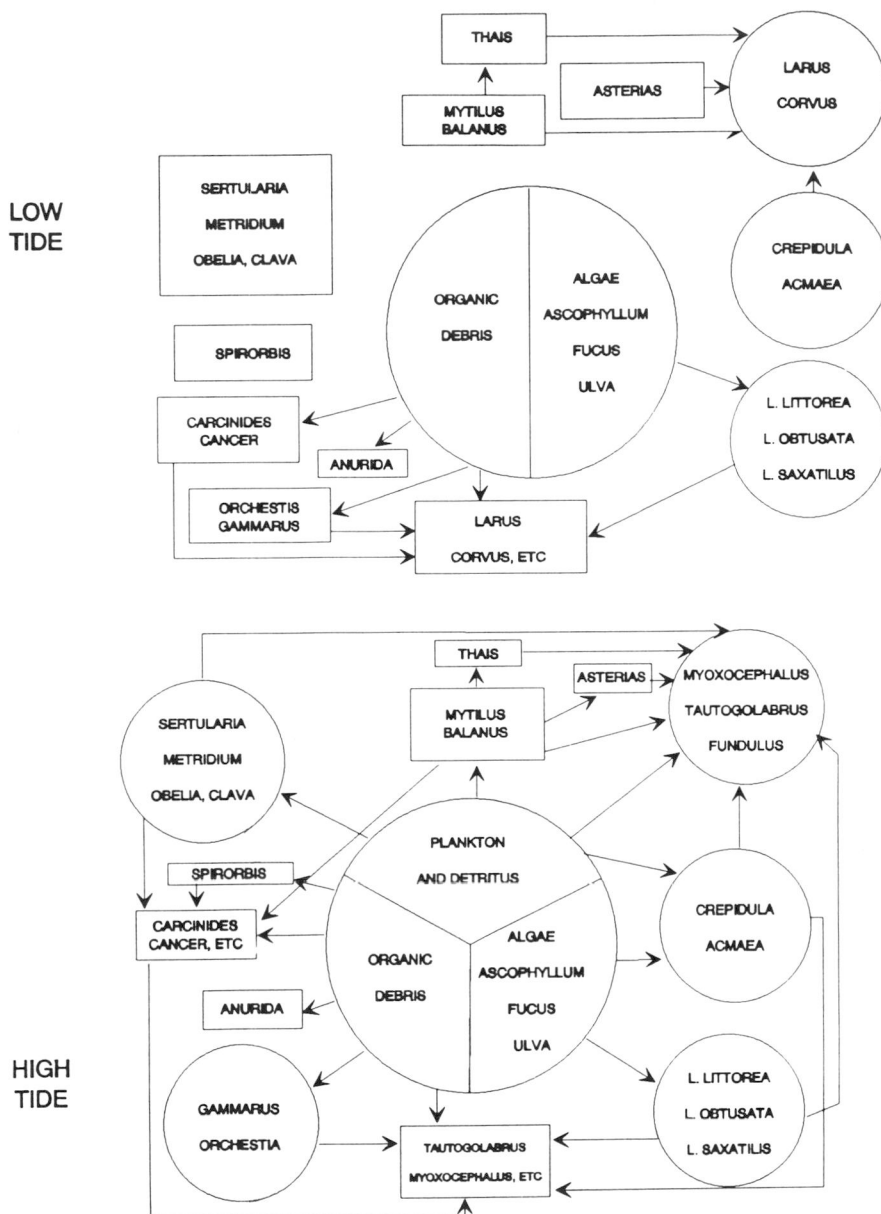

FIGURE 3.3.   Food coactions of the *Balanus–Mytilus–Littorina* biome. (After "The marine communities of a tidal inlet at Cape Ann, Massachusetts: a study in bioecology" by R. W. Dexter, *Ecological Monograph*, 1947, **17**, 261–294. Copyright © 1947 by the Ecological Society of America. Reprinted by permission.)

TABLE 3.3. *Food Preferences of Littorina littorea*[a]

Preference Ranking	Chlorophyceae (Greens)	Phaeophyceae (Browns)	Rhodophyceae (Reds)
High	*Cladophora* *Enteromorpha* *Monostroma* *Spongomorpha* *Ulothrix–Urospora* *Ulva*	*Ectocarpus–Pylaiella* *Elachistea* *Petalonia* *Scytosiphon*	*Ceramium* *Porphyra*
Medium	*Rhizoclonium*	*Dictyosiphon*	*Asparagopsis* *Cystoclonium* *Dumontia* *Halosaccion* *Phycodrys* *Polysiphonia flexicaulis* *P. lanosa*
Low	*Chaetomorpha* *Codium*	*Agarum* *Ascophyllum* *Chorda* *Chordaria* *Desmarestia* *Fucus* *Laminaria* *Ralfsia* *Saccorhiza*	*Ahnfeltia* *Chondrus* *Euthora* *Gigartina* *Polyides* *Rhodymenia*

Source: After Lubchenco (1978).

[a] Preferences were determined by laboratory two-way choice experiments. Only large individuals of any algal species were used. A group of 20–40 snails was placed in the middle of the bottom of a filled 20-gal aquarium (standing new seawater) surrounded by equal amounts of two species of algae, with the same species on opposing sides. The probability of any snail's contacting species 1 was equal to that of its contacting species 2. These periwinkles did not appear to detect food at a distance, but relied on tactile–chemical methods once plants were contacted. Once a snail contacted a piece of alga it would either move away or remain there and feed. The numbers of snails on the two species of algae were compared using χ^2 after 30–90 min. All large algae had had micro- and macroscopic epiphytic algae removed from them. Results were usually clear-cut and are arranged here in three preference categories. Most experiments were repeated at least once, rotating positions of algae and using a new group of snails.

In the low intertidal zone, *Mytilus*, *Chondrus*, and *Balanus* competed for space, with *Mytilus edulis* dominating exposed sites and *Chondrus crispus* dominating the other sites. At exposed sites in this zone, *Thais* was fairly common, whereas sea stars were more common in the protected areas (Lubchenco and Menge, 1978).

Intertidal Flats. Tides leave intertidal flats exposed for different lengths of time. Organisms that live in the flats are thus exposed to differing temperatures, water exchange rates, and desiccation, which is largely determined by the exposure time and water exchange. The exchange of water is largely determined by the vertical amplitude of the tide and the tidal cycle.

The strength of current influences the types of sediments that compose the flat. Near or at the fresh water–salt water interface in an estuary, the extremes of salinity are greatest; near the mouth of the estuary, the exposure time and scouring effects may be most important in determining the habitats of organisms.

Typically, every estuary supports a great variety of species. Many species are able to withstand wide changes in environmental factors. Others are more specifically adapted to certain types of habitats and certain degrees of salinity. In this discussion we describe the communities associated with sandy flats and bars of various types, sandy-mud communities, and communities typical of true mud habitats.

Sandy Flats.   On bars where the scouring effect is severe, the few species that can survive are surf clams and some kinds of crustacea living in among the sand grains. The dominant species of amphipod in the most exposed habitats was found to be *Amphiporeia virginiana* (Croker et al., 1975). In the moderately exposed habitats where the scouring effect was not as great, the dominants were *Psammonyx nobilis* and *Acanthohaustorius millsi*. In the least exposed habitats, the dominant species was *Haustorius canadensis*. In the sandy shores of New Hampshire and southern Maine, burrowing amphipods dominate the communities of moderately exposed intertidal shores. The dominant *Amphiporeia virginiana* was also abundant on barrier beaches. In relatively exposed sheltered habitats were *Acanthaustorius millsi, Oxyurostylis smithii, Cheridotea caeca, Scolelipis squamata, Protohaustorius deichmannae, Tellina agilis,* and *Gemma gemma.* The zonation of these organisms is set forth in Figure 3.4 (Croker et al., 1975).

In the Barnstable beaches (Massachusetts), which are high-exchange sandy beaches, Sanders et al. (1962) found 82 species of invertebrates. The species list is composed of Polychaeta (34%), Crustacea (23%), and Mollusca (23%), with all other groups represented in the remaining 20%. Hanks (1956), studying Sheepscot Bay, a Maine estuary, found that 47% of the species are Polychaeta, 32% Mollusca, and 11% Crustacea; all other groups make up about 10% of the fauna.

The density of organisms on the intertidal, sandy flats in Barnstable Harbor was very high, varying from 7000 to $35,000 \, \text{m}^{-2}$. The most common species were the small pea clam, *Gemma gemma,* and polychaete annelids (*Clymenella torquata* and *Glycera dibranchiata*). The density of the small pea clam (*Gemma gemma*) averaged about $146,000 \, \text{m}^{-2}$, with a maximum of $331,000 \, \text{m}^{-2}$.

The infauna were important in sorting sediments on the Barnstable flats (Rhoads, 1967). *Clymenella torquata* lived in a vertical tube of agglutinated sand grains approximately 20 cm long. The worm fed primarily on medium-sized particles ingested at the lower end of the tube. The sediment particles moved through the gut vertically and were ejected on the sediment surface as uncompact feces of well-sorted sand grains. The worm rejected particles too large for ingestion and these remained at the lower end of the tube. Separation of the grains of the sediment by biological processes resulted in a biogenic graded bedding. A diagram of this type of sorting is showing in Figure 3.5.

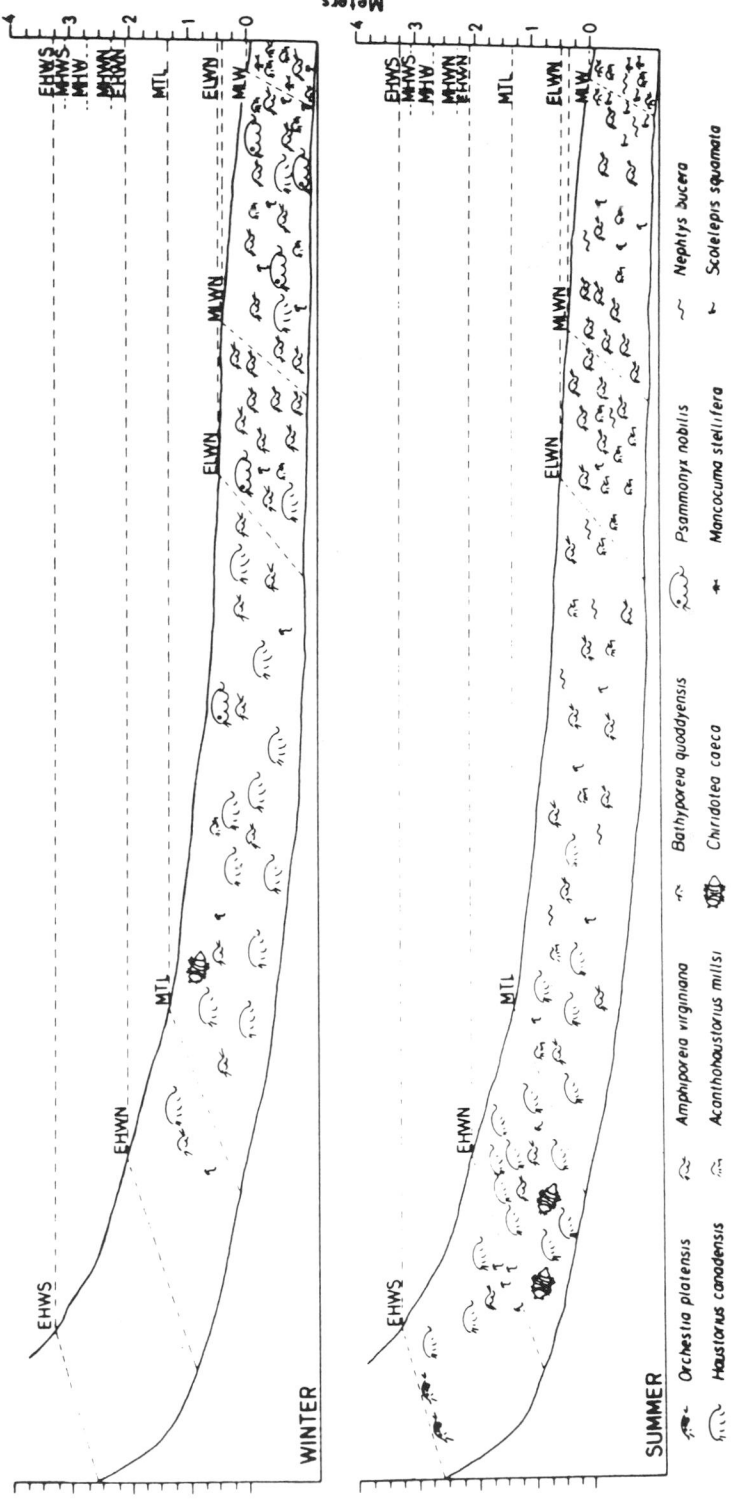

FIGURE 3.4. Intertidal zonation of a typical community in moderately exposed New England sand beaches during winter and summer. The vertical dimension is exaggerated, and the burrowing depth of species is not considered. (From Croker et al., 1975. Research Journals, National Research Council of Canada.)

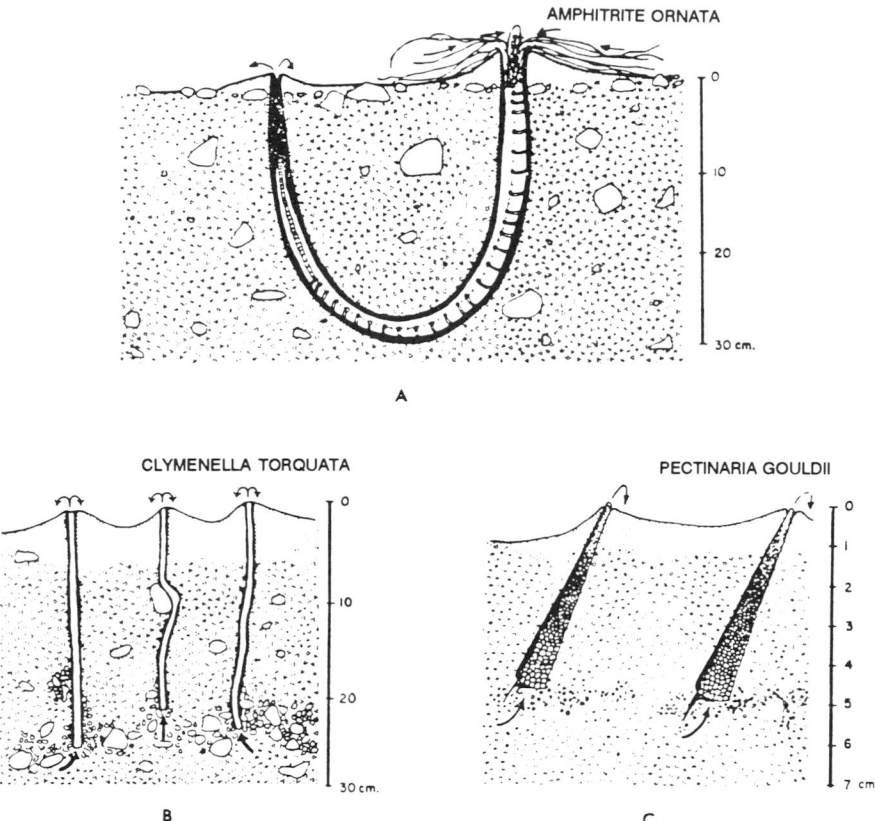

FIGURE 3.5. Reworking of intertidal sediments by three polychaete species in Barnstable Harbor, Massachusetts. (*A*) Sediment sorting by *Amphitrite ornata*. Grooved ciliated tentacles of *A. ornata* collect and transport sediment 1 mm and less in size to the mouth. Noningested (manipulated) sediment remains as a conical deposit around the anterior opening of the U-shaped mud tube. Egested sediment surrounds the anal end of the tube. (*B*) Sediment sorting by *Clymenella torquata*. The anterior end of the agglutinated sand tube is located 20 to 30 cm below the sediment surface. *Clymenella* ingests sediment 1 mm or less in size and egests this fraction at the sediment surface. Particles too large for ingestion remain as a coarse layer at the feeding depth. This vertical size sorting produces biogenic graded bedding. (*C*) Sediment sorting by *Pectinari gouldii*. The conical agglutinated sand tube of *P. gouldii* is capable of being moved through the sediment as *Pectinaria* feeds. Ingestion of particles smaller than 1 mm takes place at a depth of 5 to 6 cm. Ingested and manipulated sediment is passed to the surface. Detritus larger than 1 mm remains at a depth of 5 to 6 cm. *Pectinaria* is capable of producing biogenically graded deposits. (From Rhoads, 1967.)

Pectinaria gouldii also formed a tube of agglutinated sand grains that the worm was capable of moving through the sediment. The tube was conical in shape and lay at a slight angle to the surface during feeding. *Pectinaria* reworked most of the sediment by passing particles over the dorsal surface of its bed within the tube. The sediment (pseudofeces) had a texture very similar to sediments that pass through the gut.

The biogenic reworking of intertidal sediment extended from the surface to a depth of about 30 cm. Most biogenic activity took place in the upper 2 to 3 cm of sediment, and the subtidal community was restricted to a depth of about 10 cm. Sediment may have been recycled several times a year by the infaunal deposit feeders living in the shallow subtidal areas. If surface predator activity was high, the upper 10 cm may have been reworked extensively over a period of 2 months. Complete reworking of the sediments by polychaetes to a depth of 30 cm was estimated to require several months or years. The biogenic reworking of a habitat depended on the organisms present, their numbers, and the rate at which they recycle materials (Rhoads, 1967).

Gemma gemma is an important food for the nemertean, *Cerebratulus lactues*, polychaete worms (*Nereis virens, Diopatra cuprea, Amphitrite ornata,* and *Lepto-synapta inhaerens*), and shrimp, *Crangon septemspinosa*. These organisms are in turn eaten by ducks. Other foods of these sandy flat organisms were detritus, diatoms, and some crustaceans and small molluscs. A study by Sanders et al. (1962) lists the organisms found in the intestines of the various species from these flats (Table 3.4).

Dexter (1947) described the communities of organisms in the sandy flat habitat at Cape Ann, Massachusetts. He found a mixture of subtidal and interdidal organisms in the lowest water levels of the sandy beaches. Under small stones the annelid, *Lepidonotus*, and nudibranchs, *Aeolis* and *Onchidoris*, were found. The lower part of the zone, which is exposed at extremely low tide, was occupied by snails, *Nassarius trivittata*; bivalves, *Mulinia* and *Siliqua*; and echinoderms, *Strongylocentrotus* and *Echinarachnius*.

Penetrating the sand were the annelids, *Lumbrineris, Clymenella, Nereis,* and *Glycera*, and the bivalves, *Ensis* and *Solemya*. While most of these species were restricted to the lower level, *Ensis* may extend upward to almost midpoint on the shore, and *Lumbrineris* and *Nereis* may range up to the highest point on the bars and also on the beaches. The distribution of the soft-shelled clam, *Mya arenaria*, found on both the sandy and muddy flats, extended several inches above spring low-water line to the top of the bars, and sometimes to the level of marshlands on the beaches and flats. *Macoma*, which was more characteristic of the mud flats, had much the same limits but was found in smaller numbers. *Gemma gemma* could be spotted over the entire bar or flat, but reached greatest concentration under and among the fronds of *Chaetomorpha*, a green alga often dropped onto the flats by the receding tide.

Sandy-Mud Flats. *Littorina littorea* was found at almost any level, especially among pebbles or fragments of seaweed that have been cast on the beach. The snail may have buried itself when the tide receded, as did the amphipod, *Talorchestia*. When the flat is covered with water, sea anemones and sea cucumbers (*Leptosynapta* sp.) extend their tentacles, and certain of the hemi-chordate worms (*Balanoglossus* or *Saccoglossus*) were found building up fecal mounds. Moving over the surface in search of food on these sandy, muddy flats were various horseshoe crabs, rays, flounder, whelks, and snails, which were even more common in the submerged areas (Gray, 1974).

TABLE 3.4. *Some Benthic Invertebrates of Barnstable Harbor, Massachusetts, with Stomach Content Data*

Species	Number of Individuals	Stomach Content
Nemertinea		
Amphiporus sp.	2	Sand, benthic diatoms
	7	Empty
Cerebratulus lacteus	1	Setae of polychaete, *Gemma* shells, *Hydrobia*, *Odostomia*, young *Mytilis*, filamentous algae, diatoms, detritus sand
	1	Five *Hydrobia*, many polychaete setae, ostracod, sand
Micrura leidyi	1	Polychaete setae, sand
	3	Empty
Polychaeta		
Eteone heteropoda	1	Few diatoms, detritus, sand
	1	Few diatoms, strands of filamentous algae, sand
	1	Diatoms, sand
	1	Detritus, sand
	2	Empty
Nereis caudata	1	Sand, detritus
	2	Sand, detritus, diatoms
	4	Sand, diatoms
Nereis virens	1	Sand, diatoms, detritus, small *Gemma*, filamentous algae
Glycera dibranchiata	1	Sand, many bundles of polychaete setae
	1	Sand
	17	Empty
Lumbrinereis tenuis	1	Sand, diatoms
	2	Sand, diatoms, detritus
	1	Empty
Drilonereis longa	1	Sand, diatoms, filamentous algae
	1	Empty
Diapatra cuprea	1	Sand, *Gemma*, *Hydrobia*, much filamentous algae (*Ulva*), detritus, crustacean setae, and spines
	1	Sand, *Gemma*, 2 *Hydrobia*, much filamentous algae (*Ulva*), detritus
	1	Sand, filamentous and thallose algae, 2 *Gemma*, 4 *Hydrobia*
	1	Sand, thallose algae, diatoms, *Gemma*
	2	Sand, thallose algae, diatoms
Streblospio benedicti	5	Sand, detritus
	4	Sand, diatoms
	3	Sand, diatoms, detritus
	1	Detritus, diatoms
	2	Empty
Pygospio elegans	2	Sand, diatoms
	8	Sand
	8	Empty

TABLE 3.4.   (*Continued*)

Species	Number of Individuals	Stomach Content
Nerinides agilis	2	Sand, diatoms
	2	Sand
	13	Empty
Polydora ligni	2	Sand, diatoms
Spio setosa	1	Sand, many diatoms, filamentous algae, detritus, nematode
	1	Sand, detritus, unidentified disclike objects
Heteromastus filiformis	2	Sand, detritus
	2	Sand, detritus, diatoms
	1	Sand, diatoms
	5	Sand
Tharyx sp.	2	Sand, diatoms
	2	Sand
	3	Empty
Scolopos robustus	1	Sand, diatoms
	1	Detritus, diatoms
Scolopos fragilis	2	Sand, diatoms, detritus
	2	Sand, diatoms, detritus, macroalgae, possible animal material
Clymenella torquata	3	Sand, detritus, diatoms
	3	Sand, deritus
	3	Sand, detritus, disclike objects
	2	Sand
	9	Empty
Amphitrite ornata	1	Sand, detritus, diatoms, *Gemma*, Eteone
	2	Sand, detritus, diatoms, *Gemma*
	1	Sand, detritus, diatoms
Echinodermata		
Leptosynapta inhaerens	1	Sand, detritus, diatoms
	2	Sand, detritus
	1	Sand, detritus, diatoms, 1 *Gemma*
	1	Sand, detritus, 3 *Gemma*, 1 ostracod
	1	Sand, detritus, 3 young *Gemma*, 1 adult *Gemma*, 2 *Hydrobia*, crustacean appendage, broken shells, diatoms, disclike objects
Enteropneusta		
Saccoglossus kowalevskii	2	Sand, detritus, diatoms
	1	Sand
	4	Empty
Mollusca		
Gemma gemma	17	Empty
Mya arenaria	2	Empty
Ensis directus	1	Empty
Tellina agilis	1	Sand, diatoms, detritus
	1	Sand, diatoms
	1	Diatoms

Continued

TABLE 3.4.   (*Continued*)

Species	Number of Individuals	Stomach Content
Aligena elevata	6	Sand, diatoms, unicellular algae
	1	Sand, diatoms
	1	Sand
	2	Empty
Hydrobia minuta	1	Diatoms
	1	Empty
Retusa pertenius	4	Sand
	1	Empty
Polynices duplicata	1	Empty
Crustacea		
Edotea montosa	1	Diatoms, filamentous and thallose algae, ostracod
	1	Few polychaete seta
	4	Empty
Listriella clymenellae	4	Empty
Carinogammarus mucronotus	1	Sand, diatoms, detritus, macroalgae
	1	Sand, diatoms, detritus
	1	Empty
Crago septemspinosus	1	Sand, detritus, diatoms
	1	Sand, detritus, ostracods, small crustacean limb
	1	Sand, diatoms, ostracods, nematodes, many crustacean limbs, mollusc shells (?*Gemma*)
	1	Sand, *Gemma* shells, many diatoms, much green algae, nematodes, small crustacean fragments
	1	Sand, broken shells, 2 *Gemma*, detritus, nematodes, diatoms, much thallose algae
Eupagurus longicarpus	1	Sand, much filamentous algae of various spp., few diatoms

Source: Sanders et al. (1962).

Dexter (1947) found that the most common organism on this sandy-mud bar was the soft-shelled clam, *Mya arenaria*. Less common was the polychaete worm, *Nereis pelagica*; the bivalve, *Macoma balthica*; and the annelid, *Clymenella torquata*.

Mud Flats.   Usually, the mud flats are farther up the estuary than the sand flats and contain a great deal more organic matter than the sand flats. In general, those organisms that live in the sand or mud are subject to much less temperature variation than those that live on the surface of the flats. For example, Gray (1961) found that the midday temperature in tidal pools, on a Beaufort, South Carolina flat, registered 35 °C; the maximum temperature in 12 *Chaetopterus* worm tubes was only 29 °C.

The food webs found in these habitats are set forth in Figure 3.6. The numbers

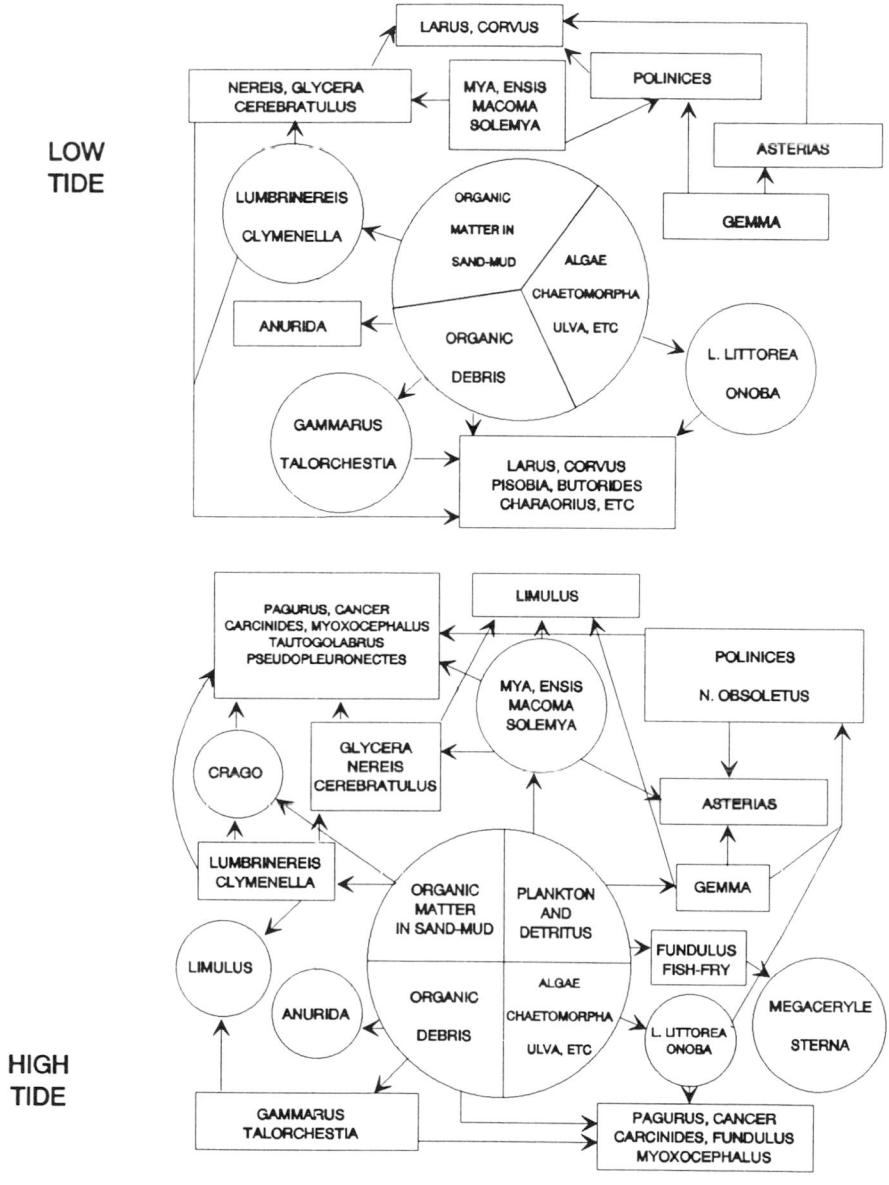

FIGURE 3.6. Food coactions at the *Mya–Nereis pelagica* biome of intertidal sediments. (After "The marine communities of a tidal inlet at Cape Ann, Massachusetts: a study in bioecology" by R. W. Dexter, *Ecological Monograph*, 1947, **17**, 261–294. Copyright © 1947 by the Ecological Society of America. Reprinted by permission.)

of species were sometimes far less on the muddy flats due to the presence of hydrogen sulfide, a result of anaerobic activity in this type of habitat. One of the more common species was *Ilyanassa obsoleta*. *Macoma* tended to be more common in the mud habitats that were less consolidated. One of the commoner polychaetes in the sandy-mud flats was *Amphitrite*, which built its tube of mud. Also, in this muddy habitat the common sea anemone, *Cerianthiopsis*, secreted a several-layered, parchment-like tube that extended 45 to 50 cm into the mud. The short razor clam, *Tagelus*, was found abundantly in the mud, but its population decreased in the transition zone of sandy mud and muddy sand. The hard-shelled clam, *Mercenaria*, was common in mud and in the transition zones and was less common in sand. The sea cucumber, *Thyone*, was often very abundant in the mud (Gray, 1974).

Thorson (1957) has pointed out that the more stable benthic communities had a number of long-lived invertebrates that did not have pelagic larvae. Gray (1974) points out that those sessile organisms that burrow deeply, such as the soft-shelled clam, *Mya arenaria*, and the polychaete worm, *Chaetopterus*, contributed more stability to the community than did the shallow burrowers, such as *Echinocardium*, *Mercenaria*, and *Nucula*.

Salt Marshes

Salt marshes are often not as well developed in New England estuaries as they are in the estuaries of more southerly states. In New England, these marshes typically occur behind barrier islands as described in Chapter 2. In defining the marshes in an estuary we usually think of two types: the low marsh, which is regularly flooded, and the high marsh, which is irregularly flooded.

In New England, the salt marsh is divided into three or four zones. The intertidal zone or lower marsh is next to the estuary, bay, or tidal creek. *Spartina alterniflora* is the dominant species. The high marsh is dominated by *S. patens*, with a mixture of *Distichlis spicata* and occasional patches of the shrub, *Iva frutescens*, and various forbes. In the *S. patens* zones and in the higher marsh are often pure stands of *Juncas gerardi*.

Low Marshes. The low marsh is covered with solid stands of the tall *Spartina alterniflora*. Intermixed on the stems of this grass are many algae, particularly diatoms. Blue-green algae common in these habitats were *Microcoleus chthonoplastes*, *Oscillatoria subuliformis*, *O. amphibia*, *Schizothrix calcicola*, *Lyngbya lutea*, *L. estuarii*, and *Hydrocoleum lyngbyaceum*. At the base of *Spartina* stems are the macroalgae such as the brown alga, *Fucus vesiculosus*, and the variety *spiralis*, *Ascophyllum nodosum*, and sometimes *A. nodosum* f. *scorpiodes*. An example of the algae in Ipswich salt marsh habitats (Massachusetts) is given in Table 3.5 (Webber and Wilce, 1971).

Feeding upon epiphytes on these macroalgae or on the algae themselves are the snails, *Littorina littorea* and *L. obtusata*. The amphipod, *Gammarus lacustris*, lived under these algae in holes in the banks. Insects were common in this marsh around the base of *Spartina*, particularly the springtail, *Anurida maitina*; the horsefly, *Tabanus nigrovittatus*; mosquitos; and midge larvae (Dexter, 1947). Mussels were often found in this habitat, particularly the rib mussel, *Brachidontes demissus*, which occurred half embedded and half exposed on the banks. The blue mussel, *Mytilus* sp., often occurred on solid substrate, attached by byssus threads. The barnacle, *Balanus balanoides*, was often present adhering to mussels,

TABLE 3.5. *Habitats of Algae in Ipswich Salt Marsh (Massachusetts)*

Algae	Habitats
Chlorophyta	
Codiolum gregarium var. *intermedius*	Endophytic in *Spartina* and *Glaux maritima* leaves
Chlorochytrium moorei	Endophytic in *Enteromorpha flexuosa* ssp. *paradoxa*
C. grande	In leaves of *Spartina patens*
Ulothrix flacca	Attached to wood pilings, marsh grasses, and littoreal fucoid algae
Ulothrix pseudoflacca	Mixed with *U. flacca*
Ulothrix subflaccida	Mixed with *U. flacca* and *U. pseudoflacca*
Pseudoendoclonium submarinum	From supralittoral wood pilings
Percursaria percursa	Most abundant along the seaward marsh edge, entangled with *Rhizoclonium riparium* in the *Spartinetum alternifloretum* zone
Capsosiphon fulvescens (1 mm × 10 cm)	Upper littoral marsh depression
Capsosiphon fulvescens (24–68 μm × 1 cm)	Small stones at the extreme head of the marsh
Enteromorpha ahlneriana (type II)	In the *Enteromorpha facies*
Enteromorpha ahlneriana (type III)	Sublittoral
Enteromorpha clathrata	Attached to stones and *Fucus visiculosus* in sublittoral
E. intestinalia (small plants 7 cm)	In *Enteromorpha facies*
E. intestinalia (large plants to 50 cm)	Stones and *Ruppia maritima*
E. linza var. *linza*	Upper sublittoral, small stones
E. linza var. *oblanceolata*	Upper sublittoral, small stones
E. flexuosa ssp. *flexuosa*	Stones and *Fucus vesiculosus*
E. flexuosa ssp. *paradoxa*	*Enteromorpha facies*
E. flexuosa ssp. *filifera*	Submerged rocks and wood, sublittoral stones
Ulvaria oxysperma (small plants)	At seaward marsh edge
Ulvaria oxysperma (larger plants)	Wood pilings and small stones
Kornmannia leptoderma	Epilithic and epiphytic on algae
Ulva gigantea	Epilithic in sublittoral
U. rigida	On submerged rocks and woodwork
Chaetomorpha linum	Epilithic in sublittoral
Rhizoclonium riparium (three forms)	From *Spartina alterniflora* through the *Juncus gerardi* zones
Cladophora albida	Epilithic in the sublittoral
C. sericea	Midlittoral mud surfaces
C. vagabunda	Drainage ditch
Bryopsis plumosa	Submerged rocks and wood
Phaeophyta	
Ecotocarpus confervoides v. *confervoides*	Epiphyte on *Fucus vesiculosus*
E. confervoides var. *arcta*	On debris in *Entermorpha facies*
E. confervoides var. *siliculosus*	Epiphytic on coarse algae
E. confervoides var. *desycarpus*	Epiphytic on *Ruppia maritima*
Giffordia sandriana	Epiphytic of *Fucus vesiculosus*
Pylaiella littoralis (highly branched)	Epiphytic on *F. vesiculosus*, sublittoral zone

Continued

TABLE 3.5. (*Continued*)

Algae	Habitats
Pylaiella littoralis (little branched)	Plant debris in *Enteromorpha facies*
Porterinema fluviatile	Epilithic on small stones
Ralfsia clavata	Rocks in the sublittoral zone
R. varucosa	Rocks in the sublittoral zone
Petroderma maculiforme	Epilithic on *Balanus* in upper sublittoral
Hyrionema aecidioides	Endophytic in worn tips of *Daminaria saccharina*
Petalonia fascia	Dominant alga in sublittoral and lower littora
Scytosiphon lomentaria	Dominant in littoral and sublittoral
Dictyosiphon chordaria	Epilithic in sublittoral
Chorda filum	Rocks and shells in sublittoral
Laminaria saccharina	Rocks, shells, and wooden pilings, sublittoral
Fucus distichus ssp. *evanescens*	Littoral–sublittoral interface, on large rocks
Fucus vesiculosus	Epilithic in sublittoral and littoral, major macroscopic alga of area
Ascophyllum nodosum	Epilithic in sublittoral and littoral
Rhodophyta	
Erythrotrichea carnea	Epiphytic on *Ceramium*, *Chondrus*, and *Polysiphonia*
Goniotrichum alsidii	Epiphytic on *Ceramium*, *Polysiphonia*, and *Ascophyllum*
Porphyra umbilicalis	Epilithic at low-tide level
Dumontia incrassata	Rocks in sublittoral zone
Hildenbrandia protytypus	Epilithic at low-tide level
Gloiosiphonia capillaria	Sublittoral
Eutnora cristata	Washed ashore from river
Agardhiella tenera	Epilithic in sublittoral zone
Gracilaria varrucosa	Epilithic in sublittoral zone
G. foliifera	Epilithic in sublittoral zone
Chondrus crispus	Sublittoral zone
Halosaccion ramentaceum	Sublittoral zone
Trailliella intricata	Sublittoral zone
Antit amnion cruciatum	Entangled in *Agardhiella*
Ceramium diaphanum	Epilithic in sublittoral zone
C. fasticiatum	Epilithic in sublittoral zone
C. rubrum	Epilithic, and epiphytic on *Gracilaria foliifera*
C. rubriforma	Epilithic in sublittoral
Ptilota serrata	Washed ashore
Phycodrys rubens	Washed ashore
Polysiphonia flexicaulis	Epilithic in sublittoral
P. urceolata	Epilithic on small stones
P. denadata	Epilithic in sublittoral zone
P. nigra	Epilithic in sublittoral

TABLE 3.5. (*Continued*)

Algae	Habitats
Chrysophyta	
Xanthophyceae	
Vaucheria compacta	Carpeting of mud and creek banks
V. arcasonensis	Mats at bases of Spartina patens
V. intermedia	At seaward edges of marsh and in
	V. arcasonensis
Dinophyceae [sic]	
Urococcus foslieanus	On Spartina debris
Chrysophyceae	
Ruttnera maritima	Soil beneath Spartina

Source: After Webber and Wilce (1971).

rocks, or plant stems, and occasionally to macroalgae or the marsh bank itself. The gastropod, *Nassarius obsoletus*, often penetrated the lower edges of this marsh community in the muddy sediment. Ranging over the surface of the marsh area were hermit crabs; the green crab, *Carcinides maenas*; and the rock crab, *Cancer irroratus*. Small minnows and *Fundulus heteroclitus*, as well as various fish fry, were often found feeding on the mud flat algae, on epiphytes of the macroscopic algae, and on smaller algae on the base of the *Spartina*. When the tide receded, many of these species moved off the mud banks or into the sediments, and the only active fauna left were snails, such as *Littorina littorea*, spider mites, and insects. Shorebirds and herons often came to feed on the exposed marsh. The food web of species living on the marsh has been roughly outlined by Dexter (1947) and is given in Figure 3.7.

High Marshes. The high marshes usually slope so gently that they are an almost level expanse. They occur between the mean high-water line, where the low marsh ends, and the spring high-water line and are formed from peaty material and the periodic deposition of debris.

The most common plant species in this region was *Spartina patens*, which may be interspersed with *Distichlis spicata* and species of *Salicornia*. *Calothrix confervicola* often formed epiphytic tufts on the leaves of dense stands of *Spartina patens* (Webber, 1967). During the cooler, damper months of autumn, winter, and spring, blue-black mounds of *Rivularia nitida* sometimes grew on the soil under stands of this grass.

Beyond the *S. patens* and at normal high tide, *Juncas gerardi* (black grass) forms pure stands. The limit of the tidal growth in the upper portions of the marsh will often be marked with *Panicum virgatum* and *Iva frutescens* along with other species. Higher plants that may be found in this area of the upper edges of the marsh, which is only inundated with spring tides, include sea lavender (*Limonium carolinianum*), aster sp., and aloe grass (*Triglochin maritima*).

One of the most ambitious studies of nutrient dynamics in salt marshes was carried out in Great Sippewissett Marsh in Massachusetts. As shown by these

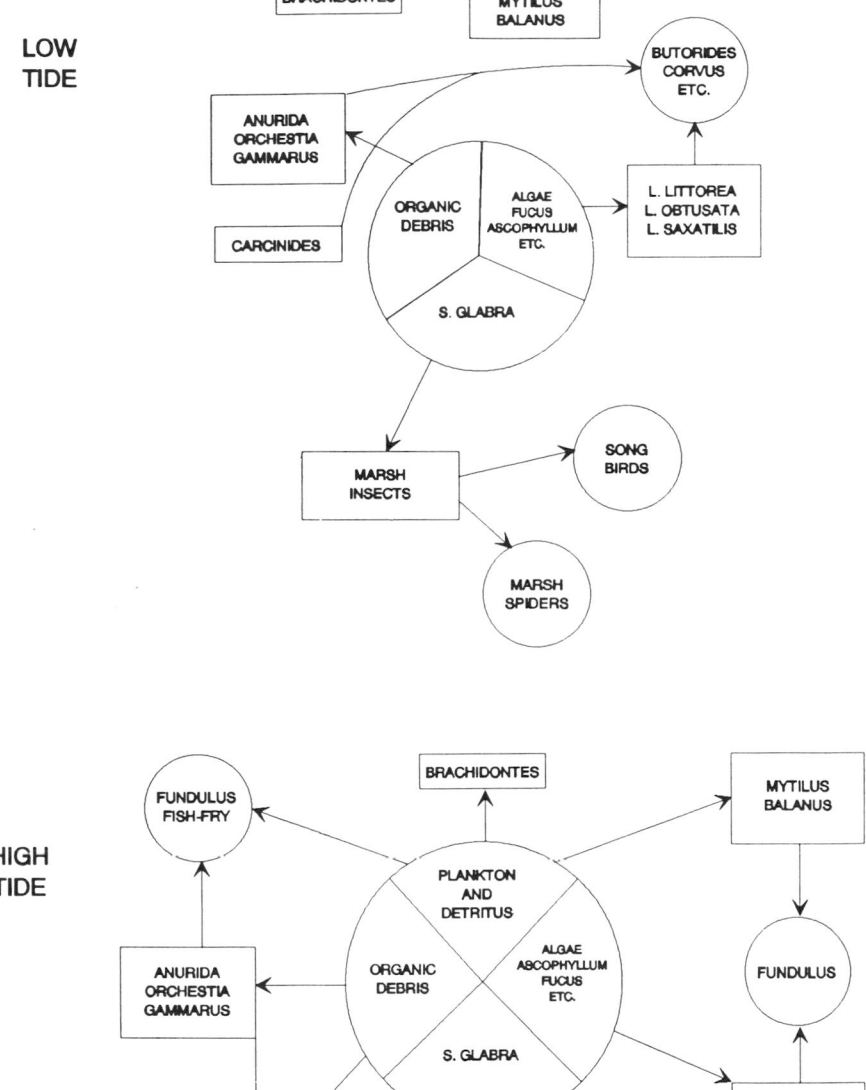

FIGURE 3.7.   Food coactions of the *Spartina glabra–Littorina sacatilis–Brachidontes* associations of low marshes. (After "The marine communities of a tidal inlet at Cape Ann, Massachusetts: a study in bioecology" by R. W. Dexter, *Ecological Monograph*, 1947, **17**, 261–294. Copyight © 1947 by the Ecological Society of America. Reprinted by permission.)

studies, nitrogen from groundwater is a primary source of nitrates. Also important is nitrogen from tidal exchanges. These two sources represent the major fluxes of nitrogens in the salt marsh. Precipitation contributes significantly less nitrogen, mostly as N as NO_3 and dissolved organic nitrogen (DON). Tidal exchange resulted in a net export of nitrogen, mostly in the form of DON. Nitrogen fixation by bacteria is significant in a marsh, whereas blue-green algae fixation is much less. Denitrification is common in the salt marsh, particularly in muddy creek bottoms and in the short *Spartina* marsh.

The beach fly (*Orchestia platensis*) and the isopod (*Philoscia vittata*) were common in the high marshes. Also found were the horsefly, midges, and the blackfly, *Coelopa frigida*. Among the dead *Spartina*, and around the roots of the living plants, were found the marsh snails, *Elampus bidentatus, Littorina littorea*, and *L. saxatilis*.

Nutrient Cycling. Marshlands are very important in the nutrient cycling of the estuary. During the summer when growth is rapid, the marshlands import nutrients, thereby reducing the concentration in tidal water. However, later in the summer there is an export of particulate nitrogen, ammonia, dissolved organic nitrogen, and carbon and phosphorus in the form of plant debris. Exports from the marsh contribute substantially to the nutrient supply of coastal waters.

Protozoans may play a significant ecological role in marshes as predators of bacteria. Ciliates play a greater role than has been realized in the flow of energy and in estuary productivity. In New Hampshire tidal marshes, Borror (1972) found a great variety of protozoans (Table 3.6).

The main sources of nitrogen entering the marshlands were groundwater and precipitation. The groundwater provided NO_3 and DON and was an important contributor to the nitrogen economy of the salt marsh. Groundwater also provided N, which was fixed by blue-green algae mats. Although the blue-green algal mat had the highest rate of fixation per unit area of the various microhabitats in the marsh (100 to 200 mg N cm^{-2} h^{-1}), the low marsh with *Spartina* covered a much greater area, so that it made a greater total contribution to the marsh as a whole even though its fixation rate was less (90 to 100 mg N m^{-2} day^{-1}). About half of the nitrogen brought into the marsh by the groundwater was converted and exported as particulate nitrogen. The marsh thus transformed the nitrogen into forms suitable for consumers, such as shellfish. Large amounts of apparently refractory DON entered the marsh through the groundwater and similar amounts were exported. Nitrogen inputs through precipitation consisted primarily of DON, N–NO_3, and N–NH_4. Particulate materials in rain had a high carbon-to-nitrogen ratio.

Nitrogen fixation on the surface of the mud and within the rhizosphere of marsh grasses was considerable (Patriquin and McClung, 1978). The fixation of nitrogen by the mud surface vegetation was mainly by blue-green algae in amounts of 10 to 20 mg N m^{-2} day^{-1}. In the rhizosphere of the roots, the fixation was about 80 mg N m^{-2} day^{-1}. Thus the total nitrogen fixed in these two areas was 90 to 100 mg N m^{-2} day^{-1} (Carpenter et al., 1978).

TABLE 3.6. *Species of Ciliates Encountered in New Hampshire Tidal Marshes*

Gymnostomatida
  Rhabdophorina
    Prorodon marinus
    Stephanopogon apogon
    Lacrymaria marina
    Loxophyllum chaetonotum
    Loxophyllum setigerum
    Litonotus cygnus
    Coleps tesselatus
    Mesodinium pulex
    Enchelyodon trepida
    Spathidium sp.
    Askenasia stellaris
    Trachelonoma oligostriata
    Metacystis striata
    Placus salinus

  Crytophorina
    Trochilia sigmoides
    Chlamydodon triquetrus
    C. obliquus
    C. lyncheiliformis n. sp.
    Trochilioides recta
    Nassula labiata
    Dysteria monostyla
    D. marina
    Cryptopharynx setigerus

Trichostomatida
  Plagiopyla nasuta
  Sonderia sinuata
  Geleia simplex
  G. orbis
  Colpoda cucullus
  Trimyema pleurispirale n. sp.

Hymenostomatida
  Paratetrahymena wassi
  Ophryoglena flava
  Frontonia marina
  F. microstoma
  F. fusca
  Paramecium calkinsi

Scuticociliatida
  Uronema marinum
  U. acutum
  U. filificum
  Uropedalium pyriforme
  Paralembus hargisi n. comb.
  P. marinus n. comb.
  Pseudocohnilembus longisetus
  Cohnilembus verminus
  Cyclidium plouneouri
  C. marinum

Paranophrys magna n. sp.
Pleuronema coronatum
P. smalli

Peritrichida
  Vorticella nebulifera
  V. striata
  Cothurnia simplex
  Zoothamnium sp.

Suctorida
  Acineta sp.

Heterotrichida
  Condylostoma arenarium
  Protocruzia depressa
  Peritromus faurei
  Gruberia lanceolata
  Parablepharisma bacteriophorum
  P. chlamydophorum

Oligotrichida
  Strombidium sulcatum
  S. latum
  S. kahli
  S. viride
  S. styliferum
  S. purpureum
  Strobilidium caudatum

Odontastomatida
  Caenomorpha sp.

Hypotrichida
  Trichotaxis pulchra n. sp.
  Holostricha diademata
  Paraholosticha polychaeta
  Oxytricha halophila
  Histriculus simulis
  Gastrostyla pulchra
  Trachelostyla pediculiformis
  Euplotes mutabilis
  E. trisulcatus
  E. crenosus
  E. bisulcatus
  E. harpa
  E. charon
  E. quinquecarinatus
  E. alatus
  E. minuta
  E. crassus
  Diophrys oligothrix
  D. scutum
  Uronychia transfuga
  Aspidisca aculeata
  A. baltica

Source: After Borror (1972).

Carbon fixation was also high in these marshes. For example, in the Great Sippewissett Marsh (Massachusetts), the plankton productivity was 2.5×10^6 to $2.5 \times 10^7 \, mg \, C \, m^{-2} \, h^{-1}$. In contrast, *Spartina alterniflora* of the low marsh fixed $9.8 \times 10^4 \, mg \, C \, m^{-2} \, h^{-1}$ to $1.3 \times 10^7 \, mg \, C \, m^{-2} \, h^{-1}$, and the algae in the unshaded areas fixed $12.5 \times 10^3 \, mg \, C \, m^{-2} \, h^{-1}$. The particulate carbon export was equivalent to 40% of the net annual production of *S. alterniflora* (Van Raalte et al., 1976).

EXAMPLE OF AN ESTUARINE COMMUNITY: SHEEPSCOT RIVER ESTUARY

General Characteristics of the Estuary

The Sheepscot River estuary is used as an example of a riverine estuary in northen New England because it is one of the best-studied estuaries (Stickney, 1959). The Sheepscot River originates in the low uplands between the Penobscot and Kennebec river valleys in Maine and flows southward to the Gulf of Maine. Where the Sheepscot intersects with the coastline, it forms a deep, narrow embayment superficially resembling a fjord. The valley is, however, river-cut rather than incised by glacier (Johnson, 1925), and therefore has no sill at the seaward end. The estuary is typical of a submerged drowned river valley, with the size of the estuary portion being much greater than that of less saline and freshwater reaches. The purpose of this discussion is to illustrate the transition in species as one moves from marine conditions, near the mouth of the estuary, to semifresh to freshwater conditions, depending on the season of the year, in the upper estuary.

Salinity. As is typical for a river estuary, the water near the mouth is 28 to 30 ppt salinity, which is similar to seawater, and a gradient in salinity is found as one progresses up the estuary. Such a transition in salinity results in various groups of species forming a community. There are those that are typically marine species, those that can tolerate fresh water to salt water, which are known as euryhaline species, and those that are characteristic of fresh water.

The town of Wiscasset, Maine (Figure 3.8), forms a dividing line between the upper and lower estuaries. The upper estuary has a channel depth of 1 to 10 m at mean low flow and is bordered by extensive mud flats and marshes. The salinity of this upper part of the estuary is greatly influenced by river flow at all times of the year, as the discharge may vary from about 0.05 to over $28 \, m^3 \, s^{-1}$. Usually, the greatest flow is after the spring thaw in April or after heavy rains. Although the salinity is low, seasonal and tidal fluctuations may vary the salt concentration as much as 15 ppt in the upper part of the estuary.

The lower estuary is characterized by deeper water and a smaller tidal exchange ratio and higher and less variable salinities than those of the upper estuaries. A narrower temperature range is also present. Below a depth of about 10 m, the salinity in the lower estuary is relatively uniform compared to the upper estuary.

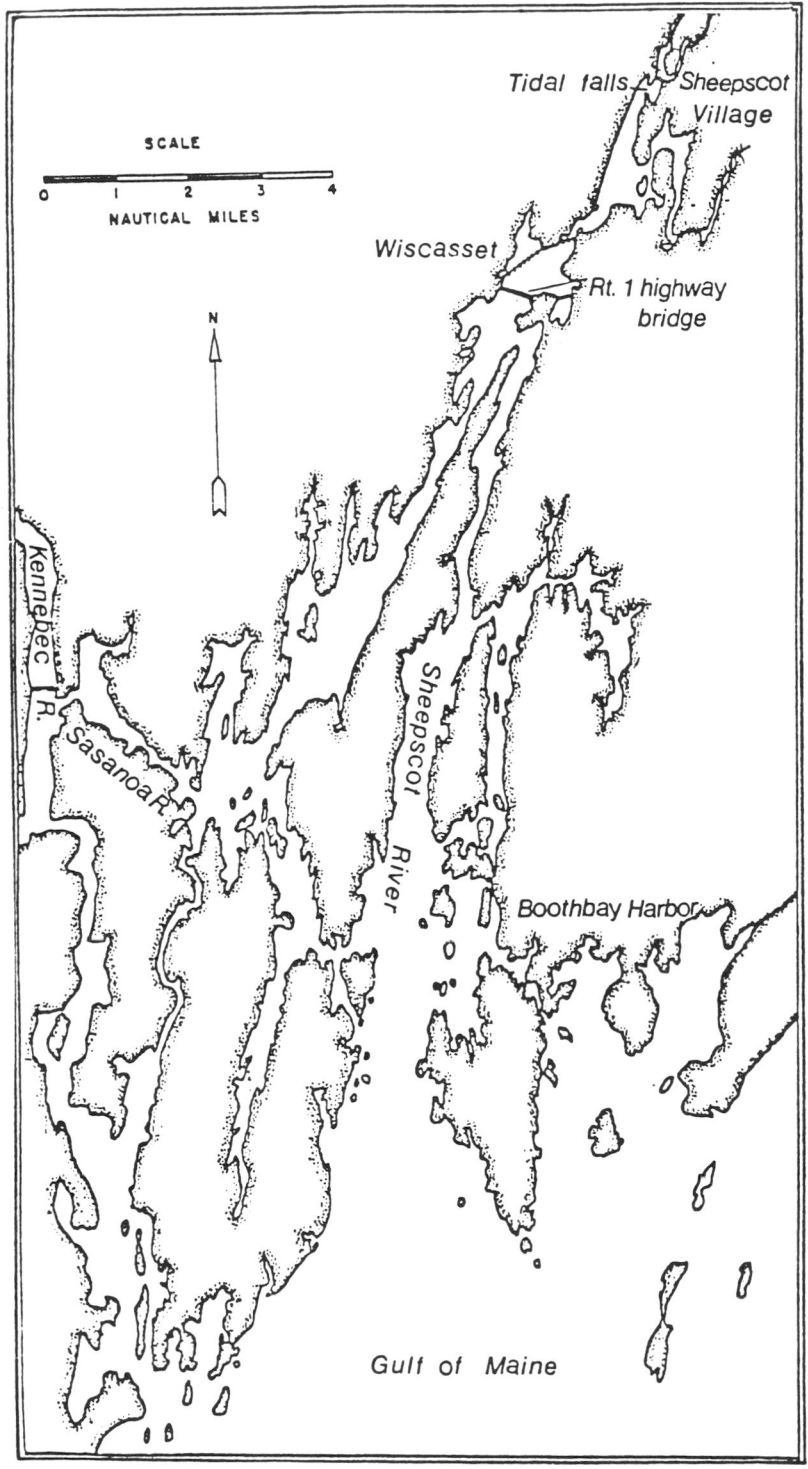

FIGURE 3.8.   Outline chart of the Sheepscot area showing locations of principal geographic features and water masses. (After Stickney, 1959.)

Tides. At the head of the estuary at Sheepscot Village (Figure 3.8), the mean tide range is 2.9 m, decreasing to 2.7 m near the mouth of the estuary. Above the falls and in the upper estuary, the tidal range is usually about 1.8 m. In the upper estuary, above the falls near the village of Sheepscot, the tide continues to ebb for a little over 2 hours after it begins to flood below the falls. The duration of the flooding tide above the falls is only about 4 hours, while the ebb lasts about 8 hours.

Temperature. There are pronounced horizontal and vertical temperature gradients in the estuaries, particularly in summer. Seasonal and tidal variations in temperature are stronger in the inner estuary or in other places where the water is shallow and protected. The greatest amount of thermal stratification occurs between April and September. After September, the mixing overcomes any surface warming, and temperatures are nearly uniform at all depths. During the coldest part of the winter, the surface waters are somewhat colder than those near the bed of the estuary (Stickney, 1959).

Bottom Sediments. Although detailed studies have not been made of bottom sediments, it appears that most of the bottom was covered by muddy sediments composed of silt, fine sand, clay, and organic detritus. Most of the organic matter was from defunct sawmills, but there was also considerable organic matter derived from the leaves, twigs, and seeds of terrestrial plants. In the narrow part of the lower estuary and in the upper estuary where the current was strong, the bottom sediments were mainly sand. Numerous and sometimes extensive outcrops of bedrock interrupted the otherwise smooth bed. Most of the intertidal area was either rock or mud flat. Sandy or gravelly flats were rare except for a few exposed beaches near the seaward end of the estuary and small sand bars in the upper estuary. The intertidal flats often showed a zonation in sediments ranging from coarse to fine from the high to the low tidewater level. The reverse was found in marginal flats between grass marshes and tidal creeks with fast current. Silt was a predominant sediment in most of the intertidal areas and may have been stirred into suspension with the flooding tide and redeposited on all exposed surfaces. The intertidal sediments also contained much organic debris, which was composed largely of fragments of *Spartina*, detritus, and sawdust (Stickney, 1959).

Fauna and Flora
The fauna and flora of the Sheepscot estuary are listed in Table 3.7 together with the preferred salinity and sediment habitats. From this list it is evident that the species were a mixture of the Acadian and Virginian fauna and flora. Organisms that prefer fresh to low-brackish water were found in the upper estuary, as were those species that prefer higher temperatures. Typically, marine species and those that preferred cooler waters were found in the lower estuary. The upper estuary contained numerous species which were limited to it by their requirments for higher temperatures or less saline waters. In general, the number of species is far greater in the lower estuary, even when an area of size comparable to that of the upper estuary was considered (Stickney, 1959).

(text continued on page 214)

TABLE 3.7. *Common Aquatic Species of the Sheepscot Estuary Arranged by Habitat*

Species	High Salinity (28–30 ppt)	Low Salinity (0–27 ppt)	Intertidal Sediments	Intertidal Solid	Subtidal Sediments	Subtidal Solid	Shallow Protected Water	Coastal Waters	Migratory Nekton	Miscellaneous Wanderers
DIVISION BACILLARIOPHYTA										
Class Bacillariophyceae										
Order Eupodiscales										
Family Coscinodiscaceae										
Melosira sp.		×								
DIVISION CHLOROPHYTA										
Class Ulothricophyceae										
Order Ulvales										
Family Ulvaceae										
Ulva lactuca	×									
Enteromorpha compressa	×									
E. clathrata		×								
E. intestinalis		×								
Order Oscillatoriales										
Family Oscillatoriaceae										
Lyngbya sp.		×								
DIVISION PHAEOPHYTA										
Order Ectocarpales										
Family Ectocarpaceae										
Ectocarpus sp.		×								
Order Chordariales										
Family Chordariaceae										
Chordaria flagelliformis	×									
Order Desmarestiales										
Family Desmarestiaceae										
Desmarestia aculeata	×									
Order Laminariales										
Family Laminariaceae										
Laminaria longicruoris	×									
L. digitata	×									
Chorda filum	×									
Order Fucales										
Family Fucaceae										
Ascophyllum nodosum	×									
Fucus evanescens	×									
F. spiralis	×									
F. vesiculosus	×									
DIVISION RHODOPHYTA										
Class Rhodophyceae										
Order Cryptonemiales										
Family Corallinaceae										

TABLE 3.7. (*Continued*)

Species	High Salinity (28–30 ppt)	Low Salinity (0–27 ppt)	Intertidal Sediments	Intertidal Solid	Subtidal Sediments	Subtidal Solid	Shallow Protected Water	Coastal Waters	Migratory Nekton	Miscellaneous Wanderers
Corallina officinalis	×									
Order Gigartinales										
Family Gigartinaceae										
Chondrus crispus	×									
Order Ceramiales										
Family Rhodomelaceae										
Polysiphonia flexicaulis	×									
P. lanosa	×									
P. subtilissima		×								
Family Dasyaceae										
Dasya pedicellata		×								
Family Ceramiaceae										
Ceramium sp.		×								
DIVISION SPERMATOPHYTA										
Class Monocotyledonae										
Order Graminalcs										
Family Graminae										
Spartina alterniflora var. *glabra*	×	×								
S. patens	×	×								
Order Helobiae										
Family Zosteraceae										
Zostera marina	×	×								
Ruppia maritima		×								
PHYLUM PROTOZOA										
Class Ciliata										
Order Tintinnida										
Family Tintinnidae										
Tintinnopsis sp.	×							×		
PHYLUM PORIFERA										
Class Desmospongiae										
Order Haplosclerida										
Family Haliclonidae										
Haliclona aculata	×					×				
(= *Chalina aculata*)										
Order Epipolasida										
Family Jaspidae										
Topsentia sp.	×					×				
(= *Halichondria* sp.)										
PHYLUM CNIDARIA										
Class Hydrozoa										

Continued

TABLE 3.7. (*Continued*)

Species	High Salinity (28–30 ppt)	Low Salinity (0–27 ppt)	Intertidal Sediments	Intertidal Solid	Subtidal Sediments	Subtidal Solid	Shallow Protected Water	Coastal Waters	Migratory Nekton	Miscellaneous Wanderers
Order Athecata										
Family Acaulidae										
Acualis primarius	×				×					
Family Clavidae										
Cordylophora lacustris		×				×				
Order Thecata										
Family Campanularidae										
Obelia longissima		×				×				
Obelia spp.	×					×				
Family Sertularidae										
Sertularia spp.	×					×				
Class Anthozoa										
Subclass Zoantharia										
Order Achnaria										
Tribe Thenaria										
Family Actinidae										
Tealia felina	×					×				
(= *Urticina crassicornis*)										
Family Metridiidae										
Metridium dianthus	×					×				
Class Scyphozoa										
Order Semaeostomeae										
Family Cyanidae										
Cyanea arctica	×							×		
Family Ulmaridae										
Aurelia aurita	×							×		
Order Actiniaria (same as Achnaria?)										
Family Edwardsiidae										
Edwardsia elegans	×				×					
Order Ceriantharia										
Cereantheopsis americana	×				×					
PHYLUM CTENOPHORA										
Class Tentaculata										
Order Cydippida										
Family Pleurobranchiidae										
Pleurobranchia pileus	×							×		
PHYLUM CHAETOGNATHA										
Sagitta sp.	×							×		

TABLE 3.7. (*Continued*)

Species	High Salinity (28–30 ppt)	Low Salinity (0–27 ppt)	Intertidal Sediments	Intertidal Solid	Subtidal Sediments	Subtidal Solid	Shallow Protected Water	Coastal Waters	Migratory Nekton	Miscellaneous Wanderers
PHYLUM ANNELIDA										
Class Polychaeta										
Order Phyllodocida										
Family Phyllodocidae										
Phyllodoce groenlandica	×				×					
Family Polynoidae										
Lepidonotus squamatus	×					×				
Harmothoe imbricata	×					×				
Hartmania moorei	×				×					
Family Sigalionidae										
Pholoe minuta	×				×					
Glycera dibranchiata		×	×							
Family Nephtyidae										
Nephtys incisa	×				×					
N. caeca	×		×		×					
Family Nereidae										
Nereis diversicolor		×	×		×					
N. virens	×		×		×					
Order Capitellida										
Family Capitellidae										
Heteromastus filiformis	×	×	×							
Family Arenicolidae										
Arenicola marina	×		×							
Family Scalibregmidae										
Scalibregma inflatum	×				×					
Family Maldanidae										
Clymenella torquata	×		×							
Maldane sarsi	×				×					
Praxillella sp.	×				×					
Rhodine loveni	×				×					
Family Opheliidae										
Ammotrypane aulogaster	×				×					
Order Sternaspidae										
Family Sternaspidae										
Sternaspis scutata	×				×					
Order Spionida										
Family Spionidae										
Polydora ligni	×	×	×							
Scolecolepides viridis		×	×		×					

Continued

TABLE 3.7. (*Continued*)

Species	High Salinity (28–30 ppt)	Low Salinity (0–27 ppt)	Intertidal Sediments	Intertidal Solid	Subtidal Sediments	Subtidal Solid	Shallow Protected Water	Coastal Waters	Migratory Nekton	Miscellaneous Wanderers
Streblospio benedicti	×		×							
Family Paraonidae										
Aricidea spp.	×				×					
Order Eunicida										
Family Lumbrinereidae										
Lumbrineris tenuis	×				×					
Ninoe nigripes	×				×					
Order Terebellida										
Family Pectinariidae										
Pectinaria hyperborea	×		×							
Family Ampharetidae										
Ampharete acutifrons	×				×					
Hypaniola grayi	×	×	×		×					
Family Terebellidae										
Amphitrite sp.	×		×							
Order Flabelligerida										
Family Flabelligeridae										
Flabelligera affinis	×				×					
Pherusa plumosa	×				×					
Diplocirrus hirsutus	×				×					
Order Sabellida										
Family Serpulidae										
Spirorbis borealis	×					×				
PHYLUM ECHINODERMATA										
Class Holothuroidea										
Order Dendrochirotida										
Family Cucumaridae										
Cucumaria frondosa	×					×				
Order Molpadiida										
Family Caudinidae										
Caudina arenata	×				×					
Class Echinoidea										
Order Echinoida										
Family Strongylocentrotidae										
Strongylocentrotus droebachiensis	×					×				
Order Clypleasteroida										
Family Echinarachnidae										

TABLE 3.7. (*Continued*)

Species	High Salinity (28–30 ppt)	Low Salinity (0–27 ppt)	Intertidal Sediments	Intertidal Solid	Subtidal Sediments	Subtidal Solid	Shallow Protected Water	Coastal Waters	Migratory Nekton	Miscellaneous Wanderers
Echinarachnius parma	×				×					
Class Stelleroidea										
Subclass Asteroidea										
Order Spinulosida										
Family Echinasteridae										
Henricia sanguinolenta	×					×				
Order Forcipulata										
Family Asteriidae										
Asterias forbesii	×					×				
A. vulgaris	×					×				
Subclass Ophiuroidea										
Order Phrynophiurida										
Family Gorgonocephalida										
Gorgonocephalus arcticus	×					×				
Order Ophiurida										
Family Ophiactidae										
Ophiopholis aculaeata	×					×				
Ophiura robusta	×				×					
PHYLUM MOLLUSCA										
Class Polyplacophora										
Order Neoloricata										
Family Ischnochitonidae										
Ischnochiton ruber	×					×				
Class Gastropoda										
Order Archaeogastropoda										
Family Acmaeidae										
Acmaea testudinalis	×			×						
Order Mesogastropoda										
Family Lacunidae										
Lacuna vincta	×				×					
Family Littorinidae										
Littorina littorea	×	×		×						
L. obtusata	×			×						
Family Hydrobiidae										
Hydrobia minuta	×	×	×		×					
(= *Paludestrina minuta*)										
H. salsa		×	×							
Family Rissoidae										
Cingula aculaeus	×				×					
Family Pyramidellidae										

Continued

TABLE 3.7. (*Continued*)

Species	High Salinity (28–30 ppt)	Low Salinity (0–27 ppt)	Intertidal Sediments	Intertidal Solid	Subtidal Sediments	Subtidal Solid	Shallow Protected Water	Coastal Waters	Migratory Nekton	Miscellaneous Wanderers
Odostomia bisuturalis	×	×				×				
Order Neogastropoda										
Family Muricidae										
Nucella lapilla	×			×						
(= *Thais lapillus*)										
Family Buccinidae										
Colus sp.	×				×					
Family Nassariidae										
Ilyanassa obsoleta	×	×	×							
(= *Nassarius obsoletis*)										
Nassarius trivittatus	×				×					
Subclass Opisthobranchia										
Order Cephalaspidea										
Family Retusidae										
Retusa obtusa	×				×					
Family Scaphandridae										
Cylichna alba	×				×					
Order Nudibranchia										
Suborder Aeolidacea										
Aeolidia papillosa	×					×				
Class Bivalvia										
Subclass Pteriomorpha										
Order Pteroconchida										
Family Nuculidae										
Nucula spp.	×				×					
Family Nuculanidae										
Yoldia limatula	×				×					
Y. sapotilla	×				×					
Subclass Pteriomorpha										
Order Pteroconchida										
Family Mytilidae										
Crenella decussata	×				×					
Mytilus edulis	×	×		×		×				
Modiolus demissus	×			×						
(= *Volsella demissa*)										
Family Ostreidae										
Crassostrea virginica		×·				×				
Family Pectinidae										
Placopecten magellanicus	×				×					
Family Anomiidae										

TABLE 3.7. *(Continued)*

Species	High Salinity (28–30 ppt)	Low Salinity (0–27 ppt)	Intertidal Sediments	Intertidal Solid	Subtidal Sediments	Subtidal Solid	Shallow Protected Water	Coastal Waters	Migratory Nekton	Miscellaneous Wanderers
Anomia aculeata	×					×				
A. simplex	×					×				
Family Hiatellidae										
Hiatella artica	×					×				
Subclass Teleodesmata										
Order Heterodontida										
Family Astartidae										
Astarte undata	×				×					
Family Thyasiridae										
Thyasira gouldii	×				×					
Family Cardiidae										
Cerastoderma pinnulatum	×				×					
Clinocardium ciliatum	×				×					
Family Veneridae										
Gemma gemma	×		×							
Family Tellinidae										
Macoma balthica	×	×	×							
Tellina agilis	×				×					
Family Solenidae										
Ensis directus	×	×	×							
Family Myidae										
Mya arenaria	×	×	×							
Subclass Anomalodesmata										
Order Eudesmodontida										
Family Thraciidae										
Thracia myopsis	×				×					
PHYLUM ARTHROPODA										
Subphylum Chelicerata										
Class Merostomata										
Limulus polyphemus		×			×					
Subphylum Mandibulatum										
Class Crustacea										
Subclass Copepoda										
Order Calanoida										
Calanus finmarchicus	×							×		
Pseudocalanus minutus	×							×		
Centropages typicus	×							×		
C. hamatus	×							×		
Temora longicornis	×							×		
Eurytemora herdmanni	×							×		

Continued

TABLE 3.7.   (Continued)

Species	High Salinity (28–30 ppt)	Low Salinity (0–27 ppt)	Intertidal Sediments	Intertidal Solid	Subtidal Sediments	Subtidal Solid	Shallow Protected Water	Coastal Waters	Migratory Nekton	Miscellaneous Wanderers
Acartia longiremis	×	×					×	×		
Tortanus discaudatus	×							×		
Order Cyclopoida										
Oithona similis	×							×		
Order Harpacticoida										
Microsetella norvergica	×							×		
Order Monstrilloida										
Eurytemora herdmani		×					×			
Subclass Branchiopoda										
Order Cladocera										
Family Polyphemidae										
Podon leuckarti	×							×		
Evadne normanni	×							×		
Subclass Cirripedia										
Order Thoracia										
Suborder Balanomorpha										
Family Balanidae										
Balanus balanoides	×	×		×						
B. crenatus	×					×				
B. improvisus		×				×				
Subclass Malacostraca										
Superorder Peracarida										
Family Leuconidae										
Eudorella sp.	×				×					
Family Distylidae										
Diastylis quadrispinosa	×				×					
Order Tanaidacea										
Family Paratanaidae										
Leptochelia rapax		×			×					
Order Isopoda										
Suborder Anthuridea										
Family Anthruidae										
Cyathura polita		×	×		×					
(= *C. carinata*)										
Suborder Valvifera										
Family Idoteidae										
Idotea balthica	×					×				
I. phosphorea	×					×				
Suborder Asellota										
Family Janiridae										

TABLE 3.7. (*Continued*)

Species	High Salinity (28–30 ppt)	Low Salinity (0–27 ppt)	Intertidal Sediments	Intertidal Solid	Subtidal Sediments	Subtidal Solid	Shallow Protected Water	Coastal Waters	Migratory Nekton	Miscellaneous Wanderers
Jaera marina		×				×				
Order Amphipoda										
Suborder Gammaridea										
Family Ampeliscidae										
Ampelisca spinipes	×				×					
Family Corophiidae										
Corophium lacustre		×				×				
C. volutator	×	×	×							
Corophium spp.	×				×					
Family Gammaridae										
Gammarus annulatus	×	×				×				
G. locusta	×	×		×						
G. marinus	×					×				
G. mucronatus		×				×				
G. tigrinus		×				×				
Casco bigelowi	×				×					
Melita nitida		×				×				
Family Lysianassidae										
Orchomonela pinguis	×				×					
Family Photidae										
Leptocheirus pinguis	×				×					
Family Phoxocephalidae										
Phoxocephalus holbolli	×				×					
Family Podoceridae										
Dulichia sp.	×				×					
Order Caprellidea										
Family Caprellidae										
Aeginella longicornis	×	×				×				
Suborder Eucarida										
Order Decapoda										
Infraorder Caridea										
Family Pandalidae										
Pandalus borealis	×				×					
Family Croingonidae										
Crangon septomspinosa	×	×			×					
(= *Crago septemspinosus*)										
Infraorder Astacidea										
Family Nephropsidae										
Homarus americanus	×									×
Infraorder Anomura										
Family Paguridae										

Continued

TABLE 3.7. (Continued)

Species	High Salinity (28–30 ppt)	Low Salinity (0–27 ppt)	Intertidal Sediments	Intertidal Solid	Subtidal Sediments	Subtidal Solid	Shallow Protected Water	Coastal Waters	Migratory Nekton	Miscellaneous Wanderers
Pagurus bernhardus	×									×
Infraorder Brachyura										
Section Oxyrhyncha										
Family Majidae										
Hyas araneus	×									×
Section Cancridea										
Family Cacridae										
Cancer irroratus	×									×
C. borealis	×									×
Section Barchyrhynca										
Family Portunidae										
Carcinus maenas	×									×
(= *Carcinides maenas*)										
Neopanope texana		×				×				
Rithropanopeus harrisii		×				×				
PHYLUM HEMICHORDATA										
Class Enteropneusta										
Saccoglossus kowalewskii	×		×							
(= *Dolichoglssus kowalewskii*)										
PHYLUM CHORDATA										
Class Ascidiacea										
Order Enterogona										
Suborder Aplousobranchia										
Family Polyclinidae										
Amaroucium sp.	×					×				
Family Didemnidae										
Didemnum albidum	×					×				
Order Pleurogona										
Suborder Stolidobranchiata										
Family Styelidae										
Dendrodoa carnea	×					×				
Family Pyuridae										
Boltenia echinata	×					×				
Subphylum Vertebrata										
Class Chondrichthyes										
Order Squaliformes										
Family Squalidae										
Squalus achanthias	×							×		
Order Rajiformes										
Family Rajidae										

TABLE 3.7. (*Continued*)

Species	High Salinity (28–30 ppt)	Low Salinity (0–27 ppt)	Intertidal Sediments	Intertidal Solid	Subtidal Sediments	Subtidal Solid	Shallow Protected Water	Coastal Waters	Migratory Nekton	Miscellaneous Wanderers
Raja erinacea	×							×		
Class Osteichthyes										
Order Clupeiformes										
Family Clupeidae										
Alosa aestivalis		×							×	
(= *Pomolobus aestivalis*)										
A. psuedoharengus		×							×	
(= *P. pseudoharengus*										
A. sapidissima		×							×	
Brevoortia tyrannus	×							×		
Clupea harengus	×							×		
Order Salmoniformes										
Family Salmonidae										
Salmo salar		×							×	
Family Osmeridae										
Osmerus mordax		×							×	
Order Lophiiformes										
Family Lophiidae										
Lophius americanus		×						×		
Order Gadiformes										
Family Gadidae										
Gadus morhua	×							×		
(= *Gadus callarias*)										
Melanogrammus aeglefinus	×							×		
Merluccius bilinearis	×									
Microgadus tomcod		×					×			
Pollachius virens	×							×		
Urophycis tenuis	×							×		
Order Atheriniformes										
Family Cyprinodontidae										
Fundulus heteroclitus		×					×			
Family Atherinidae										
Menidia sp.		×					×			
Order Gasterosteiformes										
Family Gasterosteidae										
Apeltes quadracus		×					×			
Pungitius pungitius		×					×			
Family Syngnathidae										
Syngnathus fuscus		×					×			
Order Perciformes										
Family Percichthyidae										

Continued

TABLE 3.7. (Continued)

Species	High Salinity (28–30 ppt)	Low Salinity (0–27 ppt)	Intertidal Sediments	Intertidal Solid	Subtidal Sediments	Subtidal Solid	Shallow Protected Water	Coastal Waters	Migratory Nekton	Miscellaneous Wanderers
Morone americana		×					×			
M. saxatilis		×					×		×	
(= Roccus saxatilis)										
Family Labridae										
Tautoglabrus adspersus	×							×		
Family Pholidae										
Pholis gunnellus	×							×		
Family Ammodytidae										
Ammodytes americanus	×							×		
Family Scombridae										
Scomber scombrus	×							×		
Family Strombridae										
Peprilus triacanthus	×							×		
(= Poronotus triacanthus)										
Family Cottidae										
Hemitripterus americanus	×							×		
Myoxocephalus aeneus	×							×		
Family Cyclopteridae										
Cyclopteropsis lumpus	×							×		
Liparis liparis	×							×		
Order Pleuronectiformes										
Family Pleuronectidae										
Liopsetta putnami		×					×			
Pseudopleuronectes americanus	×							×		

Source: Stickney (1959).

Lower Estuary: Submerged Fauna and Flora

Plankton.   In the lower estuary, the dominant plankton were diatoms and dinoflagellates. In the spring the chief genera of diatoms were *Thalassosira, Thalassothrix*, and *Chaetoceras*. In the summer *Skeletonema, Asterionella*, and *Rhizosolenia* occurred, often in local concentrations. Various species of *Coscinodiscus* were nearly always present. The most abundant species of dinoflagellates were *Ceratium tripos, C. longipes, C. fusus*, and several species of *Peridinium*.

The zooplankton in the lower estuary consisted mainly of copepods; however, cladocerans were often very common. The most characteristic copepods were

Pseudocalanus minitus, Acartia longiremis, and *Oithona similis. Microsetella norvegica* occurred mainly in the winter months. Other common species of copepods were *Eurytemora herdmani, Centropages hamatus,* and *Temora longicornis.* The pelagic larval stages of nonplanktonic species were abundant seasonally. In the spring and early summer the most abundant forms were pluteus larvae of brittle stars (*Ophiuroidea*), barnacle nauplii, crab zoea, and worm trochophores. Bivalve veligers and various worm larvae were common in mid and late summer. Larger plankton species, such as some of the medusae and ctenophores, were often collected. The jellyfish (*Aurelia aurita* and *Cyanea arctica*) were abundant in the early part of the summer, the former often in dense concentrations (Stickney, 1959).

Nekton. Large populations of forager fish, such as the silversides, *Menidia* sp.; mummichog, *Fundulus heteroclitus*; young blueblack herring. *Alosa aestivalis*; and young alewife, *Alosa pseudoharengus*, were common in the lower estuary. The fish species of Sheepscot estuary are listed in Table 3.7. The migratory species consisted of seasonal migrants such as the Atlantic herring (*Clupea harengus*) and Atlantic mackerel (*Scomber scombrus*); anadromous species such as the rainbow smelt (*Osmerus mordax*), the alewife (*Alosa pseudoharengus*), and the Atlantic salmon (*Salmo salar*); and catadromous species such as the American eel (*Anguilla rostrata*). The alewife and the sea lamprey (*Petromygon marinus*) ascended the river in May, blueblack herring (*Alosa aestivalis*) in June. The smelt (*Osmerus mordax*) entered the estuary in the fall, remained in the tidal creeks and upper estuary during the winter, and in April entered the freshwater river and tributary streams to spawn. The striped bass (*Morone saxatilis*) appeared in the upper estuary in the summer (Stickney, 1959).

Benthos. The benthic communities of algae in the lower estuary were dominated by species of *Fucaceae*, particularly *F. vesiculosus*, and *Ascophyllum nodosum*. Below the tide level, and sometimes exposed during extremely low spring tides, were Irish moss (*Chondrus crispus*) and kelps, such as various species of *Laminaria* (Stickney, 1959).

The invertebrate infauna consisted of many species that were abundant and important food species of many kinds of fish (Table 3.7). The more important groups were the shrimp, particularly *Crangon septemspinosus*, cumaceans, polychaete worms, small bivalves, and amphipods. Also fairly common in the lower estuary and confined to high-salinity rock or solid substrate habitats were the lobster (*Homarus americanus*), rock carb (*Cancer irroratus*), sea scallops (*Placopecten magellanicus*), sponges (*Halichondra* sp. and *Chalina oculata*), and starfish (Table 3.7). A very important predator living in these habitats was the green crab (*Carcinides maenas*). It was a serious predator of the soft-shelled clam and largely responsible for the great reduction in their populations (Stickney, 1959).

Upper Estuary: Submerged Fauna and Flora

Plankton–Zooplankton. In the upper estuary, the zooplankton consisted of species indigenous to the area and some marine species. For example, *Acartia longiremis, Eurytemora herdmani*, larvae of molluscs and worms, and nauplii of barnacles were present. In general, the harpacticoid copepods were more common in the plankton in the upper estuary than in the lower estuary. The amounts of plankton were quite variable, being typically high in August and September, although fairly large plankton populations were found in June, July, and October. This was particularly true in 1954 (Stickney, 1959).

Nekton. The nekton community is not recorded as being different from that in the lower estuary. Stickney (1959, Table 3.7) gives a list of fish found in shallow, brackish, or protected waters but does not say that they occurred in the upper estuary. The anadromous and catadromous fish occurred in the upper estuary, as did some of the seasonal migratory species.

Benthos. The benthic intertidal and subtidal organisms are mainly euryhaline species which can withstand 0 to 27 ppt salinity. Species that are fairly common infauna of upper estuary soild substrates were the mud crab (*Rhithropanopeus harrisii*), small populations of older oysters (*Crassostrea virginica*), the coelenterate, *Cordylophora lacustris*, and the amphipod, *Gammarus tigrinus*. The horseshoe crab (*Limulus polyphemus*) and polychaete worms (Table 3.7) are found living on the unconsolidated muddy sand sediments.

Algae. In the upper estuary, in low-salinity, protected waters, the most common algal species was *Enteromorpha intestinalis*. Other species of *Enteromorpha* were found very frequently. Growing on these algae or on other substrates were species of the genera *Ceratium* and *Ectocarpus*. Various species of the diatom *Melosira* were also often present.

Invertebrates. A study of Ebenecook Harbor and Jewett Cove in the Sheepscot estuary indicated that the soft sediment was dominated by a *Nephtys–Nucula* community (Hanks, 1964). This community was similar to the one identified by Sanders in Buzzards Bay. The bivalve, *Nucula proxima*, was the most abundant animal, and the polychaete worm, *Nephtys incisa*, was the most uniformly distributed species in these areas and was therefore most characteristic of this community. Second in abundance to the bivalve were the cumaceans, of which the most common genera were *Eudorella* and *Diastylis*. Next in abundance was a hemichordate, *Stereobalanus canadensis*, which lived in fragile, mucus-lined tubes and was a selective deposit feeder. These tubes offered habitat for organisms such as the amphipod, *Corophium* sp., and the polychaete, *Hartmania moorei*. Common was the small bivalve, *Volsella modiolus*. The widely distributed *Nephtys incisa* was a nonselective deposit feeder burrowing through the upper layers of the sediment and ingesting the substratum from which food materials are obtained. The polychaete worm, *Nephtys incisa*, and the acorn worm, *Stereobalanus canadensis*, provided tubes and tunnels for organisms such as the scaleworm, *Hartmania moorei*, to live in. Most of the organisms in this community were deposit feeders ingesting the organic materials from the fine ooze layers of the sediments. The occurrence and abundance of the more common species are given in Table 3.8. The association, as stated above, is common in Buzzards Bay and has also been found in the Long Island Sound area.

The community in Sheepscot estuary consisted of approximately 1500 animals per square meter, which is not nearly as dense a population as Sanders

TABLE 3.8. *Occurrence and Abundance of Selected Species, Ebenecook Harbor and Jewett Cove, Maine, July–November 1955*

Species	Ebenecook Harbor			Jewett Cove		
	Number of Specimens	Number of Stations	Average number per m²	Number of Specimens	Number of Stations	Average number per m²
Nucula proxima	619	19	325.7	1739	40	434.7
Cumacea sp. (4 + species)	828	17	487.0	1145	38	301.3
Stereobalanus canadensis	158	13	121.5	610	21	290.4
Thyasira gouldi	98	13	75.3	619	33	187.5
Phoxocephalus holbolli	5	4	12.5	618	35	176.5
Volsella modiolus	129	27	47.7	444	41	108.2
Corophium sp.	3	1	30.0	554	21	263.8
Nucula tenuis	73	11	66.3	442	35	126.1
Dulichia sp.	188	12	156.6	219	27	81.1
Scoloplos armiger	173	17	101.7	229	30	76.3
Aricidea sp.	272	19	143.1	123	24	51.2
Nephtys incisa	132	32	41.2	200	38	52.6
Orchomenella pinquis	4	4	10.0	288	24	120.0
Ampelisca spinipes	252	14	180.0	39	14	27.9
Diplocirrus hirsutus	4	4	10.0	249	15	166.0
Retusa obtusa	98	18	54.4	108	30	36.0
Sternaspis scutata	55	10	55.0	143	21	68.0
Hartmania moorei	48	13	36.9	107	26	41.1
Ampharete acutifrons	21	11	19.0	114	31	36.7
Nemertea sp.	28	16	17.5	106	33	32.1
Casco bigelowi	3	2	15.0	131	14	93.5
Nucula delphinodonta	119	11	108.1	—	—	—
Pholoe minuta	18	10	18.0	82	30	27.3
Cingula aculeus	10	3	33.3	84	15	56.0
Crenella decussata	6	3	20.0	70	21	33.3

Source: Hanks (1964).

found in the Long Island Sound community of similar type. This may be due in part to the difference in the methods of collecting (Hanks, 1964).

SUMMARY

The northern New England estuaries are dominated by the Canadian currents and therefore support a cold water fauna and flora. The shoreline is rugged, consisting of older, resistant rocks.

In Massachusetts, the rocky shore includes pocket beaches with pebbles and sand, and hence the structure of the cold water fauna and flora is most evident north of Cape Cod. In the southern part of Cape Cod and southward through the Hudson River, the fauna and flora are quite different. Not many ecosystem studies have been made of these types of estuaries. However, it is evident that the main macroscopic algae are the brown algae and that they harbor many epiphytes and are excellent shelters for a diverse invertebrate fauna. One of the most common crustaceans is *Calanus finmarchicus*. Also fairly common are larvae of crustaceans.

Zooplankton populations seem to be related to temperature and nutrients and stability of the water mass. The populations tended to be larger offshore than west of Mount Desert and smaller in the headlands east of Mount Desert and in Passamaquodi Bay. In general, the zooplankton seemed to decline from the western southern part near the end of the Gulf of Maine to the eastern end of the Gulf of Maine: that is, Machias Bay. Copepods are the dominant group at all seasons. Fish are very common in this area. Of the anadromous fish, the most common are salmon and shad. The pelagic species are the Atlantic mackerel, the Atlantic herring, the pikefish, the pollock, the alewife, the butter-fish, and the bluefish.

Benthic communities are very diverse. Many species, such as clams and some of the crustacea and polychaetes, live within the substrate. The kelps, which are macroscopic algae, furnish excellent habitats for many organisms, such as sea squirts, net-forming bryozoa, sponges, small sea anemones, fish, bivalves or molluscs, shrimp, and amphipods. Sometimes colonies of sponges and hydroids attach to islands of algae. Brittle stars are sometimes found in this habitat. Snails are common in sandy and muddy habitats. Algae and its epiphytes form an important base of the food chain as well as the plankton and detritus that are consumed by the filter feeders. Many organisms are detrital feeders, such as the annelid worms and some of the fish and crabs. The base of the food web is composed of algae, organic deris, bacteria, and plankton.

The upper intertidal zone is dominated by the brown algae, *Ascophyllum*, and *Fucus*, the green algae. *Rhizoclonium* and *Enteromorpha* are found in these reaches of the intertidal zone. Barnacles are quite common in this habitat. In the mid intertidal zone, *Fucus* and *Ascophyllum* are usually the most common algae. The most common invertebrates were barnacles and mussels and the predatory snail, *Thais lapillus*. Various anthropods and crabs are also found in this mid intertidal zone. The lower intertidal zone is dominated by the red algae, *Chondrus crispus*, accompanied by various brown and red algae. Mussels dominate this lower rocky intertidal zone.

Tide pools are often found in the intertidal area and have a rather diverse fauna and flora. Examples of the invertebrates found in this area are anemone and periwinkles, worms, and an occasional brittle star. The algae in these pools are typically a mixture of brown and green algae. *Thais lapillus* is one of the most important predators. Another important predator is the snail, *Littorina littorea*, which fed mainly on algae.

The intertidal flats support a greater variety of species than do the intertidal rocky areas. The most common organisms on the sandy-mud flats are the snail, *Littorina littorea*, and amphipods. If the flat is covered with water continually, sea anemones and sea cucumbers may be common. Also very common in the sandy mud is the soft-shelled clam, *Mya arenaria*. The diversity of species that form the food web in these habitats is large. Gray believes that the stability of the habitat is maintained by the burrowing organisms, whereas Thorson pointed out that more stabile benthic communities had a number of long-lived invertebrates that did not have pelagic larvae.

High marshes in this area are dominated by *Spartina patens*. Primary productivity is very high in these marshlands, for example *Spartina alterniflora* of the low marsh fix 9.8×10^4 to $1.3 \times 10^7 \mu g \, C \, m^{-2} h^{-1}$ and the algae fix $12.5 \times 10^3 \mu g \, C \, m^{-2} h^{-1}$. Fixation of nitrogen in the mud surface is mainly by blue-green algae and probably by various bacteria. It is estimated in amounts of 10 to $20 \mu g \, N \, m^{-2} \, day^{-1}$. In the rhizosphere of the roots of the *Spartina* the fixation was about $80 \mu g \, N \, m^{-2} \, day^{-1}$. Thus the total fix in these two areas was 90 to $100 \mu g \, N \, m^{-2} \, day^{-1}$. The Sheepscott River estuary is one of the best examples of the association of organisms in a riverine estuary in this reach.

BIBLIOGRAPHY

Borror, A. 1972. Tidal marsh ciliates (Protozoa): morphology, ecology, systematics. Acta Protozool. 10:29–72.

Carpenter, E. J., C. D. Van Raalte, and I. Valiela. 1978. Nitrogen fixation by algae in a Massachusetts salt marsh, Limnol. Oceanogr. 23:318–327.

Chenoweth, S. B. 1973. Fish larvae of the estuaries and coast of central Maine. U.S. Natl. Mar. Fish. Serv. Fish Bull. 71:105–113.

Croker, R. A., R. P. Hager, and K. J. Scott. 1975. Macro infauna of northern New England sand. Part 2. Amphipod-dominated intertidal communities. Can. J. Zool. 53:42–51.

Dexter, R. W. 1947. The marine communities of a tidal inlet at Cape Ann, Massachusetts: a study in bioecology. Ecol. Monogr. 17:261–294.

Dexter, R. W. 1950. Restoration of the *Zostera* faciation at Cape Ann, Mass. Ecology 31(2):286–288.

Fish, C. J. and M. W. Johnson. 1973. The biology of the zooplankton population in the Bay of Fundy and Gulf of Maine with species reference to production and distribution. J. Biol. Board. Can. 3:189–322.

Fogg, G. E. 1966. The extracellular products of algae. Oceanogr. Mar. Biol. Annu. Rev. 4:195–212.

Fried, S. M., J. D. McCleave, and G. W. Labar. 1978. Seaward migration of hatchery-reared Atlantic salmon, *Salmo salar*, smolts in the Penobscot River estuary, Maine: riverine movements. J. Fish. Res. Bd. Can 35:76–87.

Gosner, K. L. 1971. Guide to identification of marine and estuarine invertebrates: Cape Hatteras to the Bay of Fundy. Wiley, New York. 693 pp.
Gray, I. E. 1961. Changes in abundance of the commensal crabs of *Chaetopterus*. Biol. Bull. 120:353–359.
Gray, I. E. 1974. Worm and clam flats, pp. 204–243. *In* H. T. Odum, B. J. Copeland, and E. A. McMahan, eds., Coastal ecology systems of the United States. Vol. 2. The Conservation Foundation, Washington, D.C.

Hanks, R. W. 1956. A survey of the fauna of the level bottom from two areas in the Sheepscot River estuary. U. S. Fish Wildl. Clam Invest., Boothbay Harbor, ME. Mimeo. Rep. 6 pp.
Hanks, R. W. 1964. A benthic community in the Sheepscot River estuary, Maine. U.S. Fish Wildl. Serv. Fish. Bull. 63(2) 343–353.
Howells, G. P. and S. Weaver. 1969. Studies on phytoplankton at Indian Point pp. 231–261. *In* G. P. Howells, and A. J. Laurer eds., Hudson River ecology. Proceedings of a symposuim 2nd Sterling River Forest, Tuxedo, N.Y. Hudson River Valley Commission of New York, Tarrytown, N.Y.

Johnson, D. 1925. The New England–Acadian shoreline. Wiley, New York. 608 pp.

Labar. G. W., J. D. McCleave, and S. M. Fried. 1978. Seaward migration of hatchery-reared Atlantic salmon, *Salmo salar*, in the Penobscot River estuary, Maine, U.S.A.: open water movements. Tour. Cons. Int. Explor. Mar. 38:257–269.
Lubchenco, J. (formerly Menge, J. Lubchenco). 1978. Plant species diversity in a marine intertidal community: importance of herbivore food preference and algal competitive abilities. Am. Nat. Univ. of Chicago Press, Chicago, Illinois 112:23–39.
Lubchenco, J., and B. A. Menge. 1978. Community development and persistence in a low, rocky intertidal zone. Ecol. Monogr. 48:67–94.

Menge, B. A. 1978a. Predation intensity in a rocky intertidal community: relation between predator foraging activity and environmental harshness. Oecologia (Berlin) 34:1–16.
Menge, B. A. 1978b. Predation intensity in a rocky intertidal community: effect of an algal canopy, wave action, and desiccation on predator feeding rates. Oecologia (Berlin) 34:17–36.

Patriquin, D. G., and C. R. McClung. 1978. Nitrogen accretion and the nature and possible significance of N_2 fixation (acetylene reduction) in a Nova Scotian *Spartina alterniflora* stand. Mar. Biol. 47:227–242.

Ray. G. C. 1975. A preliminary classification of coastal and marine environments. Int. Union Conserv. Nat. Natural Resour. Occas. Pap. 14. 25 pp.
Rhoads. D. C. 1967. Biogenic reworking of intertidal and subtidal sediments in Barnstable Harbor and Buzzards Bay, Massachusetts. J. Geol. Univ. of Chicago Press, Chicago, Illinois 75:461–476.

Sanders, H. L., E. M. Goudsmit, E. L. Mills, and G. E. Hampson. 1962. A study of the intertidal fauna of Barnstable Harbor, Massachusetts. Limnol. Oceanogr. 7:63–79.
Sherman, K. 1970. Seasonal and areal distribution of zooplankton in coastal waters of the Gulf of Maine, 1967 and 1968 U.S. Fish Wildl. Serv. Spec. Sci. Rept. Fish. 594. 8 pp.
Shorey, W. K. 1973. Macrobenthic ecology of a sawdust bearing substrate in the Penobscot River estuary, Maine. J. Fish. Res. Board Can. 30:493–497.
Stickney, A. P. 1959. Ecology of the Sheepscot River estuary. U.S. Fish Wildl. Serv. Spec. Rept. Fish. 309. 21 pp.

Thorson, G. 1957. Bottom communities. In J. W. Hedgpeth, ed., Treatise on marine ecology and paleocology. Vol. 1. Ecology. Geol. Soc. Am. Mem. 67:461–534.

U.S. Geological Survey. 1970. The national atlas of the United States of America. Washington, D.C. 417 pp.

Van Raalte, C. D., I. Valiela, and J. M. Teal. 1976. Production of epibenthic salt marsh algae: light and nutrient limitation. Limnol. Oceanogr. 21:862–872.

Walburg, C. H., and P. R. Nichols. 1967. Biology and management of the American shad and status of the fisheries, Atlantic coast of the United States, 1960. U.S. Fish Wildl. Serv. Spec. Sci. Rept. Fish. 550. 105 pp.

Webber, E. E. 1967. Blue-green algae from a Massachusetts salt marsh. Bull. Torrey Bot. Club 94:99–106.

Weber, E. E., and R. T. Wilce. 1971. Benthic salt marsh algae at Ipswich, Massachusetts. Rhodora 73:262–291.

CHAPTER 4

Southern New England Estuaries

The southern New England estuary region extends along the coasts of southern Cape Cod, Rhode Island, and Connecticut and includes the Hudson estuary of New York. Southern New England estuaries are subject to warmer ocean temperatures, an effect of Cape Cod. They are protected further by small barrier islands. Because of differences in temperature and geology, the fauna and flora of southern New England differ from the more northerly species already described.

In contrast to the rocky shore of northern New England, the southern New England coast has many spits, tombolos, and sandy beaches. Beaches are formed from sand brought to the estuaries by rivers and ocean currents. The beaches of the Connecticut coast tend to the narrow and have small dunes. These barrier islands are present across the mouth of the estuaries along the coast of this region. Long Island is a barrier island across several rivers in its vicinity. The island influences salinity and flow characteristics of Long Island Sound (Figure 4.1) and causes it to resemble, to some extent, the Chesapeake Bay estuary in the middle Atlantic states. Therefore, this area, bordered by Long Island to the south and the continental coastline on the west and the north, will be considered a southern New England estuary.

The tidal marshes of southern New England were probably formed following the late Pleistocene. As the sea level rose, marshes that maintained themselves were those that could accumulate debris fast enough to hold their position between midtide and high tide. Water trapped in the marshlands enabled an inland extension of the marshes. Mud flats are often found in association with

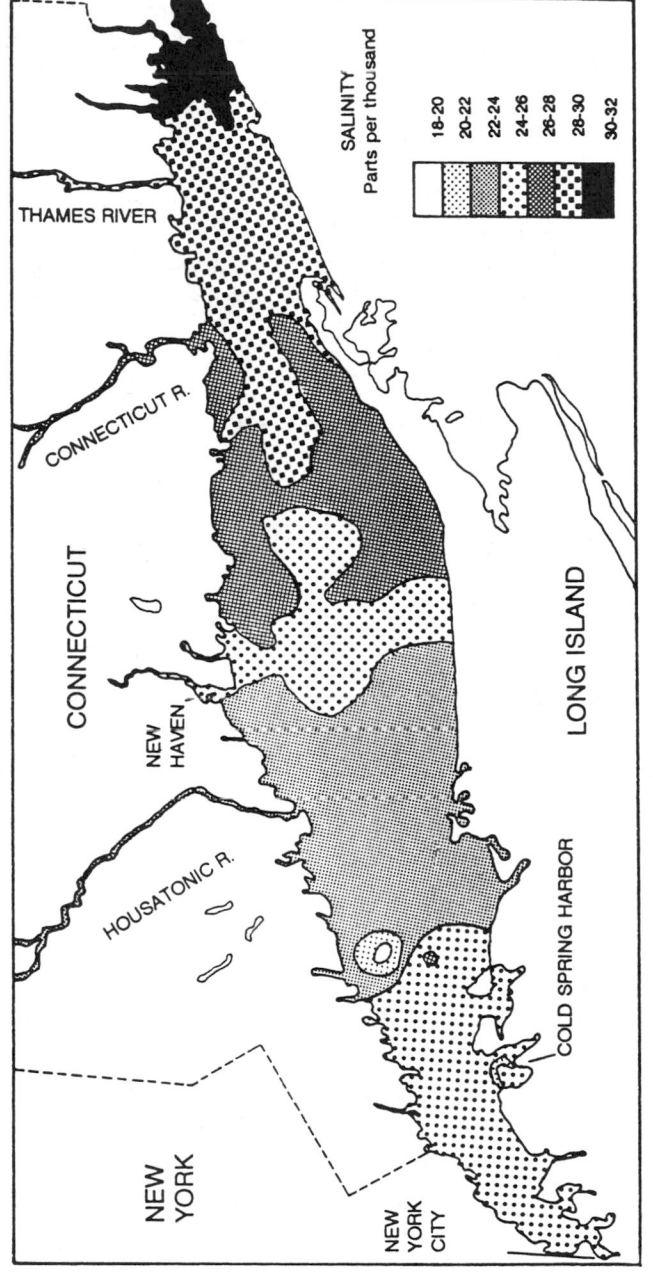

FIGURE 4.1. Surface salinity distribution in the waters of Long Island Sound. (After Coastal Area Management Program, 1977.)

tidal marshes and were formed by the accumulation of fine sediments. South of Cape Cod, the maximum tide range averages about 1.5 m, decreasing slightly near the Thames–Connecticut River mouths, and then increasing rapidly to 2.4 m going westward into Long Island Sound. Along the outer Long Island coast and the Atlantic coast the tide range is about 1.5 m, increasing to about 1.8 m around the Hudson River and the Passaic–Hackensack River mouths.

EXAMPLES OF COMMUNITIES OF AQUATIC LIFE

Submerged Fauna and Flora

Plankton. Phytoplankton has been extensively studied in Narragansett Bay by Smayda (1957) and Martin (1965, 1968). In this bay, *Skeletonema costatum*

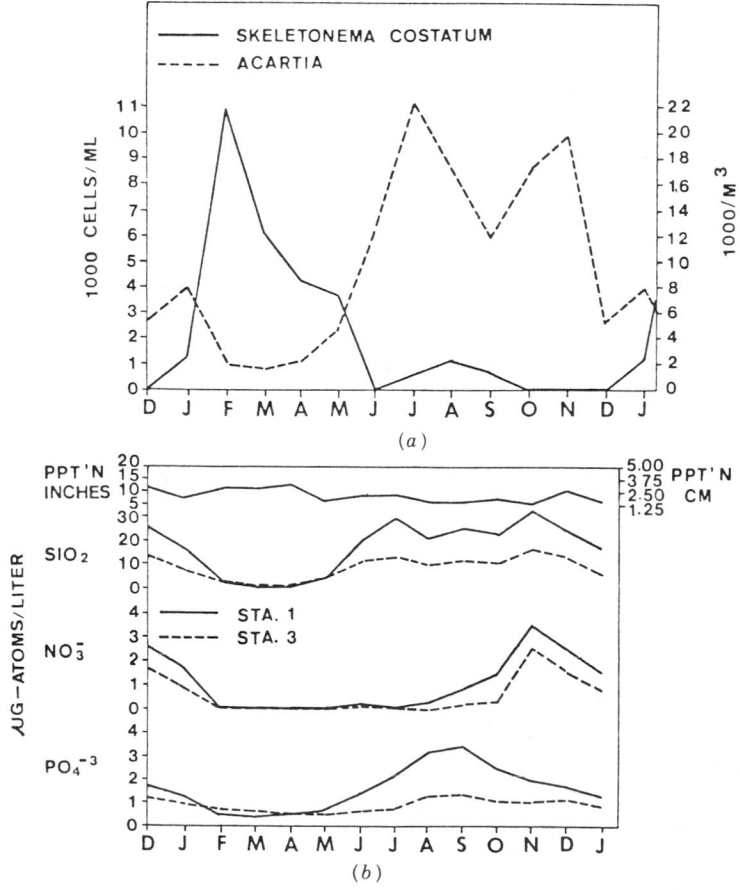

FIGURE 4.2. Phytoplankton, zooplankton, and nutrient relationships in Narragansett Bay, Rhode Island: (*a*) 3-year average of the abundance of *Skeletonema costatum* and of *Arcatia* spp. copepodites; (*b*) 3-year average of the concentrations of inorganic phosphate silicate and nitrate (μg at L^{-1}), and the 3-year average precipitation. (From Martin, 1965.)

seemed to be the dominant phytoplankton organism, with the largest populations appearing in late winter and spring. Other diatoms having large populations were the chain-forming diatoms, *Thallasiosira nordonskioldii*, and *Dentonula confervacea* (Durbin et al., 1975). From June to February 1954–1955 Smayda found that phytoplankton primary production was commonly $64 \, g \, C \, m^{-3}$, reflecting the large blooms of *Skeletonema costatum* and perhaps other diatoms occurring in late winter and early spring. Smayda found that *S. costatum* had a mean phosphorus assimilation rate of $0.87 \, \mu g \, L^{-1} \, day^{-1}$. The average rate of oxygen production was $0.43 \, mg \, O_2 \, L^{-1} \, day^{-1}$, while respiration utilized $0.32 \, mg \, O_2 \, L^{-1} \, day^{-1}$, indicating that more oxygen is produced by photosynthesis than is used in respiration.

Martin (1968) found that *Skeletonema costatum* was a favorite food for zooplankton, particularly the calanoid copepods, *Acartia clausi* and *A. tonsa*. These zooplankton increased greatly during warmer weather and their grazing put considerable pressure upon *S. costatum* (Figure 4.2). Martin (1968) found that when phytoplankton populations were large, the zooplankton feeding on them stored fat and produced eggs, resulting in the zooplankton excreting only moderate amounts of nitrogen and small amounts of phosphorus. However, when the phytoplankton populations became low, the zooplankton probably used their stored lipids for energy and the rates of nitrogen and phosphorus excretion increased. Thus the zooplankton and phytoplankton populations can be seen to have an effect on water chemistry. This interrelationship is set forth in Figures 4.3 and 4.4.

Durbin et al. (1975) found that during the fall, winter, and spring phytoplankton blooms in Narragansett Bay, the net plankton fraction was most important, while nanoplankton dominated during the summer. They believe that temperature accounted for most of this variability in the bloom, as on only two occasions did nutrient concentrations seem to provide a stress. The net plankton seemed to have a faster reproductive rate and a higher assimilation rate than the nanoplankton. Growth rates, as calculated from ^{14}C uptake and adenosine triphosphate levels, were generally high, with a maximum doubling time of 1.9 per day during some of the blooms of flagellates in the summer and *Skeletonema costatum* in the fall.

In Moriches and Great South Bay (Long Island), the diatom *Nitzschia closterium*, which grows best on nitrates and nitrites and poorly on ammonia and organic forms of nitrogen, was present in early spring. Later in the spring, summer, and early fall, the green algae, *Nannochloris atomus* and *Stichococcus* sp., were dominant. In the laboratory they grew best on ammonia, urea and uric acid, cysteine, asparagine, and glycol (Ryther, 1954). Ketchum (1954) points out that Moriches Bay was heavily fertilized by drainage from duck farms. Rapid reproduction rates in the phytoplankton were probably encouraged by the presence of such nutrients and the large population maintained by the slow circulation of water in the bay.

The phytoplankton of the shoals in the Niantic (Connecticut) estuary was greatly influenced by the source of the phytoplankton (Marshal and Wheeler, 1965). Phytoplankton populations in shoal areas were larger when the phyto-

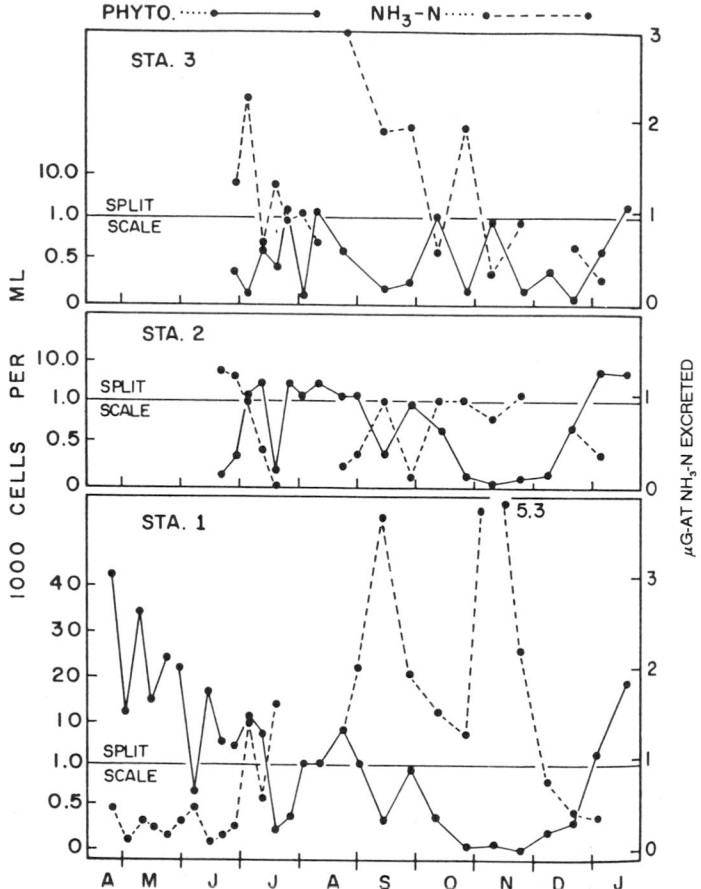

FIGURE 4.3.   Seasonal zooplankton excretion of nitrogen in µg at NH_3–N mg^{-1} dry wt day^{-1} and the abundance of phytoplankton in Narrangansett Bay. (From Martin, 1968.)

plankton was contributed mainly by up-estuary waters. When the outer basin was largely the source of plankton, the abundance fell to about one-tenth of the counts obtained when the upper estuary was the major contributor. Two periods of dominance, or blooms, of phytoplankton were noted. The winter/early spring (February through April) plankton bloom was characterized by *Thalassionema nitzschioides*, *Thallassiosira nordenskioldii*, *Asterionella japonica*, and *Plaschaetoceros bridymus*. One of these occurred in late summer/early fall (July to October). The dominant species were *Skeletonema costatum*, *Cyclotella caspia*, and *Asterionella japonica*. Of the dinoflagellates, *Exuviella baltica* was abundant in November, *Peridinium triquetrum* was most common in the winter, and in July the dominant dinoflagellate was *Prorocentrum micans*.

Nekton.   The principal nekton species in the estuaries were fish, which may be classified as estuary residents, summer migrants, local marine forms, diad-

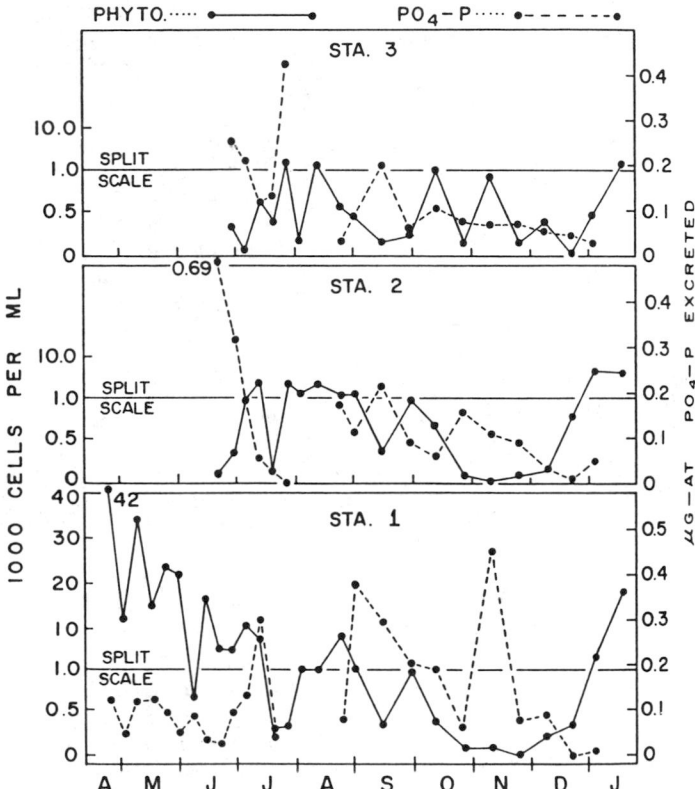

FIGURE 4.4. Seasonal zooplankton excretion of phosphorus in μg at PO_4–P mg^{-1} dry wt day^{-1} and abundance of total phytoplankton in Narragansett Bay. (From Martin, 1968.)

romous species, and sporadic freshwater species. Pearcy and Richards (1962) listed the fish in five groups, based on their use of the estuary at Mystic River, Massachusetts. They identified 51 species of fish in waters with salinity ranging from 17 to 29 ppt (Table 4.1). Most of these fish were found in the lower estuary, where the salinity averaged less than 24 ppt and where the water mixing was almost perfect.

Ninety-seven percent (all but two resident species) of the estuarine fish have demersal eggs, and 50% of all larvae were hatched from demersal eggs. Larvae from pelagic eggs tended to be more abundant in the adjoining sound. Several factors favor the survival of demersal eggs and the larvae that hatch from them. Demersal eggs are better protected against severe winter conditions because, where they rest on the bed of the estuary, they do not experience the extremes of temperature experienced by eggs in surface waters, and they are better able than pelagic eggs to resist the flow of current toward the sea. Demersal eggs are larger than pelagic eggs, so more food is available to the young larvae. The larvae from demersal eggs are larger, more completely developed when hatched, and have the advantage of parental care (Pearcy and Richards, 1962).

TABLE 4.1.   *Juvenile or Adult Stages of 51 Species of Fish Collected Within the Estuary of Mystic River, Massachusetts*

Residents
  Cyprinodon variegatus
  Fundulus heteroclitus
  Fundulus majalis
  Microgadus tomcod
  Apeltes quadracus
  Gasterosteus aculeatus
  Pungitius pungitius
  Syngnathus fuscus
  Tautogolabrus adspersus
  Gobiosoma bosci
  Gobiosoma ginsburgi (II?)
  Myoxocephalus aeneus
  Pholis gunnellus
  Menidia beryllina
  Menidia menidia
  Pseudopleuronectes americanus
  Opsanus tau

Summer migrants
  Synodus foetens
  Strongylura marina
  Pomatomus saltatrix
  Alectis ciliaris
  Seriola zonata
  Bairdiella chrysaura
  Leiostomus xanthurus
  Menticirrhus saxatilis
  Mullus auratus
  Stenotomus chrysops

  Sphyraena borealis
  Mugil cephalus
  Etropus microstomus
  Paralichthys dentatus
  Echeneis naucrates
  Alutera schoepfi
  Balistes capriscus
  Sphoeroides maculatus
  Chilomycterus schoepfi

Local marine
  Raja erinacea
  Anchoa mitchilli (I?)
  Urophycis chuss
  Urophycis regius
  Tautoga onitis (I?)
  Priontus carolinus
  Myoxocephalus octodecemspinosus
  Cyclopterus lumpus
  Liparis atlanticus
  Paralichthys oblongus
  Scophthalmus aquosus

Diadromous
  Alosa pseudoharengus
  Osmerus mordax
  Anguilla rostrata

Fresh water
  Esox niger

Source: After Pearcy and Richards (1962).

Benthos.   Distribution and the size of benthic invertebrate populations is limited by predation, competition for substrate, turbidity, salinity, water chemistry, temperature, organic matter and its conditions of decomposition, food supply, and substrate quality. Substrate is the most evident factor separating one habitat from another for the attached or burrowing species. Important substrates are sand, mud, gravel, hard rock bottoms, eelgrass (*Zostera*), *Spartina* (and the "peat" on which it grows), rocky shores, and human-made solid structures in the water (Allee, 1923a; Stickney and Stringer, 1957). Creeping, boring, or tubiculous species are less influenced by substrates (Burbank et al., 1956).

Allee (1923a) classified New England invertebrates and listed their occurrence by habitat (Table 4.2). The distribution record is the result of data amassed in 1920 and 1921. The species list was compiled from all collecting done in the area between 1912 and 1921.

(*text continues on page 244*)

TABLE 4.2 *Invertebrates Collected in Woods Hole, Massachusetts, Area, 1912–1921*

Species	Range[a]	Mud	Sand	Gravel	Eelgrass	Rocks and Rockweed	Pilings	Dredging
PHYLUM PORIFERA								
Class Calcarea								
Subclass Calcaronea								
Order Leucosolenida								
Family Homocoelidea								
Leucosolenia botryoides	N					13	24	1
Family Heterocoelidae								
Scypha ciliata	N		1			11	30	13
(=*Grantia ciliata*)								
Class Demospongiae								
Subclass Teractinomorpha								
Order Choristida								
Family Clathriidae								
Microciona prolifera	S	1			4	43	30	
Order Haplosclerida								
Family Haliclonidae								
Haliclona arbuscula	S	1				8	10	9
(=*Chalina arbuscula*)								
Order Hadromerida								
Family Clionidae								
Cliona celata	S			2	1	33	25	16
PHYLUM CNIDARIA								
Class Hydrozoa								
Order Athecata								
Family Tubulariidae								
Tubularia crocea							30	7
Family Pennariidae								
Pennaria tiarella	S				14	4	10	4
Family Clavidae								
Clava leptostyla	N					1		
Family Hydractiniidae								
Podocoryne carnea	N		2		1			
Hydractinia echinata	N	9	18	3	5	12		11
Stylactis hooperi	S							
Family Bougainvilliidae								
Bougainvillia carolinensis	S				1	2	1	
Family Eudendriidae								
Eudendrium album					2	4	6	
E. ramosum	M					7	22	7
E. tenue							1	
Order Thecata								
Family Campanularidae								
Campanularia calceolifera							1	
Campularia sp.						1	5	
Clytia grayi	L					2		
C. bicophora	N				1	2	1	
C. cylindrica							*Continued*	

TABLE 4.2   (*Continued*)

Species	Range[a]	Mud	Sand	Gravel	Eelgrass	Rocks and Rockweed	Pilings	Dredging
Obelia bicuspidata	S				1		1	
O. commissuralis	S	1			12	8	11	2
O. geniculata	N				5	6	7	
Family Sertularidae								
Sertularia pumilia	N				11	30	12	10
Abietinaria abietina	N							12
Family Plumularidae								
Schizotricha tenella	S					1	11	2
Order Limnomedusae								
Family Olindiidae								
Gonionemus murbackii	L							
Class Scyphozoa								
Order Stauromedusae								
Family Eleutherocarpidae								
Haliclystus auricula	N							
Order Semaestomeae								
Family Pelagiidae								
Chrysaora quinquecirrha	S							
(= *Dactylometra quinquecirrha*)								
Family Cyanidae								
Cyanea capillata	N							
Family Ulmaridae								
Aurelia flavidula	M							
Class Anthozoa								
Subclass Octocorallia								
Order Alcyonacea								
Family Alcyoniidae								
Alcyonium carneum	N							
Subclass Zoantharia								
Order Actinaria								
Suborder Athenaria								
Family Edwardsiidae								
Edwardsia elegans	N	1	5		1			
Family Haloclavidae								
Haloclava producta	S		3					
(= *Eloactis producta*)								
Family Sagartidae								
Actinothoe modesta	S				4	12		
(= *Sagartia modesta*)								
Family Metridiidae								
Metridium senile	N					29	24	
(= *Metridium dianthus*)								
Family Aiptasiomorphidae								
Haliplanella luciae	S	2	2		6	38	6	2
(= *Sagartia luciae*)								
Family Diadumenidae								

TABLE 4.2 (*Continued*)

Species	Range[a]	Mud	Sand	Gravel	Eelgrass	Rocks and Rockweed	Pilings	Dredging
Diadumene leucolena	S	3	3		2	37	11	4
(= *Sagartia leucolena*)								
Order Scleractinia								
Asterangia danae	G					11		7
PHYLUM PLATYHELMINTHES								
Class Turbellaria								
Order Trichladida								
Suborder Maricola								
Family Procerodidae								
Procerodes littoralis	N					1		
(= *Procerodes wheatlandi*)								
Family Bdellouridae								
Bdelloura candida	S	5	2		7			
B. propinqua								
Syncoelidium pellucidum					2			
Order Polycladida								
Suborder Acotylea								
Section Craspedommata								
Family Stylochidae								
Stylochus ellipticus	N	3	2	1	1	6	5	
S. zebra	L					1		1
PHYLUM NEMERTEA								
Class Anopla								
Order Paleonemertea								
Family Cephalothricidae								
Cephalothrix linearis	N					1		
Order Heteronemertea								
Family Lineidae								
Lineus bicolor	S	1	1			1	2	
Micrura leidyi	M	6	15		8	3		
Cerebratulus lacteus	S	7	11		2	2		
Class Enopla								
Order Hoplonemertea								
Suborder Monostylifera								
Family Amphiporidae								
Amphiporus ochraceus	S							5
Family Tetrastemmatidae								
Tetrastemma vermiculus	S	4					5	3
Family Nemathelminthes								
Pontonema movinum	S	1	1		5	6	19	6
PHYLUM BRYOZOA								
Class Gymnolaemata								
Order Ctenostomata								
Family Alcyonidiidae								
Alcyonidium sp.						3		
Family Flustrellidridae								

Continued

TABLE 4.2 (*Continued*)

Species	Range[a]	Mud	Sand	Gravel	Eelgrass	Rocks and Rockweed	Pilings	Dredging
Flustrellidra hispida	N				1	22		
Family Vesicularidae								
Bowerbankia gracilis	N					3	1	
Order Cyclostoma								
Family Crisiidae								
Crisia eburnea	N	1	1		4	21	18	12
Family Lichenoporidae								
Lichenopora verrucaria	N						2	
Order Cheilostomata								
Suborder Anasca								
Family Aeteidae								
Aetea anguina	N				5	10	12	
Family Membraniporidae								
Membranipora tenuis							6	
Family Electridae								
Electra monostachys							1	
(= *Membranipora hastingsae*)								
E. pilosa	N		1	1	6	21	13	5
(= *Membranipora pilosa*)								
Family Bugulidae								
Bugula harmsworthi	N						1	
(= *B. cucullifera*)								
B. simplex	N					1	1	
(= *B. flabellata*)								
B. turrita	S	1	2		17	17	31	14
Family Bicellariellidae								
Bicellariella ciliata	M						3	3
Family Cribrilinidae								
Cribrilina punctata	N							1
Suborder Ascophora								
Family Hippothoidae								
Hippothoa divaricata	C						1	
H. hyalina	C						1	
Hipporporina porosa	S		1		10	14	6	6
(= *Lepralia porosa*)								
Cleidochasma contractum	M						1	
(= *Lepralia serrata*)								
Family Schizoporellida								
Schizoporella unicornis	S	2	3	1	8	32	25	11
Stephanosella biaperta)								5
(= *Schizoporella biaperta*)								
Family Microporellidae								
Microporella ciliata	C					1	2	3
Family Smittinidae								
Parasmittia nitida	M		1			3		15
(= *Smittia trispinosa nitida*)								
Family Cheiloporinidae								

TABLE 4.2 (*Continued*)

Species	Range[a]	Mud	Sand	Gravel	Eelgrass	Rocks and Rockweed	Pilings	Dredging
Cryptosula pallasiana	N							
(= *Leptralia pallasiana*)								
PHYLUM ANNELIDA								
Class Polychaeta								
Order Orbiniida								
Family Orbiniidae								
Scoloplos acutus		12	1		6			
S. fragilis	S	8	19		9	1		
S. robustus	S	8	10		3	1		
Order Spionida								
Suborder Spioniformia								
Family Spionidae								
Spio setosa			1					
Polydora sp.								2
Laonice cirrata	S	3	1					
Suborder Chaetopteriformia								
Family Chaetopteridae								
Chaetopterus pergamentaceus[b]	S	2	2		5	6	2	4
Suborder Cirratuliformia								
Family Cirratulidae								
Cirratulus grandis	S	11	6	1		5		1
C. tenuis[b]								1
Order Capitellida								
Family Arenicolidae								
Arenicola cristata	S		3	6		1		
Family Maldanidae								
Maldane urceolata	S	3	9		2			
Order Phyllodocida								
Suborder Phyllodociformia								
Family Phyllodocidae								
Phyllodoce maculata	N	3	6		3	5	17	13
(= *Phyllodoce catenula*)								
Suborder Aphroditiformia								
Family Polynoidae								
Lepidametria commensalis	S					1		
Lepidontus squamatus	N	3	5	2	2	37	29	22
Harmothoe imbricata	N	2	5	1	3	26	27	11
Family Sigalionidae								
Sthenelais boa	S	6	5		4	3	4	6
(= *Sthenelais leidyi*)								
Suborder Nereidiformia								
Family Hesionidae								
Podarke obscura	S	2			4	4	7	6
Family Syllidae								
Autolytus cornutus	N				1		9	
A. varians[b]	S						1	
Family Nereidae								

Continued

TABLE 4.2   (*Continued*)

Species	Range[a]	Mud	Sand	Gravel	Eelgrass	Rocks and Rockweed	Pilings	Dredging
Platynereis magalops[b]	S				1		1	
Nereis succina	S	12	9	2	3	8	3	
(= *N. limbata*)								
N. pelagica	N	4	6			9	29	22
N. virens	N	17	20		9	3	1	
Suborder Glyceriformia								
Family Glyceridae								
Glycera americana or *dibranchiata*	SM	20	53	1	12	1		
Order Eunicida								
Family Onuphidae								
Diopatra cuprea	S	6	14		2	1		2
Family Eunicidae								
Marphysa leidyi[b]		1						3
Family Lumbrineridae								
Lumbrinereis tenuis	S	7	19	2	1	3		14
Family Arabellidae								
Arabella opalina[b]	S	8	17	2	5	1	1	7
Drilonereis longa		1	7	1				
Order Flabelligerida								
Family Flabelligeridae								
Pherusa affinis	S	4	1					6
(= *Trophonia affinis*)								
Order Terebellida								
Family Sabellariidae								
Sabellaria vulgaris	S	2	2		5	6	2	4
Family Pectinariidae								
Pectinaria gouldii	S	9	18	1	5			
Family Ampharetidae								
Amphareta setosa[b]	S							
Family Terebellidae								
Amphitrite attenuata[b]						1	9	
A. brunnea	N						1	
A. ornata	S	19	8		3	3		2
Enoplobranchus sanguineus	M	3						
Terebella rubra	S			1		4		
(= *Lepraea rubra*)								
Terebellides stroemi	N							
Nicolea simplex[b]		1	3		2	7	13	7
Polycirrus eximius	S	10	14		4	15	6	12
Pista palmata	S	3	1		1			
Thelepus cincinnatus	N					1	3	
Order Sabellida								
Family Sabellidae								
Sabella microphthalma	S	1	1	2		3	7	1
Potamilla sp.								1
Family Serpulidae								
Hydroides hexagonus[b]	S	2	3	1	3	39	17	22

TABLE 4.2 (*Continued*)

Species	Range[a]	Mud	Sand	Gravel	Eelgrass	Rocks and Rockweed	Pilings	Dredging
Spirorbis spirorbis[b]	N	3	4	2	11	26	19	
S. tubaeformis[b]	S					1		1
PHYLUM SIPUNCULA								
Phascolopsis gouldii	M	13	22		3	2		
PHYLUM MOLLUSCA								
Class Gasteropoda								
Subclass Prosobranchiata								
Order Archaeogastropoda								
Suborder Patellina								
Family Acmaeidae								
Acmaea testudinalis	N	1	2		1	26	1	3
Order Mesogastropoda								
Suborder Littorina								
Family Lacunidae								
Lacuna vincta	S	4	4	2	14	13	21	3
Family Littorinidae								
Littorina irrorata	S					2		
L. littorea	N	15	8	6	18	29	27	
L. palliata	N	4	5	3	11	24	7	1
L. rudis	N	8	4	2	12	32	6	1
Family Caecidae								
Caecum pulchellum						2		
Family Cerithiidae								
Bittium alternatum	M	6	6	2	20	17	11	8
Cerithiopsis emersonii	S				2	3		6
C. greenii	S				2	1		2
C terebralis								2
Family Crepidulidae								
Crepidula convexa	S	12	10	1	6	20	4	7
C. fornicata	S	6	15	1	2	21	12	9
C. plana	S	7	16	2	2	15	14	15
Family Naticidae								
Policines duplicata	S	2	6	1	3	1		
(=*Natica duplicata*)								
P. heros	M	2	1	1		2		
(=*Natica heros*)								
P. immaculata	N							2
(=*Natica immaculata*)								
N. pusilla	S	1			1			
Order Neogastropoda								
Family Muricidae								
Eupleura caudata	S	1	3	1		4		5
Urosalpinx cincerus	S	5	8	1	5	31	22	5
Family Columbellidae								
Anachis avara	S	3	5	1	9	13	14	19
(=*Columbella avara*)								

Continued

TABLE 4.2   (*Continued*)

Species	Range[a]	Mud	Sand	Gravel	Eelgrass	Rocks and Rockweed	Pilings	Dredging
A. lunata	S	3	7		12	20	30	21
(=*Collumbella lunata*)								
Family Melongenidae								
Busycon canaliculatum	S		7	1		2		
B. carica	S		1	1		1	1	
Family Nassariidae								
Ilyanassa obsoleta	S	35	14		3	9		
(=*Nassa obsoleta*)								
Nassarius trivittata	S	13	16	1	3	8	11	3
(=*Nassa trivittata*)								
Nassarius vibex	S	1						
(=*Nassa vibex*)								
Subclass Opisthobranchiata								
Order Bassomatophora								
Family Ellobiidae								
Melampus bidentatus	S	14	4	2				
(=*Melampus lineatus*)								
Order Sacoglossa								
Family Plakobranchidae								
Elysia chlorotica	M				4	1		
Class Polyplacophora								
Order Neoloricata								
Family Chaetopleuridae								
Chaetopleura apiculata	S					19		16
Order Nudibranchia								
Suborder Doridoida								
Family Dorididae								
Echinochila sp.	N						1	1
(=*Doris bifida*)								
Suborder Aeolioidea								
Family Favorinidae								
Cratena pymnata	N			1	1	2	15	
(=*Coryphella gymonota*)								
Class Bivalvia								
Subclass Palaeotaxodonta								
Order Nuculoida								
Family Nuculidae								
Nucula delphinodonta	N							
N. proxima	M	3	3	1	4	4		1
Family Nuculanidac								
Yoldia limatula	N							
Subclass Cryptodonta								
Order Solemioida								
Family Solemyacidae								
Solemva velum	M	10	20		4	4		
Subclass Pteriomorpha								
Order Arcoida								
Family Arcidae								

TABLE 4.2 (*Continued*)

Species	Range[a]	Mud	Sand	Gravel	Eelgrass	Rocks and Rockweed	Pilings	Dredging
Anadara pexata	S		1			5	1	7
(*Arca pexata*)								
Noetia ponderosa	S							
(=*Arca ponderosa*)								
Order Mytiloida								
Family Mytilidae								
Mytilus edulis	N	11	11	5	4	24	28	7
Modiolus demissus	S	22	15	3	6	8	3	3
M. modiolus	N	10	7		4	6	3	3
Order Pteroida								
Suborder Pteriina								
Family Pectinidae								
Aequipecten irradians	S	9	9		11	4		4
(=*Pecten irradians*)								
Family Anomiidae								
Anomia aculeata	N			1		12	4	5
A. ephippium	S	2		1		22	10	7
Family Ostreidae								
Crassostrea virginica	S	14	5			9		
Subclass Heterodonta								
Order Veneroida								
Family Astartidae								
Astarte castanea	M							3
A. undata	N							5
Family Cardiidae								
Cerastoderma pinnulatum	N							5
(=*Cardium pinnulatum*)								
Laevicarium mortoni	S	11	5	2	4	1		
Family Mactridae								
Mulinia lateralis	S		1					
(=*Mactra lateralis*)								
Mactra solidissima	N		3			2		2
(=*Spisula solidissima*)								
Family Tellinidae								
Tellina tenera	S	5	16	3	4	1		
Macoma tenta		2	2		1			1
Family Semelidae								
Cumingia tellinoides	S	10	11		6	1		
Family Solenidae								
Ensis directus	M	9	9		2	5		
Family Veneridae								
Mercenaria mercenaria	S	19	14	2	1	4		2
(=*Venus mercenaria*)								
Gemma gemma	N		3			1		
Family Petricolidae								
Petricola pholadiformis	S	3	2	3		1		
Order Myoida								
Family Myidae								

Continued

TABLE 4.2   (*Continued*)

Species	Range[a]	Mud	Sand	Gravel	Eelgrass	Rocks and Rockweed	Pilings	Dredging
Mya arenaria	N	23	21	3	6	5		
Family Corbulidae								
Corbula contracta	S		2					
Family Hiatellidae								
Hiatella arctica	N					2		
(= *Saxicava arctica*)								
Family Pholadidae								
Zirphaea crispata	N	1						
Family Teredinidae								
Teredo navalis	N		2	1	1	1	7	
Family Lyonsiidae								
Lyonsia hyalina	S		2					
Class Cephalopoda								
Subclass Coleoidea								
Order Teuthoidea								
Family Loliginidae								
Loligo peali	S		3					
PHYLUM ARTHROPODA								
Subphylum Mandibulata								
Class Crustacea								
Subclass Branchiopoda								
Division Oligobranchipoda								
Order Cladocera								
Suborder Eucladocera								
Family Polyphemidae								
Podon leuckarti	M							
Evadne nordmanni	M							
Subclass Cirripedia								
Order Thoracica								
Suborder Lepadomorpha								
Family Lepadidae								
Lepas anatifera	C					1		
Suborder Balanomorpha								
Family Balanidae								
Balanus balanoides	M	5	4	3	2	48		2
B. eburneus	S	1	3	1	6	18	19	17
Subclass Malacostraca								
Division Hoplocarida								
Order Stomatopoda								
Family Squillidae								
Squilla empusa	S					1	5	
Division Peracarida								
Order Mysidacea								
Suborder Mysida								
Family Mysidae								
Mysis stenolepis	M							
Heteromysis formosa	N	3	3		1	1		12

TABLE 4.2 (*Continued*)

Species	Range[a]	Mud	Sand	Gravel	Eelgrass	Rocks and Rockweed	Pilings	Dredging
Order Tanaidacea								
Suborder Dikonophora								
Family Tanaidae								
Tanais cavolinii	N						1	
Order Isopoda								
Suborder Anthuridea								
Family Anthuridae								
Cyanthura carinata	N		1		1			
Suborder Flabellifera								
Family Sphaeromidae								
Sphaeroma quadridentatum	S					5		
Suborder Valvifera								
Family Idoteidae								
Chiridotea coeca	S	2	2		2	2		
Idothea baltica	M	5	4		20	9	15	
I. metallica	S	3		2	5			
I. phosphorea	N					1		
Edotea triloba	M	3			2	2		
Erichsonella filiformis	N		1		2	2	2	4
Suborder Asellota								
Family Janiridae								
Jaera marina	N		2	1	4	3		
Suborder Oniscidea								
Infraorder Ligiomorpha								
Group Diplocheta								
Family Ligiidae								
Ligia oceanica	N					3		
(= *Ligyda oceanica*)								
Order Amphipoda								
Suborder Gammaridea								
Family Ampithoidae								
Ampithoe vibricata	N	1	1			6	6	8
Family Aoridae								
Lembos smithi	L		1			5	5	9
Family Corophiidae								
Corophium cylindricum[b]							2	
Unicola irrorata	N							1
Family Gammaridae								
Gammarus sp.		8	11	3	15	10	28	18
Family Haustoriidae								
Haustorius arenarius[b]	S		2					
Family Talitridae								
Orchestia agilis	S	1	33			8	2	
(= *Orchestis platensis*)								
Talorchestia longicornis	S	2	14	6	1			
Suborder Caprellidea								
Family Caprellidae								

Continued

TABLE 4.2   (*Continued*)

Species	Range[a]	Mud	Sand	Gravel	Eelgrass	Rocks and Rockweed	Pilings	Dredging
Aeginina longicornis	N					1	4	
(= *Aeginella longicornis*)								
Caprella penantis	S		1		6	13	26	1
(= *Caprella geometrica*)								
Division Eucarida								
Order Decapoda								
Suborder Natantia								
Section Caridea								
Family Hippolytidae								
Hippolyte zostericola	S	4	2		25	1		
Family Palaemonidae								
Palaemonetes vulgaris	S	9	7		16	8		
Family Crangonidae								
Crangon septemspinosa	M	3	4	4	16	3		1
Suborder Reptantia								
Section Astacura								
Family Callianassidae								
Callianassa atlantica	S	1				1		
(= *Callianassa stimpsoni*)								
Section Anomura								
Family Paguridae								
Pagurus acadianus	M		1					2
P. longicarpus	S	19	16	5	10	7	2	22
P. pollicaris	S	4	10	4	7	1	1	10
Section Brachyura								
Subsection Branchygnatha								
Infrasubsection Oxyrhyncha								
Family Majidae								
Hyas coarctatus	N							
Pelia multica	S		1					
Libinia dubia	S	14	8	1	10	3	20	16
L. emarginata	S	14	4	1	7	1	10	9
Family Parthenopidae								
Heterocrypta granulata	S							1
Infrasubsection Ocanchyrhyncha								
Family Cancridae								
Cancer borealis	N				3			
C. irroratus	M	5	7	2	4	6	2	2
Family Portunidae								
Ovalipes ocellatus	S	1	3		3	2		1
Portunus sayi	S							
Callinectes sapidus	S	1	1					
Carcinides maenas	S	16	4	4	4	8		5
(= *Carcinus maenas*)								
Family Xanthidae								
Neopanope texana sayi	S	17	12	3	12	7	27	16
Family Pinnotheridae								

TABLE 4.2   (Continued)

Species	Range[a]	Mud	Sand	Gravel	Eelgrass	Rocks and Rockweed	Pilings	Dredging
Pinnixa chaetopterana		2			2	1		
Pinnotheres maculatus	S	3					6	
Family Ocypodidae								
Uca pugilator	S	21	4	3	2	8		
U. pugnax	S		2					
Subphylum Pycnogonida								
Class Pantopoda								
Family Tanystylidae								
Tanystylum orbiculare	S					10	1	
Family Phoxichilidiidae								
Anoplodactylus lentus						4	10	2
Subphylum Chelicerata								
Class Merostomata								
Limulus polyphemus	S	12	10	2	6	1		
PHYLUM HEMICHORDATA								
Class Enteropneusta								
Family Harrimaniidae								
Saccoglossus kowalevskii	S	12	14	6	2	3		
PHYLUM CHORDATA								
Subphylum Urochordata								
Class Ascidiacea								
Order Enterogona								
Suborder Aplousobranchia								
Family Polyclinidae								
Amaraecium constellatum	N			2	3	19	29	14
A. pellucidum								
Family Didemnidae								
Didemnum lutarium	N				6	13		30
Suborder Phlebobranchia								
Family Perophoridae								
Perophora viridis	S		1		5	16	28	4
Order Pleurogona								
Suborder Stolidobranchiata								
Family Styelidae								
Styela partita	S	1	1		6	17	29	9
Botryllus schlosseri	N				13	7	5	
Family Molgulidae								
Molgula arenata	S						1	
M. manhattensis	S	3		1	6	2	24	1
M. papillosa	N						1	
Class Larvaceae								
Family Fritillaria								
Appendicularia longicauda	M							

Source: After Allee (1923a).

[a] N, north ranging (from Woods Hole); S, south ranging; M, midrange; L, local; C, cosmopolitan.

[b] Generic and specific names not found in K. L. Gosner, *Guide to Identification of Marine and Estuarine Invertebrates*, Wiley, New York, 1971.

TABLE 4.3. *Structure of the Community of Buzzards Bay at Station R[a]*

Rank by number	Species	Number	Cumulative percent by number	Percent of Fauna by number	Dry weight (g)	Percent by weight	Rank by weight	Feeding type[b]
1	Nucula proxima	9195	58.86	58.86	2.9694	13.98	4	SDF
2	Nephtys incisa	2689	76.07	17.21	6.1489	28.95	1	NSDF
3	Ninoe nigripes	671	80.37	4.30	0.3791	1.78	8	NSDF
4	Cylichna oryza	647	84.51	4.14	0.0782			?
5	Callocardia morrhuana	525	87.87	3.36	3.1803	14.97	3	SF
6	Hutchinsoniella macrocantha	307	89.84	1.97	0.0583			NSDF
7	Lumbrineris tenuis	286	91.67	1.83	0.0620			NSDF
8	Turbonilla a	145	92.60	0.93	0.0053			?
9	?Spio filicornis	135	93.46	0.86	0.0186			SDF
10	Retusa canaliculata	120	94.23	0.77	0.0440			?C
11	Stauronereis caecus	103	94.89	0.66	0.0099			?C
12	Tharyx sp.	89	95.46	0.57	0.0100			SDF
13	Unciola irrorata	58	95.83	0.37	0.0286			SDF
14	Ampelisca spinipes	54	96.18	0.35	0.0324			SF
15	Nassarius trivittata	45	96.47	0.29	0.1726	0.81	9	NSDF

16	*Bostrichobranchus pilularis*	40	96.73	0.26	4.9878	23.49	2	SF
17	*Yoldia limatula*	39	96.98	0.25	0.1084	0.51	13	SDF
18	*Nucula delphinodonta*	37	97.22	0.24	0.0060			SDF
19	*Edotea triloba*	37	97.46	0.24	0.0381			S
20	*Paraonis gracilis*	31	97.66	0.20	0.0032			SDF
21	*Melinna cristata*	25	97.82	0.16	0.0461			SDF
22	*Capitellid*	24	97.97	0.15	0.0007			NSDF
23	*Ampharete arctica*	24	98.12	0.15	0.0154			SDF
24	*Macoma tenta*	22	98.26	0.14	0.0094			SDF
25	*Arabella iricolor*	19	98.36	0.12	0.8000	3.77	6	?C
26	*Tubulanus pellucidus*	19	98.50	0.12	0.0019			?C
27	*Maldanopsis elongata*	17	98.61	0.11	0.0488			NSDF
28	*Mulinia lateralis*	12	98.69	0.08	0.0059			SF
29	*Pectinaria gouldii*	11	98.76	0.07	0.0185			NSDF
30	*Micrura leidyi*	11	98.83	0.07	1.0263	4.83	5	C

Source: Sanders (1960).

[a] The species listed are those present in 20 samples of "typical" sediment composition (78–91% silt-clay), and total abundance in column 2 represents the sum of the numbers of individuals in all 20 samples.

[b] SDF, selective deposit feeder; NSDF, non-selective deposit feeder; SF, suspension feeder; C, carnivore; S, scavenger.

Food preferences greatly influenced the distribution of invertebrates in the benthos. Scavengers were concentrated near shore where organic detritus supplies were high. Crabs, hermit crabs, sand shrimp, and *Ilyanassa* (mollusc) were typical scavengers. Detritus feeders, which included *Ampelisca spinipes* (amphipod) and *Pectinaria gouldii* (polychaete), were particularly abundant where organic content was high (Allee, 1923a). Suspended organic matter was important, especially to tentacled worms, many bivalves, and *Crepidula* (mollusc). These species required fairly active water circulation to wash sediments and put material in suspension. Some sediment-feeding bivalves (e.g., *Macoma tenta*) created a drift of sediment toward themselves. They succeed best where water circulation is less. They are found more often in muddy sediments than in sandy ones.

Life history may also be important in determining the distribution of species. For example, *Balanus* (barnacle), *Anomia* and *Modiolus* (molluscs), and *Molgula* (tunicate) have a pelagic larval phase during which they may be widely dispersed. The critical and limiting requirement for their maturation is a hard substrate for attachment. The molluscs, *Mercenaria*, *Mya*, *Mulinia*, and *Ensis*, also have pelagic larval phases, but their substrate requirements as adults are less critical. They did not cover the bottom totally each year, even in areas ostensibly suited to them, suggesting that physical factors or possibly some directed movement of the larvae toward the best sites was responsible for their uneven distribution (Stickney and Stringer, 1957).

Unlike the species noted above, *Ampelisca* (amphipod) had a continuous and extensive distribution throughout the bay. *Ampelisca* young do not have a pelagic phase but develop in the brood pouch of the female. As long as adults remain in an area, successive generations of the amphipod repopulate the same site (Stickney and Stringer, 1957).

Adults of active species are able to move to the best sites, so the range of the larval phase is not very important. For example, *Ilyanassa obsoleta* (mollusc) congregates in shallow water at the outlets of tidal creeks, where fresh supplies of organic material are in continuous supply. *Neopanope* sp. (crustacean) seeks crevices in shell beds and rocky bottoms where concealment is best. *Eupleura* (mollusc) forms patches wherever the young bivalves on which it feeds are congregated (Allee, 1923a).

Stickney and Stringer (1957) studied the invertebrate bottom communities in Greenwich Bay (Providence River estuary), which is an arm of Narragansett Bay. They found and named two groups of organisms living together: organisms that interact are designated *associations*; organisms that live together but may not interact are *communities*.

In Buzzards Bay the meiofauna (nematodes, kinorhynchs, ostracods, benthic copepods) had a density of about 930,000 m^{-2}, making meiofauna about 100 times as numerous as the macrofauna. The weight of all the meiofauna is only about 3% of that of the macrofauna.

Table 4.3 shows the main species of the community and their habitats. Most of the species (87.5%) feed on detritus which is in or on the sediments. The next most common species, composing 4.3% of the population, feed on particles or organisms suspended in the water.

Nucula proxima, a mollusc, the overwhelming dominant in terms of numbers, lay just below the sediment surface, feeding on the finer sediment immediately beneath itself. *Nephytys incisa*, a polychaete, the second most abundant species, was also a deposit feeder, but it was nonselective, ingesting both fine sediments and sand, including all the associated diatoms and organic films on these particles. The third most abundant species, *Ninoe nigripes*, another polychaete, had jaws which indicated that it was a predator, but gut analyses showed that it fed on the brown flocculant zone of sediments as a nonselective deposit feeder. It remained stationary and allowed the slow movement of the sediment mass to replenish its supply.

The fourth most abundant species, the opisthobranch gastropod, *Cylichna oryza*, could not be analyzed successfully. *Callocardia morrhuana*, a mollusc, ranked fifth in population and third by weight and was a suspension feeder, drawing in water through its siphon. *Hutchinsoniella macracantha*, a crustacean, was ranked sixth by numbers of organisms. It stirred up the surface sediments and then moved them toward its mouth. It was a nonselective deposit feeder. *Lumbrineris tenuis*, a polychaete, ranked seventh in abundance, had been considered carnivorous by some, but gut analyses showed that it was really a nonselective deposit feeder, allowing sediments to drift toward it as *Ninoe nigripes* did. *Turbonilla* (species not given) was a mollusc and the eight-ranked species. It is a member of a group that has been regarded as exclusively predatory on polychaetes and coelenterates, but this taxon was found in great abundance in samples containing no prey species, so Sanders suggests that it can be a deposit feeder. An examination of Table 4.3 indicates that most species in this community were deposit feeders. Very few were scavengers or carnivores.

Muddy Sediment Communities. The *Ampelisca* community, the most extensive in the bay, occupied the muddy central part of Greenwich Bay at a depth of 3.04 to 4.3 m. The community was characterized by the dominance of one species, in this case the amphipod, *Ampelisca spinipes* (found in densities of up to 10,000 individuals m^{-2}). All other species were considerably rarer. Moderately abundant species in the *Ampelisca* community were *Corophium cylindricum* (amphipod); *Tharyx acutus* (polychaete); *Tornatina canaliculata* (snail); the bivalves, *Macoma tenta*, *Nucula proxima*, *Pitar morrhuana*, and *Mercenaria mercenaria*; and the arthropods, *Squilla empusa* and *Upogebia affinis*. Species of variable occurrence (either in time or in space) were the molluscs, *Ilyanassa obsoleta* and *Eupleura caudata*, and the polychaetes, *Podarke obscura* and *Spiochaetopterus oculatus*.

Sand Bottom Communities. The most characteristic members of this community were *Ensis directus* (razor clam) and *Blycera dibranchiata* (bloodworm), which inhabited the sediment, and *Crangon septemspinosa* (sand shrimp) and *Pagurus longicarpus* (hermit crab), which occupied the sediment surface. Species found occasionally in abundance were the polychaete, *Spiochaetopterus oculatus*; the molluscs, *Eupleura caudata*, *Mulinia lateralis*, and *Petricola pholadiformis*;

and the bivalves, *Mercenaria mercenaria*, *Ensis directus*, and *Mya arenaria*. Occasional dense patches were formed by the polychaetes, *Spio setosa* and *Streblospio benedicti*, and by the amphipod, *Ampelisca macrocephala*. Also characteristic but less abundant were *Tellina tenera* (bivalve) and the polychaetes, *Diopatra cuprea* and *Haploscoloplos fragilis* (Stickney and Stringer, 1957).

Sanders (1960) sampled intensively at a single station about 19 m below the surface of Buzzards Bay, Massachusetts. The site was presumed to be representative of the *Nephtys incisa* (polychaete) and *Nucula proxima* (mollusc) community typical of the softer sediments in the region. Most of the sediment particles were smaler than 50 m in size and in most cases made up 78 to 91% of the sample. The macroinvertebrate community was characterized by dominance of a small number of species (*Nephtys incisa, Nucula proxima, Callacardia morrhuana, Ninoe nigripes*). Eleven species provided about 95% of the total number of individuals, and 13 species constituted about 95% of the biomass. Some species with large individuals represented significant percentages of the total weight, although the number of individuals was small and the species was not listed among the 30 most commonly found. Among the large but rare invertebrates were *Ceriantheopsis americanus* (coelenterate, 0.74% of total biomass), *Flabelligera affinis* (polychaete, 0.66% of total biomass), *Cerastoderma pinnulatum* (mollusc, 0.65% of total biomass), and *Lumbrineris tenuis* (polychaete, 1.86% of total biomass).

In shallow water the most important influences on distribution of fauna and flora are the current patterns, temperature, water chemistry, and food supply, which includes the size of the sediment particles.

Hard Substrate Communities. In Greenwich Bay the "*Crepidula–Nereis–Neopanope*" association was more or less restricted to a small portion of the bay, close to its opening, where old shells formed a hard substrate. The dominant species of this association were the molluscs, *Crepidula fornicata* and *Anoria simplex*, and the polychaete, *Nereis succinea*. Also characteristic of the association were *Neopanope texana* (mud crab), *Libinia emarginata* (spider crab), and *Urosalpinx cinerea* (oyster drill). *Mercenaria mercenaria* (hard-shelled clam) was more commonly found in the shell–sand–mud in the vicinity of the harder shell substrate. Encrusting organisms also found in this habitat were *Cliona* (boring sponge) and *Lepralia* and the tubiculous worms, *Sabella* and *Hydroides* (Stickney and Stringer, 1957).

In Buzzards Bay, too, dead bivalve shells were an excellent habitat for some invertebrate species. Driscoll and Swanson (1973) found an assemblage of 106 species composed of 53,000 individuals on 28 shells of *Mercenaria*.

Eelgrass Association. Eelgrass (*Zostera*) communities in the Niantic River (Connecticut) and in the Pettaquamscutt River (Rhode Island) areas with low current speed were studied by Tietjen (1969). Large numbers of diatoms, chrysophytes, and chlorophytes were present on sand grains around the eelgrass. Nematodes were the dominant group of meiofauna and were 58 to 90% of the total fauna. The epigrowth-feeding nematodes were dominant, although deposit-feeding nematodes were present. For most of the year, the nematode distribution was confined largely to the upper centimeter of the sediment. The availability of food and the higher oxygen levels in the top centimeter of sediment probably accounted for the concentration of nematodes in such a shallow band. Eelgrass (*Zostera*) and microscopic algae furnished most of the food for the epigrowth feeders. Other important groups, in descending order of occurrence, were copepods, ostracods, polychaetes, amphipods, and lamellibranchs.

The eelgrass association in Buzzards Bay supports as large a number of species as that supported by the Niantic River and the Pettaquamscutt River. Davis (1911) lists 42 species of plants known to occur as epiphytes upon the eelgrass. The animals associated with the eelgrass may live attached as epiphytes on the blades of the eelgrass, the eelgrass mat, or among its roots in the muck. The animals associated with eelgrass in the Woods Hole region are set forth in Table 4.2. Very common on mats of eelgrass are mud snails, *Ilyanassa obsoleta*; the hermit crab, *Pagurus longicarpus*; and the snail, *Crepidula convexa*. In places the mollusc, *Littorina litorea*, almost equals the mud snails in number.

Intertidal Communities
Some species are found in both intertidal and subtidal habitats. Polychaete species were much more common in mud and sand than in any other habitat (Allee, 1923a), but their occurrences in eelgrass and on rocks and in rockweeds were almost as great. The lowest number of polychaete species was recorded from gravel. As one might expect, eelgrass, rocks and rockweed, and pilings had many more species of bryozoa than did mud, sand, and gravel. Pilings and gravel and significantly fewer species of *Thoracostraca* than are found in other habitats. More species of gastropods were found on rocks and in rockweeds, while mud and sand had about equal numbers of individuals but ranked second in number of species. The pelecypods were represented by the largest number of species in mud, sand, rocks, and rockweed. The number of animals present in a given locality seems to be more dependent on the availability of suitable breeding places and abundance of food than on other factors, such as disturbance.

Rocky Substrates. In their studies of the Merrimack River estuary, Mathieson and Fralick (1973) found that more species of algae grew on rocky substrates or on artificial breakwaters than on soft substrates. In general, the rocks, pilings, and gravel tended to support fewer species of certain groups of invertebrates than did mud or sand. This was particularly true for bivalve molluscs. The associations on wharf pilings were similar to those on rocks. Seventy-seven percent of the animals common in the former were next in abundance on the latter. Animals common on rocks and pilings were nearly as abundant on the flats. This is probably due to the fact that the rocks extend up from the flats, often forming a belt only a few feet wide in the tidal portion of the flats. Single rocks may be surrounded by typical mud or sandy flats. Rocks, rockweeds, and pilings were a more favored habitat for the hydrozoa than were mud, sand, or gravel. This is probably because many of these species typically grow attached to a firm substrate (Mathieson and Fralick, 1973).

There are both exposed and protected rocky shores in Buzzards Bay. Exposed rocky shores had few macroscopic algae associated with them because wave action was too strong to permit heavy growth. On exposed rocky shores were found associations of organisms composed of sponges, *Microcione* and *Clione*; the actinians, *Sagartia leucolena* and *S. luciae*; the hydroid, *Metricium*; the starfish, *Asterias*; and the annelids, *Harmothoe*, *Hydroides*, *Lepraea*, and *Lepiodontus*. The encrusting forms also present on exposed rocks were bryozoans belonging to the genus *Bugula* and various barnacles, chitons, snails, and the chordate, *Amaraecium*, usually present in small clusters (Table 4.4). Zonation was not as distinct on these rocky shores as it was on dock pilings (Allee, 1923b).

On protected rocky shores the common rockweeds, *Ascophyllum* and *Fucus*, sheltered the invertebrates living among them from the scouring effect of waves, extreme temperatures, and the dangers of desiccation. Rockweed associations were characteristically found in shallow water which may have been exposed at low tide. Animals found on a protected rocky shore are listed according to tidal stratum and substrate in Table 4.5 (Allee, 1923b).

Wharves and Pilings.   In Greenwich Bay (Stickney and Stringer, 1957) solid intertidal substrates (wharf pilings) were occupied by different species according to the exposure the fauna and flora could tolerate. The barnacle, *Balanus balanoides*, was the most usually encountered species from the high-tide to midtide level. From midtide to well below the low-tide line *Balanus eburneus* was common. From low tide to the bottom of the pilings the hydroid, *Obelia*, was common. Near the bottom of the piling were large populations of the drill, *Urosalpinx cinera*. In crevices or under rocks were *Unicola errorata*, *Eupleura caudata*, and *Odostomia* sp.

In Buzzards Bay, wharf pilings supported a considerable number of species, as shown in Table 4.6 (Allee, 1923b). On these pilings a vertical distribution was quite apparent. Near high-tide level, *Littorina* and *Urosalpinx* (molluscs) and barnacles, *Balanus balanoides*, were found with an occasional *Asterias forbesi* (starfish). Nearer the water's edge at low tide were *Mytilus* clusters and *Modiolus modiolus*, which shelter *Libinia dubia* (crab) and *Lepidonotus* (polychaete). Below these, normally in water at all times, were the chordates, *Ameraecium*, *Styela*, and a few others. The sponges, *Microcione*, *Grantia*, and *Cliona*, and hydroids such as *Tubularia* and *Schizotricha* were also found below the low-tide line. Intermixed and abundant in this zone were the worms, *Lepidonotus*, *Harmothoe*, *Sthenelais*, *Nereis pelagica*, and *N. limbata*. Also abundant below the water line were sea slugs, snails, and the encrusting bryozoans, *Bugula*, *Schizoporella*, *Lepralia*, and *Membranipora*. Below these may be found some sea anemones. These associations of organisms could be recognized as distinct bands on the pilings. In Vineyard Haven, for example, as one looked down the piling one saw the Balanus band above the low-water level; the *Mytilus* band was near the low-water level; the hydroid band, which is more brilliantly colored, was below the mussels; and deeper were the sea anemones, which formed a dull brown band.

Stony Beaches.   The predominant species on stony beaches in the Greenwich

TABLE 4.4. *Animals Commonly Found in the Exposed Rock Association*

Porifera
  Cliona celata(?)
  Grantia ciliata
  Leucosolena botryoides
  Microcione prolifera[a]

Coelenterata
  Asterangia danae
  Clava leptostyla
  Hydractinia echinata[a]
  Metridium dianthus
  Sargartia leucolena
  S. luciae
  S. modesta
  Sertularia pumila

Platyhelminthes
  Stylochus ellipticus

Echinoderma
  Arbacia punctulata
  Asterias forbesi[a]

Annelida
  Harmothoe imbricata[a]
  Hydroides hexagonus[a]
  Lepraea rubra
  Lepidonotus squamatus[a]
  Nicolea simplex
  Polycirrus eximeus
  Spirorbis spirorbis[a]
  Sabellaria vulgaris[a]

Bryozoa
  Alcyonidium sp.
  Bugula turrita[a]
  Crisia eburnea[a]
  Flustrella hispida
  Lepralia pertusa
  Membranipora pilosa[a]
  Schizoporella unicornis[a]

Crustacea
  Amphithoe
  Balanus balanoides[a]

Balanus eburneus
Cancer irroratus[a]
Idothea metallica
Idothea baltica[a]
Pagurus longicarpus[a]
Panopeus sayi[a]
Sphaeroma quadridentatum[a]
  (under rocks)

Mollusca
  Anomia ephippium[a]
  A. aculeata
  Modiolus modiolus[a]
  Mytilus edulis[a]
  Acmea testudinalis
  Bittium alternatum
  Cerithiopsis emersonii
  Chaetopleura apiculata
  Columbella avara
  C. lunata[a]
  Coryphella gymnota
  Crepidula fornicata
  C. convexa
  C. plana[a]
  Eupleura caudata
  Lacuna vincta[a]
  Littorina litorea[a]
  L. palliata
  L. rudis[a]
  Purpura lapillus[a]
  Odostomia sp.
  Urosalpinx cinereus[a]

Chordata
  Amaraecium constellatum[a]
  Botryllus schlosseri[a]
  Didemnum lutarium
  Molgula manhattensis
  Perophora viridis
  Styela partita

Source: Allee (1923b).
[a] May be taken above low-tide mark.

estuary were the polychaete, *Nereis succinea*; the crab, *Neopanope texana*; and the clams, *Mya arenaria* and *Mercenaria mercenaria*.

Tidal Flats. Tidal flats are fairly common in the Woods Hole area. The zonation of these flats is not as distinct as on the pilings or even as clear as on rocky habitats. Certain associations may be recognized, however. The most

TABLE 4.5.   *Representative Animals of the Rockweed Association by Strata*

Animals on or Among the Rockweed When Left Exposed by the Tide

Coelenterata
  Clava leptostyla
  Obelia geniculata
  Sertularia pumila
  Sagartia lucioe

Echinoderma
  Asterias forbesi

Bryozoa
  Alconidium sp.?
  Bugula turrita
  Flustrella hispida

Arthropoda
  Amphithoe rubricata
  Balanus balanoides
  Caprella geometrica
  Anoplodactylus lentus
  Limulus polyphemus

Mollusca
  Littorina litorea
  Littorina palliata
  Columbella avara
  Columbella lunata
  Mytilus edulis

Animals from the Rocks Below the Rockweed Stratum from First Six Rocks Examined

Porifera
  Cliona celata (?)
  Microcione prolifera

Coelenterata
  Sagartia leucolena

Echinoderma
  Asterias forbesi

Bryozoa
  Lepralia pertusa
  Membranipora pilosa
  Schizoporella unicornis

Annelida
  Harmothoe imbricata
  Lepidonotus squamatus
  Hydroides hexagonus
  Polycirrus eximeus

Arthropoda
  Cancer irroratus

Mollusca
  Mytilus edylis

Chordata
  Styela partita

Animals Found in Brief Examination on Surface of Substratum

Crustacea
  Cancer irroratus
  Libinia dubia carrying the sponge, *Cliona celata* (?)
  Pagurus longicarpus carrying the hydroid, *Hydractinia echinata*
  Panopeus sayi

Gasteropoda
  Littorina litorea, very numerous

D. Animals Found in Sampling the Subsratum (Three spadesful were dug)

Platyhelminthes
  Lineus ochraeus

Mollusca
  Cumingia tellinoides
  Nassa trivitatta

Annelida
  Clymenella torquata
  Lepraea rubra
  Lumbrinereis tenuis
  Nereis limbata
  Pectinaria gouldii

Source: Allee (1923b).

common associations in the flats are the sandbar associations and the muddy sand community. Sandbar associations are usually separated from the open water by a sandbar, which gives them protection. Here were found practically pure cultures of *Scoloplos fragilis* (a polychaete worm) associated with various arthropods, molluscs, and other worms. A list of the animals characteristic of this eelgrass associated with Blind Gutter Flats is given in Table 4.7.

TABLE 4.6. *Invertebrate Animals Taken from Crane's Wharf Piles in Nine Years' Collecting*[a]

	Sessile	Free		Sessile	Free
Porifera			*Sabellaria vulgaris*		
Chalina arbuscula	7		*Spirorbis spirorbis*	6	
Cliona celata (?)	7		*Sthenelais leidyi*		
Grantia ciliata	7		*Thelepus* sp.		
Leucosolenia botryoides	5				
Microcione prolifera	7		Bryozoa		
			Aelea anguina	5	
Coelenterata			*Bugula turrita*	7	
Campanularia sp.	1		*Bicellaria ciliata*		
Clytia bicophora	7		*Crisia eburnea*	7	
Eudendrium album			*Lepralia pertusa*		
Eudendrium ramosum			*Membranipora pilosa*	6	
Gemmaria gemmosa	1		*Flustrella hispida*	2	
Hydractinia echinata			*Schizoporella unicornis*	6	
Metridium dianthus	6				
Obelia commissuralis	4		Arthropoda		
Obelia geniculata			*Amphithoe rubricata*		2
Pennaria tiarella	1		*Autonoe smithi*		1
Sagartia luciae	1		*Anoplodactylus lentus*		2
Sagartia leucolena	1		*Balanus balanoides*		7
Schizotricha tenella			*Balanus eburneus*		2
Sertularia pumila			*Caprella geometrica*		7
Tubularia crocea	7		*Erichsonella filiformis*		1
			Idothea baltica		2
Platyhelminthes			*Libinia dubia*		6
Tetrastemma vermiculum	1		*Libinia emarginata*		6
Lineus bicolor			*Lygidia oceanica*		2
			Orchestia agilis		
Nemathelminthes			*Palaemonetes vulgaris*		
Pontonema marinum	5		*Palene empusa*		1
			Pinnotheres maculata		2
Echinoderma			*Panopeus sayi*		6
Arbacia punctulata		3	*Talorchestia longicornis*		
Asterias forbesi		5	*Tanystylum orbiculare*		2
Asterias vulgaris		1			
Henricia sanguinolenta			Mollusca		
			Acmea testudinalis		1
Annelida			*Anomia aculeata*	1	
Arabella opalina		1	*Anomia ephippium*	4	
Amphitrite attenuata		2	*Arca pexata*		
Autolytus cornutus		1	*Bittium alternatum*		4
Harmothoe imbricata		5	*Busycon carica*		
Hydroides hexagonus	5		*Columbella avara*		6
Lepidonotus squamatus		7	*Columbella lunata*		7
Lepraea rubra			*Crepidula convexa*		
Nereis pelagica		7	*Crepidula fornicata*		3
Nicolea simplex		2	*Crepidula plana*		3
Podarka obscura		2	*Coryphella gymnota*		5
Polycirrus eximeus		3	*Lacuna vincta*		4
Polydora sp.					
Phyllodoce catenula					

Continued

TABLE 4.6.   (*Continued*)

	Sessile	Free		Sessile	Free
Littorina litorea		7	Chordata		
Littorina palleata		1	*Amaraecium constellatum*	6	
Littorina rudis		1	*Botryllus schlosseri*		
Modiolus modiolus	1		*Didemnum lutarium*	7	
Mytilus edulis	6		*Molgula arenaria*	1	
Teredo navalis		3	*Molgula manhattensis*	4	
Odostomia sp.			*Molgula papillosa*	1	
Urosalpinx cinereus		7	*Perophora viridis*	6	
			Styela partita	7	

Source: Allee (1923b).
[a]The figures give an indication of comparative abundance in 1920 and are based on the number of collecting teams reporting the several species. Absence of a figure indicates that the animal was not taken during this trip.

TABLE 4.7.   *Common Animals Found on, Among, and at the Roots of Eelgrass in the Center of N.W. and Blind Gutter Flats*

On Eelgrass

Coelenterata
  Sagartia luciae (frequently many)

Bryozoa
  Bugula turrita (much)
  Schizoporella unicornis (some)

Gasteropoda
  Bittium alternatum (many)
  Crepidula convexa (several)

Crepidula fornicata (few)
Littorina rudis (few)
Littorina litorea (many)
Littorina palliata (few)

Chordata
  Molgula manhattensis (very few)
  Botryllus schlosseri (little)

Among Eelgrass

Annelida
  Podarka obscura (frequently abundant)

Crustacea
  Virbius zostericola (very many)

Mollusca
  Pecten irradians (many)

In Muck at Roots

Echinoderma
  Thyone briareus (frequently abundant)

Annelida
  Scoloplos acutus (many)

Source: Allee (1923a).

The flat associations were represented by animals that live near high tide and animals that live near the low-tide level. The mollusc association, dominated by *Mya*, was near the low-tide level. Other animals found low on the flat were *Matica duplicata*, *Nereis virens*, and *Polycirrus eximeus* (worms) that were buried in the mud. The hermit crab, *P. longicarpus*, and the mollusc, *Ilyanassa obsoleta*, were found in this association as well. The oyster, *Crassostrea virginica*, was occasionally found growing on the rocks that jutted through the mud here and there.

The high mud shores were dominated by fiddler crabs (a species of *Uca*) and the snail, *Melampus lineatus*. This association of animals was found intermixed with *Spartina* and probably belonged to the salty marsh association.

It is evident from Table 4.7 that the flats contained by far the greatest number of species, and the largest number of species found in only one habitat were found in the flats. Characteristic of this habitat in Greenwich Bay were *Mya arenaria* (clam), *Sagartia modula* (anthozoan), and *Dolichoglossus kowalevskii*, a protochordate (Stickney and Stringer, 1957).

Muddy Sand Association. The muddy sand association is usually located between the sandbar association and the eelgrass association. The most characteristic animal of this community was the Sipunuclid worm, *Phascolosoma gouldii*. Table 4.8 lists the organisms most commonly found in this community.

Sand Communities. Perhaps the best study on sand habitats is that of Wall (1973) who studied the intertidal sand and salt marsh sod organisms around Cape Cod. He found that the species on both sides of Cape Cod were quite similar, although the tides are about 5 ft higher and the water is 6 to 11 °C colder on the north side of Cape Cod. South of Cape Cod the summer substrate temperatures ranged from 18 to 30 °C, with a few instances as high as 33 °C. The winter substrate temperatures were occasionally as low as -2 °C. The salinity in the intertidal sand varied from about 32 ppt at high tide, to 17 ppt, minimum, at low tide. At high tide in small protected estuaries of the bay

TABLE 4.8. *Animals Easily Found in the Muddy Sand or* Phascolosoma *Association*

Coelenterata	*Lacuna vincta*
Hydractinia echinata	*Laevicardium mortoni*
Sagartia luciae	*Littorina litorea*
Annelida	*Mya arenaria*
Arabella opalina	*Nassa obsoleta*
Clymenella torquata	*Venus mercenaria*
Drilonereis longa	Arthropoda
Glycera americana	*Carcinides maenas*
G. dibranchiata	*Heteromysis formosa*
Lumbrinereis tenuis	*Libinia dubia*
Nereis limbata	*Limulus polyphemus*
Nereis virens	*Palaemonetes vulgaris*
Pectinaria gouldii	*Virbius zostericola*
Phascolosoma gouldii	Chordata
Phyllodoce catenula	*Dolichoglossus*
Mollusca	
Crepidula convexa	

Source: Allee (1923b).

bay the minimum was 28 ppt. The pH of areas on the south side of Cape Cod varied from 6.8 at high tide on exposed beaches to 8.1 at low tide on protected beaches.

The numbers of nematodes were similar at depths of 5 and 7.5 cm in sand. A few isopods and polychaetes were found at these same depths. Greater numbers of organisms were taken from protected areas than from unprotected beaches subject to heavy wave action. The few organisms taken from unprotected beaches were amphipods under seaweed and a few nematodes and gastrotrichs.

Salt Marsh Fauna and Flora

Salt Marsh Meadows. In contrast to the sand organisms, the salt marsh fauna appeared to remain near or on the surface of the sod during the winter months. For example, on two occasions when the sod temperature was around $-1\,°C$, such surface forms as collembolans, delphacids, and mites were collected alive in large numbers from the surface area of the sod. The species were much the same in winter and summer. The most common organisms taken from the salt marsh sod samples were amphipods, mites, collembolans, and snails (*Melampus*). In certain samples, pseudococcid nymphs were very numerous. In most samples, doliochopodids and ceratopogonids were most common. Most of the insect larvae were found in the sand, in the sod, or associated with the salt marsh grasses growing from it. One thousand dipteran larvae of the genus *Tabanus* were collected. Of these 98% were *T. nigrovittatus*, and the remainder were *T. lineola*. Numbers of *Culicoides hollensis* were taken from the salt marsh mud during the summer months. About 2000 larvae of these species were taken. The most common organisms taken in the salt marsh mud were oligochaetes, fiddler crabs, nematodes, ciliates, gastropods, turbellarians, ostracods, and tanaidaccans (Wall, 1973). The species found in these two habitats are given in Table 4.9.

In southern New England, as in northern New England, the dominant plants of the salt marshes were *Spartina alterniflora* (formerly *Spartina glabra*) in the wetter areas and *Spartina patens* at dryer elevations. Johnson and York (1915) divided salt marshes into three belts in the Cold Spring Harbor area on the north side of Long Island. The midlittoral belt, which extended from 0.5 to 3 m (1.5 to 6.5 ft) was dominated by *Spartina alterniflora* (= *S. patens*), and numerous algae, such as diatoms and blue-green and green algae, grew around the bases of the *Spartina*. Here and there, on hard surfaces, red and brown algae were found. The upper littoral belt extended from 3 to 3.5 m, and the blue-green and green algae found there were generally growing on stems of *Spartina patens* or in the mud. The supralittoral belt was from 3.5 to 4 m and supported very little algal growth.

On the base of *Spartina alterniflora* and *S. patens* in Massachusetts marshes, Webber (1967) found the blue-green algae, *Microcoleus chthonoplastes*, *Oscillatoria subuliformis*, *O. amphibia*, *Schizothrix calcicola*, *Lyngbya lutea*, *L. aestuarii*, and *Hydrocoleum lyngbyaceum*. In the mainly freshwater upper marshes, *Tolypothrix*

TABLE 4.9.   *Taxonomic List of Adult Organisms Collected at Cape Cod*[a]

Intertidal Sand Organisms

Platyhelminthes
Turbellaria
Proporidae
Anaperus gardineri
Mollusca
Gastropoda
Littorinidae
Littorina littorea
Nassariidae
Nassarius obsoletus
Ressoidae
Hydrobia spp.
Crepidulidae
Crepidula fornicata
Pelecypoda
Myacidae
Mya arenaria
Mytilidae
Modiolus demissus
Pectinidae
Aequipecten irradians
Veneridae
Mercenaria mercenaria
Annelida
Polychaeta
Nereidae
Nereis sp.
N. succinea
Glyceridae
Glycera dibranchiata
Orbiniidae
Schroederella sp.
Scoloplos acutus
S. fragilis
Spionidae
Pygospio elegans
Streblospio benedicti

Oligochaeta
Enchytraeidae
Enchytraeus albidus
Enchytraeus sp.
Marionina elongata
Naididae
Paranais littoralis
Tubificidae
? *Tubifex pseudogaster*
Arthropoda
Merostomata
Limulidae
Limulus polyphemus
Crustacea
Cumacea
Diastylidae
Diastylis polita
Tanaidacea
Paratanaidae
Leptochelia savignyi
Isopoda
Anthuridae
Cyathura polita
Sphaeromidae
Exosphaeroma popillae
Sphaeroma quadridentatum
Idoteidae
Edotea triloba
Amphipoda
Aoridae
Microdeutopus sp.
Haustoriidae
Haustorius canadensis
Orchestiidae
Hyale sp.
Orchestia platensis

O. uhleri
Decapoda
Pilumnidae
Neopanope texana
Ocypodidae
Uca pugilator
Paguridae
Pagurus longicarpus
Portunidae
Carcinus maenas
Palaemonidae
Palaemonetes pugio
P. vulgaris
Crangonidae
Crangon septemspinosus
Insecta
Collembola
Poduridae
Annurida granaria
A. maritima
A. tullbergi
Xenylla maritima
Isotomidae
Proisotoma besselsi
Coleoptera
Staphylinidae
Bledius neglectus
Hydrophilidae
Enochrus hamiltoni
Diptera
Ceratopogonidae
Culicoides melleus
Dolichopodidae*
Otitidae*
Ephydridae*

Salt Marsh Organisms

Mollusca
Gastropoda
Littorinidae
Littorina littorea
Ellobiidae
Melampus bidentatus
Ressoidae
Hydrobia spp.
Pelecypoda
Mytilidae
Modiolus demissus
Annelida

Polychaeta
Phyllodocidae
Eteone heteropoda
Nereidae
Nereis sp.
N. succinea
Orbiniidae
Scoloplos acutus
Spionidae
Polydora sp.
Streblospio benedicti
Capitellidae

Capitella capitata
Ampharetidae
Hypaniola grayi
Sabellidae
Fabricia sabella
Oligochaeta
Enchytraeidae
Enchytraeus albidus
Marionina sp.
M. spicula
Naididae
Amphichaeta sannio

Continued

TABLE 4.9.   (*Continued*)

Salt Marsh Organisms

Nais elinguis
Paranais littoralis
Tubificidae
Monopylephorus parvus
Monopylephorus sp.
Tubifex pseudogaster
Arthropoda
Merostomata
Limulidae
Limulus polyphemus
Arachnida
Pseudoscorpionida
Chernetidae
Dinocheirus tristis
Acarina
Lycosidae
Pardosa sp.
Crustacea
Cumacea
Nannastacidae
Almyracuma proximoculi
Tanaidacea
Paratanaidae
Leptochelia savignyi
Isopoda
Anthuridae
Cyathura polita
Idoteidae
Idotea metallica
Oniscidae
Philoscia vittata
Trichoniscidae
Scyphacella arenicola
Amphipoda
Orchestiidae
Orchestia grillus
O. gammarella
U. uhleri
Gammaridae
Gammarus palustris
Decapoda
Ocypodidae
Uca pugnax
Portunidae
Carcinus maenas
Insecta
Collembola
Isotomidae
Isotoma cinerea
I. trispinata
Proisotoma besselsi
P. elongata

Poduridae
Brachystomella parvula
Micranurida furcifer
Onychiurus armatus
O. litoreus
Pseudachorutes subcrassoides
Tullbergia iowensis
Xenylla maritima
X. welchi
Entomobryidae
Entomobrya assuta
E. knaba
E. marginata
E. multifasciata
E. purpurascens
Orchesella ainsliei
Pseudosinella violenta
Seira platani
Homoptera
Delphacidae
Prokelisia marginata
Pseudococcidae
Rhizoecus maritimus
Cercopidae
Clastoptera hyperici
C. testacea
Philaenus spumarius
Cicadellidae
Amplicephalus littoralis
A. simplex
Macrosteles sp.
Scaphoideus carinatus
S. frisoni
Scaphoideus sp.
Scaphytopius sp.
Xestocephalus pulicarius
X. superbus
Hemiptera
Lygaeidae
Blissus arenarius arenarius
Saldidae
Micracanthia humilis
Thysanoptera
Thripidae
? *Pseudothrips inaequalis*
Coleoptera
Heteroceridae
*Neoheterocerus fatuus**
Coccinellidae
Coeleomegilla maculata
Curculionidae
Sphenophorus v. *venatus**

Lissorhoptrus chapini
Scarabaeidae
Aegialia arenaria
Hydrophilidae
*Enochrus hamiltoni**
Melyridae*
Diptera
Tipulidae*
Psychodidae
Telmatoscopus spp.*
Culicidae
*Aedes cantator**
*A. sollicitans**
Ceratopogonidae
*Atrichopogon levis**
Atrichopogon sp.*
*Culicoides furens**
*C. hollensis**
Dasyhelea sp.*
Chironomidae
Chironomus sp.*
Dicrotendipes sp.*
Glyptotendipes sp.*
Rheorthocladius sp.*
Scatopsidae
Parascatopse sp.
(nr. *flavida*)*
Cecidomyiidae*
Lestodiplosis sp.*
Contarinia sp.
Stratiomyiidae
Odontomyia microstoma
Stratiomys sp.*
Caloparyphus sp.*
Tabanidae
*Chrysops atlanticus**
*C. fuliginosus**
*Tabanus atratus**
*T. lineola**
*T. nigrovittatus**
Dolichopodidae*
Dolichopus sp.
Pelastoneurus lamellatus
Syrphidae
Eristalis anthophorinus
Platycheirus sp.
Otitidae*
Chaetopsis aenea
C. apicalis
C. fulvifrons
C. massyla
Euxesta scoriacea

TABLE 4.9. (*Continued*)

	Salt Marsh Organisms	
Sciomyzidae	*Hippelates nobilis*	*Tetramorium caespitum*
*Hoplodictya setosa**	*Oscinella infesta*	Scelionidae
Ephydridae*	*Oscinella* sp	*Telenomus* sp.
Dictrichophora sp.	Hymenoptera	*Cynipidae*
Parydra sp.*	Formicidae	? *Rhoptromeris* sp.
Chloropidae		

Source: After Wall (1973). Reproduced by permission of the Entomological Society of America.

tenuis was usually found in association with *Juncus gerardi. Calothrix confervicola* formed epiphytic tufts on *Spartina patens* leaves, and less frequently, on the leaves of *S. alterniflora.* Brownish-green mats of the nitrogen-fixing *Calothrix scopulorum* formed encrusted patches on exposed soils at low water during spring tides. *Microcoleus chthonoplastes* and *Broscheria* sp. apparently act as soil stabilizers of the tidal mud flats. The blue-green alga, *Anabaina torulosa,* formed bright-blue films on midlittoral mud surfaces. During the cooler and damper months of the autumn, winter, and spring, blue-black mounds of *Rivularia nitida* grew on the soil beneath the dense cover of *Spartina patens. Rivularia nitida* and *R. atra* were in the sublittoral areas on stones, usually in association with the green alga, *Chaetomorpha linum,* and the red algae, *Ralfsia* sp., *Protoderma maculiforma,* and *Hildenbrandia prototypus.*

The invertebrates associated with *Spartina* communities were *Modiolus demissus,* a pelecypod; the barnacle, *Balanus balanoides;* and the crabs, *Uca pugnax* and *U. pugilator.* Nematodes were very common in the mud of the marshes at Penzance Point (Nixon and Oviatt, 1973).

The common mummichog, *Fundulus heteroclitus,* was the dominant fish in salt marsh embayments such as Bissel Cove, Rhode Island. Large individuals were most abundant in late April through June. The proportion of small fish increased during the summer months, and during the winter the young-of-the-year were dominant. Gut analysis revealed that these small mummichogs ate mainly harpacticoid copepods, amphipods, benthic diatoms, and detritus. The large fish of the common mummichog, and the striped mummichog, *Fundulus majalis,* fed mainly on the shrimp, *Palaemonetes pugio;* the juvenile fish of their own and other species; and detritus.

Eels and the white perch fed mostly on shrimp and the juveniles and adults of other fish species. Certain of the fish showed strong migratory patterns. The common mummichog moved into the marsh in the spring and left in the fall, as did the menhaden and bluefish. The species that spent the entire year in the salt marsh embayment were the striped mummichog, silversides, sticklebacks, eels, and sheepshead minnows (Nixon and Oviatt, 1973).

Salt Marsh Creek Communities

Salinity in salt marsh creeks ranged from 17 ppt at low tide to 32 ppt at high tide on the marsh surface, in drainage ditches, and in potholes. The pH in the tidal creeks was somewhat lower than in the marshlands, ranging from 6.4 to 7.8.

During the spring, summer, and early fall most of the smaller organisms were near the surface of the sediment. A total of 2000 *Culicoides* larvae were identified and about 58% of the larvae were in the top $\frac{1}{2}$ in., 27% in the second $\frac{1}{2}$ in. 12% in the third $\frac{1}{2}$ in., and 3% in the fourth $\frac{1}{2}$ in. All the larvae collected were within 2 in. (about 5 cm) of the surface. Rarely were these larvae found at depths greater than 3 in. (about 7.6 cm) during the summer months. During the winter, when sand temperatures were as low as 0°C and bays were covered with ice, *Protozoa, Nematoda, Copepoda, Ostracoda, Polychaeta, Oligochaeta, Dolichopodida* (Diptera), and larvae of *Culicoides* were found as deep as 9 to 10 in. (22.9 to 25.4 cm). Other than *Collembola* and *Ostracoda*, no organisms were found in the top 1 in. (2.54 cm) (Wall, 1973).

Salt Marsh Productivity

Primary Productivity. The only detailed research on productivity in the southern New England estuaries has been done in the marshes. Primary productivity of the salt marsh was mainly from the algae, whereas *Spartina* was a main source of detritus. Studies of productivity in Great Sippewisset Marsh (E. J. Carpenter, cited by Van Raalte et al., 1976) showed that the marsh phytoplankton fixed 2.5×10^6 to 2.5×10^7 mg C h^{-1}. The area of the low marsh, covered by *Spartina alterniflora*, fixed about 9.8×10^4 to 1.13×10^7 mg C h^{-1} (Van Raalte et al., 1976).

During the year, the productivity of algae in Great Sippewissett Marsh beneath the *Spartina* canopy was about 105.5 ± 12.5 g m^{-2} yr^{-1} in the unshaded portion. This production was about one-fourth of the aboveground seasonal grass production in the Great Sippewissett Marsh.

Nixon and Oviatt (1973) estimate that the emergent marsh vegetation in a marsh embayment in Bissel Cove (Narragansett Bay, RI) produced about 22.7×10^6 kcal m^{-2} yr^{-1}. The greatest growth of *Spartina alterniflora* was a meter-wide bank around the periphery of the embayment which produced 2.8×10^3 kcal m^{-2} yr^{-1}.

Secondary Productivity. The productivity of invertebrates, many of which were prey for *Fundulus heteroclitus* (the common mummichog), and the productivity of the mummichog itself have been studied by Valiela et al. (1977) in Great Sippewisset Marsh, Rhode Island. They found that the invertebrates in the tidal creeks and marsh surfaces ranged from 50 to 1000 mg m^{-2} dry weight and could provide about 3 to 52 kcal if all the invertebrates were acceptable food items. Analysis of the gut content of predators indicated, however, that some prey preference was shown. During the spring and early summer, the mummichog consumed about 1.2 kcal m^{-2} day^{-1}. Toward the fall the amount decreased to about 0.3 kcal m^{-2} day^{-1}. Using these figures it appears that the standing crop in the spring would last about 2.5 to 43 days, and in the fall, 10 to 173 days. The authors determined that the prey species were not randomly distributed, and it was this clumping of the prey that determined the behavior patterns of the mummichog in feeding. Production of 1-, 2-, and 3-year-old fish for the entire growing season (June to November) was estimated to be 91 kg ha^{-1}. To get an estimate of total production of the mummichog, Valiela et al. (1977) considered 0-age class production to equal the biomass of the fish in the 1-year class at the beginning of the sampling period in the spring. This recruitment measure may underestimate the productivity by an amount dependent upon the intensity of predation on these younger fish. Predation seemed to be small over winter since the estimated number at the beginning of the sampling season was nearly identical to that observed in the 0-class in the following fall. Valiela et al. (1977) calculated the production of the 0-class to be at least 70 kg ha^{-1}, which is a total mummichog production of 160 kg ha^{-1} dry weight. This would be about 640 kg ha^{-1} as wet weight, or 64 kcal m^{-2}. This value is comparable to production of assemblages of species in the River Thames in England and to trout in the Horokiwi stream in New Zealand (Mann, 1965).

In the marsh, the ratio of the production of the mummichog to the winter standing crop was over 2. This contrasts to 1.65 in the Thames. Huet (1964) stated that for typical freshwaters, the production rate was about 0.5 for trout. The semiannual turnover for mummichog with at least a 3-year life span, indicated intense predation, presumably by larger fish and birds that fed in the salt marsh. Supposing that the entire fish production were vulnerable to predation by striped bass, bluefish, heron, egrets, terns, and gulls, Valiela et al. (1977) calculated the ecological efficiency from production and consumption figures for *Fundulus heteroclitus* shown in Table 4.10.

Nutrient Cycling. The nitrogen cycling in marshes, the only estuarine area examined in detail, shows that the sources of nitrogen for fauna and flora were precipitation, groundwater, and nitrogen fixation. The nutrient input from precipitation was primarily dissolved organic nitrogen, nitrates, and ammonia. Particulate material in rain has a high carbon-to-nitrogen ratio. Groundwater provided nitrogen primarily as nitrates and dissolved organic nitrogen and was a major factor in the nitrogen economy of the salt marsh. Large amounts of

TABLE 4.10. *Fundulus heteroclitus: Summary of Biomass, Production, and Consumption of Population for Each Month*

Date	Biomass (g m^{-2})	Production During Time Interval (g m^{-2})	Consumption During Time Interval (kcal m^{-2})	Ecological Efficiency (%)
June 16	12.8	3.8	32.3	11.8
July 14	59.6	2.8	29.1	9.6
Aug. 20	10.8	1.6	18.5	8.6
Sept. 25	8.3	1.0	12.8	7.8
Nov. 10	7.8	——	——	
	Sum	9.2	92.7	
Recruitment of 0-age class		6.9	23.0[a]	
	Annual total	16.1	115.7	

[a]On basis of respiration at 4°C for 8 winter months and no mortality.
Source: Valiela et al. (1977).

various kinds of organic nitrogen entered the marsh in the groundwater and similar amounts were exported by the tides. About half of the dissolved inorganic nitrogen brought into the marsh by the groundwater was converted to an exported particulate nitrogen. The marsh thus transformed the nitrogen, which was utilized by primary producers into forms suitable for consumers, such as shellfish.

During the summer the uptakes of nutrients by the marsh exceeded, by an order of magnitude, the exports. During August, the exports increased, which is believed to be due to the leaching of senescent marsh plants. This caused a net export of ammonia, nitrates, nitrites, dissolved organic nitrogen, particulate nitrogen, particulate carbon, and phosphates. The nutrient concentrations in coastal and marsh waters indicated that the marsh exports contributed substantially to the nutrient supply of coastal waters. The particulate carbon exported to coastal waters was equivalent to 40% of the natural annual production of *Spartina alterniflora*, the dominant marsh plant (Valiela et al., 1978).

Studies of Long Island, New York (Woodwell et al., 1979) found a net export of ammonia nitrogen from the marsh during summer and fall and a net import from the coastal waters in winter and spring. In other words, the marsh served as a sink. Nitrate was also imported in winter and lost from the marsh in summer. Three inorganic nitrogen compounds—ammonia (NH_4^+), NO_3, and NO_2—are exported. There was a net export of about 20 kg N ha^{-1} yr^{-1}. However, when compared with the uptake of nitrogen by marsh grasses, the loss was very small. The export of nitrogen from salt marshes into Long Island Sound during the summer was about one-third the amount of nitrogen that enters the sound from rivers during the same period. Whether or not there is a net loss of nitrogen from the salt marsh is an unresolved question. The study of the Great Sippewissett Marsh indicates an approximate balance between the input and output.

HUDSON RIVER ESTUARY

The Hudson River estuary has been fairly well studied and therefore serves as an example of an estuary in southern New England (Figure 4.5). The channel of this estuary has changed over time, but at present it is a drowned river valley estuary that is slowly being filled with silt. In the upper part of the estuary the river bottom is composed of soft clay that is dark gray in color. As one approaches the mouth of the estuary, sand becomes the main bottom material and is also the main material on beaches and bars.

Tidal influence is apparent 250 km upstream at Albany, New York, where the average tidal amplitude is 1.4 m. At West Point, the tidal range is only about 0.8 m, but it increases again to 1.4 m at New York City. Although tidal effects may be seen as far north as Albany, salt penetration extends only 50 to 80 km upstream to between Newburgh and Poughkeepsie. The 60-km-long wedge of salt water which is pushed back and forth by the tide extends only about 50 km north of Battery Park, New York. The freshwater input varies tenfold over the

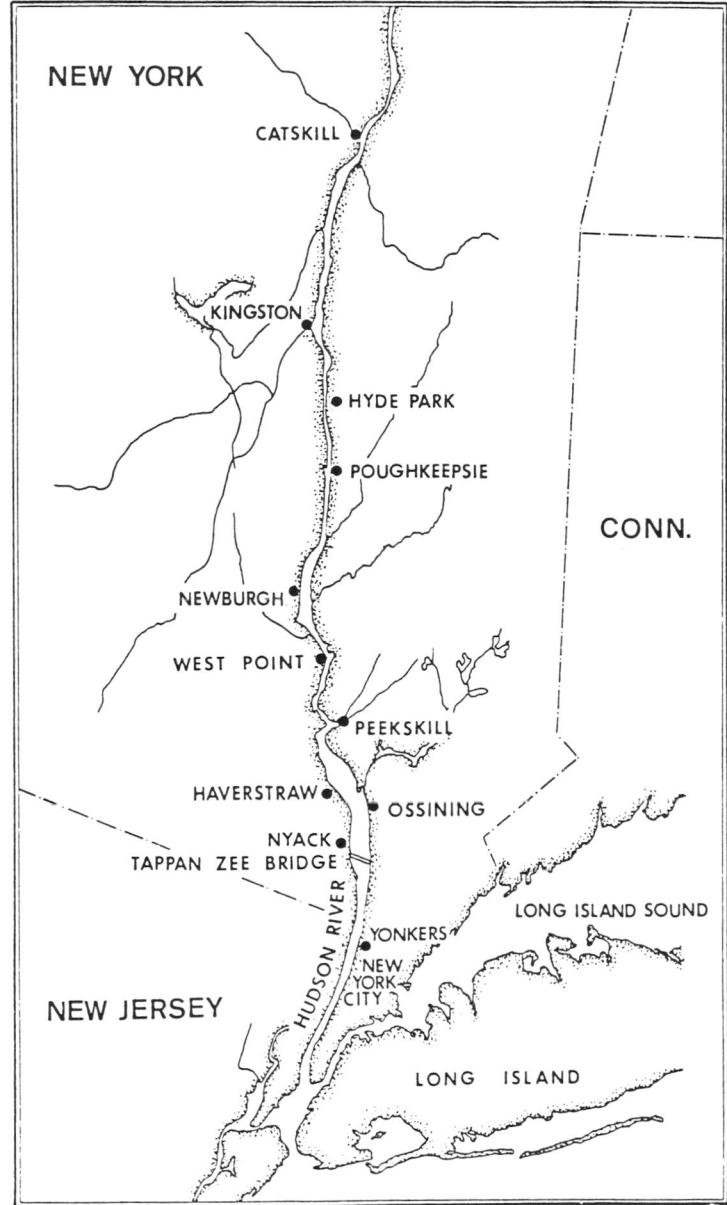

FIGURE 4.5. Hudson River from Staten Island to the town of Catskill.

course of a year, so the position of the salt front is forced up and down the estuary for fairly long distances.

There is considerable monthly variation in salinity and temperature within a given reach of the Hudson River. Below the Tappan Zee Bridge the monthly averages of salinity range between 10 and 20 ppt. At Indian Point, in the intermediate reach, the monthly averages are between 0 and 15 ppt. Salt water does not penetrate as far up the river as Hyde Park.

The monthly averages of temperature below the Tappan Zee Bridge ranges between 1 and 25 °C. Near Indian Point the temperatures range between 0 and 30 °C and the same temperatures are found at Hyde Park.

Fauna and Flora

The aquatic organisms found in the Hudson River together with their general habitat and salinity preferences are given in Tables 4.11 and 4.12. The types of communities are plankton organisms, intertidal organisms that may occur on rocky substrates or on sandy or mud flats or on sandy bars and beaches, and nektonic organisms, particularly fish.

Plankton. The seasonal cycle of phytoplankton in the Hudson varied with the temperature and salinity of the photic zone, which was 1 to 3 m deep. As seen in Table 4.11, the species of diatoms differed in various parts of the estuary. Species of the genus *Asterionella* (*A. formosa* in the fresh water and *A. japonica* in the estuary) were very common in the spring and early summer. During the summer, species belonging to the genus *Melosira* (*M. ambigua*, *M. distans*, *M. granulata*, and *M. varians*) were often very common. In the late summer/early fall, the most important species in the brackish parts of the estuary was *Skeletonema costatum*, an important food for oysters and small fish. As shown in Table 4.11, in the freshwater areas, the most common green algae in the phytoplankton were *Pediastrum*, *Scenedesmus*, and *Ankisstrodesmus*, members of the order Cholorococcales. Blue-green algae blooms that produce toxic material have been encountered in the Hudson River from time to time.

To calculate the primary productivity in the Hudson estuary, one estimates the biomass from chlorophyll a concentrations and determines the carbon fixed. Weinstein (1977) has shown a high correlation between summer maximums of chlorophyll *a* and the maximum gross primary productivity (Figure 4.6). Summer estimates of the daily primary production in areas near Nyack showed that the Hudson's productivity in this reach is comparable to that of other east coast estuaries (Weinstein, 1977; Sirois and Frederick, 1978). The area of high productivity extended from the Tappan Zee region to near Haverstraw. Farther north, near Peekskill, the greatest abundance of phytoplankton was from April to August (Howells and Weaver, 1969) (Figure 4.7).

Fresh Water. Zooplankton in the Hudson estuary was composed primarily of dinoflagellates, protozoans, rotifers, and crustaceans. In the fresh water, the dominant dinoflagellates were *Ceratium hirundinella* and *C. tripos*. The more common protozoa were the ciliates, *Colpoda*, sp., *Glaucoma* sp., *Vorticella*, and *Paramecium* (Howells et al., 1969), which were numerous in the summer and increased in diversity in the fall. The amoebas, *Difflugia* spp. and *Arcella* spp., which were present in the summer preyed on bacteria and algae (Howells et al., 1969).

Of the crustacea, the cyclopoid copepods and the cladocerans were the most important food species for newly hatched fish larvae (Weinstein, 1977). *Oithona*

(*text continues on page 279*)

TABLE 4.11. *Hudson River Fauna and Flora*

	Freshwater (0 ppt Salinity)	Oligohaline (0.5–5 ppt Salinity)	Mesohaline (5–18 ppt Salinity)	Polyhaline (18–32 ppt Salinity)
DIVISION BACILLARIOPHYTA				
Class Bacillariophyceae				
Order Eupodicales				
Family Coscinodiscaceae				
Melosira ambigua	×			
M. distans	×			
M. granulata	×			
M. italica	×	×		
M. moniliformis			×	×
M. sulcata			×	×
M. varians	×			
Melosira sp.			×	
Hyalodiscus sp.			×	×
Skeletonema costatum			×	×
Coscinodiscus excentricus		×	×	×
C. lacustris				
C. lineatus				×
C. rothii			×	
C. sublineatus				
Cyclotella aliguantula				
C. atomus	×			
C. bodanica	×			
C. compta	×			
C. glomerata	×	×	×	×
C. kutzingiana	×			
C. meneghiniana	×			
C. ocellata	×			
C. pseudostelligera	×			
C. stelligera	×			
C. stylorum				×
C. striata				
Stephanodiscus astraea	×			
S. nigarae	×			
Thalassiosira fluviatilis				
Thalassiosira sp.			×	
Actinopytchus undulatus				
Actinocyclus sp.				
Family Rhizosolenaceae				
Rhizosolenia eriensis				
R. fragilissima				
Rhizosolenia spp.			×	
Order Biddulphiales				
Family Biddulphiaceae				

Continued

TABLE 4.11   (*Continued*)

	Freshwater (0 ppt Salinity)	Oligohaline (0.5–5 ppt Salinity)	Mesohaline (5–18 ppt Salinity)	Polyhaline (18–32 ppt Salinity)
Biddulphia sp.				
Ditylum brightwelli				
Triceratium favus				
Lithodesmium sp.				
Family Chaetoceraceae				
Chaetoceros sp.				
Order Fragilariales				
Family Fragilariaceae				
Tabellaria fenestrata	×			
Meridion circulare	×			
Diatoma elongatum v. *tenuis*				
D. vulgare	×			
Fragilaria capuncina	×			
F. construens	×			
F. crotonensis	×			
F. leptostauron	×			
F. vaucheriae	×			
F. virescens	×			
Asterionella bleakleyi			×	
A. formosa	×			
A. japonica				×
Asterionella sp.		×		
Synedra toxoneides var. *curvata*				
S. pulchella	×	×		
S. rumpens	×			
S. ulna	×	×		
Synedra sp.	×	×		
Thalassionema nitzschoides			×	×
Thalassiothrix sp.			×	
Order Eunotiales				
Suborder Raphidioidineae				
Family Eunkotiaceae				
Eunotia pectinalis	×			
Order Achnanthales				
Family Achnanthaceae				
Achananthes lanceolata	×			
A. minutissima	×			
A. subhudsonis var. *kraeuselii*				
Rhoicosophenia curvata		×		
Cocconeis placentula	×			
C. scutellum	×			
Cocconeis sp.	×			
Order Naviculales				
Family Naviculaceae				

TABLE 4.11 (Continued)

	Freshwater (0 ppt Salinity)	Oligohaline (0.5–5 ppt Salinity)	Mesohaline (5–18 ppt Salinity)	Polyhaline (18–32 ppt Salinity)
Frustulia rhomboides	×			
Anomoeneis vitrea	×			
Gyrosigma acuminatum	×	×		
G. attenuatum	×	×		
G. macrum			×	
G. spencerii	×	×	×	
G. wormleyi	×			
Pleurosigma salinarum	×	×		
Pleurosigma sp.				
Stauroneis sp.				
Navicula biconica	×			
N. capitata	×			
N. cryptocephala	×			
N. enigua	×			
N. lanceolata	×			
N. peregrina	×			
N. pupula	×			
N. pygmaea	×			
N. radiosa	×			
N rhynchocephala	×			
N. viridula	×			
Navicula sp.	×			
Pinnularia bregissonii				
Family Entomoneidaceae				
Entomoneis ornata		×		
E. paludosa			×	
Family Gomphonemaceae				
Gomphonema olivaceum	×			
G. parvulum	×			
Gomphoneis herculeana				
Family Cymbellaceae				
Cymbella affinis	×			
C. sinuta	×			
C. tumida	×			
Amphora ovalis	×			
Order Ephithemiales				
Family Epithemiaceae				
Epithemia turgida	×			
Family Rhopalodioideae				
Rhopalodia gibba	×			
Family Nitzschiaceae				
Nitzschia accomodata	×			
N. acicularis				

Continued

TABLE 4.11 (*Continued*)

	Freshwater (0 ppt Salinity)	Oligohaline (0.5–5 ppt Salinity)	Mesohaline (5–18 ppt Salinity)	Polyhaline (18–32 ppt Salinity)
N. amphibia	×			
N. closterium				
N. dissapata	×			
N. fonticola				
N. kuetzingiana	×			
N. linearis	×			
N. microcephala	×			
N. palea	×			
N. seriata			×	
N. sigma				
N. tryblionella	×			
Nitzschia sp.				
Hantzschia sp.				
Bacillaria paradoxa	×	×	×	
Order Surirellales				
Family Surirellaceae				
Surirella elegans	×			
S. ovalis	×			
S. ovata	×			
S. patella		×	×	×
Campylodiscus echeneis				
DIVISION CYANOPHYTA				
Class Myxohoyceae				
Order Chroococcales				
Family Chroococcaceae				
Coccochloris aeruginosa				
(= *Synechococcus aeruginosus*				
Anacystis aeruginosa		×	×	
A. incerta		×	×	
A. cyanea				
(= *Coelosphaerum dubium*)				
Agmenellum thermali	×			
(= *Merismopoedia thermalis*)	×			
Gomphasphaeria aponina	×			
G. lacustris				
Order Oscillatorales				
Suborder Oscillatoria				
Family Oscillatoriaceae				
Schizothrix calcicola	×			
(= *Oscillatoria limnetica*)				
Schizothrix sp.	×			
Microcoleus lyngbyaceus	×			
(= *Oscillatoria limosa*)				
(= *O. tenuis*)				

TABLE 4.11 (*Continued*)

	Freshwater (0 ppt Salinity)	Oligohaline (0.5–5 ppt Salinity)	Mesohaline (5–18 ppt Salinity)	Polyhaline (18–32 ppt Salinity)
Microcoleus sp.	×			
Spirulina sp.	×			
Family Nostocaceae				
Anabaina oscillaroides		×	×	
(= *A. circinalis*)				
(= *A. flos aquae*)				
Anabaina spiroidea		×	×	
DIVISION CHRYSOPHYTA				
Class Zanthophyceae				
Order Heterosiphonales				
Family Vaucheriaceae				
Vaucheria sp.	×			
DIVISION CHLOROPHYTA				
Class Chlorophyceae				
Order Tetrasporales				
Family Tetrasporaceae				
Tetraspora sp.	×			
Order Chlorococcales				
Family Hydrodictyaceae				
Pediastrum biradiatum	×			
P. boryanum	×			
P. duplex	×			
P. glanduliferum	×			
P. obtusum	×			
P. sculpatum	×			
P. simplex	×			
P. tetras	×			
Family Coelastraceae				
Coelastrum sp.	×			
Family Botryococcaceae				
Botryococcus sp.	×			
Family Oocystaceae				
Ankistrodesmus braunii	×			
A. convalutus				
A. falcatus	×	×		
A. fractus				
A. spiralis				
Chlorella sp.				
Closteriopsis longissima	×			
Kirchneriella lunaris	×			
K. obesa	×			
Lagerheimia longiseta	×			
(= *Chodatella longiseta*)				

Continued

TABLE 4.11   (*Continued*)

	Freshwater (0 ppt Salinity)	Oligohaline (0.5–5 ppt Salinity)	Mesohaline (5–18 ppt Salinity)	Polyhaline (18–32 ppt Salinity)
Lagerheimia quadriceta	×			
(= *Chodatella quadricerata*)	×			
Planktosphaeria sp.				
Schroderia setigera	×			
Selenastrum gracile	×			
Tetraedron caudatum	×			
T. trigonum	×			
Family Scenesdesmaceae				
Actinastrum hantzschia	×			
Crucigenia fenestrata	×			
C. quadrata	×			
C. tetrapedia	×			
Micracatinium pusillum	×			
Scenedesmus abundans	×			
S. acuminatus	×			
S. acutus	×			
S. bijuga	×			
S. dimorphus	×			
S. obliquus	×			
S. opoliensis	×			
S. quadricauda	×			
Order Ulotrichales				
Family Ulotrichaceae				
Ulothrix sp.			×	×
Order Ulvales				
Family Ulvaceae				
Enteromorpha intestinalis			×	×	×
Order Zygonematales				
Family Zygonemataceae				
Spirogyra sp.				
Family Desmidiacaea				
Closterum sp.				
Staurastrum alternans	×			
DIVISION RHODOPHYTA				
Class Rhodophyceae				
Order Ceramiales				
Family Delesseriaceae				
Caloglossa leprieurii			×	×
PHYLUM PROTOZOA				
Class Mastigophora				
Subclass Phytomatigia				
Order Chrysomonadida				
Suborder Euchrysomonadina				
Family Chromulinidae				

TABLE 4.11   (*Continued*)

	Freshwater (0 ppt Salinity)	Oligohaline (0.5–5 ppt Salinity)	Mesohaline (5–18 ppt Salinity)	Polyhaline (18–32 ppt Salinity)
Mallomonas sp.	×			
Family Syncryptidae				
Synura uvella	×			
Family Ochromonadidae				
Ochromonas sp.		×		
Order Cryptomonadida				
Family Crytomonadidae				
Chilomonas sp.				
Order Phytomonadida				
Family Volvocidae				
Volvox sp.	×			
Gonium pectorale	×			
G. sociale	×			
Pandorina morum	×			
Eudorina elegans	×			
Family Carteriidae				
Polytomella sp.				
Order Euglenoidida				
Family Euglenidae				
Euglena sp.				
Phacus longicauda	×			
Order Dinoflagellida				
Suborder Prorocentrina				
Family Prorocentridae				
Prorocentrum micans			×	
Suborder Peridiniina				
Family Cystodiniidae				
Genodinium sp		×		
Family Gymnodiniidae				
Gymnodinium sp		×		
Amphidinium sp		×		
Family Polykrikidae				
Polykrikos sp.				
Family Peridiniidae				
Peridinium cinctum				
P. trochoideum				
Ceratium hirudinella	×	×		
C. tripos	×			
Family Dinophysidae				
Dinophysis sp.				
Subclass Zoomastiga				
Order Rhizomatigida				
Family Mastigamoebidae				

Continued

TABLE 4.11   (*Continued*)

	Freshwater (0 ppt Salinity)	Oligohaline (0.5–5 ppt Salinity)	Mesohaline (5–18 ppt Salinity)	Polyhaline (18–32 ppt Salinity)
Mastigamoeba sp.		×		
Class Sarcodinia				
Order Amoebida				
Family Amoebidae				
Amoeba sp.		×		×
Order Testacida				
Family Arcellidae				
Arcella sp.		×	×	
Family Difflugiida				
Difflugia sp.		×	×	
Order Foraminiferida				
Family Camerinidae				
Elphidium sp.			×	
Ammonia sp.			×	
Subphylum Ciliophora				
Class Ciliata				
Subclass Holotricha				
Order Gymnostomatida				
Family Amphilepltidae				
Loxophyllum setigerum				
Order Trichostomatida				
Family Colpodidae				
Colpoda sp.			×	×
Order Hymenstomatida				
Family Tetrahymenidae				
Glaucoma sp.			×	
Family Parameciidae				
Paramecium sp.	×			
Family Pleuronematidae				
Pleuronema sp.				
Order Hypotrichida				
Family Euplotidae				
Euplotes sp.				
Subclass Peritricha				
Order Peritrichida				
Family Vorticellidae				
Vorticella sp.			×	
Class Suctoria				
Takophyra sp.				×
PHYLUM CNIDARIA				
Class Hydrozoa				
Order Athecata				
Family Clavidae				
Cordylophora lacustris	×			
Family Bougainvilliidae				

TABLE 4.11   (*Continued*)

	Freshwater (0 ppt Salinity)	Oligohaline (0.5–5 ppt Salinity)	Mesohaline (5–18 ppt Salinity)	Polyhaline (18–32 ppt Salinity)
Nemopsis bachei			×	
Order Thecata				
Family Lovenellidae				
Blackfordia manhattensis			×	
Order Hydrina				
Hydra oligactis	×	×		
Class Anthozoa				
Order Actinaria				
Family Actinostolidae				
Paranthus rapiformis			×	
Family Aiptasiomorphiidae				
Haliplanella luciae			×	×
(= *Aiptasiomorpha luciae*				
(= *Sagartia?*)				
PHYLUM CTENOPHORA				
Class Tentaculata				
Order Lobata				
Family Mnemiidae				
Mnemiopsis leidyi				×
Class Nuda				
Order Beroida				
Family Beroidae				
Beroe cucumis			×	×
PHYLUM RHYNCHOCOELA			×	
Class Anopla				
Order Paleonemertea				
Family Carinomidae				
Carinoma tremaphoras		×		×
Order Heteronemertea				
Family Lineidae				
Lineaus sp.				
PHYLUM ASCHELMINTHES				
Class Rotifera				
Order Monogononta				
Family Branchionidae				
Keratella cochlearis		×	×	
K. quadrata			×	
Notholca sp.			×	
Family Asplanchnidae				
Asplanchna sp.			×	
Family Philodinidae				
Philodina sp.	×		×	
Family Trichocercidae				

Continued

TABLE 4.11   *(Continued)*

	Freshwater (0 ppt Salinity)	Oligohaline (0.5–5 ppt Salinity)	Mesohaline (5–18 ppt Salinity)	Polyhaline (18–32 ppt Salinity)
Trichocerca sp.			×	
Class Nematoda				
Nematodes sp.				
PHYLUM CHAETOGNATHA				
Sagitta elegans				×
PHYLUM ANNELIDA				
Class Polychaeta				
Order Phyllodocida				
Family Phylodocidae				
Eteone heteropoda			×	×
Eumida sanguinea				×
Family Glyceridae				
Glycera americana		×	×	
Family Syllidae				
Autolytus cornutus			×	×
Family Nereidae				
Nereis succinea			×	×
Nereis sp.				
Order Capitellida				
Family Capitellidae				
Capitella capitata			×	×
Heteromastus filiformis			×	×
Order Spionida				
Family Spionidae				
Spio setosa			×	×
Spio spp.				
Scolecolepides viridis	×	×	×	
Streblospio benedicti			×	×
Polydora websteri			×	×
P. concharum			?	×
P. ligni			?	
Family Sabellariidae				
Sabellaria vulgaris				
Subfamily Fabricinae				
Mangyunkia speciosa		×		
Order Euncida				
Family Onuphidae				
Lumbrineris sp.				?
Order Terebellida				
Family Pectinaridae				
Pectinaria gouldii		×	×	×
Family Ampharetidae				
Asabellides oculata			?	?
Asabellides sp.		?	?	?

TABLE 4.11 (*Continued*)

	Freshwater (0 ppt Salinity)	Oligohaline (0.5–5 ppt Salinity)	Mesohaline (5–18 ppt Salinity)	Polyhaline (18–32 ppt Salinity)
Hypaniola grayi				
Class Oligochaeta				
Peloscolex benedini	×			
Order Plesiopora				
Family Tubificidae				
Limnodrilus		×		
Ilyodrilus sp.	×			
Family Aeolosomatidae				
Aeolosoma sp.	×			
Class Hirudinea				
Order Rhynchobdellae				
Family Piscicolidae				
Pisicola puntata	×	×		
PHYLUM MOLLUSCA				
Class Gastropoda				
Subclass Prosobranchiata				
Order Mesogastropoda				
Family Valvatidae				
Valvata sincera			×	×
Family Hydrobiidae				
Hydrobia sp.	×	×		
Armnicola limosa	×	×		
Family Naticidae				
Polinices duplicatus				
Order Neogastropoda				
Family Nassariidae				
Ilynassa obsoleta			×	×
(= *Nassaruis obsoletus*)				
Nassarius trivittatus				×
Nassarius sp.	×	×		
Subclass Opisthobranchia				
Order Cephalaspidea				
Family Retusidae				
Retusa canaliculata				×
Order Basommatophora				
Family Physidae				
Physella heterostropha	×		×	
(= *Physa heterostropha*)				
Family Lymnaeidae				
Stagnicola palustris	×			
(= *Lymnaea palustris*)				
Family Planorbidae				

Continued

TABLE 4.11   (*Continued*)

	Freshwater (0 ppt Salinity)	Oligohaline (0.5–5 ppt Salinity)	Mesohaline (5–18 ppt Salinity)	Polyhaline (18–32 ppt Salinity)
Gyraulus parvus	×			
Order Nudibranchia				
Suborder Aeoliodea				
Family Cuthonidae				
Tenelia fuscata			×	×
Class Bivalvia				
Subclass Palaeoheterodonta				
Order Unionoida				
Family Unionidae				
Elliptio complanata	×			
Subclass Pteriomorpha				
Order Mytiloida				
Family Mytilidae				
Mytilus edulis			×	×
Order Pteroida				
Suborder Pteriina				
Family Ostreidae				
Crassostrea virginica			×	×
Subclass Heterodonta				
Order Veneroida				
Family Mactridae				
Spisula sp.			×	
Mulinia lateralis			×	×
Family Tellinidae				
Macoma balthica			×	×
Family Dreissenidae				
Mytilopsis leucophaeta		×	×	×
(= *Congeria leucopheata*)				
Family Sphaeriidae				
Sphaerium simile	×			
Sphaerium sp.	×			
Pisidium sp.	×			
Musculium sp.				
Family Veneridae				
Mercenaria mercenaria				×
Family Petricolidae				
Petricola pholadiformis			×	×
Order Myoida				
Family Myidae				
Mya arenaria			×	×
PHYLUM ARTHROPODA				
Subphylum Mandibulata				
Class Crustacea				
Division Oligobranchipoda				

TABLE 4.11 (*Continued*)

	Freshwater (0 ppt Salinity)	Oligohaline (0.5–5 ppt Salinity)	Mesohaline (5–18 ppt Salinity)	Polyhaline (18–32 ppt Salinity)
Order Cladocera				
Suborder Haplopoda				
Family Leptodoridae				
Leptodora kindtii	×			
Suborder Eucladocera				
Family Sididae				
Sida crystallina	×			
Diaphanosoma brachyurum	×			
Latona setifera	×			
Family Daphniidae				
Diaphanosoma brachyurum	×	×		
Ceriodaphnia reticulata				
Daphnia pulex	×			
D. retrocurva	×			
Monia sp.	×		×	×
Family Bosmidae				
Bosmia longirostrus	×	×	×	×
Family Macrothricidae				
Ilyocryptus spinifer	×			
Macrothrix spp.	×			
Family Chydoridae				
Alona affinis	×			
Alona sp.	×			
Family Polyphemidae				
Podon leuckarti	?			
P. polyphemoides	?			
Evadne normanni				
Subclass Ostracoda				
Order Podocopida				
Family Cyprididae				
Cypris sp.			×	
Subclass Copepoda				
Order Calanoida				
Family Calanidae				
Calanus finmarchicus			×	×
Family Centropagidae				
Centropages typicus			×	
C. hamatus			×	
Family Diaptomidae				
Diaptomus ashlandi	×			
D. pallidus	×			
Diaptomus sp.				

Continued

TABLE 4.11   (*Continued*)

	Freshwater (0 ppt Salinity)	Oligohaline (0.5–5 ppt Salinity)	Mesohaline (5–18 ppt Salinity)	Polyhaline (18–32 ppt Salinity)
Pseudodiaptomus coronatus				
Family Temoridae				
Eurytemora affinia	×	×	×	×
(= *hirundoides*?)				
Epischura sp.				
Temora longicornis				×
Family Pontellidae				
Labidocera aestiva				
Family Acartidae				
Acartia tonsa			×	×
Family Tortanidae				
Tortanus discaudatus				
Order Cyclopoida				
Family Oithonidae				
Oithona sp.			×	×
Family Cyclopidae				
Cyclops bicuspidatus	×	×	×	
Cyclops sp.				
Halicyclops sp.	×			
Subclass Cirripedia				
Order Thoracica				
Suborder Balanomorpha				
Family Balanidae				
Balanus balanoides				×
B. improvisus			×	
B. subalbidus				×
Balanus sp.				
Subclass Malacostraca				
Division Peracarida				
Order Mysidacea				
Suborder Mysida				
Family Mysidae				
Neomysis americana			×	
Order Cumacea				
Family Leuconiidae				
Leucon americanus				×
Pseudoleucon sp.				×
Family Nannastacidae				
Almyracuma proximoculi				×
Family Diastylidae				
Oxyurostylis smithi				
Order Isopoda				
Suborder Anthuridea				
Family Anthuridae				

TABLE 4.11 (*Continued*)

	Freshwater (0 ppt Salinity)	Oligohaline (0.5–5 ppt Salinity)	Mesohaline (5–18 ppt Salinity)	Polyhaline (18–32 ppt Salinity)
Cyathura polita		×		
Suborder Flabellifera				
Family Cymothoidae				
Livoneca ovalis				×
Family Sphaeromidae				
Cassidinisca lunifrons				
Suborder Valvifera				
Family Idoteidae				
Chiridotea almyra				
C. caeca			?	
Edotea triloba			×	×
Suborder Asellota				
Family Asellidae				
Asellus racovitzai	?	?		
Order Amphipoda				
Suborder Gammaridea				
Family Corophiidae				
Corophium lacustre	×			
Family Gammaridae				
Gammarus annulatus				
G. daiberi		×	×	×
G. fasciatus	×	×		
G. mucronatus		×		
G. palustris		×		
G. tigrinis	×	×	×	
Melita nitida		×	×	
Family Haustoriidae				
Acanthohaustorius sp.				
Family Lysianassidae				
Eucrangonyx sp.				
Family Oedicerotidae				
Monoculodes edwardsi		×	×	
Family Photidae				
Leptocheirus plumulosus		×	×	
Family Stenothoidae				
Parametopella cypris			×	?
Order Decapoda				
Suborder Natantia				
Section Penaeidea				
Family Penaeidae				
Penaeus sp.			×	
Section Caridea				
Family Paleomonidae				

Continued

TABLE 4.11   (*Continued*)

	Freshwater (0 ppt Salinity)	Oligohaline (0.5–5 ppt Salinity)	Mesohaline (5–18 ppt Salinity)	Polyhaline (18–32 ppt Salinity)
Palaemontes paludosus		×	×	
P. pugio			×	×
Family Crangonidae				
Crangon septemspinosa			×	×
Suborder Reptantia				
Section Astacura				
Family Nephropidae				
Homarus americanus			×	×
Family Astascidae				
Orconectes limosus				
Section Brachyura				
Subsection Branchygnatha				
Infrasubsection Brachyrhyncha				
Family Cancridae				
Cancer irroratus			×	
Family Portunidae				
Ovalipes ocellatus		×	×	
Callinectes sapidus		×	×	×
Family Xanthidae				
Neopanope texana				×
Rhithropanopeus harisii			×	
Family Ocypodidae				
Uca minax				
Subphylum Chelicerata				
Class Insecta				
Subclass Pterygota				
Infraclass Paleoptera				
Order Ephemoptera sp.				
Order Odonata sp.				
Order Hemiptera sp.				
Division Endopterygota				
Order Trichoptera sp.				
Order Coleoptera sp.				
Family Hydrophilidae				
Tropisternus sp.	×			
Order Diptera				
Suborder Nematocera				
Family Tipulidae				
Tipula spp.	×			
Ulomorpha sp.				
Paradelphomyia sp.				
Family Culicidae sp.				
Family Chaoboridae				
Chaoborus punctipennis	×			

TABLE 4.11 *(Continued)*

	Freshwater (0 ppt Salinity)	Oligohaline (0.5–5 ppt Salinity)	Mesohaline (5–18 ppt Salinity)	Polyhaline (18–32 ppt Salinity)
C. albipes	×			
(= *Corethra*)				
Family Psychodidae sp.				
Family Ceratopogonidae				
Bezzia sp.	×			
Culicoides sp.	×			
Dasyhelia sp				
Family Chironomidae				
Ablabesmia sp.				
Coelotanypus sp.	×			
Procladius sp.	×			
Tanypus sp.	×			
Zavrelia sp.	×			
Cricotopus sp.	×			
Calopsectra sp.	×			
Chironomus attenuatus	×			
Cryptonomus sp.	×			
Dicrotendipes sp.	?			
Glyptotendipes sp.	×			
Polypedilum sp.	×			
Suborder Brachycera				
Family Stratiomyidae				
Hedriodiscus sp.				
Stratiomys sp.	?			
Family Tabanidae				
Chrysops brimleyi	×			
Chrysops sp.	?			
Tabanus sp.	?			
Family Dolichopodidae sp.				
Suborder Cyclorrhapha				
Family Syrphidae sp.				
Family Ephydridae				
Notiphila sp.	?			

sp. was the most common copepod in May and June. *Diaphanosoma brachyurum*, a cladoceran, was very abundant in late summer and early fall. *Bosmina longirostris* was abundant along the entire length of the estuary in June. Populations reached their greatest size in fresh and brackish waters at different times in July.

In fresh waters, the common calanoid copepods were represented primarily by *Diaptomus* sp.; the cyclopoids were represented by *Cyclops* spp. (Howells

TABLE 4.12.   *Hudson River Fish Species*[a]

PHYLUM CHORDATA		
Subphylum Urochordata		
Class Ascidacea		
Order Pleurogona		
Suborder Stolidobranchiata		
Family Molgulidae		
Molgula sp.	*Enchelyopus cimbrius*	M
Subphylum Vertebrata	*Gadus morhau*	M
Class Agnatha	*Microgadus tomcod*	A
Order Petromyzontiformes	Order Atheriniformes	
Family Petromyzontidae	Family Cyprinodontidae	
Petromyzon marinus	A	*Fundulus heteroclitus*	F,M
Class Osteichthyes	*F. diaphanus*	F,M
Order Acipenseriformes	Family Atherinidae	
Family Acipenseridae	*Menidia beryllina*	F,M
Acipenser oxyrhynchus	A	*M. menidia*	F,M
A. brevirostrum	F	Order Gasterosteiformes	
Order Anguilliformes	Family Syngnathidae	
Family Anguillidae	*Syngnathus fuscus*	M
Anguilla rostrata	C	*Hippocampus erectus*	M
Family Congridae	Order Perciformes	
Conger oceanicus	M	Family Percichthyidae	
Order Clupeiformes	*Morone americana*	F
Family Clupeidae	*M. saxatilis*	A
Alosa aestivalis	A	Family Centrachidae	
A. pseudoharengus	A	*Lepomis auritus*	F
A. sapidissima	A	*L. gibbosus*	F
Brevoortia tyrannus	M	*L. macrochirus*	F
Clupea harengus harengus	M	*Pomoxis nigromaculatus*	F
Family Engraulidae	*Etheostoma nigrum*	F
Anchoa mitchilli	E	*E. olmstedi*	F
Order Salmoniformes	*Perca flavescens*	F
Family Osmeridae	Family Pomatomidae	
Osmerus mordax	A	*Pomatomus saltatrix*	M
Order Cypriniformes	Family Echeneidae	
Family Cyprinidae	*Caranax hippos*	M
Carassius auratus	F	Family Sciaenidae	
Cyprinus carpio	F	*Bairdiella chrysoura*	F,M
Notemigonus crysoleucas	F	*Cynoscion regalis*	M
Notropis atherinoides	F	*Leiostomus xanthurus*	M
N. hudsonius	F	*Menticirrhus saxatilis*	M
Family Catostomidae	Family Labridae	
Catostomus commersoni	F	*Tautoga onitis*	M
Order Silurifomes	*Tautogolabrus adspersus*	M
Family Ictaluridae	Family Mugilidae	
Ictalurus catus	F	*Mugil curema*	M
I. natalis	F	Family Ammodytidae	
I. nebulosus	F	*Ammodytes* sp.	M
Order Lophiiformes	Family Gobiidae	
Family Lophiidae	*Gobiosoma ginsburgi*	M
Lophius americanus	M	Family Stromateidae	
Order Gadiformes	*Peprilus triacanthus*	M
Family Gadidae	Family Cottidae	

TABLE 4.12. (*Continued*)

Myoxocephalus octodecemspinosus	M	Family Pleuronectidae	
Order Pleuronectiformes		*Limanda ferruginea*	M
Family Bothidae		*Pseudopleuronectes americanus*	E
Paralichthys dentatus	M	Family Soleidae	
Scophthalmus aquosus	M	*Trinectes maculatus*	E

*F, Freshwater; M, Marine; A, Anadromous; C, Catadromous; E, Estuarine.

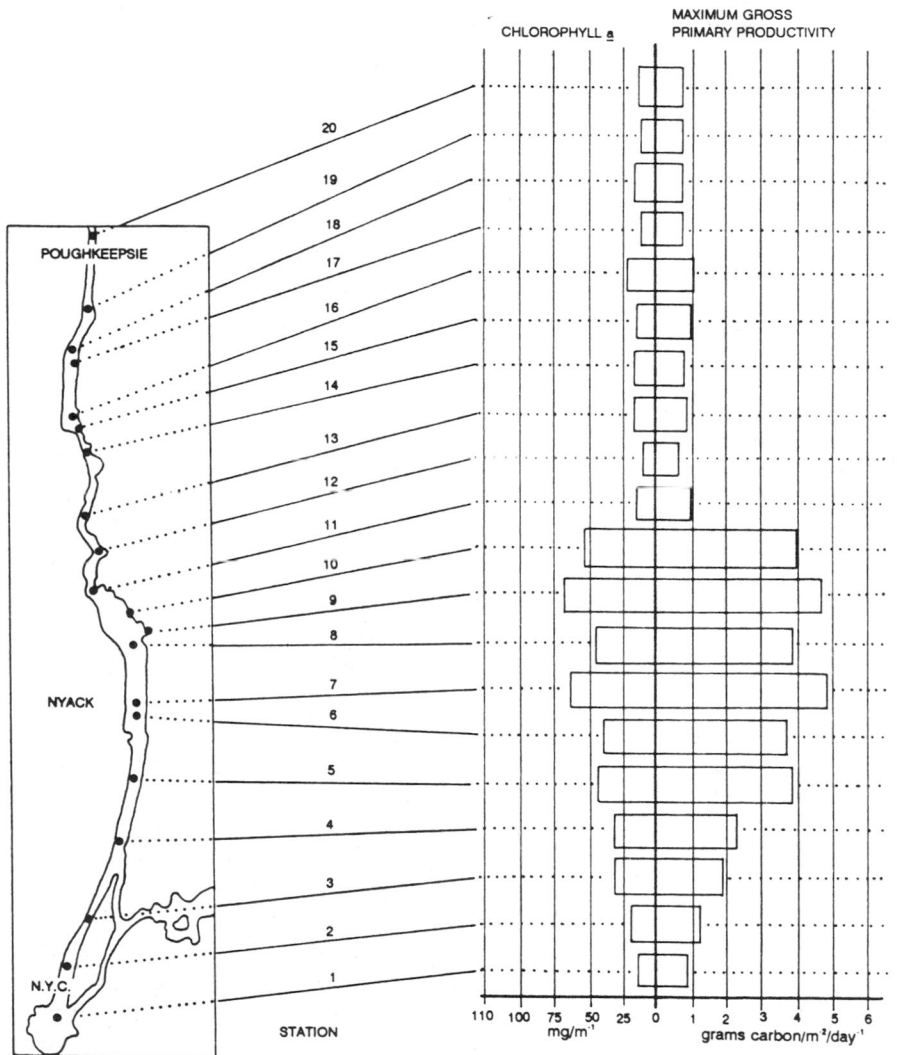

FIGURE 4.6. Maximum levels of gross primary production and chlorophyll *a* in the Hudson River estuary during 1972. (From Weinstein, 1977.)

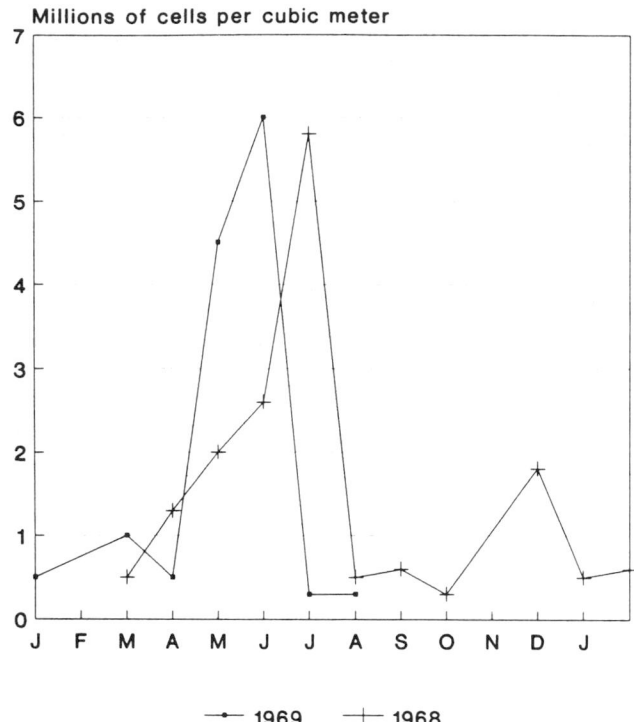

J F M A M J J A S O N D J

—•— 1969   —+— 1968

FIGURE 4.7.   Phytoplankton abundance in the Hudson River at Indian Point (near Peekskill), New York, in 1968 and 1969. Data points are the means of three stations. (After Howells and Weaver, 1969.)

et al., 1969). The amphipods, *Gammarus* sp. and *Monoculodes* sp., which were important fish food, were common from June to August. In September and October the mysid shrimp, *Neomysis mercedis*, another fish food, became more common.

Fresh-to-Brackish Water.   Rotifers were abundant in the zooplankton in fresh and slightly brackish water (Howells et al., 1969). In April 1968, near Indian Point, *Notholca* sp., *Trichocerca* sp., *Philodina* sp., and *Keratella cochlearis* were very abundant (1500 individuals L^{-1}). In March 1969, at Indian Point and Cornwall, *Asplanchna* was very common. Throughout the year, *K. cochlearis* and *K. quadrata* were common. The rotifers were important predators of bacteria, protozoa, and phytoplankton.

Brackish-to-Saline Water.   In brackish water the more common zooplankton were *Ceratium* sp., which peaked in May (Howells et al., 1969); the ciliates, *Colpoda* and *Glaucoma*; and the amoeba, *Difflugia* and *Arcella*. In higher-salinity waters the dinoflagellate of the lower Hudson estuary, *Prorocentrum micans*, was common and varied its range upriver according to the penetration of the salt front (Weinstein, 1977). Among the crustacea, the cladoceran, *Moina* spp., was extremely abundant in early fall and late winter in New York Harbor. It appeared in the lower Hudson channel in the spring and reached its greatest concentration near the mouth of the estuary (Weinstein, 1977).

In the brackish-to-marine part of the estuary, calanoid copepods were the most important prey species for fish. The most common copepods were *Acartia tonsa*, *Eurytemora affinis*, and *Temora longicornis* (Weinstein, 1977). *Acartia tonsa* attained populations up to 100,000 m^{-3} in the summer and seemed to prefer salinity of 10 to 20 ppt. Populations were low in winter near the mouth of the estuary. In late spring, the salt front moved upriver as the runoff decreased and the species began to extend its range northward. The population of *Acartia tonsa* increased with moderating temperatures. *A. tonsa* dominated throughout the brackish part of the estuary in July, August, and September. In fall, populations decreased rapidly with the return of cold weather. From November through June, *Eurytemora affinis* dominated in the lower part of the estuary, in waters up to 15 ppt salinity. Its center of distribution moved upriver in summer and early fall, but total density of individuals was less than earlier in the season due to competition with *A. tonsa*. *A. tonsa* was more successful in summer because it preferred a higher salinity (10 to 20 ppt) than *E. affinis* (12 to 15 ppt) and was better adapted to warm water. *Temora longicornis* was normally confined to New York Harbor in early fall and late winter, but it appeared in the lower Hudson channel in spring. Its populations reached as far north as the New York City/Yonkers boundary in 1972, but the greatest concentration of individuals was found toward the mouth of the estuary in spring (Weinstein, 1977).

The small (7-mm-diameter) gastropod mollusc, *Valvata sincera*, was the only member of its phylum in the plankton of the Hudson River (Weinstein, 1977). In 1972, *V. sincera* developed large populations between Dobbs Ferry and Croton during late July and early August, but was scarce or not found at all the rest of the year. Barnacles (*Balanus* spp.) were represented in the plankton by the nauplii larvae, which were abundant in the lower estuary in spring. Cypris larvae, which develop from the barnacle nauplii, were found primarily in July through September. The barnacles set when the larvae are 5 to 6 mm long and thereafter were sessile. Barnacle zooplankton were always confined to brackish-to-marine waters. Crandell (1977) found that setting of *Balanus improvisus* took place mostly between July and mid-September, with the maximal setting in the 6-week period from 1 July to mid-August in Croton Bay, near Haverstraw.

Benthic Communities. Benthic organisms are a very important part of the estuary community. The kinds of species vary according to habitat and salinity, as seen in Figure 4.8.

Fresh Water. The freshwater areas were characterized by oligochaetes, crustaceans, some insects, and various molluscs. The more common insects were craneflies, chironomids, mosquitos, and biting midges. The characteristic molluscs were the *Elliptio complanata*, *Balanus tentaculatus*, *Helisoma anceps*, *Lymnea palustris*, *Physa heterostropha*, and *Pisidium* sp.

Brackish Water (Oligohaline to Polyhaline). A large number of invertebrates have been identified from the brackish-to-marine areas, as this is the area that

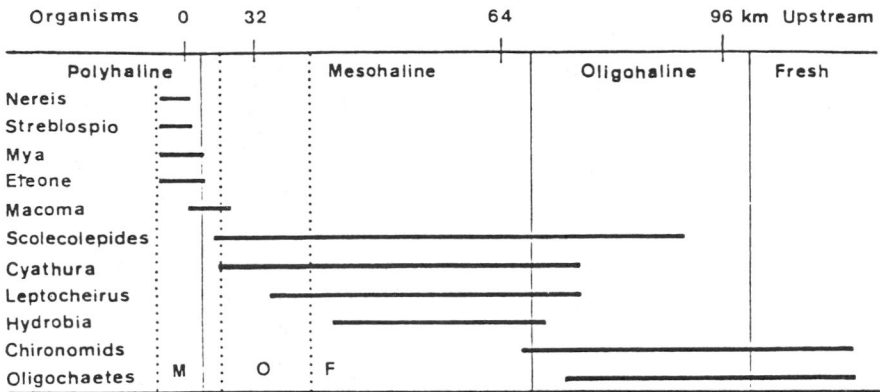

FIGURE 4.8.   Dominant genera of benthic invertebrates in the Hudson River estuary. Genera were selected from a biological index based on abundance rank and frequency of occurrence. Salinity zones (heavy vertical lines) are near levels of greatest salt penetration. The same salinity zones move far downstream in the spring (dotted vertical lines). (After Ristich et al., 1977.)

has received the greatest amount of study. The distribution according to salinity of some of the more common invertebrates is given in Figure 4.8 (see also Tables 4.11 and 4.12). Of the annelids, the more common were *Eteone heteropoda, Streblospio benedicti, Scolecolepides viridis, Polydora websteri, Polydora* spp., *Hypaniola grayi,* and several Oligochaeta genera. The Polychaeta, *Scolecolepides viridis,* was the most numerous benthic invertebrate and covered the widest range. The most important molluscs were *Macoma balthica* in the poly-mesohaline zone between the Battery and Tappan Zee Bridge, and *Mya arenaria* in the lower polyhaline and upper mesohaline areas south of Mt. St. Vincent. Between New York Harbor and south Haverstraw Bay, the more common crustacea were the isopods, *Edotea triloba,* in the mesohaline areas and *Cyathura polita,* which preferred oligohaline-to-mesohaline water. The distribution of *Edotea triloba* was discontinuous, probably because of a lack of suitable substrate in certain reaches of the river. The largest populations of *Cyathura polita* occurred between the Tappan Zee Bridge and Haverstraw Bay. The amphipods may be divided into three groups by distribution: (1) *Gammarus daiberi, Melita nitida,* and *Leptocheirus plumulosus,* which were found in the reaches from Tappan Zee to Haverstraw Bay; (2) *Monoculodes edwardsii,* which occurred in the oligohaline zone between Mt. St. Vincent and Haverstraw Bay; and (3) *Corophium lacustre,* which had two populations in the estuary, one from Mt. St. Vincent to the upper Tappan Zee, and one from the upper Tappan Zee to Peekskill (Ristich et al., 1977).

In the meso-oligohaline area south of Haverstraw, large populations of polychaetes lived within the sediments. Unionid clams lived on the sediment or burrowed only a few centimeters into it. Various crustacea, such as crabs and shrimp, moved about over the surface of the estuary bed or were free-swimming. All these taxa were preyed upon by fish.

The isopod, *Cyathura polita*, found in brackish waters, grazed on detritus, diatoms, and other crustaceans. It was eaten, in turn, by ducks and fish. The amphipods were also important in the food web and they too had various prey species. *Gammarus daiberi* preyed upon small crustaceans and did some scavenging. *Melita nitida* was often found associated with hydroids on muddy beds. *Leptocheirus plumulosus* is a tube-building amphipod with mouthparts adapted to feeding on algae and detritus. It was a prey for larval and juvenile fish. *Corophium lacustre* is also a tube builder and is both a deposit feeder and a filter feeder. *Monoculodes edwardsii* tended to be associated with burrowing or sedentary animals such as snails and nemerteans (Ristich et al., 1977). Thus we see a food chain that is common in the Hudson, based on algae and detritus, which are food for amphipods and isopods, which in turn are prey for fish. The importance of invertebrates as prey for fish is illustrated in Table 4.13 (Hirshfield et al., 1966).

Nekton. Fishes of the lower Hudson River system can be divided into three major groups: (1) those that spend their entire life within the Hudson River; (2) those that spawn in fresh waters and then go out to sea as they mature; and (3) those that spend most of their adult life in rivers but go to the sea to spawn (Weinstein, 1977).

The bay anchovy (*Anchoa mitchilli*) is a good example of the first group. In the early fall juvenile anchovy initially swam upstream but were turned back by cold water and moved downstream to deeper, warmer waters, where they spent the winter. In May, juveniles moved upstream to the area between the Tappan Zee Bridge and Croton Point to feed. In June, adults moved south of the Tappan Zee Bridge to spawn in water of salinity greater than 10 ppt and temperature higher than 14 °C (Weinstein, 1977). Large numbers of the larvae congregated in low-salinity feeding areas between the Tappan Zee Bridge and Peekskill from June to August.

The hogchoker (*Trinectes maculatus*) is another fish that spends its life in the Hudson River. Like the anchovy, it spawned in downstream areas, where salinity is greater than 10 ppt and its young moved to fresher water to feed (Weinstein, 1977). Hogchokers were particularly abundant in the Peekskill Bay area.

The mummichog (*Fundulus heteroclitus*) and its close relative, the banded killifish (*F. disphanus*), were common in small embayments along the length of the estuary (Weinstein, 1977). Mummichog and killifish were important consumers of mosquito larvae, shrimp, and other small invertebrates of calm, shallow waters.

An example of fish that spawn in freshwater and live in the sea as adults is the Atlantic tomcod (*Microgadus tomcod*). It is a small fish preferring cool-water habitats. Spawning took place in upstream freshwater during late winter, sometimes under ice. The larvae spent their first year of life in low-salinity water and usually migrated downstream from freshwater areas between January and July. They sometimes followed the low brackish-water zone upstream in the

TABLE 4.13. *Stomach Contents of the Hudson River Estuaries Fish Collected Between a Point South of Tappan Zee Bridge and Nyack State Park, New York, Summer 1964*

Fish Species	Percentage of Stomach Contents			
	90	50–90	25–50	25
Anchoa mitchilli (anchovy)	—	—	—	Dipteran larvae Tubificids
Microgadus tomcod (tomcod)	*Corophium*	—	—	Copepod remains
Menidia menidia notata (silversides)	—	Nematodes	—	*Corophium?* *Gammarus?* Tubificids
Alosa sapidissima (shad)	—	—	Copepods *Corophium* Dipteran adults Dipteran larvae *Gammarus* Insect adults Snails	Barnacles
Alosa aestivalis (blueback herring)	Copepods	—	—	—
Alosa pseudoharengus (alewife)	—	—	Copepods Dipteran larvae Dipteran adults *Gammarus*	—
Fundulus heteroclitus (saltwater killifish)	—	Filamentous algae	—	*Corophium* *Cyathura* Diatoms Dipteran larvae Fish eggs Fish larvae *Gammarus*
Roccus americanus (white perch)	—	—	Copepods *Gammarus*	*Corophium* Dipteran larvae
Roccus saxatilis (striped bass)	—	—	*Corophium* Fish eggs and larvae *Gammarus*	Copepods Crabs *Cyathura* Snails

Source: Hirshfield et al. (1966).

summer if the water was cool. They fed on various invertebrates, including shrimp, worms, amphipods, squid, snails, and immature fish. After spawning, the adults moved into the deeper, cooler water of coastal areas and Long Island Sound, but did not go into the offshore ocean (Weinstein, 1977).

The Atlantic sturgeon (*Acipenser oxyrhynchus*) and the shortnose sturgeon (*A. brevirostrum*) follow a similar pattern. The sturgeon were several years old when they first spawned in fresh water. Juveniles tended to remain in the fresher areas of the estuary. As they matured, the young sturgeon moved toward the sea. The shortnose sturgeon rarely left the estuary, but Atlantic sturgeon from the Hudson have been caught as far away as Kitty Hawk, North Carolina. The sturgeon may go as far north as Albany, but Greeley (1937) did not report any recovered from tributaries of the Hudson. The sturgeon scavenged the river bottom mud for crustacea and small fish (Weinstein, 1977).

Other species that spawned in fresh water were the American shad (*Alosa sapidissima*), the blueback herring (*A. aestivalis*), and the alewife (*A. pseudoharengus*). The alewife and blueback herring were found in tributaries, but the shad remained in the main trunk of the river. Young shad filter-fed opportunistically on zooplankton, particularly copepods.

The reproductive cycles of all three fish were similar in that they spawned in the May–June period in the freshwater part of the estuary. They spawned in the following order: alewife, blueback herring, and shad (Weinstein, 1977). The young of all three species remained in fresh water or moved into a slightly brackish portion of the estuary for their first summer. In response to cooling river temperatures most fish left the estuary and moved down the coast to stay within a water mass of acceptable temperature. In the summer they moved north along the coast, past the estuary mouth, to avoid warm river water. At 3 years of age, they returned to the estuary of their origin to spawn.

Two other species that spawn in freshwater were the white perch (*Morone americana*) and the striped bass (*M. saxatilis*). The white perch hatched in the estuary and did not leave it, but the striped bass spent most of its life in the Atlantic after it hatched in the estuary and was therefore truly an anadromous fish. Early larval and early juvenile stages of these species were found together and their movements were similar.

The young white perch remained in the Haverstraw Bay and upper Tappan Zee areas. The Hudson estuary is probably the second most important estuary, after the Chesapeake, for striped bass propagation on the east coast of North America (Weinstein, 1977). Young striped bass congregated in the lower Tappan Zee, where they fed on anchovies and other fish. Late juvenile striped bass were more active and ranged farther downstream than the white perch. The young-of-the-year remained in the lower estuary for about one year, during which time they became more and more active. They left the estuary before maturity, and did not return again until they spawned. Each spring, as the temperature rose to around 10 °C, the adult striped bass moved into the estuary to spawn in fresh water.

The third group consists of fish of the Hudson estuary that spawn in the ocean but return to the estuary for varying lengths of time (Weinstein, 1977). The American eel, *Anguilla rostrata*, spawned in the Sargasso Sea. Its year-old juveniles entered coastal estuaries and were found in all tributary streams as well as the main stem of the Hudson. The males are thought to have remained in the brackish-water areas, while the females moved upstream into fresh water. After several years of living as carnivorous scavengers, the mature eels returned in the fall to the Sargasso Sea, where they died after spawning.

The Atlantic menhaden (*Brevoortia tyrannus*) is a herring that hatched in the marine environment in fall and winter and migrated up the estuaries into fresh water when a small larva. During the summer the young, rapidly growing fish returned to the sea to feed on zooplankton. Juvenile menhaden, such as were common in the Tappan Zee–Haverstraw Bay area in spring and summer, died readily and were often the main constituent of spectacular fish kills observed in many estuaries. Weinstein (1977) reports no menhaden outside the Hudson River proper. Adult bluefish (*Potatomus saltatrix*) live in coastal waters from Cape Cod to Brazil. The juvenile phase was found in the lower Hudson estuary but not in any of the tributaries (Weinstein, 1977).

The weakfish (*Cynoscion regalis*) is a member of the croaker family, a group that uses the lower portions of estuaries during their early development. Other members of the family found in the Hudson estuary were Atlantic croaker (*Micropogon undulatus*), silver perch (*Bairdiella chrysura*), spot (*Leistomus xanthurus*), and northern kingfish (*Menticirrhus saxatilis*).

Greeley (1937) reported only one croaker species, the spot, and found it only in the Hudson itself. Members of the croaker family are more abundant now than previously in the Hudson estuary.

The winter flounder (*Pseudopleuronectes americanus*) spawned in brackish water of the estuary during late winter before water temperatures rose (Weinstein, 1977). The larvae and juveniles were found in brackish areas until late spring. Adults were rarely found in the estuary except during spawning (Greeley, 1937).

Two marine fish, the northern pipefish (*Syngnathus fuscus*) and the fourbeard rockling (*Enchelyopus cimbrius*), used the lower Hudson estuary for feeding. They did not have regular seasonal migrations and stayed well within the saline part of the estuary (Weinstein, 1977)

Hirshfield et al. (1966) studied stomach contents of a number of fish from the Hudson River to see how the results compared with invertebrate collections made by tow nets and sediment samples. The fish fed on some species (e.g., *Corophium*, amphipod, and occasionally *Cyathura*, isopod) that were virtually absent from tow net and sediment samples examined, implying that these organisms were more important in the fauna than the tow net and sediment studies indicated. As shown in Table 4.12, most fish had a varied diet, and most shared the same dietary items with other species. Shad and saltwater killifish ate a wider variety of foods than the others. Hirshfield et al. (1966) stated that, in general, fish tend to eat what is seasonally abundant in the estuary.

SUMMARY

The southern New England estuaries are mostly barrier island estuaries or otherwise sheltered areas and have, for the most part, sand or sandy mud as a substrate although rocks are present here and there. The water currents are much warmer than in northern New England and the fauna is a mixture of Virginian and New England fauna and flora. The phytoplankton has been extensively studied by Smayda. The rate of oxygen production is $0.42 \, \text{mg O L}^{-1} \, \text{day}^{-1}$ while respiration utilizes $0.32 \, \text{mg O L}^{-1} \, \text{day}^{-1}$—thus it is an autotrophic system.

Skeletonema is the most important diatom and is a favorite food for the zooplankton. There is considerable seasonal variation in the phytoplankton. Most of the fish have dimersal eggs and 50% of all larvae are hatched from the dimersal eggs. The fish fauna is very diverse. It is composed of both resident and migratory fish. Benthic invertebrate fauna contains many species. The scavengers are usually found where the organic debris supply is high. Examples are crabs and shrimp. Other detrital feeders are amphipods, tentacled worms, and many bivalves. Some species are confined to certain habitats, whereas others are widely distributed over the bay.

In Buzzards Bay, the meiofauna—that is, the nematodes, the kinorhynchs, the ostracods, and the benthic copepods—have a density of about 930,000 m^{-2}, making the meiofauna about 100 times as numerous as the macrofauna. However, the weight of the meiofauna is only about 3% that of the macrofauna. The fauna is very diverse as to both species numbers and habitats and food preferences.

The salt marshes are dominated primarily by *Spartina* and are well developed in this area. They support a characteristic fauna. Insects, particularly those that belong to the genus *Tabanus*, are very common in the salt marsh. Other very common organisms are oligochaete worms, fiddler crabs, nematodes, ciliates, gastropods, turbellaria, ostracods, and tanaidaceans. Muddy sediments support the *Ampelisca* community. This arthropod dominates the fauna. The sand bottom communities are characterized by the razor clam, the blood worm, and the sand shrimps and hermit crabs. Many other species are also found in this habitat.

The hard substrates are dominated by molluscs, whereas in the intertidal community the main species are polychaete worms, bryozoa, gastropods, and pelecypods. Rocky areas have a particular fauna. The association of organisms is composed of sponges, actinians, hydroids, and annelid worms. Bryozoans are often found encrusted on the rocks and various species of barnacles, chitons, snails, and cordates are present. Wharves and pilings present special habitats and support a great variety of species, including barnacles, oyster drills, clams, and an occasional starfish. In this habitat one may also find some of the smaller crabs. In the areas that are submerged at all times may be found sponges, various types of worms, snails, bryozoans, and sea anemones.

The tidal flats are among the most common habitats in this area. They are occupied by many different kinds of diatoms and other algae as well as by molluscs, which are the dominant in these habitats. Sand communities are rich in nematodes, various types of worms, and molluscs as well as some of the shrimps and other arthropods.

In the marshlands, blue-green algae are commonly associated with the *Spartina* and *Juncus*. Barnacles, crabs, nematodes, and the pelecypod, *Modiolus demissus*, is common. The common mumichog is the dominant fish in these areas.

The salt marsh creeks are very important communities and are often breeding and nursery grounds for many species. Production is high in these marshes. The marsh phytoplankton fix 2.5×10^6 to 2.5×10^7 mg C h^{-1}. Areas of the low marsh fix about 9.8×10^4 to 1.13×10^7 mg C h^{-1}. During the year, the productivity of the algae beneath the *Spartina* canopy was about 105.5 g m^{-2} yr^{-1} in the unshaded portion. This production was about one-fourth the aboveground seasonal grass production in the Great Sippewissett Marsh. Production of the marsh vegetation is about 22.7×10^6 kcal m^{-2} yr^{-1}. Secondary production is also very high in these marshes. Invertebrates in the tidal creeks and marsh surfaces range from 50 to 1000 mg m^{-2} dry weight per year.

Nutrients enter both the surface water and groundwater. It is estimated that about half of the dissolved inorganic nitrogen brought into the marsh by groundwater was converted and exported as particulate nitrogen. In the summer the uptake of nutrients by the marsh exceeded the exports by an order of magnitude. There was a net export of ammonia, nitrates, nitrites, and dissolved organic nitrogen, particulate nitrogen, particulate carbon, and phosphates. This occurred during August.

The Hudson River estuary represents a very different type of estuary than the small river estuaries found in southern New Jersey. It has been subject to a great deal of pollution, as has the Delaware. The tidal influence on the Hudson extends as far up as Albany. Considering the amount of pollution that has entered the Hudson, the fauna and flora are relatively normal. It is, indeed, quite comparable to the Delaware below Trenton. The greatest primary productivity occurs near Nyack. Primary productivity is measured by chlorophyll production. As in the Delaware, the more tolerant species are dominant. Worms of various types are very common, as are various species of arthropods. Fish of the lower Hudson can be divided into three groups: those that spend their entire life in the Hudson, those that spawn in fresh water and then go to sea to mature, and those that spawn in the sea and spend most of their adult life in the rivers.

Thus we find in the Hudson, as in the Delaware, a transition from fresh to mesohaline conditions as one progresses from the head of the estuary to the mouth. The aquatic life is diverse and supports an ecosystem that functions similar to a natural community in the transfer nutrients and energy through the food web. However, the species composition, as in the Delaware, is composed primarily of species that are tolerant of a wide range of environmental conditions.

BIBLIOGRAPHY

Allee, W. C. 1923a. Studies in marine ecology. I and II. Biol. Bull. 44(4): 167–197.

Allee, W. C. 1923b. Studies in marine ecology. III. Some physical factors related to the distribution of littoral invertebrates. Biol. Bull. 44(5): 205–253.

Burbank, W. E., M. E. Pierce, and G. C. Whiteley, Jr. 1956. A study of bottom fauna of Rands Harbor, Mass.: an application of the ecotone concept. Ecol. Monogr. 26: 213–243.

Crandell, M. E. 1977. Epibenthic invertebrates of Croton Bay in the Hudson River. N.Y. Fish Game J. 24: 178–186.

Davis, B. M. 1911. Part 1, Section II. Botanical biological survey of the waters of Woods Hole and vicinity. Bull. Bur. Fish 31 (1911): 443–544.

Driscoll, E. G., and R. A. Swanson. 1973. Diversity and structure of epifaunal communities on mollusc bivalves, Buzzards Bay, Mass. Palaeogeogr. Palaeoclimatol. Palaeoecol. 14: 229–247.

Durbin, E. G., R. Krawiec, and T. Smayda. 1975. Seasonal studies on the relative importance of different size fractions of phytoplankton in Narragansett Bay (U.S.A.). Mar. Biol. 32: 271–287.

Fogg, G. E. 1966. The extracellular products of algae. Oceanogr. Mar. Biol. Annu. Rev. 4: 195–212.

Gordon, D. C., Jr. 1966. The effect of the deposit feeding polychaete *Pectinaria gouldii* on the intertidal sediments of Barnstable Harbor. Limnol. Oceanogr. 11: 327–332.

Greeley, J. R. 1937. Fishes of the area with annotated list: New York State Conservation Department. A biological survey of the lower Hudson watershed. (Suppl. to 26th Annu. Rep., 1936.) New York State Biol. Surv. 11: 45–103.

Hirshfield, H. I., H. W. Rachlin, and E. Leff. 1966. A survey of the invertebrates from selected sites of the lower Hudson River, pp. 220–257. *In* M. Eisenbud and D. B. Stevens, co-chairmen, Hudson River ecology, Oct. 4–5, 1966, Onichiota Conference Center at Sterling Forest, Tuxedo, N.Y. Hudson River Valley Commission of New York, Tarrytown, N.Y.

Howells, G. P., and S. Weaver. 1969. Studies on phytoplankton at Indian point, pp. 231–261. *In* G. P. Howells and A. J. Laurer, eds. Hudson River ecology. Proceedings of a symposium. 2nd Sterling River Forest, Tuxedo, N.Y. Hudson River Valley Commission of New York, Tarrytown, N.Y.

Howells, G. P., E. Musnick, and H. I. Hirshfield. 1969. Invertebrates of the Hudson River, pp. 262–280. *In* G. P. Howells and A. J. Laurer, eds. Hudson River ecology. Proceedings of a symposium. 2nd Sterling River Forest, Tuxedo, N.Y. Hudson River Valley Commission of New York, Tarrytown, N.Y.

Huet, M. 1964. The evaluation of fish productivity in fresh waters. Verh. Intern. Verh. Intern. Limnol. 15: 524–528.

Johnson, D. S., and H. H. York. 1915. The relation of plants to tide levels. Carnegie Inst. Washington Publ. 206. 162 pp.

Ketchum, B. H. 1954. The relation between circulation and planktonic populations in estuaries. Ecology 35: 191–200.

Mann, K. H. 1965. Energy transformation by a population of fish in the River Thames. J. Anim. Ecol. 34: 253–275.

Marshall, N., and B. M. Wheeler. 1965. Role of coastal and upper estuarine water contributing phytoplankton to the shoals of the Niantic estuary. Ecology 46: 665–673.

Martin, J. H. 1965. Phytoplankton–zooplankton relationships in Narragansett Bay. Limnol. Oceanogr. 10: 185–191.

Martin, J. H. 1968. Phytoplankton–zooplankton relationships in Narragansett Bay. III. Seasonal changes in zooplankton excretion rates in relation to phytoplankton abundance. Limnol. Oceanogr. 13: 63–71.

Mathieson, A. C., and R. A. Fralick. 1973. Benthic algae and vascular plants of the lower Merrimack River and adjacent shoreline. Rhodora 75(801): 52–64.

Menge, B. A. 1978b. Predation intensity in a rocky intertidal community: effect of an algal canopy, wave action, and desiccation on predator feeding rates. Oecologia (Berlin) 34: 17–36.

Nixon, S. W., and C. A. Oviatt. 1973. Ecology of a New England salt marsh. Ecol. Monogr. 43: 463–498.

Pearcy, W. G., and S. W. Richards. 1962. Distribution and ecology of fishes in the Mystic River estuary, Connecticut. Ecology 43: 248–259.

Ristich, S. S., M. Crandall, and J. Fortier. 1977. Benthic and epibenthic macroinvertebrates of the Hudson River. I. Distribution, natural history and community structure. Estuarine Coastal Mar. Sci. 5: 255–266.

Ryther, J. H. 1954. The ecology of phytoplankton blooms in Mariches Bay and Great South Bay, Long Island. New York Biol. Bull. (Woods Hole) 106(2): 198–209.

Sanders, H. L. 1960. Benthic studies in Buzzards Bay. III. The structure of the soft bottom communities. Limnol. Oceanogr. 5: 138–153.

Sirois, D. L., and S. W. Frederick. 1978. Phytoplankton and primary production in the lower Hudson River estuary, New York. Estuarine Coastal Mar. Sci. 7: 413–424.

Smayda, T. J. 1957. Phytoplankton studies in lower Narragansett Bay. Limnol. Oceanogr. 2: 342–359.

Stickney, A. P., and L. D. Stringer. 1957. A study of the invertebrate bottom fauna of Greenwich Bay, Rhode Island. Ecology 38: 111–122.

Tietjen, J. H. 1969. The ecology of shallow-water meiofauna in two New England estuaries. Oecoiogia (Berlin) 2: 251–291.

Udell, H. F., J. Zarudsky, T. E. Doheny, and P. R. Burkholder. 1969. Productivity and nutrient values of plants growing in the salt marshes of the town of Hempstead, Long Island. Bull. Torrey Bot. Club 96: 42–51.

U.S. Geological Survey. 1970. The national atlas of the United States of America. Washington, D.C. 417 pp.

Valiela, I., J. E. Wright, J. M. Teal, and S. B. Volkman. 1977. Growth, production and energy transformations in the salt-marsh killifish Fundulus heteroclitus. Mar. Biol. 40: 135–144.

Valiela, I., J. M. Teal, S. Volkman, D. Shafer, and E. J. Carpenter. 1978. Nutrient and particulate fluxes in a salt marsh ecosystem: tidal exchanges and inputs by precipitation and ground water. Limnol. Oceanogr. 23: 798–812.

Van Raalte, C. D., I. Valiela, and J. M. Teal. 1976. Production of epibenthic salt marsh algae: light and nutrient limitation. Limnol. Oceanogr. 21: 862–872.

Wall, W. J., Jr. 1973. The intertidal sand and salt marsh invertebrate fauna associated with the bloodsucking Diptera of Cape Cod, Mass. Environ. Entomol. 2: 681–684.

Webber, E. E. 1967. Blue-green algae from a Massachusetts salt marsh. Bull. Torrey Bot. Club 94: 99–106.

Weinstein, L.H., ed. 1977. An atlas of the biologic resources of the Hudson River estuary. Bayce Thompson Institute, New York. 104 pp.

Woodwell, G. M., R. A. Houghton, C. A. S. Hall, D. E. Whitney, R. A. Moll, and D. W. Juers, 1979. The Flax Pond ecosystem study: the annual metabolism and nutrient budgets of a salt marsh, pp. 491–511. In R. L. Jeffries and A. J. Davy eds., Ecological processes in coastal environments. Blackwell, Oxford.

CHAPTER 5

Middle Atlantic Estuaries

GENERAL CHARACTERISTICS

The middle Atlantic estuary zone extends from the Passaic–Hackensack estuary south of the Hudson River to Albermarle Sound, just north of Cape Hatteras (Figure 5.1). The estuaries traversing the coastal plain represent parts of former river channels whose estuaries were on the continental shelf. The channels of these present-day estuaries may be well-defined, with steep banks consisting of clay and mud of various types, or ill defined and merging into large marshlands. Usually, the channel banks become less defined near the mouth of the estuary.

Estuaries in this region vary in size from small to the large estuaries of the Delaware and Chesapeake bays. The Delaware estuary is dominated by one large river. Many rivers empty into Chesapeake Bay, which resembles Long Island Sound in structure and salinity gradients.

The flow of most estuaries is river dominated during periods of high river flow and dominated by tidal action during periods of low river flow. In the upper parts of the estuaries the flow is usually fresh throughout the year and only during extremely low flow is there salt water intrusion. This differential in salinity has profound effects on the characteristics of the fauna and flora. An estuary typically supports freshwater communities in the upper reaches, communities tolerant of great variation in salinity in the middle reaches, and a marine fauna and flora near the mouth.

Estuarine habitats are the intertidal grasslands and mud flats of the marshes, the intertidal and subtidal benthos in the open estuary, and the water column,

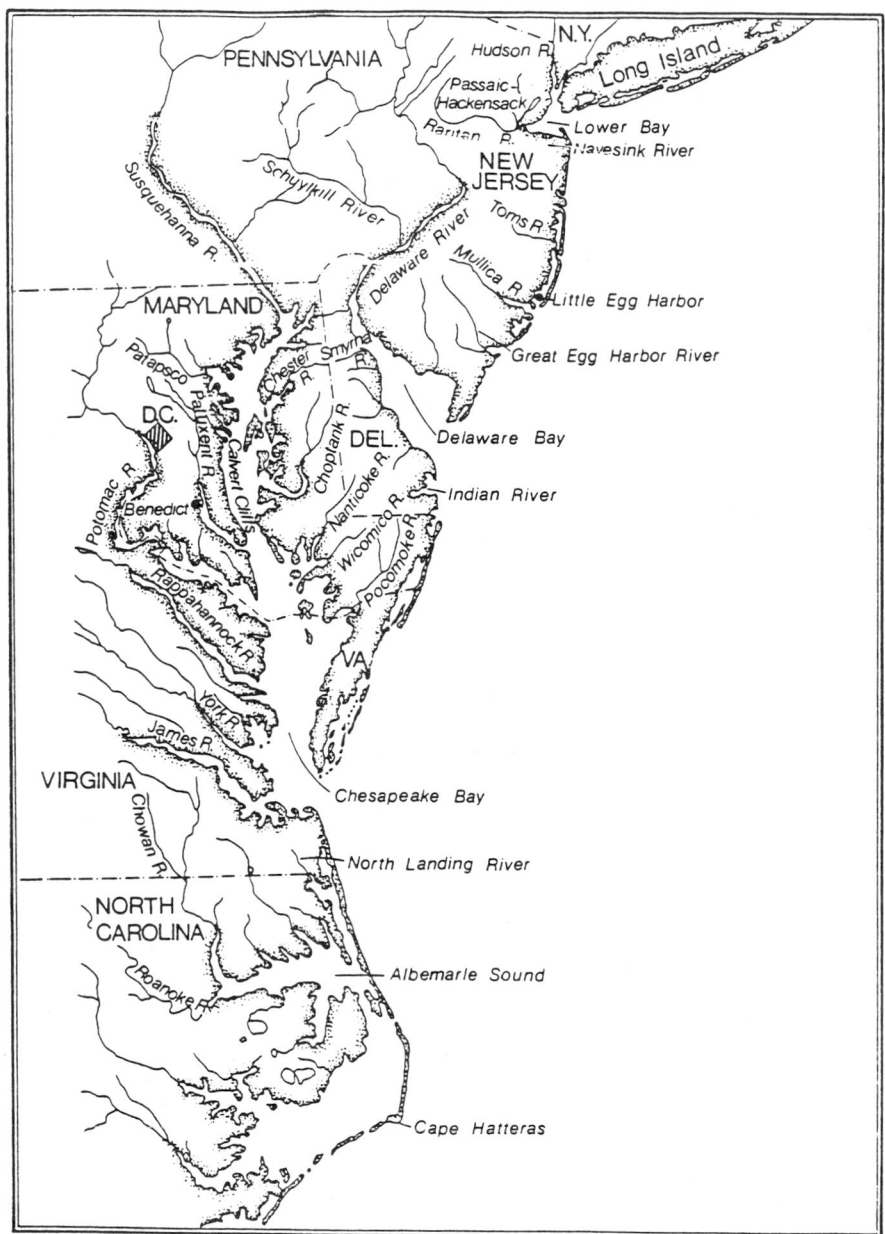

FIGURE 5.1.   Map of middle Atlantic shoreline, from Long Island to Cape Hatteras, showing major tributaries to the Delaware and Chesapeake bays.

which supports pelagic and nektonic species. The substrates are mostly sand, gravel, sandy mud, or mud. Rocky shores of the type found in New England are almost nonexistent and their nearest solid substrate counterparts are breakwaters, piers, and other manufactured structures.

The middle Atlantic estuaries are in the Virginian biotic province. Species found here are transitional between those of the northern Acadian province and the more southern species of the Carolina province.

Knowledge of the transition of communities of aquatic organisms from fresh to salt water is more complete in Delaware Bay, although associations of plants and animals in specific fresh, brackish, and marine areas have been studied in Chesapeake Bay as well. The shift in the communities of aquatic life as one passes from fresh to marine, or almost marine, water in the mouth of the bay has not been researched. However, rather complete descriptions of associations in estuaries entering the Delaware and Chesapeake bays have been made (Table 5.26).

DELAWARE BAY

Productivity
   Open Water. Many factors seem to have been postulated for the limitation of phytoplankton production in the upper estuary of the Delaware. Pennock and Sharp (1986) postulate that it is the turbidity that is the major factor limiting production in the upper estuary, despite the presence of high nutrient levels. The greatest production takes place in the lower estuary, where the turbidity is much less. They estimate the average phytoplankton production in the Delaware estuary as $307 \, \text{g m}^{-2} \, \text{yr}^{-1}$. Pennock (1985) emphasizes that the lack of production of algae in the upper Delaware, despite nonlimiting nutrient concentrations, is due to light limitations, and thus the phytoplankton does not reach nuisance levels. Grazing is an important factor in controlling phytoplankton levels in the lower estuary.

The greatest amount of algal chlorophyll a is produced by the spring *Skeletonema costatum* blooms, which are 50 to 60 μg of chlorophyll per liter. Transient blooms of 15 to 20 μg of *Skeletonema costatum* per liter occur in the fall (Pennock, 1985).

Microbial trophodynamics are important in controlling the movement of carbon through the food web in the Delaware estuary (Coffin and Sharp, 1987). The study extended from Philadelphia to the mouth of the estuary. Temperature was a major factor that regulated bacteria and microflagellates. With the exception of cold periods, bacteria and microflagellates appeared to respond to phytoplankton production. In the spring and summer in the lower estuary, where phytoplankton production was highest, bacteria production and micro-flagellate grazing were also highest.

On an average, 23% of the phytoplankton carbon production in this area of the estuary was grazed on by bacteria. Bacterivores grazed 85% of the bacterial production. Estimates of the carbon flow from phytoplankton to bacteria and, subsequently, to microflagellates suggest that the bacteria and microflagellates do not return lost phytoplankton production to the main phytoplankton–zooplankton food chain in the Delaware estuary, but the primary effect is the mineralization of organic compounds to their inorganic constituents.

Studies of the productivity of the open water of the Chesapeake indicate that the upper bay is more productive than the lower bay. In the vicinity of the Rhode River, carbon was fixed at rates varying between 2 and 200 mg C m^{-3} h^{-1} up-bay, and between 2 and 40 mg C m^{-3} h^{-1} down-bay (incubator studies). The gross annual production in the upper bay was estimated to be 73 g C m^{-2} yr^{-1} (Flemer, 1970). This is roughly similar to the productivity of a shallow estuary near Beaufort, North Carolina. Of the total carbon, 70 to 80% was fixed mainly by dinoflagellates from June to November, whereas nanoplankton and green algae together with some very small dinoflagellates were important during the rest of the year. The most metabolically active species in June were *Gymnodinium dominaus*, *Peridinium* sp., and *Procentrum mariae-lebouriae* (Faust and Corell, 1977).

Marshes. In the Delaware estuary the *Phragmites* net primary productivity (carbon fixation) varied from 989 g C m^{-2} yr^{-1} in Cedar Swamp Marsh to 1099 g C m^{-2} yr^{-1} in Smyrna River Marsh. The *Spartina* plus a small mixture of other species had a productivity of 737 g C m^{-2} yr^{-1} in Cedar Swamp Marsh and 696 g C m^{-2} yr^{-1} in Smyrna River Marsh (ANSP, 1972). In Canary Creek Marsh the productivity of the grasses, *Spartina* sp. and *Distichlis* sp., was 445 g C m^{-2} yr^{-1} (Flemer et al., 1978).

In the Delaware, the productivity of the Marsh diatoms on the mud flats in the lower estuary was 160 g C m^{-2} yr^{-1} (ash-free dry weight) (Gallagher and Daiber, 1974). In the drainage creeks of the less saline Oldmans Creek Marsh the productivity of the algae varied between 0.158 g C m^{-3} h^{-1} (7/4/73) and 0.547 g C m^{-3} h^{-1} (6/14–15/73). This study in the vicinity of Oldmans Creek showed that net productivity varied greatly with the season of the year and the amount of sun (ANSP, 1974).

Hamilton Marsh in the Delaware estuary had an estimated net aboveground production of 1286.5 g m^{-2} yr^{-1} (Whigham et al., 1978). In general, the freshwater tidal wetlands in the middle Atlantic states have a productivity varying from 1000 g C m^{-2} yr^{-1} to 3500 g C m^{-2} yr^{-1} and some may produce more than 4000 g C m^{-2} yr^{-1} (Whigham et al., 1978).

In the Chesapeake, the best estimates of the productivity of marsh phanerogams are based on grams of biomass per square mile per year. When one considers community, 11.8% by the *Typha–Pontedera–Peltandra* community, and 4.6% largest productivity (2500 g m^{-2} yr^{-1}), followed by 2160 g m^{-2} yr^{-1} for a *Spartina patens* community. The *Scirpus olneyi* community produced 894 g m^{-2} yr^{-1} and the *Typha–Scirpus* community 394 g m^{-2} yr^{-1}. Thirty-seven percent of the study area was occupied by *Spartina patens*, 37.3% by the *Scirpus olney* community, 11.8% by the *Typha–Pontedera–Peltandra* community, and 4.6% by the *Typha–Scripus* community (Flemer et al., 1978).

Productivity studies of phytoplankton in the Patuxent River near Benedict, Maryland 1968–1969 indicate that gross productivity varied from 0.65 g C m^{-2}

day^{-1} to 1.9 g C m^{-2} day^{-1}. The variation is, in part, caused by the various methods used in estimating the amount of carbon fixed (Corey, 1974). The higher estimates are similar to those found in the lower part of Chesapeake Bay.

In the lower bay the productivity near the mouth of the Patuxent River averaged 22 mg C m^{-3} h^{-1}. This is similar to the productivity in Long Island Sound (Flemer, 1970). Near Sandy Point the gross daytime primary productivity was estimated to range between 1.1 and 3.75 g C m^{-2} day^{-1} (Flemer et al., 1978). Productivity studies in the Patuxent near Benedict indicate that gross productivity of plankton varied from 0.65 to 1.6 g C m^{-2} day^{-1} in 1962–1964 and 0.53 to 1.9 g C m^{-2} day^{-1} in 1968–1969. The variation is in part caused by the different methods used in estimating the amount of carbon fixed (Corey, 1974). These estimates are higher than those found in the York River, a tributary of the lower part of Chesapeake Bay (Patton and Chabot, 1966).

Integrated gross productivity in the York River estuary near the Virginia Institute of Marine Science varied from 1.39 to 25.21 g cal cm^{-2} day^{-1} in the period from June 24, 1963 to August 14, 1963. The highest productivity was August 13–14 and the lowest July 28–30. The integrated gross productivity efficiencies were 4.0% and 0.22%, respectively. The temperature, salinity, and intregrated light intensities were quite similar. Patton and Chabot (1966) did not find a correlation between these data and types of species or population sizes.

McCarthy et al. (1974) made a study of the contribution of the nanoplankton to the productivity of the Chesapeake Bay. Their transect extended from the head to the mouth of the bay. In a 2-year study they found that nanoplankton (which could pass through a 35–μm screen) produced a median value of 89.6% of the total phytoplankton productivity. Most of the chlorophyll and carbon were produced by organisms smaller than 10 μm (McCarthy et al., 1974). After heavy rain, which reduced salinity and raised the nutrient content of the water (Table 5.1), euglenoids and blue-green algae multiplied rapidly and the dino-flagellate, *Oxytoxum* sp., become dominant. These became the food of nauplii and rotifers, which increased rapidly (Loftus et al., 1972). This bloom of *Oxtoxum* sp. is different from the bloom that occurs in the fall and consists of a community of other species. The data suggest that near the mouths of the Susquehanna and Potomac rivers the productivity of the net plankton increases relative to the nanoplankton.

McHugh (1967) states that if the primary productivity of Chesapeake Bay equals that of Long Island Sound, an estimate of carbon fixation based on Riley's (1952) Long Island Sound data would be about 1800 lb of carbon per acre per year (approximately 2046 kg hectare^{-1}). If we assume that carbon is 5% of the wet weight of phytoplankton, the biomass of the phytoplankton would be about 40,000 kg h^{-1} yr^{-1}.

Nutrient Cycling: Chemical

The photosynthetic/respiration ratios in these middle Atlantic estuaries vary greatly depending on the season of the year, the amount of algae and bacteria, and the nutrients available for algal and bacterial growth. Usually, phosphorus

TABLE 5.1. Concentrations[a] of Phytoplankton and Zooplankton at Various Locations in Chesapeake Bay, August 10, 1971

	Mouth of Rhode River	Bay 2	Bay 73	Bloom East of Bay 73	Bloom at Thomas Point at Depth: 0.05 m	0.5 m	1 m	2 m	3 m	Bay 77	Severn River Buoy 10	Bloom South of Bay 78	Bay 78	Bay Bridge
Phytoplankton														
Ultraflagellates	29	(29)	32	43	43	40	29	43	51	61	58	29	54	43
Dinoflagellates														
Gonyaulax sp.	—	0.2	0.2	3.6	0.03	0.04	0.04	0.04	0.04	0.4	0.06	0.04	—	0.04
Gymnodinium nelsonii	0.4	0.4	0.8	—	0.2	0.02	0.03	0.01	—	0.1	—	1.1	—	—
Gymnodinium splendens	—	—	0.01	—	0.02	0.02	0.03	—	0.01	—	—	—	—	—
Oxytoxum sp.	—	—	12.4	94	47	32	47	40	17	0.19	4.8	53	—	—
Polykrikos hardmanii	0.4	0.4	0.02	0.2	0.04	0.07	0.12	0.03	—	1.1	0.01	1	0.6	0.6
Prorocentrum triangulatum	—	2.3	—	0.02	—	—	0.03	—	—	1.1	0.02	0.4	0.8	0.6
Blue–green algae	—	0.02	0.001	0.001	—	—	—	—	0.002	—	0.4	0.01	0.006	0.6
Euglena spp. 10–15 μm long 2–3 μm diam.	0.76	0.4	1.1	1.1	2.3	1.1	1.5	1.1	1.5	0.4	1.1	0.8	0.4	0.6
Diatoms														
Coscinosira sp.	—	—	—	—	—	—	—	0.02	—	—	—	—	—	—
Cylindrotheca closterium	1.9	0.2	0.02	—	0.4	0.01	—	0.04	—	—	0.02	0.2	—	—
Pleurosigma sp.	—	—	—	—	0.01	—	—	—	—	—	—	—	—	—
Skeletonema costatum	7.2	0.02	0.6	0.02	—	0.4	0.02	0.01	0.08	0.03	0.04	0.04	—	0.02
Thalassiothrix frauenfeldii	—	0.2	0.04	0.04	0.02	—	—	—	—	—	0.02	—	—	—
Total chlorophyll a (μg L^{-1})	41.5	61	72	218	109	165	147	111	91	30	68	390	38	60
Zooplankton														
Ciliates	400/L	400/L	—	0.01	—	—	—	—	—	—	—	0.02	—	—
Nauplii	400/L	400/L	—	—	200/L	200/L	200/L	600/L	200/L	200/L	800/L	200/L	400/L	400/L
Rotifers	0.06	0.01	0.01	600/L	0.01	200/L	—	—	—	400/L	—	0.002	—	200/L
Tintinnids	0.02	—	—	0.01	—	—	—	—	—	—	—	—	0.01	—

Source: Loftus et al. (1972).

[a]Concentrations are in millions per liter unless specified as number per liter.

298

becomes the limiting element in the estuary, but under some late summer conditions nitrogen has been found to be limiting. However, some studies in the Delaware Bay indicate that the amount of nitrogen in salt marshes of the lower bay area is much larger than had previously been supposed. It is present in various forms and indicates hypercutrophication (Reimold, 1974).

The general chemical characteristics of the various study areas in the Delaware and Chesapeake estuaries are set forth in Tables 5.2 and 5.3. These analyses were made at different times and should be read with this in mind.

It would appear that other nonnutrient stresses related to poor drainage and low redox potential limit the ability of interim plants to assimilate ammonia nitrogen. As the result, ammonia accumulates in the substrates, although along the creek banks, nitrogen is usually low, due to the rapidly growing plants. Aurand and Daiber (1973) found a net import of inorganic nitrogen into Delaware salt marsh over a year, whereas Stevenson et al. (1977) found a net discharge of both nitrogen and phosphorus from the Chesapeake Bay salt marsh.

Phosphorus. Phosphorus concentration in the water seems to increase with the decrease in salinity, indicating the importance of runoff from the watershed in contributing to phosphorus content. There is a definite correlation between the tidal stage and phosphorus concentration in the water column. Studies of Hamilton Marsh in New Jersey indicated that $P-PO_4$ was taken up by the

TABLE 5.2. *Chemical Analyses of Surface Samples*[a]

	Mesohaline Patuxent River (ANSP, 1970)	Fresh Water Patuxent River (ANSP, 1970)	Polyhaline York River (ANSP, 1970)
Alkalinity, M.O. as $CaCO_3$	24–42	57–68	84.3–85.94
CO_2	Not measured	Not measured	Not measured
Cl	25–880	4890–6390	11,895–12,140
D.O.	4.6–7.7	7.4–8.5	7.80–8.99
Total hardness as $CaCO_3$	32–321	1664–2008	692–743
Ca	8.2–30	128–136	277–295
Mg	2.8–60	278–406	848–900
Fe	0.78–3.1	0.22–0.49	< 0.002
NH_3-N	0.07–0.13	0.18–0.223	< 0.004
NO_2-N	0.002–0.035	0.002–0.042	0.003–0.006
TKN	0.41–0.8	0.25–0.73	Not measured
PO_4-P	0.052–0.221	0.098–0.342	0.022–0.076
SiO_2	0.91–9.77	4.3–7.21	0.828–2.138
SO_4	14.6–134	569–1046	1861.4–2016.9
Turbidity	139–414	45–56	11.7–16.2
Temperature (°C)	25.5–29.0	26.5–29.0	17.8–19.0
pH	6.8–7.4	7.2–8.1	8.0–8.2

[a]All results are in ppm, except pH and temperature. For the York River, ranges of the means of high and low tides are shown.

TABLE 5.3. *Chemical Analyses of Surface Samples[a]*

	Mesohaline		
	Potomac River (ANSP, 1971)	Chesapeake Bay (ANSP, 1969)	Patuxent River (ANSP, 1970)
Alkalinity, M.O. as $CaCO_3$	40–54	64–71	24–42
CO_2	Not measured	Not measured	Not measured
Cl	3200–4300	1063–1141	25–880
D.O.	4.4–9.0	7.9–10.1	4.6–7.7
Total hardness as $CaCO_3$	1020–1460	2484–2656	32–321
Ca	72–108	170–182	8.2–30
Mg	202–305	501–536	2.8–60
Fe	0.10–0.20	0.47–0.95	0.78–3.1
NH_3–N	0.03–0.12	0.048–0.068	0.07–0.13
NO_2–N	0.007–0.016	0.010–0.055	0.002–0.035
TKN	0.25–0.75	0.048–0.068	0.41–0.8
PO_4–P	0.20–0.38	0.028–0.140	0.052–0.221
SiO_2	2.88–3.30	2.34–3.13	0.91–9.77
SO_4	420–630	1063–1141	14.6–134
Turbidity	25–50	43–124	139–414
Temperature (°C)	24.0–26.5	26.7–29.0	25.5–29.0
pH	7.6–8.4	7.2–7.5	6.8–7.4

[a]All results in ppm, except pH and temperature.

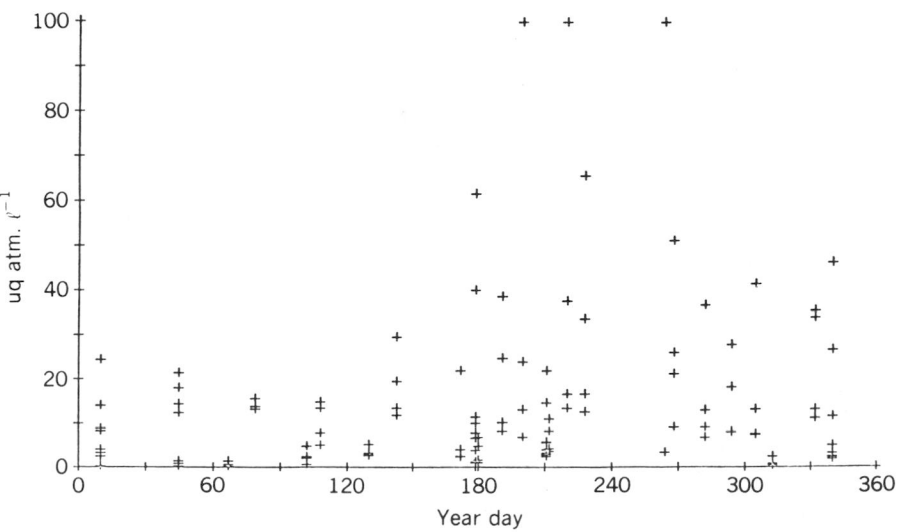

FIGURE 5.2. Inorganic phosphorous concentrations versus day of year in a natural Delaware marsh. Abscissa day of year; ordinate, inorganic dissolved phosphorus concentration, µg at L^{-1}. (From Reimold, 1974.)

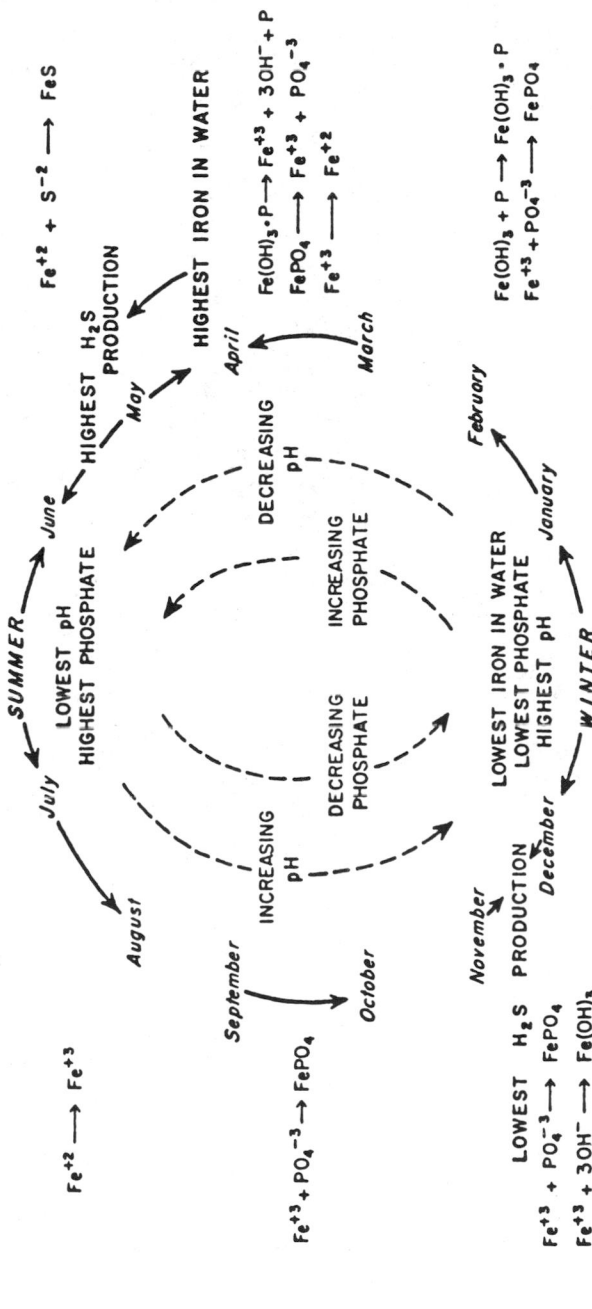

FIGURE 5.3. Chemical processes in Canary Creek Marsh (Delaware) that cause the release of inorganic phosphates. (From Gooch, 1974a.)

301

highwater tidal marsh, but also was quickly exported, as 95% of the phosphorus incorporated in the vegetation was lost within a month after the vegetation died following a frost (Simpson et al., 1978). Both nitrogen and phosphorus were retained during fall and winter in the marsh ponds if algal growth developed. Each ebb tide tended to increase the phosphorus in the bay proper, and there was a net transport from the marsh to the open water.

As seen in Figure 5.2, there are seasonal fluctuations in the abundance of inorganic phosphorus from the sediments in Canary Creek Marsh. The chemical processes that bring about the release of inorganic phosphate are set forth in Figure 5.3. The occurrence of soluble iron and its binding of sulfide ions in the sediments is the primary cause of the release of inorganic phosphorus. This commonly occurs when the redox potential is very low and often develops under anaerobic conditions. Such conditions are most common during warm weather months (Reimold, 1974).

Carbon in the organic form is closely related to the phosphorus cycle because in the presence of abundant organic carbon, anaerobic conditions often develop. Thus the cycling of the release of phosphorus from the sediments and the deposition of phosphorus in the sediments is controlled largely by the amount of anaerobic activity and the presence of oxygen, which precipitates phosphorus within the estuary muds (Gooch, 1974a).

The cyling of phosphorus in Chesapeake marshes is probably very similar to that in the Delaware marshes (Figure 5.3). The studies that have been done indicate relatively high concentrations of phosphates in Chesapeake Bay in the summer (Taft and Taylor, 1976).

Nitrogen

Nitrogen Fixation.   Nitrogen fixation in the middle Atlantic state estuaries has been studied in the Rhode River estuary (Chesapeake) (Marsho et al., 1975). Fixation is mainly by anaerobic heterotrophic bacteria with smaller contributions by blue-green algae. The fixation is greater, but more variable, in the intertidal marsh sediments than in the subtidal sediments. In the intertidal sediments the fixation rate, as measured by the reduction of acetylene, was greatest in the fall of the year, and varied between 12.1 and 37.4 µg of fixed nitrogen per gram dry weight of sediments per hour. In the subtidal sediments, the fixation rate was more uniform and lower. The average monthly rate was 2.2 to 6.8 g dry weight per hour in the sediments. It would appear that nitrogen fixation makes only a minor contribution to the nitrogen budget in the estuary (Marsho et al., 1975).

Nitrification.   Studies of Canary Creek Marsh (Delaware) indicate that nitrification takes place in the sediments at differing rates depending on the time of year, the sediment type, and the initial substrates. Favorable substrates in early spring and early autumn seem to be molecular nitrogen plus 0.5 M NH_4Cl. When 0.5 M concentrations of $NaNO_2$ formed the substrate, maximum nitrification occurred in late winter and early spring. Nitrification was inhibited with increasing amounts of NH_4^+. It is apparent that sufficient nitrification takes place to supply the nitrate needs of the marsh flora. The most rapid nitrification occurs in the autumn and spring months, and an accumulation of nitrate occurs during the winter months because utilization by organisms is so much less. Little accumulation takes place in the warmer months, however due to rapid growth of the marsh flora. It appears that very little nitrate is released from the marsh to the Delaware Bay, but rather is used within the marsh. The nitrogen form released to the bay is organic nitrogen exported as detritus. It is the breakdown of this detritus into nitrates that raises the nitrate content of the estuary waters, and nitrates are returned to the marshes with the flooding tides (Gooch, 1974b). Denitrification has also been shown to be an important process in estuaries (Seitzinger, 1988).

A study of Hamilton Marsh and Crosswicks Creek in New Jersey adjacent to the Delaware River indicated that the marsh took up a large amount of nitrogen in the summer, largely as a result of plant growth. A similar phenomenon was noted in Tinicum Marsh as nitrogen was lost from the water as it flooded through the marsh grasses (Grant and Patrick, 1970). In Hamilton Marsh within a month after the dieback in vegetation following a frost, 80% of the nitrogen in the dead vegetation was lost. Stevenson et al. (1977) found a net export of inorganic nitrogen from a low-salinity Chesapeake Bay marsh. In ponds where algal bloom developed following dieback of the vegetation, the nitrogen was retained within the algal growth during the fall and winter.

Ammonia was found to be more important than nitrates to phytoplankton. In the Delaware Bay saturated nitrogen uptake rates increased directly with water temperature and reached a maximum of $380 \, \text{nmol} \, \text{N} \, \text{L}^{-1} \, \text{h}^{-1}$ during the summer. Temperature dependence was related primarily to changes in the rate of maximum chlorophyll-specific uptake, which varied exponentially between 2 and 70 nmol of nitrogen per microgram of chlorophyll per hour over the temperature range 2 to 28 °C. Despite these high uptake rates, the balance growth carbon/nitrogen ratio was 7:1 or, in other words, despite these high uptake rates, the carbon/nitrogen ratio remains 7:1. This could be maintained over the daylight cycle only by highly efficient nitrogen uptake at low light intensities and dark uptake below the photic zone and at night. Dark uptake at night equaled 25%, the maximum uptake.

Ammonia fulfilled 82% of the annual phytoplankton nitrogen demand in the estuary despite the dominance of nitrates in the ambient dissolved inorganic nitrogen pool. The predominance of ammonia uptake occurred because of the general suppression of NO_3 assimilation at ammonia concentrations in excess of 2 μmol. This suppression, however, was not as universal as has been reported for other systems. Extremely high nitrate concentrations in the estuary may contribute to this pattern. The marsh creeks were an important source of nitrogen only during periods of high phytoplankton production in the summer and when ammonia concentrations were low at the end of the spring bloom (Pennock, 1987).

Nitrite and Ammonia Formation. Nitrite formation occurs in sediments. Its accumulation results from inhibition of the oxidation of nitrogen by bacteria (*Nitrosomonas*). This occurs when ammonia (NH_4^+) is bound to sediments, which makes the soil water more alkaline. Ammonia is formed from metabolic activity of bacteria that use organic nitrogen compounds as a nutrient source. It is often sorbed onto particulate matter.

Particulate Nitrogen.   Studies of the particulate nitrogen in the Chesapeake Bay show that the concentration forms a gradient along a longitudinal axis with maximum values found in the more northerly part of the bay. In this area the mean concentration of nitrogen in the water column ranges from 0.1 to 0.3 mg N L^{-1} in the summer, with greater values occurring in the fall and winter. In areas south of Gibson Island, the concentrations of particulate nitrogen rarely exceed 0.1 mg N L^{-1}. The Susquehanna's contribution of particulate nitrogen amounts to about 4.7×10^3 metric tons. The carbon/nitrogen atomic ratios in the water column were high in the upper study area much of the year, with values often ranging between 20 and 30. During the winter and spring the values were greater than 30. Below Tracey's Landing the C/N ratios usually averaged less than 20 in the water column. In July, August, and September the ratios were consistently less than 20 throughout the study area (Flemer and Biggs, 1971). It appears that upland drainage and production were the major sources of particulate nitrogen in the upper estuary and that processes within the estuary were the major source in the lower estuary.

Releases of N$_2$O from Sediment.   In the Potomac River in areas under the influence of releases of sewage, N$_2$O is formed rapidly and released to the atmosphere. The formation of N$_2$O occurs in shallow-water embayments, and its release to the atmosphere occurs in response to the turbulence of tidal currents. The rate of release of N$_2$O to the atmosphere takes place at a rate of about 10^3 kg day^{-1}, which is produced at a rate of 0.4 µg L^{-1} h^{-1}. About 1 to 5% of the total N from the Blue Plains sewage plant is released in this way to the atmosphere (McElory et al., 1978).

Sulfur.   The cycling of sulfur, as indicated from studies in Canary Creek Marsh in the Delaware, is carried out primarily by two genera of bacteria, *Desulfotomaculum* and *Desulfovibrio*. *Desulfotomaculum* is found in environments that may have variable salinity and sediment moisture, whereas *Desulfovibrio* is found where the salinity is more constant. Hydrogen sulfide is produced by anaerobic activity from the utilization of oxygen from SO$_4$. In the presence of soluble iron, the sulfide ion forms iron sulfide, which is a relatively insoluble salt, and thus the iron and sulfur are taken out of solution. Conditions that promote the oxidation of sulfides also promote the oxidation of ferrous iron. The high water content of the sediment, together with the excess amount of organic carbon in the Canary Creek Marsh, were the primary factors that allowed the presence of sulfide-producing bacteria (Gooch, 1947a).

Food Webs

Plants (particularly algae), detritus, and bacteria form the bases of the food web.

Detrital Food.   The importance of detritus as a nutrient source depends not only on the type of detritus, but also on the bacteria and other organisms associated with it. In the Rhode River area, the smallest sizes of detritus (2 to

5 µm in diameter) average about 64.7% of the total number of detrital particles. In general, phytoplankton average about 23.4% of the total number of water column particles throughout the year, with a summer high of 35.4%, 20.2% in fall, 18.7% in winter, 21.7% in spring. Of the phytoplankton population, 55.6% are 2 to 5 µm in size, 24.6% from 5 to 10 µm, 14.3% from 10 to 20 µm and only 5.5% are about 20.8 µm or more.

Typically, more bacteria are found on sedimented detritus particles (5 to 40 µm in diameter) than on particles in the water column. Bacterial colonies on sedimented detritus are less exposed to the effects of current and friction. There seem to be physiological differences between sedimented and water column detrital bacteria. Bacteria on the sedimented detritus seem to produce H_2S from cystine, to have a greater tolerance for low pH, and to prefer higher temperatures (Hargrave, 1972). Hood et al. (1975) found that the salt marsh sediment bacteria utilize a greater variety of carbon sources and have a shorter generation time than do those in the water column.

Hargrave (1972) found that only 1.54 to 1.83% of the surfaces of suspended detritus particles were covered with bacteria, and that the bacterial populations on similar-sized particles varied greatly. One reason for this variation in population may be that close growth is discouraged by a regulating substance secreted by some colonies (Hargrave, 1972).

In general, the biomass of bacteria on detritus in short *Spartina* areas was larger (as measured by ATP production) than the biomass of bacteria on detritus from tall *Spartina*, although the oxygen consumed was the same.

Bacteria are an excellent food source for many organisms that live in the water column. For example, it is known that many protozoa, particularly ciliates, feed on bacteria in the water column. The protozoa are, in turn, excellent food for other organisms. Berk et al. (1977) found that the copepod, *Eurytemora affinis*, which was 15 to 20 µm long, fed and survived longer on the protozoan, *Uronema nigrans*, which was 8.8 to 17.3 µm in diameter. Richman et al. (1977) found that this copepod usually lived on detrius that supported bacteria and protozoa. *Pseudocalanus menutur* ingests nonliving detritus as well as bacteria and protozoa. The copepod, *Acartia tonsa*, eats detritus derived from *Fucus*, but at a lower rate than it eats living algae.

Analysis of field samples shows that ciliates compose about 20% of the total plankton biomass. These studies, as well as the field observations, indicate that the ciliates are a very important food of copepods. Studies by Richman et al. (1977) show that copepods feed on an entire size spectrum of particles, but their filtering rate sometimes shows greater selectivity for biomass peaks than for the particles in lower concentrations. This manner of feeding has considerable effect on the diversity of the phytoplankton population. Grazing pressure on those species with higher biomass concentrations enables small phytoplankton populations to increase, thus increasing population diversity.

Algal Food. In general, detritus is the main component of the particles in the water column. However, phytoplankton is also a component of water column particles and an important food source for copepods. The species that were dominant throughout the year in the Rhode River area were the nano-planktons, *Calcycomonas ovalis*, *Ochromonas nannos*, and *Mychomaster ruminants*. *Chroomonas diplococca* and an undetermined species of *Amphidinium* were dominant throughout the summer months. *Thalassiosira pseudomana*, on the other hand, was prominent in the plankton except during the fall, and *Microcytis*, a blue-green alga, was prominent during summer and fall but occurred at no other time. *Chrysochromulina minor* was abundant only in winter and spring. Usually, the diatom, *Skeletonema costatum*, was present and was the dominant species during the spring and summer. *Paramimonas grossi* occurred in large numbers in the spring and was replaced by *P. microm* during the summer. Dinoflagellates were dominant during the winter (*Amphidinium crassum*) and were very common in the spring (*Gynodinium simplex* and *Procentrum minimus*). In the summer the dinoflagellate bloom consisted mainly of a species of the genus *Ochromonas*. They were also fairly common at other times indicating that they were probably one of the most important food sources in the water column.

Algae: Herbivores.   The copepods, which compose a major part of the zooplankton, feed mainly on the phytoplankton. Few species are only berbivores; many feed on algae and detritus.

Omnivores and Carnivores.   It is known that crustacea are a primary food source for many invertebrates and fish, although predator–prey relationships have not been particularly well studied in the Chesapeake or the Delaware. For example, the mysid shrimp, *Neomysis americana*, and the copepods, *Acartia tonsa*, *A. clausii*, *Centropages hamatus*, *Labidocera aestiva*, and *Pseudodiaptomus*, are the main food of the ctenophore, *Mnemiopsis leidyi*. In general, ctenophores prefer the smaller zooplankton and very small fish. In turn, the ctenophore, *Mnemiopsis*, is prey for the sea nettle, *Chrysaora quinquecirrha*.

Many species of fish also feed on the phytoplankton and zooplankton. The biomass of the zooplankton has been conservatively estimated by McHugh (1967) to be greater than 8,749 kg h^{-1} yr^{-1}, which was the estimate Riley (1952) gave for Long Island Sound. One of the chief predators in the Chesapeake is the menhaden, which filters enormous quantities of water. McHugh (1967) states that if all the adult menhaden in the Chesapeake Bay area were within the bay for 1 year, they could filter all the water in the Virginia portion of the bay and its estuaries twice in 24 hours, but this is probably on overestimate. Studies have shown that there is an inverse correlation between the populations of blue crab and menhaden populations which is probably caused by menhaden preying upon the larvae of blue crabs.

There are many predator–prey foods webs in the benthos. In the Rhode River area, the main predator of the barnacle, *Balanus improvisus*, is the flatworm, *Stylochus ellipticus*. Crustacea may also act as predators and one of the most common is the blue crab (*Callinectes sapidus*), which preys upon spat of the oyster. High mortality (i.e., 79 to 99%) of the spat was observed within a month after the oysters reached 3 to 40 mm in diameter, the size usually placed on the beds when they are seeded. The umbo and pediveliger larvae of the Virginia oyster are often preyed on by the sea anemone, *Diadumene leucolena*, and the barnacle, *Balanus improvisus*. It has been observed that the feeding on these

TABLE 5.4. *Rank Analysis of Dominant Species in the Natural Community from Natural Sediments, 1974*

Species[a]	Rank	Score[b]	Average Density $(N\,m^{-2})$	Variability of Density (Variance of Monthly Means About the Yearly Mean)
Peloscolex gabriellae (0)	1	96	3971	7.03
Spiochaetopterus oculatus (P)	2	80.5	890	0.36
Heteromastus filiformis (P)	3	79	1424	1.00
Streblospio benedicti (P)	4	63	1162	10.06
Phoronis psammophila (Ph)	5	50.8	436	0.68
Glycinde solitaria (P)	6	45.3	349	0.89
Polydora ligni (P)	7	27	450	11.90
Paraprionospio pinnata (P)	8	22.3	167	0.46
Scolelepis squamata (P)	9	15.5	153	0.51
Scoloplos robustus (P)	10	15.3	107	0.54
Eteone heteropoda (P)	11	13	105	1.34
Nereis succinea (P)	12	9.5	110	0.37
Acteon punctostriatus (G)	13	9	89	0.64

Source: From "The importance of predation by crabs and fishes on benthic infauna in Chesapeake Bay" by R. W. Virnstein, *Ecology*, 1977, *58*(6), 1199–1217. Copyright © 1977 by the Ecological Society of America. Reprinted by permission.

[a]O, oligochaete; P, polychaete; Ph, phoronid; G, gastropod.

[b]Maximum score is 100.

larvae by the sea anemone increases with the density of the larvae (Steinberg and Kennedy, 1979). In addition to the blue crab, sea anemone, and barnacles feeding on oyster larvae, it has been found that the mud crab preys on oyster spat and is very abundant in certain areas of the Chesapeake.

In the lower York River, Virnstein (1977) found that blue crab, *Callinectes sapidus*, and the bottom-feeding fish, spot (*Leistomus xanthurus*), are important predators of sediment infauna. Predation rather than food or space is the primary limiting factor of infauna populations. Species able to resist predation are those that can withdraw into the substrate or live deep in the sediment. Exclusion of predators brings about a large increase in density and diversity of macrobenthic invertebrates. Table 5.4 gives a list of the more important benthic organisms found and their relative abundance.

EXAMPLES OF ESTUARINE COMMUNITIES

The undisturbed marshlands surrounding the freshwater reach in the Delaware are dominated by *Nuphar advena* and *Peltandra virginica* in the wetter portion and by *Zizania aquatica* and *Typha latifolia* in wet but slightly drier areas. In disturbed areas, *Phragmites communis* is common. In fresh-to-brackish water marshes and extending into more saline areas, *Spartina alterniflora* is dominant, often intermixed with *Baccharis halimifolia* and *Iva frutescens*. In drier areas one finds *Spartina patens* and *Distichlis spicata*.

Structure of Communities in the Delaware Estuary
Freshwater: Yardley to Philadelphia

Open Water. The freshwater reach studied was the area between Yardley and the Burlington–Bristol Bridge (Figure 5.4). The fauna and flora reflect the influence of many municipalities and some industry. A fairly large number of species forming associations in this area listed in Tables 5.5, 5.6, 5.7 and 5.8. The upper end of this reach, is located above the dam of Trenton. Although the dam probably does not affect benthic and planktonic forms, it probably does affect the movement of fish. The area between Trenton and the Burlington–Bristol Bridge, however, represents a free-flowing part of the estuary.

The most common alga at Yardley was *Hydrodictyon reticulatum*, which is known to be common in eutrophic waters. Also common on rocks are *Cladophora* sp. and *Oedogonium* sp. The most common diatoms were species belonging to the genus *Nitzschia*, particularly *N. palea*. The finding of the typically saltwater diatoms, *Coscinodis decipiens*, *C. denarius*, and *Thalassionema nitzschioides*, was very unusual and probably indicates contamination. Since this part of the estuary is used in navigation, the saltwater diatoms may have been brought in on ship hulls.

The protozoa were fairly diverse in the freshwater reach. The most common were the bacteria–feeding ciliates, *Vorticella* sp. and *Stichotricha* sp. Also found were the phytoflagellates, *Gonium sociale*, *Platydorina* sp., and *Pandorina*, which were very abundant in one collection. The protozoan community showed a variety of flagellates, amoeba, and ciliates, and seems to be fairly well balanced, although it clearly indicates eutrophically enriched conditions (ANSP, 1959).

In the Burlington–Bristol Bridge area, *Pandorina* sp., *Eudorina* sp., and other colonial flagellates, together with various species of *Euglena*, *Chlamydomonas* sp., and *Carteria* sp., were very common. Particularly abundant was *Vahlkamfia limax* and the amoeba, *Amoeba dubia*. Hypotrich ciliates were very numerous. These species indicate, as at Yardley, an area that is eutrophic and received considerable nutrient loading, as one would expect from the uses of the Delaware in this region (ANSP, 1959).

At Yardley, above the dam, most of the insect orders and genera that one would expect to be representative were present (Table 5.6). However, the population sizes of many of the groups, particularly Ephemeroptera, Tricoptera, and Diptera, were small. The predominant mayfly species belong to the family Baetidae. At the Burlington–Bristol Bridge, there seemed to be more pollution and the insect fauna was not as well developed. The *Odonata* and *Diptera tenipedids* (family Chironomidae) were the only insects found.

In the Yardley area, the unionid, *Lampsilis cariosa*, was fairly common, whereas at the Burlington–Bristol station it was absent. As seen in Table 5.7, invertebrates other than insects are diversified in this area.

The fish fauna found in this reach are listed in Table 5.8. The fish in the Yardley area differed from those in the Burlington–Bristol area. It is difficult to sort out how much of this was due to the effects of pollution and how much to the presence of the dam at Trenton. At Yardley, by far the most numerous

FIGURE 5.4. Map of Delaware Bay and some of its tributaries. (Adapted from Patrick, 1988.)

TABLE 5.5. *Algae and Diatoms Recorded in the Yardley to Burlington–Bristol Bridge Stretch of the Delaware River Estuary, 1957–1959*

Green and Blue–green Algae

DIVISION CHLOROPHYTA
Class Vlothricophyceae
Order Vlotrichales
Family Microsporaceae
Microspora sp.
Order Chaetophorales
Family Chaetophoraceae
Stigeoclonium stagnatile
Order Siphonocladales
Family Cladophoraceae
Rhizoclonium hieroglyphicum
Rhizoclonium sp.
Cladophora
Class Zygophyceae
Order Zygenmatales
Family Desmidiaceae
Closterium monilferum
Cosmarium margaritatum fo. minor
Cosmarium tarpinii var. *podolicum*
Cosmarium punctulatum var. *subpunctutatum*
Class Euchlorophyceae
Family Hydroidictyaceae
Hydrodictyon reticulatum
Pediastrum duplex var. *clathratum*

Pediastrum tetras
Family Oocystaceae
Ankistrodesmus falcatus
Family Scenedesmaceae
Scenedesmus brasiliensis
Scenedesmus acutiformis
Scenedesmus sp.
DIVISION CYANOPHYTA
Class Cyanophyceae
Subclass Hormogonophycidae
Order Nostocales
Family Oscillatoriaceae
Oscillatoria chalybea
Oscillatoria okenii
Oscillatoria proboscidea
Oscillatoria splendida
Phormidium uncinatum
Lyngbya taylorii
Microcoleus rupicola
Microcoleus vaginatus
DIVISION CHROMOPHYTA
Class Xanthophyceae
Order Vaucheriales
Family Vaucheriaceae
Vaucheria sp.

Algae—Diatoms

DIVISION BACILLARIOPHYTA
Class Bacillariophyceae
Order Eupodiscales
Family Coscinodiscaceae
Coscinodiscus decipiens
Coscinodiscus denarius
Coscinodiscus radiolatus
Cyclotella kutzingiana
Cyclotella meneghiaiana
Cyclotella meneghiniana var. *rectangularis*
Cyclotella nana
Cyclotella pseudostelligera
Cyclotella striata
Melosira ambigua
Melosira borrerii
Melosira granulata
Melosira nummuloides
Melosira sulcata fo. *radiata*
Melosira varians
Stephanodiscus astera var. *minutula*
Order Fragilariales
Family Fragilariaceae

Asterionella formosa
Asterionella gracillima
Ceratoneis arcus
Cymatosira belgica
Diatoma vulgare
Fragilaria capucina
Fragilaria pinnata
Meridion circulare var. *constricta*
Rhaphoneis amphiceros var. *rhombica*
Synedra acus
Synedra notha
Synedra pulchella
Synedra pulchella var. *abnormis*
Synedra rumpens
Synedra rumpens var. *familiaris*
Synedra rumpens var. scotica
Synedra ulna
Synedra ulna var. *danica*
Synedra ulna var. *oxyrhynchus*
Synedra vaucheriae
Order Eunotiales
Family Eunotiaceae
Eunotia meisterii

TABLE 5.5. (*Continued*)

Order Achnanthales	*Gomphonema clevii*
Family Achnanthaceae	*Gomphonema commutatum*
Achnanthes lanceolata	*Gomphonema parvulum*
Achnanthes microcephala	Order Epithemiales
Achnanthes minutissima	Family Epithemiaceae
Achnanthes pseudolinearis	*Epithemia argus*
Achnanthes taeniata	Order Bacillariales
Cocconeis placentula	Family Nitzschiaceae
Cocconeis placentula var. *euglypta*	*Nitzschia acicularis*
Order Naviculales	*Nitzschia amphibia*
Family Naviculaceae	*Nitzschia capitellata*
Caloneis bacillum	*Nitzschia dissipata*
Frustulia rhomboides	*Nitzschia filiformis*
Frustulia vulgaris	*Nitzschia fonticola*
Frustulia weinholdii	*Nitzschia frustulum*
Navicula canalis	*Nitzschia frustulum* var. *perminuta*
Navicula cryptochephala	*Nitzschia frustulum* var. *perpusilla*
Navicula cryptocephala var. *intermedia*	*Nitzschia frustulum* var. *subsalina*
Navicula cryptocephala var. *veneta*	*Nitzschia frustulum* var. *subsariens*
Navicula gracilis	*Nitzschia gracilis*
Navicula gracilis var. *schizonemoides*	*Nitzschia granulata*
Navicula hungarica var. *lunburgensis*	*Nitzschia intermedia*
Navicula lanceolata	*Nitzschia kutzingiana*
Navicula minima	*Nitzschia linearis*
Navicula mutica	*Nitzschia palea*
Navicula pyomaea	*Nitzschia paleafromis*
Navicula radiosa var. *tenella*	*Nitzschia sigma*
Navicula viridula var. *linearis*	*Nitzschia tropica*
Neidium bisulcatum	*Nitzschia tryblionella*
Stauroneis cruicula	*Nitzschia tryblionella* var. *littorlis*
Family Cymbellaceae	*Nitzschia tryblionella* var. *victoriae*
Cymbella affinis	Order Surirellales
Cymbella delicatula	Family Surirellaceae
Cymbella sinuata	*Surirella augusta*
Cymbella ventricosa	*Surirella brightwellii*
Gomphonema affinis	*Surirella ovata* var. *pinnata*

Source: ANSP (1959).

fish were the golden shiner (*Notemigonus crysoleucas*), the spottailed shiner (*Notropis hudsonius*), the satinfish shiner (*N. analostanus*), the pumpkinseed sunfish (*Lepomis gibbosus*), and the black crappie (*Pomoxis nigromaculatus*). At the Burlington–Bristol Bridge, the most common fish were the banded killifish (*Fundulus diaphanus*), the blueback herring (*Alosa aestivalis*), and the Mississippi silvery minnow (*Hybognathus nuchalis*) (ANSP, 1959).

Marshlands. There are only two marshlands of any size in this area. One is on the New Jersey side of the Delaware at Crosswicks Creek and the other is on the lower Neshaminy and Rancocas Creek. The following species were more common at Crosswicks Creek: the planktonic diatoms, *Melosira varians*,

TABLE 5.6. *Insects Recorded in the Yardley to Burlington–Bristol Bridge Stretch of the Delaware River Estuary, 1957–1959*

PHYLUM ARTHROPODA	Superfamily Hydrophiloidea
Class Insecta	Family Hydrophilidae
Order Odonta	Subfamily Hydrophilinae
Suborder Zygoptera	*Berosus striatus*
Family Coenagrionidae	*Enochrus nebulosus*
Argia apicalis	*Enochrus perplexus*
Argia moesta	*Hydrophilus* sp. (larvae)
Enallagma civile	*Tropisternus glaber*
Enallagma signatum	*Tropisternus lateralis*
Suborder Anisoptera	*Tropisternus mixtus*
Family Gomphidae	Order Trichoptera
Gomphus (Stylurus) plagiatus	Superfamily Hydropsychoidea
Gomphus sp.	Family Polycentropodidae
Order Ephemeroptera	*Neureclipsis* sp.
Family Baetidae	Family Hydropsychidae
Callibaetis nr. *fluctuans*	*Hydropsyche phalerata*
Pseudocloeon sp.	Superfamily Rhyacophiloidea
Family Heptageniidae	Family Hydroptilidae
Subfamily Heptageniidae	*Hydroptilia* sp.
Stenonema (*bipunctatum* group) sp.	Superfamily Limnephiloidea
Stenonema poss. *heterotarsale*	Family Leptoceridae
Order Hemiptera	*Leptocella* sp.
Suborder Heteroptera	*Oecetis* nr. *inconspicua*
Series Gymnocerata	Order Diptera
Family Gerridae	Suborder Nematocera
Metrobates hesperius	Superfamily Culicoidea
Series Cryptocerata	Family Ceratopogonidae
Family Corixidae	*Bezzia* sp.
Trichocorixa calva	Family Chironomidae
Order Megaloptera	Subfamily Tanypodina
Family Corydalidae	Tribe Procladiini
Chauliodes sp.	*Procladius culciformis*
Order Coleoptera	*Procladius* poss. *riparius*
Suborder Adephaga	Subfamily Orthocladiinae
Family Haliplidae	*Cardiocladius obscurus*
Peltodytes edentulus	*Cricotopus bicinctus*
Peltodytes duodecimpunctatus	*Hydrobaenus paradorenus*
Family Dytiscidae	Subfamily Chironominae
Subfamily Laccophilinae	Tribe Tanytarsini
Laccophilus maculosus	*Polypedilum illinoense*
Laccophilus sp. (larvae)	*Tanytarsus* sp.
Suborder Haplogastra	*Tendipes* nr. *decorus*

Source: ANSP (1959).

TABLE 5.7. *Invertebrates (Except Insects) Recorded in the Yardley to Burlington–Bristol Bridge Stretch of the Delaware River, 1957–1959*

PHYLUM PORIFERA
Class Demospongae
Order Haplosclerina
Family Spongillidae
Spongilla lacustris
    PHYLUM COELENTERATA
Class Hydrozoa
Order Hydroida
Family Hydridae
Hydra sp.
    PHYLUM PLATYHELMINTHES
Class Turbellaria
Order Allocoela
Family Plagiostomidae
Hydrolimax grisca
    PHYLUM BRYOZOA
Class Ectoprocta
Order Phylactolaemata
Family Plumatellidae
Plumatella repens
Family Urnatellidae
Urnatella gracilis
Order Gymnolaemata
Family Paludicellidae
Paludicella articulata
    PHYLUM ANNELIDA
Class Oligochaeta
Order Haplotaxida
Suborder Tubificina
Superfamily Tubificoidea
Family Tubificidae
Peloscolex veriegatus
Limnodrilus sp.
Suborder Lumbricina
Superfamily Lumbricoidea
Family Glossoscolecidae
Sparaganophilus eiseni
Class Hirudinea
Subclass Hirudinea
Order Arhynchobdellida
Family Erpobdellidae
Erpobdella punctata
Order Rhynchobdellida

Family Glossiphoniidae
Glossiphonia complanata
Helobdella fusca
Placobdella rugosa
    PHYLUM MOLLUSCA
Class Gastropoda
Subclass Euthyneura
Order Basommatophora
Superfamily Ancylacea
Family Physidae
Physa heterostropha
Family Ancylidae
Ferrissia sp.
Family Planorbidae
Helisoma trivoluis
Gyraulus sp.
Superfamily Lymnaeacea
Family Lymnaeidae
Lymnacea humilis
Class Bivalvia
Subclass Heterodanta
Order Veneroida
Suborder Arcticina
Family Sphaeriidae
Sphaerium sp.
Pisidium sp.
Subclass Palaeoheterodonta
Order Unionoida
Superfamily Unionacea
Family Unionidae
Subfamily Lampsilinae
Lampsilus cariosa
    PHYLUM ARTHROPODA
Class Crustacea
Division Oligobranchiopoda
Subclass Malacostraca
Family Gammaridae
Gammarus fasciatus
Division Eucardia
Order Decapoda
Family Astacidae
Subfamily Cambarinae
Orionectes limosus

Source: ANSP (1959).

TABLE 5.8. *Fish Recorded in the Yardley to Burlington–Bristol Bridge Stretch of the Delaware River, 1957–1959*

PHYLUM CHORDATA
Class Osteichthyes
Order Clupeiformes
Family Clupeidae
Alosa aestivalis
(glut herring)
Alosa pseudoharengus
(alewife)
Alosa sapidissima
(American shad)
Order Cypriniformes
Family Catostomidae
Catostomus commersoni
(white sucker)
Erimyzon oblongus
(creek chubsucker)
Family Cyprindae
Hybognathus nuchalis
(gudgeon)
Notemigonous crysoleucas
(golden shiner)
Notropis analostanus
(satinfish shiner)
Notropis cornutus
(common shiner)
Notropis hudsonius
(spottail shiner)
Rhinichthys cataractae
(longnose dace)
Order Siluriformes
Family Ictalutidae
Ictalurus catus
(white catfish)
Ictalurus nebulosus
(bullhead)

Ictalurus punctatus
(channel catfish)
Order Anguilliformes
Family Anguillidae
Anguilla rostrata
(common eel)
Order Cyprinodontiformes
Family Cyprinodontidae
Fundulus diaphanus
(freshwater killifish)
Fundulus heteroclitus
(common killifish)
Order Perciformes
Family Percichthyidae
Morone americana
(white perch)
Family Centrarchidae
Ambleplites rupestris
(rock bass)
Lepomis auritus
(redbreast sunfish)
Lepomis gibbosus
(sunfish)
Lepomis macrochirus
(bluegill)
Lepomis yg. (mixed, of *gibbosus* and *macrochirus*)
Micropterus salmoides
(black bass)
Pomoxis nigromaculatus
(black crappie)
Family Percidae
Perca flavescens
(yellow perch)
Etheostoma nigrum
(Johnny darter)

Source: ANSP (1959).

M. italica, *Cyclotella meneghiniana*, and *Coscinodiscus excentricus*; and the benthic diatoms, *Achnanthese minutissima*, *Cocconeis placentula* var. *lineata*, *Nitzschia parvula*, *N. obtusa* var. *scalpelliformis*, and *N. palea*. Other common algae were *Scenedesumus quadricauda* and *Coelastrum microsporum*. The most common zooplankton were the daphnia, *Bosmina longirostris*, and the rotifers, *Lecane elasma*, *Keratella cochlearis*, and *Brachionus bidentatus*. Also present were many copepod nauplii. Of the benthic invertebrates in this area, the most common were the oligochaete, *Helobdella stagnalis*; leeches; the isopod, *Gammarus* sp.; and the freshwater mussel, *Corbicula manilensis*. The most common fish were *Hybognathus nuchalis*, *Notropis hudsonius*, *Fundulus heteroclitus*, *F. diaphanus*, and *Morone americana*.

In the Rancocas Marsh, the dominant plankton was *Melosira granulata*. Associated with it, and common, were *M. italica* and *Cyclotella meneghiniana*. Of the benthic diatoms, *Nitzschia parvula* was fairly common. Other common algae were *Actinastrum hantzschii*, *Pediastrum duplex*, and *Scenedesmus quadricauda*. The most common zooplankton were the rotifer, *Keratella cochlearis*, and the cladoceran, *Bosmina longirostris*. Of the benthic invertebrates the most frequent ones were the mussel, *Corbicula manilensis*, and the amphipod, *Gammarus* sp. Some members of the Gastropoda were common, while other snails (and leéches) were less frequently found. The oligochaete worm, *Limnodrilus*, was abundant. The most common fish in this marsh was *Cyprinodon variegatus*, and of frequent occurrence were *Alosa aestivalis*, *Notemigonus crysoleuca*, and *Hybognathus nuchalis*. Of rare occurrence were *Notropis hudsonius*, *Fundulus heteroclitus*, *Morone americana*, *Lepomis gibbosus*, *Notropis analostanus*, *Etheostoma olmstedi*, *Dorosoma cepedianum*, *Fundulus diaphanus*, *Anguilla rostrata*, *Carassius auratus*, *Lepomis macrochirus*, and *Pomoxis nigromaculatus* (ANSP, 1959).

Fresh-to-Brackish Water: Philadelphia to Marcus Hook

Freshwater. The reach of the river designated as the Philadelphia area is that region bounded by Allegheny Avenue to the north of Philadelphia and Marcus Hook to the south. It is the region of the Delaware that is most severely affected by both organic and toxic pollution. Studies conducted from 1957 to 1959 by the Academy of Natural Sciences show that the algae of Allegheny Avenue were dominated by blue-green algae and the green alga, *Stigeoclonium lubricum* (Table 5.9). Diatoms were fairly abundant in patches, the main species

TABLE 5.9. *Algae (Other Than Diatoms) Found in the Philadelphia Area of the Delaware River, 1957–1959*

DIVISION CHLOROPHYTA	*Oscillatoria anguina*
Class Vlothricophyceae	*Oscillatoria chalybea*
Order Chaetophorales	*Oscillatoria formosa*
Family Chaetophoraceae	*Oscillatoria proboscidea*
Stigeoclonium lubricum	*Phormidium favosum*
Stigeoclonium sp.	*Phormidium uncinatum*
Order Siphonocladales	*Lyngbya putealis*
Family Cladophoraceae	*Lyngbya Taylorii*
Rhizoclonium hieroglyphicum	*Symploca muralis*
Rhizoclonium sp.	*Symploca muscorum*
Chaetomorpha aerea var. *linum*	*Microcoleus paludosus*
DIVISION CYANOPHYTA	*Microcoleus rupicola*
Class Cyanophyceae	*Microcoleus vaginatus*
Subclass Hormogonophycidae	DIVISION CHROMOPHYTA
Order Nostocales	Class Xanthophyceae
Family Oscillatoriaceae	Order Vaucheriales
Spirulina major	Family Vaucheriaceae
Spirulina subsalsa	*Vaucheria* sp.
Oscillatoria amoena	

Source: ANSP (1959).

TABLE 5.10. *Diatoms Found in the Philadelphia Area of the Delaware River, 1957–1959*

DIVISION BACILLARIOPHYTA
Class Bacillariophyceae
  Order Eupodiscales
  Family Coscinodiscaceae
Actinoptychus undulatus
Coscinodiscus decipiens
Coscinodiscus denarius
Coscinodiscus lineatus
Coscinodiscus radiatus
Coscinodiscus radiolatus
Cyclotella glomerata
Cyclotella meneghiniana
Cyclotella meneghiniana var.
  rectangularis
Cyclotella operculata
Cyclotella striata
Melosira ambigua
Melosira borrerii
Melosira distans
Melosira granulata
Melosira granulata var. *angustissima*
Melosira italica
Melosira nummuloides
Melosira sulcata
Melosira sulcata fo. *coronata*
Melosira sulcata fo. *radiata*
Melosira varians
Skeletonema costatum
Stephanopyxis minutas
Stephanodiscus astrea var. *minutula*
  Order Fragilariales
  Family Fragilariaceae
Asterionella gracillima
Campylosira cymbelliformis
Ceratoneis arcus
Cymatosira belgica
Fragilaria capucina
Fragilaria pinnata
Fragilaria virescens
Meridion circulare
Rhaphoneis amphiceros var. *rhombica*
Rhaphoneis surirella
Synedra acus
Synedra minuscula
Synedra rumpens
Synedra ulna
Synedra ulna var. *oxyrhynchus*
Synedra vaucheriae
  Order Eunotiales
  Family Eunotiaceae
Eunotiogramma laeve
  Order Achnanthales
  Family Achnanthaceae
Achnanthes lanceolata
Achnanthes linearis
Achnanthes minutissima

Achnanthes taeniata
Cocconeis placentula
Cocconeis placentula var. *euglypta*
Rhoicosphenia curvata
  Order Naviculales
  Family Naviculaceae
Caloneis amphisbaena
Diploneis ovalis
Frustulia vulgaris
Frustulia weinholdii
Navicula atomus
Navicula cryptocephala var. *intermedia*
Navicula gracilis
Navicula hungarica
Navicula hungarica var. *lunburgensis*
Navicula lanceolata
Navicula menisculus
Navicula minima
Navicula mutica
Navicula pygmaea
Navicula radiosa var. *tenella*
Navicula seminuloides
Neidium bisculcatum
  Family Cymbellaceae
Cymbella perpusilla
Cymbella sinuata
Cymbella turgida
Cymbella ventricosa
Gomphonema braziliense
Gomphonema intricatum var. *dichotum*
  Family Gomphonemaceae
Gomphonema olivaceum
Gomphonema parvulum
  Order Bacillariales
  Family Nitzschiaceae
Nitzschia acicularis
Nitzschia amphibia
Nitzschia brevissima
Nitzschia clausii
Nitzschia filiformis
Nitzschia frustulum var. *perminuta*
Nitzschia frustulum var. *subsalina*
Nitzschia granulata
Nitzschia intermedia
Nitzschia kutzingiana
Nitzschia palea
Nitzschia punctata
Nitzschia sigma
Nitzschia tryblionella
Nitzschia tryblionella var. *victoriae*
  Order Surirellales
  Family Surirellaceae
Surirella angusta
Surirella ovalis
Surirella ovata

Source: ANSP (1959).

belonging to the genera *Nitzschia* and *Gomphonema* (Table 5.10); all these algae are known to be very tolerant of organic pollution, particularly of heavy metals. At Marcus Hook, the only common macroscopic alga was *Rhizoclonium hieroglyphicum*. Blue-green algae and diatoms are found in patches on pilings and scattered wood debris; however, in general, the diatoms were not very common (ANSP, 1959).

The protozoa in the Allegheny Avenue area consisted mainly of ciliates and flagellates. The ciliates, *Hypotrichida* and *Oligotrichida*, which are bacterial feeders, were very common. The small number of species of protozoans in this area indicates a toxic condition, and the abundance of the two bacterial feeders indicates that an organic load was also present. At Marcus Hook, the protozoan fauna was also very scarce; however, there were abundant numbers of a few bacterial-feeding species of *Peritrichida* and *Hypotrichida*.

The remaining invertebrates, including insects, are set forth in Table 5.11. Most of the fauna at Allegheny Avenue were freshwater fauna except for the grass shrimp, *Palaemonetes pugio*. Very abundant at this station was the bivalve, *Sphaerium (musculim)* sp., a detritus feeder. Also common were *Limnodrilus* sp.; leeches; isopods; the pulmonate snail, *Physa heterostropha*; *Ferrissia* sp.; and bryozoans. The association of fauna indicates heavy organic pollution. The North Philadelphia sewage treatment plant effluent enters the river above this area.

At Allegheny Avenue, the insect fauna consisted of only a few species, mainly very large populations of *Tendipedida* and *Chironomida* (Table 5.11). Very large populations of *Pelopia* nr. *stellata* were intermixed with a few specimens of *Tendipes* nr. *decorus*, a characteristic pattern in areas with a heavy organic load. At Marcus Hook, the only insects found were *Tendipedida* larvae.

At Marcus Hook, the invertebrate fauna was a mixture of brackish and fresh-water forms. The brackish-water species, taken primarily on the New Jersey side of the river, were the blue crab (*Callinectes sapidus*), the mud crab (*Rithropanopeus harrisii*), and the grass shrimp (*Palaemonetes pugio*). The only invertebrate taken in abundance was the leech, *Erpobdella punctata*. Other freshwater invertebrates were tubificid worms, which were common in dredge samples. On rocks the snail, *Physa heterostropha*, was found, and in the more sandy habitats the bivalve, *Sphaerium* sp., was taken (ANSP, 1959).

As seen in Table 5.12, relatively few fish were collected in the Philadelphia reach. At Allegheny Avenue, nine species were taken, but only two were very common or abundant: the blueback herring, *Alosa aestivalis*, and the mummichog, *Fundulus heteroclitus*. At Marcus Hook, the fish were a mixture of fresh- and brackish-water species. In July the common species were the American eel, *Anguilla rostrata*, and the white perch, *Morone americana*. In September the abundant fish were the bay anchovy, *Anchoa mitchilli*, and the Atlantic silversides, *Menidia menidia*.

The restricted variety of fauna and algal flora of the Philadelphia area indicates the impact of pollution. The presence of heavy metals and other toxic materials, along with a large amount of detritus, results in very low oxygen

TABLE 5.11.   *Invertebrates Found in the Philadelphia Area of the Delaware River, 1957–1959*

PHYLUM BRYOZOA
Class Ectoprocta
    Order Phylactolaemata
    Family Plumatellidae
Plumatella repens
    PHYLUM ANNELIDA
    Class Oligochaeta
    Order Haplotaxida
    Suborder Tubificina
    Superfamily Tubificoidea
    Family Tubificidae
Peloscolex veriegatus
Limnodrilus sp.
    Superfamily Enchytraeoidea
    Family Enchytraeida
Fridericia sp.
    PHYLUM ANNELIDA
    Class Hirudineoidia
    Subclass Hirudinea
    Order Arhynchobdellidae
    Family Erpobdellidae
Erpobdella punctata
Dina sp.
    Order Rhynchobdellida
    Family Glossiphonidae
Glossiphonia complanata
Helobdella stagnalis
Helobdella nephiloidea
Placobdella rugosa
    PHYLUM MOLLUSCA
    Class Gastropoda
    Subclass Euthyneura
    Order Pulmonata
    Superfamily Ancylacea
    Family Physidae
Physa heterostropha
    Family Ancylidae
Ferrissia sp.
    Family Planobidae
Helisoma trivoluis
    Class Bivalvia
    Subclass Heterodonta

Order Veneroida
Suborder Arcticina
Superfamily Corbiculiacea
Family Sphaeriidae
Sphaerium sp.
Sphaerium (musculium) sp.
PHYLUM ARTHROPODA
Class Crustacea
Subclass Branchiopoda
Division Peracarida
Order Isopoda
Suborder Asellota
Family Asellidae
Asellus communis = A. militoris
Order Amphipoda
Family Gammaridae
Gammarus fasciatus
Division Eucarida
Subclass Branchiopoda
Order Decapoda
Family Palaemonidae
Palaemonetes pugio
Family Plumnidae
Rhithropanopeus harrisii
Family Portunidae
Callinectes sapidus
Class Insecta
Order Diptera
Suborder Nematocera
Superfamily Culicoidea
Family Chironomidae
Subfamily Tanypodinae
Tribe Procladiini
Procladius culiciformis
Pelopia nr. *stellata*
Subfamily Chironomina
Tribe Chironomini
Cryptochironomus argus
Cryptochironomus nr. *fulvus*
Harnischia abortiva?
Tendipes nr. *decorus*

Source: ANSP (1959).

TABLE 5.12. *Fish Found in the Philadelphia Area of the Delaware River, 1957–1959*

PHYLUM CHORDATA	*Strongylura marina*
Class Osteichthyes	(billfish)
Order Clupeiformes	Family Cyprinodontidae
Family Clupeidae	*Fundulus diaphanus*
Alosa aestivalis	(freshwater killifish)
(glut herring)	*Fundulus heteroclitus*
Alosa pseudoharengus	(common killifish)
(alewife)	Family Atherinidae
Family Engraulidae	*Membras martinica*
Anchoa mitchilli	(rough silversides)
(common anchovy)	*Menidia beryllina*
Order Cypriniformes	(tide-water silversides)
Family Cyprinidae	*Menidia menidia*
Hybognathus nuchalis	(common silversides)
(gudgeon)	Order Perciformes
Order Siluriformes	Family Percichthyidae
Family Ictaluridae	*Morone americana*
Ictalurus catus	(white perch)
(white catfish)	*Roccus saxatillis*
Ictalurus nebulosus	(striped bass)
(bullhead)	Family Percidae
Order Anguilliformes	*Perca flavescens*
Family Anguillidae	(yellow perch)
Anguilla rostrata	Suborder Gobioidei
(common eel)	Family Gobiidae
Order Atheriniformes	*Gobiosoma bosci*
Family Belonidae	(naked goby)

Source: ANSP (1959).

levels during the summer. Because of the tidal action and the flow of the river, these pollutants can be found in a range of concentrations between Trenton and the lower bay. However, as noted in the other reaches of the river, the area between Trenton and the Burlington–Bristol Bridge and the area between the Delaware Bay canal and the mouth of the bay support diverse and fairly healthy communities of aquatic life (ANSP, 1959).

Freshwater–Oligohaline (0.5 to 5.0 ppt Salinity)

Open Water

Appoquinimink Creek and Alloway Creek. The extent of the freshwater–oligohaline zone varies depending upon the flow of the Delaware River. It may extend only as far downriver as Alloway Creek, or it may extend as far as Appoquinimink Creek. The marshes in this area, even during low-flow conditions of the Delaware, were oligohaline to fresh. These studies of the ecosystems in this area have been made by the Academy of Natural Sciences of Philadelphia from 1957 to 1959. A list of the species of algae, invertebrates, insects, and fish collected in the area are set forth in Tables 5.13 and 5.14.

TABLE 5.13.   *Algae and Diatoms Found in the Delaware River near Appoquinimink Creek, 1957–1959*

Algae

DIVISION CHLOROPHYTA
Class Chlorophyceae
Order Ulvales
Family Ulvaceae
Enteromorpha sp.
Class Ulothricophyceae
Order Ulotrichales
Family Microsporaceae
Microspora W. *Hrockii*
DIVISION CYANOPHYTA
Class Cyanophyceae
Subclass Hormogonophycidae

Order Nostocales
Family Oscillatoriaceae
Spirulina major
Oscillatoria formosa
Lyngbya putealis
Microcoleus rupicola
DIVISION CHROMOPHYTA
Class Xanthophyceae
Order Vaucheriales
Family Vaucheriacea
Vaucheria sp.

Diatoms

DIVISION BACILLARIOPHYTA
Class Bacillariophyceae
Order Eupodiscales
Family Coscinodiscaceae
Coscinodiscus decipiens
Coscinodiscus lineatus
Cyclotella glomerata
Cyclotella meneghiniana
Cyclotella meneghiniana var.
  rectangularis
Melosira nummuloides
Melosira sulcata fo. *radiata*
Family Skeletonemoiacea
Skeletonema costatum
Family Thalassiosiraceae
Thalassiosira subtilis
Thalassionema nitzschioides
Order Biddulphiales
Family Biddulphiaceae
Biddulphia laevis
Order Fragilariales
Family Fragilariaceae
Rhaphoneis amphiceros
Rhaphoneis amphiceros var. *rhombica*
Order Achnanthales
Family Achnanthaceae
Achnanthes brevipes

Cocconeis placentula var. *euglypta*
Order Naviculales
Family Naviculaceae
Caloneis bacillum
Navicula gracilis
Navicula gracilis var. *schizonemoides*
Navicula mutica
Navicula mutica var. 2W
Navicula salinicola
Order Epithemiales
Family Epithemiaceae
Denticula subtilis
Order Bacillariales
Family Nitzschiaceae
Bacillaria paradoxa
Nitzschia brevissima
Nitzschia fasciculata
Nitzschia filiformis
Nitzschia frustulum var. *perminuta*
Nitzschia frustulum var. *subsalina*
Nitzschia kutzingiana
Nitzschia lacunarum
Nitzschia palea
Nitzschia paleaformis
Nitzschia thermalis
Nitzschia tryblionella var. *littoralis*

Source: ANSP (1959).

TABLE 5.14. *Invertebrates and Fish of the Freshwater to Oligohaline* *(0.5–5.0 ppt Salinity) Zone of the Delaware River near Appoquinimink* *Creek, 1957–1959*

Invertebrates

PHYLUM ANNELIDA	Superorder Peracarida
Class Polychaeta	Order Isopoda
Order Phyllodocida	Family Bopyridae
Family Nereidae	*Probopyrus pandalicola*
Nereis limbata	Family Anthuridae
Class Oligochaeta	*Cyathura carinata*
Order Haplotaxida	Family Sphaerinudae
Suborder Tubificina	*Cassidisca lunifrons*
Superfamily Tubificoidea	Order Amphipoda
Family Tubificidae	Family Corophiidae
Limnodrilus sp.	*Corophium cylindricum*
PHYLUM MOLLUSCA	Family Gammaridae
Class Pelecypoda	*Gammarus locusta*
Order Pteroconchida	*Melita nitida*
Family Mytilidae	Order Decapoda
Modiolus demissus	Family Palaemonidae
PHYLUM ARTHROPODA	*Palaemonetes pugio*
Class Crustacea	Family Plumnidae
Order Cirripedia	*Rithropanopeus harrisii*
Family Balanidae	Family Portunidae
Balanus balanoides	*Callinectes sapidus*
Subclass Malacostraca	

Chordates

PHYLUM CHORDATA	Family Cyprinodontidae
Subphylum Vertebrata	*Fundulus heteroclitus*
Class Osteichthyes	Family Atherinidae
Order Clupeiformes	*Menidia beryllina*
Family Clupeidae	Order Gasterosteiformes
Brevoortia tyrannus	Family Syngnathidae
Family Engraulidae	*Syngnathus fuscus*
Anchoa mitchilli	Order Pleuronectiformes
Order Cypriniformes	Family Bothidae
Family Cyprinidae	*Paralichthys dentatus*
Cyprinus carpio	Family Soleidae
Order Atheriniformes	*Trinectes maculatus*

Source: ANSP (1959).

Channel.   The algae in this stretch of the river (Table 5.13) during the ANSP study were dominated by diatoms, which were very abundant in favorable habitats. The most common green alga was *Enteromorpha* sp. Some of the more common diatoms were *Melosira nummuloides, Denticula subtilis, Navicula gracilis, N. mutica, Nitzschia paleaformis,* and *N. filiformis.*

The protozoan fauna was a mixture of fresh- and brackish-water species, with the dominant species, *Stylonychia mytilus,* being euryhaline. Also common were species belonging to the genus *Aspidisca.* The species found seem to be bacteria feeders, indicating a fairly high organic load in the river.

The invertebrate fauna (Table 5.14) were almost entirely brackish-water species, mainly crustacea. Of these, the isopods, *Cyathura carinata, Cassidisca lunifrons,* and *Probopyrus pandalicola,* were identified. Among the amphipods, *Corophium cylindricum, Gammarus locusta,* and *Melita nitida,* were found. Also present were grass shrimp (*Palaemonetes pugio*), mud crab (*Rithropanopeus harrisii*), and blue crab (*Callinectes sapidus*). The most common species of fish collected during the ANSP study were the mummichog, *Fundulus heteroclitus,* and the Atlantic silversides, *Menidia menidia* (ANSP, 1959).

Marshlands

Delaware Marshes.   In 1972, a variety of species were collected in St. George's Creek, which drains the marshlands in that area (Walton and Patrick, 1973). The most common algae were the diatoms, *Nitzschia acicularis, N. reversa, N. sigmoidea,* and *Tropidoneis lepidoptera.* Other algae that were found were the blue-green alga, *Anacystis cyanea,* the green flagellate, *Euglena* sp., and the green algae, *Pediastrum boryanum, P. duplex, Scenedesmus quandricauda,* and *S. acuminatus.*

The zooplankton collected were *Keratella cochlearis* (rotifer), *Bosmina longirostris* (cladoceran), *Daphnia ambigua* (cladoceran), *Cyclops vernalis* (copepod), and *Brachionus bidentatus* (bivalve). The common benthic invertebrates were chironomid larvae, oligochaetes, and the isopod, *Cyanthura polita.* The algae present indicate organic enrichment in this area, as does the common occurrence of the rotifer, *Keratella cochlearis;* chironomids; and oligochaete worms.

The most generally distributed fish was the white perch, *Morone americana,* which was found most frequently in creeks. The brown bullhead, *Ictalurus nebulosus,* was found in creeks, too, but much more rarely. Also rare were the eel (*Anguilla rostrata*), inland silversides (*Menidia beryllina*), and black crappie

TABLE 5.15.   *Fish Collected by Seine and Trawl in Appoquinimink and Blackbird Creeks, Delaware, and Alloway and Hope Creeks, New Jersey, 1969–1970[a]*

	Type of Water[a]	Method of Collection[b] at:			
		Appoquini-mink Creek	Blackbird Creek	Alloway Creek	Hope Creek
PHYLUM CHORDATA					
Subphylum Vertebrata					
Class Osteichthyes					
Order Anguilliformes					
Family Anguillidae					
Anguilla rostrata	M & F	S, T	S, T	S, T	T
Order Clupeiformes					
Family Clupeidae					

(*Continued*)

TABLE 5.15. (*Continued*)

	Type of Water[a]	Method of Collection[b] at:			
		Appoquinimink Creek	Blackbird Creek	Alloway Creek	Hope Creek
Alosa aestivalis	M & F	S, T	S, T	S, T	S, T
A. mediocris	M & F	S	—	—	—
A. pseudoharengus	M & F	S, T	S, T	S, T	T
Brevoortia tyrannus	M & F	S, T	S, T	S, T	S
Dorosoma cepedianum	M & F	S, T	S, T	S, T	—
Family Engraulidae					
Anchoa mitchilli	M & F	S, T	S, T	S, T	S, T
Order Salmoniformes					
Family Esocidae					
Esox americanus americanus	F	S	S	—	—
E. niger	F	S	—	—	—
Order Cypriniformes					
Family Cyprinidae					
Carassius auratus	F	S, T	—	—	—
Cyprinus carpio	F	S, T	S, T	S, T	T
Hybognathus nuchalis	F	S, T	S, T	S, T	—
Notemigonus crysoleucas	F	S	S	S	—
Notropis analostanus	F	S	—	—	—
N. hudsonius	F	S, T	S, T	S	—
Rhinichthys atratulus	F	—	—	S	—
Family Catostomidae					
Catostomus commersoni	F	—	S	—	—
Erimyzon oblongus	F	—	S	—	—
Order Siluriformes					
Family Ictaluridae					
Ictalurus catus	F	T	S, T	S, T	T
I. nebulosus	F	S, T	S, T	S, T	T
I. punctatus	F	T	S, T	S, T	—
Noturus gyrinus	F	—	S	—	—
Order Atheriniformes					
Family Belonidae					
Strongylura marina	F	S	S	S	—
Family Cyprinodontidae					
Cyprinodon variegatus	M & F	—	S	S	—
F. heteroclitus	M & F	S	S	S	S
Family Poeciliidae					
Gambusia affinis	M & F	S	—	—	—

Source: Adapted from Smith (1971).

[a] M, marine water; F, fresh water.

[b] S, seine; T, trawl.

(*Pomoxis nigromaculatus*). A list of the fish of this general area is set forth in Table 5.15.

New Jersey marshes.   In the low-salinity marshes on the New Jersey side of the estuary, the dominant diatoms were *Melosira granulata*, *M. italica*, *M. granulata* var. *angustissima*, *Asterionella formosa*, *Cyclotella meneghiniana*, *Nitzschia sigmoidea*, *Coscinodiscus excentricus*, and *Cyclostella striata*. Other algae, such as phytoflagellates, were represented by *Trachlemonas hispida*, *Phacus* sp., and *Euglena acus*. The blue-green algae were represented by species of *Oscillatoria*. The green algae present were *Pediastrum* sp., *Scenedesmus* sp., *Actinastrum hantzschii*, *Ankistrodesmus* sp., *Coelastrum* sp., *Micractinium* sp., and *Coronastrum* sp. and *Mougeotia* sp. (which were probably washed out from the marshlands).

The zooplankton were represented by the crustacea, *Acartia tonsa*, *Bosmina longirostris*, *Cyclops vernalis*; and the rotifers, *Brachionus plicatilis*, *Brachionus bidentata*, *Keratella cochlearis*, *Eurytemora affinis*, *Trichocerca similis*, and *Notholca acuminata*. A species of chaetogaster was also found. The common benthic invertebrates were the oligochaetes; chironomids; larvae of the mud crab, *Rhithropanopeus harrisii*; and the fiddler crab, *Uca minax*.

Of the fish described from this area (Smith, 1971), at least 13 were life residents. Those present were the creek chubsucker (*Erimyzon oblongus*), the carp (*Cyprinus carpio*), the eastern silvery minnow (*Hybognathus regius*), the spottailed shiner (*Notropus hudsonius*), the redfinned pickerel (*Esox americanus*), the banded killifish (*Fundulus diaphanus*), the mummichog (*F. heteroclitus*), the tessellated darter (*Etheostoma olmstedi*), the white catfish (*Ictalurus catus*), the brown bullhead (*I. nebulosus*), the pumpkinseed/(*Lepomis gibbosus*), the gizzard shad (*Dorosoma cepedianum*), the goldfish (*Carassius auratus*), the satinfin shiner (*Notropus analostanus*), the channel catfish (*Ictalurus punctatus*), the chain pickerel (*Exox niger*), the bluegill (*Lepomis macrochirus*), the white crappie (*Pomoxis annularis*), the white sucker (*Catostomus commersoni*), the golden shiner (*Notemigonus crysoleucas*), the blacknosed dace (*Rhinichthys atratulus*), the tadpole madtom (*Noturus gyrinus*), the mosquitofish (*Gambusia affinis*), the largemouth bass (*Micropterus salmoides*), and the black crappie (*Pomoxis nigromaculatus*). The fish that were known to spawn in these creeks were the white perch (*Morone americana*), the blueback herring (*Alosa aestivalis*), the tidewater silversides (*Menidia beryllina*), and alewives (*Alosa pseudoharengus*). The fish using the marshes as a nursery were the bay anchovy (*Anchoa mitchilli*), the American eel (*Anguilla rostrata*), the silver perch (*Bairdiella chrysura*), the black drum (*Pogonias cromis*), the naked goby (*Gobiosoma bosci*), and the hogchoker (*Trinectes maculatus*). Few adults were found among the young fish in low-salinity nursery waters between May and August.

Mesohaline (5 to 18 ppt Salinity).   The extent of this salinity region varied greatly depending on the flow of the Delaware River. Sometimes it extended only as far down as the Cohansey River in New Jersey. At other times, under high-flow conditions, it extended down to Dividing Creek in New Jersey.

Salinity varied greatly in the marshes of the mesohaline area. Nearly freshwater salinities were found in areas remote from the river. As one approached the mouths of marsh drainage creeks, salinities began to resemble those of the main river, fluctuating as the salinity of the river fluctuated.

The marshlands in this reach of the Delaware River were very extensive, and those in the vicinity of Smyrna River and Cedar Creek (DE) have been studied in detail by the Academy of Natural Sciences (1972). Other studies in this region have been done by Walton and Patrick (1973). Mesohaline open water has been studied by Ferrante (1971), and no comprehensive studies have been made of the open-water associations of aquatic life.

Open Water

Open-water invertebrates. Ferrante's (1971) studies of zooplankton were conducted in the vicinity of Artificial Island, north of the Cohansey River. A list of species found in this reach of the river is given in Table 5.16. The most characteristic species of zooplankton found were the mysid shrimp, *Neomysis americana*; the decapod, *Rhithropanopeus harrisii*; the jellyfish, *Blackfordia manhattensis*; and the copepods, *Eurytemora hirundoides* and *Acartia tonsa*.

Neomysis americana composed about 80% of the mysid population and showed no particular variation in abundance between May and December, but did show considerable difference between day and night sampling, with the night sampling having 10 to 100 times the number of organisms as the day samples. The zoeal and earlier developmental stages of the decapod, *Rhithropanopeus harrisii*, were present from June through September. They were found most commonly where the salinity was 1 to 11 ppt and the temperature ranged between 16 and 32°C. The medusa, *Blackfordia manhattensis*, was found from the end of June to the beginning of November. The densities tended to be greater in the more saline downstream reaches of the river.

The copepod, *Eurytemora hirundoides*, was collected primarily from May to the end of July, and again from the beginning of October to the beginning of December. This bimodal distribution was probably caused by the increase in salinity in the summer months. *E. hirundoides* was collected in the salinity range 0 to 8 ppt in the spring and fall. *Acartia tonsa* was the most abundant copepod in the area and had somewhat larger populations at the surface during the dark hours. In August and September the population sizes of this species were greatly reduced by predation by the ctenophore, *Mnemiopsis leidyi*.

Marshlands

Marsh algae. Algae have been studied in the mouths of several marsh drainage creeks in this region by Walton and Patrick (1973). Samples were taken from Back Creek, Middlemarsh Creek, and Cedar Creek in New Jersey, all near the Cohansey River, in waters of salinity ranging from 12.4 to 22 ppt. Species of phytoplankton typically found there were the diatoms, *Skeletonema costatum*, *Chaetoceros subtilis*, and *C. danicus*. The benthic algae was largely dominated by the diatoms, *Nitzschia filiformis*, *N. parvula*, *Navicula pygmaea*, *N. secreta* var. *apiculata*, *N. tripunctata* var. *schizonemoides*, and *Amphipora alta*. The red-tide organisms, *Peridinum* sp., were also found, as was *Anabaena* sp. *Cyclotella meneghiniana* was found but may be a washout from fresher drainage waters. The blue-green alga, *Oscillatoria* sp., was found on the mud.

TABLE 5.16.   *Invertebrates Collected in the Vicinity of Artificial Island in the Delaware River, May–December 1970[a]*

Schizopoda
  Neomysis americana

Decapoda
  Neopanope texana sayi
  Rhithropanopeus harrisii
  Callinectes sapidus
  Palaemonetes puqio
  Cranqon septemspinosa

Amphipoda
  Corophium lacustre
  Corophium acherusicum
  Corophium cylindricum
  Gammarus fasciatus
  Gammarus daiberi
  Melita nitida
  Monoculodes edwardsi
  Probopyrus sp. (thompsoni)

Isopoda
  Chiridotea tuftsi or *almyra*
  Cirolana concharum
  Cyathura polita
  Edotea mantosa
  Livonica ovalis

Cladocera
  Leptodora kindti
  Daphnia parvula
  Daphnia schodleri
  Daphnia sp.
  Bosmina longirostris
  Bosmina coregoni
  Moina sp. (affinis)

Hydracarina
  Water mite

Copepoda
  Pseudodiaptomus coronatus
  Eurytemora hirundoides
  Cyclops vernalis
  Acartia tonsa
  Mesocyclops edax
  Mesocyclops leuckarti
  Labidocera aestiva

Coelenterata
  Nemopis bachei
  Blackfordia manhattensis
  Hydroid colony
  1. *Garveia franciscana*
  2. *Amathia vidovici*
  3. Unidentified Campulinidae

Ctenophora
  Mnemiopsis leidyi

Cirripedia
  Barnacle casts
  Balanus spp.

Chaetognatha
  Sagitta elegans

Xiposura
  Limulus polyphemus

Annelida
  Nereis succinea
  Polydora websteri (larvae)

Cumacea

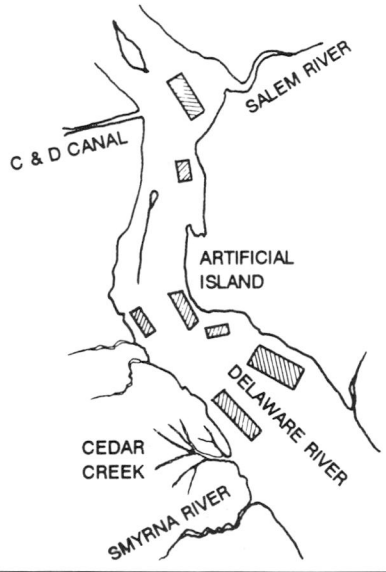

Source: After Ferrante (1971).
[a]Inset map shows sampling areas (shaded rectangles).

Algae were also studied by the Academy of Natural Sciences (1972) in the Delaware marshes surrounding Smyrna River and Cedar Creek, which feeds into the Smyrna, nearly opposite the Cohansey River of New Jersey. The phytoplankton was dominated by the very common diatom, *Stephanopyxis costatum*, from July through September. The second most common species was *Coscinodiscus pygmaeus* var. *micropunctata*. From June to mid-July *Cyclotella aliquantula* and *C. caspia* were most abundant in the areas nearest the river. *Cyclotella striata* was common in remote areas and particularly abundant from mid-July to early September. *Chaetoceros wighami* was very common in late July and again in early October. The benthic diatoms, *Nitzschia parvula* and *N. sigma* var. *rigidula*, were often present in the phytoplankton and occasionally common. The red-tide organisms, *Peridinium* sp., occasionally occurred in the plankton from June to August. The diversity of the plankton varies with the season of the year and was usually highest between April and May, again in June and August, and from September to December. The more common diatoms are listed in Table 5.17.

Among the benthic algae in the Smyrna River–Cedar Creek area (on the west side of Delaware Bay), by far the most common was the filamentous green alga, *Rhizoclonium hieroglyphicum*, which was usually present at all stations but found dependably at stations remote from the Delaware River. The unicellular green alga, *Chlorococeum* sp., was common during the summer months in all areas studied. The blue-green alga, *Microcoleus vaginatus*, was often present at the remote stations. *Schizothrix calcicola* and *Oscillatoria submembranacea* were found growing on the bases of *Spartina alterniflora* or on nearby soil. The diatom, *Nitzschia parvula*, formed 32.8% of the benthic collections, *N. diserta* formed 13%, and *Coscinodiscus pygmaeus* var. *micropunctata* formed 10 to 20%. As stated previously, the latter species was also found in the phytoplankton and supports the theory that in these shallow waters plankton are mainly scuffed-up benthic forms or are brought in from the river by tides. Many of these species indicate mesotrophic-to-eutrophic conditions in this area (ANSP, 1972).

Marsh microinvertebrates were also studied in the Smyrna River–Cedar Creek–Cedar Swamp area (ANSP, 1972). The largest and least diverse population of protozoans was found between mid-July and September, peaking between the end of August and mid-September. In stations nearest the Delaware River, protozoan populations subsided from the summer peak early in September. In remote areas of the marshes, protozoa were still abundant by late September. Phytoflagellates were most abundant in September, October, and November but absent in June at the remote stations, and were present in areas nearest the Delaware River. The zooflagellates were most common in the fall. Sarcodina were often seen in the various study areas during July but were never very abundant. The ciliates were the most common protozoans found, among which the most important species were *Codonella amorella*, *C. cratera*, *Tintinnopsis fibriata*, and *Leprotintinnus nordquist*.

The population of copepods, composed primarily of nauplius larvae, was largest from June to September and again in the early part of October. It is

TABLE 5.17.   *Diatoms Found in the Salt Marshes at Cedar Swamp, Smyrna River, Woodland Beach, and Bombay Hook in the Delaware Estuary, 1970–1971*

DIVISION CHRYSOPHYTA
Class Bacillariophyceae
Order Centrales
Suborder Discineae
Family Coscinodiscaceae
Subfamily Melosiroideae
Melosira granulata
M. nummuloides
M. sulcata
M. sulcata f. *cornata*
M. sulcata f. *radiata*
Stephanopyxis costatum
Subfamily Thalassiosiroideae
Thalassionema nitzschioides
Subfamily Coscinodiscoideae
Actinoptyschus undulatus
Coscinodiscus divisus
C. kuetzingii
C. lacustris
C. lineatus
C. lineatus f. *minor*
C. marginatus
C. pygmaeus var. *micropunctatus*
Cyclotella aliguantula
C. atomus
C. caspia
C. comta
C. meneghiniana
C. striata
Suborder Biddulphineae
Family Chaetoceraceae
Subfamily Chaetocerioidea
Chaetoceros danicus
C. pelagius
C. wighami
Order Pennales
Suborder Araphidneae
Family Fragilariaceae
Subfamily Meridionoideae
Asterionella formosa
Campylosira cymbelliformis
Cymatosira belgica
Fragilaria pinnata
Rhaphoneis amphiceros
R. minutissima

R. surirella
Suborder Monoraphidineae
Family Achnanthaceae
Subfamily Cocconeioideae
Cocconeis placentula var. *lineata*
Subfamily Achnanthoideae
Achnanthes lanceolata
A. minutissima
Suborder Biraphidineae
Family Naviculaceae
Subfamily Naviculoideae
Gyrosigma fasciola
Navicula capitata var. *hungarica*
N. decussis
N. diserta
N. mutica var. *cohnii*
N. peregrina
N. pygmaea
N. salinarum
N. secreta var. *apiculata*
N. tripunctata var. *schizonemoides*
Order Naviculales
Family Entomoneidaceae
Amphiprora alata
Order Epithemiales
Family Epithemiaceae
Subfamily Epithemioideae
Denticula tenuis
Family Nitzschiaceae
Subfamily Nitzschioideae
Bacillaria paradoxa
Nitzschia clausii
N. closterium
N. dissipata
N. filiformis
Nitzschia fonticola var. *genuina*
N. frustulum
N. frustulum var. *perminuta*
N. granulata
N. hungarica
N. parvula
N. parvula var. *terricola*
N. sigma var. *rigidula*
N. tryblionella var. *debilis*
N. tryblionella var. *levidensis*

Source: ANSP (1972).

interesting to note that areas with the largest populations of copepods have sparse populations of ciliates.

Rotifers were usually subdominant and seemed to be most common from July to early September. They were found more often in the drainage ditches of Smyrna Creek Marsh than in Cedar Swamp Marsh ditches. The mollusc veligers were most common in June, July, and August, and absent at most of the stations after early September. Uncommon microinvertebrates were foraminifera (protozoans), which were relatively scarce but widely distributed from June to October; nematode worms, which were rarely found; and some small annelids, which were found throughout the summer months from June through September (ANSP, 1972).

Seven different types of macroinvertebrate habitats have been studied within Cedar Swamp Marsh and the Smyrna River Marsh.

1. In sand and gravel mixed with clay and soft mud the nemertean, *Carinoma tremaphoros*, was found only infrequently and in small numbers. The pulmonate snail, *Melampus bidentatus*, and the beach fly, *Orchestia gammarella*, were frequently found among the roots of *Phragmites* and on the intertidal beach areas associated with the clam, *Macoma balthica*. In the lower littoral and the sublittoral areas, large populations of the grass shrimp, *Palaemonetes pugio*, an important food for fish, were encountered during the winter. The fiddler crab, *Uca minax*, was common in mud burrows in the marsh, although the closely related *U. pugnax* was rarely found. The isopod, *Cyathura polita*, was observed consistently in moderate numbers. The amphipod, *Gammarus palustris*, was found in very substantial numbers, and *Gammarus daiberi* was found in all the areas where *G. palustris* was present.

2. The organisms most consistently found in soft mud and clay included *Carinoma tremaphoros*, *Macoma balthica*, and *Cyathura polita*. Forming burrows within the soft mud was the crab, *Uca minax*. Also present within the mud were the bristle worms, *Nereis succinea* and *N. virens*. Large but fluctuating populations of amphipods consisting of *Gammarus palustris* and *Leptocheirus plumulosus* were found along with large populations of the grass shrimp, *Crangon septemspinosa* and *Palaemonetes pugio*. Present, but not so numerous, were a pulmonate snail, *Melampus bidentatus*, and the mysid shrimp, *Neomysis americana*.

3. The organisms that were most abundant and typical of soft mud fibrous material habitat were the clam, *Macoma balthica*; the grass shrimp, *Palaemonetes pugio*; the fiddler crab, *Uca minax*; the amphipod, *Leptocheirus plumulosus*; and the isopod, *Cyathura polita*. Scattered over the area were small populations of the nemertean, *Carinoma tremaphoros*; two species of bristle worm, *Nereis succinea* and *N. virens*; and the amphipods, *Gammarus palustris* and *Orchestia gammerella*.

4. The most abundant organisms in soft mud with clay and peat were the mollusc, *Macoma balthica*; the bristle worm, *Cyathura polita*; the grass shrimp, *Rhithropanopeus harrisii*; and the crab, *Uca minax*. In deeper, swifter-flowing water, but with the same type of substrate, were the amphipods, *Corophium*

lacustre, *Gammarus palustris*, *Maera danae*, and *Leptochirus plumulosus*, which were not too common. The crab, *Uca pugnax*, had a fairly large population in this area, as did its close relative *Uca minax*, but they occupied different banks in the Smyrna River Marsh.

5. In a clay fibrous peaty material mixed with soft mud and sand habitat the most frequently encountered organisms were the bristle worm, *Cyathura polita*, and the fiddler crab, *Uca minax*, followed in abundance by the bivalve, *Macoma balthica*. Scattered over the area, but never abundant, were the amphipods, *Gammarus palustris*, *Leptocheirus plumulosus*, and *Melita nitida*. The grass shrimps, *Palaemonetes pugio* and *P. vulgaris*; the snail, *Melampus bidentatus*; and *U. pugnax* were also found here.

6. Most consistently present in hard clay with some fibrous material and a little soft mud were the isopod, *Cyathura polita*, and the amphipods, *Gammarus palustris* and *Orchestia gammarella*; the grass shrimps, *Palaemonetes pugio* and *Crangon septemspinosa*; the fiddler crab, *Uca minax*; the mud crab, *Rhithropanopeus harrisii*; the bivalve, *Macoma balthica*; the snail, *Melampus bidentatus*; and the bristle worms, *Nereis succinea* and *N. virens*. These areas seem to be particularly favorable for isopods and grass shrimps.

7. The solid habitats of submerged stumps with some mud formed a substrate for the barnacle, *Balanus improvisus*. In the more sheltered habitats, the mud crab, *Rhithropanopeus harrisii*; amphipods, chiefly *Gammarus palustris*; and the bristle worm, *Nereis succinea*, were found in the more or less decayed parts of stumps. On the soft mud the most abundant organisms found in this habitat were the mud crab, *Rhithropanopeus harrisii*; the fiddler crab, *Uca minax*; the isopod, *Cyathura polita*; and the grass shrimp, *Palaemonetes pugio*. The bivalve, *Macoma balthica*, was generally present in the soft mud. In a similar substrate in Bombay Hook Marsh, the mud snail, *Ilyanassa obsoletus*, was very abundant and formed huge populations in the soft mud. The bristle worm, *Nereis succineas*, was frequently encountered. The isopod, *Cyathura polita*, and the fiddler crab, *Uca minax*, were in most collections and the populations were often quite large, as was the case with the grass shrimp, *Palaemonetes pugio*. A list of macro-invertebrates taken from these marsh areas is given in Table 5.18. In the more saline areas were found the oyster, *Crassostrea virginica*; the grass shrimp, *Palaemonetes intermedius* and *P. pugio*; the mud crab, *Rhithropanopeus harrisii*; the blue crab, *Callinectes sapidus*; the fiddler crab, *Uca minax*; and the bristle worm, *Nereis succinea* (Walton and Patrick, 1973).

Vertebrates.   Fish were collected by Walton and Patrick (1973) in the meso-haline area. The more common species were bay anchovy (*Anchoa mitchilli*), Atlantic menhaden (*Brevoortia tyrannus*), weakfish (*Cynoscion regalis*), spot (*Leiostomus xanthurus*), white perch (*Morone americana*), small mouth flounder (*Etropus microstomus*), summer flounder (*Paralichthys dentatus*), hogchoker (*Trinectes maculatus*), red hake (*Urophycis chuss*), spotted hake (*V. regius*), and striped sea robin (*Prionotus evolans*). A list of the fish species found in the marsh during 1970–1972 is given in Table 5.19.

TABLE 5.18. *Macroinvertebrates Found in Delaware Estuary Marshes*

PHYLUM NEMERTEA
Class Anopla
Order Paleonemertea
Family Cephalotrichidae
Carinoma tremaphoros
PHYLUM ANNELIDA
Class Polychaeta
Family Nereidae
Nereis succinea
Nereis virens
PHYLUM MOLLUSCA
Class Gastropoda
Subclass Prosobranchia
Order Neogastropoda
Family Nassariidae
Ilyanassa obsoletus
Subclass Pulmonata
Order Basommatophora
Family Ellobiidae
Melampus bidentatus
Class Bivalvia
Subclass Lamellibranchia
Order Anisomyaria
Family Mytilidae
Modiolus demissus
Order Heterodonta
Family Tellinidae
Macoma baltica
PHYLUM ARTHROPODA
Subphylum Mandibulata
Class Crustacea
Subclass Cirripedia
Order Thoracica
Suborder Balanomorpha
Balanus improvisus
Subclass Malacostraca
Series Eumalacostraca
Superorder Percarida
Order Mysidacea
Suborder Mysida
Family Mysidae
Neomysis americana
Order Isopoda
Suborder Anthuridea
Family Anthuridae
Cyathura polita
Suborder Oniscoidea
Family Oniscidae
Philoscia vittata
Suborder Flabellifera
Family Sphaeromidae

Cassidinisca lunifrons
Family Cymothoidae
Lironeca ovalis
Suborder Valvifera
Family Idoteidae
Idotea triloba
Idotea baltica
Chiridotea almyra
Suborder Bopyroidea
Family Bopyridae
Probopyrus pandalicola
Order Amphipoda
Suborder Gammaridea
Family Gammaridae
Gammarus palustris
Gammarus daiberi
Family Melitidae
Maera danae
Melita nitida
Family Aoridae
Leptocheirus plumulosus
Family Haustoriidae
Lepidactylus dysticus
Family Talitridae
Orchestia gammarella
Family Oedicerotidae
Monocluodes edwardsi
Family Corophiidae
Corophium lacustre
Superorder Eucarida
Order Decapoda
Suborder Natantia
Section Caridea
Family Crangonidae
Crangon septemspinosus
Family Palaemonidae
Palaemonetes intermedius
Palaemonetes pugio
Palaemonetes vulgaris
Suborder Reptantia
Section Brachyura
Subsection Brachygnatha
Superfamily Brachyrhyncha
Family Xanthidae
Rhithropanopeus harrisi
Family Ocypodidae
Uca minax
Uca pugnax
Family Grapsidae
Sesarma reticulatum
Family Portunidae
Callinectes sapidus

Source: Walton and Patrick (1973).

TABLE 5.19. *Fish Found in the Salt Marshes at Cedar Swamp, Smyrna River, Woodland Beach, and Bombay Hook in the Delaware Estuary, 1970–1971*

PHYLUM CHORDATA
Subphylum Vertebrata
Class Agnatha
    Order Petromyzontiformes
    Family Petromyzontidae
Petromyzon marinus
    Class Osteichthyes
    Order Acipenseriformes
    Family Acipenseridae
Acipenser oxyrhynchus
    Order Anguilliformes
    Family Anguillidae
Anguilla rostrata
    Family Congridae
Conger oceanicus
    Order Clupeiformes
    Family Clupeidae
Alosa aestivalis
A. mediocris
A. pseudoharengus
A. sapidissima
Brevoortia tyrannus
Clupea harengus harengus
Dorosoma cepedianum
    Family Engraulidae
Anchoa hepsetus
A. mitchilli
    Order Cypriniformes
    Family Cyprinidae
Notemigonus crysoleucas
    Order Siluriformes
    Family Ictaluridae
Ictalurus catus
I. nebulosus
I. punctatus
    Order Batrachoidiformes
    Family Batrachoididae
Opsanus tau
    Order Gadiformes
    Family Gadidae
Urophycis chuss
U. regia
    Family Ophidiidae
Ophidion marginatum
    Order Atheriniformes
    Family Belonidae
Strongylura marina
    Family Cyprinodontidae

Cyprinodon variegatus
Fundulus heteroclitus
F. majalis
    Family Atherinidae
Menidia beryllina
M. menidia
    Order Gasterosteiformes
    Family Syngnathidae
Syngnathus fuscus
    Order Perciformes
    Family Percichthyidae
Morone americana
M. saxatilis
    Family Serranidae
Centropristis striata
    Family Centrarchidae
Lepomis gibbosus
L. macrochirus
Pomoxis nigromaculatus
    Family Percidae
Etheostoma olmstedi
Perca flavescens
    Family Pomatomidae
Pomatomus saltatrix
    Family Carangidae
Caranx hippos
    Family Sciaenidae
Baridiella crysoura
Cynoscion regalis
Leiostomus xanthurus
Micropogonias undulatus
Pogonias cromis
    Family Gobiidae
Gobiosoma bosci
    Family Stromateidae
Peprilus triacanthus
    Family Triglidae
Prionotus evolans
    Family Cottidae
Myoxocephalus aenaeus
    Order Pleuronectiformes
    Family Bothidae
Etropus crossotus
Paralichthys dentatus
Scophthalmus aquosus
    Family Pleuronectidae
Pseudopleuronectes americanus
    Family Soleidae
Trinectes maculatus

Source: Walton and Patrick (1973).

The considerable movement of fish within the marsh areas may be related to current pattern and to types and abundance of food found in the various areas. The mummichog, *Fundulus heteroclitus*, was present throughout the marsh area. The largest numbers were taken during August and September 1970–1971 in the Smyrna River Marsh, mainly in the upper parts of the marsh. A downstream migration of the mummichogs to the areas nearest the river seemed to occur during the fall months. The Atlantic silversides, *Menidia menidia*, was common in the Smyrna Creek Marsh and Cedar Swamp in early spring (i.e., late February or early March through April). The first juveniles were found in June and again in July in the upper or more remote areas of the marsh, indicating an early spring spawn. The Atlantic silversides stay in the marsh throughout the year and move from the upper areas to the lower areas of the marsh in October and finally out of the marshes in November. They probably overwinter near the mouth of the bay in much deeper waters.

The tidewater silversides, *Menidia beryllina*, seems to prefer fresher waters. The greatest catch within the marsh was made in September and October. It would appear that this species tends to move into deeper waters in spring and summer (Walton and Patrick, 1973).

The white perch, *Morone americana*, lives in the marsh from March to fall. Spawning may have occurred at some other place, since the young-of-the-year came into the marsh to feed. They disappeared during December and returned in significant numbers in March. Their average length had not increased between December and March.

The weakfish, *Cynoscion regalis*, seems to use these marsh areas mainly as a feeding ground. Juveniles were reported to be common during June and July in 1970–1971. In 1971–1972, the juveniles were believed to be starting their migration to deeper water. According to Bigelow and Schroeder (1953), the migration of weakfish from the marsh to offshore waters farther down the coast is triggered by changes in temperature.

The bay anchovy, *Anchoa mitchilli*, is primarily a saltwater fish. The largest populations of bay anchovy were found in areas of Cedar Swamp Marsh near the Delaware River. The fish seemed to use the marsh only as a temporary stopping point in their migration, as no increase in the size of the fish was noted over time.

The Atlantic menhaden, *Brevoortia tyrannus*, was not found in significant numbers at any time in the Delaware Bay. Large numbers of the fish did occur, however, in the more remote parts of the marshes from June to August or September. The Atlantic menhaden may have been in the process of migration (possibly to less saline waters). Menhaden were rarely found in the more saline waters of Woodland Beach and none were taken at Bombay Hook (Walton and Patrick, 1973).

The spot, *Leiostomus xanthurus*, was most commonly found in Cedar Swamp, and rarely in Bombay Hook marshes or Woodlands Beach. During June, the spot were captured in fairly large numbers at the more remote fresher-water stations in Cedar Swamp Marsh. Most of the spot were collected in July from all of the upper collecting areas and in one area near the river on the inshore side of Cedar Swamp marsh. They were not found in deeper waters near the mouth of the marsh. During August, maturing spot occurred more frequently along the inshore side of the marsh and less frequently in more remote areas. Young spot probably congregated in shallow marsh waters because food (young *Macoma* clams and aquatic stages of terrestrial insects) was available and because there were few predators. The adult spot inhabited deeper waters of the marsh, where they could pursue their more vagile prey. During September, most spot were found in more open waters of the marsh. The few spot collected in October and November were from those areas nearest the river.

Polyhaline Zone (18 to 30 ppt Salinity). Under low-river-flow conditions, the polyhaline zone extended as far inshore as Stow Creek.

Open Water

Algae. The most extensive phytoplankton studies in the lower Delaware Bay were conducted 10 km east of the mouth of the Mispillion River (Watling et al., 1979). Most of the 113 species collected were diatoms and dinoflagellates (Table 5.20). *Cryptomonas acuta* was usually dominant or subdominant, but sometimes in the winter, spring, and fall it was replaced by *Skeletonema costatum* as dominant and *Leptocylindrus danicus* and *Rhizosolenia fragilissima*. In March, *Katodinium rotundatum* was abundant, as was *Chroomonas* sp. in November and December. Dinoflagellates may also be abundant in the phytoplankton of Delaware Bay (Martin, 1928). Common dinoflagellate species were *Exuviaella apora, Gymnodinium subrufescens, Amphidinium fusiforme, Polykrikos kofoidi, Gonyaulax spinifera,* and *Peridiniopsis leonis*. The benthic algae on the western shore of the bay consisted of blue-green, green, brown, and red algae which were attached to or growing on hard substrates (Table 5.21).

The only solid substrates in the Delaware estuary are riprap, logs, wharves, jetties, breakwaters, and other objects resulting from human activities. Maurer (1974) found the following zonation on jetties. The zone most exposed to intertidal action, or the upper zone, consisted of the blue-green algae, *Calothrix crustacea, Oscillatoria princeps,* and *Lyngbya* spp. Lower were the green algae, *Enteromorpha linza, E. minima, E. prolifera, E. intestinalis,* and *Ulothrix flacca*. The next lowest zone, which was submerged, was chiefly *E. prolifera* and *Ulva lactuca* mixed with some reds and browns. The dominant species in the lowest zone were the brown algae, *Ectocarpus siliculosus* and *Petalonia fascia,* and the red algae, *Polysiphonia harveyi, P. nigrescens,* and *Gracilaria foliifera*.

Invertebrates. The zooplankton of Delaware Bay did not show a consistent cyclic rhythm in biomass numbers comparable to that in more northern estuaries, but the general pattern of species succession was nearly the same over many years. The number of individuals of surface zooplankton ranged seasonally from 58 m^{-3} in August to 21,092 m^{-3} in June. Bottom samples ranged from 259 m^{-3} in August to 30,395 m^{-3} in October. Veligers of the clam, *Mytilus edulis,* contributed significant numbers to the zooplankton in December and January. From January to May, the dominant species were *Centropages hamatus, Temora longicornis,* and *Pseudocalanus minutus*. Larvae of bottom invertebrates composed

TABLE 5.20. *Phytoplankton Species of Lower Delaware Bay, June 1974–May 1975*

DIVISION CHLOROPHYTA
    Class Chlorophyceae
        Order Volvocales
            Family Pyramimonaceae
Pyramimonas spp.
            Family Tetraselmiaceae
Tetraselmis sp.
            Family Chlamydomondaceae
Chlamydomonas sp.
Brachiomonas submarina
        Order Chlorococcales
            Family Oocystaceae
Ankistrodesmus sp.
Kirchneriella sp.
            Family Scenedesmaceae
Scenedesmus sp.
            Family unknown
Chlorococcales sp.
    Class Prasinophyceae
        Order unknown
Prasinophyte sp.
DIVISION CHROMOPHYTA
    Class Chrysophyceae
        Subclass Heterochrysophysidae
        Order Chromulinales
            Family Chrysococcaceae
Calycomonas ovalis
            Family Pedinellaceae
Pseudopedinella pyriformis
        Order Ochromonadales
            Family Ochromonadaceae
Ochromonas sp.
            Family Synuraceae
Catenochrysis (= Chrysodidymus) *gracilis*
Ebria tripartita
        Subclass Isochrysophycidaceae
        Order Prymnesiales
            Family Prymnesiaceae
Chrysochromulina sp.
            Family Coccolithaceae
Coccolithaceae sp.
    Class Xanthophyceae
        Order Heterochloridales
Olisthodiscus sp.
    Class Diatomophyceae
        (= Bacillariophyceae)
        Subclass Centrophycidae
        Order Coscinodiscales
            Family Coscinodiscaceae
Coscinodiscus lineatus
Coscinodiscus radiatus

Coscinodiscus sp.
Cyclotella sp.
Paralia sulcata
Skeletonema costatum
Thalassiosira sp.
Thalassiosira ? *gravida*
Thalassiosira nordenskioldii
            Family Actinodiscaceae
Actinoptychus senarius
        Order Rhizosoleniales
            Family Rhizosoleniaceae
Rhizosolenia alata
Rhizosolenia delicatula
Rhizosolenia fragilissima
Rhizosolenia stolterfothii
Rhizosolenia setigera
            Family Leptocylindraceae
Leptocylindrus danicus
Laptocylindrus minimus
Schroderella delicatula
Guinardia flaccida
Detonula confervacea
        Order Biddulphiaceae
            Family Biddulphiaceae
Biddulphia sp.
Biddulphia regia
Biddulphia rhombus
Cerataulina pelagica
Lithodesmium undulatum
Streptotheca tamesis
            Family Chaetoceraceae
Chaetoceros sp.
Chaetoceros decipiens
Chaetoceros simplex
        Order Fragilariales
            Family Fragilariaceae
Asterionella glacialis
Fragilaria oceanica
Grammatophora marina
Raphoneis amphiceros
Synedra sp.
Thalassionema nitzschioides
        Order Achnanthales
            Family Achnanthaceae
Cocconeis sp.
        Order Naviculales
            Suborder Naviculineae
                Family Naviculaceae
Navicula spp.
Navicula membranacea
Diploneis sp.

Continued

TABLE 5.20.   (Continued)

Pleurosigma sp.	*Gymnodinium* spp.
Family Cymbellacea	*Katodinium rotundatum*
? *Phaeodactylum tricornutum*	*Gyrodinium* ? *carteretensis*
Amphora sp.	*Gyrodinium spirale*
Family Bacillariaceae	*Gyrodinium* ? *metum*
Cylindrotheca (= Nitzschia) *closterium*	*Gyrodinium* ? *grossestriatum*
Nitzschia seriata	*Gyrodinium* spp.
Suborder Surirellinaea	Family Noctilucaceae
Family Surirellaceae	*Noctiluca scintillans*
Surirella sp.	Family Glenodiniaceae
Order unknown	*Glenodinium danicum*
Pennatae sp.	*Glenodinium rotundum*
DIVISION PYRRHOPHYTA	Family Peridiniaceae
Class Cryptophyceae	*Scrippsiella trochoidea*
Order Cryptomonadales	Family Gonyaulacaceae
Family Cryptomonadaceae	*Gonyaulax spinifera*
Chroomonas sp.	Family Ceratiaceae
Cryptomonas acuta	*Ceratium tripos*
Family unknown	Family Warnowiaceae
Cryptomonad spp. 2	*Warnowia* (= Pouchetia) sp.
Class Dinophyceae	Order Dinophysiales
Order Prorocentrales	Family Dinophysiaceae
Prorocentrum minimum	*Dinophysis* (= Phalacroma) sp.
Prorocentrum scutellm	Order unknown
Prorocentrum micans	*Dinoflagellate*
Prorocentrum compressum	DIVISION EUGLENOPHYTA
Prorocentrum balticum	Class Euglenophyceae
Prorocentrum aporum	Order Euglenales
Prorocentrum sp.	Family Eutreptiaceae
Order Peridiniales	*Eutreptia* sp.
Family Gymnodiniaceae	Family Euglenaceae
Gymnodinium ? *roseostigma*	*Euglena* sp.
Gymnodinium ? *aurantium*	DIVISION PROCARYOTA
Gymnodinium ? *simplex*	Class Cyanophyceae
Gymnodinium ? *arcticum*	*Cyanophyceae* sp.
Gymnodinium ? *punctatum*	

Source: Watling et al. (1979).

TABLE 5.21.   *Algal Species Collected from Benthic shoreline Habitats Along the Delaware Bay Western Shore, Slightly to the South of the Bay Mouth*

DIVISION CYANOPHYTA	*Lyngbya aestuarii*
Class Cyanophyceae	*Lyngbya confervoides*
Order Chroococcales	*Lyngbya semiplena*
Family Entophysalidaceae	*Microcoleus chthonoplastes*
Entophysalis deusta	*Oscillatoria laetevirens*
Order Nostocales	*Oscillatoria princeps*
Family Rivulariaceae	*Spirulina subsalsa*
Calothrix crustacea	*Porphyrosiphon splendida*
Family Oscillatoriaceae	*Schizothrix calcicola*

Continued

TABLE 5.21. (*Continued*)

DIVISION CHLOROPHYTA
Class Ulothricophyceae
Order Ulothrichales
Family Ulotrichaccac
Ulothrix flacca
Family Chaetophoraceae
Pilinia rimosa
Order Ulvales
Family Ulvaceae
Enteromorpha intestinalis
Enteromorpha linza
Enteromorpha marginata
Enteromorpha prolifera
Blidingia minima
Percursaria percursa
Ulva lactuca var. *latissima*
Ulva lactuca var. *rigida*
Order Siphonocladales
Family Cladophoraceae
Chaetomorpha aerea
Cladophora albida
Cladophora crystalline
Cladophora expansa
Cladophora flexuosa
Rhizoclonium kerneri
Urospora collabens
Urospora penicilliformis
Family Bryopsidaceae
Bryopsis hypnoides
Bryopsis plumosa
DIVISION XANTHOPHYTA
Order Heterosiphonales
Family Vaucheriaceae
Vaucheria piloboloides
DIVISION PHAEOPHYTA
Class Phaeosporeae
Order Ectocarpales
Family Ectocarpaceae
Ectocarpus confervoides
Ectocarpus faciculatus
Ectocarpus tomentosus
Pylaiella littoralis
Sorocarpus micromorus
Order Chordariales
Family Ralfsiaceae
Ralfsia verrucosa
Family Elachisteaceae
Elachistea fucicola
Family Chordariaceae
Leathesia difformis

Order Punctariales
Family Punctariaceae
Punctaria plantaginea
Petalonia fascia
Scytosiphon lomentaria
Order Fucales
Family Fucaceae
Ascophyllum nodosum
Fucus edentatus
Fucus spiralis
Fucus vesiculosus
Fucus vesiculosus var. *laterifructus*
Fucus vesiculosus var. *sphaerocarpus*
Fucus vesiculosus var. *spiralis*
Family Sargassaceae
Sargassum hystrix var. *buxifolium*
DIVISION RHODOPHYTA
Class Bangidae
Order Bangiales
Family Bangiaceae
Bangia fuscopurpurea
Porphyra umbilicalis
Order Gigartinales
Family Solieriaceae
Agardhiella tenera
Family Hypneaceae
Hypnea musciformis
Family Gracilariaceae
Gracilaria verrucosa
Gracilaria foliifera
Family Phyllophoraceae
Phyllophora membranifolia
Family Gigartinaceae
Chondrus crispus
Order Ceramiales
Family Ceramiaceae
Callithamnion baileyi
Ceramium fastigiatum
Ceramium strictum
Ceramium diaphanum
Ceramium rubrum
Pleonosporium borreri
Spermothamnion turneri var. *variabile*
Family Rhodomelaceae
Chondria tenuissima
Polysiphonia harveyi
Polysiphonia fibrillosa
Polysiphonia subtilissima
Polysiphonia denudata
Polysiphonia nigrescens

Source: After Zaneveld (1972).

a significant percent of the zooplankton. Crab zoeae were very abundant in early summer. In the summer, the dominant surface and bottom zooplankter, *Acartia tonsa*, was occasionally replaced by *Pseudodiaptomus coronatus*. *Cyphonautes* larvae (ectoprocts) appeared in early August and disappeared by late October. In the fall most characteristic zooplankton species were *Oikopleura* sp. and *Paracalanus* spp. Polychaete larvae were found in low numbers in all seasons. There appeared to be three major peaks of zooplankton in the Delaware, which was different from more northern estuaries, where bimodal peaks in biomass occurred (Maurer et al., 1978).

Benthos. The invertebrates may be divided into groups according to habitat (Maurer, 1974; Kinner et al., 1974): near the mouth of the bay and within the bay. Near the mouth of the bay (Kinner et al., 1974), Arthropoda represent 35.2% of the invertebrate species, Annelida 22.8%, Mollusca 20.9%, Ectoprocta 10.4%, and the remaining phyla (Cnidaria, Rhynchocoela, Echinodermata, Platyhelminthes) 10.4%. In terms of numbers of individuals, the Mollusca compose 76.5% of the fauna. The most common molluscan species are *Tellina agilis*, *Gemma gemma*, and *Nucula proxima*, which composed 65.2% of individuals collected.

Near the mouth of the bay, the soft bottom (greater than 50% silt-clay) was dominated by *Nucula proxima* and *Heteromastus filiformis*. *Yoldia limatula*, *Cerebratulus lacteus*, and *Ampelisca abdita* were frequent. In mud that was high in clay content, *Petricola pholadiformis* was found. In sandy bottoms, *P. wigleyi* and *Trichophoxus epistomus* were the important species, and in the transitional zone between sand and mud, *Gemma gemma*, *Cardita borealis*, *Ampelisca verrilli*, and *T. agilis* are most common.

Oyster bed communities were better developed in the New Jersey side than on the Delaware side of the bay, but both areas contained many species associated in oyster beds. Studies by Maurer and Watling (1973) showed that the main associates of oysters include the coelenterates, *Aiptasimorpha luciae*, *Diadumene leucolena*, *Garveia franciscana*, *Obelia* spp., *Sertularia argentea*, and *Tubularia crocea*; the molluscs, *Crepidula fornicata*, *C. plana*, *C. convexa*, *Mytilus edulis*, and *Amygdalum papyria*; the polychaetes, *Sabellaria vulgaris*, *Hydroides dianthus*, and *Polydora websteri*; the amphipods, *Cerapus tubularis*, *Corophium acherusicum*, and *C. insidiosum*; the barnacles, *Balanus eburneus* and *B. improvisus*; the ectoprocts, *Membranipora tenuis* and *Conopeum tenuissimum*; and the tunicate, *Molgula manhattensis*. These sessile organisms attacted a fauna that used them for attachment or food, including the nemerteans, *Micrura rubra* and *Zygeupolia rubens*; the nudibranchs, *Tergipes despectus* and *Eubranchus pallidus*; the polychaetes, *Eumida sanguinea* and *Eteone heteropoda*; the amphipods, *Paraceprella tenuis* and *Cymadusa compta*; and the pycnogonid, *Callipallene brevirostris*.

Animals finding shelter in the crevices between shells or in the deeper parts of the oyster bed included the bivalves, *Petricola pholadiformis* and *Mysella planulata*; the xanthid crabs, *Panopeus herbsti* and *Eurypanopeus depressus*; the isopod, *Edotea triloba*; the amphipod, *Parapleustes* sp.; and the polychaete, *Nereis succinea*.

The boring sponge, *Cliona celata*, and a polychaete, *Polydora websteri*, actively burrowed into oyster shells. Active predators of adult oysters, spat, and other molluscs included the gastropods, *Uroxalpinx cinerea*, *Eupleura caudata*, *Busycon carica*, *B. canaliculatum*, *Polinices duplicata*, and *P. immaculata*; the xanthid crabs; the blue crabs, *Callinectes sapidus*; the flatworm, *Stylochus ellipticus*; and the oyster cracker fish, *Opsanus tau*. The oyster crab, *Pinnotheres ostreum*, and the pyramidellid snails, *Odostomia impressa* and *Turbonilla interrupta*, were also oyster pests.

Organisms found in the substrate between oysters, or in the mud underneath them, included the polychaetes, *Scoloplos fragilis*, *Glycera dibranchiata*, and *Heteromastus filiformis*; the bivalves, *Mercenaria mercenaria*, *Lyonsia hyalina*, *Tellina agilis*, *Mulinia lateralis*, *Solen viridis*, *Tagelus divisus*, and *Macoma balthica*; the hermit crab, *Pagurus longicarpus*; the horseshoe crab, *Limulus polyphemus*; the naked goby, *Gobisoma bosci*; and the northern pipefish, *Sygnathus fuscus*.

Organisms straying onto the oyster bed include the marsh grass molluscs, *Modiolus demissus*, *Melampus bidentatus*, and *Littorina irrorata*; the polychaete, *Hypaniola grayi*; the amphipod, *Ampelisca abdita*; and the gastropod, *Nassarius obsoletus*, from the mud flats. The gastropod, *Nassarius vibex*, and the polychaete, *Pectinaria gouldii*, may have strayed in from the sandy beaches. Two shrimp, *Neomysis americana* and *Crangon septemspinosa*, are vagile transients which sometimes lived semipermanently on oyster beds. The blue crab, *Callinectes sapidus*, was also a temporary inhabitant, in addition to being an oyster predator. The diversity of this benthic community associated with oysters seemed to decrease as the salinity decreases.

The community associated with the hard clam beds included large whelks, *Busycon carica* and *B. canaliculatum*; sea star, *Asterias forbes*; horseshoe crab, *Limulus polyphemus*; rock crab, *Cancer irroratus*; and spider crab, *Libinia emarginata*. The horseshoe crab, *Limulus polyphemus*, served as a substrate for smaller invertebrates, *Mytilus edulis*, *Crepidula plana*, *C. convexa*, *C. fornicata*, *Conopeum tennuissimum*, *Membranipora tenuis*, and *Sabellaria vulgaris*. The hermit crabs, *Pagurus longicarpus* and *P. pollicaris*, used empty whelk shells as habitats. Hyroids, *Sertularia argenta*, *Garveia franciscana*, *Obelia* spp., and *Tubularia crocea*, attached to dead clam shells, which contained many amphipod crustaceans, *Gammarus mucronatus*, *Jassa falcata*, *Parapleustes* sp., and *Caprella* spp., and polychaete worms, *Nereis succinea*, *Eteone heteropoda*, and *Harmothoe extenuata*. In addition, large populations ($200 \, m^{-2}$) of the bivalve, *Ensis directus*, were found in sandy mud (20 to 30% silt-clay) between the clams (Keck et al., 1973).

Exposed beaches in Delaware Bay and New Jersey normally were home to highly specialized species which were excellent burrowers. Haustoriid amphipods ($100 \, m^{-2}$); polychaete worms; the mole crab, *Emerita talpoida*; ($50 \, m^{-2}$); the jumping clam, *Donax fossor*; *Nephtys* spp.; and *Scolelepis squamata* inhabited the exposed beaches. Both the New Jersey and Delaware coasts supported beach hoppers, *Talorchestia megalophthalma*, along the drift line together with some marine insects. The uppermost portions of the beach were occupied by the ghost crab, *Oxypode quadrata*, which were active at night in isolated beach areas.

Many beaches along Delaware Bay are protected from wave action. Examples of protected beaches are the Cape May Flats, Cape Henlopen Flat, Broadkill, Slaughter, and Big Stone beaches (Figure 5.4). The protected nature of the Cape Henlopen soft-bottom area permitted an extensive infauna featuring the bivalves, *Mercenaria mercenaria* (3 m^{-2}), *Ensis directus*, *Tellina agilis*, and *Mulinia lateralis*; polychaetes, *Hetermostus filiformis* (25 m^{-2}), *Diopatra cuprea*, *Scolecolepides viridis* (50 m^{-2}), *Scoloplos fragilis*, and *Pectinaria gouldi*; nemerteans, *Micrura rubra* and *Cerebratulus lacteus*; and the acorn worm, *Saccoglossus kowalevskii* (20 m^{-2}). During the summer the algae, *Ulva lactuca* and *Enteromorpha* sp., and shells constitute the substrate for epifaunal species such as the amphipod, *Gammarus mucronatus*; snails, *Crepidula fornicata*, *C. convexa*, and *C. plana*; and polychaetes, *Polydora ligni* and *Hydroides dianthus*. The mud snail, *Nassarius obsoletus*, was particularly characteristic of certain portions of the Cape Henlopen Flat, where it fed on surface diatoms and dead organisms. The horseshoe crab, *Limulus polyphemus*, found these protected sand beaches important for laying eggs that incubate in the hot sun.

The lobster, *Homarus americanus*, occurred between November and April in the deep channel between Old Bare Shoal and Lower Middle Shoal for a distance of 8 miles. It preferred hard sand or, if present, a rocky substrate. The largest numbers have been caught in April and the largest in size caught in December (Maurer, 1977).

Organisms using jetties as a habitat formed associations according to exposure. The most exposed regions developed associations of isopods; gastropods, *Littorina littorea* and *L. saxatilis*; and during the summer months, possibly Diptera larvae. The next zone afforded the maximum development of the barnacle, *Balanus balanoides*. Below this a zone of blue mussels, *Mytilus edulis*, occurred associated with the amphipods, *Jassa falcata*, *Hyale plumulosa*, and *Elasmopus laevis*. In the lowest zone were the sea anemone, *Metridium senile*; the red beard sponge, *Microciona prolifera*; and the sea star, *Asterias forbesi*. Moving up and down with the tides were the spider crab, *Libinia emarginata*; mud crabs, *Eurypanopeus depressus* and *Neopanope texana sayi*; the blue crab, *Callinectes sapidus*; and the rock crab, *Cancer irroratus*.

In the Delaware estuary, the number of species and number of individuals usually decreased with lower salinities and varied with the type of sediment (Table 5.22). The decline in numbers of species and numbers of individuals was sharpest between the mesohaline and oligohaline reaches. The average population density in the mesohaline and oligohaline area of the estuary was 722 individuals m^{-2}, which was one to two orders of magnitude lower than in many temperate estuaries (Table 5.23) and may have been the result of industrial and municipal pollution coupled with physical disturbances such as dredging. The lack of suitable substrate for attachment of macroalgae affected a range of organisms. Macroalgae contributed inorganic matter to filter feeders and provided shelter and habitats for many invertebrates. In general, the benthic fauna consisted

TABLE 5.22. *Distribution by Taxon per Sediment Type in Terms of Density, Wet Weight, and Dry Weight*

	Mud	Muddy Sand	Sand	Total
		Density		
Polychaeta	535	274	43	852
Mollusca	82	395	155	632
Amphipoda	8065	8201	113	16,379
Total	8682	8870	311	17,863
		Wet Weight (no. m^{-2})		
Polychaeta	22.5	14.1	2.46	39.1
Mollusca	3.76	50.8	2.37	56.9
Amphipoda	5.44	5.5	0.26	11.2
Total	31.7	70.4	5.09	107.2
		Dry Weight ($g\,m^{-2}$)		
Polychaeta	5.89	4.49	1.0	11.38
Mollusca	0.16	3.61	0.16	3.93
Amphipoda	0.94	1.09	0.13	2.16
Total	6.99	9.19	1.29	17.47

Source: Maurer (1977).

of 45% deposit feeders, 24.8% suspension feeders, 18.3% carnivores, 10.7% omnivores, 0.6% ectoparasites, and 0.6% commensals. Typically, the highest diversity of invertebrates occurred along the New Jersey side of the Delaware Bay (Maurer et al., 1978).

Marshlands and Tributaries

Delaware marshes. Although some papers have been written concerning the use of polyhaline marshes as spawning and nursery grounds, relatively little has been written about the species that compose the aquatic communities in these areas. Cursory studies have been made of many of these marshes by the Academy of Natural Sciences of Philadelphia.

Simons and Mahon Rivers. In the marshes in the vicinity of Simons and Mahon rivers, the more common zooplankton were copepod nauplii and the crustaceans, *Tachidius littoralis*, *Cyclops vernalis*, and *Bosmina longirostris*. The benthic invertebrates were the oyster, *Crassostrea virginica*; the anthropods, *Gammarus* spp. and *Corophium lacustre*; the isopod, *Probopyrus pandalicola*; and the decapods, *Crangon septemspinosa*, *Palaemonetes pugio*, *Callinectes sapidus*, and *Rhithropanopeus harrisii*. The common or frequent fishes taken in this area were *Fundulus heteroclitus*, *Menidia menidia*, and *Leiostomus xanthurus*. The eel, *Anguilla rostrata*, and the fish, *Bairdiella chrysura*, *Opsanus tau*, *Cynoscion regalis*, and *Morone americana*, were also collected here.

TABLE 5.23. *Average Density of Benthic Invertebrates Along the Northeast Coast of the United States*

Location	Average Density (no. m^{-2})	Sieve Size (mm)
Buzzards Bay, Mass., Station R	9,000	0.2
Pocasset River, Mass.	67,000	0.21
Sally Cove, Rehoboth Bay, Del.	20,000	0.25
Long Island Sound	16,000	0.29–2.0
Penobscot River Estuary, Me.	3,600	0.5
Buzzards Bay, Mass., all stations	4,000	0.5
Charlestown Pond, R.I.	30,000	0.5
Indian River Bay, Del.	6,000	0.5
Rehoboth Bay, Del.	900	0.8
Indian River Bay, Del.	3,800	0.8
Cape Cod Bay, Mass.	15,000	1.0
Mystic River, Conn.	3,000	1.0
Shallow Shelf off Long Island, N.Y.	700	1.0–2.0
Moriches Bay, N.Y.	1,300	1.0
Mouth of Delaware Bay	100	1.0
Rehoboth Bay, Del.	4,200	1.0
Indian River Bay, Del.	1,000	1.0
Indian River Bay, Del.	7,400	1.0
Chesapeake Bay eel grass beds	14,000	1.0
Hampton Roads, Va.	2,394	1.0
Great Bay, N.J.	≅ 5,000	1.1
Barnegat Bay, N.J.	600	1.5

Source: Ralph (1977).

Obeng-Asamoa (1975) studied the diatoms from pools and marshes in the vicinity of Port Mahon. He found that *Nitzschia filiformis* and *N. frustulum* occurred frequently throughout the study period. A list of the species that he identified from this area are given in Table 5.24.

Murderkill and St. Jones marshes.   The algae in the marshes associated with the Murderkill and St. Jones rivers consisted of diatoms and blue-green and green algae. Ralph (1977) studied, in some detail, the algae associated with the St. Jones marshes and found that the blue-green algae, *Microcoleus lyngbyaceus* and *Schizothrix calcicola*, were important constituents of all collections. *Schizothrix arenaria* formed mats in among the *Spartina*. These subaerial mats were as much as several millimeters thick and extended over the bare sediments. Microscopic masses of *Microcoleus lyngbyaceus* and *Schizothrix calcicola* may have over-wintered in *S. arenaria* mats on the dead culms of *Spartina alterniflora*. Certain green algae also produced subaerial mats over the St. Jones Marsh sediment (Table 5.25). They were *Chaetomorpha aerea*, *Rhizoclonium riparium* var. *implexum*, *Ulothrix flacca*, *V. thuretti*, and *V. piloboloides*. As the blue-green algae mats seemed to exclude most secondary species, the mats formed by the green algae

TABLE 5.24. *Diatoms Found at Port Mahon, Delaware*

DIVISION CHRYSOPHYTA
Class Bacillariophyceae
Order Centrales
Suborder Discineae
Family Coscinodiscaceae
Subfamily Melosiroideae
Melosira ambiqua
M. nummuloides
Subfamily Skeletonemoideae
Skeletonema costatum
Subfamily Coscinodiscoideae
Actinoptychus senarius
Coscinodiscus excentricus
C. curvatulus
C. lineatus
C. marginatus
C. nodulifer
C. rothii
C. subtilis
Coscinosira cestrupli
Cyclotella bodanica
C. glomerata
C. meneghiniana
C. striata
Suborder Araphidineae
Family Fragilariaceae
Subfamily Fragilarioideae
Opephora pacifica
Raphoneis affinis
R. crystallina
R. fasciculata
R. gailloni
R. surirella
R. tenera
R. ulna
Staurosira mutabilis
Thalassionema nitzschioides
Suborder Monoraphidineae
Family Achnanthaceae
Subfamily Cocconeioideae
Cocconeis disculoides
Subfamily Achnanthoideae
Achnanthes brevipes
A. conspicua
A. hauckiana
A. longipes
Suborder Biraphidineae
Family Naviculaceae
Subfamily Naviculoideae
Caloneis westii
Gyrosigma fasciola

G. peisonis
Mastogloia pumila
Navicula abunda
N. accomoda
N. arenaria
N. atlantica
N. barberi
N. bremensis
N. cancellata
N. cincta
N. clementis
N. crucicula
N. cryptocephala
N. diserta
N. elegans
N. heufleri
N. gracilis
N. gregaria
N. halophila
N. halophiloides
N. lanceolata
N. meniscus
N. mutica
N. peregrina
N. plicata
N. protracta
N. pupula
N. pygmaea
N. rhynchocephala
N. rostellata
N. salinarum
N. secreta v. *apiculata*
N. serians
N. subrostellata
Scoliopleura sp.
Stauroneis amphioxys
S. salina
S. spicula
Subfamily Amphiproroideae
Amphiprora alata
A. conspicua
A. paludosa
A. similis
A. suirelloides
Family Gomphonemaceae
Subfamily Gomphonemoideae
Gomphonema parvulum
Family Cymbellaceae
Subfamily Cymbelloideae
Amphora acutiuscula
A. delicatissima

Continued

TABLE 5.24.   (*Continued*)

A. eunotia	*N. filiformis*
A. exigua	*N. fonticola*
A. granulata	*N. frustulum*
A. lineolata	*N. granulata*
A. macilenta	*N. hybridaeformis*
A. proteus	*N. hugarica*
A. quadrata	*N. intermedia*
A. sancti-martiali	*N. levidensis*
A. subangularis	*N. longa*
Family Epithemiaceae	*N. microcephala*
Subfamily Epithemioideae	*N. minutissima*
Denticula subtilis	*N. palea*
Rhopalodia musculus	*N. polaris*
Family Nitzschiaceae	*N. pseudohybrida*
Subfamily Nitzschioideae	*N. punctata*
Nitzschia acuminata	*N. sigma*
N. amphibia	*N. thermalis*
N. calida	*N. tropica*
N. commutata	*N. vermicularis*
N. dubia	*P. australis*

Source: Obeng-Asamoa (1975).

and yellow-green algae provided habitats for many microscopic forms, including some of the blue-green algae. There were many different species on or in these green and yellow-green algal mats, which were often associated with the culms of *Spartina patens* and *Distichlis spicata*.

In Delaware marsh ponds and pools where there was an influx of fresh water, submerged mats of the blue-green alga, *Oscillatoria princeps*, were found. The blue-green algae, *Microcoleus lyngbyaceus*, *Schizothrix arenaria*, and *S. calcicola*, also occurred in ponds and pools along with occasional blooms of *Anacystis montana* and *Calothrix crustacea* (Ralph, 1977). A list of the algae found in these marshes is given in Table 5.25.

The zooplankton found in this area were copepod nauplii and *Scottolana canadensis* (Walton and Patrick, 1973). Frequent to common benthic invertebrates were hydromedusa; hydroids, *Nassarius* spp.; the oyster, *Crassostrea virginica*; the isopod, *Neomysis americana*; the decapods, *Palaemonetes pugio*, *P. intermedius*, and *Crangon septemspinosa*; and the crab, *Callinectes sapidus*. Fish common to the area were *Morone americana*, *Menidia menidia*, and *M. beryllina*. The eel, *Anguilla rostrata*, and the fish, *Cyprinodon variegatus*, *Dorosoma cepedianum*, *Syngnathus fuscus*, *Gobiosoma bosci*, *Pseudopleuronectes americanus*, and *Fundulus majalis*, were rarely collected.

Cedar Creek–Mispillion.   A variety of diatoms were found in the Cedar Creek and Mispillion marshes. Among the more common were *Stephanopyxis costatum*, *Nitzschia palea*, and *Navicula secreta* v. *apiculata*. Also present and more abundant in Mispillion Marsh were *Melosira italica*, *Ditylium intricatum*, and *Asterionella formosa* (Walton and Patrick, 1973). Some blue-green algae belonging to the genus *Oscillatoria* were also found.

The protozoans in the benthic community associated with the algae were the holotrich, *Coleps* sp., and the amoeba, *Difflugia*. The zooplankton consisted of copepod nauplii, *Scottolana canadensis*, and some *Acartia clausi*. The decapods, *Palaemonetes pugio*, *P. intermedius*, *P. vulgaris*, *Callinectes sapidus*, and *Uca pugnax*, were frequent to common. The most common fish were the anchovy, *Anchoa mitchilli* and *Menidia menidia*. Fish found more rarely were *Fundulus heteroclitus*, *F. majalis*, *Morone americana*, *Bairdiella chrysura*, *Leiostomus xanthurus*, *Pogonias cromis*, *Cynoscion regalis*, and *Gobiosoma bosic*, and the eel, *Anguilla rostrata*.

Broadkill and Canary Creek.   The Canary Creek Marsh near Lewes, Delaware has been studied as extensively as any marsh in this reach. The species of green and blue-green algae found in this marsh are given in Table 5.25. No extensive study was made of the diatoms, but observations indicate that most diatoms belong either to the genus *Navicula* or *Nitzschia*. Other algae present on the surface of the sediments were species of *Oscillatoria* and are set forth by Ralph (1977). *Microcoleus lyngbyaceus*, *Schizothrix calcicola*, and *S. arenaria* formed subaerial mats over the sediments of the marshlands, as did the green and yellow–green algae, *Chaetomorpha aerea*, *Rhizoclonium riparium*, and *Vaucheria piloboloides*. *Ulothrix flacca* was also found in subaerial mats. Scattered here and there was the sea lecttuce (*Ulva lactuca*).

Among the protozoa, the amoeba, *Difflugia* sp., was fairly common. Nauplii of the copepods, *Acartia clausi* and *Pseudodiaptomus coronatus*, were also in the zooplankton. The most common benthic invertebrates were the decapods, *Palaemonetes pugio*, *Callinectes sapidus*, and *Crangon septemspinosa*. The decapods, *P. intermedius* and *P. vulgaris*, were found frequently. The mollusc, *Modiolus demissus*, was also common and worms belonging to the Oligochaeta were collected frequently. The most common fish in Canary Creek and the Broadkill were *Menidia menidia* and *M. beryllina*.

New Jersey marshes.   Fauna and flora of the marshes in the New Jersey area are not as well known, but a short study by the Academy of Natural Sciences (Walton and Patrick, 1973) at the Fortescue Marsh in 1973 gave information on the species present in this area. The planktonic diatoms were mainly *Stephanopyxis costatum* and *Thalassionema nitzschioides*. The amoeba, *Difflugia* sp., was quite common. The gastrotrich, *Chaetonotus* sp., was also fairly common. The zooplankton consisted largely of Foraminifera, copepod nauplii, and veliger larvae. The benthic invertebrates consisted of hydromedusae; the polychaetes, *Glycera dibranchiata* and *Nassarius* sp.; and the mollusc, *Modiolus demissus*. The most common fish was *Menidia menidia*. The eel, *Anguilla rostrata*, and the fish, *Fundulus heteroclitus*, *Bairdiella chrysura*, and *Pseudopleuronectes americanus*, were rare.

In the marshes surrounding Maurice and Dividing creeks, the more common benthic diatoms were *Nitzschia filiformis* and *Thalassiothrix* sp. The common dinoflagellates were *Peridinium* sp. and *Glenodinium* sp. The zooplankton

TABLE 5.25. *Cyanophycean and Macroscopic Eukaryotic Algae Observed in Two Marshes on the Western Shore of Delaware Bay*

Data for Barker's Landing on St. Jones Marsh, Kent County, Delaware, 1971–1973

	Low Marsh						Pannes and Pools						High Marsh					
	June	July	Aug.	Sept.	Oct.	Jan.	June	July	Aug.	Sept.	Oct.	Jan.	June	July	Aug.	Sept.	Oct.	Jan.
Primary species																		
Microcoleus lyngbyaceus	−	+	+++	++	++	+	++	++	++	++	++	++	+++	+++	+++	+++	++	++
Schizothrix calcicola	−	+	++	++	+	−	++	++	++	++	+	+	+	+	+	++	++	−
Oscillatoria princeps	+	+	++	+	−	−	+++	++++	+++++	+++++	+	−	++	++	+	−	−	+
Secondary species																		
Anacystis dimidiata	−	−	+	+	+	−	−	+	−	−	−	−	+	++	+	−	−	−
Anacystis montana	−	−	−	−	+	+	−	+	−	−	+	+	+	+	+	+	+	++
Arthrospira neapolitana	−	−	++	++	−	−	−	−	−	−	−	−	++	++	+	+	−	+
Minor species	0	1	5	2	3	2	2	6	5	2	1	1	9	4	1	1	1	2
Macroscopic algae																		
Chaetomorpha aerea	−	−	−	−	−	+++	−	−	−	−	−	+++	−	−	−	−	−	−
Enteromorpha sp.	−	−	−	−	−	−	−	−	−	−	−	−	++	++	−	−	−	−
Rhizoclonium riparium	−	−	−	++	++	−	−	−	−	−	−	−	−	−	−	−	−	−
Ulothrix tenuissima	−	−	−	.	−	++	++	−	−	−	++	++	−	−	−	−	−	+++
Vaucheria thuretii	−	++	++	−	−	−	+++	+++	+++++	+++	++	−	+++	+++	+++	+++	+++	−
Total species	1	5	11	8	8	6	6	12	9	6	6	5	17	12	7	6	5	6

Data for Green Hill on Canary Creek Marsh, Lewes, Sussex County, Delaware, 1971–1973

Low Marsh

	Oct.	Mar.	June	July	Aug.	Sept.	Oct.	Nov.	Jan.
Primary species									
Microcoleus lyngbyaceus	++	++	++++	+++++++	++++++	+++	++	+	+
Schizothrix calcicola	++	++	++++	+++ −	+++	+++	++	−	+
Schizothrix arenaria	−	−	−	+++	−	+	−	++	−
Secondary species									
Spirulina subsalsa	+	−	+	−	−	+	−	−	+
Anacystis montana	−	−	−	−	+	−	+	−	+
Arthrospira neapolitana	++	−	++	−	−	+	−	−	−
Anabaena torulosa	−	−	−	+	+	−	−	−	−
Anacystis dimidiata	−	−	−	−	−	+	−	−	+
Porphyrosiphon notarisii	−	−	++	+++	++	−	−	−	−
Minor species	0	0	0	0	0	1	2	1	0
Macroscopic algae									
Chaetomorpha aerea	−+++++ / −++								+++++ / +
Enteromorpha sp.									
Rhizoclonium riparium	−	−	−	++++++++	++++++++	++++++++	−	−	−
Sphacelaria sp.									
Ulothrix flacca	−++	−	−	−	−	−	−	−	+++
Ulothrix implexa									
Vaucheria piloboloides									
Total species	4	6	6	3	5	8	6	4	7

Pannes and Pools

	Oct.	Mar.	June	July	Aug.	Sept.	Oct.	Nov.	Jan.
Primary species									
Microcoleus lyngbyaceus	++	++	++++	+++++++	+++++++	++	++	+	+
Schizothrix calcicola	++	++	++++	+++++++	++++	++	++	+	+++
Schizothrix arenaria	+++++++	+++	++++	+++++++	++++	+++++	+++	+	+++
Secondary species									
Spirulina subsalsa	+	+	−	+	−	+	+	−	+
Anacystis montana	−	−	−	−	−	+	−	+	+
Arthrospira neapolitana	−	−	−	−	++	−	−	−	−
Anabaena torulosa	−	+	−	−	+	++	+	+	+
Anacystis dimidiata	−	−	−	−	−	+	−	+	−
Porphyrosiphon notarisii	−	−	−	++	−	+	−	+	−
Minor species	0	0	0	0	1	2	7	3	3
Macroscopic algae	(Macroscopic eukaryotic algae not observed.)								
Total species	4	5	3	5	6	10	13	11	9

High Marsh

	Mar.	June	July	Aug.	Sept.	Oct.	Nov.	Jan.
Primary species								
Microcoleus lyngbyaceus	++	+++	+++++++	+++++++	+++++	++	++	++
Schizothrix calcicola	−	+++	+++++++	+++++	− +	+	+++	+++
Schizothrix arenaria	−	+++	+++++++	+++++	− − +	++	+++	+
Secondary species								
Spirulina subsalsa	+	+	+	++	+	−	−	+
Anacystis montana	−	−	+	++	+	−	−	−
Arthrospira neapolitana	+	++	++	++	+	−	++	+
Anabaena torulosa	+	+	+	−	+	−	+	+
Anacystis dimidiata	+	−	−	−	+	−	−	+
Porphyrosiphon notarisii	−	++	+++	−	−	−	+	−
Minor species	0	2	1	0	2	0	1	3
Macroscopic algae								
Chaetomorpha aerea	+++++++ / ++					+++++++ / −		+++++++ / −
Rhizoclonium riparium	−	−	+++++++	+++++++	+++++++	+++++++	+++	−
Ulothrix flacca	+++++ / −	−	−	−	−	+++++ / −	+++ / ++	+++ / ++
Vaucheria piloboloides	−	−	++	+++++++	+++++++	+++++++	+++++++	+++++++
Total species	7	10	10	7	13	6	11	15

Source: Ralph (1977).

[1] Species contributed to formation of discrete subaerial mats over the surface of sediments.

+ + + +, very abundant; + + +, abundant but not dominant; + +, frequent and infrequent; +, − not observed.

consisted mainly of the amoeba, *Difflugia* sp.; the rotifer, *Brachionus plicatilis*; the cladoceran, *Bosmina longirostris*; and the copepod, *Scottolana canadensis*. The benthic invertebrates were the hydroid, *Aurelia aurita*; the polychaetes, *Nereis succinea* and *Nassarius* sp.; the mollusc, *Modiolus demissus*; and the crabs, *Callinectes sapidus* and *Rhithropanopeus harrisii*. The fish that were frequent to common were *Menidia menidia*, *Fundulus heteroclitus*, and *Leiostomus xanthurus*. *Anchoa mitchilli*, *Sygnathus fuscus*, and *Morone americana* were rare.

In Dennis Creek, which drains the marshes in this area, the dominant diatoms were *Thalassionema nitzschioides* and *Chaetoceros danicus*. Elsewhere there were scattered species belonging to the genus *Nitzschia* and *Navicula*. The dinoflagellate, *Peridinium* sp., was common, and some blue-green algae were observed. The zooplankton consisted of the amoeba, *Difflugia* sp.; nauplii and adults of the copepods, *Tachidius littoralis* and *Acartia tonsa*; and the larvae of polychaetes. Benthic invertebrates that were frequent to common were hydromedusa; the polychaete, *Nereis succinea*; the decapod, *Palemonetes pugio*; and the crabs, *Callinectes sapidus* and *Thithropanopeus harrisii*. The most common fish in Dennis Creek was *Fundulus heteroclitus*. Also frequent were *Cynoscion regalis*, *Gobiosoma bosci*, *Menidia menidia*, and *Opsanus tau*. Rarer were *Pogonias cromis*, *Menidia americana*, *Cyprinodon variegatus*, and *Trinectes maculatus* (Walton and Patrick, 1973).

CHESAPEAKE BAY AND ITS TRIBUTARIES

Aquatic life in the Chesapeake Bay has been studied on many occasions, but few studies have included algae and most of the major groups of animals, identified to the species level. The best examples of this type of study are those made in the Chesapeake Bay near Calvert Cliffs, the Patuxent River in the vicinity of Chalk Point, the Potomac River in the vicinity of Route 301, and in the mouth of the York River estuary (ANSP 1957, 1970a, b, 1971).

Salinity. The salinity of Chesapeake Bay varies in a more or less regular way from the concentration of the Susquehanna River at its head to nearly that of full seawater at its mouth in Virginia (Pritchard, 1971). The surface salinity pattern is one of gradual increase in salinity from about 1 to 3 ppt near the head of the bay to around 22 to 25 ppt near the mouth, where the gradient of increase toward seawater salinity of around 30 ppt becomes very steep. The pattern of surface salinity changes little from season to season, but the actual values are lowest in the spring when influx of fresh water is greatest. At the 12-m depth, tongues of high (up to 16 ppt)-salinity water extend northward up the bay and into all the major tributaries. Northward extensions of high salinity at depth are greatest in the fall.

Patuxent and Potomac Rivers

In the areas where studies were carried out, the salinity values of the Patuxent and Potomac rivers were very similar. Silica was higher in the Patuxent; ammonia was also higher than silica. The greatest difference was seen in the phosphate

(text continues on page 379)

TABLE 5.26. *Species of the Chesapeake and Tributary Communities*

Species	Patuxent River: Salinity 0.0054 ppt Fresh Water	Potomac River: Salinity 7.5–7.7 ppt Mesohaline	Patuxent River: Salinity 8.9 ppt Mesohaline	Chesapeake Bay: Salinity 13–15 ppt Mesohaline	York River: Salinity 18.7–20.1 ppt Polyhaline
DIVISION BACILLARIOPHYTA					
Class Bacillariophyceae					
Order Fragilariales					
Family Fragilariaceae					
Grammatophora marina				×	×
G. perpusilla					×
Licmophora abbreviata				×	
L. debilis					×
L. gracilis					×
L. lyngbyei					×
Diatoma tenuis				×	
Fragilaria construens			×		
F. pinnata	×	×	×	×	×
F. vaucheriae	×				
F. virescens fo. *clavata*		×	×		×
Fragilaria sp.*					×
Opephora marina			×		×
O. martyii	×	×	×	×	×
O. martyii v. *baikalensis*				×	
O. pacifica					×
Cyclophora tenuis					×
Cymatosira belgica					×
Dimerogramma acutum					×
Dimerogramma sp.*					×
Rhaphoneis amphiceros var. *rhombica*					×
R. surirella					×
Raphoneis sp.*					×
Synedra affinis v. *gracilis*			×		×
S. affinis v. *parva*			×		
S. fasciculata (Ag.)		×	×		
S. fasciculata v. *parva*				×	
S. fasciculata v. *truncata*		×	×		
S. pulchella	×				
S. rumpens v. *meneghiniana*	×				
Synedra sp.*					×
Trachysphenia acuminata					×
Trachysphenia sp.*					×
Thalassiothrix nitzschioides					×
T. nitzschioides var. *javanica*					×

Continued

TABLE 5.26. (Continued)

Species	Patuxent River: Salinity 0.0054 ppt Fresh Water	Potomac River: Salinity 7.5–7.7 ppt Mesohaline	Patuxent River: Salinity 8.9 ppt Mesohaline	Chesapeake Bay: Salinity 13–15 ppt Mesohaline	York River: Salinity 18.7–20.1 ppt Polyhaline
Order Eunotiales					
Family Eunotiaceae					
Eunotogramma laeve					×
Order Achnanthales					
Family Achnanthaceae					
Cocconeis disculoides					×
C. disculus v. *minor*				×	
C. latecostata					×
C. placentula v. *euglypta*		×			×
C. placentula v. *lineata*		×		×	×
C. scutellum				×	
C. scutellum var. *ornata*					×
C. scutellum var. *parva*				×	
C. thumensis				×	
Cocconeis sp.*		×			×
Achnanthes brevipes v. *intermedia*				×	
A. coarctata var.					×
A. delicatissima				×	
A. delicatula				×	
A. hauckiana	×		×	×	×
A. hauckiana v. *rostrata*			×	×	
A. lanceolata	×			×	
A. lemmermanni				×	×
A. lemmermanni var. *obtusa*					×
A. minutissima	×				
A. montana				×	
A. pinnata				×	
Achnanthes wellsiae				×	
Achnanthes sp.*	×		×		×
Rhicosphenia curvata		×			
Order Naviculales					
Family Naviculaceae					
Amphipleura micans					×
A. parasitica					×
A. rutilans			×		×
A. rutilans var. *dillwynii*	×		×		
Anomoeoneis vitrea				×	
Capartogramma crucicula	×				
Diploneis bombus					×
D. littoralis			×		

TABLE 5.26. (*Continued*)

Species	Patuxent River: Salinity 0.0054 ppt Fresh Water	Potomac River: Salinity 7.5–7.7 ppt Mesohaline	Patuxent River: Salinity 8.9 ppt Mesohaline	Chesapeake Bay: Salinity 13–15 ppt Mesohaline	York River: Salinity 18.7–20.1 ppt Polyhaline
D. oblongella					×
D. puella	×	×	×		
D. smithii		×	×		
D. vetula var. americana					×
Diploneis sp.*					×
Gyrosigma acuminatum	×				
G. distortum			×		
G. nodiferum			×		
Mastogloia exigua			×		
M. lanceolata					×
M. pumila			×	×	×
M. pusilla					×
M. pusilla var. lineata					×
Mastogloia sp.*					×
Navicula abunda			×		×
N. agnita			×		
N. amphipleuroides					×
N. aspera var. minor					×
N. bicephala	×				
N. capitata v. hungarica	×	×	×		
N. cincta		×			
N. cincta				×	
N. clamans				×	
N. complanata			×		
N. complanatula				×	
N. contenta var. parallela					×
N. contenta var. biceps	×				
N. cryptocephala	×			×	
N. cryptocephala v. veneta				×	
N. diserta	×	×	×	×	
N. expansa			×		
N. fenestrella					×
N. gregaria	×				
N. incomposita			×		
N. indifferens				×	
N. minima	×			×	
Navicula misella					×
N. mutica		×	×	×	
N. mutica var. cohnii	×	×	×	×.	
N. nyella		×		×	

Continued

TABLE 5.26. *(Continued)*

Species	Patuxent River: Salinity 0.0054 ppt Fresh Water	Potomac River: Salinity 7.5–7.7 ppt Mesohaline	Patuxent River: Salinity 8.9 ppt Mesohaline	Chesapeake Bay: Salinity 13–15 ppt Mesohaline	York River: Salinity 18.7–20.1 ppt Polyhaline
N. oculiformis		×			
N. ostrearia					×
N. pavillardi				×	×
N. pennata					×
N. peregrina	×	×		×	
N. permitis				×	
N. plicata				×	
N. pseudony					×
N. pullus					×
N. pyugmaea				×	
N. rhyncocephala v. *germainii*	×			×	
N. rostellata		×			
N. salinarum	×			×	
N. salinicola	×		×		×
N. schroederi v. *escambia*	×				
N. scopulorum var. *belgica*					×
N. secreta v. *apiculata*	×		×	×	
N. subforcipata				×	
N. symmetrica	×			×	
N. tripunctata v. *schizonemoides*	×	×	×		×
Navicula sp.	×	×	×	×	×
Pinnularia borealis				×	×
P. elongatum				×	
Pleurosigma angulatum					×
P. angulatum v. *aestuarii*				×	
Pleurosigma salinarum		×	×		
P. salinarum v. *boyeri*				×	
Stauroneis amphoroides					×
Trachyneis aspera				×	
Amphiprora alata		×	×	×	×
A. paludosa					×
Tropidoneis lepidoptera		×			
T. lepidoptera v. *minor*				×	
Family Cymbellaceae					
Amphora acutinuscula			×		
A. angusta		×		×	×
A. angustata v. *ventricosa*				×	
A. coffeaeformis		×		×	
A. cymbelloides			×		×
A. delicatissima		×		×	
A. eunotia					×

TABLE 5.26. (Continued)

Species	Patuxent River: Salinity 0.0054 ppt Fresh Water	Potomac River: Salinity 7.5–7.7 ppt Mesohaline	Patuxent River: Salinity 8.9 ppt Mesohaline	Chesapeake Bay: Salinity 13–15 ppt Mesohaline	York River: Salinity 18.7–20.1 ppt Polyhaline
A. obtusa v. rectangulata				×	
A. ostrearea v. lineata				×	
A. ovalis			×	×	×
A. ovalis var. affinis		×		×	
A. ovalis v. pediculus				×	
A. perpusilla					×
A. sublaevis			×	×	
A. tenerrima				×	
A. tenuissima			×	×	×
A. tumida				×	
A. turgida		×	×	×	
A. veneta				×	
Amhora sp.*		×		×	×
Family Gomphonemaceae					
Gomphonema boreale var.					×
G. boreale var. minor					×
G. parvulum	×				
Gomphonema sp.*				×	
Order Epithemiales					
Family Epithemiaceae					
Denticula subtilis			×		
Rhopalodia gibberula					×
R. gibberula var. succincta					×
R. musculus			×	×	×
R. musculus var. mirabilis					×
Order Bacillariales					
Family Bacillariaceae					
Bacillaria paradoxa	×	×	×		×
Fragilariopsis pseudonana				×	
Nitzschia accomodata	×				
N. acula				×	
N. apiculata				×	
N. brittonii			×		×
N. circumsuta	×				
N. clausii	×				
N. closterium					×
N. diserta	×	×	×		
Nitzschia dissipata		×		×	×
N. dissipata v. media	×		×		
N. dubioides			×		

Continued

TABLE 5.26. (*Continued*)

Species	Patuxent River: Salinity 0.0054 ppt Fresh Water	Potomac River: Salinity 7.5–7.7 ppt Mesohaline	Patuxent River: Salinity 8.9 ppt Mesohaline	Chesapeake Bay: Salinity 13–15 ppt Mesohaline	York River: Salinity 18.7–20.1 ppt Polyhaline
N. epithemioides				×	
N. epiphytica				×	
N. fasciculata		×	×		
N. filiformis	×	×	×	×	
N. fonticola		×			×
N. frustulum	×	×	×	×	
N. frustulum var. *perminuta*	×	×	×	×	×
N. frustulum v. *perpulsilla*				×	
N. frustulum v. *subsalina*		×		×	
N. hungarica	×	×	×	×	
N. ignorata	×				
N. kuetzingiana	×	×	×	×	
N. liebethruthii	×	×	×		
N. linearis		×			
N. longissima					×
N. longissima var. *parva*					×
N. microcephala			×		
N. minutissima			×		
N. obtusa v. *scapelliformis*		×	×	×	×
N. ovalis				×	
N. palea	×		×		
N. palea var. *kuetzingiana*					×
N. paleacea			×	×	×
N. paleaformis		×			
Nitzschia panduriformis var. *minor*					×
N. parvula	×		×		
N. proxima					×
N. pseudocommunis				×	
N. pseudohybrida				×	×
N. punctata				×	
N. rhombica					×
N. rhopalodioides				×	
N. romana	×				×
N. sigma				×	
N. sigma var. *dimunuta*					×
N. sigma v. *rigidula*			×		
N. sigmaformis					×
N. sigmoidea	×			×	
N. spathulata					×
N. spathulata var.					×
N. tropica		×			

TABLE 5.26. (*Continued*)

Species	Patuxent River: Salinity 0.0054 ppt Fresh Water	Potomac River: Salinity 7.5–7.7 ppt Mesohaline	Patuxent River: Salinity 8.9 ppt Mesohaline	Chesapeake Bay: Salinity 13–15 ppt Mesohaline	York River: Salinity 18.7–20.1 ppt Polyhaline
N. tryblionella v. *debilis*	×				
N. tryblionella v. *levidensis*	×				
N. tryblionella v. *victoriae*	×				
N. vidovichii					×
Nitzschia sp.*			×	×	×
Order Surirellales					
Family Surirellaceae					
Surirella angusta	×				
S. brightwelli	×				
S. angusta		×			
S. ovata		×			
Order Coscinodiscales					
Family Coscinodiscaceae					
Melosira borreri			×		×
M. borreri var. *hispida*					×
M. distans v. *alpigena*	×				
M. granulata	×				
M. nummuloides		×	×	×	×
M. sulcata				×	
M. sulcata var. *biseriata*					×
M. sulcata var. *coronata* f. *minor*					×
Melosira sulcata f. *radiata*	×			×	
M. sulcata var. *radiolata*					×
M. varians				×	
Hyalodiscus socticus					×
Pyxidicula sp.*					×
Skeletonema costatum				×	×
Skeletonema sp.*					×
Stephanopyxis costata	×		×		
Thalassiosira sp.*		×			
Coscinodiscus decipiens					×
C. excentricus	×				
C. lacustris	×				
C. lineatus	×	×			×
C. nitidus	×				
C. pygmaeus v. *micropunctata*	×	×	×	×	×
C. radiatus					×
C. rothii	×		×		
C. rothii v. *subsalsa*	×		×		
Coscinodiscus sp.*					×

Continued

TABLE 5.26.   (Continued)

Species	Patuxent River: Salinity 0.0054 ppt Fresh Water	Potomac River: Salinity 7.5–7.7 ppt Mesohaline	Patuxent River: Salinity 8.9 ppt Mesohaline	Chesapeake Bay: Salinity 13–15 ppt Mesohaline	York River: Salinity 18.7–20.1 ppt Polyhaline
Actinoptychus campanulifer					×
A. taeniatus					×
Cyclotella aliquantula	×	×	×		×
C. antiqua				×	
C. atomus	×	×	×	×	
C. caspia	×	×		×	
C. kuetzingiana			×		×
Cyclotella meneghiniana	×		×	×	
C. meneghiniana var. *rectangulata*		×			×
C. nana				×	
C. striata	×		×	×	×
C. striata var. *bipunctata*					×
C. striata var. *subsalina*					×
Cyclotella sp.*					×
Stephanodiscus dubius	×				
Order Biddulphiales					
Family Biddulphiaceae					
Biddulphia laevis	×	×	×	×	
Family Anaulaceae					
Anaulus balticus		×		×	
Family Chaetoceraceae					
Chaetoceros gracilis				×	
DIVISION CYANOPHYTA					
Class Myxophyceae					
Order Chroococcales					
Family Chroococcaceae					
Anacystis cyanea		×			
Family Entophysalidaceae					
Entophysalis deusta		×	×	×	
Order Oscillatoriales					
Family Oscillatoriaceae					
Microcoleus lyngbyaceus	×	×	×	×	×
(= *Lyngbya aestuarii*)					
Oscillatoria lutea		×	×		
O. retzii	×				
O. submembranacea		×		×	
Schizothrix arenaria		×	×		×
S. calcicola	×	×	×	×	
S. mexicana			×	×	
S. tenerrima		×		×	
Spirulina subsalsa		×	×		

TABLE 5.26. (*Continued*)

Species	Patuxent River: Salinity 0.0054 ppt Fresh Water	Potomac River: Salinity 7.5–7.7 ppt Mesohaline	Patuxent River: Salinity 8.9 ppt Mesohaline	Chesapeake Bay: Salinity 13–15 ppt Mesohaline	York River: Salinity 18.7–20.1 ppt Polyhaline
Family Nostocaceae					
Anabaina licheniformis	×				
(= *Cylindrospermum muscicola*)					
Anabaina sp.*	×		×		
Nostoc sp.*		×		×	
Family Rivulariaceae					
Calothrix crustacea		×		×	×
C. parietina				×	
DIVISION CHLOROPHYTA					
Class Chlorophyceae					
Order Ulotrichales					
Family Ulvaceae					
Enteromorpha intestinalis					×
E. plumosa					×
E. prolifera		×	×	×	
Ulva lactuca		×	×	×	×
U. lactuca var. *latissima*					×
Family Chaetophoraceae					
Stigeoclonium lubricum	×				
Order Oedogonales					
Family Oedogoniaceae					
Oedogonium sp.*	×				
Order Cladophorales					
Family Cladophoraceae					
Cladophora flexuosa					×
C. glomerata	×				
C. gracilis		×	×	×	
Rhizoclonium hieroglyphicum	×				
R. riparium	×	×	×		
Order Zygnematales					
Family Zygnemataceae					
Spirogyra sp.*	×				
DIVISION RHODOPHYTA					
Class Rhodophyceae					
Subclass Florideae					
Order Nemalionales					
Family Chantransiaceae					
Rhodochorton rothii	×				
Order Gigartinales					
Family Solieriaceae					

Continued

TABLE 5.26. (*Continued*)

Species	Patuxent River: Salinity 0.0054 ppt Fresh Water	Potomac River: Salinity 7.5–7.7 ppt Mesohaline	Patuxent River: Salinity 8.9 ppt Mesohaline	Chesapeake Bay: Salinity 13–15 ppt Mesohaline	York River: Salinity 18.7–20.1 ppt Polyhaline
Agardhiella tenera					×
Family Gracilariaceae					
Gracilaria foliifera				×	
Order Rhodymeniales					
Family Champiaceae					
Champlia parvula					×
Order Ceramiales					
Family Ceramiaceae					
Callithamnion roseum					×
C. byssoideum					×
C. diaphanum				×	
C. rubrum				×	
C. strictum					×
Griffithsia tenuis					×
Spyridia filamentosa					×
Family Delesseriaceae					
Grinnellia americana			×		×
Family Rhodomelaceae					
Bostrychia montagnei			×		
Polysiphonia harveyi					×
P. nigrescens					×
P. subtilissima		×	×	×	×
P. denudata					×
DIVISION CHRYSOPHYTA					
Class Xanthophyceae					
Order Heterosiphonales					
Family Vaucheriaceae					
Vaucheria sp.	×	×	×		
PHYLUM PROTOZOA					
Subphylum Plasmodroma					
Class Mastigophora					
Subclass Phytomastigia					
Order Chrysomonadida					
Suborder Euchrysomonadina					
Family Chromulinidae					
Chromulina pascheri				×	
Chrysapsis sagene	×			×	×
Family Syncryptidae					
Synura uvella	×				
Stylochrysalis parasitica		×			
Family Ochromonadidae					

TABLE 5.26. (*Continued*)

Species	Patuxent River: Salinity 0.0054 ppt Fresh Water	Potomac River: Salinity 7.5–7.7 ppt Mesohaline	Patuxent River: Salinity 8.9 ppt Mesohaline	Chesapeake Bay: Salinity 13–15 ppt Mesohaline	York River: Salinity 18.7–20.1 ppt Polyhaline
Monas guttula	×		×	×	
Monas sp.*					×
Suborder Rhizochrysidina					
Chrysothylakion vorax			×		
Order Cryptomonadida					
Suborder Eucryptomonadina					
Family Cryptomonadidae					
Cryptomonas compressa	×				
C. erosa	×	×			
Order Phytomonadida					
Family Chlamydomonadidae					
Chlamydomonas globosa	×				
C. monadina	×	×			
Brachiomonas westiana		×		×	×
Family Carteriidae					
Carteria cordiformis	×				
Family Chlorasteridae					
Chloraster gyrans			×		
Family Volvocidae					
Eudorina elegans				×	
Order Euglenoidida					
Family Euglenidae					
Euglena acus				×	
E. deses		×			
E. ehrenbergi	×				
E. gracilis					
E. viridis	×			×	
E. oxyuris	×				
E. spirogyra	×				
Trachelomonas hispida	×				
T. urceolata	×				
Eutreptia marina	×	×	×	×	×
E. viridis				×	
Family Anisonemidae					
Anisonema acinus	×		×	×	
A. grande		×			
A. truncatum					×
Paranema trichophorum	×	×	×		
Heteronema mutabile				×	
Entosiphon sulcatum		×		×	

Continued

TABLE 5.26. (*Continued*)

Species	Patuxent River: Salinity 0.0054 ppt Fresh Water	Potomac River: Salinity 7.5–7.7 ppt Mesohaline	Patuxent River: Salinity 8.9 ppt Mesohaline	Chesapeake Bay: Salinity 13–15 ppt Mesohaline	York River: Salinity 18.7–20.1 ppt Polyhaline
Order Dinoflagellida					
Suborder Prorocentrina					
Family Prorocentridae					
Prorocentrum scutellum		×			
P. micans			×	×	×
P. triangulatum		×	×	×	
Exuviaella apora		×			
E. compressa				×	
E. marina			×		×
Suborder Peridiniina					
Superfamily Gymnodinioidea					
Family Cystodiniidae					
Glenodinium cinctum	×	×	×	×	
G. danicum	×	×	×		×
G. neglectum				×	
Family Pronoctilucidae					
Oxyrrhis marina				×	
Family Pouchetiidae					
Nematodinium partitum		×			
Family Gymnodiniidae					
Gymnodinium agile	×		×	×	
G. filum					×
G. marylandicum	×	×	×	×	
G. nelsoni		×	×	×	
Gymnodinium pellucidum		×			
Gymnodinium rotundatum	×			×	
G. splendens		×	×	×	×
Gymnodinium sp.*	×			×	
Amphidinium klebsi					×
A. operculatum			×	×	×
Gyrodinium biconicum		×	×	×	×
G. pellucidum		×			
G. piague				×	
Cochlodinium helicoides					×
C. helix		×	×	×	×
Massartia nieuportensis					×
Family Polykrikidae					
Polykrikos barnegatensis			×	×	
P. kofoidi			×		
Superfamily Peridinioidea					
Family Peridiniidae					

TABLE 5.26. (*Continued*)

Species	Patuxent River: Salinity 0.0054 ppt Fresh Water	Potomac River: Salinity 7.5–7.7 ppt Mesohaline	Patuxent River: Salinity 8.9 ppt Mesohaline	Chesapeake Bay: Salinity 13–15 ppt Mesohaline	York River: Salinity 18.7–20.1 ppt Polyhaline
Peridinium brevipes					×
P. claudicans		×	×	×	
P. depressum				×	
P. divergens					×
P. leonis		×	×	×	×
P. obtusum					×
P. pellucidum				×	×
P. trochoideum		×	×	×	×
P. wisconsinsis	×				
Peridinium sp.*					
Peridinopsis rotunda		×			×
Diplopsalis lenticula				×	×
Ceratium minutum				×	×
C. tripos					×
Gonyaulax catenata			×		
G. scrippsae		×		×	
G. spinifer	×	×	×	×	
Kryptoperidinium foliaceum					×
Family Dinophysiidae					
Dinophysis acuta				×	
Subclass Zoomastigia					
Order Rhizomastigia					
Family Multiciliidae					
Multicilia marina					×
Order Protomonadida					
Family Phalansteriidae					
Phalansterium digitatum		×			
Family Bicosoecidae					
Coconoeca sp.*				×	
Family Bodonidae					
Bodo caudatus					×
B. obovatus	×			×	
Bodo sp.					
Pleuromonas jaculana					×
Rhynchomonas marina					×
Order Polymastigida					
Family Trimastigidae					
Trimastix marina					×
Class Sarcodina					
Subclass Rhizopoda					

Continued

TABLE 5.26.   (*Continued*)

Species	Patuxent River: Salinity 0.0054 ppt Fresh Water	Potomac River: Salinity 7.5–7.7 ppt Mesohaline	Patuxent River: Salinity 8.9 ppt Mesohaline	Chesapeake Bay: Salinity 13–15 ppt Mesohaline	York River: Salinity 18.7–20.1 ppt Polyhaline
Order Proteomyxida					
Family Vampyrellidae					
Nuclearia sp.*					×
Order Amoebida					
Family Amoebidae					
Amoeba guttulata			×		
A. limicola		×			
A. radiosa	×				
A. spumosa			×		
Vahlkampfia limax		×			×
Acanthamoeba hyalina	×				
Order Testacida					
Family Gromiidae					
Gromia ovoidea				×	×
Lieberkuhnia wagneri					×
Family Arcellidae					
Arcella vulgaris	×				
Order Foraminiferida					
Family Valvulinidae					
Eggerella advena			×		
Family Trochamminidae					
Trochammina inflata			×		
Family Globigerinidae					
Globigerina bulloides			×		
Subclass Actinopoda					
Order Helioizoida					
Family Actinophyridae					
Actinophrys sol		×			
Actinosphaerium eichhorni		×			
Oxnerella maritima		×			
Family Ciliophryidae					
Ciliophrys marina					×
Subphylum Ciliophora					
Class Ciliata					
Subclass Holotricha					
Order Gymnostomatida					
Suborder Rhabdophorina					
Family Holophryidae					
Holophrya simplex		×	×		
Placus socialis				×	
Lacyrmaria coronata		×			

TABLE 5.26. (*Continued*)

Species	Patuxent River: Salinity 0.0054 ppt Fresh Water	Potomac River: Salinity 7.5–7.7 ppt Mesohaline	Patuxent River: Salinity 8.9 ppt Mesohaline	Chesapeake Bay: Salinity 13–15 ppt Mesohaline	York River: Salinity 18.7–20.1 ppt Polyhaline
L. lagenula				×	
Trachelocera phoneicopterus		×	×	×	×
T. subviridis		×		×	
Trachelophyllum clavatum		×		×	
Family Colepidae					
Coleps elongata		×			
C. hirtus		×	×	×	
C. octospinus				×	
Family Spathidiidae					
Homalozoon vermiculare				×	
Family Didiniidae					
Didinium nastum	×		×		
Mesodinium acarus			×		×
M. pulex		×		×	
Cyclotrichium meunieri					
Family Amphileptidae					
Amphileptus claparedei				×	
Litonotus fasciola			×	×	
Loxophyllum mealagris			×	×	
L. setigerum		×		×	
Bryophyllum vorax		×	×		
Family Tracheliidae					
Dileptus anser	×				
Family Loxodidae					
Loxodes vorax				×	
Remanella rugosa			×		
Suborder Cyrtophorina					
Family Dysteriidae					
Dysteria calkinsi		×		×	
D. navicula	×				
Trochilia palustris		×			
Family Chlamydodontidae					
Chlamydodon mnemosyne				×	
Chilodonella cuculluslus	×	×	×	×	
C. fluviatilis	×	×	×	×	
Family Nassulidae					
Nassula aurea			×		×
Eucamptocerca longa				×	
Chilodontepsis vorax	×				
Order Trichostomatida					

Continued

TABLE 5.26.   (*Continued*)

Species	Patuxent River: Salinity 0.0054 ppt Fresh Water	Potomac River: Salinity 7.5–7.7 ppt Mesohaline	Patuxent River: Salinity 8.9 ppt Mesohaline	Chesapeake Bay: Salinity 13–15 ppt Mesohaline	York River: Salinity 18.7–20.1 ppt Polyhaline
Family Coelosomididae					
Pseudoprorodon farctus	×			×	
Paraspathidium trichostomum				×	
Order Hymenstomatida					
Suborder Tetrahymenina					
Family Tetrahymenidae					
Tetrahymena pyriformis	×	×	×	×	
Glaucoma scintillans		×		×	
Loxocephalus plagius		×			
Family Cohnilembidae					
Cohnilembus fusiformis	×	×		×	
Uronema marinum					×
Suborder Peniculina					
Family Parameciidae					
Paramecium aurelia		×			
P. trichium	×	×	×	×	×
Family Frontoniidae					
Fronotonia leucas	×	×			
F. marina					×
F. microstoma				×	
Lembadion bullinum			×		
L. magnum		×			
Cintochilum margarataceum				×	
Suborder Pleuronematina					
Family Pleuronematidae					
Pleuronema marinum		×			
P. setigenum				×	
Cyclidium litomesum		×		×	
Subclass Spirotricha					
Order Heterotrichida					
Family Spirostomatidae					
Spirostomum intermedium				×	
S. minus			×		×
Gruberia calkinsi			×	×	
Family Condylostomatidae					
Condylostoma patens	×	×			×
C. tardum		×			
Family Stentoridae					
Stentor igneus			×		
Climacostomum virens			×		
Family Peritromidae					

TABLE 5.26. (*Continued*)

Species	Patuxent River: Salinity 0.0054 ppt Fresh Water	Potomac River: Salinity 7.5–7.7 ppt Mesohaline	Patuxent River: Salinity 8.9 ppt Mesohaline	Chesapeake Bay: Salinity 13–15 ppt Mesohaline	York River: Salinity 18.7–20.1 ppt Polyhaline
Peritromus emmae					×
Order Oligotrichida					
Family Halteriidae					
Strombidium calkinsi		×			×
S. conicum				×	
S. sulcatum				×	
S. viride		×			
Tontonia gracillima					×
Family Strobilidiidae					
Strobilidium conicum	×	×	×		×
S. gyrans	×	×	×	×	
Strobilidium sp.			×		
Order Tintinnina					
Butintinnis pectinis			×		
Coxliella sp.					×
Eutintinnus pectinis			×	×	
E. tubulosus				×	
E. apertus				×	
Leprotintinnus bottnicus					×
L. fracknoi				×	
L. pellucidus					
Tintinnidum fluviatile		×		×	
Tintinnopsis aperta					×
T. beroidea		×		×	
T. butschilii					×
T. cylindrica				×	
T. meunierii		×			
T. minuta		×	×		×
T. plagistoma		×	×	×	
T. platensis					×
T. radix					×
T. subcuta					×
T. tocantinensis				×	
T. tubulosa			×	×	×
T. urnula					×
Codonella cratera		×		×	
Stenosomella nivalis		×	×	×	
Metacyclis angusta				×	×
M. mereschkowskii					×
Helicostomella kiliensis					×
Favella panamensis				×	×

Continued

TABLE 5.26. (*Continued*)

Species	Patuxent River: Salinity 0.0054 ppt Fresh Water	Potomac River: Salinity 7.5–7.7 ppt Mesohaline	Patuxent River: Salinity 8.9 ppt Mesohaline	Chesapeake Bay: Salinity 13–15 ppt Mesohaline	York River: Salinity 18.7–20.1 ppt Polyhaline
Parundella longa					×
Parundella sp.*				×	
Order Hypotrichida					
Family Oxytrichidae					
Oxytricha fallax	×		×	×	
Urosoma caudata	×		×		
Aphisiella thiophaga				×	
Stichotricha intermedia	×		×		
S. secunda				×	
Uroleptus halseyi				×	
Urostyla caudata		×			
U. coei				×	
U. marina					×
Holosticha vernalis		×			
Stylonychina mytilis	×				
Onychodromopsis flexilis		×		×	
Family Euplotidae					
Euplotes charon	×	×	×	×	
E. eurystomum				×	
E. harpa		×	×		
Diophrys appendiculata		×	×	×	
Uronychia setigera		×	×	×	
Family Aspidiscidae					
Aspidisca hexeres	×	×	×		
A. lynceus		×		×	
A. polystyla				×	×
Subclass Pertricha					
Order Peritrichida					
Suborder Sessilina					
Family Vorticellidae					
Vorticella campulana	×	×	×	×	
V. convallaria		×	×	×	
V. microstomum		×	×	×	
V. marina		×			
V. marinium		×		×	×
V. monilata					×
V. oceanicum		×			
Vorticella sp.					×
Carchesium polypinum			×	×	
Zoothamnium adamsi	×	×	×	×	
Z. alternans				×	×

TABLE 5.26. (Continued)

Species	Patuxent River: Salinity 0.0054 ppt Fresh Water	Potomac River: Salinity 7.5–7.7 ppt Mesohaline	Patuxent River: Salinity 8.9 ppt Mesohaline	Chesapeake Bay: Salinity 13–15 ppt Mesohaline	York River: Salinity 18.7–20.1 ppt Polyhaline
Z. nutans		×	×	×	
Family Epistylidae					
Epistylis plicatilis		×	×	×	
Campanella umbellaria				×	
Family Vaginicolidae					
Vaginicola annulata	×		×	×	
V. crystallina		×			
Cothurnia imberbis		×	×		
C. ovata	×	×	×	×	×
C. poculum				×	
Pyxicola affinis	×	×	×		
P. socialis				×	
Suborder Mobilina					
Family Urceolariidae					
Trichodina sp.*	×	×	×	×	
Class Suctoria					
Order Suctorida					
Family Acinetidae					
Acineta divisa		×			
A. tuberosa		×	×	×	
Tokophrya infusionum		×	×		
Thecacineta cothurnioides		×			
Family Podophryidae					
Sphaerophyra sp.*				×	
Family Ephelotidae					
Ephelota coronata		×			
E. gemmipara				×	
PHYLUM PORIFERA					
Class Demospongiae					
Subclass Teractinomorpha					
Order Spirophorida					
Family Tetillidae					
Tetilla laminaris					×
Order Hadromerida					
Family Suberitidae					
Suberites sp.					×
Family Clionidae					
Cliona celata					×
Subclass Ceractinomorpha					
Order Poecilosclerida					

Continued

TABLE 5.26.   (*Continued*)

Species	Patuxent River: Salinity 0.0054 ppt Fresh Water	Potomac River: Salinity 7.5–7.7 ppt Mesohaline	Patuxent River: Salinity 8.9 ppt Mesohaline	Chesapeake Bay: Salinity 13–15 ppt Mesohaline	York River: Salinity 18.7–20.1 ppt Polyhaline
Family Mycalidae					
Stylotella heliophila					×
Family Clathriidae					×
Microciona prolifera					×
Order Haplosclerida					
Family Haliclonidae					
Haliclona oculata					×
(= *Chalina oculata*)					
H. arbuscula					×
(= *Chalina arbuscula*)					
Haliclona sp.				×	
Family Spongillidae					
Spongilla sp.					×
PHYLUM CNIDARIA					
Class Hydrozoa					
Order Athecata					
Family Hydractiniidae					
Hydractinia echinata					×
Family Bougainvilliidae					
Bimeria franciscana		×			
Order Thecata					
Family Campanularidae					
Obelia sp.					×
Family Sertularidae					
Sertularia pumila					×
Sertularella gayi					×
Thuiaria argentea					×
Class Scyphozoa					
Order Semaeostomeae					
Family Cyaneidae					
Cyanea sp.					×
Family Ulmaridae					
Aurelia aurita				×	
Class Anthozoa					
Subclass Octocorallia					
Order Gorgonacea					
Family Gorgoniidae					
Leptogorgia virgulata					×
Subclass Zoantharia					
Order Actiniaria					
Family Edwardsiidae					

TABLE 5.26. (*Continued*)

Species	Patuxent River: Salinity 0.0054 ppt Fresh Water	Potomac River: Salinity 7.5–7.7 ppt Mesohaline	Patuxent River: Salinity 8.9 ppt Mesohaline	Chesapeake Bay: Salinity 13–15 ppt Mesohaline	York River: Salinity 18.7–20.1 ppt Polyhaline
Edwardsia sp.			×		
Family Diadumenidae					
Diadumene leucolena					×
(= *Sagartia leucolena*)					
Family Aiptasiomorphidae					
Aiptasiomorpha luciae		×	×		
Haliplanella luciae					×
(= *Sagartia leucolena*)					
PHYLUM ANNELIDA					
Class Polychaeta					
Order Orbiniida					
Family Orbiniidae					
Scoloplos fragilis					×
Order Spionida					
Suborder Spioniformia					
Family Spionidae					
Polydora ciliata					×
P. ligni				×	×
Polydora sp.					×
Scolecolepides viridis		×			
Suborder Chaetopteriformia					
Family Chaetopteridae					
Chaetopterus pergamentaceus					×
Order Capitellida					
Family Capitellidae					
Heteromastus filiformis		×		×	
Family Maldanidae					
Clymenella torquata					×
Order Phyllodocida					
Family Nephtydidae					
Nephtys bucera					×
N. ingens Stimpson					×
Nephtys sp.					×
Suborder Phyllodociformia					
Family Polynoidae					
Harmothoe aculeata					×
Lepidonotus sublevis					×
Family Sigalionidae					
Sthenelais leidyi					×
Suborder Nereidiformia					

Continued

TABLE 5.26.   (*Continued*)

Species	Patuxent River: Salinity 0.0054 ppt Fresh Water	Potomac River: Salinity 7.5–7.7 ppt Mesohaline	Patuxent River: Salinity 8.9 ppt Mesohaline	Chesapeake Bay: Salinity 13–15 ppt Mesohaline	York River: Salinity 18.7–20.1 ppt Polyhaline
Family Nereidae					
Laeonereis culveri		×		×	
Nereis limbata					×
N. pelagica					×
N. succinea		×		×	
Suborder Glyceriformia					
Family Glyceridae					
Glycera dibranchiata				×	×
Family Goniadidae					
Glycinde solitaria				×	
Family Sabellariidae					
Sabellaria vulgaris					×
Order Terebellida					
Family Pectinariidae					
Pectinaria gouldi		×			×
P. hyperborea		×			
Order Sabellida					
Family Serpulidae					
Hydroides hexagonus					×
Suborder Chaetopteriformia					
Family Chaetopteridae					
Chaetopterus pergamentaceus					×
Order Capitellida					
Family Capitellidae					
Heteromastus filiformis		×		×	
Family Maldanidae					
Clymenella torquata					×
Order Phyllodocida					
Family Nephtydidae					
Nephtys bucera					×
N. ingens					×
Nephtys sp.					×
Suborder Phyllodociformia					
Family Polynoidae					
Harmothoe aculeata					×
Lepidonotus sublevis					×
Family Sigalionidae					
Sthenelais leidyi					×
Suborder Nereidiformia					
Family Nereidae					
Laeonereis culveri		×		×	

TABLE 5.26. (*Continued*)

Species	Patuxent River: Salinity 0.0054 ppt Fresh Water	Potomac River: Salinity 7.5–7.7 ppt Mesohaline	Patuxent River: Salinity 8.9 ppt Mesohaline	Chesapeake Bay: Salinity 13–15 ppt Mesohaline	York River: Salinity 18.7–20.1 ppt Polyhaline
Nereis limbata					×
N. pelagica					×
N. succinea		×		×	
Suborder Glyceriformia					
Family Glyceridae					
Glycera dibranchiata				×	×
Family Goniadidae					
Glycinde solitaria				×	
Family Sabellariidae					
Sabellaria vulgaris					×
Order Terebellida					
Family Pectinariidae					
Pectinaria gouldi		×			×
P. hyperborea		×			
Order Sabellida					
Family Serpulidae					
Hydroides hexagonus					×
Class Hirudinia					
Order Rhynchobdellida					
Family Piscicolidac					
Piscicola punctata					×
(= *Pentebdella punctata*)					
Trachylobdella vividus					×
(= *Cystobranchus vividus*)					
PHYLUM CTENOPHORA					
Class Tentaculata					
Order Lobata					
Family Mnemiidae					
Mnemiopsis leidyi					×
Class Nuda					
Order Beroida					
Family Beroidae					
Beroe ovata					×
?*Beroe* sp.		×		×	
PHYLUM PLATYHELMINTHES					
Class Turbellaria					
Order Polycladida					
Suborder Acotylea					
Section Craspedommata					

Continued

TABLE 5.26.   (Continued)

Species	Patuxent River: Salinity 0.0054 ppt Fresh Water	Potomac River: Salinity 7.5–7.7 ppt Mesohaline	Patuxent River: Salinity 8.9 ppt Mesohaline	Chesapeake Bay: Salinity 13–15 ppt Mesohaline	York River: Salinity 18.7–20.1 ppt Polyhaline
Family Stylochidae					
Stylochus ellipticus					×
PHYLUM BRYOZOA					
Class Gymnolaemata					
Order Ctenostomata					
Family Victorellidae					
Victorella pavida			×	×	
Family Nolellidae					
Anguinella palmata					×
Order Cyclostomata					
Family Crisiidae					
Hemiseptella denticulata				×	
(= *Crisia denticulata*)					
Order Cheilostomata					
Family Membraniporidae					
Membranipora tenuis		×	×		
Family Electridae					
Electra crustulenta				×	
PHYLUM ECHINODERMATA					
Class Ohiuroidea					
Order Ophiurae					
Family Ophiodermatidae					
Ophiodermata brevispinum		×			
PHYLUM MOLLUSCA					
Class Gastropoda					
Subclass Prosobranchia					
Order Mesogastropoda					
Suborder Littorina					
Family Littorinidae					
Littorina irrorata		×			
Family Hydrobiidae					
Littoridinops tenuipes			×		
Family Cerithiidae					
Bittium alternum		×			
B. varium		×			
Family Triphoridae					
Triphora nigrocincta		×			
Family Crepidulidae					
Crepidula fornicata		×			
Order Neogastropoda					

TABLE 5.26. (*Continued*)

Species	Patuxent River: Salinity 0.0054 ppt Fresh Water	Potomac River: Salinity 7.5–7.7 ppt Mesohaline	Patuxent River: Salinity 8.9 ppt Mesohaline	Chesapeake Bay: Salinity 13–15 ppt Mesohaline	York River: Salinity 18.7–20.1 ppt Polyhaline
Family Columbellidae					
Anachis avara		×			
Mitrella lunata		×			
Family Muricidae					
Eupleura caudata		×			
Urosalpinx cincereus		×			
Family Melongenidae					
Busycon caniculatum		×			
Family Nassariidae					
Nassarius vibex		×			
Ilyanassa obsoleta		×			
(= *Nassarius obsoleta*)					
Order Pyramidelloida					
Family Pyramidellidae					
Odostomia impressa		×			×
(= *Menestho impressa*)					
(= *Boonea impressa*)					
Class Bivalvia					
Subclass Pteriomorphia					
Order Arcoida					
Family Arcidae					
Anadara transversa					×
A. ovalis					×
Order Mytiloida					
Family Mytilidae					
Brachiodontes recurvus		×	×	×	×
(= *Ischadium recurvum*)					
Modiolus demissus			×		×
(= *Guekensia demissa*)					
Order Pteroida					
Suborder Pteriina					
Family Anomiidae					
Anomia simplex					×
Family Ostreidae					
Crassostrea virginica		×		×	×
Subclass Heterodonta					
Order Veneroida					
Family Mactridae					
Mulinia lateralis			×		
Rangia cuneata		×		×	

Continued

TABLE 5.26. *(Continued)*

Species	Patuxent River: Salinity 0.0054 ppt Fresh Water	Potomac River: Salinity 7.5–7.7 ppt Mesohaline	Patuxent River: Salinity 8.9 ppt Mesohaline	Chesapeake Bay: Salinity 13–15 ppt Mesohaline	York River: Salinity 18.7–20.1 ppt Polyhaline
Family Dreissenidae					
Mercenaria mercenaria					×
Order Myoida					
Family Myidae					
Mya arenaria		×		×	
Family Teredinidae					
Bankia gouldii				×	
PHYLUM ARTHROPODA					
Subphylum Mandibulata					
Class Crustacea					
Subclass Cirripedia					
Order Thoracica					
Suborder Balanomorpha					
Family Chthamalidae					
Chthamalus fragilis					×
Family Balanidae					
Balanus balanoides					×
B. eburneus					×
B. improvisus		×	×	×	
Order Rhizocephala					
Family ? Sacculinidae					
?Sacculina sp.				×	
Subclass Malacostraca					
Division Peracarida					
Order Isopoda					
Suborder Anthuridea					
Family Anthuridae					
Cyathura polita		×		×	
Suborder Flabellifera					
Family Cymothoidae					
Lironeca ovalis				×	
Family Sphaeromidae					
Exosphaeroma diminutum	×			×	
Suborder Valvifera					
Family Idoteidae					
Idotea balthica				×	×
Edotea triloba		×		×	
Erichsonella attenuata					×
Order Amphipoda					
Suborder Gammaridea					
Family Ampithoidae					

TABLE 5.26. (*Continued*)

Species	Patuxent River: Salinity 0.0054 ppt Fresh Water	Potomac River: Salinity 7.5–7.7 ppt Mesohaline	Patuxent River: Salinity 8.9 ppt Mesohaline	Chesapeake Bay: Salinity 13–15 ppt Mesohaline	York River: Salinity 18.7–20.1 ppt Polyhaline
Ampithoe valida				×	
Cymadusa compta		×		×	×
(= *Grubia compta*)					
Family Bateidae					
Batea catharinensis					×
Family Corophiidae					
Corophium lacustre	×	×	×	×	
Erichthonius brasiliensis					×
Unicola irroratus					×
Family Gammaridae					
Carcinogammarus sp.					×
Carcinogammarus mucronatus				×	×
Gammarus daiberi	×				
G. mucronatus			×		
G. tigrinus	×				
Family Haustoriidae					
Lepidactylus dysticus				×	
Family Stenothoidae					
Stenothoe cypris				×	
Family Talitridae					
Orchestia platensis				×	×
O. grillus					×
Suborder Caprellida					
Family Caprellidae					
Caprella acutifrons					×
Paracaprella simplex					×
Aeginella longicornis					×
Division Eucarida					
Order Decapoda					
Suborder Natantia					
Section Caridea					
Family Palaemonidae					
Palaemonetes pugio	×	×		×	
P. vulgaris				×	×
P. intermedius				×	
Family Crangonidae					
Crangon septemspinous				×	×
C. normannia					×
(= *Alpheus normanni*)					
Suborder Reptantia					

Continued

TABLE 5.26. (*Continued*)

Species	Patuxent River: Salinity 0.0054 ppt Fresh Water	Potomac River: Salinity 7.5–7.7 ppt Mesohaline	Patuxent River: Salinity 8.9 ppt Mesohaline	Chesapeake Bay: Salinity 13–15 ppt Mesohaline	York River: Salinity 18.7–20.1 ppt Polyhaline
Section Anomura					
Family Paguridae					
Pagurus longicarpus					×
P. pollicaris					×
Section Brachyura					
Subsection Branchygnatha					
Infrasubsection Oxyrhyncha					
Family Majidae					
Libinia dubia				×	×
L. erinacea					×
Infrasubsection Brachyrhyncha					
Family Portunidae					
Callinectes sapidus	×	×	×	×	×
Family Xanthidae					
Eurypanopeus depressus				×	×
Panopeus herbstii					×
(= *Eurypanopeus herbstii*)					
Neopanoeus texana					×
Rhithropanopeus harrisii		×		×	×
Family Pinnothcridae					
Pinnotheres ostreum					×
Family Ocypodidae					
Uca pugnax					×
Family Grapsidae					
Sesarma cinereum					×
Subphylum Chelicerata					
Class Insecta					
Subclass Pterygota					
Infraclass Paleoptera					
Order Odonata					
Suborder Zygoptera					
Family Coenagrionidae					
Ischnura vericalis	×				
Order Hemiptera					
Suborder Heteroptera					
Family Gerridae					
Rheumbates sp.	×				
Trepobates inermis	×				
Family Notonectidae					

TABLE 5.26. (*Continued*)

Species	Patuxent River: Salinity 0.0054 ppt Fresh Water	Potomac River: Salinity 7.5–7.7 ppt Mesohaline	Patuxent River: Salinity 8.9 ppt Mesohaline	Chesapeake Bay: Salinity 13–15 ppt Mesohaline	York River: Salinity 18.7–20.1 ppt Polyhaline
Notonecta sp. (immature)	×				
Division Endopterygota					
Order Coleoptera					
Family Gyrinidae					
Dineutes nr. *nigrior*	×				
Cercyon sp.	×				
Order Diptera					
Suborder Nematocera					
Family Chironomidae					
Coelontanypus nr. *concinnus*	×				
PHYLUM CHORDATA					
Subphylum Urochordata					
Class Ascidacea					
Order Pleurogona					
Suborder Stolidobranchiata					
Family Molgulidae					
Mogula manhattensis				×	×
Subphylum Vertebrata					
Class Osteichthyes					
Subclass Actinopterygii					
Order Anguilliformes					
Family Anguillidae					
Anguilla rostrata	×			×	
Order Clupeiformes					
Family Clupeidae					
Alosa aestivalis	×		×		
A. pseudoharengus	×				
Dorosoma cepedianum				×	
Family Engraulidae					
Anchoa hepsetus		×	×		
A. mitchilli		×	×	×	×
Order Salmoniformes					
Family Esocidae					
Esox americanus			×		
Order Cypriniformes					
Family Cyprinidae					
Cyprinus carpio			×		
Hybognathus nuchalis	×				

Continued

TABLE 5.26. (Continued)

Species	Patuxent River: Salinity 0.0054 ppt Fresh Water	Potomac River: Salinity 7.5–7.7 ppt Mesohaline	Patuxent River: Salinity 8.9 ppt Mesohaline	Chesapeake Bay: Salinity 13–15 ppt Mesohaline	York River: Salinity 18.7–20.1 ppt Polyhaline
Notropis hudsonius	×				
Order Siluriformes					
Family Ictaluridae					
Ictalurus catus	×				
Order Atheriniformes					
Family Exocoetidae					
Hyporhamphus unifasciatus			×		
Family Belonidae					
Strongylura marina	×	×	×	×	
Family Cyprinodontidae					
Fundulus diaphanus	×	×			
F. heteroclitus	×	×	×	×	×
F. majalis		×	×	×	×
Cyprinodon variegatus					×
Lucania parva				×	
Family Atherinidae					
Membras marinica		×	×		
Menidia berylinna	×			×	×
M. menidia		×	×	×	×
Order Gasterosteiformes					
Family Gasterosteidae					
Apeltes quadracus				×	
Family Syngnathidae					
Syngnathyus fuscus		×		×	×
S. floridae					×
Order Perciformes					
Family Percichthyidae					
Monroe americana	×	×	×	×	
M. saxatilis	×	×	×	×	
Family Centrarchidae					
Lepomis macrochirus	×				
Family Percidae					
Etheostoma olmstedi	×				
Perca flavescens	×				
Family Sciaenidae					
Bairdiella chrysoura				×	
Leiostomus xanthurus			×	×	×
Cynoscion nebulosus				×	
C. regalis				×	
Family Ephippidae					

TABLE 5.26. (*Continued*)

Species	Patuxent River: Salinity 0.0054 ppt Fresh Water	Potomac River: Salinity 7.5–7.7 ppt Mesohaline	Patuxent River: Salinity 8.9 ppt Mesohaline	Chesapeake Bay: Salinity 13–15 ppt Mesohaline	York River: Salinity 18.7–20.1 ppt Polyhaline
Chaetodipterus faber					×
Family Blenniidae					
Chasmodes bosquianus				×	×
Hypsoblennius hentzi					×
Family Gobiidae					
Gobiosoma bosci	×	×		×	×
G. ginsburgi					×
Microgobius holmesi					×
Family Stromateidae					
Peprilus alepidotus				×	
Order Gobiesociformes					
Family Gobiesocidae					
Gobiesox strumosus			×	×	×
Order Pleuronectiformes					
Family Bothidae					
Paralichthys dentatus				×	
Family Pleuronectidae					
Pseudopleuronectes americanus				×	
Family Soleidae					
Trinectes maculatus	×			×	×
Family Cynoglossidae					
Symphurus plagiusa					×
Order Tetrodontiformes					
Family Tetraodontidae					
Spheroides maculatus				×	×
Family Diodontidae					
Chilomycterus schoepfi				×	×
Order Batrachoidiformes					
Family Batrachoididae					
Opsanus tau				×	×

Source: ANSP (1957, 1970a, b, 1971).
*Species not identified.

content, which was about a half an order of magnitude higher in the Potomac River. Sulfates were less in the Potomac than in the Patuxent. Both studies were carried out in August 1970 (ANSP, 1970a, b, 1971) (Table 5.26). The Station 3 in the Patuxent River and Station 3 in the Potomac are comparable as to salinity.

Patuxent River. In the Patuxent River diatoms were the most common algae (Table 5.26). Of these the more common were *Amphipleura rutilans* v. *dillwynii* and *Melosira nummuloides.* These were shallow-water forms or benthic species. Two other common benthic species were *Melosira borreri*, which was abundant in association with green algae, and *Nitzschia brittoni* which was very common on a fallen three. Another subdominant associated with other algal filaments was *Synedra fasciculata* v. *truncata.* The plankton was dominated by *Coscinodiscus excentricus.* Near the shore and associated with peat, *Nitzschia obstusa* v. *scapelliformis* was very common. In the peat along the shoreline, dark green mats of the chrysophyte, *Vaucheria* sp., were also found. Intermixed with the other algae and fairly common were the blue-green algae, *Microcoleus lyngbyaceus, Schizothrix calcicola, S. arenaria, Spirulina subsalsa,* and a species of *Anabaina.* On the fallen tree the blue-green alga, *Oscillatoria lutea,* was found intermixed with *Enteromorpha prolifera.* Also on the fallen tree were very small tufts of the red alga, *Polysiphonia subtilissima,* the only red alga encountered in this region. Red algae are characteristic of more saline waters, as seen in the collection from the York River.

Protozoa in the Patuxent River in August were dominated by dinoflagellates in both numbers of species and numbers of individuals. A bloom, or a very large growth, was present and consisted mainly of *Glenodinium cinctum, G. danicum, Exuviaella marina, Gyrodinium biconicum,* and *Cochlodinium helix* (Table 5.26). This type of aggregation is quite characteristic of the lower Chesapeake Bay drainage basin. Phytoflagellates other than dinoflagellates were represented by 6 species. Ciliates, the next most common group, were represented by 20 species of *Holotricha* and 4 species of *Spirotricha.* This group is believed to be important as a food organism in the Chesapeake, where it forms very large populations.

The macroinvertebrates were represented by relatively few species. Common on muddy sand was an undetermined species of the genus *Edwardsia*, an anthozoan called "sea onion." On hard substrates were two bryozoans, *Victorella pavida* and *Membranipora tenuis* (Table 5.26). Also very common on hard substrates was the barnacle, *Balanus improvisus.* Common to the bed of the estuary were the mussel, *Macoma balthica,* and the clam, *Mya arenaria.* The anthropod, *Gammarus mucronatus,* was also fairly common.

The most common fish among the 12 species taken in the Patuxent area of study were the blueback herring (*Alosa aestivalis*), white perch (*Morone americana*), and striped bass (*M. saxatilis*). The herring represented the largest number of individuals and was second in weight of these three commercial fish. Of the smaller fish taken in shallow water, the Atlantic silversides (*Menidia menidia*) and Atlantic menhaden (*Brevoortia tyrannus*) were also common (ANSP, 1971).

Potomac River. In the Potomac River fresh water area of study a diverse algal flora was present in August. The most common diatom was *Melosira nummuloides. Navicula mutica* was a very common subdominant most often found near the high-tide line on pilings. *Cocconeis placentula* v. *euglypta* was common on the stems of young plants in somewhat deeper water but was occasionally found in relatively shallow water. Blue-green algae were not generally as common as diatoms throughout the Potomac area, but they were quite common in some habitats, and a total of six species were taken. Associated with the peat banks were mats of the yellow-green alga, *Vaucheria* sp., and the green algae, *Ulva lactuca* and *Cladophora gracilis*. It would be hard to tell whether the green algae were really dependent on the peaty habitat or whether they occurred in shallow waters and were washed into this association via wave action.

The Potomac protozoans were represented by 75 species at Station 3. The *Holotricha*, with 24 species, were best represented. Of the species of phytoflagellates, 15 were dinoflagellates and were fairly common. Of the 12 species of *Spirotricha*, 3 were tintinnids, which is less than the number found in the Patuxent. The number of phytoflagellates (*Phytomastigina*) is similar to the number found in the Patuxent. Particularly common in the Potomogeton beds and associated with *Polysiphonea subtilissima* were large numbers of vorticellids and other sessile peritrichs. These would indicate a fairly high nutrient condition in this area.

In this area the most common macroinvertebrates were the polychaetes, crustaceans, and various bivalves. The number of bivalves was similar in the two areas of study.

Eleven species of fish were collected in the Potomac area in August. Among the most common were the young Atlantic silversides (*Menidia menidia*), the white perch (*Morone americana*), and the bay anchovy (*Anchoa mitchilli*). A number of the young of the Atlantic needlefish (*Strongylura marina*) were also collected (ANSP, 1970a).

York River

The York River empties into Chesapeake Bay near its mouth, where the influence of the Atlantic Ocean is greatest. The York estuary studies were done in 1956 before the river was polluted by industry and therefore represent a condition that may no longer exist. River waters are now used by industry and a utility. The salinity was usually in the 10 ppt to 11.5 ppt range.

Diatoms were very common among the young shoots of eelgrass and also in the older eelgrass beds. The high salinity of the water was evidenced by the common occurrence of *Melosira borreri* and *M. nummuloides*, the presence of *Hyalodiscus scoticus*, and the common occurrence of *Grammatophora marina* and *Licmorphora debilis*. As noted in Table 5.26, *Nitzschia longissima* and various species of *Polysiphonea* were common in the eelgrass beds.

Macroalgae collected from the large mud flats of the intertidal zone and from eelgrass (*Zostera*) beds also indicated that the salinity of the York River was higher than in the three other Chesapeake Bay areas studied. The green algae, *Enteromorpha intestinalis* and *Cladophora flexuosa*, were common in the intertidal zone and shallow subtidal water. *Ulva lactuca* v. *latissima*, another green alga, was common in eelgrass beds. Two red algae, *Agardhiella tenera* and *Gracilaria foliifera* v. *angustissima*, were very common in shallow subtidal waters of the mud flat and in the *Zostera* beds. Red algae collected by dredging in deeper waters were mainly *Ceramium strictum* and *C. rubrum*. The dominant algae in September were similar to those in the spring.

The protozoans in the York River were found principally in benthic habitats in the *Zostera* beds and among the algae in the intertidal and subtidal zones. Dinoflagellates found in the benthic zone were *Brachiomonas westiana*, *Ceratium minutum*, *Gymnodinium splendens*, *Peridinium leonis*, *P. divergens*, *Prorocentrum micans*, and *Amphidinium klebsi*. Other protozoans found were the zooflagellate, *Bodo caudatus*, and the foram, *Globigerina bulloydes*. The plankton was dominated by tintinnids, the most common of which were *Favella panamensis*, *Tintinnopsis platensis*, *T. radix*, *T. tubulosa*, *T. subcuta*, and *T. urnula*.

The anemone, *Haliplanella luciae*, was particularly common. *Diadume leucolena* was not quite as frequently found but was one of the more abundant anemone species. In deeper water, the Gorgonian coral, *Leptogorgia virgulata*, was abundant. During the fall in the eelgrass there was a decided increase in the number of species of polychaete worms, particularly tube dwellers.

The snails, *Nassarius vibex* and *N. obsoletus*, were the major macroinvertebrates found in the intertidal zone and shallow water subtidal zone. The oyster, *Crassostrea virginica*, was very common in subtidal areas as was the associated sponge, *Cliona celata*. Also numerous in the oyster beds was the turbellarian, *Stylochus inimicus*, which preyed on young oysters. The mussel, *Brachidontus recurvus*, was found in the area. It has been reported that the mud crab, *Neopanope texana*, preyed on the hard-shelled clam, *Mercenaria mercenaria*, and this may account for the fact that the clam is not very common in this region.

Crabs were fairly common in *Zostera* beds, particularly the blue crab, *Callinectes sapidus*, and the mud spidercrab, *Libinia dubia*. Also occurring, but not quite as commonly, was the fiddler crab, *Uca pugnax*. Two mud crabs, *Eurypanopeus depressus* and *Neopanope texana*, were common in various areas but not uniformly through the study area. Isopods were more common in the spring than in late summer.

At the time of this study (1956) the mouth of the York River provided excellent commercial fishing. The most abundant fish taken in commercial operations were the croaker, the butterfish, and the spot. Sea trout were much less common and young sea trout were scarcer than adults (ANSP, 1957).

Chesapeake Bay

The Calvert Cliffs study area was less saline (13 to 15 ppt) than the York River (18.7 to 20.1 ppt) and more saline than the Potomac (7.5 to 7.7 ppt) and Patuxent (8.9 + ppt during the period of study). Calvert Cliffs is north of the York River, farther from the mouth of Chesapeake Bay, and had much higher levels of phosphates and ammonia than were found in the York River. The fauna and flora collections did not contain the many typically marine species common to the York River (Table 5.26).

The 1969 studies were made in the vicinity of the Calvert Cliffs power plant but prior to its operation. One set of studies was made in shallow water, that is, less than 2 m of depth, and this included an analysis of the algae, the protozoa, the various invertebrates, and fish (ANSP, 1970b). Mountford et al. (1977) studied invertebrates only at depths of 3, 6, and 9 m and in association with oyster shells.

The shallow water supported a rich and diversified group of algae. In August and September the most common species of diatoms were *Synedra fasciculata* v. *parva*, *Cyclotella caspia*, *Navicula diserta*, *N. nyella*, *Cocconeis scutellum*, *Nitzschia frustulum* v. *perminuta*, *N. obtusa* v. *scapelliformis*, *Mastogloia pumila*, and *Amphipleura rutilans* v. *dillwynii*. The most common green algae were *Ulva lactuca* and *Enteromorpha prolifera*. Blue-green algae were fairly scarce. The diversity of the algal flora can be seen from Table 5.26. In deeper water, associated with eelgrass blades, were found patches of *Polysiphonia subtilissima* and *Ceramium rubrum* and *C. diaphanum*.

The protozoan fauna was dominated by flagellates and ciliates. Of the flagellates, the dinoflagellates were particularly common during August. The most common species belonged to the following genera: *Prorocentrum*, *Glenodinium*, *Gymnodinium*, *Diplopsalis*, *Ceratium*, and *Gonyaulax*. Genera of tintinnids that were common were *Leprotintinnus*, *Tintinnopsis*, *Favella*, *Metacyclis*, and *Eutinnus*. The species of these genera are given in Table 5.26. Many of these species are typically found in organically enriched water and indicated the presence of domestic sewage in the general area. These nutrients were enough to increase populations but did not alter the general diverse characteristic of the natural system.

The macroinvertebrates in the 1969 surveys may have been affected by a silt load, probably resulting from dredging, which occurred in the area. The list of invertebrates is given in Table 5.26. The most common sponge was *Haliclona* sp. Of the coelenterates, the jellyfish, *Aurelia aurita*, was very common. The most common polychaete was *Nereis succinea*, which had relatively large populations distributed throughout the area. Other polychaetes were represented by only moderately large populations. The most common gastropod was the bubble shell, *Haminoea solitaria*, which occurred in very large populations. Several species of bivalves were found, but not in large populations.

The barnacle, *Balanus improvisus*, was fairly common in the lower part of the study area. Crustaceans were very common and were represented primarily by the amphipods, *Lepidactylus dysticus* and *Orchestia plantensis*, which burrow into the soft sand of shallow water. Other common amphipods were *Gammarus mucronatus* and *Ampithoe valida*. The grass shrimp, *Palaeomonetes pugio* and *Crangon septemspinosus*, were abundant, as was the commercial blue crab, *Callinectes sapidus*. In the lower part of the study area and in deeper water, the mud crab, *Rhithropanopeus harrisii*, was found, but the size of its population was difficult to determine. The sea squirt, *Molgula manhattensis*, was very common throughout the study area. The most common fish collected in shallow

TABLE 5.27. *Numerically Dominant Invertebrate Species of the Calvert Cliffs, Maryland, Area (1973–1974) Listed as Determined by Rank Analysis*

	3-m Sand Habitat			6-m Muddy-Sand Habitat		
Season	Species	Frequency, f	Mean, $\bar{x}$ (no. m^{-2})	Species	Frequency, f	Mean, $\bar{x}$ (no. m^{-2})
Spring (May 1973)	*Scolecolepides viridis*	100	1968	*Scolecolepides viridis*	100	5232
	Macoma balthica	100	176	*Macoma balthica*	100	1660
	Heteromastus filiformis	100	138	*Heteromastus filiformis*	100	714
				Mya arenaria	100	506
				Nereis succinea	100	345
Summer (Aug. 1973)	*Scolecolepides viridis*	100	518	*Macoma balthica*	100	703
	Lepidactylus dytiscus	92	151	*Heteromastus filiformis*	100	233
	Heteromastus filiformis	100	99	*Mya arenaria*	91	82
	Macoma phenax	75	37	*Scolecolepides viridis*	100	112
Fall (Nov. 1973)	*Heteromastus filiformis*	100	49	*Heteromastus filiformis*	100	149
	Lepidactylus dytiscus	88	30	*Paraprionospio pinnata*	100	146
	Macoma phenax	100	28	*Nereis succinea*	100	164
	Micura leidyi	88	17			
Winter (Feb. 1974)	*Mulinia lateralis*	80	207	*Heteromastus filiformis*	100	331
	Mya arenaria	100	168	*Mulinia lateralis*	100	828
	Heteromastus filiformis	100	111	*Macoma balthica*	100	521
	Macoma balthica	80	214	*Mya arenaria*	100	319
	Scolecolepides viridis	100	102	*Nereis succinea*	78	175
	Lepidactylus dysticus	90	55			

9-m Mud Habitat

Season	Species	Frequency, f	Mean, $\bar{x}$ (no. m^{-2})	Species	Frequency, f	Mean, $\bar{x}$ (no. m^{-2})
Spring (May 1973)	Macoma balthica	100	660	Scolecolepides viridis	100	6882
	Scolecolepides viridis	100	257	Macoma balthica	100	2010
	Nereis succinea	100	113	Nereis succinea	100	809
	Leptocheirus plumulosus	100	81	Paraprionospio pinnata	75	643
	Paraprionospio pinnata	100	83			
Summer (Aug. 1973)	Paraprionospio pinnata	70	10	Macoma balthica	100	1488[a]
	Macoma balthica	60	8	Heteromastus filiformis	100	347
	Micura leidyi	50	13	Mya arenaria	66	100
	Heteromastus filiformis	30	4			
Fall (Nov. 1973)	Paraprionospio pinnata	100	152	Nereis succinea	100	476
	Nereis succinea	100	43	Heteromastus filiformis	100	70
	Macoma phenax	37	7	Paraprionospio pinnata	90	200
	Micura leidyi	45	5	Diadumene leucolena	80	185
Winter (Feb. 1974)	Paraprionospio pinnata	100	94	Macoma balthica	95	509
	Nereis succinea	100	49	Mya arenaria	100	444
	Mulinia lateralis	100	47	Heteromastus filiformis	100	412
	Macoma balthica	100	36	Paraprionospio pinnata	86	449
				Mulinia lateralis	75	428

Source: Mountford et al. (1977).

[a] Only 3 shell samples were obtained during this period.

water were the bay anchovy, *Anchoa mitchilli*; the Atlantic needlefish, *Strongylura marina*; the northern pike, *Syngnathus fuscus*; the spot, *Leiostomus xanthurus*; and the Atlantic silversides, *Menidia menidia* (ANSP, 1970b).

The community of invertebrates in 3-m sand, as reported by Mountford et al. (1977), was characterized by the sand-burrowing arthropods, *Lepidactylus dysticus* and *Monoculodes edwardsii*. Throughout the study one of these was always dominant in this area. As shown in Table 5.27, there was overlap between the species found at 3, 6, and 9 m. The 6-m muddy sand community was intermediate between the sandy 3-m community and the muddy 9-m community. In the sand community the total ash-free biomass ranged from 0.7 to 2 g m^{-2}. No species were restricted to the 6-m muddy sand community; however, the species more abundant in this habitat than in the other habitats were the polychaetes, *Heteromastus filiformis* and *Scolecolepides viridis*, and the bivalves, *Macoma balthica*, *Mulinia lateralis*, and *Mya arenaria*. The total ash-free biomass ranged from 1 to 11 g m^{-2}. In the 9-m mud community the most characteristic species were the polychaetes, *Nereis succinea* and *Paraprionospio pinnata*. The number of individuals m^{-2} composing the 9-m mud community was lowest, and the total ash-free biomass ranged from 0.1 to 4 g m^{-2}.

The shell community was characterized by the bivalves, *Brachiodontes recurvus* and *Doridella obscura*; the barnacle, *Balanus balanoides*; the amphipod, *Corophium lacustre*; and the anemone, *Diadumene leucolema*. The total number of individuals was highest in the shell habitat and the ash-free biomass ranged from 1 g m^{-2} to 11 g m^{-2}. Many species overlapped in the various habitats and many were ubiquitous and therefore found in waters with a range of salinities and nutrients (Mountford et al., 1977).

Comparison of Study Areas in the Chesapeake Bay and Tributaries

It is evident from the Jaccard Similarity Index (Table 5.28) that the Calvert Cliffs area of the Chesapeake Bay and the Potomac River area are more similar

TABLE 5.28.   *Jaccard Similarity Index (%) of Algae, Protozoa, Macroinvertebrates, and Fish at Pairs of Stations in the Chesapeake Bay Area*

	Patuxent–Potomac	Chesapeake–Patuxent	Chesapeake–Potomac	Chesapeake–York
Algae				
Diatoms	31	17	19	11
Blue–green	46	30	53	8
Green	100	60	75	14
Red	—	—	—	7
Protozoa	22	31	29	13
Macroinvertebrates	14	8	50	12
Fish	50	27	26	33

in species composition of algae and fish than the other areas, although their salinities are quite different. The Potomac River and the Patuxent River are more similar than the Chesapeake area and the Patuxent study area except for protozoa. The York River community is the most different.

An important factor in the difference may be that the York River is nearer the ocean and may be more easily invaded by oceanic species; the salinity is quite similar to that of the Chesapeake study area. Another factor may be that the Chesapeake and Potomac studies were made in adjacent years (1970 and 1971), whereas the York River studies were made in 1957 (ANSP, 1957, 1970a, b, 1971).

Eelgrass Beds in Chesapeake Bay

In the past, eelgrass beds were quite common in the Chesapeake estuary but rare in the Delaware estuary. The size and extent of a grass bed is determined by the depth of the water, the degree of exposure to wind and wave conditions, and the salinity range. *Zostera* beds are found at a maximum depth of 2 m at midwater low tide and are usually absent where there is heavy surf. *Zostera* is replaced by *Ruppia maritima* where the salinity is less than 10 ppt.

In 1971 the western shore of the lower Chesapeake supported approximately 4950 ha of *Zostera*. By 1974 eelgrass beds had increased in Mobjack Bay, Poguoson River, and bay areas north of New Point Comfort. In lower Chesapeake Bay, particularly around York River, Rappahonnock River, Piankatank River, Poguoson Flats, and Plum Tree Island, *Zostera marina* beds declined by as much as 36%. This significant reduction of eelgrass acreage is thought to have been caused by a combination of factors (Orth, 1976). Tropical storm Agnes, in 1972, lowered the salinity of the bay. A general warming trend in the weather increased the midwinter water temperature, which caused greater fluctuations in temperature, and, normally, extremes of temperature lead either to mass defoliation or death of the plants. Another major factor in the destruction of the eelgrass beds was thought to be the cownose ray, *Rhinoptera bonasus*, which was present in great numbers in the lower Chesapeake during the period of eelgrass decline. Rays preyed on the infauna bivalves in the grass beds by digging into the sediment with their pectoral fins, uprooting the *Zostera* in the process. Rays traveled and fed in large schools and one such school can destroy a sizable eelgrass bed.

Loss of eelgrass greatly reduced the number of animal species, many of which were favored prey of larger animals. The lower Chesapeake lost not only large beds of eelgrass but also the microfauna associated with it and the animals dependent on the microfauna. In addition, the sandy-mud bottom was destabilized by loss of eelgrass roots, and shore erosion occurred in the absence of the baffling effect of eelgrass leaves.

Common eelgrass can tolerate salinities ranging from 5 to 32 ppt (Rasmussen, 1977). It is much less tolerant of temperature extremes. An ice cover kills eelgrass. Below 10 °C there is no metabolic activity. From 10 to 15 °C vegetative growth is rapid, and between 15 and 20 °C leaf growth stops and flowering stems are formed. Above 20 °C all activities in the plants may stop, and at 25 to 30 °C the plants, including the rhizomes, may die (Rasmussen, 1977). Because of high temperature, *Zostera marina* is not found in southern waters and may be adversely affected during the summer in Chesapeake Bay.

In temperate and north temperate zones *Zostera marina*, the most common seagrass, may have a productivity of 500 to 1500 g C m^{-2} yr^{-1} with a turnover rate of one to three times a year (McRoy and McMillan, 1977).

Food Web.   The nutrient cycle in a *Zostera* bed is complex and nutrients may be derived from the sediments or water column. Ammonia was the preferred source of nitrogen for *Zostera marina*, although other forms of nitrogen might have been used, including low-molecular-weight organic compounds such as glyceine. The nitrogen requirement was estimated to be 200 to 300 mg m^{-2} day^{-1} (McRoy and McMillan, 1977).

Rather large amounts of trace metals have been found in *Zostera marina*, and the role that eelgrass played in the coastal heavy metal budget seemed to be of considerable importance. The growth of the roots in a reduced sediment layer may have facilitated the uptake. Wood (1953) and Bass-Becking and Wood (1955) stated that reducing complexes may be released by *Zostera marina*, which may regulate the Eh environment of the sediments (Burrell and Schubel, 1977).

The functioning of the eelgrass ecosystem is dependent on anaerobic processes within the detritus as well as aerobic processes on the surface of the detritus. The quantitatively dominant anaerobic biological process was sulfate reduction, because of the abundance of SO_4^{2-} in seawater. The liberation of sulfide affected the chemical and biological environment of the eelgrass bed in several important ways. The presence of H_2S provided a sink for heavy metals, especially iron, which was precipitated as black ferrous sulfide, to which reducing sediments owe their color. Under aerobic conditions, phosphate tended to precipitate as ferric or calcium phosphate. In the presence of a sulfide, phosphates were liberated from iron and again became available to the ecosystem. This is the process by which phosphate is made available in eelgrass beds and is very important in the productivity of the system.

Another important process in these sediments was the oxidation of sulfur by chemo-autotrophic bacteria in the presence of oxygen. The energy yield of these oxidation processes was utilized to assimilate CO_2 and synthesize particulate organic matter in the form of bacterial biomass, thus rendering it available to higher levels of the food chain.

Sulfides may be oxidized in three ways. Hydrogen sulfide may be oxidized abiologically in the presence of oxygen, but this method is not usually very productive. White sulfur bacteria oxidize H_2S to S, which may be further oxidized to SO_4^{2-}. When light reaches the anaerobic zone, green and purple sulfur bacteria may oxidize H_2S and utilize it as a hydrogen donor in the photosynthesis process. The end product may be sulfur or SO_4^{2-}. The importance of these anaerobic processes was seen in experiments conducted by Jorgensen and Fenchel (1974) which showed that these processes oxidized three times as much organic material as ordinary respiration did, and that SO_4^{2-} was as important as O_2 in transporting oxidation equivalents from the water to sediment (Fenchel, 1977; Jorgensen and Fenchel, 1974).

Aerobic processing of detritus occurs in several ways. Fresh and senescent leaves of *Zostera*, which contained from 12 to 20% water-soluble organics, were an important source of soluble and particulate organic matter. Some of these organics formed the air–water interface of air bubbles. Some sorbed onto inorganic particles and became a food source for organisms. Other water-soluble organics were taken up by bacteria, which, in turn, became a food source for many other organisms.

Some organisms, such as the molluscs, *Hydrobia* and *Macoma*, assimilated only a small fraction of the organic carbon in the particulate detritus they ingested. Their fecal pellets, still rich in carbon, became a substrate for bacteria. Colonization by bacteria increased the nitrogen and decreased the carbon available from the pellets, so that, with the microflora, the pellets were a good food source.

The detritus of *Zostera* was freely attacked by bacteria (particularly *Pseudomonas* and *Cytophaga*), some fungi (Chytrids), and by protozoans. Chytrids and unicellular fungi of various sorts are usually present. Ciliates and zooflagellates (*Monas*, *Bodo*, and *Rhynchomonas*) were often associated with *Zostera* detritus. Other protozoan groups, such as amoeba, colorless euglenoids, and more rarely, heliozoans, might have been present feeding on detritus and microalgae. Rotifers may have fed on bacteria or protozoa associated with eelgrass detritus. Nematodes associated with the detritus had diversified feeding habits, while the turbellarians present were mainly predators. Small crustacea fed on bacteria and microalgae. Microfauna constituted a significant amount of biomass in the detritus. Micro-faunal biomass was about the same as that of the bacteria and indicated the importance of microfauna as detritus feeders. A reasonable estimate of bacterial biomass in 1 g of detritus was 4×10^{-3} g. The average biomass of zooflagellates and ciliates, together was 5×10^{-3} g per gram dry weight of detritus (Fenchel, 1977). A schematic diagram of the detritus food web is given in Figure 5.5.

As in the case of *Spartina*, the leaves of *Zostera marina* were eaten by a very few invertebrates and some fish and turtles (den Hartog, 1977). Animals such as bryozoans, barnacles, worms, and gastropods lived as epiphytes on the leaves of *Zostera*. Algae that grew attached to *Zostera* leaves included some small red and brown algae and many green algae and diatoms. There were roughly four associations that depend upon eelgrass or its detritus. One association consisted of plants and animals that lived on or attached to eelgrass leaves, the epiphytes. Another association was composed of the animals that fed on the epiphytes. A third association of organisms lived on the detritus surface in aerobic conditions. A loosely associated group of animals, fish, crab, shrimp, and other nekton used eelgrass as shelter.

Orth (1973) identified 117 taxa, which were composed of the following groups of invertebrates; 36% of the total number of species were Polychaeta; Amphipoda

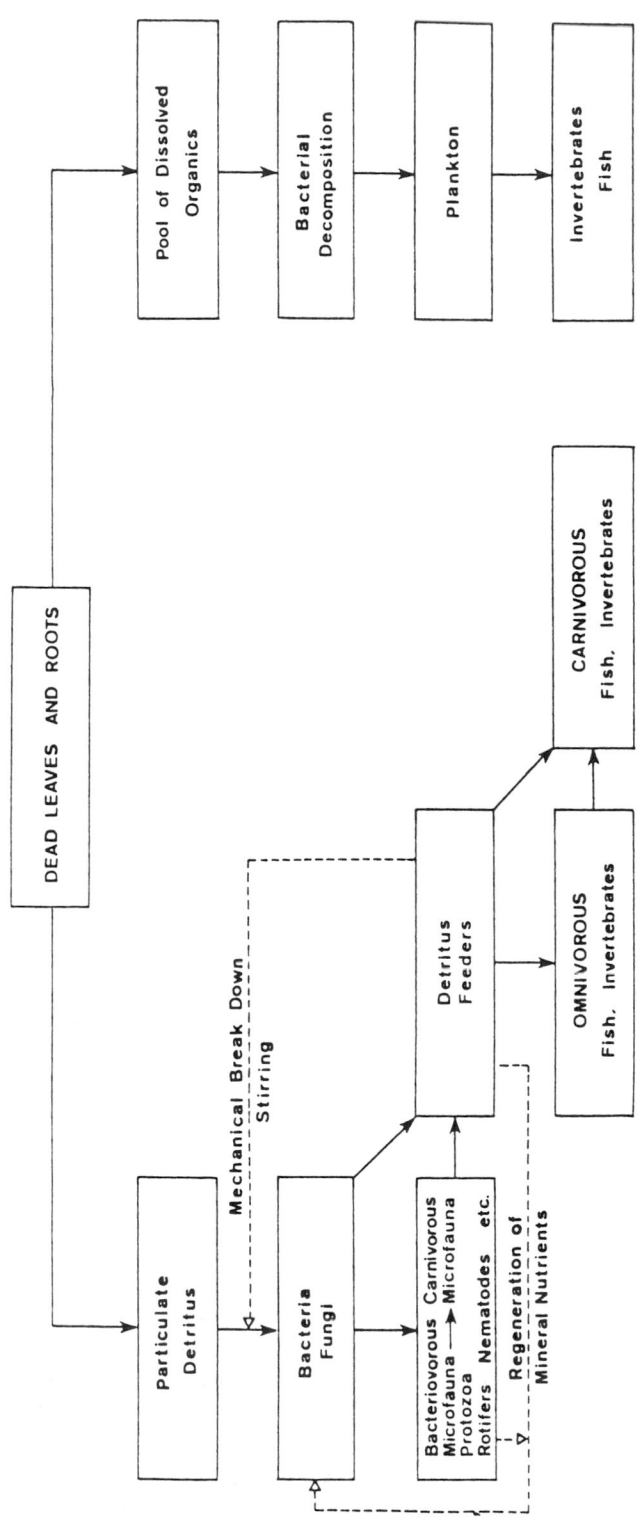

FIGURE 5.5. Schematic diagram of the detritus food web associated with *Zostera marina* beds. (Adapted from Fenchel, 1977.)

were 16%; Gastropoda were 11%; Bivalvia 7%; and the remaining percent were small numbers of other taxa. He found a significant decrease in numbers of species from the mouth of the Chesapeake estuary to the upper reaches.

Those species found living on or associated with the leaves of *Zostera* occurred in varying numbers at different seasons of the year. In other words, various species seemed to have a seasonal succession of dominance. This is best exemplified by Marsh's (1976) and Orth's (1973) studies in the York River of Chesapeake Bay. In January the snail, *Odostomia dux*, had its peak occurrence. This snail typically fed on tubicolous polychaetes. The main species of these polychaetes found living on the *Zostera* were *Sabella microphthalma* and *Hydroides hexagona*. In March *Polydora ligni* and *Streblospio benedicti* were most common. Also very common in March was *Spiochaetocerus oculatus*. This species also occurred very commonly later in the summer. Ampeliscid amphipods, *Ampelisca abdita* and *A. vadorum*, were very common at most of the stations in winter and summer, but the greatest density of *Ampelisca vadorum* occurred in March. In May and June the gelatinous egg masses of the snails, *Diastoma varium*, were found on the blades of *Zostera*. The adult snails were commonly in association with the hydrozoan, *Hydractinia arge*, and the algae, *Fosliella lejolisii*. The peak biomass of *Zostera* occurred in June. The nudibranch, *Corambe obscura* (= *Doridella obscura*), was collected from early June through July and found again in October.

In July the oligochaete, *Spiochaetopterus oculatus*, reached its peak, as did *Heteromastus filiformis*. The worm, *Nereis succinea*, was a very common species at all stations, particularly in July. Also common was the gastropod, *Bittium varium*. The amphipod, *Ampelisca abdita*, reached its peak density in July. *Polycera conyma*, a naked gastropod, found almost exclusively in July, fed on the bryozoan, *Bowerbankia gracilis*. Many of the common species in August were also found in the early fall. Among these was the gastropod, *Crepidula convexa*, which had its largest populations in August. The females of this species were often found from May to September attaching eggs to blades of *Zostera*. *Urosalpinx cinerea* had its largest populations in August. This species preyed largely on barnacles, limpets, tube worms, and encrusted bryozoa, which were very common during the summer months on the leaves of *Zostera*. The sponge, *Prosuberites microsclerus*, was found commonly on *Urosalpinx* shells during the summer. The opistobranch, *Odostomis impressa*, had its largest populations from July to October. This snail fed on other molluscs, such as *Diastoma, Crepidula,* and *Urosalpinx*. It also fed on *Molgula*. *Odostomia bisuturalis* was fairly common all year round but had its greatest densities in late summer or early fall. The snail, *Triphora nigrocincta*, was fairly common in late summer, with peak abundances occurring in October. The sacoglossan, *Elysia catula*, was found all year but reached its peak in November and December.

The most common infauna species in the Chesapeake was a clam, *Mya arenaria*, which was an important prey of the cownose ray, *Rhinoptera bonasus*. Other species spent part of their life as infauna and the rest of their life as epifauna. For example, the amphipods, *Ampelisca abdita* and *A. vadorum*, were sedimentary and bottom-dwelling amphipods as adults, but they became free-swimming plankton during their reproductive period. *Nereis succinea* was a highly mobile polychaete worm that spent part of its life as infauna and part as epifauna. Isopods such as *Edotea triloba* and the polychaete, *Exogone dispar*, were abundant infauna animals. Only rarely were they found on the blades of *Zostera*, whereas the epifaunal polychaetes, *Brania clarata* and *Podarke obscura*, were occasionally found as infauna animals (Marsh, 1976; Orth, 1973).

Many fish preyed on epifauna on *Zostera* during the summer. Most abundant were the Atlantic silversides (*Menidia menidia*), the fourspine stickleback (*Apeltes quadracus*), and the northern pipefish (*Syngnathus fuscus*). Stomach content analyses of these species revealed diets consisting chiefly of amphipods, mysids, and other small crustaceans.

The loss of *Zostera* can have several major implications to the estuarine ecosystem. *Zostera* and its associated epiphytes are an important source of primary productivity and detritus. Also, since *Zostera* binds the sediments, loss of the eelgrass may lead to serious beach erosion. The reduction of *Zostera* also results in the loss of an important nursery for finfish and shellfish.

The removal of grass beds resulted in an unstable sand habitat with low infaunal diversity and density. Recovery of the epifauna upon reestablishment of the grass bed depended on dispersal powers of the animals. The community before the decline was dominated by species that brood their young and have limited dispersal powers.

SUMMARY

The most important estuaries of the Middle Atlantic States are dominated by single rivers and are called open-mouth estuaries or estuaries formed by sunken rivers. In other words, the estuary represents a portion of a former river that extended much farther out on the continental shelf.

The rivers contributing to the Chesapeake Bay as well as the estuary of the Delaware have received varying amounts of pollution over time. Both of these estuaries have vast grass marshlands which are very important to the immediate functioning of the open waters but also maintain important ecosystems that function within them. It is the gradient of salinity which one finds in an estuary as well as the gradient of salinity which exists in the marshland that allows the development of a great number of species. These marshes are particularly important as nursery grounds for many different kinds of organisms, both fish and invertebrates. They are also very productive of oxygen and thus oxygenate the water, which often has reduced oxygen content as it drains the uplands. They also retain, through tidal invasion, many of the pollutants that are introduced into the riverine water as it flows throughout its course. In this manner, they purify the water before it enters the sea. The detritus of the marsh grasses is an excellent food source for many species. If the salinity gradients were changed in these wetlands, their value of spawning and nursery grounds for many anadromous species would be greatly reduced.

In the past people have not realized the many diverse values of the marshlands and so, in the Delaware, many of them have been destroyed. In fact, practically all of the marshlands above Philadelphia and many of them below Philadelphia have been drained, diked, filled, or otherwise destroyed.

In the Chesapeake during the last 20 years we have begun to realize the impact of human beings on the estuary as the eutrophication problem has become much more severe in recent times. There are many sources of this pollution load: drainage from the landscape, drainage from upstream areas, and fallout from the atmosphere, as well as the increased nutrients brought in by the millions of boats that utilize the estuary on the weekends and all during the summer.

In the Delaware, boating is not as popular as it is in the Chesapeake but is increasing steadily. The effects of pollution have perhaps been appreciated longer in the Delaware than in the Chesapeake. As a result, at the present time the waters of the Delaware are greatly improving as the inorganic load has been reduced. The toxic load in the sediments remains a problem. The effect of this pollution is most severe in the upper estuary and disappears almost entirely in the bay.

In the Chesapeake we are just beginning to understand the sources of pollution, which of the tributary estuaries are contributing the largest pollution load, and the types of chemicals that compose these pollution loads. It is by understanding the types of pollution and the effects on the biodiversity of the ecosystems that we will be able to manage and reduce these anthropogenic inputs.

In summary, the results of these various studies show that the pollution loads existing in the various tributaries to the Chesapeake and the Delaware are highly variable and have affected various portions of these waterways in different manners. Furthermore, the Chesapeake and the Delaware are very different in their structure and hence in the variability of types of conclusions that one can draw from studies.

The Delaware has a sequential set of water qualities, from fresh to marine waters. The ecosystems have been exposed to varying amounts of pollution. In the Chesapeake, such a sequence exists in each of the tributaries, but the Chesapeake Bay itself is a melting pot, and the effects of pollution may not be realized for a much longer period because of the great dilution factor. However, as far as the nutrients are concerned, that time has come; there is at present a very severe problem in the Chesapeake.

In both the Chesapeake and Delaware estuaries, as one studies them over time, one finds that the population sizes of various species vary greatly, sometimes caused by disease, as in the case of *Dermocystidium* (*Perkinsus marinus*) and MSX with oysters, or by sudden physical changes such as those caused by Hurricane Agnes on the Chesapeake, when large numbers of oysters were killed because of reduced salinity. The effects of introducing fresh water which have occurred in the Patuxent because of the establishment of a sewage treatment plant have resulted in a great shift in the natural equilibrium of species, causing some pest organisms to increase greatly and others to decrease. This effect has also been seen in the Delaware around Artificial Island, where large amounts of fresh water were introduced as coolant water from the power plants. This upset of the natural salinity regimes may greatly favor some species and lead to the destruction of others. Despite these pollution effects, these estuaries support very diverse ecosystems. Often the species composing them are more tolerant to pollution than would be the composition of species in an unpolluted estuary.

In the Delaware, where we have studies of the ecosystems from the head of the estuary in Trenton down to the bay, it is quite evident that the biodiversity changes greatly, as seen by the species composition in response to the pollution load. Changing the natural saltwater regimes will also greatly affect the functioning of these ecosystems. It is the maintenance of high biodiversity that is most important in maintaining the health of these ecosystems.

Until the last 20 to 30 years, few people have realized the importance of marshlands in increasing the oxygen content of water and reducing the pollution load gained from upstream activities. This was first demonstrated in the Delaware and has now been shown in many other estuaries. More recently, the important role of marshlands in cycling nitrogen and in denitrification has been discovered (Seitzinger, 1988).

BIBLIOGRAPHY

The Academy of Natural Sciences of Philadelphia (ANSP). 1957. York River, Virginia: biological, chemical, and physical studies for the American Oil Company. Philadelphia, Pa. Vol. I.

The Academy of Natural Sciences of Philadelphia (ANSP). 1959. Biological studies of the Delaware River for the Interstate Commission on the Delaware River. Philadelphia, Pa. 99 pp.

The Academy of Natural Sciences of Philadelphia (ANSP). 1969. Report for Baltimore Gas and Electric Company (Calvert Cliffs). Philadelphia, Pa.

The Academy of Natural Sciences of Philadelphia (ANSP). 1970. Patuxent River. Philadelphia, Pa.

The Academy of Natural Sciences of Philadelphia (ANSP). 1970a. Potomac River Surveys: Morgantown 1970 survey report for the Potomac Electric Power Company. Philadelphia, Pa.

The Academy of Natural Sciences of Philadelphia (ANSP). 1970b. Preoperational estuarine ecological studies for the Calvert Cliffs nuclear power plant of the Baltimore Gas and Electric Company. Vol. II. Philadelphia, Pa.

The Academy of Natural Sciences of Philadelphia (ANSP). 1971. Patuxent River, Maryland: stream survey report for the Potomac Electric Power Company. Philadelphia, Pa. 93 pp.

The Academy of Natural Sciences of Philadelphia (ANSP). 1972. Ecological studies near Smyrna, Del., for the Shell Oil Company. Annual report 1970–1971. Vol. I. Philadelphia, Pa.

The Academy of Natural Sciences of Philadelphia (ANSP). 1974. Ecological studies in New Jersey: Oldman's Creek, Raccoon Creek, Birch Creek, and the Delaware River, 1972–1973, for the Shell Oil Company. Vols. I and II. Philadelphia, Pa.

Aurand, D., and F. C. Daiber. 1973. Nitrate and nitrite in the surface water of two Delaware salt marshes. Chesapeake Sci. 14: 105–111.

Bass-Becking, L. G. M., and E. J. F. Wood. 1955. Biological processes in the estuarine environment. I and II. Ecology of the sulphur cycle. Proc. Acad. Sci. Amsterdam B58: 160–181.

Berk, S. G., D. C. Brownlee, D. R. Heinle, H. J. Kling, and R. R. Colwell. 1977. Ciliates as a food source for marine planktonic copepods. Microb. Ecol. 4(1): 27–40.

Bigelow, H. W., and W. C. Schroeder. 1953. Fishes of the Gulf of Maine. U.S. Fish Wildl. Serv. Fish. Bull. 53(74): 1–575.

Burrell, D. C., and J. R. Schubel. 1977. Seagrass ecosystem oceanography. *In* C. P. McRoy, and C. Helfferich, eds., Seagrass ecosystems. Mar. Sci. 4: 196–232.

Coffin, R. B., and J. Sharp. 1987. Microbial trophodynamics in the Delaware estuary. Mar. Ecol. Prog. Ser. 41: 253–366.

Corey, R. L. 1974. Changes in oxygen and primary production of the Patuxent estuary, Maryland, 1963 through 1969. Chesapeake Sci. 15(2): 78–83.

den Hartog, C. 1977. Structure, function, and classification in seagrass communities. *In* C. P. McRoy, and C. Helfferich, eds., Seagrass ecosystems. Mar. Sci. 4: 89–122.

Fager, E. W. 1957. Determination and analysis of recurrent groups. Ecology 38: 586–595.

Faust, M. A., and D. L. Corell. 1977. Autoradiographic study to detect metabolically active phytoplankton and bacteria in the Rhode River estuary, Chesapeake Bay, U.S.A. Mar. Biol. (Berlin) 41(4): 293–306.

Fenchel, T. 1977. Aspects of the decomposition of seagrasses, pp. 293–306. *In* C. P. McRoy, and C. Helfferich, eds., Seagrass ecosystems. Marcel Dekker, New York.

Ferrante, J. G. 1971. A quantitative study of the zooplankton in the Delaware River in the vicinity of Artificial Island, pp. 1–46. *In* V. J. Schuler, proj. leader, An ecological study of the Delaware River in the vicinity of Artificial Island. Progress report for the period Jan.–Dec., 1970, Part 2, for Public Service Electric and Gas Co., Salem Nuclear Generating Station. Ichthyological Associates, Lansing, N.Y.

Flemer, D. A. 1970. Primary production in the Chesapeake Bay. Chesapeake Sci. 11: 117–129.

Flemer, D. A., and R. B. Biggs. 1971. Particulate carbon:nitrogen relations in northern Chesapeake Bay. J. Fish. Res. Board Can. 28(6): 911–918.

Flemer, D. A., and J. Olmar. 1971. Daylight incubator estimates of primary production in the mouth of the Patuxent River, Maryland. Chesapeake Sci. 12: 105–110.

Flemer, D. A., D. R. Heinle, C. W. Keefe, and D. H. Hamilton. 1978. Standing crops of marsh vegetation of two tributaries of Chesapeake Bay. Estuaries 1(3): 157–163.

Gallagher, J. L., and F. C. Daiber. 1974. Primary production of edaphic algal communities in a Delaware salt marsh. Limnol. Oceanogr. 19: 390–395.

Gooch, E. L. 1974a. Hydrogen sulfide production and its effect on inorganic phosphate release from the sediments of the Canary Creek Marsh, pp. 117–121. *In* H. T. Odum, B. J. Copeland, and E. A. McMahan, eds., Coastal ecological systems of the United States. Vol. 2. The Conservation Foundation, Washington, D. C.

Gooch, E. L. 1974b. Production and release of nutrients from the sediments of the tidal marshes of Delaware, pp. 131–139. *In* H. T. Odum, B. J. Copeland, and E. A. McMahan, eds., Coastal ecological systems of the United States. Vol. 2. The Conservation Foundation World Wildlife Fund, Washington, D.C. For copyright information, contact WWF.

Grant, R. R., Jr., and R. Patrick. 1970. Tinicum Marsh as a water purifier, pp. 105–123. *In* Two studies of Tinicum Marsh, Delaware and Philadelphia counties, Pennsylvania. The Conservation Foundation, Washington, D.C.

Hargrave, B. T. 1972. Aerobic decomposition of sediment and detritus as a function of particle surface area and organic content. Limnol. Oceanogr. 17(4): 583–596.

Hood, M. A., W. S. Bishop, Jr., F. W. Bishop, S. P. Meyers, and T. Whelan III. 1975. Microbial indicators of oil-rich salt marsh sediments. Appl. Microbiol. 30(6): 982–987.

Jorgensen, D. B., and T. Fenchel. 1974. The sulfur cycle of marine sediment model systems. Mar. Biol. 24:189–201.

Keck, R., D. Maurer, and L. Watling. 1973. Tidal stream development and its effect on the distribution of the American oyster. Hydrobiology 42:369–379.

Kinner, P., D. Maurer, and W. Leathem. 1974. Benthic invertebrates in Delaware Bay: animal-sediment associations of the dominant species. Int. Rev. Gesamten Hydrobiol. 59(5):685–701.

Loftus, M. E., D. V. Subba Rao, and H. H. Seliger. 1972. Growth and dissipation of phytoplankton in Chesapeake Bay: response to a large pulse of rainfall. Chesapeake Sci. 13(4):282–299.

Marsh, G. A. 1976. Ecology of the gastropod epifauna of eelgrass in a Virginia estuary. Chesapeake Sci. 17(3):182–187.

Marsho, T. V., R. P. Burchard, and R. Fleming. 1975. Nitrogen fixation in the Rhode River estuary of Chesapeake Bay. Can. J. Microbiol. 21:1348–1356.

Martin, G. W. 1928. Dinoflagellates from marine and brackish waters in New Jersey. Univ. Iowa Stud. Nat. Hist. 12(9):1–32.

Maurer, D. 1974. The Delaware estuary system, environmental impacts and socio-economic effects: biological condition of the deepwater portion of lower Delaware Bay. A report to the National Science Foundation RANN Program. College of Marine Studies, Univ. Delaware, Newark, Del. 94 pp.

Maurer, D. 1977. Estuarine benthic invertebrates of Indian River and Rehoboth Bay, Delaware. Int. Rev. Ges. Hydrobiol. 62(5):591–630.

Maurer, D., and L. Watling. 1973. Studies in the oyster community in Delaware: the effects of the estuarine environment on the associated fauna. Int. Rev. Gesamten Hydrobiol. 58(2):161–202.

Maurer, D., R. Lambert, and A. Pembroke. 1978. Seasonal fluctuations of zooplankton populations in lower Delaware Bay. Hydrobiologia 61(2):149–160.

McCarthy, J. J., W. R. Taylor, and M. E. Loftus. 1974. Significance of nanoplankton in the Chesapeake Bay estuary and problems associated with the measurement of nanoplankton productivity. Mar. Biol. 24(1):7–16.

McElroy, M. B., J. W. Elkins, S. C. Wolfsy, C. E. Kolb, A. P. Duran, and W. A. Kaplan. 1978. Production and release of nitrous oxide from the Potomac estuary. Limnol. Oceanogr. 23(6):1168–1182.

McHugh, J. L. 1967. Estuarine nekton. In G. H. Lauff, ed., Estuaries. AAAS Publ. 83, pp. 581–620.

McRoy, C. P., and C. McMillan. 1977. Production ecology and physiology of seagrasses. In C. P. McRoy, and C. Helfferich, eds., Seagrass ecosystems. Mar. Sci. 4:53–87.

Mountford, N. K., A. F. Holland, and J. A. Milhursky. 1977. Identification and description of macrobenthic communities in the Calvert Cliffs region of the Chesapeake Bay. Chesapeake Sci. 18(4):360–369.

Obeng-Asamoa, E. 1975. Diatoms associated with salt marsh pools that support the breeding of the salt marsh mosquito, *Aedes solicitans*, in the state of Delaware, U.S.A. Nova Hedwigia 26:317–339.

Orth, R. J. 1973. Benthic infauna of eelgrass, *Zostera marina*, beds. Chesapeake Sci. 14(4):258–269.

Orth, R. J. 1975. Destruction of eelgrass, *Zostera marina*, by the cownose ray, *Rhinoptera bonasus*, in the Chesapeake Bay. Chesapeake Sci. 16(3):205–208.

Orth, R. J. 1976. The demise and recovery of eelgrass, *Zostera marina*, in the Chesapeake Bay, Virginia. Aquat. Bot. 2(2):141–159.

Patrick, R. 1988. Changes in the chemical and biological characteristics of the upper Delaware River estuary in response to environmental laws. pp. 332–360. *In* Ecology and Restoration of the Delaware River Basin. E. Shymal, K. Majumdar, E. W. Miller, L. E. Sage. Pa. Academy Sci. Publ. pp. 431.

Patton, B. C., and B. I. Chabot, 1966. Factorial productivity experiments in a shallow estuary: characteristics of response surfaces. Chesapeake Sci. 7(3): 117–136.

Pennock, J. R. 1985. Chlorophyll distribution in the Delaware estuary: regulation by light limitation. Estuarine Coastal Shelf Sci. 21: 711–725.

Pennock, J. R. 1987. Temporal and spatial variability in phytoplankton ammonia and nitrate uptake in the Delaware estuary. Estuarine Coastal Shelf Sci. 24: 841–857.

Pennock, J. R., and Jonathan H. Sharp. 1986. Phytoplankton production in the Delaware estuary: temporal and spatial variability. Mar. Ecol. Prog. Ser. 34: 143–155.

Pritchard, D. W. 1971. Hydrodynamic models. Part 1. Three dimensional models, pp. 5–21. *In* G. H. Ward, and W. H. Espey, Estuarine modeling: an assessment. Tracor, Inc., Austin, Texas.

Pritchard, D. W., and H. H. Carter. 1971. Estuarine circulation patterns, pp. IV-1 to IV-17. *In* J. R. Schubel, convenor, The estuarine environment, estuaries and estuarine sedimentation. AGI Short Course Lect. Notes, Oct. 30–31, 1971, Wye Institute, Md. American Geological Institute, Washington, D.C.

Ralph, R. 1977. The myxophyceae of the marshes of southern Delaware. Chesapeake Sci. 18(2): 208–221.

Rasmussen, E. 1977. The wasting disease of eelgrass (*Zostera marina*) and its effects on environmental factors and fauna. *In* C. P. McRoy, and C. Helfferich, eds., Seagrass ecosystems. Mar. Sci. 4: 1–51.

Reimold, R. J. 1974. Evidence for dissolved phosphorus hypereutrophication, pp. 113–117. *In* H. T. Odum, B. J. Copeland, and E. A. McMahan, eds. Coastal ecological systems of the United States. Vol. 2. The Conservation Foundation World Wildlife Fund, Washington, D.C. For copyright information, contact WWF.

Richman, S., D. R. Heinle, and R. Huff. 1977. Grazing by adult estuarine calanoid copepods of the Chesapeake Bay. Mar. Biol. (Berlin) 42(1): 69–84.

Riley, G. A. 1952. Phytoplankton of Block Island Sound. Bull. Bingham Oceanogr. Collect. 13(3): 40–64.

Seitzinger, S. 1988. Denitrification in fresh water and coastal marine ecosystems: ecological and geochemical significance. Limnology and Oceanography 33(4) part 2: 702–724.

Sharp, J. H. 1984. Excerpts from *The Delaware estuary*: research as background for estuarine management and development. (Originally published July 1983.) Univ. Delaware Sea Grant College Program. 221 pp.

Simpson, R. L., D. F. Whigham, and R. Walker. 1978. Seasonal pattern of nutrient movement in a freshwater tidal marsh, pp. 243–257. *In* R. E. Good, D. F. Whigham, and R. L. Simpson, eds., Freshwater wetlands: ecological processes and management potential. Academic Press, New York.

Smith, B. A. 1971. The fishes of four low salinity tidal tributaries of the Delaware River estuary. *In* V. J. Schuler, proj. leader, An ecological study of the Delaware River in the vicinity of Artificial Island. Progress report for the period Jan.–Dec. 1970, Part 5, for Public Services Electric and Gas Co., Salem Nuclear Generating Station. Ichthyological Associates, Lansing, N.Y. 291 pp.

Steinberg, P. D., and V. S. Kennedy. 1979. Predation upon *Crassostrea virginica* larvae by two invertebrate species common to Chesapeake Bay, U.S.A., oyster bars. Veliger 22(1): 78–84.

Stevenson, J. C., D. R. Heinle, D. A. Flemer, R. J. Small, R. A. Rowland, and J. F. Ustach. 1977. Nutrient exchanges between brackish water marshes and the estuary, pp. 219–240. *In* M. Wiley, ed., Estuarine processes. Vol. 2. Academic Press, New York.

Taft, J. L., and W. R. Taylor. 1976. Phosphorus dynamics in some coastal plain estuaries, pp. 79–89. *In* M. Wiley, ed., Estuarine processes. Vol. 1. Uses, stresses and adaptation to the estuary. Academic Press, New York.

Virnstein, R. W. 1977. The importance of predation by crabs and fishes on benthic infauna in Chesapeake Bay. Ecology 58(6): 1199–1217.

Walton, T. E., III, and R. Patrick, eds. 1973. The Delaware estuary system: environmental impacts and socio-economic effects. Delaware River estuarine marsh survey. Report to the National Science Foundation RANN Program. The Academy of Natural Sciences, Philadelphia, Pa. 174 pp.

Watling, L., D. Bottom, A. Pembroke, and D. Maurer. 1979. Seasonal variations in Delaware Bay phytoplankton community structure. Mar. Biol. 52: 207–215.

Whigham, D. F., J. McCormick, R. E. Good, and R. L. Simpson. 1978. Biomass and primary production in freshwater tidal wetlands of the middle Atlantic coast, pp. 3–20. *In* R. E. Good, D. F. Whigham, and R. L. Simpson, eds., Freshwater wetlands: ecological processes and management potential. Academic Press, New York.

Wood, E. J. F. 1953. Reducing substances in *Zostera*. Nature 172(4385): 916.

Zaneveld, J. S. 1972. The benthic marine algae of Delaware, U.S.A. Chesapeake Sci. 13: 120–138.

CHAPTER 6

Southeastern Estuaries

The estuaries along the southeastern part of the coast of the United States are well developed. Many of them are estuaries formed behind barrier islands. The marshes are covered in grasses dominated by a few species. Five distinct zones have been recognized in salt marshes. They are creek bank, which has very little vegetation, and is muddy or sandy. The second, the streamside marsh, which is 1 to 3 m wide and is dominated by *Spartina alterniflora*, is adjacent to the creek bank. The third is the levee marsh, in which the *Spartina* is of intermediate height on the natural levees that border the creek. The fourth, the short *Spartina* marsh, is a flat area behind the levee. This is a wide area and supports the short form of *Spartina alterniflora*. The fifth, the *Salicornia* marsh, comprises sandy areas near the upland where *Salicornia* spp. may be common. *Baetis maritima* is another species that often flourishes in association with *Salicornia* spp.

The mud flats, which are intertidal, are dominated by blue-green algae, diatoms, and green algae. Usually, the diatoms are dominant. The blue-green genera which are often found on mud flats, belong to the genera *Lyngbya* and *Rivularia*. The green algae are genera such as *Rhizoclonium*, *Chaetomorpha*, *Ulva*, and *Enteromorpha*. Numerous diatom speices are present. Succession on these mud flats is often quite rapid, as the algae have short life histories and can quickly change with changes in the chemical and physical characteristics of the water. Algae are also found around the base of the stems and on the roots of plants within the marsh (Mitsch and Gosselink, 1986).

The Newport River estuarine system near Beaufort, North Carolina (see Figure 6.1), has been studied by many investigators. Because of the mild climate,

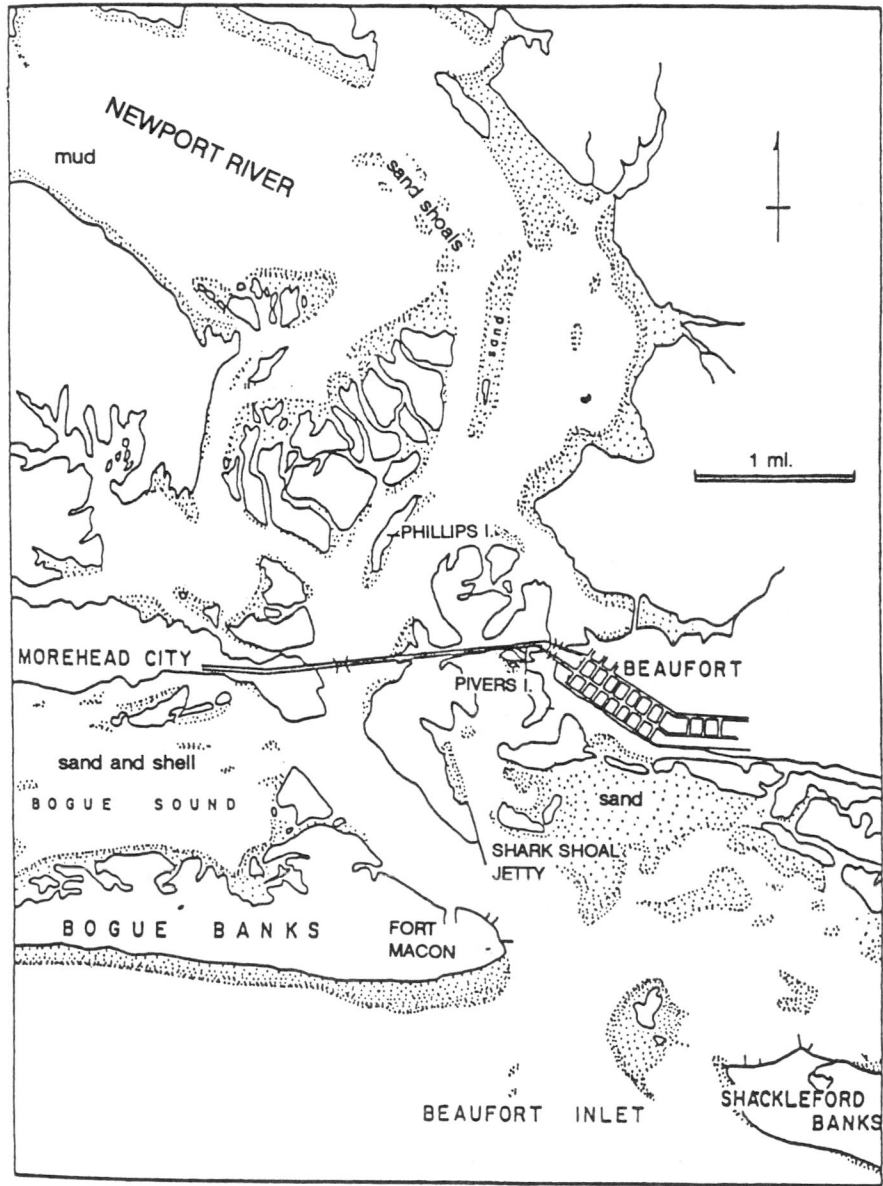

FIGURE 6.1.   Map of Beaufort, North Carolina and vicinity with notations on the bottom types. (From Maturo, 1957.)

it is a very productive area, with many species characteristic of warm-temperature estuaries. The species forming the associations in this area are listed in Table 6.1.

Salinities in the waterways adjacent to Beaufort Inlet were variable, as they were affected by fresh water entering the enclosed area as rain or from rivers

(*text continues on page 426*)

TABLE 6.1. *Species of the Newport Riben Estuary*

Species	Freshwater	Oligohaline	Mesohaline	Polyhaline
DIVISION BACCILLARIOPHYTA				
Class Bacillariophyceae				
Order Fragilariales				
Family Fragilariaceae				
Licmophora sp.				
Meridion circulare	×			
Fragilaria construens	×			
F. crotenensis	×			
F. investiens			×	
Asterionella formosa				
A. japonica			×	
Opheophora pacifica	×		×	×
Cymatosira belgica			×	
Dimerogramma minor				
D. rostratum			×	×
Rhaphoneis amphiceros		×		
R. belgica			×	
R. surirella		×	×	
Synedra gallionii		×		×
S. miniscula	×	×		
S. tabulata	×	×		
S. ulna	×	×	×	
Thalassionema nitzchoides				
Thallasiothrix frauenfeldii				
Tabellaria fenestrata	×		×	×
Plagiogramma pygmaeum		×	×	
Order Eunotiales				
Family Eunotiaceae				
Eunotogramma marinum			×	×
E. rostratum			×	×
Order Achnanthales				
Family Achnanthaceae				
Achnanthes exigua				
A. longipes	×	×	×	
Anorthoneis humii				
Cocconeis disculoides	×	×	×	×
Cocconeis spp.				
Order Naviculales				
Family Naviculaceae	×	×	×	×
Diploneis crabro		×	×	
D. bombus	×	×	×	
D. elliptica	×	×	×	
D. smithii		×	×	×
Gryosigma fasciola			×	×
G. febigerii			×	×

Continued

TABLE 6.1. (*Continued*)

Species	Freshwater	Oligohaline	Mesohaline	Polyhaline
G. peisonis		×		
G. spencerii	×	×	×	
Navicula abunda	×	×		
N. agnita				
N. meniscoides	×			
N. minima	×	×		
N. salinarum	×	×		
Navicula spp.				
Pleurosigma aestuarii			×	×
Family Cymbellaceae				
Amphipora alata		×	×	×
A. gigantea		×		
A. ornata	×	×		
A. paludosa	×	×		
Amphora acutinuscula		×	×	
A. proteoides				
Amphora spp.				
Order Epithemiales				
Family Epithemiaceae				
Denticula sp.				
Order Bacillariales				
Family Bacillariaceae				
Nitschia adducta				
N. compressa				
N. dissipata	×			
N. delicatissima				
N. hummi				
N. laevis				
N. longa				
N. penduriformis				
N. seriata				
N. sigma		×	×	
N. tryblionella	×	×		
N. vermicularis	×	×		
Nitzschia sp.				
Cylindrotheca closterium		×	×	
Order Coscinodiscales				
Family Coscinodiscaceae				
Melosira distans	×			
M. granulata	×			
M. icelandica	×			
M. moniliformis			×	×
M. sulcata			×	×
Melosira varians				
Hyalodiscus scelliger				×
Skeletonema costatum			×	×
S. tropicum			×	

TABLE 6.1. (*Continued*)

Species	Freshwater	Oligohaline	Mesohaline	Polyhaline
Coscinodiscus antiquus				×
C. gravidus				×
C. lineatus				×
C. perforatus				×
C. plicatus				×
Actinoptychus splendens				×
A. taeniatus				×
Cyclotella kutzingiana	×			
C. meneghiniana	×			
C. striata	×			
Thalassira decipiens				×
T. fluviatilis		×	×	
T. nana			×	×
T. rotula			×	×
Order Biddulphiales				
Family Biddulphiaceae				
Biddulphia alternans				
B. aurita				×
B. mobilenis				×
B. regia				×
B. rhombus				×
B. sinenis				×
Ditylum brightwelli				×
Bacteriastrum delicatulum				×
Ceratulina bergonii				
Hemiaulus sinensis			?	
Hemiaulus sp.				
Family Chaetoceraceae				
Chaetoceros affinis				×
C. borgei				×
C. curvisetus				×
C. debile				×
C. decipiens				×
C. didymus			×	×
C. gracilis				×
C. lacinisum				
C. simplex		×	×	×
C. subtilis		×	×	
C. subsecundus				×
C. teres				
C. wighami				
Order Rhizosoleniales				
Family Rhizosoleniaceae				
Rhizosolenia alternans				
R. calcar-avis				×
R. fragilissima				×

Continued

TABLE 6.1.　(*Continued*)

Species	Freshwater	Oligohaline	Mesohaline	Polyhaline
R. hebata var. *semispina*				
R. imbricata			×	×
R. robusta			×	×
R. setigera			×	×
R. stolterfathii				
Guinardia flaccide				×
Corethron criophilum				×
Leptocylindrus danicus			×	×
L. minimus				
DIVISION CYANOPHYTA				
Class Myxophyceae				
Order Chroococcales				
Family Chroococcaceae				
Anacystis aeruginosa	×			
Chroococcus sp.				
Merismopedia sp.				
Gomphosphaeria sp.				
Family Entophysalidaceae				
Entophysalis conferta			×	×
E. deusta			×	×
Order Oscillatoriales				
Suborder Oscillatorineae				
Family Oscilatoriaceae				
Arthrospira jenneri	×			
Lyngbya majuscula	×			
L. confervoides	×			
Microcoleus lyngbyaceaus	×			
(=*Oscillatoria tenuis*)				
Oscillatoria sp.				
Phoridium fragile				
Spirulina subsalsa			×	
Hydrocoleum comoides				
Suborder Nostocales				
Family Nostocaceae				
Calothrix crustacea			×	×
C. pulvinata				
DIVISION CHLOROPHYTA				
Class Chlorophyceae				
Order Tetrasporales				
Family Palmellaceae				
Dictyosphaerium sp.				
Dimorphococcus sp.				
Order Chlorococcales				
Family Hydrodictyaceae				
Pediastrum duplex	×			
Family Oocystaceae				
Ankistrodesmus falcatus	×			

TABLE 6.1. (*Continued*)

Species	Freshwater	Oligohaline	Mesohaline	Polyhaline
A. nannoselene	×			
Family Scenedesmaceae				
Scenedesmus acuminatus	×			
S. denticulatus				
S. opoliensis				
S. producto-capitatus				
S. quadracaudata	×			
Actinastrum hantzschii				
Order Ulotrichales				
Family Ulvaceae				
Monostroma oxyspermum	×		×	×
Ulva lactuca			×	×
U. lactuca var. *rigida*			×	×
Enteromorpha clathrata			×	×
E. flexuosa			×	
E. intestinalis			×	
E. linza			×	
E. lingulata			×	
E. prolifera			×	
Order Cladophorales				
Family Cladophoraceae				
Cladophora albida				
C. crystallina				
C. deliculata				
C. flexuosa		×	×	
C. gracilis		×	×	
C. refracta				
C. utriculosa				
Rhizoclonium riparium			×	
Chaetomorpha aerea				
Order Siphonales				
Family Bryopsidaceae				
Bryopsis hypnoides			×	×
B. plumosa				×
Order Desmidales				
Family Desmidaceae	×			
Cosmarium sp.				
Crucigenia crucifera				
C. fenestrata				
DIVISION PHAEOPHYTA				
Class Isogeneratae				
Order Ectocarpales				
Family Ectocarpaceae				
Ectocarpus confervoides			×	×
E. mitchellae			×	
E. confervoides f. *irregularis*			×	×

Continued

TABLE 6.1. (*Continued*)

Species	Freshwater	Oligohaline	Mesohaline	Polyhaline
Giffordia mitchellae			×	×
Order Sphacelariales				
Family Sphacelariaceae				
Sphacelaria furcigera				×
Order Dictyotales				
Family Dictyotaceae				
Dictyota dichotoma				×
Padina vickersiae				×
Class Heterogenatae				
Subclass Polystichinae				
Order Punctariales				
Family Asperococcaceae				
Punctaria latifolla				×
Class Cyclosporaceae				
Order Fucales				
Family Fucaceae				
Fucus versiculosus			×	×
Ascophyllum nodosum			×	×
Sargassum filipendula				
DIVISION RHODOPHYTA				
Class Rhodophoyceae				
Subclass Bangioideae				
Order Bangiales				
Family Bangiaceae				
Bangia fuscopurpurea				×
Goniotrichum alsidii				×
Asterocystis ramosa				×
Subclass Florideae				
Order Gelidiales				
Family Gelidiaceae				
Gelidium crinale		×	×	×
G. pusillum				×
Order Gigartinales				
Family Gigartinaceae				
Gigartina acicularis				×
G. foliifera				×
Order Rhodymeniales				
Family Rhodymeniaceae				
Lomentaria baileyana				×
Order Ceramiales				
Family Ceramiaceae				
Ceramium strictum				×
Family Rhodomelaceae				
Polysiphonia denudata				×
PHYLUM PROTOZOA				
Subphylum Plasmodroma				
Class Mastigophora				

TABLE 6.1. (*Continued*)

Species	Freshwater	Oligohaline	Mesohaline	Polyhaline
Subclass Phytomastiga				
Order Chrysomonadida				
Suborder Euchrysomonadida				
Family Chromulinidae				
Chrysochromulina sp.				
Family Ochromonadidae				
Dinobryon sertularia	×			
Pseudopedinella pyriforme				
Family Prymnesidae				
Prymnesum parvum				
Order Cryptomonadida				
Suborder Eucryptomonadina				
Family Cryptomonadidae				
Cryptomonas ovata	×	×		
Cryptomonas sp.				
Rhodomonas amphioxeia				
R. minuta				
Order Phytomonadida				
Family Chlamydomonadidae				
Chlamydomonas sp.				
Family Carteriidae				
Pyramimonas amylifera				
P. grossii				
P. obovata				
P. nanella				
P. plurioculata				
Pyramimonas sp.				
Family Volvocidae				
Pandorina morum	×			
Order Dinoflagellida				
Suborder Prorocentrina				
Family Prorocentridae				
Prorocentrum micans			×	
P. minimum				
Exuviella compressa			×	
Suborder Peridiniina				
Superfamily Gymnodiniodea				
Family Gymnodiniidae				
Gymnodinium sp.				
Amphidinium sp.				
Katodinium rotundatum				
Gyrodinium dominas				
G. estuariale				
G. glabum				
G. metum				
G. pellucidum				

Continued

TABLE 6.1. (*Continued*)

Species	Freshwater	Oligohaline	Mesohaline	Polyhaline
Superfamily Peridinioidea				
Family Peridiniidae				
Ceratium fusus		×		
Peridiniopsis rotunda				
Peridinium triquetrum				
P. trochoideum				
Class Sarcodina				
Subclass Rhizopoda				
Order Foraminiferida				
Ammonia beccari				×
Cibicides pseudoungarianus				×
Florilus atlanticus				×
Hanzawia concentrica				×
Miliammina beaufortensis				×
M. fusca				×
Psammosphaera fusca				×
Quinqueloculina poeyana				×
Q. seminulum				×
Family Silicinidae				
Ammodiscus sp.				×
Family Camerinidae				
Elphidium gunteri				×
E. incertum				×
Family Globorotaliidae				
Globigerinoides ruber				×
PHYLUM PORIFERA				
Class Demospongiae				
Subclass Teractinomorpha				
Order Choristida				
Family Craniellidae				
Craniella crania				
Order Spirophorida				
Family Tetillidae				
Tetilla laminaris				
Order Hadromerida				
Family Suberitidae				
Suberites undulatus				×
Family Spirasterellidae				
Spirastrella andrewsii				
Family Clionidae				
Cliona cellata			×	×
Poterion atlantica				
Subclass Ceractinomorpha				
Order Poecilosclerida				
Family Mycalidae				
Stylotella heliophila			×	×
Lissodendoryx carolinensis			×	×

TABLE 6.1. (*Continued*)

Species	Freshwater	Oligohaline	Mesohaline	Polyhaline
Family Clathriidae				
Microciona prolifera			×	×
Order Haplosclerida				
Family Renieridae				
Reniera tubifera			×	×
Family Spongellidae				
Pleraplysilla latens				
Order Dendroceratida				
Family Apylsillidae				
Aplysilla longispina				
PHYLUM CNIDARIA				
Class Hydrozoa				
Order Athecata				
Family Tubulariidae				
Tubularia crocea			×	×
Family Pennariidae				
Pennaria tiarella			×	×
Family Clavidae				
Cordylophora caspia	×	×	×	
Family Hydractiniidae				
Hydractinia echinata			×	×
Family Bougainvillidae				
Garveia groenlandica	×	×	×	
Family Eudendriidae				
Eudendrium carneum			×	×
E. ramosum				
Order Thecata				
Family Campanularidae				
Clytia hemisphaerica			×	
Family Lafoeidae				
Filellum expansum				×
Class Anthozoa				
Subclass Octocorallia				
Order Gorgonacea				
Family Gorgoniidae				
Leptogorgia vingulata				
Subclass Zoantharia				
Order Actinaria				
Family Diadumenidae				
Diadumene leucolena			×	
Order Scleractinia				
Astrangia danae				
PHYLUM PLATYHELMINTHES				
Class Turbellaria				
Order Polycladida				
Suborder Acotylea				

Continued

TABLE 6.1. (*Continued*)

Species	Freshwater	Oligohaline	Mesohaline	Polyhaline
Section Craspedommata				
Family Stylochidae				
Stylochus ellipticus	×	×	×	
Suborder Acotylea				
Section Schematammata				
Family Planocaeridae				
Eustylochus meridianalis				
PHYLUM BRYOZOA				
Class Gymnolaemata				
Order Ctenostomata				
Family Alcyonidiidae				
Alyconidium hauffi			×	
A. polyoum			×	
A. mammillatum			×	
A. verrilli			×	
Family Victorellidae				
Victorella pavida				
Family Nolellidae				
Anguinella palmata			×	×
Family Vesiculariidae				
Bowerbankia gracilis			×	
Amathia brasiliensis				
A. convoluta				×
A. distans				
A. vidovici				×
Family Walkeriidae				
Aeverillia armata			×	
A. setigera			×	
Family Triticellidae				
Triticella elongata				×
Family Paludicellidae				
Sundanella sibogae				
Order Cyclostomata				
Family Crisiidae				
Crisia eburnea				×
C. elongata				×
C. ramosa				×
Family Tubuliporidae				
Proboscina sp.				
Family Diaperoeciidae				
Diaperoecia floridana				
Crisulipora orientalis				
Order Cheilostomata				
Suborder Anasca				
Family Aeteidae				
Aetea anguina				
Family Membraniporidae				

TABLE 6.1. (*Continued*)

Species	Freshwater	Oligohaline	Mesohaline	Polyhaline
Membranipora tuberculata			×	×
M. savartii		×	×	
M. tenuis			×	×
Conopeum commensale				
Family Electridae				
Electra crustulenta		×	×	
E. hastingsae				
Family Hincksinidae				
Aplousina gigantea				
Family Chaperiidae				
Chaperia galeata				
Family Thalamoporellidae				
Thalamoporella falcifera				
T. gothica var. *floridana*				
Family Lunulariidae				
Discoporella umbellata				
D. doma				
Family Epistoniidae				
Synnotum aegyptiacum				
Family Bugilidae				
Bugula neritina				
B. avicularia			×	×
B. californica			×	×
B. turrita				
Family Cribrilinidae				
Colletosia radiata				
Suborder Ascophora				
Family Hippothoidae				
Hippothoa hyalina			×	×
Family Schizoporellidae				
Schizoporella cornuta				
S. floridana			×	×
S. unicornis			×	×
Family Microporellidae				
Microprella ciliata			×	×
Family Hippoporinidae				
Hippoporina contracta				
Aimulosia uvulifera				
Hippoporidra janthina				
Family Celleporinidae				
Schizmopora dichotoma				
S. magaritacea				
Holoporella magnifica				
Costazia costazii				
Family Smittinidae				
Parasmittina trispinosa			×	×
Family Cheiloporinidae				

Continued

TABLE 6.1.   (*Continued*)

Species	Freshwater	Oligohaline	Mesohaline	Polyhaline
Hippodiplosia americana				
Cryptosula pallasiana			×	×
Family Reteporidae				
Rhynchozoon rostratum				
PHYLUM ENTOPROCTA				
Family Pedicellinidae				
Pedicellina cernua			×	×
Barentsia discreta			×	×
B. laxa			×	×
PHYLUM ANNELIDA				
Class Polychaeta				
Order Orbiniida				
Family Orbiniidae				
Scoloplos sp.				
Haploscoloplos fragilis			×	
Order Spionida				
Suborder Spioniformia				
Family Spionidae				
Streblospio benedicti				
Scolelepis squamata				×
Polydora websteri				
Family Magelonidae				
Magelona rosea				×
Order Capitellida				
Family Maldanidae				
Clymenella torquata			×	
Order Opheliida				
Family Ophelidae				
Armandia agilis				
Order Phyllodocida				
Family Nephtyidae				
Nephtys picata			×	
Suborder Phylodociformia				
Family Phyllodocidae				
Eteone heteropoda			×	
Suborder Nereidiformia				
Family Nereidae				
Laeonereis culveri				
Nereis succinea		×	×	
Suborder Glyceriformia				
Family Glyceridae				
Glycera americana		×		
G. dibranchiata		×		
Order Eunicida				
Family Onuphidae				
Diopatra cuprea			×	×
Family Lumberinereidae				

TABLE 6.1. (*Continued*)

Species	Freshwater	Oligohaline	Mesohaline	Polyhaline
Lumbrinereis sp.				
PHYLUM ECHINODERMATA				
Class Holothuroidea				
Order Dendrochirota				
Family Sclerodactylidae				
Sclerodactyla briareus			×	×
(= *Thione briareus*)				
Order Apodida				
Family Synaptidae				
Leptosynapta inhaerens				×
Class Echinoidea				
Subclass Regularia				
Order Stirodonta				
Family Arbaciidae				
Arbacia punctulata			×	×
Order Clylpeasteroida				
Family Scutellidae				
Mellita quinquiesperforata			×	×
Class Ophiuroidea				
Order Ophiurae				
Family Ophiothrichidae				
Ophiothrix angulata			×	×
PHYLUM BRACHIOPODA				
Class Inarticulata				
Order Lingulida				
Family Lingulidae				
Glottidia audebarti				
PHYLUM MOLLUSCA				
Class Gastropoda				
Subclass Prosobranchiata				
Order Mesogastropoda				
Suborder Littorina				
Family Cerithiidae				
Bittium varium				×
Cerithiopsis greenii				×
C. subulata				×
Seila adamsii				
Family Triphoridae				
Triphora nigrocincta				×
Family Epitoniidae				
Epitonium angulatum				×
Family Calyptraeidae				
Crepidula convexa				×
C. fornicata				×
C. plana				×
Family Ovulidae				

Continued

TABLE 6.1.   (*Continued*)

Species	Freshwater	Oligohaline	Mesohaline	Polyhaline
Simnia uniplicata				
Family Naticidae				
Polonices duplicatus				×
Order Neogastropoda				
Family Columbellidae				
Mitrella lunata				×
Anachis avara				×
A. obesa				×
A. translirata				×
Family Muricidae				
Urosalpinx cinereus				
Eupleura candata				
Family Melongidae				
Busycon canaliculatum				
B. carica				
B. contrarium				
Family Nassaridae				
Ilynassa obsoleta			×	×
(= *Nassarius obsoletus*)				
Nassarius vibex			×	×
Family Olividae				
Olivella mutica				×
Family Terebridae				
Terebra concava				×
T. dislocata				×
Family Turridae				
Mangila cerina				×
M. plicosa				×
Order Pyramidelloida				
Family Pyramidellidae				
Odostomia impressa			×	×
O. seminuda				×
Pyramidella candida				×
P. crenulata				
Turbonilla interrupta				×
Subclass Opisthobranchiata				
Order Cephalaspidea				
Family Acteonidae				
Acteon punctostriatus				×
Family Cylichnidae				
Cylichna bidentata				×
Family Retusidae				
Retusa canaliculata				×
Order Sacoglossa				
Family Plankobranchidae				
Stiliger vanellus				
(= *Ercolania vanellus*)				

TABLE 6.1. (*Continued*)

Species	Freshwater	Oligohaline	Mesohaline	Polyhaline
Order Nudibranchia				
Suborder Doridoida				
Family Corambidae				
Doridella obscura			×	×
Class Bivalvia				
Subclass Palaeotaxodonta				
Order Nuculoida				
Family Nuculidae				
Nucula proxima				×
Family Nuculanidae				
Nuculana acuta				×
N. concentrica				×
Subclass Cryptodonta				
Order Solemioida				
Family Solemyacidae				
Solemya velum				×
Subclass Pteriomorphia				
Order Arcoida				
Family Arcidae				
Anadara brasiliana				
A. ovalis				×
A. transversa				
Noetia ponderosa				
Order Mytiloida				
Family Mytilidae				
Mytilus edulis			×	×
Modiolus demissus		×	×	×
M. modiolus			×	×
Order Pteroida				
Suborder Pteriina				
Family Pteriidae				
Pteria colymbus				
Family Pectinidae				
Aequipecten gibbus				×
Family Anomiidae				
Anomia simplex				×
Family Ostreidae				
Ostrea virginia			×	×
Subclass Heterodonta				
Order Veneroida				
Family Lucinidae				
Lucina multilineata				×
Divaricella quadrisulcata				×
Family Ungulinidae				
Diplodonta punctata				
Family Leptonidae				

Continued

TABLE 6.1.   (*Continued*)

Species	Freshwater	Oligohaline	Mesohaline	Polyhaline
Montacula elevata				×
(= *Allgena elevata*)				
Mysella planulata				×
Family Carditidae				
Cardita tridentata				×
Family Crassatellidae				
Crassinella lunulata				×
Family Cardiidae				
Laevicardium mortoni				×
Trachycardium muricatum				×
Family Mactridae				
Spisula solidissma				×
Mulivia lateralis				×
Family Solenidae				
Ensis directus				×
Family Tellinidae				
Tagelus divisus				×
T. gibbus				×
Tellina agilis				
Tellina cf. *alternata*				×
Strigilla mirabilis				×
Macoma balthica			×	×
M. phenax			×	×
M. tenta				×
Family Donacidae				
Donac variabilis				
Family Semelidae				
Abra aequalis				×
Semele purpuracens				×
Cumingia tellinoides				×
Family Dreissenidae				
Congeria leucophaeta	×	×	×	
Family Veneridae				
Mercenaria mercenaria	×	×	×	×
Chione cancellata				×
C. grus				×
Gemma gemma				×
Dosinia discus				×
Family Petricolidae				
Petricola pholadiformis				×
Order Myoida				
Family Corbulidae				
Corbula contracta				×
Family Pholadidae				
Barnea truncata				×
Family Teredinidae				
Bankia fimbriata			×	×

TABLE 6.1. (*Continued*)

Species	Freshwater	Oligohaline	Mesohaline	Polyhaline
Family Lyonsiidae				
Lyonsia hyalina				×
Family Pandoridae				
Pandora trilineata				×
PHYLUM ARTHROPODA				
Subphylum Pyncnogonida				
Class Pantopoda				
Family Phoxichilidiidae				
Anoplodactylus lentus				
Subphylum Mandibulata				
Class Crustacea				
Subclass Copepoda				
Order Calanoida				
Family Calanidae				
Parvocalanus crassirostris				×
Family Acartiidae				
Acartia tonsa				
Family Centropagidae		×	×	
Centropaages hamatus	×	×	×	×
C. typicus	×	×	×	×
Family Diaptomidae				
Pseudodiaptomus coronatus	×			
Family Temoridae				
Eurytemora affinis				
Temora turbinata				
Family Pontellidae				
Labidocera aestiva			×	×
Order Harpacticoida				
Family Peltidiidae				
Alteutha sp.				×
Family Thalestridae				
Thalestris gibba			×	×
Family Diosaccidae				
Amphiascopsis cincutus			×	×
Family Canthocamptidae				
Mesochra pygmaea	×	×		
Family Tachidiidae				
Clytemennstra rostrata		×	×	×
Family Metidae				
Metis holothuriae				
M. ignea				
Order Cyclopoida				
Family Oithonidae				
Oithona colcarva				
Oithona sp.				
Family Cyclopinidae				

Continued

TABLE 6.1.   (*Continued*)

Species	Freshwater	Oligohaline	Mesohaline	Polyhaline
Paracylcopina sp.	×	×	×	
Family Oncaeidae				
Oncaea venusta	×	×	×	
Family Corycaeidae				
Corycaeus sp.				
Subclass Cirripedia				
Order Thoracica				
Suborder Balanomorpha				
Family Chthamalidae				
Chthamalus fragilis			×	×
Family Balanidae				
Balanus amphitrite niveus			×	
B. eburneus			×	×
B. galeatus			×	×
B. improvisus		×	×	×
B. subalbidus	×	×	×	×
Subclass Malacostracá				
Division Peracarida				
Order Cumacea				
Family Bodotriidae				
Leptocuma sp.				
Family Diastylidae				
Oxyurostylis smithii			×	×
Order Isopoda				
Suborder Anthuridea				
Family Anthuridae				
Limnora lignorum	×	×		
Suborder Flabellifera				
Family Sphaeromidae				
Sphaeroma quadridentata			×	×
Exosphaeroma diminutum				×
Suborder Valvifera				
Family Idoteidae				
Chirodotea coeca				×
Chiridotea sp.		×	×	
Suborder Onsicidea				
Family Ligididae				
Ligia exotica				×
(= *Lygida exotica*)				
Order Amphipoda				
Suborder Gammaridae				
Family Ampeliscidae				
Ampelisca vadorum			×	×
A. verrilli			×	×
Family Amphithoidae				
Amphithoe longimana				
A. valida				

TABLE 6.1. (*Continued*)

Species	Freshwater	Oligohaline	Mesohaline	Polyhaline
Cyamdusa compta				
Family Argissidae				
Argissa hamatipes				
Family Atylidae				
Atylus minikoti				
Family Bateidae				
Batea catharinensis				×
Family Colomastigidae				
Colomastix halichondriae				
Family Corophiidae				
Cerapus tubularis				
Corophium acheruscium				
C. acutum				
C. insidiousum				
C. lacustre	×	×	×	
C. simile				
C. tuberculatum				
Erichthonius brasiliensis				×
Grandidierella bonnieroides				
Unicola irrorata				×
U. serrata				
Family Gammaridae				
Elasmopous laevis				
Gammarus mucronatus			×	×
G. palustris				
G. tigrinus	×			
Maera spp.				
Melita appendiculata				
M. fresnelii				
N. nitida				
Gammaropsis maculata				
Microprotopus raneyi				
Family Haustoridae				
Acanthohastorius intermedius				
A. millsi				
Amphiporeia virginiana				
Bathyporeia parkeri				
Haustorius sp.				
Lepidactylus dytiscus			×	
Neohaustorius schmitzi				
Parahaustorius attenuatus				
P. longimerus				
Protohaustorius nr. *deichmannae*				
Family Hyalidae				
Hyale plumulosa			×	
Parhyale hawaiensis				

Continued

TABLE 6.1. (*Continued*)

Species	Freshwater	Oligohaline	Mesohaline	Polyhaline
Family Ischyroceridae				
Jassa falcata			×	
J. marmorata			×	
Family Leucothoidae				
Leucothoe spinicarpa				
Family Liljeborgiidae				
Listriella barnardi				
L. clymenellae				
Family Lysinianassidae				
Lysianassa alba				
Family Oedicerotidae				
Monoculoides edwardsi				×
Synchelidium americanum n. sp.				
Family Photidae				
Gammaropsis maculata				
Family Phoxocephalidae				
Paraphoxus spinsosus				
P. floridana				
Trichophoxus epistomus			×	×
T. floridanus			×	×
Family Pleustidae				
Parapleustes aestuarius				
Family Podoceridae				
Podocerus brailiensis				
Family Stenothoidae				
Parametopella cypris				
Stenothoe gallensis			×	×
Family Taltridae				
Orchestia grillus			×	×
O. platensis			×	×
O. uhleri			×	×
Talorchestia longicornis			×	×
T. megalophthalma			×	×
Suborder Caprellida				
Family Caprellidae				
Caprella equilibra sp.			×	×
C. penantis			×	×
Paracaprella tenuis				
Luconacia incerta				
Division Eucarida				
Order Decapoda				
Suborder Natantia				
Section Caridea				
Family Hippolytidae				
Hippolysmata wurdemanni			×	×
Latreutes gibberosus				
Family Palaemonidae				

TABLE 6.1. (Continued)

Species	Freshwater	Oligohaline	Mesohaline	Polyhaline
Palaemontes carolinus				×
Family Crangonidae				
Crangon heterochaelis				×
Section Anomura				
Family Paguridae				
Pagurus longicarpus				×
Family Hippidae				
Emerita talpoida				×
Section Brachyura				
Subsection Branchygnatha				
Infrasubsection Oxyrhyncha				
Family Majidae				
Pelia mutica				
Libnia dubia			×	×
Family Portunidae				
Ovalipes ocellatus				
Portunus sayi				×
Family Xanthidae				
Neopanope texana sayi				
Rhithropanopeus harrisii	×	×	×	×
Family Pinnotheridae				
Pinnixia cylindrica				
P. chaetopterana				
P. sayana				
Family Grapsidae				
Sesarma cinereum				×
PHYLUM CHORDATA				
Subphylum Urochordata				
Class Ascidiacea				
Order Enterogona				
Suborder Aplousobranchia				
Family Didemnidae				
Didemnum lutarium				
Suborder Phlebobranchia				
Family Perophoridae				
Perophora viridis				
Family Ascidiidae			×	×
Phallusia hygomiana				
Order Pleurogona				
Suborder Stolidobranchiata				
Family Styelidae				
Styela plicata				
Family Molgulidae				
Molgula manhattensis			×	×
Class Larvacea				
Family Oikopleuridae				

Continued

TABLE 6.1. *(Continued)*

Species	Freshwater	Oligohaline	Mesohaline	Polyhaline
Oikopleura sp.				
Subphylum Leptocardia				
Family Branchiostomidae				
Branchiostoma caribaeum				
Subphylum Vertebrata				
Class Chondrichthyes				
Order Squaliformes				
Family Dasyatidae				
Dasyatis sayi				×
Class Osteichthyes				
Order Seminotiformes				
Family Lepisosteidae				
Lepisosteus ossseus	×	×	×	
Order Amiiformes				
Family Amiidae				
Amia calva	×			
Order Elopiformes				
Family Elopidae				
Elops saurus	×	×	×	×
Order Anguilliformes				
Family Anguillidae				
Anguilla rostrata	×	×	×	×
Family Congridae				
Conger oceanicus				×
Order Clupeiformes				
Family Clupeidae				
Alosa aestivalis	×	×	×	×
A. mediocris	×	×	×	×
A. pseudoharengus		×	×	×
A. sapidissima	×	×	×	
Dorosoma cepedianum	×	×	×	×
Brevoortia tyrannus	×	×	×	×
Optisthonema oglinum			×	×
Family Engraulidae				
Anchoa hepsetus		×	×	×
A. mitchilli	×	×	×	×
Order Salmoniformes				
Family Umbridae				
Umbra pygmaea	×			
Family Esocidae				
Esox americanus	×	×	×	
E. niger	×	×		
Order Myctofiformes				
Family Synodontidae				
Synodus foetus			×	×
Order Cypriniformes				
Family Cyprinidae				

TABLE 6.1. (Continued)

Species	Freshwater	Oligohaline	Mesohaline	Polyhaline
Cyprinis carpio	×	×		
Hybognathus nuchalis	×	×		
Notemigonus crysoleucas	×	×		
Notropis amoenus	×			
N. bifrenatus	×	×		
N. chalybaeus	×			
N. cummingsae	×			
N. hudsonis	×			
N. procne	×			
Family Catostomidae				
Erimyzon oblongus	×	×		
E. succetta	×	×		
Order Siluriformes				
Family Ictaluridae				
Ictalurus catus	×			
I. natalis	×	×		
I. nebulosus	×	×	×	
I. punctatus	×			
Noturus gyrinus	×	×		
Order Percopsiformes				
Family Amblyopsidae				
Chologaster cornuta	×	×		
Family Aphredoderidae				
Aphredoderus sayanus	×	×	×	
Order Gobiesociformes				
Family Gobisocidae				
Gobiesox strumosus		×	×	×
Order Gadiformes				
Family Gadidae				
Urophycis regis				×
Family Ophidiidae				
Ophidion marginatum				×
(= Rissola marginata)				
Order Atheriniformes				
Family Exocoetidae				
Hyporhamphus unifasciatus				×
Family Belonidae				
Tylosurus acus				×
(= Strongylura acus)				
Strongylura marina	×	×	×	×
Family Cyprinodontidae				
Cyprinodon variegatus		×	×	×
Fundulus heteroclitus	×	×	×	×
F. luciae				×
F. majalis	×	×	×	×
F. nothi	×	×		

Continued

TABLE 6.1. (*Continued*)

Species	Freshwater	Oligohaline	Mesohaline	Polyhaline
Luciana parva	×			
Family Poecilliidae				
Gambusia affinis		×	×	×
Family Atherinidae				
Membras martinica	×	×	×	×
Menidia beryllina	×	×	×	×
M. menidia				×
Order Gasterosteiformes				
Family Syngnathidae				
Syngnathus floridae				×
S. fuscus				×
Syngnathus sp.				
Order Perciformes				
Family Percichthyidae				
Morone americana	×	×	×	×
(= *Roccus americanus*)				
Mycteroperca microlepis				×
Family Centrarchidae				
Acantharcus pomotis	×			
Centrarchus macropterus	×	×		
Elassoma zonatum	×	×		
Enneacanthus gloriosus	×	×	×	
E. obesus	×	×		
Lepomis auritus	×	×		
L. gibbosus	×	×	×	
L. gulosus	×	×		
(= *Chaenobrythus gulosus*)				
Lepomis macrochirus	×	×		
L. marginatus	×	×		
Micropterus salmoides	×	×	×	
Pomoxis nigromaculatus	×			
Family Percidae				
Etheostoma fusiformis	×	×		
(= *E. barratti*)				
E. nigrum	×			
E. serriferum	×	×		
Perca flavescens	×	×	×	
Family Pomatomidae				
Pomatomus salatrix			×	×
Family Carangidae				
Caranx hippos			×	×
Oligoplites saurus	×	×	×	×
Selene volmer				×
Trachinotus carolinus				×
T. falcatus			×	×
Family Lutjanidae				
Lutjanus campechanus				×

TABLE 6.1. (Continued)

Species	Freshwater	Oligohaline	Mesohaline	Polyhaline
(= *Lutjanus blackfordii*)				
L. griseus		×	×	×
Rhamboplites aurorubens				×
Family Gerreidae				
Eucinostoma gula		×	×	×
Family Haemulidae				
Orthopristis chrysoptera	×	×	×	
Family Sparidae				
Lagodon rhomboides	×	×	×	×
Family Sciaenidae				
Bairdella chrysoura	×	×	×	×
Cynoscion nebulosus	×	×	×	×
C. regalis			×	×
Leiostomus xanthurus	×	×	×	×
Menticirrhus americanus				×
M. littoralis				×
M. saxatilis				×
Micropogonias undulatus	×	×	×	×
Pogonias cromis				×
Sciaenops ocellatus	×	×	×	×
Stellifer lanceolatus				×
Family Mullidae				
Pseudupeneus maculatus				×
Family Kyphosidae				
Kyphosus sectatrix		×	×	×
Family Ephippidae				
Chaetodipterus faber		×	×	×
Family Mugilidae				
Mugil cephalus	×	×	×	×
M. curema	×	×	×	×
Family Sphyraenidae				
Sphyraena barracuda				×
Family Blennidae				
Hypsoblennius hentzi				×
Chasmodes bosquianus				×
Family Gobiidae				
Gobionellus boleosoma	×	×	×	×
G. stigmaticus		×	×	×
Gobiosoma bosci		×	×	
Family Scombridae				
Scomberomorus maculatus		×	×	×
Family Trigilidae				
Prionotus carolinus				×
Order Pleuronectiformes				
Family Bothidae				
Etropus crossotus				×

Continued

TABLE 6.1. (*Continued*)

Species	Freshwater	Oligohaline	Mesohaline	Polyhaline
Paralichthus albigutta				×
P. dentatus			×	×
P. lethostigma	×	×	×	×
P. squamilentus				×
Scopthalmus aquosus				×
Family Soleidae				
Trinectes maculatus	×	×	×	
Family Cynoglossidae				
Symphurus plagiusa		×	×	×
Order Teradontiformes				
Family Balistidae				
Monocanthus hispidus				×
Family Tetradontidae				
Sphoeroides maculatus				×

and streams, by evaporation, and by tidal currents (Stephenson and Stephenson, 1952). Salinity averaged about 20 to 32 ppt in this area and ranged from 10 to 38 ppt.

The Newport River estuary showed a general pattern of sediments typical of estuaries. Fine and very fine sand were characteristic of the estuary sediments. Silt and mud accumulated at the mouths of slow-moving sloughs and in the central, deeper-water areas of the upper part of the estuary. Particle size and sorting increased downstream in keeping with increased current action. The deepest zones of the estuary were flooded by lag "gravel" of medium sand size. Finer particles were swept up the estuary or out to sea (Bird, 1970).

The estuary, which flows into Beaufort Sound, received effluents from fish-processing plants, runoff from fertilized farmland, and sewage from primary and secondary treatment plants (Williams, 1966, in Smith, 1978). The estuary was well mixed and the euphotic zone generally extended to the bottom. The functioning of estuarine aquatic communities is based on detrital and primary productivity, and the cycling of nutrients results from the functioning of the entire system.

In contrast to the Beaufort estuary, the North Inlet, South Carolina, received relatively little fresh water and is free of evident anthropogenic pollution. This salt marsh is characteristic of marshes along the southeastern coast of the United States from Georgetown, South Carolina to Jacksonville, Florida. It has a dendritic pattern of tidal creeks within broad expanses of the salt marsh cord grass, *Spartina alterniflora*. The 34-km² salt marsh consists of 70% vegetated marsh surface, 23% subtidal creek bottom, 4% oyster bars, and 3% mud flats.

It is a well-mixed, high-salinity estuary (30 to 35 ppt salt). Rainfall is approximately 1.3 m yr^{-1} which accounts for over 75% of the freshwater input into the salt marsh. The majority of the rainfall occurs in fall and winter and the remainder during summer thunderstorms. Mean freshwater input (rainfall and forest surface runoff) to the salt marsh over the year measured approximately 7.0 × 10^4 m^3 per tide. The largest creek entering the marsh is Town Creek with a mean tidal prism of 15.0 × 10^6 m^3. This creek accounts for 80 to 85% of the total tidal prism for the North Inlet marsh system. The North James Creek accounts for about 15% of the total water exchange. The smallest creek, South Jones, accounts for 1% to 2% of the total water exchange (Whitting et al., 1987).

NUTRIENT CYCLING

Concentrations of ammonia, phosphates, nitrates, and nitrites during low tide coupled with lack of stream flow during the late summer suggest that there is an internal source of generation of these species in estuaries. Ammonia and orthophosphate most likely have their source in sediment diffusion from the tidal creek sediments and/or seepage from the vegetated marsh surface during tidal exposure. The high nitrates plus high nitrite values and low values at low tide are caused by nitrification within the tidal water or tidal creek sediments. During the summer there is evidence for a source of dissolved organic nitrogen and dissolved organic phosphorus within the North Inlet system probably via diffusion from creek sediments. In general, the main source of dissolved organic nitrogen is via stream flow from adjacent watersheds. Particulate nitrogen and phosphorus concentrations are a function of wind and rain events that cause resuspension of particulate matter from the tidal creek banks, rain events that scour the marsh surface during tidal exposures, and high-tide velocities that scour the creek bottoms (Wolaver et al., 1984).

Phosphorus

Along the North Carolina coast, including the Beaufort area, the concentration of phosphorus is generally low throughout the year compared to the adjoining Pamlico Sound or the Georgia salt marsh complex. Dissolved inorganic phosphorus (DIP) was found by Thayer (1971) to range from 0.00 to 1.46 μg A L^{-1}, dissolved organic phosphorus (DOP) from 0.00 to 1.60 μg A L^{-1}, and particulate phosphorus (pp) from 0.01 to 1.36 μg A L^{-1}. Thayer also found that the average weighted DIP and DOP concentrations were fairly constant during fall and early winter, both ranging from 0.2 to 0.3 μg A L^{-1}. Peak concentrations of DOP and DIP occurred in June and July, respectively, followed by a decline during late summer and fall. The freshwater portion of the Newport River had significantly higher average DIP and PP concentrations than elsewhere (Thayer, 1971).

In another study of the Beaufort system (Thayer, 1974), inorganic phosphate was generally below concentrations reported limiting to phytoplankton growth.

The paucity of nutrients was presumably a result of little enrichment of the area by land drainage and river inflow. More important, phosphates may have been removed from the water and immobilized by bacteria growing on suspended *Spartina* detritus.

In the Pamlico River estuary of North Carolina, total phosphorus concentrations were always relatively high (Hobbie et al., 1975). Most of the phosphorus came from upstream, where concentrations were between 2 and $6\,\mu g\,A\,L^{-1}$. Highest average concentrations were found from August to October, while the lowest average values occurred from April to July. Phosphorus did not limit primary productivity. The estuary was a sink for nutrients, retaining over 60% annually of the total phosphorus, presumably in the sediments.

In the salt marsh and estuarine systems near Sapelo Island, phosphorus was not limiting. This was because large reserves of phosphorus, much of it in the form of phosphate, were sorbed in clay sediments or peat. Clay acted as the dominated binding agent and sink in the Georgia marshes. Next to the soil and sediments, the biota, primarily *Spartina* and the microorganisms, were the only other sizable standing stocks of phosphorus (Whitney et al., 1981).

Phosphorus can be mobilized from the sediments by different means. Suspended sediments or water percolating through sediments will exchange phosphate. Thus rainwater run off will increase phosphorus concentrations. *Spartina* may be engaged in the active uptake of phosphate from the sediments. Phosphate was leached out when *Spartina* was covered by high water, or was recycled as the grass died and reentered the water as detritus.

In the Georgia estuarine system, there was a large input of phosphate from the Altamaha River, but less than 1% of this reached the Duplin River. Ocean phosphate was imported to the Duplin River and marsh, and detrital phosphorus was released into the marsh. An estimated half of the annual production of *Spartina* was degraded, releasing $3\,g\,p\,m^{-2}$ into the marsh. The marsh received organic phosphorus and released inorganic phosphate, with the net flux of total phosphorus probably being into the marsh. Phosphate was exported during the warm months, and organic phosphorus was imported throughout the year. In summary, the largest single source of organic phosphorus imported into the Sapelo Island salt marshes was the ocean. The Altamaha River was the second largest contributor of phosphorus in the area.

Nitrogen

In the Beaufort, North Carolina estuarine system, the available nitrogen was low throughout the year, in comparison to Long Island Sound and the tributaries of Chesapeake Bay (Thayer, 1971). Maximum nitrate concentrations occurred in spring and early summer, with an average value of $0.35\,\mu g\,A\,L^{-1}$. Nitrite ranged from 0.00 to $0.50\,\mu g\,A\,L^{-1}$ with an average concentration of $0.03\,\mu g\,A\,L^{-1}$. Ammonia averaged $0.44\,\mu g\,A\,L^{-1}$ and the total available nitrogen was estimated at $0.82\,\mu g\,A\,L^{-1}$ (Thayer, 1971). Because of the year-round low nitrogen concentrations in the Beaufort system, nitrogen was more limiting to primary production than phosphorus. The Newport River and Pamlico Sound appeared to be major sources of nutrient-rich water entering the Beaufort system. Freshwater input seems to have provided the major source of nitrogen for the Newport River estuary.

In the Pamlico River estuary, high concentrations of ammonia were continuously produced in the planktonic part of the system (Hobbie et al., 1975). Nitrate concentrations increased in the rivers and streams in late fall and continued at high levels until spring. High concentrations of nitrate reached the middle estuary in early winter (November), usually causing an algal bloom. Nitrate concentrations were low in the estuary during July and August. The total quantity of nutrients present in the estuary was relatively constant for ammonia and dissolved organic nitrogen, but the quantity of nitrate nitrogen varied seasonally in the Pamlico River estuary (Hobbie et al., 1975).

The Pamlico River estuary was a sink for nutrients. During one year, 50% of the nitrate nitrogen remained in the estuary. The nitrate was most likely denitrified, assimilated, and trapped in the sediments (Hobbie et al., 1975).

The average concentration of ammonia in the interstitial water of high-marsh and low-marsh soils was 3 to 70 μg A L^{-1}, with little seasonal variation (Whitney et al., 1981). Nitrite and nitrate concentrations in soils averaged 2 to 3 μg A L^{-1} and 5 to 10 μ A L^{-1}, respectively.

Ammonia

In North Inlet, South Carolina, particular ammonia and phosphate seem to be generated within the system during late summer and fall, in the tidal creeks. The vegetated marsh surface was shown to be a sink for particular phosphorus and particular nitrogen. These facts were substantiated by the fact that there were consistently higher values found for these species at low tide relative to seawater entering the North Inlet. It appears that ammonia and phosphate may have some origin from runoff and seepage from vegetated marsh surfaces during tidal exposure. The high nitrate plus nitrite values found at low tide are caused primarily by nitrification. Wolaver et al., (1984) state that the more refractile constituents, DON, DOP, PN, and PP, either pass through the system moving from the forest watershed to the Atlantic Ocean reasonably unaltered or they are generated within the system; that is, detrital nitrogen and phosphorus are flushed into the tidal creeks by rain storms and wave action (Wolaver et al., 1984).

Dissolved Organic Nitrogen

At Sapelo Island, Georgia, the largest pools of nitrogen, excluding N_2, in the surrounding estuarine waters were in the form of dissolved and particulate organic nitrogen (Whitney et al., 1981). The concentrations of dissolved organic nitrogen (DON) in Georgia estuarine waters ranged from 2.5 to 20.4 μg A N L^{-1}. For particulate nitrogen (PN), this range was 0.1 to 31.0 μg A N L^{-1} (Haines, 1979). Neither DON nor PN showed seasonal variations. Concentrations of the inorganic nutrients, ammonia, nitrate, and nitrite were low, ranging from 0.0 to $2.2 \,\mu g \, A \, N \, L^{-1}$.

In the salt marshes of Doboy Sound, concentrations of DON and PN at high and low tides were more variable. Concentrations of nutrients were generally higher at low tide. For example, concentrations of DON at low tide ranged from 4.4 to $38.0 \,\mu g \, A \, N \, L^{-1}$, and for PN the range was 13.0 to $239.0 \,\mu g \, A \, N \, L^{-1}$ (Haines, 1979).

There appeared to be a net loss of DON from the marsh to the estuary. Presumably, this occurred when the nitrogen diffused into the thin layer of water left on the marsh surface at low tide, and the nitrogen was picked up by the next flood tide (Whitney et al., 1981). PN was filtered out of the water by *Spartina alterniflora*, leading to a net input of particulate matter to the marshes.

Nitrogen Fixation
Nitrogen fixation acted as a new source of nitrogen to the salt marsh soils of Sapelo Island, contributing an estimated $15 \, g \, N \, m^{-2} \, yr^{-1}$ (Hanson, 1977). Less than 1% of this fixation occurred on the marsh surface and by epiphytes on *Spartina*. Bacterial fixation in the rhizosphere was by far the major source of nitrogen fixation. Nitrogen fixation was greatest in tall $(40 \, g \, N \, m^{-2} \, yr^{-1})$ and short $(13 \, g \, N \, m^{-2} \, yr^{-1})$ *Spartina* soils (Hanson, 1977). Nitrogen fixation was a significant source of nitrogen for *Spartina* and estuarine algae (Whitney et al., 1981).

The presence of high concentrations of nitrate and nitrite in the soil relative to concentrations in tidal water suggested that nitrite and nitrate production occurred in oxidized zones near the soil surface and around roots and rhizomes of *Spartina* (Whitney et al., 1981).

Like the Great Sippewissett Marsh, however, high rates of nitrogen fixation characterized the Sapelo Island marshes, but the fixation rate was substantially exceeded by losses to denitrification. Unlike the Great Sippewissett Marsh, the Sapelo Island system did not export, but rather, imported large quantities of nitrogen yearly. This most likely occurred in the form of nitrate from seawater and the Altamaha River (Whitney et al., 1981).

The combination of several processes may contribute to the ammonia tidal concentration pattern and export observed in the present study. During low-tide exposure of the marsh surface Gardner found an enrichment of silica phosphates and bicarbonates and indicated a similar increase for ammonia in the runoff water from the marsh surface in small tidal creek basins adjacent to Town Creek. An increase in the concentration of ammonia in the tidal water leaving the marsh surface was also measured by Haines (1979) in a Georgia salt marsh. Appearance of ammonia tidal concentration patterns in export during the summer and fall is probably related to higher rates of ammonia remineralization rather than uptake from primary production. For example, a similar seasonal pattern of ammonia flux has been observed in New England salt marshes and it has been speculated that this pattern was caused by an increase in nitrogen uptake by *Spartina alterniflora* during spring and summer. Increased regeneration of ammonia from the sediments during the high temperatures of late summer coincident with the fall senescence of primary production may have produced an excess of reduced inorganic nitrogen which was exported from the marsh.

Conservative extrapolation of area-based ammonia fluxes over the year from the Town Creek Marsh drainage basin yielded $4.7 \, g \, N \, m^{-2} \, yr^{-1}$. Upper bound estimate of $5.6 \, g \, N \, m^{-2} \, yr^{-1}$ is obtained by the mean of all fluxes measured including those with net water movement. These estimates are at the upper end of the range reported for other marshes.

Nitrogen Sinks

Kenworthy et al. (1982) found that seagrass bed sediments acted as nitrogen sinks. Apparently, nitrogenase activity associated with *Zostera* reflected the active growth periods of the plant in North Carolina coastal waters. That is, during the plant's most active growth period (late winter to spring) nitrogenase activity was primarily rhizospheric with $8.47 \, \mu mol$ nitrogen fixed per square meter per day. Conversely, during the period from fall to early winter, this activity was primarily in the phyllosphere with $8.03 \, \mu mol$ nitrogen fixed per square meter per day. No nitrogenase activity was detected during the warmer summer months when the plant was dormant (Smith and Hayasaka, 1982). Nitrogen fixation in the phyllosphere contributed primarily to the epiphytic community, while fixation in the rhizosphere contributed mainly to macrophyte production (Zieman, 1982; Smith and Hayasaka, 1982).

Denitrification

Denitrification at Sapelo Island was estimated at $65 \, g \, N \, m^{-2} \, yr^{-1}$ (Whitney et al., 1981) and thus exceeded fixation. Denitrifying activity was significantly different between the high and low marsh. While rates of activity did not vary seasonally in the low marsh, activity in the high marsh was notably lower in winter (Whitney et al., 1981). Most likely, the anaerboic sediments of the salt marsh, with continuing input of organic substrates from *Spartina* production, were the site of significant denitrification.

The measurements of flux of nitrate plus nitrite indicate that the marsh exports these organic nutrients to the coastal ocean during the spring, summer, and fall months. Conservative annual export is $0.58 \, g \, N \, m^{-2} \, yr^{-1}$ from the Town Creek drainage basin. This might vary if all samples are included to an annual estimate of $0.94 \, g \, N \, m^{-2} \, yr^{-1}$.

Other studies have estimated that the uptake by the estuary marsh is in the range of 0.34 to $3.95 \, g \, N \, m^{-2} \, yr^{-1}$. Freshwater inputs via surface and groundwater from the uplands surrounding North Inlet do not appear to contribute to the export of nitrate plus nitrate in this study. The high concentrations of nitrate plus nitrite appear to indicate an active nitrification of ammonia in runoff from the marsh.

In summary, the inorganic nitrogen fluxes for the year from Town Creek drainage basin export 5.3 to $6.5 \, g \, N \, m^{-2} \, yr^{-1}$. It is estimated that the export of inorganic nitrogen from the system is 14 to 40% of the nitrogen utilized annually by the plants. Marsh surface was estimated to be exporting approximately $8 \, g \, N \, m^{-2} \, yr^{-1}$ to the adjacent tidal creeks. The nitrogen loss from North Inlet salt marsh could be balanced by an input of nitrogen through nitrogen fixation, measured in this marsh at a rate of approximately $38 \, g \, N \, m^{-2} \, yr^{-1}$.

The concentration of ammonia, nitrates, and nitrite displayed distinct tidal patterns with rising values during ebb flow. These patterns suggest the importance of biogeochemical processes in the flux of material from the salt marsh. Ammonia export peaked in the summer (15 to $20 \, mg \, m^{-2}$ per tide) during a net balance of tidal water exchange. Remineralization of ammonia within the salt marsh system appears to be contributing to the estimated annual net export of about $4.7 \, g \, A \, N \, m^{-2} \, yr^{-1}$. Nitrate plus nitrite export was higher in the fall and winter of 1979, 2 to $4 \, mg \, N \, m^{-2}$ per tide.

The winter export showed no distinct concentration patterns. The fall peak of nitrate and nitrite export occurred during a period of net water balance in tidal exchange and an insignificant freshwater input from the western forested boundary. During the summer and fall, tidal concentration patterns were particularly apparent, suggesting that nitrification within the salt marsh system was contributing to the estimated annual export amount of $0.6 \, g$ of nitrate plus nitrites as nitrogen per square meter per year (Whitting et al., 1987).

Carbon

Dissolved organic carbon (DOC) is the most abundant carbon source and drives the metabolism of most natural aquatic systems. Particulate organic carbon (POC), usually less than $0.5 \, \mu m$ in size, is also an important source of reduced carbon in estuaries. The sources of DOC and POC were described by Darnell (1967) as follows:

1. Autochthonous sources.
   a. Phytoplankton.
   b. Marginal submerged vegetation.
   c. Mud-flat diatoms and filamentous algae.
   d. Periphyton.
2. Allochthonous sources.
   a. Marginal marsh vegetation.
   b. Marginal swamp vegetation.
   c. River-borne phytoplankton and organic detritus.
   d. Windblown material—leaves and pollen.
   e. Phytoplankton from adjacent marine environments.

Larger POC particles tended to precipitate rapidly and decompose slowly. Small particles tended to remain in suspension, decomposed rapidly, and eventually went into suspensions as DOC. The processes of adsorption and agglomeration had the effect of increasing particles size.

Carbon is available to salt marsh macroconsumers in many forms, including live vascular plants, dead plants, microbes, algae (benthic and planktonic), live and dead animal tissue, and feces. Most of these, expect living *Spartina alterniflora*, are commonly ingested by the aquatic macroconsumers.

According to Zieman (1982), seagrasses released substantial amounts of DOC during growth and decomposition. Microorganisms used the DOC fraction of the seagrass organic matter most readily and assimilated it quickly. In the Newport River estuary near Beaufort, North Carolina, Penhale and Smith (1977) found that the amount of DOC excreted was a small percentage of the total carbon fixed. The overall release of total carbon fixed by colonized plants is 0.9%, 1.5% by clean plants, and 2.1% by epiphytes. Excretion rates during the light and dark periods averaged 9.7 and 1.3 $\mu g \, C \, g^{-1} \, h^{-1}$, respectively for epiphytes, and 110 and 1.3 $\mu g \, C \, g^{-1} \, h^{-1}$, respectively, for colonized plants (Penhale and Smith, 1977). On the basis of these estimates, it is clear that eelgrass and its epiphytes are an important part of the carbon cycle in the Beaufort estuarine system.

Filter feeders such as the polychaetes *Fungia*, *Clymenella*, *Nereis succinea*, *N. limnicola*, and *Golfingia*, as well as the molluscs *Mercenaria mercenaria*, *Mytilus edulis*, and *Solemya velum*; the echinoderms, *Asterias forbeso*, *Thyone briarens*, and *Leptosynapta inhaerens*; and several annelid and cnidarian genera, filtered DOC out of the water. DOC appeared to be a significant supplemental source of reduced carbon in estuaries (Stephans, 1967).

PRIMARY PRODUCTIVITY

The southern Coastal Plain tidal marshes of North America are among the most productive ecosystems in the world (Table 6.2). They produce up to 25 metric tons per hectare of plant material (2500 g N m^{-2} yr^{-1}. Three major production units of the salt marsh are the salt marsh grasses, the mud algae, and the phytoplankton in the tidal creeks. Primary production in North

TABLE 6.2. *Comparison of Annual Rates of Photosynthesis in the Area Studied with Those from Other Estuarine Environments*

Location	Method of Measurement	Rate of Production in (g C/m^{-2} yr^{-1})	Reference
Estuaries, N.C.	^{14}C	67	Thayer (1971)
	O$_2$ (gross)	100	Williams, 1966
	O$_2$ (net)	53	Williams, 1966
Long Island Sound	O$_2$ (gross)	380	Riley, 1956
	O$_2$ (net)	170	Riley, 1956
Altamaha River mouth	^{14}C	546	Thomas, 1966
Columbia River mouth	^{14}C	88	Anderson, 1964
Columbia River plume	^{14}C	61	Anderson, 1964
Charleston and Green Hill ponds	Phosphate changes	23–130	Conover, 1961
Wacasassa estuary	^{14}C	107	Putnam, 1966
Patuxent River estuary Bays, Denmark	^{14}C	193–330	Stross and Stottlemyer, 1965
	^{14}C	58	Steemann-Nielsen, 1958

Carolina and Georgia varied from 1290 g dry weight per square meter per year in the low marshes to 3700 g dry weight per square meter per year. The *Spartina alterniflora* produced these high amounts. In high marshes *Spartina alterniflora* produced from 330 g dry weight per square meter per year in North Carolina to 1300 g dry weight per square meter per year in Georgia.

Much of the higher production in the southern Coastal Plain marshes compared to the northern Atlantic states may be due to the nutrient-rich sediments carried in by the rivers in the region. The below ground productivity is often greater than the aerial production. Under unfavorable conditions, plants seem to put more of their energy into root production. Hence root/shoot ratios seem to be generally higher inland than at the streamside location.

Odum and de la Cruz (1967) estimated a net export of about 140 kg on the spring tides and 25 kg on the neap tides of organic matter. Weigert and Pomeroy (1981) estimated that on one tidal cycle from a 10- to 25-ha salt marsh in Georgia $100 \, g \, C \, m^{-2} \, yr^{-1}$ was exported if one prorated the estimate over the watershed of the tidal creek.

Marsh Grasses

The net annual productivity of marsh grasses from several southeast Atlantic coastal areas has been estimated. At the Duplin River marshes (near Sapelo Island, Georgia) the annual net aerial production of *Spartina alterniflora* averaged 2883 g dry matter per square meter or 11, 820 kcal m^{-2} (Odum and Fanning, 1973). The reported range of productivity was 970 to 3300 g m^{-2} yr^{-1} (Smalley, 1959; Odum, 1959, 1961). *Spartina* salt marshes in Georgia were more productive than those farther north, where the tidal amplitude is less. Williams and Murdoch (1969) and Stroud and Cooper (1969) gave values for the net annual aerial production of *S. alterniflora* in North Carolina ranging from 329 to 1296 g dry matter per square meter. For *Spartina cynosuroides* at Sapelo Island, the corresponding figure was 1028 g dry matter m^{-2} yr^{-1} or 4338 kcal m^{-2} (Odum and Fanning, 1973). It is apparent that *S. alterniflora* is more productive in Georgia marshes than in North Carolina, but *S. cynosuroides* is a little less productive at Sapelo Island than *S. alterniflora* is in North Carolina.

The production dynamics of the underground biomass of marsh grasses was as great and often greater than the aerial dynamics. Estimates of underground production by *Spartina alterniflora* near Sapelo Island averaged about 770 g C m^{-2} annually and 2000 g dry wt m^{-2} yr^{-1} (Gallagher and Plumley, 1979). For *Spartina cynosuroides* this figure was 1300 g C m^{-2} yr^{-1} and 3560 g dry wt m^{-2} yr^{-1}. The cycling of photosynthate to the underground pool and back to the aerial parts of the plants or to the soil detritus food web is, as yet, poorly understood.

There are many reasons why these saltwater marshes are rated among the most productive in the world. One of the main reasons is that many of the species of salt marsh plants have C_4 biochemical pathways of photosynthesis. This initial product of photosynthesis is oxaloacetic acid rather than phosphoglyceric acid, which is characteristic of C_3 plants. C_4 plants have much higher light and temperature saturation levels and therefore can live in hotter exposed areas. For example, *Spartina alterniflora*, a C_4 plant, is productive in temperatures of 30 to 35 °C, whereas *Juncus roemerianus*, a C_3 plant, is most productive at 25 °C. This means that as the temperature and light increase, the photosynthetic rate of C_3 plants goes down and hence their carbon productivity. Also, less water is respired by C_4 plants per unit of photosynthesis than by C_3 plants. Also most C_3 plants have higher levels of photorespiration than do C_4 plants. For example, the photorespiration for *Spartina alterniflora* is 11 to 40% of photosynthesis. For *Juncus reomerianus* it is 54%. Hence many of the salt marsh species in this area of *Spartina* sp. and *Distichlis* sp. are C_4 plants. This, no doubt, is one of the major reasons why they are so productive.

In North Inlet estuary (South Carolina), the net productivity varied considerably between the marshes along the creek and the high marshes. For example, it is estimated that the net aboveground primary productivity averaged 2188 g $m^{-2} yr^{-1}$ for the marshes along the creek; 724 g $m^{-2} yr^{-1}$ for the mid-marshes; and 1295 g $m^{-2} yr^{-1}$ for the high marshes. The net belowground (roots and rhizomes) primary productivity was 2363 g $m^{-2} yr^{-1}$ for the creek-side marshes and 5445 g $m^{-2} yr^{-1}$ for the high marshes (Dame and Kenney 1986).

In the North Inlet estuary it was found that the DOC (dissolved organic carbon) largely entered the marsh from the adjacent forested watershed. This assertion is supported by the observed decrease of tidal water salinity with the onset of stream flow. DOC variability is also associated with groundwater advection and/or runoff and seepage from the marsh surface. Removal from tidal water is via either (1) physical sorption or (2) biological uptake and (3) sampling location and (4) original water mass. Particular organic carbon concentrations vary seasonally, higher values found during the summer. DOC variability seems to be controlled by a series of physical and biological factors. The evidence suggests that in the smaller tidal creeks, DOC concentrations are associated with rain events scarring the marsh surfaces, phytoplankton concentrations varying as a function of tidal stage, and the removal of particulate material from the marsh surface at ebb tide.

The large tidal creeks' tidal water velocity appears to be a main factor influencing DOC values. Chrcanowski et al. (1983) estimated that the integrated annual net flux over the Town Creek drainage area yielded annual export equivalents to 416 g DOC $m^{-2} yr^{-1}$ and 533 g DOC $m^{-2} yr^{-1}$ for all data. Estimates for the net aerial production of *Spartina* are not available for the year that the transport measurements were made. However, estimates are 483 m^{-2} yr^{-1} for creek side grass and 6717 g $m^{-2} yr^{-1}$ for high marsh grass (Dame et al., 1980; Wolaver et al., 1986).

As stated earlier, these *Spartina* marshes are very extensive in the southeastern part of the United States. In higher, drier levels they give way to other shrubs and grasses. They form part of the excellent flyways for water birds in this area and are very productive of invertebrates. Excellent examples of these types of estuaries are the Newport River estuary system near Beaufort, North Carolina; Pamlico River estuary in North Carolina; and the marshlands and open estuaries in the region of Sapelo Island, Georgia (Day et al., 1989; Mitsch and Gosselink, 1986).

PHYTOPLANKTON PRODUCTIVITY

Phytoplankton productivity in the Pamlico Sound area was highly variable between the Newport River estuary, North River estuary, Jarret Bay, and within the sound. Production ranged from an average of 343 mg C day^{-1} in late spring and early summer to an average of 103 mg C day^{-1} during the rest of the year (Thayer, 1971). These results of 1967–1968 are quite similar to those obtained during 1964–1965 by Williams (1966). The seasonal shifts in phytoplankton were correlated with temperature changes and, in part, to available nutrients.

The shallow water areas were more productive than many shallow water areas. This Williams (1966) attributed to optimum light and temperature conditions as well as to the low grazing pressure of zooplankton, which over the year averaged about 12% of the phytoplankton production. The overall production of shallow water was less than that of deeper water. Production figures for the entire Pamlico Sound system ranged from 97 to 622 mg C m^{-2} day^{-1} with an average of 99.6 g C m^{-2} yr^{-1}. Williams (1966) estimated that the annual productivity was a little less than, 100 g C m^{-2} (99.6 g C m^{-2}) if Bogue Sound, Newport River, North River, and Core Sound [subsets of the area considered by Thayer (1971)] were considered (Table 6.2). Pamlico Sound productivity is similar to that of the Wacasassa estuary and of the Columbia River but less than that of several east coast estuaries.

In North Inlet, South Carolina, production estimates tended to be higher than in the North Carolina study area. Sellner et al. (1976) estimated the total annual production of phytoplankton (^{14}C method) at 346 g C m^{-2}. Total production rates followed seasonal changes in the water temperature. Production rates ranged from 6.44 to 234 mg C m^{-2} h^{-1}. At Duplin River, Georgia, near Sapelo Island, the gross annual phytoplankton production was found to be 248 g C m^{-2}. For Doboy Sound, the average was 275 g C m^{-2} (Pomeroy et al., 1981).

Annual gross phytoplankton production in the Duplin River marsh has been estimated at 200 g C m^{-2} yr^{-1} (Pomeroy, 1959). In the nearby marshes of Wassaw Sound, Georgia, average primary production of phytoplankton was 20.2 mg C m^{-2} h^{-1}, or 90 g C m^{-2} yr^{-1} (Turner et al., 1979). At Sapelo Island, Georgia, this figure was 190 g C m^{-2} annually (Pomeroy et al. 1981).

There appears to be little information regarding the productivity of the benthic algae. Thayer et al. (1975), with some unpublished data from R. B. Williams. puts the annual net production of benthic algae in the Beaufort system at 125 kcal m^{-2} yr^{-1}.

The productivity on the east coast of algae is roughly one-third to one-fourth that of the vascular productivity. This is true on the east coast but this is not true on the southern coast of California (Mitsch and Gosselink, 1986).

Zostera

Eelgrass was highly productive (Thayer et al., 1975; Penhale, 1977). Phillips (1974) reported values ranging from 10 to 1078 g dry wt m^{-2} yr^{-1} for eelgrass beds in the United States. Thayer et al. (1975) found that *Zostera* in the Beaufort area produces an average $350 \, g \, C \, m^{-2} \, yr^{-1}$. Associated plants such as *Halodule* and *Ectocarpus* together contributed an estimated additional $300 \, g \, C \, m^{-2} \, yr^{-1}$. This production was supplemented by the production of benthic microalgae and epiphytes in the beds, and by phytoplankton in the overlying water (Thayer et al., 1975).

Penhale (1977) found in the same area that the contribution of the epiphytes of *Zostera* was somewhat higher, $0.2 \, g \, C \, m^{-2} \, day^{-1}$ or $73 \, g \, C \, m^{-2} \, yr^{-1}$ (Penhale and Smith, 1977), which includes the estimate of $10 \, g \, C \, m^{-2} \, yr^{-1}$ of Driftmeyer et al. (1980). Few other studies done in this region address this aspect of primary productivity.

ENERGY FLOW

Teal (1962) made a study of the energy flow in the entire salt marsh ecosystem in a Georgia salt marsh. Whereas some of his values would be modified today, it still remains a classic. He calculated gross primary productivity to be 6.1% of the incident sunlight. However, only 1.4% of the incident sunlight was converted into net primary productivity, which was available to other organisms.

Herbivore insects, mostly plant hoppers (*Prokelisia*) and grasshoppers, (*Ochelimum*), consumed only 4.6% of the *Spartina* net productivity. The rest of the *Spartina* net productivity and that of the mud algae passed through the

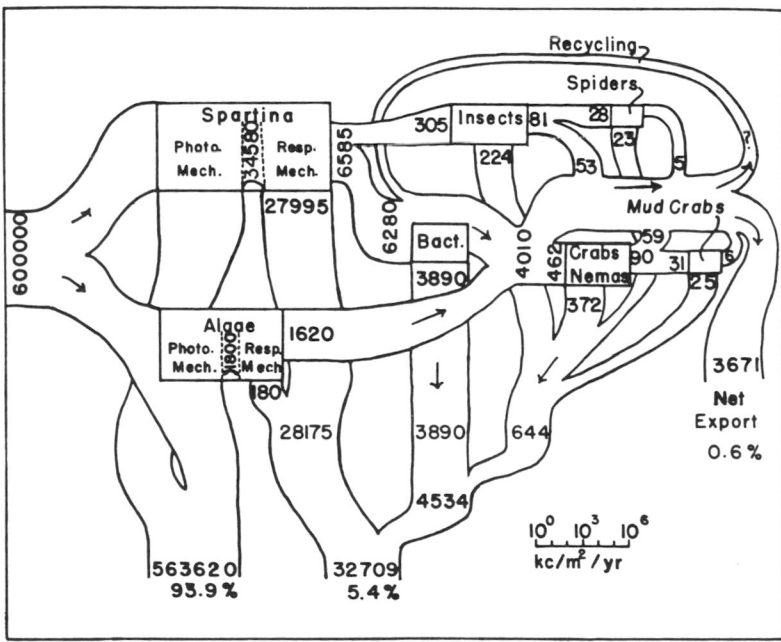

FIGURE 6.2. Energy flow diagram for a Georgia salt marsh. (From "Energy flow in the salt marsh ecosystem of Georgia" by J. M. Teal, *Ecology*, 1962, *43*(4), 614–624. Copyright © by the Ecological Society of America. Reprinted by permission.

detrital algae food chain and was exported to adjacent estuaries. Primary and secondary consumers dominated the detrital food chain. The dominated species were the fiddler crab (*Uca*) and the carnivorous mud crab (*Eurytium*). Forty-five percent of the net production was exported from the marsh into the estuary. This energy flow is shown in Figure 6.2.

FOOD WEBS: MARSHES

Detrital Productivity

In most southeastern Atlantic estuaries, particularly in the estuaries associated with the Newport River area, detritus seems to be more important than macrophytes and algae as a food source. However, recent studies of ^{13}C ratios have indicated that detritus from algae may be more important than formerly believed. This detritus consists of dissolved organic carbon, seston, and particulate detritus. In the Duplin River in Georgia the seston was found to be composed of from 5 to 50% algal detritus.

The detrital content in estuaries of this region came from land vegetation and freshwater swamps and marshes (Haines, 1977). The detrital input from land vegetation and freshwater swamps and marshes to these Georgia estuaries has been estimated to be comparable to the input from *Spartina* in salt marshes, approximately 780 to $16,060 \, g \, m^{-2} \, yr^{-1}$. The detrital potential from phytoplankton was as high as $770 \, g \, C \, m^{-2} \, yr^{-1}$ (dry weight) and from organic terrestrial material, $600 \, g \, C \, m^{-2} \, yr^{-1}$ (dry weight).

Eelgrass beds appeared to produce dead leaves year round which form detritus and thus, differed from marsh grass, paticularly *Spartina*, which was seasonal (Thayer et al., 1977). Adams amd Angelovic (1970) found that the extensive grass beds of Beaufort. North Carolina, contained at least four times as much dead plant material (detritus) as living plant material. They also concluded that the detritus itself, as well as its microbial fraction, may be an important food source for seagrass animals.

In a 30,000-m^2 eelgrass bed in an embayment on the southeastern side of Phillips Island near the mouth of the Newport Estuary in the Beaufort area, some studies regarding the productivity of eelgrass showed that in 1974–1975, $87.7 \, g \, C \, m^{-2} \, yr^{-1}$ from dead grass blades was produced (Thayer et al., 1977). In suspension, detritus particles larger than 1 mm in size contained $18 \, kcal \, C \, m^{-2}$. Detritus particles were also found in sediments to a depth of 18 cm. Sedimental detritus contained $21,160 \, kcal \, C \, m^{-2}$, of which $242 \, kcal$ was attributed to particles larger than 1 mm and $20,900 \, kcal$ to particles less than 1 mm in size (Thayer et al., 1975).

In Georgia estuaries detritus from *Spartina alterniflora* marshes was considered to be the major link between primary and secondary productivity since only a small portion of the net production of the marshgrass was consumed while it was alive (Odum and de la Cruz, 1967). About 90% of the aboveground primary production of salt marsh plants entered the detritus food web when the plants died (Reimold et al., 1975).

At Sapelo Island, Georgia, the average monthly detritus production of the tall form of *Spartina alterniflora* was $197.9\,g\,C\,m^{-2}$, significantly greater than the production of the short form of the same speceis, which was $113.6\,g\,C\,m^{-2}$. *Juncus roemerianus* had an average detrital production of $188.4\,g\,C\,m^{-2}$. In early spring (March and April) the tall form of *Spartina* produced the most detritus per month, while between May and July *J. roemerianus* was most productive. The mean annual detrital production for this watershed from marsh plants was $1845.8\,g\,C\,m^{-2}\,yr^{-1}$ (Reimold et al., 1975).

Soil detritus was also a contributing component of the detrital input and is often neglected because it is poorly understood. In Core Banks, North Carolina organic carbon was found to accumulate in the marsh sediment at the rate of 80.3 to $96.8\,g\,C\,m^{-2}$. Both bare and planted dredge spoil areas accumulated organic carbon, but the annual accumulation rate was higher where the planted *Spartina* was present (Cammen, 1975). The organic carbon in the top 13 cm of natural marsh sediments had a turnover time of about 3.7 to 4.5 years, based on the rate of accumulation (Cammen, 1975).

There is a great deal of evidence that detritus is superior to living grass tissue as a food source for aquatic organisms, because bacteria growing on the detritus concentrate and assimilate essential elements such as phosphorus and nitrogen in dissolved form from both plants and seawater. Bacteria appear to be essential for the transfer of energy between primary and secondary production levels of the marsh ecosystem since only a few higher organisms are able to digest the largely refractory organic detritus derived from plants.

Detrital Food Web

Detritus is processed by many different kinds of detritivores. Different theories have been developed over time as to the ultimate fate of detritus in marshlands of the southeast. Researchers have studied the decomposition of detritus.

Odum and de la Cruz (1967) found that *Spartina* grass was decomposed into organic matter largely by bacteria and that the organic matter increased in protein content 10 to 24% on an ashfree basis; that is, the carbon/nitrogen ratio decreased in the detritus. They concluded that the bacteria-rich detritus is nutritionally a better food source for animals than the *Spartina* tissue that originally formed the base of most of the particulate matter. In contrast, Wiebe and Pomeroy (1972) did not conclude that the detritus was colonized by large populations of bacteria, but rather, that it was grazed by nematodes and other microscopic benthic organisms, which in turn are eaten by large deposit feeders. There is no doubt that bacteria production was high but that the rapid turnover kept the populations low.

Pomeroy et al. (1977) described the importance of soluble organic matter as well as particulate organic matter in the detrital food web of a salt marsh. They concluded that soluble organic matter may make up as much as 25% of the initial dry weight of the dying grass and that both living and decomposing salt marsh vegetation were important energy sources for microorganisms in the marsh and adjacent estuary. They pointed out the importance of anaerobic microorganisms, such as nitrogen-reducing bacteria, sulfur-reducing bacteria, and methane-generating bacteria, which were important consumers of organic substance in the salt marsh, particularly below the surface. Because of anoxic conditions, the decomposition of organic matter is very slow at depths greater than 20 cm beneath the marsh surface. However, Teal (1986) reported that less than 20% of the organic litter remained after 2.5 years (Mitsch and Gosselink, 1986).

The detrital food web is composed of meiofauna (metazoa that pass through a 500-μm sieve) and macrofauna. Meiofauna in southeastern Atlantic estuaries consisted of small benthic multicellular animals of which 67 to 98% may be nematodes. These roundworms averaged about 2×10^6 individuals $m^{-2} yr^{-1}$. Peak abundance was in the early spring and the lowest values occurred in late summer and early fall. Nematode carbon was about 1% of the total carbon in the sediments, which were composed largely of detritus of *Spartina alterniflora*. Adenosine triphosphate (ATP) measurements of biomass indicated that over an annual cycle nematodes contributed 92% of the living biomass within the intertidal sediments and 78% in the subtidal sediments. On an annual basis, nematode biomass was 10 times that of the bacterial component of the sediments (Sikora et al., 1977).

Nematodes converted a diffuse substrate into a discrete, particulate, high-energy food source for the next trophic level. The higher trophic level of organisms must ingest biomass present at the instant of foraging. Sikora et al., do not indicate the turnover rate of the bacteria. The finding that bacterial mass was about 10% of that of nematode biomass lends importance to the packaging rule of meiobenthic nematodes. Detritivores such as small fish or shrimp had better success at foraging when meiofauna numbers were high because of the higher energy content obtained per unit area. It is believed that this lowering of the foraging cost may have balanced the energetic cost of the additional step in the food chain represented by foraging on nematodes (Sikora et al., 1977).

In the estuaries near Beaufort, the macrofauna played a very important part in the foodweb. Their greatest abundance was in late winter and early spring and they were least abundant in summer and early autumn. The average number of macrofauna individuals was $7600 m^{-2}$. The standing stock was $3 g m^{-2}$ ash-free dry weight (Cammen, 1979).

In the Newport estuary the most important small macrofauna were the polychaetes and the oligochaetes. The Capitellidae, *Nereis succinea* and *Streblospio benedicti*, were very common. These two species together with the Oligochaeta composed about 96% of the number of individuals found (Cammen, 1979). The macroinvertebrate infauna in the marsh were nonselective deposit feeders or omnivores, except for *Eteone heteropoda* and *Glycera americana*. Adams and Angelovic (1970) found that *G. dibranchiata* assimilated about twice as much non detritus food.

Nereis succinea ingested about $5 kg C m^{-2} yr^{-1}$ (dry weight), according to Cammen (1980). The rest of the infauna also were large consumers, which indicated that the sediments and detritus in the marsh were reworked each year by the infauna.

Predator–Prey Relationships. In the North Inlet when the larger macrofauna (i.e., the larger invertebrates and fish) were excluded, the densities of the smaller macroinvertebrates, particularly polychaetes, increased rapidly, indicating the existence of predator–prey relationships (Bell, 1980). In the exclusion studies 99% of the smaller macroinvertebrates were *Manayunkia aestuarina* and juveniles of *Streblospio benedicti*. The remaining 1% of the population was copepods, predominantly the hartacticoid copepods, *Stenhelia bifidia*, *Microarthridion littorale*, *Enhydrosoma propinquum*, and *Schizoptera knabeni*. Fleeger (1979) found that the copepod, *Microarthridion littorale*, occurred almost exclusively in the upper 3 mm of the marsh surface and therefore was the most heavily preyed upon. The principal invertebrate predator excluded in these experiments was *Palaemonetes pugio*. Detritivores are prey also for fish, fish larvae, and crab of the genera *Callinectes* and *Uca*. *Enhydrosoma propinquum* and *Stenhelis bifida* occurred through the upper 1 cm of the marsh mud and were able to escape some of the predation. The populations of *S. bifida*, a burrowing species, were probably more controlled by food limitations than by predation. The factors limiting the population of *E. propinquum* were not determined.

Nematodes were very susceptible to the predation of *Uca pugnax* and *Palaemonetes pugio*, which, as noted above, also fed on crustacea. Copepods, shrimp, mussels, and gastropods consume both herbivores and detritivores as well as some plant material directly. It is therefore difficult to categorize them as being either omnivorous or carnivorous and equally difficult to determine whether they are part of the algal or detrital food web.

Algal Food Web

Algae predators that also eat detritus include the marsh snail (*Melampus bidentatus*), the sand flea (*Orchestia*), and the isopod (*Philosia*). In the intertidal zone, the fiddler crab (*Uca*), various muscles (*Modiolus* and *Mytilus*), the periwinkle (*Littorina*), the mud snail (*Nassarius*), and various immature insects, oligochaetes, and annelid worms also feed on algae.

Living on the *Spartina* and other grasses were species of insect such as the salt marsh grasshopper (*Orchelimum*) and the plant hopper (*Prokelixia*). Muskrats (*Onclatra*) are conspicuous in some salt marshes by their many houses of piled-up vegetation in the marsh surface. They feed primarily on plant material, preferring low-salinity plants such as *Scirpus* and *Tuipha*. Secondary consumers in the salt marsh include the mud crabs (*Eurytium*) and the clapper rail (*Rallus*) (Mitsch and Gosselink, 1986).

Those species that seem to graze primarily on the algae were zooplankton, which fed on phytoplankton. The zooplankton of the estuaries in the Beaufort system were dominated by copepods (Thayer et al., 1974). Ten genera of copepods were identified, the most important of these being *Acartia tonsa*, representing 30% of the total numbers of zooplankters, species of *Oithona* (17%), *Corycaeus* (14%), and *Centropages* (6%). Secondary in importance in the zooplankton were the harpacticoids, *Enterpina acutifrons*, and species of *Temora*, barnacle larvae, and copepod nauplii. Other members of the zooplankton were the larvae of annelids, ostracods, gastropods, bivalves, cladocerans, and *Sagitta*, and the zoea of crab and shrimp (Thayer et al., 1974). The maximum abundance of zooplankton occurred between March and June and again between October and December.

Benthic and planktonic algae were found also to be an important food source for other estuary animals in the southeastern coastal marshes. When available, algae may be a more readily utilized food than decomposer microbes (Montague et al., 1981). For example, the mud snail, *Ilyanassa* sp., fed on mud flats of which the algae compose 75% of the food and the decomposer microbes 25% (Wetzel, 1976). Fiddler crabs readily assimilate benthic diatoms. Grass shrimp and mullet graze on both phytoplankton and benthic algae (Welsh, 1975; Odum, 1968). The mollusc, *Littorina irrorata*, is a detrital algal feeder and utilizes algae and other epiphytes when detritus is less available (Odum and Smalley, 1959). However, Montague et al. (1981) suggest that algae may be the preferred food of many aquatic macroconsumers rather than a dietary supplement as often believed.

When one considers the fish omnivores and carnivores it is often difficult to classify them as belonging to the algal food web or to the detrital food web. Indeed, in these stages of nutrient transfer, the organisms which they eat are often detrital or algal feeders and sometimes feed on a combination of these two nutrient sources. However, some fish, such as the cyprinodontid, *Fundulus luciae*, in the estuaries near Beaufort, preferred in the summer and fall a combination of sand, detritus, and diatoms, whereas in the winter and spring it fed mainly on small crustacea (copepods, tanaied, and amphipods) and insects (hemipterans and small dipterans) (Kneib, 1978). Fish that feed primarily on detritus are the juvenile pinfish, *Lagodon rhomboides*; juvenile pigfish, *Orthopristis chrysoptera*; spot, *Leiostomus xanthurus*; and filefish, *Monacanthus hispidus*.

Predator–Prey Reltionships. Fish larvae were heavy predators of the zooplankton. It was estimated by Thayer et al. (1974) that from November to April 8×10^8 fish larvae entered the lower Newport River estuary. Of these, pinfish represented about 64%. Of the gut content of the larval pinfish, spot, and menhaden, 76 to 99%, contained *Acartia, Centropaqes, Temora*, and harpacticoid copepods (mostly *Enteropina*). The remaining gut content consisted of copepods, barnacle larvae, crab zoea, and amphipods. Kjelson et al. (1975) linked the decrease in zooplankton abundance to the presence of the grazing larvae of *Labidesthes lepomis* and to the juveniles and adults of the species *L. sicculus*.

Other predators on the phytoplankton and zooplankton were filter-feeding invertebrates such as clams, oysters, and barnacles. Barnacles, in turn, are preyed upon by the sponge, *Microciona proliferra*, and oysters are attacked by another sponge, *Cliona celata*, which bores into their shells (de Laubenfels, 1947). The clam, *Tagelus* sp., a filter feeder, was a favorite of the snail, *Busycon* sp., in the Beaufort area. Predators on *Busycon* sp. included crabs such as *Menippe mercenaria*; hermit crabs, *Clibanarius vittatus* and *Pagurus pollicaris* and the blue crab, *Callinectes sapidus*, according to Magalhaes (1948).

Invertebrate predators upon amphipods were grass shrimp, *Palaemonetes vulgaris*; brown shrimp, *Penaeus aztecus*; and blue crab, *Callinectes sapidus*. The amphipods consumed by these organisms included *Ampelisca abdita*, *Corophium acherusicum*, *Amphithoe longimana*, *Cymadusa compta*, *Lembos websteri*, *Leasmopus lebis*, and *Melita appendiculata* (Nelson, 1979).

Most fish seem to ingest organisms that may be derived either from detritus or algae; however, often their habitat would suggest that they are detrital and benthic feeders or feeders on zooplankton and hence on phytoplankton. For example, Nelson (1979) found that the most important fish predators on amphipods associated with the benthos in the Beaufort eelgrass beds were pinfish, *Lagodon rhomboides*; mummichog, *Fundulus heteroclitus*; filefish, *Monocanthus hispidus*; gaggrouper, *Mycteroperca microleptis*; and spot, *Leiostomus xanthurus*.

Copepods dominated the spot diet with harpaticoid copepods occurring in over 88% of the stomachs examined and the calanoid copepod, *Pseudodiaptomus coronatus*, occurring in 33% of the stomachs. Other Crustacea were also present. These species of spot showed no distinct variation in diet related to season or to size (Stickney et al., 1975). The croaker, *M. undulatus*, fed on many invertebrates, including polychaetes, molluscs, ostracods, copepods, amphipods, decapods, and occasionally, some fish. The percentages of copepod types varied depending on their location in the river and, to some extent, on the season of the year (Stickney et al., 1975).

Croaker and spot showed marked differences in diet in Pamlico River. The croaker fed heavily on annelids and frequently on copepods and pelecypods. The spot fed very heavily on copepods and nematodes and frequently on annelids, bivalves, and plant material. The difference in feeding habit is partially due to the way they feed. The croaker tended to ingest more organisms living in the bed of the estuary, while the spot ingested those living on the bed (Roelofs, 1954).

In the Beaufort eelgrass, planktonic copepods were important in the diet of the silversides (*Menidia menidia*), the mojarra (*Eucinostomus gula*), and made up one-half of the diet of anchovies (*Anchoa* sp.). Calanoid copepods were a large part of the diet of juvenile pinfish and pigfish, silver perch (*Bairdiella chrysoura*), and pipefish (*Syngnathus* sp.). Polychaetes were major diet items of adult pinfish, silver perch, and spot. Juvenile and larval fish were preyed upon by silversides, silver perch, oyster toadfish (*Opsanus tau*), and flounders (*Paralichthys* sp.). Silver perch, pipefish, flounder, and the gaggrouper (*Mycteroperca microlepis*) fed heavily on crustacean groups such as amphipods and isopods, and the genera *Hippolyte* and *Palaemonetes* as well as small blue crabs (*Callinectes sapidus*). The four fish appeared to be life-long carnivores. Adult striped burrfish, *Chilomyterus schoepfi*, and the oyster toadfish fed almost exclusively (95% and 50%, respectively) on intact bay scallops, *Argopecten irradians*, and the gastropod, *Bittium varium* (Adams, 1976a).

Benthic fish species had varied diets, as is illustrated by two species of the Bothidae occurring in Pamlico Sound. The most important foods for the young flounder (100 to 200 mm total length) were mysid shrimp, particularly *Neomysis americana*, isopods, amphipods, caridean shrimp, brachyuran crab, a gastropod (*Retusa canaliculata*), and many fish of the engraulid and scaenid groups (Powell and Schwartz, 1979).

In other southeastern estuaries five species belonging to the families Scianidae and Bothidae dominated the fish population: silver perch, *Bairdiella chrysoura*; weakfish, *Cynoscion regalis*; spot, *Leiostomus xanthurus*; Atlantic croaker, *Micropogon undulatus*; and star drum, *Stellifer lanceolatus*. According to Stickney et al. (1975) these species consumed in varying amounts many diverse invertebrates and small fish. *B. chrysoura* fed near the bottom primarily on small crustaceans, especially *Neomysis americana*, and to a lesser extent, on annelids, molluscs, isopods, the polychaete worm *Nereis succinea*, and fish. In the summer the callenoid copepod, *Pseudodiaptomus coronatus*, predominated as a food item and in the fall and winter the mysid shrimp dominated (Stickney et al., 1975). Weakfish, *C. regalis*, fed mainly on fish and crustacea. The mysid shrimp, *Neomysis americana*, was present in 55% of the stomachs and fish remains occurred in 30% of the stomachs. The only polychaete worm found was *Nereis succinea*. Small *Cynoscion regalis* (30 to 49 mm standard length) preferred *Pseudodiaptomus coronatus*. At 50 mm standard length or greater, the diet was largely mysid shrimp. After *C. regalis* reached 130 mm standard length, fish appeared in its diet (Stickney et al., 1975).

In Bogue Sound, *Fundulus heteroclitus* fed primarily on small crustaceans and polychaetes with little seasonal variation. Plant materials, crabs, and insects occurred in up to 68% of the guts but were seasonal with maximums in either the summer or fall months. The size of this species of fish was found to influence its diet, as larger individuals consumed crabs, detritus, algae, and an algal–detrital conglomerate more frequently than did smaller fish (Kneib and Stiven, 1978).

In South Carolina, *F. heteroclitus* and *Menidia menidia* dominated tidal creeks in the spring. They fed almost exclusively on the larvae of the very numerous spot, croaker, and striped mullet. Also common to the South Carolina estuaries were the bay anchovy, which fed mostly on planktonic crustacea and the striped killifish, which fed only on larval fish (Cain and Dean, 1976).

Along the coast of the Carolinas the most frequently occurring snapper fish is the vermillion snapper, *Rhomboplites aurorubens*. This snapper feeds mainly on cephalopods, amphipods, pelagic gastropods, shrimp, and fish (Grimes, 1979). The diet varied with the size of the fish and with the season. For fish under 100 mm total length, copepods formed 67%, and nematodes 10% by volume of the diet. In the juveniles (100 to 175 mm total length), fish scales formed 68% of the diet and copepods 14% (Grimes, 1979).

FOOD WEB: INTERTIDAL AREA

Upper Intertidal Area

Unlike the New England coastline, the Beaufort area does not have a true rocky intertidal habitat. However, manufactured piers, pilings, seawalls, and breakwaters provide a hard intertidal substrate for many encrusting intertidal forms.

Earle and Humm (1964) have recognized six floristic zones on the basis of the distribution of algae in the intertidal zone (Figure 6.3). Algae with sharply defined upper limits and undetermined lower limits were sometimes more abundant than species confined to a given zone. The only alga found in zone 1, which was 18 to 28 in. (45.7 to 71 cm) above mean low water, was *Calothrix crustacea*. Zone 2, which was 14 to 28 in. (35.6 to 45.7 cm) above mean low water, was characterized by the blue-green algae, *Lyngbya confervoides* and *Enterophysalis deusta*, and three species of the green alga, *Enteromorpha*, of which *E. intestinalis* was the most common.

Bangia fusco-purpurea, a red alga, was found in a range corresponding exactly to zone 3, which lay between 10 and 18 in. (25.4 to 35.6 cm) above mean low water. Other algae with a zone 3 upper limit were the blue-greens, *Hydrocoleum comoides*, *Entophysalis conferta*, and *Microcoleus lyngbyaceous* (= *Lyngbya majuscula*); the green algae, *Ulva latuca* and *Chaetomorpha area*; and the red alga, *Ceramium strictum*. In addition to *Anacystis aeruginosa*, zone 4 contained the brown, *Sphacelaria furcigera*, and the red, *Asterocystis ramosa*.

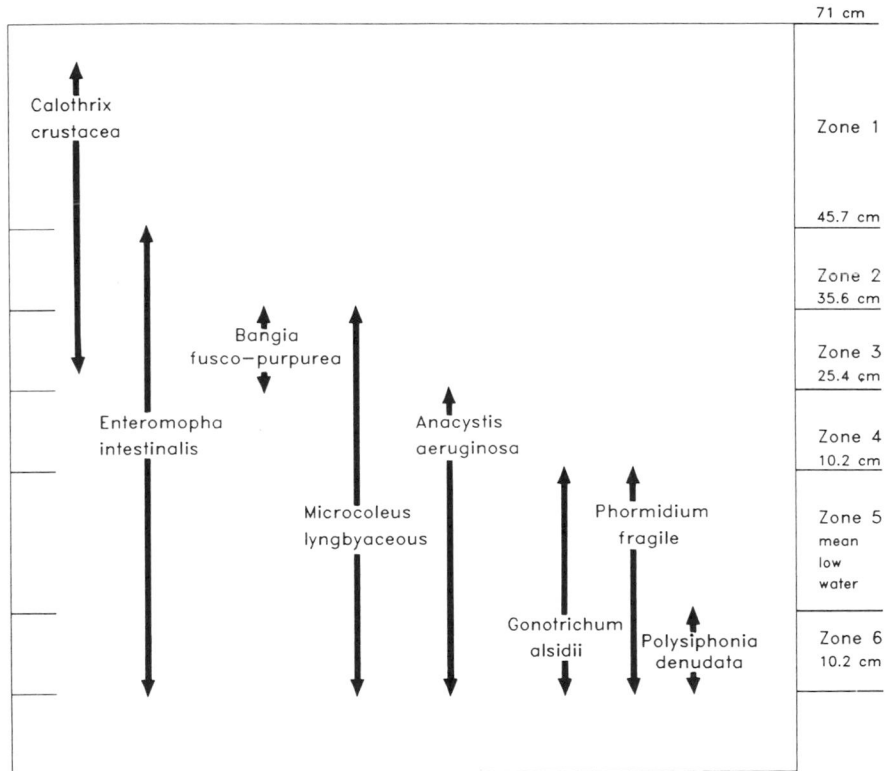

FIGURE 6.3. Some algae of Beaufort Harbor, North Carolina. Algae with sharply defined upper and lower limits are often used as zone indicators. See the text for additional algae of the area. (Adapted from Earle and Humm, 1964.)

Zone 5, with its lower limit at mean low water, was dominated by the blue-green alga, *Phoromium fragile*, although the red, *Goniotrichum alsidii*, was also confined to that 10.2-cm band. *Polysiphonia denudata*, a red alga, was limited to zone 6, a 10.2-cm band extending downward from mean low water. Five other algae reach a lower limit in zone 6 but have upper limits in other zones (Earle and Humm, 1964).

Fifteen species of sponges characterized the Beaufort region and can be found listed in Table 6.1. The five abundant and important species were *Cliona celata*, *Haliclona permollis*, *Hymeniacidon heliophila*, *Lissodendoryx isodactyalis*, and *Microciona prolifera* (de Laubenfels, 1947). The ecological situation at Beaufort favored sponges that were normally intertidal, especially those typical of the upper portion of the intertidal area. Beaufort Harbor and vicinity was notably devoid of sponge life below the low-tide mark, probably because occasional freshets caused a marked decrease in salinity.

The snail, *Littorina irrorata*, occurred on the plants in estuarine reed beds. Snails of the genus *Busycon* were among the most common marine gastropods of the eastern U.S. coast. *Busycon canaliculatum* and *B. contrarium* were both found seasonally, but *B. carica* was the most abundant species of this genus at Beaufort (Magalhaes, 1948).

The upper intertidal zone also maintained sporadically dense populations of the snails, *Ilyanassa obsoleta* and *Melampus lineatus*; the bivalves, *Modiolus demissus* and *Crassostrea virginica*; and various species of the crab, *Uca* (Bird, 1970).

The supralittoral fringe was characterized by the blue–green algae, *Entophysalis deusta* and *Calothrix pulvinata* and a species of *Plectonema*. On some break-waters the rapid isopod, *Ligia exotica*, was abundant and the small rapid crab, *Sesarma cinereum*, was also found (Stephenson and Stephenson, 1952).

Mid-Intertidal Area

Barnacles; oysters; the mussel, *Brachiodontes exustus*; and the green alga, *Enteromorpha* sp., were the main organisms occupying space at the middle and low intertidal exposed areas. The oyster, *Crassostrea virginica*, dominated Beaufort communities protected from wave action but was not found in large numbers in areas exposed directly to waves. Ortega (1981) showed that *C. virginica* did not become dominant at exposed locations because the constant wave shock at ocean sites reduced growth and increased the mortality of young and adult oysters. Under those conditions, oysters were outcompeted by the mussel, *B. exustus*. While the community structure of exposed areas was highly variable, the communities in protected areas were fairly constant. The intertidal community at protected sites was occupied by the barnacles, *Balanus amphitrite* and *Chthamalus fragilis*, and the oyster, *C. virginica*. Predation was unimportant at Beaufort because predators were absent at the exposed areas and the oyster drill, *Urosalpinx cinerea*, was restricted to the subtidal zone in the protected areas (Ortega, 1981).

Of the five prevalent sponge species at Beaufort, only *Microciona* was found growing on barnacle shells. *Microciona* was a major danger to barnacles at Beaufort. *Hymeniacidon* showed less tendency than other sponges to smother substrate organisms. It was a symbiotic host to immense numbers of nematodes, annelids, and amphipods. *Cliona* bored into oysters, often causing serious damage to whole beds. *Cliona* may bore into calcareous substances to escape low salinity (de Laubenfels, 1947).

Sandy Beach

At Beaufort, the intertidal sandy beach community is dominated by haustoriid amphipods, which composed between 91 and 97% by number of the total infauna (Dexter, 1967, 1969). Two major factors aided in separating ecological niches or in reducing competition among haustoriid amphipods in North Carolina sandy beaches: habitat isolation and reproductive isolation due to seasonal differences in breeding. Although haustoriids could be found coexisting on the same inlet sandy beach, they were characteristically associated in one of several sandy beach habitats.

The sandy beach fauna of intertidal inlets is 83% (by number) *Neohaustorius schmitzi* (Dexter, 1969). *Neohaustorius*, along with *Acanthohaustorius millsi*; the bivalve, *Donax variabilis*; the polychaetes, *Scolelepis squamata* and *Haploscoloplos fragilis*; and the isopod, *Exosphaeroma diminutum*, composed 97% of the total (Dexter, 1969). The community was thus typified by low diversity, low density, and dominance of a few species. *A. millsi* was the second most abundant haustoriid. It was usually found in greatest concentrations from the midtide zone to shallow water (Dexter, 1967).

The fauna of subtidal inlet sandy beaches were the haustoriid amphipods, *Acanthohaustorius millsi*, *A. intermedius*, and *Protohaustorius deichmannae*; the polychaetes, *Nephtys picata*, *Magelona papillicornis*, and *Armandia agilis*; the echinoid, *Mellita quinquiesperforata*; the cumacean, *Oxyurostylis smithi*; and the gastropod, *Terebra dislocata*.

Barrier island sandy beach fauna consisted of haustoriid amphipods, *Haustorius* sp. and *Amphiporeia virginiana*; the talitrid amphipods, *Orchestia platensis* and *Talorchestia megalophthalma*; the decapods, *Emerita talpoida* and *Ocypode albicans*; the bivalve, *Donax variabilis*; and the isopod, *Chiridotea caeca* (Dexter, 1967).

Adults of the crabs, *Pinnixia chaetopterana*, *P. sayana*, *P. cylindrica*, and *P. cristata*, were found in Beaufort high- and medium, salinity intertidal zones, living in the burrows and tubes of various invertebrates. *P. chaetopterana* was the most abundant crab of this genus (Dowds, 1978).

Lagoons

Lagoonal, muddy-sand beach fauna were the haustoriid amphipod, *Lepidactylus dysticus*; the polychaetes, *Clymenella torquata*, *Diopatra cuprea*, and *Glycera dibranchiata*; the holothurian, *Leptosynapta inharens*; the gastropods, *Ilyanassa obsoleta* and *Nassarius vibex*; and the bivalves, *Mercenaria mercenaria* and *Solemya velum*.

Eelgrass (Zostera)

Zostera marina, eelgrass, forms the single most important north temperate seagrass system, according to Phillips (1974). At Beaufort, North Carolina, eelgrass was the dominant seagrass. Salinity ranged from 19 to 33 ppt and averaged 26 ppt. Eelgrass covered about 17% of the estuarine area near Beaufort, where it provided an estimated 64% of the total production of algae, cord grass, and eelgrass (Thayer et al., 1975).

In their study of the Beaufort area, Thayer et al. (1975) collected only 11 species of algae. Of these, *Ectocarpus confervoides* and *Agardhiella tenera* dominated from summer through fall. Of the 45 species of epifaunal invertebrates taken, 12 species represented 90%, and 17 species represented 95% of all organisms collected. The top 12 species in order of abundance were *Bittium varium*, *Retusa canaliculata*, *Mitrella lunata*, *Carinogammarus mucronatus*, *Hippolyte pleuacantha*, *Amphithoe longimana*, *Pyramidella fusca*, *Nassarius vibex*, *Caprella geometrica*, *Macoma tenta*, *Abra aequalis*, and *Nereis pelagica*. *Bittium varium* alone represented 48.11% of the epifauna. The dominating taxa, based on total numbers collected, were gastropods (72%), amphipods (12%), bivalves (7%), and crustaceans (6%) (Thayer et al., 1975).

On an ash-free dry weight (AFDW) basis, dominance was lessened. Eighteen species represented 90% of AFDW. In this analysis, *Nassarius vibex* (18%), *Callinectes sapidus* (8.8%), *Mogula manhattensis* (8.0%), and *Bittium varium* (7.8%) were the most significant species (Thayer et al., 1975).

The infaunal population was numerically smaller than the epifaunal population, but it had a much greater biomass. Thayer et al. (1975) collected 40 species of infauna, dominated by *Nereis pelagica*, *Tellina versicolor*, *Solemya velum*, *Abra aequalis*, and *Clymenella torquata*. Bivalves represented 58% and polychaetes 41% of the individuals, with nemertines, crustaceans, and echinoderms together representing only 1%.

The infaunal population displayed a slight seasonal trend in numerical abundance, with maximum numbers during spring. Polychaetes dominated from fall through winter and bivalves dominated the rest of the year (Thayer et al., 1975).

Epifaunal deposit feeders made up 77% of the number of individuals collected and the infaunal deposit feeders made up 53%. Epifaunal suspension feeders composed 18% of the number of individuals and infaunal suspension feeders composed 42%. The preponderance of deposit and suspension feeders reflected the importance of the great quality and quantity of detritus and its associated microbes in the fine sediments of the Beaufort eelgrass beds (Thayer et al., 1975).

Of the 33 species of fish collected from the Beaufort eelgrass beds, *Lagodon rhomboides*, *Orthopristes chrysopterus*, *Menidia menidia*, *Anchoa mitchilli*, and *A. hepsetus* accounted for about 80% of the total annual biomass of fish. *L. rhomboides* was by far the dominant species, accounting for approximately 50% of the total standing crop biomass (Thayer et al., 1975).

Adams (1976b) collected 39 species of fish from the Beaufort area seagrasses (Table 6.3). He found that *L. rhomboides* was the must abundant fish during

TABLE 6.3. *Annual Average Percentage by Weight of Each Food Item in the Diet of the Major Species of Fish Inhabiting Eelgrass Beds*

Food item	Juvenile Pinfish (118)[a]	Adult Pinfish (97)	Juvenile Pigfish (105)	Silver-sides (130)	Silver Perch (77)	Spot (112)	Pipe-fish (61)	Burr-fish (26)	File-fish (87)	Anchovy (90)	Gag (26)	Mojarra (65)	Toad-fish (28)	Floun-ders (39)	Percent of Total
Detritus	30.4	27.8	46.2	4.1	18.5	67.5	37.5		65.5	50.0				1.7	21.7
Calanoid copepods	19.6	9.5	35.2	73.1		0.8				50.0		100.0			24.6
Polychaetes	3.9	10.5	0.6		13.7	6.0			0.5						2.5
Gammarid amphipods	10.9	7.2	1.2	5.5	16.8	2.6	12.5							1.8	4.2
Caprellid amphipods	6.3	9.5		3.3			31.0								3.6
Filamentous algae	7.1	9.8			2.5	0.5							3.8		1.7
Eelgrass	10.5	7.7			5.0	1.0			12.5				3.7		2.9
Eelgrass seeds		5.8	0.4												0.4
Pelecypods		0.2				14.2									1.1
Bittium		0.5		1.0	2.5			82.5					25.0	30.0	10.2
Isopods	0.6	0.5													0.1
Palaemonetes	3.6	0.8	12.5	12.3	7.5	0.3					50.0				5.3
Juvenile and larval fish		0.8			15.0			5.0			6.0		37.5	41.5	8.4
Crabs	0.7		1.8										5.0	25.0	2.3
Scallops		1.7			18.5			12.5					25.0		2.8
Hippolyte	3.0	0.7	0.6	0.3		3.3	19.0				44.0				6.2
Harpacticoid copepods	1.7	0.5	1.5						5.0						0.9
Other[b]	1.7	0.5		0.4		3.8			6.5						1.4

Source: Adams (1976b)

[a] Number of samples shown in parentheses.

[b] Includes seaweed, brittle stars, brozoans, nematodes, nemertines, flatwarms, nauplii, and megalops stages of crustacea.

449

the year. Anchovies, primarily *Anchoa mitchilli*, were the dominant species in the summer. *Orthopristis chrysoptera* was also abundant during the warmer months. The winter fish community of the eelgrass beds was dominated by *Leiostomus xanthurus*, *Menidia menidia*, and *Membras martinica*.

SUBMERGED FAUNA AND FLORA COMMUNITIES

Plankton

In the Beaufort estuarine system there was a seasonal pattern in phytoplankton abundance. Maximum cell numbers in individual samples occurred in December and minimum numbers in March and July. The average cell numbers, $1.70 \times 10^6 \, L^{-1}$ and $1.64 \times 10^6 \, L^{-1}$ for cool and warm periods, respectively, are quite similar. Diatoms dominated the algal population throughout the year, ranging between 34 and 81% of the total population. *Skeletonema costatum* and species of *Chaetoceros* and *Nitzschia* were the most abundant diatoms. Constant turbulence caused the normally benthic diatoms, such as *Amphiprora*, *Biddulphia*, *Gyrosigma*, and *Licmophora*, to be common in collections. The Dinophyceae, represented by species of *Gymnodinium*, *Katodinium*, *Peridinium*, and *Prorocentrum*, were second in abundance and represented an average of 20% of the population (Thayer, 1971).

The zooplankton in the estuary at Beaufort was dominated by copepods, which were more abundant before larval fish entered the estuary. A total of 10 genera were identified by Thayer et al. (1974). *Acartia tonsa*, *Oithona* spp., *Corycaeus* spp., and *Centropages* spp. were responsible for 30, 17, 14 and 6%, respectively, of the total zooplankton numbers. *Enterpina acutifrons*, *Temora* spp., barnacle larvae, and copepod nauplii were of secondary importance. Other organisms present in collections were annelid larvae, ostracods, gastropods, bivalves, crab and shrimp zoea, cladocerans, and *Sagitta* (Thayer et al., 1974).

Seasonal zooplankton maxima occurred between March and June and between October and December. In comparison to other estuarine systems, there was a general dearth of zooplankton in the Beaufort and Newport River estuarine systems as well as a high degree of variability in zooplankton abundance from year to year. Seasonal changes in abundance in the estuaries were much more consistent than annual changes.

Nekton

The peak migration of larval fish into the estuary was from February to March. Larval fish preyed on a wide variety of zooplankters and maximum density of larval fish coincided with zooplankton decline. The Atlantic menhaden, *Brevoortia tyrannus*, the spot, *Leiostomus xanthurus*, and the pinfish, *Lagodon rhomboides*, were the three most abundant larval fish here (Lewis and Wilkens, 1971). The pinfish alone represented 64% of the larval fish in the estuary (Thayer et al., 1974). These three species together preyed heavily on the Beaufort zooplankton.

Near Bogue Banks in the Beaufort region the gradually sloping bed consisted of fine sand and shell fragments. Salinity ranged from 24.9 to 37.8 ppt. Of the many fish collected by Tagatz and Dudley (1961), the following species were numerically dominant: Atlantic menhaden, *Brevoortia tyrannus*; striped anchovy, *Anchoa hepsetus*; and rough silverside, *Menidia martinica*.

At Piver's Island (Fig. 6.1) the habitats included a *Spartina alterniflora* salt marsh and a sandy bottom. Salinity ranged from 22.0 to 37.0 ppt. Dominant fish species here included Atlantic menhaden, *Brevoortia tyrannus*; spot, *Leiostomus xanthurus*; and Atlantic silversides, *Menidia menidia* (Tagatz and Dudley, 1961). For a complete list of Beaufort fish species, see Table 6.1.

The cyprinodonts, *Fundulus heteroclitus* and *F. luciae*, showed seasonal variation in appearance and were found primarily in the marshes (Kneib and Stiven, 1978; Kneib, 1978). The vermillion snapper, *Rhombopolites aurorubens*, was the most frequently caught snapper along the coast of North Carolina (Grimes, 1979).

Benthos

Sandy Shell Substrate. At Beaufort many species of foraminifera, a protozoan group, were found in the sandy shell substrate. *Elphidium gunteri* was the dominant foraminiferan of this area. Other abundant species included *Ammonia beccari*, *Hanzawia concentrica*, and *Quinqueloculina seminulum* (Akers, 1971). The residue where these species were found was mainly medium-to-coarse quartz sand with abundant broken and polished mollusc shells.

Hard Substrate. On hard substrates such as jetties, shells, rocks, pilings, submerged debris, and algae, the epifauna was fairly diverse. Of the 59 species of bryozoa characteristic of the Beaufort region, one, *Bugula neritina*, was by far the most common, occurring at depths of 0 to 5 ft (0 to 1.5 m) and most frequently at the mouth of the Newport River (Maturo, 1957). The species reproduced almost year round, although the period of greatest larval settling was between late June and October, with a second, smaller peak in November. The highest population of bryozoa was found on a shell substrate at the bottom of Bogue Sound in front of Morehead City Port Terminal (Maturo, 1957).

Schizoporella unicornis, another bryozoan, was the most prevalent encrusting form. Settling occurred throughout the year except in the period from January through March. Settling of larvae of this species was much greater at the mouth of the Newport River than at Bogue Sound or Piver's Island (Maturo, 1959), but most individuals did not survive after settling. Bryozoans were the first to colonize an available surface but when additional organisms, such as hydroids, began to settle and grow larger, sediment accumulated. Sediment and crowding by larger organisms smothered the bryozoans so that they were no longer a major part of the fouling fauna. Additional factors (e.g., adult tolerances to salinity changes, available food supply, and pollution) also played important roles in the establishment of bryozoan colonies at Beaufort. Most of the time current velocities in the sound were apparently too great to permit successful establishment of *Bugula neritina* and some other species. The lower the velocity, the greater the settling (Maturo, 1959).

Also common on hard substrates were the sponges, *Reneira tubifera* and *Microciona prolifera*. *Reneira* larvae settled primarily in June and July, while *Microciona* settled from mid-August through September. Both of these species were abundant (McDougall, 1943).

Five species of hydroid were conspicuous on piles in the Beaufort area: *Tubularia crocea, Eudendrium carneum, Pennaria tiarella, Hydractinia echinata,* and *Obelia* sp. *H. echinata* occurred on shells on the bottom of Bogue Sound near Beaufort at a depth of 10 to 12 ft (3 to 3.6 m). *T. crocea* was one of the most abundant Beaufort hydroids except during the summer months. The majority of pile-dwelling organisms at Beaufort exhibited marked seasonal variations in abundance. The following organisms were found in considerable abundance at all seasons in Beaufort: the sponges, *Reneira tubifera, Microciona prolifera,* and *Lissodendoryx caroliniensis;* the worm, *Hydroides hexagonus;* the ascidians, *Styela plicata* and *Phallusia hygomania;* the molluscs, *Modiolus demissus, Ostrea virginica, Urosalpinx cinereus,* and *Anachis avara;* the bryozoans, *Bugula neritina* and *Schizoporella unicornis;* and the barnacles, *Balanus eburneus, B. amphitrite,* and *Chthamalus fragilis.* Although there was a high mortality among young individuals, so many were produced that many became established (McDougall, 1943).

Salinity-Dominated Substrates. About 120 species of shelled molluscs have been collected in the Beaufort area (Bird, 1970). The single physical factor apparently exerting the most influence on distribution is salinity. Sediment type seems to have a minor role.

Outside the mouth of the Newport River estuary, near Beaufort, stations were characterized by the clams, *Spisula solidissima, Tellina alternata,* and *Lucina multilineata,* and the snails, *Retusa canaliculata, Crepidula convexa,* and *Olivella mutica.* Just inside the mouth of the estuary the dominant species were much the same except that the predator, *Olivella mutica,* was less prominent. Farther upstream *O. mutica* was not dominant (Bird, 1970).

The Beaufort area provided a nearly classic example of transition in level-bottom communities. The *Tellina* (bivalve) community of the shallow outer zone (salinity range, 35 to 26 ppt; sediment, medium to very fine sand) gave way to the estuarine bivalve, *Syndosmya* (= *Abra*), community (salinity, 27 to 26 ppt; sediment, very fine sand), which in turn give way to the bivalve, *Macoma balthica,* community (salinity, 23 to 8 ppt; sediment, fine sand to silt). The total and average number of species in each transect showed a gradual and uninterrupted decrease from the mouth to the head of the estuary. The results clearly demonstrated that estuarine communities were made up primarily of euryhaline marine species (Bird, 1970).

SUMMARY

The southeastern estuaries have not been studied as much as the Chesapeake and the Delaware estuaries. However, interest in these estuaries is growing steadily. The main areas of study have been around Sapelo Island by the

University of Georgia and around Beaufort and North Inlet by the people associated with the universities of South Carolina and North Carolina.

These estuaries are mainly classified as barrier island estuaries. They differ from those of the middle Atlantic, Delaware, and Chesapeake Bay estuaries in that a major river is not an important source of water entering the estuary.

The grasslands associated with these barrier island estuaries are very extensive and are considered among the most productive in the world. Small rivers enter the estuary and provide an inflow of fresh water. As in the middle Atlantic estuaries, there is a strong salinity gradient in each of these areas. Nutrients seem to be generated from both the outside and inside the estuary. The concentrations of ammonia, phosphate, nitrates, and nitrite vary greatly. The nitrogen cycling within these estuaries indicates that high rates of nitrogen fixation are occurring in Sapelo Island marshes. However, a substantial amount of denitrification is taking place, so the overall effect is not as large as one might expect. Undoubtedly, some nitrogen is brought in by the incoming tidal waters. It is recognized that considerable amounts of nitrogen are exported from the system.

Recycling of carbon within the system is extensive. A large amount of carbon is fixed in the marshlands. Indeed, these marshlands are considered some of the most productive in the world because of the fixation of carbon by primary production. It is believed that the higher production of the southern coastal plain marshes, compared to those of northern Atlantic states, may be due to nutrient-rich sediments carried in by the rivers in the region and to more favorable year round climates.

In North Inlet, net primary productivity varies greatly within a marshland, with the marshes along the creek being more productive than the high marshes. The phytoplankton productivity was highly variable in Pamlico Sound. Shallow-water areas were more productive than many shallow-water areas in other estuaries. However, the overall production was less than that in deep water.

On the east coast algal productivity is roughly one-third to one-fourth that of the vascular productivity. However, this is not true on the coast of southern California.

Eelgrass beds have been found to be very productive. A great deal of the carbon fixation and oxygen production is by the epiphytes that live on the eelgrass.

Some of the primary productivity in the marshes is consumed directly; for example, 4.6% of the *Spartina* net productivity is estimated to be consumed by herbivorous insects. However, the rest of the *Spartina* productivity and that of the mud algae passes through the detrital–algal food web and is exported to adjacent estuaries. The dominant species in the food web were the fiddler crab and the carnivorous mud crab.

It is estimated that 45% of the net production was exported from the marsh into the estuary. In these southern marshes and estuaries a great deal of the detrital input is from land vegetation and freshwater swamps and marshes. This amount is comparable to the input from the *Spartina* in the salt marshes. The greatest nutrient input of *Spartina* is by detritus, as not many species eat the living *Spartina*. A great many organisms are important in the detrital food web, particularly worms, copepods, shrimp, fish, and crabs.

The algal predators were mainly sandfleas, isopods, fiddler crabs, various types of mussels, snails, and various types of insects. Although not as productive as the *Spartina* detrital food web, these algal food webs are among the most productive in the world for algae.

As in the middle Atlantic estuaries, these marshlands are very productive as spawning and nursery grounds and as feeding grounds for many adult species of organisms, particularly fish and invertebrates. The communities of organisms living in the intertidal zone are very diverse; that is, many different kinds of species form the food web. The plankton, both phytoplankton and zooplankton, are very abundant in these areas. A large number of species are present. Fish are also very common as predators on the rich food supply of invertebrates and algae. The molluscs are very diverse in this area, as about 120 species have been collected in the Beaufort area. The single factor exerting the most influence on their distribution is salinity. The large amount of nutrients and energy-rich food enables the ecosystem to be very diverse in types and numbers of species.

BIBLIOGRAPHY

Adams, S. M. 1976a. Feeding ecology of eelgrass fish communities. Trans. Am. Fish. Soc. 105(4): 514–519.

Adams, S. M. 1976b. The ecology of eelgrass, *Zostera marina*, fish communities. I. Structural analysis. J. Exp. Mar. Biol. Ecol. 22(3): 269–291.

Adams, S. M., and J. W. Angelovic. 1970. Assimilation of detritus and its associated bacteria by three species of estuarine animals. Chesapeake Sci. 11(4): 249–254.

Akers, W. H. 1971. Estuarine foraminiferal associations of the Beaufort areas, North Carolina. Tulane Stud. Geol. Paleontol. 8: 147–165.

Anderson, G. C. 1964. The seasonal and geographic distribution of primary productivity off the Washington and Oregon coasts. Limnol. Oceanogr. 9: 284–302.

Bell, S. S. 1980. Meiofauna–macrofauna interactions in a high salt marsh habitat. Ecol. Monogr. 50(4): 487–505.

Bird, S. O. 1970. Shallow marine and estuarine benthic molluscan communities from the area of Beaufort, N. C. Am. Assoc. Pet. Geol. Bull. 54(9): 1651–1676.

Cain, R. L., and J. M. Dean. 1976. Annual occurrence, abundance, and diversity of fish in a South Carolina intertidal creek. Mar. Biol. 36(4): 369–379.

Cammen, L. M. 1975. Accumulation rate and turnover time of organic carbon in a salt marsh sediment. Limnol. Oceanogr. 20(6): 1012–1015.

Cammen, L. M. 1979. The macro-infauna of a North Carolina salt marsh. Am. Midl. Nat. 102(2): 244–253.

Cammen, L. M. 1980. A method for measuring ingestion rate of deposit feeders and its use with the polychaete, *Nereis succinea*. Estuaries 3(1): 55–60.

Chrcanowski, T. H., B. Stevenson, and J. D. Spurrier. 1983. Dissolved organic carbon transport through the North Inlet ecosystem. Mar. Ecol. 13: 167–174.

Conover, R. J. 1961. A study of Charlestown and Green Hill ponds, Rhode Island. Ecology 42(1): 119–140.

Dame, R. F., and P. D. Kenney. 1986. Variability of *Spartina alterniflora* primary production in the euhaline North Inlet estuary. Mar. Ecol. Prog. Ser. 32: 71–80.

Dame, R., T. Chrzanowski, K. Bildstein, B. Kjerfve, H. Mckellar, D. Nelson, J. Spurrier, S. Stancyk, H. Stevenson, J. Vernberg, and R. Zingmark. 1986. The outwelling hypothesis and North Inlet, South Carolina. Marine Ecology Prog. Ser 33(3): 217–229.

Darnell, R. M. 1967. Organic detritus in relation to the estuarine ecosystem, pp. 376–383. In G. H. Lauff, ed., Estuaries. AAAS Publ. 83.

Day, J. W., Jr., A. S. Hall, W. M. Kemp, and A. Tang-Arancibia. 1989. Estuarine ecology. Wiley, New York, 558 pp.

de Laubenfels, M. W. 1947. Ecology of the sponges of a brackish water environment, at Beaufort, North Carolina. Ecol. Monogr. 17(1): 31–46.

Dexter, D. M. 1967. Distribution and niche diversity of haustroiid amphipods in North Carolina. Chesapeake Sci. 8(3): 187–192.

Dexter, D. M. 1969. Structure of an intertidal sandy beach community in North Carolina. Chesapeake Sci. 10(2): 93–98.

Dowds, R. E. 1978. Distribution and reproduction of four species of *Pinnixia* (Crustacea: *Brachyura*) in a North Carolina estuary. Am. Zool. 18(3): 599.

Driftmeyer, J., G. Thayer, F. Cross, and J. Zieman. 1980. Cycling of Mn, Fe, Cn, and Zn by eelgrass, *Zostera marina*. Am. J. Bot. 67(7): 1089–1096.

Earle, L. C., and H. J. Humm. 1964. Intertidal zonation of algae in Beaufort Harbor. J. Elisha Mitchell Sci. Soc. 80: 78–82.

Fleeger, J. W. 1979. Population dynamics of three estuarine meiobenthic harpacticoids (Copepoda) in South Carolina. Mar. Biol. 52(2): 147–156.

Fleeger, J. W. 1980. Community structure of an estuarine meiobenthic copepod assemblage. Estuarine Coastal Mar. Sci. 10(1): 107–118.

Gallagher, J., and F. Plumley. 1979. Underground biomass profiles and productivity in Atlantic coastal marshes. Am J. Bot. 66(2): 156–161.

Grimes, C. B. 1979. Diet and feeding ecology of the vermillion snapper, *Rhombopolites aurorubens* from North Carolina and South Carolina waters. Bull. Mar. Sci. 29(1): 53–61.

Haines, E. B. 1976. Stable carbon isotope ratios in the biota, soils, and tidal water of a Georgia salt marsh. Estuarine Coastal Mar. Sci. 4(6): 609–619.

Haines, E. B. 1977. The origins of detritus in Georgia salt marsh estuaries. Oikos 29(2): 254–260.

Haines, E. B. 1979. Nitrogen pools in Georgia coastal waters. Estuaries 2(1): 34–38.

Haines, E. B., and C. L. Montague. 1979. Food sources of estuarine invertebrates analyzed using C/C ratios. Ecology 60(1): 48–56.

Hanson, R. B. 1977. Nitrogen fixation (acetylene reduction) in a salt marsh amended with sewage sludge and organic carbon and nitrogen compounds. Appl. Environ. Microbiol. 33(3): 846–852.

Hanson, R. B., and J. Snyder. 1979. Microheterotrophic activity in a salt marsh estuary, Sapelo Island, Georgia, U.S.A. Ecology 60(1): 99–107.

Harlin, M. M. 1971. Translocations between marine hosts and their epiphytic algae. Plant Physiol. 47 (suppl.): 41.

Hobbie, J., B. Copeland, and W. Harrison. 1975. Sources and fates of nutrients of the Pamlico River estuary, North Carolina. In L. E. Cronin, ed., Estuarine Res. 1: 287–302.

Kenworthy, W., J. Zieman, and G. Thayer. 1982. Evidence for the influence of seagrasses on the benthic nitrogen cycle in a coastal plain estuary near Beaufort, North Carolina (USA). Oecologia 54(2): 152–158.

Kikuchi, T. 1980. Faunal relationships in temperate seagrass beds, pp. 153–172. *In* R. C. Phillips, and K. P. McRoy, eds., Handbook of seagrass biology: an ecosystem perspective. Garland Publishing, New York.

Kjelson, M. A., D. S. Peters, G. W. Thayer, and G. N. Johnson. 1975. The general feeding ecology of post larval fishes in the Newport River estuary. U.S. Natl. Mar. Fish. Serv. Fish. Bull. 73(1): 137–144.

Kneib, R. T. 1978. Habitat, diet, reproduction, and growth of the spotfin killifish, *Fundulus luciae*, from a North Carolina salt marsh. Copeia 1978 (1): 164–168.

Kneib, R. T., and A. E. Stiven. 1978. Growth, reproduction, and feeding of *Fundulus heteroclitus* on a North Carolina salt marsh. J. Exp. Mar. Biol. Ecol. 31(2): 121–140.

Lewis, R. M., and E. P. H. Wilkens. 1971. Abundance of Atlantic menhaden larvae and associated species during a diel collection of Beaufort, North Carolina. Chesapeake Sci. 12(3): 185–187.

Lonsdale, D. J., and B. C. Powell. 1977. Composition and seasonality of zooplankton of North Inlet, South Carolina. Chesapeake Sci. 18(3): 272–283.

Magalhaes, H. 1948. An ecological study of the genus Busycon at Beaufort, North Carolina. Ecol. Monogr. 18(3): 377–409.

Maturo, F. J. S., Jr., 1957. A study of the Bryozoa of Beaufort, North Carolina, and vicinity. J. Elisha Mitchell Sci. Soc. 73: 11–68.

Maturo, F. J. S., Jr. 1959. Seasonal distribution and settling rates of estuarine Bryozoa, Ecology 40: 116–127.

McDougall, K. D. 1943. Sessile marine invertebrates of Beaufort, N.C. Ecol. Monogr. 13(3): 321–374.

Mitsch, W.J., and J. G. Gosselink. 1986. Wetlands. Van Nostrand Reinhold, New York. 539 pp.

Montague, C. L., S. M. Bunker, E. B. Haines, M. L. Pace, and R. L. Wetzel. 1981. Aquatic macroconsumers, pp. 69–85. In L. Pomeroy and R. Wiegart, eds., The ecology of a salt marsh. Springer-Verlag, New York.

Nelson, W. G. 1979. Experimental studies of selective predation on amphipods: consequences for amphipod distribution and abundance. J. Exp. Biol. Ecol. 38(3): 225–245.

Odum, E. P. 1959. Fundamentals of ecology. W. B. Saunders, Philadelphia, Pa.

Odum, E. P. 1961. The role of tidal marshes in estuarine production. N.Y. State Conserv. 15(6): 12–15, 35.

Odum, W. E. 1968. The ecological significance of fine particle selection by striped mullet, *Mugil cephalus*. Limnol. Oceanogr. 13(1): 92–98.

Odum, W. E. 1970. Utilization of the direct grazing and plant detritus food chains by the striped mullet, *Mugil cephalus*, pp. 222–240. *In* J. H. Steele, ed., Marine food chains. Univ. California, Berkley.

Odum, E. P., and A. A. de la Cruz. 1967. Particulate organic detritus in a Georgia salt marsh–estuarine ecosystem, pp. 383–388. In G. H. Lauff, ed., Estuaries. AAAS Publ. 83.

Odum, E. P., and M. Fanning. 1973. Comparison of the productivity of *Spartina alterniflora* and *Spartina cynosuroides* in Georgia coastal marshes. Bull. Ga. Acad. Sci. 31: 1–12.

Odum, E. P., and A. E. Smalley. 1959. Comparison of population energy flow of a herbivorous and a deposit feeding invertebrate in a salt marsh ecosystem. Proc. Natl. Acad. Sci. 45(4): 617–622.

Ortega, S. 1981. Environmental stress, competition and dominance of *Crassostrea virginica* near Beaufort, N.C. Mar. Biol. 62(1): 47–56.

Penhale, P. A. 1977. Macrophyte–epiphyte biomass and productivity in an eelgrass (*Zostera marina*) community. J. Exp. Mar. Biol. Ecol. 26(2): 107–224.

Penhale, P., and W. Smith, Sr. 1977. Excretion of dissolved organic carbon by eelgrass (*Zostera marina*) and its epiphytes. Limnol. Oceanogr. 22(3): 400–407.

Peters, D. S., and M. A. Kjelson. 1975. Consumption and utilization of food by various post larval and juvenile fishes of North Carolina estuaries. *In* L. E. Cronin, ed., Estuarine Res. 1: 448–472.

Phillips, R. C. 1974. Temperate grass flats, pp. 244–299. *In* H. T. Odum, B. J. Copeland, and E. A. McMahan, eds., Coastal ecological systems of the United States. Vol. 2. The Conservation Foundation, Washington, D.C.

Pomeroy, L. R. 1959. Algal productivity in salt marshes of Georgia. Limnol Oceanogr. 4(4): 386–397.

Pomeroy, L. R., K. Bancroft, J. Breed, R. R. Christian, D. Frankenberg, J. R. Hall, L. G. Maurer, W. J. Wiebe, R. G. Wiegert, and R. L. Wetzel. 1977. Flux of organic matter through a salt marsh, pp. 270–279. *In* M. Wiley, ed., Estuarine processes. Vol. 2. Academic Press, New York.

Pomeroy, L., W. Darley, E. Dunn, J. Gallagher, E. Haines, and D. Whiting. 1981. Primary production, pp. 39–86. *In* L. Pomeroy and R. Wiegert, eds., The ecology of a salt marsh. Springer-Verlag, New York.

Powell, A. B., and F. J. Schwartz. 1979. Food of *Paralichthys dentatus* and *P. lethostigma* (Pisces: Bothidae) in North Carolina estuaries. Estuaries 2(4): 276–279.

Putnam, H. D. 1966. Limiting factors for primary production in a west coast Florida estuary. Adv. Water Pollut. Res. 3rd Int. Conf. Proc. *In* J. Water Pollut. Control Fed. 38: 382–383.

Ragotzkie, R. A. 1959. Plankton productivity in estuarine waters of Georgia. Publ. Inst. Mar. Sci. Univ. Texas 6: 146–158.

Reimold, R. J., J. L. Gallagher, R. A. Linthurst, and W. J. Pfeiffer. 1975. Detritus production in coastal Georgia salt marshes. *In* L. E. Cronin, ed., Estuarine Res. 1: 217–228.

Riley, G. A. 1956. Oceanography of Long Island Sound. 1952–54. IX. Production and utilization of organic matter. Bull. Bingham Oceanogr. Collect 15: 324–344.

Roelofs, E. W. 1954. Food studies of young sciaenid fishes, *Micropogon* and *Leiostomus* from North Carolina. Copeia 1954(2): 151–153.

Sellner, K., R. Zingmark, and T. Miller. 1976. Interpretations of the C method of measuring the total annual production of phytoplankton in a South Carolina estuary. Bot. Mar. 19(2): 119–125.

Sikora, J. P., W. B. Sikora, C. Erkenbrecher, and B. Coull. 1977. Significance of ATP, carbon, and caloric content of meiobenthic nematodes in partitioning benthic biomass. Mar. Biol. 44(1): 7–14.

Smalley, A. 1959. The growth cycle of *Spartina* and its relation to the insect populations in the marsh, pp. 96–100. Proceedings of the salt marsh conference. Marine Institute, Univ. Georgia, Sapelo Island, Ga.

Smith, S. L. 1978. The role of zooplankton in the nitrogen dynamics of a shallow estuary. Estuarine Coastal Mar. Sci. 7(6): 555–565.

Smith, G., and S. Hayasaka. 1982. Nitrogenase activity associated with *Zostera marina* from a North Carolina estuary. Can. J. Microbiol. 28(4): 448–451.

Steeman-Nielsen, E. 1958. The balance between phytoplankton and zooplankton in the sea. J. Conserv. Expl. Mar. 23(2): 178–188.

Stephans, G. C. 1967. Dissolved organic material as a nutritional source for marine and estuarine invertebrates, pp. 367–376. *In* G. H. Lauff, ed., Estuaries. AAAS Publ. 83.

Stephenson, T. A., and A. Stephenson. 1952. Life between tide-marks in North America. II. Northern Florida and the Carolinas. J. Ecol. 40(1): 1–49.

Stickney, R. R., G. L. Taylor, and D. B. White. 1975. Food habits of five species of young southeastern United States estuarine Sciaenidae. Chesapeake Sci. 16(2): 104–114.

Stross, R. G., and J. R. Stottlemyer. 1965. Primary production in the Patuxent River. Chesapeake Sci. 6(3): 125–140.

Stroud, L., and A. Cooper. 1969. Color-infrared aerial photographic interpretation and net primary productivity of a regularly flooded North Carolina salt marsh. Univ. North Carolina Water Resource. Res. Inst. Rept. 14. 86 pp.

Tagatz, M. E., and D. L. Dudley. 1961. Seasonal occurrence of marine fishes in four shore habitats near Beaufort, N.C., 1957–1960. U.S. Fish Wildl. Serv. Spec. Sci. Rept. Fish. 390 19 pp.

Teal, J. M. 1962. Energy flow in the salt marsh ecosystem of Georgia. Ecology 43(4): 614–624.

Teal, J. M. 1986. The ecology of regularly flooded salt marshes of New England: a commu-profile. Fish and Wildlife Service, Division of Biological Services, Washington, D.C. Biol. Rep. 85(7.4).

Thayer, G. W. 1971. Phytoplankton production and the distribution of nutrients in a shallow unstratified estuarine system near Beaufort, N.C. Chesapeake Sci. 12(4): 240–253.

Thayer, G. W. 1974. Identity and regulation of nutrients limiting phytoplankton production in the shallow estuaries near Beaufort, N.C. Oecologia (Berlin) 14(1/2): 75–92.

Thayer, G., D. Hoss, M. Kjelson, W. Hettler, Jr., and M. LaCroix. 1974. Biomass of zooplankton in the Newport River estuary and the influence of postlarval fishes. Chesapeake Sci. 15(1): 9–16.

Thayer, G. W., S. M. Adams, and M. W. LaCroix. 1975. Structural and functional aspects of a recently established Zostera marina community. In L. E. Cronin, ed., Estuarine Res. 1: 517–540.

Thayer, G., D. Engel, and M. LaCroix. 1977. Seasonal distribution and changes in the nutritive quality of living, dead, and detrital fractions of Zostera marina. J. Exp. Mar. Biol. Ecol. 30(2): 109–128.

Thomas, C. W. 1966. Vertical circulation off the Ross Ice Shelf. Pac. Sci. 20(2): 239–245.

Turner, R., S. Woo, and H. Jitts. 1979. Phytoplankton production in a turbid, temperate salt marsh. Estuarine Coastal Mar. Sci. 9(5): 603–613.

Weigert, R. G., R. R. Christian, and R. L. Wetzel, 1981. A model view of the marsh, pp. 183–218. In L. R. Pomeroy and R. G. Weigert, eds., The ecology of a salt marsh. Springer-Verlag, New York.

Weigert, R. G. and L. R. Pomeroy. 1981. The salt marsh ecosystem: a synthesis, pp. 219–230. In L. R. Pomeroy and R. G. Weigert (eds.) The ecology of a salt marsh. Springer, New York.

Welsh, B. 1975. The role of grass shrimp, Palaemonetes pugio, in a tidal marsh ecosystem. Ecology 56(3): 513–530.

Wetzel, R. L. 1975. An experimental study of detrital carbon utilization in a Georgia salt marsh. Ph.D. thesis. Univ. Georgia, Athens, Ga.

Wetzel, R. L. 1976. Carbon resources of a benthic salt marsh invertebrate, Nassarius obsoletus (Mollusca: Nassariidae). Estuarine Process. 2: 293–308.

Whitney, D., A. Chalmers, E. Haines, R. Hanson, L. Pomeroy, and B. Sherr. 1981. The cycles of nitrogen and phosphorus. In L. Pomeroy and R. Weigert, eds., The ecology of a salt marsh. Ecol. Stud. 38: 163–181.

Whitting, G. J., H. N. McKellar, Jr., B. Kjerfbe, and J. D. Spurrier. 1987. Nitrogen exchange between the southeastern U.S. salt marsh ecosystem and the coastal ocean. Mar. Biol. 95: 173–182.

Wiebe, W. J., and L. R. Pomeroy. 1972. Microorganisms and their associations with aggregates and detritus in the sea: a microscopic study. pp. 325–352. In U. Melchiorri-Santolini and J. W. Hopton, eds., Detritus and its role in aquatic ecosystems. Proceedings of the IBP-UNESCO Symposium. Mem. 1st Ital. Idrobiol., 29 Suppl. Pallanza, Italy.

Williams, R. B. 1966. Annual phytoplankton production in a system of shallow temperate estuaries, pp. 699–716. In H. Barnes, ed., Some contemporary studies in marine science. Allen & Unwin, New York.

Williams, R. B. 1973. Nutrient levels and phytoplankton productivity in the estuary, pp. 59–89. In R. A. Chabrek, ed., Proceedings of the coastal marsh and estuary management symposium, Louisiana State Univ., Baton Rouge, La.

Williams, R., and M. Murdoch. 1966. Phytoplankton production and chlorophyll concentrations in Beaufort Channel, North Carolina. Limnol. Oceanogr. 11(1): 73–82.

Williams, R., and M. Murdoch. 1969. The potential importance of Spartina alterniflora in conveying zinc, maganese, and iron into estuarine food chains, pp. 431–439. In: D. J. Nelson, and F. C. Evans, eds., Proceedings of the 2nd national symposium on radioecology, A.S.A.E.C.

Williams, R. B., M. B. Murdoch, and L. K. Thomas. 1968. Standing crop and importance of zooplankton in a system of shallow estuaries. Chesapeake Sci. 9(1): 42–51.

Wolaver, T. G., W. Johnson, and M. Marozas. 1984. Nitrogen and phosphorus concentrations within North Inlet, South Carolina: speculation as to sources of sinks. Estuarine Coastal Shelf Sci. 19: 243–255.

Wolaver, T. G., S. Hutchinson, and M. Marozas. 1986. Dissolved and particulate organic carbon in the North Inlet Estuary, South Carolina: what controls their concentrations. Estuaries 19(1): 31–36.

Zieman, J. C. 1982. The ecology of the seagrasses of south Florida: a community profile. U.S. Fish and Wildlife Service, Office of Biological Services, Washington, D. C. FWS/BS-82/25. 158 pp.

CHAPTER 7

South Florida Seagrasses

S eagrass meadows in south Florida are highly productive, faunally rich, and ecologically important habitats. They offer plentiful shelter and food, and are perhaps the richest nursery and feeding grounds in south Florida's coastal waters.

A map of the south Florida area is reproduced in Figure 7.1. Turtle grass (*Thalassia testudinum*) is the largest and most robust of the south Florida seagrasses. Other species of seagrass include *Halophila decipiens, H. engelmanni, H. johnsonii, Syringodium filiforme,* and *Halodule wrightii*.

The seagrasses in south Florida grow on a variety of substrates, and sediment depth is important for optimum growth. Fine sediment ($<63 \mu m$) deposition increases with the density of the leaves because the leaves create a low-water-energy environment. The stages of succession in a seagrass ecosystem are diagrammed by Zieman (1982) in Figure 7.2.

PRODUCTIVITY

Primary Productivity
Typical seagrass beds produce between 500 and $1000 \, g \, C \, m^{-2} \, yr^{-1}$ (Fenchel, 1977). The south Florida beds cover an area of $8500 \, km^2$ and are the largest seagrass resource of our biosphere.

Thalassia testudinum (turtlegrass) and associated seagrasses have the potential for extremely high primary productivity, but recorded values vary enormously depending on density, season, and measurement techniques. In turtle grass 10

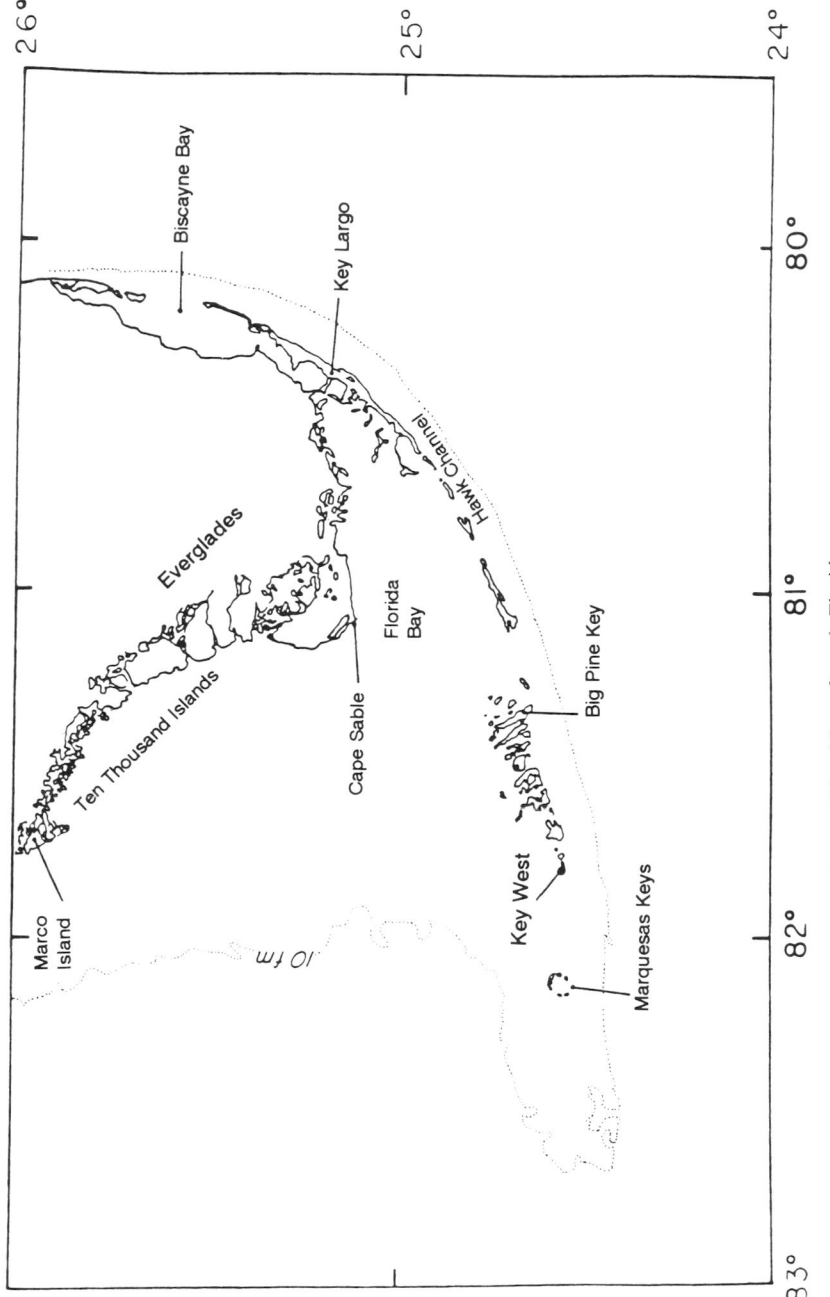

FIGURE 7.1. Map of south Florida: seagrass area.

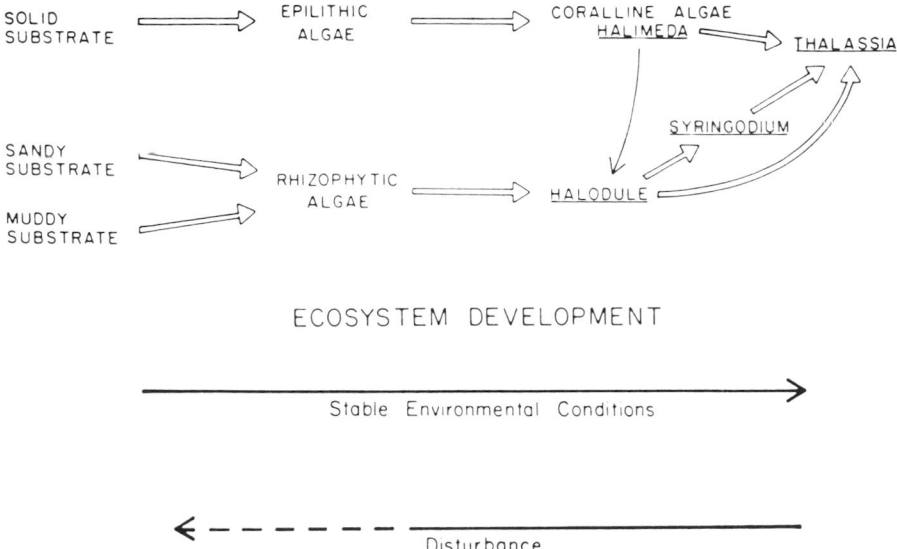

FIGURE 7.2. Ecosystem development patterns in south Florida marine waters. This is a generalized pattern and all stages may not be present. Note that in the absence of disturbance the tendency is to a *Thalassia* cleanup. (From Zieman, 1982, for U.S. Dept. of Interior.)

to 45% of the biomass is in the leaves and shoots with the remaining amount in the roots and rhizomes. In Biscayne Bay the ratio of weight of leaves and shoots to rhizomes to roots was 3:2:2 (Zieman, 1982).

At Turkey Point in Biscayne Bay *Thalassia testudinum* had a productivity of 0.92 to 4.40 g dry wt m^{-2} day^{-1}. The mean *Thalassia* growth in Biscayne Bay was 1410 g dry wt m^{-2} yr^{-1}. This was much higher than the productivity of mangrove leaf litter (300 g dry wt m^{-2} yr^{-1}) and of plankton (34 to 39 g dry wt m^{-2} yr^{-1}) or red or green algae (19.5 g and 30 g dry wt m^{-2} yr^{-1}, respectively). When this plant production was summed on an areal basis the dry weight production was more than 8×10^{11} g yr^{-1}, exclusive of microepiphytes (Thorhaug and Roessler, 1977).

Odum (1963) and Jones (1968) reported *Thalassia* productivity values of 0.9 to 16 g C m^{-2} day^{-1} in south Florida. The net aboveground production was around 1 to 4 g C m^{-2} day^{-1}, although the maximum rates can be several times these values (Zieman and Wetzel, 1980). McRoy and McMillan (1977) estimated a total annual primary production of about 1000 g C m^{-2} (or about 2000 g dry wt m^{-2} yr^{-1}) based on an assumption of a 250-day net growing season. By comparison, in the U.S. Virgin Islands, Zieman et al. (1979) estimated for one tropical turtle grass community a net export of 0.18 to 0.36 g m^{-2} day^{-1} of leaf material.

Live turtle grass leaves contained 9 to 22% protein, 6 to 31% soluble carbohydrates, and 25 to 44% ash (dry weight) (Dawes and Lawrence, 1980).

The calculated energy levels were constant over the year (4.5 to 4.8 kcal g^{-1}, organic weight) with an energy value of 1.76 to 1.8 × 10^4 joules g^{-1} organic weight (Walsh and Grow, 1972). This is comparable to the energy levels of *Spartina* which was found to be 4.4 to 4.6 kcal g^{-1} organic weight (Squiers and Good, 1974).

Green seagrass is relatively unavailable as food to many organisms because of a complex combination of factors. Seagrass contains up to 59% fiber (dry weight), and many animals lack the enzymatic capacity to assimilate it. The fiber is resistant to maceration by many organisms. The six phenolic acids detected in the leaves, roots, and rhizomes of turtle grass, manatee grass, and shoal grass are also deterrents to direct herbivory (Zapata and McMillan, 1979).

Algae. Phytoplankton production in *Thalassia* beds has not been studied very extensively. Reeve (1975) suggested for Biscayne Bay that a crude estimate of phytoplankton production might place it an order of magnitude less than in the seagrass, estimated at 95 mg C m^{-2} day^{-1}. Odum (1963) suggested that compared with benthic production, phytoplankton production played a minor role in these beds. Phytoplankton production may assume more importance in the food chain because it is rapid rather than entering after the slow process of decomposition which is necessary for the seagrasses and many macrophytic algae before they become a food source (Reeve, 1975).

Epiphytic flora was comparatively important in the seagrass community metabolism. Both Harlin (1980) and McRoy and McMillan (1977) summarize epiphytic productivity measurements made by Jones (1968) in his unpublished Ph.D. dissertation. For epiphytes on *Thalassia* in Florida, Jones found considerable seasonal variation in productivity. The average net epiphyte production was estimated to be 0.9 g C m^{-2} day^{-1} in summer and 0.2 g C m^{-2} day^{-1} in winter. The total annual production of epiphytes was estimated as 200 g C m^{-2} yr^{-1}. This value was 20% of the estimated average net production of *Thalassia* in the region.

The contribution of the benthic algae to productivity in seagrass beds has not been well explored. McRoy and McMillan (1977) suspected that the filamentous species of algae that were favored by the reduced turbulence of a seagrass bed had high rates of production and were important contributors to the community. Dawes et al. (1979) found that the benthic macroalgal component to the seagrass community was energetically equal in importance to turtle grass.

Detrital Productivity

The formation of detritus from green plant tissue is accomplished by biological and chemical activity and by physical changes. The results of these processes are particles of various sizes and the release of dissolved organic matter from the detritus itself and the organisms processing the detritus.

Biological processing of detritus is carried out primarily by bacteria, fungi, and protozoa, although some macroinvertebrates are also involved. In this activity the nutritive value of the detritus is often increased as the microorganisms obtain nutrients from other sources. For example, the nitrogen content of seagrass is usually 2 to 4%, whereas the microflora and fauna contain 5 to 10% available nitrogen. Nonprotein nitrogen may compose up to 30% of the nitrogen, but is in complex form, which is not easily available as a food source. Initially, the leaves of turtle grass contain 9 to 22% protein, but after microbial activity the detritus, with microbial biomass, contains from 30 to 40% protein. In the processes of mineralization of the detritus and the synthesis of microbial biomass, a much higher proportion of soluble compounds is formed.

Physical changes during formation of detritus result in smaller particulate matter, which offers more surface for the attachment of bacteria. The small particles with their associated microfauna are food for the abundant deposit-feeding fauna such as polychaete worms, amphipods, isopods, ophiuroids, and certain gastropods and molluscs. Detritivores consume both the detritus and its microbial components, which can be assimilated with an efficiency of 50 to 100%. In contrast, the green plant material is assimilated with less than 5% efficiency (Zieman, 1982).

Turtle grass (*Thalassia testudinum*) was the most important component of the detritus (87.1%) in Biscayne Bay. Other components were other grasses (2.1%), algae (4.6%), mangrove leaves (3.3%), terrestrial material (2.5%), and animal remains (0.4%). The detrital community of microorganisms consisted of bacteria, small zooflagellates, ciliates, diatoms, and other unicellular algae (Zieman, 1982).

NUTRIENT CYCLING

Phosphorus

Patriquin (1972) found that the sediments contain a considerable reserve of phosphate; however, there is some uptake of phosphorus from the interstitial water, which in the midroot layer, averaged 0.73 µg A L^{-1} (0.27 to 1.04 µg A L^{-1}), and from seawater, where the average concentration was 0.20 µg A L^{-1}. In the sediments there was a reserve supply equal to requirements for 300 to 1000 days of growth.

Phosphorus in the water column interacted dynamically with the upper few centimeters of the sediment. Below this, phosphorus was accumulated and particulate phosphorus, largely from organic detritus, was buried and lost from short-term circulation. Where seagrasses were found, phosphorus from the deeper sediments could be returned to the water via uptake by the roots, incorporation into the leaves, and release into the water (McRoy and Barsdate, 1970).

Nitrogen

Nitrogen was needed in much greater quantities than phosphorus, and its source was more obscure in the seagrass ecosystem (McRoy and McMillan, 1977). According to Zieman (1982), seagrasses had three potential sources of nitrogen: recycled nitrogen in the sediments, nitrogen in the water column, and nitrogen fixation. Patriquin (1972) suggested that the primary source of nitrogen for leaf

TABLE 7.1. *Nitrogen Requirements and Sources of Supply in Beds of* Thalassia testudinum *and* Zostera marina

	Thalassia testudinum (Patriquin, 1972)	Zostera marina (McRoy and McMillan, 1977)
Plant requirements		
Standing stock	~440 shoots m^{-2}	~1000 g dry m^{-2}
N content	2.3% dry wt	2–3% dry wt
Productivity	1.2–7.6 g dry m^{-2} day^{-1}	10 g dry m^{-2} day^{-1}
N requirement	21–71 mg m^{-2} day^{-1}	200–300 m^{-2} day^{-1}
Environment sources		
Interstitial (N)	6.1 μg at N L^{-1}	30 μg at N L^{-1}
Volume of interstitial H$_2$O	64 L m^{-2}	15 L m^{-2}
Total interstitial N	5.3 mg m^{-2}	6.3 mg N m^{-2}
Extractable (N)	28–863 μg at kg^{-1} day^{-1}	54–131 μg at L^{-1}
Volume of root layer	127 L m^{-2}	150 L m^{-2}
Total extractable N	340 mg m^{-2}	113–275 mg m^{-2}
N fixation		
Epiphytes	—	0
Sediments	40–251 mg N m^{-2} day^{-1}	0
Water column: total dissolved inorganic N	14 mg m^{-3}	14 mg m^{-3}

production was recycled material from sediments, but that rhizosphere fixation could supply 20 to 50% of the plant's requirements. He also suggested that the nitrogen requirement of *Thalassia* was derived from gaseous nitrogen fixed by the anaerobic bacteria *Clostridium* sp. and *Desulfovibrio* sp., and that only a 5- to 15-day supply of nitrogen was available in the sediments. Ammonia was the preferred form of nitrogen for *Thalassia*, although other forms of nitrogen were also used. No conclusive answer is possible at this time to explain apparent nitrogen deficits (McRoy and McMillan, 1977). A comparison between *T. testudium* and *Z. marina* of nitrogen requirements and sources of supply is made in Table 7.1.

Carbon

Seagrasses released substantial amounts of dissolved organic carbon (DOC) during growth and decomposition. The DOC fraction of the seagrass organic matter was most frequently used and quickly assimilated by microorganisms. DOC was available to consumers as food in significant quantities only after its conversion to microbial biomass. The utilization of seagrass DOC was functionally similar to detrital food webs based on the particulate fraction of seagrass carbon (Zieman, 1982).

The short-term release of recently synthesized photosynthate from blades of turtle grass was found to be 2 to 10% (Wetzel and Penhale, 1979). Photosynthate losses to the water column from the entire community, including belowground biomass and decomposing portions, may have been much higher. Release of DOC from detrital leaves may also have been substantial since dried turtle grass was shown to release 13% of its organic carbon content during leaching under sterile conditions. It is important to remember that carbon released as DOC was extremely labile and rapidly assimilated by microorganisms. This led to its immediate availability as a food source for secondary consumers. In most marine systems the dissolved organic carbon pool contained 100 times more carbon than the particulate organic carbon pool (Zieman, 1982).

FOODWEB

There were basically three pathways by which seagrasses and their associated epiphytes provided food for the higher trophic levels: (1) direct herbivory, (2) detrital food webs within grass beds, and (3) exported material consumed in other systems either as macrophyte material or as detritus (Zieman, 1982). The detrital pathway has usually been considered of primary importance. However, it is becoming increasingly apparent that in many locations both the direct utilization pathway and exports of material may provide more carbon to the community than was previously suspected (Zieman et al., 1979).

Direct grazing of seagrasses in south Florida was more important in the Florida Keys and the outer margin of Florida Bay than in areas to the west of the Florida Keys (Zieman, 1982). McRoy and Helfferich (1980) identified five Florida animals that grazed directly on *Thalassia*. Three of the five were sea urchins (*Eucidaris tribuloides, Tripneustes esculentus, T. ventricosus*), another was a lugworm (*Arenicola cristata*), and the fifth was a fish, the halfbeak (*Hyporhamphus unifasciatus*). Randall (1967) reported that the parrotfish (Scaridae), known to feed on Florida seagrass and associated algae, has an absorption efficiency of about 50%. *Sparisoma radians*, the bucktooth parrotfish, fed almost exclusively on turtle grass. Other parrotfish found in the grassbeds were *Sparisoma rubripinne* and *S. chrysopterum*. Additional seagrass-consuming fish identified by Zieman (1982) were surgeonfish (Acanthuridae), porgies (Sparidae), and halfbeaks (Hyporhamphus).

Urchins that Zieman (1982) found feeding on seagrass included *Eucidaris tribuloides, Lytechinus variegatus, Diadema antillarum,* and *Tripneustes ventricosus*. According to Ogden (1980), however, *T. ventricosus* and *D.. antillarum* fed exclusively on seagrasses with epiphytes. *Lytechinus variegatus* has been known to denude large areas of seagrass, although it fed mainly on detritus. The absorption efficiency of urchins feeding on seagrasses was about 50%, but the assimilation efficiency was only 3.8% for *T. ventricosus* and 3.0% for *L. variegatus* (Zieman, 1982).

The emerald nerite, *Smaragdia viridis*, a small gastropod, was another direct consumer of turtle grass blades, feeding primarily on the lower half of the leaves (Zieman, 1982).

Marine turtles and sirenians (manatees) were probably the only large vertebrates that browsed on seagrass (Kikuchi and Peres, 1977). Turtles ate only the basal part of the leaf, permitting most of the blade to float away. The Caribbean manatee of south Florida (*Trichechus manatus*) uprooted seagrass plants from soft substrate and shook them free of nonplant material. Manatees are known to consume up to 20% of their body weight (500 kg) of aquatic grasses per day. One of the main effects of these animals browsing seagrasses was the export of the freed blade or the settling of partially eaten plants on the seagrass bed.

The majority of seagrass consumers had no enzymes to digest seagrass. It is increasingly apparent that most macroconsumers of seagrass depended on cell contents of the seagrasses and the attached epiphytes for food. In fact, Zieman (1982) felt that seagrass epiphytes were important in the flow of energy within the grass carpet because many of the small, mobile epifaunal species that were food for fish fed at least in part on epiphytes. However, the detrital pathway remained of primary importance since most organisms were incapable of utilizing seagrass directly, and since about 70% of daily seagrass production went directly into the detrital system and was not available to herbivores (Zieman et al., 1979).

Many small organisms in grass beds used algal epiphytes and detritus as their food sources. Amphipods, isopods, crabs, and other crustaceans ingested a mixture of epiphytic and benthic algae as well as detritus (Odum and Heald, 1972). In a study by Zieman et al. (1979) three of the four seagrass-dwelling amphipods common in south Florida used seagrass epiphytes, seagrass detritus, and drift algae as food, in that order of preference. Epiphytic algae were the most important food source for the caridean shrimp, *Tozeuma carolinense*, and the amphipods, *Cymadusa compta*, *Gammarus mucronatus*, and *Melita nitida*. The efficiency of assimilation by the amphipods was 48, 43, and 75%, respectively, which was greater than for other food sources (macrophytic drift algae, live and detrital seagrass).

Penaeid and caridean shrimp are usually considered omnivores. The pink shrimp, *Penaeus duorarum*, ingested organic detritus, sand, polychaetes, nematodes, caridean shrimp, mysids, copepods, isopods, amphipods, ostracods, molluscs, and foraminiferans (Eldred, 1958; Eldred et al., 1961). Shrimp stripped microbes from the detritus, and reingested their own fecal pellets after microorganisms had again colonized them (Fenchel, 1970).

Several large invertebrates such as the gastropod, *Strombus gigas*, and the sea star, *Oreaster reticulatus*, were detritivores (Zieman, 1982). Detritus was a major dietary component for six species of juvenile fish: southern puffer, *Sphoeroides nephelus*; clown goby, *Microgobius glosus*; Florida blenny, *Chasmodes saburrae*; inland silversides, *Menidia beryllina*; Atlantic thread herring, *Opisthonema oglinum*; and halfbeak, *Hyporhamphus unifasciatus* (Carr and Adams, 1973).

Numerous fish ingested some plant material but few were strict herbivores (Table 7.2). Most plant and detrital material was probably taken incidentally while feeding on other organisms. The very abundant pigfish, *Orthopristis chrysoptera*, and the pinfish, *Lagodon rhomboides*, were omnivores during some feeding stages, ingesting substantial amounts of epiphytes, detritus, and seagrass

(*text continued on page 478*)

TABLE 7.2 *Direct Consumers of Seagrass*

Herbivore				
Scientific Name	Common Name	Seagrass Eaten	Part of Seagrass Eaten	Percent Seagrass in Diet	Location of Population

Scientific Name	Common Name	Seagrass Eaten	Part of Seagrass Eaten	Percent Seagrass in Diet	Location of Population
		Invertebrates			
Annelids					
Arenicola cristata	Lugworm	*Thalassia* *Halodule* *Syringodium*	Detritus	Up to 100	Florida
Capitella capitata	Polychaete	*Zostera marina*	Detritus	Up to 100	Massachusetts
Diopatra cuprea	Quill worm	*Zostera marina*	Leaf		Massachusetts Chesapeake Bay
Enchytraeus lineatus	Oligochaete	*Zostera marina*	Leaf		North Sea
Hesperonoe adventor	Scaleworm	*Zostera marina*	Leaf	Up to 10	Alaska
Lumbricillis lineatus	Oligochaete	*Zostera marina*	Leaf		North Sea
Molluscs					
Aplysia california (*Tethys californicus*)	Sea hare	*Zostera marina*	Leaf		California
Bursatella leachii	Sea hare	*Zostera nana* *Z. tasmanica* *Zostera*	Leaf (live or dead)		New Zealand
Dolabela sp.		*Zostera* sp.	Leaf		Australia
Gibbula sp.	Periwinkle	*Zostera nana*	Leaf		South Africa
Haminoea zelandiae	Bubble shell	*Z. tasmanica*	Leaf		New Zealand
Lacuna carinata	Chink snail	*Zostera marina*	Leaf	Up to 100	Alaska
Lacuna variegata	Chink snail	*Zostera marina*	Leaf	Up to 100	Alaska
Lacuna vincta	Chink snail	*Zosterc marina*	Leaf	Up to 100	Alaska
Quibulla quoyi	Bubble shell	*Zostera nana* *Z. tasmanica*	Leaf		New Zealand
Strombus gigas	Queen conch	*Thalassia* *Syringodium* *Halodule*	Leaf Leaf Leaf		West Indies

Continued

467

TABLE 7.2 (*Continued*)

Scientific Name	Herbivore Common Name	Seagrass Eaten	Part of Seagrass Eaten	Percent Seagrass in Diet	Location of Population
Crustaceans					
Amphithoe vaillanti	Amphipod	*Zostera*	Leaf	16	Black Sea
		Ruppia	Leaf	8	
Anisogammarus sp.	Amphipod	*Zostera marina*	Beached leaves		Alaska
Callinectes sapidus	Blue crab	*Zostera marina*	Leaf		U.S. Atlantic coast
		Thalassia	Leaf		Texas
		Ruppia	Leaf		
Dexamine spinosa	Amphipod	*Zostera*	Leaf	1.8	Black Sea
		Ruppia	Leaf	3	
Gammarus locusta	Amphipod	*Zostera*	Leaf	43	Black Sea
		Ruppia	Leaf	25	
Idotea baltica	Isopod	*Zostera marina*	Leaf		Black Sea
Idotea fewkesi	Isopod	*Zostera marina*	Leaf		Alaska
	Isopod	*Zostera marina*	Leaf	up to 100	Black Sea
	Isopod	*Phyllospadix*	Leaf		Black Sea
Ligia pallasii	Amphipod	*Zostera marina*	Beached leaves		Alaska
Orchestia sp.	Decorator crab	*Zostera marina*	Leaf	10	Alaska
Pugettia gracilis	Helmet crab, horsehair crab	*Zostera marina*	Stem	15	Alaska
Telmessus chieragonus			Rhizome	12	Alaska
Uca sp.	Fiddler crab	*Thalassia testudinum*	Leaf (wrack)		Texas
Echinoderms					
Astropyga radiata					Zanzibar
Diadema antillarum	Sea urchin	*Thalassia*	Leaf		West Indies
		Syringodium	Leaf		
Diadema setosum	Sea urchin	*Thalassia testudinum*		12	West Indies
					Zanzibar

468

Organism	Common name	Plant	Part	Number	Location
Echinometra lucunter	Sea urchin	*Thalassia*	Leaf	10.2	Caribbean
		Syringodium	Leaf	8.9	Alaska
Echinometra mathaei	Sea urchin	*Halodule*	Leaf	7.9	Alaska
					Mauritius
					Zanzibar
Echinothrix calamaris	Sea urchin	*Thalassia*	Leaf		Zanzibar
Eucidaris tribuloides	Sea urchin	*Zostera marina*	Leaf		Caribbean
Lytechinus anamesus	Sea urchin	*Thalassia*	Leaf		Gulf of California
Lytechinus variegatus	Sea urchin	*Thalassia*	Leaf	Up to 100	Florida
		Thalassia	Leaf		Jamaica
		Thalassia	Leaf		Caribbean
		Syringodium	Leaf		
Paracentrotus lividus	Sea urchin	*Posidonia*	Leaf		Denmark
Psammechinus miliaris	Sea urchin	*Zostera marina*	Leaf		Denmark
		Zostera marina	Dead leaf		Mauritius
Stomopneustes variolaris	Sea urchin				Zanzibar
Strongylocentrotus droebachiensis	Green urchin	*Zostera marina*	Leaf	Up to 100	Alaska
		Phyllospadix	Leaf		Denmark
		Zostera marina	Dead leaf		Maine, Puget Sound
Strongylocentrotus franciscanus	Sea urchin	*Phyllospadix*	Leaf		California
Strongylocentrotus intermedius	Sea urchin	*Phyllospadix*	Leaf	10–50	Japan
		Phyllospadix	Leaf	30–100	Japan
Strongylocentrotus purpuratus	Sea urchin	*Phyllospadix*	Leaf		California
Tripneustes esculentus	Sea urchin	*Phyllospadix*	Leaf		Oregon
Tripneustes gratilla	Sea urchin	*Thalassia*	Leaf	More than 50	Florida
					Mauritius
					Zanzibar
Tripneustes ventricosus	Sea urchin	*Thalassia*	Leaf	Up to 100	Florida

Continued

TABLE 7.2 (Continued)

	Herbivore		Seagrass Eaten	Part of Seagrass Eaten	Percent Seagrass in Diet	Location of Population
Scientific Name	Common Name					
Vertebrates						
Fishes						
Acanthostracion quadricornis	Cowfish		*Thalassia*	Leaf	3	West Indies
Acanthurus bahianus	Ocean surgeon fish		*Syringodium* *Halophila baillonis* *Thalassia*	Leaf	8.2	West Indies
Acanthurus chirurgus	Doctor fish		*Syringodium* *Thalassia* *Syringodium*	Leaf	40–80 (Thalassia) 5.7	West Indies West Indies
Acanthurus coeruleus	Blue tang		*Thalassia* *Syringodium* *Halophila baillonis* *Syringodium*	Leaf	25 6.8	West Indies West Indies
Alutera schoepfi	Orange filefish		*Syringodium* *Thalassia*	Leaf	67	West Indies
Alutera scripta	Scrawled filefish		*Syringodium* *Thalassia*	Leaf	9	West Indies
Anguilla rostrata	American eel		*Zostera marina*	Leaf		Chesapeake Bay
Archosargus oviceps	Gulf sheepshead		*Ruppia*	Leaf		Louisiana
Archosargus probatocephalus	Sheepshead		*Halodule*	Leaf		Texas
Archosargus rhomboidalis	Sea bream		*Thalassia* *Syringodium*	Leaf	44.6	West Indies
Cantherhines pullus	Orange-spotted filefish		*Thalassia* *Halophila baillonis*	Leaf	4.6	West Indies
Canthigaster rostrata	Sharp-nose puffer		*Syringodium* *Halophila baillonis*	Leaf	16.1	West Indies

470

Scientific name	Common name	Seagrass	Part	Amount	Location
Centropomus ensiferus (juvenile)	Sword fin snook	*Ruppia*	Leaf	25	Puerto Rico
Chaetodipterus faber	Spadefish	*Syringodium*	Leaf	2.3	West Indies
Diapterus olistostomus (juvenile)	Irish pompano	*Ruppia*	Leaf	Up to 100	Puerto Rico
Diapterus plumieri (juvenile)	Striped majorra	*Thalassia*	Leaf	Up to 33	Puerto Rico
Diapterus rhombeus	Sand majorra	*Thalassia*	Leaf		Venezuela
		Ruppia	Leaf	Up to 16.7	Puerto Rico
		Thalassia	Leaf	Up to 32.5	Puerto Rico
		Ruppia	Leaf		
		Halophila	Leaf		
Diplodus holbrooki	Spottail pinfish	*Thalassia*	Leaf		Florida
Halichoeres bivittatus	Slippery dick	*Thalassia*	Leaf	5	West Indies
Harengula humeralis	Red-ear sardine	*Syringodium*	Leaf	2.5	West Indies
Hemiramphus australis	Beakie, sea garfish, Australian garfish	*Zostera*	Leaf		Australia
Hemiramphus brasiliensis	Halfbeak, ballyhoo	*Thalassia*	Leaf	81	West Indies
		Syringodium			
Hyporhamphus hildebrandi	Halfbeak	*Haloduie*	Leaf		Texas
Hyporhamphus unifasciatus	Halfbeak	*Thalassia*	Leaf	49	Florida
Kyphosus incisor	Paddlefish	*Thalassia*	Leaf		West Indies
Kyphosus sectatrix	Rudder fish, Bermuda chub	*Syringodium*	Leaf		West Indies
				0.5	West Indies
Lactophrys bicaudalis	Spotted trunkfish	*Syringodium*	Leaf	8	West Indies
		Thalassia			
Lactophrys trigonus	Trunkfish	*Syringodium*	Leaf	3	West Indies
		Thalassia			
Lactophrys triquetar	Smooth trunkfish	*Thalassia*	Leaf	1.3	West Indies
		Halophila baillonis			

Continued

471

TABLE 7.2 (Continued)

| | Herbivore | | | | |
Scientific Name	Common Name	Seagrass Eaten	Part of Seagrass Eaten	Percent Seagrass in Diet	Location of Population
Lagodon rhomboides	Pinfish	Ruppia	Leaf	41	Gulf of Mexico
		Halodule			
Melichthys niger	Black durgon	Syringodium	Leaf	4.4	Florida
Melichthys radula	Trigger fish	Syringodium	Leaf		West Indies
Monocanthus ciliatus	Fringed filefish	Thalassi	Leaf	15.4	West Indies
Monocanthus setifera	Speckled filefish	Thalassia	Leaf		West Indies
Mugil cephalus	Mullet	Ruppia	Leaf		West Indies
Mugil curema	White mullet	Thalassia	Leaf		Gulf of Mexico
Pogonias chromis	Black drum	Halodule	Leaf		West Indies
Polydactylus virginicus	Threadfish	Thalassia	Leaf	17	Texas
		Ruppia			Puerto Rico
Pomacanthus arcuatus	Grey angelfish	Syringodium	Leaf	0.1	West Indies
Pomacanthus paru	French angelfish	Ruppia			West Indies
		Syringodium	Leaf	0.1	West Indies
		Halophila baillonis			
Pomacentrus fuscus	Dusky damselfish	Syringodium	Leaf	1.6	West Indies
Pomacentrus planifrons	Three-spot damselfish	Thalassia	Leaf	3.9	West Indies
Reporlampus ardelio		Zostera sp.	Leaf		Australia
Rhabdosargus globiceps	White stumpnose	Zostera	Leaf		West Africa
Rhinoptera quadriloba	Cownose ray	Thalassia	Leaf		Texas
		Halodule			
Scarus coelestinus	Midnight parrotfish	Thalassia	Leaf	1.3	West Indies
Scarus guacamaia	Rainbow parrotfish	Syringodium	Leaf	95	West Indies
		Syringodium		8	West Indies
		Thalassia			
Scarus retula	Queen parrotfish	Thalassia	Leaf	3.2	West indies

Species	Common name	Plant	Part	Value	Location
Scarus taeniopterus	Painted-tail parrotfish	*Thalassia*	Leaf	17.3	West Indies
Siganus omarin	Rabbitfish	*Enhalus* *Thalassia hemprichii*	Leaf		Philippines
Siganus striolata	Rabbitfish	*Enhalus* spp. *Thalassia hemprichii*	Leaf		Philippines
Sparisoma aurofrenatum	Redband parrotfish	*Syringodium*	Leaf	1.3	West Indies
Sparisoma chrysopterum	Redtail parrotfish	*Thalassia*	Leaf	16.8	West Indies
Sparisoma radians	Bucktooth parrotfish	*Thalassia*	Leaf	88	West Indies Jamaica
Sparisoma rubripinne	Redfin parrotfish	*Thalassia*	Leaf	7	West Indies
Sparisoma viride	Stoplight parrotfish	*Thalassia*	Leaf	2.5	West Indies
Sphaeroides spenglerii	Banded puffertail	*Halophila baillonis* *Thalassia*	Leaf	5.3	West Indies
Strongylura marina	Atlantic needlefish	*Ruppia*	Leaf		
Symphurus plagiusa	Blackcheek tonguefish	*Ruppia* *Halodule*	Leaf tips Leaf tips	19	Puerto Rico
Birds					
Ajaia ajaja	Roseate spoonbill	*Ruppia* *Halodule*	Leaf, seed Root, rhizome	3 88	Texas Texas
Anas acuta	Pintail duck	*Ruppia* *Halodule* *Ruppia* *Ruppia* *Zostera marina*	Leaf, seed Root, rhizome	4 5–10	Southeastern U.S.
Anas americana	Baldpate, American widgeon	*Ruppia* *Zostera americana*	Leaf, seed, root, rhizome Leaf, root, rhizome	10–25 5–10	U.S. Atlantic and Pacific coasts U.S. Pacific coast
Anas clypeata	Shoveller duck	*Ruppia*	Leaf, seed, root, rhizome	2–5	Southeastern U.S.
Anas crecca carolinensis	Green-winged teal	*Ruppia*	Leaf, root, rhizome	2–5	Western U.S.
Anas cyanoptera	Cinnamon teal	*Ruppia*	Leaf, seed, root, rhizome	2–5	U.S. Pacific Coast
Anas discors	Blue-winged teal	*Ruppia*	Leaf, seed, root, rhizome	5–10	Southeastern and western U.S.

Continued

473

TABLE 7.2 (Continued)

Scientific Name	Herbivore Common Name	Seagrass Eaten	Part of Seagrass Eaten	Percent Seagrass in Diet	Location of Population
Anas fulvigula	Mottled duck	*Ruppia*	Leaf, seed		Gulf Coast
Anas platyrhynchos	Mallard	*Ruppia*	Leaf, seed	2–5	Southeastern U.S.
		Zostera	Root, rhizome		
Anas rubripes	Black duck	*Ruppia*	Leaf, seed	2–5	
		Zostera	Root, rhizome		
Anas strepera	Gadwall duck	*Ruppia*	Leaf, seed, root, rhizome	10–25	Southeastern U.S.
Aythya affinis	Lesser scaup	*Zostera marina*	Leaf, seed		
		Ruppia	Root, rhizome	22	
		Ruppia	Leaf, seed, root, rhizome		
		Rupia	Leaf, seed, root, rhizome	10–15	Southeastern U.S.
		Zostera marina	Leaf, seed, root, rhizome		Northeastern U.S.
Aythya americana	Redhead duck	*Ruppia*	Leaf, seed, root, rhizome	10–25	Southeastern U.S.
		Halodule	Leaf, seed, root, rhizome		Texas
		Ruppia		10	
		Halodule		84	
Aythya collaris	Ring-necked duck	*Ruppia*	Leaf, seed, root, rhizome	2–5	Western U.S.
Aythya fuligula	Tufted duck	*Zostera marina*	Seed	25	Sweden
		Ruppia			
Arythya marila	Greater scaup	*Ruppia*	Seed	4	Sweden
		Zostera marina	Leaf, seed, root, rhizome	2–5	

Scientific name	Common name	Plant	Parts eaten	Percent	Location
		Zostera marina	Leaf, seed, root, rhizome	2–5	Northeastern U.S.
		Ruppia	Leaf, seed, root, rhizome	10–25	Southeastern U.S.
Aythya valisineria	Canvasback duck	*Ruppia*	Seed	2–5	Western U.S.
Branta bernicla bernicla	American brant goose	*Zostera marina*	Leaf, seed, root, rhizome	Up to 25	N. Carolina to Quebec
Branta bernicla hrota	American brant	*Ruppia*	Leaf, seed, root, rhizome	88	N. Carolina to Quebec
		Zostera marina	Leaf, seed, root, rhizome		
Branta canadensis	Canada goose	*Ruppia*	Leaf, seed, root, rhizome	Up to 25	Alaska
Branta nigricans	Black brant	*Zostera marina*	Leaf, seed, root, rhizome	Up to 100	Alaska
		Zostera marina	Leaf, seed, root, rhizome	Up to 100	U.S. Pacific coast
		Phyllospadix	Leaf, seed, root, rhizome	50 or more	U.S. pacific coast
Bucephala albeola	Bufflehead duck	*Ruppia*	Leaf, seed, root, rhizome	2–5	Western U.S.
Bucephala clangula	Goldeneye duck	*Ruppia*	Leaf, seed		Sweden
		Zostera marina	Root, rhizome		U.S.
Bucephala islandica	Barrow golden-eye	*Ruppia*	Leaf, seed, root, rhizome	2–5	
Calidris canutus	Red knot	*Ruppia*	Seed	2–5	U.S. (migration)
		Zostera	Seed		U.S. North Atlantic coast
Calidris fuscicollis	White-rumped sandpiper	*Ruppia*		2–5	Eastern U.S.

Continued

TABLE 7.2 (Continued)

Herbivore		Seagrass Eaten	Part of Seagrass Eaten	Percent Seagrass in Diet	Location of Population
Scientific Name	Common Name				
Calidris melanotos	Pectoral sandpiper	Ruppia			U.S.
Calidris pusilla	Semipalmated sandpiper	Ruppia			U.S. Atlantic coast
Cygnus atratus	Black swan	Zostera	Leaf, seed, root, rhizome		New South Wales south coast
Cygnus olor	Mute swan	Zostera marina	Leaf, seed		Sweden
Fulica americana	Coot	Ruppia	Root, rhizome		
		Ruppia	Leaf, seed, root, rhizome	10–25	
Himantopus mexicanus	Blackneck stilt	Ruppia	Leaf, seed, root, rhizome		
Limnodromus griseus	Eastern (short-billed) dowitcher	Ruppia	Leaf, seed		
Limnodromus scolopaceus	Long-billed dowitcher	Ruppia	Leaf, seed		
Melanitta fusca	Velvet scoter	Zostera marina	Leaf, seed, root, rhizome	2–5	U.S. Atlantic and Pacific coasts
Melanitta nigra	Black scoter	Ruppia	Leaf, seed, root, rhizome		
		Zostera marina	Leaf, root, rhizome		U.S. Atlantic and Pacific coasts
Melanitta perspicillata	Surf scoter	Ruppia	Leaf, root, rhizome		
		Zostera marina	Leaf, root, rhizome	2–5	U.S. Atlantic and Pacific coasts
Olor columbianus	Whistling swan	Ruppia	Leaf, seed		Alaska
		Zostera marina	Root, rhizome		

Species	Common name	Seagrass	Part eaten	Percent	Location
Oxyura jamaicensis	Ruddy duck	*Ruppia*	Leaf, seed, root, rhizome		
Philacte canagica	Emperor goose	*Zostera marina*	Leaf, seed, root, rhizome	5–10	Western U.S.
Phoenicopterus ruber	Flamingo	*Ruppia* / *Ruppia*	Seed / Leaf, seed		
Porphyrula martinica	Purple gallinule	*Ruppia*	Seed		Southeastern U.S.
Rallus elegans	King rail	*Ruppia*	Leaf, seed, root, rhizome		Southeastern U.S.
Reptiles					
Caretta caretta	Loggerhead turtle	*Thalassia*	Leaf		
Chelonia mydas (adult)	Green sea turtle	*Enhalus* *Posidonia* *Halodule*	Leaf	Up to 100	Indo-Pacific Red Sea Caribbean
Eretmochelys imbricata (juvenile)	Hawksbill turtle		Leaf	Up to 100	
Mammals					
Dugong dugon	Dugong	*Zostera* *Posidonia* *Halodule* *Halophila*	Leaf	Up to 100	Australia
Homo sapiens	Human (Seri Indian) (Kwakiutl Indians) (Aborigines)	*Zostera marina* *Zostera marina* *Enhalus* *Ruppia* *Zostera* (captive) (*Syringodium, Halodule, Thalassia* implicated)	Seed Shoot Seed Leaf		Mexico British Columbia Australia Florida
Trichechus manatus	Manatee				

Source: McRoy and Helfferich (1980).

(Carr and Adams, 1973). Other omnivores included some filefishes, Balistidae; porgies, Sparidae; blennies, Blennidae; and gobies, Gobiidae (Zieman, 1982).

Predator–Prey Relationships

The majority of fish within the grass beds fed on small, mobile epifauna, including copepods, cumaceans, amphipods, isopods, and shrimp. Fish with this diet included all the seasonally resident fish of the south Florida grass beds, such as the drums (Sciaenidae), grunts (Pomadasyidae), snappers (Lutjanidae), and mojarras (Gerridae), as well as many of the permanent residents, such as pipefish and seahorses (Synathidae) and clinids (Clinidae) (Zieman, 1982). Some specific examples of south Florida fish with an epifaunal diet are: hardhead silversides, *Atherinomorus stipes*; silver jenny, *Eucinostomus gula*; spotfin mojarra, *E. argenteus*; goldspotted killifish, *Floridichthys carpio*; redfin needlefish, *Strongylura notata*; pinfish, *Lagodon rhomboides*; gulf pipefish, *Syngnathus scoveli*; and dusky pipefish, *S. floridae* (Brook, 1977; Livingston, 1982).

A variety of fish, including wrasses, porcupine fishes, eagle rays, and the permit, *Trachnotus falcatus*, fed on gastropods. The white grunt, *Haemulon plumieri*, fed on the gastropod *Cerithium*. The southern stingray, *Dasyatis americana*, fed on the queen conch, *Strombus gigas*. The spring lobster, *Panulirus argus*, was an active predator on seagrass molluscs (Zieman, 1982).

Relatively few fish fed on infauna within the grass bed. Among these were the southern stingray and the spotted eagle ray, *Aetobatis narinari*, which excavated the sediments. Similar feeders were wrasses (Labridae), goatfish (Mullidae), and mojarras (Gerridae). The adult yellowtail snapper, *Ocyurus chrysurus*, has been observed foraging in seagrass sediments, as well (Zieman, 1982). It is likely that the protection from predation afforded the infauna of grass beds is great enough that few infauna-feeding species are successful (Orth, 1977).

According to Zieman (1982), the important piscivores present in south Florida grass beds included the lemon shark, *Negaprion brevirostris*: bonnethead shark, *Sphyrna tiburo*; tarpon, *Megalops atlantica*; inshore lizardfish, *Synodus foetens*; bluespotted coronet fish, *Fistularia tabacaria*; the great barracuda, *Sphyraena barracuda*; gray snapper, *Lutjanus griseus*; spotted sea trout, *Cynoscion nebulosus*; and some Carangidae.

COMMUNITY STRUCTURE

Open Water

Plankton. Information on phytoplankton in the seagrass communities of south Florida is very sparse, however, zooplankton seems to have been studied to a somewhat greater extent. Reeve (1975) found that in Card Sound, Florida, the holoplankton was dominated by the copepods, *Acartia tonsa* and *Paracalanus parvus*, the most common copepods in Florida marine waters. Annual mean numbers of these two copepods in Card Sound were 524 and $300 \, m^{-3}$, respectively. *Labidocera scotti* and *L. mirabilis* were found in numbers ranging from 22 to 47 m^{-3} on average in Biscayne Bay and Card Sound. Their significance is perhaps more appreciated when one considers their large contribution in terms of biomass. *Oithona nana* was overwhelmingly the major constituent of the cyclopoid copepod population, with a few species of the genus *Corycaeus* present at times. *O. nana* accounted for over 50% of the copepod standing stock (dry weight) in Card Sound, with a mean number of 14,000 m^{-3}. *Temora turbinata* usually occurred in small numbers and was associated with regions of lower salinity. Its mean numbers in south and central Biscayne Bay were 37 and 33 m^{-3}, respectively. *Calanopia americana* and *Metis jousseaumi* were also taken in small numbers (Reeve, 1975).

Aside from copepods, the only other plankters of quantitative significance in Card Sound were larval tunicates; tintinnids; the chaetognath, *Sagitta hispida*; and the ctenophore, *Mnemiopsis mccradyi*. *Sagitta hispida* was collected in mean numbers of 50 to 70 m^{-3}. The tintinnids, an important food source, were collected in annual mean numbers of 121,000 m^{-3}. The meroplankton was dominated by molluscan veligers and decapod larvae with occasional peaks of polychaete and echinoderm larvae (Reeve, 1975).

The general pattern of seasonal variations of the zooplankton in Card Sound and Biscayne Bay was one of rapid fluctuation throughout the year. The major constituents of the Card Sound macroplankton shared a midsummer low point of biomass and numbers (Reeve, 1975).

Nekton. It is well known that seagrass meadows are inhabited by diverse and abundant fish fauna (Table 7.3). Often the grass bed serves as a nursery or feeding ground for fish (Zieman, 1982; Carr and Adams, 1973).

Permanently resident fish were usually small, less mobile, more cryptic species. The emerald clingfish, *Acyrtops beryllina*, and members of the families Syngnathidae, Gobiidae, and Clinidae in south Florida may be included in this group (Zieman, 1982). The pipefish, *Syngnathus scovilli*, *S. floridae*, *S. louisianae*, and *Micrognatus crinigerus*, as well as the seahorses, *Hippocampus zosterae* and *H. erectus*, were abundant in seagrass throughout south Florida. *Gobiosoma robustum* was the most abundant goby in the area. The clinids were generally limited in distribution to the Florida Keys and Florida Bay. It was in these areas that *Paraclinus fasciatus* and *P. marmoratus* were most abundant. Also found in this area were the parrotfish, *Sparisoma rubripinne*, *S. radians*, and *S. chrysopterum* (Zieman, 1982).

South Florida eels included the sharptail eel, *Myrichthys acuminatus*, and the goldspotted eel, *M. oculatus* (Ophichthidae), which were common in the grass during the day. At night young moray eels, *Gymnothorax* sp. (Muraenidae), were common (Zieman, 1982).

Seasonal residents of the seagrass meadows spent their juvenile, subadult stages or their spawning season in the grass beds, and then moved on. Among these the drums (Sciaenidae), porgies (Sparidae), snappers (Lutjanidae), and mojarras (Gerridae) were the most abundant in south Florida seagrass communities (Zieman, 1982).

(text continues on page 502)

TABLE 7.3. *Fishes and Their Diets from Collections in South Florida*

Species	Abundance by Survey Number[a]										Diet
	1	2	3	4	5	6	7	8	9	10	
Orectolobidae/nurse sharks											
Ginglymostoma cirratum (nurse shark)	r	r			p						Fish: *Acanthurus* sp., clupeids, scarids *Mugil* sp., *Jenkinsia* sp., *Cantherhines pullus*; molluscs; cephalopods
Carcharhindiae/requiem sharks											
Negeprion brevirostris (lemon shark)				p							Fish: *Bagre marinus, Chilomycterus schoepfi, Galeichthys felis, Mugil* sp., *Rhinobatos lentiginosus*; octopods
Sphyrnidae/hammerhead sharks											
Sphyrna tiburo (bonnethead)				p							Crabs: *Callinectes sapidus*, stomatopods; shrimp; isopods; barnacles; bivalves; cephalopods; fish
Pristidae/sawfishes											
Pristis pectinata (smalltooth sawfish)				p							
Rhinobatidae/ guitarfishes											
Rhinobatus lentiginosus (Atlantic guitarfish)		r									
Torpedinidae/electric rays											
Narcine brasiliensis (lesser electric ray)		r				r	r				
Rajidae/skates											
Raja texana (roundel skate)			r								Annelids; crustacea; fishes
Dasytidae/stingrays											
Urolophs jamaicensis (yellow stingray)	r	r									
Gymnura micrura (smooth butterfly ray)								r	r		Fish: *Centropristis striata*, molluscs: *Solemya* sp.; annelids; shrimp; small crustaceans
Dasyatis americana (southern stingray)					p						Fishes; sipunculids; crabs; polychaetes; shrimp; hemichordates; stomatopods
Dasyatis sabina (Atlantic stingray)								r			
Elopidae/tarpons											
Elops saurus (ladyfish)					p						Fishes: *Lagodon rhomboides*; shrimp; *Penaeus setiferus*

TABLE 7.3. (*Continued*)

Species	Abundance by Survey Number[a]										Diet
	1	2	3	4	5	6	7	8	9	10	
Megalops atlantica (tarpon)				p							Fishes: *Allanetta harringtonensis, Atherinomorus stipes*
Albulidae/bonefishes											
Albula vulpes (bonefish)				p							Molluscs: *Codakia costata*; crabs; shrimp; fish
Muraenidae/morays											
Gymnothorax nigromarginatus (blackedge moray)		r									
Ophichthidae/snake eels											
Myrophis punctatus (speckled worm eel)		r			r	r		r			Crabs
Ophichthus gomesi (shrimp eel)					r			r			
Clupeidae/herrings											
Harengula pensacolae (scaled sardine)		r	r		r			r		c	Juveniles: veligers, crab megalops, amphipods, mysids, copepods, isopods, chironomid larvae
Harengula humeralis (redear sardine)		r									Fishes; polychaetes; shrimp larvae; plants: *Enteromorpha* sp., *Thalassia, Syringodium*; crab larvae
Jenkinsia sp.				r							*J. lamprotaenia*—copepods; shrimp larvae; crab larvae; amphipods; fish eggs
Brevoortia smithi (yellowfin menhaden)								r			
Opisthonema oglinum (Atlantic thread herring)				r	r					r	Veligers; copepods; detritus; polychaetes; shrimp; fishes; shrimp and crab larvae; mysids; tunicates; stomatopod larvae; eggs; gastropod larvae; other rare items
Sardinella anchovia (spanish sardine)				r				r			
Engraulidae/anchovies											
Anchoa cubana (Cuban anchovy)				r							Ostracods; copepods
Anchoa lamprotaenia (bigeye anchovy)				a	p						
Anchoa mitchilli (bay anchovy)	r			r	p	c	r		r	c	Less than 23 mm SL veligers, copepods, eggs; 31 to 62 mm SL. amphipods, detritus, ostracods, zooplankton, mysids, harpacticoid copepods, small molluscs, chironomid larvae

Continued

TABLE 7.3. (*Continued*)

Species	Abundance by Survey Number[a]										Diet
	1	2	3	4	5	6	7	8	9	10	
Anchoviella perfasciata (flat anchovy)			r								
Anchoa hepsetus (striped anchovy)					r	r		r		c	Veligers; copepods; mysids; zooea; fish; eggs
Synodontidae/ lizardfishes											
Synodus foetens (inshore lizardfish)	r	r	r	r	p	c	r	r	r	r	Fishes: gobies, killifish, silver perch, pipefish, pigfish, juvenile sea trout, puffer; shrimp; plant detritus
Ariidae/sea catfishes											
Bagre marinus (gafftopsail catfish)								r			*Callinectes sapidus*; fishes
Arius felis (sea catfish)				p	r		r	r			Crabs; *Rhithropanopeus harrissii*, amphipods; mysids; fishes; copepods; shrimp
Batrachoididae/ toadfishes											
Opsanus beta (gulf toadfish)	c	a	r	r	p	c	c	c	r		Crabs; penaeid and crangonid shrimp; *Palaemonetes* sp., *Alpheus heterochaelis*; hermit crabs; molluscs; amphipods; fish; *Logodon rhomboides*
Porichthys porosissmus (Atlantic midshipman)					r						
Gobiesocidae/clingfishes											
Acyrtops beryllina (emerald clingfish)	r		r								
Gobiesox strumosus (skilletfish)				r	p	r					Amphipods; isopods; chironomid larvae
Antennaridae/frogfishes											
Histrio histrio (sargassumfish)			r	r							
Ogcocephalidae/batfishes											
Ogcocephalus cubifrons			r								
Ogcocephalus nasutus (shortnose batfish)	r										Pelecypods; gastropods; *Nassarius vivex*; *Cerithium mucarium*; *Urosalphinx tampaensis*; *Bittium* sp.; *Mitrella* sp., *Modulus modulus*; *Olivella mutica*; *Haminoea elegans*; *Anachris avara*; polychaetes
Ogcocephalus radiatus (polka-dot batfish)											
Gadidae/codfishes											
Urophysis floridanus (southern hake)		r									Shrimps; fishes; *Lagodon rhomboides*; amphipods; copepods; crabs; gastropods

TABLE 7.3. (*Continued*)

Species	1	2	3	4	5	6	7	8	9	10	Diet
Ophididae/cusk-eels and brotulas											
Ogilbia cayorum (key brotula)		r	r		r						
Ophidion holbrooki (bank cusk-eel)	r										
Gunterichthys longipenis (gold brotula)								r			
Carapidae/pearlfishes											
Carapus bermudensis (pearlfish)				r							
Exocoetidae/flying fishes and halfbeaks											
Hemiramphys brasiliensis (ballyhoo)				r							Seagrasses: *Thalassia, Syringodium*; fishes: *Jenkinsia* sp.
Chridorus atherinoides (hardhead halfbeak)				p							
Hyporhamphus unfasciatus (halfbeak)				p	r					r	Juveniles: zooplankton; crab megalops larvae, veligers, copepods, insect remains; sub-adults and adults: epiphytic algae and detritus, seagrasses, occasional microcrustacea
Belonidae/needlefishes											
Strongylura notata (redfin needlefish)				r	r	p	r			r	Shrimp
Strongylura timucu (timucu)				r		r				r	Fishes: *Anchoa parva, Jenkinsia* sp.; shrimp; copepods; insects
Tylosurus crocodilus (houndfish)				r							Fishes: *Acanthurus* sp., *Anchoa* sp., *Cetengraulis edentulus, Harengula humeralis, Mugil* sp.; shrimp
Cyprinodontidae/ killifishes											
Flordichthys carpio (goldspotted killifish)		c	a		r						Amphipods, copepods, polychaetes, filamentous algae, diatoms, detritus, ostracods, chironomid larvae, isopods, nematodes
Adinia xenica (diamond killifish)					r						Detritus, diatoms, filamentous algae, amphipods, insects, copepods
Lucania parva (rainwater killifish)		a	r	r	p	r			r	r	Amphipods, musids, chironomid larvae, insects, molluscs, detritus, copepods, cumaceans
Fundulus heteroclitus (mummichog)		r									Small crustaceans: amphipods, isopods, tanaids, ostracods,

Continued

TABLE 7.3.   (*Continued*)

Species	Abundance by Survey Number[a]										Diet
	1	2	3	4	5	6	7	8	9	10	
											copepods; polychaetes, detritus, algae, insects, crabs, fish, gastropods, eggs
Cyprinodon variegatus (sheepshead minnow)					p					r	Detritus, filamentous green algae, filamentous blue-green algae, diatoms, crustaceans, nematodes
Rivulus marmoratus (rivulus)						r					
Poeciliidae/livebearers											
Poecilia latipinna (sailfin molly)					p					r	Detritus; filamentous algae; diatoms
Gambusia affinis (mosquitofish)						r					Amphipods; algae; hydracarina; chironomid larvae; insects
Heterandria formosa (least killifish)						r					Chironomid larvae; copepods; green algae; diatoms; cladocerans; insects
Atherinidae/silversides											
Allanetta harringtonensis (reef silversides)			c		r	p					Copepods: *Corycaeus* sp., *Labidocera scotti*, *Paracalanus crassirostris*; fish larvae; polychaete larvae
Atherinomorus stipes (hardhead silversides)			a		a						Day: copepods; plants; amphipods; tanaids; insects; polychaetes; night: amphipods; polychaetes; cumacea; copepods; isopods; ostracods; nebalids; insects; plants
Menidia beryllina (tidewater silversides)					r			r		c	Day: less than 25 mm SL: veligers, detritus, copepods; greater than 30 mm: copepods, veligers, insects, chironmid larvae, amphipods, hydracarina, algae, detritus, mysids; night: greater than 30 mm: mysids, amphipods, copepods, chironomid larvae
Membras martinica (rough silversides)					p						Copepods; insects (listed under *Membras martinica vagrans*)
Membras vagrans					r			r			
Syngnathidae/pipefishes and seahorses											
Corythoichthys albirostris (whitenose pipefish)	r	r		r							
Corythoichthys brachycephalus (crested pipefish)			r								
Hippocampus hudsonius		r									
Hippocampus zosterae (dwarf seahorse)	r	c	r	r	p	r	r	r	r		Shrimp; microcrustaceans

TABLE 7.3.　(*Continued*)

Species	Abundance by Survey Number[a]										Diet
	1	2	3	4	5	6	7	8	9	10	
Hippocampus erectus (lined seahorse)	r	r	r			r		r	r		
Hippocampus reidi (longsnout seahorse)						r					
Syngnathus dunckeri (pugnose pipefish)				r							
Syngnathus floridae (dusky pipefish)	c	r	r	r	p	r		r		r	Shrimp; amphipods; tanaids; isopods; copepods; nebalids
Syngnathus louisianae (chain pipefish)	r		r	r		r	r	r	r	r	Copepods; amphipods; shrimp
Syngnathus scovelli (gulf pipefish)	r	r	c	r	p	c	a	c	c	c	Amphipods; copepods; tanaids; isopods; shrimp; nebalids
Micrognathus crinigerus (fringed pipefish)		a	r		p		r				Copepods; microcrustaceans
Centropomidae/snooks											
Centropomus undecimalis (snook)				p							Fishes: *Eucinostomus* sp., *Mugil cephalus*, *Lagodon rhomboides*, *Anchoa* sp., *Poecilia latipinna*, and *Gambusia affinis*; caridean and panacid shrimp; crabs; crayfish
Serranidae/sea basses											
Mycteroperca bonaci (black grouper)				r							Fishes: *Fistularia tabacaria*, *Haemulon flavolineatum*
Mycteroperca microlepis (gag)	r	r		p		r	r	r			Shrimp; fish
Serraniculus pumilio (pygmy sea bass)						r					
Serranus subligarius (belted sandfish)						r					
Diplectrum bivittatum (dwarf sand perch)	r										
Diplectrum formosum (sand perch)	r					r	r	r	r	r	Caridean and palaemonid shrimps; mysids
Epinephalus morio (red grouper)	r										Crustaceans; fishes
Epinephalus itajara (jewfish)				p							Lobsters; *Panulirus argus*, *Scyllardes aequinoctialis*, fishes; *Dasyatis americana*, *Diodon* sp.; crabs; sea turtles; *Eretmochelys imbricata*
Apogonidae/ cardinalfishes											
Astrapogon alutus (bronze cardinalfish)	r	r									

Continued

TABLE 7.3.   (*Continued*)

Species	Abundance by Survey Number[a]										Diet
	1	2	3	4	5	6	7	8	9	10	
Astrapogon stellatus (conchfish)	r										
Rachycentridae/cobias											
Rachycentron canadum (cobia)			p								Fishes: *Lactophrys* sp., *Lactophrys triqueter*
Echeneidae/remoras											
Echeneis naucrates (sharksucker)				r							Fishes: larval *Catherines pullus*; isopods; crustaceans
Carangidae/jacks and pompanos											
Caranx hippos (crevalle jack)				r	p					r	Fishes: *Prionotus scitulus*
Caranx latus (horse-eye jack)		r									Fishes: atherinids, *Harengula* sp., *Myripristis jacobus*; pteropods; penaeid shrimp; isopods
Caranx ruber (bar jack)					p						Fishes: larvel *Acanthurus* sp., *Acanthurus coerulus, Anchoa hepsetus,* atherinids, engraulids, *Entomarcrodus nigricans, Harengula clueola, Jenkinsia* sp., *Monocanthus* sp., mullid, *Ophioblennius atlanticus, Pomacentrus planifrons, Pseudupeneus maculatus,* scarids, *Scarus croicensis, Sparisoma aurofrenatus, Sparisoma viride;* syngnathid; shrimps; penaeid, *Tozeuma* sp.; mysids; squids; stomatopods; gastropods; crabs
Trachinotus falcatus (permit)					r					c	Juvenile fishes; anchovies, tidewater silversides, crabs; *Petrolisthes* sp., gastropods; shrimp; mysids, adult gastropods; *Astraea longispina, Cerithium* sp., *Columbella mercatoria, Oliva* sp., *Strombus gigas, Tegula lividomaculata, Turbo castanea;* echinoids: *Diadema antillarum, Echinometera* sp.; pelecypods; *Arca zebra, Glycymeris decussata, Trachycardium magnum;* hermit crabs: *Pauristes grayi,* crabs: *Albunea gibbesii,* porcellanids.
Trachinotus carolinus (Florida pompano)								r			
Oligoplites saurus (leatherjacket)					p	r				r	Mysids; shrimp; ectoparasites; copepods

TABLE 7.3. (*Continued*)

Species	Abundance by Survey Number[a]										Diet
	1	2	3	4	5	6	7	8	9	10	
Selene vomer (lookdown)				r							Shrimp; other crustaceans, small molluscs
Lutjanidae/snappers											
Lutjanus analis (mutton snapper)	r		r								Crabs: *Calappa gallus*, calappids, *Cronius ruber, majid, Parthenope serrata, Petrolishes* sp., portunids, *Portunus* sp., *Portunus sebrae, Ranilia muricata*; fishes: *Acanthurus bahianus, Diodon* sp., *Fistularia tabacaria*, gobiids, *Haemulon* sp., *Haemulon aurolineatum, Halichoeres garnoti aurolineatum, Halichoeres garnoti, Holocentrus ascensionis, Malacanthus plumeri, Monocanthus* sp., *Monocanthus setifer, Pseudupeneus maculatus*, scarids, *Scorpaena plumeri, Sphoeroides spengleri*; gastropods: *Fasciolaria tulipa, Murex pomum, Strombus* sp., *Strombus gigas*; octopuses; hermit crabs: *Petrochirus diogenes*; penaeid shrimp; lobster: *Panulirus argus*; stomatopods: *Lysiosquilla glabriuscula*
Lutjanus apodus (schoolmaster)	r		a	p							Fishes: atherinids, *Aulostomus maculatus, Bodianus rufus, Cantherhines pullus, Chromis multilineata, Gymnothorax moringa, Haemulon* sp., *Jenkinsia* sp., *Pomcentris fuscus*, scarids, *Scorpaena plumeri*, scorpaenids, serranids, *Sparisoma* sp., *Sparisoma aurofrenatum*; crabs: *Actaea acantha*, calappids, majids, *Mithrax sculptus, Pernon gibbesi, Portunnus sebrae*, portunids; stomatopods; shrimp; octopuses; gastropods
Lutjanus griseus (gray snapper)	r	r	c	p	r	r	r	r			Crab: *Callinectes* sp., goneplacids, portunids, xanthids; *fishes: Jenkinsia* sp., penaeid shrimp; gastropods; *Strombus gigas*; scyllarid lobsters
Lutjanus jocu (dog snapper)	r										Fishes: atherinids, *Aulostomus maculatus, Clepticus parrae, Gymnothorax moringa, Haemulon*

Continued

TABLE 7.3. (Continued)

Species	Abundance by Survey Number[a]										Diet
	1	2	3	4	5	6	7	8	9	10	
											sp., *Haemulon plumeri*, *Haemulon aurolineatum*, *Holocanthus tricolor*, *Holocentrus* sp., *Holocentrus rufus*, *Jenkinsia* sp., *Myrichthys* sp., ophichthids, *Opisthonema oglinum*, *Pseudupeneus maculatus*, scarids, serranids, *Sparisoma* sp., *Sparisoma viride*, *Xanthihthys ringens*; crabs: *Carpilius corallinus*, *Cronius ruber*, *Pitho lherminieri*, portunids, *Portunus* sp.; octopuses: *Octopus vulgaris*; lobsters; *Panulirus argus*, *Panulirus guttatus*, gastropods: *Strombus gigas*; squid; fish eggs; scyllarid lobsters
Lutjanus synagris (lane snapper)	r			p	c	r	a	c		r	Crabs: goneplacids, *Leiolambrus nitidus*, portunids; stomatopods: *Lysiosquilla glabriuscula*; fish; shrimp; mysids; copepods
Ocyurus chrysurus (yellowtail snapper)	r		r								Crabs: *Callappa ocellata*, *Mithax* sp., *Mithax Mithax sculptus*, *Pitho aculeata*; shrimp: caridean, penaeidean, *Sicyonia laevigata*, *Trachycaris restirctus*; fish: *Jenkinsia* sp.; siphonophores; pterophods; *Calvolina* sp.; copepods; cephalopods; mysids; tunicates; ctenophores; gastropods: *Strombus gigas*; stomatopods: *Gonodactylus oerstedii*, *Pseudosquilla ciliata*; scyllarid larvae; heteropods; pelecypods; eggs; euphausids; gastropod larvae; amphipods; insects
Labotidae/tripletails											
Lobotes surinamensis (tripletails)			r								
Gerridae/mojarras											
Eucinostomus argenteus (spotfin mojarra)	r	c	c	r	p	r	r	r	r	c	Less than 63 mm copepods, amphipods, mysids, molluscs, detritus, chironomid larvae, 75 to 152 mm amphipods; *Hyale* sp., polychaetes; eunicids, crabs; calappids, majids, *raninids*, shrimp; alpheids, *Callianassa* sp., tanaids, pelecypods; *Tellina* sp., sipunculids, copepods, gastropods

TABLE 7.3. (*Continued*)

Species	Abundance by Survey Number[a]										Diet
	1	2	3	4	5	6	7	8	9	10	
Eucinostromus gula (silver jenny)	r	r	a	a	p	a	a	a	a	a	Less than 60 mm—polychaetes; copepods; amphipods; mysids; small shrimp; small molluscs; detritus
Eucinostomus lefroyi (mottled mojarra)			r								
Gerres cinereus (yellowfin mojarra)			r								Crabs: hippids, majids, portunids; pelecypods: *Laevicardium* sp., *Macoma cerina, Solemya occidentalis, Tellina* sp., *Yoldia perprotracta*; gastropods: *Acmaea antillarum, Fissurella barbadensis, Hemitoma octoradiata, Olivella* sp., *Tricolia tessellata*; polychaetes; sipunculids; *Aspidosiphon* sp., shrimps; alpheids; *Callianasa* sp., stomatopods; *Gonodactylus oerstedii*, hemichordates; ophiuroids; *Ophiothrix* sp., amphipods
Pomadasyidae/grunts											
Haemulon flavolineatum (French grunt)			r	r							Polychaetes: capitellids, *Eunice* sp., maldanids, terebellids; crabs, sipunculids; *Aspidosiphon* sp.; chitons; *Acanthochitona* pygmaea; holothurians; isopods; shrimps; octopuses; pelecypods: *Pitar* sp., *Tellina* sp., ophiuroids: *Ophiothrix* sp., echinoids: *Diadema antillarum*, spatangoid; scaphopods: *Cadulus* sp., *Dentalium* sp.; hermit crabs; stomatopods; amphipods, gastropods; *Arene* sp.
Haemulon parrai (sailor's choice)	r	r	r	c							Shrimps: alpheids, carideans, penaeids; crabs: majids, portunids; amphipods; gastropods; *Olivella* sp.; anemones: *Phyllattis flosculifera*; holothurians; polychaetes; pelecypods; *Gouldia cerina, Pecten* sp., *Pitar* sp., *Solemya* occidentalis, *Tellina* sp., ophiuroids; isopods; stomatopods; scaphopods: *Cadulus* sp.
Haemulon sciurus (bluestriped grunt)		r	c	r	p	r					Crabs: portunids, xanthids; pelecypods: *Macoma cerina, Pitar fulminata, Tellina caribaea*; shrimps; alpheids, axiids,

Continued

TABLE 7.3.   (Continued)

Species	Abundance by Survey Number[a]										Diet
	1	2	3	4	5	6	7	8	9	10	
											echinoids: *Diadema antillarum*; ophiuroids: *Ophiothrix* sp.; polychaetes; gastropods: *Acmaea* sp., *Anachis* sp., *Arene* sp., *Bittium varium, Cyclostremiscus ornatus, Diodora* sp., *Hyalina* sp., *Hylina albolineata, Mangelia* sp., *Melampus coffeus, Mitra barbadensis, Modulus modulus, Nitidella* sp., *Olivella* sp., *Persicula lavalleeana, Rissoina* sp., *Strombus gigas*; ciliates; sipunclids; fishes; amphipods; octopuses; isopods; tunicates; ostracods; bryozoans; scaphopods; *Cadulus* sp.; tanaids; hermit crabs
Haemulon aurolineatum (tomtate)	r	r					r				Shrimp: larvae; polychaetes: *Chloeia* sp.; eggs; hermit crabs; larvae; amphipods: *Ampelisca* sp., *Elasmopus* sp., *Eurystheus* sp., *Megamphopus* sp., *Photis* sp.; copepods: *Undinula vulgaris*; gastropods: *Alvania auberiana, Caecum pulchellum, Retusa* sp.; pelecypods: *Solemya occidentalis*; barnacle larvae; tanaids; scaphopods: *Cadulus acus*; isopods
Haemulon plumeri (white grunt)	a	r		a			a	r			Less than 40 mm copepods, mysids or shrimp, detritus. 130–279 mm crabs: *Mithrax* sp.; polychaetes; echinoids: *Diadema antillarum, Eucidaris tribuloides*; spatangoid, sipunculids: *Aspidosiphon* sp.; gastropods: *Acmaea antillarum, Strombus gigas*; shrimps; alpheids, ophiuroids: *Ophiothrix* sp.; fishes; hemichordates; holothurians: *Thyone pseudofusus*; pelecypods: *Cumingia* antillarum, chitons: *Ischnochiton papillosus*, amphipods, tanaids
Haemulon carbonarium (caesar grunt)		r									Crabs; majids, *Pisosoma* sp., gastropods; *Acmaea pustulata, Columbella mercatoria, Diodora* sp., *Emarginula pumila, Fissurella* sp., *Fissurella barbadensis, Hyalina* sp., *Nitidella* sp., echinoids; *Diadema antillarum, Echinometra* sp., *Echinometra viridis*, chitons; *Ischnochiton papillosus*, polychaetes, ophiuroids; *Ophicoma*

TABLE 7.3. (*Continued*)

Species	Abundance by Survey Number[a]										Diet
	1	2	3	4	5	6	7	8	9	10	
											echinata, Ophiothrix sp., sipunculids, shrimp; alpheids, barnacle appendages, fish; blennoid, amphipods, astracods
Anisotremus virginicus (porkfish)	r							r			Ophiuroides; *Ophiothrix* sp., crabs, shrimps; alpheids, carideans, polychaetes; *Eunice* sp., isopods; anthurids, *Asellote* sp., *Cymodoce* sp., excorallanid, sphaeromid, pelecypods; *Americardia guppyi, Americardia media,* Chione sp., *Chione cancellata, Cumingia antillarum, Papyridea semisulcata, Pecten* sp., stomatopods, gastropods; *Columbella mercatoria, Hyalina* sp., *Mitra* sp., *Modulus modulus, Olivella* sp., *Zebina browniana,* amphipods; caprellids, gammarids, lysianassids, metopids, copepods; harpacticoids, tunicates; *Tridemnun savignii,* tanaids, ostracods; *Bairdoppilata carinata, cypridinine,* chitons, hermit crabs, foraminifera, nebaliaceans; *Nebalia* sp., scaphopods: *Dentalium* sp.,
Orthopristis chrysoptera (pigfish)			r		p	c	a	a	a	r	Fish of SL 25–50 mm: copepods, ostracods, shrimps, polychaetes; SL 51–150 mm: shrimps, amphipods, copepods, polychaetes, crabs, fishes; SL greater than 150 mm: polychaetes, shrimps, crabs, molluscs, amphipods, insects
Sparidae/porgies											
Archosargus probatocephalus (sheepshead)			r		p	r	r		r		Less than 50 mm amphipods, copepods, polychaetes; larger than 50 mm molluscs, barnacles, algae
Archosargus rhomboides (sea bream)			r								Seagrass: *Syringodium filiforme, Thalassia testudinum;* algae; crabs; gastropods; eggs; pelecypods: *Pictada ladiata;* polychaetes; amphipods
Lagodon rhomboides (pinfish)	c	c	r	c	p	a	a	a	a	a	Less than 35 mm copepods; amphipods; mysids; epiphytes; polychaetes; crabs. SL 36–65 mm epiphytes; shrimps; mysids; crabs; fish; amphipods;

Continued

TABLE 7.3.   (*Continued*)

Species	Abundance by Survey Number[a]	Diet
	1 2 3 4 5 6 7 8 9 10	
		copepods; detritus. SL greater than 65 mm shrimp, fish; epiphytes; mysids; detritus; crabs; amphipods; copepods
Calamus arctifrons (grass porgy)	r r	Copepods; amphipods; mysids; shrimps; pelecypods; gastropods: *Mitrella* sp., *Bittium* sp.; polychaetes
Calamus calamus (saucereye porgy)	r	Polychaetes; ophiuroids; *Ophioderma* sp., *Ophiothrix* sp.; pelecypods; *Codakia orbicularis, Gouldia cerina, Pinna carnea*; hermit crabs; crabs: majid, echinoids: *Diadema antillarum*, gastropods: *Nassarius albus, Tequla* sp., *Tegula fasciata*; chitons; sipunculids: *Aspidosiphon* sp.
Sciaenidae/drums		
Menticirrhus focaliger (minkfish)	r c	
Sciaenops ocellata (red drum)	p r r	SL 31–46 mm mysids; polychaetes; amphipods; shrimp: *Palaemonetes intermedius*. SL 59–126 mm fish: *Micropogon undulatus*; shrimp; crabs; insect larvae; mysids. SL 100–500 mm shrimp: penaeids; crabs: xanthids, *Rithropanopeus harrisii*, portunids
Bairdiella chrysoura (silver perch)	r r c a a c c	SL 25–99 m shrimp; copepods; amphipods; molluscs; fishes, polychaetes. SL 100–130 mm shrimp, amphipods, crabs, molluscs, fish: *Anchoa mitchilli*
Cynoscion nebulosus (spotted sea trout)	p r c r r r	Juveniles; mysids; chironomid larvae; carideans; fishes; *Gobiosoma robustum*. Greater than 150 mm shrimp: *Penaeus duorarum*, fishes: *Anchoa mitchilli, Mugil cephalus, Lagodon rhomboides, Eucinostomus gula, E. argenteus, Cyprinodon variegatus, Gobiosoma robustus*
Equetus acuminatus (high-hat)	r	Shrimps: alpheids, palemonids, *Periclimenes* sp., *Processa* sp., penaeids, crabs: *Petrolisthes galathinus*; fishes; isopods; stomatopods; copepods; amphipods

TABLE 7.3. (*Continued*)

Species	Abundance by Survey Number[a]										Diet
	1	2	3	4	5	6	7	8	9	10	
Bairdiella betebana (blue croaker)							r				
Odontoscion dentex (reef croaker)	r										Shrimp: larvae, alpheids, carideans, penaeids; fishes: larvae; isopods: *Excorallana antillensis*; crabs; stomatopod larvae
Leiostomus xanthurus (spot)									c	a	Less than 40 mm copepods; ostracods; chetognaths. Greater than 40 mm filamentous algae; desmids; forams; mysids; copepods; amphipods; ostracods; isopods; chaetognaths; insect larvae; pelecypods; gastropods; polychaetes
Cynoscion arenarius (sand sea trout)							r		r	r	Fishes; shrimp: *Palaemonetes* sp.; mysids; amphipods; crab zoea
Micropogon undulatus (atlantic croaker)										r	SL 30–107 mm copepods; mysids; caridean shrimp; polychaetes; insect larvae; isopods; pelecypods
Menticirrhus americanus (southern kingfish)							r		r	c	Polychaetes; crabs; mysids; *Emerita* sp.
Mullidae/goatfishes											
Pseudupeneus maculatus (spotted goatfish)				r							Crabs: calappids, grasoid, majids, portunids, xanthids; shrimps: alpheids, carideans, palaemonid, penaeid, *Tozeuma* sp.; polychaetes; pelecypods; *Pecten* sp., *Tellina* sp., siphunculids; *Aspidosiphon cumingi*, fishes: *Coryphopterus personatus*, syngnathids, stomatopods; *Pseudosquilla ciliata*, isopods, amphipods, ophiuroids, gastropods; *Turbonilla* sp., ostracods, tanaids, eggs
Ephippidae/spadefishes											
Chaetodipterus faber (Atlantic spadefish)				r	p		r	r	r		Sponges; zoantharians; *Rhodactis sacntithomae*, Zoanthus sp., polychaetes; *Sabellastarte magnifica*, tunicates; salps, gorgonians; *Muricea laxa*, algae; gastropod eggs; holothurians; corals; *Oculina diffusa, seagrasses*; *Syringodium filliforme*, heteropods; crab larvae; amphipods; hyperiids
Chaetodontidae/butterflyfishes											
Pomacanthus arcuatus (gray angelfish)	r										Sponges, tunicates; didemnid; algae; *Caulerpa* spp., *Penicillus pyriformis*,

Continued

TABLE 7.3. (*Continued*)

Species	1	2	3	4	5	6	7	8	9	10	Diet
											Dictyota spp., zoantharians; *Zoanthus* sp., *Zoanthus sociatus*, gorgonians; *Pterogorgia* sp., eggs, hydroids, bryozoans, seagrasses; *Ruppia maritima*
Pomacentridae/ damselfishes											
Pomacentrus leucostictus (beaugregory)				r							Algae, eggs; molluscs, pomacentrid, polychaetes, fishes, coelenterate polyps, tunicates, crabs, amphipods, corals, foraminifera, hermit crabs, shrimps, copepods, gastropods, gastropods; *Arene tricarinata, Crassispira nigrescens*
Abudefduf saxatilis (sergeant major)					p						Anthozoans, copepods, algae, tunicates; appendicularians, opisthobranchs; *Tridachia crispata*, fish eggs, fishes; *Jenkinsia* sp., shrimp larvae, barnacle appendages, ants, polychaetes, siphonophores
Labridae/wrasses											
Poratonatus megalepsis (dwarf wrasse)	r			r							
Halichoeres bivittatus (slippery dick)				r	p						Crabs: majids, *Mithrax* sp., *Mithrax sculptus, Platypodia spectabilis*, portunid, xanthid, echinoid; *Diadema antillarum, Lytechinum variegatus*, polychaetes; ampharetid, gastropods; *Acmaea* sp., *Acmaea pustulata*, acteonid, *Arene* sp., *Arene tricarinata, Bittium varium, Bulla striata, Bullata ovuliformis, Cerithium* sp., *Modulus modulus, Nassarius* sp., *Olivella* sp., *Planaxis lineatus, Pseudostomatella coccinea, Seila adamsi, Smaragdia viridis, Synaptocochlea picta, Tegula lividomaculata, Tricolia bella, Tricolia tessellata*, turrid, ophiuroid; *Ophioderma* sp., *Ophiothrix* sp., pelecypods; *Adequipecten gibbus, Americardia guppyi, Brachidontes exustus, Crassinella* sp., *Cuminigia antillarum, Ervilia nitens, Isognomon* sp., *Laevicardium* sp., *Nuculana*

TABLE 7.3. (*Continued*)

Species	Abundance by Survey Number[a]										Diet
	1	2	3	4	5	6	7	8	9	10	
											sp., *Papyridea semisulcata*, *Tellina listeri*, *Trachycardium* sp., shrimps; alpheid, chitons; *Acanthochiton pygmaea*, *Ischnochiton* sp., fishes, stomatopods, hermit crabs; diogenids, pagurids, foraminiferas
Hemipteronotus martinicensis (rosy razorfish)				r							
Hemipteronotus novacula (pearly razorfish)			r								Gastropods: *Batilaria* sp., *Caecum* sp., *Drillia* sp., *Litiopa melanostoma*, *Natica* sp., pelecypods; *Eryilia nitens*, *Pitar* sp., polychaetes, shrimps, scaphopods; *Dentalium* sp., isopods; amphipods
Lachnolaimus maximus (hogfish)			c								Pelecypods; gastropods; crabs; hermit crabs; echinoids; amphipods; scaphopods; barnacles
Scaridae/parrotfishes											
Nichlsina usta (emerald parrotfish)	r		r				r				
Scarus coelestinus (midnight parrotfish)			r								Algae; seagrass; *Thalassia testudinum*, molluscs; foraminifera; coral; echinoid; sponge
Scarus croicensis (striped parrotfish)			r								Algae
Scarus quacamaia (rainbow parrotfish)			r								Algae; seagrasses; *Syringodium filliforme*, *Thalassia testudinum*
Sparisoma chrysopterum (redtail parrotfish)			r								Algae, seagrasses; *Thalassia testudinum*
Sparisoma radians (bucktooth parrotfish)			r								Algae, seagrasses; *Thalassia testundinum*
Sparisoma rubripinne (redfin parrotfish)	a	r		c							Algae, seagrasses; *Thalassia testudinum*
Sparisoma viride (stoplight parrotfish)			r								Algae, seagrasses; *Thalassia testudinum*
Mugilidae/mullets											
Mugil cephalus (striped mullet)			r		p					a	Inorganic sediments, detritus, microalgae
Mugil curema (white mullet)			r	r	p					c	Plants, diatoms, *Lyngbya majuscula*, *Rhizoclonium riparium*, *Thalassia testudinum*, *Vaucheria* sp.
Mugil trichodon (fantail mullet)			r								

Continued

TABLE 7.3.   (*Continued*)

Species	Abundance by Survey Number[a]										Diet
	1	2	3	4	5	6	7	8	9	10	
Sphyraenidae/ barracudas											
Sphyraena barracuda (great barracuda)		r	r	r	p	r					Fishes: *Ablennes hians, Acanthurus bahianus, Allanetta harringtonen-siis,* atherinids, *Canthigaster rostrata,* carnagids, *Caranx fusus,* clupeids, *Decapterus* sp., *Diodon* sp., *Echidna catenata, Haemulon* sp., *Harengula slupeola, Jenkinsia* sp., *Ocyurus scarid, Sphyraena picudilla, Trachinocephalus myops,* octopuses, scyllarid lobsters
Opistognathidae/ jawfishes											
Opistognathus maxillosus (mottled jawfish)		r									Shrimps, isopods, fishes, polychaetes, mysids, copepods
Dactyloscopidae/sand stargazers											
Dactyloscopus tridigitatus (sand stargazer)		r		r							
Uranoscophidae/ stargazers											
Astroscopus y-graecum (southern stargazer)					r						
Clinidae/clinids											
Malacoctenus macropus (rosy blenny)				r							
Paraclinus fasciatus (banded blenny)		r	r	c							
Paraclinus nigripinnis (blackfin blenny)				r							
Paraclinus marmoratus (marbled blenny)	r	r	r	r	p						
Chaenopsis ocellata (bluethroat pikeblenny)					p						
Blennidae/combtooth blennies											
Chasmodes saburrae (Florida blenny)		r	r			r	r		r	r	Amphipods, detritus, polychaetes, crabs, fish, pelecypods; *Crepidula* sp., isopods
Blennius marmoreus (seaweed blenny)					p						Algae, detritus, ophiuroides, polychaetes, hydroids
Hypsoblennius ionthas (freckled blenny)							r				

TABLE 7.3. (*Continued*)

Species	Abundance by Survey Number[a]										Diet
	1	2	3	4	5	6	7	8	9	10	
Callionymidae/ dragonets											
Callionymus pauciradiatus (spotted dragonet)	r	r	r	r	p						
Gobiidae/gobies											
Barbulifer ceuthoecus (bearded goby)				r							
Microgobius microlepis (banner goby)	r			p							
Microgobius gulosus (clown goby)					p	c	r		r		Detritus, copepods, epiphytic algae, amphipods, polychaetes, bivalves, shrimp mysids
Microgobius thalassinus (green goby)					r						Small crustaceans; amphipods, other invertebrates
Bathygobius curacao (notchtongue goby)				c							
Bathygobius soporator (frillfin goby)					r						Caridean shrimp; *Palaemonetes intermedius*, chironomids, amphipods
Gobionellus bolesoma (darter goby)				r							
Gobionellus smaragdus (emerald goby)					r						
Gobionellus shufelti (freshwater goby)							r				
Gobionellus stigmarturus (spottail goby)				r							
Gobiosoma robustum (code goby)	a	r	r	p	c	c	r	r	r	r	Amphipods, chironomid larvae, mysids, cladocerans, ostracods, small molluscs, algal filaments, detritus, cumaceans
Gobiosoma longipala (twoscale goby)						r					
Gobiosoma macrodon (tiger goby)	r	r									
Gobiosoma longum											
Lophogobius cyprinoides (crested goby)				r							Amphipods; detritus; filamentous algae; mysids; shrimp; *Neanthes*; ostracods; small bivalves; chironomid larvae; copepods; *Rithropanopeus harrisii*, snails
Coryphopterus glaucofraenum (bridled goby)	r										Algae and detritus; ostracods; ophiuroids; eggs; pelecypods; copepods

Continued

TABLE 7.3. (*Continued*)

Species	Abundance by Survey Number[a]										Diet
	1	2	3	4	5	6	7	8	9	10	
Acanthuridae/ surgeonfishes											
Acanthurus bahianus (ocean surgeon)	r		r								Algae; organic detritus; diatoms; seagrasses; *Syringodium filiforme, Halophila baillonis, Thalassia testudinum*
Acanthurus chirurgus (doctorfish)				r							Algae; organic detritus; diatoms; seagrasses; *Syringodium filiforme, Thalassia testudinum,* worm tubes; gastropods; nudibranch eggs
Stromateidae/ butterfishes											
Nomeus gronovii (man-of-war fish)			r								
Scorpaenidae/ scorpionfishes											
Scorpaena brasiliensis (barbfish)	r	r		r							Shrimps: penaeid; crustaceans; stomatopods; fishes; *Hippocampus* sp., crabs
Scorpaena grandicornis (plumed scorpionfish)	r	r		r							Shrimp: caridean, stenopid; fishes; crustaceans
Scorpaena plumeri (spotted scorpionfish)				r							Fishes: *Acanthurus* sp., congrid, *Jenkinsia* sp., crabs; majid, *Mithrax coryphe, Pitho* sp., *Portunus anceps, Portunus ordwayi;* shrimps; penaeid, *Penaepsis goodei;* octopuses; hermit crabs
Triglidae/searobins											
Prionotus salmonicolor (blackwing sea robin)					r	p					
Prionotus scitulus (leopard sea robin)	r	r	r			r	r	r	r		Small molluscs: *Solemya* sp., *Bulla* sp., *Olivia* sp.; shrimp; crabs; fishes
Prionotus tribulus			r			r	c		r	r	Shrimp; crabs; *Limulus polyphemus, Uca* sp.; fishes; amphipods; copepods; annelids; bivalves; echinoids
Bothidae/lefteye flounder											
Bothus ocellatus (eyed flounder)	r	r		r							Fishes; *Coryphopterus* sp.; crabs; *Calappa ocellata;* majid; shrimps; amphipods; isaeid; stomatopods; *Pseudosquilla ciliata*
Ancylopsetta quadrocellata (ocellated flounder)							r				

TABLE 7.3.   (*Continued*)

Species	1	2	3	4	5	6	7	8	9	10	Diet
Citharichthys macrops (spotted wiff)		r		r							
Citharichthys spilopterus (bay wiff)	r	r			r			r			Mysids; shrimp; crabs; copepods; amphipods; fishes; annelids
Paralichthys albigutta (gulf flounder)	r	r			r	r	r	r			Less than 45 mm SL: amphipods, small crustaceans. Greater than 45 mm: fishes: *Orthopristis chrysopterus, Lagodon rhomboides, Synodus foetens, Anchoa mitchilli,* crustaceans
Syacium papillosus (dusky flounder)		r									
Etropus crossotus (fringed flounder)						r					Polychaetes; copepods; shrimps; amphipods
Soleidae/soles											
Trinectes inscriptus (scrawled sole)		r		r							
Trinectes maculatus (hogchoker)	r				r	r					Amphipods; mysids; chironomid larvae; polychaetes; *Nereis pelagica;* foraminifera
Achirus lineatus (lined sole)		r	r	r	p	c	c		r	r	Polychaetes; amphipods; copepods
Cynoglossidae/ tonguefishes											
Symphurus plagiusa (blackcheek tonguefish)	r	r		r		c	c		r		Copepods; amphipods; ostracods; polychaetes; pelecypods
Balistidae/triggerfishes and filefishes											
Balistes capriscus (grey triggerfish)				r							
Monocanthus ciliatus (fringed filefish)	c	r	r	c				r	r		Algae; detritus; seagrasses; *Thalassia testudinum;* copepods; shrimp; caridean, amphipods; *Colomastix* sp.; *Leucothoe* sp.; tanaids; polychaetes; stomatopod larvae; isopods; shrimps; amphipods
Monocanthus hispidus (planehead filefish)	c	r	r	c		r	r	r	r	r	Amphipods; pelecypods; polychaetes
Alutera schoepfi (orange filefish)		r									Seagrasses: *Syringodium filiforme, Thalassia testudinum;* algae; *Halimeda* sp.; hermit crabs; *Clibanarius tricolor,* gastropods; *Columbella mercatoria*
Ostraciidae/boxfishes											
Lactophrys quadricornis	r	c	r	r	p			r	r		Sponges; tunicates; zoantharians; *Bunodosoma granulifera,*

Continued

TABLE 7.3. (*Continued*)

Species	Abundance by Survey Number[a]										Diet
	1	2	3	4	5	6	7	8	9	10	
(scrawled cowfish)											*Phyllactis flosculifera, Zoanthus pulchellus,* hermit crabs; *Pagurus bonairensis,* algae: bluegreens, *Halimeda opuntia;* gorgonians: *Muricea atlantica;* seagrasses: *Thalassia testudinum; scypho-zoans; polychaetes; eggs;* pelecypods; *shrimps; amphipods*
Lactophrys trigonus (trunkfish)	r	r		c						r	Crabs: calappid, *Emerita* sp., majids, *Mithrax* sp., *Pitho* sp., portunids, xanthids; pelecypods: *Atrina seminuda, Codakia costata, Musculus lateralis, Tellina* sp., *Trachycardium muricatum,* polychaetes: slyerid, pectinariid; echinoids: *Lytechinus variegatus;* algae; tunicates; *Microcosmus exasperatus;* seagrasses: *Syringodium filiforme, Thalassia testudinum;* holothurians; *Holothuria arenicola;* asteroids; *Oreaster reticulata;* gastropods: *Acmaea pustulata, Anachis sparsa, Arene* sp., *Bulla* sp., *Haminoea elegans, Nassarius* sp., *Elasmopus* sp.; ophiuroids; *Ophioderma brevis-pinum, Ophiothrix* sp., eggs; chitons: *Acanthochitona* sp., hermit crabs, shrimp; alpheid
Lactophrys triqueter (smooth trunkfish)	r	r									Polychaetes; onuphid, syllid, sipunculids: *Aspidosiphon spinos-scutatus;* crabs: majids, pinotherid, *Upogebia* sp.; shrimps: alpheids, carideans, gnathophyllid; tunica-tes: *Asidia nigra, Trididemnum savignii, sponges,* hemichordates; gastropods: *Balcis intermedia, Nitidella laevigata, Trivia* sp., *Turbo castanea;* hermit crabs; *Paguristes* sp.; *Spiropagurus* sp.; echinoids: *Lytechinus variegatus;* pelecypods; *Tellina* sp., amphi-pods; seagrasses: *Halophila bail-lonis, Thalassia testudinum;* algae: *Halimeda* sp., chitons, eggs, ostracods
Tetradontidae/puffers											
Sphoeroides nephalus (southern puffer)	r		r	p	r	c	r			r	Crabs, *Callinectes sapidus,* pelecy-pods

TABLE 7.3. (*Continued*)

Species	Abundance by Survey Number[a]										Diet
	1	2	3	4	5	6	7	8	9	10	
Sphoeroides spengleri (bandtail puffer)	r	r	r	r				r			Crabs: majids, *Microphrys bicorutus*, rannid; pelecypods: *Musculus lateralis*, *Pinctada radiata*; gastropods: *Bullata ovuliformis*, polychaetes; echinoids: *Diadema antillarum*, spatangoid, pohiuroids; *Ophiocoma riisei*, *Ophioderma rubicundum*, *Ophiothix* sp., *Ophiothix lineata*: amphipods; shrimps; seagrasses: *Halophila baillonis*, *Thalassia testudinum*; algae; detritus; hemichordates; eggs; chitons; isopods; copepods; tunicates; hermit crabs; fishes
Sphoeroides testudineus (checkered puffer)	r										Crustacea: *Portunid megalops*; gastropods; *Nertina* sp.
Diodontidae/ porcupinefishes											
Chilomycterus schoepfi (striped burrfish)	r	c	r	r	p	r	r	c	r	r	Molluscs: pelecypods, gastropods, *Bittium* sp., *Mitrella* sp.; echinoid; *Mellita* sp., xanthid crab
Chilomycterus antennatus (bridled burrfish)	r										Gastropods: *Anachis* sp., *Arene* sp., *Astraea* sp., *Cerithium* sp., *Cerithium litteratum*, *Columbella mercatoria*, *Crassispira fuscescens*, *Marginella* sp., *Mitrella lunata*, *Modulus modulus*, *Nitidella ocellata*, *Pusia* sp., *Pyramidella candida*, *Smaragdia viridis*, *Tegula fasciata*, *Turbo* sp., *Turbo castanaea*; hermit crabs: diogenids, pagurids; isopods: *Paracereis caudata*, crabs, shrimps
Diodon holocanthus (balloonfish)	r		r								Gastropods: *Acmaea leucopleura*, *Astraea* sp., *Calliostoma* sp., *Cerithium algicola*, *Cerithium litteratum*, *Crassostrea rhizophorae*, *Fissurella* sp., *Modulus modulus*, muricids, *Nassarius* sp., *Oliva reticularis*, *Polinices lacteus*, *Siphonaria* sp., *Pusia* sp., *Pyramidella candida*, *Smaragdia viridis*, *Tegula fasciata*, *Turbo* sp., *Turbo castanaea*; hermit crabs: diogenids pagurids; isopods: *Paracereis caudata*, crabs, shrimps

Source: Zieman (1982).
[a] r, Rare; p, present; c, common.

Of the eight Sciaenidae found in south Florida's estuaries, only the spotted sea trout, *Cynoscion nebulosus*; the spot, *Leiostomus xanthurus*; and the silver perch, *Bairdiella chrysura*, occurred commonly in the seagrasses (Carr and Adams, 1973; Zieman, 1982). The pigfish, *Orthopristis chrysoptera* (Pomadasyidae), was abundant on muddy bottoms and in the turbid waters associated with grass in Florida's variable salinity regions but was rare in the Florida Keys (Tabb and Manning, 1961). Other grunts (Pomadasyidae) occurring rarely were *Anisotrenus virginicus*, *Haemulon scirus*, and *H. aurolineatum*. *Lagodon rhomboides* (Sparidae) was the most abundant fish collected in southwestern Florida and Florida Bay. The silver jenny, *Eucinostomus gulla*, and the spotfin mojarra, *E. argenteus* were seasonally abundant Gerridae of the seagrasses. Haemulidae, including *Haemulon flavolineatum*, *H. parri*, and *H. carbonium*, were found in the clearer waters of the Florida Keys. Common snappers (Lutjanidae) included *Lutjanus griseus*, *L. syngaris*, *L. apodus*, *L. analis*, *L. jocu*, and *Ocyurus chrysurus* (Zieman, 1982).

It was not unusual to find greater densities of fish in grass bed habitats of south Florida estuaries and coastal lagoons than in adjacent, open-water habitats (Zieman, 1982). In Biscayne Bay, up to 3.5 times as many fish were captured in grass-beds as in other habitats (Roessler, 1965). Unfortunately, there is a dearth of knowledge about within-habitat distribution patterns in relation to structural complexity, prey density, and other seagrass community characteristics (Zieman, 1982).

Benthic Communities
Along the Florida Gulf coast there are few rocky outcrops on the inner shelf where most seagrasses are found. As a result, the leaves of seagrasses are the most important substrate for benthic algae in depths of less than 10 m (Ballantine and Humm, 1975; Zieman, 1982; Harlin, 1980). Harlin (1975, 1980) noted the factors influencing the distribution and abundance of epiphytes as follows:

(1) Physical substratum (algae, invertebrates, bacteria).
(2) Access to photic zone (photosynthetic algae).
(3) A free ride through moving waters (suspension feeders and algae).
(4) Nutrient exchange with host (algae).
(5) Organic carbon source (animals, bacteria, and heterotrophic algae).

Epiphytic algae that occurred in south Florida and in the Anclote estuary are listed in Table 7.4.

Macroalgae.   On tropical seagrasses the heaviest coatings of epiphytes occurred only after the leaf had been colonized by the coralline red algae, *Fosliella* or *Melobesia*. The coralline skeleton of these algae roughened the grass blade surface enough to be a suitable substrate for other epiphytes. Typically, seagrass leaves were more heavily epiphytized at their tips than at their bases. This allowed small algae attached to leaf tips to be in the photic zone. Also, the

TABLE 7.4. Algal Ephiphytes of Seagrasses

DIVISION CYANOPHYTA
Order Coccogonales
Family Chroococcaceae
Anacystis aeruginosa
A. dimidiata
A. montanta
Agmenellum thermale
Family Chamaesiphonaceae
Entophysalis conferta
E. duesta
Order Hormogonales
Family Oscillatoriaceae
Microcoleus lyngbyaceus
Oscillatoria lutea
Porphyrosiphon notarisii
Schizothrix arenaria
S. calcicola
S. mexicana
Spirulina subsalsa
Family Rivulariaceae
Calothrix crustacea
DIVISION RHODOPHYTA
Order Bangiales
Family Bangiaceae
Asterocystis ramosa
Erythrocladia subintegra
E. carnea
Goniotrichum alsidii
Order Nemalionales
Family Acrochaeticeae
Acrochaetium sargassi
A. thureti
A. crassipes
Order Cryptonemiales
Family Squamariaceae
Peyssonnelia rubra
Family Corallinaceae
Fosliella atlantica
F. farinosa
Jania adhaerans
Family Hypneaceae
Hypnea musciformis
H. spinella
Order Rhodomeniales
Family Champiaceae
Champia parvula
Order Ceramiales
Family Cermiaceae
Centroceras clavulatum
Ceramium byssoideum
C. byssoideum persimilis
Ceramium fastigiatum
Griffithsia tenuis
G. globulifera
Spyridia filamentosa

Family Dasyaceae
Dasya pedicellata
Family Rhodomelaceae
Polysiphonia havanensis
P. echinata
Herposiphonia tenella
Lophosiphonia saccorhiza
Chondria collinsiana
C. dasyphylla
C. tenuissima
Laurencia obtusa
L. poitei
DIVISION PHAEOPHYTA
Order Ectocarpales
Family Ectocarpales
Giffordia rallsiae
G. mitchellae
Order Sphacelariales
Family Sphacelariaceae
Sphacelaria furcigera
S. tribuloides
Order Chordariales
Family Chordariaceae
Cladosiphon occidentalis
Family Myrionemataceae
Ascocyclus magnusii
Order Dictyosiphonales
Family Stictyosiphonaceae
Myriotrichia subcorymbosa
Stictyosiphon subsimplex
DIVISION CHLOROPHYTA
Order Ulotrichales
Family Pleurococcaceae
Pseudotetraspora antillarum
Family Gomontiaceae
Gomontia polyrhiza
Family Chaetophoraceae
Entocladia viridis
Phaeophila dendroides
Ulvella lens
Order Ulvales
Family Ulvaceae
Enteromorpha chaetomorphoides
E. clathrata
E. prolifera
Order Cladophorales
Family Cladophoraceae
Chaetomorpha brachygona
Cladophora sericea
Rhizoclonium hookeri
R. kerneri
Order Siphonales
Family Derbesiaceae
Derbesia vaucheriaeformis
Caulerpa prolifera

Source: Ballantine and Humm (1975).

upper leaf surface was exposed to much greater water motion than were the lower portions, which was advantageous to suspension-feeding animals and algae alike. For the algae, the increased water motion reduced the gradients for photosynthesis (Zieman, 1982).

The areas inhabited by seagrasses did not offer a suitable substrate for most algae, which required hard substrates for attachment with their holdfasts. The primary substrates for benthic algae included the seagrass leaves themselves, as discussed above, the sediments, and occasional rocks or outcrops. Many macroalgae, collectively known as "drift algae," formed large unattached masses on the southern Florida sea bottom. Most drift algae belonged to the red algal genus, *Laurencia*. The only algae able consistently to use sediments as substrates were mat-forming green algae, which were members of the order Siphonales. The most important genera included *Halimeda, Penicillus, Caulerpa, Rhipocephalus*, and *Udotea*.

Macroinvertebrates. In south Florida, amphipods associated with common seagrass were *Cymadusa compta, Gammarus mucronatus, Melita nitida, Grandidierella bonnieroides, Lysianops alba, Ampelisca verrilli*, and *Chevalia aviculae* (Zieman, 1982; Nelson, 1980). Abundant within the grass beds were the carideans *Palaemonetes pugio, P. vulgaris, P. intermedius, Periclimenes longicaudatus, P. americanus, Thor floridanus, Tozeuma carolinense, Hippolyte pleuracantha, Alpheus normanni*, and *A. heterochaelis* (Zieman, 1982).

Large epibenthic organisms were among the most obvious invertebrates inhabiting south Florida seagrass beds. Some of these were the queen conch, *Strombus gigas*; Bahamian starfish, *Oreaster reticulata*; gastropods, *Fasciolaria tulipa* and *Pleuroploca gigantea*; and numerous sea urchins, such as *Lytechinus variegatus* and *Tripneustes ventricosus*. Common in the beds were juveniles of the long-spined urchin, *Diadema antillarum*. The deposit-feeding holothurians, *Actinopyqa agassizi* and *Holothuria floridana*, were found on the surface, while the large sea hare, the nudibranch, *Aplysia dactylomela*, was often found gliding gracefully over the grass canopy. The pink shrimp, *Penaeus duorarum*, and the spring lobster, *Panulirus argus*, were found foraging in the seagrass at night (Zieman, 1982).

Infauna included benthic nematodes found in the soft surface sediments of *Thalassia* beds. In Biscayne Bay, Hopper and Meyers (1967) found approximately 100 nematode taxa. Of these, the dominant species were *Metoncholaimus scissus, Theristus fistulatus, Spirinia parasitifera*, and *Gomphionema typica*, which together usually composed 87 to 95% of the total number of nematodes present.

Examples of other infauna were the rigid pen shell, *Atrina rigida*, and numerous bivalve molluscs such as *Chione cancellata, Codakia orbicularis, Tellina radiata, Lucina pennsylvanica*, and *Laevicardium laevigatum*. A variety of annelid worms were among the infauna, notably *Arenicola cristata, Onuphis magna, Terebellides stroemi*, and *Eunice longicerrata* (Zieman, 1982).

SUMMARY

The underwater seagrass beds are commonly found around the coast of southern Florida and the Keys. They occur on both the Atlantic and Gulf sides of Florida. They are very sensitive to turbidity and to disruption by boats and other equipment that dislodge them. When undisturbed, *Thalassia* becomes the dominant grass, although there are other grass associates in these beds. These grasses are fairly productive, with an annual primary production of about $1000 \, \text{g} \, \text{C} \, \text{m}^{-2}$. High turtle grass leaves contain 9 to 22% protein; however, a great deal of this is not utilizable, as the turtle grass, manatee grass, and shoal grass are C_3 plants, which are undesirable as a source of food for many organisms. Hybrids are generally higher in the rhizomes than in the leaves of the turtle grass, manatee grass, and shoal grass. The green seagrass is relatively unavailable for food because of many factors. However, the contents of the cells of these green leaves is adjustable, and the action of bacteria and fungi on these leaves as they decay makes the detritus highly desirable as a food. Epiphytes are very important as a source of nutrition for the organisms that live and feed on the seagrasses.

These seagrasses support a large diversity of epiphytes. It is believed that *Thalassia* is able to fix gaseous nitrogen by the anaerobic bacteria, *Clostridium* sp. and *Desulfobibrio* sp., that live in the sediments associated with these plants. These beds are particularly valuable because of the great diversity of aquatic animals that live in association with them. Many different types of organisms feed on these seagrasses. It is believed that the epiphytes on the seagrass are often more valuable as a food source than the seagrass itself. Marine turtles and manatees are probably the only large invertebrates that browse on seagrass. The detritus of seagrass is a very valuable source of food for many of these organisms, but it is not clearly known how much they feed on the products of detrital decomposition and on the seagrass itself.

The majority of the fish within the grass beds feed on small, mobile epifauna, including copepods, cumaceans, amphipods, isopods, and shrimps. A great variety of fish live in association with these beds. Many diatoms and algae are often found as epiphytes of the seagrasses and probably are a valuable source of food for many of the small invertebrates and some of the fish.

Because these underwater seagrass beds are so rare along the coast of the United States and form an unusual habitat for the harboring of a very diverse fauna, they should be carefully conserved and protected against the anthropogenic effects of human beings.

BIBLIOGRAPHY

Ballantine, D., and H. J. Humm. 1975. Benthic algae of the Anclote estuary. I. Epiphytes of seagrass leaves. Fla. Sci. 38(3): 150–162.

Bauersfeld, P., R. Kleer, N. Durrant, and J. Sykes. 1969. Nutrient content of turtle grass (*Thalassia testudinum*). Proc. Int. Seaweed Symp. 6: 376–645.

Brook, I. M. 1977. Trophic relationships in a seagrass community: *Thalassia testudinum* in Card Sound, Florida. Fish diets in relation to macrobenthic and cryptic faunal abundance. Trans. Am. Fish. Soc. 106(3): 219–229.

Carr, W. E. S. and C. A. Adams. 1973. Food habits of juvenile marine fishes occupying seagrass beds in the estuarine zone near Crystal River, Florida. Trans. Am. Fish. Soc. 102(3): 11– 540.

Dawes, C. J., and J. M. Lawrence. 1980. Seasonal changes in the proximate constituents of the seagrasses, *Thalassia testudinum, Halodule wrightii,* and *Syringodinum filiforme.* Aquat. Bot. 8: 371–380.
Dawes, C. J., K. Bird, M. Durako, R. Goddard, W. Hoffman, and R. McIntosh. 1979. Chemical fluctuations due to seasonal and cropping effects on an algal seagrass community. Aquat. Bot. 6: 79–86.

Eldred, B. 1958. *Meioceras lermondi* as food for *Penaeus duorarum?* Nautilus 71(4): 152.
Eldred, B., R. M. Ingle, K. D. Woodburn, R. F. Hutton, and H. Jones. 1961. Biological observations on the commercial shrimp, *Pennaeus duorarum,* in Florida waters. Fla. State Board. Conserv. Mar. Prof. Pap. Ser. 3: 1–139.

Fenchel, T. 1970. Studies on the decomposition of organic detritus derived from turtle grass, *Thalassia testudinum.* Limnol. Oceanogr. 15(1): 14–20.
Fenchel, T. 1977. Aspects of the decomposition of seagrasses. *In* C. P. McRoy, and C. Helfferich, eds., Seagrass ecosystems. Mar. Sci. 4: 123–146.

Harlin, M. M. 1975. Epiphyte–host relations in seagrass communities. Aquat. Bot. 1: 125–131.
Harlin, M. M. 1980. Seagrass epiphytes, pp. 117–151. *In* R. C. Phillips, and C. P. McRoy, eds., Handbook of seagrass biology: an ecosystem perspective. Garland Publishing, New York.
Hooks, T. A., K. L. Heck, Jr., and R. J. Livingston. 1976. An inshore marine invertebrate community: structure and habitat associations in the northeastern Gulf of Mexico. Bull. Mar. Sci. 26(1): 99–109.
Hopper, B. E., and S. P. Myers. 1967. Aspects of the life cycle of marine nematodes. Helgol. Wiss. Meersunters. 13(4): 444–449.

Jones, J. A. 1968. Primary productivity by the tropical marine turtle grass, *Thalassis testudinum,* and its epiphytes. Ph.D. dissertation, Univ. Miami, Coral Gables, Fla. 196 pp.

Kikuchi, T. and J. M. Peres. 1977. Consumer ecology of seagrass beds. *In* C. P. McRoy and C. Helfferich, eds., Seagrass ecosystems. Mar. Sci. 4: 147–193.

Livingston, R. J. 1976. Diurnal and seasonal fluctuations of organisms in a north Florida estuary. Estuarine Coastal Mar. Sci. 4(4): 373–400.
Livingston, R.J. 1982. Trophic organization of fishes in a coastal seagrass system. Mar. Ecol. Prog. Ser. 7: 1–12.

McRoy, C. P., and R. J. Barsdate. 1970. Phosphate absorption in eelgrass. Limnol. Oceanogr. 15(1): 6–13.
McRoy, C. P., and C. Helfferich. 1980. Applied aspects of seagrasses, pp. 297–343. *In* R. C. Phillips, and C. P. McRoy, eds., Handbook of seagrass biology: an ecosystem perspective. Garland Publishing, New York.
McRoy, C. P. and C. McMillan. 1977. Production ecology and physiology of seagrasses, pp. 53–87. *In* C. P. McRoy, and C. Helfferich, eds., Seagrass ecosystems. Marcel Dekker, New York.
McRoy, C. P., R. J. Barsdate, and M. Nebert. 1972. Phosphorus cycling in an eelgrass (*Zostera marina*) ecosystem. Limnol. Oceanogr. 17(1): 55–67.

Nelson, W. G. 1980. A comparative study of amphipods in seagrasses from Florida to Nova Scotia. Bull. Mar. Sci. 30(1): 80–89.

Odum, H. T. 1963. Productivity measurements in Texas turtle grass and the effects of dredging an intracoastal channel. Publ. Inst. Mar. Sci. 9: 48–58.

Odum, W. E., and E. J. Heald. 1972. Trophic analyses of an estuarine mangrove community. Bull. Mar. Sci. 22(3): 671–738.

Ogden, J. C. 1980. Faunal relationships in Caribbean seagrass beds, pp. 173–198. *In* R. C. Phillips, and C. P. McRoy, eds., Handbook of seagrass biology. Garland Publishing, New York.

Orth, R. J. 1977. The importance of sediment stability in seagrass communities, pp. 28–300. *In* B. C. Coull, ed., Ecology of marine benthos. Univ. South Carolina Press, Columbia, S.C.

Patriquin, D. G. 1972. The origin of nitrogen and phosphorus for growth of the marine angiosperm, *Thalassia testudinum*. Mar. Biol. 15(1): 35–46.

Randall, J. E. 1967. Food habits of reef fishes of the West Indies. Stud. Trop. Oceanogr. Miami 5: 665–847.

Reeve, M. R. 1975. The ecological significance of the zooplankton in the shallow subtropical waters of south Florida. *In* L. E. Cronin, ed., Estuarine Res. 1: 352–371.

Roessler, M. 1965. An analysis of the variability of fish populations taken by otter trawl in Biscayne Bay, Florida. Trans. Am. Fish. Soc. 94: 311–318.

Squiers, E. R., and R. E. Good. 1974. Seasonal changes in the productivity, caloric content, and chemical composition of a population of salt-marsh cord-grass. Chesapeake Sci. 15(2): 63–71.

Tabb, D. C., and R. B. Manning. 1961. A checklist of the flora and fauna of northern Florida Bay and adjacent brackish waters of the Florida mainland collected during the period July, 1957 through September, 1960. Bull. Mar. Sci. Gulf Caribb. 11(4): 552–649.

Thorhaug, A., and M. A. Roessler. 1977. Seagrass community dynamics in a subtropical estuarine lagoon. Aquaculture 12: 253–277.

Walsh, G. E., and T. E. Grow. 1972. Composition of *Thalassia testudinum* and *Ruppia maritima*. Fla. Sci. 35(2/3): 97–107.

Wetzel, R. G., and P. A. Penhale. 1979. Transport of carbon and excretion of dissolved organic carbon of leaves and roots/rhizomes in seagrasses and their epiphytes. Aquat. Bot. 6: 149–158.

Zapata, O., and C. McMillan. 1979. Phenolic acids in seagrasses. Aquat. Bot. 7: 307 317.

Zieman, J. C. 1975. Quantitative and dynamic aspects of the ecology of turtle grass, *Thalassia testudinum*. *In* L. E. Cronin ed., Estuarine Res. 1: 541–562.

Zieman, J. C. 1982. The ecology of the seagrasses of south Florida: a community profile. U.S. Fish and Wildlife Service, Office of Biological Services Washington, D.C. FWS/OBS-82/25. 158 pp.

Zieman, J. C. and R. G. Wetzel. 1980. Methods and rates of productivity in seagrasses, pp. 87–116. *In* R. C. Phillips, and C. P. McRoy, eds., Handbook of seagrass biology. Garland Publishing, New York.

Zieman, J. C., G. W. Thayer, M. B. Robblee, and R. T. Zieman. 1979. Production and export of seagrasses from a tropical bay. *In* R. J. Livingston, ed., Ecological processes in coastal and marine systems. Plenum Press, New York. Mar. Sci. 10: 21–34.

CHAPTER 8

Mangrove Estuaries: South Florida, Gulf of Mexico

M angrove swamps serve as ecotones between land and sea (Walsh, 1974) and are complexes of plant communities covering large areas fringing sheltered tropical shores. Mangrove vegetation varies in character from forest 30 m high or more to a poor scrub barely 2 in. high (Richards, 1964). Typically, mangroves are associated with sheltered muddy shores where the land is encroaching on the sea, but they also grow on coral reefs and on sandy shores where there is little accretion.

In the American tropics, the mangrove swamp forest consists of a series of zones each dominated by one species of tree (Golley et al., 1962). Zonation patterns in mangrove forests generally are well correlated with frequency and duration of tidal immersion, the nature of the substratum, and the salinity of the groundwater (Ball, 1980; Golley et al., 1962).

Mangroves dominate the Florida coast, although there are reports of occurrences of the black mangrove, *Avicennia nitida*, along the Texas coast on Harbor Island (near Corpus Christi) and Clark Island in the Rio Grande delta. The Florida mangrove communities have been studied more thoroughly than those anywhere else and are therefore considered here as an example of Gulf of Mexico mangrove communities.

Mangrove vegetation in Florida is developed extensively as far north as the southern limit of "killing" frosts. Figure 8.1 shows areas of mangrove growth in Florida. The mangrove forests of south Florida cover an area of 1750 km^2,

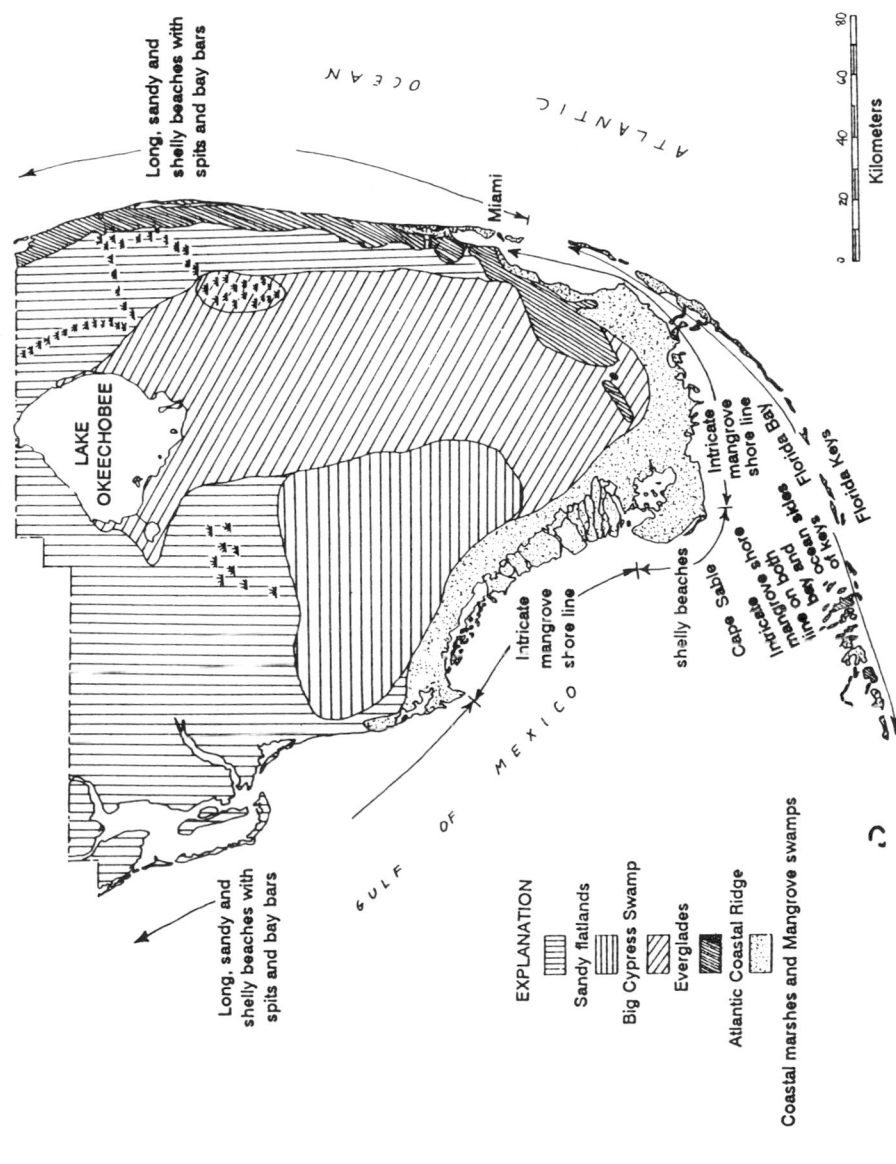

FIGURE 8.1. Topographic-ecologic map of south Florida. (After Kuenzler, 1974.)

EXPLANATION

Sandy flatlands

Big Cypress Swamp

Everglades

Atlantic Coastal Ridge

Coastal marshes and Mangrove swamps

located primarily within the boundaries of the Everglades National Park and within the region known as the Ten Thousand Islands. The four south Florida mangrove forest tree species are *Rhizophora mangle, Avicennia nitida* (= *A. germinans*), *Laguncularia racemosa*, and *Conocarpus erecta* (Lugo et al., 1975).

The following mangrove communities can be distinguished in Florida (Figure 8.2) (Richards, 1964; Chapman, 1976; Reimold, 1977):

1. The "pioneer *Rhizophora* family" is represented by young plants of *R. mangle* (20 to 30 per square foot) growing on almost continually submerged soil. Associated marine phanerogams include *Thalassia testudinum* and *Cymodocea manatorum*, and in some places the grass, *Spartina alterniflora*. Seedlings of *Avicennia* and *Laguncularia* are common.
2. The "mature *Rhizophora* consocies" develops from the pioneer family in a mature community, a forest up to 9 to 10 m high, in which a very few plants of *Thalassia* and *Cymodocea* may persist.
3. The "*Avicennia* – salt marsh associes" develops behind the outer *Rhizophora* consocies, on land that is regularly or only occasionally submerged. It is typically dominated by *Avicennia nitida*, which forms an open forest with an undergrowth of succulent shrubs, such as *Batis maritima* and *Salicornia perennis* and salt marsh grasses.
4. The "*Conocarpus* transition associes" is inundated by the very highest spring tides or only by storm tides. The semimangrove, *Conocarpus erectus*, is the most characteristic species in this community, which is located immediately inland from the *Avicennia* associes.
5. The "mature mangrove forest association" is a very luxuriant forest in which 60% of the tall trees are *Rhizophora* and about 30% *Avicennia*. The mangrove, *Laguncularia racemosa*; *Conocarpus* in small numbers; and various palms and other inland plants are also found.

Seedlings colonize areas made available by disturbances in hydrologic conditions. Any species of mangrove is able to colonize and competition is not manifest during the early phases; mixed stands (e.g., *Rhizophora* and *Laguncularia*) become established. As individuals reach maturity and require more space, competition becomes critical. At this point in the intertidal zone, *Rhizophora* outcompetes *Laguncularia* (Ball, 1980).

COMMUNITY STRUCTURE

The mangrove system in south Florida has been studied by many investigators. The species forming the associations in this area are set forth in Table 8.1.

Salinities along the south Florida coast and southern mangrove swamps are complicated and variable. Average salinity for the North River estuary is about 27 ppt but drops as low as 100 to 300 ppm in the fall (Odum and Heald, 1980). In the Old Rhodes Key lagoon, a shallow, nearshore, mangrove-lined marine lagoon with three inlets, the average salinity is 37.4 ppt (Holm, 1978).

(*text continues on page 540*)

TABLE 8.1.   *Species Associated with Mangrove Wetlands*

Species	Marquesa Keys	South Florida	North River	S. W. Florida Everglades	Ten Thousand Islands	Weeki Wachee River	Cockroach Bay	West coast Florida
DIVISION BACILLARIOPHYTA								
Class Bacillariophyceae								
Order Fragilariales								
Family Fragilariaceae								
Fragilaria sp.								×
Order Naviculales								
Family Naviculaceae								
Pleurosigma sp.		×						×
Order Bacillariales								
Family Bacillariaceae								
Bacillaria sp.								×
Nitzschia closterium		×						×
Nitzschia seriata								×
Order Surirellales								
Family Surirellaceae								
Campylodiscus sp.		×						
Order Coscinodiscales								
Family Coscinodiscaceae								
Melosira sp.		×						×
Order Biddulphiales								
Family Biddulphiaceae								
Biddulphia sp.								×
Family Chaetoceraceae								
Chaetoceros spp.		×						×
DIVISION CYANOPHYTA								
Class Myxophyceae								
Order Chroococcales								
Family Chroococcaceae								
Aphanoceapsa sp.		×						
Merismopedia sp.		×						×
Order Oscillatoriales								
Suborder Oscillatorineae								
Family Oscillatoriaceae								
Microcoleus lyngbyaceus								
(= *Lyngbya majuscula*)					×			
Schizothrix arenaria								
(= *Microcoleus tenerrimus*)					×			
Skujaella thiebautii		×						
Spirulina sp.								×
DIVISION CHLOROPHYTA								
Class Chlorophyceae								
Order Chlorococcales								
Family Chlorococcaceae								

Continued

TABLE 8.1.   (Continued)

Species	Marquesa Keys	South Florida	North River	S. W. Florida Everglades	Ten Thousand Islands	Weeki Wachee River	Cockroach Bay	West coast Florida
Tetraedron sp.								×
Order Ulotrichales								
Family Ulvaceae								
Enteromorpha sp.		×						
Monostroma sp.								
Order Cladophorales								
Family Cladophoraceae								
Cladophora repens							×	
Rhizoclonium sp.		×						
Chaetomorpha sp.								
Rhizoclonium sp.								
Order Siphonocladiales								
Family Dasycladaceae								
Acetabularia epenulate			×					
Acetabularia sp.		×		×				
Batophora oerstedi								
Family Valoniacaeae								
Cladophoropsis sp.		×	×	×				
Valonia sp.								
Order Siphonales								
Family Derbesiaceae								
Vaucheria sp.		×		×				
Family Caulerpaceae								
Caulerpa sp.		×	×	×				
Family Codiaceae								
Boodleopsis sp.		×						
Penicillus sp.		×	×	×				
Halimedia sp.			×	×				
Order Zygnematales								
Family Zygnemataceae								
Spirogyra sp.								×
Family Desmidiaceae								
Micrasterias sp.								×
Sphaerozosoma sp.								×
DIVISION PHAEOPHYTA								
Class Isogeneratae								
Order Dictyotales								
Family Dictyotaceae								
Padina vickersiae		×						
Class Cyclosporeae								
Order Fucales								
Family Fucaceae								
Sargassum sp.				×				

TABLE 8.1. (*Continued*)

Species	Marquesa Keys	South Florida	North River	S. W. Florida Everglades	Ten Thousand Islands	Weeki Wachee River	Cockroach Bay	West coast Florida
DIVISION RHODOPHYTA								
Class Rhodophyceae								
Subclass Florideae								
Order Gelidales								
Family Wurdemanniaceae								
Wurdemannia sp.		×						
Order Gigartinales								
Family Rhabdoniaceae								
Catenella repens		×				×		
Catenella sp.					×			
Family Hypnaceae								
Hypnea sp.								
Family Gracilariaceae								
Gracilaria verrucosa				×		×	×	
Gracilaria sp.		×						
Order Ceramiales								
Family Ceramiaceae								
Centroceras sp.		×						
Sphyridia filamentosa						×		
Wrangelia sp.								
Family Delesseriaceae								
Caloglossa leprieurii		×						
Caloglossa sp.					×			
Family Rhodomelaceae								
Acanthophora spicifera							×	
Bostrychia binderi						×	×	
B. montagnei		×						
B. tenella		×						
Bostrychia sp.					×			
Laurencia sp.								
Murrayella periclados		×						
Polysiphonia macrocarpa		×						
DIVISION CHRYSOPHYTA								
Class Xanthopyceae								
Order Heterosiphonales								
Family Vaucheriaceae								
Vaucheria sp.								

Continued

TABLE 8.1.   (*Continued*)

Species	North River	South Florida	Southwest Florida	Diet
PHYLUM PROTOZOA				
Subphylum Plasmodroma				
Class Sarcodina				
Subclass Rhizopoda				
Order Foraminiferida				
Family Rzehakinidae				
Milammina fusca		×		
Family Lituolidae				
Ammoastuta inepta		×		
Halophragmoides wilberti		×		
Family Trochamminidae				
Arenoparella mexicana		×		
Trochammina inflata		×		
Subphylum Ciliophora				
Class Ciliata				
Subclass Holotricha				
Order Gymnostomatida				
Suborder Rhabdophorina				
Family Holophyridae				
Prorodon sp.		×		Ciliates, flagellates
Lacrynaria sp.		×		Ciliates
Mesodinium pupula		×		
Order Hymenstomatida				
Suborder Tetrahymenina				
Family Ophryoglenidae				
Frontonia marina		×		Diatoms
Uronema sp.		×		Bacteria
Family Philasteridae				
Helicostoma sp.		×		Dead metazoa
Suborder Pleuronematidae				
Family Pleuronematidae				
Pleuronema sp.		×		Bacteria
Cyclidium sp.		×		Bacteria
Subclass Spirotricha				
Order Heterotrichida				
Family Bursariidae				
Condylostoma sp.		×		Ciliates
Family Spirostomatidae				
Parablepharisma pellitum		×		Sulfur bacteria
Family Peritromidae				
Peritromus sp.		×		Bacteria
Order Oligotrichida				
Family Helteriidae				

TABLE 8.1. (*Continued*)

Species	North River	South Florida	Southwest Florida	Diet
Strombidium sp.	×			Bacteria
Order Tintinnida				
Tintinnopsis sp.			×	
Order Hypotrichida				
Family Oxytrichidae				
Holosticha sp.	×			Bacteria
Family Euplotidae				
Uronychia transfuga	×			Ciliates
Aspidisca sp.	×			Bacteria
PHYLUM CHAETOGNATHA				
Sagitta hispida	×			
PHYLUM ANNELIDA				
Class Polychaeta				
Order Phyllodocida				
Suborder Nereidiformia				
Family Nereidae				
Nereis pelagica	×			Detritus, algae, small crustaceans
Nereis succinea	×			Detritus, algae, small crustaceans
PHYLUM MOLLUSCA				
Class Gastropoda				
Subclass Prosobranchiata				
Order Archaeogastropoda				
Suborder Pleurotomariinae				
Family Fissurellidae				
Diodora cayenensis		×	×	
Order Mesogastropoda				
Family Littorinidae				
Littorina angulifera		×	×	
L. scabra angulifera			×	
Family Turritellidae				
Turritella sp.		×	×	
Family Potamidae				
Cerithidea scalariformis		×		
Family Crepidulidae				
Crepidula acuelata			×	
C. plana		×	×	
Family Cypraeidae				
Cypraea sp.		×	×	
Order Neogastropoda				
Family Muricidae				

Continued

TABLE 8.1. (*Continued*)

Species	North River	South Florida	Southwest Florida	Diet
Urosalpinx perrugata		×	×	
Family Columbellidae				
Anchis semiplicata		×	×	
Family Buccinidae				
Pisiana tincta				
Family Melongenidae				
Melongena corona				
Family Turritellidae				
Turritella sp.				
Subclass Ophisthobranchiata				
Order Cephalispidea				
Family Bullidae				
Bulla striata		×	×	
Family Haminoeidae				
Haminoea elegans				
Order Basommatophora				
Family Melamplidae				
Melampus coffeus		×		
Order Aplysiacea				
Family Aplysidae				
Aplysia willcoxi			×	
Class Bivalvia				
Subclass Pteriomorpha				
Order Arcoida				
Arca imbricata Bruguiere				
Barbatia candida Helbling				
Order Mytilioda				
Family Mytilidae				
Brachiodontes exustus	×	×	×	Algae, detritus
Lithophaga bisculcata			×	
Musculus lateralis				
Order Pterioida				
Suborder Pteriina				
Family Ostreidae				
Ostrea frons			×	
Crassostrea virginica	×	×	×	
Subclass Heterodonta				
Order Veneroida ·				
Family Lasaeidae				
Lasea adansoni Gmelin				
Family Carditidae				
Carditamera floridana				
Family Dreissensiidae				

TABLE 8.1. (*Continued*)

Species	North River	South Florida	Southwest Florida	Diet
Mytilopsis (= *Congeria*) *leucophaeata*	×	×		Detritus, algae
Order Myoida				
Family Pholadidae				
Martesia striata		×	×	
PHYLUM ARTHROPODA				
Subphylum Mandibulata				
Class Crustacea				
Subclass Copepoda				
Order Calanoida				
Family Pontellidae				
Labidocera sp.		×		Phytoplankton, detritus, epiphytic diatoms
Family Acartiidae				
Acartia sp.		×		Phytoplankton, detritus, epiphytic diatoms
Acartia tonsa			×	Phytoplankton, detritus, epiphytic diatoms
Order Cyclopoida				
Family Cyclopidae				
Cyclops sp.		×		Phytoplankton, detritus, epiphytic diatoms
Subclass Cirripedia				
Suborder Balanomorpha				
Family Balanidae				
Balanus eburneus			×	
Subclass Malacostraca				
Division Peracarida				
Order Mysidacea				
Suborder Mysida				
Family Mysidae				
Mysidopsis almyra		×		Diatoms, detritus, copepods
M. bahia		×		Diatoms, detritus, copepods, dead amphipods
Taphromysis bowmani				
Gastrosaccus dissimilis				
Order Cumacea				
Family Bodotriidae				
Cyclaspis varians		×		Detritus, diatoms
Family Diastylidae				
Oxyuristylis sp.		×		
Order Tanaidacea				
Suborder Dikonophora				
Family Paratanaidae				*Continued*

TABLE 8.1.   (*Continued*)

Species	North River	South Florida	Southwest Florida	Diet
Leptochelia sp.	×			Detritus, diatoms
Order Isopoda				
Suborder Flabellifera				
Family Limnoriidae				
Limnoria sp.	×			Algae, detritus
Family Sphaeromidae				
Sphaeroma terebrans			×	
Suborder Onsicidea				
Infraorder Ligiamorpha				
Group Diplocheta				
Family Ligiidae				
Ligia exotica				
Order Amphipoda				
Suborder Gammaridea				
Family Ampithoidae				
Cymadusa compta	×			
Family Aoridae				
Grandidierella bonnieri	×			Detritus, microorganisms
Family Corophiidae				
Corophium lacustre	×	×		Detritus, microorganisms
Family Gammaridae				
Elasmopus sp.	×			
Gammarus mucronatus	×			
Melita nitida	×	×		Detritus, mangrove leaves, bacteria, protozoa
Division Eucarida				
Order Decapoda				
Suborder Reptantia				
Section Astacura				
Family Astacidae				
Procambarus alleni				
Section Anomura				
Family Porcellanidae				
Petrolisthes armatus			×	
Suborder Natantia				
Section Penaeidae				
Family Penaeidae				
Penaeus duorarum	×	×		Harpacticoid copepods, algae, bacteria, detritus, diatoms, ostracods, small molluscs
Section Caridea				
Family Alpheidae				
Synalpheus fritmuelleri			×	

TABLE 8.1. (*Continued*)

Species	North River	South Florida	Southwest Florida	Diet
Alpheus heterochaelis	×	×		Detritus, copepods, amphipods
Family Palaemonidae				
Palaemonetes intermedius	×	×		Detritus, ostracods, amphipods, copepods, chironomid larvae, snails, protozoa, fungi, microalgae
P. paludosus Gibbes	×			Microalgae, detritus, ostracods, amphipods, copepods, chironomid larvae, snails, protozoa, fungi
P. pugio	×			Algae, plant fragments (Kawanabe et al., unpublished manuscript, *Spartina* marshes of Georgia)
Periclimenes americanus	×			
P. longicaudatus				
Palaemon floridanus				
Section Brachyura				
Subsection Branchygnatha				
Infrasection Oxystomata				
Infrasubsection Brachyrhynca				
Family Xanthidae				
Eurytium limosum			×	
Panopeus occidentalis			×	
Eurypanopeus depressus			×	
Neopanope texana			×	
Menippe mercenaria			×	
Rhithropanopeus harrisii	×	×	×	Detritus, crustaceans, diatoms, algae
Family Portunidae				
Callinectes sapidus	×	×	×	Mussels, *Rhithropanopeus*, amphipods, fish, detritus
Family Ocypodidae				
Ocypode quadrata			×	
Uca pugilator			×	
U. speciosa			×	
U. thayeri			×	
Family Grapsidae				
Sesarma curacaoense		×	×	

Continued

TABLE 8.1.   (Continued)

Species	North River	South Florida	Southwest Florida	Diet
S. reritulatum			×	
Aratus pisonii				
Subphylum Chelicerata				
Class Insecta				
Subclass Pterygota				
Division Endopterygota				
Order Diptera				
Suborder Nematocera				
Family Chironomidae				
Cricotopus sp.		×		Plants, detritus, fungi, bacteria, protozoa
Chironomis sp.		×		Plants, detritus, fungi, bacteria, protozoa
Chironomis decorus		×		
PHYLUM CHORDATA				
Subphylum Vertebrata				
Class Chondrichthyes				
Order Squaliformes				
Family Orectolobidae				
Ginglymostoma cirratum (nurse shark)				Fish, cephalopods, molluscs, shrimp, sea urchins
Family Carcharhinidae				
Carchartinus leucas (bull shark)		×		The fish, *Galeichtys felis*; the shrimp, *Penaeus duorum*; the fish, *Lophogobius cyprinoides*; juveniles: fish (*Arius felis, Lophogobius Mugil cephalus, Brevoortia patronus, Micropogon undulatus*) crustaceans, including penaeid shrimp, blue crabs
C. limbatus (blacktip shark)				Fish: *Caranx* sp., *Centropomus undecimalis, Chilomycterus schoepfi, Arius felis, Lactophrys trigonnus, Lagodon rhomboides*; crabs
Negaprion brevirostris (lemon shark)				Young: crustaceans, fish; adults: fish, crustaceans
Family Sphyrnidae				
Sphyrna tiburo (bonnethead)				Mantis shrimp, shrimp, isopods barnacles,

TABLE 8.1. (*Continued*)

Species	North River	South Florida	Southwest Florida	Diet
				bivalve molluscs, cephalopods, fish
Order Rajiformes				
Family Pristidae				
Pristis pectinata				Fish, benthic crustaceans
(smalltooth sawfish)				
Family Rhinobatidae				
Rhinobatos lentiginosus				
(Atlantic guitarfish)				
Family Torpedinidae				
Narcine brasiliensis				
(lesser electric ray)				
Family Rajidae				
Raja texana				Crustacea, fish, annelids
(roundel skate)				
Family Dasyatidae				
Dasyatis americana				Fishes, sipunculid and
(southern stingray)				polychaete worms, crabs, bivalves, shrimp, mantis shrimp
D. sabina				Benthic invertebrates,
(Atlantic stingray)				including bivalves, xanthid and portunid crabs, shrimps, amphipods, annelids, chironomid larvae
Gymnura micrura				Fish, molluscs, annelids,
(smooth butterfly ray)				shrimp, other small crustaceans
Urolophus jamaicensis				Probably small burrowing
(yellow stingray)				invertebrates
Family Myliobatidae				
Aetobatus narinari				Clams, oysters
(spotted eagle ray)				
Class Osteichthyes				
Order Semionotiformes				
Family Lepisosteidae				
Lepisosteus platyrhincus			✕	Primarily the fish, *Gambusia*
(Florida gar)				*affinis*, and the shrimp, *Paleomenetes paludosus*; also the fish, *Lucania goodei, Jordanella floridae, Heterandia*

Continued

TABLE 8.1.   (*Continued*)

Species	North River	South Florida	Southwest Florida	Diet
				formosa, Poecilia latipinna; chironomid larvae; dragonfly and damsel nymphs
Order Elopiformes Family Elopidae				
Elops saurus (lady fish)	×	×		Copepods, caridean shrimp, small fish such as *Poecilia latipinna, Eucinostomus gula, Menidia beryllina, Anchoa hepsetus*; zooplankton, including chaetognaths, polychaete worms; penaeid shrimp
Megalops atlantica (tarpon)	×	×		The fish, *Gambusia*; ostracods; the shrimp, *Palaemontetes*; the fish, *Fundulus heteroclitus*; *Mugil cephalus* (Rickards, 1968, Georgia marshes); copepods, crabs, ctenophores (Randall, 1967), insects
Family Albulidae				
Albula vulpes (bonefish)				Clams, snails, shrimp, small fish
Order Anguilliformes Family Anguillidae				
Anguilla rostrata (American eel)	×			*Rhithropanopeus, Palaemonetes intermedius, Alpheus heterochaelis* and *Lophogobius cyprinoides*, amphipods, isopods, xanthid crabs, caridean shrimp
Family Ophichthidae				
Myrophis punctatus (speckled worm eel)				Polychaetes, *Branchiostoma caribeum*, sand crabs
Bascanichthys scuticaris (whip eel)				
Ophichthus gomesi (shrimp eel)				
Order Clupeiformes Family Clupeidae				

TABLE 8.1. (*Continued*)

Species	North River	South Florida	Southwest Florida	Diet
Brevoortia smithi (yellowfin sardine)				
B. patronus (gulf maidenhead)				Phytoplankton, zooplankton, plant fragments, detritus, organic matter, silt, diatoms, foraminiferans, copepods
Harengula pensacolae (scaled sardine)	×			Amphipods, mysids, chironomid larvae, isopods, copepods, zoea, nauplii, larval fish
Opisthonema oglinum (Atlantic thread herring)	×			Copepods, polychaetes, shrimp, fishes, crab larvae, mysids
Sardinella aurita (= *S. anchovia*) (Spanish sardine) Family Engraulidae				
Anchoa cubana (Cuban anchovy)				Ostracods, copepods
A. hepsetus (striped anchovy)				Copepods, isopods, mysids, caridean shrimp, small bivalves
A. lamprotaenia (bigeye anchovy)				
A. mitchilli (bay anchovy)	×			Microzooplankton such as copepods, copepodites, nauplii; also mysids and ostracods, amphipods, plant detritus, small molluscs chironomid larvae
Order Myctophiformes Family Synodontidae				
Synodus foetens (inshore lizardfish)				Small fish, crabs, shrimps, polychaete worms
Order Cypriniformes Family Catastomidae				
Erimyzson sucetta (lake chubsucker) Order Siluriformes Family Ictaluridae				
Ictalurus natalis (yellow bullhead)				

Continued

TABLE 8.1. (*Continued*)

Species	North River	South Florida	Southwest Florida	Diet
Noturus gyrinus (tadpole madtom) Family Ariidae				
Arius felis (sea catfish)	×			*Rhithropanopeus harrisii;* amphipods; mysids; fish; nematodes; crayfish; dragonfly larvae; tarpon and other fish scales; adult insects; the mollusc, *Brachiodontes exustus;* isopods, algae, the shrimp, *Penaeus duorarum;* *Paleomonetes* spp. and *Alpheus heterochaelis;* amphipods; chironomid larvae; crabs; copepods; zooplankton, benthic invertebrates; bark
Bagre marinus (gafftopsail catfish) Order Batrachoidiformes Family Batrachoididae	×	×		*Callinectes sapidus,* fish blue crabs
Opsanus beta (gulf toadfish)	×	×		Amphipods; chironomid larvae; mysids; isopods; shrimp, including *Paleomonetes* sp.; crabs, including *Rhithropanopeus* *heterochaelis;* fish; mangrove bark; mussels
Porichthys plectrodon (= *P. porosissimus*) (Atlantic midshipman) Order Gobiesociformes Family Gobiosocidae				
Gobiesox strumosus (skilletfish) Order Lophiiformes Family Ogcocephalidae	×		×	Amphipods, isopods, chironomid larvae
Ogcocephalus nasutus (shortnose batfish)				Small bivalves, gastropods, polychaetes
O. radiatus (polka-dot batfish) Order Gadiformes Family Gadidae				

TABLE 8.1. (*Continued*)

Species	North River	South Florida	Southwest Florida	Diet
Urophycis floridana (southern hake)				Amphipods; isopods; mysids; decapod shrimp; polychaetes; insect larvae; fishes, *Lagodon rhomboides* and *Paralichthyes albigutta*
Family Ophidiidae *Gunterichthys longipennis* (gold brotula)				
Ogilbia cayorum (key brotula)				
Ophidion holbrooki (bank cusk-eel)				
Order Atheriniformes Family Exocoetidae *Chriodorus atherinoides* (hardhead halfbreak)				
Hyporhampus unifasciatus (halfbreak)				Juveniles: zooplankton, including crab megalops, veligers, copepods; adults: epiphytic algae detritus, seagrass
Family Belonidae *Strongylura marina* (Atlantic needlefish)	×			Small fishes, insects, shrimp, small amounts of vascular plant material and algae
S. notata (redfin needlefish)	×			Juveniles: polychaete worms, cumaceans, fish; adults: primarily atherinids
S. timucu (timucu)				Anchovies, shrimp
Tylosurus crocodilus (houndfish)				Fishes, shrimp
Family Cyprinodontidae *Adinia xenica* (diamond killifish)	×	×		Detritus, algae, amphipods, terrestrial insects, copepods, diatoms
Cyprinodon variegatus (sheepshead minnow)	×	×	×	Detritus, algae, a few copepods and amphipods, diatoms, nematodes, small crustaceans

Continued

TABLE 8.1.   (Continued)

Species	North River	South Florida	Southwest Florida	Diet
Floridichthys carpio (goldspotted killifish)	×		×	Detritus, small amphipods, chironomid larvae, *Neanthes*, copepods, isopods, nematodes, ostracods, diatoms, algae
Fundulus confluentus (marsh killifish)	×	×		Chironomid larvae, amphipods, adult and larval insects, small bivalve molluscs, a few isopods, algal filaments, ostracods, mysids, copepods, small fish (*Gambusia affinis*), caridean shrimp
Fundulus chrysotus (golden topminnow)				
F. grandis (gulf killifish)	×	×		Amphipods; isopods; *Rhithropanopeus*; chironomid larvae; terrestrial insects; small snails; filaments of algae; fish, including *Gambusia affinis*; xanthid crabs
Fundulus heteroclitus (mummichog)				Small crustaceans: amphipods, isopods, ostracods, tanaids, copepod detritus; polychaete worms; insects; snails; invertebrate eggs
F. seminolis (Seminole killifish)				
Jordanella floridae (flagfish)				
Lucania goodei (bluefin killlfish)	×			Copepods, cladocerans, ostracods and chironomid larvae, other insect larvae
L. parva (rainwater killifish)	×	×		Planktonic copepods, amphipods, mysids, chironomid larvae, terrestrial insects, small molluscs, detritus, copepods, cumaceans, ostracods

TABLE 8.1. (*Continued*)

Species	North River	South Florida	Southwest Florida	Diet
Rivulus marmoratus (rivulus)	×			
Family Poecilidae				
Gambusia affinis (mosquitofish)	×	×		Amphipods, animal material, *Hydracarina*, algae, chironomid larvae, small insects, copepods, small snails, ants, adult insects, *Neanthes*, ostracods, mosquito pupae, polychaete worms, hydracarina
G. rhizophorae (mangrove gambusia)				
Heterandria formosa (least killifish)	×			Chironomid larvae, harpacticoid and planktonic copepods, filamentous algae cladocerans, terrestrial insects, algae and diatoms
Poecilia latipinna (sailfin molly)	×	×	×	Vascular plant detritus, inorganic particles, algae and diatoms
Family Atherinidae				
Hypoatherina harringtonensis (= *Allanetta harringtonensis*) (reef silversides)				Copepods, fish larvae, polychaete larvae
Membras martinica (rough silversides)				Small zooplankton crustaceans, juvenile and larval fishes, insects, detritus, snails
Menidia beryllina				Night: mysids, amphipods, chironomid larvae, harpacticoid copepods, algae; day: terrestrial insects, copepods, chironomid larvae, *Hydracarina*, algae, amphipods, ostracods, zooplankton
Order Gasterosteiformes Family Sygnathidae				

Continued

TABLE 8.1.   (*Continued*)

Species	North River	South Florida	Southwest Florida	Diet
Cosmocampus albirostris (= *Corythoichthys albirostris*) whitenose pipefish)				
Hippocampus erectus (lined seahorse)				
H. zosterae (dwarf seahorse)				
Micrognathus criniger (fringed pipefish)				Copepods, microcrustaceans
Syngnathus floridae (dusky pipefish)				Caridean shrimp, amphipods, tanaids, isopods
S. louisianae Gunther (chain pipefish)				Copepods, amphipods, small shrimp
S. scovelli (gulf pipefish)				Amphipods, isopods, tanaids, copepods, tiny caridean shrimp, gastropods (*Bittium, Mitrella*)
S. springeri (bull pipefish)				
S. dunckeri (pugnose pipefish)				
S. pelagicus (sargassum pipefish) Order Perciformes Family Centropomidae				
Centropomus parallelus (fat snook)				
C. pectinatus (tarpon snook)	×			Fish, such as *Eucinostomus* sp., *Mugil cephalus Lagadon rhomboides, Anchoa* spp., *Poecilia latipinna*, and *Gambusia affinis*; caridean and penaeid shrimp; crabs and crayfish
C. undecimalis (snook)	×	×		Juveniles: caridean shrimp, small cyprinodont fishes, gobies, mojarras; adults: fish, crabs, penaid shrimp, crayfish, snapping shrimp
Family Serrandidae *Centropristis striata* (black seabass)				Carnivorous on fish, crustaceans

TABLE 8.1.   (*Continued*)

Species	North River	South Florida	Southwest Florida	Diet
Diplectrum formosum (sand perch)				Caridean and penaeid shrimp, copepods, crabs, fish
Epinephelus itajara (jewfish)	×	×		Shrimp such as *Penaeus duorarum*; *Rhithropanopeus* Crustaceans, crabs, fishes
E. morio (red grouper)				
E. striatus (nassa grouper)				Fish, crabs, stomatopods, cephalopods, shrimp, spiny lobsters, gastropods, bivalves, isopods
Hypoplectrus unicolar (= *H. puella*) (barred hamlet)				Snapping shrimp, crabs, fish, mysids, stomatopods, isopods
Mycteroperca microlepis (gag) Family Centrarchidae				Penaeid shrimp, fish
Elassoma everygladei (Everglades pygmy fish)				
Lepomis auritus (redbrcast sunfish)				
L. gulosus (warmouth)		×		Shrimp (*Paleomenetes*) fish (*Gobieosoma bosci*, *Lepomis macrochirus*), detritus, *Vallisneria*, amphipods, xanthid crabs, blue crabs
Lepomis macrochirus (bluegill)				Amphipods, blue crab (*Callinectes sapidus*), xanthid crabs, detritus, *Vallisneria*, clams (*Rangia cuneata*), sponge (*Ephydatia fluviatilis*), barnacles, insect larvae
L. microlophus (redear sunfish)		×		Chironomid larvae, amphipods, xanthid crabs, detritus *Vallisneria*, clams (*Rangia cuneata*), sponge (*Ephydatia fluviatilis*), barnacles, insect larvae
L. punctatus (spotted sunfish)		×		Cladocerans, insects, chironomid larvae,

(Continued)

TABLE 8.1.   (*Continued*)

Species	North River	South Florida	Southwest Florida	Diet
				isopods, amphipods, small molluscs, hydracarina, adult insects, algae, *Rithropanopeus harrisii*, mysids, fish
Micropterus salmoides (largemouth bass) Family Apogonidae				Caridean shrimp, small blue crabs, crayfish, xanthid crabs, 25 species of fish, *Vallisneria*, *Cladophora*
Astropogon alutus (bronze cardinalfish) *A. stellatus* (conchfish) Family Pomatomidae				
Pomatomus saltatrix (bluefish)				Young—mainly fishes— anchovies, silversides, killifishes, menhaden, shad, spotted sea trout; shrimp, crabs, other small crustaceans, annelids, snails
Family Rachycentridae *Rachycentron canadum* (cobia)				Fish, crabs
Family Echeneidae *Echeneis neucratoides* (whitefin sharksucker)				Fish, isopods, other crustacea
Remora remora (remora) Family carangidae				Copepods, isopods, vertebrate muscle tissue, crab larvae fish remains, crustaceans, amphipods
Caranx crysos (blue runner)				
C. hippos (crevalle jack)		×	×	Penaeid shrimp, fishes, crustaceans
C. latus (horse-eye jack)				Predaceous on other fishes
C. ruber (bar jack)				Fish, shrimp, mysids, stomatopods, gastropods
Chloroscombrus chrysurus (Atlantic bumper)				
Oligoplites saurus (leatherjacket)		×		*Paleomenetes* sp., penaeid shrimp, snapping shrimp, larval anchovies, ladyfish, harpacticoid copepods

TABLE 8.1. (*Continued*)

Species	North River	South Florida	Southwest Florida	Diet
Trachinotus carolinus (Florida pompano)				Sardines (*Harengula* sp.), mole crabs (*Hippa* sp.), bivalves (*Donax* sp.)
T. falcatus (permit)				Mysids, shrimp, anchovies, silversides, crabs, snails
Selene vomer (lookdown)				Young: shrimp and other crustaceans, small molluscs
Hemicaranx amblyrhynchus (bluntnose jack) Family Lutjanidae				
Lutjanus analis (mutton snapper)				Crabs, fish, gastropods, octopods, hermit crabs, penaeid shrimp, spiny lobster stomatopods
L. apodus (schoolmaster)				Crustaceans (shrimp, snapping shrimp, blue crabs, xanthid crabs, grapsid crabs), fish
L. griseus (gray snapper)		×	×	Day: *Rhithropanopeus* *harrisii; Alpheus* *heterochaelis;* *Paleomenetes* sp.; fish, including *Lophogobius* *cyprinoides, Microgobius* *gulosus, Anchoa hepsetus,* *A. mitchilli, Gambusia* *affinis, Poecilia latipinna,* *Fundulus grandis,* and *Anguilla rostrata;* night: *R. harrisii; Alpheus* *heterochaelis;* fish, *Paleomonetes,* *Procambarus alleni,* and *P. duorarum;* young live in grass beds feeding on small crustaceans and insect larvae
L. jocu (dog snapper)				Fish, crabs, octopods, spiny lobster, gastropods
L. synagris (lane snapper)				Snapping shrimp, crabs, anchovies, annelids, molluscs

Continued

TABLE 8.1.   (*Continued*)

Species	North River	South Florida	Southwest Florida	Diet
Family Gerreidae				
Diapterus auratus (= *D. olisthostomus* (Irish pompano)				Green algae (*Enteromorpha flexuosa, Cladophora*), *Ruppia maritima*, blue-green algae (*Lyngba majuscula*)
D. plumieri (striped mojarra)	×	×		Mysids, amphipods, copepods, chironomid larvae, ostracods, bivalves, and detritus
Eucinostomus argenteus (spotfin mojarra)	×			Amphipods, harpacticoid copepods, chrionomid larvae, small molluscs, detritus, ostracods, mysids
E. gula (silver jenny)	×	×		Amphipods, harpacticoid copepods, chironomid larvae, mysids, ostracods, small molluscs, detritus
E. lefroyi (mottled mojarra)				
Gerres cinereus (yellowfin mojarra) Family Pomadasyidae				Crabs, bivalves, gastropods, polychaete worms, shrimp, ostracods
Anisotremus virginicus (porkfish)				Brittle stars, crabs, shrimp, polychaetes, isopods, bivalves, stomatopods, gastropods
Haemulon aurolineatum (tomtate)				Shrimp and shrimp larvae, polychaetes, hermit crabs, amphipods, copepods gastropods, bivalves
H. carbonarium (caesar grunt)				Crabs, gastropods, sea urchins, chitons, polychaetes, brittle stars, sipunculid worms, shrimp
Haemulon flavolineatum (French grunt)				Polychaetes, crabs, sipunculid worms, chitons, holothurians, isopods, shrimp, bivalves
H. parrai (sailor's choice)				Benthic invertebrates, including shrimp, crabs, amphipods, gastropods, polychaete worms, bivalves

TABLE 8.1. (*Continued*)

Species	North River	South Florida	Southwest Florida	Diet
H. plumieri (white grunt)				Crabs, polychaetes, sea urchins, sipunculid worms, gastropods, shrimp, brittle stars; juveniles: copepods, mysids
H. album (margate)				Benthic invertebrates, including crabs, shrimp, polychaetes, amphipods, copepods, snails, bivalves
H. sciurus (bluestriped grunt)				Benthic invertebrates, including crustaceans, molluscs, annelid worms
Orthopristis chrysoptera (pigfish)				Juveniles: plankton, including copepods, mysids, postlarval shrimp; adults: polychaetes, shrimp, amphipods
Family Sparidae *Archosargus probatocephalus* (sheepshead)	×	×	×	*Congeria leucophaeta*, *Branchiodontes exustus*, *Rithropanopeus*, algae, detritus, *Alpheus heterochaelis*, *Anomalocardia cunimeris*, *Procambarius alleni*, copepods, amphipods, chironomid larvae, mysids, molluscs, mussels, false mussels, crabs, hydrazoans
Archosargus rhomboidalis (sea bream)				Seagrasses (*Cymodocea* and *Thalassia*) algae, crabs, gastropods, invertebrate eggs, bivalves
Calamus arctifrons (grass porgy)				Copepods, amphipods, mysids, shrimp, bivalves, gastropods (*Mitrella*, *Bittum*), polychaetes
C. calamus (saucereye porgy)				Polychaetes, brittle stars, bivalves, hermit crabs, sea urchins, gastropods, chitons

Continued

TABLE 8.1. (*Continued*)

Species	North River	South Florida	Southwest Florida	Diet
Logodon rhomboides (pinfish)	×		×	*Brachiodontes exustus*, mysids, amphipods, *Congeria leucophaeta*, scorched mussels, false mussel
Family Sciaenidae				
Bairdiella batabana (blue croaker)				
B. chrysura (silver perch)		×	×	Copepods, larval fish (*Menidia beryllina*, *Anchoa mitchilli*), mysids
Cynoscion arenarius (sand sea trout)				Mostly fish, caridean shrimp, mysids, amphipods, crab zoea
Cynoscion nebulosus (spotted sea trout)		×	×	Fish (*Anchoa mitchilli*, *Eucinostomus gula*, *E. argenteus*, *Mugil cephalus*, *Lagodon rhomboides*, *Cyprinodon variegatus*, *Gobiosoma robustum*), caridean shrimp, copepods, planktonic crustaceans
Leiostomus xanthurus (spot)				Planktonic organisms, filamentous algae, desmids, forams, amphipods, mysids, copepods, ostracods, isopods, chaetognaths, bivalves, snails, polychaet worms
Menticirrhus americanus (southern kingfish)				Fish, benthic crustaceans
M. littoralis (gulf kingfish)				Polychaetes, bivalves (*Donax*), sand crab (*Emerita*), razor clams
Micropogon undulatus (Atlantic croaker)				Juveniles: copepods, mysids, caridean shrimp, polychaete worms, insect larvae, isopods, small bivalves
Pogonias cromis (black drum)				Molluscs, xanthid crabs, bivalves amphipods, blue crabs, penaeid shrimp, caridean shrimp

TABLE 8.1. *(Continued)*

Species	North River	South Florida	Southwest Florida	Diet
Sciaenops ocellatus (red drum)	×	×		Crabs such as *Rithropanopeus*, chironomid larvae, mangrove bark, copepods, crab zoeae, larval fish, mysids, amphipods, *Palaemonetes intermedius*, copepods, caridean shrimp, xanthid and portunid crabs, penaeid shrimp, small fish
Equetus acuminatus (high-hat)				Shrimp and shrimp larvae, isopods, stomatopod larvae, copepods, amphipods
Family ephippidae *Chaetodipterus faber* (Atlantic spadefish)				Worms, crustaceans, debris
Family Pomacentridae *Abudefduf saxatilis* (sergeant major)				Copepods, algae, fish eggs, fish, shrimp larvae, polychaetes
Family Labridae *Halichoeres bivittatus* (slippery dick)				Crabs, sea urchins, polychaetes, gastropods, brittle stars, bivalves, shrimp, fish, hermit crabs
Family Scaridae *Nicholsina usta* (emerald parrotfish)				Family herbivorous, feeding primarily on algae growing on hard substrates, secondarily on seagrasses
Scarus coeruleus (*blue parrotfish*) *S. croicensis* (striped parrotfish) *Sparisoma chrysopterum* (redtail parrotfish) *S. rubripinne* (redfin parrotfish) *S. viride* (stoplight parrotfish) Family Mugilidae				

Continued

TABLE 8.1. (*Continued*)

Species	North River	South Florida	Southwest Florida	Diet
Mugil cephalus (striped mullet)	×	×		Benthic diatoms, filamentous algae, plant detritus, inorganic sediments, microalgae
M. curema (white mullet)				Plant detritus, blue-green algae (*Lyngbya majuscula*)
M. trichodon (*fantail mullet*) Family Sphyraenidae				
Sphyraena barracuda (great barracuda) Family Opistognathidae	×			Fish (*E. gula, M. berylinna, Archosargus*)
Opistognathus maxillosus (mottled jawfish) family clinidae				Shrimp, isopods, fishes, polychaetes, mysids, copepods
Chaenopsis ocellata (bluethrout pickleblenny)				Family appears to be carnivorous on benthic invertebrates
Paraclinus marmoratus (marbled blenny)				
P. fasciatus (banded blenny)				
Stathmonotus hemphilli (blackbelly blenny) Family Blenniidae				
Chasmodes saburrae (Florida blenny)				Amphipods, detritus, polychaetes, snails
Parablennius marmoreus (= *Blennius marmoreus*) (seaweed blenny)				Algae, organic detritus, brittle stars, polychaetes, hydroids
Lupinoblennius nicholsi (= *Blennius nicholsi*) (highfin blenny) Family Callionymidae				
Callionymus pauciradiatus (spotted dragnet) Family Eleotridae				
Dormitor maculatus (Fat sleeper) Family Gobiidae				
Bathygobius soporator (frillfin goby)	×	×	×	*Paleomenetes intermedius,* chironomids, amphipods, caridean shrimp
Gobionellus hastatus (sharptail goby)				Filamentous algae (*Enteromorpha*),

TABLE 8.1. (*Continued*)

Species	North River	South Florida	Southwest Florida	Diet
				ostracods, copepods, insect larvae
G. shufeldti (freshwater goby)				
G. smaragdus (emerald goby)		×		Filamentous algae (*Enteromorpha*), ostracods, copepods, insect larvae
Gobiosoma bosci (naked goby)				Small crustaceans, including amphipods; annelids; fish; fish eggs
G. longipala (twoscale goby)				
G. macrodon (tiger goby)				
G. robustum (code goby)		×	×	Amphipods, chironomid larvae, mysids, cladocerans, ostracods, small molluscs, algal filaments, plant detritus, cumaceans
Lophogobius cyprinoides (crested goby)		×	×	Amphipods, plant detritus, filamentous algae, mysids, caridean and penaeid shrimp, *Neanthes*, ostracods, small bivalves, chironomid larvae, harpacticoid copepods, isopods, *Rithropanopeus harrissii*, snails, polychaete worms.
Microgobius gulosus (clown goby)		×	×	Amphiods, harpacticoid copepods, chironomid larvae, cumaceans, cladocerans, algae, detritus, mysids, planktonic organisms
M. microlepis (banner goby)				
M. thalassinus (green goby) Family Scombridae				Small crustaceans, including amphipods; other invertebrates

Continued

TABLE 8.1.   (*Continued*)

Species	North River	South Florida	Southwest Florida	Diet
Scomberomorus maculatus (Spanish mackerel)				Adults feed on penaeid shrimp from tidal streams
S. cavalla (king mackerel)				Fish
Family Scorpaenidae				
Scorpaena brasiliensis (barbfish)				Shrimp, other crustaceans, fish
S. grandicornis (plumed scorpionfish)				Shrimp, fish, unidentified crustaceans
Family Triglidae				
Prionotus salmonicolor (blackwing sea robin)				
P. scitulus (leopard sea robin)				Small molluscs, shrimp, crabs, fish, small crustaceans (ostracods, cumaceans)
P. tribulus (bighead sea robin)	×			Shrimp, crabs, fishes, amphipods, copepods, annelids, bivalves, sea urchins
Order Pleuronectiformes				
Family Bothidae				
Bothus ocellatus (eyed flounder)				Fish, crabs, shrimp, amphipods
Citharichthys macrops (spotted whiff)				
C. spilopterus (bay whiff)				Mainly mysids; also, shrimp, crabs, isopods, amphipods, fishes, annelids
Etropus crossotus (fringed flounder)				Calanoid copepods, cumaceans, amphipods, mysids, shrimp, crabs, isopods, annelids, molluscs, fishes
Paralichthys albigutta (gulf flounder)				Small crustaceans, including amphipods; fish (pigfish, pinfish, lizardfish, bay anchovy, labrids); crustaceans
P. lethostigma (southern flounder)				Mainly fishes (mullet, menhaden, shad, anchovies, pinfish, mojarras, croakers), crabs,

TABLE 8.1. *(Continued)*

Species	North River	South Florida	Southwest Florida	Diet
				mysids, molluscs, penaeid shrimp, amphipods
Syacium papillosum (dusky flounder) Family Soleidae				
Achirus lineatus (lined sole)	×			Amphipods, mysids, chironomid larvae, *Nereis pelagica*, foraminifera, polychaete worms
Trinectes inscriptus (scrawled sole)				
T. maculatus (hogchoker) Family Cynoglossidae	×	×		Amphipods, mysids
Symphurus plagiusa (blackcheek tonguefish)				Polychaete worms, ostracods, portunid crabs, *ruppia* and *Halodule* plant tips
Family Balistidae				
Aluterus schoepfi (orange filefish)				Seagrasses, algae, hermit crabs, gastropods
Balistes vetula (queen triggerfish)				Sea urchins, crabs, bivalves, brittle stars, polychaetes, hermit crabs, gastropods, algae
Monacanthus ciliatus (fringed filefish)				Algae, organic detritus, seagrass copepods, shrimp and shrimp larvae, amphipods, hermit crabs, molluscs, algae, sea urchins
M. hispidus (plain head filefish)				Detritus, bryozoans, annelids, harpacticoid copepods, amphipods, hermit crabs, molluscs, algae, sea urchins
Balistes capriscus (= *B. vetula*) (gray triggerfish) Family Ostraciidae				
Lactophrys quadracornis (scrawled cowfish)				Vegetation, algae, bivalves
L. trigonus (trunkfish)				Crabs, bivalves, polychaetes, sea urchins, algae,

Continued

TABLE 8.1.   (*Continued*)

Species	North River	South Florida	Southwest Florida	Diet
				seagrass, gastropods, amphipods
L. triqueter (smooth trunkfish)				Polychaetes, sipunculid worms, crabs, shrimp, gastropods, hermit crabs, sea urchins, bivalves
Family Tetraodontidae				
Sphoeroides nephelus (southern puffer)				Juveniles: detritus, fecal pellets, zooplankton, polychaetes, gastropods, crabs, shrimp; adults: small crabs, bivalves
S. spengleri (bandtail puffer)				Crabs, bivalves, snails, polychaetes, amphipods, shrimp
S. testudineus (checkered puffer)				Portunid megalops larvae, gastropods
Family Diodontidae				
Chilomycterus antennatus (bridled burrfish)				Gastropods, hermit crabs, isopods, crabs, shrimp
C. antillarum (web burrfish)				
C. schoepfi (striped burrfish)				Gastropods, barnacles, crabs, amphipods

Source: Holm, 1978.

Prop Root and Associated Mud Surface Communities

Algae. The aerial root systems of mangroves provide a convenient substrate for attachment of algae. These root–algal communities are particularly noticeable on red mangrove (*Rhizophora mangle*) roots, but also occur to a lesser extent on black mangrove (*Avicennia nitida*) pneumatophores located in the intertidal zone. Four phyla tend to dominate these algal prop root associations: Chlorophyta, Cyanophyta, Phaeophyta, and Rhodophyta, the last of which is usually more important in terms of biomass (Odum et al., 1982).

The following zonation of algae comes largely from Taylor (1960). Near the high-water mark, a green band usually exists which is dominated by species of *Rhizoclonium*. Below this is a zone dominated by species of the red algae, *Bostrychia*, *Catenella*, and *Caloglossa*. At brackish or nearly freshwater sites, these species are replaced by species of the green algae, *Batophora*, *Chaetomorpha*, *Cladophora*, and *Penicillus*. The pneumatophores of the black mangrove, *Avicennia*, when colonized, are often covered with species of the green algae, *Rhizoclonium* and *Monostroma*, and *Bostrychia*, a red alga (Taylor, 1960).

If there is a permanently submerged portion of the prop root, it may be covered with rich growths of the red algae, *Acanthophora*, *Spyrida*, *Hypnea*, *Laurencia*, and *Wrangelia*, and the green algae, *Valonia* and *Caulerpa*. In addition, anywhere on the moist sections of the prop roots there are epiphytic diatoms and filamentous green and blue–green algae of many genera (Odum et al., 1982).

Rehm (1974, in Odum et al., 1982) found a significant difference in the prop root algae between south and central Florida. South of Tampa Bay the standard red algal association of *Bostrychia–Catenella–Caloglossa* dominates. In the Tampa Bay area species of the orders Ulotrichales and Cladophorales are dominant.

The mud adjacent to the mangrove root community hosts a variety of algae. These can include species of the green algae, *Cladophoropsis*, *Enteromorpha*, *Vaucheria*, and *Boodleopsis* (Taylor, 1960), in addition to many benthic diatoms and dinoflagellates and other filamentous green and blue–green algae (Odum et al., 1982).

Invertebrates. The prop root and mud communities are considered together because of the large number of mobile organisms which move back and forth between tidal cycles. The aerial roots are used as a protective habitat, while nearby mud substrates are used principally for feeding.

The prop roots essentially contain two zones: an upper zone dominated by barnacles and a lower zone dominated by mussels, oysters, and ascidians. Between mean high tide and mean tide, the wood boring isopod, *Sphaeroma terebrans*, is important, both numerically and for providing numerous holes for use by other organisms.

The most complete study of the Florida mangrove prop root community is Courtney's (1975) comparison of seawall and mangrove associations. The invertebrates from mangrove prop roots at Marco Island, Florida include the gastropods, *Littorina angulifera*, *Crepidula plana*, *Diodora cayenensis*, *Urosalpinx perrugata*, and *Pisania tincta*; the bivalves, *Crassostrea virginica* and *Brachiodontes exustus*; nine species of polychaetes; the isopod, *Sphaeroma terebrans*; the shrimp, *Palaemon floridanus*, *Periclimenes longicaudatus*, *Synalpheus fritzmuelleri*, and *Thor floridanus*; the crab, *Petrolisthes armatus*, and at least eight other species of crabs. Species found only on mangrove roots and not on seawalls include the gastropods, *Turitella* sp., *Melongena corona*, *Anachis semiplicata*, and *Bulla striata*; the bivalves, *Arca imbricata* and *Carditamera floridana*; the nudibranch, *Hypselodcris* sp.; the wood-boring mollusc, *Martesia striata*; and *Pseudoirus typica* (Courtney, 1975).

Crabs that exploit the intertidal muds from the safety of burrows include *Uca pugilator*, *U. speciosa*, *U. thayeri*, and *Eurytium limosum* (Tabb et al., 1962, in Odum et al., 1982). In low-salinity mangrove forests of south Florida, the crayfish, *Procambarus alleni*, is a dominant member of the burrowing community, as is the crab, *Rhithropanopeus harrisii* (Odum and Heald, 1972). Both organisms are found in a remarkable number of fish stomachs.

It is most likely that prop root communities vary somewhat from site to site in response to a number of factors, including latitude, salinity, and proximity to other communities, such as seagrass beds and coral reefs. Consequently, further studies in mangrove areas other than south Florida are warranted.

Arboreal Communities

A surprising variety of arthropods inhabit the mangrove canopy. They are involved in direct herbivory on mangrove leaves, predator–prey interactions, and biomass export (Odum et al., 1982). The dominant group of arboreal arthropods is insects. Simberloff and Wilson (1969) and Simberloff (1976) list over 200 species of insects associated with overwash mangrove islands in the Florida Keys.

Aratus pisonii, the mangrove tree crab, is not as numerically abundant as the insects, but appears to be potentially as important in terms of grazing impact. Other invertebrates that may visit the canopy from below either for purposes of feeding or for protection from high tides include *Littorina angulifera*, *Cerithidea scalariformis*, and *Melampus coffeus*; the isopod, *Ligea exotica*; and a host of small crabs (Odum et al., 1982).

Water Column Communities

All aspects of phytoplankton, from seasonal occurrence to productivity, have been studied in mangrove ecosystems. This is particularly true in Florida. The same is true for the zooplankton. Generally, standing crops of net phytoplankton in mangrove areas are low (Odum et al., 1982). This part of the phytoplankton is usually dominated by diatoms such as *Thalassothrix* spp., *Chaetoceras* spp., *Nitzschia* spp., *Skeletonema* spp., and *Rhizosolenia* spp.

Zooplankton near mangroves are probably no different from those found in other shallow, inshore areas in south Florida. Based on Davis and Williams (1950) and Reeve (1964), Odum et al. (1982) hypothesize that the community is dominated by copepod species of the genus *Acartia*, particularly *Acartia tonsa*. In addition, they expect a few other calanoid copepods, arrow worms (*Sagitta* spp.), many fish, polychaete, and crustacean larvae and eggs.

Plankton are not the only invertebrates in the water column. Swimming crabs such as the blue crab, *Callinectes sapidus*, are abundant in most estuarine mangrove regions of south Florida. Other swimming crustaceans include: the caridean shrimp (*Palaemonetes* spp. and *Periclimenes* spp.), the snapping shrimp (*Alpheus* spp.), and the penaeid shrimp (*Penaeus* spp.).

The main vertebrate group found in the water column is the fishes. They are an important component of three mangrove community types: (1) basin forests, (2) riverine forests, and (3) fringe forests. Red mangrove prop roots offer a fairly protected habitat that is particularly suitable for juvenile fishes. Mangrove

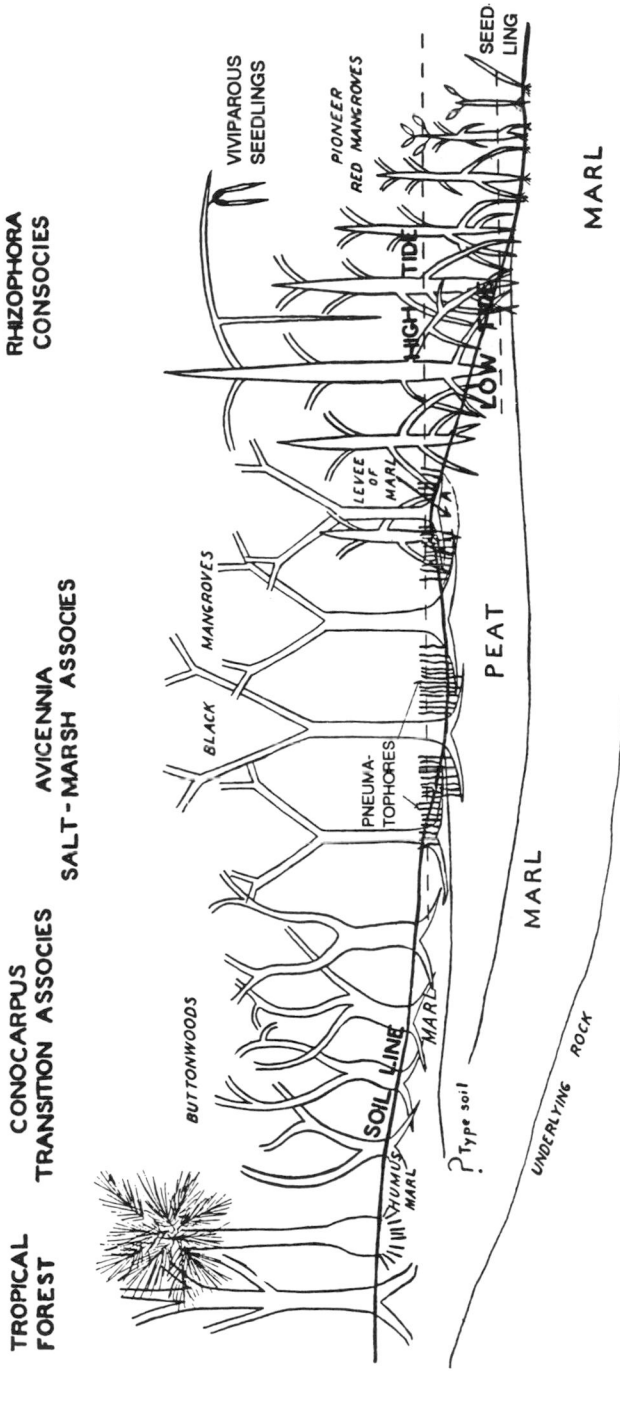

FIGURE 8.2. Zonation of Florida mangrove wetlands. Note adaptation of mangroves such as prop roots, viviparous seedlings, and black mangrove pneumatophores (Mitsch and Gosselink, 1986.)

leaves, as discussed in the later section on productivity, are the basic energy source of a detritus-based food web on which many fishes are dependent.

The infrequently flooded pools in the black mangrove–dominated zone provide an extreme habitat that few fish species can tolerate. Dissolved oxygen is low (1 to 2 ppm) and hydrogen sulfide is released from the sediments following physical disturbance. Salinities are highly variable, running the gamut from fresh to hypersaline. Thus the fish families best adapted to this environment are the euryhaline cyprinodonts, or killifishes, and the poecilids, or live-bearers (Odum et al., 1982). The most common of these are the cyprinodontids, *Fundulus confluentus*, *Rivulus marmoratus*, *Floridichthys carpio*, and *Cyprinodon variegatus*, and the poeclids, *Poecilia latipinna* and *Gambusia affinis* (Odum, 1970, in Odum et al., 1982; Heald et al., 1974).

The North River is an example of a tidal river, fringed largely by red mangroves, which connects the freshwater marshes of south Florida with the shallow estuarine bays and lagoons, in this case, with Whitewater Bay (Figure 8.3). This type of habitat exhibits extreme seasonal variability in both physical characteristics and fish community components.

During the wet season (June to November), salinities fall throughout the watercourses. Opportunistic freshwater fish may then invade the mangrove zone from the river. These include the Florida gar, *Lepisosteus platyrhincus*; several centrarchid sunfishes of the genus *Lepomis*, and the largemouth bass, *Micropterus salmoides*; the freshwater catfishes, *Ictalurus natalis* and *Noturus gyrinus*; and the killifishes, *Lucania goodei* and *Rivulus marmoratus* (Odum, 1970, in Odum et al., 1982).

During the dry season (December to early May) salinities rise as a result of decreased freshwater runoff and continuing evaporation. Marine species then invade the tidal streams primarily on feeding forays. Among these fishes are the jewfish (*Epinephelus itajara*), the stingrays (Dasyatidae), the needlefishes (Belonidae), the jacks (Carangidae), and the barracuda, *Sphyraena barracuda* (Odum et al., 1982). Fishes in this area attain a biomass of approximately $90 \, \mathrm{g\,m^{-2}}$ (Carter et al., 1973).

Embayments and Small Islands

The Ten Thousand Islands area and Whitewater Bay are fringed by dense growths of red mangroves and contain small mangrove islets. Salinities in these example estuaries tend to be higher than in the tidal streams and rivers and this, as well as the added habitat dimension of seagrass and macroalgae beds, is reflected in the fish assemblages. True freshwater fishes are rare and a greater number of marine species are present (Odum et al., 1982).

In the benthic habitat, the dominant fish families include drums (Sciaenidae), porgies (Sparidae), grunts (Pomadasyidae), mojarras (Gerreidae), snappers (Lutjanidae), and mullet (Mugilidae). Other common families include pipefishes (Syngnathidae), flounder (Bothidae), sole (Soleidae), sea robins (Triglidae), and toadfishes (Batrochoididae) (Odum et al., 1982). Species that dominated the benthic habitat were *Lagodon rhomboides*, *Bairdiella chrysoura*, and *Orthopristis chrysoptera*, and the mojarras, *Eucinostomus gula* and *E. argenteus* (Odum et al., 1982).

The numerically abundant fish families of the middle and upper waters include anchovies (Engraulidae), herrings (Clupeidae), and needlefishes (Belonidae). The most common midwater and surface species include the two anchovies, *Anchoa mitchilli* and *A. hepsetus*, and two clupeids, *Brevoortia smithi* and *Harengula pensacolae*.

PRODUCTIVITY

Detrital Productivity

Mangrove forests are among the most productive of all estuarine ecosystems. Leaves and twigs constitute a substantial portion of the annual production of mangroves and they form a major source of detritus for the aquatic food chains in Florida swamps (Kuenzler, 1974). Many marine species, such as pink shrimp, mullet, gray snapper, red drum, and blue crab, use the estuaries as nursery and feeding grounds. Consequently, the mangrove-dominated detritus food web is highly important. In place of *Spartina* found in northern salt marshes, southern tidal areas are dominated by *Rhizophora mangle* (red mangrove) and *Thalassia testudinum* (turtle grass). The dominant vegetation in both northern and southern marshes produces a virtually continuous supply of plant debris for use by detritus feeders and thus transfers carbon fixed by photosynthesis to animal consumers (Figure 8.4) (Heald et al., 1974; Heald and Odum, 1970).

Detritus can be considered a product of the breakdown of mangrove leaf, twig, and nonviable fruit debris. The plant detrital particles are about 1 to 5 mm in size and are usually protein enriched by various microorganisms (Heald et al., 1974). Both leaching and decomposition of senescent red mangrove leaves appear important in the detrital food webs of estuaries of south Florida. During the first 70 days submerged in the water column, the carbon decreases from 46.2% to 36.2% of the leaf material while nitrogen content increases from 0.51% to 0.89%. This increase in nitrogen in the decaying leaves represents the formation of microbial protein. The protein content thus increases from 3.2% to 5.6% after 70 days' submersion (Cundell et al., 1979). Heald et al. (1974) found that red mangrove leaves contain 5 to 6% protein by weight at abscission on an ash-free basis. After a month in estuarine water this has risen to 13%, increasing slowly to 21% after 12 months.

Only about 5% of the annual leaf production is consumed on the tree by terrestrial herbivores; most of it falls from the tree (Kuenzler, 1974; Heald and Odum, 1970). More leaves drop in summer than at any other season (Kuenzler, 1974). About half of the fallen leaf material is consumed by bacteria, fungi, and detritus feeders. Of the detrital material produced in the North River basin, roughly one-half is flushed out of the river system into nearby shallow coastal embayments, where it is available as food to detritus consumers in those

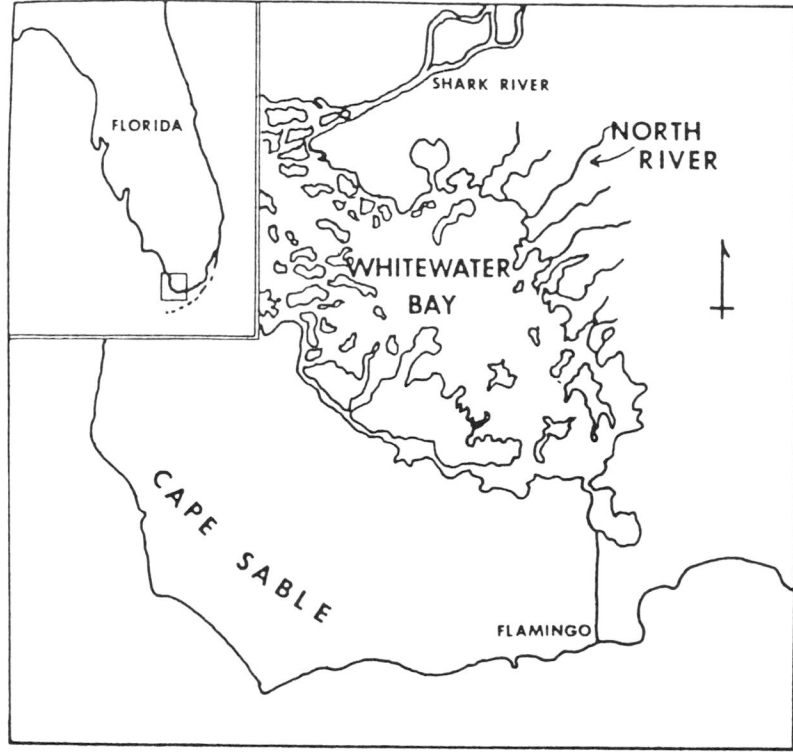

FIGURE 8.3.   Map of Whitewater Bay. (From Odum and Heald, 1975.)

ecosystems (Heald and Odum, 1970; Odum and Heald, 1975). The export of particulate organic matter is relatively large, about $1.37\,\mathrm{g\,C\,m^{-2}\,day^{-1}}$ (Kuenzler, 1974). Heald (1971) estimated that on the average, 40% of the detrital matter present in suspension in the estuarine waters of Everglades Park was of mangrove origin, and mangrove debris was the largest component of estuarine detrital materials throughout the year.

Tidal and riverine red mangrove forests in south Florida produce annually over 8 metric tons dry weight per hectare of leaf and twig debris (Heald et al., 1974). Production of mangrove leaf material in the North River estuary exceeds 2.9 dry tons per acre per year or $800\,\mathrm{dry\,g\,m^{-2}\,yr^{-1}}$ (Heald and Odum, 1970). Annual leaf fall rates for mangrove forests in Dade County in south Florida are remarkably constant. Only the scrub mangrove forest in Dade County in south Florida deviates significantly from a mean leaf-fall rate of $2\,\mathrm{g\,m^{-2}\,day^{-1}}$, or approximately $830\,\mathrm{g\,m^{-2}\,yr^{-1}}$ (Lugo and Snedaker, 1974). Heald (1971), working in the Everglades Park are in Florida, estimated leaf and twig fall in a mangrove forest to be $2.4\,\mathrm{g\,m^{-2}\,day^{-1}}$ ($876\,\mathrm{g\,m^{-2}\,yr^{-1}}$).

As stated earlier, in south Florida *Rhizophora* and *Thalassia* share the role of dominant primary producer and source of detritus. The algal food chain is less productive than the detrital food chain. For example, aquatic primary producers are nowhere abundant in the North River (Heald and Odum, 1970). Phytoplankton volumes are low and benthic algae are not abundant (Heald and Odum, 1970). Field observations in the North River basin by Odum and Heald (1975) revealed sparse growths of benthic algae, low phytoplankton standing crops ($\leqslant 10^5$ cells L^{-1}) and low rates of phytoplankton net production. These facts indicate that vascular plant detritus is the most important element of the energy base for this area. However, algae are also important, especially because their production may be much more quickly consumed by the mangrove fauna than the woody material produced by the tree (Kuenzler, 1974).

In Florida open shoal areas, algae are often very common below mean low water. These areas are often covered by tropical species of algae, such as *Caulerpa*, *Acetabularia*, *Penicillus*, *Gracillaria*, *Halimeda*, *Sargassum*, and *Batophora*. Above this region, on the intertidal muds one may find a thick growth of *Vaucheria* or *Cladophoropsis*. There is also a subterranean algal flora composed of unicellular and filamentous blue–green and green algae (Kuenzler, 1974).

Primary Productivity

The net annual productivity of mangrove trees from several Gulf coastal areas has been estimated. In general, estimates run from about 1.3 to $5.6 \, g \, C \, m^{-2} \, day^{-1}$, although some areas may be higher (see Table 8.2). Walsh (1974) found that the net photosynthetic production of organic matter from Florida mangroves is $3.4 \, g \, C \, m^{-2} \, day^{-1}$. Lugo et al. (1975) measured net daytime photosynthesis for red and white mangroves in south Florida and found that red mangroves have a higher rate of production than white mangroves (2.86 vs. $1.56 \, g \, C \, m^{-2} \, day^{-1}$, respectively). At Turkey Point, Florida and on Key Largo, net photosynthesis is estimated at 5.6 g organic matter $m^{-2} \, day^{-1}$ for sunny days and 3.5 for cloudy days with an annual average of 2.8 g organic matter $m^{-2} \, day^{-1}$. Air temperature and humidity are the most important environmental variables influencing primary production. Production decreases with increasing air temperature and humidity (Miller, 1972).

By comparison, Golley et al. (1962), in studies on the southern shore of Puerto Rico, found net daytime photosynthetic rates for mangroves of $5.2 \, g \, C \, m^{-2} \, day^{-1}$ for sunleaves. They found, with a gross production of $8 \, g \, C \, m^{-2} \, day^{-1}$, that red mangrove communities were more fertile than most marine and terrestrial communities.

Aquatic primary producers are usually not abundant (Heald and Odum, 1970). However, in some swamps, phytoplankton in the water contribute appreciably to synthesis of organic matter (Walsh, 1974). The net photosynthetic rate of periphyton growing on red mangrove roots has been reported by Lugo et al. (1975) as ranging from 0.128 to $0.189 \, g \, C \, m^{-2} \, h^{-1}$. The overall periphyton productivity is $1.1 \, g \, C \, m^{-2} \, day^{-1}$, which appears to be a significant contribution to the overall productivity of the mangrove forest.

TABLE 8.2. *Mean Estimates of Gross Photosynthesis* (P_g), *24-hr Respiration* (R_t) ($g\,C\,m^{-2}\,day^{-1}$), *and Transpiration* (T) ($g\,H_2O\,m^{-2}\,day^{-1}$), *of Mangrove Ecosystems*[a]

Ecosystem	Leaf Area Index	Leaves			Stems[b]		Surface Roots[c]		Peri-phyton $P_{(net)}$	Soil R_t	Losses Export	Total for the System			P_g/R_t
		P_g	R_t	T	R_t	T	R_t	T				P_g	R_t	T	
Rookery Bay															
Red mangrove Stand (fringe)	3.5	5.63	1.61	2.500	0.23	10	0.06	60	1.1	—	—	6.73	1.90	2.570	3.5
Black mangrove stand (inside swamp)	5.1	9.02	5.40	1.482	0.14	8	0.54	78	—	0.20	—	9.02	6.28	1.568	1.4
Puerto Rico															
Red mangrove stand	4.4	8.23[d]	5.39[d]	—	—	—	2.03	—	—	0.37	1.37	8.23	9.16	—	0.8
Key Largo, Fla.															
Red mangrove stand	2.4[e]	5.34[d]	6.05[f]	736[f]	—	—	—	—	—	—	—	5.34	6.05	736	0.8

Source: Lugo et al. (1975).

[a]Values have been corrected for leaf, trunk, and root area indices.

[b]Mean trunk area index was $0.66\,m^2\,m^{-2}$.

[c]Mean root area index was $0.67\,m^2\,m^{-2}$.

[d]Includes seedlings.

[e]Mean of three determinations.

[f]Mean of four determinations for sunny and cloudy days.

Secondary Productivity

Odum (1971) has reported that there are at least four pathways by which freshly fallen mangrove leaves are utilized by heterotrophs: (1) dissolved organic substances to microorganisms to higher consumers, (2) dissolved organic substances to sorption on sediment and aged detritus particles to higher consumers, (3) leaf material to higher consumers, and (4) leaf material to bacteria and fungi to higher consumers. This last pathway is believed by many to be the most important (Odum, 1971; Heald et al., 1974; Heald and Odum, 1970; Odum and Heald, 1975).

The most important means of energy transfer in a detrital system depends on the ability of bacteria and fungi to break down and assimilate resistant plant substances, such as cellulose and lignins. The tissues of fallen red mangrove leaves are rapidly invaded by fungi and nematodes, with attached bacteria, protozoa, and microalgae. The net result of this microbial invasion is a relative increase in the potential food value of any specific particle of disintegrating leaf (Heald et al., 1974).

The primary consumers are a small number of animal species which comprise a larger number of individuals, and are dominated by opportunistic omnivorous crustaceans (e.g., amphipods, mysids, harpacticoid copepods, caridean and penaeid shrimp, along with chironomid midge larvae and a few omnivorous fish such as the striped mullet (*Mugil cephalus*) and sheepshead minnow (*Cyprinodon latipinnia*) (Heald et al., 1974; Heald and Odum, 1970). They pass large quantities of the enriched detritus through their digestive tracts unaltered except for mechanical grinding and partial removal of adsorbed microorganisms (Odum and Heald, 1975).

Food Web

The overall food chain system for mangrove forests is solar energy → mangrove leaves → bacteria and fungi → detrital consumers (invertebrates and a few fishes) → middle carnivores (most fish) → higher carnivores (sharks, alligators, larger fish) (Odum, 1971; Heald and Odum, 1970). Odum and Heald (1975) have reported that a schematic diagram of the North River food web suggests that the principal flow of energy is along the route mangrove leaf detritus → bacteria and fungi → detritus consumers → lower carnivores → higher carnivores. Figure 8.4 reproduced from this report gives a model of this food web. Mangrove detritus serves as the energy base for an extensive food web. The plankton of mangrove areas probably contribute only a small amount to the total primary productivity, but it does constitute, with detritus, the diet of filter feeders and, after sedimentation, deposit feeders of the swamps (Kuenzler, 1974).

In the North River mangrove swamp of Florida, the critical detritus feeding link is composed of six species of fish: sheepshead killifish (*Cyprinodon variegatus*), goldspotted killifish (*Floridichthys carpio*), diamond killifish (*Adinia xenica*), sailfin molly (*Poecilia latipinna*), crested goby (*Lophiogobius cyprinoides*), and the striped mullet (*Mugil cephalus*); two nereid polychaetes (*Nereis pelagica* and *Neanthes succinea*); the amphipods, *Melita nitida*, *Grandidierella bonnieri*,

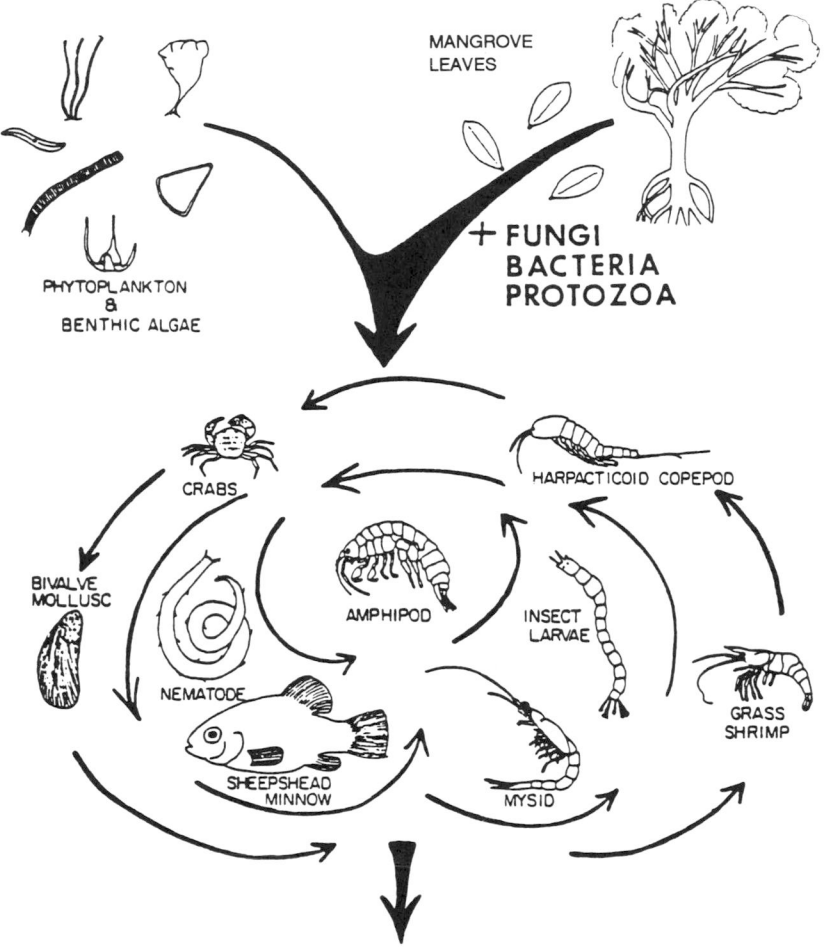

2ND CONSUMERS

FIGURE 8.4.   Detritus-based food web in south Florida estuary showing the major contribution of mangrove detritus. [After W. E. Odum, 1970 (thesis for Ph.D.); Mitsch and Gosselink, 1986.]

and *Corophium lacustre*; the mysids, *Mysidopsis almyra, Taphomysis bowmani, Mysidopsis bahia,* and *Gastrosaccus dissimilis*; two carideans; the penaeid, *Penaeus duorarum,* and the xanthid crab, *Rhithropanopeus harrisii*; several copepod and isopod species; and larval and chironomid midges (Heald et al., 1974; Odum and Heald, 1980).

Rhithropanopeus and *Melita* subject detritus to grinding and cutting, which serve to fragment leaf debris rapidly. *Cyprinodon variegatus* and *Lophiogobius* select intermediate-sized particles from benthic deposits, while *Adinia xenica*, *Palaemonetes pugio* (grass shrimp), *Nereis pelagica*, and *Neanthes succinea* select much finer particles. The finest particles, which are mostly in suspension, are ingested by filter feeders, such as *Brachiodontes exustus* (scorched mussel) and *Congeria leucophaeta* (false mussel) (Heald et al., 1974).

The most important benthic marine animals are probably crustaceans and molluscs, and most of these can be classified as either deposit or filter feeders. The crabs commonly found are *Uca pugilator*, *U. speciosa*, *U. thayeri*, and *Eurytium limosum*. *Aratus pisonii*, *Sesarma curacaoense*, and *S. reticulatum* are also abundant. The barnacle, *Balanus eburneus*, the coon oyster, *Ostrea frons*, and *Crassostrea virginica* are also important filter feeders. The snails, *Cerithium*, *Melogena*, *Cupraea*, and *Littorina angulifera*, feed on material deposited on the roots or on the mud surface (Kuenzler, 1974).

The secondary consumers include virtually all the important sport fish and most commercially important species. They are basically carnivorous and depend, directly or indirectly, on the omnivorous or herbivorous primary consumers discussed above (Heald et al., 1974).

The lower carnivores are predominantly small fish that feed on herbivores and omnivores. They include marsh killifish (*Fundulus confluentus*), Gulf killifish (*F. grandis*), rainwater killifish (*Lucania parva*), the mojarras (*Eucinostomus* and *Diapterus* spp.), frillfin goby (*Bathygobius soporator*), hogchoker (*Trinectes maculatus*), silver perch (*Bairdiella chrysura*), Gulf toadfish (*Opsanus beta*), and blue crab (*Callinectes sapidus*) (Heald et al., 1974).

The middle carnivores prey chiefly on the small fish from the lower carnivores. Included at this trophic level are most of the wading birds and sport fish species: great blue and great white herons, Louisiana heron, green heron, little blue heron, common egret, lady fish (*Elops saurus*), snook (*Centropomus undecimalis*), spotted sea trout (*Cynoscion nebulosus*), red drum (*Sciaenops ocellata*), jewfish (*Epinephelus itajarra*), crevalle jack (*Caranx hippos*), gafftopsail catfish (*Bagre marinus*), gray snapper (*Lutjanus griseus*), sheepshead (*Archosargus probatocephalus*), and juveniles of certain top carnivores (Heald et al., 1974; Heald and Odum, 1970; Kuenzler, 1974).

There are relatively few species of top carnivores and they prey chiefly on the middle carnivores. The tarpon (*Megalops atlanticus*), barracuda, and bull shark occupy this trophic level, as do bald eagles and ospreys (Heald et al., 1974; Heald and Odum, 1970).

The net annual primary productivity of mangrove trees from several Gulf coast areas varies from 1.3 to $5.6\,g\,C\,m^{-3}\,day^{-1}$. The daytime photosynthesis for red and white mangroves has been estimated and red mangroves appear to have a higher rate of production than white mangroves, $2.86\,g\,C\,m^{-3}\,day^{-1}$ versus $1.56\,g\,C\,m^{-3}\,day^{-1}$. at Key Point and on Key Largo, the net photosynthesis is estimated at 5.6 g organic matter $m^{-3}\,day^{-1}$ on sunny days and $3.5\,g\,m^{-3}\,day^{-1}$ for cloudy days.

Air temperature and humidity are the most important environmental variables influencing primary productivity. Aquatic primary productivity is not as high.

The net photosynthetic rate of periphyton growing on red mangrove roots has been reported to range from 0.128 to $0.189 \, g \, C \, m^{-3} \, day^{-1}$. Overall periphyton productivity is about $1.1 \, g \, C \, m^{-3} \, day^{-1}$.

Secondary productivity is largely dependent upon the ability of bacteria and fungi to break down and assimilate resistant plant substances such as cellulose and lignin. Leaves are rapidly invaded by fungi and nematodes with attached bacteria protozoan and microalgae. The organisms increase the food value of any particle of the disintegrating leaf. The small animals, such as omnivorous crustaceans, chironomic midges, and even a few omnivorous fish, are the primary consumers. Many species of more complex organisms are involved in the transfer of nutrients and energy to the invertebrates and from the invertebrates to the fishes.

Nutrient Cycling

The nutrient cycle is not well understood. Mangrove ecosystems appear to act as sinks for macronutrients such as nitrogen, phosphorus, trace elements, and heavy metals. A high input of nutrients into these systems leads to high storage and high primary productivity. Natural nutrient inputs for mangrove swamps come from upland and terrestrial sources. Thus, some of the most luxuriant and productive mangrove forests in south Florida occur in riverine locations or adjacent to significant upland drainage. Nitrogen fixation has been observed in the mangrove swamps and the highest rates of mangrove nitrogen fixation have been measured in association with decaying mangrove leaves.

Mangrove ecosystems act as sinks (net accumulators) for macronutrients such as nitrogen and phosphorus, trace elements, and heavy metals (Figure 8.5; Table 8.3). These elements are removed from waters flowing through mangrove prop roots, prop root algae, the associated sediments, the fine root system of the mangrove trees, and the myriad small invertebrates and microorganisms attached to these surfaces. An unknown portion of these elements is tied up or stored in wood, sediments, and peat for many years (Odum et al., 1982).

For significant nutrient storage and resultant high primary production to occur, there must be a continual input of nutrients to the mangrove forest from

TABLE 8.3.   *Distribution of Phosphorus in the Mud of a Mangrove Swamp*

	Phosphorus (ppm dry weight)
Organic phosphorus	485
Iron phosphate	29
Calcium phosphate	25
Aluminum phosphate	6
Occluded aluminum phosphate	6
Water-soluble phosphate	2
Reductant iron phosphate	0

Source: Hesse (1962).

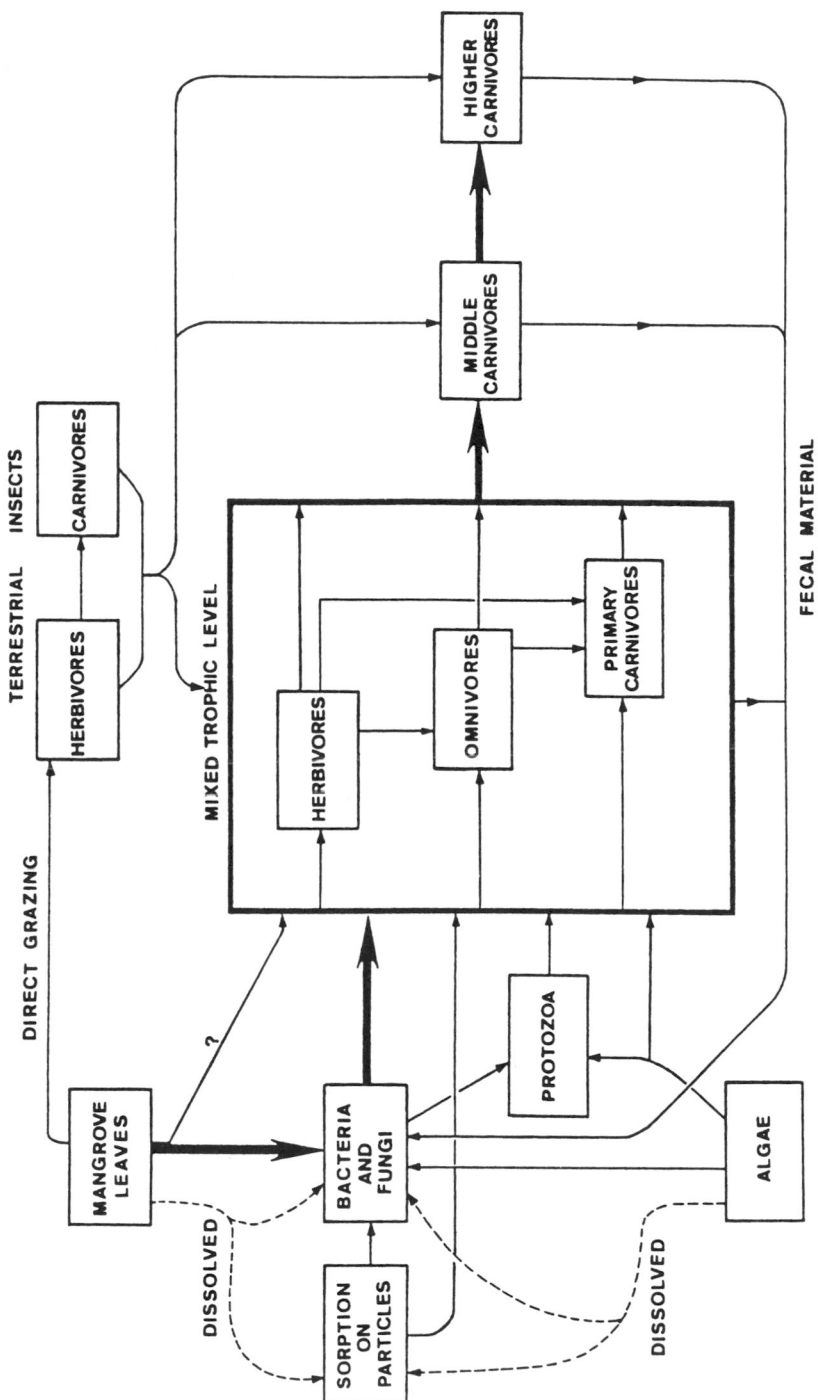

FIGURE 8.5.   Diagram of the ecosystems dependent on mangrove leaves. (After Odum and Heald, 1975.)

553

outside the system. Although sinks for these nutrients, mangrove ecosystems are subject to continual loss through export of particulate and dissolved substances. High input of nutrients leads to high storage and high primary productivity; the reverse is true when nutrient input is low (Odum et al., 1982).

Carter et al. (1973) and Snedaker and Lugo (1973, in Odum et al., 1982) hypothesized that the greatest natural nutrient inputs for mangrove swamps come from upland and terrestrial sources. This concurs with the observation that the most luxuriant and productive mangrove forests in south Florida occur in riverine locations or adjacent to significant upland drainage.

Nitrogen fixation occurs in mangrove swamps at rates comparable to those measured in other shallow, tropical marine areas (Gotto et al., 1981). Nitrogen fixation occurs in association with mangrove leaves (living and dead), mangrove sediment surfaces, the litter layer in mangrove swamps, and mangrove root systems (Odum et al., 1982). In all cases, nitrogen fixation is limited by the availability of labile carbon compounds. Thus it comes as no surprise that the highest rates of mangrove nitrogen fixation have been measured in association with decaying mangrove leaves. Nitrogen fixation within the swamp may provide much of the nitrogen needed for mangrove growth (Odum et al., 1982).

SUMMARY

Mangrove forests are typically found along the southern part of the Gulf, along the coast of Florida, and also extend upward in Florida along the Gulf coast of south Florida. There have been reports of mangrove forests in Texas. These mangrove forests are almost impenetrable because of the prop roots of the red mangrove and the pneumatophores that are necessary for growth of the black and white mangroves. Pneumatophores enable the trees to obtain oxygen from the air, as the soil in which they live is typically anaerobic.

A variety of animals live associated with these mangrove forests. Also present are many types of algae. As a result we find a fauna that lives on the surface of the mangrove forest floor, on the roots, and even in the canopy. The diversity of this fauna is very great and is highly specialized. A large number of algae, particularly diatoms, green and red algae, and some brown algae are found associated with them.

Mangroves stabilize the substrate in which they are found and thus protect the shoreline. Once the trees are destroyed the roots soon disintegrate, and often the land disappears. The detritus of the mangroves is particularly valuable as a food source for the diverse fauna that live associated with these trees. It is a particularly favorable habitat for a variety of molluscs and crustacea. It is an excellent habitat particularly for fiddler crabs. Because of the rich invertebrate and algal flora many fish are found in the mangrove forest, where they are protected from many predators and the ravages of human activities. Mangrove forests form a fairly unique habitat that is limited to a few areas on our coast. They should be carefully conserved.

BIBLIOGRAPHY

Ball, M. C. 1980. Patterns of secondary succession in a mangrove forest of southern Florida. Oecologia 44(2): 226–235.

Carter, M. R., L. A. Burns, T. R. Cavinder, K. R. Dugger, P. L. Fore, D. B. Hicks, H. L. Revells, and T. W. Schmidt. 1973. Ecosystem analysis of the Bigg Cypress Swamp and estuaries. U.S. EPA, Ecol. Rept. DI-SFEP-74-51. 375 pp.

Chapman, V. J. 1976. Mangrove vegetation. *In* J. Cramer, ed., New world mangroves. Vaduz, Germany, 447 pp.

Courtney, C. M. 1975. Mangrove and seawall oyster communities, Marco Island, Florida. Bull. Am. Malacol. Union 1975: 29–32.

Cundell, A. M., M. S. Brown, R. Stanford, and R. Mitchell, 1979. Microbial degradation of *Rhizophora mangle* leaves immersed in the sea. Estuarine Coastal Mar. Shelf Sci. 9(3): 281–286.

Davis, C. C., and R. H. Williams. 1950. Brackish water plankton of mangrove areas in southern Florida. Ecology 31: 519–531.

Davis, J. H. 1940. The ecology and geologic role of mangroves in Florida. Paper Tortuqas Lab 32, Carnegie Inst. Washington Publ. 517: 303–412.

Dawes, C. J., R. E. Moon, and M. A. Davis. 1978. The photosynthetic and respiratory rates and tolerances of benthic algae from a mangrove and salt marsh estuary: a comparative study. Estuarine Coastal Mar. Sci. 6(2): 175–185.

Egler, F. E. 1952. Southeast saline everglades vegetation, Florida, and its management. Vegetation 3: 213–265.

Golley, F., H. T. Odum, and R. F. Wilson. 1962. The structure and metabolism of a Puerto Rican red mangrove forest in May. Ecology 43: 9–19.

Golley, F. B., et al., 1975. Mineral cycling in tropical moist systems. Univ. Georgia Press, Athens, Ga. 298 pp.

Gotto, J. W., F. R. Tabita, and C. V. Baalen. 1981. Nitrogen fixation in inertidal environments of the Texas gulf coast. Estuarine Coastal Shelf Sci. 12: 231–235.

Heald, E. 1971. The production of organic detritus in a south Florida estuary. Univ. Miami Sea Grant Tech. Bull. 6.

Heald, E., and W. E. Odum. 1970. The contribution of mangrove swamps to Florida fisheries. Proc. Gulf Caribb. Fish. Inst. 22: 130–135.

Heald, E. J., W. E. Odum, and D. C. Tabb. 1974. Mangroves in the estuarine food chain. *In* P. J. Gleason, ed., Environments of south Florida: present and past. Miami Geol. Soc. Man. 2.

Hesse, P. R. 1962. Phosphorus fixation in mangrove swamp mud. Nature 193(4812): 295–296.

Holm, R. F. 1978. The community structure of a tropical marine lagoon. Estuarine Coastal Mar. Sci. 7(4): 329–345.

Kuenzler, E. J. 1974. Mangrove swamp systems, pp. 346–371. *In* H. T. Odum, B. J. Copeland, and E. A. McMahan, eds., Coastal ecological systems of the United States. Vol. 1. The Conservation Foundation, Washington, D.C.

Lugo, A. E., and S. C. Snedaker. 1974. The ecology of mangroves. Annu. Rev. Ecol. Syst. 5: 39–64.

Lugo, A. E., G. Evink, M. M. Brinson, A. Broce, and S. C. Snedaker. 1975. Diurnal rates of photosynthesis, respiration, and transpiration in mangrove forests of south Florida. *In* F. B. Golley and E. Medina, eds., Tropical ecological systems. Ecol. Stud. 11: 335–350.

Miller, P. C. 1972. Bioclimate, leaf temperature, and primary production in red mangrove canopies in south Florida. Ecology 53(1): 22–45.

Mitsch, W. J., and J. G. Gosselink, 1986. Wetlands. Van Nostrand Reinhold, New York. 537 pp.

Odum, W. E. 1970. Pathways of energy flow in a south Florida estuary. Ph.D. dissertation. Univ. Miami, Fla. 162 pp.
Odum, W. E. 1971. Pathways of energy flow in a south Florida estuary. Univ. Miami Sea Grant Program Tech. Bull. 7.
Odum, W. E., and E. J. Heald. 1972. Trophic analyses of an estuarine mangrove community. Bull. Mar. Sci. 22(3):671–738.
Odum, W. E., and E. J. Heald. 1975. The detritus-based food web of an estuarine mangrove community. *In* L. E. Cronin, ed. Estuarine Res. 1:265–286.
Odum, W. E., C. C. McIvor, and T. J. Smith III. 1982. The ecology of the mangroves of south Florida: a community profile. Bureau of Land Management, Fish and Wildlife Service, Biological Services Program, Washington, D.C. 130 pp.

Reeve, M. R. 1964. Studies on the seasonal variation of the zooplankton in a marine subtropical in-shore environment. Bull. Mar. Sci. 14:103–122.
Rehm, A. E. 1974. A study of the marine algae epiphytic on the prop roots of *Rhizophora mangle* L. from Tampa to Key Largo, Florida. Dissertation. Univ. of South Florida, Tampa. 183 pp.
Reimold, R. J. 1977. Mangals and salt marshes of eastern United States. *In* V. J. Chapman, ed., Ecosyst. World 1:157–166.
Richards, P. W. 1964. The tropical rain forest: an ecological study. Cambridge Univ. Press, Cambridge 450 pp.

Simberloff, D. S. 1976. Experimental zoogeography of islands: effects of island size. Ecology 57(4):629–648.
Simberloff, D. S., and E. O. Wilson. 1969. Experimental zoogeography of islands: the colonization of empty islands. Ecology 50:278–296.
Snedaker, S. C., and A. E. Lugo. 1973. The role of mangrove ecosystems in the maintenance of environmental quality and a high productivity of desirable fisheries. Final Rept. Contr. 14-16-008-606 to Bur. Sport Fish. Wildl. 381 pp.

Tabb, D. C., D. L. Dubrow, and R. B. Manning. 1962. The ecology of northern Florida Bay and adjacent estuaries. Fla. State Board Conserv. Tech. Ser. 39:1–81.
Taylor, W. R. 1960. Marine algae of the eastern tropical and subtropical coasts of the Americas. Univ. Michigan Press, Ann Arbor. 879 pp.

Walsh, G. E. 1974. Mangroves: a review, pp. 51–174. *In* R. J. Reimold and W. H. Queen, eds., Ecology of halophytes. Academic Press, New York.

Zaninetti, L. 1979. Study of foraminifera from current mangrove swamps: reflections on objectives and status of knowledge. Arch. Sci. (Geneva) 32(2):151–162.

CHAPTER 9

Gulf of Mexico Estuaries: Florida, Louisiana

The estuaries which are described in detail include those associated with the Apalachicola Bay, the Escambia River, and the Baritaria Bay. The estuaries that enter the Gulf of Mexico are more variable in their vegetation and general characteristics than estuaries in other regions of the United States. There are basically three types of estuaries on the Gulf of Mexico and one type that is a mixture. These types are the mangrove estuaries found mainly on the coast of Florida but also occurring on the coast of Louisiana and some places in Texas. The underwater grasslands of southern Florida typically occur where the water is clear and sedimentation is low and the nutrient level of the water is low. As a result, any human activity that increases the nutrients of the water or its turbidity tends to eliminate these *Thalassia* grasslands. The *Spartina–Juncus* grassland estuaries are typical of large areas of the gulf. These grasses are sometimes associated with the underwater beds of *Thalassia* as occurs in the Econfina and Fenholloway estuaries.

FLORIDA ESTUARIES

Apalachicola Bay–Apalachee Bay

Primary productivity. Livingston et al. (1974) determined that in the Apalachicola Bay system in Florida, into which the Apalachicola River enters, the average phytoplankton poductivity ranged from $63\,\text{mg}\,\text{C}\,\text{m}^{-2}\,\text{day}^{-1}$ in February to $1694\,\text{mg}\,\text{C}\,\text{m}^{-2}\,\text{day}^{-1}$ in April. The bay averaged 9 ft (2.7 m) in depth at mid low water.

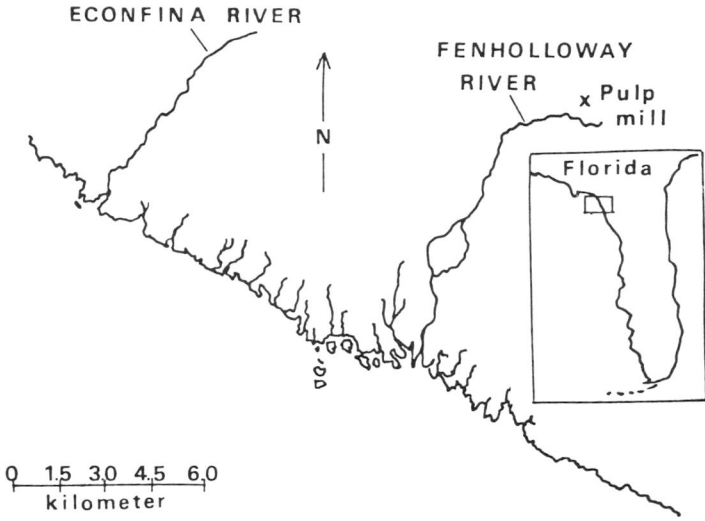

FIGURE 9.1.   Apalachee Bay and drainage area. (From Zimmerman and Livingston, 1976.)

Temperature was the primary limiting factor to phytoplankton growth, while light, turbidity, nutrients, grazing, and flushing rates were additional controlling factors. The diatoms, *Chaetoceras lorenzianum*, *Bacteriastrum delicatulum*, and *Thalassiothrix frauenfeldi*, were the dominant producers in spring and summer, while *Skeletonema costatum*, *Rhizosolenia alata*, and *Coscinodiscus radiatus* were dominant during fall and winter months.

Benthic macrophytes in Apalachee Bay were found to exist throughout the year, but exhibit distinct seasonal variation in biomass. Of this group, the dominant species were the seagrasses; *Thalassia testudinum* and *Syringodium filiforme*; the green alga, *Halimeda incrassata*; and the red algae, *Digenia simplex* and *Laurencia poitei* (Zimmerman and Livingston, 1976; Stoner, 1980a). Other macrophytes had patchy distributions, causing irregularities in biomass over time; however, they were present throughout the year. These include the vascular plant, *Halophila engelmanni*; the green algae, *Caulerpa prolifera*; *Anadyomene stellata*, *Penicillus capitatus*, and *Udotea* sp.; and the red algae, *Laurencia intricata* and *Gracilaria*. The annual mean total benthic macrophyte standing crop in Apalachee bay was found by Stoner (1980a) to range from 9.3 to 320 g dry wt m^{-2} at stations in the Fenholloway and Econfina rivers (Figure 9.1). Zimmerman and Livingston (1979) found *Thalassia testudinum* to be the dominant benthic macrophyte, ranging from 24 to 226 g dry wt m^{-2} in Apalachee Bay and total benthic macrophyte standing crop ranging from 29 to 290 g dry wt m^{-2}.

Detrital Productivity.   It is reasonable to assume, as is the case along the southeastern Atlantic coast, that the primary pathway of energy is the detritus-based food web. Whereas the southeastern Atlantic estuaries are dominated by *Spartina alterniflora*, those of the Gulf coast are dominated by a mixture of the emergent plants *Spartina alterniflora*, *S. patens*, *Juncus roemerianus*, *Distichlis* *spicata*, and *Salicornia perennis*, which are continuous along the entire coast (Livingston et al., 1977). Unfortunately, little information exists as to the production of detritus or the primary productivity of these species in the Gulf of Mexico. Livingston et al. (1977) described the Apalachicola Bay system as having "a relatively high rate of primary and secondary production."

The three major forms of macro-detritus (leaf litter, wood debris, and benthic macrophytes) in Apalachicola Bay were roughly comparable in terms of relative abundance. After a small increase in the spring, benthic macrophyte detritus peaked during the fall period. Detritus in upland (oligohaline) portions of the bay was characterized by benthic macrophytes such as *Ruppia maritima* and *Vallisneria americana* and *Gracilaria* spp., with lesser amounts of wood debris and leaf litter. River-dominated areas were characterized predominantly by wood debris and leaf detritus, with lesser amounts of *Ruppia* and *Vallisneria*. Outer bay areas that do not receive direct river runoff were dominated by detritus of benthic algal origin, notably *Gracilaria folifera*, *Halodule wrightii*, and *Ulva lactuca* (Livingston et al., 1977).

Cycling of Nutrients. Very few studies appear to have addressed the cycling of nutrients in the Gulf coast area. In Apalachicola Bay, Livingston et al. (1974) found that nitrate showed the greatest seasonal variation ($180 \mu g L^{-1}$ in February to 2 to $6 \mu g L^{-1}$ in July). Ammonia values in the bay (7 to $25 \mu g L^{-1}$) did not fluctuate to any degree during the year; there was no definite seasonal trend.

In the Escambia River estuary nitrite values ranged from < 0.001 ppm in the spring to 0.003 ppm in the fall. Nitrate ranged from 0.05 ppm to 0.14 ppm over the same period. Phosphate (PO_4 P) was below 0.001 ppm all year. Ammonia (NH_3-N) ranged from 0.05 to 0.12 ppm in the fall to 0.60 to 1.10 ppm in the spring (ANSP, 1953).

Secondary Productivity. The forms of detritus that are available to the macroconsumers in the estuary include live vascular plants, dead plants, microbes, algae (benthic and planktonic), live and dead animal tissue, and feces (Figure 9.2).

The spatial pattern in the abundance of macrobenthic animals is a function of macrophyte cover and not of the fine sediments often associated with vegetation. However, amphipod abundance was related to reproductive seasonalities and abundance of predatory fish, and the amphipod population increased in the fall when fish left the grassbeds (Stoner, 1980a).

Stoner (1980a) conducted a study of the Econfina and Fenholloway estuaries in Apalachee Bay at four collecting sites with salinities ranging from 17 to 34 ppt. The macrophytes at the three vegetated sites (annual mean standing crops of 141, 215, and $320 g dry wt m^{-2}$) were dominated by mixtures of *Thalassia testudinum* and *Syringodium filiforme*. The sparse growth at the "unvegetated" station was *Halophila engelmanni* (annual mean standing crop of $9.3 g dry wt m^{-2}$).

The total macrofauna density was clearly correlated with macrophyte standing crop since the mean density at the unvegetated station was $1754 m^{-2}$ as compared to $3107 m^{-2}$ for the vegetated stations (Stoner, 1980a). Overall, Stoner

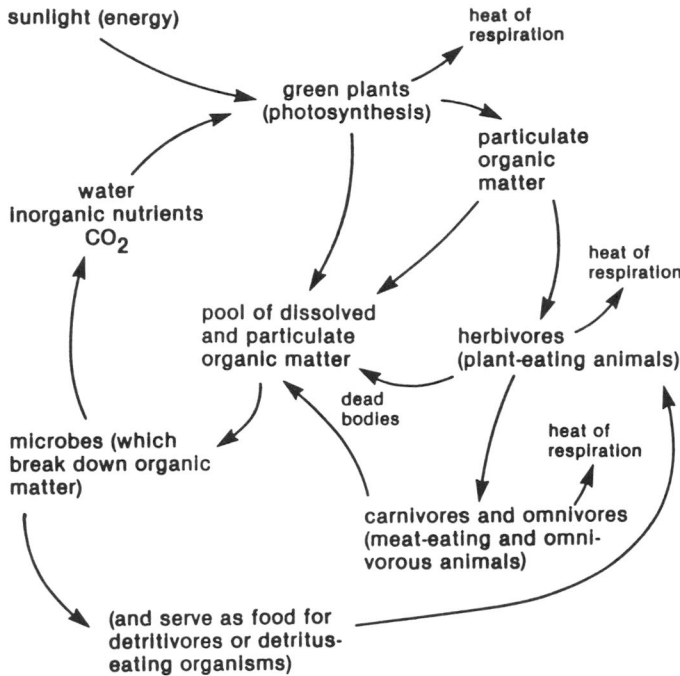

FIGURE 9.2.   Plant–microbe–animal cycle of north Gulf grassland estuaries. (From Livingston, 1983, Florida Sea Grant.)

collected 170 species, including 75 polychaete, 31 amphipod, 21 mollusc, 10 shrimp, 6 crab, and 5 isopod. He found that 33 to 45% of the total macrofauna was composed of polychaetous annelids. Of 75 polychaete species taken, only 34 were taken at the unvegetated sites, whereas up to 54 species were taken at the vegetated sites. The polychaete fauna at the unvegetated site was dominated by the capitellid, *Mediomastus californiensis*, and the arabellid, *Lumbrineris tenuis* (38.9% and 15.6% of the polychaetes, respectively). Syllids and serpulids were limited in distribution to vegetated stations, as were 41 other species. The relative abundance of epifaunal polychaetes was directly related to macrophyte abundance, whereas the inverse relation was demonstrated by burrowers (Stoner, 1980a).

In Stoner's collection 37 to 47% of the macrofaunal numbers taken were amphipods. *Elasmopus levis*, a species of *Lembos*, and *Rudilemboides naglei* were abundant. Also associated solely with the vegetated stations were *Lysianopsis hirsuta*, a species of *Cerapus*, and a species of *Colomastix*. The mean density of amphipods was highest at a vegetated station (1578 m^{-2}) and lowest at the unvegetated station (641 m^{-2}) (Stoner, 1980a).

Stoner categorized the amphipods he collected into seven classifications: (1) epifaunal free-living, (2) epifaunal domicolous, (3) infaunal tube building, (4) infaunal free burrowing, (5) motile tube dwellers, (6) commensals, and (7) both epifaunal and infaunal. He found that the percentage of the total amphipod populations falling into these different microhabitat categories differed from station to station and was especially marked between vegetated and unvegetated stations. Free-living epifaunal types were 28.9% to 34.2% of the amphipod fauna at vegetated sites, but only 12.1% at the unvegetated station. Similarly, amphipods categorized as domicolous epifauna were abundant at vegetated stations (23.5 to 49.7%) and rare at the unvegetated station (3.6%). The abundance of infaunal tube-building amphipods (mainly *Ampelisca verrilli* and *A. vadorum*) was inversely related to macrophyte abundance; that is, 67.6% of all amphipods collected at the unvegetated site were of this type (Stoner, 1980a).

Food Web. The food web is represented graphically in Figure 9.3. Isopods, amphipods, and decapods utilize estuarine grassland detritus as a substrate for shelter and food. It is likely that species such as these depend on microbial components of detritus for food; however, the actual details of the trophodynamic relationships of detritus-based systems are little known (Livingston et al., 1977). Leaf litter fauna are omnivores and detritivores and ultimately become available to higher trophic levels. The relative significance of autochthonous and allochthonous detritus in the overall energy budget of the Apalachee Bay system is still in question.

Normally in estuarine systems, the meiofaunal taxa are very important to the flow of energy through the food web to higher trophic levels, and this was the case in Apalachee Bay. Amphipoda made up approximately 37 to 47% of

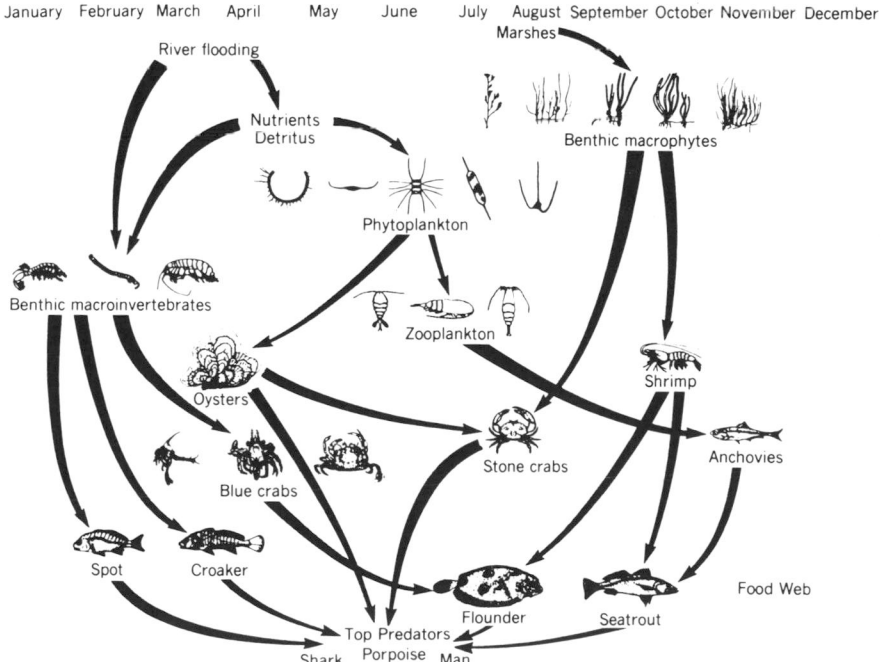

FIGURE 9.3.   Food webs of Apalachicola Bay. (From Livingston, 1983, Florida Sea Grant.)

the macrofaunal numbers taken at Fenholloway and Econfina river stations. The abundance depended on the degree of vegetation. The mean density of amphipods varied from 641 to 1578 m^2 from unvegetated to vegetated stations. Greatest abundance of amphipods was found between April and May, and densities and biomasses were lowest in the fall (Livingston, 1983).

Stoner (1980a) found that polychaetous annelids made up 33 to 45% of the total macrofauna numbers, again dependent on the degree of vegetation. In unvegetated areas, the polychaete fauna was dominated by the capitellid, *Mediomastus californiensis* (38.9%), and the arabellid, *Lumbrineris tenuis* (15.6%). *Anicidea taylori* was the only other worm that made up more than 5% of the total polychaete fauna at the unvegetated sites. However, it was the most numerous worm in vegetated areas. The mean density of polychaetes ranged from 705 to 1467 m^2 with spring peaks and fall minima.

It should be noted that macrofaunal densities in Stoner's (1980a) study were low relative to those found in other investigations. Orth (1973) reported a mean density of 14,284 macrobenthic animals per square meter associated with *Zostera marina* in Chesapeake Bay. The relatively low density of macrofaunal animals in Apalachee Bay is probably related to the high degree of tidal flow in the area (Stoner, 1980a).

Fish (Predator–Prey Relationships).   The fish of Apalachee Bay were divided into three trophic groups. According to Livingston (1982), the first such group was composed of planktiverous forms, which included early stages of anchovies, spot, and the mojarras. These species fed primarily on copepods (calanoid, cyclopoid, harpacticoid), amphipods, and plant remains or detritus. The second trophic group was composed of benthic omnivores and carnivores, such as the pinfish, *Lagodon rhomboides*, and the spotted pinfish, *Diplodus holbrooki*. These species fed on plant remains, harpacticoid copepods, invertebrate eggs, and benthic crustaceans. Polychaetes and bivalve molluscs were added to this diet by other benthic omnivores, such as the planehead filefish, *Monacanthis hispidus*, and the fringed filefish, *M. ciliatus*. Fish of the third group, which tended to feed on crustaceans such as shrimp, crabs, and amphipods, included the pigfish, *Orthopristis chrysoptera*; silver perch, *Bairdiella chrysura*; and the dusky pipefish, *Syngnathus floridae*.

The pinfish, *Lagodon rhomboides*, was the most numerous epibenthic fish predator in seagrass habitats of the Gulf of Mexico (Stoner, 1980b). Amphipods were among the most important food items consumed by pinfish, and in Apalachee Bay, amphipods consistently made up the largest portion of the stomach contents of juvenile pinfish. In stomach content analyses, Stoner (1980b) found that *Cymadusa compta* was the most frequently consumed prey species. Three other amphipods (*Lembos* sp., *Elasmopus levis*, and *Paracaprella tenuis*) individually contributed greater than 10% of the occurrence overall. Three other species, *Gitanopsis* sp., *Rudilemboides naglei*, and *Batea catharinensis*, contributed more than 4% of the total. These seven species were considered preferred prey species for *Lagodon*, and they were all epifaunal forms. Infaunal species of the genera *Ampelisca*, *Corophium*, *Lysianopsis*, and *Paraphoxus* contributed little to the diets of pinfish (Stoner, 1980b), which are known to undergo ontogenetic changes in feeding habit. Food preference by size class proceeds from largely planktiverous juveniles through benthic carnivory, omnivory, and a final (largely) herbivorous feeding mode (Livingston, 1982).

Ryan and Livingston (1980) conducted a study of the feeding habits of the dominant nocturnally active fish in Apalachee Bay. They found that silver perch, *Bairdiella chrysura*, were the most numerous of the nocturnal predators collected. The diet of this species was dominated by the shrimp *Hippolyte zostericola*, and the mysids, *Bowmaniella disimilis* and *Taphromysis bowmani*. The silver perch, in turn, was commonly preyed upon by the inshore lizardfish, *Synodus foetens*; black sea bass, *Centropristis striata*; gulf toadfish, *Opsanus beta*; and southern hake, *Urophycis floridana*.

The black sea bass, *Centropristis striata*, was found by Ryan and Livingston (1980) to be a day/night feeder whose dominant food items included the shrimp, *Hippolyte zostericola*, *Periclimenes longicaudatus*, and *Ambidexter symmetricus*, and the crabs, *Pagurus* spp., and *Neopanope texana* spp.

The diet of 31- to 90-mm southern hake, *Urophycis floridana*, consisted primarily of caridean shrimp, amphipods, and mysids. Shrimp also dominate prey taken by larger *U. floridana* (91 to 140 mm), but juvenile pigfish, spot, pinfish, and silver perch become increasingly important prey as the predator grows (Ryan and Livingston, 1980).

The dominant prey of the gulf toadfish, *Opsanus beta*, include the crabs, *Pagurus* spp. and *Neopanope texana sayi*, and the shrimp, *Alpheus normani*, *Penaeus duorarum*, and *Hippolyte zostericola* (Ryan and Livingston, 1980).

Structure of Communities. The communities that have been studied in the most detail are those, associated with the Econfina and Escambia river estuaries. In the Econfina and Fenholloway estuaries within Apalachee Bay, Florida, Hooks et al. (1976) found that at least four different habitats with associated species groups occur in different proportions: (1) seagrasses, (2) oyster reefs, (3) mud flats, and (4) red algae. The seagrass beds supported the most diverse fauna and flora (Table 9.1).

Many complex factors combined to determine the structure of the estuarine communities found in Apalachee Bay. Among these factors were seagrass and macrophyte biomass and distribution, species-specific reproductive strategies, predator–prey interactions, feeding habits (nocturnal versus diurnal feeding), species-specific seasonal cycles, habitat characteristics (physical, chemical, etc.), and seasonal climatic fluctuations.

Plankton. Salinity was a key factor in determining the distribution of plankton. In a system similar to the Apalachee Bay, where salinity ranged from 14 to 32 ppt, the diatoms, *Chaetoceras lorenzianum*, *Bacteriastrum delicatulum*, and *Thalassiothrix frauenfeldi*, were the dominant net phytoplankton during spring and summer, while *Skeletonema costatum*, *Rhizosolenia alata*, and *Coscinodiscus radiatus* were dominant during fall and winter months (Livingston et al., 1974).

(*text continues on page 585*)

TABLE 9.1.   *Species of the North Gulf Grassland Estuaries*

Species	Econfina River	Fenholloway River	Apalachee Bay	Apalachicola River	Barataria Bay
DIVISION CHLOROPHYTA					
Class Chlorophyceae					
Order Tetrasporales					
Family Tetrasporaceae					
Tetraspora lubrica				×	
Order Ulotrichales					
Family Ulotrichaceae					
Ulothrix subtilissima				×	
U. tenerrima				×	
Family Microsporaceae					
Microspora tumida				×	
Family Chaetophoraceae					
Aphanochaete repens				×	
Chaetophora attenuata				×	
C. elegans				×	
C. linum	×		×		
Chaetosphaeridium globusum				×	
Coleochaete divergens				×	
Draparnalida glomerata				×	
Stigeoclonium attenuatum				×	
S. stagnatile				×	
Family Ulvaceae					
Enteromorpha intestinalis		×			
Order Oedogoniales					
Family Oedogoniaceae					
Bulbochaete minuta				×	
Order Cladophorales					
Family Cladophoraceae					
Basicladia chelonum				×	
Cladophora sp.	×	×			
Rhizoclonium hieroglyphicum				×	
Order Siphonocladiales					
Family Valoniaceae					
Cladophoropsis membranacea	×	×	×		
Anadyomene stellata	×	×	×		
Order Siphonales					
Family Caulerpaceae					
Caulerpa ashmeadii	×	×	×		
C. fastigata	×				
C. paspaloides	×	×	×		
C. prolifera	×	×	×		
C. decorticatum	×				

TABLE 9.1. (*Continued*)

Species	Econfina River	Fenholloway River	Apalachee Bay	Apalachicola River	Barataria Bay
Codium isthmocladum	×	×	×		
Family Codiaceae					
Udotea conglutinata	×	×	×		
U. flabellum	×		×		
Penicillus capitatus	×	×	×		
P. lamourouxii	×	×			
Halimeda incrassata	×	×	×		
Order Desmidales					
Family Gonatozygaceae					
Gonatozygon monotoenium				×	
G. kinahami				×	
DIVISION PHAEOPHYTA					
Class Isogneratae					
Order Dictyotales					
Family Dictyotaceae					
Dictyota divaricata		×	×		
Padina vickersiae	×	×	×		
Class Cyclosporaceae					
Order Fucales					
Family Fucaceae					
Sargassum filipendula	×	×	×		
S. pteropleurum	×	×	×		
DIVISION RHODOPHYTA					
Class Rhodophyceae					
Subclass Florideae					
Order Cryptonemiales					
Family Corallinaceae					
Jania rubens	×				
Order Gigartinales					
Family Solieraceae					
Agardhiella ramosissima	×	×			
A. tenera	×				
Eucheuma isiforme	×				
Family Hypnaceae					
Hypnea cervicornis	×				
Family Gracilariaceae					
Gracilaria cervicornis	×	×	×		
G. cylindrica	×	×			
G. damaecornis		×			
G. foliifera	×	×	×		
C. verrucosa	×	×	×		

Continued

TABLE 9.1. (*Continued*)

Species	Econfina River	Fenholloway River	Apalachee Bay	Apalachicola River	Barataria Bay
Order Rhodymeniales					
Family Champiaceae					
Champia parvula	×				
Order Ceramiales					
Family Ceramiaceae					
Ceramium fastigum	×				
Spyridia filamentosa	×	×	×		
Family Dasyaceae					
Dasya sp.		×			
Family Rhodomelaceae					
Polysiphonia gorgoniae	×	×			
P. harveyi	×	×			
P. ramentacea	×				
P. subtilissima	×	×			
Digenia simplex	×	×	×		
Lophosiphonia saccorhiza	×				
Chondria littoralis	×	×	×		
C. tenuissima	×	×	×		
Laurencia intricata	×	×	×		
L. papillosa	×	×	×		
L. poitei	×	×	×		
PHYLUM PROTOZOA					
Subphylum Plasmodroma					
Class Sarcodina					
Subclass Rhizopoda					
Order Foraminiferida					
Ammoastuta salsa					
Ammoastuta sp.					×
Ammobaculites crassus					
A. subcantenulatus					
Ammobaculites sp.					×
Ammonia sp.					×
Ammotium dilatatum					
A. Fragile					
A. salsum					
Ammontium sp.					×
Arenoparella mexicana					
Arenoparella sp.					×
Bolivina striatula					
Elphidium gunteri					
E. limosum					
E. matagordanum					

TABLE 9.1.   (*Continued*)

Species	Econfina River	Fenholloway River	Apalachee Bay	Apalachicola River	Barataria Bay
Gaudryina exilis					
Haplophragmoides manilaensis					
H. wilberti					
Miliammina fusca					
Miliammina sp.					×
Quinqueloculina cf. *Q. lamarckiana*					
Q. rhodiensis					
Streblus parkinsoniana					
S. tepida					
Trochammina comprimata					
T. inflata					
T. macrescens					
Trochammina sp.					×
PHYLUM CNIDARIA					
Class Scyphozoa					
Order Semaeostomeae					
Family Pelagiidae					
Chrysaora quinquecirrha			×		
Order Rhizostomeae					
Suborder Daktyliophorae					
Family Stomolophidae					
Stomolophus meleagris				×	
PHYLUM PHORONIDA					
Phonronis architect				×	
PHYLUM ANNELIDA					
Class Polychaeta					
Order Orbiniida					
Family Orbiniidae					
Scoloplos fragilis				×	
(= *Haploscoloplos fragilis*)					
S. rubra				×	
Family Paraonidae					
Anicidea fragilis				×	
Anicidea taylori	×	×			
Order Spionida					
Suborder Spioniformia					
Family Spionidae					
Paraprionospio pinnata				×	
Polydora ligni				×	
Prionospio heterobranchia				×	
Spiophanes bombyx				×	

Continued

TABLE 9.1.   (Continued)

Species	Econfina River	Fenholloway River	Apalachee Bay	Apalachicola River	Barataria Bay
Streblospio benedicti				×	
Family Magelonidae					
Magelona polydentata				×	
Order Capitellida					
Family Capitellidae					
Capitella capitata				×	
Capitellides jonesi					
Heteromastus filiformis				×	
Mediomastus californiensis				×	
Family Arenicolidae					
Arenicola cristata				×	
Family Maldanidae					
? *Brachiosychis americana*				×	
Order Phyllodocida					
Family Nephtyidae					
Nephtys bucera	×				
N. picata		×			
Suborder Phyllodociformia					
Family Phyllodocidae					
Eteone heteropoda				×	
Phyllodoce fragilis			×	×	
Suborder Aphroditiformia					
Family Polyodontidae					
Polyodontes lupina				×	
Suborder Nereidiformia					
Family Hesionidae					
Podarke sp.				×	
Family Pilargiidae					
Ancistrosyllis sp.				×	
Loandalia americana				×	
Sigambra bassi				×	
Family Syllidae					
Exogone dispar			×		
Family Nereidae					
Nereis culveri				×	
(= *Laeonereis culveri*)					
N. succinea				×	
(= *Neanthes succinea*)					
Platynereis dumerili	×	×	×		
Suborder Glyceriformia					
Family Goniadidae					
Glycinde solitaria				×	

TABLE 9.1.   (*Continued*)

Species	Econfina River	Fenholloway River	Apalachee Bay	Apalachicola River	Barataria Bay
Order Amphinomida					
Family Amphinomidae					
Amphinome rostrata				×	
Order Eunicida					
Family Onuphidae					
Diopatra cuprea	×	×	×	×	
Marphysa sanguinea				×	
Onuphis sp.				×	
Order Terebellida					
Family Sabellariidae					
Sabellaria vulgaris			×		
Family Pectinariidae					
Pectinaria gouldi			×		
Family Ampharetidae					
Amphicteis gunneri				×	
Melinna maculata				×	
Family Terebellidae					
Amphitrite sp.	×				
Order Sabellida					
Family Sabellidae					
Fabricia sp.				×	
PHYLUM ECHINODERMATA					
Class Holothuroidea					
Order Dendrochirotida					
Family Cucumaridae					
Pentacta pygmae		×	×		
Pentacta sp.	×				
Class Asteroida					
Order Phanerozonia					
Suborder Paxillosa					
Family Luidiidae					
Luida alternata	×	×			
L. clathrata	×	×	×	×	
L. sagamina			×		
Order Spinnulosa					
Family Echinasteridae					
Echinaster parma			×		
E. sentus			×		
E. serpentarius	×	×			
Echinaster sp.			×		

Continued

TABLE 9.1.   (*Continued*)

Species	Econfina River	Fenholloway River	Apalachee Bay	Apalachicola River	Barataria Bay
Class Echinoidea					
Subclass Regularia					
Order Camarodonta					
Family Toxopneustidae					
Lytechinus variegatus	×	×	×		
Subclass Exocyclia					
Order Clypeasteroida					
Family Scutellidae					
Mellita quinquiesperforata				×	
Class Ophiuroidea					
Order Ophiurae					
Family Amphiuridae					
Hemipholis elongata				×	×
Family Ophiothrichidae					
Ophithrix angulata	×	×	×		
Family Ophiodermatidae					
Ophioderma brevispinum	×	×	×		
Family Ophiolepididae					
Ophiolepis elegans			×	×	
PHYLUM MOLLUSCA					
Class Gasteropoda					
Subclass Prosobranchiata					
Order Archaeogastropoda					
Suborder Pleurotomarina					
Family Fissurellidae					
Diodora cayenensis				×	
Suborder Trochina					
Family Trochidae					
Calliostoma euglylptum				×	
Family Turbinidae					
Turbo castanea				×	
Family Neritidae					
Neritina reclivata				×	
Class Polyplacophora					
Order Neoloricata					
Family Acanthochitonidae					
Chiton tuberculatus				×	
Order Mesogastropoda					
Suborder Littorina					
Family Littorinidae					
Littoridina sphinctostoma					×
Family Architectonicidae					
Modulus modulus				×	

TABLE 9.1.   (Continued)

Species	Econfina River	Fenholloway River	Apalachee Bay	Apalachicola River	Barataria Bay
Family Cerithiidae					
Bittum varium			×	×	
(= *Diastoma varium*)					
Cerithiopsis subulata			×		
Cerithium muscarum			×		
Family Epitoniidae					
Epitonium humphreysi			×		
E. rupicola			×	×	
Family Eratoidae					
Erato maugeriae			×		
Family Crepidulidae					
Crepidula fornicata			×		
C. plana			×	×	
Family Natacidae					
Polinices duplicatus	×	×	×	×	
Order Neogastropoda					
Family Muricidae					
Eupleura sulcidentata			×	×	
Murex dilectus			×		
M. rubidus	×	×			
Urosalpinx perrugata			×	×	
Family Columbellidae					
Anachis avara			×	×	
Columbella rusticoides			×		
Mitrella lunata			×	×	
Family Buccinidae					
Cantharus cancellaria				×	
C. multangulus			×		
C. tinctus			×		
Family Melongenidae					
Busycon contarium			×	×	
B. spiratum			×	×	
Melongena corona			×		
Family Nassaridae					
Nassarius vibex			×		
Family Fasaciolariidae					
Fasciolaria hunteria	×		×		
F. tulipa	×		×		
Family Marginellidae					
Prunum apicinum			×	×	
(= *Marginella apicinia*)					

Continued

TABLE 9.1.   (*Continued*)

Species	Econfina River	Fenholloway River	Apalachee Bay	Apalachicola River	Barataria Bay
Family Conidae					
Conus jaspidius steamsi			×		
Family Terebridae					
Terebra sp.			×		
Order Pyramidelloida					
Family Pyramidellidae					
Odostomia bisuturalis				×	
O. laevigata				×	
Subclass Opisthobranchia					
Order Cephalaspidea					
Family Bullidae					
Bulla striata			×		
Family Retusidae					
Retusa canaliculata				×	
Order Nudibranchia					
Suborder Doridoida					
Family Tethyidae					
Tethys willcoxi			×		
(= *Aplysia willcoxi*)					
Bursatella leachi			×		
Class Scaphopoda					
Family Dentaliidae					
Dentalium laqueatum			×		
Class Bivalvia					
Subclass Pteriomorphia					
Order Mytiloida					
Family Mytilidae					
Amygdalum papyria				×	
Brachyodontes exustus			×	×	
B. recurvus			×		
Order Pteroida					
Suborder Pteriina					
Family Pteriidae					
Pinctada imbricata			×		
Family Pectinidae					
Aquipecten irradians	×	×	×		
(= *Agropectin irradians*)					
Family Ostreidae					
Crassostrea virginica			×	×	
Subclass Heterodonta					
Order Veneroida					

TABLE 9.1.   (*Continued*)

Species	Econfina River	Fenholloway River	Apalachee Bay	Apalachicola River	Barataria Bay
Family Cardiidae					
Dinocardium robustum				×	
Laevicardium mortoni			×		
Family Mactridae					
Mactra fragilis				×	
Mulinia lateralis				×	
Rangia cuneata				×	
Spisula solidissima				×	
Family Solenidae					
Ensis directus			×		
E. minor				×	
Family Tellinidae					
Macoma mitchilli				×	
Telina texana				×	
Family Semelidae					
Abra aedualis				×	
Family Solecurtidae					
Tagelus plebeius				×	
Family Dreissenidae					
Congeria leucophaeta				×	
Family Corbiculidae					
Pseudocyrena floridana				×	
Family Veneridae					
Chione cancellata			×		
Dosinia elegans				×	
Class Cephalapoda					
Subclass Coleiodea					
Order Teuthoidea					
Suborder Myopsida					
Family Loliginidae					
Lolliguncula brevis	×	×	×	×	
PHYLUM ARTHROPODA					
Class Crustacea					
Subclass Malacostraca					
Division Hoplocarida					
Order Stomatopoda					
Family Squillidae					
Squilla empusa	×		×	×	
Division Peracarida					
Order Mysidacea					
Suborder Lophogastrida					
Family Mysidae					

Continued

TABLE 9.1. (Continued)

Species	Econfina River	Fenholloway River	Apalachee Bay	Apalachicola River	Barataria Bay
Bowmaniella dissimilis			×	×	
Mysidopsis almyra				×	
M. bahia				×	
M. bigelowi				×	
Taphromysis bowmani				×	
T. louisianae				×	
Order Tanaidacea					
Suborder Dikonophora					
Family Paratanaidae					
Leptochelia rapax			×	×	
Order Isopoda					
Suborder Anthuridea					
Family Anthuridae					
Cyathura polita				×	
Xenanthura montosa				×	
Suborder Flabellifera					
Family Sphaeromidae					
Cassidinisca ovalis				×	
Paracerceis caudata			×		
Sphaeroma quadridentatum				×	
S. terebrans				×	
Suborder Valvifera					
Family Idoteidae					
Cleantis planicaudata			×		
Edotea montosa				×	
Erichsonella filiformis			×	×	
Suborder Asellota					
Family Asellidae					
Asellus attenuatus				×	
A. militaris				×	
Family Munnidae					
Munna reynoldsi				×	
Order Amphipoda					
Suborder Gammaridea					
Family Ampeliscidae					
Ampelisca vadorum			×	×	
A. verilli			×	×	
Family Amphithoidae					
Cymedusa compta			×	×	
Family Aoridae					
Grandidierella bonnieroides				×	
Lembos sp.			×		

TABLE 9.1. (*Continued*)

Species	Econfina River	Fenholloway River	Apalachee Bay	Apalachicola River	Barataria Bay
Rubdilmboides naglei			×		
Family Bateidae					
Batea catharinensis			×	×	
Carinobatea tricarinata				×	
Carinobatea sp.				×	
Family Corophidae					
Corophium louisianum				×	
Corophium sp.			×	×	
Erichthonius sp.			×		
Family Gammaridae					
Elasmopous levis			×		
Gammarus macromucronatus			×	×	
Mellita appendiculata			×	×	
M. nitida			×		
M. quinquiesperforata		×	×		
Family Lysianassidae					
Lysianopsis allea			×		
Microprotopus sp.				×	
Family Oedicerotidae					
Synchelidium americanum			×		
Family Phoxocephalidae					
Paraphoxus sp.			×		
Family Pontogeneiidae					
Pontogeneia sp.			×		
Family Stenothoidae					
Parametopella cypris				×	
Family Talitridae					
Orchestia uhleri				×	
Suborder Caprellida					
Family Caprellidae					
Paracaprella tenuis			×	×	
Division Eucarida					
Order Decapoda					
Suborder Natantia					
Section Penaeidea					
Family Penaeidae					
Penaeus duorarum	×	×	×	×	
P. setiferus	×	×	×	×	
Sicyonia brevirostris	×	×	×		
S. dorsalis				×	
S. laevigata			×		

Continued

TABLE 9.1.   (*Continued*)

Species	Econfina River	Fenholloway River	Apalachee Bay	Apalachicola River	Barataria Bay
S. typica			×		
Trachypenaeus constrictus				×	
T. similis			×	×	
Xiphonpeneus kroyeri				×	
Section Caridea					
Family Alpheidae					
Alpheus armillatus	×	×	×	×	
A. heterochaelis	×	×	×	×	
A. normanni			×	×	
Synalpheus fritzmulleri	×	×	×		
S. minus	×	×	×		
S. townsendi	×	×	×		
Family Hippolytidae					
Hippolyte pleuracanthus	×	×	×		
H. zosterica			×	×	
Latreutes fucorum	×	×	×		
L. parvulus	×	×	×	×	
Lysmata wurdemanni	×	×	×	×	
Tozeuma carolinese	×	×	×	×	
Thor dobkini			×		
T. floridanus	×	×	×		
Family Palaemonidae					
Leander tenuicornis	×	×		×	
Palaemon floridanus	×	×	×	×	
Palaemonetes intermedius	×	×	×	×	
P. pugio	×	×	×		
P. vulgaris	×	×	×	×	
Palaemontes sp.				×	
Periclimenes americanus	×	×	×	×	
P. longicaudatus	×	×	×	×	
Periclimenes sp.			×		
Family Ogyridae					
Ogyrides limicola			×		
Suborder Reptantia					
Section Astacura					
Family Astacidae					
Procambarus paeninsulanus			×	×	
Section Anomura					
Family Diogenidae					
Clibanarius vittatus			×		
Family Paguridae					
Pagurus bonairensis	×	×	×		

TABLE 9.1.   (Continued)

Species	Econfina River	Fenholloway River	Apalachee Bay	Apalachicola River	Barataria Bay
P. longicarpus			×	×	
P. pollicaris	×	×	×	×	
Family Porcellanidae					
Petrolisthes armatus	×	×	×	×	
P. galathinus	×	×	×		
Section Brachyura					
Subsection Oxystomata					
Family Calappidae					
Hepatus pudibundus			×		
Family Leucosiidae					
Ebalia cariosa			×		
Subsection Branchygnatha					
Infrasubsection Oxyrhyncha					
Family Majidae					
Epialtus dilatatus	×	×	×		
Libinia dubia	×	×	×		
Macrocolema camptocerum	×	×	×		
Metaphorhapsis calcerata	×	×	×	×	
Mithrax pleurocanthus	×	×	×		
Pelia mutica	×	×	×		
Pitho anisodon	×	×	×		
Podochela riisei	×	×	×		
Family Parthenopidae					
Hetrocrypta granulata			×		
Infrasubsection Brachyrhyncha					
Family Portunidae					
Callinectes sapidus	×	×	×	×	
C. similis			×	×	
Ovalipes gaudalupensis				×	
Porunus gibbesii	×	×	×	×	
Family Xanthidae					
Eurypanopeus depressus	×	×	×	×	
E. turgidus	×	×			
Hexopanopeus angustifrons	×	×	×		
Mennipe mercenaria	×	×	×	×	
Micropanope pusilla	×	×	×	×	
Neopanope packardii	×	×	×	×	
N. texana	×	×	×	×	
Panopeus herbstii	×	×	×		
Pilumnus dasypodus	×		×		
P. sayi	×		×		

Continued

TABLE 9.1. (*Continued*)

Species	Econfina River	Fenholloway River	Apalachee Bay	Apalachicola River	Barataria Bay
Rhithropanopeus harrisii				×	×	
Family Pinnotheridae					
Pinnixia cylindrica				×	
Pinnotheres maculatus				×	
Family Grapsidae					
Sesarma cinereum				×	×
PHYLUM CHORDATA					
Subphylum Vertebrata					
Class Chondrichthyes					
Order Squaliformes					
Family Carcharhinidae					
Carcharhinus leucas				×	
C. limbatus				×	
Rhizoprionodon terraenovae			×		
Family Sphyrnidae					
Sphyrna tiburo			×	×	
Order Rajiformes					
Family Rajidae					
Pristis poctinata					×
Raja texana		×			
Family Dasyatidae					
Dasyatis sabina	×	×	×	×	×
Gymnura micrura			×	×	
Family Myliobatidae					
Rhinoptera bonasus				×	
Class Osteichthyes					
Order Semionotiformes					
Family Lepisosteidae					
Lepisosteus osseus		×	×	×	
L. platyrhincus	×				
L. spatula				×	
Order Amiiformes					
Family Amiidae					
Amia calva				×	
Order Elopiformes					
Family Elopidae					
Elops saurus		×		×	×
Order Anguilliformes					
Family Anguillidae					
Anguilla rostrata		×		×	
Family Muraenidae					
Gymnothorax nigromarginatus		×	×		

TABLE 9.1. (*Continued*)

Species	Econfina River	Fenholloway River	Apalachee Bay	Apalachicola River	Barataria Bay
Family Ophichthidae					
Myrophis punctatus	×	×	×	×	
Ophichthus gomesi				×	×
Order Clupeiformes					
Family Clupeidae					
Alsoa alabamae			×		×
A. chrysochloris					×
Brevoortia patronus		×	×	×	×
Dorosoma petenense				×	
Harengula jaguana	×	×	×	×	
(= *H. pensacolae*)					
Opisthonema oglinum					×
Sardinella aurita				×	
(= *A. anchovia*)					
Family Engraulidae					
Anchoa hepsetus		×	×	×	×
A. mitchilli	×	×	×	×	×
Order Myctophiformes					
Family Synodontidae					
Synodus foetens	×	×	×	×	×
Order Cypriniformes					
Family Cyprinidae					
Cyprinus carpio				×	
Hybognathus hayi				×	
Notemigonus crysoleucas	×			×	
Notropis petersoni	×				
Notropis sp.				×	
Order Siluriformes					
Family Ictaluridae					
Ictalurus catus				×	
I. natalis	×			×	
Family Ariidae					
Arius felis		×	×	×	×	×
Bagre marinus				×	×	×
Order Batrachoidiformes					
Family Batrachoididae					
Opsanus beta	×	×	×	×	×	×	×
Porichthys plectrodon			×		×
(= *P. porosissimus*)					
Order Gobiesociformes					

Continued

TABLE 9.1.   (*Continued*)

Species	Econfina River	Fenholloway River	Apalachee Bay	Apalachicola River	Barataria Bay
Family Gobiesocidae					
Gobiesox strumosus			×		×
Order Lophiiformes					
Family Lophiidae					
Ogcocephalus radiatus		×	×		
Order Gadiformes					
Family Gadidae					
Urophycis floridana		×		×	×	×
Family Ophidiidae					
Ophidion beani		×	×		×
Family Bythitidae					
Ogilbia cayorum				×	
Order Atheriniformes					
Family Exocoetidae					
Hemirhamphus brasiliensis		×			
Hyporhamphus unifasciatus	×	×	×		
Family Belonidae					
Strongylura marina		×		×	×
S. notata	×	×			
S. timucu	×	×			
Family Cyprinodontidae					
Adinia xenica	×	×	×		×	×
Cyprinodon variegatus	×	×	×	×	×	×
Floridichtys carpio	×	×			
Fundulus chrysotus	×				
F. confluentus	×	×		×	
F. grandis	×	×		×	×
F. similis	×	×		×	×
Jordanella floridae	×				
Lucania goodei	×			×	
L. parva	×	×	×	×	×
Family Poeciliidae					
Gambusia affinis	×	×			
Heterandria formosa	×				
Poecilia latipinna	×	×		×	×
Family Atherinidae					
Membras martinica					×
Menidia beryllina	×	×		×	×
Order Gasterosteiformes					
Family Syngnathidae					
Hippocampus erectus		×	×	×	
H. zosterae		×	×		
Micrognathus criniger	×	×	×		

TABLE 9.1. (*Continued*)

Species	Econfina River	Fenholloway River	Apalachee Bay	Apalachicola River	Barataria Bay
Syngnanthus floridae	×	×	×	×	×
S. louisianae	×	×	×		×
S. scovelli	×	×	×	×	×	×
Order Perciformes					
Family Percichthyidae					
Centropristis striata		×	×	×	×
(= *C. melana*)					
Diplectrum formosum		×	×		×
Mycteroperca microlepis		×			
Serranus subligarius			×		
Family Centrarchidae					
Elassoma evergladei	×				
Lepomis gulosus	×				
L. macrochirus	×				
L. microlophus	×			×	
Lepomis punctatus	×			×	
Micropterus salmoides	×				
Pomoxis nigromaculatus				×	
Family Apogonidae					
Apogon townsendi			×		
Astrapogon stellatus		×			
Family Pomatomidae					
Pomatomus saltatrix				×	
Family Echeneidae					
Echeneis naucrates			×		
Family Carangidae					
Alectis cillaris					×
Caranx bartholomaei				×	
C. hippos		×	×		×	×
Chloroscombrus chrysurus	×	×	×		×	×
Oligoplites saurus	×			×	×
Selene setapinnis					×
S. vomer		×	×		×	×
Trachinotus carolinus			×		×
T. falcatus	×				
Family Lutjanidae					
Lutjanus griseus	×	×	×	×	
L. synagris					×
Family Lobotidae					
Lobotes surinamensis			×		
Family Gerreidae					
Eucinostomus argenteus	×	×	×		×	×

Continued

TABLE 9.1.   (*Continued*)

Species	Econfina River	Fenholloway River	Apalachee Bay	Apalachicola River	Barataria Bay
E. gula	×	×	×		×
Eucinostomus sp.		×	×		×
Family Haemulidae					
Haemulon aurolineatum		×	×		
H. plumieri		×	×	×	×
Haemulon sp.		×			
Orthopristis chrysoptera	×	×	×	×	×
Family Sparidae					
Archosargus probatocephalus	×		×	×	×	×
Calamus arctifrons		×	×	×	
Diplodus hobrooki		×	×	×	×
Lagodon rhomboides	×	×	×	×	×	×	×
Stenotomus caprinus		×			
Family Sciaenidae					
Bairdiella chrysura	×	×	×	×	×	×	×
Cynoscion arenarius		×	×	×	×	×	×
C. nebulosus		×	×	×	×	×
Cynoscion sp.				×	×
Larimus fasciatus					×
Leiostomus xanthurus	×	×	×	×	×	×	×
Menticirrhus americanus		×	×		×	×
M. saxatilis		×		×	
Menticirrhus sp.		×	×		×
Micropogonias undulatus		×	×		×	×
Pogonias cromis	×		×		×
Sciaenops ocellatus	×	×	×	×		×	×
Stellifer lanceolatus				×	×
Family Kyphosidae					
Mullus auratus		×			
Family Ephippidae					
Chaetodipterus faber		×	×	×	×	×
Family Labridae					
Lachnolaimus maximus		×	×		
Family Scaridae					
Nicolsina usta		×	×		
Scarus sp.		×			
Family Mugilidae					
Mugil cephalus	×	×	×	×	×	×
M. curema	×	×		×	
M. trichodon		×			
Mugil sp.				×	

TABLE 9.1. (*Continued*)

Species	Econfina River	Fenholloway River	Apalachee Bay	Apalachicola River	Barataria Bay
Family Sphyraenidae					
Sphyraena barracuda	×		×	×	
S. borealis		×	×	×	
S. quachaucho					×
Family Polynemidae					
Polydactylus octonemus		×	×	×	×	×
Family Uranoscopidae					
Astroscopus y-graecum		×	×	×	
Family Clinidae					
Paraclinus fasciatus		×	×		
P. marmoratus		×	×		
Paraclinus sp.				×	
Family Blennidae					
Chasmodes saburrae	×	×	×	×	
Hypleurochilus geminatus			×		
Hypsoblennius hentzi		×	×	×	
H. ionthas					×
Family Gobiidae					
Bathygobius sopoprator		×	×	×	
Gobioides broussonneti					×
Gobionellus boleosoma		×	×		×	×
G. hastatus		×			×	×
Larimus fasciatus					×
Leiostomus xanthurus	×	×	×	×	×	×	×
Menticirrhus americanus		×	×		×	×
M. saxatilis		×		×	
Menticirrhus sp.		×	×	×	
Micropogonias undulatus		×	×	×	×
Pogonias cromis		×		×		×
Sciaenops ocellatus	×	×	×	×	×	×
Stellifer lanceolatus				×	×
Family Kyphosidae					
Mullus auratus		×			
Family Ephippidae					
Chaetodipterus faber		×	×	×	×	×
Family Labridae					
Lachnolaimus maximus		×	×		
Family Scaridae					
Nicolsina usta		×	×		
Scarus sp.		×			
Family Mugilidae					
Mugil cephalus	×	×	×	×	×	×

Continued

TABLE 9.1.   (*Continued*)

Species	Econfina River	Fenholloway River	Apalachee Bay	Apalachicola River	Barataria Bay
M. curema	×	×		×	
M. trichodon		×			
Mugil sp.				×	
Family Sphyraenidae					
Sphyraena barrracuda	×		×	×	
S. borealis		×	×	×	
S. quachaucho					×
Family Polynemidae					
Polydactylus octonemus		×	×	×	×	×
Family Uranoscopidae					
Astroscopus v-graecum		×	×	×	
Family Clinidae					
Paraclinus fasciatus		×	×		
P. marmoratus		×	×		
Paraclinus sp.				×	
Family Blennidae					
Chasmodes saburrae	×	×	×	×	
Hypleurochilus geminatus		×			
Hypsoblennius hentzi		×	×	×	
H. ionthas					×
Family Gobiidae					
Bathygobius sopoprator		×	×	×	
Gobioides broussonneti					×
Gobionellus boleosoma		×	×		×	×
G. hastatus		×		×	×
Gobionellus stigmaturus	×				
Gobiosoma bosci		×	×	×	×	×
G. robustum	×	×	×	×	
Microgobius gulosus	×	×	×	×	×
M. thalassimus				×	×
Family Trichiuridae					
Trichiurus lepturus					×
Family Scombridae					
Scomberomorus maculatus				×	×
Family Stromateidae					
Peprilus burti		×	×		×	×
P. paru				×	
P. triacanthus					×
Family Scorpaenidae					
Scorpaena brasiliensis		×	×		
Family Triglidae					
Prionotus rubio				×	×

TABLE 9.1.   (Continued)

Species	Econfina River	Fenholloway River	Apalachee Bay	Apalachicola River	Barataria Bay
P. scitulus				×	×
P. tribulus		×		×	×	×
Order Pleuronectiformes					
Family Bothidae					
Ancylopsetta quadrocellata			×	×		×
Citharichtys spilopterus						×
Etropus crossotus		×	×	×		×	×
Paralichthys albigutta			×	×	×	×	×
P. lethostigma			×	×	×	×	×
Paralichthys sp.				×	
Family Soleidae					
Achirus lineatus	×	×				×
Trinectes maculatus		×	×	×		×	×
Family Cynoglossidae					
Symphurus plagiusa		×.	×	×	×	×	×
Family Balistidae					
Aluterus schoepfi			×	×		×
Monacanthus ciliatus			×	×	×	×
M. hispidus	×		×	×	×	×
Family Ostraciidae					
Lactophrys quadricornis			×	×	
Family Tetraodontidae					
Lagocephalus laevigatus						×
Sphoeroides nephelus		×	×	×		×
S. parvus						×
Family Diodontidae					
Chilomycterus schoepfi			×	×		×	×

Seagrass Beds.   In Apalachee Bay, where salinities averaged between 20 and 25 ppt at most stations (35 ppt for full maximum at outermost stations), a total of 39 species of benthic macrophytes were collected by Zimmerman and Livingston (1976). Of the red algae, which provided the most species for the list, *Laurencia poitei, Digenia simplex, Gracilaria verrucosa,* and *G. folifera* had the greatest tolerance for variations in salinity and were, consequently, the most widely distributed species in Apalachee Bay (Zimmerman and Livingston, 1979).

The population and biomass of other macroalgal groups varied over time, but all were present throughout the year. The green algae, *Caulerpa prolifera, Anadyomene stellata, Penicillus capitatus,* and *Udotea* sp., and the red algae,

Laurencia intricata and species of *Gracilaria*, had seasonal biomass and population peaks (Zimmerman and Livingston, 1976, 1979).

Brown algae were found in Apalachee Bay only during the warmer months. Zimmerman and Livingston (1976) reported that *Dictyota divaricata* appeared from early spring to the fall on limestone outcroppings, and *Padina vickersiae* was most often found attached to *Digenia simplex*.

The red algae, *Neoagardhiella ramosissima*, *Eucheuma nudum*, *Halymenia floresia*, and *H. floridana* were collected only in warm months, while *Jania pumila*, *Polysiphonia harveyi*, and *Spyridia filamentosa* appeared during the winter months (Zimmerman and Livingston, 1976).

Some vascular plants showed more seasonal variation than others. The seagrasses, *Thalassia testudinum*, *Halimeda incrassata*, and *Syringodium filiforme*, existed year-long in the most saline areas but showed distinct seasonal variation in biomass. Less biomass variation was shown by *Halophila engelmanni* and *Halodule wrightii* (Zimmerman and Livingston, 1976).

The presence of seagrasses, especially *Thalassia testudinum*, seemed to affect the distribution and abundance of macroalgae. According to Humm (1956), from the Florida keys to the Mississippi sound there was generally a low macroalgal biomass where seagrasses were absent. Some macroalgae, such as the green alga, *Caulerpa prolifera*, and the red algae, *Digeria simplex*, *Laurencia poitei*, *Gracilaria cervicornis*, and *G. verrucosa*, were ubiquitous; however, in areas where seagrasses existed, these species were present in greater quantity. Interestingly, Humm (1964) found 113 species of algae epiphytic on *Thalassia testudinum*, whereas other seagrasses and benthic algae in the same area of study had few, if any, epiphytes. Thus it appears that the distribution of *Thalassia* has a profound effect on the presence of assemblages of benthic macroalgae and hence on the entire community structure.

In Apalachee Bay seagrass biomass is directly correlated with the density of benthic animals (number per square meter) and animal species' richness, relative dominance, species diversity, and indirectly the trophic organization of macrofaunal assemblages. For example, carnivorous and suspension feeding polychaetes are generally closely associated with benthic vegetation, while deposit feeders and omnivores are associated with low macrophyte cover (Stoner, 1980a).

Amphipod abundance appears not to be influenced so much by seasonal changes in macrophyte biomass, but by species-specific reproductive responses and abundances of fish predators as mediated by macrophyte biomass. Amphipod species most affected by predation are those specifically preyed upon by the pinfish, *Lagodon rhomboides*, a major dominant in the fish population (Livingston, 1980).

Seagrasses provide support for epiphytes, protection for small animals from predators, and abundant detritus. Hooks et al. (1976) found that in Apalachee Bay the seagrass-associated group was composed of the caridean shrimps, *Palaemonetes floridanus*, *Tozeuma carolinense*, and *Hippolyte pleuracantha*; the hermit crab, *Pagurus bonairensis* (the most abundant species, 43% of all the organisms collected); the scallop, *Argopectin irradians*; the majid crabs, *Libinia dubia, Metoporhaphis calcerata,* and *Podochela riisei;* and the echinoderms, *Echinaster serpentarius* and *Lytechinus variegatus.*

Dugan and Livingston (1982) found that the echinoderm, *Echinaster sentus,* and the scallop, *Argopectin irradians,* were associated with seagrass beds dominated by *Thalassia testudinum* in Apalachee Bay. They also found that certain dominant crustacean species, such as *Palaemonetes intermedius, P. pugio, Callinectes sapidus, Rithropanopeus harrisii, Eurypanopeus depressus,* and *Panopeus herbstii,* occurred primarily in low-salinity areas. The shrimp, *Penaeus duorarum,* was found in all areas, however, and abundance was inversely proportional to increased salinity (Dugan and Livingston, 1982).

Seagrass beds provide such variability and complexity of habitat for fish that it is often impossible to explain patterns of resource utilization and allocation in a general way. One aspect of fish community structure in seagrass beds that has not received much attention is the temporal structure of these communities, especially diurnal–nocturnal patterns. A review of available data indicates that roughly one-third to one-half of the fish in seagrass assemblages are nocturnally active (Helfman, 1978). Notable exceptions exist in the kelp beds of southern California, where only 13% of the fish tend to be active at night (Ebeling and Bray, 1976), and temperate seagrass beds near Beaufort, North Carolina, where only 3% of the fish were nocturnally active (Adams, 1976). In the latter, only one species was nocturnal (Ryan and Livingston, 1980).

In Apalachee Bay the pinfish, *Lagodon rhomboides,* was the most numerous epibenthic fish predator in seagrass habitats (Stoner, 1980b). Ryan and Livingston (1980) collected pinfish, spot (*Leiostomus xanthurus*), and pigfish (*Orthopristis chrysoptera*) during nocturnal collections in Apalachee Bay, although these three species are not considered nocturnal feeders. Other burrowing or demersal species, such as the speckled worm eel, *Myrophis punctatus;* the longnose cusk-eel, *Ophidion beani;* and two flat fish, the gulf flounder, *Paralichthys albigutta,* and the blackcheek tonguefish, *Symphurus plagiusa,* were captured almost exclusively at night. Stomach content analyses indicated that 17 to 59 species taken engaged in some form of nocturnal feeding (Ryan and Livingston, 1980).

The silver perch, *Bairdiella chrysura,* was the most numerous fish species taken in nocturnal collections by Ryan and Livingston (1980). They also found that the black sea bass, *Centropristis striata,* was nocturnally abundant. Other species collected at night included the southern hake, *Urophycis floridana;* gulf toadfish, *Opsanus beta;* Atlantic threadfin, *Polydactylus octonemus;* longnose cusk-eel, *Ophiodon beani;* and the speckled worm eel, *Myrophis punctatus.*

Zilberberg (1966) found that upper portions of canals in the Apalachee Bay area were dominated by the rainwater killifish, *Lucania parva,* and the mosquito-fish, *Gambusia affinis.* Killifish, *Fundulus* sp., and the sailfin molly, *Poecilia latipinna* (= *Mollienesia latipinna*), predominate in the lower regions of the canals, although striped mullet, *Mugil cephalus,* and sheepshead minnow, *Cyprinodon variegatus,* were locally conspicuous. In tidal ponds the dominant species included the sailfin molly, *Poecilia latipinna;* inland silversides, *Menidia beryllina*; longnose killifish, *Fundulus similis*; rainwater killifish, *Lucania parva*; and mosquitofish, *Gambusia affinis*. During the spring, *Mugil, Leiostomus,* and *Lagodon* became dominant (Zilberberg, 1966).

Oyster reefs.   Oyster reefs offer a sheltered habitat and hard substrate. Species found associated with oyster bars in the Econfina and Fenholloway estuarine areas included brittle stars, *Ophiothrix angulata, Ophioderma brevispinum,* and *Ophiolepis elegans*; bivalves, *Brachiodontes exustus* and *B. recurvus*; the pistol shrimp, *Synalpheus fritzmulleri*; and crabs, *Portunus gibbesi, Eurypanopeus depressus, Menippe mercenaria, Petrolisthes armatus,* and *P. galathinus* (Hooks et al., 1976; Dugan and Livingston, 1982).

Mud flats.   An abundant and dominant organism in the mud flats of the Apalachee Bay region was the polychaete, *Diopatra cuprea.* Two other species often collected in this habitat were the isopod, *Cleantis planicuada,* and the free-swimming polychaete, *Platynereis dumrilii.* The crab, *Callinectes sapidus,* was also relatively abundant (Hooks et al., 1976).

Escambia River Estuary

Freshwater.   The Escambia River estuary, like the Econfina and Fenholloway estuaries, lies in the coastal plain and has headwaters of very soft, fresh water. The water of the Escambia River has a brownish color because many small streams rich in humates drain into it.

The strong freshwater flow of the Escambia has a profound effect on the salinity of the estuary. Study areas nearest the mouth of the river (Figure 9.4) had salinities ranging between 106 ppm and 18 ppt. In the winter and spring, when there was considerable freshwater runoff, the lower part of the river was oligohaline to fresh on its upper surface, and more saline along the riverbed, where salt water from the gulf intruded. Near the mouth of the river a few euryhaline species were found on the riverbed during the entire year. During the summer months and through late fall, a saltwater tongue extended up the estuary, gradually fading away at about mile 10.

When the flow of fresh water was least, and the saltwater influence greatest, some freshwater species disappeared near the mouth of the river.

At the time these studies were made there were no towns or industries on the Escambia River or in the estuary. As a result, in the fall the level of phosphates was extremely low, less than 1 ppb, and the nitrates varied from 50 to 140 ppb. Ammonia varied from 50 to 120 ppb, and dissolved oxygen was near saturation for a brown-water river rich in humates (Table 9.2).

The study area farthest from the mouth of the estuary was completely fresh during the year. It was located at mile 12 to 12.1 (Figure 9.4), just above the point where the river divided to form the White River and the Escambia Channel. At that point the current was relatively swift (ANSP, 1953).

Structure of Community

Algae.   The banks of the river in the freshwater region of study were either tree covered or swamplands. The shallow left bank of this freshwater station provided an excellent substrate for the dominant alga, the yellow-green,

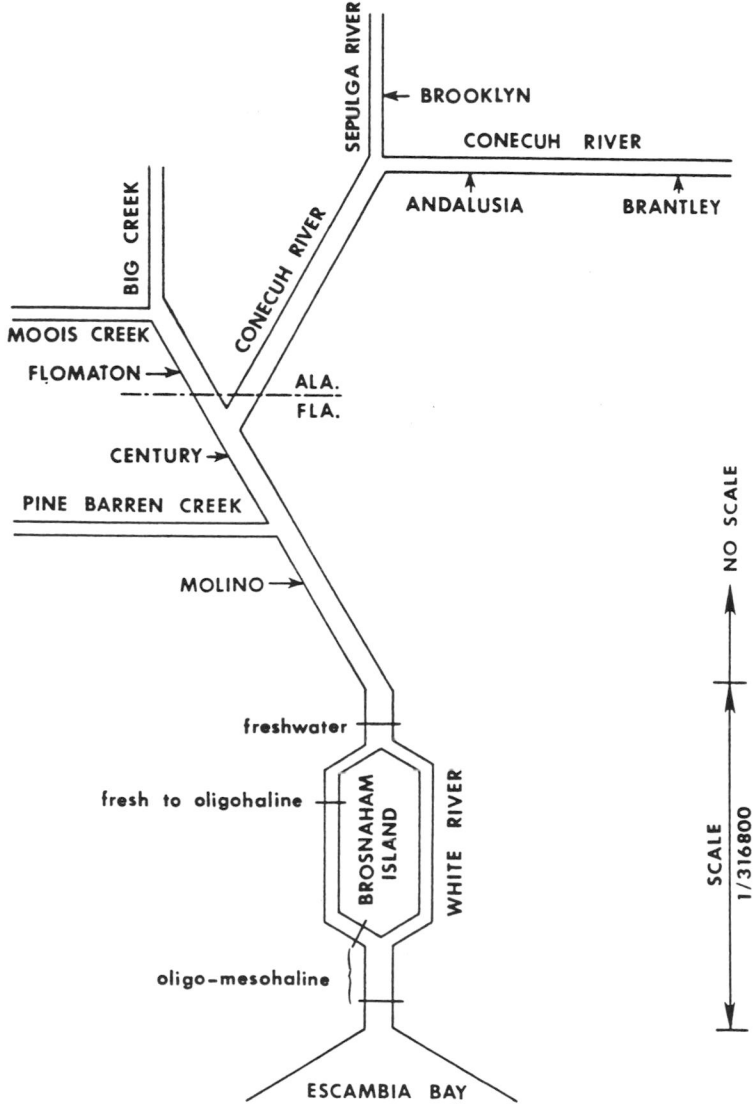

FIGURE 9.4. Diagrammatic map of the drainage basin of the Escambia River of Florida. (From ANSP, 1953.)

Vaucheria sp. A series of pilings at the upper end of the area provided some habitats dominated primarily by the red algae, *Batrachospermum moniliforme* and *B. pyramidala*. At the lower end of the freshwater region fallen willow trees provided excellent habitats for various diatoms and algae during the spring survey. The dominant species in this habitat were a red alga, *Batrachospermum pyramidala*; a green alga, *Tetraspora lubrica*; and the diatom, *Eunotia pectinalis* v. *ventralis*. There was considerable swamp drainage into the riverine system,

TABLE 9.2.   Chemical Analyses of Surface Samples of the Escambia River, Florida[a].

	Freshwater	Oligohaline	Mesohaline– Oligohaline
Alkalinity, M.O. as $CaCO_3$	27.6–29.0	32.4	41.0–39.0
CO_2	4.4–4.6	5.2	5.1–3.9
Cl	3.2–185	965	2500–2750
D.O.	8.4–8.65	8.2	7.4–7.65
Total hardness as $CaCO_3$	23.2–86.8	370	900–1000
Ca	7.44–11.0	28.0	60–68
Mg	1.12–14.4	73.0	180–200
Fe	0.26–0.28	0.07	0.01
NH_3–N	0.05–0.06	0.1	0.12–0.25
NO_2–N	0.002	0.004	0.003–0.004
NO_3–N	0.14	0.05	0.05–0.07
PO_4–P	<0.001	<0.001	<0.001
SiO_2	7.9–8.0	7.4	6.8
SO_4	3.2–25.5	240	480–570
Turbidity	8–15	9	8–9
Temperature $(°C)$[b]	22.0–22.5	16.5	19.5–22.5
pH	7.1	7.1	7.1–7.3

Source: ANSP (1953).
[a]All results in ppm, except pH and temperature.
[b]Taken at time of sampling for D.O.

as evidenced by the presence of such diatoms as species of the genera *Frustulia* and *Eunotia*, and also by *Tabelaria fenestrata*. The well-developed desmid flora also indicated the low pH value of swamp water (Table 9.3).

Protozoa.   Protozoan fauna was dominated by autotrophic flagellates. Sarcodinia (amoebae) were present in larger numbers in freshwater than in lower parts of the river that felt the effects of saltwater. Cilliates were quite common and probably reflected rainage from the swamp, as there were no known human-made sources of pollution at the time of these studies.

Invertebrates.   The invertebrate fauna was well developed in the freshwater habitat. Two species of freshwater sponges, *Meyenia crateriformis* and *Trochospongilla leidii*, were taken from wood in 10 ft of water. Tubificid worms were represented in fair numbers in spring and fall by *Brancheura sowerbyi* and species of *Limnodrilus* and *Drilocrius*. Numbers of a *Premnodrilus* species were found in the spring.

The most common bryozoan was *Plumetella repens*, found on wood in the spring. Leeches were found only in the fall of the year in this area. Of frequent occurrence were *Helobdella nepheloidea* and *Placobdella parasitica*.

The more common mollusc in this area was *Campeloma lewisii* in the spring. Several small species of gastropods were taken from wood, lily pads, and from among the roots and stalks of saw grass (*Cladium jamaicense*). Of the pulmonate

(text continues on page 615)

TABLE 9.3.   *Species of the Escambia River*

Species	Freshwater	Oligohaline	Mesohaline-Oligohaline
DIVISION BACILLARIOPHYTA			
Class Bacillariophyceae			
Order Fragilariales			
Family Fragilariaceae			
Tabellaria fenestrata	×	×	×
Opephora martyi	×	×	×
Fragilaria crotonensis	×	×	
F. leptostauron var. *rhomboides*	×		
Fragilaria spp.	×	×	×
Synedra acus var. *angustissima*	×	×	
S. affinis		×	×
S. pulchella var. *lacerata*	×	×	
S. rumpens	×		
S. ulna	×	×	
S. ulna var. *danica*	×	×	
S. ulna var. *ramesi*	×	×	
Synedra spp.	×	×	×
Order Eunotiales			
Family Eunotiaceae			
Eunotia flexosa	×	×	×
E. lunaris	×	×	
E. pectinalis var. *minor*			
E. pectinalis var. *minor* f. *impressa*			×
E. pectinalis var. *ventralis*	×	×	
E. robusta var. *tetraodon*	×		
E. veneris	×	×	×
Eunotia spp.	×	×	×
Desmogonium rabenhorstianum var. *elongatum*			×
Order Achnanthales			
Family Achnanthaceae			
Cocconeis placentula var. *lineata*	×	×	×
Cocconeis spp.	×	×	×
Achnanthes chilensis		×	
A. clevei	×		
A. coarctata var. *elliptica*	×		
A. exigua var. *heterovalvata*	×	×	×
A. lanceolata	×		
A. lanceolata var. *apiculata*	×	×	×
A. lanceolata var. *dubia*	×	×	×
A. minutissima	×	×	×
Order Naviculales			
Family Naviculaceae			

Continued

TABLE 9.3. (*Continued*)

Species	Freshwater	Oligohaline	Mesohaline-Oligohaline
Mastogloia sp.		×	
Amphipleura pellucida	×	×	×
A. rutilans		×	×
Frustulia rhomboides	×	×	×
F. rhomboides var. *crassinervia*	×	×	×
F. vulgaris	×		
F. weinholdii	×	×	×
Gyrosigma kuzingii	×	×	
G. scalproides	×		
G. spencerii	×		
G. spencerii var. *nodifera*	×	×	×
Gyrosigma spp.	×	×	×
Pleurosigma sp.		×	×
Caloneis fasciata		×	×
Diploneis didyma		×	
D. elliptica		×	×
D. ovalis	×	×	×
D. puella		×	×
Diploneis sp.		×	×
Stauroneis anceps	×		
S. crucicula	×	×	×
S. phoenicenteron	×		
Stauroneis sp.			×
Anomoeoneis exilis	×	×	×
A. serians var. *brachycera*	×	×	×
Navicula auriculata		×	×
N. canalis	×	×	×
N. confervacea			×
N. creuzburgensis		×	×
N. cryptocephala	×		
N. cryptocephala var. *intermedia*	×		
N. expansa		×	×
N. hungarica var. *capitata*	×	×	×
N. minima var. *atomoides*		×	
N. peregrina	×	×	
N. pupula			×
N. pupula var. *capitata*	×		
N. pupula var. *rectangularis*	×		
N. schroeteri	×	×	×
N. spicula			×
N. subtilissima	×		
N. symmetrica		×	
N. viridula var. *linearis*	×	×	
Navicula spp.	×	×	×
Pinnularia interrupta f. *minor*		×	

TABLE 9.3.   (Continued)

Species	Freshwater	Oligohaline	Mesohaline-Oligohaline
P. viridis	×		
Pinnularia sp.		×	
Amphiprora alata		×	×
Torpidoneis? lepidoptera	×		
Family Gomphonemaceae			
Amphora cymbiformis		×	×
A. delicatissima		×	
Amphora sp.			×
Cymbella aspera	×	×	
C. microcephala	×	×	×
C. scotica	×	×	×
C. turgida	×		
C. turgidula	×	×	×
C. ventricosa	×	×	×
Cymbella sp.			×
Gomphonema acuminatum var. coronata	×	×	×
G. elongatum	×	×	
G. gracile var. naviculoides	×	×	×
G. intricatum	×		
G. intricatum var. pulvinatum	×		
G. parvulum var. parvulum	×	×	×
Gomphonema spp.	×		
Order Epithemiales			
Family Epithemiaceae			
Rhopalodia gibberula			×
Order Bacillariales			
Family Bacillariaceae			
Bacillaria paradoxa	×	×	×
Nitzschia acicularis	×	×	
N. brevissima	×	×	
N. clausii	×	×	×
N. denticula		×	×
N. dissipata	×		
N. fasciculata		×	×
N. filiformis	×	×	×
N. fonticola		×	×
N. frustulum	×		
N. frustulum var. subsalina		×	
N. ignorata	×		×
N. kutzingiana	×	×	×
N. lanceolata		×	
N. lorenziana var. subtilis	×	×	
Nitzschia palea	×	×	
N. paleacea	×	×	×

Continued

TABLE 9.3.   (*Continued*)

Species	Freshwater	Oligohaline	Mesohaline-Oligohaline
N. panduriformis var. *continua*			×
N. romana	×	×	×
N. sigma	×	×	×
N. tryblionella var. *levidensis*	×		×
N. tryblionella var. *victoriae*	×	×	×
Nitzschia spp.	×	×	×
Order Surirellales			
Family Surirellaceae			
Stenopterobia intermedia	×		
Surirella angusta	×		
S. guatimalensis	×		
S. ovalis	×		
S. ovata var. *salina*		×	
S. striatula		×	×
S. suecica	×	×	
S. tenera var. *nervosa*	×		
Surirella spp.	×	×	×
Order Coscinodiscales			
Family Coscinodiscaceae			
Melosira varians	×	×	
Melosira spp.		×	×
Cyclotella meneghiniana		×	
C. pumila			×
C. stelligera	×	×	×
C. striata var. *ambigua*		×	
Order Biddulphiales			
Family Biddulphiaceae			
Terpsinoe muscica			×
Terpsinoe sp.			×
DIVISION CYANOPHYTA			
Class Myxophyceae			
Order Chamaesiphonales			
Family Chamaesiphonaceae			
Chamaesiphon incrustans			×
Order Oscillatoriales			
Suborder Oscillatorineae			
Family Oscillatoriaceae			
Spirulina subsalsa	×		
Oscillatoria geminata	×		
O. limosa	×	×	
O. probaoscidea	×		
Oscillatoria splendida	×	×	×
Phormidium retzii	×	×	
P. subuliforme		×	
P. valderianum	×		

TABLE 9.3.   (Continued)

Species	Freshwater	Oligohaline	Mesohaline-Oligohaline
Lyngbya aerugineo-caerulea		×	
L. putealis	×	×	
Microcoleus chthonoplastes			×
M. paludosus	×		
M. tenerrimus		×	×
Suborder Nostocineae			
Family Nostacaceae			
Nostoc muscorum	×		
Family Scytonemataceae			
Scytonema javanicum	×		
Family Stigonemataceae			
Hapalosiphon pumilus		×	
Family Rivularaceae			
Calothrix parietina		×	
DIVISION CHLOROPHYTA			
Class Chlorophyceae			
Order Tetrasporales			
Family Tetrasporaceae			
Tetraspora sp.	×	×	
Tetraspora lubrica	×		
Order Chlorococcales			
Family Scenedesmaceae			
Scenedsemus bijuga	×		
Order Ulotrichales			
Family Ulotrichaceae			
Ulothrix tenerrima	×		
Family Microsporaceae			
Microspora tumidula		×	
Family Chaetophoraceae			
Stigeoclonium sp.	×		
Stigeoclonium stagnatile		×	
Chaetophora attenuata	×		
C. elegans	×	×	
C. pisiformis	×	×	
Draparnaldia glomerata	×	×	
Aphanochaete repens	×		
Chaetosphaeridium globosum	×		
Order Oedogoniales			
Family Oedogoniaceae			
Bulbochaete spp.	×		
Bulbochaete minuta		×	
Oedogonium spp.	×	×	×
Order Cladophorales			
Family Cladophoraceae			

Continued

TABLE 9.3. *(Continued)*

Species	Freshwater	Oligohaline	Mesohaline-Oligohaline
Rhizoclonium sp.		×	
Rhizoclonium hieroglyphicum	×		
Basicladia chelonum	×		
Order Desmidales			
Family Gonatozygaceae			
Gonatozygon monotaenium	×		
Order Zygnematales			
Family Zygnemataceae			
Mougeotia spp.	×	×	×
Spirogyra spp.	×	×	×
Zygnema sp.	×	×	
Family Desmidaceae			
Closterium moniliferum	×		
C. parvulum	×		
Cosmarium sp.	×		
Cosmarium octhodes	×		
C. punctulatum var. *subpunctulatum*	×		
Spondylosium pulchrum	×		
Hyalotheca dissiliens	×		
H. mucosa	×		
Desmidium baileyii	×		
D. swartzii	×		
Class Charophyceae			
Order Charales			
Family Characeae			
Nitella sp.	×		
Nitella flexilis		×	
DIVISION RHODOPHYTA			
Class Rhodophyceae			
Subclass Bangioideae			
Order Bangiales			
Family Bangiaceae			
Bangia atropurpurea	×		
Family Compsopogonaceae			
Compsopogon coeruleus	×	×	×
Subclass Florideae			
Order Nemalionales			
Family Chantransiaceae			
Audouinella violacea	×		
Acrochaetium sp.			×
Family Batrachospermaceae			
Batrachospermum sp.	×		
? *B. globosporum*		×	
B. louisianae		×	×
? *B. macrosporum*	×		

TABLE 9.3.   (*Continued*)

Species	Freshwater	Oligohaline	Mesohaline-Oligohaline
? B. moniliforme	×		
B. pyramidale	×		
Family Lemaneaceae			
Tuomeya fluviatilis	×	×	
Order Ceramiales			
Family Delesseriaceae			
Caloglossa (prob. *leprieurii*)		×	
Family Rhodomelaceae			
Bostrychia sp.		×	
DIVISION CHRYSOPHYTA			
Class Xanthophyceae			
Order Heterosiphonales			
Family Vaucheriaceae			
Vaucheria sp.	×		
Vaucheria geminata		×	
V. schleicheri	×		
PHYLUM PROTOZOA			
Subphylum Plasmodroma			
Class Mastigophora			
Subclass Phytomastigia			
Order Crysomonadida			
Suborder Euchrysomonadida			
Family Chromulinidae			
Chromulina sp.	×		
Oikomonas ocellata	×		
Oikomonas sp.	×		
Family Syncryptidae			
Hymenomonas sp.	×		
Family Ochromonadidae			
Anthophysa steinii	×		
A. vegetans	×		
Dinobryon sp.	×	×	
Monas sociabilis		×	
Ochromonas crenata	×		
O. variabilis	×		
Poteriochromonas stipitata	×		
Suborder Rhizochrysidina			
Chrysarachnion insidians		×	
Chrysothylakion vorax			×
Order Cryptomonadida			
Suborder Eucryptomonadina			
Family Cryptomonadidae			
Chilomonas paramecium	×	×	×
Cryptomonas lucens	×		

Continued

TABLE 9.3.   (*Continued*)

Species	Freshwater	Oligohaline	Mesohaline-Oligohaline
C. ovata	×		
Family Nephroselmidae			
Nephroselmis olvacea	×		
Order Phytomonadida			
Family Chlamydomonadidae			
Brachiomonas sp.	×		×
Chlamydomonas autumnalis	×		
C. elongata		×	
C. globosa	×		
C. intermedia	×		
C. nasuta		×	
Chlamydomonas sp.	×	×	
Sphaerellopsis fluviatilis	×		
Family Carteriidae			
Carteria caudata	×		
C. cordiformis		×	
C. ellipsoidalis		×	
Carteria sp.	×		
Family Chlorasteridae			
Chloraster sp.			×
Family Volvocidae			
Gonium pectorale		×	
Order Euglenoidida			
Family Euglenidae			
Euglena agilis			×
E. anabaena		×	
E. dicentra	×		
E. ehrenbergii	×		
E. fusca	×		×
E. gracilis			×
E. intermedia		×	
E. oxyuris		×	
E. pisciformis	×		
E. pyrum	×		
E. spirogyra	×	×	
E. suecica	×		
E. viridis	×		×
Euglena sp.	×		×
Lepocinclis buetschlii	×		
L. fusiformis	×		
L. sphagnophila	×	×	
L. texta			×
Phacus auminata			×
P. anacoelus	×		
P. helikoides	×		

TABLE 9.3.   (*Continued*)

Species	Freshwater	Oligohaline	Mesohaline-Oligohaline
P. margaritatus	×		
P. pyrum		×	
P. triqueter			×
Trachelomonas acanthostoma		×	
T. annulata		×	
T. armata	×		
T. caudata		×	
T. fluviatilis	×		
T. hispida		×	
T. incerta		×	
T. volgensis	×	×	
Trachelomonas sp.		×	×
Family Astasiidae			
Menoidium incurvatum	×		
Peranema granulifera	×		
P. trichophorum	×	×	×
Petalomonas mira			×
P. prototheca	×		
Petalomonas sp.		×	×
Scytomonas pusilla	×		
Sphenomonas teres		×	
Urceolus sp.	×		
Family Anisonemidae			
Anisonema emarginatum		×	
A. ovale		×	
Entosiphon obliquum	×		
Entosiphon sp.		×	
Heteronema acutissimum	×		
Notosolenus apocampus		×	
Order Dinoflagellida			
Suborder Prorocentrina			
Family Prorocentridae			
Exuviaella apora			×
Prorocentrum triangulatum			×
Suborder Peridiniina			
Superfamily Gymnodiniodea			
Family Cystodiniidae			
Glenodinium neglectum			×
G. pulvisculum		×	
Glenodinium sp.			×
Family Pronoctilucidae			
Pronoctiluca tentaculatum			×
Family Polykrikidae			
Polykrikos barnegatensis			×

Continued

TABLE 9.3.   (*Continued*)

Species	Freshwater	Oligohaline	Mesohaline-Oligohaline
Superfamily Peridinioidea			
Family Peridiniidae			
Peridinium globulus			×
Subclass Zoomastigia			
Order Rhizomastigida			
Family Mastigamaebidae			
Mastigamoeba aspera	×		
Order Protomonadida			
Family Bodonidae			
Bodo alexeieffii			×
B. amoebinus	×	×	
B. angustus	×		
B. caudatus	×	×	×
B. cruzi		×	
B. edax	×	×	
B. globosus	×		
B. lens			×
B. triangularis	×		
Bodo sp.	×	×	
Class Sarcodina			
Subclass Rhizopoda			
Order Amoebida			
Family Amoebidae			
Amoeba actinophora	×		
A. gorgonia	×		
A. proteus	×	×	
A. striata			×
A. vespertilio	×		
Amoeba sp.	×		
Vahlkampfia limax	×	×	
Order Testacdia			
Family Gromiidae			
Gromia sp.	×		×
Family Arcellidae			
Arcella catinus	×		
A. dentata	×		
A. vulgaris		×	
Arcella sp.	×		
Hyalosphenia cuneata	×		
Family Difflugiidae			
Difflugia acuminata		×	
D. bacillariarum	×		
D. corona	×		
D. oblonga	×		×
D. oviformis			×

TABLE 9.3. (*Continued*)

Species	Freshwater	Oligohaline	Mesohaline-Oligohaline
Difflugia sp.		×	
Phryganella acropodia		×	
Family Euglyphidae			
Corythion pulchellum	×		
Euglypha cristata	×		
E. scutigera	×		
E. strigosa	×		
Euglypha sp.	×	×	
Nebela sp.	×	×	
Subclass Actinopoda			
Order Heliozoida			
Family Actinophryidae			
Actinophrys sol	×		
A. vesiculata			×
Family Lithocoelidae			
Astrodisculus radians	×		
Family Acanthocystidae			
Acanthocystis aculeata	×	×	
Subphylum Ciliophora			
Class Ciliata			
Subclass Holotricha			
Order Gymnostomatida			
Suborder Rhabdophorina			
Family Holopohryidae			
Lacrymaria olor		×	
Family Colepidae			
Coleps hirtus		×	
Family Spathidiidae			
Spathidium vermiforme	×		
Family Didiniidae			
Mesodinium pulex	×		
Family Amphileptidae			
Hemiophrys bivacuolata		×	
Lionotus trichocystus	×		
Lionotus sp.	×	×	×
Family Tracheliidae			
Dileptus amphileptoides	×		
D. anser	×		
D. bivacuolatus	×		
Family Loxodidae			
Loxodes rostrum	×		
L. vorax	×		
Suborder Cyrtophorina			
Family Dysteriidae			

Continued

TABLE 9.3.   (*Continued*)

Species	Freshwater	Oligohaline	Mesohaline-Oligohaline
Dysteria distyla		×	
Trochilioides recta		×	
Family Chlamydodontidae			
Chilodonella cucullulus	×	×	
Family Nassulidae			
Nassula aurea	×		
N. gracilis	×		
Order Hymenostomatida			
Suborder Peniculina			
Family Parameciidae			
Paramecium aurelia	×		×
Family Frontoniidae			
Cinetochilum margaritaceum	×	×	
C. marinum			×
Colpidium campylum		×	
Frontonia sp.		×	
Glaucoma avellana	×		
G. macrostoma	×		
Pseudoglaucoma muscorum		×	
Urocentrum turbo	×	×	
Suborder Pleuronematina			
Family Pleuronematidae			
Cyclidium citrullus	×		
Cyclidium sp.	×		
Pleuronema coronatum		×	
Subclass Spirotricha			
Order Heterotrichida			
Family Metopidae			
Metopus ridiculus			×
Family Condylostomatidae			
Condylostoma remanei			×
C. tardum			×
Family Stentoridae			
Climacostomum virens		×	
Stentor niger			×
Order Oligotrichida			
Family Halteriidae			
Halteria grandinella	×	×	
Strombidium conicum		×	
S. styliferum		×	
Strombidium sp.	×		
Strombilidium caudatum			×
Order Hypotrichida			
Family Oxytrichidae			
Gastrostyla pulchra			×

TABLE 9.3. (*Continued*)

Species	Freshwater	Oligohaline	Mesohaline-Oligohaline
Gastrostyla sp.			×
Gonostomum strenuum	×		
Holosticha intermedia	×		
Oxytricha bifaria	×		
O. fallax		×	
O. furcata	×		
O. marina			×
O. procera	×		
Oxytricha sp.		×	
Stylonychia mytilus		×	×
Tachysoma pellionella			×
Uroleptus dispar	×		
U. limnetis	×		
U. violaceus	×		
Urosoma cienkowskii		×	
Family Euplotidae			
Euplotes eurystomus			×
E. muscicola	×		
E. novemcarinatus	×		
Euplotes sp.	×		
Family Aspidiscidae			
Aspidisca aculeata			×
A. costata	×	×	
A. lynceus	×		
Aspidisca sp.	×		
Subclass Peritricha			
Order Peritrichida			
Suborder Sessilina			
Family Vorticellidae			
Vorticella campanula		×	
V. citrina		×	
V. floridensis			×
V. globosa		×	
V. monilata	×		
V. picta		×	
V. similis			×
Vorticella sp.	×	×	
Family Epistylidae			
Rhabdostyla vernalis	×		
Class Suctoria			
Order Suctorida			
Family Acinetidae			
Acineta tuberosa			×

Continued

TABLE 9.3.   (*Continued*)

Species	Freshwater	Oligohaline	Mesohaline-Oligohaline
PHYLUM PORIFERA			
Class Demospongiae			
Subclass Ceractinomorpha			
Order Haplosclerida			
Family Spongillidae			
Meyenia crateriformis	×		
Trochospongilla leidii	×	×	
T. horrida	×	×	
PHYLUM CNIDARIA			
Class Hydrozoa			
Order Athecata			
Family Clavidae			
Cordylophora lacustris			×
PHYLUM PLATYHELMINTHES			
Class Turbellaria			
Order Tricladida			
Suborder Proburalia			
Family Planariide			
Dugesia tigrina	×		
PHYLUM ASCHELMINTHES			
Class Rotifera			
Subclass Monogononta			
Order Flosculariacea			
Family Testudinellidae			
Pompholyx complanata	×	×	
Testudinella discoidea		×	
Order Ploima			
Family Notommatidae			
Cephalodella gibba	×		
C. poitera		×	
Family Synchaetidae			
Ploesoma hudsoni	×		
P. lenticulare	×		
P. truncatum	×	×	
Polyarthra minor		×	
P. remata	×	×	×
P. vulgaris	×	×	
Family Trichocercidae			
Trichocerca longiseta		×	
Family Asplanchnidae			
Asplanchnopus multiceps		×	
Family Brachionidae			
Anuraeopsis fissa		×	
Brachionus mirabilis		×	
Kellicottia bostoniensis	×	×	
K. cochlearis	×	×	×

TABLE 9.3. (*Continued*)

Species	Freshwater	Oligohaline	Mesohaline-Oligohaline
K. crassa	×	×	
K. gracilenta	×	×	
K. quadricornis		×	
Colurella colurus		×	×
Lecane brilla	×		
L. lunaris	×	×	
L. scutata		×	
L. stokesii		×	
L. sylvatica	×		
Lepadella ovalis	×	×	
L. patella	×	×	
Macrochaetus subquadratus	×		
Trichotria tetractis		×	
PHYLUM BRYOZOA			
Class Phylactolaemata			
Order Plumatellina			
Family Plumatellidae			
Plumatella repens	×	×	
Fredericella sultana		×	
PHYLUM ANNELIDA			
Class Polychaeta			
Order Spionida			
Suborder Spioniformia			
Family Spionidae			
Polydora sp.			×
Order Phyllodocida			
Suborder Nereidiformia			
Family Nereidae			
Laeonereis culveri		×	×
Order Eunicida			
Family Arabellidae			
Drilonereis sp.			×
Class Hirudinea			
Order Rhynchobdella			
Family Glossiphoniidae			
Helobdella stagnalis	×		
H. nepheloidea	×	×	×
Placobdella parasitica	×		
Family Piscicolidae			
Piscicola sp.			×
Illinobdella sp.	×		
Order Arhynchobdellida			
Family Erpobdellidae			
Erpobdella punctata	×		

Continued

TABLE 9.3.   (*Continued*)

Species	Freshwater	Oligohaline	Mesohaline-Oligohaline
Dina microstoma	×		
Class Oligochaeta			
Order Plesiopora			
Family Naididae			
Stylaria lacustris	×		
S. fossularis	×		
Family Tubificidae			
Limnodrilus sp.	×		
Monopylephorus sp.	×	×	
Branchiura sowerbyi	×		
Order Prosopora			
Family Lubriculidae			
Premnodrilus ? sp.	×	×	
PHYLUM MOLLUSCA			
Class Gastropoda			
Subclass Prosobranchiata			
Order Archaeogastropoda			
Suborder Trochina			
Family Neritidae			
Neritina reclivata		×	×
Order Mesogastropoda			
Suborder Littorina			
Family Viviparidae			
Campeloma lewisii	×		
Family Valvatidae			
Valvata bicarinata	×		
Family Amnicolidae			
Amnicola sp.	×		
Lyrodes ? sp.	×		
Pomatiopsis lapidaria		×	
Order Basommatophora			
Family Lymnaeidae			
Pseudosuccinea columella	×	×	
Family Ferrissiidae			
Ferrissia fusca	×	×	
Family Planorbidae			
Menetus alabamensis	×		
Family Physidae			
Physa sp.	×	×	×
Class Bivalvia			
Subclass Palaeoheterodonta			
Order Unionida			
Family Unionidae			
Micromya vibex	×		
M. lienosa	×		

TABLE 9.3.   (Continued)

Species	Freshwater	Oligohaline	Mesohaline-Oligohaline
Lampsilis claibornensis	×		
L. anodontoides	×		
Anodonta gibbosa	×		
A. imbecillis	×		
Quadrula succissa	×		
Q. nr. *succissa*	×		
Quadrula sp.	×		
Elliptio crassidens	×		
E. arctatus	×		
Family Sphaeriidae			
Sphaerium sp.	×		
Pisidium sp.	×		
Subclass Heterodonta			
Order Veneroida			
Family Mactidae			
Rangia sp.		×	×
Family Dreissenidae			
Mytilopsis leucophaeatus	×	×	×
PHYLUM ARTHROPODA			
Class Crustacea			
Subclass branchiopoda			
Division Oligobranchipoda			
Order Cladocera			
Suborder Eucladocera			
Family Chydoridae			
Eurycercus lamellatus	×		
Subclass Branchiura			
Family Argulidae			
Argulus sp.			×
Subclass Cirripedia			
Order Thoracica			
Suborder Balanomorpha			
Family Balanidae			
Balanus amphitrite niveus		×	×
Subclass Malacostraca			
Division Peracarida			
Order Mysidacea			
Suborder Mysida			
Family Mysidae			
Mysos stenolepis	×	×	×
Order Isopoda			
Suborder Flabelifera			
Family Sphaeromidae			
Cassidisca lunifrons	×	×	×

Continued

TABLE 9.3. (*Continued*)

Species	Freshwater	Oligohaline	Mesohaline-Oligohaline
Sphaeroma destructor		×	×
Suborder Asellota			
Family Asellidae			
Asellus attenuatus	×	×	
Order Amphipoda			
Suborder Gammaridea			
Family Corophiidae			
Corophium crassicorne	×	×	×
Erichthonius brasiliensis		×	×
Family Gammaridae			
Carinogammarus mucronatus	×	×	×
Crangonyx gracilis	×		
Melita nitida		×	×
Family Talitridae			
Hyalella azteca	×		
Division Eucarida			
Order Decapoda			
Suborder Natantia			
Section Caridea			
Family Palaemonidae			
Macrobrachium ohione	×		×
Palaemonetes pugio	×	×	
Suborder Reptantia			
Section Astacura			
Family Callianassidae			
Callianassa sp.			×
Section Brachyura			
Subsection Branchygnatha			
Infrasubsection Brachyrhyncha			
Family Portunidae			
Callinectes sapidus	×	×	×
Family Xanthidae			
Rithropanopeus harrisii		×	×
Family Ocypodidae			
Uca pugnax	×	×	
Subphylum Chelicerata			
Class Arachnida			
Order Acari			
Family Lebertiidae			
Lebertia sp.	×		×
Class Insecta			
Subclass Pterygota			
Infraclass Paleoptera			
Order Ephemeroptera			
Family Baetidae			

TABLE 9.3. (*Continued*)

Species	Freshwater	Oligohaline	Mesohaline-Oligohaline
Isonychia sp.	×	×	
Paraleptophlebia volitans	×		
Blasturus poss. *intermedius*		×	
Ephemerella hirsuta	×		
E. trilineata	×	×	
Tricorythodes sp.	×		
Brachycercus nitidus	×		
Baetis spinosus	×	×	×
Pseudocloeon prob. *parvulum*	×	×	
Pseudocloeon sp.	×		
Neocloeon prob. *alamance*		×	×
Cloeon poss. *rubropictum*		×	
Callibaetis sp.			×
Family Heptageniidae			
Stenonema sp.	×	×	
Stenonema pulchellum	×		
Heptagenia flavescens		×	
H. nr. *julia*	×		
Family Ephemeridae			
Hexagenia munda elegans?	×	×	
Order Odonata			
Suborder Anisoptera			
Family Aeshnidae			
Negomphoides ambigua		×	
Gomphus lividus	×		
G. nr. *notatus*	×		
G. nr. *spicatus*	×		
G. nr. *dilatatus*	×		
Boyeria vinosa		×	
Nasiaeshna sp.	×	×	
Family Libellulidae			
Macromia sp.	×		
Neurocordulia sp.	×		
Tetragoneuria sp.	×		
Somatochlora sp.	×		
Libellula spp.	×	×	×
Pachydiplax longipennis	×		
Suborder Zygoptera			
Family Coenagrionidae			
Argia tibialis	×	×	
A. moesta	×		
A. sedula	×	×	
Enallagma sp.	×	×	×
Enallagma weewa	×	×	

Continued

TABLE 9.3. (*Continued*)

Species	Freshwater	Oligohaline	Mesohaline-Oligohaline
E. signatum	×	×	
E. pallidum	×	×	
Ischnura posita			×
Order Plecoptera			
Family Perlidae			
Neoperla clymene	×		
Perlesta placida	×	×	
Togoperla sp.	×		
Order Hemiptera			
Suborder Heteroptera			
Family Hydrometridae			
Hydrometra hungerfordi	×		
Family Gerridae			
Metrobates hesperius	×		
Rheumatobates tenuipes	×		×
Trepobates inermis		×	×
Family Nepidae			
Ranatra australis	×		
Ranatra nigra	×		
Family Naucoridae			
Pelocoris femoratus		×	
Family Corixidae			
Trichocorixa sp.		×	
Trichocorixa kanza	×		
Division Endopterygota			
Order Neuroptera			
Family Sisyridae			
Sisyra sp.	×		
Order Megaloptera			
Family Corydalidae			
Chauliodes sp.	×		
Corydalis cornutus	×		
Family Sialidae			
Sialis sp.	×		
Order Trichoptera			
Family Philopotamidae			
Chimarra feria	×		
Family Psychomyiidae			
Polycentropus nr. *remotus*	×		
Phylocentropus placidus	×		
Family Hydropsychidae			
Macronemum carolina	×		
Family Hydroptilidae			
Oxytheira sp.	×	×	
Family Leptoceridae			

TABLE 9.3. (*Continued*)

Species	Freshwater	Oligohaline	Mesohaline-Oligohaline
Leptocella sp.	×		
Triaenodes injusta ?	×	×	
Athripsodes nr. *alagmus*	×	×	
Oecetis inconspicua	×		
Order Lepidoptera			
Family Pyralidae			
Catoclysta sp.	×		
Order Coleoptera			
Family Gyrinidae			
Gyrinus spp.	×	×	
Gyrinus borealis	×		
G. lugens	×		
G. pectoralis		×	
G. analis	×		
Gyretes sinuatus	×		
Family Dytiscidae			
Desmopachria convexa	×	×	
Coelabus spp.	×		
Coelambus inaequalis	×		
Coptotomus interrogatus	×		
Family Hydrophilidae			
Helophorus sp.	×		
Hydorbius tesselatus	×		
Family Elmidae			
Stenelmis spp.	×		
Stenelmis grossa	×		
S. fuscata	×		
S. antennalis	×		
Machronychus glabratus	×		
Ancyronyx variegatus	×		
Simsonia sp.	×		×
Family Chrysomelidae			
Donacia sp.	×	×	
Donacia palmata	×		
Order Diptera			
Suborder Nematocera			
Family Culicidae			
Chaoborus punctipennis		×	
Family Ceratopogonidae			
Palpomyia spp.	×	×	×
Family Simuliidae			
Simulium nr. *jenningsi*	×		
Family Chironomidae			
Pentaneura spp.	×	×	

Continued

TABLE 9.3.   (Continued)

Species	Freshwater	Oligohaline	Mesohaline-Oligohaline
Pentaneura nr. *flavifrons*	×		
Procladius adumbratus		×	×
Clinotanypus pinguis ?	×	×	×
Coelotanypus concinnus	×	×	×
Corynoneura sp.	×		
C. nr *suctellata*	×	×	
Cricotopus nr. *exilis*		×	
Hydrobaenus spp.	×	×	×
Hydrobaenus prob. *minoriundus*	×		
H. prob. *flavus*		×	
Calopsectra nr. *exigua*	×		
C. curticornis ?	×		
Calopsectra spp.	×	×	
Tendipedini spp.	×		×
Stenochironomus spp.	×		×
Polypedilum sp.		×	
Polypedilum illinoense	×	×	×
P. fallax	×		
P. halterale	×		
P. prob. *scalaenum*	×	×	
Tanytarus spp.	×		×
T. nr. nigricans	×	×	×
Cryptochironomus sp.	×	×	
Cryptochironomus nr. *psittacinus*	×		
Tendipes sp.	×	×	
Glyptotendipes spp.	×		×
G. nr. *senilis*	×	×	
Harnishia sp.			×
Suborder Brachycera			
Family Tabanidae			
Tabanus spp.	×		
PHYLUM CHORDATA			
Subphylum Vertebrata			
Class Osteichthyes			
Order Semionotiformes			
Family Lepisosteidae			
Lepisosteus osseus	×	×	×
L. oculatus	×	×	×
(= *L. productus*)			
L. spatula	×		×
Order Amiiformes			
Family Amiidae			
Amia calva	×		
Order Anguilliformes			
Family Anguillidae			

TABLE 9.3.   (*Continued*)

Species	Freshwater	Oligohaline	Mesohaline-Oligohaline
Anguilla rostrata	×	×	
Family Ophichthidae			
Myrophis punctatus	×	×	
Order Clupeiformes			
Family Clupeidae			
Alosa chrysochloris	×	×	×
(= *Pomolobus chrysochloris*)			
Brevoortia sp.		×	×
Dorosoma cepedianum	×		
D. petenense	×		
Family Engraulidae			
Anchoa mitchilli	×		
A. hepsetus		×	×
Order Salmoniformes			
Family Esocidae			
Esox americanus			
E. niger			
Order Cypriniformes			
Family Cyprinidae			
Notemigonus crysoleucas	×	×	
Hybognathus hayi	×		
Hybopsis amblops winchelli	×		
Notropis emiliae	×	×	
(= *Opsopoeodus emiliae*)			
N. chalybaeus	×		
N. maculatus	×		
N. petersoni	×	×	×
N. texanus	×	×	×
(= *N. roseus roseus*)			
N. venustus	×	×	
Family Catostomidae			
Erimyzon oblongus	×		
E. tenuis	×		
Minytrema melanops	×		
Moxostoma poecilurum	×		×
Carpiodes sp.	×		
Order Siluriformes			
Family Ictaluridae			
Noturus gyrinus	×		
(= *Schilbeodes mollis*)			
N. leptacanthus	×		
(= *Schilbeodes leptacanthus*)			
Ictalurus catus	×		
I. natalis	×		

Continued

TABLE 9.3.   (Continued)

Species	Freshwater	Oligohaline	Mesohaline-Oligohaline
(= *Ameiurus natalis*)			
I. punctatus	×	×	
Family Ariidae			
Galeichthys felis			×
Order Percopsiformes			
Family Aphredoderidae			
Aphredoderus sayanus	×	×	
Order Atheriniformes			
Family Cyprinodontidae			
Fundulus grandis			×
F. confluentus			×
F. jenkensi			×
F. olivaceus	×		
F. notti	×	×	
Lucania parva		×	×
Cyprinodon variegatus			×
Family Poeciliidae			
Gambusia affinis	×	×	×
Poecilia latipinna			×
(= *Mollienesia latipinna*)			
Heterandria formosa			×
Family Atherinidae			
Labidesthes sicculus	×	×	×
Menidia beryllina		×	×
Order Gasterosteiformes			
Family Synganthidae			
Syngnathus scovelli		×	×
Order Perciformes			
Family Centrarchidae			
Micropterus salmoides	×	×	×
Lepomis gulosus			
(= *Chaenobryttus coronarius*)			
Pomoxis nigromaculatus	×	×	
Lepomis punctatus	×	×	×
L. macrochirus	×	×	×
L. microlophus	×	×	×
L. megalotis megalotis	×	×	
Enneacanthus gloriosus	×	×	
Elassoma zonatum	×		
Family Percidae			
Etheostoma fusiforme	×	×	
(= *Etheostoma barratti*)			
E. proeliare	×		
E. stigmaeum	×		
(= *E. saxatile*)			

TABLE 9.3. (*Continued*)

Species	Freshwater	Oligohaline	Mesohaline-Oligohaline
Percina caprodes	×		
Family Gerridae			
Eucinostomus argenteus	×		
Family Scianenidae			
Bairdiella chrysoura			×
Leiostomus xanthurus		×	×
Micropogon undulatus		×	×
Cynoscion nebulosus	×	×	
C. arenarius			×
Family Mugilidae			
Mugil cephalus	×	×	×
Family Eleotridae			
Eleotris pisonis		×	×
Dormitator maculatus		×	
Family Gobiidae			
Microgobius gulosus		×	
Gobionellus shufeldti	×	×	
G. boleosoma	×	×	×
Gobiosoma robustum			×
G. bosci		×	
Order Pleuronectiformes			
Family Bothidae			
Paralichthys lethostigmus	×		×
Family Soleidae			
Trinectes maculatus	×	×	×

snails, only *Physa* sp. was common. Many freshwater unionids (bivalves) were found in this area (Table 9.3). These were bottom-dwelling burrowers and, probably because of their sensitivity to salinity, found only in this area. Careful study of the freshwater distribution of these unionids indicated that the most downstream population was at about 10.6 miles from the mouth of the Escambia River. Small bivalves of the family Sphaeridae were more tolerant of salinity/ Two sphaerid genera, *Pisidium* sp. and *Sphaerium* sp., were found in freshwater and also in slightly more saline waters.

An undetermined species of crayfish (family Astacidae) was found in the debris in shallow water. The isopod, *Asellus attenatus*, was fairly common in both spring and fall studies, whereas the amphipod, *Crangonyx gracilis*, was found in fairly well developed populations only in the spring of the year.

Insects. The insect fauna was best developed in this freshwater area. The number of species collected was highest in the spring when the river had a greater freshwater flow, and lowest in the fall when river flow was low and the water temperatures warmer. Many of the species seemed to have life histories that made them collectible from the water during the spring and not collectible during the fall (because they had emerged and left the water). Mayflies were represented by more species and larger populations in the spring, as were Coleoptera, Trichoptera, and Diptera. In the fall, or low-flow periods, the Odonata were more commonly collected in this area and were the only group that had more species present in the fall than in the higher-river-flow conditions of spring. This predominance in the fall may have been due partially to the fact that Odonata were bottom dwellers and more easily collected during low-flow conditions. Downstream from the freshwater area, insect fauna became more scarce and was generally found in spring or freshwater flow conditions.

Fish.   The largest number of fish species was taken in the freshwater area. The species were typically freshwater forms, although some that tolerated brackish water were also found. The fish taken most commonly in the fall were the weed shiner, *Notropis texanus* (= *Notropis roseus roseus*); mosquitofish, *Gambusia affinis*; bluegill, *Lepomis machrochirus*; and the cypress minnow, *Hybognathus hayi*. In the spring the most common species were the American eel, *Anguilla rostrata*, and the bluegill. The weed shiner, common in the fall, was of only frequent occurrence in the spring.

Fresh to Oligohaline

Structure of Community

Algae.   The next area of study downstream (mile 8.75 to 8.9) had a salinity that varied from 5.04 ppm in the spring to 333 ppm in the fall. Thus it could be characterized as fresh to oligohaline. In this area the right bank of the river was a mud shelf covered with yellow water lilies, or spatterdock, and upland from the lilies was saw grass. The submerged roots of saw grass and the stems and undersides of water lily leaves formed suitable habitats for a great many algae, including the diatoms, *Eunotia lunaris*, *Achnanthes minutissima*, and *Anomoeoneis exilis*. As in freshwater areas, *Vaucheria* was the dominant alga on the mud banks.

In this area acid drainage from the swamplands was indicated by the very common occurrence of the diatoms, *Stenopterobia intermedia* and *Pinnularia viridis*. In the fall of the year a fairly large number of blue-green algae species was found in small pockets. Intermixed with the blue-green algae were species of *Spirogyra*. In the spring, on the left bank of the river, *Batrachospermum* (red algae) species were very common, and some blue-green algae were found along the mud banks.

Invertebrates.   As in the freshwater area, the protozoan fauna was dominated by autotrophic flagellates. The distribution of the amoebas and cilliates was similar to that found in freshwater. The sponge, *Trochospongilla horrida*, was fairly common in the spring but was not found in the fall. Although no sponge was collected, the spongilla fly, *Sisyra*, was taken and therefore the sponge must have been present.

In the spring the flatworm, *Dugesia tigrina*, was frequent but it was not found during the fall studies. In the spring the leeches, *Helobdella stagnales*, *H.*

nepheloidea, Dina microstoma, Stylaria lacustris, and *S. fossularis,* and an unidentified species of *Illinodella* were found attached to wood, dead leaves, and saw grass stalks. They were "present" to "frequent" in occurrence. *Placobdella parasitica* was present in both spring and fall. *Erpobdella punctata* was found only in the fall. The tubificid, *Limnodrilus* sp., was common in mud in the fall.

Bivalve molluscs were represented in the spring by *Pisidium* sp., which is thought to be very tolerant of salinity, and *Sphaerium* sp., which is typically found in fresh water. On hard substrates such as wood, lily pads, and the roots and rhizomes of saw grass, various small Gastropoda were found in the spring and the fall (Table 9.3). *Lyrodes* sp. was found only in the spring, and *Pseudozirecinea columella* was collected only in the fall. *Physa* sp. was represented by populations larger than those of the other Gastropoda.

An undetermined species of crayfish (Astacidae) occurred frequently. During the fall the blue crab, *Callinectes sapidus,* and the fiddler crab, *Uca pugnax,* were taken. The isopod, *Asellus attenuatus,* was fairly common in both the spring and fall. In both surveys the amphipod, *Hyatella azteca,* was of frequent occurrence. This species is characteristic of freshwater. Also characteristic of freshwater and found in the spring and the fall was the amphipod, *Crangonyx gracilis.* Of frequent occurrence in both spring and fall was the mysid shrimp, *Mysis stenolepis.*

Insects.   Saw grass and lily pads provided excellent habitats for the spring insect fauna. There were seven species of Ephemeroptera, eight species of beetles (Coleoptera), and five species of Odonata. The most diverse fauna was the Diptera, represented by 21 species. At this time the water was slightly more fresh than during the late summer and early fall months. In the fall fewer species were collected from some groups: Ephemeroptera, 2 species; Coleoptera, 5 species; and Diptera, 13 species. A few more species of Odonata were collected in the fall than in the spring.

Fish.   The fish fauna was a mixture of fresh and brackish water species. In the fall the dominant species were the bay anchovy, *Anchoa mitchilli;* pugnosed minnow, *Notropis emiliae* (= *Opsopocodus emiliae*); bluegill, *Lepomis machrochirus;* black crappy, *Pomoxis nigromaculatus;* and the taillight shiner, *Notropis maculatus.* In the spring the two common species were bluegill, *Lepomis machrochirus,* and threadfin shad, *Dorosoma petenense.*

Oligohaline to Mesohaline

Structure of Community

Algae.   The two study areas (1 to 1.5 and 3.5 to 4 miles) above the mouth of the river were very similar in salinity and may both be classed as oligohaline in the spring (106 ppm) and mesohaline in the fall (18 ppt). Among the saw grass rhizomes were moderate-sized populations of *Nitella flexilis.* Yellow water lilies which had been common in fresh waters were absent in these more saline areas.

Numbers of floating logs and branches in this region formed excellent habitats for the algae and diatoms (Table 9.3). On the branches occurred the red alga, *Batrachospermum,* probably *globosporum,* which was found in fairly large patches in the spring. In the fall this species was replaced by *B. louisianae.* Among the culms of saw grass the blue-green algal growth consisted of *Oscillatoria retzii* (= *Phormidium retzii*), *Schizothrix arenaria* (= *Phormidium subuliforme*), *Microcoleus vaginatus* (= *Lyngbia aerugineo-caerulae*), *Schizothrix mexicana* (= *Lyngbia putelais*), and *Schizothrix tenerrima* (= *Microcoleus tenerrimus*). The green alga, *Spirogyra* sp., was also present in this habitat, which included pilings as well as saw grass stems. Common diatoms, which indicated the higher salinities of this area, were *Navicula expansa, Diploneis didyma, Mastogloia smithii* v. *lanceolata, Surirella ovata* v. *salina*, and *Amphiprora alata*. These salinity-indicating species were particularly common in the fall, low-flow conditions.

Protozoa.   There were 32 species of protozoa present. Some were freshwater species and were associated with debris, as often happens when freshwater species occur in slightly saline areas, but most were oligohaline or brackish-water species. Seventeen species of flagellates were found, of which 16 were autotrophs. The ciliate population was much larger in this region; 12 species were collected in the fall and 11 species in the spring (Table 9.3). Two species of vorticellids were represented by fairly large populations and indicate more bacteria present in this area than in the other study areas. This is substantiated by the total bacteria count, which was 1800 per milliliter, as opposed to 400 per milliliter in the upper estuary (ANSP, 1953).

Invertebrates.   In the spring of the year this area was almost fresh (oligohaline), due to the heavy flow of the Escambia River. The sponge, *Trochospongilla horrida*, was widely distributed. Only one species of leech, *Helobdella nepheloidae*, was found in the spring and fall. Also in the fall, indicating more saline conditions, were the hydroid, *Cordylophora lacustris*, and two species of unidentified jellyfish belonging to the families Ulmaridae and Hydractinidae. Four species of polychaete worms were found in October, indicating the more saline fauna. Only one species, *Laeonereis culveri*, was found in the spring. Of the gastropoda the more common one was a brackish-water species, *Neritina reclivata*, which was associated with wood and saw grass. A single species of the genus *Physa* was present. Some species of this genus may withstand seawater if introduced slowly. Of the clams, or Pelecypoda, two brackish water species, *Mytilopsis leucophaetus* and *Rangia* sp., were common.

Of the Arthropoda the barnacle, *Balanus amphitrite*, was found more commonly in the fall. Common in both early spring and fall (March and October) was the mysid shrimp, *Mysis stenolepis*. During the fall studies the blue crab, *Callinectes sapidus*, was fairly common in shallow water and the mud crab, *Rhithropanopeus harrisii*, was abundant among the saw grass roots. The fiddler crab, *Uca pugnax*, was found only in the spring but was probably present in the fall. It was of frequent occurrence particularly at the mouth of the estuary.

Insects.   The insect fauna in this area consisted of very few species. This was particularly true in the fall of the year when the salinity was much higher. None of the insects were common (Table 9.3). The Diptera and Coleoptera were fairly well established in the spring of the year, whereas the Odonata was the only group that was represented by more species under brackish fall conditions than in the oligohaline spring conditions.

Fish.   During the spring of the year the common fish in this area was the inland silversides, *Menidia beryllina*, whereas the common species in the fall were the mosquitofish, *Gambusia affinis*, and the coastal shiner, *Notropis petersoni*. The hogchoker, *Trinectes maculatus*, was also common in the spring of the year. In this area several fish were found that were fairly common in the entire study area (i.e., in fresh to mesohaline conditions). These were the longnose gar, *Lepisosteus osseus*; channel catfish, *Ictalurus punctatus*; spotted sea trout, *Cynoscion nebulosus*; and sand seatrout, *C. arenarius*. In the backwaters of this area were also found the spotted gar, *Lepisosteus oculatus* (= *L. productus*); starheaded top minnow, *Fundulus notti*; and the cypress darter, *Etheostoma proeliare*. During the fall there were many specimens of the migratory striped mullet, *Mugil cephalus*, in this area. The female striped mullet contained ripe eggs. They were apparently migrating upstream to spawn. Associated with the mullet, which was probably its predator, was the longnose gar, *Lepisosteus osseus*. In the spring the only migratory fish was the American eel, *Anguilla rostrata*. Perhaps migratory, and common in the fall were the bay anchovy, *Anchoa mitchilli*, and the seatrout, *Cynoscion nebulosus* and *C. arenarius*.

BARATARIA BAY, LOUISIANA

The Barataria Bay estuary (Louisiana) is a typical grass estuary associated with black mangrove (*Avicennia germinaus*) and, in the drier areas, *Salicornia virginica*.

Marshes
Primary Productivity
Emergent Vascular Plants.   Standing crops of *Spartina alterniflora*, which was an important detrital source for the bay, followed distinct season patterns. In a study by Day et al. (1973) of Barataria Bay, live streamside grass attained maximum biomass of 925 g dry wt m^{-2}, while the inland area reached a maximum of 600 g dry wt m^{-2}; both reached their maximum in September. The dead standing crop had the highest biomass in February and March, with almost 1500 g dry wt m^{-2} streamside and 1200 g dry wt m^{-2} for the inland area. Minimum levels of approximately 925 g m^{-2} streamside and 750 g m^{-2} inland occurred in August. The total annual gross production of grasses in Barataria Bay has been estimated as 14,000 g m^{-2} streamside and 9,750 g m^{-2} inland.

The total annual net production of *Spartina* was 1484 g dry wt m^{-2} inland and 2960 g dry wt m^{-2} streamside (Kirby, 1972) (Table 9.4). Using Smalley's technique, these figures are 1006 and 1410 g dry wt m^{-2}, respectively (Kirby and Gosselink, 1978). This figure was very similar to 2883 g dry wt m^{-2} streamside at Sapelo Island, Georgia (Odum and Fanning, 1973), but higher than the 329 to 1296 g dry wt m^{-2} production in North Carolina (Williams and Murdoch, 1969; Stroud and Cooper, 1969). Generally speaking, the data for Louisiana showed much higher production than other areas farther north, probably due to the extended growing season (Day et al., 1973).

TABLE 9.4. *Production and Use of Organic Matter in the Barataria Bay Area of Louisiana*[a]

	Production		Consumer Respiration	Community Net Production
	Gross	Net[b]		
		Marsh		
Grass				
Streamside	14,000	2,960	—	—
Inland (50 m)	9,750	1,484	—	—
Average over marsh	8,418[c]	1,518[c]	754[c]	764[c]
Epiphytes				
Streamside	103.9	—	—	60
Inland (2 m)	27.3	—	—	− 18.4
Average (to 2 m)	32.2	25.8	—	
Totals	32,331.4	5,987.8	754	805.6
		Water		
Phytoplankton	598	418	—	—
Benthic plants	698	488	—	—
Water column[d]	—	—	450	—
Benthos and nekton	—	—	798	—
Totals	1,296	906	1,248	48

Source: Day et al. (1973).
[a] Data for marsh are g dry wt m^{-2} marsh yr^{-1} and data for water are g dry m^{-2} water yr^{-1}.
[b] Net production is less respiration of plants.
[c] Takes into consideration bare areas of marsh.
[d] Phytoplankton, zooplankton, and bacteria.

Algae.   Chlorophyll *a* levels corresponded to phytoplankton production. The common spring bloom of phytoplankton has not been found to occur in the shallow waters of Barataria Bay, although there seemed to be some discrepancy as to when it does occur. Day et al. (1973) found that both chlorophyll *a* and phytoplankton production were highest in midsummer, while Morrison (1978) found the highest production in the winter, with an overall average of 9.8 mg m^{-2} chlorophyll *a*. The gross primary production of phytoplankton in Barataria Bay was estimated by Day et al. (1973) to be 598 g wt m^{-2} annually. Net production was determined to be 418 g dry wt m^{-2}.

Benthic algae are not especially abundant in this area; however, production has been measured. The gross primary production of benthic algae in Barataria Bay has been measured at 698 g dry wt m^{-2} annually, and the net production was estimated at 488 g dry wt m^{-2} yearly (Day et al., 1973).

The epiphytic community was divided into filamentous and nonfilamentous algae. The filamentous algae existed in two distinct seasonal forms, *Bostrychia* and *Polysiphonia* in the summer, and *Enteromorpha* and *Ectocarpus* in the winter. The annual gross primary production of epiphytes in Barataria Bay was

103.9 g dry wt m^{-2} streamside and 27.3 g dry wt m^{-2} inland. The average gross production over the marsh was 32.2 g dry wt m^{-2}. Annual net primary production of epiphytes was estimated at 60 g dry wt m^{-2} stream-side and 25.8 g dry wt m^{-2} average over the marsh (Day et al., 1973).

Detrital Productivity.   In the Barataria Bay (Louisiana) estuarine system the dominant angiosperm is the cord grass, *Spartina alterniflora*. It composed 65% of the biomass of higher plants in the entire salt marsh area of Barataria Bay. In some spots 93 to 95% of the higher plant biomass was *Spartina alterniflora*. Other significant higher plants included the salt warts, *Batis maritima* and *Salicornia virginica*, and the black mangrove, *Avicennia germinans* (Day et al., 1973).

Much of the fertility of Louisiana waters was detritus based and most of the detritus in Barataria Bay's shallow, marsh-fringed estuary came from decaying marsh vegetation. Tides and rain washed this material off the marsh surface into the water column, where it was made available to aquatic organisms (Happ et al., 1977). Production by phytoplankton, zooplankton, and bacteria alone did not appear to account for the amount of organic carbon contained in open coastal waters. This suggested enrichment, or net export of organic carbon, from riverine, estuarine, or terrestrial sources. This was probably especially true for the Gulf of Mexico because organic matter was added from the Mississippi River and from over 3 million hectares of fringing estuaries (Happ et al., 1977).

Day et al. (1973) estimated from Mulkana's (1968, 1969) data on suspended matter in Barataria Bay that the seston varied from 0.09 to 0.52 g m^{-2} and the nannoseston ranged from 10 to 30 g m^{-2}. Overall, Day et al. (1973) estimated that the net estuary production available for export or sedimentation was 260 g C m^{-2} yr^{-1} for Barataria Bay. The detritus was rich in carbohydrate and admixed with plankton by constant turbulence (Mulkana, 1969). Average values of DOC (dissolved organic carbon) ranged from 6.5 mg L^{-1} in the upper bay to 3.9 mg L^{-1} in the lower bay to 2.4 mg L^{-1} offshore (Happ et al., 1977). Corresponding to this trend, there was a general trend of decreasing amounts of phytoplankton gulfward (Morrison, 1978).

The dead standing crop of *Spartina alterniflora*, primary component of detritus in the bay, peaked in January–March. The spring months were the period when the dead standing crop was removed from the marsh most rapidly in the form of suspended detritus, and this high rate of detritus loss from the marsh corresponded to peaks in biomass of zooplankton, larval shrimp and fishes, foraminifera, and other organisms that fed on the detritus (Kirby, 1972). Many organisms used this pulse of organic material as a food source. Thus, in contrast to many areas where the spring pulse is phytoplankton based, it seemed to be mainly detrital based in Barataria Bay. Detritus from the marsh grasses represented from 50 to 70% of the total organic production available to the water areas of the estuary (Day et al., 1973).

Estimates of production of organic matter in the marsh and waters of Barataria Bay are given in Table 9.4. The production and path of organic matter from the marsh to the bay and hence to the gulf are given in Figure 9.5. It is

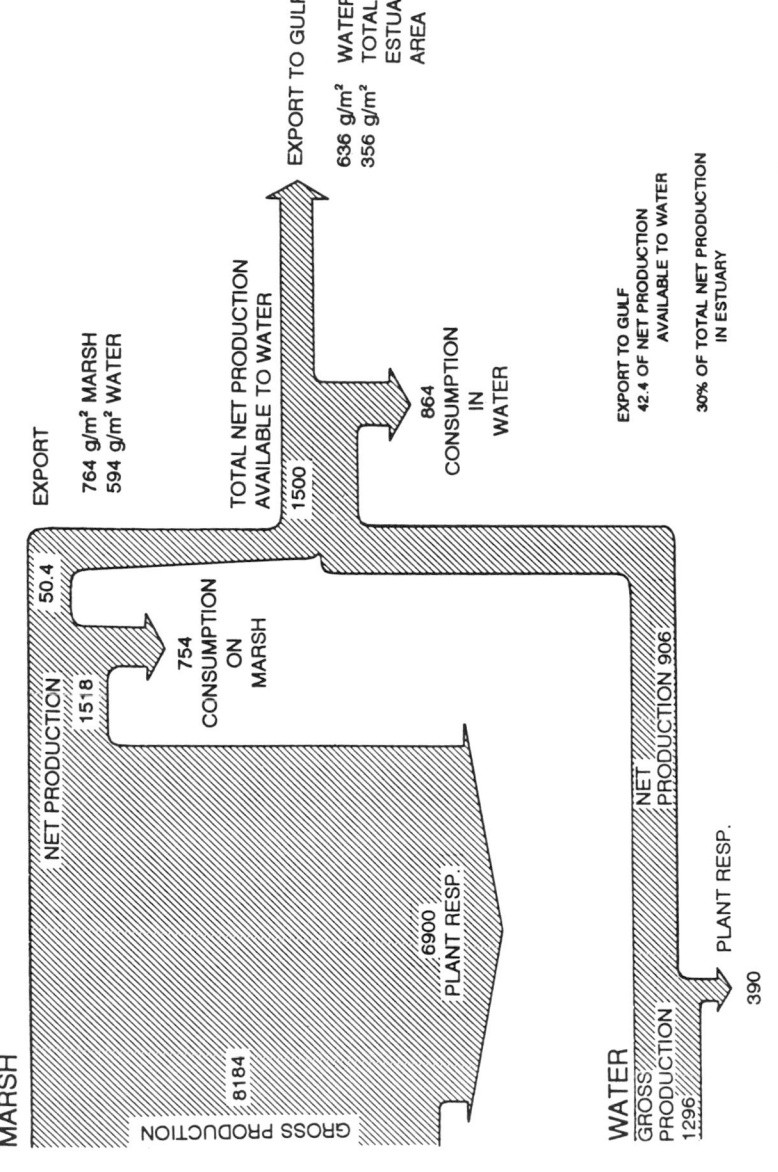

FIGURE 9.5. Production and flow of organic matter in Barataria Bay. Numbers for marsh are g dry wt m^{-2} marsh/yr^{-1} and g dry wt m^{-2} water yr^{-1} for water areas. (From Day et al., 1973.)

evident that although the gross production is much higher in the marsh, the percent of gross that is net production is a little higher in the water.

Secondary Productivity.   The food chain in the Barataria Bay marshes was based, in large part, on detritus from the marsh grasses. The principal factor which seemed to determine density of marsh organisms is tidal inundation or proximity to tidally affected water bodies. Feeding directly on the detritus–bacteria–algae base of the food web were meiobenthos and protozoa. The meiobenthos included nematodes, ostracods, amphipods, harpaticoid copepods, and small polychaetes and oligochaetes. Ciliates and foraminifera were common protozoa in the marshes (Day et al., 1973).

Ciliates have been observed both in marsh soil and submerged sediments, but they appeared to be more abundant in the marsh soil. The food of these organisms included other ciliates, flagellates, diatoms, bacteria, and dead metazoa (Day et al., 1973). Johannes (1965) found that regeneration of dissolved phosphate proceeded faster and more completely in the presence of ciliates than in the presence of bacteria alone. It appeared that a significant fraction of benthic regeneration of phosphorus from organic detritus was attributable to protozoa and that, by extension, most of the meiobenthic organisms may have had a dual role of nutrient regeneration in conjunction with the bacteria and "packaging" of small particles so that they were available to higher trophic levels.

The foraminifera, another group of protozoans, were important in the trophic structure of the marsh. Foods taken by these organisms included algae, bacteria, yeasts, and probably detrital particles (Day et al., 1973).

Most zooplankters were considered to be herbivorous filter feeders (with the exception of some carnivorous forms described below) on any small particulate material. Since detritus was the most abundant suspended particulate material in the waters of Barataria Bay, it was probably the primary food of filter-feeding zooplankters such as copepods, which were most numerous near eroding marshes (Day et al., 1973).

Acartia tonsa represented about 83% of all zooplankton organisms collected in Barataria Bay. There was a large biomass peak in April and a smaller one in August. Day et al. (1973) calculated that the average amount of organic material produced by the total population was $25 \, \text{g m}^{-2} \, \text{yr}^{-1}$. *Arcatia* alone produced $20 \, \text{g m}^{-2} \, \text{yr}^{-1}$. Feces production was calculated to be $150 \, \text{g m}^{-2} \, \text{yr}^{-1}$ for *Acartia* and $187.5 \, \text{g m}^{-2} \, \text{yr}^{-1}$ for the total zooplankton population.

The greatest amount of the biomass of the submerged sediments in Barataria Bay is represented by meiofaunal organisms. With populations ranging between 685,000 and $4,165,000 \, \text{m}^{-2}$, nematodes represented about 90% of the total numbers of meiobenthic organisms in the submerged sediments. Some nematodes were epigrowth feeders and some were deposit feeders. The latter showed peaks in abundance when detrital washout from the marshes was greatest.

The average annual total biomass (foraminifera, nematodes, and other meiobenthic organisms) was $1.47 \, \text{g dry wt m}^{-2}$. The production was estimated at $14.7 \, \text{g org m}^{-2} \, \text{yr}^{-1}$ and feces production is $60.6 \, \text{g org m}^{-2} \, \text{yr}^{-1}$ (Day et al., 1973).

The average standing crop of polychaetes in the marsh was $0.17\,g\,org\,m^{-2}$. Fecal production was estimated at $4\,g\,org\,m^{-2}\,yr^{-1}$ and production was $0.62\,g$ $org\,m^{-2}\,yr^{-1}$ (Day et al., 1973). Polychaetes were most likely omnivores, feeding on diatoms, fine detritus, sand, mud, and even small crustaceans such as harpacticoid copepods and amphipods (Odum, 1971).

The average annual population level of amphipods was found by Bennet (unpublished data) to be $3080\,m^{-2}$ and that for copepods was $6832\,m^{-2}$. He estimated that amphipods and harpacticoid copepods made up, on average, about 8% of the total meiofaunal population and 9% of the biomass in submerged sediments. In all cases, the meiofauna fed on the substrate itself; that is, they were deposit feeders.

At distances greater than 10 m from the water line into the marsh, molluscs were the predominant larger organisms. Snails fed on the epiphytic algal film on the plants and on the marsh floor. The snail diet consisted of diatoms, filamentous algae, detritus, and small animals living in the epiphytic film (Day et al., 1973). The average biomass of snails (*Neritina*, *Melampus*, and *Littorina*) was $9.80\,g\,dry\,wt\,m^{-2}$. Day et al. (1973) estimated that $134\,g\,org\,m^{-2}\,yr^{-1}$ was feces of these snails and that production averaged $19.5\,g\,org\,m^{-2}\,yr^{-1}$. *Modiolus demissus*, a filter-feeding mollusc, was common in the marsh fauna. The average biomass of this species was $3.19\,g\,org\,m^{-2}$ and production is $6.4\,g\,org\,m^{-2}$ (Day et al., 1973).

The American oyster, *Crassostrea virginica*, was the subject of a very large fishery industry in Barataria Bay. Although most of the oyster beds were artificially planted, the oysters themselves cannot be ignored in terms of their function in the food web. Oysters are filter feeders that take deteritus, phytoplankton, bacteria, and other small particulate matter from the water column. This feeding process resulted in a large amount of suspended material being sedimented as feces and pseudofeces. Day et al. (1973) suggested that oysters may be important in removing phosphorus and other mineral and organic material from the water and depositing it on the bottom in fecal material, where it can be used by rooted vegetation and benthic algae.

Brown shrimp averaged $0.075\,g\,dry\,wt\,m^{-2}$ per year, whereas white shrimp were estimated at $0.03\,g\,dry\,wt\,m^{-2}$ yearly (Day et al., 1973). The yearly production of brown shrimp was calculated as $0.7 + g\,org\,m^{-2}$ and for white shrimp $0.32\,g\,dry\,m^{-2}\,yr^{-1}$. These shrimp were generally omnivorous, eating plants, animals, inorganic, and organic detritus (Farfante, 1969). Shrimp along the Louisiana coast have been found to consume detritus, small molluscs, microcrustacea, chitin, annelids, blue-green filamentous algae, diatoms, bryozoans, coral, roots, and stems (Day et al., 1973).

Herbivorous members of the Barataria Bay area fish community (i.e., those that feed primarily on organic detritus, vascular plants, algae, and phytoplankton) included *Mugil cephalus* (striped mullet), *Poecilia latipinna* (sailfin molly), *Adinia xenica* (diamond killifish), *Cyprinodon variegatus* (sheepshead minnow), and *Brevoortia patronus* (gulf menhaden).

Predator–Prey Relationships. *Labidocera aestiva* is a predatory copepod that seemed instrumental in controlling the population size of *Acartia tonsa.* Ctenophores seemed to be the most important zooplankton predators, due to their local abundance and voracious feeding habits. The most common species were *Beroe ovata* and *Mnemiopsis mccradyi.* These jellyfish and ctenophores fed mainly on zooplankton and, to a lesser extent, on small fishes. In turn, they were fed upon by several fishes, crabs, and shorebirds (Day et al., 1973).

The average biomass of the crabs in the Louisiana marsh (fiddlers, *Sesarma,* and blue crabs) was $3.60 \, \mathrm{g\,org\,m^{-2}\,yr^{-1}}$. Feces production was calculated by Day et al. (1973) at $73.7 \, \mathrm{g\,org\,m^{-2}\,yr^{-1}}$ and net production at $7.44 \, \mathrm{g\,org\,m^{-2}\,yr^{-1}}$ (average for streamside marsh). Fiddler crabs sorted through mud and ingested nematodes, bacteria, and detritus (Teal, 1958, 1962). Mud crabs fed on plant detritus, animal matter (including mostly copepods and amphipods), diatoms, and filamentous algae (Odum, 1971).

The blue crab, *Callinectes sapidus,* was common along the Louisiana coast and its biomass was found to average $0.23 \, \mathrm{g\,dry\,wt\,m^{-2}}$ during the winter. Food habits of the blue crab have been discussed by Darnell (1958), who found that in percent by volume the adult diet consisted of 63% molluscs, 10.4% crabs and crustacea, 5.4% fish remains, and 8% organic detritus. Crabs and crustaceans were the most important diet component for younger crabs, while molluscs and fish were less important. For blue crabs in oligohaline areas, the clam, *Rangia cuneata,* represented 46% of the total diet. In higher-salinity areas, molluscs may not have been as important in the diet. The crabs, in turn, were preyed upon by fishes.

The major primary carnivore of this area was the bay anchovy, *Anchoa mitchilli,* which preyed on copepods (largely *Acartia tonsa*), mysids, amphipods, ostracods, and crab megalops larvae in the zooplankton, and also on small molluscs, chironomid larvae, small fishes, and plant detritus. The fact that little utilization of phytoplankton was observed strengthens the picture that nutrition in this system was based on allochthonous organic detritus such as *Spartina* and other marsh macrophytes.

The middle carnivores included the marsh killifish, *Fundulus confluentas;* gulf killifish, *F. grandis;* rainwater killifish, *Lucania parva;* bay whiff, *Citharichthys spilopterus;* inland silversides, *Menidia beryllina;* spot, *Leiostomus xanthurus;* Atlantic croaker, *Micropogonias undulatus;* and hardhead catfish, *Arius felis.* These species fed extensively on the meiobenthos. More specifically, *F. confluentus* fed on *Palaemonetes,* small fish, amphipods, isopods, copepods, mysids, ostracods, adult and larval insects, and algal filaments. The diet of *F. grandis* was similar, with the addition of small xanthid crabs and gastropods. *Menidia beryllina* preyed on zooplankton, insect larvae, and fish, while *Micropogon undulatus* preyed on amphipods, annelids, copepods, fish, insect larvae, and organic detritus (Day et al., 1973).

The top carnivores of this area were the sand seatrout, *Cynoscion arenarius,* and the spotted sea trout, *C. nebulosus.* These two species were predaceous primarily on fish of lower trophic levels but also consumed macrobenthic forms, such as blue crabs and penaeid and caridean shrimp, microbenthos, vascular plants, zooplankton, and organic detritus (Day et al., 1973).

Birds, along with certain mammals and fish, represented the top of the food chain in the estuarine ecosystem. Wading birds such as herons, egrets, and ibis took mostly small fishes, crustaceans, molluscs, and insects. Waterfowl (e.g., ducks and coots) fed primarily on plant material, although some snails, insects, and fish were found in their diets. In general, diving ducks tended to take a larger proportion of animal material than did puddle ducks. The shorebirds (plovers, sandpipers, and willets) fed mainly on bare mud flat, taking small worms, crustaceans, and so on. The fishing birds such as gulls and terns fed exclusively on fish and shrimp. In Louisiana, clapper rails (*Rallus longirostris*) were one of the most important top consumers in the marsh. In percent by volume 74% of their prey consisted of crabs, 14% of snails, 9% of insects, and the remainder was spiders, fishes, and plants (Day et al., 1973).

Structure of Community. Many marshes are present in this part of the Gulf and furnish breeding and nursery grounds for various species. Since the marshes vary greatly in salinity, they support different flora and fauna.

Flora. The dominant plant of Barataria Bay marshes was cord grass, *Spartina alterniflora*, especially where mean salinity was 20 ppt (Kirby and Gosseling, 1978; Happ et al., 1977; Day et al., 1973). Approximately 93% to 95% of the biomass of higher plants in the Airplane Lake region of the bay, and about 65% of the total salt marsh was *S. alterniflora*. Other significant emergent macrophytes included the salt worts, *Baetis maritima* and *Salicornia virginica*, and the black mangrove, *Avicennia germinans* (Day et al., 1973).

Algae that were epiphytic on these plants were either filamentous or non-filamentous. *Enteromorpha* (green), *Ectocarpus* (brown), and the red algae, *Bostrychia* and *Polysiphonia*, were the major filamentous epiphytes. The non-filamentous algal community was composed almost exclusively of diatoms. Blue-green algae were conspicuously absent (Day et al., 1973). Temperature was the major factor affecting the epiphytic population although there was a distinct correlation between water levels and species composition of filamentous growth. When tide levels were high, *Bostrychia* and *Polysiphonia* dominated. When tide levels were at winter lows, *Enteromorpha* and *Ectocarpus* dominated (Day et al., 1973).

The density of epiphytic diatoms on *Spartina* was greater at the water's edge than 5 ft inland. Forty to sixty percent of the diatom population was composed of *Amphora*, *Cocconeis*, and *Melosira*. *Nitzschia* was 10 to 20% of the diatom population on inland *Spartina*.

Fauna. Foraminifera were important protozoans of the marsh community in the Airplane lake area of Barataria Bay. Some of the genera listed by Cruz-Orozco (1970) were *Ammoastuta*, *Arenoparella*, *Trochammina*, *Ammobaculities*, *Milammina*, *Ammotium*, and *Ammonia*. Generally, the highest populations were located at the interface between the marsh and open water, where *Spartina alterniflora* dominated. Also, more foraminifera were associated with mud than with sand. The lowest populations were associated with backmarsh stands of *Salicornia* (Day et al., 1973).

The first 3 m of marsh adjacent to open water generally showed a greater diversity of species and higher populations than areas more distant from the water's edge. More than 90% of the total meiobenthic population consisted of nematodes, copepods, amphipods, polychaetes, and oligochaetes. Nematodes and crustacea dominated bottom sediments. The numbers of *Turbellaria* and *Gastrotricha* were relatively small. The density of marsh meiofauna is principally a result of water level and tidal inundation (Day et al., 1973).

The most common larger meiobenthic organisms, excluding the nematodes, were harpacticoid copepods and amphipods, which represented a combined 80% of the total number of organisms in the sediments. Specifically, the most common amphipods were *Corophium lacustre* on *Spartina* roots near shore, and *Ampelisca* in the submerged sediments adjacent to the shore. The next most common groups were ostracods, chironomid larvae, and polychaetes, which composed more than an additional 15% of the meiobenthos. The submerged sediments of Barataria Bay are mainly soft peat or muddy materials. Consequently, there was a scarcity of large sessile organisms, which need a more stable substrate for attachment (Day et al., 1973).

The macrofauna of the Barataria Bay marshes was dominated by the snails, *Littorina*, *Neritina*, and *Melampus*. *Neanthes succinea* was the dominant poly-chaete associated with the marsh. Common crabs found were the fiddler crab, *Uca pugnax*, the square-backed crab, *Sesarma reticulatum*, and small (less than 25 mm) blue crabs, *Callinectes sapidus*. Crabs were generally associated with the marsh edge habitat, but fiddler and blue crab populations extended inland as far as 50 m in October (Day et al., 1973). Mud crabs common to this area included *Panopeus herbstii*, *Rithropanopeu harisii*, and *Menippe mercenaria*. The hermit crab, *Clibanarius* sp., has also been observed associated with the shore (Wagner, 1970).

Associated with the marsh at greater than 10 m inland were the molluscs, which dominate the macrofauna. Commonly occurring snails in this habitat included the marsh periwinkle, *Littorina irrorata*; the smooth periwinkle, *Neritina reclivata*; and the snail, *Melampus bidentata*. These snails were found both on grass stalks and on the marsh floor (Day et al., 1973).

The ribbed mussel, *Modiolus dismissus*, was another common representative of the marsh fauna, which lived in groups associated with clumps of *Spartina*, attached to the roots by their byssal threads (Day et al., 1973). In the Airplane Lake region of Barataria Bay, the mussel was found only in the marsh edge habitat.

Cyprinodonts (killifishes) were generally associated with interior marsh areas, or "prairie" as it is called in south Louisiana. In addition, they were generally found in shallow marsh ponds and tidal creeks with bottoms of mud, clay, and organic detritus (Day et al., 1973).

Open Water
  Structure of Community
  Plankton
Phytoplankton. Apparently, very few studies have been conducted on the composition of the phytoplankton in Barataria Bay. Day et al. (1973) included the following species among the major primary producers of the area: blue-green alga, *Merismopedia*; protozoan, *Actinophychus*; diatoms, *Biddulphia, Chaetoceras, Coscinodiscus, Skeletonema, Rhizosolenia, Thalassiosira, Ditylum brightwellii, Cylindrotheca closterium*, and *Nitzschia pungens*; and dinoflagellates, *Ceratium fusus, C. hircus, C. trichoceros, C. tripos, C. vultur, Dinophysis caudata, Gonyaulax monilata, Prorocentrum gracile, P. maximum*, and *Peridinium* sp. Day et al. described these as "some of the common species" in the bay.

Zooplankton. Gillespie (1978) found that almost every phylum was represented in the Barataria Bay zooplankton. The most abundant hydromedusae found were *Liriope tetraphulla, Nemopsis bachei*, and *Obelia* sp. Ctenophora occasionally accounted for 100% of the samples. Species collected were *Beroe ovata, Mnemiopsis maccradyi*, and *Pleurobrachia* sp. (Gillespie, 1978; Day et al., 1973). The larvae of oysters, of the snail, *Thais laemastoma*, and the polychaete, *Nereis succinea*, were collected occasionally. The cladocerans, *Evadne tergestina, Penilia avirostris, Daphnia longispans*, and *Ceriodaphnia* sp., were common (Gillespie, 1978).

The presence of copepods in the zooplankton was associated with surface waters characterized by mixing of water masses, bottom roiling, and proximity to eroding marshes (Darnell, 1961). The dominant member of the zooplankton community in Barataria Bay was the copepod, *Acartia tonsa*, a euryhaline and eurythermal organism often found to be a major component of zooplankton in coastal areas from Massachusetts to the gulf (Day et al., 1973). Together with other species of the genus *Acartia*, and exclusive of Ctenophora, these copepods accounted for 60% of the samples (Gillespie, 1978; Day et al., 1973). Common copepods besides *Acartia tonsa* were *Labidocera aestiva, Centropages hamatus, Temora turbinata, Tortanus* sp., *Undinula vulgaris, Halicyclops fosteri, Eurytemora hirundoides, Eucalanus* spp., *Onacaea mediterranea*, and *Corycaeus* sp. (Gillespie, 1978; Day et al., 1973; Cuzon du Rest, 1963).

The pericarideans, *Gammarus mucronatus, Cerapus tubularis*, and *Corophium* sp., were occasionally found in samples by Gillespie (1978). She also identified one mysid, *Mysidopsis alm*, in the samples. Decapods were dominant in late summer and early fall samples, and consisted of Brachyuran zoea and the megalops larvae of the benthic crab, *Callinectes sapidus* (Gillespie, 1978). Other important decapod components include protozoeal stages of the penaeid larvae of *Palaemonetes* sp., pagurid larvae, sergestid larvae, *Lucifer faxoni, Acetes americanus carolinae*, and the caridean, *Leander tenuicornis* (Gillespie, 1978; Day et al., 1973).

Three species of the holoplanktonic Chaetognatha, *Sagitta hispida, S. englata*, and *Oikopleura* sp., were taken by Gillespie (1978). Fish larvae in the plankton were dominated by gulf menhaden, *Brevoortia patronus*; bay anchovy, *Anchoa mitchilli*; inland silversides, *Menidia beryllina*; and striped mullet, *Mugil cephalus*.

Nekton. In their study of Barataria Bay, Day et al. (1973) collected 97,223 fish of 100 species from 82 genera representing 46 families. The following 16 species, in order of relative abundance, represent 88.7% of the total numbers collected: *Anchoa mitchilli* (bay anchovy), *Brevoortia patronus* (gulf menhaden), *Leiostomus xanthurus* (spot), *Micropogonias undulatus* (Atlantic croaker), *Cyprinodon variegatus* (sheepshead minnow), *Adinia xenica* (diamond killifish), *Fundulus grandis* (gulf killifish), *F. confluentus* (marsh killifish), *Lucania parva* (rainwater killifish), *Poecilia latipinna* (sailfin molly), *Arius felis* (hardhead catfish), *Menidia beryllina* (inland silversides), *Cynoscion arenarius* (sand sea trout), *Citharichthyes spilopterus* (bay whiff), *Mugil cephalus* (striped mullet), and *Cynoscion nebulosus* (spotted sea trout). Of these species, only *A. mitchilli*, *M. beryllina*, and the killifishes, *A. xenica*, *F. grandis*, *F. confluentus*, and *L. parva*, were indigenous, truly estuarine species. The others were marine species that used the estuary as a nursery area, usually spawning in the gulf and moving into the bays as postlarvae and returning to the gulf as subadults (Day et al., 1973).

Species diversity of the fish was directly correlated with temperature. The greatest number of species occurred in later summer–early fall, and the lowest number of species in winter. There was also a direct correlation between size distribution and salinity. That is, smaller juvenile fishes tolerated lower salinities and lower temperatures than adult conspecifics. Postlarval fishes of many species moved into upper, fresher sections of the estuary and gradually moved gulfward as they matured (Day et al., 1973).

Benthos. Although the Gulf of Mexico has been described as being a region barren of benthic marine algae (Taylor, 1960), Barataria Bay and surrounding areas had some macroscopic algal flora. In the marsh, the most common genera were the green alga, *Enteromorpha*, and the brown alga, *Ectocarpus*, which were abundant on the banks of streams and lakes. The red alga, *Gracilaria follifera*, was found in only one area west of the Mississippi, in a small bayou near the gulf. Filamentous algae associated with the benthos and mudflats included the green algae, *Ulvella* sp., *Ulothrix* sp., *Cladophora*, and *Rhizoclonium*. *Rhizoclonium* was found in thick mats growing in shallow (less than 10 cm) tidal pools. *Vaucheria*, another green alga, was found infrequently growing on the banks of small tidal streams, and *Ulva lactuca* was rare, growing on oyster shells and abandoned boats (Day et al., 1973).

In Barataria Bay three genera of Oscillatoriaceae were common: *Lyngbya*, *Oscillatoria*, and *Spirulina* (Day et al., 1973). The benthic blue-green mats were dominated by *O. princeps*, with *Lyngbya* and *Spirulina* making up the majority of other species in the algal mats (Day et al., 1973). Common benthic diatoms included species of the genera *Amphora*, *Denticula*, *Diploneis*, *D. interrupta*, *Gyrosigme*, *Navicula directa*, *Nitzschia*, *Opephora*, *Paralia*, *Amphiprora*, *Caloneis*, *Mastogloia*, *Pleurosigma*, *Surirella*, and *Cylindortheca closterium* (Day et al., 1973).

SUMMARY

The estuaries in the Gulf of Mexico are very similar to those in southeastern United States. The main vegetation of the marshlands are grasses of similar species to those in southeastern United States. The Apalachicola Bay and the Apalachee Bay have been thoroughly studied by Livingston and represent some of the best examples of the ecosystems in these environments.

In this area one finds various types of estuary habitats, such as the grasslands, the tidal areas, and submerged areas. In contrast to the submerged areas being dominated by *Thalassia* around the coast of southern Florida, they are dominated by macroscopic algae, particularly reds and brown algae, but also some green algae. This is probably because of the disturbance of the area by human beings, and the rooting out of the *Thalassia*. As in the southeastern part of the United States, the *Spartina* marshes are very productive varying from $63 \, \text{mg} \, \text{C} \, \text{m}^{-2} \, \text{day}^{-1}$ in February to $1640 \, \text{mg} \, \text{C} \, \text{m}^{-2} \, \text{day}^{-1}$ in April. Because of the very dense growths of macroscopic algae and rooted and floating aquatics and the large areas of *Spartina* marshes, the detrital productivity is very large.

In the Apalachicola area the nutrients are in larger concentrations than they are in the Escambia River, where they were studied. The Escambia River studies were done before there were any human habitations in the watershed area. Thus they represent truly natural conditions, whereas the Apalachee Bay area represents natural functional conditions but not necessarily pristine areas.

Macrofauna density is clearly correlated with the macrophyte standing crop. The mean density in unvegetated stations was $1754 \, \text{m}^{-2}$, compared to $3107 \, \text{m}^{-2}$ for the vegetated areas. The fauna is composed of polychaete annelids, but there are large numbers of shrimp, crab, molluscs, and various other crustacea. It should be noted that the meiofauna taxa are a very important flow of energy to the higher trophic levels. In the Apalachee Bay, the *Amphipoda* made up approximately 37 to 47% of the macrofauna. The mean density of amphipods varied from 641 to $1578 \, \text{m}^{-2}$, the difference being unvegetated to vegetated sites. Thus the greatest abundance was where the vegetation was highest.

The fish of Apalachee Bay are divided into three trophic groups. The first group, planktivorous forms, fed primarily on copepods, amphipods, and detritus. The second group were the benthic omnivores and carnivores. These species fed on plant detritus, harpacticoid copepods, invertebrate eggs, and benthic crustacea. Polychaetes and bivalve molluscs were also eaten by the omnivores. The third group were mainly carnivorous and fed on shrimp, crabs, and amphipods.

The seagrass beds were dominated by macroalgae, particularly green algae and red algae. Some brown algae were also found. In some places *Thalassia* did occur. It seemed to affect the distribution and abundance of the macroalgae. Where the seagrasses occurred, they provided support for many epiphytes and organisms that feed upon them. It is in these areas that one finds many shrimp, the hermit crab, scallops, and majid crabs.

The seagrass beds also formed habitats for many species of fish. Oyster reefs were found here and there in the area and supported by a large number of associated organisms. This was also true in the Delaware.

In structure the Escambia River estuary greatly resembles the Delaware estuary except that at the time of the study, no anthropogenic pollution was entering it. The nutrient levels were very low, whereas in the Delaware they were often very high. As a result, we see a much greater diversity of all groups of organisms in the Escambia than we did in the Delaware, which for years had been subject to pollution. Although the Delaware seemed to be functioning as a natural ecosystem with a variety of species in each stage of nutrient transfer, biodiversity was not nearly as great as in the Escambia. Of course, the Delaware is in the temperate zone, whereas the Escambia is in a semitropical zone. Also, the Escambia water contains more lignates and fulvates than the Delaware estuary.

One finds a gradual transition from a freshwater fauna and flora at the head of the estuary to oligohaline and mesohaline conditions at the mouth. Indeed, the flow of the river was so strong that during the winter, typically freshwater insects, with very short life cycles, were able to live near the mouth of the Escambia River. The algae seemed to be about equally diverse in the freshwater, oligohaline, and mesohaline areas. The *Chlorophyta* appeared to be more diverse in the freshwater areas than in the other parts of the estuary. The protozoans were most diverse in the freshwater areas, whereas the rotifers were a little more diverse in the oligohaline reach of the estuary. Molluscs were also more diverse in the freshwater areas. As would be expected, the insects were most diverse in the freshwater areas, whereas the arthropods were about equally numerous in all areas. Fish diversity was also highest in the freshwater areas, but was relatively high in the mesohaline and oligohaline reaches of the estuary. Actually, the oligohaline area, which is often a transition zone from fresh to more saline waters at the time of high low tide, has a rigorous environment and is not inducive to the growth of many species. In many estuaries this is the area where euryhaline species live and diversity is less than in either the freshwater reaches or the truly mesohaline to euryhaline reaches.

BIBLIOGRAPHY

The Academy of Natural Sciences of Philadelphia (ANSP). 1953. Escambia River, Florida: vicinity of the Chemstrand Corporation Plant, fall 1952 to spring 1953. Stream survey report for E. I. DuPont de Nemours and Co.

Adams, S. M. 1976. Feeding ecology of eelgrass fish communities. Trans. Am. Fish. Soc. 105(3): 514–519.

Bennett, H. J. 1972. Unpublished data on meiofaunal populations. Louisiana State Univ., Baton Rouge, La.

Cruz-Orozco, R. 1970. A general comparison between the Foraminifera assemblages found on a marsh in the Pacific coast, in Scofield Bayou, and on the marshland in Barataria Bay region. Class report submitted for MRSC coastal swamps and marshes.

Cuzon du Rest, R. P. 1963. Distribution of the zooplankton in the salt marshes of southeastern Louisiana. Publ. Inst. Mar. Sci. 9:132–155.

Darnell, R. M. 1958. Food habits of fishes and larger invertebrates of Lake Pontchartrain, La, an estuarine community. Publ. Inst. Mar. Sci. 5:353–416.
Darnell, R. M. 1961. Trophic spectrum of an estuarine community based on studies of Lake Pontchartrain, La. Ecology 42(3):553–568.
Day, J. W., W. G. Smith, P. R. Wagner, and W. C. Stowe. 1973. Community structure and carbon budget of a salt marsh and shallow bay estuarine system in Louisiana. Publ. LSU-SG-72-04. Center for Wetland Resources, Louisiana State Univ., Baton Rouge, La.
Dugan, P. J., and R. J. Livingston. 1982. Long-term variations of macroinvertebrate assemblages in Apalachee Bay, Fla. Estuarine Coastal Shelf Sci. 14(4):391–403.

Ebeling, A., and R. N. Bray. 1976. Day versus night activity of reef fishes in a kelp forest off Santa Barbara, California. Fish. Bull. 14. 13 pp.
Elliott, P. B., and S. S. Bamforth. 1975. Interstitial protozoa and algae of Louisiana salt marshes. J. Protozool. 22(4):514–519.

Farfante, I. P. 1969. Western Atlantic shrimps of the genus *Penaeus*. U.S. Fish Wildl. Serv. Fish. Bull. 67:461–591.

Gillespie, M. C. 1978. Zooplankton analysis. *In* B. B. Barrett, J. L. Merrell, T. P. Morrison, M. C. Gillespie, E. J. Ralph, and J. F. Burdon, eds., A study of Louisiana's major estuaries and adjacent offshore waters. La. Dept. Wildl. Fish. Tech. Bull. 27:27–80.

Happ, G., J. G. Gosselink, and J. W. Day, Jr. 1977. The seasonal distribution of organic carbon in a Louisiana estuary. Estuarine Coastal Mar. Sci. 5(6):695–705.
Helfman, G. S. 1978. Patterns of community structure in fishes: summary and overview. Environ. Biol. Fish. 3:129–148.
Hooks, T. A., K. L. Heck, Jr., and R. J. Livingston. 1976. An inshore marine invertebrate community: structure and habitat associations in the northeastern Gulf of Mexico. Bull. Mar. Sci. 26(1):99–109.
Humm, H. J. 1956. Seagrasses of the northern Gulf coast. Bull. Mar. Sci. Gulf Caribb. 6:305–308.
Humm, H. J. 1964. Epiphytes of the seagrass *Thalassia testudinum* in Florida. Bull. Mar. Sci. Gulf Caribb. 14:306–339.

Johannes, R. E. 1965. Influence of marine protozoa on nutrient regeneration. Limnol. Oceanogr. 10(3):434–442.

Kirby, C. J. 1972. The annual net primary production and decomposition of the salt marsh grass *Spartina alterniflora*. Loisel in the Barataria Bay estuary of Louisiana. Unpubl. Ph.D. dissertation. Louisiana State Univ., Baton Rouge, La.
Kirby, C. J., and J. G. Gosselink. 1978. Primary production in a Louisiana Gulf coast *Spartina alterniflora* marsh. Ecology. 57(5):1052–1059.

Livingston, R. J. 1980. Community structure and trophic interactions in a coastal seagrass system: evaluation of short- and long-term variability, water quality, and biological response. Final Rept. Proj. R805288–01, Mar. Div. U.S. EPA.
Livingston, R. J. 1982. Trophic organization of fishes in a coastal seagrass system. Mar. Ecol. Prog. Ser. 7(1):1–12.
Livingston, R. J. 1983. Resource atlas of the Apalachicola Estuary. Florida Sea Grant College Program (project T/P-1, Grant NA80AA-D-00038), Rept. 55.
Livingston, R. J., R. L. Iverson, R. H. Estabrook, V. E. Keys, and J. Taylor, Jr. 1974. Major features of the Apalachicola Bay system: physiography, biota, and resource management. Fla. Sci. 37(4):245–271.

Livingston, R. J., P. S. Sheridan, B. G. McLane, F. G. Lewis III, and G. G. Kobylinski. 1977. The biota of the Apalachicola Bay system: functional relationships. Fla. Mar. Res. Publ. 26: 75–100.

Maples, R. S., and J. C. Watson. 1979. Occurrence of micro-algae in southwestern Louisiana coastal salt flats. Gulf Res. Rept. 6(3): 301–303.
Morrison, T. P. 1978. Chlorophyll a analysis. In B. B. Barret, J. L. Merrell, T. P. Morrison, M. C. Gillespie, E. J. Ralph, and J. F. Burdon, eds. A study of Louisiana's major estuaries and adjacent offshore waters. Louisiana Dep. Wildl. Fish. Tech. Bull. 27 pp.
Mulkana, M. S. 1968. Winter standing plankton biomass in Barataria Bay, Louisiana, and its adjacent estuarine systems. Proc. La. Acad. Sci. 31: 65–69.
Mulkana, M. S. 1969. An annual nannoplankton carbohydrate cycle in Barataria Bay, Louisiana, and its adjacent waters. Proc. La. Acad. Sci. 32: 62–68.

Odum, W. E. 1971. Pathways of energy flow in a south Florida estuary. Univ. Miami Sea Grant Program Tech. Bull. 7.
Odum, E. P., and M. Fanning. 1973. Comparison of the productivity of Spartina alterniflora and Spartina cynosuroides in Georgia coastal marshes. Bull. Ga. Acad. Sci. 31: 1–12.
Orth, R. J. 1973. Benthic infauna of eelgrass, Zostera marina, beds. Chesapeake Sci. 14(4): 258–269.

Ryan, J. D., and R. J. Livingston. 1980. Temporal patterns of food habits of fishes in Apalachee Bay with an emphasis on nocturnal trophic relationships, pp. 259–291. In R. J. Livingston, ed., Community structure and trophic interactions in a coastal seagrass system: evaluation of short- and long-term variability, water quality, and biological response. Final Rept. Proj. R805288–01, Mar. Div. U.S. EPA.

Stoner, A. W. 1972. The macrobenthos of seagrass meadows in Apalachee Bay, Florida, and the feeding ecology of Lagodon rhomboides (Pisces: Sparidae). Ph.D. dissertation. Florida State Univ., Tallahassee.
Stoner, A. W. 1980a. The role of seagrass biomass in the organization of benthic macrofaunal assemblages. Bull. Mar. Sci. 30(3): 537–551.
Stoner, A. W. 1980b. Species-specific predation on amphipod crustacea by pinfish (Lagodon rhomboides): mediation by macrophyte standing crop. Mar. Biol. 55(3): 201–208.
Stroud, L., and A. Cooper. 1969. Color-infrared aerial photographic interpretation and net primary productivity of a regularly flooded North Carolina salt marsh. Univ. North Carolina Water Resourc. Res. Inst. Rept. 14. 86 pp.

Taylor, W. R. 1960. Marine algae of the eastern tropical and subtropical coasts of the Americas. Univ. Michigan Press, Ann Arbor. 822 pp.
Teal, J. M. 1958. Distribution of fiddler crabs in Georgia salt marshes. Ecology 39(2): 185–193.
Teal, J. M. 1962. Energy flow in the salt marsh ecosystem of Georgia. Ecology 43(4): 614–624.

Wagner, P. R. 1970. An annotated list of the crabs of the Barataria Bay area. Class report submitted for MRSC coastal swamps and marshes.
Waldron, R. P. 1963. A seasonal ecological study of foraminifera from Timbalier Bay, Louisiana. Gulf Res. Rept. 1(4): 132–188.
Williams, R., and M. Murdoch. 1969. The potential importance of Spartina alterniflora in conveying zinc, manganese, and iron into estuarine food chains, pp. 431–439. In D. J. Nelson and F. C. Evans, eds., Proceedings of the 2nd national symposium on radioecology, A.S.A.E.C.

Zilberberg, M. H. 1966. Seasonal occurrence of fishes in a coastal marsh of northwest Florida. Contrib. Mar. Sci. 11: 126–134.
Zimmerman, M. J., and R. J. Livingston. 1976. Seasonality and physiochemical ranges of benthic macrophytes from a north Florida estuary (Apalachee Bay). Contrib. Mar. Sci. 20(1): 33–45.
Zimmerman, M. J., and R. J. Livingston. 1979. Dominance and distribution of benthic macrophyte assemblages in a north Florida estuary (Apalachee Bay, FL). Bull. Mar. Sci. 29(1): 27–40.

CHAPTER *10*

Southern California Estuaries

S ince San Francisco Bay, which is part of the San Joaquin estuary, is heavily
polluted, and little literature is available, to obtain a comprehensive picture,
it is necessary to consider several similar, smaller estuaries. Newport Bay, Alamitos
Bay, and Anaheim Bay are not only in reasonably natural conditions and near
each other, but also have many characteristics in common (Figure 10.1). Cluster
analyses have shown that the fish species of Newport Bay and Anaheim Bay
are closely associated.

Anaheim Bay and Alamitos Bay have similar surface areas and mouth widths
and share common climates and tidal characteristics. In addition, all three bays
rely on runoff, and/or small creeks as their primary source of freshwater and
maintain marine salinities except during the rainy winter season. The three bays
also share a somewhat similar flora and fauna (Table 10.1). Thus, by examining
the three bays, one can acquire a more complete picture of southern California
estuaries than from studying any one bay.

The California bays differ from Atlantic coast estuaries in that the movement
of water is dependent more on tidal action than on riverine flow. The structure
of eastern and western estuarine communities is similar, though the species
present are different. The western bays show no transition from fresh to mesohaline conditions and, for that reason, the fauna and flora of their communities
are more similar to those of the mesohaline communities of eastern and gulf
estuaries.

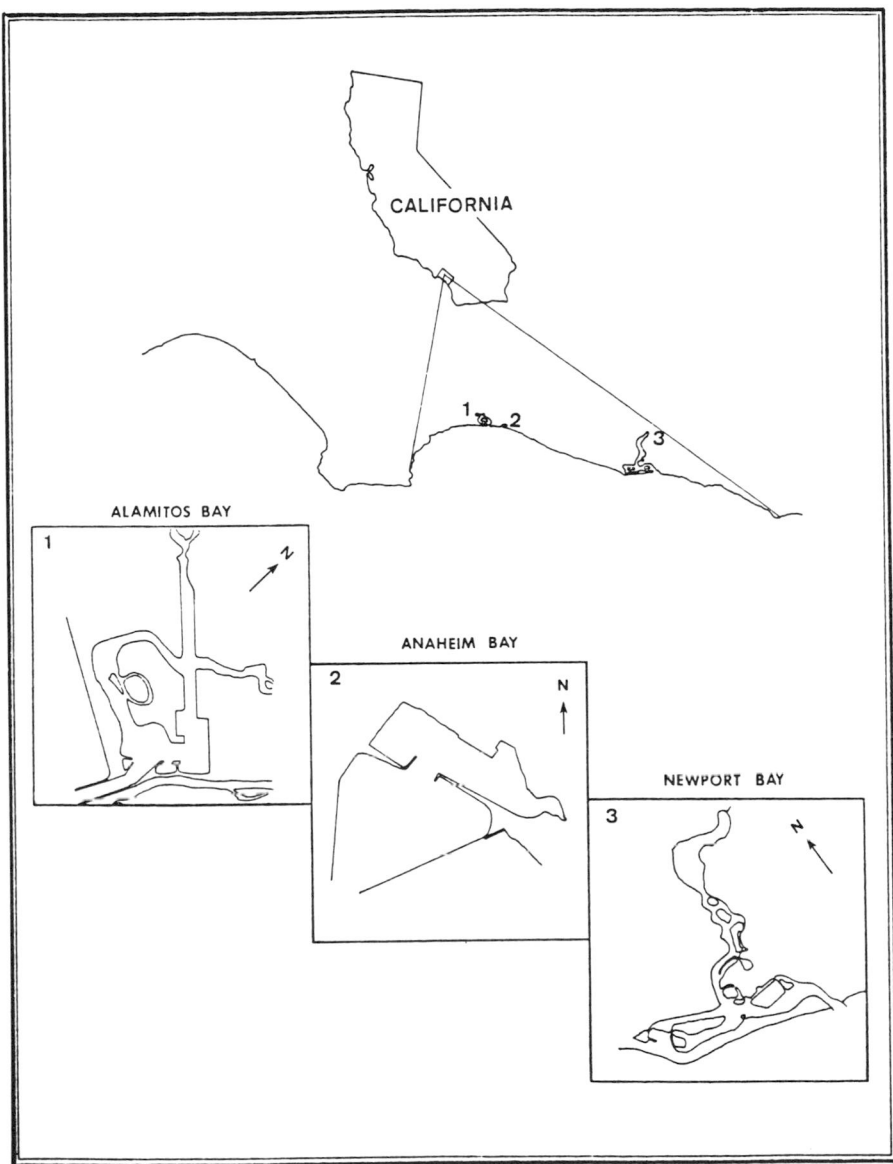

FIGURE 10.1.   Maps of Alamitos Bay, Anaheim Bay, and Newport Bay. (After Horn and Allen, Fish and Game Commission, 1981.)

NEWPORT BAY

Newport Bay is a shallow body of water located in Orange County in a heavily populated area approximately 35 miles southeast of Los Angeles, California. It receives relatively little fresh water, which is sporadic runoff from drainage channels to the north. It is considered a bay-estuary (Figure 10.2) (Trinast, 1975).

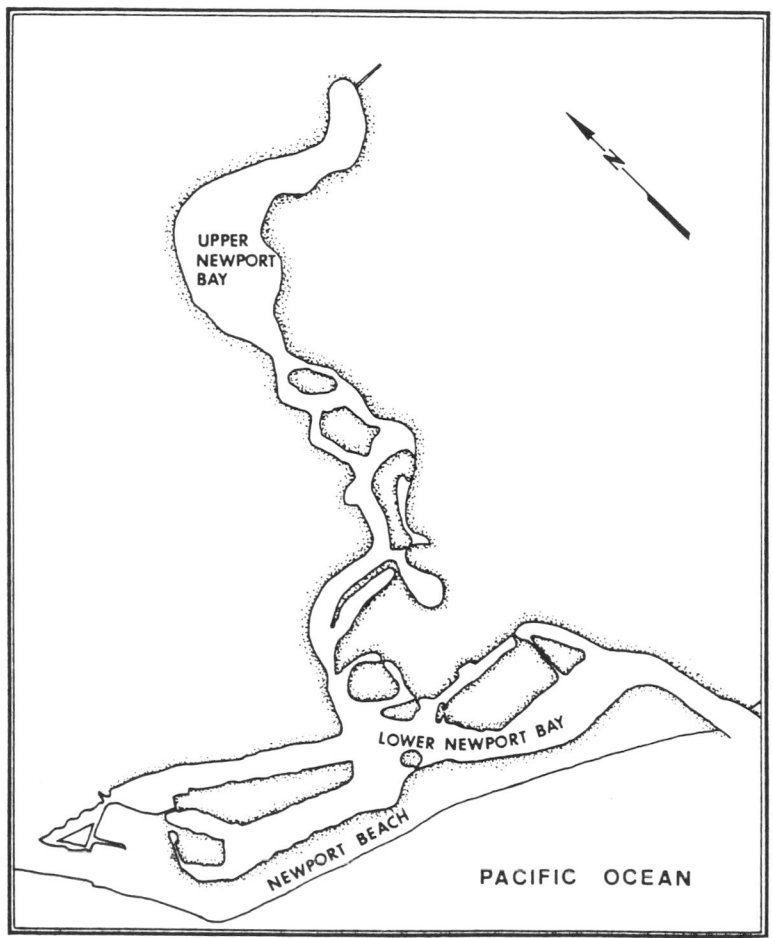

FIGURE 10.2.   Map of Newport Bay. (After Barnard and Reish, 1959. Allan Hancock Publications, Hancock Library of Biology and Oceanography, University of Southern California 90089–0372.)

The southern portion of the bay is a nearly landlocked lagoon used extensively for recreation, while the northern portion is one of the largest bay-estuaries in southern California (Vogl, 1966; Allen, 1982). The estuary extends about $2\frac{1}{2}$ miles inland and is surrounded by marsh vegetation and mudflats (Allen, 1982). Two islands and the northern portion of Shellmaker Island are the major marsh areas in the Upper Bay. In addition, marshlands run from the base of the bluffs into the bay at several locations. Mud flats are found north of the Narrows, and salt ponds occur in the northeastern part of the bay (Frey, et al., 1970; Barnard and Reish, 1959).

Originally, at least until the time of the Spanish exploration of California, the Santa Ana River entered the bay (Barnard and Reish, 1959). Longshore drift and periodic flooding, however, shifted the river 5 miles upcoast from the

(*text continues on page 660*)

TABLE 10.1. Species of the Southern California Estimates

Species	Alamitos Bay	Newport Bay	Anaheim Bay
PHYLUM CHLOROPHYTA			
Class Chlorophyceae			
Order Ulvales			
Family Ulvaceae			
Enteromorpha crinata			×
E. intestinalis		×	
E. tubulosa		×	
Enteromorpha sp.	×	×	×
Ulva lactuca		×	×
U. lobata	×	×	
Ulva sp.		×	
Order Siphonales			
Family Bryopsidaceae			
Bryopsis hypnoides			×
Order Cladophorales			
Family Cladophoraceae			
Cladophora sp.	×		
PHYLUM PHAEOPHYTA			
Class Isogeneratae			
Order Ectocarpales			
Family Ralfsiaceae			
Ralfsia sp.		×	
Family Ectocarpaceae			
Ectocarpus confervoides	×		
E. c. forma *parva*	×		
E. granulosoides		×	
Ectocarpus spp		×	
Class Heterogenerate			
Subclass Haplostichineae			
Order Chordariales			
Family Corynophloeacea			
Leathesia difformis	×		
Subclass Polystichineae			
Order Punctariales			
Family Encoeliaceae			
Colpomenia sinuosa	×	×	
Scytosiphon lomentaria	×		
Order Laminariales			
Family Lessoniaceae			
Macroystis integrifolia		×	
M. pyrifera		×	
Family Alariaceae			
Egregia laevigata	×		
PHYLUM RHODOPHYTA			
Class Rhodophyceae			

Continued

TABLE 10.1.   (*Continued*)

Species	Alamitos Bay	Newport Bay	Anaheim Bay
Subclass Bangioideae			
Order Bangiales			
Family Bangiaceae			
Porphyra perforata	×	×	
Subclass Florideae			
Order Ceramiales			
Family Delesseriaceae			
Nienburgia andersoniana		×	
Family Ceramiaceae			
Antithamnion occidentale	×		
A? secundatum	×		
Antithamnion sp.		×	
Family Rhodomelaceae			
Lophosiphonia villum		×	
Lophosiphonia sp.		×	
Polysiphonia pacifica	×		
Polysiphonia sp.		×	
Pterosiphonia bipinnata		×	×
P. dendroidea		×	
Order Cryptonemiales			
Family Dumontiaceae			
Cryptosiphonia sp.		×	
Family Corallinaceae			
Corallina sp.	×		
Order Gigartinales			
Family Gigartinaceae			
Gigartina canaliculata		×	
Rhodoglossum affine	×		
Family Gracilariaceae			
Gracilaria verrucosa			×
Gracilariopsis sjoestedii		×	
Gracilariopsis sp.		×	
Order Gelidiales			
Family Gelidiaceae			
Gelidium coulteri	×		
PHYLUM PROTOZOA			
Subphylum Ciliophora			
Class Suctoria			
Order Suctorida			
Family Ephelotidae			
Ephelota sp.		×	
PHYLUM PORIFERA			
Class Calcarea			
Family Homocoelidea			

TABLE 10.1. (*Continued*)

Species	Alamitos Bay	Newport Bay	Anaheim Bay
Leucosolenia sp.	×		×
Class Desmospongiae			
Order Haploscleridae			
Family Haliclonidae			
Haliclona permollis	×		
Haliclona sp.			×
Order Halichondrida			
Family Halichondriidae			
Halichondria panicea		×	
Family Hymeniacidonidae			
Hymeniacidon sinapium		×	
Order Sycettida			
Family Grantiidae			
Leucandra (= *Leuconia*) *barbata*		×	
L. heathi		×	
Order Spirophorida			
Family Tetillidae			
Tetilla mutabilis		×	
PHYLUM CNIDARIA			
Class Anthozoa			
Subclass Zoantharia			
Order Actiniaria			
Family Actiniidae			
Anthopleura elegantissima	×	×	×
A. xanthogrammica		×	
Family Diadumenidae			
Diadumene franciscana		×	
D. leucolena	×		×
Order Cerianthidae			
Family Ceriantharia			
Ceriantus aestuari			×
Order Corallimorpharia			
Family Corallimorphidae			
Corynactis sp.		×	
Subclass Alcyonaria			
Order Pennatulacea			
Family Virgularidae			
Stylatula elongata		×	×
Class Scyphozoa			
Order Semaeostomaea			
Family Ulmaridae			
Aurellia sp.		×	
Class Hydrozoa			
Order Thecata (Leptomedusae, Calyptoblastea)			
Family Campanularidae			

Continued

TABLE 10.1. (*Continued*)

Species	Alamitos Bay	Newport Bay	Anaheim Bay
Obelia dichotoma		×	
Obelia sp.	×		
Family Plumularidae			
Aglaophenia diegensis		×	
Aglaophenia sp.	×		
Order Athecata (Anthomedusae, Gymnoblastea)			
Family Tubulariidae			
Tubularia crocea		×	
Tubularia sp.	×		
Family Corymorphiidae			
Corymorpha palma		×	
Family Bouganvillidae			
Bouganvilla sp.	×		
PHYLUM CTENOPHORA			
Class Tentaculata			
Order Cydippa			
Family Pleurobrachiidae			
Pleurobranchia bachei	×		
PHYLUM NEMERTEA			
Class Enopla			
Order Hoplonemertea			
Family Emplectonematidae			
Emplectonema gracilis	×		
PHYLUM ANNELIDA			
Class Polychaeta			
Family Saccocirridae			
Saccocirrus papillocercus		×	
Order Ctenodrilida			
Family Ctenodrilidae			
Ctenodrillis serratus	×		
Order Phyllodocida			
Family Nephtyidae			
Nephtys caecoides	×	×	×
N. californiensis			×
N. cornuta franciscana			×
Suborder Aphroditiformia			
Family Polynoidae			
Arctonoe vittata		×	
Halosydna brevisetosa			×
H. johnsoni	×	×	×
Harmothoe sp.			×
Harmothoe imbricata			×
Harmothoe lunulata	×		
Family Sigalionidae			

TABLE 10.1. (Continued)

Species	Alamitos Bay	Newport Bay	Anaheim Bay
Sthenelais verruculosa			×
Sthenelanella uniformis		×	
Family Chrysopetalidae			
Paleonotus bellis	×		×
P. chrysolepis		×	
Suborder Phyllodocidiformia			
Family Phyllodocidae			
Anaitides madeirensis		×	
A. medipapillata	×		
A. williamsi	×	×	×
Anaitides sp.	×	×	
Eteone californica			×
E. dilatae	×	×	×
E. pacifica	×		×
Eteone sp.		×	×
Eulalia (=Hypoeulalia) bilineata	×		
Eulalia sp.			×
Eumida sanguinea	×	×	×
Suborder Nereidiformia			
Family Hesionidae			
Glyptis arenicola glabra			×
Leocrates sp.	×	×	
Podarke (=Ophiodromus) pugettensis	×	×	×
Family Pilargiidae			
Ancistrosyllis bassi	×	×	
A. hamata			×
Sigambra tentaculata			×
Family Syllidae			
Brania limbata		×	
Eusyllis sp.		×	
Exogene sp.	×		×
Exogene lourei	×		×
Odontosyllis phosphorea	×		
Sphaerosyllis pirifera	×		×
Syllis gracilis	×		×
S. (Ehlersia) gracilis near cornuta			×
Typosyllis fasciata			×
Typosyllis sp.	×		
Family Nereidae			
Neanthes arenaceodentata	×		×
N. caudata	×	×	
N. succinea	×		×
Neanthes sp.	×		
Nereis eakini		×	
N. procera	×	×	×
N. grubei	×	×	

Continued

TABLE 10.1. (*Continued*)

Species	Alamitos Bay	Newport Bay	Anaheim Bay
N. latescens	×		
N. neonigripes	×		
Nereis sp.		×	
Platynereis bicanaliculata	×	×	×
Suborder Glyceriformia			
Family Glyceridae			
Glycera americana	×	×	×
G. convoluta			×
G. robusta			×
G. tesselata			×
Glycera sp.			×
Hemipodus borealis	×		
Family Goniadidae			
Glycinde armigera			×
Glycinde sp.			×
Goniada acicula			×
G. littorea	×	×	
G. uncinigera			×
Order Eunicida			
Family Eunicidae			
Marphysa sanguinea	×	×	×
M. stylobranchiata		×	
Family Onuphidae			
Diopatra splendidissima	×		×
Nothria elegans			×
Family Lumbrineridae			
Lumbrineris erecta	×	×	×
L. minima	×	×	×
L. tetraura			×
L. zonata	×		×
Lumbrineris sp.	×	×	×
Family Arabellidae			
Drilonereis nuda		×	
Family Dorvilleidae			
Dorvillea articulata	×	×	
Ophryotrocha puerilis	×		
Protodorvillea gracilis			×
Stauronereis gracilis			×
S. rudolphi	×		×
Order Orbiniida			
Family Orbiniidae			
Haploscoloplos elongatus	×	×	×
Naineris dendritica	×	×	×
Naineris sp.		×	
Family Paraonidae			

TABLE 10.1. (*Continued*)

Species	Alamitos Bay	Newport Bay	Anaheim Bay
Paraonis gracilis oculata	×	×	
Order Spionida			
Suborder Spionoformia			
Family Spionidae			
Boccardia polybranchia			×
B. proboscidea			×
B. redeki	×		
B. uncata	×		×
Laonice cirrata	×		×
Nerinides acuta	×	×	×
N. maculata	×	×	
N. pigmentata	×	×	×
Polydora brachycephala			×
P. ligni	×		×
P. limnicola	×		×
P. nuchalis	×		
P. paucibranchiata		×	×
P. socialis	×		
P. websteri			×
Polydora sp.	×		
Prionospio cirrifera	×	×	×
P. near *kroyeri*	×		
P. malmgreni	×		×
P. near *malmgreni*	×		
P. heterobranchia newportensis	×	×	×
P. pinnata	×	×	×
P. pigmaeus	×		×
Prionospio sp.		×	
Pseudopolydora kempi			×
P. (= *Polydora*) *paucibranchiata*	×	×	×
Rhynchospio arenicola			×
Spiophanes fimbriata			×
S. missionensis	×	×	×
S. pigmentata	×		
Spiophanes sp.	×	×	
Streblospio benedicti	×	×	×
Family Magelonidae			
Magelona californica	×	×	×
Suborder Chaetopteriformia			
Family Chaetopteridae			
Chaetopterus variopedatus	×	×	
Spiochaetopterus sp.	×		
Telepsavus costarum	×		×
Suborder Cirratuliformia			
Family Cirratulidae			

Continued

TABLE 10.1. (*Continued*)

Species	Alamitos Bay	Newport Bay	Anaheim Bay
Chaetozone corona	×	×	×
C. multioculata			×
Cirriformia luxuriosa	×	×	×
C. spirabrancha	×		×
Cirriformia sp.	×		×
Thayrx multifilis	×		×
T. parvus	×	×	×
Thayrx sp.	×		
Order Cossura			
Family Cossuridae			
Cossura candida	×	×	×
C. longicirrata	×		
Polyopthalmus pictus	×		×
Order Flabelligerida			
Family Flabelligeridae			
Pherusa capulata	×		
P. inflata		×	
P. papillata			×
Order Opheliida			
Family Opheliidae			
Armandia bioculata	×	×	×
Family Scalibregmidae			
Scalibregma inflatum			×
Order Capitellida			
Family Capitellidae			
Capitella capitata	×	×	×
Capitita ambiseta	×	×	×
Dasybranchus lumbricoides			×
Notomastus magnus			×
N. (= *Clistomastus*) *tenuis*	×	×	
Notomatus sp.			×
Scyphoproctus oculatus		×	
Family Maldanidae			
Asychis disparidentata	×	×	
A. similis	×		
Asychis sp.			×
Axiothella rubrocincta	×	×	×
Nichomache personata			×
Praxiella affinis pacifica		×	×
Order Oweniida			
Family Oweniidae			
Owenia collaris			×
O. fusiformis collaris	×	×	
Order Terebellida			
Family Sabellariidae			
Sabellaria gracilis		×	×

TABLE 10.1. (*Continued*)

Species	Alamitos Bay	Newport Bay	Anaheim Bay
Family Pectinariidae			
Pectinaria californiensis	×		×
Family Ampharetidae			
Amage anops	×	×	
Ampharete arctica	×		
A. labrops			×
Ampharete sp.	×		
Amphicteis glabra			×
A. scaphobranchiata	×		×
Melinna oculata			×
Family Terebellidae			
Amaeana occidentalis	×	×	×
Eupolymnia heterobranchia		×	
Pista alata	×	×	×
P. cristata	×		×
P. disjuncta			×
Streblosoma crassibranchia			×
Thelepus setosus			×
Order Sabellida			
Family Sabellidae			
Chone sp.			×
Chone mollis		×	
Euchone.limnicola	×	×	×
Euchone sp.	×		
Eudistyla polymorpha		×	
Fabricia limnicola	×	×	
Megalomma pigmentum	×	×	×
Megalomma sp.	×	×	
Myxicola infundibulum	×		
Sabella media	×		
Family Serpulidae			
Crucigera zygophora	×		
Eupomatus gracilis		×	
Eupomatus sp.	×		
Hydroides norvegica	×		
Spirabranchus spinosus	×		
PHYLUM SIPUNCULA			
Family Sipunculidae			
Sipunculus nudus		×	
PHYLUM ECHIURA			
Order Xenopneusta			
Family Urechidae			
Urechis caupo		×	×
PHYLUM MOLLUSCA			
Class Polyplacophora			

Continued

TABLE 10.1.   (*Continued*)

Species	Alamitos Bay	Newport Bay	Anaheim Bay
Order Neoloricata			
Suborder Ischnochitonina			
Family Ischnochitonidae			
Cyanoplax hartwegi		×	
Family Mopaliidae			
Mopalia muscosa	×		
Class Gastropoda			
Subclass Prosobranchiata			
Order Archaeogastropoda			
Family Trochidae			
Tegula funebralis	×	×	
Tegula sp.			×
Family Littorina			
Littorinia planaxis	×		
L. scutulata	×		
Littorina sp.			×
Family Olividae			
Olivella sp.			×
Family Fissurellidae			
Diodara aspera		×	
Lucapinella callomarginata		×	
Megathura crenulata	×		
Family Acmaeidae			
Acmaea fenestrata		×	
A. limatula	×		
A. pelta		×	
A. scabra	×	×	
Lottia gigantea	×		
Order Mesogastropoda			
Family Potamididae			
Cerithidea californica	×	×	×
Family Vermetidae			
Serulorbis (= *Aletes*) *squamigerus*	×		
Family Calyptraeidae			
Crepidula onyx	×	×	×
Crepidula sp.	×	×	
Crepipatella lingulata		×	
Crucibulum spinosum		×	
Family Naticidae			
Polinices reclusianus	×		×
Family Columbellidae			
Mitrella carinata		×	
Family Lamellariidae			
Lamellaria stearnsii		×	
Family Vermetidae			
Serpulorbis squamigerous		×	

TABLE 10.1. (Continued)

Species	Alamitos Bay	Newport Bay	Anaheim Bay
Family Rissöidae			
Barleeia sp.		×	
Family Caecidae			
Caecum californicum		×	
C. crebricinctum		×	
Family Cerithiopsidae			
Cerithiopsis carpenteri		×	
Cerithiopsis sp.		×	
Order Neogastropoda			
Family Muricidae			
Ceratostoma nuttalli	×	×	
Maxwellia gemma		×	
Pteropurpura (= *Pterynotus*) *trialata*		×	
Roperia (= *Ocenebra*) *poulsoni*	×	×	
Family Thaisidae			
Acanthina spirata	×		
Family Olividae			
Olivella biplicata	×	×	
Family Nassariidae			
Nassarius fossatus	×	×	
N. mendicus	×	×	
N. tegula		×	×
Family Conidae			
Conus californicus		×	
Family Collumbellidae			
Mitrella carinata		×	
M. gausapata		×	
Subclass Opisthobranchiata			
Order Nudibranchia			
Suborder Doridacea			
Family Discodorididae			
Anisodoris nobilis		×	
Dialula sandiegensis	×	×	
Doriopsilla (= *Dendrodoris*) *albopunctata*		×	
Suborder Aeolidacea			
Family Facelinidae			
Hermissenda crassicornis	×		
Order Anaspidea			
Family Aplysiidae			
Aplysia californica	×	×	
Aplysia sp.		×	
Family Archidoridae			
Archidoris montereyensis	×		
Order Cephalaspidea			
Family Atyidae			

Continued

TABLE 10.1. (*Continued*)

Species	Alamitos Bay	Newport Bay	Anaheim Bay
Haminoea vesicula		×	
Haminoea sp.			×
Family Acteonidae			
Acteon punctocoelata	×		
Rictaxis (= *Acteon*) *punctocaelatus*	×		
Family Acteocinidae			
Acteocina smira	×		
Family Bullidae			
Bulla gouldiana	×	×	
Bulla sp.			×
Family Aglajidae			
Navanax inermis	×	×	
Family Retusidae			
Acteocina (= *Retusa*) sp.		×	
Class Bivalvia			
Subclass Pteriomorpha			
Order Mytiloida			
Family Mytilidae			
Modiolus (= *Volsella*) *capax*		×	
M. demissa	×	×	
M. flabellata		×	
Mytilus californianus	×		
M. edulis	×	×	×
Mytilus sp.		×	
Geukensia desmiss			×
Order Pterioida			
Family Ostreidae			
Ostrea lurida	×	×	
Family Pectinidae			
Hinnites giganteus (= *H. multirugosus*)	×		
Leptopecten latiauratus		×	
Pecten sp.		×	
Subclass Heterodonta			
Order Veneroida			
Family Veneridae			
Chione californiensis	×	×	
C. fluctifraga	×	×	×
C. undatella	×	×	×
Protothaca laciniata		×	
P. staminea	×	×	×
P. tenerrima		×	
Saxidomus nuttalli	×		
Tivela stultorum			×
Family Tellinidae			
Leporimetis obesa		×	
Macoma acolasta		×	

TABLE 10.1. (*Continued*)

Species	Alamitos Bay	Newport Bay	Anaheim Bay
M. nasuta	×	×	×
M. secta	×	×	×
Tellina buttoni	×		
T. carpenteri	×		
T. modesta		×	
Family Psammobiidae			
Gama californica		×	
Heterodonax pacificus		×	
Nuttallia (= Sanguinolaria) nuttallii	×	×	
Tagelus californianus	×	×	×
Tagelus sp.			x
Family Cardiidae			
Clinocardium nuttalli		×	
Laevicardium substriatum	×	×	
Laevicardium sp.			×
Trachycardium quadragenarium		×	×
Family Montacutidae			
Mysella (= Rochefortia) spp.	×		
Family Solenidae			
Solen rosaceus	×	×	
Family Mactridae			
Mactra californica		×	
Spisula catilliformis		×	
S. hemphilli		×	
Tresus nuttallii (= Schizothaerus nuttalli)	×	×	×
Family Chamidae			
Chama arcana (= C. pellucida)	×	×	
Psuedochama exogyra	×		
Family Donacidae			
Donax californicus		×	
Order Myoida			
Family Myidae			
Cryptomya californica			×
Family Hiatellidae			
Hiatella arctica	×	×	×
Panope generosa		×	
Saxicava sp.		×	
Family Teredinidae			
Lyrodus pedicellatus	×		
Subclass Anomalodesmata			
Order Pholadamyoida			
Family Lyonsiidae			
Lyonsia (= Lysonia) californica	×	×	
Class Cephalopoda			
Order Decapoda			

Continued

TABLE 10.1.   (Continued)

Species	Alamitos Bay	Newport Bay	Anaheim Bay
Suborder Teuthoidea			
Family Loliginidae			
Loligo opalescens			×
Order Octopoda			
Family Octopodidae			
Octopus bimaculatus		×	
Octopus sp.			×
PHYLUM ARTHROPODA			
Class Crustacea			
Subclass Cirripedia			
Order Thoracica			
Suborder Balanomorpha			
Family Balanidae			
Balanus amphitrite	×		×
B. aquila		×	
B. concavus pacificus		×	
B. crenatus	×		×
B. glandula	×	×	
B. tintinnabulum	×	×	
Family Chthamalidae			
Chthamalus fissus	×		×
Family Tetraclitidae			
Tetraclita squamosa	×		
Suborder Lepadomorpha			
Family Scalpellidae			
Pollicipes (= *Mittela*) *polymerus*	×		
Subclass Copepoda			
Order Calanoida			
Family Calanidae			
Calanus sp.	×		×
Family Acartiidae			
Acartia californiensis		×	
A. tonsa			×
Order Cyclopoda			
Clausidium vancouverense			×
Family Chondracanthidae			
Acanthochondria soleae			×
Acanthochondria sp.			×
Family Taeniacanthidae			
Taeniacanthodes haakeri			×
Family Ergasilidae			
Ergasilis lizae			×
Family Bomolochidae			
Bomolochus cuneatus			×
Holobomolocus embiotocae			×
H. prolixus			×

TABLE 10.1. (*Continued*)

Species	Alamitos Bay	Newport Bay	Anaheim Bay
Family Taeniacanthidae			
Taeniacanthodes haakeri			×
Order Caligoida			
Family Caligidae			
Lepeophtheirus bifidus			×
Family Pandaridae			
Achtheinus oblongus			×
Subclass Malacostraca			
Superorder Peracarida			
Order Cumacea			
Family Diastylidae			
Oxyurostylis pacifica	×		×
Order Isopoda			
Suborder Flabellifera			
Family Sphaeromatidae			
Cilocoela gilliana	×		
Paracerceis cordata		×	
P. gilliana		×	×
P. sculpta		×	
Sphaeroma quoyana (− *S. pentadon*)		×	
Family Limnoriidae			
Limnoria tripunctata	×		×
Family Cymothoidae			
Braga sp.		×	
Lironeca (= *Livoneca*) *californica*			×
L. vulgaris			×
Lironeca (= *Livoneca*) sp.			×
Nerocila californica		×	
Suborder Valvifera			
Family Idoteidae			
Edotea sp.	×		
Idotea resecata		×	
Suborder Oniscoidea			
Family Ligiidae			
Ligia occidentalis	×		
Ligia sp.			×
Order Amphipoda			
Suborder Gammaridea			
Family Lysianassidae			
Aruga holmesi		×	
Family Ampeliscidae			
Ampelisca cristata	×	×	
A. cristata forma *microdenta*		×	
Family Phoxocephalidae			

Continued

TABLE 10.1.   (*Continued*)

Species	Alamitos Bay	Newport Bay	Anaheim Bay
Paraphoxus spinosus		×	
Family Amphilochidae			
Amphilochus neapolitanus		×	
Family Colomastigidae			
Colomastix pusilla		×	
Family Leucothoidae			
Leucothoe alata	×	×	
L. pacifica		×	
Leucothoides pacifica	×		
Family Pontogenidae			
Pontogenia minuta	×		
Family Anamixidae			
Anamixis linsleyi	×	×	
Family Stenothoidae			
Stenothoe valida		×	
Family Calliopiidae			
Incisocalliope newportensis		×	
Family Pontogeneiidae			
Pontogeneia minuta		×	
Family Gammaridae			
Elasmopus rapax	×	×	×
Maera simile		×	
M. inaequipes		×	
Metaceradocus occidentalis		×	
Family Hyalidae			
Allorchestes angustus		×	
Allorchestes sp.		×	×
Hyale frequens		×	×
H. plumulosa		×	×
Hyale sp.	×		×
Family Liljeborgiidae			
Listrella sp.			×
Family Aoridae			
Acuminodeutopus heteruropus		×	
Amphidentopis sp.			×
Rudilemboides stenopropodus		×	
Microdeutopus schmiti?		×	
Aoroides columbiae		×	
Family Photidae			
Amphideutopus oculatus	×	×	
Eurystheus thompsoni	×	×	
Family Ampithoidae			
Ampithoe longimana		×	
A. plumulosa	×	×	×
A. pollex		×	

TABLE 10.1. (*Continued*)

Species	Alamitos Bay	Newport Bay	Anaheim Bay
Family Ischyroceridae			
Jassa falcata	×	×	
Family Corophiidae			
Corophium acherusicum	×	×	×
C. baconi		×	
C. insidiosum	×	×	
C. uenoi		×	
Corophium sp.	×		
Erichthonius brasiliensis		×	
E. crenulata		×	
Family Podoceridae			
Podocerus brasiliensis		×	
Podocerus sp.		×	
Family Oedicerotidae			
Monoculodes sp.			×
Suborder Caprellidae			
Family Caprellidae			
Caprella californica	×	×	×
C. equilibra	×	×	×
Caprella sp.			×
Family Aeginellidae			
Metacaprella sp.	×		
Superorder Eucarida			
Order Decapoda			
Suborder Reptantia			
Section Palineura			
Family Palinuridae			
Panulirus interruptus	×		
Section Macrura			
Family Callianassidae			
Callianassa californiensis	×	×	×
C. gigas			×
Callianassa sp.	×		×
Upogebia pugettensis	×	×	×
Section Brachyura			
Family Majidae			
Pyromaia tuberculata		×	
Family Xanthidae			
Lophopanopeus frontalis		×	
Lophopanopeus sp.		×	
Family Grapsidae			
Hemigrapsus nudus		×	×
H. oregonensis	×		×
Hemigrapsus sp.			×

Continued

TABLE 10.1.   (*Continued*)

Species	Alamitos Bay	Newport Bay	Anaheim Bay
Pachygrapsus crassipes	×	×	×
Family Pinnotheridae			
Pinnixa franciscana	×		×
P. tubicola		×	
Pinnixia sp.			×
Family Cancridae			
Cancer antennarius	×		×
C. gracilis			×
C. jordani	×		
Family Ocypodidae			
Uca crenulata	×	×	
Section Anomura			
Family Paguridae			
Isocheles (= *Holopagurus*) *pilosus*			×
Pagurus samuelis		×	
Pagurus sp.		×	
Suborder Natantia			
Section Caridea			
Family Crangonidae			
Crangon californiensis	×	×	×
C. stylirostris	×		
Crangon sp.			×
Family Alpheidac			
Alpheus sp.		×	
Subphylum Pycnogonida			
Class Pantopoda			
Family Phoxichilidiidae			
Anoplodactylus erectus			×
PHYLUM ECTOPROCTA			
Class Gymnolaemata			
Order Cheilostomata			
Suborder Anasca			
Family Bicellariellidae			
Bugula californica	×		
B. neritina	×	×	×
B. pacifica		×	
Family Membraniporidae			
Membranipora tuberculata		×	
Family Scrupariidae			
Eucratea clavata		×	
Family Scrupocellariidae			
Scrupocellaria bertholetti	×		
S. b. tenuirostris		×	
S. californica		×	
S. diegensis		×	
Family Thalamoporellidae			

TABLE 10.1. (*Continued*)

Species	Alamitos Bay	Newport Bay	Anaheim Bay
Thalamoporella californica	×		
Suborder Ascophora			
Family Schizoporellidae			
Schizoporella unicornis	×	×	
Family Cheiloporinidae			
Crypotsula pallasiana	×	×	
Family Reteporidae			
Phidolopora pacifica	×		
Rhincozoon rostratum	×		
R. tumulosum		×	
Family Celliporidae			
Celleporaria (=Holoporella) brunnea	×		
Holoporella aperta		×	
Suborder Articulata			
Family Crisiidae			
Crisulipora occidentalis	×	×	
Order Cyclostomata			
Suborder Tubuliporina			
Family Diastoporidae			
Diaperoecia floridina	×	×	
Suborder Articulata			
Family Crisiidae			
Filicrisia geniculata		×	
Order Ctenostomata			
Suborder Stolonifera			
Family Vesiculariidae			
Zoobotryon venticillatum	×		
PHYLUM PHORONIDA			
Phoronis sp.			×
Phoronis vancouverensis	×		
PHYLUM ECHINODERMATA			
Class Asteroidea			
Order Spinulosida			
Family Asterinidae			
Patiria minuta	×	×	
Order Paxillosida			
Family Astropectinidae			
Astropecten armatus	×		
Order Forcipulatida			
Family Asteriidae			
Pisaster giganteus	×		
P. ochraceus	×		
Class Holothuroidea			
Order Apodid			
Family Synaptidae			

Continued

TABLE 10.1.   (*Continued*)

Species	Alamitos Bay	Newport Bay	Anaheim Bay
Leptosynapta albicans	×		
Order Aspidochirotida			
Family Stichopodidae			
Parastichopus (= *Stichopus*) *parvimensis*	×		
Class Echinoidea			
Order Echinoida			
Family Strongylocentrotidae			
Strongylocentrotus franciscanus	×	×	
S. purpuratus	×		
Order Temnopleuroida			
Family Toxopneustidae			
Lytechinus anamesus (= *L. pictus*)		×	
Order Clylpeasteroida			
Family Dendrasteridae			
Dendraster excentricus	×		
Class Ophiuroidea			
Order Ophiurida			
Suborder Gnathophiurina			
Family Ophiactidae			
Amphipholis pugetana		×	
A. squamata		×	
Ophiactis simplex		×	
Family Ophiothricidae			
Ophiothrix spiculata	×		
PHYLUM CHORDATA			
Subphylum Urochordata			
Class Ascidiacea			
Order Enterogona			
Suborder Phlebobranchia			
Family Cionidae			
Ciona intestinalis (Linnaeus)	×	×	
Suborder Aplousobranchia			
Family Polyclinidae			
Amaroucium (= *Aplidium*) *californicum*	×	×	×
Amaroucium sp.	×	×	
Order Pleurogona			
Suborder Stolidobranchia			
Family Styelidae			
Botrylus sp.	×		
Styela clava Herdman (= *S. barnharti*)		×	
S. montereyensis	×	×	×
S. plicata	×		×
S. truncata		×	
Family Pyuridae			
Pyura haustor (= *Halocynthia johnsoni*)		×	

TABLE 10.1. (*Continued*)

Species	Alamitos Bay	Newport Bay	Anaheim Bay
Family Mogulidae			
Eugyra arenosa			×
Subphylum Vertebrata			
Class Chondrichthys			
Order Heterodontiformes			
Family Heterodontidae			
Heterodontus francisci			×
Order Squaliformes			
Family Carcharhinidae			
Mustelus californicus		×	×
M. henlei			×
Triakis henlei		×	
T. semifasciata		×	×
Family Squatinidae			
Squatina californica			×
Order Rajiformes			
Family Rhinobatidae			
Platyrhinoidis triseriata		×	
Rhinobatos productus	×	×	×
Family Dasyatidae			
Dasyatis dipterura		×	
Gymnura marmorata		×	
Urolophus halleri	×	×	×
Family Myliobatidae			
Myliobatis californicus	×	×	×
Class Osteichthyes			
Order Elopiformes			
Family Albulidae			
Albula vulpes		×	
Order Clupeiformes			
Family Clupeidae			
Dorosoma petenense		×	×
Opisthonema libertate		×	
Sardinops caerulea		×	
S. sagaz		×	
Family Engraulidae			
Anchoa compressa	×	×	×
A. delicatissima	×	×	×
Engraulis mordax	×	×	×
Order Gobiesociformes			
Family Gobiesocidae			
Gobiesox rhessodon	×	×	
Order Gadiformes			
Family Ophidiidae			

Continued

TABLE 10.1.   (*Continued*)

Species	Alamitos Bay	Newport Bay	Anaheim Bay
Otophidium scrippsi			×
Order Atheriniformes			
Family Cyprinodontidae			
Fundulus parvipinnis	×	×	×
Family Poeciliidae			
Gambusia affinis		×	
Family Atherinidae			
Atherinops affinis	×	×	×
Leuresthes tenuis (*Ayres*)	×	×	
Order Gasterosteiformes			
Family Sygnathidae			
Syngnathus californiensis		×	
S. griseolineatus	×	×	
S. leptorhynchus			×
Order Perciformes			
Family Centrarchidae			
Lepomis cyanellus		×	
L. macrochirus		×	
L. tenuis		×	
Family Pomadasyidae			
Anisotremus davidsoni	×	×	×
Xenistius californiensis		×	
Family Serranidae			
Paralabrax clathratus	×	×	×
P. maculatofasciatus	×	×	×
P. nebulifer		×	×
Family Mugilidae			
Mugil cephalus	×	×	×
Family Percichthyidae			
Morone (= *Roccus*) *saxatilis*		×	×
Family Kyphosidae			
Girella nigricans	×	×	×
Family Scombridae			
Sarda chiliensis			×
Scomber japonicus		×	
Family Stromateidae			
Paprilus (= *Palometa*) *simillima*		×	×
Family Scorpaenidae			
Sebastes serranoides			×
Family Sciaenidae			
Cheilotrema saturnum		×	×
Cynoscion nobilis		×	×
Genyonemus lineatus	×	×	×
Menticirrhus undulatus	×	×	×
Roncador stearnsi	×	×	×

TABLE 10.1. (*Continued*)

Species	Alamitos Bay	Newport Bay	Anaheim Bay
Seriphus politus	×	×	×
Umbrina roncador		×	×
Family Embiotocidae			
Amphistichus argenteus		×	×
Cymatogaster aggregata	×	×	×
Embiotoca jacksoni	×	×	×
Hyperprosopon argenteum	×	×	×
H. ellipticum		×	
Hypsurus caryi			×
Micrometrus minimus			×
Phanerodon furcatus	×	×	×
Rhacochilus toxotes		×	
R. vacca	×	×	×
Family Gobiidae			
Acanthogobius flavimanus		×	
Clevelandia ios	×	×	×
Gillichthys mirabilis	×	×	×
Quietula y-cauda	×	×	×
Ilypnus gilberti		×	×
Lepidogobius lepidus			×
Family Clinidae			
Gibbonsia elegans	×		
Heterostichus rostratus	×	×	×
Paraclinus integrippinis		×	
Family Blenniidae			
Hypsoblennius gentilis		×	×
Family Stichaeidae			
Xiphister mucosa	×		
Family Sphyraenidae			
Sphyraena argentea		×	
Family Cottidae			
Clinocottus analis	×		
Leptocottus armatus	×	×	×
L. a. australis		×	
Scorpaenichthys marmoratus	×		
Order Batrachoidiforme			
Family Batrachoididae			
Porichthys myriaster	×	×	×
P. notatus		×	
Order Pleuronectiformes			
Family Bothidae			
Citharichthys sordidus		×	
C. stigmaeus		×	×

Continued

TABLE 10.1. (*Continued*)

Species	Alamitos Bay	Newport Bay	Anaheim Bay
Paralichthys californicus	×	×	×
Family Pleuronectidae			
Hypsopsetta guttulata	×	×	×
Parophrys vetulus			×
Pleuronichthys ritteri		×	×
P. verticalis			×
Family Cynoglossidae			
Symphurus atricauda		×	×

Newport Bay entrance, where it now enters the ocean directly (Barnard and Reish, 1959; Trinast, 1975). An artificial entrance channel now joins the Newport Bay to the Pacific Ocean (Trinast, 1975).

The lower harbor area has been dramatically altered by dredging, landfills, and bulkheads (Allen, 1982). From 1950 to 1966 one-third of the salt marsh vegetation was removed (Vogl, 1966). The channels have been deepened and the islands in the harbor are densely crowded with homes (Barnard and Reish, 1959). The upper bay remains in a relatively natural condition, while the lower portion of the bay suffers moderate to low pollution levels (Allen, 1982; Barnard and Reish, 1959).

Water Quality Characteristics

Salinity. Salinity averaged over one year at five stations varied from a low of 33.33 ppt to a high of 34.39 ppt (Stevenson and Emery, 1958). From January to March, 1978 low salinities were recorded in the Upper Bay, while higher salinities (25 ppt to 32 ppt) occurred after May (Allen, 1982). Salinities of water flowing around the Narrows were reported to differ by 1 ppt to 3 ppt from that of the lower reaches of the bay, due to freshwater runoff. The water column around the Narrows tended to be isohaline, due to mixing caused by the turbulence of waters flowing over the shallow channels of the northern sector of the bay. Weak vertical salinity gradients were observed near the Dunes, in the lower portion of the Upper Bay (Trinast, 1975).

Water Temperature. Water temperatures were extremely variable in the bay, due to its shallowness (Stevenson and Emery, 1958). Water temperatures of the littoral zone in the Upper Bay were observed to increase from 14 to 15 °C in January to 26 to 28 °C in June. Through the summer, temperatures remained above 25 °C. In the fall, temperatures declined gradually until November and December, when they fell sharply to 15 °C or below. In general, temperatures were higher than those in the adjacent open ocean except from December to February (Frey et al., 1970). Temperatures could vary as much as 15 °C in one day (Trinast, 1975). Mean yearly air temperature was 16 °C, with an average range of approximately 7 °C (Stevenson and Emery, 1958).

pH. The average pH of the bay waters was 7.78, with the highest pH of 8.79 being measured at a temperature of 33 °C in shallow water. The lowest, found over foul mud (H_2S) was 7.22. The normal pH. range, however, was between 7.3 and 8.2 (Stevenson and Emery, 1958).

Chlorinity. Chlorinity, measured at 55 stations in the bay in January, 1954, ranged from 15.2 ppt to 19.7 ppt on the surface and from 17.9 ppt to 20.0 ppt at depth. Chlorinity was measured at 23 stations in January 1953 and ranged from 16.5 ppt to 19.2 ppt at the surface and from 16.7 ppt to 19.1 ppt at depth (Barnard and Reish, 1959).

Dissolved Oxygen; Transparency. Dissolved oxygen in January, 1953 ranged from 5.9 to 8.1 ppm at the surface and from 5.5 to 8.1 ppm at depth. Water transparency measurements at this time varied from a low of 6 ft to a high of 23 ft (Barnard and Reish, 1959).

Hydrography. There was no continuous inflow of freshwater into Newport Bay. Estuarine conditions prevailed in Newport Bay only during winter rain storms (Seapy and Kitting, 1978). The principal drainage into the bay was from San Diego Creek, which received runoff from a 109-square-mile area of mountains, farmland, and urban developments. Maximum peak flood discharge from the San Diego Creek was estimated at 10,000 ft per second. In addition, both Big Canyon and Delhi Drainage Ditch discharged into the central and northwest portions of the bay, respectively (Frey et al., 1970).

Due to the narrowness of the bay there was little tidal mixing observed (Stevenson and Emery, 1958). The northernmost portion of the bay was cut off from normal tidal circulation by a series of dikes and basins (Stevenson and Emery, 1958). The principal currents were reported to be from the ebb and flow of tides, with only minor surface currents occurring from winds. The tidal pattern was of the mixed, semidiurnal type, typical of the Pacific Coast of North America (Seapy and Kitting, 1978). Due to this tidal pattern, current conditions and duration of slack tide varied from month to month (Trinast, 1975). In addition to daily tides, the bay's waters were influenced by coastal plain runoff and occasional floods and strong tides (Stevenson and Emery, 1958).

The tide range of the bay was 3.4 ft, with a diurnal range of 4.9 ft. Average tidal current velocity was approximately 2.3 ft per second during spring tides and 0.80 ft per second during neap tides. Current velocity at the mouth of the bay was greater than in other areas of the bay, with velocities up to 5.8 ft per second recorded (Stevenson and Emery, 1958).

Waves in the bay rarely exceeded 15 cm in height except during the Santa Anas (seasonal sandstorms driven by warm winds), when waves reached 61 cm. Under normal conditions the prevailing wind was a southwesterly afternoon sea breeze from 1 to 8 knots (Stevenson and Emery, 1958).

Sediments

An extensive study of sediments in Newport Bay was conducted by Stevenson and Emery (1958). Coarse sediments were found in the major channel, the coarsest (median diameter ranging from 3 to 0.96 mm) being found from the entrance of the bay to where the channel bends northward. Median size sediments were found on tidal flats (0.11 to 0.052 mm), on marsh beaches (0.031 to 0.0016 mm, with the majority skewed to the coarse limit), and in bottom deposits of the basins. Finest sediments were found on the marsh surfaces. Although median marsh surface sediments ranged in size from 0.010 to 0.0016 mm, most (97%) had median diameters less than 0.016 mm (Stevenson and Emery, 1958).

In general, sediments in the main channel and on the flats ranged from fine sand to coarse silt, although the majority of channel sediments were silt. Tidal flats bordering the main channel had sediments of fine sand, although occasionally, pebbles and cobbles from adjacent cliffs were found on silt mud flats. Beaches ranged from sand to fine silt and clay, while tidal creek sediments were sandy. Marsh sediments were sandy in the center with silt and clay borders (Stevenson and Emery, 1958). Beneath the surface sediments, grain size, percent sand, and sorting tended to increase with depth. At 1.21 m deep, 95% of the sediment was sand with a median diameter of 0.75 mm (Stevenson and Emery, 1958).

The sandy beach sediments, as well as those sediments whose median diameters were in the clay fraction, were well sorted. Poorest sorting was found in sediments within the silt fraction. Sediment color varied from light buff-brown in the coarser sands to blue-black in nearshore clays (Stevenson and Emery, 1958). Variation in color is caused by the amount of organic matter in the sediments and the degree of oxidation. A light yellow-brown color is characteristic of sediments that contain little organic material and a high level of oxygenation. Darker sediments are characteristic of anaerobic conditions, and anaerobic activity in the sediment often produces H_2S.

Organic material in the sediments of Newport Bay varied from finely divided fragments in areas where active decomposition was occurring to undecomposed areas in the Upper Marsh. Percent organic matter varied from 0.1% in channel sand to 27.7% in a thick stand of a community composed mainly of the salt marsh phanerogram, *Monanthocloe littoralis*. Basin samples were low in organic materials (1.3% average), while adjacent tidal flats had an average of 6.5% (Stevenson and Emery, 1958).

Calcium carbonate in sediments was low except in the North and South Basins and the tidal flats, where the sediments were largely composed of shell fragments. The percentage of calcium carbonate tended to be around 2% (Stevenson and Emery, 1958).

pH in the sediments averaged 7.28 in the barren sand beaches, 6.94 in silt beaches, 6.41 in silty marsh, and 5.91 in clayey marsh (Stevenson and Emery, 1958).

Primary Production

Little information is available on primary productivity in Newport Bay. A recent study of macrophyte production in the Upper Bay found the salt marsh in the bay to be floristically diverse, low in stature, and to cover 85 ha. Net production was quite high and estimated at $2150 \, g \, m^{-2} \, yr^{-1}$ (Eilers, 1981).

Secondary Production

Littoral fish abundance and diversity fluctuated markedly during the 13 months of the study. Fish species numbers increased from 10 in January to 16 in July 1978, and declined throughout the fall. Diversity values reached a high of 1.76 in May. Biomass was highest in June (21.7 kg), decreasing from then until a January low of 0.42 except for a slight increase in September and October. Numbers of individuals followed the same pattern as biomass values, with a peak of 21,907 individuals in June (Allen, 1982).

Annual littoral fish production of the Upper Bay was 9.35 g dry wt m^{-2}. This high rate of production was due primarily to rapid growth of the large number of juveniles in the area. *Atherinops affinis* young of the year contributed 85.1% of the total production and formed a direct link through their herbivorous/detritivorous diet to the high primary productivity of the Upper Bay. Productivity was highly seasonal, with 75.9% of productivity occurring in the spring–summer period. Average standing stock for Upper Bay fish in 1978 was 784 kg dry weight based on an estimate of 50 ha of habitable littoral zone in Upper Newport Bay (Allen, 1982).

Structure of Submerged Communities

Zooplankton.   The total biomass of zooplankton in the Upper Newport Bay was measured in terms of displacement values for surface, middepth, and near-bottom water samples. Surface values ranged from approximately 5 mL m^{-3} to less than 1 mL m^{-3}. For middepth samples, biomass varied from 4 to 1 mL m^{-3}, and near-bottom samples ranged from almost 6 to 2 mL m^{-3}. Samples collected from the Lower Bay showed consistently lower biomass levels through all phases of the tidal cycle than did samples collected at stations in the Upper Bay (Trinast, 1975).

The most dominant species in Upper Newport Bay zooplankton was the copepod, *Acartia californiensis*, which was responsible for approximately 90% of the total number of zooplankton in spring and summer samples. Conditions in Newport Bay appeared to be favorable for *Acartia californiensis*. Hydrological conditions favored the retention and breeding of *Acartia californiensis*, and the variable salinity in the bay seemed to restrict competitor species from entering the bay. The high nutrient levels and warm temperatures in the bay probably increased primary productivity in the area and provided an abundant food source for *A. californiensis*, producing a higher respiratory and reproductive rate for the species (Trinast, 1975).

Adult copepods tended to spend daylight hours in the lower regions of the water column in the Upper Bay, although they appeared to rise to the surface during flood cycles. At the dunes, in the lower part of the Upper Bay, most of the copepods rose to surface waters at sunset, although a few remained in the lower waters. In the Lower Newport Bay, on the other hand, copepods rose slowly to the surface during the day and sank at night. The majority of immature copepods tended to remain in the lower waters at most stations except in the lowermost regions of the Upper Bay, where they were most often found in the upper layers of the water. At sunset, immature copepods at the Dunes and other lower Upper Bay stations congregated in surface waters, returning to lower waters around midnight. Dune copepods remained in the lower portion of the water column for the rest of the day, while Lower Bay and other immature copepods in the Upper Bay migrated upward again at low-water slack (Trinast, 1975).

Benthic Invertebrates

Amphipods and Polychaetes. A study of the benthic animals collected in Newport Bay in January 1951 and January 1953 reported four species of amphipods and seven species of polychaetes to be common. The relative abundance of species in the Upper and Lower bays are given in Tables 10.2 and 10.3. Common amphipods included *Amphideutopus oculatus*, which was found on or in bottoms of black mud and plant debris, on or in sand and fine shell fragments, and on or in gray and brown sand with mud in the Lower Bay. In both the upper and lower bay, *Acuminodeutopus heteruropus* was very common on or in mud and sand bottoms, including those with fine shell fragments, plant fragments, and eelgrass. Another common species, *Rudilemboides stenopropodus*, was found in the inner part of the Upper Bay and throughout the Lower Bay. *Paraphoxus* sp. was also common, although numbers collected and location were not reported (Barnard and Reish, 1959).

Of the seven common polychaete species in Newport Bay, *Lumbrineris minima*, which lived on mud or muddy-sand bottoms, was the most abundant species in the survey of the bay. It was also collected from areas with sand and shell bottoms, sand bottoms, or shell fragment bottoms. *Dorvillea articulata* was widely distributed and common in the Lower and Upper bays. *Haploscoloplos elongatus* was the most nearly ubiquitous polychaete species in the bay. It was found on or in virtually all substrate types except black sulfide mud and at almost all stations with mud or muddy-sand substrates. It was especially common on or in bottoms with fine mud. *Prionospio* sp., a tube-building polychaete unique to Newport Bay, was widespread throughout the bay, although it was not particularly abundant at any one station. It was taken from nearly every type of substrate, including muddy-sand, mud, mud and clay mixture, sand, sand and shell fragments, and shell fragments. (A total of 211 specimens were found.) The polychaete, *Armandia bioculata*, was one of the most common polychaetes and appeared to be able to exist on many substrate types but was taken most frequently from muddy-sand bottoms. The burrowing polychaete, *Capitata ambiseta*, was very common in the Lower Bay on or in mud or muddy-sand substrates but was rare in the Upper Bay. *Cossura candida*, another common species, was found almost exclusively in the Lower Bay on or in substrates of muddy sand and occasionally on or in mud, clay, shell fragments, or sand bottoms. A total of 792 specimens were found, only one in the Upper Bay (Barnard and Reish, 1959).

Lower Bay. In Newport's Lower Bay, hard substrates were found at two stations. The amphipods, *Acuminodeutopus heteruropus* and *Rudilemboides stenopropodus*, were observed on or in this substrate, while only one species of polychaete, *Dorvillea articulata*, was found in any number (Barnard and Reish, 1959).

At the one station in the Lower Bay with a substrate of eelgrass, eelgrass fragments, and small shell fragments, the polychaetes, *Dorvillea articulata* and *Capitata ambiseta*, were common (Barnard and Reish, 1959). Three types of muddy sand were found in the Lower Bay: gray muddy sand at two stations, brown-gray muddy sand at two stations, and brown muddy sand at six stations. This variation in sediment color was due primarily to the oxidizing or reducing conditions of the particular sediment. Oxidized sediments had a light brown color, while reduced sediments had a darker color.

Amphipods found fairly commonly on or in the gray muddy-sand substrate were *Acuminodeutopus heteruropus*, *Microdeutopus schmitti*?, and *Amphideutopus oculatus*. Polychaetes taken from Lower Bay gray muddy sand were *Lumbrineris minima*, *Haploscoloplos elongatus*, *Cossura candida*, *Tharyx multifilis*, *Capitata ambiseta*, *Pista alata*, and *Megalomma* sp. (Barnard and Reish, 1959).

Thirteen species of amphipods were found on or in brown muddy-sand substrates. Of these, the most common species were *Hyale frequens*, *Acuminodeutopus heteruropus*, *Ampithoe plumulosa*, *Corophium acherusicum*, *C. baconi*, and *Ericthonius brasiliensis*. The most common species of polychaetes taken from brown muddy sand in the Lower Bay were as follows: *Eteone dilatae*, *Nephtys caecoides*, *Lumbrineris erecta*, *L. minima*, *Dorvillea articulata*, *Haploscoloplos elongatus*, *Polydora paucibranchiata*, *Prionospio* sp., *P. cirrifera*, *Spiophanes* sp., *Chaetozone corona*, *Cossura candida*, *Tharyx multifillis*, *T. parvus*, *Armandia bioculata*, and *Capitata ambiseta* (Barnard and Reish, 1959).

On or in brown-gray muddy sand, only one amphipod, *Rudilemboides stenopropodus*, was found. Polychaetes taken from brown-gray muddy sand in the Lower Bay were *Nephtys caecoides*, *Lumbrineris minima*, *Dorvillea articulata*, *Haploscoloplos elongatus*, *Polydora paucibranchiata*, *Cossura candida*, *Tharyx parvus*, *T. multifilis*, and *Capitata ambiseta* (Barnard and Reish, 1959).

Various clay substrates were found at three stations in the Lower Bay. At one station, black clay with a layer of sand on top was predominant, while brown clay was found at another Lower Bay station and gray clay at the third. At the black clay station, the amphipods, *Paraphoxus spinosus*, *Acuminodeutopus heteruropus*, and *Rudilemboides stenopropodus*, were found. Polychaetes found at this station in large numbers were the following: *Lumbrineris minima*, *Dorvillea articulata*, *Haploscoloplos elongatus*, *Prionospio* sp., *Cossura candida*, and *Capitata ambiseta* (Barnard and Reish, 1959).

On or in gray clay in the Lower Bay only two species of amphipods were found: *Acuminodeutopus heteruropus* and *Rudilemboides stenopropodus*. The polychaetes, *Lumbrineris minima*, *Haploscoloplos elongatus*, *Cossura candida*, and *Tharyx multifilis*, were common on this substrate (Barnard and Reish, 1959).

On brown-gray clay, the following species of amphipods were common: *Hyale frequens*, *Ampithoe plumulosa*, *A. pollex*, and *Corophium acherusicum*. The common polychaetes on this substrate were *Lumbrineris erecta*, *L. minima*, *Haploscoloplos elongatus*, *Cossura candida*, and *Tharyx parvus* (Barnard and Reish, 1959).

TABLE 10.2. *Amphipods of Newport Bay. Numbers recorded for floats, docks, and pilings are the largest sample found in 3 years of collecting. Benthic collections were made in 1951 (lower number) and 1954 (upper number).*

AMPHIPODS	Intertidal	Floats, docks, pilings	Hard sand	Hard, black sand	Brown mud, sand, eelgrass	Eelgrass, shell fragments	Black mud	Black mud, plant debris	Sand, shell fragments	Gray mud, eelgrass	Gray mud	Gray mud, sand	Brown muddy sand	Brown-gray muddy sand	Black mud, H$_2$S
Acuminodeutopus heteruropus		23						19	34	2/17	2/22	2/15	4/18		
Ampelisca cristata											1				
Amphiceutopis oculatus		2						2	1/9		3	2/2 2	11/2		
Amphilochus neopolitanus	1												3		
Ampithoe longimana	7														
Ampithoe plumosa	12	25								94			15		
Ampithoe pollex										12					
Anamixis linslevi		4													
Aoroides columbiae					4										
Aruga holmesi															
Colomastix pusilla	2	47													
Corophium acherusicum		12								21			15		
Corophium baconi		22								17			22		
Corophium insidiosum													1		
Elasmopus rapax	8	135								177					
Ericthonius brasiliensis	4	5				1				6	1		29		
Eurystheus thompsoni		4													
Hyale frequens	32									11			10		
Incisocalliope newportensis		9													
Jassa falcata	1	19								2			7		
Leucothoe alata		51											1		
Leucothoides pacifica	1	19													
Maera inaequipes		4													
Maera simile		5													
Metaceradocus occidentalis															
Microdeutopus schmitti										2		15	1		
Paraphorus spinosus				1						10	1	1	6		
Podocerus brasiliensis	3	49								1					
Podocerus sp.	1														
Rudilemboides stenopropodus		38		1	1			13	23	9/6	6	5/4	5/6		
Stenothoe valida	50	24											7		

Source: Barnard and Reish, 1959.

Upper Newport Bay

Gray sand, mud, clay	Brown-gray clay	Gray-brown mud, sand, wood chips	Gray clay	Sand on black clay	Brown sand, shell fragments	Gray sand	Sand, shell fragments	Gravel, shell	Shell	Shell, mud, stone	Shell, red algae	Shell, sand, red algae	Gray mud, sand	Sand, shell, sponges, algae	Gray mud, sponges, algae	Sand, black mud	Shell, rock, black sand	Brown mud on black clay	Sand on black clay	Sand, clay
		2	13	1	29	7							1			4			3	
			2	2	1															
6	1				1						1			3	4			9		6
									2											
	50																			
	21																			
							1								10					
					1															
							20				4	2		11	10					
6	35			2					4		3				2		1			
20	5						1							1						
42	3						80		6		22	2		27	178	1	7			
8	2						8													
1	30						1													
	1																			
							17		3					2	73					
							1													
														2	10					
							1	3	2	1										
2	1	1																		1
	2			14			2				2			1	6		1		5	3
7							5													
							1				1	1		3	3					
	1	13	9	9	12		1				1					8	6	14	3	
27	4						1													

TABLE 10.3. Polychaetes of Newport Bay. Samples collected in 1954.

Lower Newport Bay

POLYCHAETES	Hard sand	Hard black sand	Brown mud, sand, eelgrass	Eelgrass, shell fragments	Black mud	Black mud, plant debris	Sand, shell fragments	Gray mud, eelgrass	Gray mud	Gray mud, sand	Brown mud, sand	Brown-gray mud, sand	Black mud, H₂S	Gray mud, sand, clay	Brown-gray clay	Gray brown mud, wood chips, sand	Gray clay	Sand on black clay	Brown mud, shells	Gray sand
Amaea occidentalis																				
Amaae anops											5									
Anaitides williamsi										1										
Anaitides madeirensis																				
Ancistrosyllis hassi										1	2									
Armandia bioculate			2	22				17	12		37			13	2	7				
Asychis disparidentata					10															
Axiothella rubrocincta		1	1	4																
Brania limbata			1	4																
Capitita ampiseta		2	2			12		63	157	54	156	9	157						6	
Capitella capitata	10	14		22	10	12	30	65	160	54	220	9	116	33	226	71	1	43	6	3
Chaetozone corona							1												1	1
Chone mollis											1			1		1				
Cossura candida						2	6	18	160	9	220	10	1	28		20	10	62		
Dorvillia articulata	10	14		9		6	3	32	54	4	120	3	9	28	18	28	3	31	1	1
Drilonereis nuda						1		1				2						2		
Eteone dilatae														4		4		2		
Eumida sanguinea																				
Eupolymnia heterobranchia																				
Exogone lourei																				
Fabricia limnicola				1		1		1	1	1										
Glycera americana			1					1												
Goniada littorea			1				1	2		1	1									

Upper Newport Bay

POLYCHAETES	Sand, shell fragments	Gravel, shells	Shells	Shells, mud, stone	Shells, red algae	Shells, sand, red algae	Gray mud, sand	Sand, shell, sponges, algae	Gray mud, sponges, algae	Sand, black mud	Shell, rock, black sand	Brown mud on black clay	Sand on black clay	Sand, clay
Amaea occidentalis	19				4			3			1			
Amaae anops														
Anaitides williamsi				1					1					
Anaitides madeirensis														
Ancistrosyllis hassi														
Armandia bioculate														
Asychis disparidentata														
Axiothella rubrocincta									1					
Brania limbata														
Capitita ampiseta	26		5	2	19	6	10	37	10	17	7	8	38	28
Capitella capitata	26		5	2	19	6	10	37	10	17	7	8	38	28
Chaetozone corona			1		4	9			2		1	4	1	
Chone mollis														
Cossura candida			12	1				6	3	2		5		
Dorvillia articulata	1			1				6	3	2		3		
Drilonereis nuda	1			1										
Eteone dilatae			1	2										4
Eumida sanguinea														
Eupolymnia heterobranchia	29	1			49			7	41					
Exogone lourei					4			2	1		1			
Fabricia limnicola			2	9	1			2	1	2	1			
Glycera americana			2	9						11	13			
Goniada littorea	1			11						1	11			

668

Species																																				
Halosydna johnsoni																													1							
Haploscoloplos elongatus		2	1				3	24	81	27	201	13	36	14	63	8	36	3	6	51	2	24	11	3			7	19	3	10	6	16	37	13
Leocrates sp.			1								32	5	38	8	3				4		1	1						1	3		1			
Lumbrineris erecta		2	5	6	5		45	115	53	412	62	37	13	73	19	42	8	13	3		8			2	1	6	2	3	8	1	10	1	3
Lumbrineris minima		2	3				3				3				3						3			1									
Magdelona californica				1			3	9	2	3						2		2		1				1		1		1		1	2	2	
Megalona sp.																				1								1					
Marphysa sanguinea																		1															
Naineris dendritica	1		6				1	23	2	64		17	6		2				3	1		4	2	1				29	3	
Neanthes caudata																				1				4								
Nephtys caecoides			9	5			3	3	2	2		1			2	1									5	2	8	1	8	
Nereis grubei					1		3				2				2	1		2													
Nereis procera	1	1																				2	2							
Nerinides acuta																					2	2									
Notomastus (Clistomastus) tenuis		1					1		4	1		4	5						1			1	2	3					
Owenia fusiformis collaris							1	2	2	5	1																			
Paleanotus chrysolepis							3					1			1					1	2	3		2						
Paronis gracilis oculata							2	1	4	196	3	1		72	2		1	7	3	3	1	1	2	2	3			2	4	
Pherusa inflata																														
Pista alata		2	1	1			6	20	1	4			4		4		5		1		91	2	1		1	6	2	2	33	12	6	22	24
Platynereis bicanaliculata	13	2	1	5			11	3	8	32	1	2	6	13	3	13		4		1	1			6	2				
Podarke pugetensis	1	2	1				11	10	2	6	2	2	2	2		1	2	8	1	7		2	6						
Polycora (Carazzia) paucibranchiata							2														99								
Praxillella affinis							2	44		12		1		5		1		5		14		2	53						
Prionospio cirrifera							1	1		1										1		1							
Prionospio sp.								4	4	1			2	2							8		1						
Prionospio pinnata							1	16	4	108	4	65	27	8	2			26	1	10	6					13	2	4
Tharyx parvus			1				10	4	49	250									1	8								

Source: **Barnard** and **Reish**, 1959.

669

Sandy substrates were common in the Lower Bay. Types of sand were gray sand, brown sand, hard sand, and sand of an unspecified type. On or in sand of unspecified type with shell fragments found at one station, three species of amphipods were collected: *Acuminodeutopus heteruropus, Rudilemboides stenopropodus,* and *Amphideutopus oculatus.* The most common polychaete taken from this substrate was *Capitata ambiseta* (Barnard and Reish, 1959).

On or in gray sand in the Lower Bay, only one amphipod specimen was found. Polychaetes were also scarce, but *Lumbrineris minima* was fairly common (Barnard and Reish, 1959). On or in gray sand with mud, plant debris, and clay, the following amphipods were common: *Stenothoe valida, Elasmopus rapax, Corophium baconi,* and *Ericthonius brasiliensis.* Polychaetes common on this Lower Bay substrate were *Lumbrineris erecta, L. minima, Haploscoloplos elongatus, Cossura candida,* and *Armandia bioculata* (Barnard and Reish, 1959).

Only one amphipod, *Rudilemboides stenopropodus,* and one polychaete, *Lumbrineris minima,* had populations of more than seven individuals on brown sand with shell fragments (found at one station) (Barnard and Reish, 1959).

On or in the hard sand found at three stations, the amphipods, *Acuminodeutopus heteruropus* and *Rudilemboides stenopropodus,* were fairly common. No polychaete species were present. At one Lower Bay station with hard black sand a single specimen of the amphipod, *Rudilemboides stenopropodus,* and one polychaete population of *Dorvillea articulata* were present (Barnard and Reish, 1959).

Mud substrates in the Lower Bay were either black, gray, brown, or gray-brown. A brown mud substrate with sand, eelgrass, and debris was found at one station. Amphipods were scarce but two polychaete populations, *Dorvillea articulata* and *Podarke pugettensis,* were found (Barnard and Reish, 1959).

On or in gray mud found at four stations, there was a population of the amphipod, *Acuminodeutopus heteruropus.* Large populations (over 75 individuals) of the polychaetes, *Lumbrineris minima, Haploscoloplos elongatus, Cossura candida,* and *Capitata ambiseta,* were also found here. Smaller populations of *Armandia bioculata, Dorvillea articulata, Megalomma* sp., and *Tharyx multifilis* were present (Barnard and Reish, 1959).

On or in the gray mud substrate with eelgrass and plant debris, which was found at two Lower Bay stations, the amphipods *Paraphoxus spinosus, Elasmopus rapax, Hyale frequens, Acuminodeutopus heteruropus, Rudilemboides stenopropodus, Ampithoe plumulosa, A. pollex, Corophium acherusicum,* and *C. baconi* were found. The polychaetes taken from this substrate were *Lumbrineris minima, Dorvillea articulata, Haploscoloplos elongatus, Prionospio* sp., *P. cirrifera, Cossura candida, Tharyx multifilis, T. parvus, Armandia bioculata,* and *Capitata ambiseta* (Barnard and Reish, 1959).

On or in black mud, found at one station in the Lower Bay, no amphipods were found, and the only polychaete with a substantial population was *Capitata ambiseta.* On or in black mud with plant debris, found at one station, populations of the amphipods, *Acuminodeutopus heteruropus* and *Rudilemboides stenopropodus,* were collected. Only one polychaete, *Capitata ambiseta,* had a population greater than seven on or in this substrate. On or in black mud with a sulfide odor, found at one Lower Bay station, no amphipods and only one large population (116 individuals) of *Capitella capitata* were found (Barnard and Reish, 1959).

At the one station with gray-brown mud with sand and wood chips, only one population of amphipods, *Rudilemboides stenopropodus*, was found. The more common polychaetes on this substrate were *Nephtys caecoides*, *Lumbrineris erecta*, *L. minima*, *Dorvillea articulata*, *Haploscoloplos elongatus*, *Polydora paucibranchiata*, *Cossura candida*, *Thayrx multifilis*, and *Capitata ambiseta* (Barnard and Reish, 1959).

Upper bay. Substrates in the Upper Bay included sand, shell fragments, gravel, mud, and clay. Only one station in the Upper Bay had a gravel substrate. At this station both amphipods and polychaetes were scarce (Barnard and Reish (1959).

On gray mud with sand found at one station in the Upper Bay, the only population larger than seven individuals was the polychaete *Armandia bioculata*. On fine gray mud with sponges, oysters, and algae, a large population of the amphipod, *Elasmopus rapax*, was found. Smaller populations of *Colomastix pusilla*, *Leucothoides pacifica*, Anamixis linsleyi, and *Maera simili* were identified. Polychaetes on this substrate were *Syllis gracilis*, *Armandia bioculata*, and *Eupolymenia heterobranchia* (Barnard and Reish, 1959).

Shell substrates found at three stations in the Upper Bay did not have many amphipods in residence. Four polychaetes, *Brania limbata*, *Haploscoloplos elongatus*, *Syllis gracilis*, and *Syllis* nr. *cornuta*, had populations of greater than seven individuals. On shell substrates with mud and stones found at one station in the Upper Bay, no numerous amphipod species were found. The polychaetes, *Polydora paucibranchiata* and *Spiophanes* sp., had large populations. Smaller polychaete populations were *Exogene lourei*, *Lumbrineris minima*, *Haploscoloplos elongatus*, and *Fabricia limnicola*.

On or in a substrate of shells with red algae at two stations in the Upper Bay, the amphipod, *Elasmopus rapax*, was found. In addition, the following amphipods were found: *Syllis gracilis*, *Armandia bioculata*, and *Eupolymenia heterobranchia*. On shells with rocks and black sand found at one station in the Upper Bay, no more than a few amphipods were present. Three polychaetes, *Exogene lourei*, *Prionospio*, sp., and *Fabricia limnicola*, were found in populations greater than seven individuals (Barnard and Reish, 1959).

On or in shells with sand and algae, amphipods and polychaetes were scarce. From the shell fragment substrate found at one station in the Upper Bay, no amphipod populations were collected, but several polychaete populations, *Brania limbata*, *Syllis gracilis*, *S.* (*Ehlersia*) nr. *cornuta*, and *Haploscoloplos elongata*, were found (Barnard and Reish, 1959).

There were two stations in the Upper Bay with black clay substrates, one covered with brown mud and one with sand. The sand substrate covered with black clay had few amphipods. The polychaetes, *Neanthes caudata*, *Haploscoloplos elongata*, *Prionospio* sp., and *Armandia bioculata*, were present in populations ranging from 2 to 38 individuals. On the station with black clay covered with brown mud, the amphipods, *Acuminodeutopus heteruropus* and *Rudilemboides stenopropodus*, were found, as well as representatives of the polychaetes, *Lumbrineris minima, Haploscoloplos elongatus, Nerinides acuta, Thayrx parvus,* and *Armandia bioculata* (Barnard and Reish, 1959).

Several types of sand substraes were found in the Upper Bay. At the one station that had a sand and black mud substrate, the amphipod, *Rudilemboides stenopropodus,* and the polychaetes, *Exogene lourei, Haploscoloplos elongatus, Prionospio* sp., and *Armandia bioculata,* were collected. On or in the sand and clay substrate at another station, amphipods were scarce. Populations of the polychaetes, *Haploscoloplos elongatus, Nerinides acuta, Prionospio* sp., and *Armandia bioculata,* were present. Five stations had a sand substrate with shell fragments. On or in this substrate the amphipods, *Colomastix pusilla, Leucothoides pacifica, Elasmopus rapax,* and *Erichthonius brasilienisis,* were found. In addition, the polychaetes, *Nerinides acuta, Haploscoloplos elongatus, Prionospio* sp., and *Armandia bioculata,* were taken from this substrate. On sand substrate with shells, sponges, algae, and mussels, found at one Upper Bay station, the amphipod, *Colomastix pusilla,* was found. The polychaetes, *Haploscoloplos elongatus, Armandia bioculata,* and *Scyphoproctus oculatus,* were also found there (Barnard and Reish, 1959).

According to Barnard and Reish (1959), the correlation between the distribution of polychaetes and the substrate types was not clearly defined in the bay, especially in the upper portion. The polychaetes, *Lumbrineris minima, Dorvillea articulata, Haploscoloplos elongatus, Prionospio* sp., *Armandia bioculata,* and *Cossura candida,* were found together in 22 of the stations in the Lower Bay and appear to form a loose assemblage (Barnard and Reish, 1959).

Intertidal Molluscs. A study of an intertidal molluscan assemblage was conducted on the −0.46 to 1.8-m portion [relative to 0.0 tidal datum at mean lower low water (MLLW) tidal level] of an uninterrupted stretch of sandy beach in lower Newport Bay. Balboa Island was selected as the site for this study, as it was determined to have the highest molluscan diversity in the bay (Seapy and Kitting, 1978).

No macro-invertebrates were found above the 1.5-m level on the beach, while no crustaceans or polychaetes were found above the MLLW line. Bivalves were found to be the most abundant molluscs with *Leporimetis obesa* (41.2%), and the little neck clam, *Protothaca staminea* (23.7%), numerically dominating the molluscan population (Seapy and Kitting, 1978).

Other molluscs found were *Nassarias mendicus* (Nassa shell); *Conus californicus* (California cone shell); *Olivella biplicata* (purple dwarf olive shell); *Mitrella carinata* (dove shell); *Bulla gouldiana* (cloudy bubble shell); *Heterodonax pacificus* (donax shell); *Sanguinolaria nuttallii* (mahogany clam); *Chione undatella* (wavy cockle); *Diplodonta orbellus* (orb diplodon); *Tagelus californicus* (California jackknife clam); *Saxidomus nuttalli* (common Washington clam); *Laevicardium substriatum* (eggshell cockle); *Macoma nasuta* (bent-nosed clam); *M. secta* (white sand clam); *Tresus nuttallii* (Pacific gaper); the clams, *Macoma acolastras, Tellina modesta,* and *Protothaca lacinitata;* and the bivalve, *Cumingia californica* (Seapy and Kitting, 1978).

Species found in the 0.61 to 1.5 m level were *Heterodonax pacifica, Protothaca staminea,* and *Sanguinolaria nuttallii.* From 0.30 to 0.61 m, *Protothaca staminea, Sanguinolaria nuttallii,* and *Leporimetis obesa* were found. The majority of species, however, were found below 0.30 m MLLW. From 0 to +3.0 m, *Protothaca staminea, Sanguinolaria nuttallii, Leporimetis obesa, Cumingia californica, Chione undatella, Diplodonta orbellus, Tagelus californianus, Saxidomus nuttalli, Bulla gouldiana, Laevicardium substriatum, Tellina modesta,* and *Macoma nasuta* were found. From 0 to −0.30 m, all species reported in this study except *Heterodonax pacificus, Tresus nuttallii,* and *Macoma carinata* were observed. From −0.30 m to −0.46 m, all species except *Heterodonax pacificus, Cumingia californica, Chione undatella,* and *Bulla gouldiana* were found (Seapy and Kitting, 1978).

Protothaca staminea had the widest range of distribution of the molluscs found on the beach, being found from −0.46 to +1.22 m. *Sanguinolaria nuttallii* had the second widest range and was found from −0.46 to +0.76 m. *Leporimetis obesa* had the third widest range, from −0.46 to +0.30 m. This species was the only mollusc in the study to have a statistically significant contiguous distribution. *Diplodontus orbellus, Tagelus californianus, Saxidomus nuttalli, Laevicardium substriatum, Tellina modesta,* and *Macoma nasuta* all had ranges of −0.46 to +0.15 m, while *Cumingia californica* and *Chione undatella* were found from −0.30 to −0.15 m. *Bulla gouldiana* was found from −0.30 to 0 m. *Nassaruis mendicus, Conus californicus,* and *Olivella biplicata* were found from −0.46 to −0.30 m. These three mobile gastropods, as well as *Mitrella carinata,* were observed moving higher on the beach, however, during periods of tidal submersion. *Mitrella carinata* was found mainly at −0.46 m or below, while *Heterodonax pacificus* was found only from +0.91 m to +0.46 m (Seapy and Kitting, 1978).

A marked change of substrate occurred at about 0.15 to 0.30 m in the study area, the higher zone having a larger silt-clay fraction than the lower. This substrate difference corresponded roughly to the habitat difference between the midlittoral zone and the higher infralittoral fringe and provided a vertical separation of the molluscan assemblage. It is likely that the beach above 0.15 to 0.30 m represented a physically limiting environment for the molluscs. The limiting factor was probably desiccation, as the upper beach drained during periods of tidal exposure to a depth that could be deeper than many bivalves can burrow. Most species that were found in the upper tidal range demonstrated the ability to burrow deeply into the sand (Seapy and Kitting, 1978).

Total wet biomass of molluscs, including shell, also showed a correlation with tidal level, averaging less than 175 g m^{-2} above 0.15 m and increasing steadily below this level to 2.65 g m^{-2} at −0.46 m (Seapy and Kitting, 1978).

Intertidal Piling Communities. *Anamacis linsleyi,* one of the more abundant amphipods in the bay, was found in the washings of sponges from pilings. *Stenothoe valida* was found in association with calyptoblastic hydroids. *Elasmopus rapax* and *Corophium acherusicum* were among the most abundant amphipods found in pilings in the Lower Bay. Other amphipods found on pilings were *Leucothoe alata*, *Maera simile*, *M. inawquipes*, *Eurystheus thompsoni*, *Ampithoe plumulosa*, *Corophium baconi*, *Ericthonius brasiliensis*, and the tube-building *Podocerus brasiliensis* (Barnard and Reish, 1959).

Nekton.   Newport Bay has a large and varied fish population with as many as 61 different species reported in the Upper Bay alone (Frey et al., 1970). One of the most abundant fish in Upper Newport Bay was the topsmelt, *Atherinops affinis*. This species dominated samples in one study in both biomass (79.9%) and numbers (76.7%). *Atherinops affinis* has been described as both a herbivore and a detritivore, as well as a low-level carnivore (Allen, 1982).

Ranking second in number and biomass in this study was the California killifish, *Fundulus parvipinnis*, constituting 12.1% of numbers collected and 7.6% of the biomass (Allen, 1982). This species was often found in isolated tide pools and on tidal flats, especially around marsh islands and peninsulas (Bane, 1972). *F. parvipinnis* was a low-level carnivore that fed on small crustaceans and insects (Allen, 1982).

The shiner perch, *Cymatogaster aggregata*, formed a significant percentage of the ichthyofauna of the Upper Bay, according to Bane and Robinson (1970) and was commonly found around pilings, docks, beds of the eelgrass, *Zostera marina*, and in shallow areas of the bay as well as in deeper midchannel waters. This species was an omnivore and fed mostly on green plants, crustaceans (especially amphipods), and often ingested sand and mud. Occasionally, samples of annelid worms, fish eggs, and green, red, and brown algae were retrieved from *C. aggregata* stomachs. *C. aggregata* fed both on the bottom and in beds of algae and eelgrass and did not appear to change its diet during the year (Bane and Robinson, 1970; Bane, 1972). The bay appeared to be used as a nursery for *Cymatogaster aggregata*. In the spring, adult females entered the bay to mate and spawn. In the summer after breeding, nearly all adults left the bay (Bane and Robinson, 1970).

Other abundant fish in the Upper Bay included the round stingray, *Urolophus halleri*, which was found in densities of 1 per 300 square yards in some areas of the bay. This species was most often found on the bottom feeding predominantly on polychaete worms, decapods, and bivalves (Bane, 1972).

Bane (1972) found the deepbody anchovy, *Anchoa compressa*, to be one of the most abundant fishes in the Upper Bay. According to Bane, it is found in large schools throughout the year, although in a study by Allen (1972) it composed only 1.2% of the total number of fish collected. This species fed on plankton and algae (Bane, 1972; Allen, 1982).

Other common fish in the bay were the mosquito fish, *Gambusia affinis*, which composed 5.5% of the total number of fish collected, and the arrow goby, *Clevelandia ios*, which composed 2.4% of the total number. These fish were low-level carnivores, feeding mainly on insects, benthic microinvertebrates, and zooplankton (Bane and Robinson, 1970). *Clevelandia ios* was often found on mud flats and around the marsh islands in the Upper Bay buried in both mud and sand substrates (Bane, 1972). Allen (1982) reports that the striped mullet, *Mugil cephalus*, probably constituted a large part of the biomass in the bay during his study but was not sampled accurately. *M. cephalus* adults fed mainly on detritus and pennate diatoms.

Bane lists many other fish as being common in Newport Bay. The kelp pipefish, *Syngnathus californiensis*, was commonly found in eelgrass and algae beds throughout the Upper Bay. The spotted sand bass, *Paralabrax maculatofaciatus*, was common in *Zostera* beds, while the barred sand bass, *P. nebulifer*, was common in the midchannel and deeper backwaters of the Upper Bay. *P. nebulifer* appeared to feed on anchovies and other fish, as well as crabs, worms, and molluscs. Another frequently sighted fish was the Atlantic croaker, *Menticirrhus undulatus*, which fed on clam siphons. The black perch, *Embiotoca jacksoni*, was found consistently in the bay, usually in deeper waters but occasionally in eelgrass beds. This species appeared to feed on the limpet, *Crucibulum spinosum*, the slipper shell, *Crepidula fornicata*, and polychaete worms. *E. jacksoni* specimens were often found infested with parasitic isopods. The Pacific staghorn sculpin, *Leptocottus armatus australis*, was common on the bottom of the Upper Bay, near areas of abundant plant growth, feeding on small fish, crustacea, and plant material such as the green algae, *Enteromorpha intestinalis*. This species was often parasitized by marine leeches. The spotted turbot, *Pleuronichtys ritteri*, was consistently found in the midchannel area and fed on bottom invertebrates. In the deeper channels of the bay, the diamond turbot, *Hypsopsetta guttulata*, was often found feeding on invertebrates. The California halibut, *Paralichtys californicus*, utilized the bay as a nursery and fed on small fish and invertebrates. In April, May, and June, 140 samples of this species were collected. The specklefin midshipman, *Porichthys miriaster*, was also abundant and fed on invertebrates (Bane, 1972).

Bane found some fish only rarely in Newport Bay. These included the California butterfly ray, *Gymnura marmorata*, which fed in invertebrates and lived on the bottom, as did the thornback, *Platyrhinoides triseriata*, which fed on mysid larvae, amphipods, and crustacea. The shovelnose guitarfish, *Rhinobatus productus*, fed on worms, crustacea, and molluscs and was also considered rare in the bay. The bat ray, *Myliobatis californicus*, was seldom seen in the Upper Bay, although it was more common in the Lower Bay, where it fed on sipunculid worms, octopus, and crabs. The threadfin shad, *Dorosoma petenense*, was also rare in the bay. This species fed on algae and small plankton. The Pacific sardine, *Sardinops sagax*, was taken only once from the Upper Bay. This species fed on copepods, eggs, and other planktonic organisms.

The northern anchovy, *Engraulis mordax*, was found only rarely in the Upper Bay, although it was common in the Lower Bay. *E. mordax* fed on eelgrass and algae. The kelp bass, *Paralabrax clathratus*, was found occasionally in the Upper Bay feeding on other fish and crustaceans. *Morone* (= *Roccus*) *saxatilis*, the white perch, fed on anchovies and smelt and was found three times in the bay.

All specimens of *A. saxatilis* captured had heavy infestations of parasitic isopods on the skin, mouth, and operculum. The polychaete-eating *Cheilotrema saturnum* (the black croaker), as well as the *Ulva*-eating *Umbrina roncador* (the yellowfin croaker), were also rare in the bay. The walleye surfperch, *Hyperprosopon argenteum*, was found occasionally in the bay and fed on crustacea. *Rhacochilus vaccas*, the pile perch, was sometimes found feeding along the bottom on *Chione undatella* (wavy cockle) and worms. Occasionally, in the deeper parts of the bay, *Symphurus atricauda*, the California tonguefish, was found. *Citharichthys stigmaeus*, the speckled sanddab, was occasionally found over sandy bottoms. One specimen of *Gobiesox rhessodon* (California clingfish) was found in an eelgrass bed. *Scomber japonicus* (chub mackerel), *Xenistius californiensis* (salema), *Anisotremus davidsoni* (sargo), *Paraclinis integripinnis* (reef finspot), *Amphisticus argenteus* (barred surfperch), *Roncador stearnsi* (spotfin croaker), *Genyonemus lineatus* (white croaker), and *Peprilus simillimus* (Pacific pompano) were also occasional inhabitants of the bay (Bane, 1972).

Other fish found in the bay but with no abundances recorded were *Triakis semifasciata* (leopard shark), *Sphyrna zygaena* (smooth hammerhead shark), *Seriphus politus* (queenfish), *Girella nigricans* (opaleye), *Phanerodon furcatus* (white seaperch), *Heterostichis rostratus* (giant kelpfish), *Gillichthys mirabilis* (longjaw mudsucker), and *Quietula y-cauda* (shadow goby) (Bane, 1972).

Five assemblages of fish species were suggested for the bay. Group I was defined as resident species that maintain year-round populations in the littoral zone. These were *Atherinops affinis*, *Clevelandia ios*, *Gillichthys mirabilis*, *Fundulus parvipinnis*, and *Gambusia affinis*. Group II was made up of midwater schooling species: *Anchoa delicatissima* (slough anchovy), *Cymatogaster aggregata*, and *Anchoa compressa*. Group III was composed of the distinctly seasonal benthic species: *Quietula y-cauda*, *Ilypnus gilberti* (cheekspot goby), and *Leptocottus armatus*. Group IV was made up of species that were seasonally present in mid to late summer and only loosely associated. These species were *Engraulis mordax*, *Hypsopsetta guttulata*, and *Syngnathus* sp. Group V was found at times of low salinities and consisted of *Lepomis macrochirus* (bluegill), *Lepomis cyanellus* (green sunfish), *Leuresthes tenuis* (California grunion), and juveniles of *Mugil cephalus*. Group IV was made up of rare species that were found in the littoral zone periodically in the summer of 1978. These rare fish were *Umbrina roncador* (yellowfin croaker), *Urolophus halleri* (round stingray), *Paralichthys californicus* (California halibut), *Mustelus californicus* (gray smoothhound), *Cynoscion nobilis* (white seabass), *Acanthogobius flavimanus* (yellowfin goby), *Sphyraena argentea* (Pacific barracuda), *Girella nigricans* (opaleye), *Symphurus articauda* (California tonguefish), *Porichthys myriaster* (specklefin midshipman), *Morone saxatilis* (striped bass), and *Seriphus politus* (queenfish) (Allen, 1982).

Predator–Prey Relationships. A study of shorebirds whose primary prey items include benthic polychaetes and oligochaetes found that shorebirds—the dowitchers, *Limnodromus griseus* and *L. scolopaceus*; the western sandpiper, *Calidris mauri*; the dunlin, *C. alpina*; and the American avocet, *Recurvirostra americana*—reduced densities of their prey 26 to 80% on mud flats, where substrates contained 8% sand. Shorebirds had no effect on benthic polychaetes and oligochaetes, where substrates had higher sand concentrations of 42 to 80% (Quammen, 1982).

Intertidal Piling Communities

A 1943–1945 study of marine fouling communities in the Lower Bay found six marine communities of sedentary organisms on submerged structures, including floats and pilings. It appeared that a definite sequence of progression occurred in lower Newport Bay fouling communities. An algal community represented the initial assemblage found on clean surfaces. Either the bryozoan or *Ciona* community eventually replaced the algal community. Occasionally, a *Styela* community displaced the bryozoan community before being itself displaced by a *Mytilus* community. Usually, however, the bryozoan or *Ciona* community gave way directly to the climax *Mytilus* community. Annelids, *Balanus*, *Erichthonius*, and other crustaceans and *Pecten* appeared irregularly without relation to the duration of exposure. Although the establishment of *Ciona* and *Styela* appeared to depend at least in part on seasonal factors, the algae–bryozoan–*Mytilus* sequence appeared to be an example of true succession (Scheer, 1945).

Algae. The algae community, usually the first community to settle on clean surfaces, included small sedentary diatoms; colonial diatoms (*Licophora*); one or more species of the green alga, *Ectocarpus* (including *E. granulosoides*) and *Enteromorpha* sp.; the red alga, *Lophosiphonia villum*; and *Pterosiphonia bipinnata*. Other species typical of this community included a sedentary protozoan resembling *Zoothamnion*, the suctorian *Ephilota*, seven or eight unidentified species of hydroids, and *Obelia dichotoma*. The bryozoans, *Bugula neritina*, *Membranipora tuberculata*, *Eucratea clavata*, and young unidentified bryozoan colonies were also found in the algal community (Scheer, 1945).

Bryozoa. The principal species in the bryozoan community were the encrusting bryozoans, *Schizoporella unicornis*, *Cryptosula pallasiana*, *Rhynchozoon tumulosum*, and *Holoporella aperta*. Erect bryozoans included *Bugula neritina*, *Eucratea clavata*, *Crisulipora occidentalis*, and *Scrupocellaria diegensis*. Other organisms in this community were the serpulid worm, *Eupomatus gracilis*; the amphipod, *Erichthonius brasiliensis*; the ascidians, *Styela barnharti*, *Halocynthia johnsoni*, and *Ciona intestinalis*; and the mussel *Mytilus* sp. In addition, many crustaceans, annelids, and other motile forms used the bryozoan clumps for shelter (Scheer, 1945).

Molluscs. Dominating float bottoms was the *Mytilus* community, often on a substrate of old and decayed bryozoans. Other organisms found in this community included old specimens of *Styela* or *Ciona* (Scheer, 1945).

Amphipods. Numerous amphipod species were also found on pilings in Lower Newport Bay. The amphipods, *Colomastix pusilla*, *Leucothothoides pacifica*, and *Incisocalliope newportensis*, were found in washings of tunicates and/or sponges taken from pilings, and *Amphilochus neapolitanus* was found on pilings with red algae.

Chordata. The *Ciona* community was composed almost entirely of the ascidian, *Ciona intestinalis*, with only a few other organisms, including colonial ascidians, crustaceans, and annelids. The *Styela* community was poorly defined and intermediate in composition between the bryozoan and *Mytilus* communities. This community contained the encrusting bryozoans found in the bryozoan community, which served as a substratum for stalks of *Styela*. *Mytilus* were attached to the stalks in large numbers along with an unidentified sponge (Scheer, 1945).

ANAHEIM BAY

Anaheim Bay is located in southern California just south of Seal Beach in the floodplain of both the San Gabriel and Santa Ana rivers. Although neither river flows through the bay at this time, both have had a significant effect on the bay. During the flood of 1862, for example, the Santa Ana River shifted its course and seized much of the drainage area of the bay. As a result, much of the marsh area in the bay was eliminated. The San Gabriel River has had a strong influence on the sediments and salinity of the entire region surrounding the bay, as well as the bay itself (Lane and Woods, 1975).

The urbanization of the area surrounding Anaheim Bay has also influenced the bay. The combined effects of the bay's transition to a metropolitan area and natural changes have shrunk its tidal marshes as much as 30% since 1980 (Lane and Woods, 1975). Remaining marshlands in the bay total about 3 km^2 and are relatively unchanged (Chan and Lane, 1975; Lane and Woods, 1975).

In the early 1960s the southern portion of the bay was dredged and filled to construct a residential and recreational area known as Huntington Harbor. Channels that had been dredged were lined with concrete walls, and virtually all mudflats and vegetation were eliminated (Kauwling and Reish, 1975). Huntington Harbor will not be considered here.

Water Quality

Water samples taken from the bay throughout the year revealed that salinity in the bay varied seasonally. From May to October salinity ranged from 34.2 to 34.5 ppt. With the onset of the rainy season in December, salinity was reduced to approximately 30 ppt, although salinities as low as 10 ppt were occasionally recorded. A horizontal salinity gradient of increasing salinity toward the lower marshland often occurred but was only temporary. Heavy rains often created a vertical salinity gradient. After several tidal cycles, internal turbulence and mixing restored vertical homohaline conditions (Chan and Lane, 1975).

Maximum mean monthly water temperature was 23.7 °C and the minimum was 12.4 °C. The maximum temperature recorded between 1969 and 1971 was 26 °C on August 1969, and the minimum was 11 °C on January 10, 1971. A fluctuation of 1 to 3 °C daily was common, due to the influx of outer harbor water. Strong mixing action due to the shallowness of the water produced homothermal condition in the bay, although during the summer, surface water temperature tended to be approximately 0.5 °C warmer than bottom water. In general, upper marsh water was cooler in the winter and warmer in the summer than were lower marsh waters (Chan and Lane, 1975).

Oxygen concentration in the channels was vertically uniform and within 10% of air saturation levels. Dissolved oxygen was about 6 to 7 ppm in the summer and 7 to 11 ppm in the winter. Daily variations in photosynthetic activity caused a variation in oxygen concentration of 1 to 2 ppm in any one day. Freshwater runoff did not appear to affect O_2 concentrations and there were no significant stagnant or anaerobic areas in the bay (Chan and Lane, 1975).

The primary source of nutrients was from runoff through erosion, leaching of fertilized lawns, and urban drainage. Nitrogen/phosphorus ratios of 1:1 to 5:1 were much lower than normal seawater ratios of 15:1. Phosphorus ranged from 0.6 to 3.6 µg at L^{-1}, nitrate from 0.5 to 6.4 µg at L^{-1}, nitrite from 0.2 to 0.7 mg L^{-1}, and silicon from 4.4 to 28.3 µg at L^{-1}. Tidal flushing appeared to keep nutrient levels in the bay relatively low and stable. No eutrophication was evident in the area (Chan and Lane, 1975).

The average depth of water in the bay was approximately 2 to 3 m at high tides and 1 m at low tide. Secchi disc transparency estimates in the middle of the bay indicated that the euphotic zone extended throughout the entire water column in the summer and 1.7 m deep in the winter. Tidal prism volume was estimated at 50 to 60% of the total high tide volume and tidal range was approximately ±1.5 m. Average current velocity, determined for one station only, was about 0.5 knot, with a maximum of more than 3 knots (Chan and Lane, 1975).

Sediments
In the middle arm of the bay, clayey silt predominated in the back bay area with a gradual change to silty sand in the direction of the channel mouth. Marsh sediments tended to be sandy, clayey silt (Chan and Lane, 1975).

Communities
Algae. The literature is very sparse on the algae of Anaheim Bay. Only a few species were reported in the bay by Shubin (1975). The green algae, *Enteromorpha*, was the most abundant genus found, with *E. crinita* being the most common species. *Enteromorpha* was found on most substrates, especially around the bases of marsh plants and on the upper edges of channel banks. Although rare in winter, this genus formed dense mats on all surfaces in summer. These mats were often found floating in the water when the tide was in and occasionally occupied areas of as much as 7 m² (Shubin, 1975).

The red alga, *Gracilaria verrucosa*, was found in constant abundance on the upper edges of banks from the mouth of the middle arm to opposite the north end of Oil Island. The green alga, *Bryopsis hypnoides*, and the red alga, *Polysiphonia* sp., were found in the bay in areas of strong current and on hard surfaces. These algae were most abundant as a tidal waterfall at the head of the middle arm. Except for a slight decrease in the summer, the abundance of these species was constant throughout the year. In addition, the sea lettuce, *Ulva lactuca*, was found in small quantities on sheltered rocks in moderately silt-free water and on plastic bottles suspended experimentally in the water (Shubin, 1975).

Invertebrates

Benthic Invertebrates.   Benthic invertebrates found in Anaheim are listed in Table 10.1. One study found 152 benthic invertebrate species, 71% of which were Polychaete, 12% Crustacea, and 11% Mollusca (Reish, 1975). Another study of benthic polychaetes found 550 individuals in a January sampling of the benthos and 391 individuals in a July sampling with a total of 44 different species. *Cossura candida, Streblospio benedicti,* and *Capitata ambiseta* were the most abundant polychaetes found, comprising 70% of all worms taken from the bay. Polychaete species considered secondary were *Prionospio cirrifera, Armandia bioculata, Rhynchospio arenicola, Capitella capitata,* and *Cirriformia luxuriosa. Rhynchospio arenicola* and *Armandia bioculata* both demonstrated seasonality, with *R. arenicola* showing a marked increase in numbers in the summer and *A. bioculata* increasing in abundance in the winter. *C. luxuriosa* appeared to prefer a substrate of fine sand and mud, interspersed with cobble (Kauwling and Reish, 1975).

In mussel beds, various unidentified flatworms and nemerteans were found as well as the polychaetes, *Halosydna johnsoni, Polydora websteri, Paleonotus bellis, Armandia bioculata*; the mollusc, *Hiatella artica* (little gaper); the isopod, *Paracereis gilliana*; and the amphipod, *Ampithoe plumulosa* (Reish et al., 1975). Additional species found in the bay were the polychaetes, *Halosydna brevisetosa, Glycera americana, Glycera convoluta, G. robusta, Glycinde armiger, Glycinde* sp., *Protodorvillea gracilis,* and *Magelona californica*; and the ribbed horse mussel, *Ischadium* (= *Geukensia*) *demissa* (Reish et al., 1975).

Intertidal Areas.   Intertidally, three species were particularly abundant. These species were the polychaete, *Streblospio benedicti*; the *Cerithidea californica,* California horn snail; and the ghost shrimp, *Callianassa californiensis.* In addition, various unidentified nematodes and oligochaetes were found as well as the polychaetes, *Eteone* sp., *Ophiodromus pugettensis, Glycera americana, Lumbrineris erecta, Stauroneris gracilis* (*Dorvillea gracilis*), *Haploscoloplos elongatus, Boccardia proboscidea, B. uncata, Prionospio cirrifera, Capitella capitata, C. ambiseta, Dasybranchus lumbricoides, Notomastus magnus, N.* (*Cistomastus*) *tenuis,* and *Pectinaria californiensis*; the molluscs, *Polinices reclusianus* (snail), *Nassarius tegula* (covered lip tegula), *Haminoea* sp. (opisthobranch), *Chione fluctifraga* (smooth cockle), *Chione undatella* (wavy cockle), *Macoma nasuta* (bent-nosed clam), *Tagelus californianus* (California jackknife clam), and *Cryptomya californica* (false mya); various unidentified ostracods; the cumacaean, *Oxyurostylis pacifica*; unidentified tanaids; the amphipod, *Corophium acherusicum*; and the phoronid, *Phoronis* sp. (Reish et al., 1975).

The yellow shore crab, *Hemigrapsus oregonensis,* was found burrowing into the banks of the channels in the high-tide horizon. Various nematodes were found parasitizing many California horn snail (*Cerithidea californica*) specimens (Reish et al., 1975).

Salt Marshes. A study of invertebrates in the salt marsh area of the bay found 116 species, 65% of which were Polychaete, 15% Crustacea, and 13% Molluscs. These invertebrates can be grouped according to the substrates or tidal zones on which they were found.

On intertidal salt marshes the polychaetes, *Streblospio benedicti, Marphysa sanguinea, Lumbrineris minima,* and *Polydora websteri;* an unidentified Cephalocarid; unidentified copepods; and the blue mud shrimp, *Upogebia pugettensis,* were found. Between intertidal rocks the polychaete, *Cirriformia spirabranchiata,* was found, and the moon snail, *Polinices reclusianus,* was found on an intertidal muddy beach. On rocky substrates the anemones, *Anthopleura elegantissima* and *Diadume leucolena;* the bay mussel, *Mytilus edulis;* the barnacles, *Balanus amphitrite, B. crenatus,* and *Chthamalus fissus;* and the ascidian, *Styela plicata,* were found (Reish et al., 1975).

Floats, Docks, Pilings. On buoys in the bay the polychaetes, *Armandia bioculata, Eumida sanguinea, Halosydna johnsoni, Paleonotus bellis,* and *Polydora websteri,* were found as well as the bay mussel, *Mytilus edulis;* the barnacles, *Balanus amphitrite, Balanus crenatus* and *Chthamalus fissus;* the amphipod, *Caprella equilibra,* and the ectoproct, Bugula neritina (Reish et al., 1975).

On one dock in the bay the polychaete, *Polydora websteri;* the bay mussel, *Mytilus edulis;* the barnacles, *Balanus amphitrite, B. crenatus,* and *Chthamalus fissus;* the isopod, *Paracereis gilliana;* and the gribble, *Limnoria tripunctata,* were found (Reish et al., 1975).

Subtidal Areas

Invertebrates. Subtidally, a wide variety of invertebrate species were found. These were the polychaetes, *Eumida sanguinea, Ophiodromus pugettensis, Exogene lourei, Goniada uncinigera, Marphysa sanguinea, Lumbrineris erecta, L. minima, Haploscoloplos elongatus, Naineris dendritica, Boccardia uncata, Nerinides acuta, N. maculata, N. pigmentata, Polydora brachycephala, P. ligni, P. limnicola, Prionospio cirrifera, P. heterobranchia newportensis, P. pinnata, P. pygmaeus, Pseudopolydora kempi, Rhynchospio arenicola, Spiophanes missionensis, Streblospio benedicti, Telepsavus costarum, Chaetezone corona, C. multioculata, Cirriformia luxuriosa, Tharyx parvus, Armandia bioculata, Polyophthalmus pictus, Capitata ambiseta, Axiothella rubrocincta, Nicomanche personata, Owenia collaris, Sabellaria gracilis, Amphicteis glabra, Amaeana occidentalis, Pista alata, Thelepus setosus, Chone* sp., *Euchone limnicola, Megalomma pigmentum;* the molluscs, *Chione fluctifraga* (the smooth cockle), *Chione undatella* (wavy chione), *Protothaca staminea* (white sand clam), *Macoma nasuta* (bent-nosed clam), *M. secta, Tagelus californianus* (California jackknife clam), *Cryptomya californica* (false mya), unidentified ostracods, unidentified copepods, the cumacaean, *Oxyurostylis pacifica;* the amphipods, *Corohium acherusicum,* and *Caprella equilibra,* the bay ghost shrimp, *Callianassa californiensis;* and *Pinnixa franciscana* (pea crab) (Reish et al., 1975).

Fish or nekton. A great deal of research has been conducted on the fish of

Anaheim Bay. Lane (1975c) compared species found in the bay from 1919 to 1928 to those found after the 1944 construction of jetties and dredging of the harbor. This dredging added hard substrate and deep water, removed eelgrass beds, and changed current patterns. In addition, tidal circulation was probably increased since dredging kept the mouth of the bay open. Fish found prior to major alterations to the bay but not since were coastal open-water forms found immediately offshore. These were *Gymnura marmorata* (California butterfly ray), *Hyporhamphus rosae* (California halfbeak), *Strongylura exilis* (California needlefish), *Chromis punctipinnis* (Blacksmith), *Oxyjulils californica* (Senorita), and *Scorpaena guttata* (California scorpian fish). *Albula vulpes* (bonefish), *Ilypnus gilberti* (cheekspot goby), and *Sardinops sagax caeruleus* (sardine) were once common but were rarely captured in later studies. *Menticirrhus argeneum* (kingfish), *Genyonemus lineatus* (white croaker), *Paralabrax maculatofasciatus* (spotted sand bass), *Hyperprosopon argenteum* (walleye surfperch), *Rhacochilus* (= *Damalichtys*) *vacca* (pile perch), *Phanerodon furcatus* (white surfperch), and *Heterostichus rostratus* (giant kelpfish) were taken in recent studies but were not recorded before the construction of the jetties. The topsmelt, *Atherinops affinis*, the most common fish in the bay, was not recorded in early studies of the bay (Lane, 1975c).

Five thousand specimens of *Atherinops affinis* were taken in a recent survey of the fish in the bay. No seasonal variation in abundance was observed. The topsmelt spent its entire life cycle in the bay, spawning in April and May. Larger topsmelts ingested mainly detritus and sediment, although ostracods, cumaceans, tanaidaceans, and amphipods were the most common food items found in the digestive tracts. Minor food items were foraminiferans, small gastropods, polychaetes, harpacticoid copepods, isopods, *Callianassa* sp. larvae, dipterans. *A. affinis* eggs, and algae. Smaller topsmelt fed mainly on planktonic crustaceans, with detritus and sediment forming only a minor part of gut conents. Other food items of smaller topsmelt included foraminiferans, other protozoans, ostracods, amphipods, dipteran adults, and larvae and algal fragments (Klingbeil et al., 1975).

Anchoa compressa, the deepbody anchovy, spawned in the bay and was one of the most abundant fish in the bay, particularly from May through November. A total of 1355 specimens were captured throughout the year. Gut analysis indicated a diet of small crustaceans, including ostracods, copepods, cumaceans, amphipods, and *Callianassa* sp. larva. Additional food items were small polychaetes and gastropods, mysids, tanaidaceans, isopods, crab zoea, dipterans, and small gobies, probably *Clevelandia ios* (Kingbeil et al., 1975).

Cymatogaster aggregata, the shiner surfperch, was the most abundant surfperch in the bay (Klingbeil et al., 1975). The catch of this fish totaled 1234 specimens, with approximately equal numbers of males and females recorded. Maximum age recorded for the bay population of this species was $2\frac{1}{2}$ years. Young shiner surfperch first appeared in April, although most were born in May. This species was eurythermal, with a temperature range from 4 to 21 °C, although on days when water temperature exceeded 18.5 °C, the number of specimens captured decreased markedly. The shiner surfperch fed on the green algae, *Enteromorpha* sp.; the sea lettuce, *Ulva* sp.; polychaetes; the gastropopds, *Tegula* sp. and *Olivella* sp.; the bay mussel, *Mytilus edulis*; eggs of *Athernops affinis*; and zooplankton, including amphipods, mysids, ostracods, caprellids, copepods, and shrimp. During spring and summer, zooplankton composed 60% of the diet of *C. aggregata*. A high incidence of mud and detritus in stomach contents indicated that these fish were bottom feeders. In spring, approximately 20% of shiner surfperch stomachs examined were empty (Odenweller, 1975).

Among the more abundant fish in the bay was the round stingray, *Urolophus halleri*. This was the most common elasmobranch in the bay, with 761 specimens captured. This species fed primarily on *Callianassa* sp. and on clams. Secondary food items were small polychaetes, amphipods, and pea crabs (Klingbeil et al., 1975).

Mustelus californicus, the gray smoothhound, was fairly abundant in the bay, with 313 specimens captured. This species was most abundant in the spring and summer. The middle arm of the bay appeared to be a congregating place for the smoothhound, probably for mating. This fish fed on invertebrates, particularly benthic invertebrates such as *Callianassa* sp. and *Hemigrapsus oregonensis*. Polychaetes and echiuroid worms were eaten occasionally by all sizes of fish, while larger individuals fed on clams and fish (Klingbeil et al., 1975).

The shovelnose guitarfish, *Rhinobatus productus*, was moderately abundant (54 specimens) and was captured throughout the year, with a slight decline in numbers in the winter. This fish fed on bottom invertebrates, especially *Callianassa* sp. (Klingbeil et al., 1975).

Porichthys miriaster, the specklefin midshipman, was common in the bay from March to November. Digestive tracts of a portion of the fish captured were examined and found to be empty, probably due to the onset of spawning activity. Juveniles were far more common than adults (Klingbeil et al., 1975).

The California killifish, *Fundulus parvipinnis*, was also common in the bay. Total population of the west arm of the bay was estimated at 24,055 ± 1900 adults and subadults. This species exhibited tidally induced movement traveling from the shallows to deeper channels and following the rising waterline at midflood. When the marsh grass flats were inundated by water, the killifish was found throughout the bay. *F. parvipinnis* spawned from April to September, with three distinct periods of spawning activity occurring in April, May, and June. Spawning probably occurred in the permanent pools in the tidal flats. The killifish lived to 11 to 18 months and died after spawning. *F. parvipinnis* fed primarily on amphipods, copepods, ostracods, and dipteran insects, with a secondary diet of annelids, gastropods, fish eggs, and algae. Fish fed throughout the water column, mostly during high slack tide, probably because feeding grounds were most accessible at this time (Fritz, 1975).

Clevelandia ios, the arrow goby, was the most abundant goby in the bay and was found in the middle and low intertidal and subtidal zones of the bay. It also lived free and commensally in the burrows of the echiuroid worm, *Urechis caupo*; the ghost shrimp, *Callianassa* sp.; and the blue mud shrimp, *Upogebia pugettensis.* Concentrations of this fish averaged 3 to 4 individuals m^{-3} over wide areas, although as many as 20 individuals m^{-3} were found in several areas. The arrow goby was most active at low light levels. Peak spawning occurred between February and June. Larger arrow gobies (over 14 mm) were primarily benthic carnivores feeding on ostracods, nematodes, oligochaetes, and cyclopoids, while very large arrow gobies fed on amphipods, caprellids, and larger oligochaetes. Fish reached a maximum length of 45 mm and lived over 2 years. Sex ratios of females to males averaged 3.3:1 (Macdonald, 1975).

Quietula y-cauda, the shadow goby, was also fairly abundant in the bay. Often the shadow goby was found in close association with the arrow goby in the middle, low, and subtidal zones living free and commensally in the burrows of the echiuroid worm, *Urechis caupo;* the ghost shrimp, *Callianassa* sp.; and the blue mud shrimp, *Upogebia pugettensis.* Unlike the arrow goby, however, the larger shadow gobies did not burrow in intertidal zones and were restricted to subtidal regions during low tide. Some specimens of the shadow goby lived more than 3 years and reached a length of 55 mm. The shadow goby had a prolonged breeding season similar to that of the arrow goby. The diet of the shadow goby was similar to that of the arrow goby, although larger fish, polychaetes, oligochaetes, caprellids, and amphipods were more common in the stomach contents of the *Quietula y-cauda* (Macdonald, 1975).

The Pacific staghorn sculpin, *Leptocottus armatus,* was found throughout the bay (Klingbeil et al., 1975). These fish left the bay soon after spawning. As a result, the population in the bay was almost entirely juvenile. The largest specimen captured in the bay was 172 mm long, while the largest ever recorded for this species was 305 mm. The staghorn sculpin was a continuous feeder and was able to ingest large prey due to its extremely large mouth. The sculpin was primarily a night feeder feeding on the yellow shore crab, *Hemigrapsus oregonensis;* the ghost shrimp, *Callianassa* sp.; pea crabs, *Pinnixia* sp.; the gobies, *Clevelandia ios,* and *Quietula y-cauda;* the killifish, *Fundulus parvipinnis;* gammarideans of the genera *Corophium, Ampithoe,* and *Hyale;* and the polychaetes, *Goniada littorea* and *Eulalia* sp. (Tasto, 1975).

The California halibut, *Paralichthys californiensis,* was quite abundant in the bay and used the bay as a nursery. After maturation, these fish emigrated into deeper offshore waters. Smaller California halibut ate mostly small crustaceans, such as amphipods, cumaceans, copepods, and mysids, as well as small gobies, including *Clevelandia ios* and *Quietula y-cauda,* and young longjaw mudsuckers, *Gillichthys mirabilis.* Larger specimens over 55 mm in length but less than 230 mm ate large crustaceans, including *Crangon* sp. and *Callianassa* sp., and fish such as the topsmelt, *Atherinops affinis;* the California killifish, *Fundulus parvipinnis;* and gobies. The California halibuts over 230 mm in length fed almost exclusively on fish, especially the topsmelt, the California killifish, the northern anchovy (*Engraulis mordax*), and gobies (Haaker, 1975).

The diamond turbot, *Hypsopsetta guttulata,* was the most common flatfish in the bay. This fish probably migrated out of the inner bay to spawn in or near the outer harbor of the bay, beginning in September and continuing through

February. Peak spawning occurred from November through January. Population estimates for the middle arm of the bay varied from 2286 in July 1970 to 5509 in September 1970, with a yearly average of 3417. The entire bay population of diamond turbot was estimated to be between 5000 and 7000 individuals over 50 mm long. The largest specimen of this species was 295 mm SL (standard length) or 258 mm TL (total length).

Most *H. guttulata* live 1 to 2 years, although one 4-year-old specimen was tagged in the bay. Diamond turbots were day feeders, consuming small crustaceans such as larval decapods; the skeleton shrimp, *Crangon* spp.; large crustaceans such as pistol shrimps; *Crangon* spp.; and crabs, including the shore crab, *Hemigrapsus* spp., young *Cancer*, and especially pea crabs of the family Pinnotheridae. The tunicate, *Eugyra arenosa*, was eaten occasionally, as well as many benthic polychaetes, molluscs including the olive shell, *Olivella* spp., siphons of clams (especially the Bullidae clam, *Tagelus* spp.), the echiuroid (*Urechis caupo*), the arrow goby (*Clevelandia ios*), and the shadow goby (*Quietula y-cauda*). Forty-one percent of the diamond turbots' stomach contents were Mollusca, 34.85% clam siphons, 18.8% Polychaeta, and 14.04% Crustacea. Young diamond turbots tended to eat more small Crustacea and polychaetes than did larger fish, which relied more on clam siphons and large crustaceans. An estimate of consumption by the diamond turbot population in the bay was 4587 kg^{-1} yr^{-1}. Annual production of the diamond turbot was approximately 457.8 kg^{-1} yr^{-1} (Lane, 1975a).

The pile surfperch, *Damalichthys* (*Rhacochilus*) *vacca*, was caught frequently throughout the bay, although rarely in summer or fall. This fish fed primarily on small molluscs (*Crepidula*, *Cerithidea*, *Bulla*, *Polinices*, *Macoma*, *Chione*, *Laevicardium*, and *Tagelus*) as well as decapods, including *Callianassa* sp., *Hemigrapsus* sp., and pinnotherids (Klingbeil et al., 1975).

Only 25 white croakers, *Genyonemus lineatus*, were captured in the bay, mostly at night. This fish probably was an indiscriminate bottom feeder, as stomach contents of captured fish revealed 22 different food items. The most common food items were polychaetes and *Callinassa* sp. adults, although amphipods, small molluscs, clam siphons, pinnotherid clams, ostracods, and gobies were also found consistently (Klingbeil et al., 1975).

Thirty-six specimens of the white surfperch, *Phanerodon furcatus*, were captured in the bay. None were captured in the summer. This species ate *Callianassa* sp. primarily, with polychaetes, pinnotherid crabs, and adult *Callianassa* sp. composing minor parts of its diet (Klingbeil et al., 1975).

Menticirrhus undulatus, the California corbina, was captured sporadically in the bay, most often in the spring and fall. Corbina moved offshore during the winter and when spawning in the summer. Digestive tracts revealed that *Callianassa* sp. was the most common food, with polychaetes, molluscs, clam siphons, shrimp, pinnotherid crabs, *Hemigrapsus* sp., and gobies being occasionally ingested (Klingbeil et al., 1975). The longjaw mudsucker, *Gillichthys mirabilis*, was the largest goby found in the bay and was found in the burrow of the yellow shore crab, *Hemigrapsus oregonensis*, along the channel banks. This species occupied one of the highest tidal zones inhabited by fish in the bay. The mudsucker had an extended spawning season and fed on *Callianassa* sp. and the yellow shore crab, *Hemigrapsus oregonensis* (Macdonald, 1975).

The brown smoothhound, *Mustelus henlei*, was captured only twice in the bay. Stomach contents were primarily *Hemigrapsus oregonensis* and clam remains. The stomachs of three leopard sharks, *Triakis semifasciata*, captured in the bay contained mostly *Callianassa* sp., unidentified clam remains, and polychaetes. Sixty juvenile barred seabass, *Paralabrax nebulifer*, were captured in the bay, but no investigation of gut contents was conducted (Klingbeil et al., 1975).

Fish species captured in the bay only occasionally were the *Squatina californica* (Pacific angel), *Platyrhinoidis triseriata* (thornback), *Myliobatis californica* (bat ray), *Dorosoma petenense* (threadfin shad), *Engraulis mordax* (northern anchovy), *Syngnathus leptorhynchus* (bay pipefish), *Roccus* (*Morone*) *saxatilis* (striped bass), *Paralabrax maculatofasciatus* (spotted sand bass), *Cynoscion nobilis* (white seabass), *Seriphus politus* (queenfish), *Roncador stearnsi* (spotfin croaker), *Umbrina roncador* (yellowfin croaker), *Embiotoca jacksoni* (black surfperch), *Hyperprosopon argenteum* (walleye surfperch), *Hypsurus caryi* (rainbow surfperch), *Mugil cephalis* (striped mullet), *Hypsoblennius gentilis* (bay blenny), *Ilypnus gilberti* (cheekspot goby), *Lepodogobius lepidus* (bay goby), *Sarda chiliensis* (Pacific bonito), *Parilus simillimus* (Pacific butterfish), *Citharichthys stigmaeus* (speckled sanddab), *Pleuronichthys verticalis* (hornyhead turbot), *Parophrys vetulus* (English sole), and the *Symphurus atricauda* (California tonguefish) (Klingbeil et al., 1975; Macdonald, 1975).

ALAMITOS BAY

Alamitos Bay is located in the city of Long Beach, California at the southeastern boundary of Los Angeles County. It is used as a recreational area for swimming, fishing, and boating. Originally, Alamitos Bay was a marsh and shared a common opening into the ocean with the San Gabriel River. However, in the 1920s the Bay and the San Gabriel River were separated from each other by a rock jetty. A side channel connected the bay with the river until the flood of 1938 silted the area in. The area known as the Marine Stadium was dredged from tidal flats and marshland in the early 1930s (Reish and Winter, 1954).

Beginning in 1955, bulkheads were built and the enclosed land area dredged to a depth of -3.65 m mean low water in the process of constructing a marina. Additonal dredging to -4.57 m, beginning in 1959, widened the marina and connected it to the Marine Stadium (Reish, 1963b). No major alterations have occurred since then.

Reish and Winter (1954) report that no waste discharges are emptied into the bay. They found some materials deleterious to fish and aquatic life in the bay but claim that none was serious at the time of their study. The cite storm drains, public dumps, oil fields, and the proximity of the bay to the heavily polluted San Gabriel River as potential sources of pollution. Their study, however, found no evidence of seepage from the San Gabriel River and no areas of benthic sterility or sludge beds (Reish and Winter, 1954).

Water Quality

Reish (1968) found that freshwater runoff entered the bay through storm drains in the winter, the largest amount entering the bay via Cerritos Channel. Salinity was that of seawater except following winter rains. Recovery to normal seawater salinity was rapid (Reish, 1968). Allen and Horn (1975), reported salinities in Colorado Lagoon, in the northwest portion of the bay, ranging from 30.0 ppt in February to 33.5 ppt in October.

Sediments

Substrates in the basin tended to be uniform—primarily gray clay with small fragments of mica (Reish, 1961). Black sulfide mud was found in several substrate samples in the marina, as well as in Colorado Lagoon (Reish, 1961; Allen and Horn, 1975). The organic content of the substrate ranged from 0.4 to 1.6%, with an approximate mean around 1.0% reported in 1957 and 1958, after the second dredging of the marina (Reish, 1961).

Communities

Benthic Fauna. Except for the marina area, which we discuss later, the bay supported a fairly uniform invertebrate population. Four species of polychaetous annelids found throughout the bay were *Lumberineris erecta, L. minima, Haploscoloplos elongatus,* and *Spiophanes missionensis.* Species found in several areas of the bay were *Nephtys caecoides, Armandia bioculata, Stauroneris rudolphi, Neanthes succinea, Capitella capitata,* and *Pista alata.* Two species, *Pectinaria californiensis* and *Diopatra splendissima,* were found in only one area other than the marina.

Bivalve molluscs found throughout the muddy/sandy bay bottom were *Chione undatellum* (wavy cockle), *Macoma nasuta* (bent nose clam), and *Tagelus californianus* (California jackknife clam). Three other cockles, *Laevicardium substriatum* (eggshell cockle), *Chione californiensis,* and *C. fluctifraga* (smooth cockle), were found less widely, as was the rosy razor clam, *Solen rosaceus.* Two other bivalves, *Saxidomus nuttalli* (common Washington clam) and *Tellina buttoni,* were found only in offshore peninsula waters and in the marina (Reish, 1968).

Benthic echinoderms were the echinoid, *Dendraster excentricus* (sand dollar), and the holothurian, *Leptosynapta albicans* (sea cucumber). The red ghost shrimp, *Callianassa pacifica,* and the crab, *Pinnixia franciscana,* were in association in all benthic areas.

Two fish were predators on benthic animals. *Rhinobatus productus* (shovelnose guitarfish) fed on crustaceans and bivalves. *Urobatus halleri* (round stingray) preyed on a range of animals that included worms, bivalves, crustaceans, and fish (Reish, 1968).

Marina. The earliest sampling of the benthos in 1952, before dredging of the marina began, revealed results differing from both later studies, which were made in dredged areas. Seventy species of animals were collected from a wide range of substrates. Polychaeta, Crustacea, and Mollusca were represented by 34, 15, and 13 species, respectively (Reish and Winter, 1954).

Only one station (number 3) had a substrate of gray sand with small shell and gravel fragments. A total of 48 specimens were taken there, although the only abundant species found (10 or more specimens) at this station was the polychaete, *Prionospio* near *malmgreni.* Thirty-two specimens of *P.* near *malmgreni* were found (Reish and Winter, 1954).

Seven sample sites (numbers 4, 6, 10, 11, 13, 17, and 21) had a substrate of fine mud with plant debris and shell fragments. A total of 945 specimens were found on or in this substrate. The most abundant species included the polychaetes, *Capitata ambiseta* (370 specimens found), *Tharyx* sp. (160), *Streblospio benedicti* (99), *Haploscoloplos elongata* (51), *Amphicteis scaphlobranchiata* (41), *Lumbrineris minima* (36), *Prionospio* near *malmgreni* (14), *Nerinides acuta* (14), *Cossura longicirrata* (14), *Prionospio* near *koyeri* (10), and *Spiophanes missioniensis* (10); 17 nemerteans; the California jackknife clam, *Tagelus californicus* (16); and 14 caprellids.

A total of 449 specimens were found on or in fine mud with plant debris at 10 stations (5, 7, 8, 9, 14, 15, 16, 18, 24, 25). These included 395 polychaetes. These were *Cossura longicirrata* (105), *Capitata ambiseta* (99), *Tharyx* sp. (91), *Capitella capitata* (84), *Haploscoloplos elongata* (16), and 11 nemerteans.

On or in the fine mud of one station (station 12), 203 specimens were found. This included the polychaetes *Cossura longicirrata* (71), *Lumbrineris minima* (16), and *Capitata ambiseta* (12) (Reish and Winter, 1954).

On or in the fine mud with gravel, plant debris, and shell fragments at one sample station (station 19), 12 specimens were taken. *Lambrineris minima* was the most abundant species, although only five specimens were found (Reish and Winter, 1954).

At the one station with a substrate of sand with plant debris (station 22), 193 specimens were found. The most abundant species included the polychaetes, *Streblospio benedicti* (128 specimens), *Capitella capitata* (29), *Spiophanes missioniensis* (13), and *Neanthes succineis* (12) (Reish and Winter, 1954).

On or in fine mud with gravel and shell fragments at one station (station 23), 43 specimens were found. The polychaete, *Haploscoloplos elongatus*, was the most abundant species with 13 specimens recorded, followed by *Lumbrineris minima* with 11 specimens found (Reish and Winter, 1954).

At the one station with black sand with filamentous algae (station 26), 1120 specimens were found. These included the polychaetes, *Corophium acherusicum* (397), *Streblospio benedicti* (357), *Polydora ligni* (126), *Capitella capitata* (60), *Hypoeulalia bilineata* (22), *Neanthes succinea* (17), *Nerinides acuta* (15), and *Eteone dilatae* (13); 67 tubificids; 10 turbellarians; the California jackknife clam, *Tagelus californianus* (13); and 26 caprellids (Reish and Winter, 1954).

At the one station with a hard bottom (station 32), *Polydora ligni*, a polychaete, was the most abundant species, with 63 specimens found. Ten specimens of *Neanthes succinea* formed the second largest population (Reish and Winter, 1954).

On or in asphalt and clay surface with sand beneath found at one station (station 27), 161 specimens were taken, of which 150 specimens were of the polychaete, *Polydora ligni*; 49 of *Streblospio benedicti*; 11 each of *Neanthes succinea* and tubificids; and 10 specimens of the polychaete, *Capitella capitata*. The crustacean, *Corophium insidiosum*, was represented by 115 individuals (Reish and Winter, 1954).

Fine mud with filamentous algae was found at one station (station 30). This station had sulfur and oil odors. A total of 162 specimens were found, including 107 specimens of the polychaete, *Streblospio benedicti*, 16 specimens of the polychaete, *Capitella capitata*, and 11 tubificids (Reish and Winter, 1954).

On or in fine mud with plant debris and a strong sulfide odor (station 28), tubificids were most abundant. Fifty specimens were found at the one station with this substrate. (Reish and Winter, 1954).

On or in fine mud with a strong sulfide odor and filamentous algae (station 30), 43 specimens included 26 tubificids and 11 specimens of the polychaete, *Capitella capitata* (Reish and Winter, 1954).

After First Dredging. A sampling of the benthos was conducted from 1956 to 1959, after the first dredging for the marina but prior to the joining of the marina to Marine Stadium. The study yielded 186 specimens representing 94 species. Polychaete annelids composed 87% of the specimens; unidentified nemerteans were responsible for 6% of the total collected. Mollusca comprised 3% of the specimens, and crustaceans, 2%. Sixty percent of the species were polychaetes, 19% were molluscs, and 16% were crustaceans (Reish, 1961).

Of those species considered by Reish to be principal species in this study, the annelids, *Lumbrineris erecta* (126 specimens found), *L. minima* (644), and *Capitata ambiseta* (359), and the mollusc, *Leptosynapta albicans*, were found living freely in the substrate. Principal species maintaining burrows in the substrate were the annelids, *Dorvillea articulata* (145) (also found crawling on the substrate) and *Tharyx parvus* (55), and the mollusc, *Macoma nasuta*.

Three of the principal benthic species built mud tubes. These were the annelids, *Prionospio cirrifera* (217), *Acmaea occidentalis* (83), and *Euchone sp.* (127). The annelid, *Spiophanes missionensis* (55), also constructed mud tubes but used a larger grain size. Also found in the benthos of the bay was *Pectinaria californiensis* (46), which constructed conical tubes from sand grains, burrowing its anterior end into the substrate while leaving its posterior end up (Reish, 1961).

There was no apparent pattern of succession in the area. Species composition in the benthos remained relatively constant, although numbers of specimens varied greatly. One severe drop in population in 1957 was probably due to the effect that the lack of circulation of water in the marina had on the amount of oxygen in the sediment (Reish, 1961). The connection of Marine Stadium to the marina in 1959 doubtlessly improved water circulation in the bay.

After Final Dredging. A 3-year study of the benthos was conducted by Reish

(1963b). After the final dredging for the marina in 1959. He found 78 species, of which 63% were polychaetes, 17% molluscans, and 12% crustaceans. The remaining 8% were sea anemones, turbellarians, nemerteans, sipunculids, phoronids, and echinoderms. No animals were encountered until 7 weeks after dredging began (Reish, 1963a).

The polychaetes, *Polydora ligni, Prionospio heterobranchia newportensis, P. pinnata*, and *Nerinides pigmentata*, were early inhabitants of the marina but later disappeared from the bay completely. The population of the polychaete, *Euchone limnicola* (found exclusively in Alamitos Bay), and the populations of *Eteone dilatae, Chaetozone corona, Tharyx parvus*, and *Macoma nasuta* were growing rapidly at the onset of the study but soon after declined sharply (Reish, 1963a).

The polychaetes, *Dorvillea articulata* and *Haploscoloplos elongatus*, showed a seasonal pattern of abundance, with two population peaks in the warmer months of the year followed by a drop in numbers with the onset of winter. The polychaete, *Nephtys caecoides*, also demonstrated two population peaks, although seasonality could not be demonstrated conclusively for this species (Reish, 1963a).

At the conclusion of the study, in 1963, populations of *Goniada littorea* and *Capitata ambiseta* were still increasing, whereas *Lumbrineris minima, Prionospio cirrifera, Cossura candida*, and the unidentified nemerteans appeared to have reached a stable population (Reish, 1963a).

Other species with relatively small populations are listed in Table 10.1. The wide range of results from samples before dredging began, after the first dredging, and after the final dredging indicate that the benthos of the bay was significantly altered from its original state by dredging.

In his book, *Marine Life of Alamitos Bay*, Reish (1968) reported that after the dredging many different benthic assemblages were found at various locations in the bay. At the marina the polychaete, *Nephtys caecoides*, was found in muddy sand. The polychaete, *Glycera americana*, was found in both sand and mud. *Harmothoe lunulata*, also a polychaete, was found in the burrows of the ghost shrimp, *Callianassa californiensis*, while the polychaete, *Ophiodromus pugettensis*, was found living commensally with the starfish, *Patira miniata*. Subtidally in the benthos of the marina, the polychaetes, *Stauronereis rudolphi* and *Pista alata*, as well as the mollusc, *Tellina buttoni*, were found. In the soft sediments of the marine the pistol shrimp, *Crangon californiensis*, was found. Polychaetes found in or on the bottom of the marina were *Armandia brevis, Polyophthalmus pictus, Capitella capitata, Asychis disparidentata, A. similis, Amphicteis scaphobranchiata, Amage anops, Ampharete arctica*, and *Megalomma pigmentum*. Molluscs were *Chione californiensis*, banded cockle; *Saxidomus nuttali*, common Washington clam; *Tagelus californianus*, California jackknife clam; and *Lyonsia californica* and *Tellina carpenteri*. Crustaceans included the amphipod, *Corophium acherusicum*, and the ghost shrimp, *Callianassa californiensis* (Reish, 1968).

Intertidal Fauna.   Reish (1968) divides the tidal zones of Alamitos Bay into the splash zone, high-tide zone, midtide zone, minus-tide zone, and subtidal zone. The acorn barnacle, *Balanus amphitrite*, is found at the lower limits of the splash zone and high-tide zone. The bay mussel, *Mytilus edulis*, was typical of the midtide zone, although it often extended into the subtidal waters. In the midtide zone, *M. edulis* was often covered with the acorn barnacle. The lower limits of the midtide zone often contained the tunicate, *Styela plicata*, and the bryozoan, *Bugula neritina*. In the low-tide zone the tunicate, *Styela montereyensis*, was often found. Less conspicuous organisms such as smaller worms and crustaceans were found throughout the zones (Reish, 1968).

Sandy or Muddy Areas. Sandy or muddy substrate provides a poor substrate for macroalgae, but a few patches of the green alga, *Enteromorpha* sp., and the red algae, *Corallina* sp., were identified on the shores of Alamitos Bay. The intertidal area of the peninsula supported the largest number of invertebrate species, most of which were either annelids or molluscs. The species present were *Nephtys caecoides*, *Hemipodus borealis*, *Goniada littorea*, *Cirriformia spirabrancha*, *Owenia fusiformis*, and *Lumbrineris zonata*. Additional species, *Neanthes succinea*, *Polydora nuchalis*, and *Streblospio benedicti*, were found in Cerritos Channel.

Two gastropod molluscs, *Bulla gouldiana* (cloudy bubble shell) and *Crepidula onyx* (onyx slipper shell), were found intertidally throughout the bay. *Polinices reclusianus* (southern moon snail), *Nassarius fossatus* (channeled basket shell), *Olivella biplicata* (California purple olive shell), *Navanax inermes* (striped sea hare), and *Aplysia californica* (sea hare) were found on the peninsula, and both sea hares were found at Belmont Shore as well. *Cerithida californica* (California horn snail) was found in Cerritos Channel, Colorado Lagoon, and the marina.

Two bivalve molluscs, *Macoma secta* (white sand clam) and *Sanguinolaria nuttalli* (purple clam), were found only on Peninsula intertidal slopes. *Ostrea lurida*, the native mussel, was taken on the intertidal sands of Colorado Lagoon. At Marine Stadium the common Washington clam, *Saxidomus nuttalli*, was collected. *Chione fluctifraga*, the smooth cockle; *C. undatellum*, the wavy cockle; *Protothaca staminea*, the little neck clam; *Schizothaerus nuttalli*, the gaper clam; *Macoma nasuta*, bent-nosed clam; and *Tagelus californicus*, the California jackknife clam, were found intertidally on the peninsula and at other locations in the bay (Reish, 1968).

The few echinoderms of sandy intertidal areas were collected from the lowest tide level. One asteroids, *Astropecten armatus* (southern sea star), one echinoid, *Dendraster excentricus* (sand dollar), and one holothuroid, *Leptosynapta albicans* (sea cucumber), were found.

The one cumacean, *Asyurostylis pacifica*, collected intertidally, was found on the mudflats of Cerritos Channel. The red ghost shrimp, *Callianassa californiensis*, and the crab, *Pinnixia franciscanus*, were found together throughout Alamitos Bay. *Uca crenulata*, a hermit crab, was common on nearly all tidal slopes (Reish, 1968).

Rocks, Walls, and Jetties. The rocky intertidal areas of Alamitos Bay provided a solid base for macroalgal attachment. (Many species found on the jetty or rock walls were also found on floats, docks, or pilings.) The brown algae, *Egregia laeviga* (feather boa) and *Scytosiphon lomentaria*, were common on rocks along the jetty. Red algae included species of *Corallina*, *Gelidium caulteri*, *Gigartina canaliculata*, *Polysiphonia pacifica*, *Porphyra perforata*, and *Rhodoglossum affine*.

The bryozoan, *Thalamoporella californica*, was observed in the lower intertidal zone as the jetty was exposed.

The nemertean, *Emplectonema*, was found on an alga anchored to the rocks. The annelids, *Anaitides medipapillata*, *Naineris dendritica*, *Odontosyllis phosphorea*, and *Owenia fusiformis*, were found intertidally, while *Diopatra splendissima* and *Pectinaria californiensis* were located subtidally (Reish, 1968).

Many echinoderms, particularly asteroids, seem to have preferred rocky areas. Species found in a rocky habitat were *Patiria miniata*, the sea bat; Pisaster ochraeceus the ochre starfish; *P. giganteus*; *Strongylocentrotus franciscanus*, the giant red urchin; and *S. purpuratus*, the purple sea urchin. The brittle star, *Ophiothrix spiculata*, and the sea cucumber, *Stichopus parvimensis*, were found under and between rocks at low tide (Reish, 1968).

Gastropod molluscs of the mid to high intertidal area were *Acmaea scabra*, the rough limpet; *Lottia gigantea*, the owl limpet; *Megathura crenulata*, the giant keyhole limpet; *Crepidula onyx*, the onyx slipper shell; *Ocenebra poulsoni*, Poulson's rock shell; *Acanthina spirata*, angled unicorn shell; *Aletes squamigerus*, the scaly worm; *Littorina planaxis*, the gray littorine; and *Aplysia californica*, the sea hare. Gastropods of the low-tide zone included *Tegula funebralis*, the black turbon snail; and the nudibranchs, *Sochidoris montereyensis* and *Diadula sandigensis*.

Bivalve molluscs attached to the rocky substrate were *Modiolus demissus*, the ribbed horse mussel; *Mytilus californianus*, the California mussel; *M. edulis*, the bay mussel; and *Hinnites multirugosis*, the purple-hinged pecten. Bivalves found in the sand between intertidal rocks, or in the immediate vicinity of the jetty, were *Protothaca staminea*, the little neck clam; *Saxidomus nuttalli*, the common Washington clam; and *Sanguinolaria nuttalli*, the purple clam.

Three barnacles (Cirrepedia) were residents of the rocky high- and midtide zones. *Balanus amphitrite* usually occupied the highest intertidal zone, while *Tetraclita squamosa*, the thatched barnacle, and *Mitella polymerus*, the goose-necked barnacle, occupied the lower strata.

The isopod, *Ligia occidentalis*, was another occupant of the highest zones. The copepod, *Modiolicola gracilis*, was found as a commensal in the mantle cavity of the mussels, *Mytilus edulis* and *Modiolus demissus*. The common rock crab, *Cancer antennarius*, because of its great mobility, was found everywhere in the rocky intertidal zone (Reish, 1968).

Floats, Docks, and Pilings. Throughout Alamitos Bay, including Marine Stadium, the large communities associated with floats, docks, and pilings were quite similar.

Algae.   The algae of the community were *Ulva lactuca* and *Cladophora* sp. (green); *Hydroclathrus clathratus* (brown); and *Antithamnion occidentale* (red).

Invertebrates.   The single protozoan associated with docks, floats, and pilings, reported by Reish (1968), was *Gonyaulax polyhedra*, the dinoflagellate whose bloom can produce a red tide. Two sponges, *Haliclona permolis* and *Leucosolenis* sp., were found in this habitat. The Cnidaria were represented by three species: the hydrozoan, *Obelis* sp.; and the anthozoans, *Diadumene leucolena* and *Anthopleura elegantissima* (Reish, 1968). Bryozoans (ectoprocts, or "moss animals") were common. *Haloporella brunnea* and *Schizoporella unicornis* were found often on mussel shells attached to docks, floats, or pilings. Other bryozoans identified were *Zoobotryton verticillatum*, *Bugula californica*, *B. neritina*, *Scrupocellaria bertholeti*, and *Cryptosula pallasianna*.

A large number of annelids were found in this habitat. The three tube builders, *Anaitedes medipapillata*, *Nereis grubei*, and *N. latiscens*, were found among the thalli of *Ulva lobata*. Annelids which specialized according to water levels rather than attachment site were *Cirriformia luxuriosa*, found subtidally, and *Stauronereis rudolphi*, an intertidal organism. Other annelids of this habitat were *Naineries dendritica*, *Polyopthalmus pictus*, *Polydora ligni*, *Chaetopterus variopedatus*, *Armandia bioculata*, *Halosydna johnsoni*, *Podarke* (= *Ophiodromus*) *pugettensi*, *Platynereis bicanaliculata*, *Lumbrineris erecta*, *Sabella media*, *Hydroides norvegica*, and *Spirobranchus spinosus* (Reish, 1968).

The 22 species of Polychaeta in the float and dock community exhibited definite population peaks in the summer and lows in the winter. Mucoid tubes constructed by *Halosydna johnsoni* and *Platynereis bicanaliculata* were found most frequently on the thalli of *Ulva lobata*. *Polydora ligni* built mud tubes on the thalli of *Ulva lobata* and in the midst of *Mytilus edulis* colonies. Other polychaetes found included *Armandia bioculata*, *Capitella capitata*, *Dorvillea articulata*, *Neanthes caudata*, *Naineris dendricata*, *Nereis grubei*, *N. latescens*, *Ophiodromus pugettensis*, *Paleonotus bellis*, *Pista alata*, *Polyopthamalus pictus*, *Spirabranchus spinosus*, and *Typosyllis* (Reish, 1964b).

Echinoderms were represented by three sea stars, *Paliria miniata* (the sea bat), *Pisaster gigantea*, and *P. ochraeus* (the ochre sea star), and two urchins, *Strongylocentrotus franciscanus* (the giant red sea urchin) and *S. purpuratus* (the purple sea urchin).

The only polyplacopheran mollusc found on Alamitos Bay floats, docks, and pilings was *Mopalia mucosa*, the mossy chiton. Gastropod molluscs were represented by *Acmaea limulata*, the file limpet; *A. scabra*, the rough limpet; *Littorina planaxis*, the gray littorine; *Crepidula onyx*, the onyx slipper shell; *Ceratostoma nuttalli*, Nuttal's hornmouth shell; and *Bulla gouldiana*, the cloudy bubble shell. The eight bivalve species recorded by Reish (1968) were *Modiolus demissus*, the ribbed horse mussel; *Mytilus edulis*, the California mussel; *Hinnites multirugosis*, the purple-hinged pecten; *Leptopecten latiauratus*, the broad-eared pecten; *Ostrea lurida*, the native mussel; *Chama pellucida*, the agate chama; *Pseudochama exogura*, the California reverse chama; and *Hiatella arctica*, the little gaper.

More species were found within the community during periods of high temperature than during periods of lower temperature. While the biomass of *M. edulis* fluctuated only slightly, that of the associated organisms varied from 50 g from January to March to a high of 260 g from July to September each year (Reish, 1964b). The barnacle, *Balanus amphitrite*, was usually found in association with the small acorn barnacle, *Chthamalus fissus*, and another barnacle, *Balanus crenatus* (Reish, 1968).

Amphipods common on and around floats, docks, or pilings were the tube-building *Corphium acherusicum*, the free-swimming species *Ampithoe plumulosa*, *Scrupocellaria bertholeti*, and *Elasmopus rapax*. Three caprellids, *Ciliocella gilliana*, *Caprella californica*, and *C. equilibria*, were usually found together.

The yellow shore crab, *Hemigrapsus oregonensis*, and the striped shore crab, *Pachygrapsus crassipes*, were commonly part of this community, as were the urochordates (tunicates), *Aplidium* (= *Amaroucium*) *californicum* (sea pork) and *Styela montereyensis*, which sometimes appeared in dense colonies.

Amphipod populations dominated the Alamitos Bay float and dock community. Populations peaked in the summer, with one collection numbering 17,450 individuals. Winter population lows reached only 1690. *Jassa falcata* constructed parchment tubes to which mud particles adhered. Their tubes were found on the thalli of *Ulva lobata* and between and on the shells of *Mytilus edulis*. Other amphipods of the community were *Ampithoe plumulosa*, *Ericthonius brasiliensis*, *Leucothoides pacifica*, and *Pontogenia minuta*.

Ciona intestinalis was the most abundant tunicate. Other tunicates found from May to September were *Diplosoma pizoni*, *Styela plicata*, and *Botryllus* sp. (Reish, 1964b).

Fish Fauna.   The only fish in consistent close association with the community on docks and floats was *Syngnathus griseolineatus*, the bay pipefish (Reish, 1968). A study of fish in Colorado Lagoon in the northwest portion of Alamitos Bay was undertaken by Allen and Horn (1975). The high productivity of Colorado Lagoon appeared to support large numbers of fish. The lagoon was used as a feeding and nursery ground by fish during the summer months when primary productivity was highest. A total of 152,169 fish were captured during the 12 sampling dates. The most abundant fish were the northern anchovy, *Engraulis mordax*; topsmelt, *Atherinops affinis*; slough anchovy, *Anchoa delicatissima*; and the shiner surfperch, *Cymatogaster aggregata* (Allen and Horn, 1975). The northern anchovy was the most abundant of all fish in the lagoon, composing 90% of all fish captured. This species was considered seasonal, reaching peaks in abundance in August and September. Northern anchovies ranged in size from 23 to 135 mm standard length (SL), with most in the size range 40 to 60 mm. This indicates that most were in the 0-age class. Northern anchovies fed on plankton.

Topsmelt were represented in the lagoon by age classes 0, I, and II and ranged in size from 9.0 to 175.5 mm SL with a mean size of 104.8 mm, while slough anchovies ranged in size from 46.5 to 93.0 mm SL with a mean of 69.7. Shiner surfperch ranged in size from 26.4 to 132 mm SL. All three fed at least partially on plankton. Topsmelt and shiner surfperch were present in the lagoon year round, while slough anchovies were present 8 months of the year. These three species, as well as the California killifish, *Fundulus parvipinnis*, and the staghorn sculpin, *Leptocottus armatus*, were considered to be residents of the lagoon (Allen and Horn, 1975).

Diversity values for the lagoon, based on the Shannon–Wiener information function, ranged from 1.11 in April and June to 0.03 in September, when the northern anchovy dominated the catch, with an overall value of 0.47 (Allen and Horn, 1975).

Special Studies. Studies on boat docks in the bay revealed a definite progression of organisms on "clean" areas (areas where all life had been scraped off by researchers). The initial inhabitants of floats scraped in October were invariably bacterial-algae scum followed approximately a month later by the bryozoan, *Bugula neritina*. About 3 months after the float was scraped, the tube-building polychaete, *Hydroides norvegica*, dominated the community. The green algae, *Ulva lobata*, replaced *H. norvegica* as the dominant organism a month later, until—about $1\frac{1}{2}$ years after the initial scraping—the bay mussel, *Mytilus edulis*, appeared. Within the next 6 months, *M. edulis* became the dominant organism and formed the climax community (Reish, 1964a).

Further experiments where floats were introduced to the bay water, then scraped clean once each season, revealed that seasonal progression keyed to temperature, not true succession, occurs in the bay. Although *Mytilus edulis* invariably represented the dominant organism in the climax community, the time of year at which the float was put in the water determined the progression of organisms that preceded the climax community. If a clean surface was exposed to winter and spring low temperatures, *Mytilus edulis* immediately dominated the area and a mature community of several species developed rapidly (Reish, 1964a).

Effects of Red Tide. Red tides occur occasionally in Alamitos Bay when blooms of the dinoflagellate, *Gonyaulax polyhedra*, off southern California are swept into the bay. One such red tide that occurred from September to November 1962 was studied extensively. The red tide destroyed the *Mytilus edulis* community in the marina either by killing the mussels outright or by affecting their ability to close. A fungus rapidly attacked the decaying mussels and associated sessile organisms (Reish, 1963a, 1968).

After November, living fouling community organisms in the bay were the sea anemone, *Diadume leucolena*; polychaetes, including *Hydroides norvegica*; and the limpet, *Acmaea limatula*. Numbers of benthic species decreased from 37 to 16 species in the outer marina and from 22 to 11 in the inner marina during the red tide. Whereas 14 benthic species decreased in number, including *Capitata ambiseta* (from 653 to 213), *Haploscoloplos elongatus* (from 46 to 12), and *Tharyx parvus* (from 29 to 7), eight species increased in number, including *Dorvillea articulata* (from 16 to 31), *Prionospio cirrifera* (from 190 to 693), *Callianassa californiensis* (from 36 to 76), and *Macoma nasuta* (from 15 to 28) (Reish, 1963a).

The die-off of the dinoflagellates and ensuing decomposition of the organisms depleted the dissolved O_2 levels to as low as 0.1 ppm in October. This fungal growth plus decay and dropping off of mussels probably caused the elimination of associated organisms. Benthic organisms were affected by the accumulation of organisms killed by the tide as well as decaying dinoflagellates. Substrates that were originally gray mud became black mud with a sulfide odor and killed off many benthic species. Increases in numbers of some species probably resulted from reduction or elimination of competitor species (Reish, 1963a, b).

Although areas other than the marina were less affected by the tide, most areas showed at least some evidence of *Mytilus edulis* death and subsequent death of associated species. Numbers of species in the channel, for example, declined from 42 species to 23 species. Areas with reduced circulation permitting large numbers of *Gonyaulax* to accumulate were most affected (Reish, 1963a). Organisms affected by the tides took as long as 6 to 8 months to become reestablished (Reish, 1968).

SUMMARY

Compared with the east and Gulf coasts, the estuaries about which we have any scientific knowledge are relatively few on the west coast. The most characteristic estuaries are those that have been formed by tectonic movements or, as in the case of Puget Sound, are fjords. In our effort to find sufficient information to describe the community's aquatic life living within the estuaries that were in fairly natural states, we had to resort to three small estuaries that are close together in southern California: the Newport Bay, Anaheim Bay, and Alamitos Bay estuaries. These small estuaries, which are relatively close together, have been somewhat disturbed by human activity. All three have had some alteration due to dredging. The types of estuaries into which a large river enters and greatly influences tidal action and shape and salinity patterns do not exist in this part of the world except for the San Francisco Bay area, which is badly polluted. Of course, another limiting factor was lack of sufficient information to describe the ecosystem.

With these limitations we selected three estuaries about which there was enough knowledge to enable us to present the structure of the ecosystem and how it functions. The Newport Bay estuary has a range of chlorinity from 15.2 to 19.7 ppt; the Anaheim estuary, a chlorinity of approximately 17 ppt. Alamitos Bay has a salinity of around 34 ppt, very similar to that of the Newport estuary. There is no regular river flow entering these estuaries.

BIBLIOGRAPHY

Allen, H. L. 1972. Phytoplankton photosynthesis, micronutrient interactions, and inorganic carbon availability in a soft-water Vermont lake. *In* G. E. Likens, ed., Nutrients and eutrophication: the limiting-nutrient controversy. Special symposium. Am. Soc. Limnol. Oceanogr. 1: 63–83.

Allen, L. G. 1982. Seasonal abundance, composition, and productivity of the littoral fish assemblage in upper Newport Bay, California. Fish Bull. 80(4): 769–790.

Allen, L. G., and M. H. Horn. 1975. Abundance, diversity, and seasonality of fishes in Colorado Lagoon, Alamitos Bay, California. Estuarine Coastal Mar. Sci. 3: 371–380.

Baker, P. C. 1975. The plants: the vascular plants of the salt water marsh. *In* E. D. Lane and C. W. Hill, eds., The marine resources of Anaheim Bay. Calif. Dep. Fish Game Fish Bull. 165: 37–39.

Bane, G. W. 1972. Fishes of the upper Newport Bay. Museum of Systematic Biology, Univ. California, Irvine, Res. Ser. 3. 114 pp.

Bane, G. W., and M. Robinson. 1970. Studies on the shiner perch, *Cymatogaster aggregata*, in Newport Bay, California. Wasmann J. Biol. 28(2): 259–268.

Barnard, J. L., and D. J. Reish. 1959. Ecology of Amphipoda and Polychaeta of Newport Bay, California. Occas. Pap. Hancock Found. 21: 1–103.

Chan, K. M., and E. D. Lane. 1975. Physical and chemical parameters of the Anaheim Bay salt marsh. *In* E. D. Lane and C. W. Hill, eds., The marine resources of Anaheim Bay. Calif. Dep. Fish Game Fish Bull. 165: 175–183.

Dixon, R. L., and W. J. Eckmayer. 1975. A checklist of the elasmobranchs and teleosts inhabiting the outer harbor of Anaheim Bay. *In* E. D. Lane and C. W. Hill, eds., Calif. Dep. Fish Game Fish Bull. 165: 175–183.

Eilers, H. P. 1981. Production in coastal salt marshes of southern California. EPA Proj. Summary 600/S3-81-023. 5 pp.

Frey, H. W., R. Hein, and J. L. Spruill. 1970. Report on the natural resources of upper Newport Bay and recommendations concerning the bay's development. California Department of Fish and Game. 68 pp.

Fritz, E. S. 1975. The life history of the California killifish, *Fundulus parvipinnis*, in Anaheim Bay, California. *In* E. D. Lane and C. W. Hill, eds., The marine resources of Anaheim Bay. Calif. Dep. Fish Game Fish Bull. 165: 91–106.

Haaker, P. L. 1975. The biology of the California halibut, *Paralichthys californicus*, in Anaheim Bay. *In* E. D. Lane and C. W. Hill, eds., The marine resources of Anaheim Bay. Calif. Dep. Fish Game Fish Bull. 165: 137–151.

Hanan, D. A. 1976. A new species of cyclopoid copepod parasitic on shiner surfperch, *Cymatogaster aggregata*, in Anaheim Bay and Huntington Harbor with notes on *Bomolochus cuneatus* and *Ergasilus lizae*. Bull. S. Calif. Acad. Sci. 75(1): 22–28.

Ho, Ju-shey. 1972. Copepod parasites of California halibut, *Paralichthys californicus* in Anaheim Bay. Calif. J. Parasitol. 58(5): 993–998.

Ho, Ju-shey. 1975. Parasitic crustacea: *In* E. D. Lane and C. W. Hill, eds., The marine resources of Anaheim Bay. Calif. Dep. Fish Game Fish Bull. 165: 69–72.

Horn, M. H., and L. G. Allen. 1981. Ecology of fishes in upper Newport Bay: seasonal dynamics and community structure. Calif. Dep. Fish Game Mar. Res. Tech. Rept. 45. 102 pp.

Kauwling, T. J., and D. J. Reish. 1975. A quantitative study of the benthic polychaetous annelids of Anaheim Bay and Huntington Harbor, California. *In* E. D. Lane and C. W. Hill, eds., The marine resources of Anaheim Bay. Calif. Dept. Fish Game Fish Bull. 165: 57–68.

Klingbeil, R. A., R. Sandell, and A. W. Wells. 1975. An annotated checklist of the elasmobranchs and teleosts of Anheim Bay. *In* E. D. Lane and C. W. Hill, eds., The marine resources of Anaheim Bay. Calif. Dep. Fish Game Fish Bull. 165: 79–90.

Lane, D. L. 1975a. Quantitative aspects of the life history of the diamond turbot, *Hypsopsetta guttulata*, in Anaheim Bay. *In* E. D. Lane and C. W. Hill, eds., The marine resources of Anaheim Bay. Calif. Dep. Fish Game Fish Bull. 165: 153–173.

Lane, D. L. 1975b. Additional invertebrates taken from fish stomachs in Anaheim Bay. *In* E. D. Lane and C. W. Hill, eds., The marine resources of Anaheim Bay. Calif. Dep. Fish Game Fish Bull. 165: 53–55.

Lane, D. L. 1975c. Early collections of fish from Anaheim Bay made between 1919 and 1928. *In* E. D. Lane, and C. W. Hill, eds., The marine resources of Anaheim Bay. Calif. Dep. Fish Game Fish Bull. 165: 13–15.

Lane, J. M., and A. Woods. 1975. A history of Anaheim Bay. *In* E. D. Lane and C. W. Hill, eds., The marine resources of Anaheim Bay. Calif. Dep. Fish and Game Fish Bull. 165:9–12.

Macdonald, C. K. 1975. Notes on the family Gobiidae from Anaheim Bay. *In* E. D. Lane and C. W. Hill, eds., The marine resources of Anaheim Bay. Calif. Dep. Fish Game Fish Bull. 165:117–121.

Odenweller, D. B. 1975. The life history of the shiner surfperch, *Cymatogster aggreata*, in Anaheim Bay, California. Calif. Dep. Fish Game Fish Bull. 165:107–117.

Quammen, M. L. 1982. Influences of subtle substrate differences on feeding by shorebirds on intertidal mudflats. Mar. Biol. 71(3):339–343.

Reish, D. J. 1961. A study of benthic fauna in a recently constructed boat harbor in southern California. Ecology 42(1):84–91.
Reish, D. J. 1963a. Mass mortality of marine organisms attributed to the "red tides" in southern California. Calif. Fish Game 49(4):265–270.
Reish, D. J. 1963b. Further studies on the benthic fauna in a recently constructed boat harbor in southern California. Bull. S. Calif. Acad. Sci. 62(1):23–32.
Reish, D. J. 1964a. Studies on the *Mytilus edulis* community in Alamitos Bay, California: development and destruction of the community. Veliger 6(3):124–131.
Reish, D. J. 1964b. Studies on the *Mytilus edulis* community in Alamitos Bay, California: population variations and discussion of the associated organisms. Veliger 6(4):202–207.
Reish, D. J. 1968. Marine life of Alamitos Bay. Forty-niner Shops, Long Beach, Calif. 92 pp.
Reish, D. J. 1975. Invertebrates, especially benthic annelids in outer Anaheim Bay. *In* E. D. Lane and C. W. Hill, eds., The marine resources of Anaheim Bay. Calif. Dept. Fish Game Fish Bull. 165:73–78.
Reish, D. J., and H. A. Winter. 1954. The ecology of Alamitos Bay, California, with special reference to pollution. Calif. Fish Game 40(2):105–121.
Reish, D. J., T. J. Kauwling, and T. C. Schreiber. 1975. Annotated checklist of the marine invertebrates of Anaheim Bay. *In* E. D. Lane and C. W. Hill, eds., The marine resources of Anaheim Bay. Calif. Dep. Fish Game Fish Bull. 165:41–51.

Scheer, B. T. 1945. The development of marine fouling communities. Biol. Bull. 89(1):102–121.
Seapy, R. R., and C. L. Kitting, 1978. Spatial structure of an intertidal molluscan assemblage on a sheltered sandy beach. Mar. Biol. 46(2):137–145.
Shubin, B. A. 1975. Plants of Anaheim Bay: the algae. *In* E. D. Lane and C. W. Hill, eds., The marine resources of Anaheim Bay. Calif. Dep. Fish Game Fish Bull. 165:35–36.
Speth, J. W., B. M. Browning, K. A. Smith, and E. C. Fullerton. 1977. The natural resources of Anaheim Bay, August, 1976. Calif. Dep. Fish Game, U.S. Wildl. Serv. Coastal Wetlands Ser. 18.
Stevenson, P. W., and K. O. Emergy, 1958. Marshlands at Newport Bay, California, pp. 1–109. *In* Allan Hancock Foundation Publications. Vol. 20. Univ. Southern California Press, Los Angeles.

Tasto, R. N. 1975. Aspects of the biology of the Pacific staghorn sculpin, *Leptocottus armatus*, in Anaheim Bay. *In* E. D. Lane and C. W. Hill, eds., Calif. Dep. Fish Game Fish Bull. 165:123–135.
Trinast, E. M. 1975. Tidal movements and *Acartia* distribution in Newport Bay, California. Estuarine Coastal Mar. Sci. 3(2):165–176.

Vogl, R. J. 1966. Salt marsh vegetation of upper Newport Bay, California. Ecology 47(1):80–87.

CHAPTER 11

Puget Sound

P uget Sound is a large estuarine inlet in the northwest corner of Washington State. Glaciers carved the many small channels, sounds, sills, and inlets of the sound and are responsible for its remarkable depth. The main basin is as deep as 250 m in some areas and is embraced bathymetrically by two shallow sills. The northern sill is located near Admiralty Inlet and the southern sill below the Narrows (Lie, 1968; Strickland, 1983). The water behind these sills in Juan de Fuca Strait and the sills near Admiralty straits and the Narrows is usually quite stable.

The unique topography of the sound as regards its structure and hydrology gives it the characteristics of a fjord (Chapter 2). Vigorous mixing is typical of much of the sound, but mixing is weaker within the main basin except near the two sills.

Mixed, nutrient-rich water enters the basin through the narrows; and highly stratified water, especially in the spring, enters from several freshwater sources in the central and southern sound. The Skagit and Snohomish rivers, which enter the main basin via the Whidbey basin, are the main freshwater sources, and the Duwamish and Puyallup rivers contribute significant amounts of strati-fied water. The less stratified, nutrient-rich narrows water and stratified river waters form two discrete masses of surface water which flow northward side by side until they reach the sill at Admiralty Inlet, where they are mixed with deeper waters. Much of this water is diverted back into the main basin and joins the deep current of cold saline ocean water and flows toward the narrows, where it resurfaces. Water may be recirculated in this manner several times before flowing out of the main basin through the Strait of Juan de Fuca (Strickland, 1983). Refluxing is more common during spring tides than during neap tides (Winter et al., 1975). This unique circulation pattern provides a highly diverse environment within the main basin (Strickland, 1983).

Tides in the sound are mixed and semidiurnal, with a diurnal range of approximately 3.3 m. This variable tidal amplitude results in strong tidal currents (Lie, 1968). Near the sills, tidal currents of up to 5 knots are common, although in the open waters of the main basin tidal currents are generally less than 1 knot (Winter et al., 1975).

Pacific tides affecting the San Juan Archipelago ebb and flow through the Strait of Juan de Fuca. The strongest current is at about midtide. The tidal pattern varies, but the amplitude is about 15 ft (4.57 m), from 12 ft (3.66 m) above mean lower low water (MLLW) to 3 ft (1 m) below MLLW. The salinity of the water is less than 32 ppt, from the surface to a depth of about 150 m (Herlinveaux and Tully, 1961). A sill separates the lower waters of the Juan de Fuca Strait from the waters surrounding the San Juan Archipelago (Figure 11.1).

NUTRIENT CYCLING

Sediment samples taken at 200 m near Richmond Beach revealed the occurrence of denitrification in the sediment. Results indicated that nitrates lost through denitrification were replaced by an unknown biochemical source. There was little or no sulfate reduction at depths below 25 to 30 cm. Normally, interstitial

FIGURE 11.1. Map of Puget Sound, the San Juan Archipelago, and the Strait of Juan de Fuca in the state of Washington.

silica concentrations increase exponentially with depth and approach a constant value. Silica profiles in this study showed a minimum silica concentration in the nitrification zone. This indicated that silica was being precipitated in the nitrification zone. This sink was probably caused by the injection of low-silica bottom water by burrowing benthic organisms.

NO_3 concentrations ranged from $0 \mu g L^{-1}$ (taken from a sample deep in the sediment) to $27.7 \mu m$ (at the sediment surface). NO_2 concentrations ranged from 0 to $2.3 \mu m$ and NH^{4+} concentrations ranged from 0 at the sediment surface to $1980 \mu m$ from a sample taken very deep in the sediment, indicating that oxygenation was occurring at the sediment surface. SO_4^{2-} concentrations ranged from zero from a deep sample to $22.7 \mu g L^{-1}$ from a middepth sample, and $SI(OH)_4$ ranged from 57 at the surface to $818 \mu g L^{-1}$ at middepth. Eh ranged from less than 78 to 225 millivolts (Grundmanis and Murray, 1977).

PRODUCTIVITY

Primary Productivity

The phytoplankton of Puget Sound undergoes intense blooms in the spring, a series of intermittent blooms during the summer and occasional less intense blooms in the fall. Species found in the area are listed in Table 11.2. During these blooms, oxygen concentrations at the surface can reach 150% saturation. Surface nitrate concentrations, usually between 15 and $25 \mu g L^{-1}$, can fall to undetectable levels for 36 to 48 hours. During the winter there is limited plant life (Strickland, 1983). Nevertheless, concentrations of phytoplankton in the sound rarely fall below 0.2 mL of chlorophyll a per cubic meter, even at depth, at any time of the year (Winter et al., 1975).

In the spring, sunlight and surface stratification (due to freshwater runoff) are at their peak, providing ideal conditions for phytoplankton growth. Water entering the main basin through the narrows is vigorously mixed along its route to the main basin. This results in supressed primary production at the narrows. Mixing is also responsible for the delay of blooms until April and May in the sound. Blooms begin in March at areas with similar runoff and sunlight characteristics, such as Long Island Sound. Once water has entered the main basin, vigorous mixing is patchy and limited. Phytoplankton growth is relatively undisturbed and productivity is remarkably high—at least one-third higher than at Long Island Sound. Productivity might be even higher if it were not for the disruptive effect of high runoff, which flushes nascent blooms out of the basin. The stronger tides during the spring also flush out blooms. Primary production at the mouth of the Duwamish River is two-thirds that of the remainder of the main basin, despite nutrient enrichment from sewage effluent, because runoff waters flush out blooms (Strickland, 1983).

The mixing of water prevalent at Admiralty Inlet has several consequences to primary production. Much of the deep water flowing through the main basin is brackish because the fresher surface water has been mixed with the low-nutrient oceanic water. Thus the salinity and nutrient content are lower than would be expected if water came primarily from the Strait of Juan de Fuca. Surface-water stratification, nutrient content, and productivity are lower in late spring and summer. The lower productivity, however, is partially offset by other factors. Downward mixing at the sill carries some of the phytoplankton with it (Table 11.1). The surface concentration of chlorophyll *a* may be less than $15\,mg\,L^{-1}$. The concentration at depth (below 50 m) is often between 0.5 and 1.5 mg of chlorophyll *a* per cubic meter (surface concentration is less than 15 mg of chlorophyll *a* per cubic meter). Cells that survive the journey back to the narrows upwell to the surface along with nutrients, and seed the surface water (Strickland, 1983; Winter et al., 1975).

Phytoplankton were the most important organisms for primary production in the area, even though the blooms were visible only as patches and streaks. The blooms of diatoms were usually greatest in the spring of the year and occurred when the sunlight, nutrients, and temperature were optimum. The best phytoplankton growth occurred at the interface of the nutrient-rich fresh (surface) water and upwelling deeper waters, which also had considerable nutrients. Green stripes in some parts of the sound occurred where two streams of water with different qualities ran side by side. Around the upper part of the sound in late summer these green stripes were found, in some cases, to be due to dinoflagellates (Strickland, 1983).

The year of highest productivity was 1969, when there was bright sun, moderate runoff, and considerable stability of the water. There was a gentle north wind and neap tides were present. This condition produced, on May 10, the highest productivity ever measured in marine phytoplankton; nearly $10\,g\,C$ m^{-2} day^{-1}. The lowest productivity from the area was recorded near the neap-tide period in 1975, when there was very low sun and high runoff and turbulence. An average year for productivity was 1966. During this period the productivity in the sound was estimated to be about $465\,g\,C\,m^{-2}\,yr^{-1}$. The period from April through August usually accounted for about 86% of the yearly productivity, with May generally the most productive month (Strickland, 1983).

The dominant organisms in a spring bloom in 1967 were the centric diatoms, *Skeletonema, Thalassiosira*, and *Chaetoceros*. There are few documented occurrences of flagellates (Strickland, 1983).

The bays of Puget Sound were often not as productive as the main basin. Elliott Bay, for example, received sanitary waste and might be thought to have a much higher nutrient level and more phytoplankton production, but its production rate was only about two-thirds that of the open sound.

Stockner et al. (1979) found that annual production in the waters between the islands of the San Juan Archipelago ranged from 200 to $300\,g\,C\,m^{-2}$ (Figure 11.2). The area surrounding the islands had a rate of productivity lower than $200\,g\,C\,m^{-2}\,yr^{-1}$, while the productivity of nearby areas off Vancouver Island was as high as $511\,g\,C\,m^{-2}$ Figure 11.3, Table 11.1).

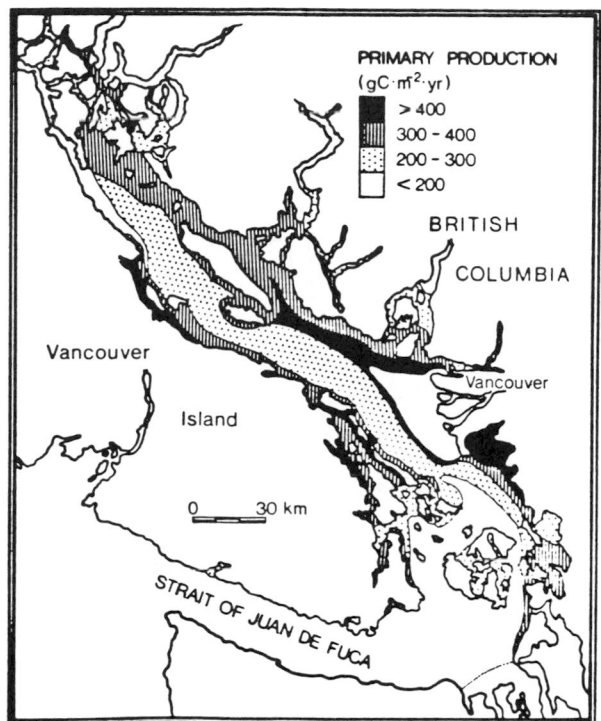

FIGURE 11.2. Generalized spatial pattern of annual phytoplankton production in the Strait of Georgia. (From Stockner et al., 1979, Figure 8.)

Stockner attributed this discrepancy to the incoming colder and more saline oceanic water, creating vertical instability and turbulence in the passages. Phytoplankton production in the San Juan Islands was reduced by such turbulence (Stockner et al., 1979). It was also probable that the presence of sills contributed to the low production in the area. The water behind the sills is typically stable water with constant phytoplankton biomass. Data from the San Juan Islands indicated that sills created a vertical homogeneity in the surrounding waters (Strickland, 1983).

Secondary Productivity
No data were found on secondary productivity in the San Juan Archipelago. In the main basin of Puget Sound, however, Lie (1968) and Lie and Evans (1973) have collected data that may resemble Archipelago conditions.

Central Basin. The standing crop on the soft mud substrate in the middle of the main basin was dominated by the echinoid, *Brisaster townsendi*. *Brisaster*, larger than the other common echinoid species, was represented by the greatest biomass and fewest individuals when all months were considered. The complete

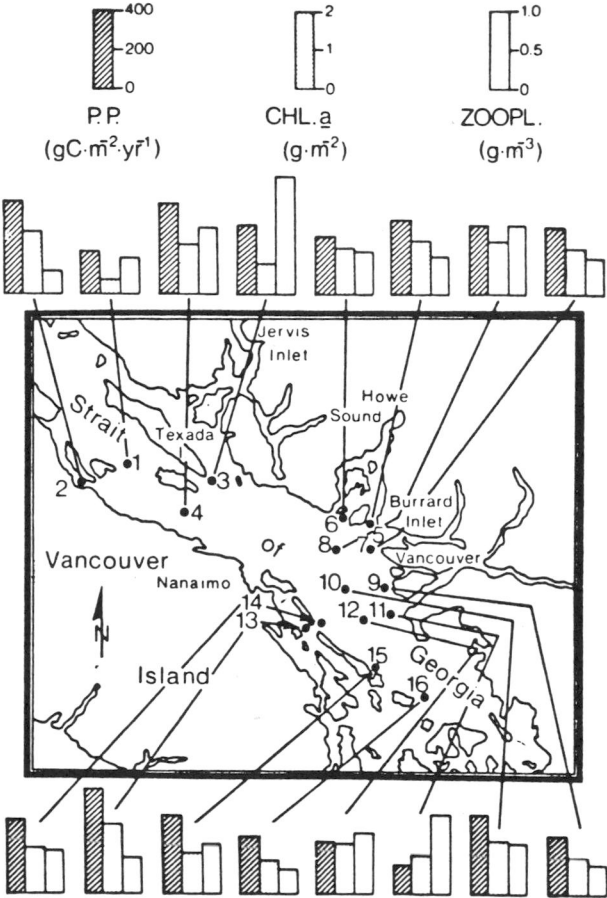

FIGURE 11.3.   Mean annual integrals of phytoplankton production, chlorophyll *a*, and zooplankton biomass by station in the Strait of Georgia. (From Stockner et al., 1979, Figure 5.)

absence of this species from areas with even small portions of sand demonstrated its preference for soft mud substrates. The polychaetes, *Travisia brevos* and *Glycera capitata*, were also dominant in terms of weight (Lie, 1968; Lie and Evans, 1973). Molluscs were fewer in number in January and April. Their biomass was always very low compared to *Brisaster*, but intermediate between the crustacea and the polychaetes other than *Pectinaria*.

Annual production of *Pectinaria*, excluding excretion and mucus production, ranged from 2.02 to 2.798 cm^2 yr^{-1} at the two stations in the main basin. At the station in the central main basin, *Pectinaria* utilized 1.2% of the carbon produced in the surface layers by primary production; 0.6% of the carbon from primary production was passed on to consumers. *Brisaster* utilized 3.2% of the

(*text continues on page 774*)

TABLE 11.1.   *Diatoms Collected at Different Depths in and Near the San Juan Archipelago*
(Diatoms mL⁻¹)

Station: Friday Harbor
Date: 6/23/28
Time:

Diatom	1 m	5 m	10 m	25 m	50 m	75 m	100 m
Chaetoceras debile	3.8	10.6	11.7	11.0	11.4	4.1	1.0
Chaetoceras scolopendra	0.2	1.1		0.1	1.2	0.7	2.2
Paralia sulcata	0.4	1.8	0.7	2.2	3.8	3.4	2.4
Rhizosolenia delicatula	1.5	2.2	3.0	1.5	1.2	1.2	2.3
Rhizosolenia stolterfothii	0.4	1.8	2.3	3.0	1.6	0.4	0.6
Skeletonema costatum	6.8	9.4	6.2	3.4	8.5	7.2	7.4
Thalassiosira condensata	1.8	0.7	1.8	2.3	5.2	1.4	1.6
Thalassiosira decipiens		0.2	0.9	0.4	1.0	0.7	
Thalassiosira nitzschioides	0.6	1.4	1.3	0.4	2.4	0.5	1.1
Thalassiosira nordenskioeldii	0.2	0.4	0.7	0.8	0.8	0.6	0.2
Thalassiosira rotula	1.3	1.6	2.5	1.7	1.7	2.3	0.5

Station: Friday Harbor
Date: 6/30/28
Time:

Diatom	1 m	10 m	25 m	50 m	80 m	130 m
Chaetoceras compressum	13.5	15.7	28.6	5.6	6.7	13.4
Chaetoceras constrictum	1.9	0.7	3.8			1.3
Chaetoceras debile	14.3	27.3	58.5	11.2	16.5	12.3
Chaetoceras decipiens		1.4				0.3
Chaetoceras diadema	2.5	0.5	4.8		1.6	0.9
Chaetoceras didymum			1.3		0.4	
Chaetoceras laciniosum	1.8	0.7	1.4		0.1	
Chaetoceras pseudocrïnitum	0.4	1.2	2.0			0.4
Chaetoceras scolopendra	0.6	0.8	3.2	2.2	2.1	1.9
Eucampea zoodiacus		2.3			0.4	1.0
Leptocylindrus danicus	1.1	1.5	1.7			0.5
Nitzschia seriata	3.8	0.4	2.0	1.1	0.5	1.1
Paralia sulcata	2.2	1.3	1.9	0.4	1.1	2.5
Rhizosolenia stolterfothii	1.0	1.0	2.8	0.2	0.8	0.6
Skeletonema costatum	103.7	63.3	60.7	6.5	23.9	71.6
Thalassiosira condensata	6.3	9.4	9.6	3.0	1.9	3.7
Thalassiosira nitzschioides	2.5	1.8	2.4	0.7	1.2	0.8
Thalassiosira nordenskioeldii	2.0	0.9	1.2	0.3	1.2	0.3
Thalassiosira rotula	8.5	9.5	11.9	7.7	4.6	4.5

Continued

TABLE 11.1.   (*Continued*)
Station: San Juan Channel
Date: 7/13/28
Time:

Diatom	1 m	5 m	10 m	20 m	35 m.	50 m	100 m	225 m
Biddulphia longicruris				1.2				
Chaetoceras affinis	0.6	1.2	0.3			0.6		
Chaetoceras compressum		1.1	0.9		0.5	0.5		
Chaetoceras constrictum				1.7	0.2	2.0	0.2	
Chaetoceras debile	0.6		0.4			1.5		
Chaetoceras lorenzianum	1.4	2.7	1.4	1.9	2.6	1.5	0.6	
Chaetoceras scolopendra	1.9	2.7	1.1	0.8	1.8	1.1		
Nitzschia seriata	1.8	0.4	0.6	161.0	3.7	2.5	0.7	0.6
Paralia sulcata	0.5	0.3	0.9	1.0	0.7	0.7	0.4	2.0
Rhizosolenia semispina				1.2				
Skeletonema costatum	7.6	12.3	6.1	13.8	4.2	7.4	0.6	9.2
Thalassiosira condensata	0.4	0.3	1.1	0.3		4.4	0.2	
Thalassiosira nitzschioides	0.3	0.9	0.5	2.2	0.8	3.1	0.2	1.4
Thalassiosira rotula	0.5	0.4	1.2	0.2	0.9	0.7	1.5	

Station: San Juan Channel
Date: 7/11/28
Time:

Diatom	0 m	5 m	20 m	100 m	200 m
Ceratulina bergonii	1.2				
Chaetoceras affinis	1.6	1.3			
Chaetoceras compressum	7.4	5.3			
Chaetoceras constrictum	1.3	0.6			
Chaetoceras diadema	2.6	0.4			
Chaetoceras didymum	1.7				
Chaetoceras laciniosum	1.0	1.1	0.4		
Chaetoceras lorenzianum	3.7	1.1			
Chaetoceras scolopendra	17.8	9.4			
Eucampea zoodiacus	3.7				
Nitzschia seriata	5.0	1.2	1.8	0.6	0.7
Skeletonema costatum	37.0	55.8	2.9	3.0	5.9
Thalassiosira condensata	0.6		1.2		
Thalassiosira nitzschioides	1.7	2.5	3.9	0.4	0.6
Thalassiosira nordenskioeldii	0.7	1.1	0.2		
Thalassiosira rotula	1.6	0.3	1.3	0.3	0.4

TABLE 11.1. (*Continued*)
Station: East Sound/Southern
Date: 7/21/28
Time: 4:00 P.M.

Diatom	1 m	5 m	10 m	20 m	40 m
Asterionella japonica					
Biddulphia longicruris	6.5	3.3	1.9	1.7	0.5
Chaetoceras affinis					
Chaetoceras approximatum					
Chaetoceras compressum					
Chaetoceras constrictum	1.9	0.8	1.6	3.7	
Chaetoceras convolutum	4.0	1.4	0.7		
Chaetoceras debile	10.2	6.8	5.7	9.0	0.6
Chaetoceras decipiens					
Chaetoceras densum					
Chaetoceras diadema	4.6	2.3	0.5	1.5	
Chaetoceras didymum					
Chaetoceras laciniosum					
Chaetoceras lorenzianum	0.6	1.1	1.4		
Chaetoceras scolopendra					
Ditylum brightwelli					
Eucampea zoodiacus	13.1	2.2	3.2	0.5	
Leptocylindrus danicus					
Nitzschia closterium	1.3	0.4	0.5	0.1	
Nitzschia longissima	5.6	1.1	0.7	0.5	0.1
Nitzschia seriata	9.1	4.1	1.4	0.8	0.6
Paralia sulcata	1.6	1.2		2.6	2.5
Rhizosolenia delicatula					
Rhizosolenia faeroenis (i.e., *Rhizosolenia fragilissima*)					
Rhizosolenia semispina	1.1	0.2			
Rhizosolenia stolterfothii	0.3	1.0	0.5	0.1	0.8
Skeletonema costatum	3.9	5.0	4.2	3.8	2.4
Stephanopyxis palmeriana					
Thalassiosira condensata	23.5	37.1	30.2	26.2	7.5
Thalassiosira decipiens					
Thalassiosira nitzschioides					
Thalassiosira nordenskioeldii	4.5	5.9	1.9	4.0	0.7
Thalassiosira rotula	2.3	4.2	3.5	4.3	2.8

Continued

TABLE 11.1.   (*Continued*)
Station: East Sound/Southern
Date: 7/13/28
Time:

Diatom	1 m	5 m	10 m	20 m
Asterionella japonica				
Biddulphia longicruris	3.9	48.4	77.5	4.1
Chaetoceras affinis			10.0	
Chaetoceras approximatum				
Chaetoceras compressum		0.2	17.0	2.0
Chaetoceras constrictum		41.2	150.0	58.3
Chaetoceras convolutum	0.1	7.4	49.0	
Chaetoceras debile		3.8	35.0	18.3
Chaetoceras decipiens		1.5		
Chaetoceras densum		0.8	2.0	
Chaetoceras diadema		29.8	103.0	32.3
Chaetoceras didymum			2.0	0.6
Chaetoceras laciniosum			4.0	1.2
Chaetoceras lorenzianum		1.2	7.0	0.4
Chaetoceras scolopendra		2.4		7.7
Ditylum brightwelli				
Eucampea zoodiacus	1.7	18.3	14.5	16.8
Leptocylindrus danicus	0.6	1.7	0.3	12.6
Nitzschia closterium			3.0	
Nitzschia longissima	21.2	17.0	48.0	8.4
Nitzschia seriata	44.1	64.1	290.0	190.3
Paralia sulcata			34.0	
Rhizosolenia delicatula	1.1	1.1		0.3
Rhizosolenia faeroenis (i.e., *Rhizosolenia fragilissima*)				
Rhizosolenia semispina	0.7	4.7	21.0	2.9
Rhizosolenia stolterfothii		1.5	3.0	0.6
Skeletonema costatum		2.9	10.0	
Stephanopyxis palmeriana	1.3	1.5	2.4	7.5
Thalassiosira condensata	4.7	44.0	108.2	4.6
Thalassiosira decipiens				
Thalassiosira nitzschioides	0.1	4.7	3.1	
Thalassiosira nordenskioeldii	2.5	13.6	6.9	9.0
Thalassiosira rotula	0.5	1.0	8.2	0.2

TABLE 11.1. (*Continued*)
Station: East Sound/Southern
Date: 8/8/28
Time: 4:00 P.M.

Diatom	1 m	5 m	10 m	20 m
Asterionella japonica	9.0	1.2	4.8	7.7
Biddulphia longicruris	10.0	1.5	0.5	
Chaetoceras affinis				
Chaetoceras approximatum	23.0	0.8	3.9	2.7
Chaetoceras compressum				2.9
Chaetoceras constrictum		1.6	3.8	1.3
Chaetoceras convolutum				
Chaetoceras debile	26.0	8.9	37.0	28.2
Chaetoceras decipiens		1.5	2.5	7.1
Chaetoceras densum				
Chaetoceras diadema	4.0	0.5	3.5	1.5
Chaetoceras didymum				
Chaetoceras laciniosum	4.0		0.5	0.2
Chaetoceras lorenzianum	11.0	1.3	4.2	4.2
Chaetoceras scolopendra				
Ditylum brightwelli	28.0	6.6	5.3	3.1
Eucampea zoodiacus	109.0	16.4	53.8	17.4
Leptocylindrus danicus				
Nitzschia closterium	5.0	0.9	1.5	1.9
Nitzschia longissima	1.0	0.2	0.2	0.3
Nitzschia seriata	3.0	1.6	2.8	2.3
Paralia sulcata				
Rhizosolenia delicatula				
Rhizosolenia faeroenis (i.e., *Rhizosolenia fragilissima*)	5.0	0.2	0.5	0.6
Rhizosolenia semispina				
Rhizosolenia stolterfothii	9.0	2.0	2.2	3.5
Skeletonema costatum	129.0	20.1	17.0	39.3
Stephanopyxis plameriana				
Thalassiosira condensata	4.0	0.3	0.5	1.5
Thalassiosira decipiens			0.2	1.0
Thalassiosira nitzschioides	3.7	7.2	16.3	15.2
Thalassiosira nordenskioeldii				
Thalassiosira rotula				

Continued

710   RIVERS OF THE UNITED STATES

TABLE 11.1. (Continued)
Station: East Sound/Middle
Date: 7/21/28
Time: 2:00 P.M.

Diatom	1 m	5 m	10 m	25 m
Biddulphia longicruris		9.7	3.2	1.0
Chaetoceras constrictum		0.5	1.6	2.9
Chaetoceras convolutum		1.3	1.9	0.2
Chaetoceras debile		13.3	4.0	5.1
Chaetoceras densum		4.8	1.6	
Chaetoceras diadema	0.2	0.7	1.5	0.6
Eucampea zoodiacus		35.1	3.9	3.1
Nitzschia longissima	11.3	6.1	3.0	0.8
Nitzschia seriata	0.6	13.7	7.7	1.4
Paralia sulcata	0.4		1.1	6.1
Rhizosolenia semispina	1.3	2.6	0.5	0.1
Rhizosolenia stolterfothii		2.1		
Thalassiosira condensata	2.9	3.1	0.9	4.0
Thalassiosira nitzschioides	0.1	1.2	0.1	1.2
Thalassiosira nordenskioeldii	1.1	1.3	1.1	1.4
Thalassiosira rotula	0.1	0.5	0.2	1.8

Station: East Sound/Middle
Date: 8/8/28
Time: 6:35 A.M.

Diatom	1 m	5 m	10 m	20 m
Asterionella japonica	13.0	0.5	0.7	3.7
Biddulphia longicruris	4.0		1.7	0.2
Ceratulina bergonii				
Chaetoceras affinis				
Chaetoceras approximatum	10.0	2.3	3.4	0.4
Chaetoceras compressum	4.0	1.7	1.7	1.3
Chaetoceras constrictum	1.0		0.9	7.1
Chaetoceras convolutum				
Chaetoceras debile	18.0	4.3	12.2	43.6
Chaetoceras decipiens	2.0		1.5	1.6
Chaetoceras densum				
Chaetoceras diadema	5.0	1.4	2.3	0.2
Chaetoceras didymum			0.6	1.2
Chaetoceras laciniosum				
Chaetoceras lorenzianum	3.0	0.9	3.7	2.5
Chaetoceras pseudocrinitum				
Chaetoceras scolopendra				
Chaetoceras secondum				
Chaetoceras teres				
Coscinodiscus exentricus				
Ditylum brightwelli	20.0	3.6	3.6	5.0
Eucampea zoodiacus	106.0	11.8	21.3	15.6
Leptocylindrus danicus	3.0	0.4		0.4
Nitzschia closterium	8.0	1.6	1.0	0.8
Nitzschia delicatissima				

TABLE 11.1. (Continued)

Diatom	1 m	5 m	10 m	20 m
Nitzschia longissima	3.0	0.3	1.0	0.1
Nitzschia seriata	9.0	0.4	2.1	3.9
Paralia sulcata ᐧ		1.4		3.0
Rhizosolenia delicatula				
Rhizosolenia faeroenis (i.e., Rhizosolenia fragilissima)				
Rhizosolenia semispina				
Rhizosolenia stolterfothii	4.0		1.3	
Skeletonema costatum	70.0	12.1	23.0	31.9
Stephanopyxis palmeriana				
Thalassiosira condensata	5.0	0.1	0.8	0.5
Thalassiosira decipiens			2.1	5.3
Thalassiosira nitzschioides	30.0	17.5	16.1	18.0
Thalassiosira nordenskioeldii				
Thalassiosira rotula	2.0	0.1	0.2	0.1

Station: East Sound/Northern
Date: 7/21/28
Time: 11:00 P.M.

Diatom	1 m	5 m	10 m	20 m
Asterionella japonica				
Biddulphia longicruris		27.3	1.1	
Chaetoceras approximatum				
Chaetoceras compressum				
Chaetoceras constrictum		1.5	0.6	1.6
Chaetoceras convolutum		1.2	1.5	1.1
Chaetoceras debile	0.4	12.9	4.1	2.1
Chaetoceras diadema		0.9	1.1	5.8
Chaetoceras laciniosum				
Chaetoceras lorenzianum				
Chaetoceras scolopendra				
Ditylum brightwelli				
Eucampea zoodiacus		6.9	5.6	3.5
Leptocylindrus danicus				
Nitzschia closterium				
Nitzschia delicatissima				
Nitzschia longissima	16.8	9.2	1.9	1.1
Nitzschia seriata	0.1	13.2		0.6
Paralia sulcata				
Rhizosolenia semispina	0.9	2.9	0.7	
Rhizosolenia stolterfothii				
Skeletonema costatum		0.9	5.8	0.5
Stephanopyxis plameriana				
Thalassiosira condensata	1.3	0.4	1.2	2.5
Thalassiosira decipiens				
Thalassiosira nitzschioides		1.0	1.8	0.9
Thalassiosira rotula		0.6	1.3	2.4

Continued

TABLE 11.1.   (*Continued*)
Station: East Sound/Northern
Date: 8/8/28
Time: 5:30 P.M.

Diatom	1 m	5 m	10 m	20 m
Asterionella japonica	6.0		0.3	2.9
Biddulphia longicruris	3.0		0.2	
Chaetoceras approximatum	169.0			
Chaetoceras compressum	14.0			0.9
Chaetoceras constrictum	52.0		1.0	
Chaetoceras convolutum				
Chaetoceras debile	93.0	0.3	1.6	11.2
Chaetoceras diadema	51.0	0.8	1.1	1.7
Chaetoceras laciniosum	6.0			0.1
Chaetoceras lorenzianum	11.0	2.2	1.3	2.6
Chaetoceras scolopendra	16.0			1.2
Ditylum brightwelli	5.0	2.6	1.3	0.7
Eucampea zoodiacus	36.0	3.2	1.1	13.6
Leptocylindrus danicus	3.0	0.5	0.4	3.0
Nitzschia closterium	1.0	1.4	1.9	1.1
Nitzschia delicatissima			0.6	1.1
Nitzschia longissima	3.0	0.4		0.5
Nitzschia seriata	1.0	0.9	0.6	3.6
Paralia sulcata		0.4	1.6	1.2
Rhizosolenia semispina				
Rhizosolenia stolterfothii		0.2	1.2	1.3
Skeletonema costatum	162.0	2.8		19.2
Stephanopyxis palmeriana				
Thalassiosira condensata	4.0		0.5	0.1
Thalassiosira decipiens		1.2	1.7	1.5
Thalassiosira nitzschioides	13.0	10.8	11.7	12.1
Thalassiosira rotula				

TABLE 11.1. (*Continued*)
Station: Strait of San Juan deFuca
Date: 7/28/28
Time: 1:45 P.M.

Diatom	1 m	10 m	25 m	50 m	100 m
Asterionella japonica	9.0	4.4	3.0	0.6	0.5
Biddulphia longicruris	2.0				
Ceratulina bergonii					
Chaetoceras affinis		11.2	0.3		
Chaetoceras approximatum	21.0	16.3			
Chaetoceras compressum	28.0	32.7	0.3		
Chaetoceras constrictum	17.0	12.7	1.0		0.1
Chaetoceras convolutum		1.3			
Chaetoceras debile	48.0	49.3	4.1	0.3	
Chaetoceras decipiens					
Chaetoceras densum					
Chaetoceras diadema	33.0	23.1	1.2	0.4	
Chaetoceras didymum	2.0	8.8	0.6		
Chaetoceras laciniosum	18.0	11.6	3.5	0.1	0.9
Chaetoceras lorenzianum	26.0	10.8	2.5	0.6	
Chaetoceras pseudocrinitum		2.6			
Chaetoceras scolopendra	43.0	169.3	1.3	0.8	0.2
Chaetoceras secondum	27.0	7.5	0.4		
Chaetoceras teres					
Coscinodiscus exentricus					
Ditylum brightwelli	8.0	0.5	0.8		
Eucampea zoodiacus	48.0	8.1	4.2	0.6	
Leptocylindrus danicus					
Nitzschia closterium	9.0	1.8	0.9	0.2	0.5
Nitzschia delicatissima		1.6	0.9	0.1	
Nitzschia longissima	1.0	0.3	0.2		
Nitzschia seriata	9.0	2.8	1.2	0.3	0.2
Paralia sulcata		0.8	0.2	1.0	1.6
Rhizosolenia delicatula					
Rhizosolenia faeroenis (i.e., *Rhizosolenia fragilissima*)					
Rhizosolenia semispina					
Rhizosolenia stolterfothii	2.0		0.5		
Skeletonema costatum	445.0	128.7	41.4	10.3	3.9
Thalassiosira condensata	38.0	1.2	3.4		
Thalassiosira decipiens	2.0	4.9	6.9	2.3	3.1
Thalassiosira nitzschioides	24.0	117.0	6.1	0.9	0.6
Thalassiosira nordenskioeldii	17.0	0.2	1.0	0.4	0.1
Thalassiosira rotula	31.0	6.4	2.3	1.0	0.3

Continued

Station: Strait of San Juan deFuca
Date: 7/28/28
Time:

Diatom	1 m	10 m	25 m	50 m	100 m	150 m
Asterionella japonica	5.5	78.0	90.0	3.7		
Biddulphia longicruris	4.5	0.1	2.0			0.1
Ceratulina bergonii	5.0	0.5	10.0	0.3		
Chaetoceras affinis		2.4	51.0	1.8	0.3	0.5
Chaetoceras approximatum		10.9	134.0	6.9	1.0	0.9
Chaetoceras compressum	2.0	4.3	58.0	3.1	0.4	0.2
Chaetoceras constrictum	2.0	14.6	57.0	5.2	0.2	0.5
Chaetoceras convolutum						
Chaetoceras debile	6.0	7.4	59.0	9.4	0.3	
Chaetoceras decipiens						
Chaetoceras densum						
Chaetoceras diadema	2.0	2.7	55.0	4.9	0.3	0.2
Chaetoceras didymum	1.0	2.4	12.0	2.2		
Chaetoceras laciniosum	16.5	5.3	19.0	2.8		
Chaetoceras lorenzianum		6.5	33.0	3.7	1.2	0.3
Chaetoceras pseudocrinitum			4.0			
Chaetoceras scolopendra	6.0	3.6	114.0	29.3	1.7	0.7
Chaetoceras secondum		4.2	29.0	0.2		0.4
Chaetoceras teres			3.0	0.3		
Coscinodiscus exentricus	1.5	0.2	0.2	0.2	0.1	
Ditylum brightwelli	10.0	5.6	3.6	0.7	0.1	0.1
Eucampea zoodiacus	35.0	24.3	9.7	9.2		0.8
Leptocylindrus danicus	2.0	2.6				0.3
Nitzschia closterium	9.0	2.5	25.0	0.4	0.5	0.3
Nitzschia delicatissima	9.5	0.4	6.0	0.2		
Nitzschia longissima	1.5	0.4	3.0	0.1	0.1	
Nitzschia seriata	8.0	1.3	7.0	2.4	0.6	
Paralia sulcata				0.6	1.0	3.4
Rhizosolenia delicatula	6.0	4.7	5.0	0.7	1.2	0.3
Rhizosolenia faeroenis (i.e.,						
Rhizosolenia fragilissima)						
Rhizosolenia semispina						
Rhizosolenia stolterfothii	3.5	0.6	2.0	0.1		
Skeletonema costatum	371.5	446.0	579.0	47.5	18.6	12.0
Thalassiosira condensata	21.0	14.7	10.0	1.5		
Thalassiosira decipiens	7.0		20.0	0.4	0.6	4.4
Thalassiosira nitzschioides	14.0	2.7	19.0	1.9	0.8	1.0
Thalassiosira nordenskioeldii	11.0	2.3	7.0	0.2		
Thalassiosira rotula	15.0	11.4	19.0	3.0	0.9	0.1

Source: Gran and Thompson (1930).

TABLE 11.2. *Species of the Puget Sound*

Species	Habitat Unknown	San Juan Islands	Near Seattle	Habitat Location[a]	Mud	Mixed Sediment	Sand	Shell, Gravel, or Cobble	Rocky Substrate or Boulders	Tide Pools	On Macrophytes Pilings, Reefs, Floats, etc.
DIVISION BACILLARIOPHYTA											
Class Bacillariophyceae											
Order Fragilariales											
Family Fragilariaceae											
Asterionella japonica	×	×		p							
A. kariana	×	×		p							
Dimeregramma minor		×		b				×			
Fragilaria sp.		×		b				×			
Fragilaria construens var. *venter*		×		b				×			
F. cylindrus		×		b				×			
F. pinnata		×		b				×			
F. pinnata var. *lancettula*		×		b				×			
F. striatula		×		p, i			×				
F. striatula var. *californica*		×		b				×			
F. virescens var. *subsalina*		×		b				×			
Grammatophora angulosa		×		b				×			
Licmophora ebrenbergii f. *grunowii*	×	×									
L. gracilis	×	×									
Opephora pacifica		×		b				×			
O. marina		×		b				×			
Plagiogramma staurophorum		×		b				×			
Rhabdonema arcuatum var. *robusta*		×		b				×			
Rhaphoneis amphiceros		×		b				×			
Synedra sp.		×		b				×			
Synedra camtscatica		×		b				×			
S. camtscatica var. *finmarchica*		×		b				×			
S. fasciculata		×		b				×			
S. tabulata		×		b				×			
Tabellaria flocculosa		×		b				×			
Thallasiothrix nitzschoides	×	×		p							
T. longissima	×	×		p							
Order Eunotiales											
Family Eunotiaceae											
Eunotia monodon var. *major*		×		b			×				
Order Achnanthales											
Family Achnanthaceae											
Achnanthes sp.		×		b			×				

[a]b, benthic; o, in open water; n, in top 5 cm of water (neuston); s, subtidal; i, intertidal; p, plankton; mllw, mean lower low water.

Continued

TABLE 11.2.   (Continued)

Species	Habitat Unknown	San Juan Islands	Near Seattle	Habitat Location[a]	Mud	Mixed Sediment	Sand	Shell, Gravel, or Cobble	Rocky Substrate or Boulders	Tide Pools	On Macrophytes Pilings, Reefs, Floats, etc.
Achnanthes brevipes		×		b, i			×	×			
A. diplopunctata		×		b			×				
A. groenlandica		×		b			×				
A. haukiana		×		b			×				
A. lanceolata f. *capitata*		×		b			×				
A. longipes		×		i							
A. obliqua		×		b			×				
A. stromi		×		b			×				
Cocconeis californica		×		b			×				
C. costata		×		b			×				
C. costata var. *pacifica*		×		b			×				
C. disculus		×		b			×				
C. distans		×		b			×				
C. maxima		×		b			×				
C. pellucida		×		b			×				
C. placentula		×		b			×				
C. placentula var. *euglypta*		×		b			×				
C. scutellum		×		b			×				
Rhoicosphenia curvata		×		b			×				
Order Naviculales											
Family Gomphonemaceae											
Gomphonema kamtschaticum		×		b			×				
G. olivaceum		×		b			×				
Family Naviculaceae											
Amphipleura rutilans		×	×	b, i			×				
Amphiprora alata		×		i			×	×			
Amphora abludens		×		b			×				
A. acutiuscula		×		b			×				
A. angusta		×		b			×				
A. coffeaeformis		×		b			×				
A. cymbifera		×		b			×				
A. holsatica		×		b			×				
A. laevis		×		b, i			×	×			
A. laevis var. *laevissima*		×		b			×				
A. libyca var. *baltica*		×		b			×				
A. lineolata		×		b			×				
A. macilenta		×		b			×				
A. mexicana		×		b			×				
A. ocellata		×		b			×				
A. proteus var. *oculata*		×		b			×				
A. rutilans	×		×	i							

[a]b, benthic; o, in open water; n, in top 5 cm of water (neuston); s, subtidal; i, intertidal; p, plankton; mllw, mean lower low water.

TABLE 11.2. *(Continued)*

Species	Habitat Unknown	San Juan Islands	Near Seattle	Habitat Location[a]	Mud	Mixed Sediment	Sand	Shell, Gravel, or Cobble	Rocky Substrate or Boulders	Tide Pools	On Macrophytes Pilings, Reefs, Floats, etc.
A. stauropohora		×		b			×				
Caloneis brevis		×		b			×				
Diploneis interrupta		×		b			×				
D. subovalis		×		b			×				
Gyrosigma arcticum		×		b			×				
G. fasciola		×		b			×				
Navicula sp.		×		i			×	×			
Navicula abunda		×		b			×				
N. aequorea		×		b			×				
N. agnita		×		b			×				
N. aspera		×		i				×			
N. cancellata		×		b		×					
N. cluthensis forma rostrata		×		b		×					
N. crucicula f. *rostrata*		×		b		×					
N. crucifera		×		b		×					
N. cryptocephala		×		b		×					
N. digito-radiata		×		b		×					
N. directa		×		b, p, i		×					
N. distans	×	×		p							
N. diversistriata		×		b		×					
N. finmarchia		×		b		×					
N. flanatica		×		b		×					
N. forcipata var. *densistriata*		×		b		×					
N. gelida		×		b		×					
N. gracilis		×		b		×					
N. granulata		×		b		×					
N. hamulifera		×		b		×					
N. insociabilis		×		b		×					
N. jamalinensis		×		b		×					
N. kriegeri		×		b		×					
N. lanceolata		×		b		×					
N. litoricola		×		b		×					
N. longa		×		b		×					
N. lyra		×		b		×					
N. menisculus var. *schumanni*		×		b		×					
N. ramosissima var. *ramosissima*	×		×	i							×
N. rhombica		×		b			×				
Navicula rhyncocephala		×		i			×	×			
N. rhyncocephala var. *elongata*		×		b			×				
N. ramosissima var. *ramoissima*	×		×	i							
N. rostellata		×		b			×				

[a] b, benthic; o, in open water; n, in top 5 cm of water (neuston); s, subtidal; i, intertidal; p, plankton; mllw, mean lower low water.

Continued

TABLE 11.2. (*Continued*)

Species	Habitat Unknown	San Juan Islands	Near Seattle	Habitat Location[a]	Mud	Mixed Sediment	Sand	Shell, Gravel, or Cobble	Rocky Substrate or Boulders	Tide Pools	On Macrophytes Pilings, Reefs, Floats, etc.
N. salinarum		×		b			×				
N. similis		×		b			×				
N. subinflatoides		×		b			×				
Pinnularia ambigua		×		b			×				
P. cruciformis		×		b			×				
P. quadratarea		×		b			×				
Pleurosigma sp.		×		b			×				
Pleurosigma balticum		×		i			×	×			
P. fasciola	×	×		p							
P. formosum		×		i			×				
P. strigosum		×		b			×				
Stauroneis amphioxys		×		b			×				
S. dubitabilis		×		b			×				
S. elata		×		b			×				
S. wislouchii		×		b			×				
Trachyneis aspera		×		b			×				
Tropidoneis anarctica	×	×		p							
T. anarctica var. *polyplasta*	×	×		p							
T. vitrea		×		b			×				
Order Bacillariales											
Family Coscinodiscaceae											
Actinocyclus ehrenbergii	×	×		p, i							
Arachnoidiscus ehrenbergi		×		p, i							×
Aulacodiscus oregonus	×	×		p, i							
Coscinodiscus sp.		×		b			×				
Coscinodiscus angstii	×	×		p							
C. angstii var. *granulomarginata*	×	×		p							
C. argus		×		b			×				
C. centralis	×	×		p							
C. centralis var. *pacifica*	×	×		p							
C. concinnus	×	×		p							
C. curvatulus		×		b, p			×				
C. divisus		×		b			×				
C. excentricus	×	×		p							
C. granii	×	×		p							
C. kutzingii		×		b			×				
C. nitidus		×		b			×				
Coscinosira radiatus		×		b, p			×				
C. rothii		×		b			×				
C. stellaris	×	×		p							
C. sublineatus		×		b			×				

[a]b, benthic; o, in open water; n, in top 5 cm of water (neuston); s, subtidal; i, intertidal; p, plankton; mllw, mean lower low water.

TABLE 11.2. (*Continued*)

Species	Habitat Unknown	San Juan Islands	Near Seattle	Habitat Location[a]	Mud	Mixed Sediment	Sand	Shell, Gravel, or Cobble	Rocky Substrate or Boulders	Tide Pools	On Macrophytes Pilings, Reefs, Floats, etc.
C. wailesii	×	×		p							
C. polychorda	×	×		p							
Hyalodiscus subtilis	×	×		p, i							
Melosira juergensi	×	×		i							
M. moniliformis	×	×		p, i							
M. numuloides		×		i			×	×			
Melosira sp.	×		×	i							
Paralia sulcata	×	×		p, i							
Planktoniella sol	×	×		p							
Skeletonema costatum	×	×		p							
Stephanopyxis palmeriana	×	×		p							
S. nipponica	×	×		p							
Thalassiosira aestivalis	×	×		p							
T. bioculata	×	×		p							
T. condensata	×	×		p							
T. decipiens	×	×		p							
T. eccentrica		×		b		×					
T. nitzschoides	×	×		p							
T. nordenskioeldii		×		b, p		×					
T. pacifica	×	×		p							
T. rotula	×	×		p							
Family Actinodiscaceae											
Actinoptychus heliopelta		×		i			×	×			
A. senarius		×		b			×				
A. splendens		×		p, i			×	×			
A. undulatus	×	×		p, i							
Asteromphalus heptactis		×		p	×						
Family Auliscaceae											
Auliscus caelatus		×		b			×				
Family Bacillariaceae											
Nitzschia closterum		×		p, i			×	×			
N. constricta		×		b			×				
N. delicatissima	×	×		p							
N. distans		×		b			×				
N. kutzingiana		×		b			×				
N. longissima		×		p, i				×			
N. palea		×		b			×				
N. paradoxa	×	×		i							
N. seriata	×	×		p							
Order Surirellales											
Family Surirellaceae											

[a]b, benthic; o, in open water; n, in top 5 cm of water (neuston); s, subtidal; i, intertidal; p, plankton; mllw, mean lower low water.

Continued

TABLE 11.2.   (*Continued*)

Species	Habitat Unknown	San Juan Islands	Near Seattle	Habitat Location[a]	Mud	Mixed Sediment	Sand	Shell, Gravel, or Cobble	Rocky Substrate or Boulders	Tide Pools	On Macrophytes Pilings, Reefs, Floats, etc.
Surirella fastuosa		×		i				×			
S. ovata		×		b			×				
Order Rhizosoleniales											
Family Corethronaceae											
Corethron hystrix	×	×		p							
Family Leptocylindraceae											
Dactyliosolen mediterraneus	×	×		p							
Lauderia annulata	×	×		p							
Leptocylindrus danicus	×	×		p							
L. minimus	×	×		p							
Family Rhizosoleniaceae											
Rhizosolenia alata	×	×		p							
R. delicatula	×	×		p							
R. semispina	×	×		p							
R. setigera	×	×		p							
R. stolterfothii	×	×		p							
R. styliformis	×	×		p							
Family Bacteriastraceae											
Bacteriastrum delicatum	×	×		p							
Order Biddulphiales											
Family Biddulphiaceae											
Biddulphia sp.	×	×		p							
Biddulphia artica	×	×		p, i							
B. (Odontella) aurita		×	×	p, i							
B. laevis	×	×		p, i							
B. longicruris	×	×		p							
B. (Odontella) obtusa	×	×		p							
B. roperiana	×	×		p, i							
Ceratulina bergonii	×	×		p							
Ditylum brightwelli	×	×		p							
Eucampia zodiacus	×	×		p							
Triceratium pentacrinus		×		b			×				
T. pentacrinus f. *quadratum*		×		b			×				
Trigonium alternans		×		b			×				
Family Anaulaceae											
Anaulus balticus		×		b			×				
Family Chaetoceraceae											
Chaetoceros sp.	×	×		p							
Chaetoceros affine	×	×		p							
C. anastomosans var. *externa*	×	×		p							
C. approximatus	×	×		p							

[a]b, benthic; o, in open water; n, in top 5 cm of water (neuston); s, subtidal; i, intertidal; p, plankton; mllw, mean lower low water.

TABLE 11.2. (*Continued*)

Species	Habitat Unknown	San Juan Islands	Near Seattle	Habitat Location[a]	Mud	Mixed Sediment	Sand Shell, Gravel, or Cobble	Rocky Substrate or Boulders	Tide Pools	On Macrophytes Pilings, Reefs, Floats, etc.
C. atlanticus	×	×		p						
C. compressum	×	×		p						
C. concavicornis	×	×		p						
C. constrictum	×	×		p						
C. convolutum	×	×		p						
C. crucifer	×	×		p						
C. danicus	×	×		p						
C. debile	×	×		p						
C. decipiens	×	×		p						
Chaetoceros densum	×	×		p						
C. diadema	×	×		p						
C. didymum	×	×		p						
C. eibenii	×	×		p						
C. gracilis	×	×		p						
C. laciniosum	×	×		p						
C. lorenzianum	×	×		p						
C. psuedocrinitum	×	×		p						
C. radicans	×	×		p						
C. scolpendra	×	×		p						
C. secundum	×	×		p						
C. seiracanthus	×	×		p						
C. similis	×	×		p						
C. socialis	×	×		p						
C. teres	×	×		p						
C. vanheurckii	×	×		p						
DIVISION CHLOROPHYTA										
Class Chlorophycaeae										
Order Chlorococcales										
Family Endosphaeraceae										
Chlorochytruim inclusum	×		×	i, s						
Order Ulotrichales										
Family Ulotrichaceae										
Ulothrix flacca	×		×	i						
U. subflacca	×		×	i						
Family Chaetophoraceae										
Phaeophila polymorpha			×	s						×
Family Gomontiaceae										
Gomontia polyrhiza	×		×	i						
Family Ulvaceae										
Blidingia minima var. *minima*	×		×	i						

[a]b, benthic; o, in open water; n, in top 5 cm of water (neuston); s, subtidal; i, intertidal; p, plankton; mllw, mean lower low water.

Continued

TABLE 11.2.   (Continued)

Species	Habitat Unknown	San Juan Islands	Near Seattle	Habitat Location[a]	Mud	Mixed Sediment	Sand	Shell, Gravel, or Cobble	Rocky Substrate or Boulders	Tide Pools	On Macrophytes Pilings, Reefs, Floats, etc.
Enteromorpha compressa	×		×	i							
E. clathrata	×		×	i							
E. intestinalis		×	×	b, s					×		
E. intestinalis var. *clavata*	×		×	i							
E. intestinalis var. *cylindracea*	×		×	i							
E. intestinalis var. *intestinalis*	×		×	i							
E. linza		×	×	b, s, i					×		
E. tubulosa	×		×	i							
Monostroma sp.			×	i					×		
Monostroma arcticum	×		×	i							
M. fracatum	×		×	s, i							
Ulva sp.			×	i					×		
Ulva expansa			×	i, s					×		
U. fenestrata			×	i					×		
U. lactuca			×	i					×		
U. rigida			×	i							
U. vexata	×		×	i							
Order Cladophorales											
Family Cladophoraceae											
Cladophora sp.		×	×	b, s							
Cladophora albida var. *albida*	×		×	i, s							
C. gracilis	×		×	l							
C. microcladioides var. microcladioides	×		×	i, s							
C. stimpsoni		×	×	i					×		
C. trichotoma		×		i					×		
Chaetomorpha sp.			×	i					×		
Chaetomorpha californica	×		×	i							
C. cannabina	×		×	i, s							
Rhizoclonium rigparium var. riparium	×		×	i							
Spongomorpha arcta	×		×	i							
S. coalita		×	×	b, s, i							
S. saxatilis			×	i					×		
S. saxatilis var. *saxatilis*	×		×	i							
S. spinescens	×		×	i							
Urospora mirabilis var. *mirabilis*	×		×	i							
U. wormskjoldii	×		×	i							
Order Siphonales											
Family Derbesiaceae											

[a]b, benthic; o, in open water; n, in top 5 cm of water (neuston); s, subtidal; i, intertidal; p, plankton; mllw, mean lower low water.

TABLE 11.2 (*Continued*)

Species	Habitat Unknown	San Juan Islands	Near Seattle	Habitat Location[a]	Mud	Mixed Sediment	Sand	Shell, Gravel, or Cobble	Rocky Substrate or Boulders	Tide Pools	On Macrophytes Pilings, Reefs, Floats, etc.
Derbesia marina	×		×	i							
Family Bryopsidaceae											
Bryopsis corticulans	×		×	s							
Bryopsis spp.		×		s					×		
Family Codiaceae											
Codium spp.		×		s					×		
Codium fragile	×		×	i							
DIVISION PHAEOPHYTA											
Class Isogeneratae											
Order Ectocarpales											
Family Ectocarpaceae											
Ectocarpus sp.	×	×		b, s							
Ectocarpus simulans			×	i							×
Pylaiella littoralis f. *littoralis*	×		×	i							
P. littoralis f. *rupincola*	×		×	i							
P. tenella			×	i							×
Streblonoma sp.			×	s, i							×
Family Heterochordariaceae											
Heterochordaria abietina	×	×		i					×		
Order Sphacelariales											
Family Sphacelariaceae											
Sphacelaria subfusca			×	i							×
Class Heterogeneratae											
Subclass Haplostichinae											
Order Chordariales											
Family Ralfasiaceae											
Ralfsia sp.		×		i					×		
Ralfsia californica		×		i						×	
R. pacifica			×	i					×		
Family Elachisteaceae											
Elachistea fucicola			×	i							×
Family Corynophloeaceae											
Leathesia difformis			×	i							×
Family Chordariaceae											
Haplogloia andersonii	×		×	i							
Order Desmarestiales											
Family Desmarestiaceae											
Desmerestia sp.		×		s, b					×		
Desmerestia aculeata			×	i					×		

[a]b, benthic; o, in open water; n, in top 5 cm of water (neuston); s, subtidal; i, intertidal; p, plankton; mllw, mean lower low water.

Continued

TABLE 11.2. (*Continued*)

Species	Habitat Unknown	San Juan Islands	Near Seattle	Habitat Location[a]	Mud	Mixed Sediment	Sand	Shell, Gravel, or Cobble	Rocky Substrate or Boulders	Tide Pools	On Macrophytes Pilings, Reefs, Floats, etc.
D. ligulata	×	×									
D. ligulata var. firma	×		×								
D. ligulata var. ligulata	×		×								
D. media	×	×									
D. viridis	×		×	i, s							
Subclass Polystichinae											
Order Punctariales											
Family Punctariaceae											
Alaria tenuifolia	×		×	i, s							
Colpomenia sp.			×	i					×		
Colpomeria bullosus	×		×	i							
C. peregrina	×		×	i							
C. sinuosa	×	×		i					×		
Petalonia fascia	×		×	i, s					×		
Scytosiphon lomentaria	×		×	i							
Order Laminariales											
Family Laminariales											
Costaria costata		×	×	s, b, i					×		
Laminaria spp.		×		s, b					×		
Laminaria ephemera	×		×	i							
L. farlowii	×		×								
L. saccharina		×	×	b, s, i					×		
L. sinclairii	×		×	i							
Nereocystis luetkeana		×									
Family Alariaceae											
Alaria sp.			×	s, b					×		
Alaria marginata			×	b, s					×		
Agarum cribrosum			×	s, b					×		
A. fimbriatum			×	s, b					×		
Pterygopohora californica			×	s, b					×		
Class Cyclosporeae											
Order Fucales											
Family Fucaceae											
Fucus sp.			×	s, i					×		
Fucus distichus	×	×		i					×		
F. gardneri			×	i, s					×		
Pelvetiopsis limitata	×	×		i					×		
Family Sargassaceae											
Sargassum muticum			×	i					×		

DIVISION
RHODOPHYTA

[a]b, benthic; o, in open water; n, in top 5 cm of water (neuston); s, subtidal; i, intertidal; p, plankton; mllw, mean lower low water.

TABLE 11.2. (*Continued*)

Species	Habitat Unknown	San Juan Islands	Near Seattle	Habitat Location[a]	Mud	Mixed Sediment	Sand	Shell, Gravel, or Cobble	Rocky Substrate or Boulders	Tide Pools	On Macrophytes, Pilings, Reefs, Floats, etc.
Class Rhodophyceae											
Subclass Bangioideae											
Order Bangiales											
Family Bangiaceae											
Bangia fuscopurpurea		×	×	i					×		
Porphyra spp.		×	×	b, i					×		
Erythrotrichia parksii var. *minor*			×	i							×
Porphyra abottae	×		×	i							
P. kanakaensis	×		×	i							
P. miniata			×	i					×		
P. nereocystis			×	i							×
P. perforata		×	×	i					×		
P. torta	×		×	i							
Subclass Floridaceae											
Order Nemalionales											
Family Acrochaetiaceae											
Acrochaetium densum			×	i							×
A. pacificum			×	i							×
Rhodoglossum californicum	×		×								
Family Bonnemaisoniaceae											
Bonnemaisonia nootkana		×		s					×		
Order Gelidiales											
Family Gelidiaceae											
Gelidium sp.		×		i					×		
Gelidium coulteri	×		×	i							
Order Cryptonemiales											
Family Dumontiaceae											
Constantinea subulifera		×	×	s, b, i					×		
Cryptosiphonia woodii			×	i					×		
Pitkea californica	×		×	i							
Family Endocladiaceae											
Endocladia muricata		×		i					×		
Gloiopeltis furcata		×		b, s, i					×		
Family Squamariaceae											
Hildenbrandia prototypus			×	i					×		
H. rosea		×		i					×		
Family Cruriaceae											
Petrocelis middendorfii	×		×	i							
Family Corallinaceae											
Lithophyllum sp.	×		×	i							
Family Grateloupiacceae											

[a]b, benthic; o, in open water; n, in top 5 cm of water (neuston); s, subtidal; i, intertidal; p, plankton; mllw, mean lower low water.

Continued

TABLE 11.2. *(Continued)*

Species	Habitat Unknown	San Juan Islands	Near Seattle	Habitat Location[a]	Mud	Mixed Sediment	Sand	Shell, Gravel, or Cobble	Rocky Substrate or Boulders	Tide Pools	On Macrophytes Pilings, Reefs, Floats, etc.
Grateloupia doryphora	×		×	i							
Halymenia sp.		×		s, b					×		
Prionitis lyallii		×		i					×		
Family Kallymeniaceae											
Callophyllis sp.		×		s, b					×		
Callophyllis firma		×		s, b					×		
C. violacea	×		×	i, s							
Order Gigartinales											
Family Memastomaceae											
Schyzimenia pacifica	×	×		b, s							
Family Gracilariaceae											
Gracilaria verrucosa	×		×	i, s							
Family Plocamiaceae											
Plocamium pacificum		×		s, b					×		
Family Sphaerococcaceae											
Caulacanthus ustulatus	×		×	i							
Family Soleriaceae											
Agardhiella coulteri		×		s, b					×		
Agardhiella tenera	×	×									
Callymenia phyllophora	×	×									
Neoagardhiella baileyi	×	×		b, s							
Opuntiella californica		×		s, b					×		
Sarcodiotheca furcata		×		s, b					×		
Family Phyllophoracaeae											
Gymnogongrus norvegicus	×		×	i							
Stenogramme interrupta		×		s, b					×		
Family Gigartiaceae											
Gigartina spp.		×		s, b					×		
Gigartina californica	×		×	i							
G. exasperata	×	×	×	b, s, i							
G. papillata		×	×	b, s, i					×		
Iridaea spp.		×		s, i					×		
Iridaea cordata		×	×	b, s, i					×		
I. heterocarpa		×	×	b, s, i					×		
Order Rhodymeniales											
Family Rhodymeniaceae											
Botryocladia pseudodichotoma		×		s, b					×		
Fauchea spp.		×		b, s							
Fauchea laciniata	×		×	i							
Fryella gardneri		×		s, b					×		
Halosaccion glandiforme		×		s, b					×		

[a]b, benthic; o, in open water; n, in top 5 cm of water (neuston); s, subtidal; i, intertidal; p, plankton; mllw, mean lower low water.

TABLE 11.2. (Continued)

Species	Habitat Unknown	San Juan Islands	Near Seattle	Habitat Location[a]	Mud	Mixed Sediment	Sand	Shell, Gravel, or Cobble	Rocky Substrate or Boulders	Tide Pools	On Macrophytes Pilings, Reefs, Floats, etc.
Laurencia spectabilis		×		b, s							
Laurencia spectabilis var. diegoensis	×		×	i							
L. spectabilis var. *spectabilis*	×		×								
Odonthalia flocossa	×	×	×	i					×		
O. semicostatum	×	×									
O. washingtoniensis	×		×	i, s							
Polysiphonia sp.			×	i					×		
Polysiphonia hendryi		×		i					×		
Polysiphonia hendryi var. deliquescens	×		×	i							
P. hendryi var. *gardneri*	×		×	i							
P. hendryi var. *luxurians*	×		×	i							
P. pacifica var. *determinata*	×		×	i							
P. pacifica var. *distans*	×		×	i							
P. pacifica var. *disticha*	×		×	i							
P. pacifica var. *gracilis*	×		×	i							
P. pacifica var. *pacifica*	×		×	i							
P. paniculata	×		×	i					×		
Pterosiphonia bipinnata var. bipinnata	×	×	×	i					×		
P. bipinnata var. *robusta*	×		×	i							
P. dendroidea	×		×	i					×		
Rhodomela larix		×	×	i					×		
Rhodymenia palmata		×		s, b							
R. pertusa		×	×	s, b, i					×		
Order Ceramiales Family Ceramiaceae											
Antithamnion defectum	×		×	i							
A. kylinii	×		×	i							
Antithamnionella glandulifera	×		×	i							
Ceramium sp.			×	i					×		
Ceramium californicum	×		×	s							
C. eatonianum	×		×	i							
C. pacificum		×	×	i					×		
C. rubrum	×		×	i							
C. washingtoniense			×	i					×		
Griffithsia pacifica		×		s, b					×		
Microcladia borealis		×		b, s							
Pleonosporium spp.		×		s, b					×		

[a]b, benthic; o, in open water; n, in top 5 cm of water (neuston); s, subtidal; i, intertidal; p, plankton; mllw, mean lower low water.

Continued

TABLE 11.2.   (Continued)

Species	Habitat Unknown	San Juan Islands	Near Seattle	Habitat Location[a]	Mud	Mixed Sediment	Sand	Shell, Gravel, or Cobble	Rocky Substrate or Boulders	Tide Pools	On Macrophytes Pilings, Reefs, Floats, etc.
Pleonosporium vancouveranum	×		×	i, s							
Ptilota spp.		×		i					×		
Family Delesseriaceae											
Botryoglossum ruprechtianum		×		b, s							
Cryptopleura sp.	×		×	i							
Membranoptera spp.		×		i					×		
Membranoptera platyphylla	×		×	i							
Myriogramme spp.		×		s, b					×		
Nienburgia borealis		×		b, s					×		
Nitophyllum latissimum	×	×									
Polyneura latissima		×	×	s, b, i					×		
Family Dasyaceae											
Dasyopsis plumosa	×	×									
Rhodoptilum plumosum		×		b, s					×		
Family Rhodomelaceae											
DIVISION											
CYANOPHYTA											
Class Myxophyceae											
Order Chamaesiphonales											
Family Pleurocapsaceae											
Xenococcus sp.			×	i							×
Pleurocapsa sp.			×	i							×
Family Dermocarpaceae											
Dermocarpa sp.			×	i							×
Order Oscillatoriales											
Family Oscillatoriacea											
Arthrospira breviarticulata	×		×	i							
Lyngba? confervoides			×	i							×
Lyngba sp.	×		×	i							
Oscillatoria sp.			×	i							×
PHYLUM PROTOZOA											
Subphylum Plasmodroma											
Class Mastigophora											
Subclass Phytomastiga											
Order Dinoflagellida											
Family Cystodiniidae											
Glenodinium sp.			×	s							×
Family Noctilucidae											
Notiluca scintillans	×	×		n							
Family Gymnodiniidae											

[a]b, benthic; o, in open water; n, in top 5 cm of water (neuston); s, subtidal; i, intertidal; p, plankton; mllw, mean lower low water.

TABLE 11.2. (*Continued*)

Species	Habitat Unknown	San Juan Islands	Near Seattle	Habitat Location[a]	Mud	Mixed Sediment	Sand	Shell, Gravel, or Cobble	Rocky Substrate or Boulders	Tide Pools	On Macrophytes Pilings, Reefs, Floats, etc.
Gymnodium sp.		×		s	×						
Family Peridiniidae											
Ceratium furca	×	×		n							
C. fusus	×	×		n							
C. lineatum	×	×		n							
C. macroceros	×	×		n							
C. tripos	×	×		n							
Gonyaulax alaskiensis	×	×		n							
G. catentata	×	×		n							
G. digitale	×	×		n							
G. polyedra	×	×		n							
G. spinifera	×	×		n							
G. triacantha	×	×		n							
Peridinium depresseum	×	×		n							
P. divergens	×	×		n							
Family Dinophysidae											
Dinophysis acuata	×	×		n							
Dinophysis sp.	×	×		n							
Order Phytomonadida											
Family Carteriidae											
Pyramimonas aff. *disomata*	×	×									
P. aff. *plurioculata*	×	×									
P. amylifera	×	×									
P. orientalis	×	×									
P. parkeae	×	×									
Class Sarchodina											
Order Amoebida											
Family Amoebidae											
Amoeba sp.		×		s							×
Amoeba guttala		×		s	×						
Subphylum Cilioiphora											
Class Ciliata											
Subclass Holotricha											
Order Gymnostomatida											
Family Holophryidae											
Lacrymaria coronata		×		s							×
Trachelocerca phoenicopterus		×		s							×
Family Didiniidae											
Mesodinium sp.		×		s							×

[a]b, benthic; o, in open water; n, in top 5 cm of water (neuston); s, subtidal; i, intertidal; p, plankton; mllw, mean lower low water.

Continued

TABLE 11.2. (Continued)

Species	Habitat Unknown	San Juan Islands	Near Seattle	Habitat Location[a]	Mud	Mixed Sediment	Sand, Shell, Gravel, or Cobble	Rocky Substrate or Boulders	Tide Pools	On Macrophytes Pilings, Reefs, Floats, etc.
Family Amphileptidae										
Loxophyllum setigerum		×		s, i	×					×
Family Dysteriidae										
Dysteria lanceolata		×		s	×					×
Family Chlamydodontidae										
Chilodon cucullulus		×		s						×
Order Hymenstomatida										
Family Cohnilembidae										
Lembus (Cohnilembus) infusionum		×		s, i						×
Uronema marinum		×		s						×
Family Philasteridae										
Helicostomella subulata	×	×		n						
Family Pleuronematidae										
Pleuronema marinum		×		s						×
Order Astomatida										
Family Anoplophyridae										
Anoplophyra sp.		×		s						×
Subclass Spirotricha										
Order Heterotrichida										
Family Condylostomidae										
Condylostoma platens		×		s, i	×					×
Family Peritromidae										
Peritronus sp.		×		s						×
Order Tintinnida										
Tintinnopsis beroidea	×	×		n						
T. cylindrica	×	×		n						
T. davidoffi	×	×		n						
T. lobiancoi	×	×		n						
T. nitida	×	×		n						
T. parvula	×	×		n						
Order Hypotrichida										
Family Eluplotidae										
Diophrys sp.		×		s, i	×					×
Euplotes charon		×		s, i	×					×
E. harpa		×		s, i	×					×
Uronychia setigera		×		s						×
Subclass Peritricha										
Order Peritrichida										
Family Vorticellidae										
Vorticella patellina		×		s						×

[a]b, benthic; o, in open water; n, in top 5 cm of water (neuston); s, subtidal; i, intertidal; p, plankton; mllw, mean lower low water.

TABLE 11.2 *(Continued)*

Species	Habitat Unknown	San Juan Islands	Near Seattle	Habitat Location[a]	Mud	Mixed Sediment	Sand	Shell, Gravel, or Cobble	Rocky Substrate or Boulders	Tide Pools	On Macrophytes Pilings, Reefs, Floats, etc.
V. robusta		×		s							×
Soothamnion sp.		×		s							×
Family Vaginicolidae											
Cothurnia sp.		×		s	×						×
Class Suctoria											
Order Suctoria											
Family Acinetidae											
Acineta divisa		×		s							×
PHYLUM PORIFERA											
Class Desmospongiae											
Order Haplosclerida											
Family Haliclonidae											
Haliclona permollis			×	mllw				×	×		
Family Desmacidonidae											
Esperella (Mycale) adhaerens		×									
Order Halichondrida											
Family Halichondridae											
Halichondria panicea			×	mllw				×	×		
Class Calcarea											
Family Heterocoelidae											
Grantia (?) sp.		×		b							×
Order Poecilosclerida											
Family Myxillidae											
Myxilla parasitica		×						×			
PHYLUM CNIDARIA											
Class Hydrozoa											
Order Athecata											
(Anthomedusae,											
Gymnoblastea)											
Family Hydridae											
Protohydra leuckarti	×		×	s, i			×				
Family Corymorphiidae											
Euphysa tentacula	×	×									
Euphysa sp.	×	×									
Family Tubulariidae											
Hybocodon prolifer	×	×									
Family Corynidae											
Sarsia spp.		×		s, i				×	×	×	×
Family Bougainvilliidae											
Bougainvilla princips	×	×									×

[a]b, benthic; o, in open water; n, in top 5 cm of water (neuston); s, subtidal; i, intertidal; p, plankton; mllw, mean lower low water.

Continued

TABLE 11.2. (Continued)

Species	Habitat Unknown	San Juan Islands	Near Seattle	Habitat Location[a]	Mud	Mixed Sediment	Sand	Shell, Gravel, or Cobble	Rocky Substrate or Boulders	Tide Pools	On Macrophytes Pilings, Reefs, Floats, etc.
B. ramosa		×									
Trichydra pudica	×	×									
Family Rathkeidae											
Rathkea octopunctata	×	×									
Family Calycopsidae											
Calycopsis nematophora	×	×									
Family Cladonemidae											
Cladonema californicum	×	×									
Family Pandeidae											
Catablema nodulosa	×	×									
Halitholus sp.	×	×									
Leuckartiara spp.	×	×									
Leuckartiara ? foersteri	×	×									
Neoturris breviconis	×	×									
Stomatoca atra	×	×									
Family Polyorchidae											
Polyorchis minuta		×									×
P. penicillatus	×	×									
Order Thecata											
(Leptomedusae,											
Calyptoblastea)											
Family Dipleurosomatidae											
Dipleurosoma typicum	×	×									
Family Melicertidae											
Melicertum octocostatum	×	×									
Family Laodiceidae											
Laodicea sp.	×	×									
Ptychogena lactea	×	×									
Staurophora mertensi	×	×									
Thaumantias(Laodicea) cellularia		×									×
Family Aequoreidae											
Aequora forskalia		×									×
A. victoria	×	×									
Family Mitrocomidae											
Mitrocoma cellularia	×	×									
M. polydiademata	×	×									
Tiaropsidium ?Kelseyi	×	×									
T. multicirrata	×	×									
Family Campanulariidae											
Obelia spp.	×	×									

[a]b, benthic; o, in open water; n, in top 5 cm of water (neuston); s, subtidal; i, intertidal; p, plankton; mllw, mean lower low water.

TABLE 11.2. (Continued)

Species	Habitat Unknown	San Juan Islands	Near Seattle	Habitat Location[a]	Mud	Mixed Sediment	Sand	Shell, Gravel, or Cobble	Rocky Substrate or Boulders	Tide Pools	On Macrophytes	Pilings, Reefs, Floats, etc.
Orthopyxis(Eucpopella) compressa		×						×		×	×	×
Phialidium gregarium		×							×			×
Family Eutimidae												
Eutonina indicans	×	×										
Family Plumularidae												
Aglaophenia struthionides	×	×		s								
Order Limnomedusae												
Family Olindiadidae												
Eperetmus typus	×	×										
Gonionemus vertens		×							×			
Family Proboscidactylidae												
Proboscidactyla flavicirrata	×	×										
Order Narcomedusae												
Family Aeginidae												
Aegina citrea	×	×		s								
Cunina sp.	×	×										
Solmissus marshalli	×	×										
Order Trachymedusae												
Family Aglauridae												
Aglantha digitale	×	×		s								
Order Siphonophora												
Family Agalmidae												
Nanomia cara	×	×										
Family Muggiaea												
Diphyes sp.		×										×
Class Scyphozoa												
Order Stauromedusae												
Family Eleutherocarpidae												
Haliclystus sp.		×		i							×	
Order Semaeostomeae												
Family Pelagidae												
Chrysaora fuscescens	×	×										
Family Cyanidae												
Cyanea capillata	×	×										
Family Ulmaridae												
Aurelia sp.		×										×
Aurelia aurita	×	×										
Phacellophora camtschatica	×	×										
Class Anthozoa												
Subclass Zoantharia												

[a]b, benthic; o, in open water; n, in top 5 cm of water (neuston); s, subtidal; i, intertidal; p, plankton; mllw, mean lower low water.

Continued

TABLE 11.2.   (Continued)

Species	Habitat Unknown	San Juan Islands	Near Seattle	Habitat Location[a]	Mud	Mixed Sediment	Sand	Shell, Gravel, or Cobble	Rocky Substrate or Boulders	Tide Pools	On Macrophytes Pilings, Reefs, Floats, etc.
Order Actiniaria											
Family Actinidae											
Anthopleura artemisia			×	i	×	×					
A. elegantissima		×	×	i				×	×		
Cribina(Anthopleura) anthogrammica		×							×		
Epiactus prolifera		×		i							×
Tealia coriaea			×	mllw					×		
T. crassicornis			×	mllw					×		
Family Halcampidae											
Halcampa decementaculata			×	mllw		×					
Family Metridiidae											
Metridium senile			×	mllw					×		
Family Aiptasiomorphidae											
Haliplanella luciae			×	mllw				×			
Order Scleractinia											
Caryophyllia sp.		×		i					×		
Order Pennatulacea											
Family Pennatulacea											
Ptilosaurcus gurneyi			×	s			×				
P. quadrangularis	×	×									
PHYLUM CTENOPHORA											
Class Tentaculata											
Order Cydippida											
Family Pleurobrachiidae											
Hormiphora sp.	×	×									
Hormiphora cucumis	×	×									
Pleurobranchia spp.		×									×
Pleurobranchia bachei	×	×									
Order Thecata (Leptomedusae, Calyptoblastea)											
Family Dipleurosomatidae											
Dipleurosoma typicum	×	×									
Family Melicertidae											
Melicertum octocostatum	×	×									
Family Laodiceidae											
Laodicea sp.	×	×									
Ptychogena lactea	×	×									
Staurophora mertensi	×	×									

[a]b, benthic; o, in open water; n, in top 5 cm of water (neuston); s, subtidal; i, intertidal; p, plankton; mllw, mean lower low water.

TABLE 11.2. (Continued)

Species	Habitat Unknown	San Juan Islands	Near Seattle	Habitat Location[a]	Mud	Mixed Sediment	Sand	Shell, Gravel, or Cobble	Rocky Substrate or Boulders	Tide Pools	On Macrophytes Pilings, Reefs, Floats, etc.
Thaumantias(Laodicea) cellularia		×									×
Family Aequoreidae											
Aequora forskalia		×									×
A. victoria	×	×									
Family Mitrocomidae											
Mitrocoma cellularia	×	×									
M. polydiademata	×	×									
Tiaropsidium ?Kelseyi	×	×									
T. multicirrata	×	×									
Family Campanulariidae											
Obelia spp.	×	×									
Orthopyxis(Eucpopella) compressa		×						×		×	×
Phialidium gregarium		×							×		×
Family Eutimidae											
Eutonina indicans	×	×									
Family Plumularidae											
Aglaophenia struthionides	×	×		s							
Order Limnomedusae											
Family Olindiadidae											
Eperetmus typus	×	×									
Gonionemus vertens		×							×		
Family Proboscidactylidae											
Proboscidactyla flavicirrata	×	×									
Order Narcomedusae											
Family Aeginidae											
Aegina citrea	×	×		s							
Cunina sp.	×	×									
Solmissus marshalli	×	×									
Order Trachymedusae											
Family Aglauridae											
Aglantha digitale	×	×		s							
Order Siphonophora											
Family Agalmidae											
Nanomia cara	×	×									
Family Muggiaea											
Diphyes sp.		×									×
Class Scyphozoa											
Order Stauromedusae											
Family Eleutherocarpidae											
Haliclystus sp.		×		i							×

[a]b, benthic; o, in open water; n, in top 5 cm of water (neuston); s, subtidal; i, intertidal; p, plankton; mllw, mean lower low water.

Continued

TABLE 11.2.   (*Continued*)

Species	Habitat Unknown	San Juan Islands	Near Seattle	Habitat Location[a]	Mud	Mixed Sediment	Sand	Shell, Gravel, or Cobble	Rocky Substrate or Boulders	Tide Pools	On Macrophytes Pilings, Reefs, Floats, etc.
Order Semaeostomeae											
Family Pelagidae											
Chrysaora fuscescens	×	×									
Family Cyanidae											
Cyanea capillata	×	×									
Family Ulmaridae											
Aurelia sp.		×									×
Aurelia aurita	×	×									
Phacellophora camtschatica	×	×									
Class Anthozoa											
Subclass Zoantharia											
Order Actiniaria											
Family Actinidae											
Anthopleura artemisia		×	i		×	×					
A. elegantissima	×	×	i					×	×		
Cribina(Anthopleura) anthogrammica	×								×		
Epiactus prolifera	×		i								×
Tealia coriaea		×	mllw						×		
T. crassicornis		×	mllw						×		
Family Halcampidae											
Halcampa decemtentaculata		×	mllw		×						
Family Metridiidae											
Metridium senile		×	mllw						×		
Family Aiptasiomorphidae											
Haliplanella luciae		×	mllw				×				
Order Scleractinia											
Caryophyllia sp.		×	i						×		
Order Pennatulacea											
Family Pennatulacea											
Ptilosaurcus gurneyi		×	s			×					
P. quadrangularis	×	×									
PHYLUM CTENOPHORA											
Class Tentaculata											
Order Cydippida											
Family Pleurobrachiidae											
Hormiphora sp.	×	×									
Hormiphora cucumis	×	×									
Pleurobranchia spp.		×									×

[a]b, benthic; o, in open water; n, in top 5 cm of water (neuston); s, subtidal; i, intertidal; p, plankton; mllw, mean lower low water.

TABLE 11.2. (Continued)

Species	Habitat Unknown	San Juan Islands	Near Seattle	Habitat Location[a]	Mud	Mixed Sediment	Sand	Shell, Gravel, or Cobble	Rocky Substrate or Boulders	Tide Pools	On Macrophytes Pilings, Reefs, Floats, etc.
Pleurobranchia bachei	×	×									
Family Coelogynoporidae											
Coelogynopora cochleare	×		×								
C. falcaria		×		i			×	×	×		
C. frondifera		×		i			×				
C. nodosa		×					×				
C. scalpri		×					×	×			
Inventa parachida		×	×				×		×		
Vannuccia rotundouncinata		×		i			×				
V. tripapillosa americana		×					×	×			
Order Polycladida											
Suborder Acotylea											
Family Leptoplanidae											
Leptoplana sp.		×		i					×		
Class Trematoda											
Subclass Digenea											
Family Opeloelidae											
Helicometra pugetensis	×	×									
Family Fellodistomatidae											
Faustula gasterostei	×	×									
Hexagrammia longistestis	×	×									
PHYLUM ASCHELMINTHES											
Class Gastrotricha											
Order Macrodasyoida											
Family Turbanellidae											
Paraturbanella intermedia			×	s, i			×				
Turbanella cornuta			×	s, i			×				
T. mustela			×	s, i			×				
Family Macrodasyidae											
Macrodasys cunctatus			×	s, i			×				
Class Nematoda											
Subclass Adenophora											
Order Enoplida											
Family Anticomidae											
Anticoma acuminata			×	s, i			×				
Family Lauratonematidae											
Lauratonema mentulatum			×	i			×				
L. pugiunculus			×	i							
Family Enoplidae											
Enoplaimus lenunculus			×	i			×				

[a] b, benthic; o, in open water; n, in top 5 cm of water (neuston); s, subtidal; i, intertidal; p, plankton; mllw, mean lower low water.

Continued

TABLE 11.2. (Continued)

Species	Habitat Unknown	San Juan Islands	Near Seattle	Habitat Location[a]	Mud	Mixed Sediment	Sand	Shell, Gravel, or Cobble	Rocky Substrate or Boulders	Tide Pools	On Macrophytes Pilings, Reefs, Floats, etc.
E. paralitoralis			×	s, i			×				
Enoploides harpax			×	s, i			×				
Enoplus paralittoralis			×	i			×				
E. velatus			×	s, i			×				
Hyalacanthion multipapillatum			×	s, i			×				
Mesacanthion arcuatilis			×	i			×				
M. cricetoides			×	s			×				
M. pali	×		×								
M. pannosum			×	s			×				
Mesacanthoides sinuosus			×	s, i			×				
Oxyonchus sp.			×	s			×				
O. culcitatus			×	i			×				
Rhabdodemania illgi			×	i			×				
Trileptium iacobinum			×	s, i			×				
Family Ironidae											
Dolicholaimus benepapillosus			×	i			×				
Metoncholaimus uvifer			×	s, i			×				
Oncholaimium vesicarium			×	s, i			×				
Oncholaimus brachycercus			×	i			×				
O. campylocercoides			×	i, s			×				
O. martini			×	s, i			×				
Viscosia tumida			×	s, i			×				
Family Eurystomidae											
Calylptronema pachyderma			×	i			×				
Eurystomina repanda			×	s, i			×				
Pareurystomina pugetensis			×	s, i			×				
Order Chromadorida											
Family Chromadoridae											
Actinonema longicaudata			×	i			×				
Atrochromadora obscura			×	s			×				
Chromadorina germanica			×	s, i			×				
Chromadora undecimpapillata			×	s			×				
Chromadorella edmondsi			×	i			×				
C. galeata			×	i			×				
Graphonema clivosa			×	i			×				
G. flaccida			×	s, i			×				
Neochromadora appiana			×	i			×				
N. bicornata		×	×								
N. poecilosoma			×	i			×				
N. pugilator			×	i			×				
Prochromadorella trianularis			×	s, i							

[a]b, benthic; o, in open water; n, in top 5 cm of water (neuston); s, subtidal; i, intertidal; p, plankton; mllw, mean lower low water.

TABLE 11.2. (Continued)

Species	Habitat Unknown	San Juan Islands	Near Seattle	Habitat Location[a]	Mud	Mixed Sediment	Sand	Shell, Gravel, or Cobble	Rocky Substrate or Boulders	Tide Pools	On Macrophytes Pilings, Reefs, Floats, etc.
Spilophorella paradoxa			×	s, i							
Family Comesomatidae											
Sabatiera spp.			×	s, i			×				
Sabatiera americana			×	i			×				
S. clavicauda			×	s, i			×				
S. cupida			×	s, i			×				
S. jubata			×	s, i			×				
Family Cyatholaimidae											
Acanthonchus (Seuratiella) rostratus			×	s, i			×				
Biarmifer gibber			×	s, i			×				
Choniolaimus macrodentatus			×	s, i			×				
Cyatholaimus dentatus			×	mllw			×				
Gammanema ferox			×	i			×				
Latronema sertata	×		×								
Longicyatholaimus quadriseta			×	s, i			×				
Metacyatholaimus (?) sp.			×	i			×				
Paracanthonchus mutatus	×		×								
P. quinquepapillatus	×		×								
P. serratus			×	i			×				
Pomponema segregata			×	i			×				
Order Desmodorida											
Family Desmodoridae											
Ceramonema carinatum	×										
Subfamily Richtersiinae											
Chromaspirina spinulosa			×	i			×				
Onyx rugata			×	s, i			×				
Spirina laevis			×	s, i			×				
Subfamily Monoposthiinae											
Monposthia costata			×	s, i			×				
Nudora armillata			×	s, i			×				
Family Microlaimidae											
Microlaimus cochleatus			×	i			×				
M. dentatus			×	i			×				
M. dixiei			×	i			×				
Paramicrolaimus spirulifer			×	s			×				
Order Araeolaimida											
Family Axononolaimidae											
Subfamily Axonolaiminae											
Axonolaimus interrogativus			×	i			×				
Odontophora lituifera			×	s			×				

[a]b, benthic; o, in open water; n, in top 5 cm of water (neuston); s, subtidal; i, intertidal; p, plankton; mllw, mean lower low water.

Continued

TABLE 11.2.   (*Continued*)

Species	Habitat Unknown	San Juan Islands	Near Seattle	Habitat Location[a]	Mud	Mixed Sediment	Sand	Shell, Gravel, or Cobble	Rocky Substrate or Boulders	Tide Pools	On Macrophytes Pilings, Reefs, Floats, etc.
O. mercurialis			×	s, i			×				
O. peritricha			×	s, i			×				
Parascolaimus ungulataus			×	s, i			×				
Subfamily Cylindrolaiminae											
Araeolaimoides botulus			×	i			×				
Araeolaimus boomerangifer			×	s			×				
Family Tripyloididae											
Bathylaimus australis			×	i			×				
B. bicoronatus			×	i			×				
Tripyloides gracilis			×	i			×				
T. imitans			×	s, i			×				
Family Linhomoeidae											
Eleutherolaimus obtusicaudatus			×	s, i			×				
E. stenosoma			×	i			×				
Filipjevinema doliolum			×	s, i			×				
Linhomoeus buculentus			×	s, i			×				
Metalinhomoeus setosus			×	s, i			×				
Order Desmoscolecida											
Family Monhysteridae											
Cobbia truncata			×	s, i			×				
Monhystera disjuncta			×	i			×				
M. refringens			×	s			×				
Paramonhystera (Leptogastrella) elliptica			×	i			×				
Rhynchonema cinctum			×	i			×				
Steineria gerlachi	×		×								
S. phimifera			×	s, i			×				
Theristus acer			×	s, i			×				
T. (Mesotheristus) circumscriptus			×	s			×				
T. (Cylindrotheristus) ecphygmaticus			×	i			×				
T. (Cylindrotheristus) kornoensis			×	s, i			×				
T. modicus			×	i			×				
T. (Cylindrotheristus) resimus			×	i			×				
T. (Cylindrotheristus) trecuspidatus			×	s, i			×				
T. (Daptonema) uncinatus			×	s, i			×				
T. wimmeria			×	s, i			×				
PHYLUM NEMERTA											
Class Anopla											

[a]b, benthic; o, in open water; n, in top 5 cm of water (neuston); s, subtidal; i, intertidal; p, plankton; mllw, mean lower low water.

TABLE 11.2. (Continued)

Species	Habitat Unknown	San Juan Islands	Near Seattle	Habitat Location[a]	Mud	Mixed Sediment	Sand	Shell, Gravel, or Cobble	Rocky Substrate or Boulders	Tide Pools	On Macrophytes Pilings, Reefs, Floats, etc.
Order Paleonemertea											
Family Tubulanidae											
Tubulanus sexlineatus			×	mllw					×		
Order Heteronemerta											
Family Lineidae											
Cerebratulus californiensis			×	i		×	×				
C. marginatus			×	i		×	×				
C. montgomeryi	×			s	×						
Class Enopla											
Order Hoplonemerta											
Suborder Monostylifera											
Family Emplectonematidae											
Emplectonema gracile		×	×	i		×	×	×			
Paranemertes peregrina		×	×	i		×	×	×			
Family Amphiporidae											
Amphiporus formidabilis			×	mllw					×		
PHYLUM ANNELIDA											
Class Polychaeta											
Order Orbiniida											
Family Orbiniidae											
Haploscoloplos pugettensis			×	b, s		×	×				
Naineris denritica			×	i		×					
Phylo (Orbinia) felix			×	b, s		×					
Scoloplos acmeceps			×	i			×				
S. armiger			×	i			×				
S. pugettenis			×	i			×				
Family Paraonidae											
Aricidea sp.			×	b, s		×					
Aricidea lopezi			×	b, s	×	×	×				
A. ramosa			×	b, s			×				
Paraonella platybranchia			×	i			×				
Paraonis ivanovi			×	b, s	×		×				
P. lyra			×	b, s			×				
Order Ctenodrila											
Family Parergodrilidae											
Stygocapitella subterranea			×	i			×				
Order Spionida											
Suborder Spioniformia											
Family Apistobranchidae											
Apistobranchus ornatus			×	b, s			×				
Family Spionidae											

[a]b, benthic; o, in open water; n, in top 5 cm of water (neuston); s, subtidal; i, intertidal; p, plankton; mllw, mean lower low water.

Continued

TABLE 11.2. (Continued)

Species	Habitat Unknown	San Juan Islands	Near Seattle	Habitat Location[a]	Mud	Mixed Sediment	Sand	Shell, Gravel, or Cobble	Rocky Substrate or Boulders	Tide Pools	On Macrophytes, Pilings, Reefs, Floats, etc.
Boccardia sp.			×	i, s			×				
Laonice sp.			×	b, s	×	×	×				
Laonice cirrata			×	b, s	×	×	×				
Malacoceros glutaeus			×	i		×					
Paraspio sp.			×	b, s			×	×			
Polydora caeca			×	b, s			×	×			
P. caulleryi			×	i	×						
P. columbiana			×	i			×				
P. natrix			×	mllw, b, s			×	×			
P. proboscidea			×	i			×				
Prionospio sp.			×	b, s	×	×					
P. cirrifera			×	b, s, i	×	×	×				
P. malmgreni			×	b, s	×	×	×				
P. pinnata			×	b, s	×		×				
P. steenstrupi			×	i			×				
Pygospio elegans			×	i			×				
Rhynchospio (cf. *arenincola*)			×	b, s, s			×				
Scolepis? squatamata			×	i		×					
Spio flilcornis			×	i		×					
Spiophanes berkeleyorum			×	b, s			×				
S. bombyx			×	i			×				
Family Magelonidae											
Magelona spp.			×	b, s	×	×	×				
M. longicornis			×	mllw			×				
M. pitelkai			×	mllw			×				
M. sacculata			×	mllw			×				
Family Trochochaetidae											
Trochochaeta multisetosa			×	b, s		×					
Suborder Chaetopteriformia											
Family Chaetopteridae											
Mesochaetopterus taylori			×	b, s			×				
Phyllochaetopterus prolifica			×	b, s				×	×		
Phyllochaetopterus sp.	×					×					
Spiophaetopterus costarum			×	mllw					×		
Telepsavus costarum			×	b, s				×	×		
Suborder Cirratuliformia											
Family Cirratulidae											
Caulleriella alata			×	b, s	×	×					
Chaetozone sp.			×	b, s			×				
C. setosa			×	b, mllw	×	×	×				
Cirratulus cirratus			×	i		×	×				

[a]b, benthic; o, in open water; n, in top 5 cm of water (neuston); s, subtidal; i, intertidal; p, plankton; mllw, mean lower low water.

TABLE 11.2. (Continued)

Species	Habitat Unknown	San Juan Islands	Near Seattle	Habitat Location[a]	Mud	Mixed Sediment	Sand	Shell, Gravel, or Cobble	Rocky Substrate or Boulders	Tide Pools	On Macrophytes Pilings, Reefs, Floats, etc.
Cirriformia sp.			×	i		×					
Tharyx sp.			×	b, s	×	×	×				
T. multifilis			×	b, s		×	×				
T. secundus			×	b, s			×				
Order Capitellida											
Family Capitellidae											
Capitella capitata			×	i		×					
Mediomastus capensis			×	i		×					
Notomastus tenuis			×	i		×					
N. lineatus			×	i		×					
Family Arenicolidae											
Abarenicola pacifica			×	i		×					
Arenicola claparedi	×			i	×		×	×			
Branchiomaldane vincente			×	i		×					
Family Maldanidae											
Axiothella rubrocincta			×	b, s		×	×				
Clymenella rubrocincta	×				×						
Clymenura columbiana			×	b, s		×	×				
Euclymene zonalis			×	mllw		×	×				
Isocirrus longiceps			×	b, s			×				
Macroclyme sp.			×	b, s	×						
Praxillella sp.			×	b, s	×						
Praxillella affinis			×	b, s	×		×				
P. gracilis			×	b, s		×	×				
Maldane glebifex			×	b, s			×				
Nichomachre lumbricalis			×	b, s			×				
Petaloproctus tenuis			×	b							
Rhodine bitorquata			×	b, s			×				
Order Opheliida											
Family Opheliidae											
Ammotrypane aulogaster			×	b, s	×		×				
Armandia brevis			×	b, s, i	×	×	×				
Ophelia limacina			×	i			×				
Travisia brevis			×	b, s			×				
T. pupa			×	b, s		×					
Family Scalibregmidae											
Soalibregma inflatum	×	×		b, s	×		×				
Order Phyllodocida											
Family Nephtyidae											
Nephtys sp.			×	s, i		×					
Nephtys assignis			×	b, s	×						

[a]b, benthic; o, in open water; n, in top 5 cm of water (neuston); s, subtidal; i, intertidal; p, plankton; mllw, mean lower low water.

Continued

TABLE 11.2. (Continued)

Species	Habitat Unknown	San Juan Islands	Near Seattle	Habitat Location[a]	Mud	Mixed Sediment	Sand	Shell, Gravel, or Cobble	Rocky Substrate or Boulders	Tide Pools	On Macrophytes, Pilings, Reefs, Floats, etc.
N. caeca			×	i		×	×				
N. caecoides			×	i		×	×				
Nephtys? californiensis			×	i		×	×				
N. cornuta			×	b, s	×						
N. ferrugina			×	b, s	×	×	×				
Nephtys? longosetosa			×	i		×	×				
Nephtys? punctata			×	b, s	×						
Family Sphaerodoridae											
Sphaerodoridum sphaerulifer			×	b, s			×				
Sphaerodorum minutum			×	i			×				
Suborder Phyllodocidiformia											
Family Phyllodocidae											
Eteone sp.			×	s, i			×				
E. longa			×	i		×					
Eulalia sp.			×	b, s			×				
E. bilineata			×	b, s		×	×				
E. levicornuta			×	b, s		×					
E. quadrioculata			×	i		×					
E. sanguinea			×	b, s		×	×				
Phyllodoce sp.			×	b, s		×	×				
P. castenea			×	b, s			×				
P. groenlandica			×	b, s		×	×				
P. maculata			×	i		×	×				
P. multiseriata			×	b, s	×	×					
P. polynoides			×	b, s		×	×				
P. williamsi			×	b, s		×					
Suborder Aphroditiformia											
Superfamily Aphroditacea											
Family Polynoidae											
Antinoella macrolepida			×	b, s	×						
Arctonoe fragilis	×		×	mllw							
A. vittata	×		×	mllw							
Eunoe sp.			×	b, s	×						
Gattyana sp.			×	b, s	×						
G. cirrosa			×	b, s			×	×			
G. treadwelli			×	b, s	×						
Halosydna brevisetosa			×	i		×					
Harmothoe imbricata			×	b, s		×	×				
H. lunulata			×	mllw		×					
Hesperonoe complanata			×	b, mllw	×						

[a]b, benthic; o, in open water; n, in top 5 cm of water (neuston); s, subtidal; i, intertidal; p, plankton; mllw, mean lower low water.

TABLE 11.2. (*Continued*)

Species	Habitat Unknown	San Juan Islands	Near Seattle	Habitat Location[a]	Mud	Mixed Sediment	Sand	Shell, Gravel, or Cobble	Rocky Substrate or Boulders	Tide Pools	On Macrophytes Pilings, Reefs, Floats, etc.
Lagisca multisetosa			×	b, s			×				
Lepidonotus squamatus			×	b, s	×						
Malmgrenis lunulata			×	b							
Polyeunoa tuta	×		×	mllw							
Polynoe squamata	×	×									
Polynoida sp.			×	b, s		×	×				
Family Pholoididae											
Pholoides (*Peisidice*) *aspera*			×	b, s			×				
Family Sigalionidae											
Pholoe minuta			×	b, s, i	×	×	×				
Superfamily Chrysopetalacea											
Family Chrysopetalidae											
Paleonotus bellis			×	mllw		×					
Superfamily Pisionacea											
Family Pisionidae											
Pisione cf. *remota*			×	i			×				
Suborder Nereidiformia											
Family Hesionidae											
Gyptis brevilpalpa			×	b, mllw	×		×				
Micropodarke dubia			×	b, s, i		×	×				
Nereis agassizi	×	×									
N. virens			×	i	×		×	×			
Ophiodromus pugettensis			×	b, s		×	×				
Podarke pugettensis	×	×									
Podarke sp.			×	s, i			×				
Family Pilargidae											
Pilargis berkeleyae			×	b, s			×				
Sigambra tentaculata			×	i			×				
Family Syllidae											
Exogene gemmifera			×	b, mllw	×						
E. lourei			×	b, s	×						
Odontosyllis phosphorea			×	b, s	×						
Pionosyllis sp.			×	b, s	×						
Syllis sp.			×	b, s	×						
S. adamantea adamantea			×	i	×						
S. alternata			×	mllw	×						
S. harti			×	b, s	×	×					
S. heterochaeta			×	i	×	×					
S. pulchra			×	i	×						

[a]b, benthic; o, in open water; n, in top 5 cm of water (neuston); s, subtidal; i, intertidal; p, plankton; mllw, mean lower low water.

Continued

TABLE 11.2.   (Continued)

Species	Habitat Unknown	San Juan Islands	Near Seattle	Habitat Location[a]	Mud	Mixed Sediment	Sand	Shell, Gravel, or Cobble	Rocky Substrate or Boulders	Tide Pools	On Macrophytes Pilings, Reefs, Floats, etc.
Syllides longocirrata			×	mllw		×					
Family Nereidae											
Micronereis nanaimoensis			×	b, s			×				
Nereis sp.			×	b, s		×	×				
Nereis brandti			×	i		×					
N. limnicola			×	i		×					
N. procera			×	i		×					
N. vexillosa			×	i		×					
N.? zonata			×	i		×					
Pectinaria californica	×		×	b, s							
P. granulata			×	mllw		×					
Platynereis bicanaliculata			×	i, b, s		×	×	×			
P. malmgreni	×		×								
Suborder Glyceriformia											
Family Glyceridae											
Glycera sp.		×	×	b, s	×						
Glycera americana			×	i		×	×				
G. capitata			×	b, s, i	×	×	×				
G. robusta			×	b, s	×						
G. siphonostoma			×	b, s	×						
Hemipodus borealis			×	i		×					
Family Goniadidae											
Goniada brunnea			×	b, s	×						
G. maculata			×	b, s		×	×				
Glycinde sp.			×	b, s		×	×				
Glycinde armigera	×		×	b, s	×		×				
Glycinde picta			×	b, s, i		×	×				
Order Eunicida											
Superfamily Eunicea											
Family Onuphidae											
Diopatra californica	×					×					
D. ornata			×	b, s, i		×	×				
Nothria sp.			×	b, s	×	×	×				
Onuphis elegans			×	mllw			×				
Family Lumbrineridae											
Lumbrineris sp.			×	b, s		×	×				
Lumbrineris bicirrata			×	b, s		×					
L. californiensis			×	b, s	×		×				
L. cruzensis			×	b, s	×	×	×				
L. limicola			×	b, s			×				
L. luti			×	b, s	×	×	×				

[a]b, benthic; o, in open water; n, in top 5 cm of water (neuston); s, subtidal; i, intertidal; p, plankton; mllw, mean lower low water.

TABLE 11.2. (Continued)

Species	Habitat Unknown	San Juan Islands	Near Seattle	Habitat Location[a]	Mud	Mixed Sediment	Sand	Shell, Gravel, or Cobble	Rocky Substrate or Boulders	Tide Pools	On Macrophytes Pilings, Reefs, Floats, etc.
L. zonata			×	i		×					
Ninoe gemmea			×	b, s	×						
Family Arabellidae											
Notocirrus californiensis			×	b, s		×	×				
Family Dorvilleidae											
Dorvillea gracilis			×	i				×			
D. pseudorubrovittat			×	b, s				×			
Protodorvilleas gracilis			×	i		×					
Schistomeringos longicornis			×	i		×					
Order Sternaspida											
Family Sternaspidae											
Stauronereis sp.			×	b, s				×			
Schistomeringos (Stauroneis)			×	i				×			
Sternaspis fossor	×		×	b, s	×			×			
Order Oweniida											
Family Oweniidae											
Owenia sp.			×					×			
Owenia fusiformis			×	i	×	×	×				
Order Flabelligerida											
Family Flabelligeridae											
Brada sachalina			×	b, s	×						
Flabelligera sp.			×	b, s				×			
Order Terbellida											
Family Sabellariidae											
Idanthyrus armatus			×	b, s				×			
Sabellaria cementarium			×	b, s		×	×				
Family Pectinariidae											
Pectinaria brevicornis	×			b, s	×						
P. californiensis			×	s	×			×			
P. granulata			×	s, mllw			×	×			
Family Ampharetidae											
Ampharete acutifrons			×	s	×						
A. arctica			×	s				×			
A. gagerea			×	s	×	×	×				
Amphicteis alaskensis	×					×					
Amphisamytha bioculata			×	i				×			
Asabellides littoralis			×	b, s				×			
Melinna ellisabethae			×	s			×	×			
Schistocomus hiltoni			×	s				×			
Family Terebellidae											
Amphitrite robusta	×			b, s, i	×						

[a]b, benthic; o, in open water; n, in top 5 cm of water (neuston); s, subtidal; i, intertidal; p, plankton; mllw, mean lower low water.

Continued

TABLE 11.2.   (Continued)

Species	Habitat Unknown	San Juan Islands	Near Seattle	Habitat Location[a]	Mud	Mixed Sediment	Sand	Shell, Gravel, or Cobble	Rocky Substrate or Boulders	Tide Pools	On Macrophytes Pilings, Reefs, Floats, etc.
A. spiralis	×	×		i							
Artacama conifera			×	b, s			×				
Eupolymenia heterobranchia			×	mllw				×	×		
Lanassa venusta			×	b, s			×				
Lysilla pacifica			×	b, s			×				
Neoamphitrite edwardsii			×	b, s	×						
N. robusta			×	b, s, mllw			×	×	×		
Pista sp.			×	b, s			×				
Pista cristata			×	b, s	×		×				
P. fasciata			×	b, s	×						
P. moorei			×	b, s	×						
Polycirrus spp.			×	b, s			×				
Proclea graffi			×	b, s			×				
Streblosoma bairdi			×	b, s			×				
Terebellides stroemi			×	b, s	×		×				
Trichobranchus glacialis			×	b, s			×				
Order Sabellida											
Family Sabellidae											
Chone sp.			×	b, s		×					
Chone bimaculata			×	b, s			×				
C. duneri			×	i		×					
Eudilsylia? polymorpha			×	mllw					×		
E. vancouveri			×	mllw					×		
Laonome kroyeri			×	b, s			×				
Megalomma splendida			×	b, s			×				
Potamilla oculata			×	b, s			×				
P. reniformis			×	b, s			×				
Pseudopoptamilla occelata			×	mllw					×		
Schizobranchia insignis			×	mllw					×		
Sabella media			×	b, s			×				
Family Serpulidae											
Serpula columbiana		×							×		
S. vermicularis			×	mllw				×			
Order Archiannelida											
Family Saccocirridae											
Saccocirrus eroticus			×	i			×				
Family Protodrilidae											
Protodrilus flabelliger			×	i			×				
P. chaetifer			×	i			×				
Family Dinophilidae											
Trilobodrilus nipponicus			×	i			×				

[a]b, benthic; o, in open water; n, in top 5 cm of water (neuston); s, subtidal; i, intertidal; p, plankton; mllw, mean lower low water.

TABLE 11.2. (*Continued*)

Species	Habitat Unknown	San Juan Islands	Near Seattle	Habitat Location[a]	Mud	Mixed Sediment	Sand	Shell, Gravel, or Cobble	Rocky Substrate or Boulders	Tide Pools	On Macrophytes Pilings, Reefs, Floats, etc.
Family Nerillidae											
Nerilla antennata			×	i			×				
PHYLUM ECHINODERMATA											
Class Holothuroidea											
Order Dendrochirotida											
Family Psolidae											
Psolus chitonoides	×	×		s							
Family Phyllophoridae											
Pentamera spp.			×	b, s	×	×	×				
Family Cucumariidae											
Cucumaria chronhejelmi		×		s, b	×						
C. japonica		×		i, s					×		
C. miniata		×	×	mllw					×		
C. lubrica	×	×		s							
C. populifera		×			×						
C. pulcherrima	×	×									
Eupentacta quinquesemita		×		mllw					×		
Family Stichopodidae											
Parastichopus californicus		×		mllw		×					
Stichopus californicus	×	×		b, s							
Order Apodida											
Family Synaptidae											
Leptosynapta clarki			×	b, s, i		×	×				
L. inhaerans		×					×				
Family Chiridotidae											
Chirodota laevis	×	×		s		×					
Order Molpadiida											
Family Molpadiidae											
Molpadia intermedia			×	b, s	×						
Family Caudinidae											
Caudina obesacauda	×	×		s							
Class Echinoidea											
Order Echinoida											
Family Strongylocentrotidae											
Strongylocentrotus drobachiensis		×	×	b, s, i				×	×		
S. franciscanus	×	×		b, s							
S. purpuratus		×									×
Order Clypesteroida											
Family Echinarachnidae											

[a]b, benthic; o, in open water; n, in top 5 cm of water (neuston); s, subtidal; i, intertidal; p, plankton; mllw, mean lower low water.

Continued

TABLE 11.2. (Continued)

Species	Habitat Unknown	San Juan Islands	Near Seattle	Habitat Location[a]	Mud	Mixed Sediment	Sand	Shell, Gravel, or Cobble	Rocky Substrate or Boulders	Tide Pools	On Macrophytes Pilings, Reefs, Floats, etc.
Echinarachnius excentricus		×		i	×	×					×
Family Dendrasteridae											
Dendraster excentricus			×	i			×				
Order Spatangoida											
Family Schizasteridae											
Brisaster latifrons			×	b, s	×						
B. townsendi			×	b, s	×						
Class Stelleroidea											
Subclass Asteroidea											
Order Platyasterida											
Family Luidiidae											
Luida foliolata		×		s	×				×		
Order Valvatida											
Family Goniasteridae											
Ceramaster granularis		×		s							
Hippasteria spinosa			×	mllw			×				
Mediaster aequalis		×	×	mllw			×		×		
Order Spinulosida											
Family Solasteridae											
Solaster dawsoni		×		s, b					×		
S. endeca	×	×		s							
S. galaxides		×		s					×		
S. (Crossaster) papposus		×		s					×		
S. stimpsoni		×	×	s, mllw				×	×		
Family Pterasteridae											
Pteraster tesselatus		×		s							
Family Echinasteridae											
Henrica leviuscula		×	×	s, mllw				×	×		
Henrica leviuscula lunula		×		s					×		
Order Forcipulatida											
Family Asteriidae											
Asterias victoriana		×		s							
Dermasterias imbricata		×		s, i					×		
Evasterias acanthostoma		×		s							
E. troschelii		×	×	s, b, i				×	×		
E. troschelii densa	×	×									
E. troschelii rudis	×	×		s							
E. troschelii subnodosa	×	×		s, i							
Leptasterias aequalis	×	×		i							
L. epichlora alaskensis	×	×		i							
L. hexactis		×		i					×		

[a]b, benthic; o, in open water; n, in top 5 cm of water (neuston); s, subtidal; i, intertidal; p, plankton; mllw, mean lower low water.

TABLE 11.2. (Continued)

Species	Habitat Unknown	San Juan Islands	Near Seattle	Habitat Location[a]	Mud	Mixed Sediment	Sand	Shell, Gravel, or Cobble	Rocky Substrate or Boulders	Tide Pools	On Macrophytes Pilings, Reefs, Floats, etc.
Orthasterias columbiana	×	×		i, s							
O. forreri forcipulata	×	×		b, s							
O. koehleri		×							×		
Pisaster brevispinna	×	×									
Pisaster confertus	×	×									
P. ochraceus		×	×	i, mllw				×			
Pycnopodia helianthoides		×	×	i, s	×			×	×		
Stylasterias forreri		×							×		
Subclass Ophiuroidea											
Order Phrynophiurida											
Family Gorgonocephalida											
Gorgonocephalus eucnemis	×	×		s, b							
Order Ophiurida											
Family Ophiuridae											
Ophiura brevispinna	×	×		s, b							
O. lutkeni			×	b, s		×	×				
O. sarsii		×			×						
Family Ophiactidae											
Ophiopholis aculeata		×		s							×
O. aculeata var. *kennerlyi*		×			×						
Family Amphiuridae											
Amphiodia occidentalis		×	×	mllw	×		×				
A. perierita		×						×			
PHYLUM BRACHIOPODA											
Class Articulata											
Order Telotremata											
Family Terebratulidae											
Terebratulina unguicula	×	×		s							
Family Terebratellidae											
Laqueus californicus	×	×		s							
vancouverensis	×	×		s							
Terebratula transversa	×	×		s							
T. transversa caurina	×	×									
Family Rhynchonellidae											
Hemithyris psittacea	×	×		s							
PHYLUM MOLLUSCA											
Class Polyplacophora											
Order Neoloricata											
Family Acanthochitidae											

[a]b, benthic; o, in open water; n, in top 5 cm of water (neuston); s, subtidal; i, intertidal; p, plankton; mllw, mean lower low water.

Continued

TABLE 11.2. (Continued)

Species	Habitat Unknown	San Juan Islands	Near Seattle	Habitat Location[a]	Mud	Mixed Sediment	Sand	Shell, Gravel, or Cobble	Rocky Substrate or Boulders	Tide Pools	On Macrophytes Pilings, Reefs, Floats, etc.
Cryptochiton stelleri		×	×	s, i					×		×
Suborder Ischnochitonina											
Family Ischnochitonidae											
Cyanoplax dentiens			×	i				×	×		
Ischnochitonidae interstinctus	×	×									
I. mertensii	×	×									
I. retiporosus	×	×									
Lepidochitona hartwegii	×	×									
L. lineata	×	×									
L. submarmorea	×	×									
Tonicella lineata		×	×	mllw				×	×		×
Family Mopaliidae											
Katherina tunicata		×	×	i, mllw				×	×		
Mopalia cilata		×	×	i				×	×		
M. cilata wosnessenskii	×	×									
M. goniura	×	×									
M. lignosa			×	i				×	×		
M. muscosa		×	×	i				×	×		
M. muscosa hindsii	×	×									
Ṁ. muscosa laevior	×	×									
M. sinuata	×	×									
Class Gastropoda											
Subclass Prosobranchia											
Order Archaeogastropoda											
Family Acmaeidae											
Acmaea sp.			×	i				×	×		
A. cassis			×	i							
A. cassis pelta	×	×									
A. cassis nacelloides	×	×									
A. digitalis			×	i				×	×		
A. digitalis umbonata	×	×		i							
Acmaea mitra	×	×									
A. paradigitalis	×	×		i							
A. patina			×						×		
A. pelta			×	i					×		
A. scutum	×	×		i							
A. scutum patina	×	×									
A. scutum pintadina	×	×									
Collisella digitalis			×	i					×		
C. pelta			×	i				×	×		
C. strigatella			×	i				×	×		

[a]b, benthic; o, in open water; n, in top 5 cm of water (neuston); s, subtidal; i, intertidal; p, plankton; mllw, mean lower low water.

TABLE 11.2. (*Continued*)

Species	Habitat Unknown	San Juan Islands	Near Seattle	Habitat Location[a]	Mud	Mixed Sediment	Sand	Shell, Gravel, or Cobble	Rocky Substrate or Boulders	Tide Pools	On Macrophytes	Pilings, Reefs, Floats, etc.
Notoacmea persona			×	i				×	×			
N. scutum			×	i				×	×			
Family Lepetidae												
Lepeta concentrica	×	×		s								
Family Cocculinidae												
Solariella obscura	×	×										
S. peramablis	×	×										
Family Trochidae												
Calliostoma annulatum	×	×		s								
C. costatum	×	×		s								
C. variegatum	×	×		s								
Cidarina cidaris	×	×										
Margarites lirulatus	×	×										
M. lirulatus obsoletus	×	×										
M. parcipictus	×	×										
M. succinctus	×	×										
Family Turbinidae												
Leptothyra bacula	×	×										
L. carpenteri	×	×										
L. lurida	×	×										
Family Fissurellidae												
Diadora aspera			×	i				×	×			
Puncturella cucullata	×	×		s								
P. galeata	×	×		s								
Order Mesogastropoda												
Family Lacunidae												
Lacuna carinata	×	×										
L. divaricata	×	×										
L. marmorata olla	×	×										
L. porrecta		×										×
L. solidula	×	×										
L. univasciata	×	×										
L. variegata		×	×	i				×				×
Family Littorinidae												
Littorina planaxis	×	×										
L. scutulata		×	×	i				×	×			
L. sitchana		×	×	i				×	×			
Family Rissoidae												
Alvania carpenteri	×	×										
A. compacta	×	×										
A. filosa	×	×										

[a]b, benthic; o, in open water; n, in top 5 cm of water (neuston); s, subtidal; i, intertidal; p, plankton; mllw, mean lower low water.

Continued

TABLE 11.2.   (*Continued*)

Species	Habitat Unknown	San Juan Islands	Near Seattle	Habitat Location[a]	Mud	Mixed Sediment	Sand	Shell, Gravel, or Cobble	Rocky Substrate or Boulders	Tide Pools	On Macrophytes Pilings, Reefs, Floats, etc.
A. montereyensis	×	×									
A. sanjuanensis	×	×									
Alvinia sp.			×	mllw			×				
Barleeia sanjuanensis	×	×									
Family Caecidae											
Fartulum occidentale	×	×									
Family Vermetidae											
Aletes squamigerus pernatus	×	×									
Family Turritellidae											
Tachyrynchus lacteolus	×	×		s							
Family Cerithiidae											
Bittium challisae	×	×									
B. eschrichtii	×	×									
B. sanjuanense	×	×									
Cerithiopsis columna	×	×		s							
C. onealensis	×	×		s							
C. paramoea	×	×		s							
C. signa	×	×		s							
C. stephensae	×	×		s							
C. willetti	×	×									
Family Epitonidae											
Epitonium indianorum	×	×		s							
E. wroblewskii	×	×		s							
Family Pyramidellidae											
Balcis (= *Melanella macra*)	×	×									
B. micans	×	×									
Odostomia columbiana	×	×		s							
O. engbergi	×	×									
O. ? quadre			×	mllw			×				×
O. sanjuanensis	×	×									
O. skidegatensis	×	×									
O. talpa	×	×									
O. tenuisculpta	×	×		s							
O. vancouverensis	×	×									
O. washingtonia	×	×									
O. youngi	×	×									
Turbonella aurantia	×	×									
T. engbergi	×	×									
Family Trichotropidae											
Trichotropis cancellata	×	×		s							
Family Calyptraeidae											

[a]b, benthic; o, in open water; n, in top 5 cm of water (neuston); s, subtidal; i, intertidal; p, plankton; mllw, mean lower low water.

TABLE 11.2. (*Continued*)

Species	Habitat Unknown	San Juan Islands	Near Seattle	Habitat Location[a]	Mud	Mixed Sediment	Sand	Shell, Gravel, or Cobble	Rocky Substrate or Boulders	Tide Pools	On Macrophytes Pilings, Reefs, Floats, etc.
Calyptraea fastigiata	×	×									
Crepidula aculeata	×	×		s							
C. adunca			×	b, s					×		
C. nivea	×	×		s							
Crepipatella lingulata			×	mllw					×		
Family Naticidae											
Natica aleutica	×	×		s							
N. clausa	×	×		s							
Polinices draconis	×	×									
P. groenlandica			×		×						
P. lewisii		×	×	mllw		×	×				
P. pallida			×	s	×						
Family Lamellariidae											
Marsenina (= *Lamellaria*) *rhombica*	×	×		s							
Velutina prolongata	×	×									
V. laevigata	×	×									
Family Cymatiidae											
Argobuccinum oregonense			×	s							×
Family Vitrinellidae											
Cyclostrenella concordia	×	×									
Leptogyra alaskana	×	×									
Order Neogastropoda											
Family Muricidae											
Ceratostoma foliatum	×	×		i							
Purpura foliata	×	×									
Micella (= *Thais*) *canaliculata*			×	i				×	×		
M. emarginata	×	×		i							
M. emarginata projecta		×	×	i				×	×		
M. lamellosa		×	×	s, i				×	×		
M. lamellosa cymica	×	×									
M. lamellosa hormica	×	×									
Tritonalia (*Ocenebra*) *interfossa*	×	×									
T. lurida	×	×									
T. michaeli	×	×									
Trophon (= *Boreotrophon*) *orpheus*		×	×								
T. pacificus	×	×									
T. stuarti	×	×		s							
T. tenuisculptus	×	×									
Family Columbellidae											

[a]b, benthic; o, in open water; n, in top 5 cm of water (neuston); s, subtidal; i, intertidal; p, plankton; mllw, mean lower low water.

Continued

TABLE 11.2.   (Continued)

Species	Habitat Unknown	San Juan Islands	Near Seattle	Habitat Location[a]	Mud	Mixed Sediment	Sand Shell, Gravel, or Cobble	Rocky Substrate or Boulders	Tide Pools	On Macrophytes Pilings, Reefs, Floats, etc.
Amphissa columbiana	×	×								
Columbella carinata californica	×	×								
C. gausapata	×	×								
Nitidella gouldii	×	×		s						
Family Buccinidae										
Beringus crebricostatus undatus	×	×		s						
Buccinum plectrum	×	×		s						
Chrysodomus liratus	×	×		s						
C. tabulatua	×	×		s						
Searlesia dira	×	×		i	×		×	×		
Family Nassariidae										
Nassarius mendicus			×	mllw		×	×			×
Family Cancellariidae										
Admete couthouyi	×	×		s						
A. couthouy laevior	×	×		s						
Cancellaria modesta	×	×		s						
C. unalashkensis	×	×		s						
Family Turridae										
Antiplanes perversa	×	×		s						
C. halcyonis	×	×								
Lora miona	×	×								
L. rosea	×	×		s						
L. turricula	×	×		s						
Family Olividae										
Olivella boatica	×	×								
Subclass Opisthobranchia										
Order Cephalaspidea										
Family Acteocinidae										
Acteocina eximia	×	×		s						
Family Retusidae										
Retusa harpa	×	×								
Family Scaphandridae										
Cylichnella attonsa	×	×		s						
Diaphana brunnea	×	×								
Family Atyidae										
Haminoea olgae										
H. vesicula		×								×
Order Nudibranchia										
Suborder Doridacea										
Family Lamellidorididae										
Acanthodoris nanaimoensis			×	mllw			×	×		

[a] b, benthic; o, in open water; n, in top 5 cm of water (neuston); s, subtidal; i, intertidal; p, plankton; mllw, mean lower low water.

TABLE 11.2. (*Continued*)

Species	Habitat Unknown	San Juan Islands	Near Seattle	Habitat Location[a]	Mud	Mixed Sediment	Sand	Shell, Gravel, or Cobble	Rocky Substrate or Boulders	Tide Pools	On Macrophytes Pilings, Reefs, Floats, etc.
Onchidoris bilamellata			×	mllw				×			
Family Dorididae											
Archidoris montereyensis			×	mllw				×	×		
S. odhneria			×	mllw				×	×		
Aglaja diomedea			×	mllw			×				
Anisodoris nobilis		×		i							
Diaulula sandigensis			×	mllw					×		
Suborder Dendronotacea											
Family Dendronotidae											
Dendronotus giganteus		×				×					
Suborder Dendronotacea											
Family Tethyidae											
Melibe lenina		×									×
Family Dolabriferidae											
Phyllaplysia sp.		×									×
Suborder Aeolidiacea											
Family Aeolidiidae											
Aeolis (= *Aeolidia*) *papillosa*			×	mllw				×	×		
Aeolis (= *Aeolidia*) sp.		×									
Family Favorinidae											
Hermissenda crassicornis			×	mllw				×	×		
Class Scaphopoda											
Family Dentaliidae											
Dentalium rectus		×				×					
Class Bivalvia											
Subclass Prionodesmata											
Order Protobranchia											
Family Nuculidae											
Leda cellulita	×	×		s							
L. fossa	×	×		s							
L. hamata	×	×		s							
L. minuta	×	×		s							
Nucula bellotii			×	b, s	×	×					
N. (= *Acilia*) *castrensis*		×	×	b, s	×	×					
N. linki		×				×					
N. tenuis	×	×		s							
Nuculana cellulita			×	b, s			×				
N. minuta			×	b, s							
Yoldia ensifera		×	×	s, b	×						
Y. limatula		×			×						
Y. myalis		×		s							

[a]b, benthic; o, in open water; n, in top 5 cm of water (neuston); s, subtidal; i, intertidal; p, plankton; mllw, mean lower low water.

Continued

TABLE 11.2.   *(Continued)*

Species	Habitat Unknown	San Juan Islands	Near Seattle	Habitat Location[a]	Mud	Mixed Sediment	Sand	Shell, Gravel, or Cobble	Rocky Substrate or Boulders	Tide Pools	On Macrophytes Pilings, Reefs, Floats, etc.
Y. scissurata		×		s	×						
Y. seminuda			×	b, s	×	×	×				
Y. thraciaeformis		×	×	s, b	×						
Yoldia sp.			×	b, s			×				
Subclass Pteriomorpha											
Order Prionodontida											
Family Glycymeridae											
Glycymeris subobsoleta	×	×		s							
Order Pteroconchida											
Family Mytilidae											
Crenella columbiana		×	×	s, b			×	×			
C. decussata	×	×									
Modiolaria laevigata	×	×		s							
Modiolus flabellatus	×	×		s							
M. modiolus		×	×	s, b			×				
M. nigra	×	×		s							
M. rectus			×	mllw					×		
Musculus substriatus			×	b, s			×	×			
Mytilus californianus		×		i				×	×		
M. edulis		×	×	i				×	×		×
Family Ostreidae											
Alectrion (Lopho) mendicus	×	×		s							
Crassostrea gigas			×	i			×				
Family Pectinidae											
Chlamys hericius			×	b, s			×	×			
Hinnites giganteus	×	×		s							
Pecten caurinus	×	×		s							
P. hericius			×	s, i	×				×		
P. hindsii	×	×		s, i							
P. hindsii kincaidi	×	×		s							
P. hindsii navarchus	×	×									
P. islandicus			×	s	×						
P. islandicus pugetensis	×	×		s							
P. jordani	×	×		s							
P. randolphis	×	×		s							
Family Anomiidae											
Pododesmus cepio			×	mllw, b				×	×		
P. macroschisma	×	×		s							
Subclass Teleodesmata											
Order Heterodontidae											
Family Crassatellidae											

[a] b, benthic; o, in open water; n, in top 5 cm of water (neuston); s, subtidal; i, intertidal; p, plankton; mllw, mean lower low water.

TABLE 11.2. (Continued)

Species	Habitat Unknown	San Juan Islands	Near Seattle	Habitat Location[a]	Mud	Mixed Sediment	Sand	Shell, Gravel, or Cobble	Rocky Substrate or Boulders	Tide Pools	On Macrophytes Pilings, Reefs, Floats, etc.
Astarte compacta	×	×		s							
A. alaskensis	×	×		s							
A. esqyuimalti	×	×		s							
Family Carditidae											
Venericardia prolongata		×						×			
V. ventricosa		×		s	×						
Family Lelptonidae											
Bornia sp.			×	b, s		×					
Kellia laperousii	×	×									
K. suborbicularis	×	×									
Lasaea rubra	×	×									
Pseudopythina rugifera	×	×		s							
Rochefortia tumida	×	×									
Family Lucinidae											
Lucinoma annulatus			×	b, s	×	×	×				
Mysella tumida			×	b, s, i	×	×	×				
Parvalucina teniusculptus			×	b, s	×	×	×				
Family Thyrasiridae											
Axinopsis sericatus		×	×	b, s	×	×	×				
Thyasira barbarensis	×	×		s							
T. gouldii			×	b, s				×			
Family Ungulidae											
Diplodonta orbella	×	×									
Family Lucinidae											
Phacoides annulatus		×		i				×			
P. teniusculptus		×				×					
Family Cardiidae											
Cardium aliatum		×			×						
C. californiense		×		s	×						
C. ciliatum		×			×						
C. corbis		×		s, i	×				×		
C. (= Clinocardium) fucanum		×	×	b, s				×			
Clinocardium nuttallii			×	b, s, i	×	×	×				
Nemocardium centifilosum			×	b, s	×	×	×				
Serripes groenlandicus		×		s	×						
Family Veneridae											
Compsomyax subdiaphana			×	b, s		×	×				
Gemma gemma	×	×									
Humilaria kennerleya			×	b, s				×			
Marcia kennerleyi	×	×		s							
M. subdiaphana	×	×									

[a]b, benthic; o, in open water; n, in top 5 cm of water (neuston); s, subtidal; i, intertidal; p, plankton; mllw, mean lower low water.

Continued

TABLE 11.2.   (Continued)

Species	Habitat Unknown	San Juan Islands	Near Seattle	Habitat Location[a]	Mud	Mixed Sediment	Sand	Shell, Gravel, or Cobble	Rocky Substrate or Boulders	Tide Pools	On Macrophytes Pilings, Reefs, Floats, etc.
Paphia staminea		×		s, i	×				×		
P. staminea petitii	×	×									
P. staminea ruderata	×	×									
Protothaca staminea			×	i		×					
Psephidia lordi		×	×	s, b		×	×				
Saxidomus giganteus		×	×	s, i	×	×	×				
S. giganteus brevis	×	×									
Tapes japonica			×	i		×					
Transennella tantilla		×	×	i		×					×
Family Petricolidae											
Petricola carditoides	×	×									
Family Mactridae											
Mactra california			×	b, s	×						
Schizothaerus (Tresus) nuttalli			×	s, i	×			×			
Spisula alaskana	×	×		s							
S. ? falcata			×	mllw			×				
Tresus capax			×	b, s		×					
Family Tellinidae											
Macoma alaskana			×	b, s		×	×				
Macoma balthica	×	×		s							
M. brota	×	×		s							
M. calcarea		×	×	s, b	×	×	×				
M. carlottensis			×	b, s	×	×	×				
M. incongrua	×	×									
M. inconspicua			×	b, s	×	×	×				
M. indentata	×	×									
Macoma inflantata			×	s							
M. inquinata		×	×	s, i	×	×			×		
M. inquinata arnheimi	×	×									
M. irus			×	b, s			×				
M. nasuta		×	×	s, i	×	×	×	×			
M. obliqua			×	i		×					
M. secta		×	×	s, i	×		×	×			
M. yoldiformis		×	×	s, b		×	×				
Tellina buttonis		×	×	b, s		×	×				
T. modesta			×	mllw			×				
T. nuculoides			×	mllw		×					
T. salmonea	×	×		s							
Family Semelidae											
Semele rubropicta		×	×	b, s			×				
Family Psammobiidae											

[a]b, benthic; o, in open water; n, in top 5 cm of water (neuston); s, subtidal; i, intertidal; p, plankton; mllw, mean lower low water.

TABLE 11.2. (Continued)

Species	Habitat Unknown	San Juan Islands	Near Seattle	Habitat Location[a]	Mud	Mixed Sediment	Sand	Shell, Gravel, or Cobble	Rocky Substrate or Boulders	Tide Pools	On Macrophytes Pilings, Reefs, Floats, etc.
Psammobia californica	×	×									
Family Solenidae											
Solen sicarius		×	×	b, s, i	×		×				
Family Myidae											
Cryptomya californica		×	×	i		×					
Mya arenaria		×	×	b, s	×	×	×				
Mya truncata		×	×	s, b, mllw		×	×				
Family Hiatellidae											
Hiatella artica			×	mllw				×	×		
Panomya ampla		×	×	b, s			×				
Panope generosa	×	×									
Saxicava arctica	×	×									
Family Pholadidae											
Xylophaga washingtona	×	×									
Zirfoea pilsbryi	×		×	mllw							
Family Teredinidae											
Bankia setacea		×									
Subclass Anomalodesmata											
Order Eudesmodontida											
Family Pandoridae											
Pandora filosa		×	×	s, b	×	×	×				
P. glacialis	×	×		s							
P. grandis	×	×		s							
Family Lyonsiidae											
Lyonsia californica	×	×		s							
L. pugetensis		×	×	s, b		×	×				
Mytilimeria nuttallii	×	×		s							
Family Thraciidae											
Thracia challisiana	×	×		s							
T. curta	×	×		s							
T. trapezoides	×	×		s							
Order Septibranchida											
Family Cuspidariidae											
Cuspidaria oldroydi		×	×	b, s			×				
Class Scaphopoda											
Family Dentaliidae											
Dentalium rectus		×			×						
PHYLUM ARTHROPODA											
Subphylum Pycnogonida											
Class Pantopoda											

[a] b, benthic; o, in open water; n, in top 5 cm of water (neuston); s, subtidal; i, intertidal; p, plankton; mllw, mean lower low water.

Continued

TABLE 11.2. (*Continued*)

Species	Habitat Unknown	San Juan Islands	Near Seattle	Habitat Location[a]	Mud	Mixed Sediment	Sand	Shell, Gravel, or Cobble	Rocky Substrate or Boulders	Tide Pools	On Macrophytes Pilings, Reefs, Floats, etc.
Family Nymphonidae											
Nymphon pixellae			×	b, s		×					
Subphylum Mandibulata											
Class Crustacea											
Subclass Ostracoda											
Order Mycodocipida											
Suborder Myodocopa											
Family Cylindroleberididae											
Cylindroleberis mariae			×	b, s	×	×	×				
Family Cypridinidae											
Cypridina squamosa			×	i			×				
Family Rutidermatidae											
Rutiderma rostrata			×	b, s		×	×				
Order Podocopida											
Suborder Podocopa											
Family Cytheridae											
Cytheridea papillosa			×	i			×				
Cytherois vitrea			×	i			×				
Cytherura gibba			×	i			×				
Xestoleberis rara			×	i			×				
Family Paradoxostamatidae											
Paradoxostoma pulchellum			×	i			×				
Family Leptocytheridae											
Leptocythere tenera			×	i			×				
Subclass Copepoda											
Order Calanoida											
Family Euchaetidae											
Euchaeta japonica	×	×		o							
Family Acariidae											
Acartia clausi	×	×									
A. longiremis	×	×		o							
Family Tortanidae											
Paralabidocera elongatus	×	×		o							
Tortanus discaudatus	×	×		o							
Family Calanidae											
Calanus cristatus	×	×		o							
C. finmarchus	×	×		o							
Order Cyclopoida											
Family Corycaeidae											
Corycaeus affinus	×	×		o							

[a]b, benthic; o, in open water; n, in top 5 cm of water (neuston); s, subtidal; i, intertidal; p, plankton; mllw, mean lower low water.

TABLE 11.2. (Continued)

Species	Habitat Unknown	San Juan Islands	Near Seattle	Habitat Location[a]	Mud	Mixed Sediment	Sand Shell, Gravel, or Cobble	Rocky Substrate or Boulders	Tide Pools	On Macrophytes Pilings, Reefs, Floats, etc.
Order Harpacticoida										
Family Ectinosomidae										
Arenosetella sp.			×	i			×			
A. fissilis			×	i			×			
A. germanica			×	i			×			
Ectinosoma finmarchicum			×	i, s			×			
E. gothiceps			×	i			×			
E. normani			×	s			×			×
E. melaniceps			×	s			×			×
Microsetella rosea	×	×		o						
Pararenosetella gracilis			×	s			×			
Pseudobradya robusta			×	i			×			
Family Canthocomptidae										
Ameriopsis brevicornis			×	i			×			
Ameria longipes			×	s			×			×
Leptastacus sp.			×	i, s			×			
Nitocra platypus			×	i			×			
Paraleptastacus sp.			×	i						
Family Laophonitidae										
Heterolaophonte discophora			×	s, 1			×			
H. littoralis			×	s, i			×			×
H. stromi			×	i			×			×
Laophonte sp.			×	i			×			×
Paralaophonte hyperborea			×	s, i			×			×
P. macera			×	s			×			×
Family Thalestridae										
Dactylopodia glacilias			×	s, i			×			×
Thalestris rufoviolascens			×	i			×			×
Family Tachidiidae										
Robertsonia propinqua			×	i			×			
Family Cletodidae										
Acrenhydrosoma perplexum			×	s			×			
Enhydrosoma sp.			×	s, i			×			
Huntemannia jadensis			×	i			×			
Rhizothrix curvata			×	i			×			
Family Diosaccidae										
Amphiascella debilis			×	i			×			
Subclass Cirripedia										
Order Thoracica										
Suborder Lepadomorpha										
Family Scalpellidae										

[a]b, benthic; o, in open water; n, in top 5 cm of water (neuston); s, subtidal; i, intertidal; p, plankton; mllw, mean lower low water.

Continued

TABLE 11.2.   (*Continued*)

Species	Habitat Unknown	San Juan Islands	Near Seattle	Habitat Location[a]	Mud	Mixed Sediment	Sand	Shell, Gravel, or Cobble	Rocky Substrate or Boulders	Tide Pools	On Macrophytes Pilings, Reefs, Floats, etc.
Mitella (Polliceps) polymerus		×		i				×	×		
Suborder Balanomorpha											
Family Balanidae											
Balanus aquilla	×		×	b							
B. balanus pugetenisis	×	×		s							
B. balanoides	×	×		i							
B. cariosus		×	×	i				×	×		
B. crenatus		×	×	i				×	×		
B. engbergi	×	×									
B. evermanni	×	×									
B. glandula		×	×	i				×	×		
B. hesperius laevidomus	×	×									
B. nubilis	×	×		s							
B. pugetensis	×	×									
B. rostratus	×	×		s							
Family Chthamalidae											
Chthamalus dalli		×	×	i				×	×		
Subclass Malacostraca											
Superorder Phyllocarida											
Order Leptostraca											
Family Nebaliidae											
Epinebalia (Nebalia) pugettensis			×	b, s		×	×				
Superorder Peracarida											
Order Cumacea											
Family Diastylidae											
Diastylopsis dawsoni			×	mllw		×	×				
D. tenuis			×	s, i			×				
Family Leuconidae											
Eudorellopsis sp.			×	b, s	×						
Eudorellopsis biplicata			×	b, s			×	×			
Eudorella pacificus			×	b, s	×	×	×				
Leucon sp.			×	b, s	×						
Leucon nasica			×	b, s	×						
Family Lampropidae											
Lamprops quadriplicata			×	i		×	×				
L. quadriplicata krasheninikova			×	b, s			×				
L. krasheninikova			×	s, i			×				
Family Nannastacidae											
Campylaspis sp.			×	b, s		×					
Campylaspis canaliculata			×	b, s		×	×				
C. (papillata)?			×	b, s		×	×				

[a] b, benthic; o, in open water; n, in top 5 cm of water (neuston); s, subtidal; i, intertidal; p, plankton; mllw, mean lower low water.

TABLE 11.2. (Continued)

Species	Habitat Unknown	San Juan Islands	Near Seattle	Habitat Location[a]	Mud	Mixed Sediment	Sand	Shell, Gravel, or Cobble	Rocky Substrate or Boulders	Tide Pools	On Macrophytes Pilings, Reefs, Floats, etc.
Family Diastylidae											
Diastylis alaskensis			×	b, s	×	×	×				
D. paraspinulosa			×	b, s			×				
D. pellucida			×	b, s	×	×	×				
Diastylopsis dawsoni			×	b, s			×				
Leptostylis villosa			×	b, s	×	×	×				
Order Tanaidacca											
Suborder Dikonophora											
Family Paratanidae											
Leptochelia dubia			×	b, i, s		×	×				
Leptognathia longiremis			×	b, s			×				
Order Isopoda											
Suborder Epicaridea											
Family Bopyridae											
Bopyrid sp.	×	×									
Suborder Flabéllifera											
Family Cirolanidae											
Exocirolana kincaidi			×	i			×				
Family Aegidae											
Rocinela belliceps			×	b, s		×	×				
Family Limnoridae											
Limnoria lignorum			×	b, s			×				
Family Sphaeromatidae											
Exosphaeroma amplicauda			×	i		×	×				
E. ?media			×	i		×	×	×	×		×
E. oregonensis			×	i			×				
E. octoncum			×	i		×		×			×
Gnorimosphaeroma oregonensis			×	i		×	×	×	×		×
Suborder Gnathiidea											
Family Bopyridae											
Hemiarthrus abdominalis	×		×	mllw							
Phyllodurus abdominalis	×		×	i							
Suborder Valvifera											
Family Idoteidae											
Idotea wosnesenskii			×	i		×		×	×		
Suborder Onoscoidea											
Family Ligididae											
Ligia pallasii			×	i					×		
Family Munnidae											
Munna chromatocephala			×	i		×		×	×		×
Order Amphipoda											

[a]b, benthic; o, in open water; n, in top 5 cm of water (neuston); s, subtidal; i, intertidal; p, plankton; mllw, mean lower low water.

Continued

TABLE 11.2.   (Continued)

Species	Habitat Unknown	San Juan Islands	Near Seattle	Habitat Location[a]	Mud	Mixed Sediment	Sand	Shell, Gravel, or Cobble	Rocky Substrate or Boulders	Tide Pools	On Macrophytes, Pilings, Reefs, Floats, etc.
Suborder Gammaridea											
Family Ampeliscidae											
Ampelisca brevisimulata			×	b, s			×				
A. compressa			×	b, s	×	×	×				
A. cristata			×	b, s		×	×				
A. lobata			×	b, s		×	×				
A. macrocephala			×	b, s	×	×	×				
A. venetiensis			×	i			×				
Byblis veleronis			×	b, s	×	×	×				
Family Amphithoidae											
Amphithoe sp.			×	b, s			×				
Amphithoe lacertosa			×	i			×		×		×
A. simulans			×	i			×		×		
Family Aoridae											
Aoroides columbiare			×	b, s, mllw		×	×				×
Family Atylidae											
Atylus collingi			×	i			×				
Family Calliopiidae											
Callioipiella sp.?			×	i			×				×
Calliopiella pratti			×	i			×				×
Calliopius laeviusculus			×	s			×				
Family Corophiidae											
Corophium acherusicum			×	i		×	×				×
C. brevis			×	i		×					
C. crassicorne			×	b, s		×					
C. salmonis			×	i			×				
Erichtionus brasiliensis			×	b, s			×				
E. hunteri			×	b, s			×				
Family Eusiridae											
Eusirus sp.			×	b, s			×				
Paramaera sp.			×	i		×					
Pontogeneia cf. rostrata			×	b, s, mllw		×	×				
P. cf. ivanovi			×	i		×					×
Family Gammaridae											
Anisogammarus sp.			×	i, s			×				
Anisogammarus confervicolus			×	i		×	×				×
A. pugettensis			×	mllw		×					×
Melita dentata			×	mllw		×		×			
M. desdicha			×	b, s	×	×	×				
M. oregonensis			×	b, s		×					
Family Haustoriidae											

[a] b, benthic; o, in open water; n, in top 5 cm of water (neuston); s, subtidal; i, intertidal; p, plankton; mllw, mean lower low water.

TABLE 11.2. *(Continued)*

Species	Habitat Unknown	San Juan Islands	Near Seattle	Habitat Location[a]	Mud	Mixed Sediment	Sand	Shell, Gravel, or Cobble	Rocky Substrate or Boulders	Tide Pools	On Macrophytes Pilings, Reefs, Floats, etc.
Eohaustorius washingtonianus	×		×	mllw							
Family Hyalidae											
Hyale sp.			×	i			×				
Hyale frequens			×	i		×	×				×
H. plumosa			×	i		×					
H. pugettensis			×	i			×	×			
Family Ischyroceridae											
Ischyrocerus cf. *anguipes*			×	i			×				
Ischyrocerus sp.			×	b, s		×	×				×
Family Lysianassidae											
Anonyx sp.			×	b, s			×				
Anonyx carinatus			×	b, s	×	×	×				
Hippomedon denticulans			×	b, s		×	×				
Orchomene sp.			×	b, s	×						
O. decipiens			×	b, s		×	×				
O. pacifica			×	b, s	×						
Orchomene cf. *pinguis*			×	i	×						
Family Oedicerotidae											
Monoculodes cf. *zernovi*			×	b, s, i			×				
Synchelidium sp.			×	s, i			×				
Synchelidium shoemakeri			×	b, s, i		×	×				×
S. rectipalmum			×	b, s		×	×				
Westwoodilla caecula			×	b, s	×	×	×				
Family Photidae											
Photis sp.			×	s			×				
Photis brevipes			×	b, s, i		×	×				×
P. californica			×	s			×				
Podoceropsis inaequistylis			×	i		×					×
Family Phoxocephalidae											
Metaphoxus fultoni			×	b, s		×	×				
Paraphoxus daboius			×	b, s		×	×				
Paraphoxus cf. *epistomus*			×	mllw			×				
P. milleri			×	mllw			×				
P. oculatus			×	b, s	×						
P. robustus			×	b, s			×				
P. similis			×	b, s		×	×				
P. spinosus			×	b, s, mllw			×				
P. variatus			×	b, s		×	×				
Family Pleustidae											
Parapleustes pugettensis			×	i		×					
Family Podoceridae											

[a]b, benthic; o, in open water; n, in top 5 cm of water (neuston); s, subtidal; i, intertidal; p, plankton; mllw, mean lower low water.

Continued

TABLE 11.2. (*Continued*)

Species	Habitat Unknown	San Juan Islands	Near Seattle	Habitat Location[a]	Mud	Mixed Sediment	Sand	Shell, Gravel, or Cobble	Rocky Substrate or Boulders	Tide Pools	On Macrophytes Pilings, Reefs, Floats, etc.
Dulichia sp.			×	b, s		×					
Dulichia arctica			×	b, s			×				
D. tubercata			×	b, s			×				
Family Taltridae											
Allorchestes angustus			×	i		×		×			×
Orchestoidea pugettensis			×	i		×	×				
Orchestia georgiana			×	mllw		×					
Family Tironidae											
Tiron biocellata			×	b, s		×					
Order Mysida											
Family Mysidae											
Neomysis kodiakensis		×		b, s	×						
Suborder Caprella											
Family Caprellidae											
Caprella sp.		×	×	b, s		×	×				×
Caprella californica		×									×
C. irregularis	×	×		s							
C. laeviuscula			×	s, i		×					×
C. mendax	×		×								
C. natalensis			×	s, i							×
Duetella californica	×		×								
Mayerella banksia	×		×	s							
Metacaprella anomala			×	i		×					×
M. kennerlyi			×	s							
Tritella pilimana			×	s							
Superorder Eucarida											
Order Decapoda											
Suborder Caridea											
Family Hippolytidae											
Heptacarpus brevirostris			×	mllw						×	
H. sitchensis			×	i						×	
Spirontocaris prionota	×	×		s							
Family Pandalidae											
Pandalus borealis	×	×		s							
P. danae		×	×	mllw, s						×	
P. jordani	×	×		s							
P. montagui tridens	×	×		s							
P. platyceros			×	i						×	
P. stenolepis	×	×		s							
Family Crangonidae											
Crangon (= *Crago*) *alaskensis*		×	×	mllw, b, s	×	×	×				

[a]b, benthic; o, in open water; n, in top 5 cm of water (neuston); s, subtidal; i, intertidal; p, plankton; mllw, mean lower low water.

TABLE 11.2. *(Continued)*

Species	Habitat Unknown	San Juan Islands	Near Seattle	Habitat Location[a]	Mud	Mixed Sediment	Sand	Shell, Gravel, or Cobble	Rocky Substrate or Boulders	Tide Pools	On Macrophytes Pilings, Reefs, Floats, etc.
C. communis		×		b, s	×						
C. dalli		×		b, s	×						
C. franciscorum		×	×	mllw, b, s	×	×	×				
C. minuta	×	×									
C. nigricauda			×	mllw		×	×				
Suborder Anomura											
Family Callianassidae											
Callianassa sp. juv.			×	b, s		×	×				
Callianassa californiensis	×	×									
C. gigas			×	mllw		×					
Family Upogebiidae											
Upogebia pugettensis		×	×	i	×	×	×				
Upogebia sp.	×	×									
Family Paguridae											
Paguristes turgidus		×	×	b, s		×	×				
Pagurus sp. juv.		×	×	b, s	×						
P. alaskensis	×	×									
P. aleuticus	×	×									
P. beringanus		×		mllw	×			×			
P. brandti	×	×									
P. dalli	×	×									
P. gilli	×	×									
P. gransosimanus		×	×	mllw	×			×			
P. hirsutiusculus		×	×	mllw	×			×			
P. kennerli	×	×									
P. ochotensis	×	×									
P. setosus	×	×									
P. splendescens	×	×									
P. tenuimanus	×	×									
Pyloplagurus schmitti	×	×									
Family Lithodidae											
Haplogaster mertensii	×	×									
Family Porcellanidae											
Pachycheles rudis		×		s				×			
Petrolistes eriomerus		×	×	b, s, mllw		×	×	×			
Suborder Brachyura											
Family Majidae											
Hyas lyratus		×	×	b, s	×		×				
Pugettia gracilis		×	×	mllw				×			
P. producta		×	×	mllw, s				×		×	×
Scyra acutifrons		×	×	b, s			×				

[a]b, benthic; o, in open water; n, in top 5 cm of water (neuston); s, subtidal; i, intertidal; p, plankton; mllw, mean lower low water.

Continued

TABLE 11.2. (*Continued*)

Species	Habitat Unknown	San Juan Islands	Near Seattle	Habitat Location[a]	Mud	Mixed Sediment	Sand	Shell, Gravel, or Cobble	Rocky Substrate or Boulders	Tide Pools	On Macrophytes Pilings, Reefs, Floats, etc.
Family Cancridae											
Cancer sp. juv.			×	b, s			×				
C. gracilis	×	×		b							
C. magister		×	×	mllw, s, i	×		×	×			×
Cancer oregonensis		×	×	i					×		
C. productus		×	×	i, s			×	×			×
Family Xanthidae											
Lophopanopeus bellus		×	×	mllw, b, s			×	×	×		×
L. diegenes			×	b, s			×	×			
Family Pinnotheridae											
Fabia subquadrata		×	×	b, s	×						
Pinnixa barnharti	×		×	i							
P. eburna		×									
P. faba		×	×	b, s, i			×	×			
P. littoralis	×	×									
P. schmitti		×	×	b, s			×	×			
P. tubicola		×									
Pinnotheres (*Faba*) *concharum*			×	b, s			×				
Pinnotheres pugettensis			×								
Scleroplax granulata			×								
Family Grapsidae											
Hemigrapsus nudus		×	×	i				×	×		×
H. oregonensis		×	×	i, s			×	×			×
Oregonia gracilis		×	×	b, s			×	×			
PHYLUM CHORDATA											
Subphylum Urochordata											
Class Ascidiacea											
Order Enterogona											
Suborder Phlebobranchia											
Family Corellidae											
Chelysoma productum		×		b	×						
Corella willmeriana		×		b							×
Order Pleurogona											
Family Styelidae											
Styela gibbsii		×	×	mllw	×				×		×
S. stimpsoni		×							×		×
Family Pyuridae											
Boltenia villosa			×	mllw					×		
Pyura (= *Cynthia*) *haustor*		×	×	mllw, s, i							×
Subphylum Vertebrata											
Class Chondrichtyes											

[a] b, benthic; o, in open water; n, in top 5 cm of water (neuston); s, subtidal; i, intertidal; p, plankton; mllw, mean lower low water.

TABLE 11.2. (*Continued*)

Species	Habitat Unknown	San Juan Islands	Near Seattle	Habitat Location[a]	Mud	Mixed Sediment	Sand Shell, Gravel, or Cobble	Rocky Substrate or Boulders	Tide Pools	On Macrophytes Pilings, Reefs, Floats, etc.
Order Squaliformes										
Family Squalidae										
Squalus acanthias			×							×
Order Rajiformes										
Family Rajidae										
Raja binoculata		×	×	b						×
Order Chamaeriformes										
Family Chimaeridae										
Hydrolagus colliei			×							×
Order Clupeiformes										
Family Clupeidae										
Clupea harengus pallasi			×							×
C. pallasii	×	×								
Order Salmoniformes										
Family Salmonidae										
Onchorhyncus spp.			×							×
Onchorhyncus gorbuscha	×	×	×							
O. keta	×		×							
O. kisutch	×	×	×							
O. nerka	×	×	×							
O. tshawytscha			×							×
Salmo clarki	×		×							
S. gairdneri	×		×							
Salverlinlus malma	×		×							
Family Osmeridae										
Allosmerus attenuatus	×	×								
Hypomesus pretiosus	×	×								
Spirinchus starksi	×	×								
Order Batrachoidiformes										
Family Batarachoididae										
Porichthys myriaster			×			×				
P. notatus			×			×				
Order Gobiesociformes										
Family Gobiesocidae										
Gobiesox (= *Caularchus*) *meandricus*		×	×	mllw				×		
Order Gadiformes										
Family Gadidae										
Gadus macrocephalus			×							×
Microgadus proximus	×		×							
Theragara chalcogramma	×		×							

[a]b, benthic; o, in open water; n, in top 5 cm of water (neuston); s, subtidal; i, intertidal; p, plankton; mllw, mean lower low water.

Continued

TABLE 11.2. (*Continued*)

Species	Habitat Unknown	San Juan Islands	Near Seattle	Habitat Location[a]	Mud	Mixed Sediment	Sand	Shell, Gravel, or Cobble	Rocky Substrate or Boulders	Tide Pools	On Macrophytes Pilings, Reefs, Floats, etc.
Family Ophidiidae											
Ophidion elongatus		×	×	s							×
Family Zoarcidae											
Lycodopsis brevipes		×				×					
L. pacifica		×	×			×					
Order Gasterosteiformes											
Family Gasterosteidae											
Aulorhynchus flavidus			×								×
Family Syngnathidae											
Syngnathus griseolineatus		×		s							×
Order Perciformes											
Family Embiotocidae											
Cymatogaster aggregata		×	×	i	×			×			×
Embiotoca lateralis			×								×
Rhacochilus vacca			×								×
Family Bathymasteridae											
Ronquilus jordani		×				×					
Family Stichaeidae											
Anoplarchus atropurpurescens		×		i				×	×		
A. purpurescens			×								×
Bryostemma decoratum	×	×									
Chirolophis polyactocephalus	×		×								
C. nugator	×		×								
Lumpenus anquillaris		×		s, i						×	
L. sagitta			×								×
Xiphister mucosus	×		×								
Family Pholidae											
Apodichthys flavidus			×	mllw				×			×
Pholis laeta		×	×	mllw				×		×	×
P. ornata		×	×	s, i	×			×		×	
Family Anarhichididae											
Anarrhichthys ocellatus	×		×								
Family Cryptacanthodidae											
Lyconectes aleutensis		×				×					
Family Ammodytidae											
Ammodytidae hexapterus			×								×
Family Gobiidae											
Coryphoptous nicholsi	×		×								
Lepidogobius lepidus	×		×								
Family Scorpaenidae											
Sebastes auriculatus			×								×

[a]b, benthic; o, in open water; n, in top 5 cm of water (neuston); s, subtidal; i, intertidal; p, plankton; mllw, mean lower low water.

TABLE 11.2. (*Continued*)

Species	Habitat Unknown	San Juan Islands	Near Seattle	Habitat Location[a]	Mud	Mixed Sediment	Sand	Shell, Gravel, or Cobble	Rocky Substrate or Boulders	Tide Pools	On Macrophytes	Pilings, Reefs, Floats, etc.
S. caurinus		×	×	s							×	×
S. emphaeus	×		×									
S. flavidus	×		×									
S. maliger		×	×	s							×	
S. melanops		×	×	s							×	×
S. nebulosus		×	×	i	×			×				
S. nigrocinctus	×		×									
S. paucispinis	×		×									
S. pinniger	×		×									
S. ruberrimus	×		×									
Family Hexagrammidae												
Gilbertidia sigalutes	×	×										
Hexagrammos decagrammos		×	×									×
H. stelleri			×									×
Oxylebius pictus			×									×
Family Cottidae												
Ascelichthys rhodorus		×	×									×
Artedius fenestralis			×									×
A. harringtoni			×	mllw						×		×
A. lateralis			×									×
Blepsias cirrhosus	×	×	×									
Chinotus pugetensis			×									×
Clinocottus acuticeps			×	i						×		
C. embryum			×	mllw				×				
Enophys bison			×									×
Hemilepidotus hemilepidotus			×									×
Icelinus borealis	×	×	×									
Jordania zonope	×		×									
Leptocottus armatus			×									×
Oligocottus maculosus		×	×	s, i	×		×	×			×	×
Nautichthys oculofasciatus		×	×									×
Myoxocephalus polyacanthocephalus	×	×	×									
Radulinus asprellus	×		×									
Rhamphocottus richardsoni		×	×									×
Scorpaenichthys marmoratus			×									×
Synchirus gilli	×		×									
Triglops pingeli	×		×									
Family Agonidae												
Agonus acipenserinus			×									×
Agonopsis emmelane	×		×									

[a]b, benthic; o, in open water; n, in top 5 cm of water (neuston); s, subtidal; i, intertidal; p, plankton; mllw, mean lower low water.

Continued

TABLE 11.2. (Continued)

Species	Habitat Unknown	San Juan Islands	Near Seattle	Habitat Location[a]	Mud	Mixed Sediment	Sand	Shell, Gravel, or Cobble	Rocky Substrate or Boulders	Tide Pools	On Macrophytes Pilings, Reefs, Floats, etc.
Aspicottus bison	×	×									
Asterotheca alascana	×	×									
Bothragonus swani	×		×								
Hypsagonus quadricornis	×		×								
Odontopoyxis trispinosa	×	×	×								
Pallasina aix		×		s							×
P. barbata	×		×								
Xeneretmus latifrons	×		×								
Family Cyclopteridae											
Eumicrotremus orbis	×		×								
Liparis pulchellus	×		×								
Order Pleuronectiformes											
Family Bothidae											
Citharichthys sordidus	×		×								
C. stigmaeus	×		×								
Family Pleuronectidae											
Glyptocephalus zachirus	×		×								
Hippoglossoides elassodon	×		×								
H. stenolepis	×		×								
Isopsetta isolepis	×		×								
Lepidopsetta bilineata		×	×	s				×			×
Lyopsetta exilis	×		×								
Microstomus pacificus		×	×	s				×			
Parophyrs vetulus			×								×
Platichthys stellatus			×								×
P. s. rugosus		×		i				×			
Pleuronichthys coenosus			×								×
Psettichthys melanosticus		×	×	s				×			

[a]b, benthic; o, in open water; n, in top 5 cm of water (neuston); s, subtidal; i, intertidal; p, plankton; mllw, mean lower low water.

primary production at this station for respiration alone, while *Molpadia* utilized 0.7% also for respiration. These estimates may have been high. Nevertheless, all three species are energetic dominants in the Puget Sound benthic community (Nichols, 1975).

At the fine mud station in the center of the main basin, the total standing crop was 18,910 g m^{-2}. The standing crop near the beach at Port Madison was 11,050 g m^{-2} (Lie, 1968).

Golden Gardens. In terms of standing crop (number of individuals), the polychaetes, *Lumbrineris californiensis* and *Diopatra ornata*; the ostracod, *Euphi-*

lomedes carcharodonta; and the sipunculid, *Golfingia pugettensis*, were the most important species at Golden Gardens, although the weight of the biomass of each species was similar and the difference was not high enough to indicate the dominance of any one species (Lie, 1968; Lie and Evans, 1973). Mean total standing crop of invertebrates at Golden Gardens was 8730 g m^{-2} (ash-free dry weight).

Port Madison. In general, the Polychaeta, Mollusca, and Crustacea were represented by fewer numbers and less biomass in the center of the basin than at Port Madison. The exceptions were *Brisaster* and *Molpadia*. The polychaetes, *Travisia brevis* and *Laonice cirrata*, and the bivalve, *Macoma calcerea*, dominated at Port Madison, but as at Golden Gardens, no particular species was highly dominant in terms of weight.

The most important contributors to standing crop on the silty sand substrate in the subtidal region at the Port Madison Beach were the polychaetes, *Nephtys ferrugina*, *Diopatra ornata*, *Haploscoloplos pugettensis*, and *Platynereis bicanaliculata*; the brachyuran, *Pinnixa schmitti*; the bivalve, *Nucula bellotii*; and the ophiurid, *Amphiodia urtica* (Lie, 1968).

Mollusca at Port Madison were similar throughout the year in numbers but greatest in biomass in July and least in October, This was probably caused by species of different sizes having population peaks at different times. Polychaetes other than *Pectinaria* were most common in numbers and biomass in July. In October the crustaceans reached their largest occurrence in biomass but not in individuals. This indicates a considerable difference in the size of the species present. In October, polychaetes were most common and had the highest biomass. They were followed by Mollusca in number of individuals, and then *Pectinaria*. However, in biomass *Pectinaria* was more than that of the molluscs. *Compsomyax* was represented by the greatest biomass and lowest numbers. The total standing crop in the center of Port Madison was 9690 g m^{-2}.

One of the more abundant intertidal species at Richmond Beach and Golden Gardens (not included in Armstrong, 1976) was the copepod, *Huntemannia jadensis*. *H. jadensis* was most abundant around MLLW (mean lower low water). Biomass was highest in the summer and fall. Biomass at Richmond Beach averaged 231 μg C m^{-2}, and at Golden Gardens, 212 μg C m^{-2}. Cohort production for this species measured by Crisp's method at Richmond Beach for a one-year study was $1.748 \text{ g C cm}^{-2} \text{ day}^{-1}$ and by the Allen Curve method was $1.628 \text{ g C cm}^{-2} \text{ day}^{-1}$ (Feller, 1982).

FOOD WEBS

Food chains, or predator–prey relationships, in the San Juan area of Puget Sound formed a web of interactions between the plankton, nekton, intertidal, and subtidal communities. In each of these habitats were primary producers, herbivores, herbivore–detritivores, omnivores, and carnivores.

Zooplankton change food habits depending on their age and size. Copepod nauplii, for instance, began feeding on the smallest of the phytoplankton and later fed on diatoms. Planktivores as larvae and juvenile fish, and to some extent as adults, fed on small epibenthic organisms that lived in the sediment surface near shore. The epibenthic group included harpacticoid copepods, mysid shrimp, gammarid amphipods, shrimp and cumaceans, and polychaete worms, which were the same size classes as the zooplankton. Small epibenthic organisms, in turn, fed on benthic algae, bacteria, and detritus. True zooplankton and the micronekton were, in part, dependent on the benthos as well as on plankton for their food (Strickland, 1983).

Open Water
The largest segment of the zooplankton standing crop of crustaceans comprised the copepods. Numerically, during the spring, the dominant copepod was the small *Acartia*, which ate phytoflagellates and small diatoms. Dominating the biomass, however, were the larger copepods, particularly *Calanus pacificus*, although other species were present.

The suspension feeding crustacea fed on diatoms, which dominated the spring bloom. *Calanus* ate mainly phytoplankton of intermediate size, although it sometimes captured stray larvae or protozoans.

Secondary to the copepods in importance were the micronekton, which consisted of euphausiids, amphipods, and mysid shrimp. The euphausiids fed mainly on filament-forming diatoms and microzoa. The mysid shrimp were omnivores, and the amphipods were carnivores feeding on protozoa in the plankton. Carnivorous zooplankton included the predatory copepods, micronekton, chaetognaths, and gelatinous zooplanktors such as ctenophores and medusas. However, they were relatively few in number; the main carnivores in the community were the true nekton, or fish (Strickland, 1983).

Pelagic fish roughly 50 to 200 mm in length were the principal predators of zooplankton. This size class of fish included juvenile and adult herring (*Clupea* sp.), smelt (*Hypomesus* sp.), sand lances (*Ammodytes* sp.), sticklebacks, and juveniles of larger animals such as salmon (*Onchorhynchus* sp.), cod (*Gadus* sp.), hake (*Merluccius* sp.), pollock (*Theragra*), ling cod (*Ophiodon elongatus*), sablefish (*Anoplopoma fimbria*), and dogfish (*Squalus acanthias*). This size class also included juvenile and adult shrimps.

As the fish matured, they used an increased proportion of plankton. Small juveniles of such fish as herring, smelt, and pink and chum salmon (*Onchorhynchus gorbuscha* and *O. keta*) ate principally copepods and crustacean larvae. Larger salmon juveniles ate both micronekton and smaller larval fish. Pink and sockeye salmon (*O. nerka*) ingested swarms of micronekton or larger crustacea, in contrast to the adult coho and chinook salmon (*O. kisutch* and *O. tshawytscha*), which pursued bait fish such as herring and smelt as their common food. This food chain was based primarily on diatoms in the phytoplankton. The diatoms were eaten by crustacean zooplankton (copepods, euphausiids, and larvae), which in turn were eaten by young fish.

Tidal and Intertidal Benthos

Herbivores.   The two sea urchins, *Strongylocentrotus drobachiensis* (green sea urchin) and *S. franciscanus* (red sea urchin), are the dominant subtidal animals throughout the San Juan Archipelago. These sea urchins are herbivores, feeding on various algae. Vadas (1977) found that the brown alga, *Nereocystis leutkeana*, was the single most important food item of both sea urchins. It composed 40% of the diet of *S. franciscanus* and 27% of the diet of *S. drobachiensis*.

Ranking second and third, respectively, in the diets of these sea urchins were the green algae, *Monostroma fuscum* and *Ulva lactuca*. Three species of brown algae, *Agarum cribosum*, *Alaria marginata*, and *Laminaria saccharina*, formed an intermediate group, ranging from 3.4 to 8.6% of the sea urchin's diet. *S. franciscanus* fed less on the brown alga, *Alaria*, than did *S. drobachiensis*, which reflected the depth distribution of both algae and urchins. *S. franciscanus* frequented deeper waters than *S. drobachiensis*, and thus was less likely to encounter *Alaria*, which grew in the subtidal fringe.

Finally, algae, which was fed upon by *S. franciscanus* only occasionally but composed more than 1% of its diet, included the brown algae, *Costaria costata*, *Laminaria groenlandica*, and *L. complanata*. Occasional food for *S. drobachiensis* included filamentous diatoms, *L. groenlandica* and *L. complanata*; another brown alga, *Costaria*; crustose red coralline algae; the red alga, *Opuntiella californica*; and the bryozoan, *Membranipora* sp. Vadas found an additional 12 food items, but these amounted to only 5.8% of all feeding observations (Vadas, 1977).

Sea urchin feeding was a combination of urchin preference and algal availability. For example, *Nereocystis*, *Laminaria saccharina*, and filamentous diatoms were disproportionately grazed in relation to their abundance. These were probably fed upon preferentially. On the other hand, *Alaria*, *Laminaria groenlandica*, and *L. complanata* were all very abundant and were probably fed upon as the result of availability. Some species (*Agarum* sp. and *Opuntiella*) were actively avoided by the urchins, despite high availability and have probably evolved chemical or physical defenses against the sea urchins (Vadas, 1977).

Omnivores.   The polychaete, *Podarke pugettensis*, was found intertidally in several areas on San Juan Island, sometimes in densities of hundreds per square meter. *P. pugettensis* was an omnivore and consumed a wide variety of small benthic invertebrates. Gut and fecal analysis by Shaffer (1978) revealed various polychaetes; crustaceans, including ostracods, harpacticoid copepods, tanaids, and isopods; kinorhynchs; nematodes; individuals and chains of centric and pennate diatoms; one filament of *Enteromorpha*; and some sediment and debris. Most of the organisms found in *Podarke*'s gut were probably prey items, although diatoms may have been ingested accidentally by suction feeding or by being in the guts of those animals eaten.

Shaffer's estimates of the field feeding rate of *Podarke pugettensis* on copepods indicated that a population of 380 *Podarke* per square meter (the average number of *Podarke* observed) would consume about $9.5\,g\,C\,m^{-2}\,yr^{-1}$ of copepods and would have a significant effect on the population of co-occurring benthic copepods (Shaffer, 1978).

Carnivores. Limpets were consumed by the asteroids, *Lepatasterias hexactis* and *Pisaster*, and the snail, *Searlesia dira*, as well as by the nemertean, *Emplectonema gracile*, and various polychaete worms. The carnivorous gastropod, *Thais*, preyed selectively on the barnacles, *Balanus glandula* and *B. cariosus*, giving the competitively inferior barnacle, *Chthamalus dalli*, an increased chance for survival. Those *B. cariosus* that settled in the fall, however, were more likely to survive predation by *Thais*. *Thais emarginata* and *T. canaliculata* tended to be relatively inactive in the winter, while *T. lamellosa* ceased feeding in order to breed. Thus fall-settling *B. cariosus* were not consumed at such a great rate and were able to grow large enough (13 to 15 mm) to be a poor risk for *Thais* to prey upon. In addition, the *B. cariosus* that settled high in the tidal zone had an increased chance of survival because the ability of *Thais* to drill and consume the barnacle depended on sufficient submergence time. *Mytilus californicus* also seemed able to avoid predation by *Thais* with increased size. Occasionally, individuals over 3 cm appeared to escape *Thais*, although larger *Thais* seemed able to eat individuals at least as large as 8 cm. When *Mytilus* survived predation by *Thais*, it was by numerically swamping the local *Thais* populations (Dayton, 1971).

The sea star, *Pisaster*, preferentially fed on mussels until late in the summer, when the absence of mussels forced *Pisaster* to prey on barnacles. *Pisaster* fed on limpets as a secondarily preferred prey. This appeared to have a beneficial side effect for the sea star. By removing limpets (which grazed voraciously on the red alga, *Endocladia*) *Pisaster* ensured the presence of the most important settling space for the sea star's preferred prey, *Mytilus* (Dayton, 1971). Sea stars have also been found feeding on sponges, anemones, bivalves, and ascidians.

Other potential predators of barnacles and mussels included the sea star, *Leptasterias*, whose generalized diet included various molluscan herbivores as well as small barnacles. This sea star appeared to be very susceptible to dessication and foraged only in the lower intertidal zone. *Onchidoria bilamellata*, a dorid nudibranch, also preyed on barnacles although its preferred habitat was protected bays, pilings, and floats rather than rocky intertidal regions (Dayton, 1971).

The carnivorous gastropod, *Searlesia dira*, seemed to prefer a solid rock substrate with medium exposure, where it fed on a variety of organisms, including barnacles, limpets, chitons, and littorines (Louda, 1979). Barnacles were the most important prey items in the upper intertidal zone, limpets the most important in the middle intertidal zone and "other" species, collectively, were important in the lowest intertidal zone. The composition of *S. dira*'s diet tended to follow the pattern of abundance of prey items in the summer and overlapped with that of *Leptasterias hexactis*, *Pisaster ochraceous*, and various species of *Thais*. Through partitioning by prey size, prey mobility, behavior, differing distribution, different periods of activity, and different preferences or feeding success, competition was reduced to a minimum (Louda, 1979).

In general, asteroid echinoderms fed on a greater variety of foods than did many other species (Mauzey et al., 1968). For example, *Luidia foliolata* was observed feeding on holothurians, bivalves, crabs, sponges, and shrimp. *Hippasteria spinosa* fed almost exclusively on sea pens (pennatulid cnidarians) and to a much lesser degree on polychaetes, anemones, and egg masses of nudibranchs.

Mediaster aequalis on sandy bottoms fed about equally on sea pens and partially damaged drift algae, and to a much lesser extent on planktonic diatoms, colonial ascidians, nudibranchs, bryozoans, and scyphomedusae. Dead crabs and starfish were also scavenged by *Mediaster*. On mud substrates this species fed on various types of detritus, including diatoms, dinoflagellates, and barnacles. Other foods were drift algae, dead fish, and in one case a small bivalve. When *Mediaster* was found on pilings it fed on ascidians (*Hermissenda*), hydroids, bryozoans, and barnacles. On rocky or gravelly areas this species fed on sponges, hydroids, and bryozoans.

Gyphyreaster swifti fed on anemones. *Solaster stimpsoni* fed mostly on holothurians but also, in relatively small amounts, on sea cucumbers (*Psolus*), bryozoans, ascidians, brachiopods, and amphipods. *Solaster dawsonii* fed mostly on *S. stimpsoni* but also ate other sea stars, holothurians, and barnacles. *Solaster endica* fed mostly on holothurians and to a lesser extent on bryozoans and ascidians.

Crossaster papporus, found on sandy bottoms, fed mostly on sea pens (pennatulid cnidarians), sea slugs, and sea hares (opisthobranchs) but also fed on *Stomphia* (the "dancing anemone of Puget Sound"), other anemones, barnacles, and gastropod egg masses. On cobbles, *Crossaster* fed on nudibranchs, ascidians, and bivalves.

Dermasterias imbricata fed in subtidal areas on anemones. In the San Juan Archipelago it fed on holothurians, anemones, and tunicates. In other areas *Dermasterias* fed on colonial tunicates, hydroides, bryozoans, clams, barnacles, and crabs. *Evasterias troschelii* fed on barnacles, tunicates, bivalves, gastropods, and polychaetes.

NEAR SEATTLE AND SOUTH PUGET SOUND

Physical Characteristics

Salinity. Salinity in the main basin near Seattle ranges from 27 to 31 ppt (Armstrong et al., 1976). Seasonal variation recorded at a station at the bottom of the central main basin was small, ranging from 29.44 to 30.82 ppt (Lie, 1968). During periods of heavy runoff, shallow lenses of relatively fresh water appear near the mouths of rivers flowing into the main basin. These lenses can remain intact for several days until they reach the northern sill at Admiralty Inlet. Generally, however, land runoff and river discharge are mixed with marine water in the central main basin and form a brackish surface zone. A layer of more saline marine waters flows northward under the brackish surface water as stated above (Winter et al., 1975).

Temperature. Near bottom temperature in a 1963 study ranged from 8 to 12 °C at stations from 12 to 70 m deep and from 8 to 11 °C at a depth of 200 m (Lie, 1968). Surface temperatures averaged about 14 °C in summer and 8.5 °C in winter (Wieser, 1959a). In winter temperatures varied little from surface to bottom (Nichols, 1975).

Oxygen. While Winter et al. (1975) report that water in the central basin of Puget Sound tends to be undersaturated due to low oxygen concentrations in the Strait of Juan de Fuca, Nichols (1975) reports relatively high oxygen concentrations in the same area. Winter et al. found saturation values at a depth of 60 ft and Nichols found concentrations of 4.0 m L^{-1}. Both report high oxygen levels during algal blooms, exceeding 150% saturation according to Winter et al., and 8.0 m L^{-1} was found by Nichols (1975).

Sediments. River transport, shore erosion, and erosion of submarine banks are largely responsible for the character of bottom sediments in the sound. Sediments tend to be a soft silty clay on basin floors, fine sand to gravel on the slopes and boulders, and gravel in the narrows and sills where currents are strong (Lie, 1968).

Community Structure Near Seattle

Open Water. Migratory zooplankters in the sound have been observed to form sonic scattering layers near the surface at night and at approximately 200 m during the day. Many planktivorous fish in the sound form tight layers corresponding to the scattering layers.

Although the smaller copepods reproduced all year, there was a generalized increase in zooplankton in the spring corresponding to the bloom season. These zooplankton continued reproducing throughout the summer while the food supply lasted. Meroplankton larvae exhibited similar timing as planktivorous larval and juvenile fish proliferating in March. During fall and winter, zooplankton populations decline in surface waters and in the deep waters of poorly sheltered areas. Scattering layers disappeared from the main basin due to predation, starvation, and increased winter turbulence and flushing. Sheltered locations such as Carr Inlet and Whidbey basin did not lose their scattering layers, which suggests the possibility that some zooplankton migrate with the help of currents to these areas and overwinter there. This would also give the zooplankton access to the earlier blooms in the warmer waters of these protected areas, and seaward currents in the spring would carry them back to the main basin (Strickland, 1983).

Nekton. The open-water carnivore community was dominated by nekton, which fed primarily on zooplankton. Principal predators on zooplankton were pelagic fish between 50 and 200 mm long. Canivorous zooplankters, although less important than nekton, also fed on smaller zooplankters, such as chaetognaths, ctenophores, and medusae (Strickland, 1983).

An artificial reef constructed in 2.8 m of water about 30 miles south of Seattle afforded the opportunity to study the fish fauna in Puget Sound. The reef, constructed of large rocks from the immediate area, was built on sand and gravel–rock substrate. Eelgrass was abundant in patches in the sandy area surrounding the reef.

Fish abundance was least from December to February. Areas surrounding the reef were barren of fish during this period, although at least 40 species of fish were counted on the reef itself. Beginning in March, fish abundance began to climb, reaching a peak from June to September.

The striped sea perch, *Embiotica laterialis*, dominated the study area in both numbers and biomass, especially on or near the reef and in areas with bouyant kelps. The shiner perch, *Cymatogaster aggregata*, was second in numbers, frequenting both the reef and surrounding area.

Fish found primarily at night were young buffalo sculpin, *Enophorys bison*; the cabezon, *Scorpaenichthys marmoratus*; the English sole, *Parophrys vetulus*; the Pacific cod, *Gadus macrocephalus*; the roughback sculpin, *Chitonotus pugetensis*; the sailfin sculpin, *Cymatogaster aggregata*; the shiner perch, *Cymatogaster aggregata*; the Pacific staghorn sculpin, *Leptocottus armatus*; and the white spotted greenling, *Hexagammos stelleri*.

Small fish such as the copper rockfish, *Sebastes caurinus*; the penpoint gunnel, *Apodichthys flavidus*; and small sculpin, *Oligocottus maculus*, appeared to use the interstices of the reef for protective cover.

The lowest density of fish in the study area was over sand. Rocky bottoms hosted a less dense fish population in the tidal zone than in the subtidal zone. Bottoms with large boulders appeared to be more attractive to fish than did bottoms of smaller rocks (Patton, 1981).

At the Sound's edge in the vicinity of West Point Beach, Carkeek Beach, and Lincoln Beach, several species of fish were found. The tidepool sculpin, *Oligocottus maculosus*, was common (2 to 100 m^2) in tide pools near these sand, cobble, and mixed sand–gravel beaches at depths ranging from 0 to 6 ft below MLLW level. The sharpnose sculpin, *Clinocottus acuticeps*, was common in tide pools from 0 to 3 ft above MLLW, while the smoothhead sculpin, *Artedius laterialis*, was found in densities of 1 m^{-2} or less at MLLW.

Under cobbles at these beaches the high cockscomb, *Anoplarchus purpurescens*, and the northern clingfish, *Gobiesox meandricus*, were common, while the calico sculpin, *Clinocottus embryum*; the penpoint gunnel, *Apodichthys flavidus*; and the saddleback gunnel, *Pholis ornata*, were found in densities of less than 1 m^{-2}.

At Richmond Beach, where cobble and mixed sand–gravel substrates prevailed, the tidepool sculpin, *Oligocottus maculosus*, was common in tidepools, while the calico sculpin, *Clinocottus embryum*, was found in densities of less than 1 per square meter in tide pools. Under cobbles at Richmond Beach, the sharpnose sculpin, *Clinocottus acuticeps*, was common.

At Alki Point, where substrates were cobble and mixed sand–gravel with few areas of sand, the tidepool sculpin, *Oligocottus maculatus*, was again common in tide pools, while the sharpnose sculpin, *Clinocottus acuticeps*, was rare. Both the high cockscomb, *Anoplarchus pupurescens*, and the northern clingfish, *Gobiesox meandricus*, were common under cobbles. The crescent gunnel, *Pholis laeta*, was also found under cobbles but was considered rare (less than 1 per square meter).

Benthos

Algae. A total of 157 algae taxa were found during the study period. Red algae had the highest number of representatives (78), followed by green algae (40), brown algae (27), blue-green algae (7), and diatoms (4) (Thom et al., 1976).

Substrates supporting the largest number of species were the rock-clay bench at Alki Beach, sea walls at Carkeek and West Point beaches, and the boulders at Lincoln Park Beach (Thom et al., 1976).

The greatest number of species (Table 11.2) were recorded in the spring and summer and the fewest in the winter. A spring bloom of brown algae was characterized by fast-growing massive species such as *Alaria tenuifolia*, *Costaria costata*, *Desmarestia* spp., *Laminaria saccharina*, *Petalonia fascia*, and *Scytosiphon lomentaria*. As this bloom declined in July, numbers of species of green algae peaked. In autumn red algae species numbers peaked (Thom et al., 1976).
Invertebrates.   A wide array of benthic faunal assemblages were found in the main basin, inhabiting a great variety of substrates. The substrates which had distinct associations of species were soft mud habitats, mixed sandy habitats, and silty sand habitats.

The absence of large variations in the water temperature, salinity, and oxygen in all seasons resulted in a stable environment that promoted a high degree of species diversity in the subtidal benthos of the central basin (Lie and Evans, 1973). Dominant species varied from substrate to substrate.

Main Basin.   Samples of main basin sediments taken from an average depth of 195 m were characterized by fine soft mud with a high percentage of sand and clay. Dominating the fauna on this substrate were the bivalves, *Macoma carlottensis*, *Axinopsis sericata*, and *Nucula bellotii*; the polychaetes, *Glycera capitata*, *Pectinaria californiensis*, *Phloe minuta*, *Lumbrineris luti*, *Nephtys ferrugina*, and *Malmgrenia lunulata*; the ostracod, *Euphilomedes producta*; the cumacean, *Eudorella pacifica*; and the echinoid, *Brisaster townsendi*. The polychaete, *Travisia pupa*; the holothurian, *Molpadia intermedia*; the echiuroid, *Nellobia eusoma*; and an unidentified nemertean were frequently found at this station, although in low numbers (Lie, 1968; Lie and Evans, 1973).

Although relative numerical dominance remained fairly constant in the 1963 study period, abundances of individual species sometimes fluctuated markedly. *Macoma carlottensis*, *Euphilomedes producta*, *Axinopsis sericata*, *Glycera capitata*, *Phloe minuta*, and *Pectinaria californiensis* all demonstrated dramatic reductions in numbers from February to August 1963. In addition, there was a slight decrease in the number of *Eudorella pacifica* and a distinct increase in numbers of the amphipod, *Cyphocaris challengeri*, from 1963 to 1969 (Lie, 1968; Lie and Evans, 1973).

Golden Gardens and Port Madison
Subtidally, mixed sandy substrates were found offshore near the Golden Gardens Beach and in the center of Port Madison. At Golden Gardens the sandy substrate contained large amounts of debris, such as wood and bottles, while at Port Madison the sediment was mixed with fine shell fragments. Despite these differences in substrate composition, both substrates were of similar coarseness and relatively similar in particle size and can be considered as one substrate in investigating assemblages. These two substrates were ranked closely in terms

of sediment size and considered mixed sandy bottoms (Lie, 1968; Lie and Evans, 1973). The benthic fauna in these stations indicate this similarity in sediment type.

Samples at Golden Gardens were taken at an average depth of 23 m, while samples at Port Madison were taken at a depth of 22 m. Numerically dominant organisms at both mixed sandy stations were the ostracods, *Euphilomedes carcharodonta* and *E. producta*, and the bivalve, *Axionopsis sericata*. The bivalve, *Crenella columbiana*, although not numerically dominant at Golden Gardens in a 1963 study, showed a slight increase in numbers in later studies at this site. *C. crenella* was dominant in the Port Madison benthos (Lie, 1968; Lie and Evans, 1973).

Organisms dominant at Golden Gardens, but not dominant at Port Madison, were the polychaetes, *Lumbrineris californiensis*, *Platynereis bicanaliculata*, *Prionospio malmgreni*, and *Glycera capitata*. The bivalves, *Mysella tumida* and *Axinopsis sericata*, were codominant. The crustacean, *Leptochelia dubia*, was dominant at Golden Gardens (Lie, 1968) but showed a significant reduction in numbers in studies conducted over the next 6 years (Lie, 1968; Lie and Evans, 1973).

Species common at Port Madison but not at Golden Gardens were the amphipod, *Byblis veleronis*; the polychaetes, *Prionospio pinnata*, *Travisia brevis*, and *Trichobranchus glacialis*; and the bivalve, *Psephia lordi* (Lie, 1968; Lie and Evans, 1973).

At the beach at Port Madison subtidal sediments consisted of fine sand mixed with silt and wood debris. This silty sand substrate was dominated by the bivalves, *Axinopsida sericata*, *Nucula bellotii*, and *Mysella tumida*; the polychaetes, *Nephtys ferruginea*, *Platynereis bicanaliculata*, and *Prionospio malmgreni*; the ostracod, *Euphilomedes carcharodonta*; the amphipod, *Paraphoxus variatus*; and the brachyuran, *Pinnixia schmitti*. Over a period of 6 years, *Macoma carlottensis* decreased noticably in number while *Eudorella pacifica* decreased slightly (Lie, 1968; Lie and Evans, 1973).

Intertidal Zone. Puget Sound offers a wide variety of intertidal environments. In the vicinity of Seattle, three types of intertidal beach have been studied, and the flora and fauna typical of these environments have been recorded. One such environment was characterized by cobble and mixed sand–gravel sediment with areas of sand. Boulders were usually encountered near the Mean Lower Low Water (MLLW) level. This mixed sediment and sand beach was found at Carkeek Beach, West Point, Lincoln Beach, and Golden Gardens. Another intertidal environment was found at Alki Point. Cobble and mixed sand–gravel was again predominant, but there were a few areas with only sand. Boulders were common at the MLLW level, while clay and rock benches were found from MLLW to 1.82 m tidal level. Richmond Beach represented another Puget Sound intertidal environment with a cobble and mixed sand–gravel beach but no boulders (Armstrong et al., 1976; Thom et al., 1976).

Algae. A 1974–1976 study of the percentage cover areas of various low intertidal benthic algae species within 0.25 m^2 quadrants on rocky substrata reported *Ulva fenestrata* to cover 20% or more of the study area in July and October 1974 and 1975. *Enteromorpha linza* covered between 5 and 20% in July and October 1974 and 1975. *Ulva lactuca* covered between 5 and 19.9% of the study area in July and October 1974 and between 10 and 19.9% in April and July 1975. Species with cover percentages between 5 and 9.9% at various times throughout the year were *Ceramium washingtoniense, Gigartina papillata,* and *Pterosiphonia bipinnata. P. bipinnata* was the only algae to cover more than 4.9% of the study site in January of any year (Thom, 1980).

At the three beaches with similar environments (Carkeek, West Point, and Lincoln beaches) more than 20% of winter samples taken in the intertidal zone contained *Fucus gardneri, Ralfsia pacifica, Rhodomela larix, Gigartina papillata,* and *Pterosiphonia bipinnata* var. *bipinnata. Ulva fenestrata, Antithamnionella glandulifera, Caulacanthus ustulatus, Cryptosiphonia woodii, Hildenbrandia prototypus, Irideae heterocarpa,* and *Odonthalia floccosa* were present in 6 to 20% of intertidal winter samples. In more than 20% of subtidal samples *Fucus gardneri* and *Gigartina papillata* were found, while in 6 to 20% of these samples *Ulva fenestrata* and *Hildenbrandia prototypus* were found (Thom et al., 1976).

More than 20% of intertidal spring samples at the three beaches contained *Fucus gardneri* and *Pterosiphonia bipinnata* var. *bipinnata.* Species in 6 to 20% of spring intertidal samples included *Odontella aurita, Enteromorpha linza, Spongomorpha saxatilis* v. *saxatilis, Ulva fenestrata,* and *U. lactuca* v. *lactuca.* Other species in 6 to 20% of the spring samples were *Petalonia fascia, Scytosiphon lomentaria, Gigartina papillata, Hildenbrandia prototypus, Porphyra miniata,* and *Rhodomela larix.* More than 20% of subtidal spring samples at Lincoln, Carkeek, and West Point contained *Fucus gardneri,* while from 6 to 20% of subtidal samples from these areas contained *Gigartina papillata* and *Hildenbrandia prototypus.*

Algae found in more than 20% of intertidal summer samples at the three areas were *Enteromorpha intestinalis* var. *intestinalis, Ulva expansa, U. fenestrata, Ralfsia pacifica, Gigartina papillata,* and *Porphyra perforata* f. *perforata.* From 6 to 20% of intertidal samples had *Enteromorpha linza, Spongomorpha saxatilis* v. *saxatilis, Fucus gardneri, Nereocystis leutkeana, Hildenbrandia prototypus, Odonthalia floccosa, Porphyra abottae, Pterosiphonia bipinnata* var. *bipinnata, Scagelia occidentale,* and *Antithamnionella glandulifera. Ulva fenestrata* and *Gigartina papillata* were in more than 20% of subtidal summer samples, while *Nereocystis luetkeana, Hildenbrandia prototypus,* and *Antithamnionella glandulifera* were in 6 to 20% of the subtidal samples (Thom et al., 1976).

Species found in more than 20% of the fall intertidal samples at Carkeek, West Point, and Lincoln were *Ulva fenestrata, U. lactuca* v. *lactuca, Fucus gardneri, Ralfsia pacifica, Gigartina papillata, Hildenbrandia prototypus,* and *Pterosiphonia bipinnata* var. *bipinnata.* In 6 to 20% of intertidal samples at the three sites, *Enteromorpha intestinalis* var. *intestinalis, E. linza, Ulva expansa, Caulacanthus ustulus, Iridea heterocarpa, Polysiphonia paniculata, Porphyra perforata* f. *perforata,* and *Rhodomela larix* were found. *Fucus gardneri, Gigartina papillata,* and *Hildenbrandia prototypus* were in more than 20% of the subtidal samples, while *Ulva expansa* was in 6 to 20% of the subtidal samples.

Invertebrates. In the intertidal zone a rich array of species were found on the many substrates in the cobble, mixed sediment, and sand intertidal environment of Carkeek, West Point, Lincoln, and Golden Gardens. At Golden Gardens, substrate studies included only sand and were restricted to macro invertebrates. The mixed sand–gravel substrate supported the greatest number of species at these beaches. Abundant (densities of more than 100 m^{-2}) species found in mixed sand–gravel sediments were the polychaetes, *Notomastus tenuis, Portodorvillea gracilis, Hemipodus borealis, Capitella capitata, Armandia brevis, Eteone longa, Pectinaria granulata, Eulalia guadrioculata, Phyllodoce maculata, Sigambra tentaculata, Syllides longocirrata,* and *Polydora proboscidea,* and the tube-dwelling *Owenia fusiformis.* Bivalves found in abundance in mixed sand–gravel substrates were *Macoma inquinata, Transennella tantilla,* and *Mysella? tumida.* Other abundant species in the sand–gravel sediment of cobble, mixed substrate, and sand beaches were the isopods, *Exosphaeroma? media* and *Gnorimosphaeroma oregonensis.* The amphipods, *Corphium acerusicum* and *Photis brevipes,* were found in abundance in tubes buried in the mixed substrate (Armstrong et al., 1976).

Among common (densities between 2 and 100 m^{-2}) species in mixed substrate at Carkeek, West Point, Lincoln, and Golden Gardens were the cnidarian, *Anthopleura artemisia,* and the polychaetes, *Mediomastus capensis, Notomastus lineatus, Nereis? zonata, Malacoceros glutaeus, Polydora collumbiana, Pygospio elegans, Branchiomaldane vicentii, Nereis vexillosa, Nereis procera, Nephtys caeca, N. caecoides, Lumbrineris zonata, Micropodarke dubia, Glycinde picta, Glycera americana, G. capitata, Cirratulus cirratus, Phloe minuta, Prionospio cirrifera, P. steenstrupi, Scolelpis? squamata, Paleonotus bellis, Spio filicornis, Spiophanes bombyx, Syllis pulchra, Syllis adamantea adamantea,* and the tube-dwelling polychaete, *Pectinaria granulata.* Common bivalves in mixed substrate were *Macoma balthica, M. obliqua, M. nasuta, Mya arenaria, Clinocardium nuttallii, Protothaca staminea, Saxidomus giganteus,* and *Tresus capax.* Other common species were the phoronid *Phoronopsis harmeri;* the cnidarian, *Amthopleura artemisia;* the holothurian, *Leptosynapta clarki;* and the decapods, *Upogebia pugettensis, Cancer productus,* and *Crangon nigricauda* (Armstrong et al., 1976).

Mixed sediments. On (rather than in) mixed sediment, the isopods, *Exosphaeroma? media* and *Gnorimosphaeroma oregonensis,* and the amphipods, *Allorchestes angustus* and *Pontogenia* cf. *ivanovi,* were abundant. Common on mixed sediment were the nemerteans, *Emplectonema gracile* and *Paramertes peregrina,* and the amphipods, *Hyale plumulosa, Aoroides pugettensis, Orchestoidea pugettensis, Anisogammarus confervicolus, Ampithoe simulans, Calliopiella pratti, Anisogammarus pugettensis, Hyale frequens,* and *Paramaera* sp. Also common on mixed sediment were the caprellid, *Caprella laeviuscula;* the cumacean, *Cumella vulgaris;* the isopods, *Exosphaeroma octoncum* and *Idotea wosnesenskii;* and the decapod, *Pagarus hirsutiusculus* (Armstrong et al., 1976).

Boulders. On the boulders at MLLW level the sponges, *Haliclona permollis* and *Halichondria panicaea,* and the cnidarian, *Anthopleura elegantissima,* were found in abundance. Common polychaetes were *Pseudopotamilla occelata, Schizobranchia insignis, Eudistylia? polymorpha,* and *E. vancouveri.* Also common

was the tube-dwelling polychaete, *Neoamphitrite robusta*, living commensally with the polychaete, *Polyeunoa tuta*. The gastropods, *Collisella strigatella, C. digitalis*, and *Thais lamellosa*, and the bivalve, *Mytilus edulis*, were also abundant, as was the serpulid, *Serpula vermicularis*. Also abundant on boulders in these areas were the barnacles, *Balanus glandula, B. cariosus, B. crenatus*, and *Chthamalus dalli*, and the isopods, *Dynamenella sheareri, Exosphaeroma? media*, and *Gnorimosphaeroma oregonensis*. Common on boulders were the cnidarian, *Metridium senile*, and the nemerteans, *Amphiporus formidabilis, Emplectonema gracile*, and *Paranemertes peregrina*. The molluscs *Cyanoplax dentiens, Katherina tunicata, Thais emarginata, Tonicella lineata, Mopalia muscosa*, and *M. lignosa*, were also common, while common gastropods on boulders were *Collisella pelta, Notoacmea persona, N. scutum, Thais emarginata*, and *Onchidella borealis*. Bivalve molluscs common on boulders included *Hiatella arctica* and *Pododesmus cepio*. In addition, the arachnid, *Lohmannella* sp.; the isopods, *Idotea wosnesenskii* and *Ligia pallasia*; the decapod, *Cancer oregonensis*; and the ascidian, *Pyura haustor*, were common on boulders. Under boulders the holothurians, *Cucumaria minuta* and *Eupentacta guinguesmita*, were common (Armstrong et al., 1976).
On cobbles. On cobble substrates at beaches such as Golden Gardens, Carkeek, West Point, and Lincoln, the sponges, *Halichondria panicea* and *Haliclona permolis*, were abundant. Also abundant were the cnidarian, *Anthopleura elegantissima*; the gastropods, *Collisella strigatela, Littorina scutulata, Thais lamellosa*, and *Lacuna? variegata*; and the bivalve, *Mytilus edulis*. Other abundant species were the barnacles, *Balanus glandula, Balanus cariosus, B. crenatus*, and *Chthamalus dalli*, and the isopods, *Exosphaeroma? media, Gnorimosphaeroma oregonensis*, and *Allorchestes angustus*.
    Common species on cobble included the cnidarian, *Haliplanella luciae*; the nematodes, *Emplectonema gracile* and *Paranemertes peregrina*; the polychaete, *Platynereis bicanaliculata*; and the tube-dwelling polychaete, *Neoamphitrite robusta*; and its commensal polychaete, *Polyeunoa tuta*. Other common species included the molluscs, *Cyanoplax dentiens, Katharina tunicata, Tonicella lineata, Mopalia ciliata, M. lignosa*, and *M. muscosa*; the gastropods, *Thais emarginata, Onchidoris bilamellata, Onchidella borealis, Collisella pelta, Notacmea persona*, and *Littorina sitkana*; and the bivalve, *Hiatella artica*. The asteroid, *Evaserias troschelli* (and its commensal polychaete, *Arctonoe fragilis*), was common as well as the arachnid, *Lohmanella* sp.; the isopods, *Idotea wosnesenskii* and *Exosphaeroma octoncum*; and the amphipods, *Hyale frequens* and *Ampithoe simulans*. Common decapods on cobble were *Pagurus hirsutiusculus, Pugettia producta*, and *P. gracilis*.
Under cobbles. Under cobble no species was abundant, although several species were common. These included the ophiuroid, *Amphiodia occidentalis*, and the decapods, *Hemigrapsus oregonensis, Lophopanopeus bellis, Pugettia gracilis, P. producta, Petrolisthes eriomus*, and *Cancer productus*, and the fish, *Gobiesox meandricus* and *Anaplarchus purpurescens* (Armstrong et al., 1976).
In sand. In the sandy areas of mixed sand–gravel, cobble, and sand beaches the cnidarian, *Protohydra leuekarti*, was abundant as well as the polychaetes,

Rhyncolspio c.f. arenicola, Armandia brevis, and *Syllides longicirrata.* The bivalve, *Macoma inquinta,* was also abundant in sand. Abundant crustaceans included the amphipods, *Corophium acherusicum* and *Photis brevipes,* and the copepod, *Huntmannia jadensis* (Armstrong et al., 1976).

Common species in sand at beaches such as Golden Gardens, West Point, Carkeek, and Lincoln were the cnidarians, *Anthopleura artemisia* and *Ptilosarcus gurneyi.* The gastrotrichs, *Turbonella cornuta, T. mustela, Macrodasys cunctatus,* and *Paraturbanella intermedia,* were frequently found in sand, as were the nematodes, *Oncholaimus brachycercus, O. campylocercoides, Spirina laevis, Onyx rugata, Mesacanthoides sinuosus, Sabatiera clavicauda, S. jubata, Anticoma acumata, Longicyatholaimus guadriseta, Monoposthia costata, Chromadornia germanica,* and *Odonthophora peritricha.* Polychaetes commonly found were *Spiochaetopterus costarum, Nephtys caeca, N. caecoides, Cirratulus cirratus, Ophelia limacina, Onuphis elegans, Scoloplos armiger, S. pugettensis, Paraenella platybranchia, Phyllodoce maculata, Spiophanes bombyx, Protodrilus flabelliger,* and *Saccoccirrus eroticus.* The polychaetes, *Glycinde picta, Rhyncospio c.f. arenicola, Podarke* sp., and *Sphaerodorum minuta,* were frequently found, as were the cumaceans, *Lamprops krasheninikova, Cumella vulgaris,* and *Diastylopsis tenuis.* Copepods frequently found in sand included *Leptastacus* sp., *Pararenosetella gracilis, Amphiascella debilis, Ameira longipes, Thalestris rufoviolascens, Heterolaophonte discophora, Robertsonia propingua,* and *Huntemannia jadensis.* The isopod, *Exosphaeroma oregonensis,* was often found in sand, as were the amphipods, *Westwoodilla caecula, Monoculodes c.f. zernovi, Photis californica,* and *Synchelidium shoemakeri,* and species of *Ischyrocerus, Hyale* and *Anisogammarus.* The amphipods, *Euhaustorius washingtonius, Orchestoidea pugettensis, Cumella vulgaris, Diastylopsis dawsoni, Lamprops guadriplicata,* and *Anisogammarus confervicolus,* were found in densities between 2 and 100 m^{-2}, as was the isopod, *Exocirolana kincaidi,* and the tube-dwelling crustacean, *Leptochelia dubia* (Armstrong et al., 1976; Wieser, 1959a).

On sand.　On sand, the isopods, *Exosphaeroma? media* and *Gnorimosphaeroma oregonensis,* were abundant, while the cumacean, *Cumella vulgaris,* and the amphipods, *Orchestoidea pugettensis* and *Anisogammarus confervicolus,* were common (Armstrong et al., 1976).

On algae.　On algae found growing on mixed sediment, abundant species were the isopods, *Exosphaeroma? media* and *Gnorimosphaeroma oregonensis,* and the amphipods, *Corophium acherusicum, Allorchestes angustus,* and *Photis brevipes.* Common species included the arachnid, ?*Lohmanella* sp.; the isopod, *Exosphaeroma octoncum*; the amphipods, *Ampithoe simulans, Aoroides columbiae, Calliopiella pratti, Pontogenia c.f. ivanovi, Anisogammarus confervicolus, A. pugettensis, Synchelidium shoemakeri, Hyale frequens,* and *Caprella laeviscula*; and the cumacean, *Cumella vulgaris.*

The arachiannelid, *Nerilla antennata,* was typically found on algae at cobble, mixed-sediment, and sand beaches, as were the copepods, *Ameira longipes* and *Thalestris rufoviolascens,* and the amphipod, *Photis californica.* In tide pools the decapod, *Pandalus danae,* was common (Armstrong et al., 1976; Wieser, 1959a).

Alki Point. The substrate at Alki Point represented another intertidal beach environment. Although it was similar in many ways to that of Golden Gardens, Lincoln, Carkeek, and West Point beaches, it had fewer areas of sand and, in addition to boulders, had clay and rock benches from MLLW to 1.82 m tidal level (Armstrong et al., 1976).

Algae. At Alki Point, no species of algae was in more than 6% of samples taken in the winter. In more than 20% of the spring intertidal samples, *Ulva lactuca, Fucus gardneri, Odonthalia floccosa,* and *Pterosiphonia bipinnata* var. *bipinnata* were found. In from 6 to 20% of the spring intertidal samples, *Spingomorpha saxatilis* v. *saxatilis, Ulva fenestrata, Colpomenia bullosus, C. peregrina, Petalonia fascia, Scytosiphon lomentaria, Gigartina papillata,* and *Iridaea cordata* were found. More than 20% of subtidal samples at Alki Point contained *Fucus gardneri* while from 6 to 20% of subtidal samples contained *Gigartina papillata* and *Iridaea cordata* (Thom et al., 1976).

Invertebrates

On boulders. On boulders at Alki Point the sponges, *Haliclona permollis* and *Halichondria panicea,* were abundant. In addition, the cnidarian, *Anthopleura elegantissima* and the serpulid, *Serpula vermicularis,* were common. The gastropods, *Thais lamellosa* and *Collisella strigatella,* were abundant on boulders as was the bivalve, *Mytilus edulis.* The barnacles, *Balanus glandula, B. cariosus, B. crenatus,* and *Chthamalus dalli,* were also abundant. Other abundant species were the isopods, *Dynamella sheari, Exosphaeroma? media,* and *Gnorimosphaeroma oregonensis.*

Common species on boulders included the nemerteans, *Amphiporus formidabilis, Emplectonema gracile,* and *Paranemertes peregrina* the polychaetes, *Eudistyla vancouveria, Pseudopotomilla occelata,* and *Schizobranchia insignis;* and the tube-dwelling *Neoamphitrite robusta.* The molluscs, *Cyanoplax dentiens, Mopalia ciliata, M. lignosa, M. muscosa,* and *Tonicella lineata,* were common. Common gastropods were *Collisella digitalis, C. pelta, Notoacmea persona, N. scutum, Onchidella borealis,* and *O. polymorpha,* while common bivalves were *Hiatella arctica* and *Pododesmus cepio.* Only the holothurians, *Cucumaria miniata* and *Eupentacta guinquesemita,* were common under boulders. Other common species included the isopods, *Idotea wosnesenskii* and *Ligia pallasi;* the decapod, *Cancer oregonensis;* and the ascidean, *Pyura haustor* (Armstrong ct al., 1976).

On cobbles. On cobbles at Alki Point the sponges, *Haliclona permollis* and *Halichondria panicea;* the cnidarian, *Anthopleura elegantissima;* the gastropods, *Thais lamellosa, Lacuna? variegata,* and *Littorina scutulata;* and the bivalves, *Mytilus edulis* and *Collisella strigatella,* were abundant. The barnacles, *Balanus glandula, B. cariosus, B. crenatus,* and *Chthamalus dalli,* were abundant, as were the isopods, *Exosphaeroma? media* and *Gnorimosphaeroma oregonensis,* and the amphipod, *Allorchestes angustus.*

Common on cobbles at Alki Point were the nemerteans, *Emplectonema gracile* and *Paranemertes peregrina;* the tube-dwelling polychaetes, *Platynereis bicanaliculata* and *Neoamphitrite robusta;* and the molluscs, *Cyanoplax dentiens, Mopalia ciliata, M. lignosa,* and *M. muscosa.* The gastropods, *Onchidoris bilamellata, Nassarius mendicus,* and *Onchidella borealis,* and the bivalves, *Hiatella arctica, Collisella pelta, Notacmea persona,* and *N. scutum,* were also common. Other common species were the asteroid, *Evasterias troschelli;* the arachnid, ?*Lohmanella* sp.; the isopods, *Idotea wosnesenskii* and *Exosphaeroma octoncum;* the amphipods, *Ampithoe simulans* and *Hyale frequens;* and the decapods, *Pugettia gracilis, P. producta,* and *Pagarus hirsutiusculus* (Armstrong et al., 1976).

Under cobbles. No species were abundant under cobble at Alki Point. Common species under cobble included the gastropod, *Onchidoris bilamellata;* and the decapods, *Hemigrapsus oregonensis, Cancer productus, Pugettia gracilis, P. producta,* and *Petrolisthes eriomerus.*

In sand. In sand at Alki Point the polychaete, *Armandia brevis,* was abundant as well as the isopods, *Exosphaeroma?* media and *Gnorimosphaeroma oregonensis,* and the tube-dwelling amphipod, *Photis brevipes* (Armstrong et al., 1976). Common species (in densities between 2 and $100 \, \text{m}^{-2}$) in sand at Alki Point were the cnidarians, *Anthopleura artemisia* and *Ptilosarcus gurneyi,* as well as the polychaete, *Saccocirrus eroticus,* and the tube-dwelling polychaete, *Spiophanes bombyx.* The tube-dwelling crustacean, *Leptochelia dubia,* and the cumacean, *Cumella vulgaris,* were common. The amphipod, *Corophium acherusicum,* was common in sand, as was the decapod, *Crangon nigricauda* (Armstrong et al., 1976; Wieser, 1959a).

On sand. On sand at Alki Point, the isopods, *Exosphaeroma?* media and *Gnorimosphaeroma oregonensis,* were abundant, while the cumacean, *Cumella vulgaris,* and the amphipod, *Anisogammarus confervicolus,* were common.

On algae. Abundant on algae at Alki Point were the gastropods, *Lacuna?* variegata, the isopods, *Exosphaeroma?* media and *Gnorimosphaeroma oregonensis,* and the amphipods, *Photis brevipes* and *Allorchestes angustus* (Armstrong et al., 1976). Common on Alki Point algae was the gastropod, *Nassarius mendicus;* the arachnid, ?*Lohmanella* sp.; the isopod, *Exosphaeroma octoncum;* the amphipods, *Ampithoe simulans, Aoroides columbiae, Pontogenia c.f. ivanovi, Anisogammarus pugettensis, A. confervicolus, Synchelidium shoemakeri, Hyale frequens,* and *Caprella laeviuscula;* and the cumacean, *Cumella vulgaris.* The crustacean, *Zirfoea pilsbryi,* was common on rocks at Alki Point (Armstrong et al., 1976).

Richmond Beach. Intertidal substrates were cobble, mixed sand–gravel, and sand, like those of Carkeek, Lincoln, West Point, and Golden Gardens but differed in having no boulders (Armstrong et al., 1976).

Algae. No species of algae was found in more than 20% of samples taken from Richmond Beach. *Gigartina papilatta* and *Pterosiphonia bipinatta* var. *bipinnata* were found in from 6 to 20% of the intertidal samples taken in the winter. *Gigartina papillatta* was also found in from 6 to 20% of the subtidal winter samples at Richmond Beach (Thom et al., 1976).

At Richmond Beach, 6 to 20% of spring intertidal samples contained the following species: *Ulva lactuca* var. *lactuca, Petalonia fascia, Iridea cordata, Palmeria palmata, Porphyra miniata,* and *Pterosiphonia bipinnata* var. *bipinnata* (Thom et al., 1976).

Enteromorpha intestinalis var. *intestinalis* and *Ulva lactuca* v. *lactuca* were present in more than 20% of summer intertidal samples at Richmond Beach. In 6 to 20% of intertidal spring samples, *Enteromorpha linza*, *Spongomorpha saxatilis* var. *saxatilis*, *Ulva fenestrata*, *Fucus gardneri*, *Nereocystis leutkeana*, *Gigartina papillatta*, *Porphyra perforata* f. *perforata*, and *Pterosiphoia bipinnata* var. *bipinnata* were present. In 6 to 20% of summer subtidal samples *Fucus gardneri*, *Nereocystis leutkeana* and *Gigartina papillatta* were present (Thom et al., 1976).

More than 20% of fall intertidal samples at Richmond Beach had *Pterosiphonia bipinnata* var. *bipinnata*, *Ulva fenestrata* and *U. lactuca* var. *lactuca*. At Richmond Beach, 6 to 20% of fall samples contained *Enteromorpha intestinalis* var. *intestinalis*, *Ulva expansa*, *Ralfsia pacifica*, *Gigartina papillata*, and *Porphyra perforata* f. *perforata*. *Enteromorpha intestinalis* var. *intestinalis* and *Gigartina papillata* were in 6 to 20% of fall samples taken subtidally.

Invertebrates

Mixed sediments.   Mixed sediment was substrate for the greatest number of faunal species. Abundant (more than $100 \, \text{m}^{-2}$) polychaetes were *Notomastus tenuis*, *Micropodarke dubia*, *Lumbrineris zonata*, *Protodorvillea gracilis*, *Armandia brevis*, and *Owenia fusiformis*. Abundant bivalves were *Macoma inquinata*, *Transennella tantilla*, and *Mysella? tumida*. Also abundant were the isopods, *Exosphaeroma? media* and *Gnorimosphaeroma oregonensis*, and the amphipod, *Allorchestes angustus* (Armstrong et al., 1976).

Many polychaetes were common (2 to $100 \, \text{m}^{-2}$) in mixed sediment. The cnidarian, *Anthopleura artemisia*, was common on this substrate. Common polychaetes were the following: *Capitella capitata*, *Mediomastus capensis*, *Notomastus lineatus*, *Glycera capitata*, *Hemipodus borealis*, *Glycinde picta*, *Nephtys caeca*, *N. caecoides*, *Nereis procera*, *N. vexillosa*, *N.? zonata*, *Eteone longa*, *Eulalia quadrioculata*, *Sigambra tentaculata*, *Phyllodoce maculata*, *Phloe minuta*, *Malcoceros glutaeus*, *Polydora columbiana*, *P. proboscidea*, *Prionospio cirrifera*, *P. steenstrupi*, *Pygospio elegans*, *Scolelepis? squamata*, *Spio filicornis*, *Syllis adamantea adamantea*, *S. alternata*, *S. heterochaeta*, *S. pulchra*, and the tube-dwelling *Pectinaria granulata*. The phoronid *Phoronopsis harmeri*, and the bivalves, *Clinocardium nuttallii*, *Macoma balthica*, *M. obliqua*, *Mya arenaria*, *Tresus capax*, *Protothaca staminea*, and *Saxidomus giganteus*, were common. The tube-dwelling crustacean, *Leptochelia dubia*; the amphipod, *Photis brevipes*; and the decapods, *Crangon nigricauda*, and *Synchelidium shoemakeri*, were also common in mixed sediment.

On mixed sediment at Richmond Beach the isopods, *Exosphaeroma? media* and *Gnorimosphaeroma oregonensis*, and the amphipods, *Allorchestes angustus* and *Caprella laeviscula*, were abundant. Common species on mixed sediment were the nemerteans, *Emplectonema gracile* and *Paranemertes peregrina*; the amphipods, *Ampithoe simulans*, *Anisogammarus pugettensis*, *Hyale frequens*, *Paramaera c.f. ivanovi*, and *Paramaera* sp.; and the decapod, *Pagurus hirsutiusculus* (Armstrong et al., 1976).

On cobbles.   The cobble substrate at Richmond Beach supported many species. The cnidarians, *Haliclona permollis*, *Anthopleura elegantissima*, and *Halichondria panicea*, and the tube-dwelling polycheate, *Platynereis bicanaliculata*, were abundant on cobble. Other abundant species included the gastropods, *Lacuna variegata*, *Littorina scutulata*, and *L. sitkana*, and the bivalves, *Mytilus edulis* and *Collisella strigatella*. The barnacles, *Balanus glandula*, *B. cariosus*, *B. crenatus*, and *Chthamalus dalli*, were abundant, as were the isopods, *Exosphaeroma? media* and *Gnorimosphaeroma oregonensis*, and the amphipod, *Allorchestes angustus* (Armstrong et al., 1976).

The cnidarian, *Haliplanella luciae*; the nemerteans, *Emplectonema gracile* and *Paranemertes pergrina*; and the polychaetes, *Paleonotus bellis* and *Neoamphitrite robusta*, were all common on cobble at Richmond Beach. The molluscs, *Cyanoplax dentiens*, *Mopalia ciliata*, *M. lignosa*, and *M. muscosa*, were all common on cobble at Richmond Beach. The gastropods, *Callisella pelta*, *Notoacmea persona*, *N. scutum*, *Thais emarginata*, *T. lamellosa*, *Onchidella borealis*, and *Onchidoris bilamellata*, and the bivalve, *Hiatella arctica*, were also common. Common isopods were *Exosphaeroma octoncum* and *Idotea wosnesenskii*. The asteroid, *Evasterias troschelii*; the arachnid, *?Lohmannella* sp.; the amphipods, *Ampithoe simulans* and *Hyale frequens*; and the decapods, *Pugettia gracilis*, *P. producta*, and *Pagarus hirsutiusculus*, were also common.

Under cobbles. Under cobble at Richmond Beach no species was abundant. The gastropod, *Onchidoris bilamellata*, was common, as were the decapods, *Hemigrapsus oregonensis*, *Pugettia gracilis*, and *P. producta* (Armstrong et al., 1976).

In sand. In sand at Richmond Beach the polychaete, *Armandia brevis*; the arachiannelid, *Protodrillus flabelliger*; and the isopods, *Exosphaeroma? media* and *Gnorimosphaeroma oregonensis*, were abundant (Armstrong et al., 1976).

Common in Richmond Beach sand were the cnidarians, *Anthopleura artemisia* and *Ptilosarcus gurneyi*. Common polychaetes were *Nephtys caeca*, *N. caecoides*, *Scoloplos armiger*, *Paraonella platybranchia*, *Phyllodoce maculata*, and *Ophilia limacina*. The tube-dwelling polychaetes, *Spiochaetopterus costarum*, *Onuphis elegans*, and *Spiophanes bombyx*, were also common in sand at Richmond Beach. In addition, the bivalves, *Clinocardium nuttallii*, *Macoma balthica*, and *Tellina modesta*, were common.

The arachiannelid, *Saccocirrus eroticus*, was common in Richmond Beach sand. The tube-dwelling crustacean, *Leptochelia dubia*, was also common in sand, as were the copepods, *Arenosetella fissulus*, *Nitocra platypus*, *Heterolaophonte littoralis*, *H. stromi*, *Dactylopodia glacialis*, *Paraleptastacus* sp., *Paraleptocaris* sp., *Leptastacus* sp., and *Enhydrasoma* sp. The isopod, *Excirolana kincaidi*, and the decapod, *Crangon nigricauda*, were also common (Armstrong et al., 1976; Wieser, 1959a).

On sand. On sand at Richmond Beach the isopods, *Exosphaeroma? media* and *Gnorimosphaeroma oregonensis*, were abundant, while the amphipod, *Calliopus* sp., was common (Armstrong et al., 1976).

On algae. On algae at Richmond Beach the gastopod, *Lacuna? variegata*; the isopods, *Exosphaeroma? media* and *Gnorimosphaeroma oregonensis*; and the amphipods, *Allorchestes angustus* and *Caprella laeviuscula*, were abundant.

Common species on algae at Richmond Beach were the isopods, *Exosphaeroma octoncum* and *Lohmanella* sp.; the amphipods, *Ampithoe simulans, Calliopius* sp., *Paramaera c.f. ivanovi, Anisogammarus pugettensis, Synchelidium shoemakeri,* and *Hyale frequens*; and the tube-dwelling amphipod, *Photis brevipes.* Typical on algae at Richmond Beach were the arachjannelid, *Nerilla antennata,* and the copepods, *Dactylopodia tisboides, Heterolaophonte littoralis, H. stromi,* and *Dactylopodia glacialis* (Armstrong et al., 1976; Wieser, 1959a).

SAN JUAN ARCHIPELAGO

Habitats in the archipelago are varied; the shoreline may be rocky shores, sandy beaches, or quiet bays. Most rock formations are of sedimentary origin, such as sandstone, shale, or limestone; however, some rocks of igneous origin (granite and basalt) are present. The rocks are affected differentially by winds, currents, and wave action. Over time, these abrading forces produce formations as different as steep cliffs and gentle slopes. Sandy beaches may be exposed to high-energy wave action or protected in a bay. In some quiet bays erosion of the land has turned the beaches into mud or muddy sand.

Some of the animals and plants (Table 11.2) prefer areas with relatively strong wave action, whereas others like areas in which there is an accumulation of sediments as a result of little wave action. The habitats that have been studied are the supratidal or splash zone, the upper intertidal, the lower intertidal, and the subtidal or benthic zones. The intertidal zone is most subject to variation in moisture. Organisms living in the upper limits of the intertidal zone and the splash zone, such as periwinkles and small snails of the genus *Littorina,* must be able to withstand considerable desiccation (Kozloff, 1973).

Open Water

Phytoplankton in the main basin of Puget Sound, the various inlets, and the San Juan area consisted mainly of small phytoflagellates, dinoflagellates, and diatoms. The phytoflagellate population began to increase in the warm waters of late summer, especially in the shallow waters of some inlets. The phytoflagellate bloom usually started near the shore and reached a peak in the early winter months. Diatom blooms started in the cool waters of inlets in the spring and continued in the main basin, which remained cool, throughout the summer (Strickland, 1983).

Phytoplankton must stay in the euphotic zone in order to live and to be able to fix carbon. Therefore, they preferred waters with a small amount of circulation that ensured some nutrients being present, as well as optimum light and temperature (Strickland, 1983). The average number of diatom cells in the San Juan Archipelago during the productive season was $100 \, mL^{-1}$ and the peak number was $400 \, mL^{-1}$ (Phifer, 1958).

The bouyancy of phytoplankton was often improved by adaptations of morphology. A common adaptation was a large surface-to-volume ratio that could be increased further by spiny extensions. These modifications to enhance floating were displayed by the dominant diatom genera, *Thalassiosira*, *Chaetoceras*, and *Skeletonema*. During periods when the water was less dense, floating could be enhanced by the excretion of heavy ions such as magnesium, copper, and sulfates; and by the intake of lighter ions such as potassium, sodium, nitrogen, and chloride. Diatoms also promoted their ability to float by the production of oil, a product of photosynthesis. Diatoms with a high oil content tended to float better than those with low oil content.

The composition of the phytoplankton during the period 1923–1929 was somewhat different in Friday Harbor from that in the waters around the San Juan Archipelago. In Friday Harbor, in April, the dominant species belonged mainly to the genera *Thalassiosira* and *Chaetoceras*. In April and May the most common *Biddulphia* species was *aurita*. In the transitional period between spring and summer *Chaetoceras convolutus* was of frequent occurrence and *Eucampia zoodiacus* was common to frequent. *Thalassiosira condensata* and *T. rotula* had maximum development in June and July. *Thalassiothrix nitzschoides* was nearly always present but not very common. In June, July, and August, *Asterionella japonica* was more common. *Tropidoneis antartica* v. *polyplasta* was most frequently found from March to November (Gran and Thompson, 1930).

In 1930, throughout the San Juan Archipelago area, the dominant species of diatoms were quite similar to those of Friday Harbor. From late May to early June the dominant species were *Chaetoceras debile*, *C. radicans*, and *Skeletonema costatum*. These three species formed 65% of the total specimens counted. *S. costatum* continued to be very common in early July, forming about 55% of the total number of cells counted (Phifer, 1958). *C. debile* and *Thalassiosira condensata* practically disappeared in July, whereas the southern species, *Chaetoceras scolopendra*, *C. affine*, *C. compressum*, and *C. lorenzianum*, were common. At a depth of 100 to 200 m during this early July period, *S. costatum*, *Nitzschia seriata*, *N. vacillaria*, *T. rotula*, and *T. nitzschoides* were found (Gran and Thompson, 1930).

The phytoplankton standing crop was influenced by the dietary preferences of the local zooplankton. Two thorough studies of Puget Sound zooplankton were the Friday Harbor study by Johnson (1932) and Strickland's (1983) study of the entire sound but more particularly the main basin and the mouths of tributaries affecting it.

The zooplankton of Puget Sound consists of numerous rare and common species with varying life cycles, and they live in various areas of the sound. Some species, such as some of the flagellates, are primary producers; others are herbivores, while some are omnivores.

Zooplankton consists of those organisms that float or move only short distances. These are often divided into microplankton (protozoa), mesoplankton (certain crustaceans), and meroplankton (fish larvae). Affecting the plankton and being part of it during certain stages in their life histories are the nekton, organisms that move or swim over considerable distances.

Unlike phytoplankton, most zooplankton demonstrated a pattern of daily and seasonal vertical migration. Protozoan plankters were characterized by very short life cycles. Some microzooplankton (such as the protozoans) and the poor swimmers (such as many of the larvae) stayed near the surface. Eddy (1925) found that the protozoans in Friday Harbor were much less numerous in deeper water. He counted 0.86 organism per liter at 50 m depth, and 28 organisms per liter at the surface.

Johnson (1932) and Shelford et al. (1935) found that dinoflagellates, tintinnids, rotifers, copepods, and larval stages of various invertebrates were the main components of zooplankton. In Friday Harbor from 1923 to 1929 the protozoans in the zooplankton were mainly ciliates belonging to the Tintinnida and the Dinoflagellida (Johnson, 1932). Tintinnids were fairly common throughout the year, with some species showing population peaks. *Stensolella expansa* was a very common species; however, the most persistent and widespread tintinnid in this area was *S. ventricosa*. In the spring and summer *Tintinnopsis nitida* was common, while the less common *T. parvula* and *T. rectus* had maximums in May. In the summertime the most frequent to common species were *Favella franciscana*, *Tintinnopsis cylindrica*, and *Helicostomella sublata*. *Tintinnopsis pectinalis* was never very common but had a population peak in the autumn. *Parafavella gigantea* and *P. parumdentata* were found mainly from November through February.

Of the dinoflagellates (considered phytoplankton by some authors) *Ceratium furca* and *Peridinum depressum* were present but not necessarily abundant throughout the year. Other species of *Peridinium* were numerically an important part of the zooplankton but because of their small size were only a small portion of the zooplankton biomass. *Dinophysis* spp. was most plentiful in the summer, and *Noctiluca scintillans* was must abundant in June, July, and August. *Ceratium fuscus*, *C. lineatus*, and *C. macroceros* were most common in the autumn, while in the winter months *C. tripos* was at its largest population but never truly common (Johnson, 1932).

Most of the mesozooplankton (larger copepods) migrated into deeper water during the day and came to the surface to feed at night. The migratory zooplankton congregated in "sonic scattering layers" which were narrow, discrete depth strata detectable with high-frequency sonar. These layers have been observed to a depth of 200 m during the day. Euphausiids, amphipods, and the larger copepods were found at these depths.

Zooplankton fauna varied from one area to another of Puget Sound. *Metridia* and *Calanus marshallae*, for instance, were found in deeper water and in the more stratified water of Dabob Bay and the Strait of Juan de Fuca. By the shores the smaller, nonmigratory mesozooplankton and the macrozooplankton assumed a much more important role as the larger migrators were usually not found.

The peaks of zooplankton abundance appeared to follow the peaks of phytoplankton, as would be expected (Strickland, 1983). In spring the copepod larvae floated to the surface and back into the main basin, where the food was developing. Also, it should be pointed out that the inlets are warmer in wintertime and phytoplankton blooms develop earlier (Strickland, 1983).

The dominant herbivores in the zooplankton (copepods and euphausiids) adapted their seasonal rhythm to the species of phytoplankton on which they preferred to feed. The smallest copepods tended to reproduce continually all year, whereas the larger ones reproduced generally during the spring months. Most of the zooplankters reached sexual maturity and released eggs when food was abundant, and continued feeding and reproducing through the summer as long as the food lasted. As an example, the medium-sized copepod, *Calanus pacificus*, swam to the surface and fed on the first spring blooms. They produced eggs near the surface, where several generations matured and reproduced before the summer food supply waned (Strickland, 1983). In the winter when food was scarce, most of the copepod activity was restricted and some zooplankters went into diapause. The large copepod, *Neocalanus*, released its eggs deep in the Strait of Georgia in February, regardless of the state of the phytoplankton. *Neocalanus* nauplii floated to the surface, fed on early spring blooms, and returned to the depths in July (Strickland, 1983).

During fall and winter a reduction of zooplankton populations, in both surface and deep waters, seemed to be linked to the increased winter turbulence and flushing. However, concentrations of these zooplankton were found in deep scattering layers in locations such as Carr Inlet and Whidbey Basin. It is possible that the larger zooplankton conserved energy and their population by horizontal, seasonal migration, sheltering from turbulence and seaward current in the depths of protected inlets (Strickland, 1983).

Larvae of invertebrates were a year-round component of zooplankton. Copepods, in either adult or larval stages, constituted the main bulk of the zooplankton. The copepod, *Calanus finmarchius*, was found from March to May but never very frequently, while *C. tonsus* was present in large numbers in May. *Paralabidoceras elongatus* was common in all seasons but most abundant in spring and autumn. The copepod, *Microstella resea*, was more frequent in winter. The copepods, *Corycaeus affinis* and *Tortanus discaudatus*, were fairly common at all times without peaking (Johnson, 1932).

Meroplankton larvae exhibited a synchronization similar to that of the copepods. Planktivorous larvae and juvenile fish came into Puget Sound in March when the larval herring began to feed and they all stayed there through August.

Euphausia sp. produced one or possibly two generations each year, with a dramatic increase in their production in April and May during the spring bloom of diatoms. During the growing season euphausiids were more or less commonly maturing, producing young, and dying (Strickland, 1983).

Spring was the season for barnacle nauplii, sea urchin larvae (echinoplutei), and holothurian larvae. Bivalve larvae were more abundant in summer and autumn, whereas gastropod and bryozoan (cyphonautes) larvae flourished from September to November. The larvae of polychaetes and the copepod, *Acartia longiremes*, were fairly common during all seasons but had no period of maximum abundance (Johnson, 1932).

Rotifers were always present in the zooplankton although they never dominated.

Two large species of rotifer provided most of the rotifer biomass. Some fairly large pelagic tunicates were a small but consistent part of the zooplankton. Jellyfish, especially *Aequorea forskalea*, *Phialidium gregarium*, and *Thaumantias cillularia*, were common. In midsummer *Sarsia stomata* and other species of *Sarsia* and *Polyorchis* were common. Ctenophores were also common (Johnson, 1932).

The migration of planktivorous fish and their predators parallel the movement of the zooplankton. Figure 11.3 is a diagrammatic illustration of the interrelationship of the phytoplankton and the zooplankton (Strickland, 1983).

Floating Docks, Boat Floats, and Pilings

Floating docks and boat floats are common in the San Juan Islands and provide a submerged habitat for a wide variety of fauna and flora ordinarily found subtidally. Pilings, to which the floating docks are connected, support many of the same life forms and may have additional intertidal species at levels where submersion is not constant.

Algae.   The algal flora on floating docks was not as varied as it was on the rocky coast, but at least one diatom species, *Navicula*, which formed branched gelatinous tubes, was common on the floats in this area. In many cases the green alga, *Ulva lactuca*, "sea lettuce", was decidedly the dominant alga. An alga similar to *Ulva lactuca*, and often intermixed with it on floats, was *Monostroma*, usually of the species *fuscum*. Another green alga that was often present was *Enteromorpha*, a euryhaline genus tolerant of low salinities as well as fairly high amounts of salt. The semimicroscopic green alga, *Derbesia marina*, is sometimes common on these floats in its spore-producing form. This phase was called *Halicystis ovalis* until it was found to be a life stage of *D. marina* (Kozloff, 1973).

The most conspicuous seaweed, in terms of mass, on these floats was the brown alga or kelp, *Laminaria saccharina*. Often growing on the *Laminaria* or attached to it was the kelp, *Costaria costata*. Another brown alga, not as large as the above-mentioned species but commonly found on floats, was *Desmarestia viridis* (= *D. media*).

Polyneura latissima was one of the relatively few larger red algae found on floats. Like many other float organisms, *P. latissima* was more characteristic of low-tide levels of rocky shores. Red algae that were common on floats were typically small and finely branched species that were members of a complex of genera that included *Antithamnion*, *Antithamnionella*, *Hollembragia*, and *Scagellia* (Kozloff, 1973).

Invertebrates.   One of the most common protozoans found associated with these floating docks was the suctorian, *Ephelota gemmipara*. It grew on hydroids such as *Obelia* and *Tubularia*. It also grew attached to worm tubes, tunicates, wood, and occasionally on exoskeletons of planktonic crustacea. When it was very abundant it formed a conspicuous white fuzz on the surface to which it was attached. The shelled protozoans, the Foraminifera, were generally abundant wherever detritus accumulated. In material that had been scraped from the surface of a float, the foraminiferan, *Gromia oviformis,* was found. This foraminiferan fed by means of long, slender pseudopodia which engulfed bacteria, small diatoms, and other microscopic organisms.

Scypha, an upright, vaselike calcareous sponge, and the encrusting siliceous sponges, *Haliclona* and *Halichondria,* were common on floats and docks (Kozloff, 1973).

In addition to the protozoan, *Ephelota,* diatoms and other hydroids were often tightly attached to the stalks of *Obelia* colonies. Various kinds of small worms and crustacea wandered in and out of the stalks of these hydroids or remained in the coating of diatoms and sediment stuck to the *Obelia.* Two distinctive types of organisms that were part of almost every *Obelia* colony were the caprellid amphipods and the sea slug.

The predominant athecate hydroid in the San Juan Archipelago was *Tubularia marina.* The hydroid, *Proboscidactyla flavicirrata,* often attached to the lips of the tubes of the polychaetes, *Schizobranchia insignis* and *Pseudopotamilla ocellata.* Common, particularly in the spring, was the polyp phase of the scyphozoan medusa. These polyps, scyphistomae, preferred to attach to the shaded underside of floats, where they were occasionally extremely abundant. They probably were the polyp phase of *Aurelia* (Kozloff, 1973).

The most common sea anemone attached to floats was the carnivorous *Metridium senile,* which fed on small organisms. Another sea anemone, *Telia crassicornis,* was also fairly common.

Turbellarian flatworms of different species were often seen crawling over and around organisms attached to floats. However, neither these species nor their habitats and ecological relationships were well known. The most common nemertean found in material scraped off the floats was *Tubulanus sexlineatus,* an animal about 50 cm long. This species inhabited a parchmentlike tube and fed on polychaetes and perhaps other small organisms (Kozloff, 1973).

The most common sabellid encountered on floats was *Schyzobranchia insignis,* which sometimes formed huge masses, which, in turn, provided hiding places or a substrate for other animals. Other sabellids of this habitat were *Pseudopotamilla ocellata, Eudistylia vancouveri,* and *Myxicola infundibulum.* Small serpulids of the genus *Spirorbis* were often found on hard substrates associated with these floats. *Spirorbis* sp. was common on shells of mussels and other molluscs, on the holdfasts of seaweeds, or associated with clumps of worm tubes. Two nearly ubiquitous polychaetes, *Halosydna brevisetosa* and *Harmothoe imbricata,* were commensal, particularly with polychaetes of the family Terebellidae. They were carnivores feeding on a variety of invertebrates, including other polychaetes.

The arborescent bryozoan, *Bugula,* was regularly represented on floats. It appeared to be soft, but because it was somewhat calcified, was brittle and gritty. An encrusting bryozoan, *Membranipora membranacea,* was common only during late spring and summer and found on the flat blades of brown algae such as *Laminaria saccharina.* Sea slugs were found here and there on *Membranipora.* Another encrusting bryozoan, *Schizoporella bicornis,* was found at all seasons on the shells of mussels and barnacles or other hard substrates. *Dendrobeania lichenoides*, which formed a leaflike growth, was often found on floats mixed with *Bugula*, hydroids, sponges, and other organisms (Kozloff, 1973).

Mollusca were a part of the community living on floating docks, boat floats, and pilings. The chitons, *Tonicella lineata*, *Mopalia muscosa*, *M. ciliata*, and *M. lignosa*, were fairly common. The only limpet that one could expect to find in this habitat was *Callisella pelta*. Nudibranch gastropods, the sea slugs, were perhaps the most ubiquitous molluscs on floats. The most common species, *Hermissenda crassicornis* (an eolid nudibranch), consumed hydroids, ascidians, other molluscs, eggs of various sorts, and pieces of fish. Another eolid, *Aeolidia papillosa*, fed almost exclusively on anemones, particularly *Metridium* and *Telia* species. The tiny eolid, *Eubranchus olivaceus*, preyed on the *Obelia* colonies among which it lived, partially destroying the colonies by nipping off the polyps. The dendronotid nudibranch, *Dendronotus frondosus*, fed to a large extent on the scyphistomae of jellyfish. Another common nudibranch found on floats was *Archidoris montereyensis*, the sea lemon, which fed almost entirely on sponges, especially *Halichondria*.

The prevailing bivalve on floats was the edible mussel, *Mytilus edulis*. It formed dense masses and thus provided protection for other organisms. The shells served as substrate for barnacles, hydroids, bryozoans, and ascidians. The pink scallop, *Chlamys hastata hericia*, was frequently found on floats. *Bankia setacea*, a bizarre mollusc known as the shipworm, often burrowed into wooden floats, causing considerable damage.

The chief predators of float fauna were the sea stars, which were either *Pisaster ochraceus* or *Evasterias troschelii*. They preyed upon mussels and other bivalves as well as barnacles.

The principal sea cucumber on floats was *Eupentacta quinquesemita*. *Cucumaria miniata* was occasionally found on floats, although its usual habitat was the lowest intertidal zone of rocky areas (Kozloff, 1973).

Barnacles were common to float habitats and pilings. The most nearly ubiquitous barnacle was *Balanus glandula*, which was typically found in high-salinity water. Also common on floats was *B. cariosus*. These two species differed in their habitats on floats, as *B. cariosus* was found below the low-water line, whereas *B. grandula* often formed sizable populations at or even slightly above the water line, where the surface was wet only by agitation. Because *B. grandula* did not need total submersion it was also found intertidally on pilings.

Amphipods and isopods were common arthropods of the float habitat. The largest amphipods, members of the genus *Ampithoe*, were about 3 cm long. In among the detritus and silt were found small amphipods of the genus *Corophium*, which formed masses of soft muddy tubes. This detritus-feeding genus was particularly common on floats where salinity was reduced and the silting heavy. The most common and conspicuous isopod was *Idotea wosnesenskii*. This isopod hung onto holdfasts, stalks and blades of seaweed, and onto worm tubes. Besides being abundant in this habitat, it was also common under rocks on the shore. A tiny burrowing isopod common on floats and pilings was *Limnoria lignorum*, the gribble. *Limnoria* caused enormous damage and could be referred to as one of the "termites of the sea." Another isopod found on floats and pilings was *Gnorinosphaeroma oregonensis*. It was often found living under mussels, among barnacles or in cavities in wood mined by the shipworm and the gribble. Large populations of *G. oregonensis* usually indicated that the salinity was a little below the full strength of seawater (Kozloff, 1973).

Associated with the floats and clinging to the attached seaweed were the "broken back shrimp" of the genus *Heptacarpus*. Other shrimp found in the float community were the straight bodied shrimp, *Pandalus* sp., and the coon-striped shrimp, *P. danae*. The largest crab associated with floats was the kelp crab, *Pugettia producta*. Two species of decorator crab found on floats were *Pugettia gracilis* and *Oregonia gracilis*.

Chordates. Five solitary ascidians, urochordates, were found fairly commonly on floats. These five were *Ascidia callosa*, *Pyura haustor*, *Corella willmeriana*, *Boltenia villosa*, and *Chelysoma productum*. The compound ascidian, *Distaplia occidentalis*, was more or less ubiquitous on floats, floating docks, and pilings (Kozloff, 1973).

Benthos

The submerged benthos areas are exposed only by extremely low tides and merge into deeper water. The habitats vary from high energy (strong wave action) on exposed rocks, to moderate wave action on rocky shores, to quiet areas between rocks. There are also sandy areas which are quiet zones resembling tidal pools and areas that have muddy sand deposits. Each of these habitats has a characteristic fauna and flora.

Rocky Areas. Brown algae growing on exposed, rocky areas were *Laminaria setchellii*, *L. saccharina*, *L. groenlandica*, and *Costaria costata*. The kelp, *Egretia menziesii*, grew in more protected areas. Tightly attached to the exposed rocks were the red coralline algae, *Corallina*, *Calliarthron*, *Bossiella*, and *Lithothamnion*. Of the noncoralline red algae, *Antithamnion* was most common. Other red algae in this habitat were stipes and fronds of *Constantinea simplex*, *C. rubulifera*, *Gigartina exasperata*, and *Iridaea cordata* (Kozloff, 1973).

In very exposed areas hydroids with a thick perisarc were found. They included species of *Aglaophenia* and *Abietinaria* associated with the common mollusc of this area, the California mussel. In this habitat were the nemerteans, *Tubulanus polymorphus* and *Micrura verrilli*, which secreted parchment tubes usually on the underside of rocks. Nemerteans ate worms (especially polychaetes), small mollusc crustacea, and other animals. The brittle star, *Ophiopholis aculeata*, was found in this habitat as well as the purple sea urchin, *Strongylocentrotus purpuratus* (Kozloff, 1973).

In rocky areas with less wave action were found the large brown algae, *Pteryogophora californica* and *Alaria marginata*. Associated with them were the kelp, *Nereocystis leutkeana*, and the smaller brown algae, *Desmarestia ligulata* and *D. viridis*. The brown alga, *Sargassum muticum*, which was introduced from Japan, has become established in this area. Resembling *Sargassum* was the brown alga, *Cystoseira geminata*, which has a brown algal epiphyte, *Coilodesme californica.* In these fairly exposed areas are hydroids belonging to the genera *Obelia, Coryne,* and *Tubularia.*

Living in and associated with the rocks in areas of fairly high wave action, but also in regions of moderate to low wave action, were the chiton, *Katharina* sp. and *Cryptochiton stelleri.* Grazing on the coralline algae, *Lithothamnion,* were the chiton, *Tonicella lineata,* and the white cap limpet, *Acmaea mitra* (Kozloff, 1973).

Particularly associated with this region of moderate wave action were the sea slugs, *Hermissenda crassicornis, Aeolidia papillosa, Archidoris montereyensis,* and *Diaulula sendiegensis.* Other slugs in this area were *Archidoris odhneri* and *Acanthodoris brunnea. Onchidoris bilamellata, Triopha carpenteri,* and *Laila cockerelli* were found in this zone. Predators were the sponge eater, *Cadlina luteomarginata,* and *Dirona albolineata,* which fed on ascidians, small snails, and bryozoa, and *Dirona surantio,* which fed on bryozoa.

Sometimes submerged and sometimes in the lower intertidal zone was found the sea star, *Pycnopodia helianthoides,* often referred to as the sunflower star, and the blood star, *Henricia leviuscula.* These two stars were also found in deeper water. The sea cucumbers (holothurians) found here were *Parastichopus californicus, Cucumaria miniata,* and *Eupentacta guinquesemita,* the latter being found in crevices and spaces between rocks (Kozloff, 1973).

Between crevices of rocks and under rocks where there was very little wave action were found a variety of crabs. The predominant hermit crabs were *Pagurus granosimanus, P. hirsutiusculus,* and *P. beringanus.* The latter species used the shells of *Thais lamellosa, T. canaliculata,* and *Searlesia dira.* The smaller specimens of *P. beringanus* used the shells of *Amphissa columbiana* and *Calliorstoma ligatum* and *Bittium eschrichtii.* Clinging to the kelp or hiding under it was the kelp crab, *Pugettia producta,* which was common in this habitat. *Pugettia gracilis,* a smaller crab, was also characteristic of this habitat. Other crabs in this area were the sharpnosed crab, *Scyra acutifrons,* and the red crab, *Cancer productus. Oregonia gracilis,* the spider crab, occurred here as well as in the more exposed intertidal waters.

Quiet Waters.   The surf grass, *Phyllospadix scouleri,* and the eelgrass, *Zostera,* were found in quiet waters. The red alga, *Smithora naiadum,* grew on the leaves of these plants. Another alga in these quiet waters was the green alga, *Codium fragile.* The red corraline alga, *Lithothamnion,* grew on the surfaces of rocks, as did three other red corallines, *Corallina, Calliarthron,* and *Bossiella.* Also present were the red algae, *Odonthalia floccosa* and *Rhodomela larix.* These algae often sheltered smaller organisms, particularly amphipod crustaceans. Growing on the surfaces of these red algae was the brown alga, *Soranthera ulvoidea* (Kozloff, 1973).

Anemones were common in quiet waters. The green anemone, *Anthopleura xanthogrammica,* supported a sizable population of symbiotic microscopic algae composed of zooxanthellae and zoochlorellae. In among shell fragments or fine gravel were the anemones, *Tealia crassicornis* and *T. coriacea.*

Deep Water.   In the deeper waters which merge with the shallower benthic areas the northern abalone, *Haliotis kamtschatkana*, and the ascidian, *Styela gibbsii*, were found. The latter was often attached to stones or shells of the snail, *Trichotropis*. The sipunculan, *Phascolosoma agassizii*, was found in muddy sand sometimes associated with rocks, but more often just in muddy sand. The sipunculan, *Themeste pyroides*, was sometimes found in burrows excavated by rock-boring bivalve molluscs. In many sand or gravelly areas there was not a very distinct fauna. The sea pen (a cnidarian), *Ptilosarcus gurneyi*, and the nudibranch, *Armina californicus*, were found in deeper water (Kozloff, 1973).

Eelgrass (*Zostera*) Beds.   Eelgrass beds were found in the very shallow benthic area and sometimes in the lower intertidal zone. The leaves and stems of eelgrass were colonized by diatoms and bacteria. Algae other than diatoms, such as the red alga, *Smithora naiadum*, live in this habitat.

Herbivores found on the eelgrass included ciliated protozoans, some turbellarian flatworms, and crustacea. Carnivores that frequented the *Zostera* beds included some ciliates and most of the turbellarians and nemerteans, particularly *Tetrastemma*. The sessile jellyfish, *Haliclystus*, and the hydroid, *Obelia longissima*, were often found in great numbers on eelgrass. Common jellyfish within the eelgrass beds were *Gonionemus vertens* and *Haliclystus auricula*. *Gonionemus* fed on small crustacea and fish larvae, while *Haliclystus* fed on caprellid amphipods, which were abundant in this area. Sea anemones, including *Epiactis prolifera*, were very common in eelgrass beds, as were the nudibranch gastropods, *Melibe leonina*, *Hermissenda crassicornis*, and *Aeolidia papillosa*. *Hermissenda* fed on the hydroids and *Aeolidia* upon sea anemones.

In summer the bubble shell, *Haminoea virescens* (a gastropod mollusc), was often abundant in muddy eelgrass beds. Also found in this habitat were the clams, *Macoma nasuta* and *M. irus*. The seastar, *Lepasterias hexactis*, was common in eelgrass, where it lives among the rhizomes, moving out to feed on the leaves at night. Isopods were also common in the eelgrass, particularly *Idotea resecata*, *I. aculeata*, and *I. wosnesenskii*. Common on or around eelgrass were the crabs, *Pugettia gracillis* and *P. producta*, and the hermit crab, *Telmessus cheiragonus*, all of which were common in deeper water as well.

Intertidal Areas

Splash Zone.   The splash zone, or supratidal zone, had a lower limit of about 7 ft (2.1 m) above MLLW. The habitat was dampened by wave spray and rain but inundated by only the highest tides. Lichens were plentiful. A common, bright orange lichen was *Caloplaca*. *Verrucaria*, which formed black bands on the rocks, was crusted with blue–green algae. In this area the green alga, *Prasiola meridionalis*, which had blades about 1 cm long, was found. Where water seeped through fissures in these vertical rocks, bright yellow–green *Enteromorpha intestinalis* grew. When *E. intestinalis* died, it turned white, so that the yellow–green of this alga was splotched with white.

Two species of periwinkles, *Littorina sitkana* and *L. scutulata*, and the limpet, *Collisella* (= *Acmaea*) *digitalis*, were found commonly in the splash zone. All three animals were herbivores that fed on algae scraped from the rocks. They were frequently found clustered in cracks where moisture collected and algae grew a little more heavily. Hiding under lower edges of boulders was often found the large limpet, *Notoacmea* (= *Acmaea*) *persona*. This limpet sometimes reached a length of about 5 cm and in some places was very common in the splash zone and upper intertidal zone. At night it fed on the surface film of algae and diatoms (Kozloff, 1973).

Two species of barnacles, *Chthamalus dalli* and *Balanus glandula*, were found in the splash zone. The latter barnacle often grew very large because the range of its predator, snails of the genus *Thais*, did not extend as far above MLLW as the barnacles grew. These barnacles were filter feeders and therefore dependent on high tides for sufficient water to obtain their food, but they survived being left high and dry for a long while without feeding.

In deep crevices and under ledges in areas that were rarely drenched with seawater the isopod, *Ligia pallassii*, was found. The isopod was a scavenger and fed on decaying algae (Kozloff, 1973).

Upper Intertidal Zone.   The upper intertidal zone extended from the lower limit of the splash zone to about 4 ft (1.22 m) above MLLW. Thin green sheets of "sea lettuce," the green alga, *Ulva*, were quite abundant in the upper intertidal zone, particularly in tide pools. *Fucus distichus*, a brown alga, was most abundant in late spring and summer. Another common brown alga was *Ralfsia*, which formed a brown–black crust on the rocks and resembled two common encrusting red algae. The red algae, *Hildenbrandia* and *Petrocelis*, were purplish, brownish, or blackish in color when dry. When wet, *Hildenbrandia* turned red and *Petrocelis* became reddish brown. Recently, *Petrocelis* was determined to be a phase in the life cycle of *Gigartina papillata*. Another red alga, *Endocladia muricata*, was also characteristic of the upper intertidal zone. It was small and rather delicate and formed tufts not over 3 cm high. The color of these tufts was brownish red to greenish brown or blackish brown. *Cumagloia andersonii*, a red, was more common on exposed rocky areas. It grew several stems that were as much as 30 cm long with rather short side branches. It was most commonly a greenish red or purplish red in color and was slimy to the touch. A red alga that was noticeable on the upper surfaces of smooth boulders was *Bangia fuscopurpurea*. It was a rusty purplish brown or blackish color and grew in rather fine filaments. During the ebb tide the filaments spread out over the rocks. *Porphyra perforata*, another red alga, was also found in this zone, forming broad sheets that were sometimes grayish to brownish purple. The sheets appeared to be ruffled and somewhat perforated near their edges (Kozloff, 1973).

The barnacles, *Balanus glandula* and *B. cariosus*, were often found associated with algae. The limpet, *Collisella digitalis*, was present but more typical of this zone were *C. strigatella*, *C. pelta*, and *Notacmea scutum*. Larger snails common in this area were *Thais emarginata* and *T. canaliculata*. Unlike the limpets and littorines, these two species of *Thais* were carnivores and very important predators of barnacles. The barnacle, *Balanus glandula*, seemed to be preferred as food over *B. cariosus*. The *Thais* ate the barnacle by drilling a small hole through its shell and then injecting through the hole a toxic substance that relaxed the barnacle's valve-closing muscles. Also living in this zone, on the lower edges of rocks set on gravel and mud, was the spindle shell, *Searlesia dira*. This snail had rather catholic, carnivorous tastes, eating littorines, barnacles, worms, and other animals.

The only hermit crab in the upper intertidal zone was *Pagurus hirsutiusculus*, which was found in tide pools and under rocks and macroalgae. When rocks occurred on gravelly or sandy substrate, and where decaying seaweed accumulated, two species of isopod, *Idotea wosnesenskii* and *Gnorimosphaeroma oregonensis*, were abundant (Kozloff, 1973).

Sandy Beaches and Quiet Bays. Sandy beaches of the upper and lower intertidal zones were of relatively pure fine sand, sand mixed with gravel or gravel and cobblestones, or muddy sand. Beaches tended to be low-energy areas with waves usually only 1 or 2 ft high; however, some San Juan Archipelago beaches were in areas that are steep, and they were very narrow.

The Pools. Tide pools formed in hollows and crevices of intertidal rocks provided a sheltered habitat in which organisms typical of subtidal habitats were often found. An example is the surf grass, *Phyllospadix*, a member of the Zosteriaceae, which typically lived in subtidal zones but was found in tide pools and gullies where water was always present.

In the splash zone, depressions in the rock occasionally held miniature tide pools containing a "pea soup" mixture of microscopic green algae and diatoms. In these pools bright red copepods belonging to the genus *Tigriopus* were frequently seen.

Tide pools were common in both upper and lower intertidal zones. As mentioned above, the green alga, *Ulva*, and the hermit crab, *Pagurus hirsutiusculus*, were abundant in these tide pools. The largest specimens of the hermit crab preferred the shells of *Thais emarginata* and *Searlesia dira*. The smaller specimens were most often found in the shells of two species of *Littorina* that were common in this area. The hermit crab fed mainly on detritus but scavenged dead animals and plant material to some extent. The tidepool sculpin, *Oligocottus maculosus*, was the only fish found frequently in upper and lower intertidal pools (Kozloff, 1973).

Lower Intertidal Zone. This zone occupied the area between 4 ft (1.22 m) above MLLW and mean low tide.

The algae of this zone consisted mainly of species of *Ulva* and *Spongomorpha coalita*, two green algae, and the brown algae, *Fucus*, *Lethesia difformis*, and *Hedophyllum cessile*, which was the dominant species. Also present was the red alga, *Halosaccion glandiforma* (Kozloff, 1973).

The sea anemone, *Anthopleura elegantissima*, was found everywhere in this zone where water accumulated. It was usually found growing on rocks where sand and fragments of shell gathered around the animals. *A. elegantissima* was a carnivore and probably fed on crustaceans.

Where there was considerable wave action, as on the west side of San Juan Island and in the southern part of Lopez Island, there were beds of the California mussel, *Mytilus californianus*. Colonies of the goose barnacle, *Pollicipes polymerus*, were often present within the beds of California mussel or alternate with them. Other organisms, including the sea cucumber, *Cucumaria pseudocurata*, and the annelid worm, *Mereis vexillosa*, formed an interesting assemblage in the California mussel beds. Also characteristic of this zone was the black chiton, *Katharina tunicata*, which grazed on a film of diatoms and other algae that coated the rocks. The molluscs, *Thais lamellosa*, *T. emarginata*, *T. canaliculata*, and *Searlesia dira*, were common in the lower intertidal zone.

The most conspicuous sea star in the rocky lower intertidal area was the purple phase of *Pisaster ochraceus*. It fed mainly on the California mussel when available, but consumed any edible mussel, the acorn barnacle, limpets, and other snails. This sea star moved into the upper intertidal zone with rising tide and moved back down to the lower intertidal zone after the tide ebbed (Kozloff, 1973).

Under loose rocks and in cracks, the crabs, *Hemigrapsus nudus* and *H. oregonensis*, were frequently found. *H. nudus* occupied the more exposed rocky situations, whereas *H. oregonensis* was typical of quiet water and a rocky habitat. The most common hermit crab of this zone was *Pagurus granosimanus*. This species generally used the shells of *Searlesia dira* and *Thais emarginata*. The porcelain crab, *Petrolisthes eriomerus*, has as its preferred habitat individual rocks that rested tightly on an accumulation of sand or rather fine gravel. Under rocks, and especially those set on muddy gravel, was the black claw crab, *Lophopanopeus bellus*. This species sometimes occurred with the porcelain crabs (Kozloff, 1973). In the lower part of the intertidal zone the lugworms, *Abarenicola pacifica* and *A. claparedii*, were quite common.

Sandy Areas. In the protected sandy beaches there were many microscopic organisms that lived between the particles of sand. In this area the amphipod, *Orchestia traskiana* (beach hopper); the scavenging isopod, *Cirolana kincaidi*; Crago shrimps; nemerteans of the genus *Cerebratulus*; and very commonly, polychaetes of the genus *Nephtys* were found (Kozloff, 1973).

In clean sand areas the common organisms were the sand dollar, *Dendraster excentricus* (an echinoderm), and the moon snail, *Polinectes lewisii*. The sand dollar was a detritivore and the moon snail was a carnivore that feeds on clams by drilling a hole in the valve and sucking out the tissue. In the winter the moon snail moved into deeper water.

The burrowing cucumber, *Leptosynapta clarki* (a holothurian), and the cockle and bent-nosed clam were more common in muddy sand, but occurred in clean sand. The detritivorous sand clam, *Macoma secta*, was found here on the surface or burrowed into the sand as deep as 40 cm (Kozloff, 1973).

On sand flats, in pools or depressions that held a little water during low tide, the sand sole, *Psettichthys melanostictus*, as well as the staghorn sculpin, *Leptocottus armatus*, were found. The sculpin was often found also in mud flats and thrived in relatively low saline waters.

On the mud and gravel flats diatoms and other small plants were abundant. Because of the richer organic matter the organisms tended to increase. Here the bent-nosed clam, *Macoma nasuta*, and *M. irus*, were found more abundantly. *Macoma inconspicua* was usually found near the surface of the muddy sand it burrowed into.

The gaper clam, or horse clam, *Tresus capax*, was found occasionally in a stiff clay but was usually in a substrate mixed with mud and gravel and shell fragments. The clam was found at less than 30 cm below the surface in stiff clay and down to 50 cm in mud. *T. capax* received air and water through its siphon, on which lived colonies of barnacles, hydroids, and the anemone, *Epiactis prolifera*. Small tufts of the red alga, *Polysiphonia* sp., were sometimes also found growing on the siphons. Pairs of small crabs, either *Pinnaxa faba* or *P. littoralis*, were often found in the mantle cavity. It is known that the females of these two species feed upon diatoms and other material brought into the mantle cavity by the clam. The diet of the male crabs is unknown. These two species of small crab also inhabited the clams, *Mya arenaria*, *Clinocardium nuttallii*, and *Saxidomus gigantus*. Other organisms found in this habitat are listed in Table 11.4 (Kozloff, 1973).

Quiet Bays. In quiet bays with gravelly sand and mud there were large numbers of little neck clams, *Protothaca staminea*, as well as the Japanese little neck clam, *Venerupis japonica*, which has been imported. The horse mussel, *Modiolus rectus*, was commonly found in these muddy areas among old shells. This species formed aggregates by attaching to others with its byssal threads.

Two oysters imported into the area were growing well in areas of low salinity. They were the Japanese oyster, *Crassostrea gigas*, and *C. virginica*, the Atlantic oyster. The native Olympia oyster, *Ostrea lurida*, was found on the undersides of rocks or, in muddy areas, sometimes on the tops of rocks. The native oyster was being crowded out by the imported species.

The detritus-feeding ghost shrimp, *Callianassa californiensis*, was found in burrows in a muddy, sandy substrate. These burrows also housed pea crabs; the scaleworm, *Hesperonoe adventor*; and the clam, *Cryptomya californica*. In even muddier areas the blue mud shrimp, *Upogebia pugettensis*, lived. Sometimes the clam, *Pseudopythina rugifera*, attached to the underside of this shrimp (Kozloff, 1973).

On the surface of these muddy habitats were found patches of the green algae, *Ulva*, *Monostroma*, and *Enteromorpha*. Sometimes associated with them was the nemertean, *Paranemertes peregrina*, which fed upon *Platynereis bicanaliculata* and other small and medium-sized polychaetes. *Platynereis* built and lived in little tubes attached to *Ulva* blades, which also served as its food. Other worm species found in quiet intertidal areas were the free-living *Ophiodromus pugettensis* and *Eupolymnia heterobranchia*, a tube builder preferring a pebbly substrate. These species ate detritus, diatoms, decaying polychaetes, and occasionally, living polychaetes.

The mollusc, *Aglaja diomeda*, was found on soft mud and muddy sand. Under algae, particularly on substrates with small pebbles, was found the brittle star,

Amphipholis squamata, which fed on diatoms and protozoans (especially ciliates and foraminifera) as well as on turbellarian flatworms (Kozloff, 1973).

The crustacea in these sediments included harpacticoid copepods, cumaceans, tanaids, small isopods, and amphipods. An odd little crustacean, *Nebalia pugettensis*, was found in pools, among seaweed, or in decaying detritus in these habitats.

In hard-packed muddy sand with no algal cover the bamboo worm, *Axiothella rubrocincta*, was often found. Other worms that preferred a muddy substrate were *Notomastus tenuis*, *Hemipodus borealis*, and *Glycera* sp. (Kozloff, 1973).

SUMMARY

The Puget Sound is a large fjord and is unique in the United States. Other smaller fjords exist in New England, but some of them do not have the typical nutrient cycle and water exchange that exists in a true fjord. Nutrients were very variable, depending on the depth of the water in which they were taken. Nitrate concentrations range from undetectable micrograms per liter from a sample deep in the sediment to $27.7\,\mu g\,L^{-1}$ at the sediment surface. Concentrations of ammonia range from 0 to $2.3\,\mu g\,L^{-1}$. Primary production was always evident in the sound and concentrations of phytoplankton in the photosynthetic zone rarely fell below 0.2 L of chlorophyll per cubic meter of water. Diatoms were largely responsible for this productivity. The highest productivity was in 1969, when the productivity of the marine phytoplankton was nearly $10\,g\,C\,m^{-2}\,day^{-1}$. The lowest productivity occurred in 1975, when there was very low sun and high runoff and turbulence. The average year productivity was 1966, when the productivity was $465\,g\,C\,m^{-2}\,yr^{-1}$. Diatoms were the dominant organisms causing this productivity.

Secondary productivity in the soft mud was dominated in the main basin by the echinoid, *Brisaster townsendi*. Polychaetes were dominant in terms of weight. Molluscs were fewer. In Golden Gate, the more important species in productivity were polychaetes, ostracod, and the Sipunculid (*Golfingia pugettensis*). At Port Madison, polychaetes and bivalves were dominant.

The food web is formed by the interaction between plankton, nekton, intertidal, and subtidal communities. Zooplankton seemed to change their food habits depending on their age and size. Copepods were the dominant organisms in the zooplankton. Pelagic fish were the principal predators on the zooplankton. Herbivores were mainly two species of sea urchins. Their main food was brown algae. Ranking second and third in diets for these sea urchins were green algae, *Monostroma fuscum* and *Ulva lactuca*. Omnivores were mainly polychaetes and copepods. The carnivores were asteroids and snails and various polychaete worms. Limpids were an important food. The gastropod, *Thais*, fed selectively on barnacles. The sea star, *Pisaster*, fed preferably on mussels until late in the summer when the lack of mussels forced them to feed on barnacles. Barnacles were also very important prey of a carnivorous gastropod, *Searlesia dira*. The specific foods for various invertebrates were given.

Puget Sound can be divided into several areas from a biological standpoint. They are the area near Seattle, South Puget Sound, and the San Juan Archipelago. The area near Seattle is divided into the Golden Gate Garden and Port Madison area, Alki Point, and Richmond Beach area. The associations of organisms were described for each of these areas.

The San Juan Archipelago is physically a very different area than Puget Sound near Seattle. The habitats are much more varied. The associations in the following habitats were described: the benthos, floating docks, boat floats, pilings, quiet waters, deep waters, eelgrass beds, and intertidal areas (which are divided into splash zones, upper intertidal zones, beach, quiet bays, tide pools, lower intertidal zones, and sandy areas).

BIBLIOGRAPHY

Armstrong, J. W., C. P. Staude, R. M. Thom, and K. K. Chew. 1976. Habitats and relative abundances of the intertidal macrofauna at five Puget Sound beaches in the Seattle area. Syesis 9: 277–290.

Ax, P., and R. Ax. 1967. *Turbellaria proseriata* von der Pazifikkuste der U.S.A. (Washington). 1. Otoplanidae. Morph. liere 61: 215–255.

Ax, P., and B. Sopott-Ehlers. 1979. *Turbellaria proseriata* from the Pacific coast of the U.S.A. (Washington). Part II. Coelogynoporidae. Zool. Scr. 8(1): 25–36.

Banse, K. 1963. Polychaetous annelids from Puget Sound and the San Juan Archipelago, Washington. Proc. Biol. Soc. Washington 76: 197–208.

Bovard, J. F., and H. L. Osterud. 1920. Partial list of the animals yielding embryological material at the Puget Sound Biological Station. Puget Sound Biol. Stn. Publ. 2: 127–138.

Bush, M. 1918. Key to the echinoderms of Friday Harbor, Washington. Puget Sound Biol. Stn. Publ. 2: 17–44.

Caine, E. A. 1977. Feeding mechanisms and possible resource partitioning of the Caprellidae from Puget Sound, Washington. Mar. Biol. 42(4): 331–336.

Dayton, P. K. 1971. Competition, disturbance and community organization: the provision and subsequent utilization of space in a rocky intertidal community. Ecol. Monogr. 41: 351–389.

Dethier, M. N. 1981. Heteromorphic algal life histories. The seasonal pattern and response to herbivory of the brown crust, *Ralfsia californica*. Oecologia 39(3): 333–339.

Eddy, S. 1925. The distribution of marine protozoa in the Friday Harbor waters (San Juan Channel, Washington Sound) Trans. Am. Microsc. Soc. 44: 97–108.

Feller, R. J. 1982. Empirical estimates of carbon production for a meiobenthic harpacticoid copepod. Can. J. Fish. Aquat. Sci. 39(11): 1435–1443.

Gran, H. H., and E. C. Angst. 1931. Plankton diatoms of Puget Sound. Publ. Puget Sound Biol. Stn. 7: 417–516.

Gran, H. H., and T. G. Thompson. 1930. The diatoms and physical and chemical conditions of the sea water of the San Juan Archipelago. Univ. Washington Publ. Puget Sound Biol. Stn. 7: 169–204.

Grundmanis, V., and J. W. Murray. 1977. Nitrification and denitrification in marine sediments from Puget Sound. Limnol. Oceanogr. 22(5): 804–813.

Herlinveaux, R. H., and J. P. Tully. 1961. Some oceanographic features of Juan de Fuca Strait. J. Fish. Res. Board Can. 18: 1027–1071.

Hruby, T. 1975. Seasonal changes in two algal populations from the coastal waters of Washington State. J. Ecol. 63(6): 881–889.

Johnson, M. W. 1932. Seasonal distribution of plankton in Friday Harbor, Washington. Univ. Washington Publ. Oceanogr. 1: 1–38.

Kozloff, E. N. 1973. Seashore life of Puget Sound, the Strait of Georgia and the San Juan Archipelago. University of Washington Press, Seattle. 282 pp.

Landry, M. R. 1978. Population dynamics and production of a planktonic marine copepod, *Acartia clausii*, in a small temperate lagoon on San Juan Island, Washington. Int. Rev. Gesamten Hydrobiol. 63(1): 77–119.
Lariviere, M. G., D. D. Jessup, and S. B. Mathews. 1981. Lingcod, *Ophiodon elongatus*, spawning and nesting in San Juan Channel, Washington. Calif. Fish Game 67(4): 231–239.
Lie, U. 1968. A quantitative study of benthic infauna in Puget Sound, Washington, U.S.A., in 1963–1964. Fiskeridir. Skr. Ser. Havunders. 14: 229–556.
Lie, U. 1974. Distribution and structure of benthic assemblages in Puget Sound, Washington. Mar. Biol. 26: 203–223.
Lie, U., and R. A. Evans. 1973. Long-term variability in the structure of subtidal benthic communities in Puget Sound, Washington, U.S.A. Mar. Biol. 21: 122–126.
Louda, S. M. 1979. Distribution, movement, and diet of the snail, *Searlesia dira*, in the intertidal community of San Juan Island, Puget Sound, Washington. Mar. Biol. 51(2): 119–132.

Mauzey, K. P., C. Birkland, and P. K. Dayton. 1968. Feeding behavior of asteroids and escape responses of their prey in the Puget Sound region. Ecology 49(4): 603–619.
Mills, C. E. 1981. Seasonal occurrence of planktonic medusae and ctenophores in the San Juan Archipelago. Wasmann J. Biol. 39(1–2): 6–29.
Muenscher, W. C. 1917. A key to the Phaeophyceae of Puget Sound. Publ. Puget Sound Biol. Stn. 1(25): 249–284.

Neushul, M. 1967. Studies of subtidal marine vegetation in western Washington. Ecology 48(1): 83–93.
Nichols, F. H. 1970. Benthic polychaete assemblages and their relationship to the sediment in Port Madison, Washington, U.S.A. Ecol. Monogr. 45(2): 57–82.
Nichols, F. H. 1975. Dynamics and energetics of 3 deposit feeding benthic invertebrate populations in Puget Sound. Ecol. Monogr. 45(1): 57–82.
Norris, R. E., and R. N. Pienaar. 1978. Comparative fine structural studies on five marine species of *Pyramimonas*. Phycologia 17(1): 41–52.

Oldroyd, I. S. 1924. Marine shells of Puget Sound and vicinity. Publ. Puget Sound Biol. Stn. 4: 1–271.

Patton, B. G. 1981. Observations of fish on and around an artificial reef in Puget Sound. Northwest Sci. 55(2): 136–144.
Phifer, L. D. 1929. Littoral diatoms of Argyle Lagoon. Publ. Puget Sound Biol. Stn. 7: 137–149.
Phifer, L. D. 1958. Periodicity of diatom growth in San Juan Archipelago. 5th Pacific Science Congress, pp. 2047–2049.
Pilsbry, H. A. 1921. Barnacles of the San Juan Islands, Washington. Proc. U.S. Nat. Mus. 59: 111–115.

Rao, V. N. R., and J. Lewin. 1976. Benthic marine diatoms flora of False Bay, San Juan Island, Washington. Syesis 9: 173–214.

Schell, S. C. 1973. Three new species of digenetic trematodes from Puget Sound fishes. Proc. Helminthol. Soc. Wash. 40(2): 227–230.

Shaffer, P. L. 1978. The feeding biology of *Podarke pugettensis* (Polychaeta:Hesionidae). Biol. Bull. 156: 343–355.

Shelford, V. E., and E. D. Towler. 1925. Animal communities of the San Juan Channel and adjacent areas. Publ. Puget Sound Biol. Stn. 5: 33–73.

Shelford, V. E., A. O. Weese, L. A. Ricc, D. I. Rasmussen, A. Maclean, N. M. Wismer, and J. H. Swanson. 1935. Some marine benthic communities of the Pacific coast of North America. Ecol. Monogr. 5: 249–354.

Somerton, D., and C. Murray. 1976. Field guide to the fish of Puget Sound and the northwest coast. 70 pp.

Stevens, B. A. 1925. Hermit crabs of Friday Harbor, Washington. Publ. Puget Sound Biol. Stn. 3: 273–310.

Stevens, B. A. 1928. Callianassidae from the west coast of North America. Publ. Puget Sound Biol. Stn. 6(2): 315–370.

Stockner, J. G., D. D. Cliff, and K. R. S. Shortreed. 1979. Phytoplankton ecology of the Strait of Georgia, British Columbia. J. Fish. Res. Board Can. 36: 657–666.

Strickland, R. M. 1983. The fertile fjord. Univ. Seattle Press, Seattle. 145 pp.

Thom, R. M. 1980. Seasonality in low intertidal benthic marine algal communities in central Puget Sound. Bot. Mar. 23(1): 7–12.

Thom, R. M., J. W. Armstrong, C. P. Staude, K. K. Chew, and R. E. Norris. 1976. A survey of the attached marine flora at five beaches in the Seattle, Washington area. Syesis 9: 267–275.

Towler, E. C. 1930. An analysis of the intertidal barnacle communities of the San Juan Archipelago. Publ. Puget Sound Biol. Stn. 7: 225–232.

Vadas, R. L. 1977. Preferential feeding: an optimization strategy in sea urchins. Ecol. Monogr. 47(4): 337–372.

Wells, W. W. 1928. Pinnotheridae of Puget Sound. Publ. Puget Sound Biol. Stn. 6(2): 283–314.

Wieser, W. 1959a. The free-living nematodes and other small invertebrates of Puget Sound beaches. Univ. Washington Press, Seattle. Publ. Biol. 19: 179 pp.

Wieser, W. 1959b. The effect of grain size on the distribution of small invertebrates inhabiting the beaches of Puget Sound. Limnol. Oceanogr. 4: 181–194.

Winter, D. F., K. Banse, and G. C. Anderson. 1975. The dynamics of phytoplankton blooms in Puget Sound, a fjord in the northwestern U.S.A. Mar. Biol. 29(2): 136–176.

Index